THE WORLD ENCYCLOPEDIA OF CARTOONS

THE WORLD
ENCYCLO

PEDIA OF CARTOONS

Maurice Horn, Editor

CHELSEA HOUSE PUBLISHERS
Philadelphia

Cover Art Copyrights

Second edition, 1999

Library of Congress Cataloguing in Publication Data

The world encyclopedia of cartoons / Maurice Horn, editor : Richard E.
Marschall, assistant editor. — 2nd ed.
p. cm.
Includes bibliographical references and index.
ISBN 0-7910-4853-5 (seven volume set). — ISBN 0-7910-4855-1 (single volume)
1. Caricatures and cartoons. 2. Comic books, strips, etc. 3. Wit and humor, Pictorial. I. Horn, Maurice. II. Marschall, Richard.
NC1325.W67 1998
741.5'03—dc21 98-37201
CIP

Chelsea House Publishers
A Division of Main Line Book Co.
1974 Sproul Road, Suite 400
Broomall, PA 19008-091

www.chelseahouse.com

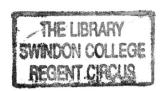

Acknowledgments

The editors of *The World Encyclopedia of Cartoons* wish to express their sincere thanks to the following persons: Herbert Block, Mary Beth Calhoun, André Carpentier, Jacky Chalard, Barrett Clark, Frank Dunay, Franco Fossati, Vasco Granja, George Griffin, Manuel Halffter, Burne Hogarth, Jud Hurd, Jim Ivey, Heikki Kaukoranta, Isidore Klein, Fred Ladd, Eric Leguèbe, Jay Leyda, Ranan Lurie, Michel Mandry, Ernie McGee, Dušan Makavejev, Mario Marchetti, Yvonne Mason, Nancy Marschall, Alvaro de Moya, Sophie Niestadt, Kosei Ono, Sheldon Oppenberg, André Parinaud, Dominique Petitfaux, Professor Leonello Ricci, H.F. Broch de Rothermann, John Ryan, Erna Schoaf, Ronald Schwarz, David Smith, Kate Steinberg, Jessie Straut, Greg Suriano, Ernesto Traverso, Bernard Trout, and Russell Young.

We also want to extend our appreciation to the following organizations: ASIFA, American Film Institute, Bibliothèque Nationale, Comic Research Library, Editoriale Corno, Gutenberghus Publishing Service, King Features Syndicate, Macmillan Educational Corporation, National Cartoonists Society, New York Times, Smithsonian Institution, Universal Press Syndicate, Walt Disney Archives, Walt Disney Productions, Warner Communications, Washington Post and Wilhelm Busch Museum.

THE CONTRIBUTORS

Stanley Appelbaum, *Germany*
Bill Blackbeard, *U.S.*
Richard Calhoun, *U.S.*
Clube Português de Banda Desenhada, *Portugal*
Jared Cook, *Japan*
Bill Crouch, *U.S.*
Giulio Cesare Cuccolini, *Italy*
Wolfgang Fuchs, *Germany*
Denis Gifford, *Great Britain*
Hongying Liu-Lengyel, *China*
Maurice Horn, *U.S./France/Eastern Europe*
Pierre Horn, *France*
Bill Janocha, *U.S.*
Serge Jongué, *Canada*
Francisco Tadeo Juan, *Spain*
Doug Kendig, *Canada*
John A. Lent, *Asia/Eastern Europe*
Vane Lindesay, *Australia*
Augusto Magalhaes, *South America*
Richard Marschall, *U.S.*
Alvaro de Moya, *Brazil*
José Muntañola, *Spain*
Saseo Ono, *Japan*
Fred Patten, *Japan*
Maria-Grazia Perini, *Italy*
Jukka Rislakki, *Finland*
Carlo Scaringi, *Italy*
Frederik Schodt, *Japan*
Luciano Secchi, *Italy*
Jørgen Sonnergaard, *Scandinavia*
Joseph Szabo, *Russia*
Sergio Trinchero, *Italy*
Dennis Wepman, *U.S.*

Contents

Foreword

The World Encyclopedia of Cartoons is the first book to survey on an international scale the entire cartoon field: caricature, editorial and political cartoons, sports cartoons, syndicated panels and animated cartoons. It examines and evaluates all aspects of caricature and cartooning—historical, ideological, aesthetic, sociological, cultural, commercial. To give unprecedented depth and scope to this undertaking, a team of contributors from a dozen different countries has been assembled, each with personal knowledge and experience of the field (see Notes on the Contributors). The exhaustive data compiled for this book has, for the most part, been obtained firsthand from a reading of the sources and from interviews with cartoonists, animators, editors, publishers and producers. In conjunction with its companion volume, *The World Encyclopedia of Comics* (Chelsea House, 1976), this encyclopedia constitutes a unique overview of all the cartooning arts; by itself it provides fascinating reading and deep insight into a field that has touched all important phases of human history for the past 200 years.

The core of the encyclopedia is comprised of close to 1,200 alphabetical entries. These are cross-referenced and fall into two classifications: biographical and bibliographical. The biographical entries summarize succinctly the careers of individual cartoonists, animators, editors and producers, with emphasis on their cartoon work, their stylistic, thematic and sociological contributions, their influence on other artists and their cultural significance. The bibliographical entries deal with the works themselves (animated cartoons, cartoon series, weekly or monthly panels, etc.) and contain a brief history, a summary of theme or plot, an evaluation of the place of the work in the history and development of its medium, and a discussion of its adaptation to other media. The entries also include anecdotal material and comparisons that further illuminate their subjects.

To supplement the bio-bibliographical entries, and to give the reader a general perspective on the subject, the encyclopedia also contains a number of informative articles, including an overview of caricature and cartoons, a brief history of humor magazines, a world summary of animated cartoons, a chronology of important events in the history of cartooning, and an extensive glossary of cartooning terms. Together with the entries, these articles make *The World Encyclopedia of Cartoons* the definitive study of one of the most influential and significant art forms of this century. It is an invaluable tool for historians, sociologists, political analysts, educators and anyone curious about one of mankind's liveliest arts.

For those interested in further research, a bibliography and a number of appendixes are also included. Particularly helpful are the indexes, which provide ready access to additional information on thousands of names and titles not treated in individual entries. Almost a thousand illustrations (some reprinted in a special color section) add visual excitement to the work and constitute the most extensive and representative anthology of cartoons ever assembled. In addition to its value as straight reference work, the text makes for lively, enjoyable and informative reading.

The data contained in *The World Encyclopedia of Cartoons* covers developments in the cartooning fields through December 1979. It is the intention of the publisher to update, revise and enlarge this encyclopedia at regular intervals.

The Editors

Preface to the Second Edition

This is an updated, enlarged edition of what has become since its publication almost twenty years ago the standard reference work in the field: *The World Encyclopedia of Cartoons.* Building upon that foundation we have conserved all the entries as originally written, only updating those (some 500 of them) that needed updating. Additionally well over 200 entries on features, artists and writers that have come to the fore in the past twenty years have been contributed to this edition, bringing the total number of entries to about 1400. Written by experts from around the world, some of them former contributors, some of them new to the Encyclopedia, these additional entries paint in bold colors the panorama of world cartoon art as it has evolved over the last two decades. We are particularly proud to have made this edition even more encyclopedic and even more universal with the inclusion of entries on countries, mostly from Asia and eastern Europe that, for political or practical reasons, were absent from the first edition.

The front and back matter (history, chronology, bibliography, various essays) have also been updated to reflect the changes that have intervened since the first publication of the Encyclopedia. This will provide the reader with a global perspective and a current timeline to a living art form that doesn't cease reinventing itself. More than 120 black-and-white illustrations and an additional color section will further enhance the usefulness and pleasure provided by this Encyclopedia.

This edition of *The World Encyclopedia of Cartoons* has been conceived not only as a scholarly reference tool, the most comprehensive survey of the medium ever realized, but also as an endless source of enjoyment for the reader. The data contained in this Encyclopedia covers the developments in the fields of print and animated cartoons through April 1998. It is the intention of the publisher to further update and revise the work at periodic intervals.

The World in Cartoons

Caricature and Cartoon
Humor Magazines
The Animated Cartoon
From Cartoon to Comic Strip
A World Chronology of Cartoon Art

Caricature and Cartoon:

An Overview

The nature of the cartoon has always been difficult to circumscribe. Most definitions are either too broad (making it impossible to distinguish cartoon from illustration) or too narrow (making appearance on the printed page a sine qua non). It is precisely its protean quality that has made the cartoon such an overwhelmingly popular graphic form. Liberated from the constraints of literalism and slavish representation, it embodies freedom of expression at its simplest and most direct.

The desire to communicate thoughts by drawing predates, of course, written language and may even lie at its origin. Every culture seems to have felt a need for such an eidetic language; in this context any drawing that encapsulates a complete thought can be called a "cartoon." This brief study attempts to retrace the history of the cartoon (and its relative, caricature) in broad outlines and to draw some tentative conclusions.

"Alexomenos Worshipping His God." This first-century A.D. graffito, found on the Palatine Hill in Rome, satirizes Christian doctrines

The origins

In what was possibly the first "how-to" cartooning book ever published, *Rules for Drawing Caricaturas* (1788), Francis Grose wrote: "The sculptors of ancient Greece seem to have diligently observed the forms and proportions constituting the European idea of beauty. . . . These measures are to be met with in many drawing books; a slight deviation from them, by the predominancy of any feature, constitutes what is called *character*. . . . This deviation or peculiarity, aggravated, forms *caricatura*." Such exaggeration of forms, already evident in Greece, flourished even more in Roman culture (as some of the bawdier frescoes in Pompei attest) and found expression in a great number of satirical drawings, many of which were displayed during Roman festivals.

The Middle Ages, despite its proclaimed piety, indulged widely in the representation of farcical or satirical themes, even in the churches (the gargoyles are the best-known manifestations of this mocking spirit). Indeed, so prevalent had the trend toward putting comic sculptures in the churches become by the 13th century that Saint Bernard felt called upon to inveigh against the practice. The medieval figures in turn inspired the first satirical engravings of the 15th century, particularly the remarkable drypoint etchings of the anonymous German artist known simply as "the E.S. master," whose works (dating from 1466) include a "grotesque alphabet" that is very modern in outlook. From there the thread leads through Dürer, Bosch, Bruegel, Da Vinci (in his drawings of heads) and Callot into modern times.

Early Cartooning in Japan

Chōjūgiga *("Animal Scrolls") is a series of four monochrome paper scrolls from Japan's 12th and 13th centuries. It primarily depicts animals engaged in human activities. The scrolls, preserved in the Buddhist temple of Kōzan in the city of Kyoto, were for years attributed to the priest-artist Toba Sōjō (also known as Kakuyu), but present evidence indicates that there may have been more than one artist and that the last two scrolls may actually have been drawn a hundred years later than the first two.*

Irrespective of authorship, Chōjūgiga *is one of Japan's earliest examples of cartooning, and with its scroll format it almost straddles the line between cartoon and animation. Predating Walt Disney by well over a thousand years, the first scroll is a humorous depiction of rabbits, frogs and monkeys behaving as humans would—swimming rivers, hunting with bow and arrow, praying in mock religious ceremonies. It is the best drawn and consequently the most famous of the four scrolls. The second scroll depicts horses, oxen, chickens, lions, dragons and other fanciful animals, while the third and fourth are mainly humorous scenes of Buddhist priests engaged in competitive games with each other and with laymen.*

Unfortunately, if any text ever existed, it has since been lost, and the exact meaning of the Chōjūgiga *scrolls is open to question. The most common interpretation is that they are a satire on Japanese society of the Heian period, focusing particularly on the abuses of the Buddhist church of that time, which was notorious for its corruption. Nonetheless, the pictures alone, especially those in the first scroll, are powerful enough to have a universal appeal, and even today they evoke laughter. The artist worked with sumi ink on white paper and had a steady hand and a keen eye; parts of* Chōjūgiga *are regarded by some experts today as representative of the best in Japanese brush painting. The artist's appreciation of animal shape and motion were uncanny, and in viewing the scrolls one is immediately struck by their realism and fluidity.* Chōjūgiga *is a designated national treasure of Japan today.*

F.S.

E.S. Master, letter D from "A Fantastic Alphabet."

Modern caricature

It is customary to ascribe credit for the development of modern caricature to the brothers Annibale and Agostino Carracci. Indeed, they are credited with coining the very word *caricature*, which derives from their *ritrattini carichi* ("loaded portraits") satirizing well-known personages and ordinary individuals alike. The Carraccis, whose caricatural work was done chiefly during the last decade of the 16th century, had been preceded in their experiments by another Italian, Giuseppe Arcimboldo, who painted amazing portraits of legendary beings, using inanimate objects, plants and vegetables to make up his fantastic "composite heads." Arcimboldo, however, labored in semi-obscurity in Prague, while the Carracci brothers' work was widely known and soon imitated. In 1646, using Annibale Carracci's own pronouncements on the subject, A. Mosini in his Trattato ("Treatise") established the definition of *caricatura* as the art of following nature's disfigurements in an attempt to arrive at *la perfetta difformità*, "the perfect deformity."

The art of caricature was for a long time the almost exclusive preserve of the Italians, who fielded such redoubtable practitioners as Pier Leone Ghezzi, Giovanni Bracelli and Gian Lorenzo Bernini. Bernini is also credited with bringing the concept to France when he settled there in the middle of the 17th century. The English historian Thomas Browne introduced the term in England, and by the beginning of the 18th century the term as well as the practice of caricature was widespread all over Europe.

Caricature as a graphic shorthand (as distinct from caricature as a well-defined graphic form) was enthusiastically seized upon by many artists who saw it as a liberation from the straitjacket of conventional art rules. Even Rembrandt in his self-portraits indulged this penchant towards mockery and fantasy. The rules of caricature have become firmly codified since the 18th century, and there is a direct line from the Frenchman Raymond La Fage (1656-1690) and the Dutchman Cornelius Dusart (1660-1704) to such modern caricaturists as Miguel Covarrubias, Al Hirshfeld and even Saul Steinberg.

From caricature to cartooning: England

It was the universal acceptance of prints that led to the phased transition from caricature to what would later be called "cartoons," a form no longer devoted simply to cataloguing external human idiosyncrasies, but one with an enlarged field of vision encompassing the whole political, social and cultural scene—indeed, the human condition itself.

Perhaps no artist embodied this vision so completely as William Hogarth (1697-

William Hogarth, plate from "A Harlot's Progress," 1732.

Thomas Rowlandson, "The Genius's Room," 1806.

1764). As Werner Hofmann noted in his study *Die Karikatur,* "Leaving aside a few prior attempts to adapt caricature to current events, we must regard Hogarth as the first truly artistic practitioner of this genre, which in the concave mirror of the deformed image encapsulates the vision of life in its entirety." Hogarth is the first artist to whom the term *cartoonist* can be legitimately applied. He was the first to draw humorous scenes without recourse to grossly caricatural effects or physical deformities. Background and detail were sufficient to bring out the humor of his compositions. His effects were primarily dramatic, not graphic, and his aims moral or social when they were not overtly political. He can thus be regarded as the first editorial cartoonist as well as the forerunner (in his series of narrative cartoons) of the comic strip.

The first manifestations of the cartoon in print took the form of the broadside, a single sheet with picture and caption printed together. This in turn led to more specialized prints, of which the copperplate became the most common. Hogarth worked chiefly in this medium, as did most of his followers and imitators.

If Hogarth can be said to have had a direct disciple, it was Thomas Rowlandson (1756-1827), who enlarged the popular audience for the cartoon with his caustic and at times bitter criticism of the inequities of his time, and with his satirical depictions of contemporary fads and foibles. Rowlandson found a kindred spirit in James Gillray (1757-1815), who specialized in mordant attacks on the monarchy and the nobility—at least, until the time of the French Revolution, when his patriotism led him away from social criticism into rabid denunciations of the French peril. (For biographies of Hogarth, Rowlandson and Gillray, see *The World Encyclopedia of Comics,* Chelsea House, 1976.)

In the course of the 18th century cartooning found a function as well as a form. The subject of the cartoonist's pen was now the whole world, and especially society, whose most telling failings the cartoonists felt themselves obliged to represent. A tradition was thus born: for a long time to come, cartooning would be a means of social protest (possibly the most effective yet devised) as well as an art of political persuasion. By linking the resources of traditional art to the immediacy of popular illustration, the English cartoonists struck a responsive chord with even the least sophisticated audiences. The lesson was not lost on other Europeans: soon the cartoon was one of the most potent weapons in the political battles of the 19th century.

The spread of the cartoon

The techniques of cartooning slowly spread outside England, although the term cartoon was in limited use among artists and only became generalized in the 1830s. In Germany Daniel Chodowiecki began his contributions to the Berlin almanacs around 1770 (and later to the Göttingen almanacs) with satirical and

Francisco Goya, "Till Death . . . ," from "Los Caprichos," 1824.

Honoré Daumier. "The Orchestra While Tragedy Is Being Played," 1852.

political drawings and commentaries on contemporary German society. His work was carried on by J.H. Ramberg, who had studied in London and who further spread the tradition of the Hogarthian cartoon in Germany. Cartoons even penetrated Russia in the early years of the 19th century, when Polish-born Aleksander Orlowski settled in St. Petersburg after fleeing from Prussian-occupied Poland because of his anti-Prussian cartoons.

Louis Boilly and Philibert Debucourt transferred the techniques of the English cartoonists to France in the waning years of the French monarchy. After an eclipse during the revolutionary and Napoleonic periods, cartooning in France found a definite footing with the drawings of Carle Vernet, which blazed the way for a recognizable French cartooning style whose most celebrated practitioner was Honoré Daumier. Cartooning did not find favor with the despotic monarchy in Spain, however; only in 1799, when the regime relaxed its grip slightly, could Goya have his *Caprichos* published. Goya's powerful depiction of the wretched human condition, his sardonic humor ("black humor" before its time) and his use of jarring imagery proved decisive in the 19th-century transformation of European cartooning into an art of protest.

Outside Europe cartooning developed fastest and most significantly in the American colonies. American cartoonists (most of them remaining prudently anonymous) took to attacking with mounting savagery the privileges of the British Crown. Their cartoons were not all political, however. Some reflected the purely domestic concerns of the colonists; others were homiletic in tone and didactic in nature. But the indisputable fact was that cartooning was flourishing in 18th-century America, and its most famous practitioner was that man-of-all-talents Benjamin Franklin. Unlike the English cartoons that inspired them, the American versions gave less importance to purely artistic considerations (drafts-

John T. McCutcheon, 1920. © Chicago Tribune.

manship, composition, perspective) and concentrated more on the main point of the argument. This predilection for the "punch line" marked American cartooning from its inception and contributed in no small measure to its phenomenal growth in the 20th century.

Cartoons became established in Latin America towards the middle of the 19th century (although there were sporadic attempts in the early years of the century). The initial impulse came mainly from immigrant Spanish and Portuguese cartoonists; in Argentina, however, there was a strong French influence, chiefly due to the presence of two expatriate French cartoonists, Henri Meyer and Henri Stein.

The art of the cartoon was brought to China by the British in the 1840s and penetrated into Japan after the opening of the country in 1867. Faithful to their approach to modernization, the Japanese then endeavored to learn the new techniques from representatives of the two dominant powers in the field of cartooning at the time: an Englishman, Charles Wirgman, and a Frenchman, Georges Bigot.

"Join or Die," Ben Franklin's famous 1754 cartoon.

The editorial cartoon

For a long time political cartooning (and editorial cartooning generally) was at the very heart of the fledgling medium. The time-honored cliché "A picture is worth a thousand words" never rang so true as during the latter part of the 18th century and most of the 19th, when competing doctrines and ideologies battled fiercely for the minds of people who were still largely illiterate. The potency of the cartoon lay in its ability to make a point sharply and quickly, without the semantic ambiguities inherent in the written word. Nowhere was this lesson as quickly grasped and enthusiastically applied as in 18th-century England and 19th-century France.

Hogarth was, if not the first, certainly the foremost artist to engage in explicit social criticism. His attacks on the English class system mounted in savagery as the century wore on, and his advocacy of social change found a powerful echo on the Continent in later years. Rowlandson redefined political cartooning as less concerned with ultimates and more narrowly focused on topical issues with his jibes at the aristocracy, the Cabinet and sometimes the Crown.

The British, who are rightly credited with inventing the social protest cartoon, did a complete about-face after the French Revolution and the Napoleonic Wars. Some of the greatest English cartoonists of the 19th century (George Du Maurier, John Leech, John Tenniel), while sniping at the more egregious shortcomings of the British social and political system, expressed a broad agreement (indeed a smug satisfaction) with the established order. In current times this conservative tradition is best represented (ironically enough) in the Soviet Union, where cartoonists are asked to uphold the existing order and content themselves with satirizing its more trivial or ridiculous aspects.

The tradition of social protest inherited from Hogarth was carried on most effectively in 19th-century France. Daumier towers over French (and world) cartooning in his embodiment of the cartoonist as prophet. His messianic fervor in the promotion of social change made him a feared figure in French politics, and his example was emulated by a host of talented cartoonists (Gavarni, Grandville, Monnier, Traviès and others).

By the middle of the 19th century, then, European political cartooning was set on two widely divergent paths. On the other side of the Atlantic, it took a slightly different course. Political cartoons played a part in the turmoil leading to the American War of Independence. Paul Revere was especially outspoken in his denunciations of British rule, and Franklin's famous "Join or Die" cartoon epitomized the colonists' plight in one telling image. In the 19th century American cartoonists fell into raucous political argumentation and were often guilty of blind partisanship. Their power was demonstrated when Thomas Nast almost singlehandedly destroyed the Tweed Ring in the early 1870s and when Bernard Gillam helped defeat James G. Blaine in the presidential election of 1884. As the century rushed on, however, a new breed of editorial cartoonist came to prominence. More skeptical, less prone to knee-jerk reactions, they injected a welcome dose of evenhandness into cartooning by attacking all comers; Homer Davenport and John McCutcheon can be counted among this group. Eventually the trend grew as

The Angels of Peace Descend on Belgium

One of David Low's famous World War II cartoons. © London Evening Standard.

American newspaper cartoonists, thanks to the generalization of the syndicate system, freed themselves to a large extent from a party (or publisher's) line.

It would be futile to go into the evolution of editorial cartooning throughout the 20th century; suffice it to say that the pattern set in the preceding century has, with minor exceptions, held fast to this day. For all practical purposes, editorial cartoonists can be grouped in two categories: the ideologues (whether of the right or the left) and the agnostics. The former are generally more persuasive, but the latter are usually funnier and more often tellingly accurate.

The late 1980s and early 1990s witnessed a series of momentous events, from the desintegration of the Soviet bloc to the birth or restoration of democracy in large parts of the globe; and these dramatic changes found immediate echoes in the cartooning world. There was a flowering of inspiration among hitherto shackled cartoonists. Of special importance in this regard are the Chinese Liao Bingxiong, whose self-portrait, "Reborn after Mao," showing him coming out in the fetal position from the womb of oppression, is world-famous; and the Russian Mikhail Zlatkovsky, whose depiction of a glum Gorbachev trying vainly to hold together a Soviet Union literally coming apart at the seams, received worldwide circulation.

In the United States a new crop of editorial cartoonists has emerged, including Jim Borgman, Mike Ramirez, Tom Toles, and Signe Wilkinson (a woman). If the widespread syndication of editorial cartoons has made some cartoonists, such as Pat Oliphant, Don Wright, and especially Ranan Lurie, internationally famous, it has also resulted in the loss of cartooning positions at a number of newspapers. Cartoonists have tried to fight these unfavorable developments by going into "video cartoons" or creating their own websites on the Internet.

Albert Dubout. © Dubout.

The humor cartoon

The humor or gag cartoon is a relative newcomer to the cartooning firmament. The drawings and scenes of the early cartoonists were often funny, but they also tried to make a social, political or moral point. Certainly, versatile artists like Gavarni in France, Leech in England, Heinrich Hoffmann in Germany or David Claypool Johnston in the United States were capable of turning out a funny drawing without being too self-conscious about its ultimate meaning, but humor cartoons as a generally accepted genre can be said to have originated in the 1860s.

The birth and flowering of the gag cartoon can be directly traced to the growing popularity of illustrated magazines (a detailed study of humor magazines follows the present survey). Magazine editors discovered that entertainment was more likely to attract a readership than were polemics, and at the turn of the century there arose a new generation of cartoonists. Men like A.B. Frost, T.S. Sullivant, Caran d'Ache and Shisui Nagahara, to mention a few, may have come from different backgrounds and traditions, but they all aimed to amuse first and foremost.

This emphasis on entertainment led to a reexamination of the role of humor in the cartoon, and graphic humor came under the scrutiny of sociologists, philosophers and even a few artists. There was also a resurgence of caricature in cartoons, a technique that had been neglected by the socially conscious cartoonists of the 19th century, who leaned heavily on realism. Simplification of line (already apparent among American cartoonists of the early 20th century) bred increasing stylization, just as the paring down of lengthy captions resulted in growing terseness. One has only to compare the elaborate and prolix "he/she" cartoons of Charles Dana Gibson to the bare, almost wordless drawings of James Thurber to see the astonishing distance covered in a few decades.

Though the taboos and prohibitions of governments and editors alike once restricted the freedom of humor cartoonists, there is now no subject they cannot deal with. In their treatments, the gag cartoonists range all the way from gentle, middle-class fun (Syd Hoff in the United States, Jacques Faizant in France and Orla Getterman in Denmark are a few examples among many) through the raucous humor of the likes of Albert Dubout, George Price and Gerard Hoffnung to the sardonic black humor of Chaval, Ronald Searle, Charles Addams, Chumy-Chumez and Toshio Saeki.

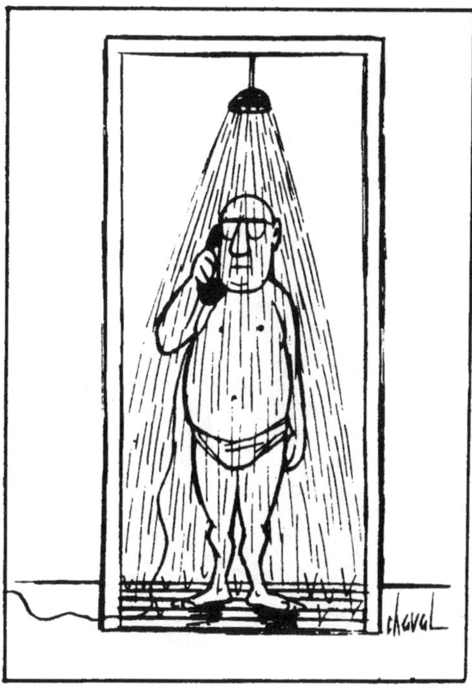

Yvan Le Louarn ("Chaval"). © Paris-Match.

A world of cartoons

While the chief trend in 20th-century cartooning has been towards the fusion of the form as a universal language, a strong opposite current toward specialization of theme or subject has also been evident. There have always been cartoons addressed to a single issue (such as the cartoons of Louis Raemakers during World War I and those of David Low during World War II); there are also groups of cartoons centering on the universal themes—women, fashion, money, medicine, etc.—dear to satirists of every country and every era. In recent times, with the growing number of specialized magazines, cartoons aimed exclusively at stamp collectors, yachting enthusiasts and racetrack devotees have appeared. Of all the special interests reflected in cartoons, however, sports remains the most enduring.

There has been a scattering of sports cartoonists abroad, but the breed is most impressively represented in the United States. In the late 19th and early 20th centuries no American newspaper of any size was without its regular sports cartoonist, usually warming up for better things. Some, like Willard Mullin and Tom Paprocki, remained in the field and became household names, but sports was usually regarded by cartoonists as a springboard to a wider audience: T.A. Dorgan, Robert Ripley and Rube Goldberg are among the cartoonists who started on the sports pages. Today the field has narrowed to a few syndicated cartoonists.

The cartoon series is almost as old as the cartoon form itself: Hogarth, Daumier, Gavarni and others all saw the advantage of having their drawings sequentially issued over a period of time, either as separate plates or in successive magazine numbers. From this practice derives the modern-day panel feature, a cartoon published in regular daily, weekly or monthly installments in the pages of newspapers or magazines. These panels encompass a wide range of styles and topics. They can be grouped around a common theme (*Side Glances* and *Metropolitan Movies* in the United States, *La Vie en Images* in Canada), a social type (Rube Goldberg's *Lunatics I Have Met,* Pont's *British Character),* a recognizable locale *(Right Around Home* in the United States, *St. Trinian's* in Britain), a single protagonist (Ted Key's *Hazel,* Jean Bellus's *Clémentine Chérie*) and sometimes nothing more than the artist's own style and concerns (Giampaolo Chies's *Monodia,* Guillermo Mordillo's *Crazy Crazy*). In fact, panels need not be cartoons at all, as Ripley's illustrative *Believe It or Not!* demonstrates.

In their periodicity, their use of a permanent cast of characters, their utilization of speech balloons, many panels constitute a bridge between the cartoon and the comic strip. Even closer to the strip in format is the magazine series, a genre pioneered in Europe in the mid-19th century by such artists as Adolf Schrödter (*Herr Piepmeyer),* Nadar (*La Vie Publique et Privée de Môssieu Réac)* and J.F. Sullivan (*The British Working Man).* These series (varying in duration from a few weeks to many

Giampaolo Chies. © Editoriale Corno

A Journal of the Cartooning Arts: Cartoonist PROfiles

Cartoonist PROfiles, *a quarterly magazine, was founded in February 1969 by Jud Hurd. From 1965 to 1969 Hurd edited the newsletter of the National Cartoonists Society and later that organization's magazine, the* Cartoonist. *With* Cartoonist PROfiles *he launched his own magazine, and during the ten years since, it has been the only regularly issued U.S. publication devoted exclusively to articles about cartoonists in all branches of the profession–syndicated comic strips, magazines, advertising, sports and political cartoons, comic books and animation. Drawing on his years of experience in the various fields of cartooning, Hurd usually sits down with a longtime cartoon acquaintance and talks shop in order to produce the* PROfiles *stories. So, as a rule, the information comes directly from a currently active cartoonist rather than from research relying on previously printed material.*

The magazine's readership consists of professional cartoonists, young people aspiring to the profession, syndicate editors, newspaper feature buyers, collectors and public libraries, as well as school and college libraries. There are currently subscribers in more than twenty-five countries, in addition to the United States. Because the magazine and its editors take no stand as to the artistic status of the cartoonists reviewed, Cartoonist PROfiles *does not completely fulfill the function of an aesthetic journal. It nevertheless constitutes the most comprehensive record of the state of American cartooning today.*

M.H.

"Citizen Smith," a daily panel by Dave Gerard. © Register and Tribune Syndicate.

TURF TERROR . . . . by Pap'
AMERIGO
–THE ENGLISH-BRED WINNER OF THE HIALEAH TURF CUP IS THE MOST TEMPERAMENTAL EQUINE RACING STAR IN ACTION –HE NIPS, KICKS AND BULLIES HIS TRAINERS, WORKS WHEN HE FEELS LIKE IT AND RUNS WHEN HE IS IN THE MOOD
!!
HIS VIOLENT OBJECTIONS TO BEING SADDLED OFTEN LEAVE HIM TOO WORN OUT TO RUN HIS BEST RACE
AMERIGO HAS WON $288,831 JUST TO PROVE THAT HE CAN RUN
PAP'
AP Newsfeatures 47

A sports panel by Tom Paprocki ("Pap").
© AP Newsfeatures.

months) used a multi-panel format with a lengthy running text underneath each panel; they can be considered the direct forerunners of the comic strip. The form was further refined and generalized by the American humor magazines of the turn of the century. Some of the most prominent cartoonists of the time tried their hands at cartoon series, among them J.M. Flagg, who created *Nervy Nat.* F.B. Opper, who drew *The Suburban Resident* in *Puck,* and C.W. Kahles, who did The *Yarns of Captain Fibb* for *Judge*, later became recognized masters of the comics.

We are now approaching a field where the boundaries between the cartoon proper and the comic strip become blurred. Many cartoonists use a typical multi-panel comic strip layout to extend the point they are making, while gag strip artists sometimes condense their strips into one cartoon panel. In those countries (Japan, Italy) where the comics represent the predominant form of graphic expression, practically no distinction is made between the cartoon and the humor strip.

In his autobiography, *Drawn from Memory* (1950), John McCutcheon wrote, "The cartoon differs from any other picture in that the idea alone is the essential requirement, whether it is meant to inform, reform, or solely to amuse. This idea should be brought out with directness and simplicity, in such a way that people will know it is a cartoon and not a work of art. It has little to do with beauty or grace; it has much to do with strength and uniqueness. It is a peculiar form of art for a peculiar purpose, and presupposes the ability to say things trenchantly, humorously, or caustically, in terms of line."

McCutcheon's definition is very important in that it represents the majority

THE IMAGINATIVE RESPONSE TO THE CONDITIONS HERE PRESENTED MAY JUST HAPPEN TO PROCEED FROM THE INTELLECTUAL EXTRAVAGANCE OF THE GIVEN OBSERVER. WHEN THIS PERSONAGE IS OPEN TO CORRUPTION BY ALMOST ANY LARGE VIEW OF AN INTENSITY OF LIFE HIS VIBRATIONS TEND TO BECOME A MATTER DIFFICULT EVEN FOR HIM TO EXPLAIN.
NUTTY
SURE!
DECK HAND
H. JAMES
F. Opper

A 1906 cartoon by Frederick Opper combining the traditions of caricature. cartoons and comics (not to mention literary criticism).

Like every self-respecting country, Turkey will divide her people into two classes: those who work and those who watch others work.
A 1908 cartoon by Juan Gris.

Cartooning in Brazil

Manoel Araújo de Porto-Alegre is supposed to be the first cartoonist in Brazil. On December 14, 1837 he published a cartoon under the title "A Campainha e o Cujo." It was a separate paper from the newspaper to be sold at request. From then on, the political cartoon (the French notion of "charge"), and the costume cartoons were the same in Brazil. No boundaries between the two mediums. It followed a notable collection of brave artists in the tradition of criticism. Angelo Agostini immigrant from Italy; Raphael Bordallo Pinheiro a Portuguese-born living for some time in Brazil (Portugal has a museum bearing his name); the painter Pedro Americo; his brother Aurelio Figueiredo; the writer Aluizio Azevedo—the Emile Zola of Pompéia; Alvarus (Alvaro Cotrim); Voltolino; Belmonte; Henrique Fleuis; Cândido de Faria; K. Lixto (Calixto Cordeiro); Raul Pederneiras; the Portuguese Julião Machado; the immigrant from Paraguay Andres Guevara and even the famous painter Di Cavalcanti did cartoons and children illustrations.

In between we have Nelo, Jayme Cortez, Messias de Mello Álvaro de Moya, Rosasco, Brito, Hilde, Luís Sá, Péricles, Carlos Estêvão and others.

The new generation is rich: Ziraldo, Millôr Fernandes, Fortuna, Borjalo, Luís Fernando Veríssimo, the twins Chico and Paulo Caruso, Henfil, Jaguar, Claudius Cláudia Lévay, Zélio (Ziraldo's brother), Lor, Vasqs, Verde, Morini, Fausto, Angeli, Miguel Paiva, Novaes, Santiago, Jal, Glauco, Nani, Redi, Spacca, Ique, Ota (Octacílio Assumpção) Edgar Vasques, Negreiros, great cartoonists in a tropical country.

A.d.M.

From Hokusai's "Shashin Gwafu." In this drawing, Hokusai blends the traditions of Japanese art, Western art, and the art of the cartoon into a single visual statement.

This extract from William Hogarth's "Analysis of Beauty" (1753) seems a fitting summation to the aesthetic debate on the art of cartooning.

James Ensor, "The Good Judges," 1894.

view of practicing cartoonists (particularly American cartoonists) on their art. It is, however, fallacious on several levels. It ignores the origin of the cartoon in art history. Hogarth, Rowlandson and Daumier were artists of the first rank who happened to work primarily in the cartoon idiom. Closer to us, many of the leading figures of modern art have also been cartoonists: Juan Gris, Jacques Villon, Heinrich Kley, John Sloan—the list could go on and on. More important, the cartoon works of artists like James Ensor, Félicien Rops and Saul Steinberg are considered, and rightly so, works of art. What McCutcheon fails to consider is that if the cartoon has "little to do with beauty or grace" as these are taught in academic art schools, so has most modern art. Artists and cartoonists have learned different lessons, or more precisely, have applied different interpretations to the lesson taught by the masters of the Renaissance: that under the surface order of the world there lurks a frightening disorder of forms. While painters and sculptors have drifted into ever simplified abstraction in their search for "pure form," cartoonists have engaged in ever wilder depictions of the human figure. They represent the allegedly absent but actually very much alive figurative tradition in 20th-century art.

Maurice Horn

Gustave Doré, "Musical Evening," 1655.

Humor Magazines:

A Brief History

The humor magazine, more than any other medium, has contributed to the universal acceptance and wide popularity of the cartoon. The cartoon—and to a lesser extent caricature—has been tied to the print media from the earliest beginnings. The broadsheets carrying Hogarth's *Rake's Progress* or *Marriage á la Mode* were only a prefiguration of things to come; in the 18th century the proliferation of almanacs in Europe and North America further established the cartoon form as an integral part of print publications. At the same time, caricatures and cartoons began to be collected in albums (an early form of the modern cartoon anthology): in London in 1740 Arthur Pond published *25 Caricatures,* an album of prints after Ghezzi, the Carraccis, Raymond La Fage and others. Towards the end of the century albums reprinting the work of a single author (such as Rowlandson or Gillray) began to make their appearance.

In the meantime contemporary gazettes used the new graphic medium sparingly. Text in the early newspapers predominated overwhelmingly, with only an occasional woodcut (not necessarily humorous) thrown in for good measure. It soon became apparent that a new vehicle would be needed to absorb the work of the cartoonists, whose ranks had swelled considerably in the course of the century.

Early humor magazines

Like the cartoon, the humor magazine also found its modern roots in England. The forerunners of this new development were the gossip sheets that flourished all over England at the end of the 18th century. The *Political Register,* the *London Magazine* and the *Town and Country Magazine* were among the titles of these publications. In order to circumvent the draconian libel laws of the time, they soon fell into the habit of adding a telling illustration to their innuendos, thus giving birth to the modern concept of the magazine cartoon.

After the turn of the century, the second generation of gossip magazines became noticeably more sophisticated, and their cartoons more acerbic as well as more artistically executed. The best known of these publications were the *Satirist, Town Talk* and, foremost among them, the *Scourge,* an avowedly political monthly whose chief claim to immortality was the cartoon work of George and Robert Cruikshank, better known to their readers under their *nom de plume,* "Tom and Jerry." The younger of the two, George, was the more innovative, and his name is one of the most important in cartooning history. As stated in The *World Encyclopedia of Comics* (Chelsea House, 1976), "George Cruikshank was the last cartoonist of note to follow in the footsteps of Rowlandson and Gillray, and provided the link between the 18th-century school of violently contrasted etchings and the realistic style of *Punch* wood engravings. . . . (He) continued and consolidated the work of the early English cartoonists, contributing further innovations to the medium."

Young Gentlemen in the Dress of the Year 1798

A magazine caricature by George Cruikshank, 1821.

More humor magazines came to the fore after the end of the Napoleonic Wars, such as the *Humorist, Life in London* and *Life in Paris,* and they further contributed to the universalization of the magazine cartoon in Britain. More important, their success spawned imitators on the Continent and especially in France, where the cartoon medium was to find its most fertile ground.

Le Charivari and the French school of cartooning

Charles Philipon may well be called the father of the modern magazine of humor and caricature. In 1830 he founded *La Caricature,* taking advantage of the newly introduced lithographic process. *La Caricature* was strongly political (in its pages Philipon himself attacked King Louis-Philippe, and his drawings of the king as a pear-head" are classics), and as a result it was shut down by the authorities; but a sister publication that Philipon had launched in 1832 under the title *Le*

MANNERS. AND. CVSTOMS. OF Ye. ENGLYSHE. IN. 1849.
Ye FASHONABLE. WORLDE. TAKYNGE. ITS EXERCYSE IN HYDE. PARKE.

Richard Doyle in "Punch."

Charivari (a *charivari* was a noisy student demonstration) endured and became a paragon of humor publications.

Le Charivari, although strongly oriented towards the left, was less openly political than *La Caricature.* Manners, mores and customs were as keenly observed as policies and institutions were satirized. *Le Charivari* became a platform for cartoonists and artists, and for almost half a century it dominated the field in France, as every cartoonist of distinction flocked to its pages. Its success prompted Philipon to embark on more publishing ventures; he founded *Le Journal pour Rire* (which later became *Le Journal Amusant)* and revived *La Caricature* (at first calling it *Provisoire)* in 1837.

In Philipon's journals there reigned an atmosphere of artistic freedom and heady experimentation that was conducive to the cartoonists' best efforts. Daumier created his first acknowledged masterpieces for its pages, Gustave Doré took his first steps there, and the contributions of such artists as Gavarni, Grandville, Henri Monnier, Charles Traviès and others greatly helped to make cartooning an art. The artists' seriousness of purpose was often reflected in their drawings, which were more figurative or romantic than humorous. The sting lay in the captions, in the loaded dialogues that provided an ironic or bitter counterpoint to the seeming amiability or respectability of the visual goings-on (Daumier's gun merchant surveying with unconcealed glee a battleground strewn with corpses represents the epitome of this approach).

Paul Gavarni, "Thomas Vireloque."

Only after reading the captions could the reader discover that the drawings were just as subversive (and possibly more so) in their subtlety and their shock value. Figures were only slightly distorted (but in a telling way, as when one of Daumier's characters extended his hand unobtrusively yet unmistakably for a bribe); and faces revealed upon examination all varieties of vice (greed, stupidity, arrogance, lust, philistinism, opportunism, pettiness, servility), which their bourgeois owners tried vainly to conceal under a show of hypocritical dignity. The object of the French cartoonists' scorn was the triumphant middle class (King Louis-Philippe himself was proud to be called *le roi bourgeois*), which was savagely satirized in the form of stock figures: Monnier, for instance, created the character Joseph Prudhomme, while Traviès focused on his misshapen Mayeux.

Scene: Westminister Bridge.
Time: Two on a foggy morning.
Reduced Tradesman (to a little party returning home): "Did you want to buy a good razor?"

John Leech, 1853.

Satirical magazines flourished in the two decades from 1835 to 1854. Often cartoonists founded their own journals: Gavarni launched *Le Journal des Gens du Monde* in the late 1830s, Daumier and Philipon teamed up to create *Le Robert-Macaire,* and Nadar brought out the short-lived *La Revue Comique* (1848-49) while he was still in his twenties. At mid-century French cartooning was at its zenith, and its practitioners enjoyed worldwide fame and recognition.

Punch and the British tradition

Philipon's journals soon found an echo in the rest of Europe and especially in the British Isles, where humor publications were already well established, as we have seen. In 1830 there appeared the London *Monthly Sheet of Caricatures* (also called the *Looking Glass*), a close imitation of *La Caricature.* During the 1830s it was followed by more magazines of the same ilk, such as *Figaro in London* (soon giving rise to *Figaro in Birmingham, Figaro in Sheffield,* etc.), the *Devil in London* and *Punchinello,* all of them closely copying the French magazines, down to the minutely detailed style and the use of lithographic printing.

These magazines enjoyed a raucous, somewhat freak success for more than a decade, until a more typically British publication emerged in 1841: *Punch,* founded by the prolific publicist Henry Mayhew. Subtitled "the London Charivari," *Punch* first went in for the same sort of social criticism that was prevalent in French cartoon magazines; soon, however, it found its role as the upholder of the British Empire and the English way of life, at the same time sniping at its most glaring shortcomings. Its tone was one of good-natured ribbing and gentlemanly fun, as befits a slightly sarcastic member of the family. *Punch* was undeniably part of the Victorian establishment, whose leading lights delighted in being caricatured (but ever so courteously) in its pages. *Punch*'s practitioners of the gentle rebuff included such luminaries as John Leech, one of the more political, and especially Richard Doyle, father of Arthur Conan Doyle. It was Doyle who designed *Punch*'s

The Sacred Elephant: This animal is sure to win, if it is kept pure and clean, and has not too heavy a load to carry.

Thomas Nast in "Harper's Weekly."

famous cover, and Leech is credited with having popularized the term *cartoon* in his 1843 "Cartoons for the Walls of the Houses of Parliament." In later years other talented artists were added to the ranks of *Punch,* such as John Tenniel, Charles Keene and the quintessential *Punch* cartoonist, George Du Maurier.

After the 1850s, at the same time that French cartooning was peaking, *Punch* was entering its most glorious phase. It had become, in fact, a school for the British nation, holding up to it a set of values and attitudes that prevailed almost until the British Empire began to dissolve. The magazine editors themselves were conscious of this fact and in 1856 announced in a mock-serious tone that they held "a lively belief that the world will feel the benignant influence of MR. PUNCH's teaching through its civilised and regenerated rules. In the meantime the Briton will be . . . proud . . . that MR. PUNCH as the Schoolmaster, is Abroad."

Throughout the 19th century *Punch*'s preeminent position remained assured, despite the efforts of other publications to rival it in the field of cartooning. Over the decades many humor journals came to life, such as *Fun, Judy* and *Tomahawk* (the most politically radical of the lot, advocating, among other things, the establishment of a republic), but they could not compete and were soon forgotten. The same fate awaited *Vanity Fair* (founded in 1868), notwithstanding the brilliant cartoons of its two most distinguished contributors, "Ape" (Carlo Pellegrini) and "Spy" (Leslie Ward), and its tone of sophistication and worldliness. To the solidly middle-class Britons who were the readers of newspapers and magazines, *Punch* was an institution almost as hallowed as the monarchy.

The Goose that Lays the Golden Eggs.
Democratic politician (to Workingman):
"Kill the Goose and get all your eggs at once."

Bernard Gillam in "Judge," 1888.

The 19th century in cartoons

To the public of the 19th century the cartoon was the most popular art of the times. It was propagated in countless magazines whose circulation soon extended throughout Europe and to many other parts of the globe as well. Politically, sociologically and in almost every other way, the century is best illustrated through the drawings of the thousands of cartoonists who plied their trade in its midst.

Humor magazines flourished all over Germany from the 1840s on. In 1844 the *Fliegende Blätter* was founded in Munich and over the years became a hospitable haven for all varieties of graphic artists. In its pages Wilhelm Busch published some of his most celebrated series; Adolf Oberländer developed his comic pages there, and it also boasted the cartoons of Carl Spitzweg and Moritz von Schwind. The *Fliegende Blätter* introduced a whimsical style of drawing and an innovative technique of graphic narration that would evolve into the comic strips of the late 19th century. Other German-language humor journals of note before the 1890s were the Berlin-based *Kladderadatsch* (founded in 1848), the Munich-based *Punsch* (the most political in its outspoken anti-Prussian cartoons) and *Kikeriki* (Joseph Keppler published his first cartoons there), *Der Floh* and the *Wiener Witzblatt,* all published in Vienna. The German school of cartooning thus established itself alongside the French and British schools.

"By Jove! It is slippery."

A Slippery Day
"Oh, hang these slanting pavements!"

"A man does have to have command of his feet on these bad spots."

An 1883 multi-panel cartoon by A.B. Frost.

The Power of the Human Eye
E.W. Kemble in "Puck," 1895.

The rest of Europe was not long in following suit. In Spain there appeared *El Sol* and especially *Don Quijote*; in Italy *Il Fischietto, L'Arlecchino* and *Don Perlino* were the more notable publications; and humor journals sprang up in Prague *(Humoristické Listy)*, Budapest (*Ustökös*), Warsaw (*Mucha*) and Amsterdam (*Notenkraker*), among many other places. The ferment was felt even in Russia, with the founding in the 1850s of *Svistok* (1859-65) and *Iskra* (1859-73), two satirical magazines that sometimes made fun of Russian institutions, but without questioning their legitimacy.

From Europe the humor magazine format migrated to the Americas. In the United States it remained largely unexploited until the 1870s, cartoons instead appearing mainly in almanacs derived from the English tradition and in such periodicals as *Leslie's Illustrated* and *Harper's Weekly*. (The remarkable flowering of American humor magazines in the last third of the 19th century will be treated in a separate part of this essay.) In Latin America the influence came from Spain and Portugal, and to a lesser extent from France (in Argentina, however, the leading humor publication of the time, *El Mosquito*, was founded in 1863 by a Frenchman, Henri Meyer, and later edited by another Frenchman, Henri Stein).

The British tradition was upheld in the most far-flung provinces of the empire, even traveling to Australia, where the *Melbourne Punch* appeared in 1855 and *Table Talk* in 1885. There was also a *Punch in Canada.* After the opening of Japan, there was inevitably a *Japan Punch*, founded in 1857 by the English-born Charles Wirgman, and mainly read by Englishmen in Japan. Japanese-language humor magazines soon followed, among them *Nipponchi* (1874), *Marumaru Chinbun* (1877) and *Tobae* (1888). By the last decade of the 19th century the humor magazine was an established institution in almost all parts of the globe.

The American humor magazines

American cartooning experienced a renaissance after the Civil War, and a number of humor magazines on the European model sprang up across the land. Titles included Frank Leslie's *Budget of Fun, Wild Oats, Jolly Joker, Phunny Phellow, Yankee Notions* and *Phunniest Kind of Phun*; all of them were short-lived.

It took Austrian-born Joseph Keppler to establish the first long-lasting, genuinely American humor magazine. It was called *Puck*, and after several false starts, it began publication in German in 1876, adding an English version the next year. The success of *Puck* was assured when it went into full-color reproduction a few years later, thus adding sparkle and dazzle to the cartoons. These were contributed primarily by Keppler himself, who later added James Wales and F.B. Opper to his staff. In its early years *Puck* was chiefly a magazine of political opinion, and its fervor reached a pitch every four years during presidential elections (its notorious campaign against Blaine is recounted elsewhere in this encyclopedia). *Puck*'s popularity continued unabated throughout the 1880s as more talented cartoonists were added to its ranks, among them C.J. Taylor, A.B. Frost, Louis Dalrymple, E.W. Kemble and Michael Angelo Woolf. By the end of the decade the magazine had achieved a balance between political concerns and purely humorous subjects, a mix that was subsequently retained.

Spurred on by *Puck*'s success, more humor magazines began to appear: *Chic, Truth, Tid-Bits, Rambler, Wasp*, etc. They all soon vanished from the scene with the exception of *Judge*, which started publication (as *The Judge*) in 1881. *Judge* relied on its cartoonists even more than *Puck*, which also employed some good humor writers. Its editors were able to gather a fine staff, including Wales (who came over from *Puck*), Frank Beard, Thomas Worth, Grant Hamilton and Frank Bellew. The contents were too close to *Puck*'s, however, and it was decided to reorganize the publication. Bernard Gillam was brought over from *Puck*, *Judge* took on a Republican hue (*Puck* had Democratic leanings), and the late 1880s witnessed a resurgence in *Judge's* sales and popularity.

Judge was soon followed (in January 1883) by *Life*, the brainchild of architect and illustrator John Ames Mitchell. The new magazine was an unmitigated disaster for the first several issues, but Mitchell persisted and *Life* began to turn a profit after a few years. In contrast to its competitors, *Life* had no color pages, depending on its staff of writers and above all on its cartoonists to attract a readership. Its early artists included Palmer Cox, F.G. Attwood, W.A. Rogers and C.G. Bush, all excellent draftsmen. It was, however, a young newcomer to the profession who made *Life's* fortune: Charles Dana Gibson, who sold his first cartoon to the magazine in 1886 and soon established himself as one of America's leading cartoonists.

By 1890 the trinity of *Puck, Judge* and *Life* had achieved unchallenged preeminence in the humor field. Their outlook, at first inspired by the English, French and German schools, had become typically American; the style and the tone of their cartoons were distinctly indigenous. With their emergence, the United States took its place in the front rank of world cartooning.

The golden age of the cartoon: 1890-1914

The decades around the turn of the century witnessed an extraordinary surge in the number, quality and popularity of humor magazines and of cartoons generally. There were literally hundreds of cartoon publications flourishing all over the world, and they reached unheard-of heights of success. Of necessity this study will limit itself to the more popular or distinguished of these publications.

Nowhere was there greater demand for graphic humor than in Paris. The years following the establishment of the Third Republic had seen a flowering of new publications which now reached maturity. *Le Rire, La Vie Parisienne, Le Journal Amusant, Gil Blas, Le Chat Noir* and *Le Courrier Français* were the most celebrated, but there were countless others. In their pages, exceptionally talented cartoonists like Jean-Louis Forain, Caran d'Ache, Alexandre Steinlen and Adolphe Willette gave free rein to their fantasies and convictions. In addition, some of the greatest artists of the time often contributed (sometimes pseudonymously) to these journals, including Toulouse-Lautrec, Jacques Villon, Felix Vallotton, Jules Pascin, Kees van Dongen and Juan Gris. The most impressively artistic of all the magazines was *L'Assiette au Beurre,* which in the course of its ten-year existence (1901-12) featured the work of the most illustrious names in the profession and also gave such newcomers as the Czech František Kupka and the Greek Dimitrius Galanis a start.

L'Assiette's most outstanding rival in these years was *Simplicissimus,* which had been founded in Munich in 1896. *Der Simpl* (as it was affectionately known) was not as radical as its French counterpart, but it nonetheless ran into difficulties with

Studies in Expression: When women are jurors.
One of the famous Gibson Girl cartoons drawn by Charles Dana Gibson for "Life" at the turn of the century.

Good Advertisement: "I used your soap two years ago: since then I have used no other."
Harry Furniss in "Punch," 1884.

the authorities on a few occasions. Some remarkable cartoonists worked for the publication: T.T. Heine, Bruno Paul, Eduard Thöny, Rudolf Wilke, Heinrich Zille and Heinrich Kley are probably the best known. *Der Simpl* also attracted talent from other countries, artists like the Norwegian Olaf Gulbransson, the Czech Alfred Kubin and the Austrian Ferdinand von Reznicek. Other humor magazines also flourished on German soil, among them *Jugend, Pan* (both employed many of the *Simplicissimus* artists) and *Ulk* (which published the first cartoons of Lyonel Feininger), in addition to the established periodicals of earlier periods.

In England *Punch* was enjoying one of its richest periods. To its prestigious roster of talented artists were added the likes of Bernard Partridge. Harry Furniss, Phil May, Leonard Raven-Hill and Max Beerbohm. Together they wove a scintillating tapestry of British life, all the way from May's slum shenanigans to Beerbohm's upper-class snobberies. Comic papers proliferated in this period, the most notable being *Comic Cuts* and *Illustrated Chips* (both born in 1890) and *Larks* (1893).

In the rest of Europe there were *such* innovative publications as *Cu-Cut!, L'Esquella de la Torratxa* and *Es Quatre Gats* (the young Pablo Picasso published his first drawings there) in Barcelona, and *Madrid Cómico* (where Juan Gris made his debut); Italy had *L'Asino* and *Il Travaso,* Switzerland *Nebelspalter;* even Russia had its first satirical magazine in decades, the short-lived *Zhupel,* which appeared for one year after the abortive revolution of 1905.

In the United States *Puck, Judge* and *Life* were thriving. The talent that was in evidence in their pages was never to be surpassed, not even in the heyday of the *New Yorker. Puck* could boast L.M. Glackens, J.S. Pughe, Rose O'Neill, Will Crawford and A.Z. Baker; *Judge* had Emil Flohri, Victor Gillam, T.S. Sullivant and James Montgomery Flagg (who created *Nervy Nat* there), not to mention Johnny Gruelle and Zim; while the staff of *Life* included Hy Mayer, "Chip" Bellew, Harrison Cady and of course Gibson, whose "Gibson Girl" was sweeping America. Art Young also worked for these magazines, but he gave the best of himself in his drawings for the *Masses* (1911-17), a radical publication that also attracted John Sloan, Boardman Robinson and George Bellows.

After the Strike: "Glad to see you back . . . so you're the fellows who wanted to starve us out!"
Alexandre Steinlen in "L'Assiette au Beurre," 1901.

Humor magazines were spanning the globe in an unprecedented outburst of creativity—*Grip* in Canada, *D. Quixote, O Malho* and *O Tagarela* in Brazil, *Caras y Caretas* and *Don Quijote* in Argentina, *Cómico* and *La Tarantula* in Mexico, the *Rambler* (where Norman Lindsay first appeared) in Australia and *Tokyo Puck* in Japan, to name some of the more notable. This brilliant epoch (of which the cartoons were often a reflection) came to an end with the opening shots of World War I, never to return.

Between the wars

In the course of the hostilities most humor magazines either disappeared or became shrilly patriotic (such was the case with *Simplicissimus* and *Punch*). The few publications that were born in this period reflected the grimness of the times; none survived, with the exception of the iconoclastic *Le Canard Enchaîné* in Paris. *Puck* lived its last years in the shadow of the war, and it is fitting that its star car-

Art Young in "The Masses."

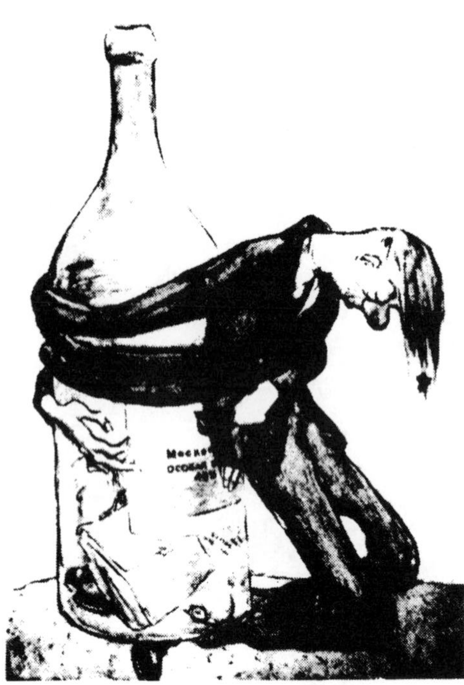

Strong Attachment
A Kukryniksy cartoon from "Krokodil."

toonist from 1917 until its demise in 1918 was the Dutch artist Louis Raemakers, whose savage anti-German cartoons helped swing American opinion to the side of the Allies.

The end of the war provided a general release and an outburst of renewed optimism and jollity. In France such magazines as *Le Rire* and *La Vie Parisienne* experienced a rebirth of creativity (before turning more and more into "girlie" magazines). In England *Punch* replenished its stable of talented cartoonists with the likes of Frank Reynolds, George Belcher, Heath Robinson, Rowland Emett and C.K. Bird ("Fougasse"). *Simplicissimus,* with George Grosz as its leading artist, continued on a more somber course in Germany, and even in Fascist Italy there was a flowering of new humor publications such as *Bertoldo* before Mussolini cracked down on cartoonists. In the Soviet Union *Krokodil* made its appearance in 1922.

The greatest activity in the field took place in the United States. *Vanity Fair,* which saw the light of print in the early 1920s, boasted the work of Miguel Covarrubias, Ralph Barton and John Held. This was also the time of *Ballyhoo* and *College Humor* and, with such memorable creations as *Hazel, Butch, Little Lulu* and *The Mountain Boys,* of an explosion of cartoon humor in such established publications as the *Saturday Evening Post, Collier's, Esquire, Look* and *Liberty.*

The most important magazine in the field, however, proved to be the *New Yorker,* founded by Harold Ross in 1925. While not a humor magazine in the strict sense (most of its prose is deadeningly humorless, and its style of reporting arch if not downright fatuous), the *New Yorker* changed the tone and tenor of the magazine cartoon. "The *New Yorker,*" Ross announced in messianic tones, "will be a magazine which is not edited for the old lady in Dubuque," and his cartoonists reflected the sophisticated, irreverent aims of the magazine. The drawings of Carl Rose, James Thurber, Charles Addams and above all Peter Arno were symbolic of a time and a mood that managed to last (at least in pages of the *New Yorker*) well into World War II.

The Depression left the *New Yorker* relatively unscathed but played havoc with the rest of the magazines. *Life* ceased publication and sold its title to Time, Incorporated, in 1936, though *Judge* managed to limp along, a ghost of its former self, into the late 1940s. In Germany, in Italy, in Japan, the dictators clamped down on humor, while the rest of the world waited joylessly for the storm to break.

The current scene

Many of the magazines that had weathered the Depression did not survive the war. In France the humor publications were turned into vehicles of Nazi and anti-

Secondhand Shop: Military and courtly goods are being disposed of cheaply.
Heinrich Kley in "Simplicissimus," 1918.

Black humor by "Siné." © Siné.

Semitic propaganda or disappeared one by one into the long night of the German occupation. In Italy *Bertoldo* was soon gone; and in Germany *Simplicissimus* and the hoary *Kladderadatsch* both stopped publication in 1944.

After the end of the war there was a concerted effort all over the world to go back to the old magazine format, with varied results. Revived versions of *La Vie Parisienne* and *Simplicissimus* did not last long. *Punch* continued a seemingly unflappable career, bringing to the fore such new talent as Ronald Searle, Gerald Scarfe and "Anton" (all of whom it often had to share with the upstart *Lilliput*). In the United States the *New Yorker* suffered a marked decline in quality after the death of Ross in 1952. Its new cartoonists (such as Dana Fradon, Frank Modell and Jack Ziegler) are a talented lot, and Saul Steinberg is in a class by himself, but the vaunted *New Yorker* humor is now largely unfocused, and its themes have been allowed to grow increasingly stale.

The new development in magazine humor has come in the form of the black humor magazines, a trend that developed fully after the 1950s. In France *Bizarre* (where Siné held sway) was a forerunner of the genre, which is best represented today in the pages of *Hara-Kiri* and *Charlie* (J.M. Reiser and Gébé are two of its mainstays). Italy has *Il Male,* and Spain *Hermano Lobo.* Their counterpart in England is *Private Eye.* The form never caught on in the United States, with the possible exception of the *National Lampoon,* where black humor is definitely a minority trend, drowned in torrents of sophomoric pranks, bad taste and scatology.

Signs of trouble, however, became apparent as early as the 1960s with humor magazines closing one after the other. The loss of the *Saturday Evening Post* was particularly troublesome. (It underwent a revival in the 1990s, but has so far proved only a pale shadow of its former self.) The "adult" magazines, *Playboy,* chief among them, took up some of the slack, and such cartoonists as Eldon Dedini and Gahan Wilson were made famous in its pages.

The state of the humor magazines today is as uncertain as the future of Western civilization, but it is safe to assume that a form that has been able to weather all the calamities of the 20th century will survive, no matter what happens next.

Maurice Horn

After the Orgy: "Give a belch, Ted, poverty tears my heart out!"

A 1926 George Grosz cartoon that seems to announce the horrors to come. © Simplicissimus.

Humor Cartooning In Russia: *Krokodil*

Krokodil *began publication in 1922 as the humor supplement to the weekly newspaper* Rabochaia Gazeta *("The Workers' Journal"). The Communist party editor and humor writer K.S. Eremeev was its founder and first editor. Humor writing was the weekly's forte, but it is for its cartoons that* Krokodil *is best known. In its pages appeared the works of such talented Soviet cartoonists as D.S. Moor, Mikhail Cheremnykh, Boris Efimov, Deni and Kukryniksy. In 1932 its success prompted Pravda Publishing House (its parent company) to issue Krokodil as an independent publication three times a month, and it has continued in that format ever since.*

The Soviet Encyclopedia *states that "*Krokodil *played a large part in establishing the principles of Soviet satire." These principles preclude any criticism of the Soviet government, the Communist party and established policies.* Krokodil's *humor, according to one of its own editorials, is aimed at "exposing bourgeois ideology and imperialistic reactionism." At the domestic level it pokes fun at the shortcomings and absurdities of Soviet life and bureaucracy, thereby providing an inoffensive safety valve for the citizenry's grievances. Over the years, two directives aimed at insuring that* Krokodil *would not overstep its bounds were issued from on high: "Decree of the Central Committee on the Magazine* Krokodil*" (1948) and "On the Shortcomings of the Magazine* Krokodil *and the Steps Needed to Eliminate Them" (1951).*

M.H.

Humor Cartooning In Denmark: *Hudibras*

A Danish magazine inspired by the examples of the New Yorker *and* La Vie Parisienne, Hudibras *was founded by Siegfried Cornelius and Asger Jerrild in 1943. From the start it was a forum for young, talented Danish cartoonists at a time when German censorship had cut off all contacts between Denmark and the outside world.*

Hudibras *(which comes out on the 13th of each month) had more ambitious aims than it could sustain for long. After the war it brought the newest trends in French and American humor to Scandinavia–spiced with what in those benighted times was considered pornography. In a cheerful, relaxed, broad-minded style, it blazed the way for changing views on sexual mores. It is still published monthly, but it no longer carries on the proud tradition of the 1940s.* Hudibras *today is merely a collection point for stale jokes, but as an institution and as the springboard for many talented Scandinavian cartoonists, its importance cannot be ignored.*

J.S.

The Animated Cartoon:

A World Summary

Frames from an early animated cartoon by Emile Cohl.

This encyclopedia provides the first comprehensive survey of cartoon animation throughout the world. Although there have been prior attempts at a worldwide history of the form, the results have always been fragmentary and largely inaccurate. Their fault lay in trying to fit the history of the animated cartoon (and of its extensions, the silhouette, cutout, painted and collage films) into the general history of the movies. The animated cartoon is part of the cinema in only a superficial and mechanical way—because it is preserved on film stock and usually projected onto a screen. Its aesthetics, however, differ markedly, and sometimes radically, from those of the film. Unlike the live cinema, animated films are created manually, prior to the photographic process; they are *reproduced,* not created on film. The animated cartoon derives not only etymologically but also artistically, historically and conceptually from the cartoon and the comic strip. This point was made in *The World Encyclopedia of Comics* (Chelsea House, 1976) but bears reiterating here. In the term *animated cartoon, cartoon* is the operative word, *animated* only the qualifier.

The origins

Man has tried from time immemorial to animate images. The first efforts gave rise to the Chinese shadow theater, early flip books and, closer to us, the magic lanterns of the 17th and 18th centuries. In the course of the 19th century, as the phenomenon known as persistence of vision came to be scientifically understood, it was inevitable that inventors would try to construct a device producing the optical illusion of movement. In 1834 W.G. Horner, a British watchmaker, invented the zoetrope, a revolving drum with slits allowing a spectator to look at moving images within the device. Horner had been preceded, however, by the Belgian scientist Joseph Plateau and his phénakistiscope (or phenakistoscope), a viewing device that was fitted with mirrors, and through which passed drawings painted on a cardboard disc. This 1832 invention allowed more realistic animation effects than had hitherto been achieved and is now regarded as the first successful try at genuine animation. (In 1974 the Japanese animator Taku Furukawa paid Plateau a deserved homage in the form of an animated color cartoon simply called *Phenakistoscope.*)

The French inventor Emile Reynaud took the process one step further with his praxinoscope; he was also the first to organize animation into a spectacle, in 1892 opening a special theater, the Théâtre Optique, where he projected a show completely consisting of skits enacted with animated drawings. His invention, however, could not keep pace with the rapid development of the movie camera, and on the level of simple entertainment, he found himself unable to compete with the trick films of Georges Méliès. Thus, the optical simulation of movement had apparently led to a dead end.

The heroic period: 1906-1918

Despite Reynaud's efforts, it therefore seemed inevitable that animation should go in the direction of the moving picture. The reproduction of images by the movie camera was much more reliable than the results achieved through mechanical means, and Méliès's films had shown that an almost infinite variety of tricks could be accomplished through judicious cutting and editing. It fell to J.S. Blackton, who was both a newspaper cartoonist and a filmmaker, to consummate the marriage between the cartoon and the cinema; with the making in 1906 of the first cartoon film, *Humorous Phases of Funny Faces,* he indisputably earned the title "father of modern animation."

Blackton's discovery—"one turn (of the camera crank), one picture"—was also being explored in Europe at about the same time. In England Walter Booth made the 1906 *Hand of the Artist* (in which a hand is seen tracing a figure that later comes

These cave drawings found near Tassili-n-Ajjer in the Sahara desert capture the essence of motion in an uncanny way.

to life) and other film cartoons. The most important cartoonist of this early period, however, was the Frenchman Emile Cohl, who made over two hundred films between 1908 and 1918 and created *le fantôche,*the first hero of a cartoon film series.

In 1912 Cohl went to New York in recognition of the fact that leadership in film animation was passing from France to the United States, thanks to the enthusiastic efforts of pioneers such as Blackton, J.R. Bray, Earl Hurd, Raoul Barré (a Canadian working in New York) and, above all, Winsor McCay. It was the public showing in 1914 of McCay's *Gertie, the Trained Dinosaur* that crystallized the diffuse aspirations of the early animators. Cohl, who was there along with every other cartoonist in New York, later reported the event in these terms: "On the stage, in front of the screen, McCay stood, in evening dress, whip in hand. He started a little speech; then, going back to the screen, like a lion tamer he gave an order to the beast, which came out from behind the rocks. Always under the command of the tamer, it gave an exhibition of acrobatic skill; the dinosaur jumped,

...utour d'une Cabine" ("Around a Cabin"), an early animated cartoon by Emile Reynaud.

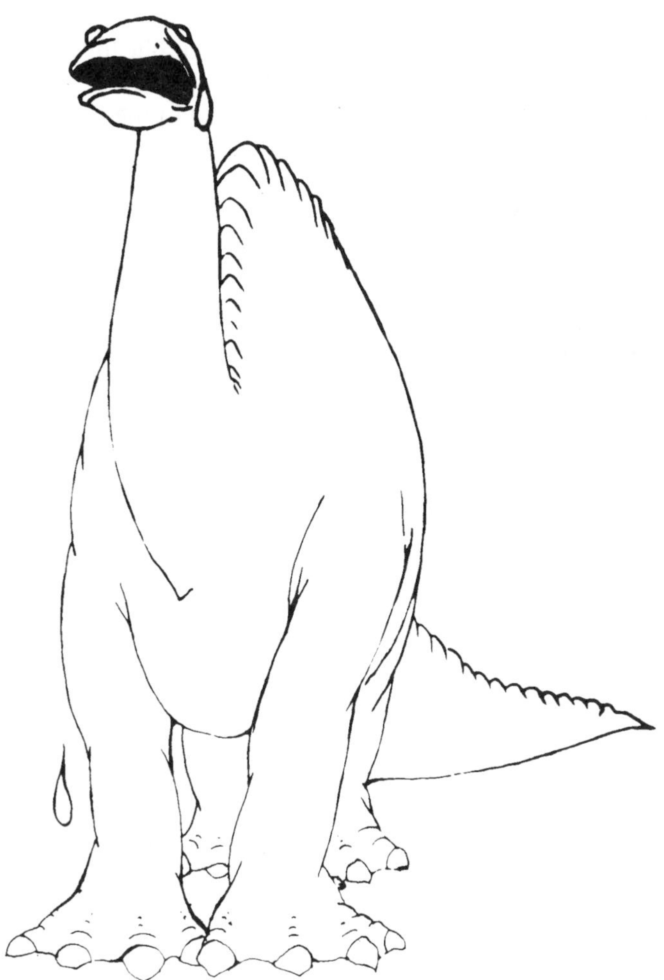

"Gertie the Trained Dinosaur," Winsor McCay's trailblazing animated film. © Winsor McCay.

danced, uprooted trees and finally took a bow in front of the wildly applauding audience."

McCay's cartoon proved that animation had the potential to become a genuine art form. Just as important, other American animators sought ways of making it a viable commercial enterprise as well. The key was to reduce the tremendous amount of labor involved in a few minutes of screen animation. Gradually, economies were realized through the introduction of technical innovations like the peg system, cel transparency, in-betweening and rotoscopy, which dramatically cut the costs of producing an animated cartoon. So did the generalization of the studio system, with its rational organization of work and its consistency of output. The first true animation studios were established by Bray and Barré in the mid-1910s. W.R. Hearst, always attracted by new media, formed the short-lived International Film Service in 1916. Others (Pat Sullivan, W.A. Carlson, the Fleischer brothers) soon followed. Despite some competition from Europeans (Cohl in France, Dudley Buxton in England, Victor Bergdahl in Sweden) the American animators seemed to have taken the lead in the budding field.

The studio system had its commercial corollary in the star system (also adopted from the film industry). Animation's "stars" were either borrowed from the newspaper comics (the Katzenjammer Kids, Krazy Kat, Mutt and Jeff) or developed by studio artists (Colonel Heezaliar, Bobby Bumps, Dreamy Dud). In either case their function was to establish the immediate rapport of recognition and familiarity between the cartoon and its audience. Thus was the concept of the cartoon series firmly entrenched in commercial practice.

Towards an art of animation

The early cartoons were of course silent. To convey dialogue, they had recourse to the word balloon, a device borrowed from the comic strip. After 1918, however, these balloons were gradually abandoned in favor of intertitles (borrowed from the movies), which could be more easily translated for sales to foreign markets—

Otto Messmer's "Felix the Cat." © King Features Syndicate.

Aleksandr Ivanov's "Zay and Chick."

a recognition of the growing internationalization of the animation medium, its practitioners and its public following World War I.

World War I also proved that the animated cartoon had definite advantages over live-action films in the teaching of new skills and methods: Bray, Hurd, the Fleischers, all honed their craft by making instructional films for the armed forces, as did Buxton and Anson Dyer in England and Benjamin Rabier in France. There was now an extraordinary flowering of animation filmmaking throughout the world: if American animators were still the most productive, they were no longer unchallenged.

France and England remained two hotbeds of activity, the former with the winsome cartoon fables of Rabier and the witty confections of O'Galop, the latter with the achievements of Dyer, Buxton and especially G.E. Studdy, who created the successful canine character Bonzo. Even more striking was the burst of creativity in the USSR following the appearance of the first Soviet cartoon, Aleksandr Bushkin's *Soviet Toys* (1924). Nikolay Khodataev, Aleksandr Ivanov, Ivan Ivanov-Vano, Mikhail Tsekhanovsky and the Brumberg sisters were among the innovative artists working in the Soviet Union in the 1920s. Animation also came to Japan, spearheaded by the pioneering efforts of Sanae Yamamoto; and Aurel Petrescu founded the Romanian animation industry almost single-handed in 1920. There were animators at work in Germany, Italy, Spain, Argentina, China, everywhere.

In the United States the animated cartoon was enjoying unprecedented popular success. By the 1920s production was booming; in addition to the established series (*Mutt and Jeff, Colonel Heezaliar),* there were new characters coming to the fore. Max Fleischer brought the bouncing Ko-Ko the Clown to the screen, Paul Terry was moderately successful with Farmer Al Falfa, and J.R. Bray was constantly trying out new characters, such as Dinky Doodle, while continuing the cartoon adventures of such earlier Hearst favorites as the Katzenjammers and Krazy Kat. None was as successful, however, as Pat Sullivan's *Felix the Cat* series, ably animated and directed by Otto Messmer. Felix was the indisputable screen cartoon star of the 1920s, as well as the first widely merchandised cartoon character.

Parallel with commercial production, avant-garde animation was springing up all over Europe. The Dadaists and later the Surrealists enthusiastically embraced the medium of animation as they had earlier embraced the medium of film. Experimental animation especially flourished in Germany in the hands of Viking Eggeling, Walter Ruttmann, Hans Richter and Julius Pinschewer, among others. The most seminal animated film, however, proved to be Fernand Léger's *Ballet Mécanique* (1924), which was later called "the ultimate poem of motion."

The innovations wrought by the experimental animators were not lost on the commercial cartoonists. On the threshold of sound, the silent cartoon had achieved a harmonious equilibrium of action, imagery and symbol that was as accomplished as anything in the contemporary cinema. (The most dramatic and convincing illustration of this development is Ronald Schwarz's remarkable screen compilation of silent cartoons, *Early American Cartoons 1900-1920.*)

Walt Disney and the era of sound

Most of the early animation activity in the United States centered on the East Coast. Laboring in Los Angeles, a young cartoonist named Walt Disney was turning out such silent series as *Alice in Cartoonland* and *Oswald the Rabbit* when he became convinced that sound animation was the only way his studio could forge ahead of the competition. There had been a number of American and European experiments (some of them successful) in bringing sound to the animated cartoon, but Disney produced the first cartoon with a synchronized sound track: "Steamboat Willie," the first *Mickey Mouse* cartoon. Upon its release in 1928, it caused as great a sensation as *Gertie* had more than a decade earlier. The following year, not content to rest on his laurels, Disney brought out *Skeleton Dance,* the first of his *Silly Symphonies.* He later produced the first animated cartoon entirely shot on color film stock (earlier efforts had been hand-colored) and crowned his studio's achievement with the release in 1937 of *Snow White and the Seven Dwarfs,* the first successful feature-length animated film. This period was indeed "the reign of Disney."

The Prize Dance," a 1920 cartoon produced by the Bray studio. © Bray Studios.

Mickey Mouse in "Shanghaied," 1934 © Walt Disney Productions.

Betty Boop coming out of the inkwell. © Max Fleischer.

There has been a tendency in recent times to downgrade Disney's personal role in the success of his studio. Granted that he left most of the actual animation work to others (notably to the talented Ub Iwerks), the decisions at the studio were chiefly his, if not his alone. He was the one with the vision to constantly innovate and diversify. Under his guidance, his studio attracted the most brilliant and talented artists and writers; the characters they created—Mickey, Donald Duck, Pluto, Goofy—were the equals of any Hollywood star. Not only were the Disney cartoons wildly popular (many of them outdrew the feature films they shared the bill with), but they were also outstanding in style and content. It is no coincidence that Disney won every Academy Award in animation from the inception of the category in 1932 until 1940. A major share of the credit for all these achievements must go to Disney himself.

The effects of the Disney revolution were felt throughout the world, but chiefly in Europe. The commercial studios in England and France could not withstand the competition, while the animators in the Soviet Union were instructed to slavishly copy the American style and methods. Outside the United States the field was left pretty much to individuals, such as the New Zealander Len Lye and the Canadian Norman McLaren working in Britain, Alexandre Alexeieff and Berthold Bartosch in France, and Kenzo Masaoka in Japan. In Germany, Oskar Fischinger began his research on sound and color animation, and Pinschewer pursued his in Switzerland.

With the exception of Mary Ellen Bute and a few other experimenters, U.S. animation remained the sole province of the cartoon studios. The success of the Disney shorts had created a demand for cartoon shorts to play alongside live features, and several former Disney employees set up their own production units: Hugh Harman and Rudolph Ising produced *Bosko* and the Happy Harmonies cartoons, and Ub Iwerks created *Flip the Frog,* among other series, before returning to the Disney fold. Among earlier animators, Walter Lantz was turning out *Oswald the Rabbit* (taken over from Disney) and *Andy Panda* cartoons. Leon Schlesinger, the most enterprising of the new producers, was intent on turning out a cheap version of the Disney product. ("Disney can make the chicken salad," he is reported to have said. "I wanna make chicken shit.") In the course of the years he assembled a cast of cartoon characters (Porky Pig, Bugs Bunny, Daffy Duck) and a team of animators (Friz Freleng, Bob Clampett, Chuck Jones) that were later to rival Disney's.

Sound brought a new dimension to cartoons. It added dialogue, music, sound effects, characterization and punctuation to the visual goings-on. It also added costs, however, and almost spelled disaster for the older East Coast studios. Sullivan had died, Bray had left animation entirely, and Terry barely survived with his Terrytoons. The only one to hold his own in the 1930s was Fleischer; his diminutive cartoon vamp, Betty Boop, was a favorite of the public, while his *Popeye* cartoons vied in popularity with those of Disney. Encouraged by his success, Fleischer decided in the late 1930s to challenge Disney on his own ground—the animated feature—and this eventually led to his downfall.

Feature animation

Snow White was not the world's first animated cartoon feature. A 60-minute cartoon, *El Apóstol*, had been released in Argentina as early as 1917. In 1926 Lotte Reiniger had produced *The Adventures of Prince Achmed*, but it was a silhouette film, not a cartoon. In the 1930s stirrings were felt all over the world—in France, England, Italy, the Soviet Union, Japan, Argentina—but the various efforts at full-length animation either were left incomplete or received only limited distribution. The success of *Snow White* changed all that.

An animated feature (generally defined as 60 minutes or more in duration) differs from a cartoon short not only in terms of length, increased production costs and expanded manpower but also, and more fundamentally, in aesthetic terms. Because of its time frame, a feature requires greater integration of the parts with the whole, and therefore a sharper definition of the characters, a more consistent story line and a heavier reliance on cinematic (as differentiated from animation) techniques. The feature cartoon is infinitely closer to the live cinema in style, nar-

A frame from "Pinocchio." © Walt Disney Productions.

"Gerald McBoing Boing." © UPA.

rative and dramatic technique than is the cartoon short, and is probably as close as the cartoon will ever come to film. Disney understood this: he planned *Snow White* as if it were a live feature, with separate direction of his cartoon "actors" and camera treatment of the various "shots."

Disney enjoyed for a long time a near monopoly on feature cartoon filmmaking. He refined and perfected his technique in *Pinocchio* (1940), *Dumbo* (1941) and *Bambi* (1942). *Fantasia* (1940) marked a departure for the studio in that it was commercially unrewarding but artistically successful. By the late 1940s the Disney studio had the formula down pat and was able to turn out feature after feature without interruptions, even after Disney's death in 1966. Fleischer was the only other American producer to turn to feature animation: in 1939 *Gulliver's Travels* was completed in his new Florida studio. It was moderately successful, but the 1941 *Mr. Bug Goes to Town* was a disaster, leading to the takeover of the Fleischer studio by Paramount. It was a long time before another American studio (UPA with *1001 Arabian Nights* in 1959) challenged Disney's supremacy in the field.

Disney's undisputed dominance also inhibited the growth of theatrical feature cartoons in the rest of the world (though a full-length animated cartoon was made for propaganda purposes in Japan in 1943). A few dates suffice to prove the point: the first Soviet feature (*The Hunchbacked Horse*) came out in 1948, as did the first two Italian features. France followed in 1950 with *Jeannot l'Intrépide,* and the British *Animal Farm* was released only in 1954. As the 1950s rolled along, Disney's grip on the public relaxed and more features came out. Today animated features are produced in many of the countries of the world.

The golden age of American animation: 1940-1959

Film historians are fond of referring to the 1930s as "the golden age of American animation," but the period should more properly be called "the golden age of Disney," with the other studios (except Fleischer) riding on his coattails. The two decades following the 1930s, by contrast, saw an explosion in both quantity of output and excellence of execution from almost all the cartoon studios as Disney's leadership in the animation field slowly slipped away. The first cracks appeared in the early 1940s, underlined by the symbolic loss of the Oscar in 1940 (to Ising's

"Tom and Jerry." © MGM.

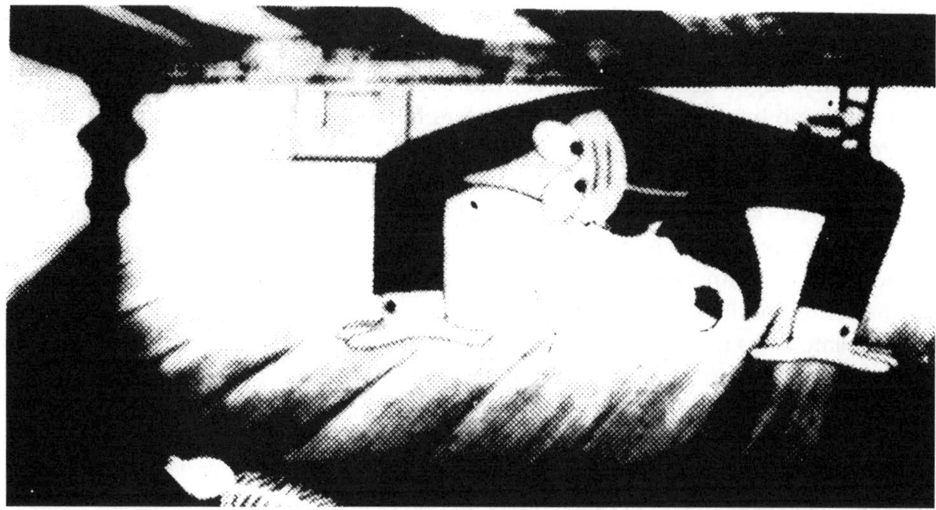

"The Devil on Springs."

"The Devil on Springs." © Barandov Studio. In the post-World War II period, many animators attempted to explore the nature of totalitarianism. Jiří Trnka's "The Devil on Springs" (1946) examined the evils of Nazism, while the 1954 "Animal Farm," based on George Orwell's novel, focussed on the Stalinist variety.

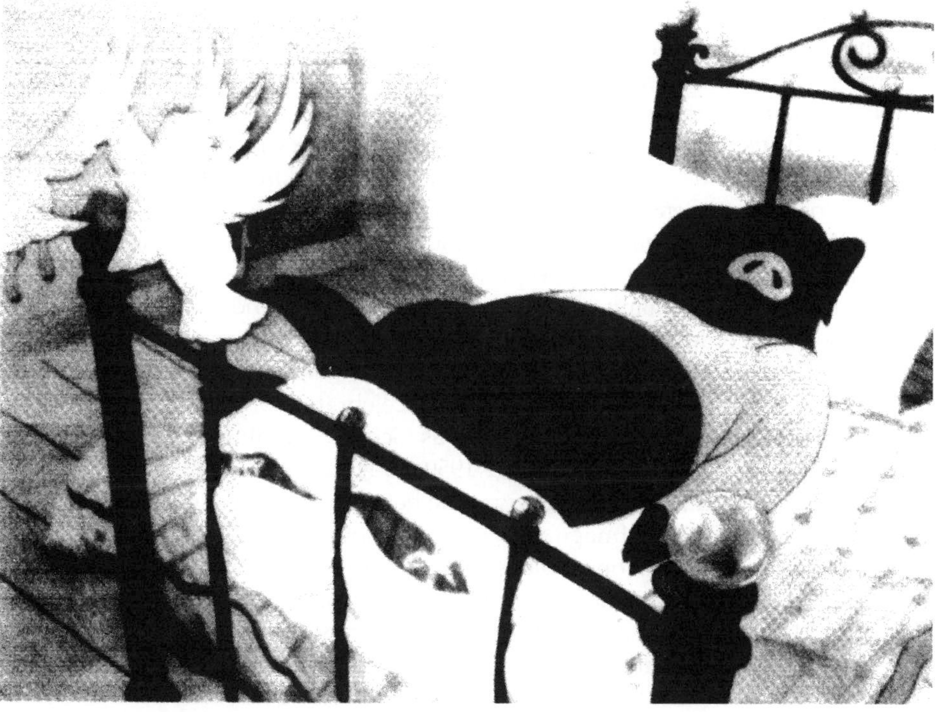

"Animal Farm." © Halas and Batchelor.

Milky Way) and the bitter animators' strike in 1941. In feature animation Disney remained supreme, but in the short subject department his rivals slowly began to overtake him in popularity, style and invention.

At Warner Brothers, animation directors were displaying a verbal wit, visual outrageousness and outlandish humor that the more sedate Disney animators were unwilling to match. At MGM Joe Barbera and Bill Hanna's *Tom and Jerry* cartoons were out-Disneying Disney in lavishness of production and excellence of draftsmanship, while Tex Avery was creating a much-admired style of animation based on frenetic pacing and endless gag building. At Columbia Frank Tashlin was developing the trailblazing *Fox and Crow* series, while Walter Lantz created Woody Woodpecker for Universal. Even Terry emerged from his somnolence with two winning creations: Supermouse (later renamed Mighty Mouse, to Disney's everlasting annoyance) and Heckle and Jeckle.

In the 1950s the upstart UPA (United Productions of America) came to the fore and established itself by contradicting all the tenets of animation filmmaking taught by Disney (to add insult to injury, UPA was chiefly staffed with Disney defectors). UPA gave free rein to the imagination and talent of its directors (John

John Hubley, "The Hat." © Storyboard, Inc.

Hubley, Pete Burness and others), who responded with some of the most innovative cartoons ever produced and created such outlandish characters as the nearsighted Mr. Magoo and the weird-sounding Gerald McBoing Boing.

At the same time, independent producers felt free to establish their own styles and to pursue their own research, thus bridging the gap between commercial and experimental animation. The most notable were John Hubley (who had left UPA in the mid-1950s) and his wife, Faith, and Gene Deitch (director of animation for Terrytoons/CBS), who created memorable, if isolated, works of animation. Avant-garde cartoon filmmaking was also on the rise, with Robert Breer perhaps the most talented of the experimental animators.

In the late 1950s television definitively replaced movie theaters as the main outlet for animated cartoons. The cheapened standards of TV animation (limited movement, paucity of backgrounds, sloppy draftsmanship, tedious repetition) spelled the end of the golden age of animation.

Animation: a universal language

World War II disrupted the distribution and production channels of animated cartoons, but the resultant constriction of the world market also brought some benefits. The war created a huge domestic demand for propaganda and instructional cartoons, especially in the United States, Canada, Britain, the Soviet Union and Japan. It also shielded most countries from United States competition, which in turn gave rise to a great many national centers of production operating in isolation, a situation that lasted well into the 1950s. By the end of that decade animation had thus become a worldwide medium of expression.

Animation made its greatest strides during this period in Britain, where the animation unit of the General Post Office (established in the 1930s) had molded a good many young animators. Several studios were formed, chief among them Halas and Batchelor, which was responsible for the first British animated feature, *Animal Farm,* and for many other creations. The Halas and Batchelor studio is today one of the oldest animation units in existence. Perhaps even more startling was the creation almost from scratch of a Canadian animation industry centered around the National Film Board. Its most celebrated practitioner is Norman McLaren, but it also fostered such talents as George Dunning and Grant Munro. In France animation in the 1940s and 1950s was dominated by two men: Paul Grimault and Jean Image. Grimault was the better craftsman and produced some remarkable cartoons, but Image was the better organizer and achieved greater popular success with cartoons unabashedly patterned on the Disney formula.

The Soviet Union, despite an enormous output, was by this time mired in sterility. The earlier animators were still active but largely contented themselves with repeating the same themes over and over again. Not so the Eastern European countries, especially Czechoslovakia, where a flourishing animation industry had been developing since the war around Jiří Trnka (better known for his later puppet films). Trnka and other Czech animators (Bretislav Pojar, Eduard Hofman, Jiří Brdecka) brought a new freshness and a more exuberant style to the animated film, and the genial Karel Zeman has also distinguished himself. Poland also developed a remarkable group of animators that included Witold Giersz, Wladyslaw Nehrebecki and, above all, Walerian Borowczyk and Jan Lenica. Romania had Ion Popescu-Gopo, and a brand-new cartoon industry sprang up in Bulgaria under the tutelage of Todor Dinov.

In the 1950s Japanese production came out of the doldrums, and a number of new studios (Nihon Dōga, Toei Dōga) were established. China also enjoyed a rebirth of animation, spearheaded by the Wan brothers, who carried on their work even under the Japanese occupation and later nurtured a new generation of Chinese animators.

By the end of the 1950s all sorts of cartoons were being produced in almost every part of the world—Italy, Spain, Latin America, Belgium, Scandinavia. Most remarkable of all was the rise of animation in Yugoslavia, where a group of young newcomers revolutionized the art of cartoon filmmaking and founded what came to be called the "Zagreb school." The leader in these developments was Dušan Vukotić, the author of *Cowboy Jimmy, Concerto for Sub-machine Gun* and *Ersatz,* the first foreign cartoon ever to win an Oscar.

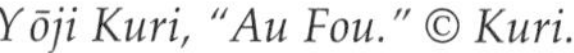

Yōji Kuri, "Au Fou." © Kuri.

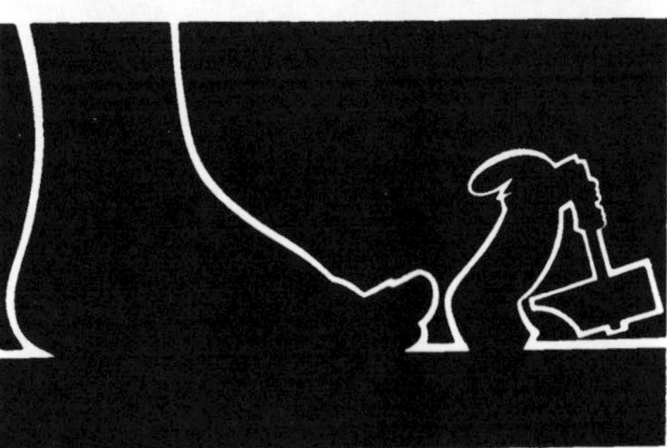

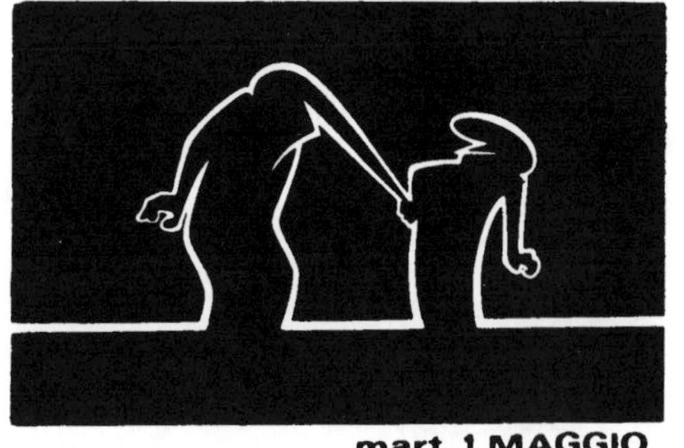

Osvaldo Cavandoli, "Lo Linea." © Cavandoli.

One world of animation

In the 1960s through the 1970s two major trends have surfaced in animation: the emergence of the *auteur* and the growing internationalization of the industry. The latter is dramatically symbolized by those artists who have voluntarily expatriated themselves, such as Gene Deitch, who has permanently settled in Prague, and Lenica and Borowczyk, who have consistently worked in Western Europe; but it is also evidenced by the increasing number of animated film co-productions and by the constant flow of animators from one country to another. Moreover, there is a growing tendency in countries with high labor costs (chiefly the United States) to contract production to studios located in less expensive countries.

The *auteur* has become the dominant figure in the animation medium, except among the studios busily engaged in churning out animation footage on an assembly line basis, mostly for television (Hanna-Barbera in the United States and Jean Image in France are two prime examples). There has been such an abundance of gifted animators in recent years that only a few of the more exalted can be cited here. Without a doubt Borowczyk (*Le Jeu des Anges, Le Théâtre de M. et Mme. Kabal*) and Lenica (*Adam II, Ubu-Roi*) are the two towering figures of contemporary animation and the creators of what might be called "animation of the absurd." In contrast, the Australian Bob Godfrey (*The Do-It Yourself Cartoon Kit, Great*) and the Canadian Dick Williams (*The Little Island, Love Me Love Me Love Me*), working in England, have created cartoons in the burlesque tradition of the early animators.

Buffoonery and slapstick are the keys to the animation work of the Italian Bruno Bozzetto (*The SuperVIPS, Allegro Non Troppo*), while the Japanese Yōji Kuri revels in black humor and sadistic themes. John Hubley (who died recently) and Ernest Pintoff (who no longer does animation work) were the most prominent *auteurs* in the United States. Only the Yugoslavs have preserved a semblance of cohesion (although their work has been declining lately), with Vukotić and such artists as Vatroslav Mimica, Borivoj Dovniković and Nedeljko Dragić trying to keep the Zagreb school alive.

Another striking feature of those two decades is the increase in the number of animated features being released. Every country seems intent on bringing out at least one full-length cartoon. The audience for such films has been considerably broadened with the introduction in recent times of "adult cartoons," notably Osamu

Dušan Vukotić's "Cowboy Jimmy." © *Zagreb Film.*

Tezuka's *A Thousand and One Nights* (1969) and Ralph Bakshi's *Fritz the Cat* (1972).

Experimental animation was also going strong in many places. Stan VanDerBeek (United States), Piotr Kamler (France), Osvaldo Cavandoli (Italy) and Taku Furukawa (Japan) are perhaps the best-known artists working in this mode. The lines between regular, experimental and underground animation are becoming more and more blurred, however, as the tendency towards one world of animation, conceptual as well as geographical, asserts itself. This tendency has been furthered by the proliferation of international animation festivals. While such festivals perform a useful function in bringing animators from all parts of the world together, they have also done a grave disservice by giving out a plethora of awards that have become as meaningless as they are numerous.

Animation at century's end

After the prolonged slump of the 1970s, the producers of theatrical cartoons started to rebound in the 1980s. Nowhere was the upsurge as marked as in the U.S., beginning with the Disney studio. With a new, younger generation at the helm, Disney embarked on an ambitious program of feature-length cartoon production based on its traditional strength, the musical fairy tale. This policy climaxed in the clamoring success of *The Little Mermaid* (1989), followed in the next decade by the no less acclaimed *Beauty and the Beast, Aladdin, The Lion King,* and *Toy Story.*

Other American studios tried to challenge Disney on its own grounds. Most successful was the company founded by former Disney animator Don Bluth; among its releases were *The Secret of NIMH, An American Tail, The Land Before Time,* and *Anastasia.* Steven Spielberg's animation arm, Amblimation, has produced *An American Tail, Fievel Goes West,* and *Balto.* Independently produced features of note have included *Fern Gully* and *The Adventures of Mark Twain.*

There has been production of full-length animated features going on in such countries as Britain (*Watership Down*), Canada (*Heavy Metal*), and Japan (*Little Nemo*), but none of these could stand up to American dominance in this field. In the short-subject department, however, the Europeans (and Canadians) have more than held their own in recent years, with such Oscar-winning films as *Creature Comforts* and *The Wrong Trousers* by the Englishman Nick Park and *The Fly* by the Hungarian Ferenc Rofusz. On television, while programs aimed at children on Saturday mornings ("kidvid"), a genre for which Americans and Japanese share equal responsibility, have remained for the most part mired in mediocrity, there have been efforts to upgrade the level of wit and sophistication in such prime-time offerings as *The Simpsons.*

Animation has never been as popular as it is today, in the waning years of the 20th century. Viewers flock to theatrical animated films in numbers not seen since the 1940s and 1950s; network and cable television alike churn out cartoon programs by the mile; and in 1993 Ted Turner was able to launch the very successful Cartoon Channel (followed in 1998 by Toon Disney). Special exhibitions on animation art and history have been held at such prestigious venues as the Museum of Modern Art and the Whitney Museum in New York and the Centre Pompidou in Paris. All these developments have led some enthusiastic supporters of the form to hail animation—perhaps prematurely—as "the art of the next century."

Maurice Horn

From Cartoon to Comic Strip:

A Pictorial Survey

In the second half of the 19th century, cartoons were organized into progressively more complex sequences of drawings. Such sequences were early antecedents of the comic strip, which evolved into an independent and distinct art form in the early years of the 20th century. Representative examples of this transition process follow.

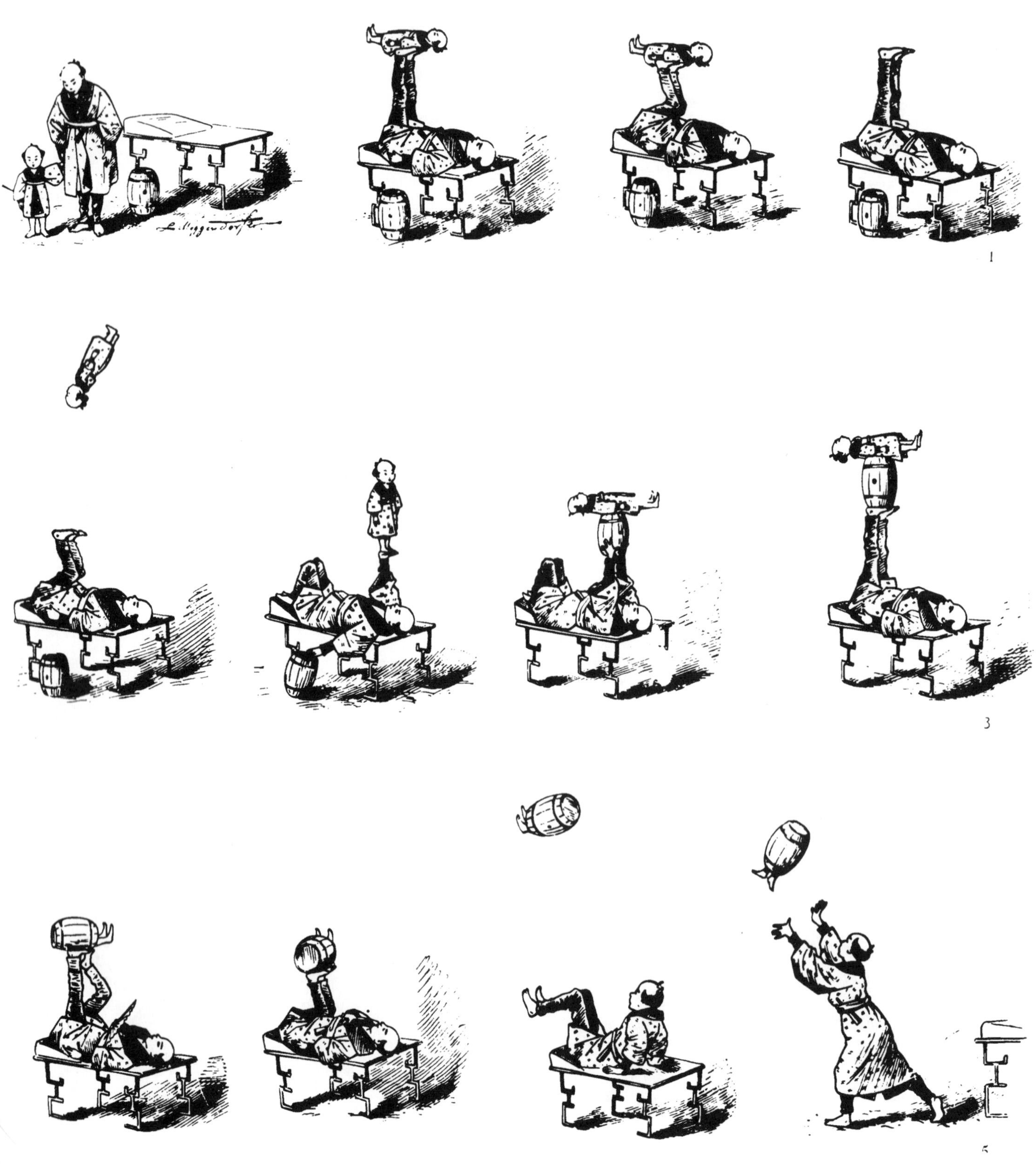

Meggendorfer, "Intermission," ca. 1875.

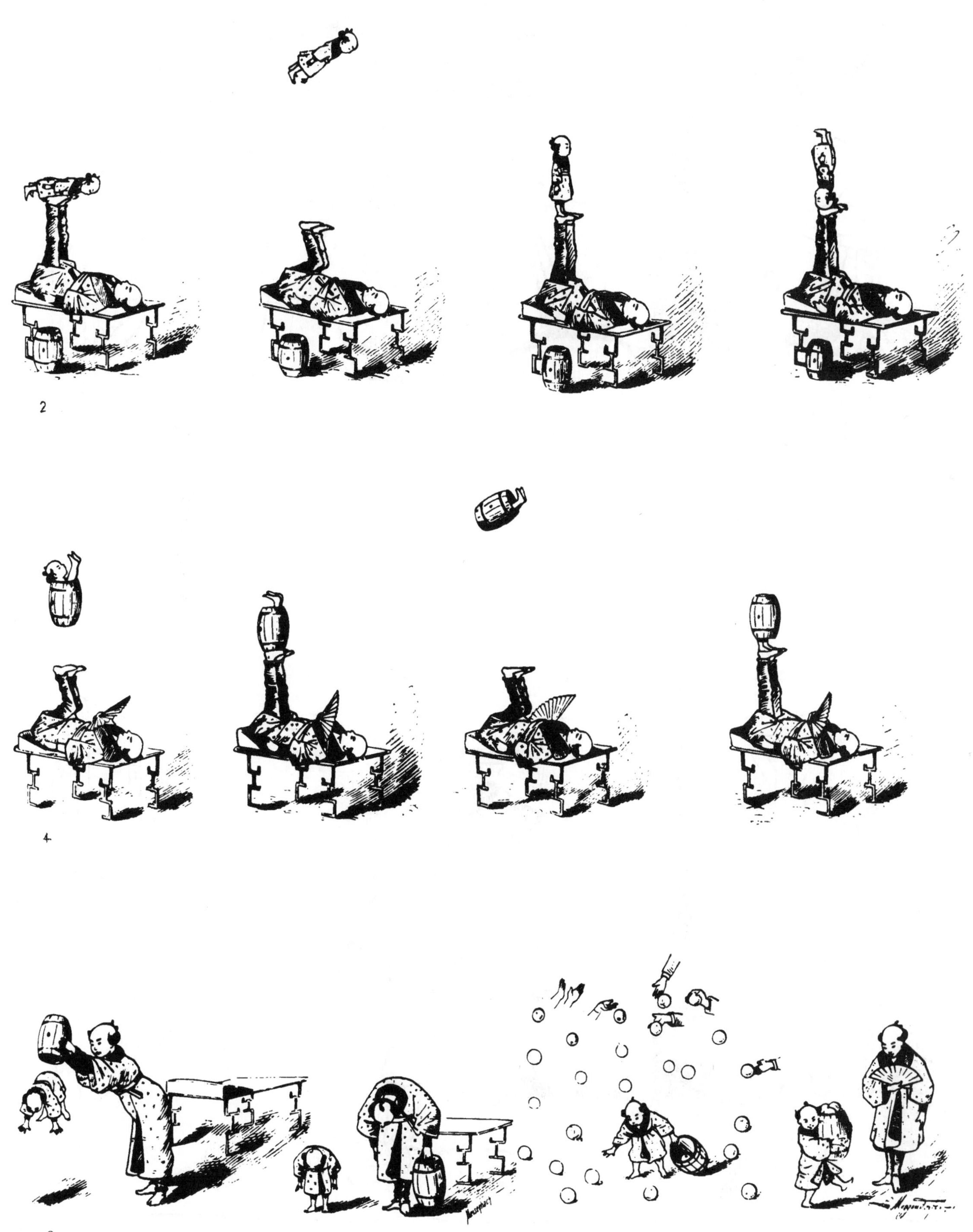

FROM CARTOON TO COMIC STRIP:

d'Ache, "The Arkansas Trapper's Mistake," ca. 1875.

3

4

FROM CARTOON TO COMIC STRIP:

5

6

7

8

FROM CARTOON TO COMIC STRIP:

1

2

5

6

'Ache, "The Cow Who Watched Trains Go By," ca. 1875

3

4

7

8

'Chip") Bellew, "The Tail Maketh the Dog," ca. 1880.

Frank ("Chip") Bellew, "An Explosive Hug," ca. 1880.

The
Fatal · Mistake ·

A · Tale · of · a · Cat ·

t, “The Fatal Mistake,” 1884.

1.

2.

3.

4.

FROM CARTOON TO COMIC STRIP:

6.

5.

7.

8.

9.

10.

11.

…rlander, "The Duel with the Fashionable Pointed Shoes," ca. 1885.

Alexandre Steinlen, "Love Story," ca. 1885.

A World Chronology of Cartoon Art

From the Renaissance to the Present

Francisco Goya, "Old Man on a Swing."

1563
Giuseppe Arcimboldo starts painting the first of his "composite heads."

1590-1600
The brothers Annibale and Agostino Carracci give birth to the term *caricature* with their *ritrattini carichi* ("loaded portraits").

1600-1700
Caricature as a genre flourishes in Italy, France, Germany, England and the Low Countries.

1734
William Hogarth publishes *A Harlot's Progress.*

1735
W. Hogarth publishes *A Rake's Progress.*

1745
W. Hogarth publishes *Marriage à la Mode.*

1754
Benjamin Franklin publishes "Join or Die," widely regarded as America's first national cartoon, in the *Pennsylvania Gazette.*

Guiseppe Arcimboldo, "Fire," 1566.

"The Tammany Tiger loose—what are you going to do about it?"

A Tammany cartoon by Thomas Nast, 1871.

1784
Thomas Rowlandson's first cartoons appear in England.

1788
Francis Grose's *Rules for Drawing Caricaturas* is published in London.

1790-1815
James Gillray publishes his series of patriotic and anti-French cartoons.

1799
Francisco Goya's *Los Caprichos* is published in Spain.

1809
T. Rowlandson produces his most famous cartoon series, *The Tour of Doctor Syntax.*

1814
The first volume of *Hokusai Manga* ("Hokusai's Cartoons") is published in Japan.

1829
Grandville's *Les Métamorphoses du Jour* is published in Paris.

1830
Charles Philipon founds *La Caricature* in Paris.

1831
Honoré Daumier is jailed for his caricatures of King Louis-Philippe of France.

1832
C. Philipon starts *Le Charivari* in Paris.
Joseph Plateau invents the phénakistiscope in Belgium.

1835
The first Currier and Ives lithographs are published in the United States.

1841
Punch magazine is founded in England as "the London Charivari."

Scenes of Family Life No. 2:
"Papa, what do you want to be when you grow up?"
A cartoon by T.T. Heine for "Simplicissimus" in its first year, 1896

1843
John Leech's "Cartoons for the Houses of Parliament" are published in *Punch.*

1844
Grandville's *Un Autre Monde* is published in France.
The *Fliegende Blätter* is founded in Munich.

1846
The first U.S. comic weekly, *Yankee Doodle,* is established in New York.

1848
Le Musée Philipon is published in Paris.
Kladderadatsch starts publication in Berlin.

1851
The Lantern, a humorous weekly, is started in New York, with Frank Bellew listed as one of the founders.

1857
Charles Wirgman founds *Japan Punch* in Tokyo.

1859
Vanity Fair (first version) is published in New York.
The satirical magazine *Iskra* starts publication in Russia.

1863
El Mosquito is established in Buenos Aires by Henri (Enrique) Meyer.

1868
Vanity Fair is founded in London.

1870
Thomas Nast's first Tammany cartoons start appearing in *Harper's Weekly*.
1874
Funny Folks is established in London.
La Caricature (third version) is founded in Paris by Albert Robida.
1877
The English-language version of the comic weekly *Puck* is published in the United States.
The *Maru Maru Chinbun* starts publication in Japan.
1881
Judge is founded in the United States (as *The Judge*).
1883
Life magazine appears in New York.
1884
Bernard Gillam's "Tattoed Man" series of cartoons appears in *Puck*.
Ally Sloper's *Half-Holiday* is started in England.
Don Quijote is established in Argentina.
1890
Comic Cuts and *Illustrated Chips* start publication in London.
1892
Emile Reynaud opens his Théâtre Optique in Paris.

"We're not the ones who stink the most, Missus!"

Cover by Adolphe Willette for "L'Assiette au Beurre" in its first year, 1901.

Cover for "Marc' Aurelio" by Gioacchino Colizzi ("Attalo"). © Marc' Aurelio.

1896
Albert Langen founds *Simplicissimus* in Germany.

1898
Caras y Caretas is published in Argentina.

1900
J.S. Blackton releases his *Enchanted Drawings.*

1901
L'Assiette au Beurre begins publication in Paris.

1902
The "Teddy bear" is created by C.K. Berryman.

1904
The comic weekly *L'Illustré* (later changed to *Le Petit Illustré*) is started in Paris.

1905
Rakuten Kitazawa starts *Tokyo Puck* in Japan.

1906
J.S. Blackton's *Humorous Phases of Funny Faces* is released in the United States.

1908
Emile Cohl starts his long career in animation in France.

1912
J.R. Bray produces his first animated cartoon, *The Artist's Dream,* in the United States.

1914
J.R. Bray starts his famous animation series *Colonel Heezaliar.* Winsor McCay's *Gertie, the Trained Dinosaur* is given its first public showing.
Louis Raemakers begins his famous series of anti-German cartoons in the Netherlands following the outbreak of World War I.

1915
Earl Hurd creates *Bobby Bumps* in the United States.

1917
El Apóstol, the first full-length animated cartoon, is released in Argentina.

1918
Robert Ripley conceives his first *Believe It or Not!* panel.
The first professional association of cartoonists, the Manga Kourakukai, is organized in Japan.

1920
Walt Disney produces his first work of animation, the Newman Laugh-O-Grams, in Kansas City.

1922
The first Pulitzer Prize for cartooning is awarded to Rollin Kirby.
The Soviet humor magazine *Krokodil* is founded in Moscow.

1923
Max Fleischer produces an animated film called *The Einstein Theory of Relativity.*

1924
Fernand Léger's animated *Ballet Mécanique* is shown in France.
The first Soviet cartoon, *Soviet Toys,* is produced by A. Ivanov and A. Bushkin.

1925
The *New Yorker* magazine is founded by Harold Ross.

1926
Lotte Reiniger's *Die Abenteuer des Prinzen Achmed* is released in Germany.

1928
The first *Mickey Mouse* cartoon, "Steamboat Willie," is exhibited in the United States.

1929
Walt Disney releases *Skeleton Dance,* first of the *Silly Symphonies.*
The first Soviet sound cartoon, M. Tsekhanovsky's *Posta,* is produced.

1930
Betty Boop makes her first appearance.
Marc Aurelio magazine is started in Italy.

1932
The first Academy Award for a short subject (animation) is given to Disney's *Flowers and Trees.*

"Ersatz," Dušan Vukotić's Oscar-winning cartoon. © Zagreb Film.

Berthold Bartosch's *L'Idée* is released and subsequently banned in France.

1933

Max Fleischer adapts *Popeye the Sailor* to animated cartoons.

1937

The first Walt Disney animated feature, *Snow White and the Seven Dwarfs*, is released.

1938

Bugs Bunny makes his first appearance in "Porky's Hare Hunt."

1939

The first *Tom and Jerry* cartoon, "Puss Gets the Boot," is released by MGM.

1940

Walt Disney's *Fantasia* opens to mixed reviews.

1941

Frederick ("Tex") Avery starts his association with the MGM animation studio.

Animators strike the Walt Disney studios.

1943

Hudibras starts publication in Denmark.

1944

Both *Kladderadatsch* and *Simplicissimus* cease publication within days of each other (September).

1945

Stephen Bosustow founds United Productions of America (UPA).

1946

The National Cartoonists Society (NCS) is organized in New York.

1949

UPA releases the first *Mr. Magoo* and *Gerald McBoing Boing* cartoons.

1952

MAD magazine is started in New York.

Biographic Films is founded by Bob Godfrey and Keith Learner in London.

1953

Paul Grimault's *La Bergère et le Ramoneur* is released in France.

1956

The animation unit of Zagreb Film is established in Yugoslavia.

1959

Stephen Becker's *Comic Art in America* is published in New York.

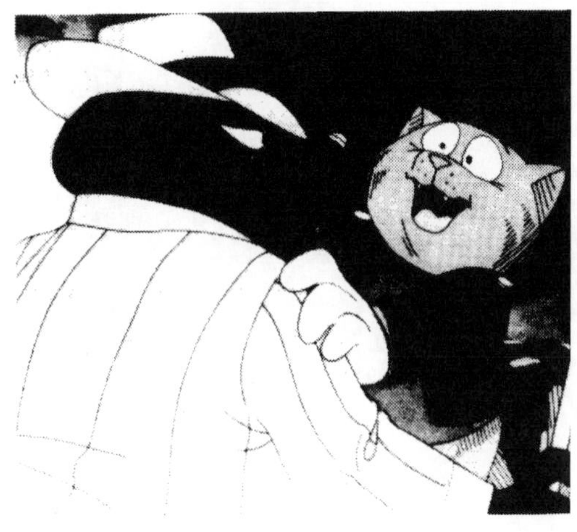

"Fritz the Cat." © Steve Krantz.

1961
Dušan Vukotić's *Ersatz* becomes the first foreign cartoon to receive an Academy Award for animation.

1962
David Low is knighted by the Queen of England.

1966
The City Museum of Cartoon Art opens in Omiya, Japan.

1969
Cartoonist PROfiles starts publication in the United States.

1971
An exhibition called Le Dessin d'Humour is organized by the Bibliothèque Nationale in Paris.

1972
The first X-rated cartoon, *Fritz the Cat,* is released.

1974
The Museum of Cartoon Art opens in Greenwich, Connecticut (later moving to Rye, New York).

1975
The Cartoon Museum opens in Orlando, Florida.

1976
The World Encyclopedia of Comics is published in New York.

1978
A Saul Steinberg retrospective is held at the Whitney Museum in New York.

1979
Herbert Block ("Herblock") receives his third Pulitzer Prize

1980
The original edition of *The World Encyclopedia of Cartoons* published.

1982
First International Salon of Editorial and Humor Cartoons held at St. Just le Martel, France.

1983
The Cartoon Museum opens in Warsaw.

A Silly Symphony: "The Tortoise and the Hare." © Walt Disney Productions.

1985
Cartoon & Karikaturen Museum opens in Basel, Switzerland.
1987
WittyWorld, first international cartoon magazine, starts publication.
1989
Disney's *The Little Mermaid* signals a renaiscence of feature-length cartoon filmmaking.
late 1980s-early 1990s
The fall of Communism opens the countries of eastern Europe to the West. Political cartooning undergoes an upsurge of activity with the rebirth of freedom.
1990
First International Cartoon Convention held in Budapest.
1992
Punch magazine ceases publication in London. (It will reappear some years later in attenuated form.)
1993
Ted Turner's Cartoon Network, first cable channel entirely devoted to showing animated cartoons, starts operation.
1994-96
John A. Lent's four-volume *International Bibliography of Comic Art* published.
1996
The International Museum of Cartoon Art opens in Boca Raton, Florida.
1998
Disney launches Toon Disney, a 24-hour cartoon cable channel.
1999
Revised and enlarged edition of *The World Encyclopedia of Comics* published.

Alphabetical Entries

Aa

ABBEY, EDWIN AUSTIN (1852-1911) American cartoonist, magazine artist and painter born in Philadelphia, Pennsylvania, on April 1, 1852. Edwin Abbey drifted from seminary to a variety of art-related activities: study, engraving, antique collecting. On December 3, 1870, his first published drawing appeared: "The Puritans' First Thanksgiving," a full page in *Harper's Weekly*. The next year Abbey joined the staff of Harper Brothers as an illustrator under Charles Parsons (with whom he was soon to collaborate on drawings) and C.S. Reinhart, and with A.B. Frost, Howard Pyle, W.A. Rogers, Winslow Homer, Gray-Parker and others.

As Willam Murrell points out, many of these artists, especially in their first years on the staff, doubled as rough-sketch artists and cartoonists. The cartoons in *Harper's Weekly* and *Monthly* appeared in the back pages and were often unsigned. Sometimes poems were illustrated, and occasionally humorous series (early strips) ran.

Abbey soon graduated to more dignified stature, however, and became the preeminent artist in American pictorial literature. As Homer depicted the everyday lives of Americans, Abbey introduced readers to the past few centuries of the English-speaking people. He became recognized as a fine artist and was the greatest American illustrator before Pyle (indeed, Pyle's sense of history seems strongly derived from his senior).

After a leave from Harper, study in England and freelance work for *Scribner's Monthly*, Abbey in the mid-1880s produced the finest pen-and-ink work of his early career: illustrations for Herrick's poems "She Stoops to Conquer" and "Old Songs." In the context of a time when photoengraving had just been introduced and was being lovingly refined, his work of this period stands as delicate, thoughtful and masterful.

About this time Abbey moved to England, where he spent most of the rest of his life; he sought to be close to the elements of his inspiration, the trappings of old England. However, he still continued to work on American projects, including the Boston Public Library, for which he painted the mural *The Quest of the Holy Grail;* the state capitol of Pennsylvania; Knickerbocker Hotel in New York; and Harper's Shakespeare series in 1905, in which the greatest pen-and-ink work of his later career appeared.

A member of the National Academy, the Royal Academy, the Legion of Honor and other groups, he died on August 1, 1911, in his studio in Chelsea. In 1921, a definitive biography was published in two volumes by Scribner's (and Methuen in England): *Edwin Austin Abbey, Royal Academician. The Record of His Life and work,* by E.V. Lucas.

R.M.

"Die Abenteuer des Prinzen Achmed." © *Lotte Reiniger.*

ABENTEUER DES PRINZEN ACHMED, DIE (Germany) Lotte Reiniger's *Die Abenteuer des Prinzen Achmed* ("The Adventures of Prince Achmed") falls midway between the animated cartoon and the silhouette film. It was created by cutting silhouettes out of black paper and photographing them frame by frame. It took Lotte Reiniger, assisted by Karl Koch (her husband) and a team of animators made up of Walter Ruttmann, Berthold Bartosch and Alexander Karadan, fully three years to complete this 65-minute film, which was released in 1926.

The story line for the feature was based on tales from the *Arabian Nights*. Fired by his love for a beautiful princess, *Achmed*, a poor little tailor, goes in search of the Magic Lamp and with the help of the White Spirits defeats the evil Djinns and the monstrous Afreets. As befits a fairy tale, the little tailor, now hailed throughout the land as "Prince Achmed" for his prowess, marries the princess at the close.

The story, simple and straightforward, was told with a great deal of spontaneity and charm. The figures were skillfully animated and seemed to move with ease in a setting of Oriental splendor with more than a touch of art deco design. A modern-day version of traditional shadow theater, the film did not set a trend among cartoon filmmakers. A new color version of *Prince* Achmed made by Primrose Productions on directions by Lotte Reiniger was shown on British television in 1954.

M.H.

ABLITZER, ALFRED G. (1889-1968) American artist born in Brooklyn, New York, on July 4, 1889. "Al Zère" (as he is better known), of Alsatian lineage, decided at the age of 12 to be a cartoonist and attended evening art school as a youngster. He later studied at Brooklyn's Adelphi College Art School and, after World War I, at the

Sorbonne. At 15 he made his first sale to *Judge* and was soon contributing there, to *Puck* and to the *Brooklyn Eagle*. For the *Eagle*, as a staffer, he created the comic strip *Buttons and Fatty*, which ran for years under a succession of artists, including M.E. Brady.

During the war he served as business manager and cartoonist for the American Expeditionary Force magazine *The Martian* and won awards for his work in its pages and for his posters. In the postwar months he traveled across Europe, sending back sketches to several American magazines. By this time Zère had a mature and breezy style, with lush pen lines delineating character and action.

Zère was one of the first cartoonists to mine the rich lode of material in America's suburban exodus; he also pioneered several "little man" themes, such as the henpecked simp who is married and harried. In the 1920s and 1930s this became a standard device in comics and humorous literature, but Zère masterfully defined the genre in such features as *Man the Master*, a panel for the *Evening Post* (which he joined in 1920) and *So This Is Married Life*, a strip for the *New York Journal* (which he joined in 1924). He married at this time the daughter of Hearst's multitalented art editor, Al Biederman.

Through the 1920s Zère also drew frequently for *Judge* and contributed editorial cartoons to labor newspapers. Thereafter he drew various features for smaller syndicates and busied himself with sculpture, at which he was accomplished. (He had spent two years in Africa seeking inspiration for his handsome plaques and busts.) Titles include: *Flossie*, which ran in 85 newspapers starting in 1935 for the Bell Syndicate; *Ella the Maid; Two Orphans; You've Got Something There*, a Hatlo imitation; and two World War II features—*Rookie Joe*, a panel for United Feature, and *Jerry, Junior Air Warden* for Bell. The widowed Ablitzer ended his full career living near the famous Niederstein's Restaurant in Queens Village, New York, which was operated by his new wife, the former Adelaide Lardon. He died on November 11, 1968.

It remains for Zère to be recognized more fully for his liberation of cartoons from stylistic stiffness and for the affirmation of married and suburban themes in the comics. His cartoons and comics stand out even today as fresh, lively treatments of what have become American stereotypes, thanks in part to him.

R.M.

ABRAHAM, ABU (1924-) Abu Abraham (Abu) was born in the south Indian state of Kerala in 1924. A mathematics graduate of Travancore University, he worked first as a reporter at the *Bombay Chronicle*, drawing cartoons in his spare time. His cartooning breakthrough came in 1950 when famous cartoonist Shankar Pillai asked him to come to New Delhi to draw for his periodical, *Shankar's Weekly*. Then, a 1953 holiday in England turned into a 16-year stay when *Punch* liked and published his work. He became the first staff cartoonist for *The Observer* in 1956, and a decade later, moved to a similar position at *The Guardian*.

Between 1969 and 1981, he worked at *The Indian Express*, making famous his signature caricaturing of tall and short politicians in *Private View*. He left the *Express* to take up freelancing and to seek syndication for his work, the latter made available through the *Sunday Observer*. Abu was also a member of the Indian Parliament during his stay in New Delhi. In 1989, he returned to Kerala, where he writes a fortnightly column for several newspapers and does a couple of cartoons monthly.

Abu's drawing style, readily recognizable throughout India, is simple, two-dimensional, and without perspective and unnecessary detail—almost childlike. In his view, "cartooning is a highly-sophisticated folk form" that should be kept simple to get messages across. He credits his influences to be Egyptian and folk art, Steinberg, and Tim. In recent years, Abu has soured on drawing political cartoons because of the "brutishness" that has entered politics and everyday life.

J.A.L.

ABU

See Abu, Abraham.

ADDAMS, CHARLES FRANCIS (1912-1988) American cartoonist born in Westfield, New Jersey, on January 7, 1912. Upon completing high school, Charles Addams attended Colgate University for one year (1929-30) and spent another at the University of Pennsylvania (1930-31). He then bade the academic grind adieu and enrolled in the Grand Central School of Art in New York City, where, according to his established custom, he spent one year (1931-32). This completed his formal schooling; Addams was ready to embark upon his art career, and in 1935 his cartoons began appearing regularly in the *New Yorker*, the magazine with which he has become most closely identified. Such has been the popularity of his work for this magazine that he has joined the select group of cartoonists who have had television series built around their characters. Indeed, The *Addams Family*

"The makers of Sun-Glo Toilet Soap bring you an entirely different type of quiz program."
Charles Addams. © The New Yorker.

enjoyed wide popularity as a prime-time network sitcom from 1966 to 1968.

Exhibitions of Addams's work have been mounted at the Fogg Art Museum in Cambridge, Massachusetts, the Rhode Island School of Design Museum, the Museum of the City of New York, the University of Pennsylvania Museum and the Metropolitan Museum of Art in New York City (as part of the War and Print exhibitions). His published work, in addition to his representation in the *New Yorker* albums, includes the collections *Drawn and Quartered* (1942); *Addams and Evil* (1947); *Monster Rally* (1950); *Home Bodies* (1954); *Night Crawlers* (1957); *Dear Dead Days* (1959); *Black Maria* (1960); *The Groaning Board* (1964); *The Charles Addams Mother Goose* (1967); *My Crowd* (1970); *Favorite Haunts* (1976); and *Creature Comforts* (1982).

Even to those unfamiliar with *The Addams Family* from television, a reading of these titles suggests that Addams is very much the black humorist. And so he is. Besides the outré members of the Addams family, one frequently encounters in his work skeletons, assorted demons, various monsters and depraved humans, and one recurrent, round-headed, evil-looking little man whose resolutely antisocial behavior seems to mark him as the cartoonist's graphic representation of the id.

Yet Addams is more than a macabre wit. There is, for example, his innocently childlike fascination with the notion of smallness—a preoccupation that gives rise to small, scholarly men living inside computers, eskimos building ice-cube igloos in refrigerator freezer compartments, musicians hauling their tiny instruments up into Muzak boxes, and cardinals in bird feeders (the kind of cardinal, that is, that might one day become history's smallest pope). Addams also devotes some attention to the upper realms—not equal time, perhaps, but then, why alter a winning formula? Thus, the sculptor of an angel figure calls upward out of his open studio window after his departing model to confirm the next sitting time, and a small, hovering cherub squeegees the stained-glass lights of a cathedral tower. Addams is finally capable of a whimsy that at its best ranks him with his late colleague Thurber—as in the cartoon of da Vinci being asked about a Mondrian-like geometric canvas found by a visitor browsing through his assorted altarpieces and portraits. "That?" answers the master. "Oh, that's nothing. Just something I was fooling around with." (That Leonardo, Addams seems to be saying; as if he weren't satisfied with anticipating the SST!)

For his work, Addams has been honored with the *Yale Humor Award* (1954) and—not surprisingly, given his more than nodding acquaintance with drafty old mansions—with a special award from the Mystery Writers of America (1961). And if it is a mark of his worldly success that he collects vintage automobiles, it seems rather more in character that he also possesses a notable collection of arms and armor. He died in New York City in September 1988.

R.C.

ADDIS, DONALD GORDON (1935-) One of the most versatile and consistently witty cartoonists in the field, Don Addis has been turning out both trenchant political commentary and genial humor for some four decades.

Don Addis, "Bent Offerings." © Creators Syndicate.

The content of his work includes everything from social and political commentary (Leutze's George Washington crossing a garbage-clogged Delaware River; a gigantic Ship of State propelled by the oars of galley slaves) to broad wordplay (a waitress asking a fur-clad barbarian warrior, "What'll it be, Hun?"), and his pictorial style shifts with equal facility according to his subject and place of publication from a bold, slashing line to the goofy bigfoot manner of the 1940s.

Born in Hollywood, California, on September 13, 1935, Addis won 16 Armed Force Press Service awards for his work on an army newspaper in Germany from 1954 to 1957, and went on to major in advertising design at the University of Florida, where his editorship of the *Orange Peel* earned it the rating of number-one college humor magazine in the U.S. After graduating in 1962, he spent a year managing the school's publications laboratory and then went to work as a promotion copywriter and ad designer for the *St. Petersburg* (Florida) *Evening Independent*, while doing news cartoons on the side. Cartooning soon became his full-time occupation, along with a weekly page-one humor column, "Addis Alley." As the staff editorial cartoonist for the *St. Petersburg Times*, he comments on a wide variety of subjects, leavening his political jabs with whimsy and good-natured humor.

His cartoons in the field of education earned him the Florida School Bell Award from the Florida Education Association in 1969, 1970, 1971, and 1972, and he was named Florida Cartoonist of the Year in 1974. In 1966 the St. Petersburg Times Co. published a collection of his work, *Don Addis Vs. 1966,* and in 1976 the *Evening Independent* published another, *Don Addis, No One Else.*

Addis introduced a comic strip, *Briny Deep,* on May 5, 1980. Featuring the crew of a ship combining elements of the *Bounty* and the *H.M.S. Pinafore,* it was distributed by United Feature Syndicate through 1983. Another foray into the strip scene was *The Great John L,* syndicated by Newspaper Enterprise Association (NEA) from 1981 to 1986 (and renamed *Babyman* on October 29, 1984), dealing with the fantasy world of children. At the height of the strip's popularity, NEA reported sales to some 200 papers, and Ballantine Books published a collection of *The Great John L* in 1983.

Since 1964 Addis has also been a successful freelance, contributing gag cartoons to national magazines ranging from *Playboy* (for which he created the feature "Symbolic Sex") and the *National Lampoon* to *Popular Boating, Teen, Clothed with the Sun* (a nudist periodical), and *Chess Life.* In 1987, Creators Syndicate began distribution of his gag-cartoon feature *Bent Offerings,* whose name reflects the singularity of its tone and its use of ingenious puns. Uniformly inventive and original, *Bent Offerings* was awarded the National Cartoonists Society's award for Best Newspaper Panel in 1993.

Whatever their market or subject, Don Addis's gag and editorial cartoons have always retained a breezily anarchic spirit. As noted in *Contemporary Graphic Artists* (1988), "Never sardonic or biting, [his] slightly skewed vision tends toward the wry and antic observation."

D.W.

ADVENTURES OF THE CLOTHESLINE
See Bugville Life.

ADVICE TO THE MENTALLY FEEBLE (U.S.) Throughout his career Charles Dana Gibson—who always insisted on being called a cartoonist and not a caricaturist, social artist or some other supposedly more polite euphemism—delighted in the depiction of embarrassing moments, uncomfortable situations and awkward interludes. This device made possible the fullest exploitation of his talent for capturing expression and emotion. Though love themes seemed to be what was expected of Gibson, it can be argued that his most successful creations are those that document the realm of the *faux pas,* startling discoveries and strong personality studies/contrasts. He developed this genre—one which was copied by many, even down to George Herriman's newspaper panel *Embarrassing Moments* in the 1930s—around the turn of the century and used it strongly in the succeeding years in *Life* and *Collier's.*

Only in 1912, after his self-imposed exile to Europe and temporary abandonment of pen and ink, did Gibson give this theme a title, and it was an amusing one: *Advice to the Mentally Feeble.* The series of double-page cartoons in *Life* began on December 12, 1912, and featured mainly the trials of dealing with bores, unexpected guests, wealthy relatives and the naive placed in unfamiliar situations. He relied on a favorite theme of young girls marrying rich old men with "By All Means Marry for a Home" and "Sleep Whenever You Can; It Will Protect Your Talking." "Go Back to the Stable As Soon As Possible" focused on a boor, while "Go Down to the Street" and "Keep Out of Politics" dealt with amateur stockbrokers and politicians, respectively.

"Aesop's Fables." © Paul Terry.

The cartoon series, actually a burlesque of etiquette manuals and guides to propriety, ran intermittently through the 1910s. In 1920 a similar series, *People We Can Do Without,* ran in *Life.*

R.M.

AESOP'S FABLES (U.S.) Paul Terry started his cartoon series *Aesop's Fables* (also known as *Aesop's Film Fables* and sometimes simply as *Fables*) in 1921. The first one was "The Cat and the Mice," and true to the series title, it followed the ancient tale of the mice trying to decide who would hang a bell around the cat's neck. The series continued with more fable adaptations, but starting in the mid-1920s, it was enlarged to include any subject under the sun. There were fairy tales like "Red Riding Hood" (1931), familiar Bible stories ("Noah Had His Troubles," 1925), prehistoric jokes ("Bonehead Age," 1925) and cartoon musicals ("Mad Melody," 1931). After the mid-1930s the series became indistinguishable from other catchall series at Warners or MGM.

Aesop's Fables was first distributed by Pathé Exchange (1921-31), then by RKO Pictures (1931-33) and finally by the Van Beuren Corporation. It was merged into Terrytoons in the late 1930s and disappeared as an independent title.

Although not quite distinguished, *Aesop's Fables* provided some fine moments of entertainment in its early days. The coming of sound proved fatal, however, as

Paul Terry never made up his mind about the direction he wanted the series to take. Among the more notable directors of the *Fables* were Frank Moser, Eddie Donnelly and Terry himself.

M.H.

AGE OF HANDBOOKS, THE (U.S.) The year 1886 saw the first inklings of *Puck* magazine's change from a primarily political-satire magazine to one more genteel, focusing on social subjects. Perhaps the shift was due to the pressure applied by the success of *Life* (which was by design a social commentary magazine), or to the changing times, or to the business office's entreaties that partisanship offended half the potential audience—or to all three factors. In any event, *The Age of Handbooks,* which ran between February 24 and May 12, 1886, is also representative of another transformation, that of Frederick Burr Opper from a gadfly to a sage social commentator. *The Age of Handbooks* was the first sustained series, drawn in a sophisticated illustrator's style, in which he examined the harebrained fads and silly mores of his day.

This series was a lampoon of compendia—those promise-all how-to books that still plague us today. Opper was already employing his lifelong cartoon formula of zeroing in on something slightly daffy, stretching it to a bit more ridiculous length, depicting an inevitable complication and reminding us in the end that many commonplace things are really quite useless or pretentious.

The first panel—they all ran in single panels in black and white—dealt with a deluded Sunday painter whose monstrosity on canvas was the proud result of reading *How to Become a Perfect Portrait Painter in Two Hours.* The succeeding weeks chronicle the mishaps generated by advice from the following handbooks: *Manual of Infants' Diseases and Their Cure; The Complete Sportsman's Guide; How to Avoid the Perils and Pitfalls of a Great City; The Parlor Joker and Humorist; The Graceful Guide to Dancing; The Young Housekeeper's Infallible Cookbook; The Handbook of High-Toned Etiquette; The Peerless Parlor Prestidigitateur; The Doctor Dispensed With, or Every Man His Own Physician* (in which a fellow can't figure out whether he has heart disease, chronic dyspepsia or St. Vitus's dance); *The Rhyming Dictionary, or the Poet's Guide to Immortal Song;* and *The Peerless and Perfect Horse-Trainer's Handbook.*

Opper's newfound art style combined well with his formula for what were twisted logical extensions of everyday elements. All was fair game to him. The device was used constantly in Puck in the following 13 years, though seldom in series format, and led the way to similar examinations of life by Rube Goldberg, Milt Gross and others.

R.M.

AGOSTINI, ANGELO (1843-1910) Italo-Brazilian cartoonist and author of picture stories, or *histoires illustrés* (as the French say), Angelo Agostini was born in Vercelli, Italy, 1843. Agostini spent his childhood with his grandmother in Paris and in 1859, when he was sixteen, he moved to S. Paulo, Brazil, with his mother. In 1864, Angelo started to illustrate for the magazine *O Diabo Coxo.* Two years later, he went to work for *O Cabrião.* In 1867, he printed his first *histoires illustrés,* titled *As Cobranças.* It was a story with captions, three strips, and seven illustrations. In the same year, he moved to Rio de Janeiro, where he illustrated for *O Mosquito* and *Vida Fluminense.* On January 30, 1869, he created his first character, *Nhô Quim,* and published 15 chapters until 1872. On January 1, 1876, he founded his own weekly, *Revista Ilustrada,* which he directed until 1888. In the 331st edition of his *Revista,* he started the second serial, *Zé Caipora* (1883-1905), which ran for 75 chapters.

In 1888, after obtaining Brazilian citizenship, marrying, and having two children, he fell in love with a pupil named Abigail who became pregnant. The affair became a scandal. In his cartoons, he was a harsh critic of crooked politicians and the "sex-depraved priests" of the Church. As a result of his personal life and his cartoons, he had to sell his property and escape to Paris with his pregnant lover. In France, his daughter Angelina was born. On January 25, 1895, he returned to Brazil and combined reprinted material from *Zé Caipora* with new material form his new weekly, *Don Quixote.* When *Don Quixote* closed, he relocated to work with *O Malho,* which launched the first magazine in color for kids on October 11, 1905. Agostini created the logo for the children's weekly, and some two-paged *histoires illustrés.* Until December 15, 1906, he again reprinted up to 75 pages of *Zé Caipora.* Agostini died in Rio on June 10, 1910, as a pioneer in comics the likes of Rudolf Toepffer, Wilhelm Busch, and others.

A.d'M.

AIN'T IT A GRAND AND GLORIOUS FEELIN'? (U.S.) *Ain't It a Grand and Glorious Feelin'?* is among Clare Briggs's most fondly remembered slice-of-life newspaper panels. It appeared in sequential form (usually six panels to the page) on an irregular basis, alternating with such other Briggs creations as *When a Feller Needs a Friend* and *The Days of Real Sport.* There was no continuing cast of characters.

Ain't It a Grand and Glorious Feelin'? started appearing in the *New York Tribune* around 1917 (although the concept had undergone a dry run as early as 1912 under another title in the *Chicago Tribune*). The panel celebrated those small, everyday moments of serendipity that come as a sharp relief after a moment of fright, embarrassment or frustration. Thus, "ain't it a grand and glorious feelin'" when some housewife discovers that her lost wallet was found at the grocer's, or when some poor bookkeeper goes to bed with a clear mind after the error in his books has been rectified? The feature addressed itself directly to the reader ("When you've been reading about a terrible kidnapping, . . ." Briggs would intone in the beginning, for instance) and always concluded on an upbeat note. *Grand and Glorious Feelin'* was tremendously popular during the 1920s, a decade whose mood it seemed to match perfectly, and the title became a popular catchphrase of the time.

After Briggs died in 1930 the panel was discontinued, although some newspapers would reprint it occasionally. Long runs of the feature have been republished regu-

"Ain't It a Grand and Glorious Feelin'?" © New York Tribune.

larly over the years in cartoon anthologies, as well as in collections of Briggs's works.

M.H.

AISLIN

See Mosher, Christopher Terry.

AKASEGAWA, GENPEI (1937-) Japanese avant-garde artist and cartoonist born in Yokohama, Japan, in 1937. After graduating from high school in Nagoya, where he was able to major in art, Genpei Akasegawa entered art school in Tokyo but quit in his third year. From 1958 to 1963 he entered artworks in the Yomiuri Independente exhibit. In 1960 Akasegawa and some friends formed the Neo Dada group, whose name reflected his budding sense of humor and parody. Then, in 1963, at the peak of this phase, he began "wrapping" art and also making imitation thousand-yen notes and burning them in public. At the same time, though not completely seriously, he drew cartoons for magazines such as *Doyō Manga* and *Asahi Sonorama.*

Akasegawa achieved his greatest notoriety in 1965, when he was indicted on counterfeiting charges stemming from his period of experimentation with imitation money. After a five-year trial he was given a three-month prison sentence, suspended for a year. He then became serious about cartooning and did a parody series for *Gendai no Me* ("Modern Eye") in 1969, just at the climax of Japan's student unrest; it dealt with riot police and student radicals, among other things. A rather long comic called *Ozashiki* ("The Living Room") ran in the magazine *Garo* in May 1970. In March 1971 his series *Sakura Gahō,* which ran in the *Asahi Journal,* embarrassed the publisher to the point of recalling it from the newsstands.

Genpei Akasegawa is one of Japan's more provocative cartoonists. His art, in fact, has often been a happening in its own right, and he constantly uses parody to a maximum effect to create humor and a personal political statement. He is an admirer of Yoshiharu Tsuge and often does parodies of his work. Books by Akasegawa include *Obuje of Motta Musansha* ("Proletarian Who Had an *Objet*"). Much more than a cartoonist, today he is a prolific artist, novelist and essayist. His 1981 novel, *Chichi ga kieta* ("Father Disappeared") won the prestigious Akutagawa award. In 1997 he had over 56 books listed in print.

F.S.

AKI, RYŪZAN (1942-) Japanese cartoonist born in Ito, Shizuoka Prefecture, Japan, in 1942. Ryūzan Aki's career has been amazingly varied. Upon graduation from junior high school he worked as a fisherman for several years. He then worked for the local post office, and began drawing cartoons for the post office newsletter on the side.

In 1965 he sent several cartoons to *Bessatsu Shukan Manga Times* (a weekly comic). Around the same time, according to one source, he read a short story by Gogol that so influenced him that he quit his job and moved to Tokyo to make his debut as a professional cartoonist. He actively contributed to comic books such as *Doyō Manga* and *Manga Tengoku* in this period and in 1969 achieved considerable popularity with series like *Ryūzan no Gera Gera Baka* ("Ryūzan the Laughing Fool") and *Oh! Jareezu.* In 1971 he won the 16th Shogakkan award for cartoons for *Oyabaka Tengoku* ("Paradise for Doting Parents") and *Gyagu Oyaji* ("Gag Daddy"); in 1975, he received the Bungei Shunju award for cartoons, a reflection of his broad popularity.

Aki's comics fall into a genre known in Japan as "nonsense." His characters generally possess such bizarre countenances that one almost has to look twice, yet they are drawn with clear, simple lines. He revels in reversing human logic and emphasizing the absurd in a black humor style that is absolutely unique. As comic critic Kosei Ono points out, Aki is a sort of Oriental Don Martin. Two of his most representative works are *Ryūzan no Fuzakketta Sekai* ("Ryūzan's Crazy World") and *Aki Ryūzan no Issen Mai* ("One Thousand Pictures by Ryūzan Aki"). Among his more recent works mention should be made of *Mujinto no Kairaku* ("Pleasures of a Deserted Island").

F.S.

AKIYOSHI, KAORU (1912-1989) Japanese cartoonist born in Tokyo, Japan, in 1912. After graduating from high school, Kaoru Akiyoshi joined the Shinei Manga Gurūpu ("New Sharp Cartoon Group") in 1934 but soon switched to the Shin Mangaha Shudan ("New Cartoonists' Group"), which was founded to give new artists greater access to Japan's newspapers and magazines. As a member of the Shin Mangaha Shudan, Akiyoshi began to draw for Hidezo Kondo's cartoon publication, *Manga* ("Cartoon"). It was there that he introduced the prototype of his best-known work, *Todoro Sensei* ("Professor Thunder"), but the strip did not become a hit until after World War II.

After the end of the war, Akiyoshi drew for *Van,* one of the most popular humor magazines then appearing. Most of his cartoons of this period were bits of social satire and glimpses of the difficult era of postwar reconstruction. Akiyoshi also contributed to such postwar publications as *Comet* (1946), but most of these, including *Van,* were short-lived enterprises, and Akiyoshi eventually rejoined Hidezo Kondo when he revived the wartime magazine *Manga.* Akiyoshi brought back *Todoro Sensei,* and this time it became an instant success with the public.

The popularity of *Todoro Sensei* had a lot to do with the timing of its presentation. Its humor was derived from the contrast between the main character's traditional ways and the modernization that was going on about him. Professor Todoro was always dressed in traditional Japanese kimono, and his very appearance suggested conservatism. The other characters, however, were always preoccupied with the fashions and fads of the present. The encounters between old and new in *Todoro Sensei* reflected the rapid changes in postwar Japan. It skillfully captured the spirit of the times, and a faithful following as well. *Todoro Sensei* ran from 1948 to 1950 in *Manga* and was then picked up by the *Yomiuri* newspaper, where it enjoyed a long and successful run. He died March 25, 1989.

Akiyoshi was also an active contributor to children's cartoon magazines such as *Kodomo Manga Shimbun* ("Children's Cartoon News"), for which he drew *Tara-chan* from 1946. *Tara-chan* was a typical six-to-eight-panel cartoon strip that was cast in the mold of "nonsense" cartoons. The strip primarily contained silly gags and pranks whose sole purpose was to amuse young readers. The *Kodomo Manga Shimbun* and its imitators, the *Kodomo Manga Times* and *Junior Shimbun,* performed a valuable service, because there were very few children's readers available in the years just after the war. Many Japanese of the postwar generation have expressed their gratitude for these cartoon books, which helped sharpen their reading skills.

J.C.

ALADDIN (U.S.) Having mined with profit the rich lode of fairy tales with *The Little Mermaid* and *Beauty and the Beast,* Disney next turned to the Arabian Nights for inspiration. The result was *Aladdin,* which was released 1992. Directed by John Musker and Ron Clements (the team that had earlier been responsible for *The Little Mermaid*), the animated feature looks back towards Persian miniatures for atmosphere and local color and to the drawings of Al Hirschfeld for simplicity of line and uncluttered design.

In the movie version, Aladdin is a thief, a young, resourceful rascal in the fictional city of Agrabah, and he is charged by the scheming wizier Jafar to steal a magic lamp. After taking hold of the lamp, Aladdin decides instead to keep it for himself. With the help of the wisecracking genie inside it, he defeats Jafar's plot to become the new sultan of Agrabah and gains the hand of the legitimate sultan's daughter, Princess Jasmine, in the process. Through the judicious use of computer-generated imagery the film created some spectacular three-dimensional effects, notably the magic carpet ride through the Cave of Wonders, in contrast to the more cartoony elements around them. In this latter respect, particular mention should be made of the shape-changing shenanigans of the crowd-pleasing genie (voiced by Robin Williams in an over-the-top performance) who could metamorphose at will into caricatures of Groucho Marx, Arnold Schwarzenegger or Cab Calloway, among others.

Despite protests from Arab-American groups who objected to some of the lyrics referring to the cutting off of ears in the "Arabian Nights" song, *Aladdin* went on to achieve unprecedented success, beating all attendance records for an animated picture.

This in turn led to a sequel, the 1996 *Aladdin and the King of Thieves* (released on video only), in which the hero, now married, confronts the Forty Thieves and their wily king. In addition, an animated TV series, simply called *Disney's Aladdin*, started airing with great success on CBS in 1994.

M.H.

ALAJALOV, CONSTANTIN (1900-1987) American cartoonist and painter born in Russia in 1900. Constantin Alajalov studied at the University of Petrograd but left for the United States in the aftermath of the Russian Revolution and ensuing war and civil war. His progress as an artist in his new country was steady, and all the more impressive when one considers that he was going against the artistic temper of the era. Starting out in the 1920s, with the various postimpressionist movements at full tide, Alajalov was (and remains) true to the classical mode in style and technique. Yet he has coupled this traditionalism with a wit that has enabled him to find commercial outlets for works that might otherwise have languished in the dark corners of galleries and lofts. Ultimately, it has gained him consideration as a serious artist.

His formal credits include commissions to do murals for the *S.S. America* and to paint *The Hands of Leonard Bernstein* (1967). His paintings are included in the permanent collections of the Brooklyn Museum, the Philadelphia Museum, the Museum of Modern Art in New York City and the Dallas Fine Arts Museum. He has been represented in many national exhibitions and has had one-man shows in Hollywood, New York City, Dallas, and Wichita, Kansas. He has also designed sets for the Michael Mordkin Ballet Company. He is currently a member of the faculty at the Phoenix Art Institute and also teaches at Archipenko's Ecole des Beaux-Arts.

The commercial side of his art has included a bit of cartooning for the *New Yorker*, as well as many covers for the *New Yorker* and the *Saturday Evening Post* (the heartland's answer to the *New Yorker*). He has also done illustrations for many books and national magazines. One of Alajalov's cartoons, reproduced in the *New Yorker*'s 50th-anniversary album, exhibits a wonderful fusion of excellent technique with an infectious sense of humor: two graceful antelopes, noses raised haughtily in the air, prance across a field before the friendly advance of a bulky, hairy fellow-ruminant. "Good lord!" remarks one to the other. "Here comes that impossible yak again."

But Alajalov is noted less for his cartoons than for the comic painting he has done for magazine covers—painting which tells little anecdotes at the same time that it represents subjects or places. On this level Alajalov must be appreciated not only as a witty craftsman, but as a man who never forgets the nature of the audience to whom he addresses a particular work. Thus, *New Yorker* readers are treated to scenes from the stage of the Metropolitan Opera House while *Saturday Evening Post* subscribers encounter the homier environment of the local soda fountain.

Alajalov's published work as an illustrator includes *The George Gershwin Songbook, Our Hearts Were Young and Gay, Nuts in May, Bottoms Up,* and Alice Miller's *Cinderella.* He died in October 1987.

R.C.

ALAN FORD (Italy) *Alan Ford,* created in 1969 by Max Bunker (Luciano Secchi), was one of the most spectacular successes among Italian comics of the 1970s (see *The World Encyclopedia of Comics,* Chelsea House, 1976). In 1977 it was adapted to television for the *Supergulp, Fumetti in TV* program; the three stories that were presented—"Gommaflex, il Bandito della Faccia di Gomma" ("Gommaflex, the Rubber-Faced Bandit"), "Il Caso dei Prosciutti Scomparsi" ("The Case of the Vanished Appetizers") and "Ipnos"—were especially scripted by Max Bunker and drawn by Paolo Piffarerio. All three centered on the hapless special agent Alan Ford and his TNT group of gumshoes. They were pitted against Gommaflex, a gangster who, because of cell mutation, was able to transform himself into any person, animal or inanimate object.

In 1978 Alan Ford returned to the TV screen in four new adventures. This time the protagonist and his associates had to deal with Superciuk, a bandit also known as "the alcoholic menace" because of the superpowers he acquired through guzzling liquor. The success of these stories led to the undertaking of an *Alan* Ford series of 13 animated cartoons, executed by Paolo Piffarerio under the direction of Guido De Maria. A third series of new Alan Ford animated cartoons (along with some older ones) began airing on RAI-TV in the fall of 1996.

M.H.

ALDIN, CECIL (1870-1935) Remembered and much collected as an animal artist, both in color and line, Cecil Charles Windsor Aldin was also a prolific cartoonist and illustrator. He was born the son of a builder on April 28, 1870, in Slough, England, and was educated at Solihull Grammar School and Eastbourne College. His interest in art led him to study anatomy at South Kensington Art School under Frank Calderon. Here he came under the influence of John Leech's illustrations for *Handley Cross*, a countryside book by Surtees. He would eventually illustrate an edition himself in 1912.

Aldin's first published work was for *The Graphic* (1891), followed by five years with the *English Illustrated Magazine* (from 1892), and twenty years with the *Illustrated London News* (1892-1911). Other magazines of the period which published his black-and-white cartoons and illustrations were *Pall Mall Budget*, the *Sporting and Dramatic News*, *Punch*, *Sketch*, and *Pick-Me-Up*. In 1898, he became a founding member of the famous institution, the Sketch Club, where he was elected President in 1905. His color posters were very popular, advertising Cadbury's Cocoa and Colman's Mustard.

Aldin was Master of the South Berkshire Foxhounds from 1914, and retired from ill health in 1930. He illus-

"Alan Ford." © Editoriale Corno.

trated and/or wrote some twenty-four books, beginning with *Everyday Characters* (1896), and continuing with *A Dog Day* (1902), *The Black Puppy Book* (1909), *Old Inns* (1921), *Dogs of Character* (1927), *Romance of the Road* (1928), *Mrs. Tickler's Caravan* (1931), *Who's Who at the Zoo* (1933), and *How to Draw Dogs* (1935). He died on January 6, 1935.

D.G.

ALEXANDER, FRANKLIN OSBORNE (1897-1993) American cartoonist born in St. Louis, Missouri, in 1897. F.O. Alexander was educated at Northwestern University and the Chicago Academy of Fine Arts; night schools and correspondence courses completed his cartoon training. In World War I he served in Europe with the Camouflage Engineers.

Alexander took over the *Hairbreadth Harry* comic strip upon the death of its creator, C.W. Kahles, in 1931; he continued writing and drawing the strip until its demise in 1939. He then tried two strips of his own—*Finney of the Force* and *The Featherheads*—and drew editorial cartoons for United Feature Syndicate before becoming staff political cartoonist of the *Philadelphia Bulletin* in 1941. He retired in 1967, spending the remainder of his long life in quiet pursuits and an occasional reminiscence. He died in 1993 at his home in Springfield, Pennsylvania.

Following Kahles was a tough act. Alexander added his own flavor to *Hairbreadth Harry,* modernizing the gags and artwork but losing the almost surreal wackiness that the great Kahles achieved in his last few years. As a political cartoonist Alexander was conservative and drew in a handsome, uncluttered brushstroke style shad-

F.O. Alexander, humorous Christmas card.

Alexandre Alexeieff, "Le Nez." © Alexeieff.

ed with careful, clean crayon additions on pebbleboard.

R.M.

ALEXEIEFF, ALEXANDRE (1901-1982) French animator and producer born in Kazan, Russia, on April 18, 1901. Alexandre Alexeieff went to Cadets School and later attended the Naval Academy in St. Petersburg. He emigrated to France in the aftermath of the Russian Revolution, settling in Paris in 1919. There he studied painting and design, and embarked on a promising career as a book illustrator and stage designer.

In 1933 Alexeieff saw Fernand Léger's fabled avant-garde film of animation *Ballet Mécanique,* and under this influence he made a cartoon short, *A Night on Bald Mountain,* using Modest Moussorgsky's music. This film was based on Alexeieff's famous "pin-board technique"—patterns and images created by means of rows of pins fastened to a board and moved either mechanically or by hand. Turning his attention to puppets, Alexeieff then produced *La Belle au Bois Dormant* ("Sleeping Beauty") to music by Francis Poulenc. He also made numerous cartoon commercials for products ranging from perfume to underwear.

During World War II Alexeieff went first to England and then to the United States. With the help of his second wife, Claire Parker (whom he had married in 1941), he experimented further with the pin-board technique and made several films for the National Film Board of Canada, the most notable being *En Passant,* a delightful romp through Canadian folk songs. Returning to France after the war, Alexeieff again took up commercial animation but later made three impressionistic films with Georges Violet: *Fumées, Masques* and *Nocturnes* (1951-54).

Alexeieff then came back to the pin-board, producing *Le Nez,* ("The Nose," 1963), a film version of Nikolai Gogol's famous tale of a man haunted by his own nose. Turning to Moussorgsky's music once more, he directed *Pictures at an Exhibition.* Dreamy, almost ethereal, this last effort was greeted almost as much with incomprehension as with praise when it was released in 1971. Alexeieff has been the recipient of countless honors over the years; his cartoons (he prefers to call them "animated engravings") have won many international awards. He himself has been called "the Einstein of animation," and he has been a perennial member of juries at animation festivals around the world. His last work was *Trois Themes* (1981), on music by Modest Mussorgsky. He died in Paris in 1982.

M.H.

ALHO, ASMO (1903-1975) Finnish cartoonist born in Helsinki, Finland, on August 2, 1903. Asmo Alho might well be the most prolific cartoonist who ever worked in Finland. His gag cartoons and comic strips were published by many large magazines, and he also did some political cartooning. He was active until his death, and his works are still being published regularly.

After finishing school in 1923, Alho went to work for Otava, the big publishing company, doing layouts and artwork. He mainly designed the covers and layouts of the books and magazines published by his company, and to further his knowledge he traveled to Denmark and Germany in 1929. He later worked on the newspaper *Uusi Suomi,* and until 1969 for the large magazine publishing concern Yhtyneet Kuvalehdet, where he became head of the art department.

Alho illustrated a widely used alphabet book and produced several of the most beloved children's books in Finland, some in collaboration with the noted poet and ethnographer Martti Haavio (among them *Porsas Urhea* and *Little Red Riding Hood*). Starting in 1933, he also drew some of the longest-running comics (with academician Mika Waltari writing verse for *Kieku and Kaiku).*

Alho's cartoons were regularly published in *Joulukärpänen, Pippuri, Radiokunntelija, Kotiliesi* and *Suomen Kuvalehti.* He also did advertising work and was

Asmo Alho. © Alho.

president of the Union of Graphic Illustrators. He wrote two books, *Tutustumme Helsinkiin* ("Getting to Know Helsinki") and *Helsinki Ennen Meitä* ("Helsinki Before Us").

After retirement Alho sometimes taught seminars for young cartoonists. The man behind the work remained largely unknown to the general public, however. The Finnish Comics Society awarded him its highest honor, the Puupäähat, just before his death in Helsinki in 1975.

J.R.

ALICE IN CARTOONLAND (U.S.) When he left Kansas City for Los Angeles in 1923, Walt Disney brought with him a copy of his latest effort, *Alice's Wonderland,* a partly animated, partly live-action short. Among the people who saw his sample was Margaret Winkler, an independent distributor, who commissioned a series of cartoons (to be called *Alice in Cartoonland*) from Disney later that same year.

With the help of his brother Roy, Walt Disney set to work with alacrity and in a few months in 1924 turned out six *Alice* cartoons (for which he was paid fifteen hundred dollars apiece). The returns, however, were disappointing, and Charles Mintz (who had married Margaret Winkler earlier that year and taken over the business) asked the Disney brothers to discontinue production. In desperation Disney sent for his former Kansas City partner, Ub Iwerks; Iwerks, an accomplished draftsman, is credited with putting the series back on its feet. Thus propped up, *Alice in Cartoonland* continued on its way until late in 1926, when everybody agreed that the series had played itself out (after a run of some fifty separate titles).

Alice in Cartoonland was not very distinguished. Its live action was rudimentary, the parts being played by neighborhood kids (Virginia Davis was the first Alice, later replaced by Margie Gay), its gags feeble, and the drawing stiff, even after the addition of Iwerks. It represents, however, Walt Disney's first successful venture into animation, and it allowed him to refine his animation and storytelling techniques. It also provided him with the nucleus of his animation team (made up of himself, his brother Roy, Iwerks, and three more associates from his Kansas City days, Rudolph Ising and Hugh and Walker Harman).

M.H.

"Alice in Cartoonland." © Walt Disney Productions.

The "Prelude to the Afternoon of a Faun" sequence of "Allegro Non Troppo." © Bruno Bozzetto.

ALLEGRO NON TROPPO (Italy) To produce a full-length animated film entirely based on musical works might sound like a hopeless gamble after *Fantasia;* yet that is exactly what Bruno Bozzetto attempted with *Allegro Non Troppo,* released in 1976.

As could be expected, the animation content was as much of a mixed bag as the musical program. The wittiest (and shortest) piece showed a bunch of uncouth louts first falling in step with, and later rebelling against, their would-be "leader," to the lusty strains of Dvorak's *Slavonic Dances.* Bozzetto's animation for Debussy's *Prelude à l'Après-Midi d'un Faune* was conventional, with a ridiculous satyr in hapless pursuit of a cute young nymph; and his recreation of man's evolution from the earth primeval (to the rhythm of Ravel's *Bolero*) looked too much like a copy of Disney's prehistoric sequence in *Fantasia.* The closing piece—depicting a barren, desolated urban landscape seen through the eyes of a starving alley cat, and set to the music of Sibelius's *Valse Triste*—was probably the feature's most gripping, as well as most original, moment.

The live-action skits connecting the different segments of animation were sophomoric and poorly acted, and the film also suffered from the lack of a live score (the music was culled from records). All in all, Allegro Non Troppo was markedly but not disgracefully inferior to *Fantasia.* (It should be noted that the film received first prize at the 1977 Sydney Film Festival.)

M.H.

ALLEN, T.S. (ca. 1870-1930) American cartoonist born in Fayette County, Kentucky, around 1870. T.S. Allen was raised in Kentucky, attended James Kane Allen's school, was a classmate of William H. Walker (later a stablemate at *Life* magazine) and graduated from Transylvania University in Lexington, where he studied classical languages. In the 1890s Allen moved to New York, where his father had established a law office, and worked there as a clerk. He moonlighted as an author and joke writer

His wife: "Do you know, John, this is the first time I've really enjoyed riding in this thing since you got it?"

T.S. Allen, 1909.

for magazine cartoonists and eventually sketched his own drawings to accompany his breezy captions.

Allen's style—obviously untutored, but showing shrewd native talent—was as flippant as his light jokes. He was among the first cartoonists to break away from the rigid illustrators' look of magazine cartoons and was perceived as the American Phil May. Thematically, many of Allen's single-panel cartoons dealt with street urchins and working-class or immigrant subjects.

When the very first Sunday supplements were issued, in the days when there were as many text jokes and panel cartoons as strip series, T.S. Allen was a prominent fixture on both the *World* and Hearst sections. Otherwise *Life* was his major outlet well into the 1910s.

R.M.

ALLEY, CALVIN LANE (1915-1970) American artist born in Memphis, Tennessee, on October 10, 1915. Cal Alley was raised in an artistic environment—his father, J.P. Alley, drew editorial cartoons for the *Memphis Commercial Appeal* and created the *Hambone* panel—and attended the American Academy and the Chicago Academy of Fine Arts in 1935-36. For two years thereafter Alley was a cowboy and sketch artist in Arizona and Texas. In 1939 Alley became editorial cartoonist of the *Kansas City Journal* and remained there until its demise in 1942. He then held a similar position on the *Nashville Banner* until 1945, when he joined his father's paper, the *Memphis Commercial Appeal,* as editorial cartoonist. Here he remained until his death on November 10, 1970.

The younger Alley, along with his brother Jim, inherited the Bell Syndicate panel *Hambone's Meditations* in 1934. Their method of working was largely unknown to the general public: they alternated weeks, drawing it in a virtually indistinguishable style. The stereotyped title character, a philosophical "darky," no matter how sympathetic, sage and harmless, was nevertheless deemed offensive by many in the race-conscious 1950s, so the panel died in 1954.

That same year Cal Alley began a family comic strip, *The Ryatts,* modeled on his own home life. Picked up by the Hall Syndicate, it premiered in October 1954 in 24

Calvin Alley, "The Ryatts." © The Hall Syndicate.

papers and soon, thanks to its empathy, engaging drawing style and thematic appeal, ran in several hundred papers. In 1967, because of ill health and the crush of daily editorial cartoon production, Alley relinquished the strip to Jack Elrod, who also assists on the *Mark Trail* strip for the successor syndicate, Field.

Alley had an extremely attractive, old-time pen-and-ink drawing style reminiscent of his father's and the Chicago Tribune school's. He very seldom used crayon shading. In politics he was a conservative.

R.M.

ALLEY, JAMES PINCKNEY (1885-1934) American cartoonist born near Benton, Arkansas, on January 11, 1885. J.P. Alley was educated in the public schools of Benton and in 1916 became the cartoonist for the *Memphis Commercial Appeal* in Tennessee; he was to remain there until his death.

Besides his editorial cartoons, which were drawn in the popular mid-South style of Carey Orr and Billy Ireland, Alley drew the widely enjoyed and long-running *Hambone's Meditations.* This syndicated panel about a rural black's observations was in the tradition of Josh Billings and other cracker-barrel humorists; Hambone's commonsense aphorisms were quoted frequently and collected in book form in 1917 and 1919 (McClure, and later Bell, was the distributor in newspapers). Alley also wrote and illustrated *Distinguished Folks* in 1928.

Alley died on April 16, 1934; his sons J.P., Jr., and Cal continued *Hambone,* and Cal was later to draw editorial cartoons in Memphis and Nashville.

R.M.

REASON I LAKS TO HEAH KUN'L BOB READ OUT DE PRES'DINT'S SPEECH_I KIN GIN'LY PICK OUT SUMP'N WHUT FIT ME !!

James Alley, "Hambone's Meditations," ca. 1900.

ALONSO, JUAN CARLOS (1886-1945) Argentine cartoonist and painter born in El Ferrol, Spain, on July 6, 1886. Juan Carlos Alonso came to Argentina in 1899 with his parents. He studied art in Buenos Aires and started his career as a cartoonist around 1905. He first worked for *Caras y Caretas,* then went over to the humor magazine *Plus Ultra.* He contributed many cartoons and illustrations to *Plus Ultra,* becoming its most noted collaborator. In the 1920s he became the director of the magazine.

Alonso was also a noted painter who specialized in genre scenes and picturesque compositions. He exhibited widely, not only in Argentina but also in France, Italy and Spain, and won first prize at the 1933 Santa Fe Salon. He was named a Knight of the Royal Order of Alfonso XIII and made a member of the Royal Academy of his native Galicia (a province of Spain). He died on February 15, 1945, in Buenos Aires.

A.M.

ALTAN, FRANCESCO TULLIO (1943-) Italian cartoonist and illustrator born in Treviso, Italy, in 1943. Francesco Altan left for Brazil after finishing his art studies in Italy; while in Latin America, he contributed cartoons and comic strips to a great number of publications. Returning to his native Venetia in the early 1970s, he freelanced for various Italian magazines.

Altan enjoyed his first success with Trino, a kind of bungling demiurge busy with the creation of the world on orders of an omnipotent boss, himself not quite sure of his intentions. This story first appeared in the monthly *Linus* in 1974 and was later collected in book form. It contained nothing irreverent, but it displayed Altan's wit and irony and indulged in some good-natured ribbing of famous characters from the past, a feature it shares with his political cartoons. These often focus on workingmen—an important aspect of Altan's satirical work, and one common to many other contemporary Italian political cartoonists. Where Chiappori, for instance, pillories the men in power, Altan makes his point indirectly, through the seemingly genuine and spontaneous comments of assembly-line workers: this is a means of putting the political cartoon in a simpler, more immediate context. In the 1980's his fame spread to France, where his editorial cartoons have been appearing in the weekly *L'Express* and where many collections of his works have been published. Since 1988 he has also become a screenwriter, adapting some of his stories to film.

Altan is also an illustrator who, in the pages of *Il Corriere dei Piccoli* and in children's books, depicts fabulous and fantastic worlds midway between unreality and poetry. Both in his political cartoons and in his children's stories Altan always displays the same sparse style, without frills and somewhat *naïf.*

C.S.

Juan Alvarez © Juan Alvarez Montalban.

ALVAREZ MONTALBAN, JUAN (1960-) Spanish cartoonist and animator, Juan Alvarez Montalban was born in 1960 in Mazarron, province of Murcia, but grew up in neighboring Mula. Alvarez showed a great love for comics and cartoons since an early age, and soon abandoned his studies to use his talent for drawing by publishing cartoons that dealt with the treatment of youth in universities and in the military. His cartoons put him at the vanguard of a new generation of artists, and his pungent drawings about teenagers and later about all kinds of social problems provided the start of his meteoric career.

In 1978 Alvarez moved to Madrid, and three years later he won first prize from the popular magazine *1984.* This opened a postion for him in an animation studio working for Hanna-Barbera in the United States. Later he became a member of the staff that produced animated cartoons for Spanish Television, including the popular series *Don Quijote de la Mancha.* After winning top awards from Spanish TV in 1985, he entered a new phase of his career, contributing comics to such magazines as *TBO, Zona Z,* and *Totem.* At the same time he produced storyboards for German, Canadian, and U.S. animation series.

Starting in 1990, Alvarez created his best known series, *M.M., el loco del claustro* ("M.M., the Madman of the Cloister"), which won him fame as soon as it appeared in the pages of the magazines *El Jueves, Putamili,* and *Los Madrugos,* all dealing with the lifestyles of college students. Later came *La Capitana,* about a beautiful woman company leader and the unruly bunch of youngsters in her charge.

Alvarez is currently working for the Italian magazine *Totem* and for the daily *La Verdad,* (and occasionally for other publications). Despite his success he also finds time to contribute to amateur publications such as *Comicguia,* the oldest Spanish fan magazine devoted to comics.

F.T.J.

ALVARUS
See Cotrim, Alvaro.

ALVIN AND THE CHIPMUNKS (U.S.) Cartoon characters have often been the inspiration for popular songs (e.g. *The Woody Woodpecker Song, Snoopy and the Red Baron, Felix Keeps on Walking,* and others), but it is a rare occurrence when a single tune gives rise to an entire animated TV series. This, however, is what happened with *The Chipmunk Song.*

Ross Bagdasarian, under the stage name David Seville, wrote the tune (also known as *Christmas Don't Be Late*) in 1958, and it was allegedly sung by a trio of chipmunks (all voiced by Seville) led by bad boy Alvin who had to be repeatedly called to task ("All-vinn! Aalvi-inn!") for his shenanigans. The novelty song became a multi-million dollar seller and gave rise in 1961 to a cartoon program on CBS-TV called *The Alvin Show.* The self-impressed Alvin, sporting a baseball cap and a large red sweater emblazoned with a big yellow "A," led his two companions, the voracious Theodore and the nerdy Simon, into numerous scrapes at home and aboard. It all ended in song (naturally) with the three chipmunks croaking one novelty number or other. The show was popular enough to last until 1965, after which it went into wide syndication.

NBC revived the show, using the old cartoons, in 1979. Four years later the performing trio made its reappearance on broadcast TV with a new, original cartoon show called *Alvin and the Chipmunks,* also on NBC. In this version the three lived with David Seville, making rock-and-roll music together. In 1988 the show was retitled simply *Chipmunks,* as the three male characters were joined by "the Chipettes," Brittany, Eleanor and Jeannette. In 1990 the title was changed (again) to *Chipmunks Go to the Movies,* in which the characters parodied famous film classics. The show ended its long run in September, 1991. There also was an animated theatrical feature, *The Chipmunk Adventure,* which came out in 1986.

M.H.

AMARAL, CRISPIM DO (1858-1911) Brazilian cartoonist born in Olinda, in the state of Pernambuco, Brazil, in 1858. Crispim do Amaral showed an early predisposition toward art, and his parents sent him to Pernambuco (now Recife) to study under the French painter Léon Chapelin. Amaral's artistic career started in 1876, when he designed sets for the stage, first in Pernambuco, then in Manaus. Towards the end of the 19th century Amaral moved to Paris, where he worked as a designer and also contributed cartoons to several French publications, notably *L'Assiette au Beurre.*

Amaral returned to Brazil in 1901, briefly staying in Pernambuco, then permanently settling in Rio de Janeiro in 1902. He pursued a flourishing career as a set designer and as a cartoonist, working variously for *O Malho* (of which he was the first art director), *A Avenida* (a magazine he founded in 1903 and ran until 1905), *O Pau* and finally *O Século.* He died in Rio in 1911.

Crispim's brother, Amaro do Amaral (1873-1922), was also a cartoonist.

A.M.

AMERICAN TAIL, AN (U.S.) In the 1980's Disney found itself successfully challenged on its home ground—the animated cartoon feature, and most galling of all the upstart had come out from the studio's own ranks. He was Don Bluth, who had defected in 1979, and now formed his own animation unit. The first feature made by the new outfit, *The Secret of NIMH,* was well received critically and fared reasonably well at the box-office when it came out in 1982. Thus encouraged, Bluth produced an even more ambitious project, *An American Tail,* which was released by Steven Spielberg's Amblin Productions in 1986.

It was an animal allegory set in Czarist Russia wherein the Mousekowitz family lived in a mousehole in the home of the Moskowitz family. The little hero of the piece, young Fievel (so named in honor of Spielberg's real-life Russian grandfather), his sister Tanya, his violin-playing papa, and his entire family were forced to leave their *shtetl* following a pogrom instigated by "Cossack cats." On their way to America, "where there are no cats," but "where there are mouseholes in every wall," their ship was buffeted by a storm, and young Fievel was washed overboard. But the doughty little rodent managed to reach shore. After many an adventure and countless perils he was reunited with his family in the shadow of the newly-erected Statue of Liberty.

Dripping in symbolism and awash in good sentiments, the film ultimately did not achieve its purpose. Technically it was an awesome work of cinematic animation, replete with spectacular effects, incident-filled sequences, and masterful compositions. The message, however, was heavy-handed and suffered from the same conceptual weakness that also flawed Art Spiegelman's *Maus,* which also tried to tell the story of murderous anti-Semitism in funny-animal guise. Charles Solomon put his finger squarely on the problem when he wrote: "Cats chasing mice were an inappropriate metaphor for religious persecution. Oppression is not a conflict between predator and prey, but the willful cruelty members of a single species inflict on each other in the name of a spurious ideology." Despite its faults, *An American Tail* set a box-office record for an animated feature up to that time, racking in close to fifty million dollars in North American movie theaters alone.

The film's success prompted Spielberg to attempt a sequel, *An American Tail: Fievel Goes West,* in which all the Western stock situations were revisited to a fare-thee-well. The plot was desultory, and the animation not on a par with the original (Bluth having left in the meantime). Released in 1991, the film fared badly with public and critics alike.

M.H.

"No, no, nurse! The tranquilizer is for ME!"
Bradley Anderson, "Marmaduke." © National Newspaper Syndicate.

ANDERSON, BRADLEY (1924-) American cartoonist born in Jamestown, New York, on May 14, 1924. Brad Anderson sold his first cartoon to *Flying* magazine in 1940, while still in high school, and continued to freelance cartoons until he was drafted in 1942. After three years in the navy during World War II, Anderson enrolled at the University of Syracuse and continued to draw cartoons, for the *Syracusan Magazine.*

Upon graduation in 1951 Anderson worked in the university's audiovisual department, contributing a number of cartoons to such publications as the *Saturday Evening Post* and *Collier's* all the while. In 1953 he decided to devote himself to cartooning full time, and the following year he created *Marmaduke,* a newspaper panel about a Great Dane and the havoc caused by his well-meaning but catastrophic exertions. From eight papers at its inception, *Marmaduke* has grown to a list of over 500 client newspapers in 1996.

Brad Anderson is a competent, if somewhat dull, draftsman who is able to achieve some moments of inspired lunacy in the course of *Marmaduke.* He fails, however, to give as good an account of himself in his newest feature, a comic strip titled *Grandpa's Boy.*

M.H.

ANDERSON, MARTIN (1854-1918?) British cartoonist born in Leuchars, Fife, Scotland, in 1854. The caricaturist who signed his work "Cynicus" was the last of the long line of independent graphic satirists who made social, political and topical attacks through the medium of the colored print, a British tradition dating back to Gillray and Hogarth.

Martin Anderson received a local education, then attended Madras College in St. Andrews. After school he went to Glasgow as an apprentice to a designer and attended the Glasgow School of Art as an evening student. His first cartoon ("The Transit of Venus") was published in the magazine *Quiz,* and he obtained a job as staff artist on John Leng's *Dundee Advertiser.*

He came down to London in 1891, converting a fish-and-chips shop at 59 Drury Lane into a studio. From there, under the imprint of the Cynicus Publishing Company, he produced a long series of caricature plates, hand-colored, which he sold as separate sheets, cards and, occasionally, in book form. His caricatures and topical or political cartoons attacking or commenting on matters of the immediate moment were captioned with couplets, and although crude in technique and basic in style, they continued the tradition of the old satirists, becoming quite popular. He returned to Scotland and set up a studio in Tayport, where, aided by a staff of women colorists, he produced cartoon postcards in series. Anderson died during or shortly after World War I.

Books: *The Satires of Cynicus* (1890); *The Humours of Cynicus* (1891); *Symbols and Metaphors* (1892); *The Fatal Smile* (1892); *Social and Political Cartoons* (1893); *The Blue Button* (1896); *Selections from Cynicus* (1909); and *Who Shall Rule, Briton or Norman* (1911).

D.G.

ANDERSSON, OSKAR EMIL (1877-1906) Swedish cartoonist, better known as O.A., born in Stockholm, Sweden, on January 11, 1877. In the tradition that a number of Swedish cartoonists, led by Albert Engström, started in the satirical magazines *Søndagsnisse* and *Strix,* O.A. stands out with a special radiance. Actually, he was Engström's greatest competitor among cartoonists, but his early death at his own hands meant that he was not to be popular among his contemporaries; rather, it is later historians who have discovered his outstanding qualities.

He was a cartoonist of the restaurants and the salons, especially; the backs of menus served as his drawing pad, and with his elegant looks one could have taken him for the son of a rich man, an officer or a rising politician. His self-portrait, which hangs in the National Museum in Stockholm, confirms the impression of a highly gifted, elegant artist. Had he had the desire and the will, he could have become one of the world's great portrait painters. But he felt he was misunderstood and sought refuge in cartoons in order to make ends meet; nobody saw his greatness. Typical of his art and mentality was the cartoon of an office clerk who says, "I'd like to ask permission to have the afternoon off." "For what purpose?" asks his fat employer. "I intend to commit suicide," he answers. Andersson did indeed commit suicide on November 28, 1906.

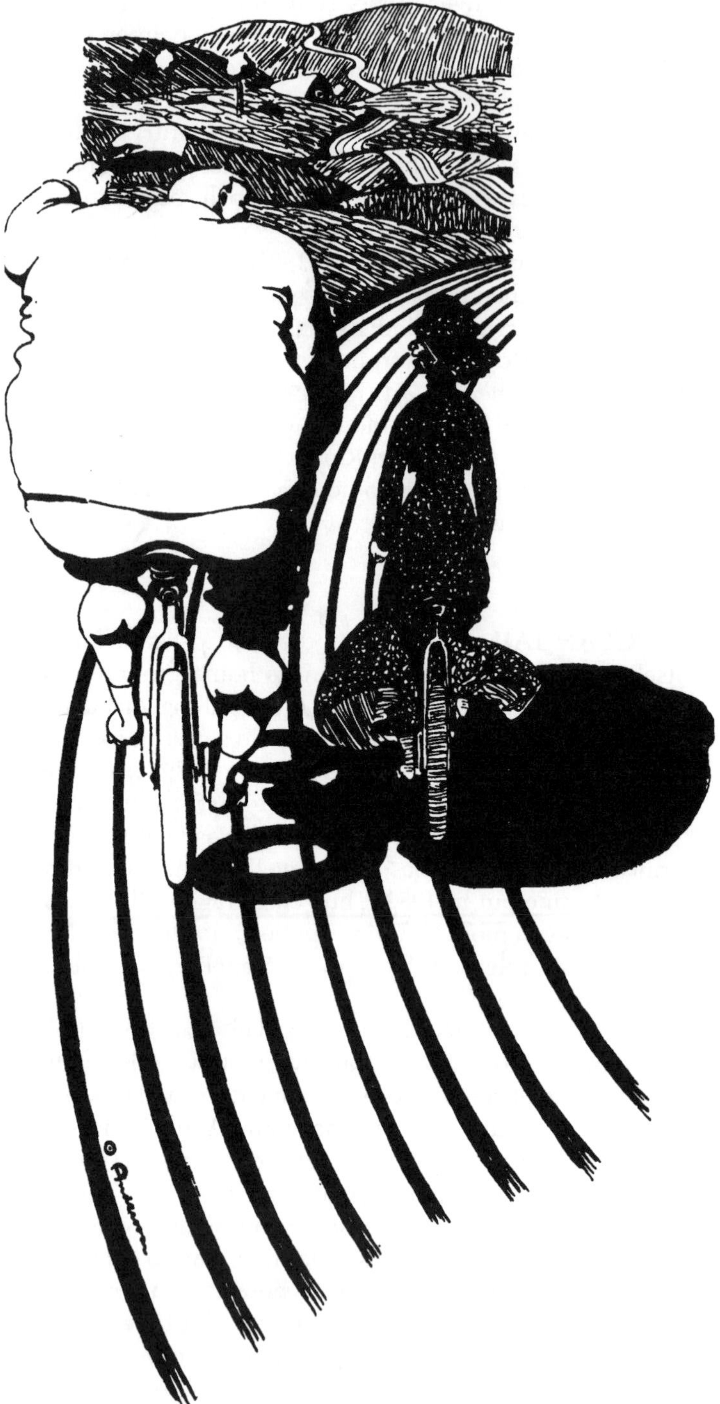

An opener: "Excuse me, miss.
Would you permit me to afford you some shade?"
Oskar Andersson ("O.A.").

The young O.A.'s drawings, scattered among Stockholm's small restaurants, have become classics: his captions are familiar quotations, his abbreviations and technique of omissions were trend-setting, his feel for composition was brilliant. (For a description of O.A.'s career as a comic strip artist, see *The World Encyclopedia of Comics,* Chelsea House, 1976.)

J.S.

ANDY PANDA (U.S.) With the popularity of Oswald the Rabbit fading fast as the 1930s wore on, Walt Lantz had the task of finding a new cartoon character who would prove attractive to moviegoers. After trying out several other animals (such as a pup, a mouse and a duck) Lantz

"Andy Panda." © Walter Lantz.

finally settled on a cuddly little panda bear named Andy Panda who made his appearance around 1938. Every hand at the Lantz studio seems to have worked on the *Andy Panda* series, James Culhane and Alex Lovy being the most notable.

Andy was a well-intentioned, not overly bright creature, and he always managed to get involved in various scrapes with other animal characters. In "Nutty Pine Cabin," Andy tried to put up a log cabin in the woods, only to be thwarted at every turn by all kinds of forest animals; in "Meatless Tuesday," he went out to catch a rooster for supper, but the hardy fowl proved too strong and crafty for him. One of the best entries in the series, "Poet and Peasant," starred Andy as the conductor of the Hollywood Washbowl Orchestra in a raucous rendition of Franz von Suppé's famous overture, amid complete chaos and mayhem.

Andy Panda was popular enough to last into the 1960s, although with diminishing invention and wit. In the cartoons of the later period (by which time he had acquired a girl friend, Miranda), Andy's role became smaller and smaller. In "Fish Fry," for instance, he was relegated to playing second banana—to a goldfish, yet!

Andy Panda was featured in comic books from 1943 to 1962, and in 1973 Gold Key started releasing a new *Andy Panda* title.

M.H.

ANGELETTI, SERGIO (1947-   ) Italian political cartoonist born in Rome in 1947, better known under his art name Angese. He studied at a commercial school and then he devoted himself to graphic satire. In 1973 he started drawing humorous cartoons which were printed in the magazines *Aut, L'Avventurista* and *Rinascita* and in the dailies *Voce Repubblicana* and *Momento sera.* In 1975 he became a steady contributor of the daily *Paese Sera* and from 1978 to 1981 he also made regular contributions to the satirical magazine *Il Male* which was a milestone in the history of Italian political satire.

During the 1980s and 1990s his cartoons have appeared in several magazines such as *Linus*, *Zut* (1987), *L'Espresso*, *L'Eco della Carogna* (of which he became the editor), and *Il clandestino* (1994-1995). Angese's style is intentionally careless, clumsy and clownish. Though politically leftist, Angese has always looked with a critical eye at the organized left political movements as well as at the conservative government.

At present he contributes to some periodicals such as *Boxer* (satirical supplement of the daily *Il manifesto*) and he is in charge of the school for graphic journalism in Perugia.

Some of his cartoons have been collected in book format: *Cento disegni* (1977), *Avventure di Craxi e Martelli* (1984), and *La qualità va male* (1992). In 1983 Angese was awarded the Prize Forte dei Marmi for Political Satire.

G.C.C.

ANGESE
See Angeletti, Sergio.

ANGOLETTA, BRUNO (1899-1954) Italian cartoonist born in Belluno, Italy, in 1899. From an early age Bruno Angoletta showed a talent for drawing, and he sold his first cartoons to the humor magazine *L'Asino* when he was not yet twenty. He later collaborated on *Pasquino*

Bruno Angoletta, caricature.

and *La Tribuna Illustrata.* In 1921 he staged Shakespeare's *Romeo and Juliet* and also illustrated several books and designed book covers. After drawing a number of pages for the weeklies *La Domenica* and *Il Giornalino,* Angoletta went over to *Il Corriere dei Piccoli* in 1928, creating for that magazine many comic strips, among them the famous *Marmittone.* Other Angoletta strips include *Il Professor Tubo, Girometto, Pancotto, Pam-pan della Micragna, Calogero Sorbara* (1930) and *Centerbe Ermete* (1934-41).

During the 1930s and early 1940s Angoletta also contributed cartoons to a great number of publications, such as *Girotondo, Novella, Donna, L'Ardita* and *Il Balilla,* the Fascist youth organization newspaper, for which he created at the time of the Ethiopian war the two famous fez-topped twins Romolino and Romoletto. He also drew many anti-British and anti-American cartoons during World War II. After the defeat of Fascism, Angoletta went into a long period of silence, from which he emerged in 1950 to collaborate on Giovanni Guareschi's newly created satirical weekly, *Il Candido.* Angoletta's cartoons appeared in its pages until his death in Milan in 1954.

M.G.P.

ANIMALAND (G.B.) *"Animaland* Cartoons created in Britain by David Hand: Gay, Lovable, Laughable and Brightly-Coloured." This was how the first fully studio-backed series of animated cartoons to be produced in the United Kingdom was advertised in the trade press on Monday, December 13, 1948. Gaumont British Animation had been set up by the millionaire flour miller Joseph Arthur Rank as part of his campaign to fill the screens of his British cinemas (the Odeon and Gaumont circuits) with British films of every kind, from features to newsreels, shorts, documentaries and, of course, cartoons.

In charge of the project was David Hand, hired from the Walt Disney organization, where he had been a top producer for many years. The studio was created in a country mansion, Moor Hall, in the village of Cookham, Berkshire, and Ralph Wright was made story supervisor. Their initial trial releases were very short cartoon commercials for Spa toothbrushes (for which they invented *Sparky*) and Rowntree's cocoa (for which they created *Coco and the Bear*). They also produced a sing-song short for Rank's Saturday morning children's clubs, called *Bound for the Rio Grande.* Two series were then planned, *Animaland* and *Musical Paintbox,* and releases alternated from 1948 to 1950.

The first *Animaland* release was *The Lion* (1948), directed by Bert Felstead from a script by Pete Griffiths. Music was by Henry Reed (as it would be for the series), and the story was narrated by radio character-actor Richard Goolden. As an old professor, he studied the life and habits of "Felis Leo" from cubhood to maturity, finally getting eaten for his pains! *The Cuckoo* (1948) was funnier, introducing a fat hero who was indeed "cuckoo." *The House Cat* (1948), written by Reg Parlett and Nobby Clark, again featured Goolden as narrator, this time with songs by The Radio Revellers to brighten the proceedings. *The Platypus* (1949) introduced two funny birds, Katie and Kobber Kookaburra, as well as the hero and heroine, Digger and Dinkum Platypus. *The Ostrich* (1949) told the life and times of Oscar and was the last of the somewhat formal—certainly as far as titles go—series. A change of policy produced a deliberately created cartoon star, Ginger Nutt the Squirrel, who starred in the remaining four releases (see the entry "Ginger Nutt"). Director for the series was Bert Felstead, and animators included Stan Pearsall, Ted Percival, Bill Hopper, John Wilson and Chick Henderson, with backgrounds by George Hawthorne and Betty Hansford.

D.G.

ANIMATED GROUCH CHASERS, THE (U.S.) *The Animated Grouch Chasers* is the collective title of a series of cartoons produced by the French-Canadian cartoonist Raoul Barré for Edison Company in New York. Conceived according to the technique of animation on paper, this series of thirty-odd cartoons was subdivided into eleven thematically related films, all released within the single year 1915: *Cartoons in the Kitchen* (April 21), *Cartoons in the Barber Shop* (May 22), *Cartoons in the Parlor* (June 5), *Cartoons in the Hotel* (June 21), *Cartoons in the Laundry* (July 8), *Cartoons on Tour* (August 6), *Cartoons on the Beach* (August 25), *Cartoons in a Seminary* (September 9), *Cartoons in the Country* (October 9), *Cartoons on a Yacht* (October 29) and *Cartoons in a Sanitarium* (November 12). Structured along the line of "Chinese boxes," these films blend animation and live action: the sudden appearance of a comic book titled *The Grouch Chaser* signals the start of the animation after a burlesque introduction played by live actors.

In addition to a series of animated fables featuring a group of insects (notable among them Ferdinand the fly and his "flyancée"), Barré created three heroes for his cartoons: Kid Kelly, Hercule Hicks and Silas Bunkum. The crafty owner of a boardinghouse, Silas is pictured as a potbellied teller of tales whose absurdity invariably gets him thrown out of the local general store by his outraged audience. Silas philosophically crowns each of his evictions with the resigned comment "Folks don't believe nothing no more!" In contrast to Silas, Hercule

Kid Kelly and his dog Jip in "The Animated Grouch Chasers," 1915. © Thomas A. Edison, Inc. and La Cinémathèque Québécoise.

Hicks is a henpecked little man who escapes from his redoubtable wife by means of dreaming. His intense oneiric activity gives rise to some interesting animation effects, like the dream balloon taking up the entire screen. The mischievous Kid Kelly is unquestionably the most interesting of the three characters. *Cartoons on a Yacht,* in which Barré satirizes office employees, and *Cartoons in the Country* both highlight the complicity between Kid Kelly and his sidekick, the larcenous dog Jip.

Several innovations were brought to bear on *The Animated Grouch Chasers:* depth of field ("Suburbanite Life," "Kid Kelly Has a Lollypop"), use of moving backgrounds ("Hicks in Nightmareland"), foreground effects ("Kid Kelly's Bathing Adventures"). In this respect the series, although badly dated, represents a giant step in terms of organization of labor and announces the imminent industrialization of American cartoon film production.

S.J.

ANTHONY, NORMAN (1893-1968) American cartoonist and editor born in Buffalo, New York, in 1893. Norman Anthony studied art at the Albright Art Gallery in Buffalo after worshiping at the pages of *Puck, Judge* and *Life* as a boy. In 1910, he sold his first cartoon to *Life* and for ten years thereafter freelanced as a cartoonist and editor on such papers as the *Lamb,* a short-lived Wall Street sheet.

As a cartoonist he was always weak; his strength was in gags. His cartoons sold on their humor, and in the early 1920s, the struggling *Judge* hired him as an idea man—often to write captions for artwork accepted on its visual merits and without gags! He analyzed *Judge*'s problems—too much text, very little real humor—and put in a bid to reform the magazine. On November 17, 1923, one of his concepts was tried, an advertising lampoon number, and was a wild success. Immensely funny (and foreshadowing his later *Ballyhoo,* and even *MAD* magazine), it assured him a name on the masthead and an editorship beginning with the December 8 issue.

Anthony literally revolutionized American cartooning. The he-she captions were out, irreverence was in; new artists like Dr. Seuss, S.J. Perelman and Jefferson Machamer were discovered; lampoon issues appeared frequently; and honest, belly-laugh humor was king. Slapstick, puns, ethnic humor, sophisticated drollery, political satire—all romped through *Judge*'s pages. As he discovered artists, writers, entertainers and the like—including such names as Jimmy Durante and Pare Lorentz—he raised the circulation from thirty thousand to more than a hundred thousand a week.

His efforts attracted the attention of the *Life* owners, smarting from *Judge*'s success and the efforts of Harold Ross at the new *New Yorker.* (Ross was a protégé of Anthony's in 1924 on *Judge;* they didn't see eye to eye on percentage of text or style of humor.) *Life* offered Anthony $35,000 a year and ten percent of the profits. He switched in 1929, but all the promises made by *Life*'s Charles Dana Gibson, after Anthony's radical changes in the magazine's format, were broken, and Anthony was out of a job (he later successfully sued for breach of contract).

Soon he conceived an idea that George Delacorte at Dell Publishing brought out as a magazine: it was truly an early *MAD,* only zanier. The magazine, *Ballyhoo,* had a bright patchwork-quilt cover, was wrapped in cellophane and contained the wildest ad lampoons and bawdiest jokes the country had seen. The weekly print runs sold out—first 150,000 copies, then 300,000 . . . 600,000 . . . 1,000,000 . . . 1,500,000 . . . 2,000,000. It was a national craze and spawned a score of imitators within a month. Anthony backed the *Ballyhoo Revue* on Broadway, starring a newcomer named Bob Hope; the critics panned it, but it was a moderate success.

The *Ballyhoo* craze died after six years. Anthony tried other magazines—*Manhattan, Mr., Helzapoppin, Der Gag,* the *Funnybone*—a radio show (*The Village Grocery*) and several books, including *The Drunk's Blue Book,* illustrated by Otto Soglow, and *What to Do Until the Psychiatrist Comes.* His autobiography, a Rabelaisian journey through his successes, failures, women and binges, was entitled *How to Grow Old Disgracefully.* Anthony, a comic genius who left a huge mark on American cartooning and humor, died on January 21, 1968.

R.M.

ANTON (G.B.) "Anton came into being in 1937, and we—brother and sister—have been partners since then. But please don't ask us how it works out." This explanation served to introduce *Anton's Amusement Arcade,* the first collection of Anton cartoons, published in 1947 to mark the first decade of this unique collaboration between Harold Underwood Thompson and his sister Beryl Antonia ("Anton" is an abbreviation of her middle name). Percy V. Bradshaw, interviewing this "double act" for his *Lines of Laughter* (1946), considered their mutual understanding uncanny. "They each scrawl their loose shading on to figures and backgrounds in precise-

"I'm happy to say the danger is passed."

Anton. © Lilliput.

ly the same way. I am convinced that if the sister did the rough sketches and the brother the finished drawings (instead of the other way around), the results would be just the same."

Time proved the acute Bradshaw right: the brother dropped out, but Anton continued until Antonia's death in June 1970. In addition to the aforementioned *Anton's Amusement Arcade,* several more Anton books were published, including *Streamlined Bridge* (1947), *Low Life and High Life* (1952) and *Entertaining Singlehanded* (1968).

D.G.

APA

See Elies i Bracons, Feliu.

APE

See Pellegrini, Carlo.

APÓSTOL, EL (Argentina) Many countries claim to have been first in the feature-length cartoon sweepstakes, but *El Apóstol,* a 60-minute cartoon produced in Argentina as early as 1917, seems to take pride of place. El Apóstol ("The Apostle") was Argentine president Irigoyen, who had recently assumed office and was then at the peak of his popularity. Adapted from a book by Alfredo de Laferrere, the film depicted the president leaving in a dream for Mount Olympus, where he was given Jupiter's thunderbolts to destroy the corrupt politicians and vice barons of the republic. The president and his ministers were actually portrayed on the screen by means of drawings based on photographs—a kind of rotoscopy.

The film was produced and directed by Frederico Valle, with Diogenes Taborda and Quirino Cristiani as assistant directors and key animators. From all accounts *El Apóstol* was an intriguing and revolutionary movie; unfortunately for posterity, the negative was destroyed in a studio fire in the 1950s, and no copy has been located so far.

(President Irigoyen was the subject of another Argentinian cartoon feature in 1931. He was then satirized as a tired old man who had run out of ideas. The title of the film was *Peludopolis,* and it was produced, written and directed by Quirino Cristiani, a veteran of the earlier—and kindlier—*El Apóstol.*)

M.H.

ARA MA OKUSAN (Japan) *Ara Ma Okusan* was a four-panel Japanese cartoon that ran in the *Yomiuri* newspaper during the early 1930s. It was drawn by Senpan Maekawa, who was born in Kyoto in 1889. Maekawa was a well-known *Yomiuri* newspaper artist who was fond of working-class themes and fumbling types. *Ara Ma Okusan* centered on a middle-aged housewife who was partial to the common Japanese exclamation "Ara Ma!," which she repeated with great frequency; hence the title of the cartoon, "Mrs. Ara Ma." Her husband was an artist, and they had one son. In short, they were a typical middle-class family that Maekawa's readers could easily identify with.

Reflecting the economic hardships of the 1930s, *Ara Ma Okusan* frequently took up the topic of the need for frugality. In fact, this was the main source of humor in the cartoon. Mrs. Ara Ma was a lover of the arts and a perpetual do-gooder. The cartoons often revolved around the conflict between her desire to go to the movies, visit museums or help out a friend in need and her recognition that her family's budget did not allow such extravagances. Her plight was the same as that of millions of Japanese, and Maekawa's gentle treatment of Mrs. Ara Ma's situation gained him a loyal following.

Ara Ma Okusan is somewhat reminiscent of Maekawa's earlier work *Awate no Kuma-san,* in which much of the humor is also derived from the interesting predicaments of a well-meaning housewife. *Ara Ma Okusan* is most significant, however, because it was the last cartoon series that Maekawa drew before he retired to spend the rest of his life making woodblock prints.

J.C.

ARCADY, JEAN

See Brachlianoff, Arcady.

ARCIMBOLDO, GIUSEPPE (1527-1593) Italian artist and caricaturist born in Milan, Italy, in 1527. Giuseppe Arcimboldo (or Arcimboldi) was a pupil and disciple of Leonardo da Vinci. He worked on the Milan cathedral, and in 1562 he went to Prague as titular portrait painter to the imperial court. For 27 years he indefatigably depicted the faces, tastes and manners of the emperors Ferdinand I, Maximilian II and Rudolph II, and their

Giuseppe Arcimboldo, "The Vegetable-Man," 1590.

wives, children and retainers. For his services he was made a margrave. He returned to his native Milan toward the end of his life and died there in 1593.

Arcimboldo was remembered as the inventor of a "color keyboard," but his work was for a long time relegated to obscurity. He was rediscovered after World War I by the Surrealists, who regarded his fantastic paintings as one of the links in the chain leading to surrealism. Arcimboldo's "composite heads" can also be seen as both a statement on the art of caricature and an attempt to transcend it; his grotesque animals are forerunners of one of the more fertile trends in cartooning. Obviously Arcimboldo was not a cartoonist in the strict sense, and his favorite medium was oil, not pen and ink. He has nonetheless left us a legacy upon which to ponder, and echoes of his work can be found in some of the research carried on by modern cartoonists like Saul Steinberg and Michel Folon.

M.H.

ARIAS BERNAL, ANTONIO (1914-1960) Mexican cartoonist born in Aguas Calientes, Mexico, in 1914. Antonio Arias Bernal was taught to draw by his mother, an amateur artist. He was a fighter against injustice from the earliest age: his first cartoon of note, published when he was 15, savagely attacked the minister of education of his native state of Aguas Calientes. In 1933 Arias Bernal moved to Mexico City, studying briefly at the Academy of San Carlos. His cartoons, which *México al Día* published regularly from 1935 on, created a sensation. He helped found the satirical magazines *Vea, Don Ferruco, El Fufurufu* and others, and his works appeared in such publications as *Hoy, Mañana, Todo* and *Siempre,* as well as in the daily newspapers *Excelsior* and *El Universal,* among others.

Gone with the Wind . .
Antonio Arias Bernal. © Arias Bernal.

Arias Bernal was already a legend when World War II broke out. He relentlessly attacked Latin American dictators, fascist and Nazi regimes, and demagoguery and corruption at home. His books of cartoons were distributed in the hundreds of thousands throughout Latin America by the U.S. Office of the Coordinator of Inter-American Affairs. In 1952 he received a Maria Moors Cabot journalism award from Columbia University for his "distinguished contribution as an artist . . . toward the advancement of friendship in our hemispere."

Antonio Arias Bernal died of cancer in Mexico City on December 31, 1960.

M.H.

Let's laugh a bit.
Othon Aristides ("Fred"). © Aristides.

ARISTIDES, OTHON (1932-) French cartoonist of Greek origin born in Paris, France, in 1932. Othon Aristides—better known under his *nom de plume,* "Fred"—embarked upon a cartooning career soon after graduation from high school in 1950. During the 1950s he contributed countless gag cartoons to the French publications *Ici-Paris* (where his first cartoon appeared), *Le Rire* and *Le Journal du Dimanche,* as well as to *Punch* in England and *Quick* in Germany.

When the satirical monthly *Hara-Kiri* was founded in 1960, Fred was among its first collaborators. There, in addition to his cartoons, he drew his first comic strips, *Les Petits Métiers* ("Odd Occupations"), *Tarsinge l'Homme Zan* ("Tarape the Zanman") and the poetic *Le Petit Cirque* ("The Little Circus").

In 1965 Fred went over to the weekly *Pilote,* where he created *Philémon,* a marvelously inventive fantasy strip, and contributed a number of full-page cartoons depicting topical subjects and contemporary situations. Fred is also a prolific scriptwriter and lyricist. The awards and distinctions he has received as a cartoonist are many and richly deserved. One of the most imaginative and wittiest cartoonists on the French scene today, Fred can be counted on to spring even more (felicitous) surprises on his readers in the future.

The decades of the 1980's and 1990's have been partucularly fruitful for Fred. He published two albums under his own imprint, Magic Palace Hotel (1981) and Parade (1982). He also regularly contributed cartoons to the daily *Le Matin de Paris,* and has written more than 40 teleplays. His latest work has been *L'Histoire du Conteur Electrique* ("The Tale of the Electric Storyteller," 1995); and the following year he was the subject of an important traveling exhibition, shown notably in Budapest and Rome.

M.H.

ARMITAGE, JOSEPH (1913-1998) From the mid-1940s onwards, the cryptic signature "Ionicus" began to pop up more and more frequently in England's leading humor magazine, *Punch.* This odd pen name disguised Joseph Charles Armitage, who was born on September 26, 1913, in Hoylake, Cheshire, England, the son of a fisherman. He attended the Liverpool School of Art (1929) after which he became an art teacher himself, except for a time in the Navy during World War Two.

Ionicus's signature first appeared in *Punch* in 1944, where his style was so approved by the art editor that he would remain with that journal for 44 years. His cartoons also appeared in the monthly *Lilliput,* a popular pocket magazine, the upper-class weekly *Tatler,* and such diverse periodicals as *The Countryman, The Dalesman, The Financial Times, Medical News* and *Amateur Gardening.*

In 1950 Ionicus left the teaching profession to become a full-time freelance, adding book illustration to his repertoire with *How to Become a Headmaster* and the children's story, *Adventures of Pinocchio* (both 1960). He also branched out into oil painting. His other books: *Survive with Me* (1962), *A Boy and His Room* (1964), *The Untold Adventures of Santa Claus* (1965), *Tom Ass* (1972), *The Good Little Devil* (1978), and *Sweet Nutcracker* (1985). He died on January 29, 1998.

D.G.

ARMSTRONG, HAROLD BARRY (1902-198?) Australian cartoonist born in Paddington, near Sydney, in March 1902.

It was not without considerable anguish that some Australian newspapers finally adopted comic strips and cartoons in their pages. But during the mid-1930s a gradual increase in strips and cartoons, along with the introduction of political cartoonists, resulted in every metropolitan newspaper competing for circulation with these novel features.

Of the sedate newspapers, the *Argus,* one of Melbourne's oldest (founded in 1846), was published every morning for 90 years before it accepted its first and only political cartoonist—Harold Barry ("Mick") Armstrong. "I was not so much appointed," Armstrong has said, "as insinuated into the *Argus,* where my cartoons were mixed in and buried among photo-pictures."

Harold Barry Armstrong—Mick is a family nickname—was the son of a teacher at Sydney High School, who later was the first headmaster of Wagga High School, which Mick Armstrong attended. He completed his education at Orange High School in New South Wales. Mick Armstrong's first published contribution in the *Bulletin* was drawn when he was a 16-year-old high school student. When he left school he worked in Orange as a survey-draftsman with the New South Wales Lands Department for nine years, continuing to submit his self-taught drawings to *Smith's Weekly,* the *Bulletin, Aussie* (a wartime soldier-produced magazine which went into civilian life in the 1920s) and other publications, steadily building a reputation as a cartoonist.

In 1931, cartoonist Tom Glover of the Sydney *Sun* recommended Armstrong as his stand-in while he was on holiday. In 1932, Armstrong joined the *Melbourne Herald* at a wage of £17 ($34) a week, a princely sum for those times. He turned out illustrations, political cartoons on the leader page, and for about a month in 1934 drew the *Ben Bowyang* comic strip—a feature still running in the *Herald* since its introduction more than 40 years ago. He was offered a position as a political cartoonist with the *Star* evening newspaper in 1935, but after its failure he was placed on the *Argus* staff in 1936 (the *Argus* had owned the *Star*).

It was at the *Argus* that Armstrong's flair and potential proved him a top-class political cartoonist. His cartoons

"Tell that to the Marines."
H.B. "Mick" Armstrong. © The Argus.

appeared prominently featured on the leader page in the late 1930s, through the war years and up until the *Argus* ceased publication in 1957. Not surprisingly, most of Mick Armstrong's best work was produced during World War II. He was a "grand-manner cartoonist, making much use of labeled, symbolic figures such as "Peace," "Prosperity," or "The Spirit of Anzac."

One of his wartime cartoons was reproduced on 25,000 flags and sold during an army march through the Melbourne streets—and the original drawing, titled "I've Got a Date," showing a determined Australian "Digger" thumbing at a picture of Hitler, was auctioned and sold for £115 ($230). Mick Armstrong's cartoons enjoyed enormous popularity during the war years and later; he could with satisfaction swell his clippings book with examples of his work published in overseas newspapers and journals.

For the interested collector, Armstrong had ten books of his cartoons published: *Cartoon Cavalcade* (the *Star* cartoons, 1935), *Cartoon Cavalcade No. 2* (1936) and the wartime volumes *Havoc, Mein Kranks, Army Stoo, Blitzy, Stag at Bay, Taxi!, War Without Tears,* and *Civvy Symphony.* In his later years Armstrong produced cartoon strips and features for various house journals and illustrated books for children. He died in the late 1980s.

V.L.

"Have you read any good books lately?"
Peter Arno. © The New Yorker.

ARNO, PETER (1904-1968) American cartoonist and writer born Curtis Arnoux Peters in Rye, New York, on January 8, 1904. Peter Arno was the son of a prominent family whose head was at the time a justice of the state supreme court. Raised as the typical scion of aristocratic lineage, he attended Hotchkiss Preparatory School and then went on to Yale. Despite his upbringing, it soon became apparent to the young man that his destiny lay in the field of show business. He played the banjo and piano and was part of a band at Yale. It only seemed natural to him that he make use of these talents in a professional way, so he dropped out of school in 1923, organized a band (which for a time featured a young vocalist named Rudy Vallee) and set off for New York City—a world of smoky speakeasies, hot jazz and even hotter flappers. About this time he changed his name to Peter Arno (allegedly to avoid embarrassing his family with the somewhat outré career he had chosen) and plunged into the life of a Jazz Age bohemian.

Tall, urbane and handsome, Arno was the very image of the aristocratic Fitzgerald hero fascinated by the underworld. Unlike Fitzgerald's characters, however, Arno was not destroyed by his fascination but instead used it (and his frequent annoyance with the New York demimonde) as material for his cartoons. Thus, for 43 years he mixed his visions of life—high and low—with color and vigor and spread them out on the pages of the *New Yorker,* to which he'd sold his first drawing in 1925, thereby launching a wholly unlooked-for career.

Arno had no formal training in art, but his inspirations were of the noblest sort—Rouault and Daumier, with strong elements of Picasso-Braque postimpressionism—and he was a disciplined craftsman, gay-blade image notwithstanding. He worked from idea to cartoon by first making some rough sketches in an easy medium like charcoal or pencil and then taking five minutes to a half hour to concentrate his efforts on the principal figures—facial expressions, postures, etc. Backgrounds were filled in later, and the finished cartoon—generally a bold, broad-lined watercolor—was produced from this rough.

Arno was above all an urbanite (if Harold Ross's little old lady from Dubuque ever *had* looked at the *New Yorker,* Arno's work would have been as likely as anything to cause her to shake her head and cluck over wicked city ways). Crowded speakeasies, scantily clad flappers, exotic dancers, boors, fools and drunks were the elements of his work. Yet he always maintained that he was able to portray that environment so well because it made him angry to see so much energy and intelligence wasted in the pursuit of dubious pleasure. Whatever the inspiration, the product was certainly one for which there was a demand among *New Yorker* readers. Ten years after selling his first drawing to Ross for ten dollars, Arno was reputedly commanding a thousand dollars per cartoon.

Besides cartooning and illustration work, Arno maintained an interest in music, and he wrote and produced a number of reviews. He also served as a writer and screen consultant to Paramount Pictures. He wrote voluminously, contributing articles, fiction and newspaper feature material to a wide range of publications, including the *Saturday Evening Post, Harper's Bazaar, American Magazine, Cosmopolitan, London Opinion,* the *Tatler* and the *Bystander.* His art has been exhibited in New York, Paris and London. Arno died in New York City on February 22, 1968, after a long illness.

Books: *The Whoops Sisters* (1927); *Peter Arno's Parade* (1929); *Peter Arno's Hullabaloo* (1930); *Peter Arno's Circus* (1931); *Peter Arno's Favorites* (1932); *For Members Only* (1935); *Man in the Shower* (1945); *Sizzling Platter* (1949); and *Hell of a Way to Run a Railroad* (1957).

R.C.

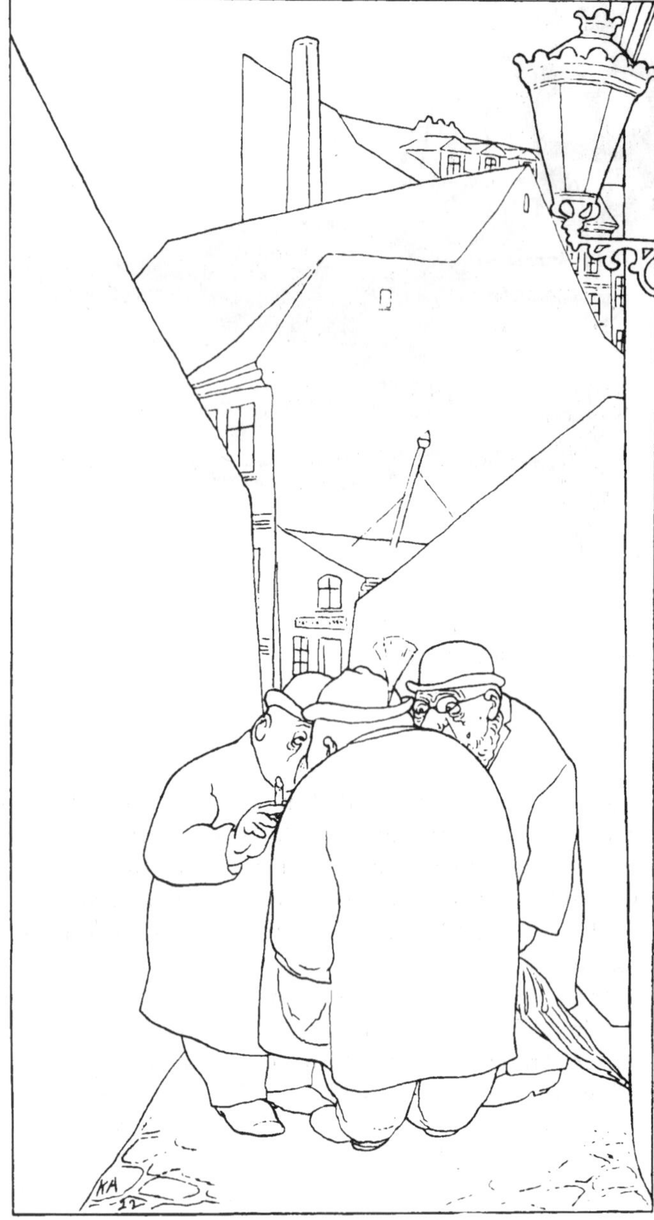

Citizens of Munich discuss Hitler's propaganda.
Karl Arnold, 1922. © Simplicissimus.

ARNOLD, KARL (1883-1953) German cartoonist and painter born in Neustadt, near Coburg, Upper Franconia, on April 1, 1883. The son of a democratic member of Parliament, Karl Arnold long preserved his liberal views in life and art, although circumstances forced him into the directorship of the Munich satirical magazine *Simplicissimus* between 1934 and 1936, when it was under the thumb of Hitler.

Arnold studied under Stuck and others at the Munich Academy, and in 1907 he began his long association with *Simplicissimus.* He also contributed to *Jugend* and *Lustige Blätter,* visited Paris in 1910, became a founding member in 1913 of the artistic group known as the New Munich Secession and, as a soldier in the German-occupied French city of Lille, illustrated the *Liller Kriegszeitung* ("Lille Wartime Newspaper") from 1914 to 1917. In 1917 he became a profit-sharing partner in *Simplicissimus.*

During the 1920s Arnold traveled to Berlin (many of his *Simplicissimus* cartoons of that period were submitted from there) and to several other European cities. In the course of his work for *Simplicissimus* his style shifted from strong dependence on shading and hatching to reliance on pure linear contours, and his model for this was obviously George Grosz. Arnold also extensively adopted Grosz's seamy subject matter of selfish bourgeois and disowned proletarians, especially in his Berlin reportage, but in Arnold everything is softened and relatively commercialized. As an observer of Munich, Arnold noted the antidemocratic leanings of the bulk of the population and warned against Nazism from its inception.

Other publications for which Arnold worked were the Zurich humor magazine *Nebelspalter* and the Copenhagen *Aftenbladet.* He was also known as an illustrator of books; an edition of the works of meistersinger Hans Sachs with Arnold's drawings was especially successful. Late in his life he published an album called *Der Mensch Ist Gut–Aber die Leut San a Gsindl* ("Man Is Good—But People Are a Bunch of Crooks"). During the 1940s Arnold's health failed him, and he had less and less to do with the operation of *Simplicissimus.* He died in Munich on November 29, 1953.

S.A.

ARTIS GENER, AVELÍ (1912-) Spanish cartoonist born in Barcelona, Spain, in 1912. Avelí Artis (better known under the pseudonym "Tisner") studied art at the Fine Arts School in Barcelona. His first drawings were published in the early 1930s in the satirical weeklies *L'Esquella de la Torratxa* and *Papitu.* From August 1933 to July 1936 he published cartoons in the *Bé Negre,* the most politically radical magazine of the time. Prior to the Spanish civil war, Artis had cartoons running regularly in such newspapers and publications as *Diari Mercantil, L'Opinió, La Publicitat* and *La Rambla.* During the war, together with other cartoonists and writers, he managed to keep *L'Esquella de la Torrotxa* going. At the same time he drew cartoons for the lesser-known magazines *Gracia-Ramblas* and *Merida.*

At the end of the civil war in 1939, Artis was interned in a concentration camp in France, from which he escaped to Mexico. There he worked for several magazines published for exiled Catalans, the most important being *La Nostra Revista.* During that time he also wrote a novel, *556 Brigada Mixta,* dealing with the civil war. In 1965 Artis returned to Barcelona, and he is currently publishing a daily cartoon in the newspaper *Tele/Express.* In 1972 he won the Catalan literary contest of San Jordi.

As a cartoonist, Tisner (as he still signs his work) uses a bitter, clear and politically radical humor. His style is more modern and abstract than that of other cartoonists of his generation. He characteristically uses people to symbolize such things as nations, freedom or tyranny, much as the cartoonists of the 19th century did. He is now retired. His last work was the 1997 *Ciris Trencat* ("Broken Circles").

J.M.

ARTUR, J.
See Bevilacqua, José Artur.

ART YOUNG'S INFERNO
See Hell.

"Aru Machikado no Monogatari." © Mushi Productions.

ARU MACHIKADO NO MONOGATARI (Japan) *Aru Machikado no Monogatari* ("Story of a Certain Street Corner") was the first animated film production of the legendary but now defunct Mushi Productions; it was released in November 1962. One year and 12 million yen (approximately $34,000) were required to make this full-color 38-minute film, but today it represents something of a classic in Japanese animation.

Produced by Osamu Tezuka with a small staff, *Aru Machikodo no Monogatari* was an experiment in creating quality animation without following the usual Disney formula of using prodigious amounts of money and personnel (which were unavailable anyway). The result is a uniquely lyrical work that has been characterized by some as antiwar, but which Tezuka prefers to describe as representing the vitality of life. Like Disney's *Fantasia,* it is entirely set to music, and it has received several awards.

As the title implies, the setting is a street in a city of an unspecified nation. The film opens on an autumn afternoon, and the details of the peaceful street—a balloon seller, a little girl and her teddy bear, a group of house mice—are all charmingly depicted. The focus then shifts to a wall of posters, the pictures on which are themselves animated in time to the music: a young violinist plays to a ballerina. Suddenly, however, the world changes. The posters are torn from the wall and replaced with those of a dictator; war comes, and the town is destroyed. Nonetheless, in the end spring arrives, and life emerges triumphant from the ashes—a favorite theme of Tezuka's.

Aru Machikado no Monogatari is a work of universal appeal that, by emphasizing music and images, transcends both time and culture. Tatsuo Takai was in charge of the music, and he used the entire Tokyo Philharmonic Orchestra.

F.S.

ASMUSSEN, ANDREAS (1913-) Danish cartoonist born in Ordrup, Denmark, in 1913. Andreas ("Des") Asmussen was born into an academic, artistic environment. His brother Johan is a well-known lawyer; his youngest brother is the world-famous jazz violinist Svend Asmussen. A cartoonist and illustrator, Des made a name for himself, as did so many other illustrators in the 1930s, in *Magasinet,* a supplement to the daily *Politiken.* He got his great following during the German occupation, when the need for artists to express themselves freely in words and pictures was greater than ever before—or since. Lack of fuel literally made people move closer together—and gave the cartoonists an opportunity to illustrate this intimacy. Blackouts during the occupation (1940-45)—and what might follow—were also excellent topics on which to base cartoons. The underground magazine *Muldvarpen* ("The Mole") nourished talents which were given freer rein than in the "legal" political yearly booklets. And Des's line drawings got an extra dimension when used satirically.

As an illustrator of short stories in Danish weekly magazines (*Hjemmet* and *Søndags B.T.*) and of book covers, Asmussen gradually became internationally known, and he has made remarkable contributions to, among others, the *Saturday Evening Post,* where his artistic drawing style, far closer to the French than to the true Danish tradition, resembles character humor.

Among the batch of young talents who blossomed in the Danish humor magazine *Hudibras,* Des Asmussen is without a doubt the most aesthetic. To him the drawing is more important in a cartoon than merely providing a pretty illustration to a good gag. The joy of drawing always shines through and has placed him today in the elite of acknowledged illustrators—from the lightest humorous novels (his *Woodhouse* book covers are unsurpassed) to anniversary booklets for top banks and public institutions.

J.S.

ASTÉRIX (France) In 1959 René Goscinny (writer) and Albert Uderzo (artist) created *Astérix,* a comic strip

"Astérix." © Dargaud.

depicting the exploits of a feisty little Gaul able to hold Julius Caesar's legions at bay virtually single-handed. The strip became an international success, and it was inevitable that it should be transposed into the animated cartoon medium.

In 1967 Belvision produced *Astérix le Gaulois* ("Astérix the Gaul"). The feature had been intended for television but was released theatrically at the last minute. The animation, done by Nic Broca, André Paape and Henri Verbeeck among others, was crude, and the story was clumsily adapted from the original. This was followed in 1970 by the far more successful *Astérix et Cléopâtre,* which was animated with more verve and spirit than the first film. In 1973 Dargaud, publisher of the *Astérix* comic strips, broke with Belvision. A new animation studio, Idéfix, was formed under the direction of Henri Gruel and Pierre Watrin, and it released a third *Astérix* feature in 1975, *Les Douze Travaux d'Astérix* ("The Twelve Labors of Astérix"). This was not an adaptation, but the development of an original story by Goscinny and Uderzo. The result, however, proved disappointing.

Having been produced under the overall supervision of the creators, the *Astérix* cartoons remained faithful to the original concept. They were, on the whole, entertaining, although they contributed little to the art of animation. Several new Astérix cartoons were produced in the 1980s and 1990s, after the Idéfix studio folded following Goscinny's death in 1977, by the major French film company Gaumont.

M.H.

ATAMANOV, LEV KONSTANTINOVICH (1905-) Animator and producer born in Moscow, Russia, on February 21, 1905. Lev Atamanov graduated from the First State School of Cinematography in 1926. One of the pioneers of Soviet cartoon animation, he worked first in Armenia, where he directed the early sound cartoon *Crossroads* (1931) and produced *The Dog and the Cat* (1938) and *The Magic Carpet* (1948), two features combining strong elements of regional folklore with a style almost slavishly derived from Disney's.

Lev Atamanov, "Dog and Cat."

In 1949 Atamanov was appointed head of the All-Union Animated Cartoon Film Studios; as such, he was the man most responsible for the sorry state of modern Soviet animation. While some of his productions, such as *The Yellow Stork* (1950), *The Golden Antelope* (1954), *Dog and Cat* (second version, 1955), *The Snow Queen* (1957) and *The Bench* (1968), have been fairly well-crafted features and have won some prizes, it can be said that most of the Soviet output lagged far behind in style, imagination and inventiveness, and had quite a way to go before matching the brilliant achievements in such Eastern European countries as Yugoslavia, Czechoslovakia and Poland. Atamanov died in Moscow on February 12, 1981. His last film, a tall tale titled *Who Narrates the Incredible,* was completed by his wife and released posthumously in 1982.

M.H.

ATTALO

See Colizzi, Gioacchino.

ATTILIO

See Mussino, Attilio.

ATTWELL, MABEL LUCIE (1879-1964) British cartoonist and illustrator born in London, England, on June 4, 1879. Creator of the most cuddly, lovable little children in picture books, postcards, dolls, toys, advertising and comic strip art, Mabel Lucie Attwell is still a household name in the United Kingdom. The continuing stream of books featuring Attwell's familiar style of full-color pictorial stories is, in fact, continued under her name by her daughter, Peggy, for her original publisher, Dean.

Mabel Lucie Attwell was educated at Cooper's Company School, then studied painting and drawing at the Regent Street Art School and Heatherley's Art School, London. Her first folio of watercolor sketches of fairies, babies and animals was left with an unenthusiastic art agency but sold almost immediately. The teenage artist struck a chord with the sentimental Victorians, and she never had to look for work again. Her chubby kiddies appeared in magazines for both children and adults, on many series of picture postcards, nursery china and pottery, textiles, handkerchiefs, toys and almost every kind of merchandise.

A few regular characters emerged from the multitude—Diddums, who became a best-selling doll; the Boo-Boos, charming little baby gnomes; and others. She also illustrated many editions of popular children's books—Charles Kingsley's *Water Babies,* Hans Christian Andersen's *Fairy Tales,* Grimm's *Fairy Tales, Peter Pan*—and executed many posters, including one of the first for London's Underground Railway. She summed up her style: "I see the child in the adult and then I draw the adult as a child." Attwell died in Cornwall on November 13, 1964.

Books: *Peeping Pansy* (1919); *Peter Pan and Wendy* (1921); *The Boo-Boos* (1921); *Lucie Attwell's Alice in Wonderland* (1922); *Lucie Attwell's Annual* (1922-57); *Rainy Day Tales* (1931); *Quiet Time Tales* (1932); *Rockabye Tales*

(1931); *Great Big Midget Book* (1934); and innumerable others.

D.G.

ATTWELL, MICHAEL (ca. 1940-) Michael Attwell is a name better known as an actor, while his pen name "Zoke" is better known as a cartoonist. Both careers form the twin lives of this talented man, and he keeps them quite separate. He originally wanted to be an actor, his pleasure in cartooning being strictly a schoolboy hobby. He studied acting at the Royal Academy of Dramatic Art, graduating and turning professional in 1962. He spent three years in the company at the Playhouse Theatre in Newcastle, followed by four years as resident leading man at the Haymarket Theatre in Leicester. He came down to London in a production of *Oliver* in which he played the hulking villain Bill Sykes. His next success was acting in the famous Young Vic Company. Spotted by Independent Television, he was offered the tough-guy role of "Razor Eddie" in the new series, *Turtle's Progress*. Excited by the prospect, Attwell bought himself out of the Young Vic, and attained immediate success with television viewers.

In his spare time during his long periods in repertory theatre, Attwell began to draw comic strips, freelancing to various D.C. Thomson-published children's weeklies including the girls' comic, *Bunty*. He continued for some years, giving up when he started to act for television. His former agent then contacted him when Franklin, the topical cartoonist of the tabloid daily newspaper, *The Sun*, departed for a holiday. Not wishing to confuse his two careers, Attwell devised the pen name of "Zoke", combining the names of his two children, Zoe and Jake. He was an immediate success, and after Franklin returned he was contacted by the Sunday newspaper, *People*. From 1982 he became their regular cartoonist, finding a once-a-week cartoon easier to fit in with his acting career.

"The hardest part of drawing cartoons is waiting for the ideas to come," he says, and on his double career he comments, "In a way, cartooning is a bit like acting. In both cases you have the responsibility of putting your performance in front of an audience and waiting for a reaction."

D.G.

ATTWOOD, FRANCIS GILBERT (1856-1900) American artist born in Jamaica Plain, Massachusetts, on September 29, 1856. Francis Attwood enrolled at Harvard with the class of 1878 and, although he left without a degree after three years, contributed more to the school than many others with sheepskins. He founded—with E.S. Martin, John T. Wheelwright, Edmund M. Wheelwright and Frederick J. Stimson (J.S. of Dale)—the *Harvard Lampoon* and was its chief artist for years, even after he was no longer a student. While on the *Lampoon* staff, he was responsible for two satirical series that were later published in book form and achieved wide notice: *Rollo's Journey to Cambridge* and *Manners and Customs of Ye Harvard Student*. At Harvard he was the official artist of the Hasty Pudding Club.

Even when he drew professionally, Attwood took art instruction, in the late 1870s and early 1880s, under Dr. William Rimmer and at the Boston Art Museum school. In 1883 he joined other Harvard alumni in establishing a grown-up *Lampoon: Life* magazine, the first issue of which contained Attwood's work. Here he was a mainstay until his death, and his work was an integral part of the magazine's character. In January 1887 he began his monthly page of drawings that summarized current events—a feature that remained, in the hands of Frederick T. Richards and later Charles Sykes, into the 1920s. Attwood also became a busy book illustrator and contributed cartoons, illustrations and decorations to the pages of the early *Cosmopolitan* magazine.

Attwood drew elaborate, almost miniature-style cartoons in a wispy but confident manner. In his *Life* years his anatomy was sound, and he employed a unique form of toning and crosshatching; his focal figures received delicate, dark shading for emphasis. He died at his birthplace on April 30, 1900.

R.M.

AUERBACH-LEVY, WILLIAM (1889-1964) American caricaturist, painter, etcher and author born William Auerbach in Brest-Litovsk, Russia, in 1889. His parents adopted the surname Levy after they emigrated to the United States when he was five.

His artistic ability was recognized by a teacher in the elementary school he attended in New York City's Lower East Side, an urban ghetto for many recent immigrants of the period. With the teacher's help William Auerbach-Levy was enrolled at the youthful age of 11 in the National Academy of Design. During high school he was noted as much for his checkers playing as his art. At age 15 he won the citywide public school checkers championship. In later years he was a regular among checkers players at the outdoor tables in Washington Square Park in Greenwich Village, where he lived most of his life.

Following graduation from City College in New York, he won an art scholarship to Paris. Upon his return to New York he joined the faculty of the National Academy's School of Fine Arts and the Educational Alliance Art School. By the time he was 25, his caricatures had earned him fame, and his career was established. A prize-winning painter and etcher, Auerbach-Levy received a Guggenheim Fellowship in 1929 for one of his paintings. His work was traditional in style, as he thought modern art had little merit.

His caricatures appeared in numerous publications including the *New Yorker, Collier's, Theatre Arts, Vogue, Vanity Fair, McCall's,* and *Ladies' Home Journal.* Originally he drew for the old *New York World,* but after the demise of that newspaper he was closely associated with the drama page of the *New York Post* and the *Brooklyn Eagle.* In 1948, assisted by his wife, Florence Von Wien, he summed up his career in *Is That Me? A Book About Caricature.* The book is a classic on the subject and contains sections about his career, along with a brief history of caricature and instructions on how to draw caricatures. A reviewer noted that William Auerbach-Levy had, with caricature, "the same indisputable authority as Freud on sex, Tilden on tennis, or Fanny Farmer on cookery."

Tony Auth. © The Philadelphia Inquirer, The Washington Post Writers Group.

"It's the first quick impression that counts," said William Auerbach-Levy. He cautioned students, "Good draughtsmanship is indispensable. . . . Caricature is an art of simple line, so faults in drawing are not easily concealed." His own style was a masterpiece of the economical use of line, resulting in drawings with power and dignity. He emphasized the need for drawing for the specific type of reproduction used in a publication. For newspaper reproduction he recommended "pure black line or solid black tone" with some use of benday dot patterns for shading. Thousands of William Auerbach-Levy caricatures were published over his long and prolific career: not only famous people in the theater, but in the fields of literature, sports, politics, and finance.

He died of a heart attack at age 75 on June 30, 1964, in Ossining, New York.

B.C.

AUTH, TONY (1942-) American cartoonist born in Akron, Ohio, on May 7, 1942. Tony Auth moved to California with his family in 1949. He was raised in Los Angeles and majored in biological illustration at UCLA, graduating in 1965. While in college, Auth contributed to campus publications, and even after graduation he drew for the campus *Daily Bruin;* his cartoons were syndicated by Sawyer Press. He was the chief medical illustrator at Rancho-Los Amigos Hospital from 1965 to 1971, when he became editorial cartoonist for the *Philadelphia Inquirer.*

Auth's handsome style is one of understatement and economy of line. He presents his powerful concepts in a horizontal format and shades with mechanical tones. In 1976 he received the Pulitzer Prize and a Sigma Delta Chi Award, and he won the Overseas Press Club award in 1975, 1984 and 1986. His work is syndicated by Universal Press Syndicate. Concerning his working philosophy he declared to John Lent in 1988, "One of the really wonderful things about the medium is to have this space to fill and you can fill it any way you want; there is no need to be hung up on style or continuity."

R.M.

AUTRE MONDE, UN (France) Grandville's *Un Autre Monde* ("Another World") came out in 36 installments published in the course of the year 1844. Unlike other books illustrated by Grandville, *Un Autre Monde* used already existing cartoons for which the prolific writer Taxile Delord provided an improvised narrative.

Un Autre Monde probably represents the epitome of Grandville's cartoon work. As Stanley Appelbaum says in his introduction to *Bizarreries and Fantasies of Grandville* (New York, 1974), "*Un Autre Monde* is the work in which Grandville's oneiric leanings receive fullest expression (leading to his adoption by the Surrealists as one of their multitude of spiritual progenitors and giving psychoanalytically minded art critics a field day)." Indeed, there is a host of disturbing and even frightening images in this work: demons cavorting under a full moon, animals disguising themselves as human beings, threatening objects and strange excrescences coming out of the earth; but there is also a multitude of finely observed social and psychological details, from the anglomania of the upper

"Un Autre Monde."

classes to the general passion for carnivals and merry-go-rounds. The attitudes, the institutions, the morals and the passions of the reign of Louis-Philippe are depicted with an unfaltering pen and a somewhat jaundiced eye.

Un Autre Monde ranks high in Grandville's canon. Its concerns and visions are probably closer to our own time than to the mid-19th century. Drawings from *Un Autre Monde* have been used over and over again in publications throughout the world, cumulatively contributing to the posthumous fame and mythical reputation of their author.

M.H.

AVERY, FREDERICK BEAN (1908-1980) American animator born in Taylor, Texas, on February 26, 1908. Frederick Bean ("Tex") Avery, a distant relative of the notorious Judge Roy Bean, "the law west of the Pecos," went to North Dallas High School and graduated in 1927. After a summer course at the Chicago Art Institute and several unsuccessful attempts at creating a newspaper strip, Avery moved to California in 1929. The following year he joined Walter Lantz's animation studio as an in-betweener and later was promoted to full animator status. (Some of the cartoons he worked on during this period include *Ham and Eggs, Elmer the Great Dane* and *Towne Hall Follies.*)

In 1935 Avery moved over to the Warner Brothers studio. During his stay at Warners he directed a number of *Porky Pig* cartoons ("Picador Porky," "Porky the Wrestler," and especially "Porky's Duck Hunt," in which the character of Daffy Duck first appeared, are among the more notable). He was also the artist most responsible for the definitive characterization of Bugs Bunny in the 1940 "A Wild Hare." Other notable Avery-Warners cartoons include *The Penguin Parade* (1938), *Thugs with Dirty Mugs* (1939) and *Cross Country Detours* (1940).

Tex Avery's most creative period came after he had moved over to MGM in 1942. The first cartoon he directed at his new studio was *The Blitz Wolf,* a retelling of the "Three Little Pigs" fable in the context of the Allied fight against Hitler (who appears as the Big Bad Wolf). This was followed by the creation of Avery's most lovable character, Droopy the Dog, who made his first appearance in the 1943 "Dumb-Hounded." Droopy proved more popular than such other Avery characters as Screwy Squirrel, and the two bears, George and Junior.

Avery's fame rests primarily on a number of cartoons which depend less on characterization than on inexhaustible gag building and frenetic action. These include *Who Killed Who?* and *Red Hot Riding Hood* (both 1943), *Bad Luck Blackie* (1949) and, above all, *King-Size Canary,* a 1947 cartoon involving a cat, a mouse, a dog and a canary grown to giant size, which is widely regarded as Avery's masterpiece.

In 1954 Avery left MGM for a short stint back at Lantz (where he directed four cartoons). He has been directing and producing advertising cartoons (including, ironically, the Bugs Bunny Kool-Aid commercials) for Cascade Studios ever since 1955. Looking back on his career in the course of a 1971 interview, he declared, "I do miss the theatricals, but I'd never go back to them."

Tex Avery has been hailed as one of the most gifted and imaginative of American cartoon directors. He has been called "a Walt Disney who has read Kafka" by some critics and blasted for the violence of his cartoons by others. Walter Lantz once admiringly stated, "The thing about Avery is that he can write a cartoon, lay it out, time it, do the whole thing himself." No Avery cartoon ever received an Oscar (an oversight for which the Academy has been castigated time and again), although several of his films were nominated. Avery has been honored at a number of international film festivals, and in 1974 he received the Annie Award for Best Cartoonist from ASIFA. He died August 26, 1980, in Los Angeles.

F.B. ("Tex") Avery, "Who Killed Who?" © MGM.

A book-length study of Avery's career, Joe Adamson's *Tex Avery: King of Cartoons,* was published in 1975 by Popular Library. An even more lavish study on the artist and his work, written by John Canemaker, came out in 1996.

M.H.

AZIMZADE, AZIM ASLAN OGLY (1880-1943) Cartoonist born in Novkhany, near Baku, in Azerbaijan, Russia, on May 7, 1880. The son of a village craftsman, Azim Azimzade had no formal art education, but he exhibited a flair for cartooning and caricature at an early age. His first cartoons, about local politics and everyday incidents, were published in such humor magazines as *Molla Nasreddin* and *Mazali.* (According to Azimzade's biographer, M. Nadzhofov, this marked the beginning of Azerbaijani graphic humor and satire.)

In 1914 Azimzade illustrated a collection of satirical poems by A. Sabri (one of the founders of *Molla Nasreddin)* entitled *Khop-Khopname,* and this spread his reputation beyond the borders of Azerbaijan. After the Russian Revolution, Azimzade contributed a great many illustrations to books and magazines, at the same time continuing to draw cartoons. His most notable works are: *Characters of Old Baku* (1937); *Ramazan Among the Poor* and *Ramazan Among the Rich* (both 1938); and the savagely satirical *The Fuehrer's Trophies* (1941) and *The Crow in Peacock Plumage* (1942).

A member of the Communist Party of the Soviet Union since 1923, Azimzade received many honors and distinctions from the Soviet regime, including the title People's Artist of the Azerbaijani Soviet Socialist Republic (1927). He died in Baku on June 15, 1943.

M.H.

Bb

BABA, NOBORU (1927-) Japanese cartoonist, comic book artist and children's book illustrator born in Sannohe, Aomori Prefecture, Japan, in 1927. After graduating from junior high school, Noboru Baba was caught up in the wartime draft and served in the Imperial Navy Air Corps. When peace finally came, he tried his hand at pioneer farming in mountainous Iwate Prefecture, but gave up after a year and returned to his home, where he worked as a substitute teacher. At the same time he began studying art. On the side, Baba drew signs and posters for theaters, and in 1948 he worked as an artist for a U.S. military base near Hachinohe. In addition to drawing posters, he began experimenting with cartoons, and in 1949, at the urging of children's book expert Shigeru Shiraki, he left for Tokyo to seek his fortune.

Baba began his cartoon career drawing for educational magazines put out by Shogakukan for children, and he received considerable attention with works such as *Posto Kun* ("Young Post") and *Yama Kara Kita Kappa* ("Kappa from the Mountains"). In 1956 his *Būtan,* which ran in *Yōni Bukku* ("Children's Book") from 1954 to 1957, won him the first Shogakkan award for children's cartoons. Būtan was a cute little piglet who was always involved in a variety of adventures, but it was his mild-mannered misfit character that accounted for his appeal among children. Most of Baba's works at this time featured animals as main characters.

In 1958 Baba joined the Manga Shūdan (Cartoonists Group) and made a transition to adult comics, producing popular works such as *Chokkusen Bāsan* ("Straight Ahead Granny"), *Makkana Dorobō* ("Crimson Thief") and *Roku San Tengoku* ("Elementary and Junior High School Paradise"). Today, in addition to creating adult comics, Noboru Baba remains active in the illustration of children's books. His *Jūippiki no Neko* ("Eleven Cats") is something of a classic and won him yet another award. It also generated multiple sequels, one the more recent coming out in 1996. Several of the works in the series have also been animated. In 1984 Baba also began drawing political cartoons for the *Yomiuri* newspaper.

F.S.

BACH, FERDINAND-SIGISMOND (1859-1952) French cartoonist, watercolorist and lithographer born in Stuttgart, Germany, on August 15, 1859. Better known as Ferdinand Bac, he started his cartooning career in 1880 by contributing first to *La Caricature* and *La Vie Parisienne* and then to *Le Rire* and *Le Journal Amusant.*

Many of his fine, even elegant illustrations depicting the Parisian life of the 1880s and 1890s were published in albums, the better known being *Femmes Honnêtes!* ("Honest Women!," 1885), *La Femme Intime* ("Intimate Woman," 1894), *Le Triomphe de la Femme* ("The Triumph of Woman," 1899) and *Le Paradis Terrestre* ("Earthly Paradise," 1903). He illustrated his own books as well, among them *La Volupté Romaine* ("Roman Pleasures," 1922) and *Jardins Enchantés* ("Enchanted Gardens"), and wrote numerous books on history, travel, biography.

Ferdinand Bac died on November 18, 1952, in Compiègne, where he had lived in retirement since the late 1920s.

P.H.

Renate Bachem, fantasy drawing. © Bachem.

BACHEM, RENATE GABRIELE (1916-) German cartoonist, illustrator, painter, printmaker and designer born in Dusseldorf, Germany, on May 17, 1916. After studying with her father, a painter descended from a famous old Rhineland publishing family, Bele Bachem (as she is best known) attended the Arts and Crafts School at the Schlesischer Bahnhof in Berlin (1934-37). From 1937 to 1939 she drew for the women's magazines *Die Dame, Elegante Welt* and *Die Neue Linie* and did book illustrations. During the war her art was considered degenerate, and she was not permitted to exhibit or publish, although her important career as a stage designer began with a 1943 production. In the late 1940s, living in Munich (as she still does), she contributed drawings to the resuscitated *Simplicissimus* then being published.

Her first illustrated book of the postwar period, *Manege-Zauber* ("Circus Magic"), was published in 1954. The individual drawings in it, some in watercolor and some in pen, are separately dated between 1942 and 1947 and represent a broad span of years during which Bachem's style approached full maturity. Already in evidence are the strong influence of Chagall, Klee, Grosz and the Surrealists (Bachem herself cites many more influences, from North Indian painting to Magnasco); the theatrical use of space, with "sets" and "props"; and the theme of odd, isolated people in out-of-the-way situations, epitomized by the nomadic circus performer. The people have the unsettling, wide-eyed stare that is practically a Bachem trademark. But the pen work is still more spiky and tentative than it later became.

In 1959 Bachem did the text as well as the pictures for *Magisches Taschentuch* ("Magical Handkerchief"), a cheerful disquisition on the use of handkerchiefs and related cloths through the ages. Because of the nature of the subject, most of the illustrations are cartoonlike versions of great works of art in many media from ancient times to the present. The renderings, which attest to her wide-ranging knowledge of art history, have all the winsomeness that generally characterizes her work, and the feminine-fashion subject suits her to a tee. The 1960 volume *Ausverkauf in Wind* ("Clearance Sale of Winds") contains original fantasy stories and her most intriguing pictures up to that time. In these surrealistic pen drawings there is real anguish and disquiet. The draftsmanship is skillful in the extreme, and it is clearly a matter of the artist's taste (and not a fault in technique) that even this fine book suffers from a tinge of greeting-card cuteness; the male figures are nearly as wasp-waisted and curvaceous as the female. This tendency is largely overcome in her later paintings.

The startlingly versatile Bachem has also done murals, calendar art, posters, textile and porcelain design, film animation and illustrations for the *Arabian Nights,* texts by Latin and Chinese authors, and other books. In the 1960s and 1970s painting and printmaking have occupied most of her time, and she has had numerous successful exhibitions in Germany and elsewhere in Europe. Since the early 1980s, in addition to her other activities, she has written several novels.

S.A.

BAIRNSFATHER, BRUCE

See Old Bill.

BAKER, ALFRED ZANTZINGER (1870-1933) American cartoonist born in Baltimore, Maryland, on January 4, 1870. "Baker-Baker" (as he became known from his monogrammed signature of two *B*s back to back) was educated in private schools and studied art at the Charcoal School of Baltimore, the Académie Julian and the Ecole des Beaux-Arts in Paris.

Baker pursued serious art and was exhibited at age 23 in the National Academy (later exhibitions were sponsored by the Société des Artistes Français and the Salon des Artistes Humoristes), but he joined the staff of *Puck* in 1898. As a cartoonist he did not confine his work to one outlet, and at the turn of the century Baker was appearing frequently in the pages of *Puck, Judge, Life, Scribner's, Harper's, Century* and *St. Nicholas.* His books include *The Moving Picture Book* (1911), *The Moving Picture Glue Book* (1912) and *The Torn Book* (1913). His innovations—such as die-cutting and 3-D drawings with glasses—are surpassed in the children's book genre only by those of the imaginative Peter Newell.

A.Z. Baker stated that he was influenced by French and Japanese cartoons (indeed, he often worked Japanese motifs into his drawings), but whatever the influences, it must be recorded that his work was among the freshest and cleverest of American cartooning at the turn of the century—and retains these characteristics even under modern scrutiny. He rejected the fine-line illustrator's style then threatening to stifle freedom of line and rendered his cartoons—which were almost exclusively animal gags—with a lush brush line, shaded in crayon on a coarse board. He had a delightful and visually agreeable sense of design and anatomy; his funny animals romped with animation among the stolid society drawings in the magazines. In this sense he helped forge a new spirit of amiable looseness in American magazine cartooning and was soon in the company of such men as Art Young, Leighton Budd and Hy Mayer. He died in 1933.

R.M.

BAKER-BAKER

See Baker, Alfred Zantzinger.

BAKER, JULIUS STAFFORD (1869-1961) British cartoonist born in Whitechapel, London, England, in 1869. Julius Stafford Baker, who created the most enduring characters in British comics, was the nephew of John Philip Stafford (1851-99), painter and cartoonist for *Funny Folks,* who taught the boy to draw and paint theatrical scenery. As a boy, Baker appeared on the music hall stage as "Vidocq, the Child Caricaturist." He began to freelance cartoons to the weekly comics and magazines quite early, and was perhaps the first British humorous artist to set out to follow the American cartoonists' style.

In 1891, he created Hooligan, an Irish laborer, and featured him in a weekly panel in *Funny Folks.* The "cod" Irish (or "Oirish") dialogue in the captions caught on with the public and made the character extremely popular. In 1897, he produced a similar series for the *Garland,* featuring Schneider, a funny German.

Baker was one of the first British cartoonists to sell his work in the United States, his cartoons of tramps appearing regularly in *Judge* from 1895 through 1899. For the weekly comic *Illustrated Chips* he created a large humorous panel called *Casey Court* (May 24, 1902), modeled on R.F. Outcault's *Yellow Kid* panels (see *The World Encyclopedia of Comics,* Chelsea House, 1976). This series

A.Z. Baker, "A Dire Threat," 1904.

ran to 1953. On April 16, 1904, the *Daily Mirror* ran its first strip, *Mrs. Hippo's Kindergarten,* in which Tiger Tim appeared. This character is now the oldest in British comics, and it is still running in *Jack and Jill.*

Baker transferred his character to the *Playbox,* a children's supplement to *The World and His Wife* (1904), *New Children's Encyclopedia* (1910), *Playbox Annual* (1912), and the weekly *Rainbow* (1914). Other cartoons he created included *Billy Smiff's Pirates* and *Buzzville,* two panels in *Puck* (1904); *Dr. Ding Dong* in *Woman's Life* (1904); *Swiss Family Robinson* in *Jester* (1904); *Stone Age Peeps* in *Chips* (1904); *Hans the Double Dutchman* in *Comic Home Journal* (1904); *Inventions of Pat* in *Nuggets* (1905); *Playtime at the Zoo* in *Sunday Circle* (1905); *Comic Cuts Colony* in *Comic Cuts* (1910); *Mrs. Jumbo's Junior Mixed* in *Southend Graphic* (1911); *Addums Academy* in *Merry and Bright* (1913); *Ragg's Rents* in *Merry and Bright* (1915); *Little Nigs of Tiny Town* in *Rainbow* (1915); *Prehistoric Pranks* in *Funny Wonder* (1919); *Nutty and Sam* in *Red Letter* (1919); *Dr. Croc's College* in *Sunday Fairy* (1919); *Jacko* in *Children's Newspaper* (1919); *Silas and His Circus* in *Wizard* (1924); and *Sambo Sue and Jolly Golly* in *Sunbeam* (1928).

His son, Julius Stafford Baker II, was born in 1904 and was trained by his father to become his assistant and to take over his strips and panel series. Baker II also drew many strips of his own, signing them "B.S.B." to avoid confusion with his father, whose style he imitated perfectly. Baker II became the official war artist for the Royal Air Force in World War II, resuming his strip career after demobilization. The elder Baker died in September 1961, at age 92. Baker II retired from commercial cartooning and is currently in the antique trade. His son, Julius Stafford Baker III, works in printing. However, *his* son, Julius Stafford Baker IV, is still too small to show artistic talent!

D.G.

BAKHTADZE, NAKHTANG (1914-1987) Russian animator born in Georgia in 1914. The film studios in Tiflis, Georgia, are among the most important producers of animated cartoons in Russia, second only to the Moscow studios; yet these cartoons are rarely shown abroad, or even outside Georgia. Nakhtang Bakhtadze is probably one of the most gifted and best known of Georgian animators (he is an Honored Artist of the Georgian Republic), but information is spotty and hard to get, and his career can be documented only through sporadic

Nakhtang Bakhtadze, "Adventures of Samodelkin."

showings of his films at international festivals and through the interpretation of Russian commentators.

Bakhtadze studied art in local schools, and in 1933 he went to work in the animation department of Georgia Film in Tiflis. He seems to have mainly contributed layouts and designed backgrounds until the 1950s, when he was given credit as an animator on *Nedjenka* (1950), *Jaffana* (1952) and *The Poor Man's Happiness* (1954). He made his directorial debut in 1952 with *Zuriko and Meriko,* in collaboration with K. Mikabadze, another fabled Georgian animator of whom surprisingly little is known. Other films that he directed include *Kursha* (1954), *After the Whistle Blows* and the satirical and much-praised *Narcissus* (1964). Bakhtadze also directed a series of animated shorts starring a plucky little hero, Samodelkin, beginning with the 1958 *Adventures of Samodelkin.* He retired at the beginning of the 1980s and died in 1987.

Bakhtadze often used Georgian themes and stories for his cartoons. The few that were shown in the West exhibited a fluid style and a lively sense of humor and situation, particularly the witty *Narcissus.*

M.H.

BAKSHI, RALPH (1938-) American animator born in the Brownsville section of Brooklyn, New York, on October 29, 1938. After studies at Thomas Jefferson High School, Ralph Bakshi attended the Industrial Arts School, graduating in 1956. In the late 1950s and early 1960s he worked at CBS-Terrytoons on such series as *Heckle and Jeckle* and *Mighty Mouse.* (Later Bakshi confided, "I spent years drawing mice from every imaginable angle.") From there he went on to Famous Studios-Paramount, where he directed countless *Casper the Friendly Ghost* and *Little Audrey* cartoons, among others. During that same period Bakshi also animated Peter Max's commercials.

When Famous Studios closed in 1967, Bakshi went into partnership with Steve Krantz, whom he had met several years earlier. Their first venture was *Fritz the Cat,* a cartoon feature Bakshi directed from Robert Crumb's original stories and drawings. Produced by Krantz, the picture was released in 1972. The success of *Fritz* prompted the duo to follow suit with *Heavy Traffic* (1973), a funny-sad chronicle of life in New York's slums. Striking out on his own, Bakshi then produced the sometimes brilliant, often disappointing *Coonskin* (1974) and the ill-starred *Wizards* (1977), a nebulous saga of times long forgotten, on which a number of comic book artists (Mike Ploog, Gray Morrow, Jim Starlin) labored to little effect. His latest work of animation, *Lord of the Rings,* came out at the end of 1978.

Ralph Bakshi occupies a somewhat ambiguous position in today's animation world. Neither *Fritz the Cat* nor *Heavy Traffic* has elicited the kind of unanimous acclaim that he has obviously been craving. His visuals are often dazzling, but he seems to lack a strong story sense, and he appears unsure of his direction. These failings became even more evident in his latter efforts, American Pop (1982) and Fire and Ice (1984), which were almost unanimously panned by reviewers.

Discouraged by the poor public reception made to his films, he went into seclusion,briefly coming back in 1986 to direct cartoons for television, including the ill-starred revival of Mighty Mouse for CBS. Bakshi retired from animation for a second time in the early 1990's and in his own words "spends all his time painting and drawing now, with no deadlines to worry about."

M.H.

BĂLAŞA, SABIN (1932-) Romanian animator born in the Carpathian region of Romania on July 17, 1932. Sabin Bălaşa studied at the N. Grigorescu Institute of Art in Bucharest, graduating in 1954. He worked first as a cartoonist for various Romanian publications and also had a promising career in book illustration.

In the early 1960s Bălaşa gravitated toward animation while continuing his work as a graphic artist. The films he directed and often drew himself were shown sporadically throughout the 1960s and 1970s. The story lines were often cryptic or nonexistent; notable among his films are *The Drop* (1965), *The Wave* (1966) and *Fascination,* which won the 1968 silver prize at the Mamaia Festival. Bălaşa tried to tell a more coherent story in his 1971 science fiction cartoon *Return to the Future,* but again the refinement of the settings and the brilliance of the design were offset by a muddled script. In recent years Bălaşa has gone into experimental and abstract animation, a field for which he seems best suited. In this domain *Windows* (1977), *Exodus to the Light* (1979), and *Games and Toys* (1980) are best noted. He has not been heard from since the Romanian revolution of 1990.

M.H.

BALLESTER, ANSELMO (1897-1974) Italian caricaturist, cartoonist and poster designer born in Rome, Italy, of a Spanish father, in 1897. Anselmo Ballester contributed theatrical caricatures to Rome newspapers while still a teenager. One of the best-known personalities in the world of show business, he never set foot on a movie set; yet he depicted every known star of silent and sound pictures in his 34 years as a movie poster designer, a career which he started in 1913.

Whether he dealt with Charlie Chaplin or Marlene

Dietrich, Marlon Brando or Mary Pickford, Ballester's drawings were not simple publicity posters but really portraits, hardly caricatured and charged with evocative expression. He turned them out at the rate of a hundred a year and did thousands in the course of his career. Italo Mussa wrote that Ballester captured in the expression of Douglas Fairbanks, say, or Betty Grable, "the invisible mood of the plot." His sketches, some four thousand of them, reveal a desire to zero in on the imagination and fantasies of the spectator. "I must suggest," the artist once said. "The rest is up to the movie."

In 1944, at a time when war was over for half of Italy, the humor weekly *Il Pupazzetto,* finding too little to laugh about, transformed itself into a comic magazine. The front page featured Ballester's *La Scimmiottino d'Oro* ("The Golden Ape"), a story full of violence, adventure and heroism, which perhaps represented the sum of Ballester's experiences as an interpreter of popular dreams. He also drew a few cartoons in the period following the war, but his heart remained with the movies. Just before his death in 1974, Ballester confessed, "With so many porno films, one doesn't rightly know what to draw."

S.T.

BARBERA, JOSEPH ROLAND (1911-) American animator and producer born in New York City in 1911. Despite a flair for drawing, Joe Barbera decided after high school to become a banker, and he attended the American Institute of Banking. He briefly worked as an accountant for a law firm but found himself out of a job at the start of the Depression. After trying unsuccessfully to begin a new career as a magazine cartoonist, he became associated with the Van Beuren studio in 1932, working as an animator and scriptwriter, notably on the *Tom and Jerry* series (which featured two zany human characters in all kinds of weird situations).

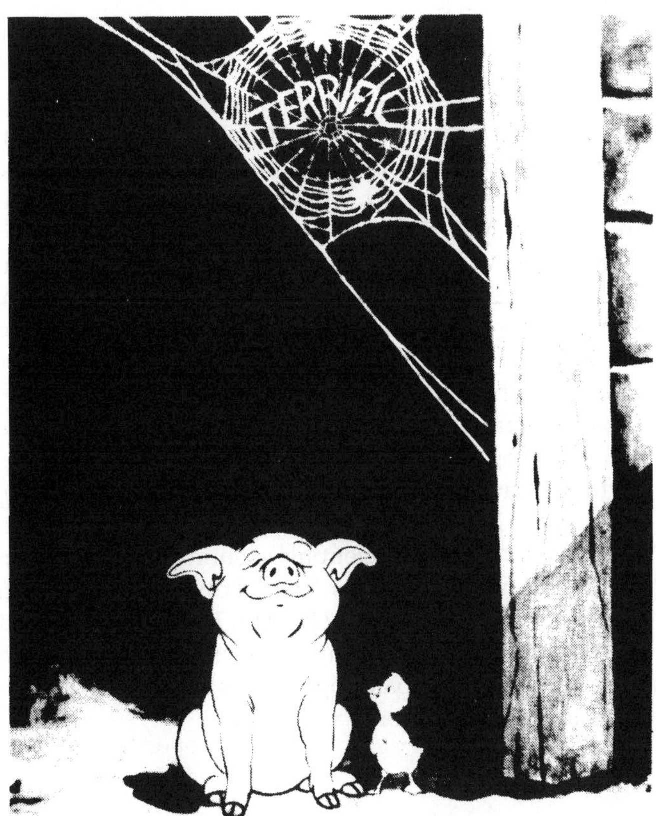

Joseph Barbera (and William Hanna), from the animated version of "Charlotte's Web." © Hanna-Barbera Productions.

In 1937 Barbera went west and joined the newly formed MGM cartoon unit, first as a scriptwriter, then as an animator. He teamed up with William Hanna the following year to direct *Gallopin' Gals;* the association proved mutually satisfying, and in 1939 Barbera and Hanna collaborated again on "Puss Gets the Boot," the first entry in the *Tom and Jerry* series. (While the title was probably inspired by the Van Beuren characters, the protagonists in this one were a cat and a mouse, and very different from their namesakes.) The *Tom and Jerry* cartoons went on to dizzying success, and from 1939 until his retirement in 1996 the professional career of Joe Barbera became inseparable from that of William Hanna (see the entry "Hanna, William").

M.H.

BARLACH, ERNST (1870-1938) German sculptor, printmaker, author and cartoonist born in Wedel, in the Lower Elbe region, on January 2, 1870. The son of a country doctor, Ernst Barlach studied at the Hamburg School of Applied Art (1888-91), at the Dresden Academy (1891-95) and in Paris (1895-96). Back in Hamburg, he worked for a few years in conjunction with the successful sculptor Carl Garbers; the two executed numerous private and civic commissions in a grandiose style. In the same years Barlach, a remarkable draftsman, submitted many drawings to the Munich art magazine *Jugend,* pliantly adapting to several of the styles then in vogue, especially art nouveau (he later felt that he had to rid himself of this "pernicious" influence).

Shortly after the turn of the century, although already in his mid thirties, Barlach found himself aesthetically and psychologically at sea. He lived for awhile in his small hometown, taught at a little school of ceramics while filling ceramic commissions himself, and moved in and out of Berlin, a major art center but no spiritual home for him. Finally, in August and September 1906, he visited one of his brothers, an engineer practicing in Kharkov, Russia. This trip is usually seen as a turning point in his life. The Russian peasants—in his eyes simple, majestic, religious—decisively turned his thoughts to a spare, monumental style. Even the loose and ample Russian peasant smock was to reappear constantly as a garb for his drawn or sculpted figures.

In 1907 and 1908, still in need of funds, Barlach sent several drawings chiefly on Russian subjects to *Simplicissimus,* where they were published with glib, rather unamusing captions. Important as his brief association with this Munich magazine is in retrospect, it was unhappy for him—although at the time there were few other publications where he could freely express the sympathy for the poor and contempt for their oppressors that he managed to convey in some of his *Simplicissimus* work.

Late in the century's first decade, Barlach's financial worries were eased by the Berlin art dealer and publisher Paul Cassirer, and his rich career really took wing. His

"Now we drink for sorrow, little brother, because they've dissolved our Duma. But when we have a new Duma, little brother, we'll drink for joy."

Ernst Barlach. © Simplicissimus.

cartooning days were over, for he turned to other forms of expression. His work in wood, bronze and other media places him securely among the great sculptors of the century. As a woodcut artist, too, he has few equals, and his lithographs are of high quality. Amazingly, from 1912 on, a parallel career in literature—and at a high level—opened up for Barlach. His harsh but powerful expressionistic plays were performed when new and have been revived since World War II (Barlach's art, both visual and verbal, was uncongenial to the Nazis). He also wrote a brief autobiography in 1928.

From about 1910 on, Barlach resided chiefly at Güstrow in the Mecklenburg region. He died at Rostock on October 24, 1938.

S.A.

BARLETTA, SERGIO (1934-) Italian cartoonist born in Bologna, Italy, on November 20, 1934. At the age of 23 he started his freelance career with contributions to such publications as *L'Illustrazione, Fotografia* and *Graphic Designer,* later becoming the art director of a number of magazines and also working for ad agencies.

Between 1960 and 1976 Barletta devoted himself exclusively to the graphic arts, producing magazine illustrations as well as political cartoons. In 1968 he created a comic strip, *Mr. Manager,* which was scheduled to appear in the weekly *Rinascita;* the magazine editor turned it down, however, because of its leftist orientation. It then was picked up by Italy's first underground publication, *Cabalá,* where it remained until the magazine folded in 1975; it has since been appearing regularly in the pages of the monthly *Eureka.*

Barletta has also contributed political cartoons to the German magazine *Pardon* since 1973, and some of his cartoons have appeared in *Fortebraccio* and *Hara-Kiri,* starting in 1974. Barletta, who has been compared to Jules Feiffer in his unrelenting examination of modern reality, has had many of his satirical cartoons collected in four books: *Homo* (1967), *Uno* (1971), *D.C.* (1976) and *Clericus* (also 1976). Recently the artist has also been active in the field of painting and has had several exhibitions in galleries in Rome and Milan.

L.S.

BARLOW, PERRY (1892-1977) American cartoonist born in McKinney, Texas, near Dallas, in 1892. Perry Barlow,

"Aunt Claire asked you a question, dear. Are you the pitcher or the catcher?"
Perry Barlow. © The New Yorker.

who was most famous for his many *New Yorker* cartoons and covers, was raised on his family's farm and spent his boyhood in Texas. He traveled to Illinois to attend the Art Institute of Chicago and there was part of a remarkable class that included Helen Hokinson and Garrett Price, also destined to be *New Yorker* greats. He met his wife, Dorothy Hope Smith, at the art school; she later became a famous portraitist of children best known for drawing the baby on the Gerber trademark.

Around 1920 the Barlows moved to New York, and he began a career of freelance cartooning and illustrating. At the Art Institute of Chicago he had discovered he was color blind, so his color work, featuring soft muted pastels, was done by his wife (and after her death by watercolorist Catherine Barr). As success came the family joined the growing artists' community of Westport, Connecticut.

James Geraghty, art editor of the *New Yorker* from 1939 to 1973, has commented that Perry Barlow was "a quiet, shy, aloof man" but still "a great artist with children." The *New Yorker*'s editor, William Shawn, regarded Barlow as "one of our three or four most prolific people." Ironically, although he had an opportunity to publish an anthology of his cartoons, Barlow was always lukewarm on the project, and no anthology exists. From the 1920s until the early 1970s, however, his cartoons appeared in a variety of magazines, including the *Saturday Evening Post* and *Collier's*. Fortunately the general cartoon anthologies of such magazines contain generous samplings of his works.

Barlow's cartoons have a loose, sketchy style and soft, understated wash. Children were a favorite theme in his cartoons, which were usually geared more for a chuckle than a belly laugh and always displayed a refined, educated sense of humor. His accomplishments as a *New Yorker* cover artist helped set the style of the magazine, along with covers by Peter Arno, Helen Hokinson and others. A Barlow cover was a humorous cartoon that needed no caption and captured some of the joy of living that appears to a cartoonist with an eye for it. Today, when the *New Yorker*'s covers are often devoted to design sans humor, one can appreciate Perry Barlow's gentle cartoon covers all the more.

He died of natural causes at his Westport home on December 26, 1977, at age 85.

B.C.

BARNEY BEAR (U.S.) Barney Bear, the prototypical dumb bear (indeed, in one cartoon Barney is handed a business card reading "Joe Scarecrow—special rates for dumb bears") made his debut in the 1939 "The Bear That Couldn't Sleep," in the course of which the rotund and slightly obfuscated plantigrade grew more and more desperate in his efforts to silence a variety of forest animals seemingly bent on disrupting his peaceful slumber.

"The Bear That Couldn't Sleep" was made by Rudolph Ising and started a trend. MGM, the producers, felt encouraged enough to turn out more *Barney Bear* shorts, which they alternated with the more popular *Tom and Jerry* series, also born around this time. The pattern hardly varied over the years: as other animals take advantage of Barney's gullibility, the bear becomes aware he is being put upon and then lashes out at his tormentors, usually with unhappy results. In "The Impossible Possum," Barney vainly tries to chase an obdurate opossum away from his honey tree and finally ends up demolishing his own cabin. In "Cobs and Robbers," in a futile attempt to get back at the crows who feed on his corn, Barney burns down his entire cornfield. And in "Barney's Hungry Cousin," the hapless bear falls victim to his relative's ravenous appetite and superior wits—the ultimate disgrace.

The *Barney Bear* shorts were directed in the fast-paced, crisp style of the MGM school of cartooning by such stalwarts as Dick Lundy, Michael Lah and Preston Blair. Barney's personality remained somewhat undefined, however, and he never transferred to other media the way Tom and Jerry did. When MGM closed down their animation studios in 1957, the *Barney Bear* series was dis-

"Barney Bear." © MGM.

continued. However, the slow-moving, slow-witted bear still occasionally appears on television in the course of *The Tom and Jerry Show.*

M.H.

For a Christmas Dinner . . .
Raoul Barré, first French-Canadian comic strip, 1902. © La Presse.

BARRÉ, RAOUL (1874-1932) French-Canadian cartoonist born in Montreal, Quebec, on January 29, 1874. Raoul Barré studied art at the Mont St.-Louis Institute in Montreal; moving to Paris in 1891, he attended courses at the Ecole des Beaux-Arts and the Académie Julian. He also started contributing cartoons to such humor publications as *Le Rire* and *L'Assiette au Beurre;* his caricatures in the satirical *Le Sifflet* were especially noteworthy.

From 1898 to 1902 Barré stayed mainly in Quebec. In 1901 his album of satirical reminiscences, *En Roulant Ma Boule* ("Bumming Around"), was published in Montreal. In 1902 he created what is regarded as the first Canadian comic page for the Montreal daily *La Presse.* During this period Barré also contributed numerous drawings and illustrations to such publications as *La Revue Nationale, La Revue des Deux-France* and *Le Monde Illustré.*

Settling in New York in 1903, Barré for a time kept his ties with the Montreal daily *La Patrie,* to which he contributed two comic strips. *Les Contes du Père Rhault,* a feature in the tradition of *The Katzenjammer Kids,* ran from 1906 to 1908; and, under the pseudonym "Varb," Barré also drew *A l'Hôtel du Père Noé* (1913), the French version of *Noah's Ark,* which he had created the preceding year for McClure Newspaper Syndicate.

In 1909 Barré got involved for the first time in the animation field. From 1910 to 1913 he made advertising films in collaboration with W.C. ("Bill") Nolan. In 1913 he founded the Raoul Barré Studio, the first animation unit organized along commercial lines. Among other famous beginners, the young Pat Sullivan first learned the secrets of his trade with Barré. Barré perfected the "peg system" in 1914 and contributed a number of other technical innovations to the craft of animation. In 1915 he realized one of the first film cartoon series, *The Animated Grouch Chasers,* for Edison, and shared with Frank Moser and George Stallings the production of Tom Powers's *Phables* (also known as *Joys and Glooms*).

Founding with Thomas Bowers the Barré-Bowers Studio in 1916, Barré produced the famous series of *Mutt and Jeff* film cartoons for the next three years. Personal and financial disputes between the partners led to Barré's withdrawal in 1919. He then devoted himself to advertising and illustration. In 1926-27 he came back to animation, notably working on Pat Sullivan's *Felix the Cat* series. Plagued by ill health, Barré returned to Montreal at the end of the 1920s. He resumed his painting activities and briefly drew caricatures and illustrations for his son-in-law's publication, *Le Taureau,* under the pseudonym "E. Paulette." Barré died on May 21, 1932, before he was able to make his planned comeback in animation.

A study of Barré's oeuvre, *Barré l'Introuvable* ("Barré the Unfindable") by André Martin, was published in Ottawa in 1976. The following year an exhibition of Barré's graphic works was organized by the International Pavilion of Humor in Montreal.

S.J.

BARRETO, BENEDITO BASTOS (1897-1947) Brazilian cartoonist and newspaperman born in São Paulo, Brazil, in 1897. Better known as "Belmonte," Benedito Barreto started his career as a humor columnist in the second decade of the century, creating, among other things, the popular character Juca Pato, a pompous know-it-all, in the São Paulo newspaper *Fôlha da Noite.* In 1912 he drew his first professional cartoons for the magazine *D. Quixote;* he later contributed more cartoons to *Carêta* (starting in 1922), *O Cruzeiro, Revista da Semana* and the humor publication *Fon-Fon!,* where he also doubled as writer and art director. In 1936 he started a cartoon campaign against the Nazis in the *Fõlha da Manhã* of São Paulo, and these cartoons were reprinted in newspapers all over South America. Belmonte also did book illustration, notably for *Povos e Trajes de América Latina* ("Peoples and Costumes of Latin America") and *História do Brasil para Crianças* ("The History of Brazil for Children).

Belmonte's cartoons were collected in book form under the titles *Angústias de Juca Pato* ("The Anxieties of Juca Pato," 1926), *O Amor Através dos Séculos* ("Love Through the Centuries," 1928) and *No Reino da Confusão* ("The Kingdom of Confusion," 1939). His humor columns (illustrated by himself) were also collected in the anthologies *Assim Falou Juca Pato* ("Thus Spake Juca Pato," 1933) and *Idéias de João-Ninguem* (1935).

Belmonte died, covered with honors and distinctions, in 1947 in São Paulo.

A.M.

BARTÁK, MIROSLAV (1938-) Miroslav Barták grew up in Prague, Czechoslovakia, with a desire early on to be a painter. His parents, wanting him to be an engineer, took the most expeditious way of realizing this dream and enrolled him in the military school. Upon graduation, Barták accepted a chance to study at a navy academy in Bulgaria. By the time he finished his studies, he owed the government five years of service as payment for his schooling.

He left his wife and child behind and began work on a

Miroslav Barták, © M. Barták.

merchant ship, traveling the world for the next ten years. He said that during this time, he started painting big pictures which evolved into small drawings which eventually changed into cartoons. In 1968, with a year's vacation due him, he returned to Prague to draw fulltime. For a short time after the Prague Spring, he lived freely, submitting his work to contra-revolutionary magazines, especially *Literany Noveni*. But in 1970, regulations tightened again and periodicals dried up, forcing Barták to send most of his work abroad to *Nebelspalter*, a Swiss humor magazine. He sought Czech outlets again in the early 1980's, mainly magazines not bound up with Communist officialdom, while still making a substantial part of his living from *Nebelspalter*. From time to time, Czech officials harassed him with threats and interrogations about his work abroad.

Barták's fame as a mirthmaker has spread worldwide since then. He has had at least 50 one-man shows in Czechoslovakia, Canada, and throughout Europe and has published at least 6 books of his cartoons. When the Union of Czech Cartoonists was formed in 1990, he was elected its first president.

Barták prides himself in his immediately-funny drawings, achieved through the use of a simple style with very few lines, single-panel format, no words, and easily-recognized subjects as themes. Occasionally, he does cartoons on social themes, but not too often, for as he said, he is interested in "things that make people common, not pull them apart as some social message cartoons do."

J.A.L.

BARTON, RALPH (1891-1931) American cartoonist, caricaturist and critic born in Kansas City, Missouri, on August 14, 1891. The young Barton studied art in Paris before entering the cartooning profession in 1910 with early work in *Judge* and *Life.*

Due no doubt to his youth, Barton's early work seems to have received its stylistic impulses from impressions of others: trendy European styles of the prewar days and American advertising art, particularly that of Laurence Fellows. Actually, his early work was consistent and handsome in an extremely stylized way (the young John Held, Jr., among others, drew similarly).

Soon his work was seen in many magazines— particularly *Vanity Fair* and *Smart Set*. In 1915, Barton was sent to Paris to cover the war for *Puck* and dispatched some witty and sophisticated copy and art about the effects of the war on the Parisian café set.

The Seven Infallible Signs of Senility. Diagram showing the average age at which man begins to sputter and fume about.

Modern Art — Modern Youth — Modern Books — Modern Dress — Modern Dancing — Modern Inventions — Modern Anything

Ralph Barton. © Liberty.

In the early 1920s, Barton was extremely influential in the field of caricature. His cartoon work had now lost the early willowy, fashion-catalog appearance and was rendered in confident pen lines and richly graded gray tones. His double-page caricatures graced the pages of *Vanity Fair;* news spoofs lightened both *Judge* and the *New Yorker;* illustrations appeared in *Cosmopolitan* and *Women's Home Companion;* and book contracts were many. For a time Barton also was drama editor for *Life.*

Included among Barton's many humorous book illustrations are the following titles: *Nonsensorship* by Heywood Broun, George S. Chappell et al. (1922); *More Letters of a Japanese Schoolboy* by Wallace Irwin (1923); *Science in Rhyme Without Reason* (1924); *Gentlemen Prefer Blondes* by Anita Loos (1925); *Droll Stories* by Balzac (1925); *But Gentlemen Marry Brunettes* by Anita Loos (1928); and his own popular history of the United States, *God's Country* (1929).

A chevalier of the Legion of Honor (1927), Barton died a suicide on May 10, 1931.

R.M.

BARTOSCH, BERTHOLD (1893-1968) Czech animator and artist born in Bohemia, then a crown land of the Hapsburg empire, in 1893. From 1911 to 1913 Berthold Bartosch worked as an apprentice and draftsman for an architectural firm in Vienna. He studied architecture and fine arts in Vienna from 1913 to 1917 and there became interested in film through his association with Professor E. Hunslik, director of the Cultural Research Institute. With Hunslik's sponsorship he opened an animation studio for educational films, first in Vienna (1918-19), then in Berlin.

In Berlin Bartosch met Lotte Reiniger and worked on some of her silhouette films, including *The Ornament of the Lovestruck Heart* and *The Adventures of Prince Achmed.* He also made several advertising films for Julius Pinschewer in Zurich. At the same time he produced a number of animated films of his own, often on political or social themes. Of these, *Communism, Animated Cards* (both 1919), *The Battle of Skagerrak* (1922) and *The Occupation of the Rhineland* (1925) are the best known.

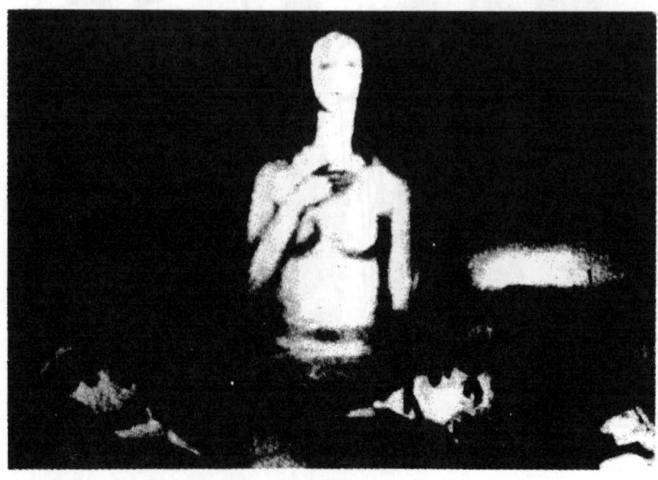

Berthold Bartosch, "L'Idée," © Bartosch.

Bartosch married in 1930 and settled in Paris. There he made the film for which he is most famous, the 30-minute *L'Idée* ("The Idea"), based on a book of woodcuts of the same title by the Belgian artist Frans Masereel. In it Bartosch used every possible kind of animation (cutout figures, drawings, collages), as well as a score by Arthur Honegger, to tell the allegory of the Artist who tries to lead the workers in their fight against Church, State and Capital with the help of the eternal Idea (represented as a nude woman). The film, released in 1932, was soon banned as scandalous, and Bartosch had to close down his studio. *L'Idée* is now regarded as a landmark in the history of animation.

In the 1930s Bartosch subsisted by working on advertising cartoons. In 1940 he fled the Nazi invasion and went into hiding. After the war he again made a few advertising films but mainly concentrated on his paintings, which were exhibited (although not widely) in galleries in Europe and America. He died in 1968.

M.H.

BASSET, GENE (1927-) American cartoonist born in Brooklyn, New York, on July 24, 1927. Gene Basset studied at the University of Missouri, Brooklyn College (where he received a B.A. degree in design), Cooper Union, the Pratt Institute and the Art Students League. He drew for the *Honolulu Star-Bulletin* in 1961 and 1962 and then switched to Scripps-Howard political headquarters in Washington, D.C. He became chief political cartoonist for the chain's *Washington Daily News,* and from there his cartoons were distributed to the Scripps-Howard papers. In 1972, and after the *News* folded, Basset was syndicated by United Feature Syndicate. He later worked for the *Atlanta Journal* and retired in 1995.

Basset's style seems at once derivative and startlingly original; there is something of the zaniness of *MAD* magazine in his concepts, and his lines are very loose without being sketchy or superfluous. He draws in the now-standard horizontal format on doubletone paper.

Brian Basset, the cartoonist's son, joined the staff of the *Detroit Free Press* as editorial cartoonist in 1978. In the 1990's he created *Adam,* a family strip for Universal Press Syndicate.

R.M.

BATCHELOR, CLARENCE DANIEL (1888-1978) American Pulitzer Prize-winning cartoonist born in Osage City, Kansas, in 1888. C.D. Batchelor attended local public schools and Salina (Kansas) High School before studying at the Chicago Art Institute from 1907 to 1910.

His first drawings were on chalk plate for the *Salina Journal.* In 1911 he was hired by the *Kansas City Star* but fired six months later. He then worked briefly with his father on a railroad and began freelancing for *Puck, Life* and *Judge* magazines. He traveled to New York around 1912 and was variously employed on the *New York Mail* (whose practice it was to solicit talent from around the country), the *New York Tribune* (where he was to return intermittently) and the *New York Journal,* where he remained for four years as a staff artist and occasional

"Come on in, I'll treat you right. I used to know your Daddy."
C.D. Batchelor, Pulitzer Prize-winning cartoon, 1937. © New York Daily News.

political cartoonist. He became the political cartoonist of the liberal *New York Post* (1923-31) and drew a panel, *Once Overs,* for the Ledger Syndicate during that time.

In 1931 he joined the staff at the *New York Daily News* and became its chief editorial cartoonist. The *News* at first supported the New Deal, but the paper and its cartoonist eventually grew disenchanted with liberalism and bureaucracy to the point that their political complexion changed; Batchelor wound up his career, after retiring from the *News* in the early 1970s, on the staff of the *National Review,* a journal of the political right. He died at his Connecticut home in 1978.

His Pulitzer Prize in 1937 was a powerful plea against what was already shaping up, for those who wished to see, as a European conflagration with American involvement. Batchelor's strong cartoons were drawn with irony, a moralizing viewpoint and direction; with labels and captions written on scrolls, they have the appearance of documents. In effect, with his crisp style and strong ideas, they are proclamations in cartoon form.

Batchelor's style is one of lilting brushstrokes graced by wisps of shading. He always had a firm grasp of anatomy and composition; he definitely relied on a newspaper artist's portraiture rather than caricature. One of his most effective series, running for years in the *News,* was *Inviting the Undertaker,* telling arguments mainly against reckless driving that won him many public service awards.

R.M.

BATCHELOR, JOY (1914-1991) English animator born in Watford, England, on May 22, 1914. After art school Joy Batchelor worked in design, creating everything from lampshades to fashions for *Harper's Bazaar* and *Queen.* Fascinated by animation, she took a job with Denis Connolly, one of the independent animators of the prewar period, and worked on *Robin Hood* (1935) and a cartoon featuring a koala bear. Moving to British Animated Films for the color short *Music Man* (1938), she met John Halas.

After completion of the film, the pair went to Hungary and attempted to set up their own studio, but the political climate and the lack of financing brought them back to England. Halas contributed cartoons to *Lilliput,* the pocket humor magazine, while drumming up potential customers for commercial advertising. Soon they were Halas and Batchelor, producing short theatrical commercials in color for the J. Walter Thompson Agency: *Carnival in the Clothes Cupboard* for Lux soap (1941), *Train Trouble* for Kellogg's Corn Flakes (1943) and *The Big Top* for Rinso (1944). They got married in 1941 and in the same year made their first entertainment short, *The Pocket Cartoon.* She died in London in 1991. (For further information on Joy Batchelor's career see the entry "Halas, John.")

D.G.

Joy Batchelor, "Ruddigore." © Halas & Batchelor.

BAUER, ROLF PETER (1912-1960) German cartoonist born in Konstanz, Germany, in 1912. The son of an architect, Rolf Bauer moved to Munich with his family when he was 11. By the time he was 19, he was already submitting sports cartoons to such newspapers as the *Münchener Abendblatt* and the *Neue Augsburger Zeitung,* and his reputation in this field was extremely high in the 1930s. His interest in sports was more than merely graphic, however, for Bauer became the tennis champion of Bavaria. Later in the 1930s, without abandoning sports as a cartoon subject, he turned increasingly to celebrity caricatures, especially of theater and film personalities.

In 1939 he became a soldier, but even in the barracks and at the front he continued to draw. About this time he also created a children's book called *Hupfauf der Gummiball* ("Hopup the Rubber Ball"). After the war he found that his Munich home had been bombed out, so he lived by the Tegernsee for awhile.

In 1946 he published a book of original pictures and verse that he had completed in 1943, *Das Spiel um die Meisterschaft* ("The Championship Game"). Here, with a large number of amusing vignettes, he did for German soccer something similar to what Ernest L. Thayer (more briefly and minus the pictures) had done for American baseball in "Casey at the Bat." Other Bauer books based on sports are *Das Grosse Spiel* ("The Big Game") and *Spiel, Satz und Sieg* ("Game, Stake and Victory").

After the war his work with celebrity caricatures became paramount. Two collections of this kind of material are *Im Konzertsaal Karikiert* ("Caricatured in the Concert Hall") and *Flimmerstars und Fürstlichkeiten* ("Stars of the Flicks and Royal Personages"). After Bauer's untimely death in 1960 at the age of 48, an excellent posthumous volume, *Unterwegs Karikiert* ("Caricatured Along the Way"), gathered together a sizable number of his gentle, likable and genuinely funny caricatures. Bauer also did film posters and television graphics.

S.A.

BAXTER, GLEN (1944-) One of the most original cartoonists, Glen Baxter currently works in England. His style consists of a rather shaky drawing copied, or inspired, by some illustration lifted from a 1920's-1930's annual for boys, to which he adds a highly incongruous caption. The result is a comment or satirical effect that touches both today and yesterday in one clever stab.

Glen was born in Leeds, England, on March 4, 1944, the son of a welder. He attended Leeds College of Art from 1960 to 1965, then taught at the Victoria and Albert from 1967 to 1974, when he became a lecturer at Goldsmith's College until 1986. His first published work, illustrated poems, was printed in the United States magazine *Adventures in Poetry* (1970), and his first exhibition of artwork was also in New York at the Gotham Book Mart Gallery. The *New Yorker* was first to publish his cartoons, followed by the London *Observer*. He also draws greetings cards and has published a dozen books of drawings, including *The Falls Tracer* (1970), *The Handy Guide to Crazy People* (1974), *The Works* (1977), *Impending Glen* (1981), *Glen Baxter His Life* (1983), *Jodhpurs in the Quantocks* (1986), *The Billiard Table Murders* (1990), *Glen Baxter Returns to Normal* (1992), and *The Collected Blurtings of Glen Baxter* (1993).

D.G.

BAXTER, WILLIAM GILES (1856-1888) British cartoonist born in America in 1856. W.G. Baxter was the creator, or rather recreator, of Ally Sloper, the first great British comic strip hero (see *The World Encyclopedia of Comics,*

Poor Pa summoned to Windsor: "My wretched Father, having, as usual made himself supremely ridiculous in the House of Commons, Her Majesty thought fit to summon him to Windsor, when, upon making a proper apology, he was taken out for a drive. He sat behind, and, I am told, made a great impression."
W.G. Baxter, "Ally Sloper's Half-Holiday," 1886.

Chelsea House, 1976). Remarkably little has been written about this giant of the popular pen, perhaps because little is known. And what little has been written is largely inaccurate. His initials stand for William Giles, according to his death certificate, and not William George, as claimed in the only major piece of writing about him ("A Great Comic Draughtsman" by W.G. Thorpe, in *Print Collectors Quarterly,* February 1938). Nor did he create Ally Sloper (as claimed in the same article); rather, he recreated him from the original cartoons by Charles Henry Ross and his wife, Marie Duval.

Commissioned by publisher-engraver Gilbert Dalziel to draw a new series of front-page cartoons featuring Ally for the new weekly comic *Ally Sloper's Half-Holiday,* Baxter exaggerated the simple hack cartoon figure into a monstrous, grotesque Micawber of the lower classes, complete with ever-expanding family (Queen Victoria's Jubilee produced a topical offspring, Jubilee Sloper!). Although Baxter only worked a short while on *Half-Holiday,* his version of Ally Sloper prevailed throughout English comic history, first continued by W.F. Thomas and revived in the original image in 1976 for *Ally Sloper* magazine by Walter Bell, who learned to draw Sloper at Thomas's elbow in 1920.

Baxter came to live in Buxton, Derbyshire, England, when still a child. As a teenager his sketches of local notables earned him admiration and a small living. John Andrew Christie, a provincial publisher, noticed Baxter's work, and when he started a new Manchester satirical weekly, *Momus,* he hired the 22-year-old artist as his chief (and only) staff cartoonist. The first issue, published March 7, 1878, had a caricature of the dean of Manchester on the cover, and for the second Baxter drew the mayor. Number 5 featured Baxter's first comic strip, *The Perils of Our Streets.* Baxter became joint editor of *Momus,* and when the paper folded in 1883, he went to London to try his luck as a freelance newspaper artist. His first cartoon for *Ally Sloper's Half-Holiday* appeared in number 10 and showed Lord Randolph Churchill at the

Henley races. Three weeks later, his first cartoon of the "new" Sloper appeared: "Sloper the Friend of Man," page 1, number 13, July 21, 1884. With the special extra edition of *Alley Sloper's Christmas Holidays,* Baxter truly flowered: he executed superb double-page center spreads of Christmas with the Sloper family.

He died on June 2, 1888, at age 31, of, it is said, alcohol and tuberculosis. He left £286 to his wife, Eleanor. His image of Ally Sloper, produced in merchandise galore, is now immortalized in the annual Ally Sloper awards presented to the top British comic artists. His books include *Fifty Sloper Cartoons* (1888), *Elijer Goff's Complete Works* (1889) and *Strange But True* (1889).

D.G.

BEAR (G.B.) "Caution, Keep Out of Reach of Children!" reads the warning notice on the cover of *The Posy Simmonds Bear Book,* published in 1969. The charming cartoon on the cover shows a slightly sly bear smiling at a slightly embarrassed child. Turn the page, and the drawing is repeated with the "adults only" caption: "Aren't you going to sleep with me tonight?" And it is Bear saying it, not Girl! This book of saucy, even shocking (for 1969) cartoons featuring a teddy bear the likes of which Christopher Robin never knew, a girl, a doll and a rabbit with a decidedly phallic carrot, took a new look at the well-loved nursery characters of old, giving them a Permissive Age twist that really could not offend, so sweefly were they drawn.

Posy Simmonds, their equally sweet creator, says with a smile, "It's all in the mind." The phrase is echoed by Bernard Shrimsley, editor of the daily tabloid the *Sun,* in his introduction to a paperback reprint of *Bear.* It was Shrimsley who, spotting the first Simmonds book, signed her to produce a daily cartoon panel entifled *Bear by Posy.* The series began in the first revamped *Sun,* November 17, 1969, and continues to delight daily.

Rosemary Simmonds, nicknamed "Rosy-Posy," hence "Posy," was born on August 9, 1945, in Cookham Dean, Berkshire. Educated at Caversham, she studied painting at the Ecole des Beaux-Arts in Paris, and graphics at the Central School of Art in London. Her first published cartoons, "little excrescences" she calls them, were thumbnails for the *Times* woman's page and *New Society.* Since 1974 she has been featured regularly in the *Guardian* and also teaches illustration at Middlesex Polytechnic. Her books include *Posy Simmonds Bear Book* (1969), *Bear by Posy* (1974) and *More Bear* (1975). Her *Guardian* strips, *The Silent Three* and *Mrs. Weber's Diary* have been reprinted in book form, and she was named "Cartoonist of the Year" by Granada Television in 1980.

D.G.

BEARD, DANIEL CARTER (1850-1941) American cartoonist, illustrator, outdoorsman and organizer born in Cincinnati, Ohio, on June 21, 1850. Dan Beard moved with his family to Covington, Kentucky, and as a boy studied art with his father, a portrait painter. He followed his brother, Frank Beard (a cartoonist with the Leslie publications), to New York and from 1880 to 1884 studied at the Art Students League.

In 1882 his first illustrated article, "How to Camp Without a Tent," appeared in *St. Nicholas* magazine, and he was soon one of America's major freelance cartoonists and comic illustrators, drawing for *Life* and many other publications. He was certainly Mark Twain's favorite, working on some of Twain's most notable books.

Beard's style was tight and tended toward the realistic, although he could achieve flights of fancy and had a real decorative sense. His cartoons were always executed neatly but boldly. As his career progressed and his interests became focused, his subjects increasingly followed the outdoors themes.

"Uncle Dan" Beard was the organizer of the Boy Scouts of America, a distinction that has sometimes obscured his achievements as a comic artist. In 1878 he began organizing boys in outdoor activities, and his first published article and first book, *The American Boys' Handy Book* (appearing in 1882), dealt with this theme. It was in 1905, when he was editor of *Recreation* magazine, that he undertook full-scale organization of the group that was to become the Boy Scouts.

For many years he was national scout commissioner, an honorary vice-president of the BSA, and chairman of its National Court of Honor. The year before his death, fifty thousand Boy Scouts gathered before him at the New York World's Fair to sing happy birthday to "Uncle Dan." At the time of his death he was still drawing and writing; he produced a monthly illustrated article for *Boys' Life* for years. At his funeral, honorary pallbearers included Franklin Roosevelt, Charles Dana Gibson and Theodore Roosevelt, Jr. Among a host of honors dedicated to his ideals, the Daniel Carter Beard Medal for Boys of Kentucky, endowed for a hundred years, is a special one. He died at his home, Brooklands, in Suffern, New York, on June 11, 1941.

Books: *Little People and Their Homes in the Meadows, Woods and Waters* (1888); *A Connecticut Yankee in King Arthur's Court* by Mark Twain (1889); *The American Claimant* by Twain (1892); *The One-Million Pound Bank Note* by Twain (1893); *Journey into Other Worlds* by John Jacob Astor (1894); *Tom Sawyer Abroad* by Twain (1894); *Following the Equator* by Twain (1897); *The Hat and the Man* (1906); and his autobiography, *Hardly a Man Is Now Alive* (1939).

R.M.

BEARD, FRANK (1842-1905) American cartoonist born in 1842, brother of illustrator Dan Beard. Eight years his brother's senior, Frank Beard took off on his cartooning career like a rocket. When only 18, he drew a cartoon, "Why Don't You Take It?," that was published by Currier and Ives lithographers and distributed by the Republicans as a campaign document; one hundred thousand were ordered, and the cartoon also graced envelopes.

During the Civil War, Beard was a special artist for *Harper's Weekly* and contributed cartoon ideas for the back page between assignments on the battlefronts. In the 1870s Beard was one of the most prolific cartoonists for the various short-lived comic papers like *Phunny Phellow, Wild Oats* and the Leslie comic magazines. One of his most important acts was his kind sponsorship of and advice to young Frederick Burr Opper in the early 1870s; Opper was influenced by Beard's techniques and helped by hours of unselfish guidance.

Beard returned to lithography when *Judge* was founded in 1881. For that Republican paper he drew some very striking, handsome and sophisticated material; sadly, he and the magazine parted ways when the Republicans took an actual financial interest in the sheet and Bernard Gillam and Zim (Eugene Zimmerman) headed up a restructured art staff in 1886.

Frank Beard is credited with being the originator of the chalk-talk, a widely popular form of public entertainment for a generation; cartoonists wore a second hat as stage comics when they entertained with lightning caricatures, sketches and humorous patter. Beard traveled the Chautauqua circuit for 17 years.

The serious—and substantial—side of his talent is revealed by the fact that Beard was for years a professor of fine arts at Syracuse University. Eventually, he gave up politics but not cartoons and joined the staff of the *Ram's Head,* a Chicago religious publication. For it he championed, via cartoons, the cause of temperance. A collection of his religious and temperance cartoons, *Fifty Great Cartoons,* was published by the Ram's Horn Press in 1899. Beard died in Chicago of a cerebral hemorrhage on September 29, 1905.

R.M.

BEAUTY AND THE BEAST (U.S.) Spurred on by the unprecedented success of *The Little Mermaid* in 1989, Disney's animators, then working on an animated version of *Beauty and the Beast,* decided to expand the fairy tale into yet another musical extravaganza. Released in 1991, *Beauty* proved an even greater box-office hit than its predecessor, and it garnered rave reviews comparing it to Jean Cocteau's 1946 movie classic.

This claustrophobic tale of a maiden abducted into an evil nobleman's castle who was transformed into a loathsome beast for his transgressions was considerably modernized and opened up. Belle, the heroine, was no longer a passive victim but an outspoken young woman, almost an early feminist, while the Beast was made into a complex character given almost equally to animal rage and human kindness. Belle's crackpot inventor of a father, Maurice, and her loutish suitor, Gaston, provided comedic counterpoint to the main situation, as did the animated household objects, notably Mrs. Potts, the teapot, (voiced by Angela Lansbury) and Lumiere the candlestick, (impersonated by Jerry Orbach in his patented Maurice Chevalier mode). As in the original tale, Belle, touched by the Beast's clumsy devotion, finally reciprocated his love and thereby broke the spell, bringing the groom back to human form.

There were dazzling sequences of animation, as in the storming of the Beast's castle by the aroused townspeople, and particularly in the ballroom scene, in which computer-generated imagery and hand-drawn animation were combined to produce an atmosphere of almost surreal enchantment. *Beauty and the Beast* was the first animated feature ever nominated for a Best Picture Academy Award; it lost to *Silence of the Lambs,* but won Oscars for best song and best original score. In both technical achievement and sophistication of plot and dialogue, it is Disney's most ambitious cartoon film, and it accordingly received wide praise from movie reviewers. Its critical success led to a long-running stage version that opened on Broadway in 1994.

M.H.

BEAVIS AND BUTTHEAD (U.S.) To paraphrase famed American journalist H.L. Mencken's quote from 1926, no one ever went broke underestimating the intelligence of the American people. *Beavis and Butthead,* the half-hour animated cartoon show about two high school-aged losers, is proof of that.

Beavis and Butthead were created in December 1991 by Mike Judge to star in his animated short film *Frog Baseball.* Blond Beavis, who favors Death Rock T-shirts, and brown-haired Butthead, who has braces on his teeth and likes Skull T-shirts, are devoted heavy metal rock fans. They also enjoy substituting live frogs for baseballs. It's splatter baseball.

Mike Judge finished his first animated film *Office Space* about disgruntled office workers in June 1991. A graduate of University of California-San Diego with a degree in physics, he abandoned a career in electrical engineering to work as a blues guitar bassist. His interest in comedy and film blossomed. Borrowing a how-to-draw-animated-cartoons book from the library, he bought second-

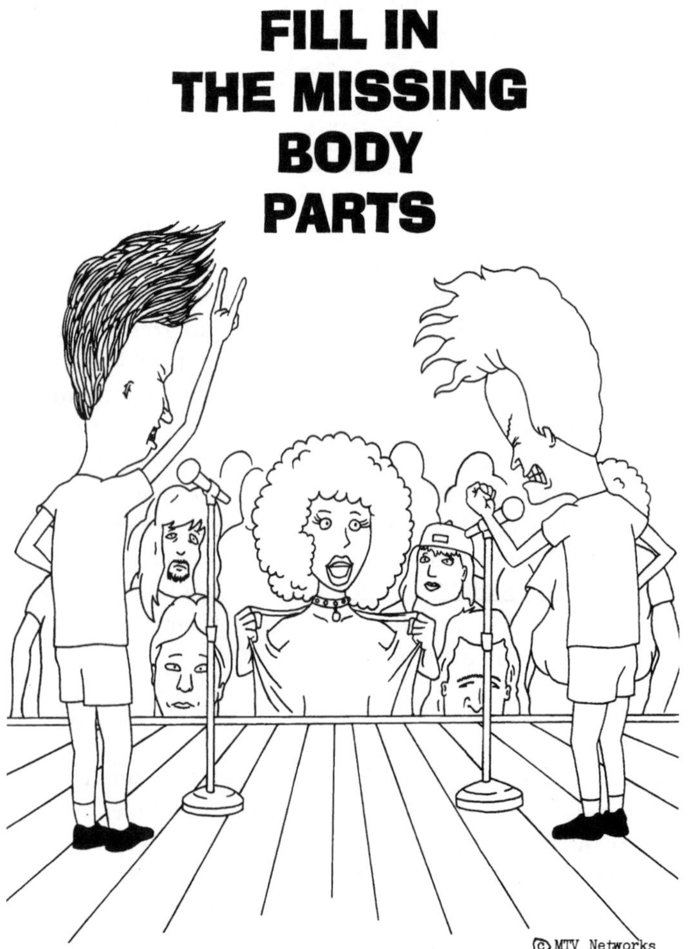

"Beavis and Butthead," © *MTV Networks.*

hand equipment and taught himself to do limited crude animation. By the time *Frog Baseball* appeared, Music Television (MTV) had taken an interest in Judge's work. The show quickly became MTV's most popular in 1993, with 35 episodes aired that year.

Beavis and Butthead play heavy-metal air guitar and frog baseball, ogle women, revel in body function jokes, put a dog in a washing machine, threaten to urinate in a neighbor's swimming pool, and make huge amounts of money for Mike Judge and MTV. Quoted in the February 28, 1994 *New Yorker*, James Wolcott noted *Beavis and Butthead* "represents another non-advance in the art of animation."

Although similar in mood, the live-action duo in *Saturday Night Live* spin-off, *Wayne's World*, are rocket scientists compared to Beavis and Butthead, and not nearly as gross and offensive. MTV executives realized teenagers and Generation X, its core audience, viewed cartoons as the equivalent of rock music. They grew up with television cartoons, and now the MTV cartoons became the humor video that entertained just as the music video did.

Early on, one of Beavis's less lovable activities, being a pyromaniac, brought public relations heat to the MTV series when a youth caught setting a fire to a building blamed the influence of *Beavis and Butthead*. MTV considers *Beavis and Butthead* to be relief from today's politically correct world.

In 1995, MTV and Judge spun off the thirty minute animated show *Daria*, from *Beavis and Butthead*. It's named for Daria Morgendorffer, the only girl on earth willing to talk to Beavis and Butthead. Bespectacled Daria was born alienated, smart, and sharp-tongued. Both *Daria* and Judge's half-hour animated comedy for the Fox Television Network *King of the Hill*, about a Texas good ol' boy and his family and friends, are much better animated products that *Beavis and Butthead*.

The last original episode of *Beavis and Butthead* aired November 28, 1997. However, MTV plans to show reruns in the future. Following the $63 million gross of the theatrical release film *Beavis and Butthead Do America* in 1997, is a new feature film with the boys, *The Stinky Cheese Man*, due out late 1998.

Although broadcast at 10 p.m., *Beavis and Butthead* became the schoolyard rage among grammar school children. In the age of the video recorder, it makes no difference how late a show is broadcast. Kids will see it. The entry of Mike Judge in the 1996 National Cartoonists Society Album notes he has two young daughters and, "Neither are allowed to watch their father's show."

Actually funnier than the MTV *Beavis and Butthead* cartoon series are two unofficial spin-offs. One is the comedy skit *Beavis and Bubba*, heard mornings by 30 million Americans on the nationally syndicated *Imus In The Morning* radio show. Bubba is a parody of President Bill Clinton, who often has a quick comment about some woman's breasts. The other is the porno-parody *Beaver and Butt-face* in which boys' wildest dreams of sexcapades come true. The actors are in *Beavis and Butthead* makeup and sets are made to look like the simplistic backgrounds used in the cartoons.

Millions of dollars of *Beavis and Butthead* licensed products have been sold, including a classic *Beavis and Butthead* toilet paper. As long as there's an audience willing to spend money to see them, expect periodic appearances of *Beavis and Butthead*, who are always quick to utter their immortal line, "Heh-heh. This sucks."

B.C.

BECKERMAN, HOWARD (1930-) American animator born in the Bronx, N.Y., on December 25, 1930. Howard Beckerman displayed a taste for drawing at an early age and decided on a cartooning career while still in grammar school. As a student of the famed School of Industrial Art (now High School of Art and Design) he elected to focus on animation, figuring he could always go back to cartoon drawing later on. After graduation he served a brief apprenticeship at the Terrytoons and Paramount animation studios before being shipped to Korea where he served in the Army from 1951 to 1953.

Upon his return to civilian life he resumed his career, freelancing as a storyman and animator for a variety of studios, from UPA to Electra. After a brief interlude as a designer for the Norcross Greeting Card Company, he came back to animation for good in 1964, returning to Paramount as head animator. Once more Beckerman experienced the vagaries of the animation business when Paramount closed the doors of its animation unit in 1967. This time he determined to weather the storm, and after a period of freelancing, he set up his own animation studio. Since then his clients have included Public Television's *Sesame Street*, the Xerox Corporation, Exxon, and Black Flag insecticide (for which he has done the

Howard Beckerman, animation sketches. © Howard Beckerman.

memorable "Roach Motel" commercials). His best work, however, is done in what he calls "personal animation," in which he serves in the multiple capacities of director, layout man, scriptwriter, and producer. His short films of this type have garnered a good number of awards and have also received popular and critical acclaim. Perhaps the best-liked of his films is *Boop-Beep*, an endearing little fable about a cat, a miser, and an old woman." The whole story is deftly visualized to the on-and-off rhythm of a lighthouse beacon.

In addition to his credits as an animator, Beckerman is also the creator of the short-lived comic strip *Miss Chipps*, about a Chaplinesque female character. Of longer duration has been his own experience as a teacher, and his courses at the School of Visual Arts and Parsons School of Design have helped form a whole generation of young animators. Equally influential have been his monthly articles in *Filmmakers Newsletter*, and later his weekly contributions to *Back Stage*, in which he shared his intimate knowledge of the history and techniques of animation with his readers. In 1995 his experience led him to write *Animation: The Whole Story*, which he describes as "a book for those thousands interested in animation."

In recognition of the many awards and distinctions he has received for his work, Beckerman was elected vice-president of ASIFA, the International Association of Film Animation, in 1985, and he has served with distinction in this position for the last decade.

M.H.

Sir Max Beerbohm, "The Rare, the Rather Awful Visits of Albert Edward, Prince of Wales, to Windsor Castle," ca. 1895.

BEERBOHM, SIR MAX (1872-1956) British caricaturist and essayist born in London, England, on August 24, 1872. Henry Maximilian Beerbohm was educated at Charterhouse School and Merton College, Oxford. His elder half-brother was Herbert Beerbohm Tree, the eminent actor-manager of the Victorian stage. An enthusiastic sketcher from the age of seven, he published his first caricature (of Rudyard Kipling) in his school magazine, the Horsmunden *School Budget.* His literary abilities developed at Oxford and blossomed professionally in the controversial magazine *Yellow Book* (1894). Two years later his first collection of cartoons, *Caricatures of 25 Gentlemen* (1896), was published. Cartoonist E.T. Reed introduced the volume: "Since 'Ape' there has been no-one with such an awful instinct for the principal part of a man's appearance. He is a psychologist in drawing if ever there was."

Caricatures signed "Max" appeared in the *Strand Magazine,* and in 1899 he was appointed drama critic of the *Saturday Review.* In 1910 he left England for Rapallo, Italy, where he made his home for the rest of his life. He occasionally returned to England for exhibitions of his color work (Leicester Galleries in 1913 and 1921) and for witty broadcasts for the BBC, particularly during World War II. He was knighted in 1939 and died in Rapallo on May 20, 1956.

Books: *Caricatures of 25 Gentlemen* (1896); *The Happy Hypocrite* (1897); *The Works of Max Beerbohm* (1897); *More* (1899); *More Theatres* (1903); *Caricatures* (1904); *Poets Corner* (1904); *Max Beerbohm in Italy* (1906); *Book of Caricatures* (1907); *Yet Again* (1909); *Last Theatres* (1911); *Second Childhood of John Bull* (1911); *Zuleika Dobson* (1911); *Christmas Garland* (1912); *50 Caricatures* (1913); *The Guerdon* (1916); *Seven Men* (1919); *And Even Now* (1920); *Herbert Beerbohm Tree* (1920); *Survey* (1921); *Rosetti and His Circle* (1922); *A Peep into the Past* (1923); *Things New and Old* (1923); *Observations* (1925); *The Dreadful Ogre of Hay Hill* (1928); *The Stuffed Owl* (1930); *Works and More* (1930); *Heroes and Heroines of Bitter Sweet* (1931); *Lytton Strachey* (1943); *Mainly on the Air* (1946); *Seven Men and Two Others* (1950); *Around Theatres* (1953); *A Variety of Things* (1953); *Max's Nineties* (1958); *The Incomparable Max* (1962); *Max in Verse* (1964); *Letters to Reggie Turner* (1964); and *The Bodley Head Max Beerbohm* (1970).

D.G.

BEHRENDT, FRITZ (1925-) Dutch editorial cartoonist born in Berlin, Germany, on February 17, 1925. By the early 1960s, with his drawings printed in such far-flung publications as the *Algemeen Handelsblad* and *Vrij Nederland* in his adoptive country, *Die Welt* and the *Süddeutsche Zeitung* in Germany, *Der Nebelspalter* and *Weltwoche* in Switzerland, the *Svenska Dagbladet* in Sweden, the *Shimbun* in Japan, the *West Australian* and the *New York Herald-Tribune,* Fritz Behrendt was the world's best-known Dutch journalist, with a readership of some fifty million.

In 1937, when Behrendt was 12, his family left

Germany for political reasons. From 1943 to 1945 he studied at the Amsterdam School of Applied Art and in 1948 was a guest student for one semester at the Academy in Zagreb, Yugoslavia. He started working for the Amsterdam publications *Algemeen Handelsblad* and *Vrij Nederland* in the early 1950s. In 1958 he moved from Amsterdam to the nearby town of Amstelveen, and in 1962 he began a monthly television series of "graphic commentary." Behrendt, a Dutch citizen, has also done posters and book illustrations.

His album *Ondanks Alles* ("In Spite of Everything," late 1962 or early 1963) contains 100 political drawings done in a pleasant cartoon pen style with many benday areas. The subject matter is of both local and international import, and there is also some mild social commentary—on frantic weekend pleasures, the inroads of motorcycling, the prevalence of television viewing, etc. Other Behrendt albums include *Geen Graples, a.u.b.* ("No Jokes, Please") and *Kijken Verboden* ("No Peeking"). In addition to having his cartoons published all around the world (including the United States), Behrendt has since 1980 increased his global reach writing articles on cartoonists past and present for the specialized press.

Politically speaking, it may be suggested that Behrendt's unusually widespread popularity is connected with the comfortable, traditional majority position he adopts—unlike most of the major Dutch and German editorial cartoonists, who have tended to join the intellectual opposition of their period. Behrendt's clear-cut defense of American actions and his condemnation of Russian policies might not be out of place in any conservative Midwestern paper. And, although many postwar European cartoonists have been surprised at the emergence of the Third World as a power to be reckoned with, Behrendt's cartoons on the subject seem to contain a special tinge of resentment that this should have come to pass.

S.A.

BELCHER, GEORGE FREDERICK ARTHUR (1875-1947) Cartoonist, etcher, painter, R.A., born in London, England on September 19, 1875. Educated at Berkhampstead School, George Belcher studied art at the Gloucester School of Art, becoming an exhibitor at the Royal Academy from 1909. His first cartoon accepted by *Punch* appeared in 1911, and he was a regular contributor to *Tatler, Vanity Fair* and other top periodicals.

His cartoon work was executed in charcoal at amazing speed, capturing Cockney and working-class life to perfection. He prowled the streets with his sketchbook and was adept at persuading characters who caught his eye to accompany him to his studio for more formal sittings. His colorful portraits were of the common man (and woman, especially charwoman) rather than of social notables; his common cornet player rendering "I dreamt that I dwelt in marble halls" was a popular classic. His jokes were basically illustrations of dialogue gags, more often supplied to him than created. It is reported that he often failed to understand these joke scripts and once made nonsense out of a gag by changing its setting from a fishmonger's shop to a greengrocer's because "there's a very good green-grocer's near my home"! He died on October 3, 1947.

Books: *The Lighter Side of English Life* (1913); *Characters* (1922); *Odd Fish* (1923); *Taken from Life* (1929); *The Table in a Roar* (1933); *and Potted Char* (1933).

D.G.

BELIEVE IT OR NOT! (U.S.) One week before Christmas a long time ago, *New York Globe* sports cartoonist Robert L. Ripley was trying to devise a way to fill up the blank space that was his daily assignment. He suddenly decided to draw a series of weird sports happenings around the world—such as the Canadian who ran the 100-yard dash backwards, the Frenchman who stayed underwater for 6 minutes 29.2 seconds, the Australian who jumped rope 11,810 times, etc. Thus, on December 18, 1918, was *Believe It or Not!* born.

Ripley went on drawing his sports oddities for the *Globe* until the paper closed in 1924. He then moved over to the *New York Telegram* and later to the *Post,* which started to syndicate his panel nationally. By that time *Believe It or Not!* no longer confined itself to sports but was venturing as far afield as geology, history, botany and numismatics. In 1929 King Features Syndicate picked up the panel and gave it worldwide distribution (and fame).

The first feature of its kind, *Believe It or Not!* has enjoyed tremendous popularity for over half a century. Its facts—dwelling heavily on the bizarre, the absurd, the incredible and the outlandish—are not always accurate (every critic has a favorite error or fallacy from *Believe It or Not!*, be it the flight time of Lindbergh's solo journey over the Atlantic or the distance from Earth to the sun), but this never fazed Ripley. Good newspaperman that he was, he knew that unadorned facts and bare statistics make for poor copy, and his aim was to entertain, not to enlighten. Indeed, much more accurate fact panels, such as John and Elsa Hix's *Strange As It Seems* and R.J. Scott's *Did You Know?*, have not even approached the success of Ripley's feature.

The popularity of *Believe It or Not!* prompted Ripley to become the national curator of odd facts and freak happenings, with a radio program, numerous motion pictures, books, lectures and even a string of wax museums. All this activity left him scant time for drawing, and the *Believe It or Not!* panel was ghosted by many other hands from the 1930s on. Eventually Paul Frehm became the exclusive artist on the feature, and he later took it over completely, signing it after Ripley's death in 1949. Frehm carried on the panel with very little change in content or style. Upon his retirement in 1978 he was succeeded by his brother Walter Frehm who drew and wrote the feature up to the time of its acquisition by United Feature in 1990. Since that time it has been done (as *Ripley's Believe It or Not*) by anonymous staffers at the syndicate.

M.H.

BELLEW, FRANK HENRY TEMPLE (1828-1888) American cartoonist born in Cawnpore, India, on April 18, 1828. Frank Bellew, born of an English family, came to America from England in 1850 and immediately

"Believe It or Not!" © King Features Syndicate.

embarked on a career in cartooning and humorous illustration.

Settling in New York City, he contributed cartoons to the new illustrated monthlies, most notably *Harper's*, and to the *Illustrated American News* and children's books. He was founder of cartoon and humor magazines like the *Lantern*, *Vanity Fair* and *Nick Nax;* he contributed frequently to sheets like the *Fifth Avenue Journal*, *Wild Oats* and the various Leslie comic papers. In the 1870s he was a mainstay of the *New York Graphic*, the first illustrated daily in America, a paper that relied heavily on cartoons and often featured them on its front page.

Bellew wrote and illustrated *The Art of Amusing* in 1866, an interesting treatise on his craft. He died, still active, in New York City on June 29, 1888. His son, Frank P.W. Bellew, was just then gaining fame as a cartoonist, signing his work "Chip," evidently in deference to and in honor of his father.

Bellew was as important to his field—the magazine panel cartoon, which he practically created—as Nast was to the editorial cartoon. Bellew was among the earliest and most prolific of woodcut cartoonists, and his subjects ranged from politics to social comment. He was one of the first celebrities among cartoonists, one who broke the bonds of anonymity and whose signature (a triangle) became as famous as the names of writers who shared magazine space with him. Among his most famous cartoons is the caricature of Abe Lincoln after his 1864 victory: "Long Abe a Little Longer." His contribution to cartoon iconography is highlighted by the 1872 rag doll baby, a Frankenstein's monster that taunted the Greenbackers.

What sustained Bellew through this period—a time span in which he could trace his career from a lonely pioneer cartoonist to a veteran viewing the progress of others such as Thomas Nast, Joseph Keppler and Frederick Opper—was the fact that he was good. His humor is typical of the period but still contains spontaneity and imagination. His drawing—and this is evident especially in the period of photoengraving—is supple and agile. He was more than a plotter who let the wood engraver make him look good—he was a gifted composer, a masterful caricaturist. To him belongs the mantle of father of American cartooning, and a resurrection of his work is deserved and long overdue.

R.M.

Frank Bellew ("Chip").

BELLEW, FRANK P.W. (ca. 1860-1894) American cartoonist, son of pioneer cartoonist Frank Bellew, known by his pen name "Chip" (as in "chip off the old block"). Obviously overshadowed by his father's long and distinguished career, Chip nevertheless made his own mark with an entirely different style. His father, a pioneering and prominent woodcut cartoonist, was identified with the tight, mechanical crosshatch look necessary for woodcut reproduction. With the advent of photoengraving, most artists used the new freedom merely to copy the look of the earlier process. Chip was among the first to simplify, to drop details and shading, to round his outlines; the characters in his drawings were cartoon figures, not stiff, illustrated models with captions beneath. Hence he formed an important link between two vital schools of American cartooning.

Chip is also significant on his own merits, as his work was enormously popular over his brief, decade-long career. His best-liked subjects were kids and dogs; these personae filled a world of wisecracks, pranks, bad puns and pantomime adventures. Before his death in November 1894, Chip developed a technique of parodying ancient friezes, mixing historical and contemporary subject matter cleverly but without the charm of his dog-and-kid cartoons. He drew mostly for *Life,* which published a posthumous collection, *Chip's Dogs,* through R.H. Russell in 1895.

R.M.

BELLUS, JEAN (1911-1967) French cartoonist born in Toulouse, France on July 22, 1911. After finishing his secondary studies at the Lycée Arago in Paris, Jean Bellus went to work as a bank clerk. Three years later (1933) he started cartooning and contributed thousands of drawings mainly to such periodicals and newspapers as *France-Dimanche, Le Figaro, Jours de France* and *Ici Paris.*

Although his first album, *Humour Verboten!* (1945), seemed a prelude to a satirist's career, dealing as it did with POW camp life, most of his other cartoons show a more gentle popular humor. Bellus indeed has created the prototypical 20th-century middle-class Frenchman and his family: a bald, roly-poly, middle-aged man (not without resemblance to his creator); his plump and charming wife; and Clémentine, his daughter—the star of the series—a vivacious and lovely young woman typical of the younger generation. Whether riding with one of her many boyfriends, dancing until the early hours of the morning or kissing in the dark, she is viewed by her parents with characteristic broad-mindedness and indulgence. These cartoons, which depict the daily events,

"That does it, in new francs, I am no longer a millionaire."
Jean Bellus. © Bellus.

joys and worries in the life of an average French family, have been released as albums: *Clémentine Chérie* ("Clémentine Chérie, the Rage of Paris," 1955), *Oh! Clémentine* (1963), *Une Famille Bien Française* ("A Very French Family," 1966) and *Vivre avec Son Temps* ("To Live with the Times," 1967).

Jean Bellus suffered a heart attack in the summer of 1966 but continued to work until November of that year. He died at his home in Paris on January 14, 1967.

P.H.

BELMONTE
See Barreto, Benedito Bastos.

BELTRAME, ACHILLE (1871-1945) Italian illustrator and cartoonist born in Arzignano, near Vicenza, Italy, on March 19, 1871. Achille Beltrame studied art at the Brera Academy, in his youthful days winning a number of awards and competitions. Later he decorated several buildings in Turin and Milan. Beltrame's name is indissolubly tied to the weekly *La Domenica del Corriere,* the covers of which he drew from the beginning weeks of this century to the closing weeks of World War II.

At a time when the objectivity of the camera was gradually supplanting the news drawing, Beltrame, instead of giving a detached account of events (assassinations of crowned heads, shoot-outs between bandits and the forces of order, bloody strikes, earthquakes, shipwrecks, trench warfare, etc.), drew them as the public wanted them to appear, adding dignity and virility to the happenings. As Dino Buzzati astutely observed in his preface to *Trieste e il Carso,* a collection of Beltrame's World War I drawings, the artist's truth, often objectively inaccurate, was "truer" than the camera's truth in that it gave the reality of movement where photography only recorded the immobility of things.

Beltrame also tried his hand at cartooning and caricaturing, but these activities pale in comparison to his achievements in the illustration field. He died on February 19, 1945, covered with honors. Newspapers heralded his death with headlines like this one: "For 46 Years He Illustrated the World." He indeed illustrated the world, perhaps in a rhetorical form, but always with humanity and optimism.

S.T.

BEN BOWYANG (Australia) A god's-eye view of Australian graphic humor today reveals that Australia is the last remaining country in the world celebrating her rural origins in comic art.

Al Capp's *Li'l Abner* and his since-vanished *Long Sam* are reminders of the American rural theme. But in Australia at present, five professional cartoonists are busy drawing humor with such rural and outback themes. Since the mid-1850s successive generations of cartoonists and humorists have reinforced the traditional stereotype of the "country dweller" with particular characteristics and ways of living, a stereotype that has become legendary. Continuing this "backblocks" theme made popular first by the *Bulletin,* then by *Smith's Weekly,* the Melbourne *Herald* introduced *Ben Bowyang,* also known in some states as *Gunn's Gully.*

The hayseed Ben, together with his corpulent mate Bill Smith and the mean Scots shopkeeper Wilson, has provided the fun in this daily feature since October 1933. No less than seven artists have drawn the strip, by and large preserving its rural flavor. Sam Wells was the first artist to delineate the character, but it was the gifted cartoonist Alex Gurney who first drew the feature, followed by Daryl (now Sir Daryl) Lindsay, Mick Armstrong, Keith Martin, Alex McCrae (whose tenure lasted for 25 years) and Bevyn Baker. In the 1970s and 1980s it was done by Peter Russell-Clarke who had taken over in December 1969. It is still going at century's end, drawn by diverse hands..

V.L.

BENGOUGH, JOHN WILSON (1851-1923) Canadian cartoonist and journalist born in Toronto, Ontario, on April 7, 1851. John Bengough grew up in Ontario and, after finishing school, worked in a local law office for a short time. Instead of going on to a legal career, Bengough started working as printer's devil and at age 20 went to the Toronto *Globe* as city reporter. Enrolling in evening classes at the Ontario Society of Artists, he developed his artistic skills and at the same time began learning about the ease and accuracy of lithographic reproduction.

At 22, Bengough left the *Globe* and founded the weekly magazine *Grip.* From May 1873 until September 1892, he edited and did most of the writing and illustrating for

"Help! Save me! I'm drowning! Glub! Glub!"
Stanley and Janice Berenstain, "It's All in the Family. © McCall's.

"La Bergère et le Ramoneur." © *Les Gémeaux.*

this successful publication. Political scandal broke out during its first year and gave *Grip* a theme which led to immediate increases in circulation. Bengough's cartoons attacked most current views, sparing only those he championed himself—the single tax, women's suffrage, antivivisectionism and prohibition of alcohol and tobacco. Working before the era of newspaper photographers and widely recognized public figures, Bengough portrayed the basic features of his subjects, using them to express what he considered to be their essential nature. At times his drawings were quite cruel, but they were also very influential. His friends credited him with contributing to the defeat of the Conservative government in the 1896 federal election.

Bengough's career included cartoon work for various other Canadian and English newspapers. His books include cartoon collections, political treatises and poetry. Starting in 1874, he gave illustrated lectures and chalk-talks. For more than forty years he sketched and spoke on political and moral subjects across Canada, the United States, the United Kingdom, Australia and New Zealand. He declined to run for Parliament for the Prohibition party but was an alderman for a term in Toronto starting in 1907. He died on October 2, 1923. In the 1950s a bronze plaque commemorating him was set up in Toronto. He was the second Canadian journalist to be so honored.

D.K.

BERENSTAIN, JANICE
See Berenstain, Stanley.

BERENSTAIN, STANLEY (1923-) American cartoonist born in Philadelphia, Pennsylvania, on September 29, 1923. Educated at the Philadelphia Museum School of Industrial Art and the Pennsylvania Academy of Fine Arts, Stanley Berenstain served as a medical artist with the army before teaming up with his wife, Janice, to draw cartoons. Around 1950 this was not uncommon; Vi and George Smith and Linda and Jerry Walter had formed cartooning teams as well.

The Berenstains drew humorous covers for *Collier's*, a newspaper feature called *Sister*, and the long-running *It's All in the Family* for *McCall's* and later *Good Housekeeping*. In 1962 the couple began designing cards and calendars for Hallmark. They have produced a score of books, mostly featuring their regular magazine family characters. Titles include *Are Parents for Real?* (1971), *What Dr. Freud Didn't Tell You* (1971), *How to Teach Your Children About Sex* (1972), *Lover Boy* (1972) and *Bedside Lover Boy* (1972).

The couples' insights into and depictions of suburban living are as telling as any produced in the comics. A frenzied, laughing atmosphere pervades their cartoons, which are drawn in simple, flowing lines and usually colored in one or two flat shades.

About two-score more of Berenstain Bears books have been published in the last 20 years, along with a number of coloring books. The couple has also issued a number of books for adult readers in that same period, their latest being *What Your Parents Never Told You about Being a Mom or Dad* (1995). A Stanley and Janice Berenstain manuscipt collection has recently been established at Syracuse University.

R.M.

BERGÈRE ET LE RAMONEUR, LA (France) Following their success with *Le Petit Soldat,* Paul Grimault and André Sarrut (founders and partners of Les Gémeaux animated studio) decided in 1947 to bring out a full-length animated cartoon on a story by Jacques Prévert, itself derived from a Hans Christian Andersen tale, *La Bergère et le Ramoneur* ("The Shepherdess and the Chimney Sweep"). Technical difficulties, production delays and a legal fight between the two partners plagued the film, and when it finally came out on May 30, 1953, both Grimault and Prévert expressed their public disapproval of the final version of the cartoon.

The story takes place in the fictional kingdom of Tachykardia, ruled by a ruthless tyrant. The shepherdess and the chimney sweep are relentlessly hounded by the king's secret police, then imprisoned and humiliated. They escape with the help of friendly animals led by a strange bird wearing a silk hat, a frock coat and spats. The music, moody and expressive, is by Joseph Kosma, and some of the most distinguished actors of the French cinema lend their voices to the characters, including Pierre Brasseur (the bird), Serge Reggiani (the chimney sweep) and Anouk Aimée (the shepherdess).

Despite its checkered history, *La Bergère et le Ramoneur* fared well with the public. It did not do well with the critics, however, and it signaled the end of Grimault's innovativeness in the field of the cartoon. It is France's finest full-length animated film and, although flawed, a milestone in the history of film animation.

M.H.

BERNARDINI, PIERO (1891-1974) Italian cartoonist, illustrator and painter born in Florence, Italy, on June 23, 1891. Piero Bernardini started his career as a painter (his self-portrait hangs in Florence's Galleria degli Uffizi), but as he himself wrote in his autobiography, "I have used more paper than canvas, more ink than varnish."

Piero Bernardini, illustration for Alphonse Daudet's "Tartarin of Tarascon." © UTET.

In sixty years of feverish activity Bernardini collaborated on some fifty different magazines and newspapers, among them *Il Corriere dei Piccoli, Le Grandi Firme, La Voce, La Gazzetta del Popolo, Il Ballilla, Il Travaso* and *La Lettura.* In addition to his humorous drawings, Bernardini illustrated over one hundred fifty books in the course of his long career, including fables, fairy tales and novels by Rudyard Kipling, Charles Dickens and Jules Verne. He also illustrated a number of textbooks and occasionally designed a few posters.

The Italian writer Bruno Cigognani was the first to single out Bernardini as an acute observer of human nature in his caricatures. Augusta Calabri wrote in 1926, "Man is to Bernardini the most important object. Man in his gestures and his clothes more than man in his face and his sentiments." Whether criticizing or exalting them, Bernardini indeed observed his fellow men, not through their physiognomies but through an investigation of their gestures. He would synthesize these gestures on paper in a few nervous lines. His style was elegant and discontinuous, as Paola Pallotino observed.

Bernardini died in October 1974, in the midst of a multitude of books and drawings. He said toward the end of his life, "I've consumed gallons of ink, truckloads of paper. The pencils I've used up would top in height any television antenna."

S.T.

BERRY, JIM (1932-   ) American editorial cartoonist born in Chicago, Illinois, on January 16, 1932. Jim Berry, the creator of a new type of editorial-page social commentary cartoon, *Berry's World,* received his art training from the Famous Cartoonists Course of Westport, Connecticut. Prior to that, his education was received at the University School in Shaker Heights, Ohio, Dartmouth College (two years) and Ohio Wesleyan University, where he minored in art and earned a degree in business administration in 1954.

In 1957, after various odd jobs, Berry joined Altamira Productions, an animation studio, where he mastered all phases of animation. His *Berry's World,* when introduced at the Newspaper Enterprise Association (NEA) in 1963, was something new in the field of editorial cartooning, even in its media: Berry uses pencils and felt-tip pens, working with originals the same size or smaller than their reproductions. Berry's World is still being published weekdays and Sundays, and in 1998 it passed the 35th-anniversary mark.

Berry's success led to a preeminent position at NEA: a comic strip creation, *Benjy,* based on a recurring tramp character in the panel, was separated from the NEA sales package and sold on its own. With art by Bill Yates (signing himself Yale), however, it was short-lived. Berry's commentary is sharpest in his comfortable panel format.

The politically independent cartoonist was three times voted the Best Syndicated Panel Cartoonist by the National Cartoonists Society (NCS) and twice received the NCS Best Special Feature award. Berry was awarded the National Headliners prize in 1967 for "consistently outstanding editorial cartoons." He served as president of the Association of American Editorial Cartoonists in 1981-82.

R.M.

©1976 by NEA, Inc.
"This is planet Earth. Remember, we should not breathe its air, drink its water or eat any of its junk food!"

Jim Berry, "Berry's World." © NEA.

Wonder how long the honeymoon will last?

Clifford Berryman. © C.K. Berryman.

BERRYMAN, CLIFFORD KENNEDY (1869-1949) American Pulitzer Prize-winning cartoonist born in Kentucky in 1869. C.K. Berryman undoubtedly acquired a penchant for cartooning from his father, who used to amuse his 11 children by drawing funny pictures. Berryman's first job in art was with the U.S. Patent Office in Washington, D.C., delineating patent entries for $30 a month. When a cartoon submitted to the *Washington Post* paid $25, his career was chosen. Berryman joined the staff of the *Post* as an editorial cartoonist in 1891; in 1907 he switched to the *Washington Star*, then a larger paper, and remained there until a stroke felled him in his office on November 17, 1949. (His last wish was to live long enough to prevent the pall his death would have cast over Washington's Gridiron Dinner. He died on December 11, 1949, several hours after the dinner.)

Berryman is remembered as a Washington institution. His cartoons were largely without malice, and his caricatures were belabored, betraying a lifelong amateurish tint to his work. He took stands—sometimes very determined—but his primary thrust was toward gentility. He always drew with pen and ink and relied on the crosshatch.

His most famous cartoon contribution to Americana came in 1902, on the subject of one of Theodore Roosevelt's bear hunts. After a hard day with no luck, a misguided guide brought a bear cub on a rope for TR to bag; he sent the man away in disgust. Berryman depicted the incident and began including the little bear as a mascot in his TR cartoons; in a day when almost every cartoonist had a mascot, the "Teddy bear" struck the public. On the basis of the president's popularity, the bear was mass-produced and became an essential element of childhood. Berryman, its originator, never realized a cent from its success.

Among Berryman's other honors was his presidency of the Gridiron Club; he was the first cartoonist to hold the position.

R.M.

BERRYMAN, JAMES (1902-1976) American Pulitzer Prize-winning cartoonist born in Washington, D.C., on June 8, 1902. The son of *Washington Star* cartoonist Clifford Berryman, Jim Berryman studied at George Washington University and at the Corcoran Art School,

Jim Berryman. © Washington Star.

and began his career as a reporter on the New Mexico *State Tribune* in 1923. He joined his father's paper as a staff artist the next year, after returning to Washington because of his mother's illness; he contributed general art and retouching work. In 1931 he was promoted to editorial art and illustration, continuing in that department for two years, when he became a sports cartoonist; Berryman also drew for the *Sporting News* between 1934 and 1941.

On May 29, 1935, Clifford Berryman suffered a stroke at his drawing board with his Memorial Day cartoon half finished. Jim finished the cartoon and intermittently drew political cartoons thereafter. He became a full-fledged substitute in 1941, and in 1944 his three cartoons a week were picked up by King Features Syndicate. He retired in the late 1960s and died in 1976.

Berryman was also a magazine illustrator and wrote and illustrated articles on arms for sport and hunting. He was an honorary lifetime member of the National Rifle Association and for years was art director of their publications. His drawing style was more polished than that of his father; he was both a better draftsman and a better advocate. His political cartoons, Republican and conservative mostly, were stronger and more incisive. The Berrymans form the only *père et fils* act to cop Pulitzers.

R.M.

BERRY'S WORLD (U.S.) In 1963 editorial cartoonist Jim Berry started a new daily panel for the Newspaper Enterprise Association simply titled *Berry's World* (a Sunday feature was later added).

A syndicate press release once termed *Berry's World* "a satirical, sociopolitical cartoon," and it does indeed lampoon (or at least mildly spoof) topical events and personages in the news. Berry has declared that he was highly influenced by the British cartoonists in their approach and by the *New Yorker* cartoonists in their style." The cross between the two is not without merit (as when President Nixon suddenly appears on his daughter's television set, unctuously intoning, "I come to you on White House closed-circuit TV to tell you I've vetoed your request for an increased allowance, Tricia"). The resemblance to editorial cartoons is further enhanced by Berry's use of one-line captions under the drawings.

In his Sunday feature, on the other hand, Berry uses a freer approach (as well as balloons for dialogue), bringing it closer to the comic strip. He also occasionally breaks down the Sunday *Berry's World* into several interrelated panels, often on a given theme ("Berry's World Goes to San Francisco, to Los Angeles," etc.). The feature has happily survived three decades of syndication and eight different U.S. presidents and is still very much alive and thriving. In 1995 it was described as capturing "the essence of life as it is shaped by technology, politics, the economy and social change."

M.H.

BERTHELOT, HECTOR (1842-1895) French-Canadian cartoonist, newspaperman and humorist born in Trois-Rivières, Quebec, on March 4, 1842. Hector Berthelot is justly regarded as the founding father of cartooning in the province of Quebec. Save for a stay in Quebec City (1861-65) and another in Ottawa (1865-70), Berthelot worked almost exclusively in Montreal.

Berthelot made his debut in 1861 as a translator and reporter for the liberal newspaper *Le Pays.* He also worked during that year for *La Guêpe, L'Ordre* and *Le Courrier de St-Hyacinthe.* He broke into cartooning in 1863. His first drawings were published anonymously in the humor publication *La Scie,* where they appeared until 1865. From 1874 he did investigative reporting for a number of Canadian newspapers, including *Le Bien Public, Le Courrier de Montréal,* the *Star, La Patrie, Le Monde, La Presse* and *La Minerve.*

In 1878 Berthelot decided to devote all his time to his humor magazine, *Le Canard,* founded in 1877. From a circulation of 500 at its inception, *Le Canard* jumped to 10,000 in a few months. This phenomenal success (which

Return from Quebec: Ladébauche, astride the "Duck," gets himself towed by three steamships of the Richelieu and Ontario Company.
Hector Berthelot, first appearance of "Le Père Ladébauche," 1878.

spawned innumerable imitators) was due almost entirely to Berthelot, who was the author of most of the cartoons that appeared unsigned in the pages of the magazine. Berthelot's most original creation was Baptiste Ladébauche. Père Ladébauche ("Pops Debauchery") appeared officially for the first time in November 1878. One of the most famous characters in French-Canadian cartooning, Ladébauche was successively drawn by Racey, Joseph Charlebois (1904-05) and especially Albéric Bourgeois, who was to immortalize him.

In 1879 Berthelot left *Le Canard* (which he had sold the preceding year) to found *Le Vrai Canard*. This publication was renamed *Le Grognard* in 1881 and *Le Violon* in 1886 before reverting to the original name, *Le Canard*, in 1893. Berthelot died in September 1895. *Le Canard*, which proved to be his most memorable contribution to cartooning, survived him by a number of years.

S.J.

BERTHIAUME, ROLAND (1927-) French-Canadian cartoonist born in Montreal, Quebec, on December 12, 1927. Better known as "Berthio," Roland Berthiaume attended Ste. Marie College (now the University of Quebec) in Montreal before embarking on a commercial art career. After attending night classes at the Montreal School of Arts, Berthiaume spent a year in Paris (1951-52).

In 1953 Berthiaume started his career with editorial cartoons in the weekly *L'Autorité du Peuple*, also contributing occasionally to such publications as *La Semaine à Radio-Canada* and *Le Travail*. He finally found his métier with the cartoons he published in the political weekly *Vrai*. There Berthiaume was responsible for two pages of cartoons, usually four in number, dealing mainly with city problems. Berthiaume collaborated on *Vrai* from its inception in October 1954 to its demise in May 1959. He then went to the Montreal daily *La Presse*, where until 1967 he contributed *Drôle de Journée* ("Some Funny Day"), a column in the form of caricatural drawings and cartoons commenting on daily happenings.

In 1967 Berthiaume returned to editorial cartooning, first for the daily *Le Devoir*, then for the pro-independence daily *Le Jour* (1974-76) and finally for *Montréal-Matin*. He has also worked for several news magazines (*Time, MacLean's*). Two collections of his caricatures have been published: *Un Monde Fou* ("A Mad World," 1961) and *Les Cent Dessins du Centenaire* ("The One Hundred Drawings of the Centennial," 1967).

Like Robert La Palme, Berthiaume has always been concerned with form as well as with content. He was the first Canadian cartoonist to engage in caricature with a social thrust. Twice a winner at the International Salon of Caricature in Montreal (1964 and 1966), Berthiaume was the recipient of the Olivar Asselin Journalism Award in 1973. He is now retired.

S.J.

The National Renovation
Roland Berthiaume. © La Patrie.

BERTHIO
See Berthiaume, Roland.

BERUSAIYU NO BARA (Japan) *Berusaiyu no Bara* ("The Rose of Versailles") is a fictionalization in comic book form of the life of France's Marie Antoinette. It was serialized weekly in *Margaret*, a young girls' magazine, from 1972 to 1973. Created and drawn by the talented woman artist Ryōko Ikeda, it is regarded as a classic of the genre known in Japan as *shōjō manga* ("young girls' comics"). As a comic book, it has no parallel in the Western world in either length or scope. It consists of over fifteen hundred pages (sold today as several paperback or hardcover volumes) and could be more aptly characterized as literature. While not a work of cartooning in the strict sense, *Berusaiyu no Bara* deserves recognition for its ground-breaking attempt to open hitherto unexplored fields to talented cartoonists and graphic artists.

Berusaiyu no Bara is a fascinating mix of French and Japanese cultural values. Oscar François de Jarjayes is a beautiful woman who, amusingly, always wears men's clothes and is the captain of the palace guard. She is so stunningly beautiful/handsome, moreover, that not only men but also the court ladies swoon over her. Oscar, Marie Antoinette, and Marie Antoinette's lover Hans Axel Fersen are the central characters, and their continuous romances and infatuations are skillfully woven into the context of unfolding French history and the divided loyalties created by the Revolution. In the end Marie Antoinette loses her head, of course; Oscar is killed while storming the Bastille with a troop of rebel soldiers, and Fersen is stoned to death by a mob in his native Sweden. Save for Oscar, nearly all characters are historical, Ikeda having studied French history in school and used Stefan Zweig's book *Marie Antoinette* as a major reference. The genre, however, demands a heavy emphasis on romance, and as a result both the graphics and the story line are syrupy at times. Nonetheless, the overall work is gripping.

Berusaiyu no Bara was the first "girls" comic in Japan to break outside a schoolgirl readership. In 1974 it was dramatized and presented by Japan's unique all-female performing group, Takarazuka, under the direction of Ichio Hasegawa. The play was a smash success and captured the imagination of all Japan. A film version was produced in location in France with Mataichiro Yamamoto in charge of direction and released in 1980. In addition an animated television series has been produced and shown to great acclaim not only in Japan, but also in Europe, where the story has also won many fans. In 1981 Tokyo-based publisher Sanyu-sha began issuing an English-language version of the books (tranlated by Frederik L. Schodt) for the Japanese market, but publication of the long series stopped at only the second volume.

F.S.

BETTY BOOP (U.S.) Betty Boop was first created as a dog character by Grim Natwick and appeared as the girl friend of the equally canine Bimbo in the *Talkartoons* series produced by Max and Dave Fleischer for Paramount. She was featured in "Dizzy Dishes," "Barnacle Bill," and other cartoons through 1930.

Betty Boop finally came into her own with "Betty Co-Ed," when she shed her doggy identity. Natwick later recalled this transformation: "She (Betty) started out as a little dog with long ears, but the rest of her was extremely feminine. After a few pictures the long ears developed into earrings, and she was nothing but a cute little girl." Betty's figure was modeled after Mae West's, and her singing style on that of Helen Kane (the "Boop Boop a-Doop Girl"), who sued Max Fleischer but lost. (Betty's actual voice was, after several women tried the characterization, that of Mae Questal, who also impersonated Olive Oyl.)

On the screen Betty was a tiny but resolutely feminine vamp who threw kisses and hearts at the audience, lifted her skirt and batted her long eyelashes in suggestive provocation. Her success was nothing short of fabulous: there were more than one hundred *Betty Boop* cartoons produced (including ninety in the official *Betty Boop* series). Among the most noteworthy are the 1932 "Stopping the Show" and "Betty Boop for President," the 1933 "Boilesk" (which was banned in Philadelphia), "Betty Boop's Birthday Party" (1933), "Red Hot Mama" (1934), "Betty Boop and the Little King" (1936), the 1937 "Zula Hula" and the Oscar-nominated "Riding the Rails" (1938). In all of them Betty Boop sang and danced her way through a variety of farfetched plots, in a surreal world of anthropomorphized clocks, flowerpots, toy trains and furniture.

A wave of puritanical attacks (mostly from women's clubs) against the Betty Boop persona, and a costly strike in 1937, persuaded Fleischer to drop the *Betty Boop* cartoons (whose popularity was waning, anyway). They came to an end in 1939 with the defiantly titled "Yip, Yip, Yippy!"

"Betty Boop." © Max Fleischer.

Betty Boop was made into toys and dolls in the 1930s, and in 1934, King Features Syndicate started distribution of *Betty Boop*, a newspaper strip (drawn by Bud Counihan). After a long eclipse, a Betty Boop craze occurred in the 1970s, with revivals of the old cartoons on television (with color added by a special process), countless toys, T-shirts, and tote bags, as well as a number of Betty Boop cartoon festivals held in the United States and abroad.

M.H.

BEVILACQUA, JOSÉ ARTUR (1880-1915) Brazilian cartoonist and illustrator born in Fortaleza, Ceará, Brazil, in 1880. After completing his high school studies, José Bevilacqua went to Rio de Janeiro in 1900 to attend the National School of Fine Arts. From 1901 to 1906, under the pen name "J. Artur," he collaborated as illustrator and cartoonist on the Rio publications *O Malho, A Avenida, Revista da Semana and O Papagio.* In 1907 he took a position as a drawing teacher in an Acre high school, remaining until 1910, when he decided to return to his home state of Ceará.

Bevilacqua moved from Ceará to Belém in 1913 and worked for the newspaper *Pronvíncia de Pará* for awhile. Back in Rio the next year, he resumed his collaboration on *Revista da Semana* and also drew cartoons for *El Imparcial.* A sick and troubled man, he returned to Granja, in his native Ceará, for the last year of his life. He died in Granja in 1915.

Almost a forgotten figure for over fifty years, Bevilacqua has been rediscovered of late, and his work is now being evaluated in a new light. He is hailed today as one of the pioneers of Brazilian cartooning.

A.M.

BEYER, MARK (1950-) Few contemporary cartoonists have staked out a territory and made it so exclusively their own as Mark Beyer, whose ghastly gallows humor carries human suffering *ad absurdum*. His brief episodes of disaster and woe reflect both despair and stoic endurance. Bleak as they are, they suggest something of the indomitable human spirit.

Born in 1950 in Pennsylvania, Beyer holds a degree from Franconia College, but prides himself on never having taken a single art lesson or held an art-related job. His defiantly naïve style, with its rudimentary figuration, its lack of perspective, and its surreal distortion, derives as much from German Expressionism as from *art brut*. Deceptively childlike, it conceals its sophisticated complexity and provides a perfect pictorial complement for the nightmare-like content of his tales.

Its astonishing inventiveness of format, each page organized and decorated in a unique design, is almost unparalleled in the field. A compulsive perfectionist, Beyer works slowly and deliberately, often re-doing a strip many times before it satisfies him, and finds publication of his art painful because, as he has expressed it, "there is no way to retract it." Beyer's original paintings, which are visually in much the same style and reflect the same existential angst as his cartoons, have been exhibited in Toronto, Stockholm, Milan, and Heidelberg, and have received solo shows in Amsterdam, Paris, Berlin, New York, and Tokyo. The Art Directors Club voted him its Merit Award in 1988, and his work is in the permanent collection of the Library of Congress.

Beyer is best known for his series featuring Amy Tilsdale and Jordan Levine, whose identities vary but whose relationship is unflaggingly one of supportive friendship. Victims of every conceivable misfortune, and many never conceived before, they somehow survive, regenerating lost limbs and heads as needed. C. Carr wrote of the series in the *Voice Literary Supplement* (December 1987) that it is "about innocent creatures trapped in a world of injustice and ignorance and cruelty, where they control nothing. But, as Beyer describes it, they feel 'this kind of apocalyptic sense that you've got to just keep doing what you're doing no matter how bad things get.'" Other characters created by Beyer include Tony Target (a natural target) and Thomas House (a house).

Beyer's cartoons and illustrations have been published widely in England, France, Germany, and Japan as well as in Art Spiegelman's *Raw*, Ben Katchor's *Picture Story*, the *Village Voice*, and the *New York Press*. As befits so anarchic and innovative a feature, it does not appear regularly in any newspaper except the independent *San Diego Times*, but several collections have been issued. His first, *A Disturbing Evening* (including stories entitled "We're Depressed," "Intense Pain," and "No Hope") was published in 1978, followed by *Death* and *Amy and Jordan at Beach Lake* (1980), *Dead Stories* (1982), *The Joke*, and *Agony* (1987). In 1993 an anthology of "Amy and Jordan" strips appeared in Paris, and three years later another in Germany. Beyer has also done a series of animated features for MTV and the *Liquid Video* television show.

D.W.

BIDSTRUP, HERLUF (1912-) Danish satirist and social cartoonist born in Copenhagen, Denmark, in 1912. His subject matter, when not directly political and topical, is human and social weakness, the constant conflict between pretext and reality: pretense, conceit, bureaucracy, etc.

With abstract satire as a base, he developed himself into a political chastiser of the first order. As "house cartoonist" at the morning paper *Socialdemokraten* (1936-45), and at the magazine *Kulturkampen*, his unsentimental drawings (trimmed Prussian necks, fat, self-satisfied collaborationists) became so provoking that the censors demanded he be dismissed. His underground cartoon of a public urinal where a German officer stands alone in the middle of eight receptacles while a long line of Danes waits in a far corner to use one is world famous. After some years as an underground cartoonist—and when the illegal communistic *Land og Folk* became the official daily for the Danish Communist movement after the Liberation in 1945—he became the daily's "house cartoonist." During the 1950s he produced first-rate caricatures and satires, merciless toward opponents, scathing and biting (his signature, "Bid," an abbreviation of his surname, means "biting").

In the 1960s and to the present his political aim has become more blatant, and his impression of the blessings of communism versus capitalism is rather stereotyped. He is still drawing factory owners with top hats, fur col-

More Space Outside

Herluf Bidstrup. © Bidstrup.

Secondo Bignardi, promotion piece.

lars and moneybags in their hands, while the workers are young, with determined expressions and fists ready for a fight. His cartoons are printed in hundreds of newspapers behind the iron curtain. He has received the Lenin prize and various other Eastern European honors for having kept his political line unbroken and active.

J.S.

BIGNARDI, SECONDO (1925-) Italian cartoonist and animator born in Modena, Italy, on April 1, 1925. Secondo Bignardi graduated in 1943 from the Adolfo Venturi Art School in Modena and then went to the Bologna Art Academy, graduating in 1949.

Bignardi started in animation as early as 1948, drawing the backgrounds for two full-length animated films by Paolo Campani, *Alí Califfo di Bagdad e Dintorni* ("Ali Caliph of Baghdad and Suburbs") and *L'Asino e la Pelle del Leone* ("The Donkey and the Lion's Hair"). In 1950 he became a member of Campani's permanent staff, and along with Angelo Benevelli, he inked the numerous comic strips that Campani (under the pseudonym "Paul") was then supplying for the Argentinian publisher Civita of Buenos Aires. Notable among the many features Bignardi dealt with are *Misterix, Tita Dinamita, Bull Rockett* and *Ted Patton.* At the same time, first as background man and later as director and head animator, Bignardi worked for Paul Film, the animation studio founded by himself, Campani, Max Massimino Garnier, Angelo Benevelli and others.

In 1962 Bignardi moved to Milan, where he worked as chief animator and director at the Cartoon Film studio, alongside Jimmy Murakami, Harry Hess, George Singer and other well-known American animators. In 1963 he became the director of the animated cartoons produced by Union Film, and in 1965 he decided to return to Modena to work for himself. Putting to good use his vast knowledge of the animated field, Bignardi has produced hundreds of advertising cartoons and has also made a number of entertainment films, among them *Alan Ford* and *Corto Maltese,* produced for Italian television. He has also worked with Guido De Maria on the first series of *Nick Carter* cartoons, also for television. In 1978 his twelve-minute cartoon, *Sandrone, la Pulonia é Sgorghello* ("Alex, the Toilet Is Plugged Up"), was greeted with much acclaim. Through the 1980s into the 1990s his main efforts have been directed toward helping turn out the new series of hugely popular *Nick Carter* cartoons.

M.G.P.

BIJLSMA, RONALD (1934-) Dutch animator born in Rotterdam, the Netherlands, in 1934. After graduation from the Netherlands Academy of Arts in 1955, Ronald Bijlsma first worked in stained glass and etching. In 1957 he turned to animation and joined Marten Toonder Studios, working on such forgettable productions as the *Tom Poes* series. In the early 1960s Bijlsma worked with Jim Hiltz at the Cartoon Center in Hilversum, producing some of the wittiest cartoons ever shown on Dutch television.

In 1966 Bijlsma founded his own company, Animated

Films, and his first independent production was the very short *The Duel,* a violent, frenetically paced cartoon that was released in 1967. In 1968 came *In the Void,* an innovative color film that Bijlsma painted directly in gouache, followed the next year by *Planet of Peace,* a satire on science fiction, the generation gap, totalitarianism and well-meaning but hollow pacifism. In 1970 Bijlsma collaborated with the Hungarian Isván Belai on the lighthearted *Parada,* which has been his last entertainment film to date. His efforts are now directed mainly toward producing commercial and promotional films and spots. In this field he won a number of awards in the 1980s and 1990s. He has been widely hailed as Holland's most original cartoonist.

M.H.

BI KEGUAN (1931-) Born in 1931 in Shandong province, Bi Keguan began cartooning in 1950. After graduating from the Chinese Art Academy in 1956, he worked as editor of *Cartoon Monthly* and *Fine Art* magazine, before becoming a researcher in the Art Research Institute in 1974. His cartoons were selected for exhibition in China and abroad; his cartoon collections and his theoretical works on cartooning include *Bi Keguan's Cartoon Selection, Ten Theories of Cartooning, Historical Comments on Chinese Cartoons,* and (in collaboration with Huang Yuanlin) *The History of Chinese Cartoons.*

Bi's creative style of cartooning usually maintains a tone of light humor or satire, sometimes with extra text to help explain the background to the readers. Some of his cartoons were made experimenting with brush and ink, and the majority of them contain some mild criticism of the wrongdoings in Chinese society, or illustrate the innocent pranks of children in their daily lives. His artistic style, and perhaps also the contents of his cartoons, were inspired by the pioneering cartoonist Feng Zikai (1898-1975). Bi Keguan is regarded as one of the most important practitioners and theorists of cartooning in China today.

H.Y.L.L.

Bi Keguan. © Bi Keguan.

BILEK, FRANZISKA (1906-1991) German cartoonist and illustrator born in Munich in 1906. Franziska Bilek started drawing for *Simplicissimus* in 1936, and she illustrated her first books a few years later.

The title of one of her albums, *München und Ich* ("Munich and I," 1969), could serve as a motto for the bulk of her production, which might be even more precisely characterized as "I and Munich." Unabashedly catering to local patriotism and the tastes of the less sophisticated Munich citizenry, one book after another celebrates the city's annual festivities, special customs and amusements (Carnival, finger wrestling, the zoo) and street scenes (construction work, hookers), but each volume turns into an even more detailed celebration of Franziska Bilek. Depicting herself as a small, unprepossessing hausfrau, she draws in a conventional cartoon style much diluted from that of her teacher Olaf Gulbransson (her *Künstlervater,* as her ads for *München und Ich* put it, exploiting his friendship for her long after his death). She subjects herself to numerous slapstick misadventures—her first Carnival ball, her first attempt at rock 'n' roll—or describes her appearances on local radio and television, her wonderful old apartment house, her hobbies, and so on.

Franziska Bilek worked for *Simplicissimus* until 1943, during its clouded last years, and then turned to book illustration. A late *Simplicissimus* cartoon by her, "Medusa at the Hairdresser's," points toward the realm of her early book *Der Heitere Olymp* ("Humorous Mount Olympus"), in which the Greek gods are shown as ordinary folk. In 1944 Bilek treated antiquity once again in her illustrations for Lucian's *Hetärengespräche* ("Dialogues of Courtesans"), but the same year saw her resolutely embracing her cult of Munich with *Das Kann Nur München Sein* ("That Can Only Be Munich"). Other volumes (some with text by her) include *Vom Brettl Unserer Tage* ("On the Cabaret of Our Day," ca. 1946), *Franziskas Blumenstrauss* ("Franziska's Bouquet"), *Franziska Bileks Heitere Welt* ("Franziska Bilek's

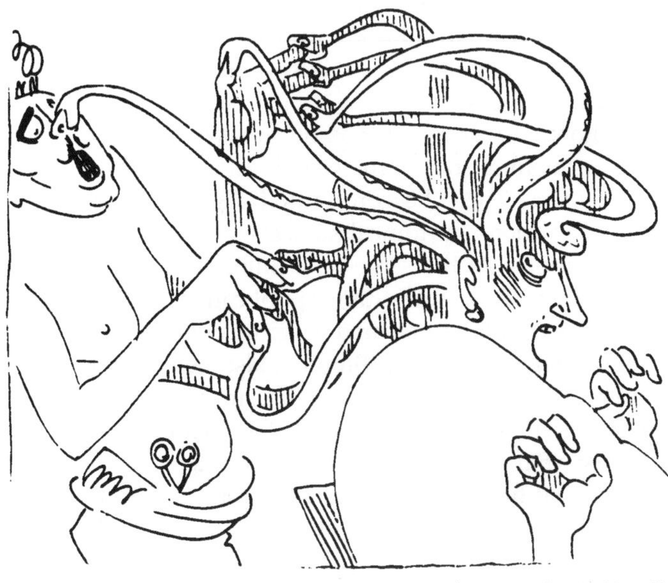

Franziska Bilek, "Medusa at the Hairdresser's," 1943. © Simplicissimus.

Humorous World"), *Mir Gefällts in München* ("I Like It in Munich," 1958) and *Bayrischer Jahrmarkt* ("Bavarian Fair," ca. 1960). She is still present in Munich's *Abendzeitung* with the cartoon character of Herr Hirnbeiss she created in 1961. Her cartoons are getting new life with new gag lines although, alas, she passed away November 11, 1991, in Munich at the age of 85.

S.A.

BILIBIN, IVAN IAKOLEVICH (1876-1942) Russian cartoonist, illustrator and designer born in Tarkhovka, near St. Petersburg, Russia, on August 16, 1876. Ivan Bilibin studied art in Munich in 1898, then in St. Petersburg from 1899 to 1904, first with I.E. Repin and later at the Academy of Arts. He started his cartooning career in 1905 with regular contributions to the satirical magazines *Adskaia Pochta* and *Zhupel.* His caricatures and lampoons of czarist society brought censure upon him, and several of his cartoons were banned from publication. In addition to his cartooning, Bilibin also illustrated books and taught at the Society for the Encouragement of Fine Arts.

Bilibin took no direct part in the Russian Revolution. In 1920 he left the Soviet Union, first for Egypt, then for France, where he pursued his career as a book illustrator. Returning to Russia in 1936, Bilibin became a professor at the Leningrad Academy of Art. He created the "Bilibin style" of book illustration, relying heavily on the discipline of the cartoon, and also designed sets and costumes for theater and opera. Although his contributions were fewer in later years, he never quite abandoned cartooning, and his drawings sporadically appeared in *Pravda* and other Soviet publications.

Bilibin died on February 7, 1942, during the siege of Leningrad. A book-length study of his career by I.N. Lipovich was published in Leningrad in 1966.

M.H.

BILLON, DANIEL (1927-) French cartoonist born in Paris, France, on July 7, 1927. After completing his college studies Daniel Billon started his career in 1948 as a cartoonist on the French women's magazine *Filles de France.* Moving to Editions Vaillant a little later, he contributed a large number of illustrations to the magazines *Vaillant* and *Caméra.*

Billon's career really took off in 1967, when he joined the cartooning staff of the weekly (now monthly) magazine *Pilote.* There he contributed a great many single-panel cartoons on topical subjects, as well as countless illustrations. At the same time Billon continued to freelance cartoons to such humor publications as *Marius* and *Le Hérisson,* and he created several comic strips as well, all of them short-lived. Billon is also noted for his children's book illustrations, as well as for his magazine covers. His illustrations for the 1981 sequel to Jean-Claude Forest's Barbarella aroused renewed interest in his work. Since that time he has been illustrating children's books for all the major french publishers, and he has also turned out a number of comic strips, notably Marie de Bois ("Wooden Marie," 1982) and Force 9 (1986).

Billon's style is competent, perhaps a little too tight, but excellent in its craftsmanship. (Daniel Billon's father, Pierre Billon, was also a cartoonist and the creator of countless short-lived humor strips in the 1940s and 1950s.)

M.H.

BILLY BROWN OF LONDON TOWN (G.B.) "I trust you'll pardon my correction/That stuff is there for your protection!" The rhymed admonishment came from a neatly dressed, bowler-hatted office clerk and was addressed to his traveling companion in a London omnibus. The windows were covered with a close-weave netting designed to prevent splintering and shattering during an air raid, and it was the special delight of London travelers to peel this adhesive away from the glass. *Billy Brown of London Town* was created by London Transport to prevent this curious habit, and the artwork was executed by David Langdon. The character caught on, and his comical couplets and cartoon messages continued throughout the war and after. There was even a Noel Coward song that went, "Mr. Brown of London Town had a job to do, thought he'd see it through, and he did it too. . . .

David Langdon, a cartoonist who had come up in *Punch* just prior to World War II, somehow made a specialty of creating comic cartoons out of London's transport system: tubes, buses, railway trains and their personnel seemed special bait to him and were (and still are) a regular source of amusement for him and his readers. As a flying officer in the war he added the RAF, its airplanes and personnel, to his gallery, becoming its special spokesperson in humor. He illustrated a number of popular handbooks on RAF slang and a strip, *Joe,* in the *RAF Journal,* which he edited from 1945.

His style, always simple, is distinctive and popular, and he claims to have invented the "open mouth" in gag cartoons. He was born on February 24, 1914, and worked in the architects' department of the London County Council from 1931 to the war. His first cartoon was published in *Time and Tide,* and he has been contributing a strip of topical gags to the *Sunday Pictorial,* now the *Sunday Mirror,* for many years.

Books: *Home Front Lines* (1941); *It's a Piece of Cake* (1943); *All Buttoned Up* (1944); *Meet Me Inside* (1946); *Slipstream* (1946); *The Way I See It* (1947); *Let's Face It* (1951); *Look at You* (1952); *Wake Up and Die* (1952); *All in Fun* (1953); *Laugh with Me* (1954); *More in Fun* (1955); *Funnier Still* (1956); *Little Cabbages* (1956); *Banger for a Monkey* (1957); *Puff and Wuff* (1957); *Langdon at Large* (1958); *I'm Only Joking* (1960); *Punch with Wings* (1961); *Best of Mikes* (1962); *How to Play Golf and Stay Happy* (1964); *David Langdon's Casebook* (1969); and *Uber Allies* (1969).

D.G.

BILLY PLONKIT (G.B.) "By the way, fellers," said Billy Plonkit, the dance band leader, "In view of the feeling between the Ministry of Labour and the American Federation of Musicians, I think we'll drop our American accent!"

Billy Plonkit was the hero (or sorts) of the first joke cartoon series addressed to musicians. He made his debut in March 1933 in the weekly trade paper, *Melody Maker,* where he lasted until the beginning of World War Two. Whether paper shortage killed him, or whether his creator, Richard Empson was called up, is not certain.

Billy Plonkit and his Band consisted of Cyril the pianist, Stanley the drummer, and Billy himself, who played not the banjo as you might suspect, but the clarinet or saxophone. Occasionally they were augmented by Red Rogers on the trumpet when a special gig was featured at their regular venue, the Daffodil Road School Hall.

Enormously popular with their professional readers, Billy and his Band were featured in a one and only *Billy Plonkit Annual* (at the price of one shilling for 100 pages of reprints), and, even more surprisingly, on a double-sided ten-inch gramophone record issued by Decca (number F.5640, at the price of one shilling and sixpence). This was entitled "Billy's Big Job" and featured a special cartoon label and the band's byline, "Four Boys without a Guitar." Issued in 1935, the names of the actual performers remain a closely guarded secret.

D.G.

"Do Be Careful Boys," a Biographic cartoon film. © Biographic.

BIMROSE, ART (1912-) American editorial and political cartoonist born in Spokane, Washington, on March 18, 1912. Art Bimrose graduated from high school and took a job arranged by his father with the Southern Pacific Railroad. But he left the job to attend the San Francisco Art Institute and follow his first love, comic strips and cartoons. When he left art school to enter the profession, he landed a job as a staff artist on the *Portland Oregonian.* This was in 1937, and Bimrose handled everything from retouching photos to drawing cartoon spots. In 1947, when the paper's cartoonist retired, Bimrose became chief editorial cartoonist, a position he retains as of this writing. His cartoons are syndicated by the *Oregonian.*

Bimrose's style is a handsome blend of pebbleboard shading and benday tones. His early interest in comics is evidenced by his humorous style and resultant gentleness. This nonpartisan, independent cartoonist is the recipient of Freedoms Foundation awards for 1952, 1961 and 1965. He received the Bronze Smoky Award from the U.S. Forest Service in 1981; he retired in 1983.

R.M.

Art Bimrose. © The Oregonian.

BIOGRAPHIC CARTOON FILMS (G.B.) "A British Film Made with British Labour." The closing caption to *The Do-It-Yourself Cartoon Kit* (1961) capped a riotous six-minute send-up of all that animation holds dear. Ironically, the gag, which burlesqued the famous wartime end-title to the prestigious Ealing Studios productions, covered up an equally fierce and patriotic determination to prove that British animators could create and produce cartoon films to equal anything the rest of the world could offer. And despite the constant cost-cutting and corner-cutting that British animators have suffered throughout their seventy-year history, whether their backers have been film companies or television organizations, it is thanks to such small pockets of resistance as Biographic Cartoon Films that Great Britain continues to be recognized and to win awards throughout the world of animation.

Biographic was formed by Bob Godfrey and Keith Learner in 1952 as a spare-time reaction to the dullness of their animation work for the Larkins Studio. Laboring by day on diagram films, by night, working in Godfrey's basement, they produced *The Big Parade.* Their second film, *Watch the Birdie* (1953), a triumph of limited animation, won the Ten Best award of the *Amateur Cine World,* the leading home movie magazine. On the strength of this 16mm production they were commissioned to make a commercial for Gillette razor blades, on the proceeds of which they moved to 11 Noel Street, Soho. There they hit the build-up period prior to the opening of Independent Television in England; on the first night the first cartoon commercial transmitted was a Biographic production for Crompton Parkinson lamps (1955). Commercials for television have continued to be the outfit's main production line, ranging from a Quaker macaroni 15-second job animated over a single hectic weekend to the longest-running series, Esso Blue, which began in 1959 and has won a number of awards.

Their first entertainment work was inserts and sequences for the Michael Bentine television comedy series *After Hours* (1956), which led to the Spike Milligan/Dick Lester series *A Show Called Fred* and *Son of Fred* (1956), and the BBC Bentine series, *It's a Square* (1957). These segments, made at less than cost, attracted attention to the new company. Vera Linnecar and Nancy Hanna, colleagues from the Larkins Studio, were invited to join the expanding company in 1957, and a large, old house was taken over on Dean Street, Soho. In 1960 came the company's first American commission, commercials for Olde Frothingslosh Stale Pale Ale of Pittsburgh, Pennsylvania. Biographic also entered entertainment cartoons with Bob Godfrey's personal production, *Polygamous Polonius,* in 1960. It was selected for a Royal Film Performance. Godfrey followed with *The Rise and Fall of Emily Sprod* (1962) and *The Plain Man's Guide to Advertising* (1963).

In 1963 the group split into individual animators to handle their own personal films. Biographic 1 (Nancy

Reginald Birch, "If They Reined In Their Horses," 1895. World

Hanna) made *Aquarius* (1963), an abstract space journey; Biographic 2 (Keith Learner) made *Goldwhiskers* (1964), about a "James Bond" mouse; Biographic 3 (Vera Linnecar) made *Springtime for Samantha* (1965), a "little girl" cartoon; and Biographic 4 (Bob Godfrey) made *Alf, Bill and Fred* (1964). Godfrey left to set up on his own, leaving Learner, Linnecar and Hanna to continue Biographic. *Do Be Careful Boys* (1965), their first three-handed cartoon, won a British Film Academy award for its humorous handling of safety advice from the Fruit Producers Council. The women have been the most productive in entertainment cartoons: *Quodlibet* (Hanna, 1968), *The Trendsetter* (Linnecar, 1970) and *A Cat Is a Cat* (Linnecar, 1971). All three directed *I'm Glad You Asked That Question* (1970) for the Gas Council and their longest cartoon to date, *I'm Sorry You've Been Kept Waiting* (1976), a 16-minute instructional cartoon sponsored by IBM. Biographic has also animated titles for the feature films *Inn for Trouble* (1960), *The Road to Hong Kong* (1962), *Hand of Night* (1966), and *The Ghost Goes Gear* (1966). Their main line continues to be television commercials, and they are proud of their claim to being the first British animation company organized to produce animated TV commercials.

D.G.

BIRCHANSKY, LEO (1887-1949) Russian-American cartoonist born in Odessa, Russia, in 1887. Lev (Leo) Birchansky studied art at a private school in his native Odessa. In 1907 he became the editorial cartoonist and later the art director of *Odesskaia Novosti*, one of the city's leading newspapers, and he continued in these positions until 1917. He then took part in the Russian Revolution and published sketches depicting scenes of the revolution.

In 1922 Birchansky left the Soviet Union for western Europe and later came to the United States, finally settling in New York. There he freelanced cartoons and illustrations, also illustrating books in Russian by his fellow émigrés. He worked for 12 years (1931-43) in the art department of the *New York News*. In 1943 he moved to Miami, where he worked for various local publications as a cartoonist and illustrator. He died in Miami on March 8, 1949.

Leo Birchansky was a noted political cartoonist in his native Russia, but his style of cartooning never found favor in the United States. His career spanned two continents and two vastly different political systems, and this fact makes his contribution worthy of acknowledgment.

M.H.

BIRCH, REGINALD BATHURST (1856-1943) American artist born in London, England, on May 2, 1856. Reginald Birch grew up in San Francisco and received his art training at the Art Academy of Munich, Germany. In 1881, Birch began to illustrate for the popular illustrated monthlies and to focus his work on the children's magazine *St. Nicholas*, originally published by Scribner's, later by the Century Company. Birch soon became about the most published illustrator in the United States, contributing to all the magazines of these firms as well as to *Harper's, Collier's, Youth's Companion* and *Life;* for his children's drawings he earned the title "the Children's Gibson"; he illustrated nearly two hundred books, including his most notable, *Little Lord Fauntleroy*, by Frances Hodgson Burnett. His drawings for the latter influenced a generation of boys' clothes—ultimately worn by Buster Brown.

His cartoons, principally in *Life* and the back sections of the monthlies, often dealt with society subjects. Birch looked the upper-class type and obviously moved in those circles. His style was always bold and handsome, a precise knowledge of anatomy and skillful use of pen-and-ink crosshatching resulting in arresting and lively representations. In later years his line grew thicker—though not stiffer—and exactitude and detail gave way to economy and exaggeration. His illustrations of Edward Lear's nonsense rhymes are classics of the genre.

Besides the many books for which he drew, a collection of story excerpts and illustrations of fifty years of work was published as *Reginald Birch—His Book* by Harcourt Brace in 1939.

R.M.

BIRD, CYRIL KENNETH (1887-1965) British cartoonist born on December 17, 1887. Cyril ("Fougasse") Bird was the Isaac Pitman of British cartooning: he was the first to invent and use a visual shorthand. His early cartoons in *Tit-Bits* and other weeklies just after World War I are average. But during the 1920s he evolved a dot-and-dash code of cartooning that by the 1930s was one of the most widely recognized individual styles in England.

Fougasse studied at Cheltenham College, obtaining his bachelor of science degree. He studied cartooning by mail through Percy V. Bradshaw's Press Art School until going to war in 1914. In 1916 he was invalided out after having been shot in the spine at Gallipoli and crippled for life. He began to assault magazines with cartoons, signing himself "Fougasse," the name of a small French land mine. Bradshaw, with whom he continued to study, sold Fougasse's first cartoon to *Punch* in 1917, and a destiny was created. Fougasse became the art editor of that famous weekly in 1937 and was appointed full editor in 1949. He retired in 1953 but kept busy by writing his definitive "Survey of Modern British and American Humorous Art," *The Good Tempered Pencil.*

His shorthand style and handwritten lettering became extremely well known (and liked) through his advertising work (Pyramid handkerchiefs, etc.) and his many war posters for the Ministry of Transport and others (1939-45). He often lectured on cartooning and humor on radio and the club circuits and was one of the pioneers of the school of cartooning that believed humor to be more important than art: "It is really better to have a good idea with a bad drawing than a bad idea with a good drawing." He died June 11, 1965.

Books: *A Gallery of Games* (1921); *Drawn at a Venture* (1922); *So This Is Golf* (1923); *A Book of Drawings* (1926); *The World's Workers* (1928); *E. and O.E.* (1928); *P.T.O.* (1930); *Southern Ways and Means* (1931); *Fun Fair* (1934); *Aces Made Easy* (1934); *You Have Been Warned* (1935); *Exploring the Avenues* (1936); *Luck of the Draw* (1936);

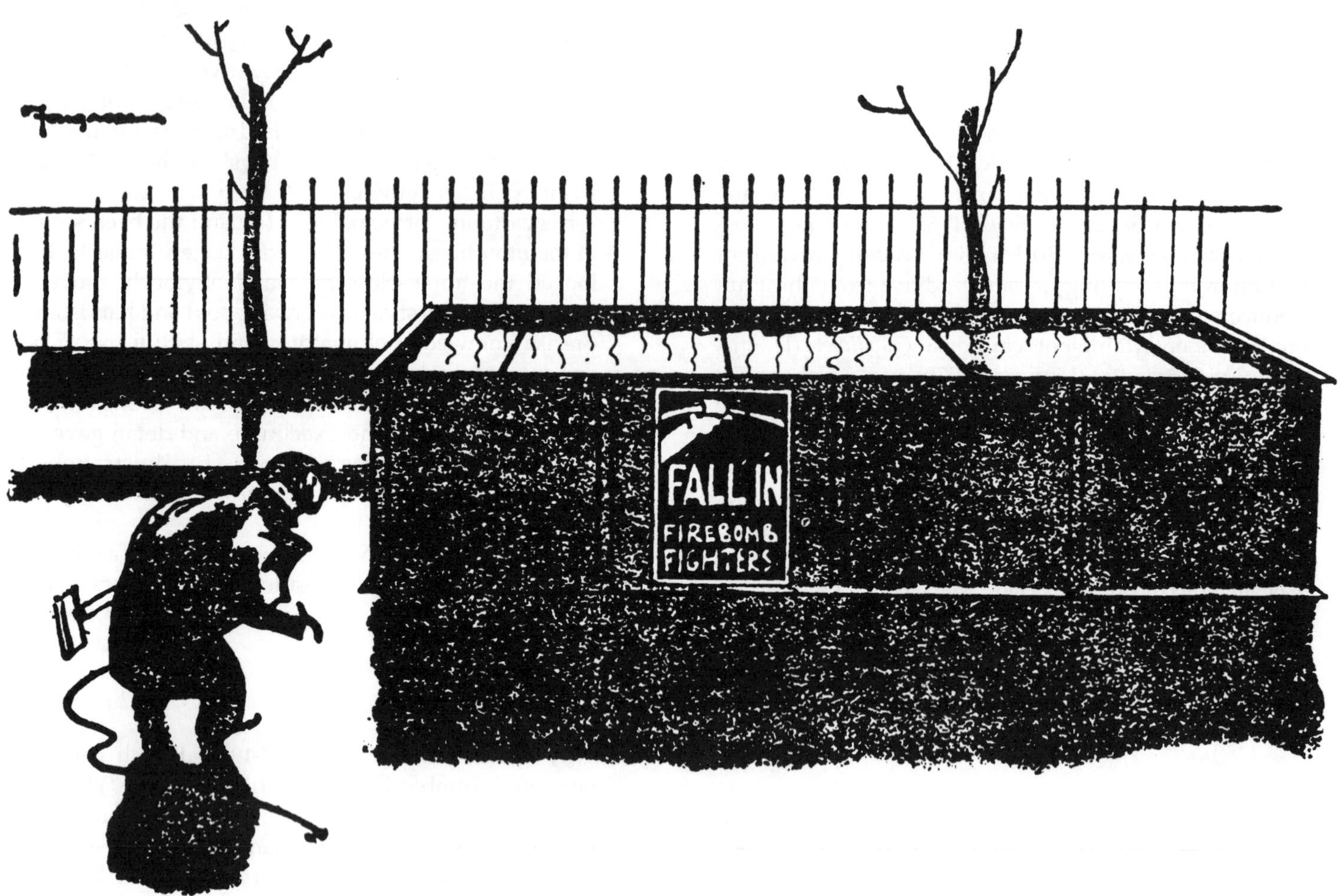

C.K. Bird ("Fougasse"), World War II cartoon. © Fougasse.

Drawing the Line Somewhere (1937); *Stop or Go* (1938); *Jotsam* (1939); *The Changing Face of Britain* (1940); *And the Gatepost* (1940); *Running Commentary* (1941); *The Little Less* (1941); *Dear Turley* (1942); *Sorry No Rubber* (1942); *Fougasse Painting Book* (1942); *Just a Few Lines* (1943); *Family Group* (1944); *Home Circle* (1945); *A School of Purposes* (1946); *You and Me* (1948); *Us* (1951); *The Neighbours* (1954); *The Good Tempered Pencil* (1956); *Wall Pictures* (1957); *Between the Lines* (1958); *Ballet Exercises* (1960); and *Guided Composition* (1961).

D.G.

BIRDSALL, TIMOTHY (1936-1963) British cartoonist born in Cambridge, England, in 1936. Timothy Birdsall, who signed himself "Timothy," was not only a brilliant and witty political cartoonist on paper, he was a budding and engaging television personality, the first cartoonist to fully use his talents "live." A rocketing career was tragically cut short when he died suddenly of leukemia at the age of 27.

Birdsall came down to London from Cambridge in 1960 and was immediately taken on by the *Sunday Times* to draw the front-page "Little Cartoon." He satirized the newspaper as the *Sunday Tome* in one of his brilliant burlesques for the satirical weekly *Private Eye,* for which he became a regular contributor from 1962. The same year he was appointed political cartoonist of the more serious weekly *Spectator.* With more time and space to play with, his drawing style expanded to become fantastically detailed in the rococo traditions of Ronald Searle, Rowland Emett and Michael Ffolkes. But his wit was always more barbed than his mentors'. He illustrated books, including Michael Frayn's collection *The Day of the Dog;* in a different vein, he drew 49 pictures of theaters for *London Theatres* by Raymond Mander and Joe Mitchenson. A book of his own creation, *This Book Is Good for You,* was never completed due to his illness, but his rough page layouts were printed in a collection of his work, *Timothy,* published as a tribute in 1964.

In the last few months of his life, Timothy became one of the team of young satirists who took the world to pieces every Saturday night on BBC television in Ned Sherrin and David Frost's series *That Was the Week That Was* (1963). For his weekly spot he developed a totally new, live, on-camera cartooning technique, with drawing and commentary linked in one inseparable five-minute flow of spontaneous comedy. His sudden death at the height of his success (June 1963) shocked the British nation.

D.G.

BISSELL, PHILIP (1926-) American cartoonist born in Worcester, Massachusetts, on February 1, 1926. Phil Bissell was a cartoonist on his high school monthly mag-

Philip Bissell, "Obliging Ted." © *Bissell.*

azine; graduating in 1944, he went directly into the army. Back in civilian life, he studied in a Boston art school on a GI bill for two years. In 1948, after completing his studies, he went to work for the *Boston Traveler,* first as a copy boy, then as a cartoonist drawing sports, entertainment and editorial cartoons. But Bissell's heart was set on sports exclusively, and when he learned in 1953 that the *Boston Globe* was looking for a new sports cartoonist he applied for the job and was accepted. Bissell drew sports cartoons (and an occasional editorial cartoon) for the *Globe* with such gusto that he soon gained national recognition. In 1965 he resigned from the *Globe* and started his own syndicate. He later joined the staff of the *Worcester Gazette,* and in 1975 he became the sports cartoonist of the *Boston Herald-American.* He then worked for the Lowell (Mass.) Sun from 1980 to 1987. Since that time he has been freelancing, sometimes under the pseudonym "Chuck Phillips."

Bissell has also contributed many cartoons and illustrations to magazines, mostly on sports subjects, and he originated the insignia of the New England Patriots. He has won many awards in the sports cartoon category, and his works are on permanent display in the basketball, football and baseball halls of fame.

M.H.

BIZARRO (U.S.) American cartoonist Dan Piraro titled his comic panel *Bizarro* because it rhymes with his name, not because it is sublimely bizarre. The panel was launched by Chronicle Features in 1985, but Piraro switched syndicates in 1995 to aggressive powerhouse Universal Press Syndicate. Several years after beginning *Bizarro,* a Sunday page was added to the six daily panels. Piraro has described his strip as "bizarre, surreal explanations for everyday events." His artistic influences as a kid were not comic books but the paintings of Salvador Dali, Italian Renaissance Masters, and *MAD* magazine.

Of the so-called "weird panel" genre, *Bizarro* is possibly the best drawn. Piraro's style is distinctive with strong pen and ink line and short curved shading lines mixed with solid black areas. It makes the *Bizarro* panel project from the comics page. In the age of *The Far Side* wannabes, *Bizarro* is not. Piraro's creation is not at all a derivative of Gary Larson's concept of humor. It is uniquely Piraro's, who along with Charles Rodriques and Bill Griffith, is a leading cartoon surrealist.

Bizarro features word balloons and often a caption underneath. There are few pure sight gags although wordplay is a common instrument of humor. Piraro finds nothing sacred in popular culture. One cartoon features an ordinary woman in a bar pitching this pickup line to a guy in a bowling shirt, "The bad new is—I'm not built like a Barbie doll. The good news is—unlike her, I'm anatomically correct." In another cartoon an attorney addresses what the caption notes is "The Supremes Court." The three female justices in beehive hairstyles hear him say, "We intend to prove, your honors, that despite numerous warnings, the defendant refused to stop—in the name of love, or otherwise."

Piraro makes better use of the extra space in his Sunday page than many panel cartoonists who just do a bigger version of their stock drawing. This also holds true for his inventive use of color.

Dan Piraro, whose official publicity photo from Universal Press Syndicate is a photo portrait of the cartoonist titled "Portrait of Me as Frida Kahlo," the Mexican painter and wife of muralist Diego Rivera, is

"Bizarro." © *Universal Press Syndicate*

hip enough that he scares the hell out of many newspaper editors. The 40-year-old cartoonist isn't putting on an act, it is just who he is. In cartooning he hates cute, poorly drawn and stupid. Possibly Universal Press Syndicate can promote *Bizarro* well beyond the 200-plus newspapers it's currently published in.

However, there is a comparison to be made between editorial daring in publishing cutting-edge comic panels and the *Bizarro* panel captioned "When Cats Rule the Earth." An irate cat customer in a fast food joint screams, "Hey! I'm ready to order. Hey you! HELLO!?" Meanwhile the service cat snores away, asleep on the order counter.

B.C.

BLACKTON, JAMES STEWART (1875-1941) American cartoonist and filmmaker born in Sheffield, England, on January 5, 1875. J.S. Blackton came to the United States as a child and started his cartooning career on Joseph Pulitzer's *New York World.* In 1896 he was the subject of an early Edison short titled *Blackton, The Evening World Cartoonist.* Fascinated by the new medium of film, Blackton, in partnership with others, established the Vitagraph Company. Among the early films he directed were "historical reconstructions" such as *Tearing Down the Spanish Flag* (1897) and *The Battle of Santiago Bay* (1899).

In 1900 Blackton produced *Enchanted Drawings,* an early attempt at animation, in which inanimate objects appeared to jump on the screen (the method is called "pixillation"). Blackton next produced what is probably the first genuine animated film, *Humorous Phases of Funny Faces* (1906), in which he discovered the formula of "one turn, one picture," a process still followed today. With this innovation the animated cartoon became irrevocably tied to the camera. Other animated films followed: *The Haunted Hotel* (1907), *Princess Nicotine, True Life, The Magic Fountain Pen,* etc.

In the period following World War I Blackton went back to England to try and recoup his fortunes (he had been ousted from Vitagraph in a bitter power struggle), and there he made several elaborate but unsuccessful live-action features, *The Glorious Adventure* and *Passionate Quest* being the most notable. Upon his return to the United States several years later, Blackton could not find work in the changed climate of the early "talkies." He spent the rest of his life exhibiting his silent films at country fairs, attired in the costume of a turn-of-the-century filmmaker. Blackton died in utter obscurity and poverty in Hollywood on August 14, 1941.

J.S. Blackton, "Humorous Phases of Funny Faces," 1906.

One of the forgotten figures of the early cinema, James Stewart Blackton can be called the father of film animation. His work, in both the animation and the live-action fields, is worthy of rediscovery and reevaluation.

M.H.

BLANCHOT, GUSTAVE (1885-1968) French cartoonist, illustrator and publisher born in central France in 1885. Drawing first for small magazines, he became, under the pen name "Gus Bofa," assistant editor of *Le Rire,* one of the most important humor journals of the 20th century. During World War I, he published *La Baïonnette.*

Bofa also published many albums, such as *Chez les Toubibs* ("At the Medicos'," 1918), *Malaises* (1930), *La Symphonie de la Peur* ("The Symphony of Fear," 1937), and *Slogans* (1939), in which his sophisticated but bitter taste was balanced by a certain comic zaniness. He illustrated dozens of works, from Courteline (1923), *Don Quixote* (1926-27) and Thomas De Quincey (1930) to Edgar Allan Poe (1941), wrote a fine and witty book of "literary and extraliterary theses" (1923) and founded with Jean-Gabriel Daragnès the Salon de l'Araignée. Despite all these accomplishments, however, Bofa is best remembered for a poster he designed for a coal and wood company. It showed a poor fellow condemned to burn at the stake who exclaims, on seeing the excellent quality of the wood and coal briquettes, "Vous me gastez!" ("You're spoiling me!").

Gustave Blanchot died in 1968.

P.H.

BLASHFIELD, ALBERT DODD (1860-1920) American cartoonist and illustrator born in Brooklyn, New York, on July 30, 1860. A.D. Blashfield's brother, Edwin H. Blashfield, was a famous muralist, and the family was an artistic one. Educated at the Brooklyn Collegiate and Polytechnic Institute and the Alexander Military Institute, Blashfield received art training from the Art Students League in New York. In the early 1890s, Blashfield joined the staff of *Life* and became a fixture there until his death. A personal favorite of *Life*'s founder and editor J.A. Mitchell, Blashfield was to illustrate several of Mitchell's books, including *The Pines of Lory* and *The Last American.*

Blashfield's major contribution was his delineation of *Life*'s cupid. Thousands of these beings floated through *Life*'s pages throughout Blashfield's tenure there (although he also drew occasional gag cartoons as he had done, crudely and on a freelance basis, before joining *Life*). His drawing style was one of most comfortable and friendly in all of cartooning; gentle, rounded lines were softly shaded by precise, willowy highlight and shadow lines. His work was striking, handsome and never frilly for all its charm. His covers for *Life* betrayed a masterful command of pastel shades, and his decorative work on title pages and in-house ads is a delight to behold.

Albert Blashfield, 1906.

Blashfield died at the age of 59 on February 7, 1920.

R.M.

BLAŽEKOVIĆ, MILAN (1940-) Yugoslavian cartoonist and animator born in Zagreb, Yugoslavia, in 1940. Milan Blažeković taught himself the art of cartooning by visiting the neighboring studio of Zagreb Film. In 1959 he joined the famed studio as an assistant animator, later graduating to head animator on such films as *Twist Again* (1964). He also animated and occasionally directed many of the cartoons in the *Slučaj . . .* and *Inspektor Masku* series. In the 1960s he became noted for his witty mini-cartoons, of which he directed more than a score.

Milan Blažeković, "Largo." © Zagreb Film.

After directing *Gorilla Dance* (1968) under the close supervision of Dušan Vukotić, Blažeković produced in 1970 his first independent cartoon, *The Man Who Had to Sing,* a droll saga of a little man who went through life singing off-key, to the annoyance and downright hostility of his neighbors. He followed this success with the equally amusing *The Collector* (1972) and did one of the cartoon sketches of *Man the Polluter* (1975). His forte, however, remains the mini-cartoons, and he continues to contribute a goodly number of them. Blažeković is also noted for his gag cartoons, which have appeared in such humor publications as *Kerempuh* and *Rajvitak.*

M.H.

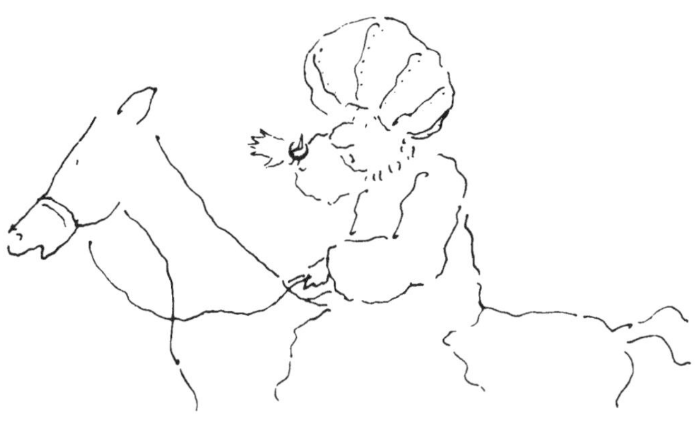

R.O. Blechman, "No Room at the Inn." © PBS.

BLECHMAN, ROBERT O. (1930-) American cartoonist and illustrator born in Brooklyn, New York, in 1930. R.O. Blechman attended Oberlin College, graduating in 1952. He started freelancing cartoons two years later in New York City, and his work appeared in the *New York Times, Look* and *Graphis,* among other publications.

Blechman is best known, however, for his work in animation. While not an animator himself, he designs the stories upon which the animation is based and works closely with the animators. His first signal success in the field came in 1957, when he did the drawings for Gene Deitch and Al Kouzel's acclaimed *The Juggler of Our Lady.* In the 1960s Blechman opened his own graphic studio and started providing hilarious advertising cartoons for print media as well as for TV. His "talking stomach" ads for Alka-Seltzer and "attack of the car" ads for Volvo have become fabled examples of witty TV commercials. Blechman occasionally returns to entertainment animation, as with *The Emperor's New Armor,* which he did in 1969 with Kouzel. His latest effort, *No Room at the Inn,* is a wry retelling of the Nativity story; it was shown on public television in 1978. In 1980 he produced an award-winning animated version of Igor Stravinsky's A Soldier's Tale. However, a feature film that was scheduled for release in 1987, The Golden Ass, unfortunately fell through.

Blechman has also illustrated a number of books in his

well-recognized, wiggly, amorphous style. A much-imitated cartoonist, he has taught a course in humorous art at the School of Visual Arts in New York City since 1960, and he occasionally lectures on his craft at college campuses around the country.

M.H.

BLIX, RAGNVALD (1882-1958) Norwegian satirical cartoonist born in Oslo, Norway, on September 12, 1882. Ragnvald Blix was one of Scandinavia's, and maybe the world's, greatest satirical cartoonists. He studied in various places throughout Europe, making a name for himself in Paris with his caricatures of the Louvre's art treasures. Among his greatest admirers was Mark Twain, who introduced him to the German satirical magazine *Simplicissimus.*

His real breakthrough occurred in Copenhagen and Oslo (1919-21), where he published *Exlex* ("Outlaw"), the first inter-Scandinavian magazine of quality. Here, world-famous cartoonists such as Adolf Hallman and Oscar Jacobsson ("Adamson") later made their debuts. World politics was the target of their sharp-witted pens, and Blix was one of the first to see the Nazi danger in Germany in the years between the wars. His devastating satire of Hitler's and Mussolini's dictator-states was frequently quoted in the world press.

When Norway was occupied by the Germans, Blix moved to Sweden, where *Göteborgs Handels-och Sjöfarts Tidning* secured him as their most talented employee, under the pen name "Stig Höök." Although Sweden officially was neutral, it was Stig Höök's cartoons that showed the Swedish view of the Germans to the outside world, and as they were smuggled out of Sweden they found their way into the underground press of other countries. Classic is the cartoon about Vidkun Quisling's audience in Berlin, where he greets *der Führer with a "Heil"* and says, "I am Quisling!" *"Jawohl,"* says Hitler, "and your name, please?" Seeing Blix's cartoons 20 years after his death confirms the belief that he was a master and possibly never will be surpassed by others in the accuracy of his caricatures and the sharpness of his captions.

J.S.

When the Socialists come:—"The new members of government are here, Your Majesty. May I show them in?"
—"Yes, but through the servants' entrance."

Ragnvald Blix. © Simplicissimus.

Herbert Block ("Herblock"). From "Herblock Special Report, W.W. Norton & Co., Inc., 1974. © Herblock.

BLOCK, HERBERT LAWRENCE (1909-   ) American cartoonist, Pulitzer Prize winner and author born in Chicago, Illinois, in 1909. "Herblock" is undoubtedly the most famous signature in cartooning. The son of a Chicago chemist, Herblock won a scholarship to the Chicago Art Institute at the age of 12. Thereafter he briefly attended Lake Forest College before becoming editorial cartoonist for the *Chicago Daily News* in 1929, at age 20.

Five years later Herblock became the syndicated cartoonist for the Newspaper Enterprise Association, winning a Pulitzer there in 1942. He then joined the army to produce GI information material. In 1945 he returned to civilian life to become the *Washington Post*'s political cartoonist, with a charge to be simply as brilliant and freewheeling as he could. What happened is virtually legend—Washington, the paper and Herblock were suited to each other, and Herblock became the most influential cartoonist of his time. His impact was felt as much in his profession—where a generation of imitators followed—as throughout the country, where politicians nervously opened their morning papers to see if they'd been scored or spared by Herblock that day.

His cartoons were widely syndicated by the Hall Syndicate and its successors. Herblock has opposed a wide array of enemies, including Senator Joe McCarthy, Richard Nixon, and the iconographic Mr. Bomb, while drawing in a conventional vertical format with crayon shading. Today especially, his roots in the label era of cartooning sometimes show, but he remains a prime exponent of devastating partisanship, uncompromising advocacy and brilliant presentations. His work is now syndicated by Creators Syndicate.

As personally modest and friendly as his work is brutal, Herblock is a celebrity who shies from public appearances. Many collections of his work have appeared, including *Herblock Looks at Communism* (1950), *The Herblock Book* (1952), *Herblock's Here and Now* (1955), *Herblock's Special for Today* (1958), *Straight Herblock* (1964), *Herblock's State of the Union* (1972) and *Special Report* (1974). His first Pulitzer has been joined by two more (1954 and 1979), and he has also won four Sigma Delta Chi awards, the National Cartoonists Society Reuben, the National Headliners Club award and the Heywood Broun award for 1950. More awards came Herblock's way in the 1990s. He won the Exceptional Merit Award from the National Women's Political Caucus in 1990, and the Maggie Award from the Planned Parenthood Federation of America in 1992; and in 1994 he was the first cartoonist to receive the Medal of Freedom. He published his memoirs, fittingly called *A Cartoonist's Life*, in 1993.Well into his eighties, Herblock gives no sign of slowing down: in 1996 he marked his 50-year tenure at the *Washington Post.*

R.M.

BLONDEAU, GEORGES (1929-) French cartoonist born in Villeneuve-Saint-Georges, a suburb of Paris, France, in 1929. After his high school studies, Georges ("Gébé") Blondeau became an industrial draftsman for the French railway system. He published his first cartoons in the house organ of the company. In 1958 Blondeau left the railways for a career as a freelance cartoonist under the pseudonym Gébé (the phonetic rendition in French of the two initials of his name). He has since contributed countless cartoons to such publications as *Paris-Presse, Le Journal du Dimanche, Arts, Pilote* and *Bizarre.* Gébé's most consistent body of work, however, has been done for the satirical weekly *Hara-Kiri,* for which he created the weird character Berck. Gébé is now the editor of *Hara-Kiri Mensuel* (the monthly version of the magazine), and he continues to work for other publications.

Parallel with his work as a cartoonist, Gébé has also known a fruitful career as a radio and television writer and producer, has been the editor of several short-lived

Georges Blondeau ("Gébé"), "The Arrival of the Chestnut Vendor." © *Gébé.*

magazines, and has created a several of comic strips. He has also written a number of songs (some interpreted by Yves Montand) as well as a mystery novel.

Gébé is one of the most imaginative (and one of the most representative) artists of the new school of French cartooning. His dark humor has a disturbing, even neurotic tone, and he crowds his compositions with strange contraptions, eerily disjointed backgrounds and a motley assortment of bizarre, threatening characters. He is the poet of the squalid, the tawdry and the horrible, and his sardonic drawings exude a leering, unsettling quality.

M.H.

BLUTH, DON (1937?-) American animator and animation producer born in El Paso, Texas, on September 13, 1937 (some sources say 1938). After attending Brigham Young University for a short period, Don Bluth joined the Disney organization in 1955 and worked on *Sleeping Beauty*. He left the studio in 1957, after only 18 months, to pursue other interests in art. After an absence of ten years, he returned to animation work, joining the Filmation studio in 1967.

In 1971 he rejoined Disney at a time when the studio was hiring new animators to replace the "Nine Old Men" who had assured its success for four decades and were now retiring. The new recruits were soon dubbed the "Nine Young Men," and Don Bluth, being older and more experienced, became their informal leader. On his second term of duty at Disney, Bluth animated, among other films, *Robin Hood* and *Winnie the Pooh and Tigger Too*, and was one of the animating directors on *The Rescuers* (1977), and directed the animation on the mostly live-action *Pete's Dragon* (also 1977). In 1979 he left Disney for the second (and last) time with a blast at the studio's hidebound policies and went on to form his own company in association with two other Disney defectors, Gary Goldman and John Pomeroy.

The new company's beginnings were not auspicious: projected as a full-length feature, *Banjo the Woodpile Cat*, a sappy story about a lost country kitten and a hip jazz-playing alley cat, suffered from money and production problems and had to be released as a television short in 1980. That same year, however, Bluth and associates struck a deal with Aurora Productions which financed their next project, the feature-length *The Secret of NIMH*. Released in 1982, the film told the lachrymose saga of Mrs. Frisby and her brood of laboratory mice fleeing from the National Institute of Mental Health (NIMH). It garnered good reviews and made a respectable showing at the box office. The follow-up features, *An American Tail* (1986) and *Land Before Time* (1988), did even better, and for a time it looked as though the Bluth studio would prove a worthy rival for the Disney organization.

The 1989 *All Dogs Go to Heaven* was both a critical and commercial disappointment. Bluth subsequently seemed to spend more time trying to arrange financing for his animation ventures than turning out outstanding, or even enjoyable, films. *Rock-a-Doodle* (1992), about a rooster who thinks he can make the sun rise, *Hans-Christian Andersen's Thumbelina* (1994), a retelling of the familiar tale, and A *Troll in Central Park* (1995), featuring a Nordic gnome's wanderings in New York City, all had their moments but hardly qualified as great animation. The redoubtable Bluth has demonstrated his resiliency and resourcefulness through the years and the last word is still not out on him. As if on cue around Thanksgiving 1997 he came out with *Anastasia*, a full-length animated feature about the putative Russian princess who allegedly alone escaped the massacre of the entire Romanov royal family at the hands of the Bolsheviks in 1918. It was extremely well-received by reviewers and proved a strong draw at the box-office, thus restoring Bluth as Disney's major rival.

In addition to animated pictures, Bluth has also produced video games and children's videos.

M.H.

BOBBY BEAR (G.B.) "Bobby, a small brown bear, has been my pet ever since I met the jolly little fellow playing in the street." So claimed "Aunt Kitsie" in her editorial introduction to the 1924 edition of *Bobby Bear Annual*. The truth, of course, is slightly different. Kitsie Bridges created *Bobby Bear* for the Children's Corner of the new daily paper published by the Labour party, the *Daily Herald* (although Bobby, of course, in no way reflected the politics of his proprietors!). Bobby appeared in the first issue of the new newspaper on March 31, 1919, in fact predating the more famous *Rupert Bear* in the *Daily Express* by 20 months (see *The World Encyclopedia of Comics*, Chelsea House, 1976).

The original format of the feature was a single panel cartoon illustrating a serialized story, and this gradually expanded pictorially, first to two panels, then to a proper comic strip of four. The first artist was Dora McLaren, who was followed by "Meg" (1930), Wilfred Haughton (1933), and Rick Elmes (1939). The cast of the series included Mother and Father Bear, the adopted orphan Maisie Mouse, Ruby Rat, Aunt McMouse, Percy Porker the Pig and Dr. Deer, the teacher.

In the first paperback publication, *The Daily Herald Bobby Bear Book* (1920), Bobby himself wrote: "I must say it is a very grate privlidge for me to have a rele book ritten about miself, but I have alwaze been a very forchnit little bear, tho I have my trubbles." A Bobby Bear Club was formed, with an enamel membership badge and club song (written by "Tomfool"), and by 1931 there were four hundred thousand members. The annual reprints went into hardback from the 1932 edition, and the books continued to be published long after the feature was dropped from the newspaper. *The Bobby Bear Annual* was published from 1922 to 1943.

D.G.

BOBBY BUMPS (U.S.) Pioneer animator Earl Hurd created his best-known character, Bobby Bumps, in 1915. Bobby was a mischievous little boy clearly inspired by R.F. Outcault's highly popular comic strip character Buster Brown. The resemblance was evident in the little hero's physical appearance, the initials of his name and the fact that Bobby, like Buster, had a bulldog for a companion—named Fido in this case.

In the early entries of the series, such as "Bobby Bumps and His Goat Mobile," "Bobby Bumps' Detective Story" and "Bobby Bumps' Hypnotic Eye" (all 1916), Hurd seemed content to spin routine stories around Bobby's pranks, often played on his parents or his little companions. The cartoons became wilder and wilder as the series progressed, however. The year 1918 is indicative in this respect, as Hurd moved from the banal antics of "Before and After" to the more outlandish "Bobby Bumps and the Speckled Death" before finishing the year with the almost surrealistic "Bobby Bumps Puts a Beanery on the Bum." The 1919 "Bobby Bumps' Film Company" pulled out all stops, blending live action and animation, alternately using word balloons and intertitles and even having the animated characters talk back to the director.

The *Bobby Bumps* series was discontinued in the early 1920s, thus ending one of the more curious experiments in commercial animation.

M.H.

BOBBY SOX

See Emmy Lou.

BOEVOI KARANDASH (Russia) Boevoi Karandash ("The Militant Pencil") was the name of a Leningrad group of artists and writers who banded together to produce a number of political posters (usually in broadsheets) and several collections of cartoons during the days of the Finno-Russian War (1939-40). They took on special importance during World War II, and especially in the course of the Leningrad siege, during which their posters and cartoons kept the morale of the population high despite the rigors of the blockade. The Boevoi Karandash collective has included at one time or another the artists V.I. Kurdov, I.S. Astapov, G.N. Petrov, G.S. Vereiskii, V.A. Serov and N.A. Tyrsa, and the writers V.M. Saianov and N.S. Tikhonov.

Boevoi Karandash dispersed in 1945 at the end of the war. However, another group of the same name formed in 1956, and they issued a number of satirical posters and cartoon collections on topical themes dealing not only with international issues but with situations of everyday Soviet life as well.

M.H.

BOFA, GUS

See Blanchot, Gustave.

BOILLY, LOUIS LEOPOLD (1761-1845) French painter, engraver and caricaturist born in La Bassée, in northern France, on July 5, 1761. Louis Boilly received his art education from his father, the wood-carver Arnould Boilly, who wanted his son to become a house painter. In 1775 the young Boilly went to live with one of his relatives in Douai, where he perfected his talents. Moving to Arras in 1779, he painted over three hundred portraits before settling in Paris in 1784.

Boilly became famous at age 27 as a painter of love scenes and portraits. During the French Revolution he almost lost his life because of a series of satirical drawings of revolutionary leaders, but he soon regained his position with a number of patriotic and political paintings. Boilly survived the Directory, the Empire, the Restoration and three revolutions without losing his footing. His paintings and engravings remained popular through every change of political regime, though the artist himself stayed poor throughout his life.

Boilly is best known for his satirical drawings, and especially for his *Grimaces,* a series of grimacing heads which he drew over the years and grouped allegorically, often round a didactic or moralistic theme (i.e., "Avarice," "Sloth," "The Perils of Ignorance"). He has been hailed as an acute observer of his times and a forerunner of the French school of social criticism.

Boilly died in Paris on January 4, 1845. Several of his children were also artists, notably Julien-Léopold (1796-1874), Edouard (1799-1854) and Alphonse (1801-1867).

M.H.

BOJESEN, BO (1923-) Danish artist born in Aabenrå, Denmark, on March 22, 1923. As the permanent satirical

Louis Boilly, "Thirty-five Heads."

cartoonist at the Copenhagen daily *Politiken* for almost thirty years, Bo Bojesen has established himself as Denmark's number one caricaturist, considered among the world elite of satirical artists. His line is clean, his caricatures accurate and incomparably funny.

Each year he draws three to four panels a week as commentaries on the politics, happenings and whims of the day. His captions are as hard-hitting as his drawing style. Every year a collection of that year's best Bo Bojesen drawings is published. He is also an active book illustrator.

J.S.

In Rothenburg, Germany, there are plans for establishing a degree in humor: "Will Herr Rumpelmayer please attend the lectures more regularly so that he can keep pace with his fellow students!"

Bo Bojesen. © Bojesen.

BOK, L. ARTHUR III (1952-) American cartoonist born in Dayton, Ohio, on July 25, 1952. L. Arthur "Chip" Bok, who graduated from the University of Dayton in 1974, always wanted to be a cartoonist. In fact, starting in high school, from his own admission, he drew hilarious caricatures of teachers and classmates in the style of the gang of idiots at *Mad* magazine. After drawing cartoons for several years for the Clearwater, Florida, *Sun* and illustrations for Dave Barry's columns in the *Miami Herald*, Bok returned to Ohio in 1987 in order to become the *Akron Beacon Journal*'s editorial cartoonist. In addition, he also contributes to *Reason*, a libertarian opinion journal.

Since he considers political cartoonists to be self-appointed watchdogs and cartoons their weapons, Bok is irreverent toward politicians and average Joes alike and unforgiving about their myriad shenanigans, though

Chip Bok, © Akron Beacon-Journal.

never bitter. His work, at first influenced by Mike Peters, is full of zest and humor, albeit sometimes macabre as in a March 1997 depiction of President Clinton in a wheelchair being pushed down a flight of stairs for a $50,000 contribution, or of a hospitalized Boris Yeltsin attended by an all-too enthusiastic Dr. Kevorkian.

Important social issues, too, get the full treatment from Bok's acerbic wit. Whether he pokes fun at the citizenry's ignorance of Latin American affairs ("I don't care about any rap group [Peru's Tupac Amaru]... Especially ones that have left the country"), or at their inimitable brand of stupidity: A smoker puffing away explains with a smile that his iron lung is "part of the settlement, they're free with every pack," Bok always seems to be surprised by people's inability to catch on to the powerful forces allied against them for political or financial gain.

Mostly interested in scoring points and making readers think through his captions and balloon dialogues, Bok draws characters with chubby faces and flabby bodies. It is no surprise then to see how much he enjoys deflating Bill Clinton and Newt Gingrich—although in the end their actions and statements speak for themselves.

Chip Bok has received a number of awards, including the C.K. Berryman Award. He is distributed by Creators Syndicate to newspapers and magazines nationwide.

P.H.

BOLEK I LOLEK (Poland) *Bolek i Lolek* is one of the most popular series of Polish animated cartoons. It was started in the early 1960s by Alfred Ledwig for Polish television. Bolek and Lolek, the two little heroes of the series, are mischievous young boys whose natural curiosity and sense of fun lead them into many adventures and discoveries. They often daydream their way into wild fights against Indians, perilous descents into waterfalls and horse rides into the countryside. Among the artists working on the series mention should be made of Leszek Lorek, Waclaw Wasjer, and especially Wladyslaw Nehrebecki.

Bolek i Lolek has been a hit with children (and their parents) ever since its inception. The fun is controlled and seldom violent, the direction very professional, and while the appeal is to young children, there are some nice pieces of animation that can be enjoyed by adults. (In the United States the cartoons can be seen on *The Polish Hour,* broadcast by WBTB-TV in Newark, New Jersey, among other stations.)

The success of the TV show prompted the release in 1975 of a full-length animated feature, *Around the World with Bolek and Lolek,* in which the two venturesome boys followed in the footsteps of Phineas Fogg, Jules Verne's famous globe-trotter. This Bielsko-Biala production was directed by Nehrebecki, assisted by Leszek Mech, and provided some eighty minutes of innocent fun reminiscent of simpler and less troubled times.

M.H.

BOLLES, ENOCH (1883-1976) American cartoonist and cover artist born in Boardman, Florida, on March 14, 1883. Enoch Bolles was raised in Florida and Newark, New Jersey, as his family changed residences with the seasons. Following an early interest in art, he studied at the National Academy of Design and at the Art Students League, where Robert Henri was a teacher.

Bolles's first job was with the Hammerschlag Company, a firm that designed packages and labels for various products. Around 1913 he began to contribute to *Judge* and its sister publication, *Film Fun.* Most of his work was in oil and consisted of illustrated puns; the cover was nearly always his showcase, and he devoted himself to boy-girl themes. One of his first pieces for *Judge* became his most popular: "Steady Work," which sold for years as a print. In the 1920s Bolles began to expand his markets and extended the illustrated puns to the realm of the pinup—*Film Fun,* still, and *Spicy Stories, Tattle Tales, Gay Broadway* and *Breezy Stories.* Almost all this work was done anonymously or signed by an occasional *EB* monogram. He also worked in advertising, with Famous Fain, Best Foods and cigarette companies as his major accounts.

In 1938 Bolles was felled by a stroke and retired to a rest home, where he continued to paint for his own pleasure and that of his friends. He died on March 16, 1976.

Over the years, Bolles was one of the most prolific cover artists in his field. He continued his work on *Film Fun* long after *Judge* sold control, into the days when future *New Yorker* cartoonist Chuck Saxon edited the pinup mag. His work was realistic and shone with personality, and among his distinctions was a bronze medal awarded by the National Academy of Design.

R.M.

BONZO (G.B.) The canine star of the only fully developed, fully animated series of cartoons made in Great Britain during the silent film period was Bonzo. "Who put the pepper in the Tom Cat's milk?" asked a popular song called "How's Bonzo," the chorus of which concluded, "He's the pet of everybody. Gee, is he a clever Study!" This last was a cunning pun on the name of Bonzo's creator, George Ernest Studdy, one of the best-known British cartoonists of his day.

Studdy was born in Devon, England, on June 23, 1878,

"Bonzo." © G.E. Studdy.

and tried both engineering and stockbroking before becoming a cartoonist. He churned out illustrations for the early boys' story papers, and for the weekly comic *The Big Budget* he created several regular strips, including *Professor Helpemon* (1903). By the outbreak of World War I he had risen to the status of caricaturist-cartoonist for the Sketch, a glossy weekly for which he executed full-page wash "plates." During this time he debuted in animation: for Gaumont he produced a series of three short cartoon films, *Studdy's War Studies,* which were released monthly from December 1915.

After the war he created Bonzo, almost by chance. Drawing weekly cartoon plates about dogs, his favorite characters, he found that one spotty pup kept recurring and finally christened him Bonzo. Soon Studdy realized he was on to a good thing and began to exploit his bull pup hero in all kinds of merchandise. The idea of a cartoon film series came through Gordon Craig and his New Era Films. No fewer than 26 were made for fortnightly release from October 1924 to January 1926, under the production supervision of William A. Ward. (Little is known of "Billy" Ward, save that he passed his last years drawing Disney serials for *Mickey Mouse Weekly* (1937) and various strip series for *New Funnies* (1940) and other Gerald G. Swan publications.)

The first Bonzo was rapturously received by the trade press: "Although the action is exceedingly funny, there is still more humor in the extraordinarily expressive face and body movements of the mischievous pup. The subtlety of some of the effects is, in fact, remarkable." Some of the cartoons have been preserved in the National Film Archive, and considered in context with average American animation of the period, they are fully comparable.

Not all the titles are known, but some are: "Playing the Dickens in an Old Curiosity Shop"; "Bonzolino"; "Detective Bonzo and the Black Hand Gang"; and "Tally Ho Bonzo." Scriptwriter on several was Adrian Brunel, who became a noteworthy director of feature films. Animators were Percy Vigas, H. McCready, M. Matheson, H. Brian White, M. Jork, Marjorie Drawbell, Charles de Mornay, P.G. Tobin, Kevin Moran, S.G. Castell and Sid

Griffiths. The series was supported by a weekly comic strip in *Tit-Bits,* which ran from February 6, 1926. This was followed by a daily and Sunday strip, produced for syndication in the USA.

Books: *Fishing* (1914); *The Studdy Dogs Portfolios* (1922); *The Bonzo Book* (1922); *Bonzo's Star Turns* (1923); *Uncle's Animal Book* (1923); *Bonzo Painting Book* (1924); *Bonzo's Country Holiday* (1925); *Bonzo's Seaside Holiday* (1925); *The Bonzo Book* (1925); *Lucky Bonzo* (1926); *Sportsman Bonzo* (1927); *Bonzo at the Party* (1927); *Bonzo's Little Trip* (1927); *Sea Breezy Bonzo* (1927); *The New Bonzo Book* (1927); *The Bonzoloo Book* (1929); *Bonzo and Us* (1931); *Bonzo's Happy Day* (1932); *Bachelor Bonzo* (1932); *Bonzo's Happy Family* (1932); *Bonzo's Bran Pie* (1932); *Bonzo's Little Holiday* (1932); *Bonzo's Leap Year* (1932); *Bonzo Colouring Book* (1934); *Bonzo Great Big Midget Book* (1934); *Bonzo's Annual* (1934); *Bonzo's Laughter Annual* (1935);*Bonzo Annual* (1936);*Bonzo's Story Book* (1940); *The Jeek* (1940); and *Bonzo Annual* (1950-51).

D.G.

BOOTH, FRANKLIN (1874-1948) American artist born in Carmel, Indiana, in 1874. A major factor in the new sophisticated look achieved by *Life* magazine in the early 1920s, Franklin Booth nonetheless was born on a farm. He studied the work of the great cartoonists and illustrators, and without knowing that woodcutting was the only method of reproduction and that it was one step removed from an original drawing, he mastered by lonely study the flow and composition of minute woodcut elements.

Staying with this style, he glorified pen and ink as much as did Charles Dana Gibson. Rich textures, vivid tones, lush contrasts: all these he achieved with pen and ink by meticulous handling of line work. He became a noted book illustrator and decorative artist; in his striking work in *Life* he decorated articles and poems and executed handsome covers in line and color. Booth died in 1948.

Books: *Lady Geraldine's Courtship* by Elizabeth Barrett Browning (1907); The *Boys of the Old Glee Club* by James Whitcomb Riley (1907); *Riley Roses* (1907); and A *Hoosier Holiday* by Theodore Dreiser (1916).

R.M.

BOOTH, GEORGE (1926-) American cartoonist born in Fairfax, Missouri, on June 28, 1926. George Booth graduated from Fairfax High School in 1944 and enlisted in the Marine Corps. After basic training at Camp LeJeune, he was assigned to a Corps printing operation as a result of some previous experience in lithography. It was during this assignment that his talent for caricature was noticed by his commanding officer. Shortly thereafter, he was transferred to Washington, D.C., and assigned to the staff of the *Leatherneck*, the Corps newspaper, as a cartoonist.

After his discharge he entered the Chicago Academy of Art, but upon the outbreak of the Korean conflict he was recalled to active duty. Once again he was assigned to the *Leatherneck*. Discharged a second and final time, he enrolled in the Corcoran School of Art in Washington, D.C., before moving to New York, where he completed his education at Adelphi University on Long Island. Booth worked for a New York-based communications firm for eight years before deciding in the early 1960s to try his hand as a freelance cartoonist. This gamble paid off when he landed the prestigious position of staff cartoonist at the *New Yorker* and set about familiarizing readers of that magazine with his memorable dogs, cats and people.

Like all the most interesting cartoonists, Booth not only has a distinctive style but also a particular cosmos to which he returns again and again for the raw stuff of his humor. His comic talent is thus accented by the element of familiarity he introduces through the recurrent use of certain images: the dogs and cats; a lower-class philosopher who thinks best in the bathtub; the neo-Goldbergian inventions; the fiddling Granny and her ensemble; and the miserable old couple in a cluttered, deteriorating flat, forever exchanging the most unlikely observations. Booth's selection of images, along with his highly idiosyncratic rendering of them, creates a sense of *déjà vu* which makes his already funny drawings even more hilarious.

Booth is an exceptionally collectible artist, to date having published two volumes of his work, taken mainly from the *New Yorker.* They are *Think Good Thoughts About a Pussy Cat* and *Rehearsal's Off* (1978).

While he is best known for his humorous drawing in *The New Yorker* (many of which have appeared on tee shirts and coffee mugs for the magazine's various promotional campaigns), he has also done commercial work (animated ad campaigns for Delta Airlines and Neiman Marcus, as well as movie posters) and written and illustrated two children's books. Of his chosen metier, he observed to an interviewer from *The New York Times* in 1993: "You do it long enough, and you're not fit for anything else."

R.C.

BOOTH, WALTER R. (18—?-19—?) British cartoonist, animator, conjuror, film producer, director, writer, actor, comedian, special effects creator and mystery man of British films. For a man who did so much in the pioneering period of the British cinema, it is extraordinary how little is known about Walter R. Booth. Between 1899 and 1916 Booth created, scripted, directed and sometimes acted in literally hundreds of short comedy and fantasy films, most involving some kind of photographic trick work, some including the animation of his own drawings. Many of his films were made for R.W. Paul, an early producer who acknowledged Booth in a 1936 address to the British Kinematograph Society: "With the valuable aid of Walter Booth and others, hundreds of humorous dramatic and trick films were produced in the studio." A veteran cameraman, F. Harold Bastwick, wrote in 1938: "I was lucky enough to start my career as a cameraman (in 1908) with W.R. Booth, a pioneer producer and genius at trick photography. He was originally with Maskeleyne and Cook (magicians) at the Egyptian Hall, so was literally steeped in the art of illusion."

Booth applied the art of the stage magician to the motion picture in much the same way that Georges Méliès did in France. His film methods ranged from the simple trick of an inverted camera in *Upside Down or the Human Flies* (1899) to the more elaborate techniques of the science fiction picture *The Airship Destroyer* (1909). His first use of animated drawing was in *The Devil in the Studio* (1901), closely followed by *The Famous Illusion of De Kolta* and *Artistic Creation. Political Favourites* (1904) used an undercranked camera to show Booth caricaturing 6 contemporary politicians in 280 feet of film.

Then Booth joined the Charles Urban Trading Company, and for this American pioneer in London he produced the first fully animated cartoon made in England, *The Hand of the Artist* (1906). This was made in the style of J. Stuart Blackton's *Humorous Phases of Funny Faces* and showed Booth's hand drawing a Coster and his Donah, who then danced the cakewalk, among many other "living cartoons." *Comedy Cartoons* came a year later and was more elaborate: "The most amazing and amusing magic, mirth and mystery film ever published!" Booth used animation occasionally thereafter but never again made a film that was purely cartoon.

D.G.

BORDALLO PINHEIRO, RAFAEL (1846-1905) Portuguese cartoonist born in Lisbon, Portugal, on March 21, 1846. Rafael Bordallo was born into a family of artists—his father, brothers and sons distinguished themselves in engraving, painting, sculpture, drawing, and the decorative and ceramic arts. He studied at the Academy of Fine Arts from 1868 to 1874. At first attracted to dramatic acting, he performed in the Garrett Theatre but soon abandoned this career. After his marriage in 1866, Bordallo began drawing and illustrating anecdotes. He started caricaturing in 1870 with a lithograph called "O Dente da Baronesa."In the same year he published the album *Calcanhar de Aquiles,* in which great literary personalities of the time were satirized, and started *O Binóculo,* a magazine of theatrical criticism, of which four numbers were issued. In 1870 and 1871 he sold seven pages of *A Berlinda,* a series of humorous notes of social events. In 1872 Bordallo published an album totally illustrated in comic strip form, thus becoming the creator of the Portuguese comic strip. Titled *Apontamentos Sobre a Picaresca Via gem do Imperador de Rasilb pela Europa* ("Notes on the Roguish Voyage of the Emperor of Rasilb Through Europe"), it was a satire on the Brazilian emperor, and it went through three printings.

In 1875 Bordallo started the magazine *Lanterna Mágica,* where for the first time the typical figure of the poor and exploited Portuguese, "Zé Povinho," appeared; in 1876 he published the *Album de Caricaturas-Frases e Anexins da Lfngua Portuguesa.* Meanwhile he published several independent lithographs and three volumes of the *Almanaque de Caricaturas* (1874-76), where he returned to the comic strip format. Also in 1876 he emigrated to Brazil, where he often worked for the magazines *Besouro* (1976), *Mosquito* (1877) and *Pst (1879).* Following a mysterious brawl in which he was stabbed, Bordallo returned to Portugal in 1879. Thereafter several illustrated anecdotes, caricatures and comic strips that gave him even greater fame appeared in *António Maria (1879), Album das Glórias* (1880), *Pontos nos Iis* (1885) and *A Paródia* (1900); he drew for the latter until his death on January 23, 1905. It is remarkable to find in some of his cartoons produced after 1880 the use

Taking Advantage of His Gift

of balloons and onomatopoeia. Iconic signs can be found as far back as 1874.

Bordallo participated widely in the illustration of books, magazine covers, and decorated menus, apart from hundreds of separate lithographs and his sketches of the first Portuguese artistic posters. He also worked for the *Illustración Española y Americana* and the *Illustración* de *Madrid,* two Spanish magazines, and from 1873 for the *Illustrated London News.* He directed the construction of the Portuguese pavilion in the Paris Exhibition of 1889, where he displayed some of his ceramics, the main artistic activity of the final phase of his career. There is a museum in Lisbon that bears Bordallo's name; here the several branches of his work, including drawings, caricatures, illustrated newspapers, lithographs and ceramics, are exhibited.

C.P.

BORGMAN, JAMES MARK (1954-) American cartoonist born in Cincinnati, Ohio, on February 24, 1954. After brilliant studies at Kenyon College, where he earned high honors in art, Jim Borgman decided to go into cartooning in his senior year and upon graduation in 1976 began his career as editorial cartoonist at his home newspaper, the

Jim Borgman © Cincinnati Enquirer.

Cincinnati Enquirer. There, his talent and pointed humor, combined with a long acquaintance with the issues and politicians of the Greater Cincinnati area and the state, made him an instant success with his readers. Whether he satirized ill-conceived curfew ordinances or elected officials once again fleecing Ohio taxpayers, his drawings revealed a forceful style and an irony that at first owed much to such greats as Jeff MacNelly and Mike Peters.

However, he soon came into his own both as artist and political and social commentator and expanded his barbs to include national and foreign affairs and personalities, from perennial unfair Japanese trade practices and attacks on the environment to Bill Clinton the philanderer, and from a whining Newt Gingrich to mean-spirited presidential candidate Bob Dole. Even the *Enquirer's* conservative editorial board accepts Borgman's mostly liberal views, for he not only brings readers to the op/ed page but he gets them to think also about their world and those who rule it, adding in a published interview, "My cartoons are not final pronouncements. They are works in progress." In addition, since 1994, he has been drawing a weekly strip of inside-the-Beltway satire, appropriately titled *Wonk City* and distributed by King Features Syndicate. Again for King, and in collaboration with Jerry Scott, he originated in July 1997 *Zits*, a sarcastically humorous daily strip which has become one of the fastest-growing syndicated strips of recent years.

His cartoons, which are distributed by King Features as well, present the important problems of the day with great drama and impact and an irony that sometimes borders on the absurd. Not unexpectedly, therefore, Borgman's work has been recognized: for example, he received the Sigma Delta Chi Award (twice), the Reuben Award in 1993, and the Thomas Nast Prize. Furthermore, his National Cartoonists Society colleagues voted him the Best Editorial Cartoonist four times, and in 1991 he was awarded the prestigious Pulitzer Prize.

Collections of his political cartoons have been reprinted, first in the 1982 *Smorgasborgman* and then in its 1985 sequel, *The Great Communicator*, while *Disturbing the Peace* (with an introduction by Bill Watterson) appeared in 1995. Moreover, he has contributed sketches to *The Ohio Almanac* (1992), a compendium of facts about the Buckeye State. Finally, his drawings often grace the pages of *Newsweek*, *Time*, and the "Week in Review" section of the *New York Times*.

P.H.

BORN, ADOLF (1930-) Adolph Born was born June 12, 1930, in Czechoslovakia. He attended the High School of Applied Arts and studied in the "Illustrations and Cartoons" program of the Academy of Fine Arts. Born began his career as a magazine cartoonist but soon felt there was a more lasting, more serious art of humor, which he found in book illustrations, free black-and-white drawings with humor implications, and cartoon films. He has said that the word "cartoon" should be used sparingly in discussing his works; he prefers instead the label "grotesque black-and-white drawings."

His works number in the hundreds; already by 1982, he had illustrated 146 books, produced 47 animated films, worked on film strips and puppet shows, and drawn hundreds of cartoons and black-and-white drawings. His first film was a puppet production, *When I Grow Up* (1963), and his first cartoon film, *The Double* (1965). By 1972, the team of Doubrava-Born-Macourek became one of the most prolific and important animation collaborations in Czechoslovakia. Born has won nearly every major cartoon award, including the grand prix at Montreal and Bordighera's Palma d'Oro.

A type of originality that is uncompromising, timely, and ridiculing characterizes all of Born's work. His drawings are full, with every nook drawing attention to itself, sometimes with dramatic tricks, and every line revealing typical qualities of his protagonists's character, behavior, and morality. Decorative stylization, good-natured irony, biting sarcasm, and a positive philosophy of life are other traits common to his work. Born has said that he does not differentiate between working for adults and children and aims to deal with human relationships in all their good and bad aspects.

J.A.L.

Marguerita Bornstein, "How to Make Your Child Schizophrenic." © TV Globo.

BORNSTEIN, MARGUERITA (1950-) Brazilian cartoonist and animator born of Polish parents in Sydney, Australia, in 1950. Marguerita Bornstein's parents took her to Brazil in the mid-1950s. One of the brightest stars in Brazilian cartooning, she had her first drawing published at age nine. Signing simply with her first name, she soon found herself working for major newspapers and magazines in Brazil and winning prizes left and right. She went to Australia in 1970, did drawings, worked for Australian television and had her first experience with drawing animated cartoons. Since her return to Brazil in 1973, she has contributed cartoons on a regular basis to the daily *Jornal do Tarde* and the weekly *Manchete.*

Marguerita is also an internationally known cover designer who has done covers for *Graphis* and *Design,* among other publications. She is equally proficient in the animation field and has directed several animated cartoons for British television *(How to Make Your Child Schizophrenic* is perhaps the best known). Through the 1980s and into the 1990s she has consolidated her international reputation as a cartoonist and animator, winning prizes and awards at such prestigious venues as Annecy, Locarno and Lucca.

A.M.

BOROWCZYK, WALERIAN (1923-) Polish animator and filmmaker born in Kwilcz, Poland, on October 21, 1923. After studying at the Polish Academy of Fine Arts, Walerian Borowczyk became a painter and graphic artist. His works were frequently exhibited in Poland and abroad. In the late 1950s Borowczyk struck up a friendship with Jan Lenica; working together in 1957 and 1958, they made three animated films of considerable merit: *Once upon a Time, Love Requited* and *Dom* ("House").

In 1958 Borowczyk left for Paris. There he made *L'Ecole* ("The School," 1958), about a soldier engaged in absurd maneuvers, followed by *Les Astronautes* (1959), a work that mixed animation and live action. Also typical of Borowczyk's preoccupation with the absurdities and horrors of modern society are *L'Encyclopédie de Grand' Maman* ("Grandma's Encyclopedia"), a spoof of Victorian learning methods; *Le Jeu des Anges* ("The Game of Angels," 1964), a terrifying allegory of the concentration camp universe; and *Renaissance,* an exercise in live-object animation.

In 1963 Borowczyk introduced the slightly sinister couple Mr. and Mrs. Kabal in his cartoon *Le Concert de M. et Mme. Kabal.* He followed this with his first feature film, released in 1967, *Le Théâtre de M. et Mme. Kabal,* in which he elaborated further on the games of cruelty, repression and frustration engaged in by this repellent couple. Since the late 1960s Borowczyk has only sporadically worked in animation, concentrating instead on live-action films (*Goto, l'Ile d'Amour* and *Blanche,* for example).

Walerian Borowczyk is one of the most significant animators of the postwar era. His innovative and thought-provoking films have been honored with a number of awards and distinctions at movie festivals around the world. His record in live-action films, however, is less dis-

Walerian Borowczyk, "Le Théâtre de M. et Mme. Kabal." © Les Cinéastes Associés.

tinguished. He has directed mostly erotic movies, such as *Lulu* (1980), *Emmanuelle* (1987) and *Ceremony of Love* (1988), where most critics consider his talents to have been wasted.

M.H.

BOSC, JEAN (1924-1973) French cartoonist, poster designer and animated cartoon director born in Nimes, France, on December 30, 1924. After his military service in France and Indochina, Jean Bosc joined the weekly magazine *Paris-Match* in 1952 and contributed cartoons to other publications as well *(Punch, Esquire, France Observateur).* Many of his drawings have been published in the albums *Gloria Viktoria, Homo Sapiens, Mort au Tyran* ("Death to the Tyrant"), *Les Boscaves* ("Bosc's Fools," 1965), *Si De Gaulle Etait Petit* ("If De Gaulle Was Short," 1968), and *La Fleur dans Tous Ses Etats* ("Two Flowers," 1968).

All his cartoons show absurd and often cruel incongruity, portraying look-alike, almost interchange-able long-nosed men and children who wait on long lines or walk in funeral corteges or interminable parades. Bosc's long stint in the army is probably responsible for the strong antimilitaristic slant in his work, with officers depicted as heartless fools, sometimes reduced to beribboned and bemedalled jackets only, and privates seen as inoffensive, mechanical dunces forever performing menial and useless chores. Bosc also directed a few animated cartoons: *Le Voyage en Boscavie* ("Travels in Bosc Country"), which won the Emile Cohl Prize in 1959, and *Le Chapeau* ("The Hat").

Like Chaval, Bosc saw no escape from the absurdity of the human condition: in 1973, at 49, he killed himself in Antibes, on the French Riviera. That same year, the Wilhelm Busch Museum in Hanover, Germany, held a two-month exhibit of his work, along with that of Chaval and Sempé.

P.H.

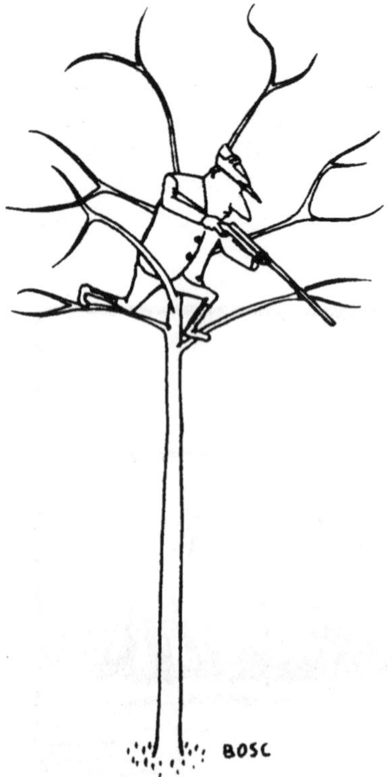

Jean Bosc. © Bosc.

"Bosko." © Harman-Ising.

BOSKO (U.S.) Bosko, a bright little black lad, was created by Hugh Harman and Rudolph Ising in a 1930 cartoon short titled "Bosko, the Talk-ink *(sic)* Kid," released by Warner Brothers. Harman and Ising, busy working on other cartoon concepts, left the subsequent *Bosko* cartoons in the hands of other Warner animators, notably Friz Freleng and Robert McKimson. Early entries in the series (included under the overall Looney Tunes banner) were "Bosko's Dizzy Date," "Bosko the Speed King" and "Bosko's Knight Mare," all released in 1933.

When Harman and Ising left Warners for MGM they took their creation with them. They gave the character more scope, directing him in a number of charming cartoons such as "Bosko's Parlor Pranks" (1934) and "Bosko's Easter Eggs" (1937). These were very much in the Mickey Mouse tradition, with Bosko getting into all kinds of predicaments and having only his wits to get him out of trouble. Bosko's appearances became rarer and rarer as the 1930s wore on, and he finally bowed out around 1940. (*Bosko* should not be confused with a similar-sounding series, *Bosco,* which featured a pup by that name and ran in the 1940s.) A *Bosko* newspaper strip, drawn by Win Smith, ran briefly in the mid 1930s.

M.H.

BOSUSTOW, STEPHEN (1911-1981) American animator and film producer born in Victoria, British Columbia, Canada, on November 6, 1911. Stephen Bosustow won first prize in a watercolor contest while he was still in grammar school. At the age of 11 he was taken by his parents to Los Angeles, where he attended Lincoln High School. After graduation in 1930 he played drums with local bands and held a variety of odd jobs.

In 1932 Bosustow started his career in the animation field as an assistant to Ub Iwerks on *Flip the Frog,* moving over the next year to Walter Lantz's studio as an in-betweener on the *Oswald the Rabbit* series. Bosustow's next big move was to the Walt Disney studios, where he remained for seven years, from 1934 to 1941, leaving in the aftermath of the famous Disney strike. After a short stint as head of production control for Hughes Aircraft Company and a brief try at making slide films for industrial purposes, Bosustow founded Industrial Film and Poster Service in 1941, making films for government agencies and corporations. In 1944 his cartoon short *Hell Bent for Election,* made for the United Auto Workers on behalf of Franklin Roosevelt's presidential campaign, won him fame and recognition.

Changing his corporate name to United Productions of America (UPA) in 1945, and with the help of other talented refugees from the Disney studios (John Hubley, Peter Burness, Bob Cannon, Bill Hurtz), Bosustow started revolutionizing the art of American cartoon filmmaking. *Robin Hoodlum* (1947), nominated for an Academy Award, was the first UPA release to attract popular and critical attention. Bosustow abandoned active filmmaking after *Swab Your Choppers* (1947) to devote himself to his duties as president and chairman of the board of UPA. As a producer, Bosustow initiated the highly successful *Mr. Magoo* and *Gerald McBoing Boing* cartoon series. He allowed his directors great freedom of expression, and this resulted in such masterpieces as *Rooty Toot Toot* (1952),*The Tell-Tale Heart* and *Unicorn in the Garden* (both in 1953).

In 1961 Bosustow sold his interest in UPA. He has since devoted his time to producing travel and educational films, although he released an entertainment cartoon, *Joshua in a Box,* in 1970, and also produced the Oscar-winner of that year, *Is It Always Right to Be Right?*

The most influential cartoon producer after Disney, Stephen Bosustow helped create a new style of cartooning, sharp, sparse and witty, which has come to be known as "the UPA style." He died in 1981.

M.H.

BOTTOM LINERS (U.S.) Newspaper editors decided years ago that comics can be as important on the business, sports, or classified ad page as on the official comics page.

When Tribune Media Services ended syndication of Henry Martin's *Good News/Bad News,* it needed a replacement panel to market to business page editors. Martin and one of the regulars published in the *New Yorker* had brought a level of sophistication to the look of his panel.

Bill and Eric Teitelbaum's *Bottom Liners* debuted in Spring, 1993. The Teitelbaum brothers were veteran cartoonists and graphic designers. Their "Finale" cartoon is a feature of the monthly *Los Angeles Magazine*. Bill's cartoons have been published in *Forbes*, the *New Yorker*, and *Penthouse.*

Downsizing is as much a reality on the newspaper page as in business. In 1993 and during the early years of the strip, *Bottom Liners* had considerably more complicated magazine cartoon style art than the brothers Teitelbaum now create. But *Bottom Liners* is more often than not published on the bottom of the business page as virtually a micro-cartoon one column wide by three inches high. Often it is squeezed smaller. Gradiated screening is successfully used to give the tiny artwork depth and add to the semi-*New Yorker*-style. The gags mostly deal with business, although personal relationships and dating sometimes are themes. Often "Dilbert" is published on the same business page.

A typical *Bottom Liners* shows two monsters devouring highrise buildings. One says to the other, "Concentrate on the financial district... it may qualify as a business lunch." Or a married couple visiting a marriage counselor are told "And you, Richard. Couldn't you give Doreen more reassurance than saying you're bullish on her over the long term?"

B.C.

BOUCQUEY, OMER (1921-) French animator born in Dunkirk, in northernmost France, on August 17, 1921. After studying drawing in high school, Omer Boucquey worked as an animator for advertising films. In 1942 he created the character Choupinet, a feisty little boy living in medieval times. Choupinet helped build the cathedrals, settled the fighting between rival barons and even took on the devil himself in a series of nicely animated, wittily constructed cartoons, the 1945 "Choupinet aux Enfers" ("Choupinet in Hades") being the most notable.

After World War II, Boucquey asserted his position as one of the leading new French animators with *Troubadour de la Joie* ("Troubador of Joy," 1949) and the enchanting *Les Dessins S'Animent* ("Drawings Spring to Life," 1952). Since this effort, however, discouraged by the shrinking market for theatrical cartoons, Boucquey has devoted most of his not inconsiderable talent to the making of advertising and commercial shorts. From time to time he has gone back to making entertainment cartoons, as with the recent *Drôles* de *Croches* ("Funny Quavers"), in which musical notes come to life in a frenzy of movement and sound. His work was rediscovered in 1987 and at that time a retrospective of his cartoons was done.

M.H.

BOUREK, ZLATKO (1929-) Yugoslav cartoonist and animator born in Slavomića Požega, Yugoslavia, in 1929. Even before his graduation from the Zagreb Art Academy in 1952, Zlatko Bourek had been contributing cartoons to Yugoslav magazines, notably the humor and satirical publication *Kerempuh.* He joined Zagreb Film in 1955, working as a background designer for many of the cartoons directed by Dušan Vukotić (*Cowboy Jimmy, The Playful Robot*), Boris Kolar (*The Boy and the Ball, Boomerang),* Vatroslav Mimica *(Happy End, The Egg)* and others.

In 1961 Bourek directed his first animated cartoon, *The Blacksmith's Apprentice,* for which he also wrote the script. This was followed by the stunning, if gruesome, *I Videl Sem Daljine Meglene i Kalne* ("Far Away I Saw Mist and Mud," 1964), a chronicle of the Turkish atrocities against the Croats in the 16th century. Bourek was now one of the most acclaimed of Zagreb animators, and he reinforced his position with a long string of distinguished works, including the folkloric *Dancing Songs* (1966), the grim *Captain Arbanas Marko* (1967) and the charming, pop-art-inspired

Zlatko Bourek, "The Cat." © Zagreb Film.

Schooling (1970). Bourek also worked on the *Profesor Balthasar* series, and in 1966 he directed a live-action film, *Circus Rex*. In the 1970s his work as a director of animated cartoons has somewhat diminished, although *The Cat*, which he wrote and directed in 1971, showed him at his peak. He also directed one of the cartoon sketches of the 1975 Canadian-Yugoslav production *Man the Polluter*. His latest effort, the ten-minute cartoon film *Ručak*, was released in 1978.

Bourek is a master of form and color, and his cartoons have a distinctive, art-oriented flavor to them. They have earned him many prizes and awards, at Belgrade, Oberhausen and Mamaia, among other places. He is also a stage designer and painter, one of the finest painters in the former Yugoslavia.

M.H.

BOURGEOIS, ALBÉRIC (1876-1962) French-Canadian cartoonist born in Montreal, Quebec, on November 29, 1876. Albéric Bourgeois won first prize at his graduation from the Montreal School of Fine Arts in 1899; the following year he left for the United States to pursue his studies at the Boston School of Art. During his stay in Boston he contributed a number of cartoons to the *Boston Post* and painted the murals of the now-destroyed Boston Opera House.

In 1903 Bourgeois was enticed back to Montreal by the publisher of the daily *La Patrie*. In addition to drawing political cartoons for the paper, he also created the first regular newspaper strip in Quebec, *Les Aventures de Timothée* (1904). In 1905 Bourgeois joined the staff of the major Montreal daily, *La Presse*, where he was to remain for over fifty years. Bourgeois's variety and versatility (he would indifferently pass from editorial cartooning to comic strip work from one week to the next) testifies to the freedom granted the artist. Bourgeois created a number of comic strips for the paper, notably *Les Aventures de Toinon* (1905-08) and *Les Fables du Parc Lafontaine (1906-08)*. At this time, however, he was looking for a more flexible format that would provide greater scope for his energies.

Bourgeois found his niche with *En Roulant Ma Boule* ("Bumming Around"), a feature centered on the character Baptiste Ladébauche. If, in the editorial cartoons that he published in *La Presse* from 1909 on, Bourgeois still used stereotypes such as John Bull, Uncle Sam or the Soviet bear, he was entirely original in his reinterpretation of Ladébauche, first created in 1878 by Hector Berthelot. In Berthelot's mind, the vindictive Père Ladébauche ("Pops Debauchery") was only a polemical tool; Bourgeois, transforming him into a sly patriarch, forged a character in whom the French-Canadian community was able to recognize itself.

In February 1905 Bourgeois took over the *Père Ladébauche* newspaper strip from Joseph Charlebois. Blending text and illustration, he arrived at a definitive format in 1911. The feature, whose title derives from a famous folk song, rapidly became an institution and today represents an irreplaceable document of the political, social and cultural life of Quebec. Aside from Ladébauche himself (to whom he gave a woman companion, Catherine), Bourgeois invented a number of Québécois types such as Marie Scapulaire or Père Gédéon. He published a collection of his *Ladébauche* texts and drawings toward the end of the 1920s.

Bourgeois brought Ladébauche to the stage as early as 1906, and he adapted *En Roulant Ma Boule* into a musical show in the 1930s. He was also a cabaret performer, and in 1932 he produced a humorous radio serial, *Joson Josette*, that lasted for seven years. Bourgeois retired in 1957 (the last installment of his feature appeared on March 23) and died on November 17, 1962. Forgotten for almost twenty years, he was rediscovered through his comic strip work. In 1977 the Montreal Museum of Fine Arts organized a

Albéric Bourgeois, "En Roulant Ma Boule." © La Presse.

traveling exhibition devoted to Bourgeois's political cartoons and drawings.

S.J.

BOVARINI, MAURIZIO (1934-) Italian cartoonist and illustrator born in Bergamo, Italy, on July 31, 1934. Maurizio Bovarini went to Milan with his parents while he was still a child. He is self-taught, and his love for drawing led him into a cartooning career. His first works in this field were published in the French magazines *Siné-Massacre, Bizarre* and *Adam,* starting in 1962. In 1969 Bovarini became the editor of the Italian edition of *Hara-Kiri,* the French satirical magazine; and between 1963 and 1970, his cartoons were exhibited in international group shows held in Milan, Rome, Paris, Berlin and Montreux, Switzerland.

Bovarini authored a cartoon book, *Ricco Ridens,* in 1970 for Edizioni Morgan, and in 1972 the same publisher brought out Bovarini's hilarious spoof, *Ultimo Tango a Fumetti* ("Last Tango in Comics"). Since then Bovarini has mainly been doing comic strips, such as *Philadelphia Killer* and *Kariplo for Linus.* In 1974 he was one of the authors featured in an anthology of horror comic strips, *Il Piacere della Paura* ("The Pleasure of Fear"), and in 1975 he started his collaboration on the comic monthly *Eureka.* After the demise of that magazine in the 1980s he has freelanced for various publications, including Linus and the Italian edition of *Playboy.*

Bovarini is one of the best contemporary Italian cartoonists, noted as much for his violent, incisive drawing style as for the antiestablishment themes he likes to deal with. He has won many cartooning awards, including the Unità prize at Reggio Emilia (1964) and first prize at the Tolentino Biennial (1967).

M.G.P.

BOWERS, THOMAS (1889-1946) American cartoonist and producer born in Cresco, Iowa, in 1889. Tom Bowers was born into a traveling circus family, and he appeared in a tightrope act at the age of six. During the next ten years he performed in circus acts and stock companies. Bowers also had a talent for drawing, and it was during his years on the road that he perfected it, drawing circus posters and painting signs and later murals.

In 1905 Bowers secured a job as a cartoonist on the *Chicago Tribune,* later going over to the *Chicago Star.* Moving east in the 1910s, he became the editorial cartoonist of the *Newark News* and later went into the budding field of animated cartoons. In 1916 he founded, with pioneer animator Raoul Barré, the Barré-Bowers Animated Cartoon Studio, which produced the *Mutt and Jeff* shorts under contract to Bud Fisher. The association, by all accounts, was not a happy one, and late in 1918 or early in 1919 Barré accused his partner of financial irregularities and broke with him. Bowers continued to produce the *Mutt and Jeff* cartoons until the mid-1920s, despite a later dispute with Fisher, again over alleged manipulation of funds.

After leaving the animated cartoon field, Bowers went into writing and illustrating books (*The Bowers Movie Book,* 1923), puppet animation, and later live-action comedy, producing under the name Charley Bowers Comedy Corporation. He also drew cartoons for the *Jersey City*

Thomas Bowers, "The Bowers Movie Book." © Harcourt, Brace & Co.

Journal. In 1941 he suddenly became ill and had to stop working (his wife took over for awhile). He died at St. Joseph's Hospital in Paterson, New Jersey, on November 24, 1946.

A colorful personality sometimes referred to as "the modern Baron Munchausen," Tom Bowers was well remembered by all who met him. He epitomized the entrepreneurial spirit of the early days of the animated cartoon.

M.H.

BOŽINOVSKA, SUNČICA (1949-) Born in Kumanova, Yugoslavia, February 16, 1949, Sunčica Božinovska for years has been the only woman cartoonist in Macedonia. Her work first appeared in 1967, in the satirical magazine *Osten,* where, since 1983, she has been employed in the editorial office. Before 1983, she worked strictly as a freelancer.

Božinovska's cartoons are also published weekly by the Skopje daily *Nova Macedonia,* as well as by periodicals abroad, such as *Je, Pardon, Szpilki,* and others. She has exhibited her cartoons individually in Macedonia and cities of former Yugoslavia, and participated in international exhibitions in Italy, Turkey, Japan, Belgium, Canada, and elsewhere. Among her awards is the Vasilie Popovíc-Cico, the top honor of the Association of Macedonian Cartoonists.

Although Božinovska varies her cartoons among social commentary, gag, and sex types, the latter have brought her much recognition; in that regard, she has been called the successor of Desa Glišic, considered Yugoslavia's most important cartoonist. In each issue of *Osten,* Božinovska's sex cartoon is carried in her column "Cicino Coše" ("Cicino's Corner)." She said she draws sex cartoons

Sunčica Bažinovska, © S. Bažinovska.

because she has experiences and, she wants to give a woman's perspective on the subject.

Married with two children, Božinovska thinks about cartoon ideas while doing household chores such as cooking and cleaning, but reserves the late night for drawing. She said that despite carrying two full-time jobs—one as wife and mother, one at the *Osten* office—she does not reflect these problems common to women in her cartoons.

Božinovska's style depends upon the visual, using simply drawn, but expressive faces and funny depiction's of sexual activity. Cleverness marks much of her work, both in content and style. For example, her characters are often drawn with shaky lines which reflect their state of being.

J.A.L.

BOZZETTO, BRUNO (1938-) Italian cartoonist and animator born in Milan, Italy, on March 3, 1938. After finishing high school in Milan, Bruno Bozzetto attended the Milan School of Law but did not complete his studies. In 1958, out of his love of drawing, he started on his cartooning career with an animated short titled *TAPUM la Storia delle Armi* ("TAPUM the History of Weapons"), which won a number of awards in festivals around the world. Thus encouraged, Bozzetto went on to produce more shorts, including *The History of Inventions* (1959), in the same vein as *TAPUM; Alpha Omega* (1961); *The Two Castles,* a much acclaimed fantasy spoof; *Ego* (1969); and *Pickles* (1971).

Bozzetto has also produced three feature-length animated films: *West and Soda,* a 1965 western spoof; *VIP, Mio Fratello Superuomo* ("VIP, My Brother Superman"), a hilarious account of the life and times of a family of superbeings (1968); and the musical *Allegro Non Troppo* (1976). Bozzetto is also the creator of the *Mr. Rossi* series, a group of about a dozen twenty-minute cartoons produced for Italian television; he is also active in the advertising cartoon field and has sporadically produced a number of comic books, usually adapted from his films, with the help of his three chief collaborators, Guido Manuli, Maurizio Nichetti and Giancarlo Rossi.

The most prolific and the best known of all Italian animators, Bozzetto has been the recipient of countless awards, from foreign and Italian organizations alike. His latest cartoon film was the ten-minute short *La Piscina* ("The Swimming Pool," 1978). He later turned to live-action and documentary filmmaking. His most notable efforts in these fields have been *Sotto il ristorante cinese* ("Under the Chinese Restaurant," 1987), *Mr. Tao* (Golden Bear winner at the Berlin Film Festival, 1988), and *Cavalette* ("Grasshoppers," nominated for an Academy award, 1991).

L.S.

BRAAKENSIEK, JOHAN (1858-1940) Dutch political cartoonist, illustrator and painter born in Amsterdam, the Netherlands, on May 24, 1858. At the turn of the century, Johan Braakensiek was considered in other European countries to be the outstanding Dutch political cartoonist. Some of his own countrymen later complained of his very careful academic draftsmanship (less a valuable rarity than now!) and his tendency to think in terms of visual clichés for nations, political parties and supernatural beings (few editorial cartoonists avoid this altogether). Nevertheless, his solid artistic merits and the obvious popularity that kept him before the public for at least forty years make his position in Dutch cartooning history unassailable.

Braakensiek studied at the Amsterdam Academy from 1876 to 1881. Soon he was drawing for the publication *Het Politienieuws,* and he later contributed to many other magazines, but he found his real niche when *De Amsterdammer Weekblad voor Nederland* was founded in 1883. For decades Braakensiek did one large and one small drawing for each weekly issue. Over the years he covered not only events in Dutch politics (such as the menace, in liberal eyes, of Dr.

Bruno Bozzetto, "The SuperVIPS." © Bozzetto.

Queen Victoria washes her hands of responsibility on seeing the Boer War casualty lists.

Johan Braakensiek.

Abraham Kuyper's severely Calvinist party), but also every important occurrence in Europe and the world (he published an album consisting entirely of his cartoons on the Spanish American War). Pathos was a frequent ingredient in his work, so that he was especially effective on such topics as the plight of the poor at home in the Netherlands, the injustice done to Dreyfus in France and the situation of Oom Kruger's people in South Africa during the Boer War.

Illustration was another important part of Braakensiek's oeuvre. He did pictures for numerous books, including works by Justus van Maurik, editor of *De Amsterdammer.* Early in his career he did a great deal of documentary drawing and was noted for his ability to render street life and characters. His much-admired pictures for Klikspaan's book *Studententypen* are in this vein. He also did genre paintings.

Braakensiek died in Amsterdam on February 27, 1940. Other artists in his immediate family were his father, Albertus, and his brother, Albertus Berend.

S.A.

BRACHLIANOFF, ARCADY (1912-) French animator and producer born in Sofia, Bulgaria, on January 12, 1912. After graduating from art school in Sofia, Arcady Brachlianoff moved to Paris in the 1930s. He soon joined a commercial animation unit and became an assistant animator under the name "Jean Arcady." The studio produced animated ads for showing at intermissions in movie theaters, and Arcady soon animated and later directed some of the wittiest cartoons, such as the one for La Pie Qui Chante, a candy manufacturer.

After World War II Arcady became a naturalized French citizen and opened his own animation studio; there he produced some of the finest French animated cartoons of the 1940s and 1950s by judiciously blending traditional and experimental elements. *Kaléidoscope, Guitares* and *Mouvement Perpétuel* ("Perpetual Motion") are some of the notable Arcady cartoons of the period. His *Prélude pour Voix, Orchestre et Caméra* ("Prelude for Voice, Orchestra and Movie Camera," 1959) earned the Special Award at the 1960 Annecy Festival. Arcady further explored the fusion of sound and image in *L'Ondomane* (1962).

Animation is not only an art, however, but also an industry; Arcady's animated cartoon production is still overwhelmingly devoted to advertising and commercial films. His work in this field is often witty and always distinctive. He retired early in 1990, but his studio still continues. (His son, Olivier Arcady, is also a filmmaker).

M.H.

BRADLEY, LUTHER DANIELS (1853-1917) American cartoonist born in New Haven, Connecticut, on September 29, 1853. Luther Bradley moved with his family to Chicago in 1857 and received his early education at Lake Forest Academy and Northwestern University; he attended Yale University until 1875, when he began to work in his father's real estate office.

In 1882 wanderlust and illness—apparently he was sick of ledger work—combined to lure Bradley on a round-the-world cruise. On his Australian stopover he was inadvertently stranded. He became interested in newspaper work and was soon contributing cartoons—having until then shown no particular interest in or talent for drawing—to *Australian Tidbits* (later the Australian *Life)* and the Melbourne *Punch,* where he eventually drew cartoons, wrote criticism and edited the paper for a year. His cartoons achieved worldwide republication.

The elder Bradley became gravely ill in 1892, and his son returned to America from Australia the following year. In Chicago he freelanced and illustrated two children's books, originally penned for his own nieces and nephews: *Wonderful Willie: What He and Tommy Did to Spain;* and *Our Indians: A Midnight Visit to the Great Somewhere-or-Other.* The drawings are stunning masterpieces of fantasy using period poster effects. In the late 1890s Bradley attached himself to *the Journal* and *Inter-Ocean,* both of Chicago, before becoming art director and cartoonist of the *Chicago Daily News;* his first editorial cartoon there appeared on July 5, 1899. Bradley's cartoons ran mainly on the front page, and the pioneering *News* comic section was among his editorial responsibilities.

Luther Bradley's editorial cartoons achieved wide circulation and respect. Using careful but lush and textured shadings, he developed a reserved style in which the sophistication of execution mirrored the maturity of comment. He was regarded as a statesman of the drawing

Design for a Union Station
Luther Bradley, 1907.

board for his fairness and reasoned partisanship—a difficult reputation to attain with John McCutcheon down the block. Bradley's cartoons were uniformly horizontal; he and Ole May of the Cleveland Leader were virtually alone in utilizing such a format at that time.

It has been recorded, incorrectly, that Bradley was the only American cartoonist to oppose the United States entry into the Great War. American cartoonists were divided into two camps: out-and-out jingoes like W.A. Rogers, and those who expressed the horrors of war, urged preventive or preparatory arming and highlighted the offenses of both sides. Bradley was certainly not alone in the latter category, but he was perhaps the most eloquent in illustrating his arguments. While he called attention to the British naval outrages that were easily as offensive as German activities against the United States prior to 1917, he also urged vigorous rearmament programs. Bradley was a Republican, and was honestly exasperated with President Wilson's policy of vacillation and appeasement. He rejoiced at armed retaliation against Mexico. One of Bradley's most popular series had Uncle Sam showing to young people paintings that illustrated lessons to be derived from American history.

Bradley, truly a statesman-cartoonist, died at his home in Wilmette on January 9, 1917, four months before the American entry into the war. Rand McNally published a posthumous collection, *Cartoons by Bradley,* later that year. His own cartoon lessons deserve to be reintroduced to America.

R.M.

BRADSHAW, PERCIVAL VANNER (1878-1965) British cartoonist born in Hackney, London, England, in 1878. Percy V. Bradshaw, who signed his cartoons and strips "P.V.B.," was educated at Aske's School and Hatcham. At the age of 14 he became a clerk in an advertising agency and sold his first cartoon to the *Boy's Own Paper,* his favorite childhood reading, receiving half a guinea from the editor, G.A. Hutchinson. This success prompted his transfer to the agency art department, and with evening art study at Goldsmith's and Birkbeck, he was able to freelance full-time at the age of 18. One of the Alfred Harmsworth comic publications sponsored a competition through the *Artist* magazine to find new strip cartooning talent. The first prize of five pounds for a sketch of a jester's head was won anonymously by Percy Bradshaw. Cartoon contributions for the Harmsworth periodicals began to flow; *Home Chat* and the *Sunday Companion* published Bradshaw's work, and finally he won a post on the art staff of the *Daily Mail.*

Bradshaw began writing to back up his drawing, and his first contribution in this field, 20 lines for the *Daily Graphic,* brought him a check for one shilling and eightpence—which he never cashed! Then came a series of articles about cartooning, "Black and White Drawing as a Profession," which ran in the *Boy's Own Paper.* So much correspondence came in to him—questions, sample drawings, requests for advice and criticism—that Bradshaw was inspired to create The Press Art School (1905). Organizing this pioneering correspondence course in cartooning from his home in London, Bradshaw soon had a success on his hands. His first pupil was Leo Cheyney, who capped a considerable career as a cartoonist by creating the familiar trademark figure Johnnie Walker for the whiskey of that name. The cartoonists who sprang from Percy V. Bradshaw's course were legion: Ern Shaw, Peter Fraser, W.L. Ridgewell, Alan D'Egville, Bertram Prance, "Fougasse" (Cyril Bird) and many more.

Other important Bradshaw contributions include the foundation of the London Sketch Club on April 1, 1898, with Phil May, Tom Browne, John Hassall and Dudley Hardy; the publication of 20 portfolios under the blanket title *The Art of the Illustrator* in 1918 (Frank Reynolds, Harry Rountree, Warwick Reynolds, Lawson Wood, Heath Robinson, Dudley Hardy, H.M. Bateman, Bert Thomas, etc.); and the major monthly series *They Make Us Smile,* which ran in *London Opinion* through the 1940s. In 1936 he published a special six-lesson supplement to his course, *Caricature and Humorous Drawing,* written by the contemporary stalwarts of the art, Tom Webster, H.M. Bateman, Bert Thomas, J.A. Shepherd, Alfred Leete and "Poy" (Percy Fearon).

Bradshaw's own artwork grew less frequent over the years; in 1930 he was working part time with Royds' Advertising Agency, and in 1933 as the London sales organizer to Sun Engravings, a printer in Watford. He died on October 13, 1965, at age 87, leaving a small fortune of £25,000 and an enormous legacy as a cartoonist. He probably did more for the furtherance of the art than any other English cartoonist.

Books: *Art of the Illustrator* (1918);*Art in Advertising* (1925); *Fashion Drawing and Designing* (1936); *I Wish I Could Draw* (1941); *They Make Us Smile* (1942); *Marching On* (1943); *Draw for Money* (1943); *Nice People to Know (1944); I Wish I Could Paint (1945); Lines of Laughter (1946); Seen in Perspective* (1947); *Come Sketching (1949); The Magic of Line* (1949); *Water Colour Painting (1949); Water Colour* (1952);

Sketching and Painting Indians (1956); and *Brother Savages and Guests* (1956).

D.G.

BRANDT, GUSTAV (1861-1919) German cartoonist born in the free city of Hamburg on June 2, 1861. Like Wilhelm Scholz, whose principal successor he became, Gustav Brandt had a career completely dedicated to the Berlin satirical magazine *Kladderadatsch.* In the early decades of the magazine's history, that is, from 1848 to about 1880, Scholz worked almost unaided, but in his old age a pleiad of fresh talent moved in for longer or shorter stints. Franz Jüttner and Arthur Wanjura, for instance, arrived about the same time as Brandt but soon left the staff, whereas Brandt (always just one artist among many on the magazine) kept contributing up to the time of his death early in 1919.

Brandt, who had thought he wanted to paint, studied at the academies of Düsseldorf and Berlin but went right from art school to a desk at *Kladderadatsch.* His contributions, which began in 1884, at first consisted of full pages in the supplement containing a host of vignettes on a given general topic (something like a Nell Brinkley page). His draftsmanship was brilliant, bustling and snappy from the very first, and he soon worked these vignette pages into interesting allover compositions (such as the 1890 page about the interviewers crashing the privacy of Bismarck's retirement).

By the turn of the century, however, Brandt had become a specialist in celebrity caricatures. These appeared in *Kladderadatsch* under the heading of *Unsere Zeitgenossen* ("Our Contemporaries"), a series that was continued by others after Brandt's death. (An anthology album by the same name was published separately in 1902.) For his caricatures, which spoofed prominent Germans and other Europeans, Brandt generally used full-length figures with little or no background, the figures themselves being carefully shaded and modeled, with the faces finely rendered. Eduard Fuchs, a historian of humorous art, declared early in this century that Brandt was the greatest living German caricaturist and the first one of world rank. In the 1910s a contributor to the Thieme-Becker (artists' lexicon) flatly stated that Brandt was the outstanding artistic talent on *Kladderadatsch* in his generation—an opinion difficult to dispute.

In his last years Brandt, who also did posters for *Kladderadatsch,* was obviously fascinated by the great artists of the Munich *Simplicissimus* and drew full-page cartoons that are too strongly reminiscent of Gulbransson, Heine and Thöny but are nevertheless at a comparable technical level.

S.A.

Bismarck, in retirement, plagued by interviewers.
Gustav Brandt, 1890.

BRANSOM, PAUL (1885-1979) American cartoonist and illustrator born in Washington, D.C., in 1885. Paul Bransom left school at 13 to work *on* technical drawings for the Patent Office. He enjoyed sketching at Washington's National Zoo, and his familiarity with the natural world led to his first work in cartooning.

In 1903 Gus Dirks committed suicide, and the Hearst papers needed someone to continue his very popular feature, *The Latest News from Bugville.* Young Bransom was the replacement for the Sunday cartoon, and he continued the bugs-and-small-animal doings for nearly a decade. Seeking more "serious" work, Bransom set up a studio at the lion house of the Bronx Zoo on breaks from the *New York Journal.* His portfolio of animal art became respectable enough to impress several magazine art directors, and his career as a magazine and book illustrator was launched.

Bransom gave his cartooning influences as T.S. Sullivant and Walt Kuhn, who used to draw little bird cartoons for *Life.* He also admired the work of Charles Livingston Bull and followed Gus Dirks's delightful style very closely throughout his association with *Bugville.* With Bull, Bransom was probably the consummate animal illustrator in the American school. He died on July 12, 1979.

Books: *Kings in Exile* (1909); *Neighbors Unknown* (1910); *The Call of the Wild* by Jack London (1912); *Children of the Wild* (1913); *The Wind in the Willows* by Kenneth Grahame (1913); *The Secret Trails* (1916); *Over Indian and Animal Trails* (1918); *An Argosy of Fables* (1921); *Jungle Babies* (1930); and *Just-So Stories* by Rudyard Kipling (1932).

R.M.

BRAUN, CASPAR (1807-1877) German cartoonist born in Aschaffenburg, Bavaria, on August 13, 1807. Although Caspar Braun's draftsmanship was never first-rate, his services to German humorous art as printer and publisher as well as cartoonist are immeasurable. He studied art at the Munich Academy under Peter von Cornelius, the

Eisele and Beisele find peasants planting roadside trees hurridly and carelessly because a bigwig's visit is expected.
Caspar Braun.

developer of so many graphic talents, and was preparing to become a historical painter with a special interest in such subjects as romantic landscapes peopled by highwaymen. However, the great book illustrations of the French cartoonist Grandville attracted him to the field of wood engraving—then highly developed in Paris but practically unknown in Germany. Braun went to Paris in 1838, met Grandville and was introduced by him to the master wood engraver Henri Brevière, with whom he proceeded to study.

Back in Munich, Braun went into partnership with court councillor Dessauer to create a wood-engraving printshop (the Xylographische Anstalt) that soon made a name for the excellence of its illustrated books. In 1843 Dessauer sold his share to a Leipzig businessman named Friedrich Schneider (1815-1864), and thus one of the greatest publishing firms in the history of graphic art was established: Braun and Schneider of Munich. On November 7, 1844, Braun and Schneider issued the first number of the *Fliegende Blätter,* the most important German magazine of pictorial satire and humor until the founding of *Simplicissimus* in 1896 (both magazines continued publication until the 1940s). Among the artists who worked for the *Fliegende Blätter* and Braun and Schneider's other famous publication, the *Münchener Bilderbogen,* were Busch, Oberländer, Spitzweg, Pocci, Schwind, Hengeler, Stuck and a host of others.

In the first years of the *Fliegende Blätter,* years of political unrest culminating in the events of 1848, Braun himself was represented by several important contributions. His series *Des Herrn Barons Beisele und Seines Hofmeisters Eisele Kreuz-und Querzüge durch Deutschland* ("The Travels All Over Germany of Baron Beisele and His Tutor Dr. Eisele") was a sharply satirical commentary on the political and social shortcomings of many regions. He also drew a series featuring the antagonism of the democratic agitator Wühlhuber and the dismayed reactionary Heulmeier, who eventually emigrated to America, and contributed other items about communists, produce-market manipulators and various characters in the news. Braun helped guide the fortunes of his enterprise until his death in Munich on October 22, 1877.

S.A.

BRAY, JOHN RANDOLPH (1879-1978) American cartoonist, animator, producer and businessman born in Addison, Michigan, on August 25, 1879. J.R. Bray studied at Alma College in Michigan in 1895-96 but soon decided upon a career in cartooning. In 1901 he joined the *Detroit News as* a cub reporter and cartoonist. Moving to New York in 1903, he worked first for the *Brooklyn Eagle,* then went on to a successful freelance career as a regular contributor to *Judge, Life* and *Harper's.* For *Judge* he created the popular cartoon series *Little Johnny and His Teddy Bears* (1903-10); he also drew a comic strip, *Mr. O.U. Absentmind,* for McClure Newspaper Syndicate.

Bray became involved in animation in 1911. After working for almost a full year, he brought out his first animated cartoon, *The Artist's Dream,* in 1912 (in his *Who's Who* biography, he claimed somewhat disingenuously that it was the first animated cartoon). In collaboration with another animation pioneer, Earl Hurd, he formed the Bray-Hurd Processing Company in 1914. Later that year he also founded Bray Studios, for which he created his innovative cartoon series *Colonel Heezaliar,* releasing first through Pathé and later through Paramount. In addition, Bray produced four animated films a week for Paramount, including Hurd's *Bobby Bumps,* Max Fleischer's *Out of the Ink-well* and Paul Terry's *Farmer Al Falfa.* By the early 1920s, however, Bray had completely abandoned animation work to concentrate on production and business matters. "I could have gone on being just a cartoonist," he stated in a 1925 interview, "but I chose to tackle the business

Santa Monk: "Great Caesar's ghost! What the Dickens do they take me for? A moving van?"
J.R. Bray, 1908.

job because I believed it was another Big Chance."

In the 1920s the Bray studio continued to turn out cartoon films (*Colonel Heezaliar, Lampoons, Dinky Doodle, Hot Dog Cartoons, etc.),* but Bray had already shifted his emphasis to documentaries and technical films (a trend that began in World War I when he produced instruction films for the U.S. Army). In the 1930s he produced the Goldwyn-Bray Pictographs and a series of comedy shorts, the *McDougall Alley Comedies,* whose title was clearly inspired by R.F. Outcault's early cartoon panels. More instruction work for the army followed during World War II. In recent years the studio has been producing documentary, safety, health and travel films for schools and television, many narrated in French and Spanish as well as English. Bray himself remained active well into his eighties. Only in 1963 did he step down as president of Bray Studios (to become its chairman of the board); he retired in the late 1960s to a nursing home in Bridgeport, Connecticut, where he died in October 1978, several months short of his 100th birthday.

J.R. Bray is one of the most important figures in early animation. His work proved pivotal in the rational organization of the American cartoon film industry. His technical contributions to the field are many; he pioneered the transparency cel process and the photographed background, among many other innovations, He received a citation for patriotic services in 1956 and a special mention for his early work in the field at the World Retrospective of Animation held in Montreal in 1967.

M.H.

BRDECKA, JIŘÍ (1917-1982) Czechoslovakian animator born in Hravice, Bohemia, Czechoslovakia, on December 24, 1917. Jiří Brdecka attended the University of Prague, where he studied art history from 1936 until the university was closed by the Nazis in 1939. During World War II he pursued a career as journalist and art critic, and in 1940 he wrote a parodic novel, *Limonadovy* Joe ("Lemonade Joe"), which was turned into a stage play in 1964.

Brdecka started his long association with animation in 1943 at the Prague Cartoon Film Studio, which he joined as a scriptwriter. After World War II he wrote the scripts for some of Jiří Trnka's cartoons, and in 1947 he directed his first animated film, *Love and the Dirigible,* a period piece about a lover eloping with his sweetheart aboard an airship. Moving over to the Barandov Studio, also in Prague, Brdecka again worked mainly as a scriptwriter on most of the cartoons turned out by the studio. These included most of Trnka's films, notably *The Devil on Springs* and *The Czech Year.*

Brdecka returned to film directing in 1957 with *How Man Learned to Fly,* a *comic* look at aviation, followed by *Attention, Clementine* (1959) and *Our Red Riding Hood* (1960). *Man Under Water (1961),* another look at one of man's inventions, the submarine, and *Sentiment and Reason* (1962), a rather sophomoric contrast between the traditional and the romantic viewpoints, were not very successful. However, Brdecka rose to the ranks of first-rate animators with *Gallina Vogelbirdae* (1963), a light and lyrical tale of a paper bird and its wild flights of fancy. Since then Brdecka has become one of the most prolific animators in Czechoslovakia. *Minstrel's Song* (1964), *The Deserter* (1965), *Why Do You Smile, Mona Lisa? (1966), Hunting in the Forest* (1967), *The Power of Fate* (1969), *Metamorpheus* (1971), *The Logger* (1974) and *The Miner's Rose* (1975) are among his more notable efforts. In 1981 he made *Mysterious Castle in the Carpathians,* after the novel by Jules Verne. He died in Prague on June 2, 1982. His last work, *Laaaska* ("Looove"), was a caustic fable of fickleness and betrayal.

Jiří Brdecka is one of the most respected names in international animation. He has won many prizes and awards in his own country and in film festivals around the world.

M.H.

BREER, ROBERT (1926-) American animator and painter born in Detroit, Michigan, on September 30, 1926. Robert Breer studied painting at Stanford University and moved to Europe in 1949. He exhibited his paintings in many group shows in Europe. Breer became interested in animation in the early 1950s and produced his first films, *Form Phases I* and *Frame by Frame,* in 1952.

Encouraged by the reception of his first efforts, Breer continued his explorations into animated forms with such outstanding abstract films as *Form Phases II-V* (1955-56), *Jamestown Baloos* (1957) and *Blazes* (1961). Of the more representational (but hardly less baffling) *A Man and His Dog out for Air* (1958), the artist said in an interview: "This film, like most of my films, begins in the middle and goes toward the two ends His early works, as well as more recent films such as *Horse over Tea Kettle* (1963), *BLP 3* (1970) and *Fuji* (1974), have increasingly come to be recognized as original and innovative works of art. His 1980 *Swiss Army Knife with Rats and Pigeons* was his last animation work of note.

Breer returned to the United States in 1959. In addition to his work as an animator he continues to paint and also creates kinetic sculptures. His work in the field of experimental animation has earned the Creative Film Foundation Award twice (in 1957 and 1961), as well as the Bergamo Festival Award in 1960 and the Max Ernst Award in 1969. He has also been teaching kinetic art at the Cooper Union in New York City since 1971. He has exhibited widely and was the subject of retrospectives at the Whitney Museum of American Art in 1977 and 1980. He received a major award from the American Film Institute in 1986.

M.H.

BRESSY, ROBERT (1922-) French cartoonist and animator born in Avignon, in southeastern France, on September 5, 1922. Robert Bressy studied at l'Ecole des Beaux-Arts in Paris and upon graduation joined the animation studio of Les Gémeaux, under the direction of Paul Grimault and André Sarrut. There, from 1946 to 1949, he worked on most of the Gémeaux projects, including *Le Petit Soldat* ("The Little Soldier") and *La Bergère et le Ramoneur* ("The Shepherdess and the Chimney Sweep").

Robert Breer, "Fist Fight." © Breer.

After a short stint as a freelancer, Bressy joined the staff of Opera Mundi (one of France's largest press syndicates) in 1952. *Since* that time he has been turning out cartoons and comic strips for a variety of French and Belgian publications. His contributions include comic strip adaptations of Sax Rohmer's *Fu-Manchu* (1962) and other popular novels, as well as the condensation in strip form of several Walt Disney movies *(Mary Poppins* being the most memorable). Following a serious illness in 1983, he has restricted his activities mainly to illustrating textbooks and reference works for a number of French publishers.

Bressy has been the recipient of a number of distinctions, including the 1972 Best Cartoonist Award given by the French Union of Newspaper Cartoonists.

M.H.

BRÉTECHER, CLAIRE (1940-) French cartoonist born in Nantes, a town in western France, in 1940. Claire Brétecher, who describes herself as the daughter of "a bourgeois family with no money," was educated in a Catholic convent and later studied fine arts. After failing to get a job as an art teacher, she went to Paris *in* the early 1960s. She started her cartooning career in 1964 with the weekly magazine *Record,* to which she contributed spot cartoons and illustrations as well as a short-lived comic strip, *Molgaga,* about a court jester.

Moving to the Belgian weekly *Spirou* in 1968, she drew two new but unsuccessful comics, *Les Gnan-Gnans* (a kid strip) and *Les Naufragés* ("The Castaways"). Her first success came in 1969 with *Cellulite,* a hilarious comic strip about a homely spinster princess, which was created for *Pilote. Brétecher* received further recognition when the intellectual magazine *Le Nouvel Observateur* asked her to create a weekly satirical strip for them. This turned out to be *Les Frustrés* ("The Frustrated Ones"), a savage, brilliant, often bitter indictment of modern civilization and the whole human race.

Claire Brétecher is the only European woman cartoonist whose professional fame is equal to that of her male colleagues. She is a writer, an illustrator and an editor as well as a successful cartoonist. She has received many distinctions and awards, and her fame has reached American shores: her cartoons have appeared in *Esquire* and *Ms.* magazine, and she was the subject of a 1977 article in the *New York Times.* A collection of her cartoons titled *The National Lampoon Presents Claire Brétecher* was published in New York in 1978.

From 1980 on Brétecher has contributed almost exclusively to the *Nouvel Observateur;* her weekly page of cartoons has been reprinted into numerous collections (some of them translated into English). She also published in 1983 *Portraits,* a series of watercolors depicting famous and not so famous French and foreign personalities she had met. In 1996-97 she visited college campuses across the United States on a lecture tour sponsored by the French government.

M.H.

BRIGHTWELL, LEONARD ROBERT (1889-1954) Leonard Robert Brightwell became fascinated by animals from a very early age, spending most of his spare time sketching them from life at the Zoological Gardens in Regents Park, London. His keenness and excellence made him a Fellow of the Zoological Society at the age of sixteen.

Brightwell was born in London in 1889 and attended the Lambeth School of Art. His love of animals combined with his strong sense of humor soon made him the leading animal cartoonist of his period. He drew cartoons for such adult magazines as *Bystander, Graphic, Humorist, Pall Mall, Punch, Sketch, Strand,* and *Tatler,* while at the same time contributing comic strips to children's weeklies including *Puck* ("The Zoo Boys" 1939), *Happy Days* ("Peter Panda" 1939), and the newspaper supplement *Boys and Girls Daily Mail* ("Effie Elephant" 1933). He also contributed to *Boys*

Own Paper, Little Folks, and his longest running strip for the children's page of the Cooperative Wholesale Society magazine, *Wheatsheaf.* "Little Oliver", a bear, ran from the Twenties to the Fifties, and was reprinted in book format.

He served in the army during the Great War (1914-1918) on the Western Front, and as a member of the Marine Biological Society he took part in a number of expeditions. He published 20 books including *A Cartoonist Among Animals* (1921), *The Zoo You Knew* (1936) and *Zoo Story* (1952).

D.G.

BRITISH CHARACTER, THE (G.B.) That which we call "the British character"—the modes, the manners, the class structure, the life-style—had no finer depicter during the 1930s and 1940s than the cartoonist who signed himself "Pont." The weekly panels under that title in *Punch* still come alive on the page, preserving for all time that which the British (and the rest of the world) regard as "British." "A tendency to put off until the last minute," "A disinclination to sparkle," "An ability to be ruthless": these captions alone speak truth, without the brilliantly drawn and hilarious illustrations that are inseparable from them.

"Pont," a pseudonym reduced from *Pontifex Maximus,* disguised Gavin Graham Laidler, A.R.I.B.A. He was born on July 4, 1908, in Jesmond, Newcastle upon Tyne, the son of a painter and decorator. He was educated at the `local preparatory school and then at Trinity College, Glenalmond, Perth. He preferred caricaturing the school's staff to compulsory games, and also studied at the London School of Architecture. In 1930 he started a strip for *Woman's Pictorial, The Twiff Family,* running it for seven years before it was taken over by Fred Robinson. In 1932 he illustrated the Christmas catalogue for the Glendenning wine merchants, and in August of the same year a long run of rejection slips was broken by the appearance of his first cartoon in *Punch,* titled "An Uninterrupted View of the Sea.

His first episode in the *British Character* series appeared on April 4, 1934: "Adaptability to Foreign Conditions" showed the impeccable English playing a rubber of bridge in the African bush. In 1937 a new weekly, *Night and Day,* lured him, or tried to. Editor E.V. Knox quickly signed him for *Punch* on that paper's first exclusive contract. He died quite suddenly, of poliomyelitis, on November 23, 1940, at 32 years of age.

Books: *The British Character* (1938); *The British at Home* (1939); *The British Carry On* (1940); *Pont* (1942); *The British Character* (1956); and *Pont* (1969).

D.G.

BRITISH WORKING MAN, THE (G.B.) "The British Working Man, by Someone Who Does Not Believe in Him" began his comic strip career by driving a nail into the top of a post, an act that took him so long that he was bearded by the time he abandoned the task because he was too old for the job! The six-picture incident filled half a page of *Fun,* dated August 14, 1875. The following week, when "Phase Two, Piece-work" took place (the Working Man builds a house that falls down), the strip occupied a full page, and it continued to do so for 17 weeks. The Working Man was replaced by the British Domestic and the British Bumpkin and the British Thief, and ever onwards. The artist, "J.F.S.," had carved an original niche that would in later years be profitably occupied by Pont's *The British Character.*

James Francis Sullivan, one of the first British cartoonists to employ strip technique with consistency, was born in 1853. His publishers, the brothers Dalziel, wrote, "He was a student at South Kensington when he first forwarded sketches for our inspection. We at once availed ourselves of his drawings." The Dalziels published *Fun,* a *comic* weekly rival to *Punch* (and a far livelier, indeed better, publication), and its editor, Tom Hood, used "Jasef" (as Sullivan often signed himself) a lot. Sullivan also drew for *Tom Hood's Comic Annual* and ran a feature called *The Queer Side of Things* in George Newnes's *Strand Magazine.* He drew with a hard line and indeed took a hard line against the people and things that annoyed him: bureaucrats, navvies, servants, shopkeepers. His revenge on human stupidity was often grotesque, fantastic, even ugly. But his was the style of his time, and he was experimenting with a very new form, the strip cartoon. He died in 1936, long after his heyday, at the age of 83.

Books: *The British Working Man* (1878); *The British Tradesman* (1880); *Among the Freaks* (1896); *Belial's Burden* (1896); *The Flame Flower* (1896); *Here They Are* (1897); *Here They Are Again* (1899); *The Great Water Joke* (1899); *Queer Side Stories* (1900); and *Glimpses of English History* (1901).

D.G.

BRITO E CUNHA, JOSÉ CARLOS DE (1884-1950) Brazilian cartoonist born in Rio de Janeiro, Brazil, in 1884. After art studies in Rio, José de Brito started his career as a cartoonist on *O Tagarela* in 1902. Alternately using pen-and-ink, crayon and etching techniques, "J. Carlos" (as he signed his works) became one of the most prolific and admired cartoonists in Brazil.

J. Carlos's long career spanned almost half a century, with contributions to all the major publications in Brazil. From 1902 to 1921, his most fecund period as a cartoonist, he worked successively or simultaneously for the following Rio magazines: *O Tagarela* (1902-03); *A Avenida* (1903-04); *O Malho, Século XX, Leitura para Todos* and *O Tico-Tico* (1905-07); *Fon-Fon!* (1907-08); *Carêta* (1908-21); *O Filhote da Carêta* (1910-11); *O Juquinha* (1912-13); and *Revista da Semana, Revista Nacíonal* and *Eu Sei Tudo* (1918-21). In this same period he also found time to contribute cartoons, illustrations and caricatures to magazines published outside Rio, such as *A Cigara, A Vida Moderna, Illustração Brasileira, Cinearte, D. Quixote, A Noite, A Hora* and others.

In 1922 J. Carlos was appointed art director for all the publications of the *O Malho* group, a position he retained until 1930. In the 1930s he drew comic strips for *O Tico-Tico,* where he created the characters Melindrosa and Almofadinha. In 1933 he published a children's book, *Minha Babá,* which he wrote and illustrated himself. In 1935 he returned as the regular cartoonist of *Carêta,* to which he contributed countless cartoons, caricatures and illustrations until the time of his death in Rio in 1950.

J. Carlos received many awards and honors for his

"José Carlos de Brito e Cunha, model drawings for "Lamparina" series. © O Tico-Tico.

work. An anthology of his cartoons was published by the Ministry of Education just before the artist's death, and a posthumous exhibition of his works was organized some months later.

A.M.

BROOKS, CHARLES GORDON (1920-) American political cartoonist born in Andalusia, Alabama, on November 22, 1920. Chuck Brooks was educated in local public schools and attended Birmingham Southern College, which he left in 1941 to attend the Chicago Academy of Fine Arts. In Chicago his teacher, Vaughn Shoemaker, taught him editorial cartooning.

Brooks enlisted in the army and won four battle stars for action in such campaigns as Normandy. After the war he freelanced in Chicago for a year, married and returned to Alabama, where he became editorial cartoonist on the *Birmingham News* in 1948. He remains there today as one of the South's strongest political cartooning voices.

Traditional-style figures and conventional crayon shading have been Brooks's visual forte throughout his career. In concepts he is strong and has always vigorously upheld the Southern point of view. One of his frequent themes, and one most tellingly presented, was of Northern hypocrisy during the desegregation years. Politically, Brooks is an independent with definite Republican-conservative leanings.

Brooks has won ten Freedoms Foundation awards, the Sigma Delta Chi Distinguished Service Award in 1960 and the Grover C. Hall Award for Excellence in Alabama Journalism from Troy State University in 1974. He also edits annual compilations of the best American editorial cartoons. He retired from his position in the early 1980s to devote his full time to his publishing venture, Pelican Press.

R.M

BROTHER JUNIPER (U.S.) "I wish I had a whole forest of

"You can rest easy—they'll be running the CIA from now on!"
Charles Brooks. © The Birmingham News.

"Brother Juniper." © Field Newspaper Syndicate.

Junipers," St. Francis of Assisi is said to have punned about a short, kindly colleague. This historical anecdote inspired Father Fred McCarthy, art editor of the *Friar* magazine, to create *Brother Juniper* in 1953. This panel cartoon about a monastery's well-meaning cook attracted notice outside Franciscan circles, and in 1957 Doubleday collected the gentle, clever gags into a book. In December 1958 Publisher's Syndicate of Chicago introduced *Brother Juniper* as a daily panel.

Brother Juniper features other regular characters, but most, like the tall Brother Superior, are unnamed. The dog, Bernard, does have a name and is a fixture of the panel, as are cute conventions like Juniper's car with stained-glass windows. All in all, it is a warm, whimsical world that McCarthy, now laicized, has created. His art style is competent, appropriate and witty. In recent years the gags have appeared a bit obtuse at times because of a ridiculous syndicate preference that McCarthy recaption old gags instead of drawing new ones. The panel, which has never been transformed into a Sunday version, has been collected in book form several times and was later distributed by Field. It was discontinued in the late 1980's.

R.M.

BROWN, BUCK (1936-) American cartoonist born in Morrison, Tennessee, in 1936. After high school Buck Brown served in the air force and upon his discharge settled in Chicago. There he joined the Chicago Transit Authority and worked as bus driver from 1958 to 1963, meanwhile attending Wilson Junior College, from which he received an associate of arts degree. Moving on to the University of Illinois, he obtained his B.F.A. in 1966.

The extent to which Brown's job as a bus driver provided him with an appreciation for human foibles can only be surmised, but it can be said that Chicago was during these years a good place to be a young apprentice cartoonist with a risqué sense of humor and a healthy attitude toward sexual topics—Chicago being the home (since 1953) of a magazine devoted to celebrating precisely these new "virtues." Capitalizing on his assets, Brown was soon a regular contributor to *Playboy,* as well as to *Esquire* and other male-oriented magazines. By 1970, he was sufficiently well known in Chicago to be named one of Chicago's ten most outstanding young men by the local chapter of the JayCees. The same year he wound up a two-year term as a member of the President's Task Force on Youth Motivation—an appointment probably less whimsical than it sounds.

In his approach to cartooning, Brown recalls Peter Arno—at least as one imagines that Arno, freed of Rossian restraints, might have painted—even to the bold signature figured along the border of each work. With their vivid colors, each of Brown's pieces is a complete, full-page picture, including central characters, supporting characters and a finished, detailed backdrop—a virtual showcase of the caricaturist's art. He likes to spoof period pieces and exploit topical situations, and his subjects range from French aristocrats of the 18th century to young modern swingers to dirty old men and women of any era—all appropriately endowed.

Unlike many "stag-magazine" artists, Brown rarely descends to the use of crude captions, preferring to let his pastels do the titillation. And titillate they do, as in the assault by a bespectacled, moustachioed super-market manager on a Junoesque young housewife-shopper, amidst a tumbled display of toilet tissue. Captioned "Mr. Whipple, please! Don't squeeze the shoppers," the piece is a masterful exploitation of one of Madison Avenue's sillier attempts to merchandise a commodity that by itself inspires the scatologist in all of us to snicker.

As Jackie Gleason's Ralph Cramden character might have observed with some envy, not many bus routes lead to the destination achieved by Buck Brown. The artist has consolidated his position at *Playboy* in recent years with his famed "Granny" cartoons, featuring a feisty (and ribald) old lady caustically commenting on the usually racy goings-on around her. As a prominent African-American cartoonist, Brown in the 1990s has been enlisted by civil-rights organizations into giving talks to racially mixed groups.

R.C.

BROWN, ROBERT (1906-1996) American cartoonist born in Pennsylvania in 1906. Robert ("Bo") Brown attended the University of Pennsylvania, graduating in 1928. He planned on a career as an attorney and was a law school student when the *Saturday Evening Post* accepted one of his drawings; he renounced forthwith the perquisites of the "Philadelphia lawyer" to become a gag cartoonist, a vocation he has been pursuing successfully ever since. Working in ink, lines and washes, Brown calls cartooning a "relaxing" profession and claims to do his best work when he is tired.

Brown's style is adequate to his purpose but hardly distinctive, being a derivative mélange of the early 20th-century styles upon which he was raised. His gag lines are generally acceptable, but much of his humor is topical and without noticeable bite or recurrent imagery, and so does not stand up as well as the humor of the greatest of his contemporaries—artists like Peter Arno or George Price. When he avoids the topical and exploits the cliché, Brown is at his best. For example, in a late-1940s panel a prospective customer points angrily to his children, sitting rapt before the console radio, and exclaims to the television salesman who has dropped by to make a pitch, "You mean I'll even have to *look* at Oatsy-Woatsies?" In this case, Brown proved rather prophetic, for it was precisely "Oatsy-Woatsy"-supported television programming that ultimately killed off the mass-circulation general-interest weeklies like the *Post* and *Look* that provided the main market for his bland, middle-of-the-road art and humor. He claimed to be "still at it, though pace has slowed" shortly before his death in August 1996.

R.C.

"I wonder what Herb is up to now?"

Robert ("Bo") Brown. © Brown.

BROWNE, CHRISTOPHER KELLY (1952-) American cartoonist born in South Orange, New Jersey, on May 16, 1952. The son of cartoonist Dik Browne, Chris Browne was raised in Connecticut and lists his only formal artistic training as one month at the Philadelphia College of Art. He had his first cartoon published by the YMCA when he was 13: a Christmas card design distributed regionally by the organization. He entered the cartooning field in 1970 with the help of his father's associates, assisting Dick Hodgins in slide and filmstrip preparations, and penciling for Frank Johnson on such comic books as *Barney Rubble* (Charlton) and *Bullwinkle* and *Road Runner* (Gold Key). For two years he pursued such work, until the elder Browne began producing *Hagar* the *Horrible,* which debuted in February 1973. Since then he has played an active role in the strip, writing gags, assisting on art chores, and penciling *Hi and Lois* for a stretch as well.

Apart from his work with his father, Browne's independent career and individual style, not to mention his zany sense of humor, mark him as one of the upcoming generation's brightest talents. In 1974 he was associate editor of the *Funny Papers,* a short-lived but highly innovative tabloid that utilized reprints of classic comics and new work by underground artists; while there, Browne created the *Mr. Nostalgia* strip. Since 1976 he has drawn regularly for the *National Lampoon* (spots and parodies including *Funny the Bunny),* and since 1978 for *Playboy,* where his creations included *Benny Juice, Born Toulouse, Tom Morrow, The Kinky Report* and *Cruiser,* a gibe at the Playboy philosophy. He also made sales to *Head* and *Esquire* magazines. Following his father's death in 1989, he took over the drawing of *Hagar the Horrible,* which he has been doing to this day.

Browne's style is either a handsome refinement or a sympathetic caricature of the "Connecticut school" bigfoot look, depending on his thematic material. He tends toward economical simplicity, well-spotted blacks and a wild, anarchical humor that seems even wilder when set against his reserved drawings.

R.M.

BRUMBERG, VALENTINA (1899-) and ZENAYEDA (1900-) A sister team of Russian animators, both born in Moscow, Russia, in 1899 and 1900 respectively. Valentina and Zenayeda Brumberg studied art in Moscow and were drawn into animation in the mid 1920s. In 1925 they were part of the collective that turned out some of the earliest Soviet cartoons. Their first solo film appears to have been *The Young Samoyed* (1929), the adventures of a plucky little seal-hunter in the Arctic.

After the Brumbergs joined the newly created Soyuzmult'film in 1935, their career picked up. They directed a great number of animated films, including the excellent *Tale of Czar Duranda,* a 1935 effort in which they joined forces with Ivanov-Vano, *The Tailor Hare* (1937) and a rather nicely animated version of *Puss in Boots* (1938);

Valentina and Zenayeda Brumberg, "Puss in Boots."

there followed *Little Red Riding Hood* (also 1938), *Ivashko* and *Baba Yaga* (both 1939). Like many other animators and filmmakers, the Brumberg sisters devoted most of their talents during World War II to turning out patriotic films, though they did succeed in making a 1943 entertainment short, *Tale of Czar Zoltan.* The period after the end of the war witnessed a flurry of activity, starting with the whimsical *Lost Certificate* (1945), and culminating in the enchanting and much-awarded *Fedya Zaytsev* (1949).

The 1950s and 1960s were a time of intense activity for the sisters. Notable among their many films of this period are *The Night Before Christmas* (1951), *Flight to the Moon* (a classic theme of science-fiction animation, 1953), *Stepa the Sailor* and *The Island of Mistakes* (both 1955), *Great Troubles* (1961), *Three Fat Men* (1963), *The Brave Little Tailor* (1964), *Golden Stepmother (1966), The Little Time Machine* (another science fiction effort, 1967) and *The Capricious Princess* (1969). Little has been heard from the Brumbergs in the last ten years, and it is assumed that they are in retirement. They were reported as still living at the time of this writing.

The Brumberg sisters have been among the most prolific animators in Russia. Their subjects have often been fairy tales and other material directed at children, but they have managed to remain fresh and reasonably innovative. Their work has been widely seen in the West and has received a fair share of awards and honors.

M.H.

BRUNA, FRANCO (1935-) Italian graphic designer, etcher and caricaturist born in Turin, on December 15, 1935. After graduating from the local art school he started working as a graphic designer at the local newspaper *La Stampa*. From 1972 to 1992 he produced for the same daily caricatured portrayals of VIP's in many fields: sport, economy, music, movie and television. From 1993 to 1995 he did the same for the Milan daily, *Corriere della Sera.* Then in 1996 he moved to the weekly magazine *L'Espresso*, illustrating also some of its covers.

From 1992 he has been a steady contributor to the daily sport newspaper *Gazzetta dello Sport*. His caricatures have also appeared in several Italian magazines for boys and adults like *Corriere dei Ragazzi, Topolino, Airone, Excelsior, Epoca* and *Playboy.* Bruna's caricatures are accurate and incisive, thanks to his powerful graphic style based on pen and crosshatch drawing. His wordless caricatured portrayals are basically benevolent, but they never lack a slight satirical innuendo which is suggested mostly through minor details. His style is very much reminiscent of David Levine's. Some of his caricatures have been collected in books and catalogues.

Bruna has been awarded the Dattero d'Oro at Bordighera (1993), the Grolla d'Oro at Saint Vincent (1996), the Prize Forte dei Marmi for Political Satire (1997) and many other prizes.

G.C.C.

BRUNHOFF, JEAN DE (1899-1937) French cartoonist, writer and painter born in Paris, France, on December 9, 1899. Jean de Brunhoff studied painting in Paris, and he later became a pupil of Othon Friesz. He was commissioned to do several paintings for industrial corporations and also started contributing cartoons and drawings to French magazines such as *Excelsior* in the mid-1920s.

Jean de Brunhoff and his wife Cécile enjoyed telling tales to their two sons, Laurent and Mathieu. One day Cécile told the children the fabulous story of a little elephant in a big forest. Elaborating on this premise, Jean de Brunhoff wrote and illustrated his first children's book, *L'Histoire de Babar le Petit Eléphant* ("The Story of Babar the Little Elephant"), which was published in Paris in 1931. The first story was so well received and successful that it was soon translated into several foreign languages (including English) and spawned four more *Babar* books, published between 1932 and 1936. That same year de Brunhoff was commissioned to decorate the children's dining room of the *Normandie* ocean liner. At the same time, *Babar* was scoring a hit in New York and running serially in the London *Daily Sketch.*

Amid all the acclaim, Jean de Brunhoff died suddenly, of

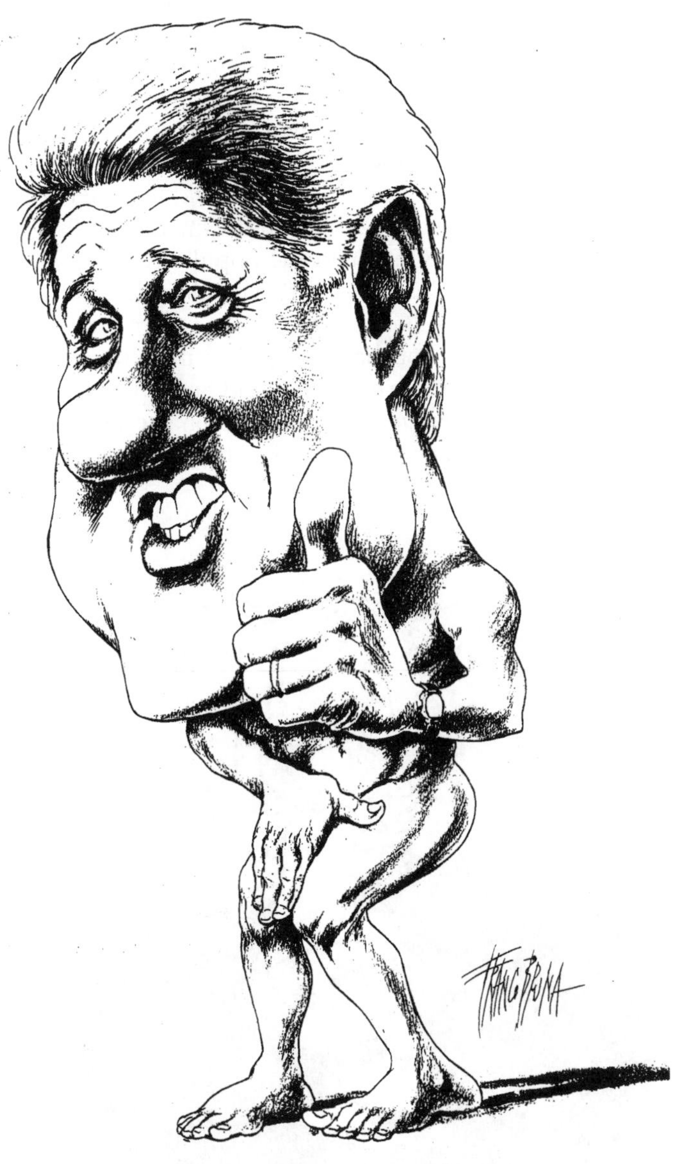

Franco Bruna. © Franco Bruna.

a heart attack, in October 1937. The two books he was then working on, *Babar en Famille* ("Babar Among His Family") and *Babar et le Père Noël* ("Babar and Santa Claus") were completed by his editor, in collaboration with de Brunhoff's brother Michel, and published in 1938 and 1939 respectively.

M.H.

BRUNHOFF, LAURENT DE (1925-) French cartoonist and writer born in Paris, France, on August 30, 1925. The son of famed *Babar* creator Jean de Brunhoff, Laurent de Brunhoff was literally raised in the company of Babar, the little elephant, and his friends: his father would tell him the stories and show him the drawings before the *Babar* books went to press. Laurent himself would often sketch Babar for his own amusement. After the death of his father in 1937, Laurent de Brunhoff went on to complete his studies at Lycée Pasteur; in 1945 he decided to devote himself to painting and studied art at the Académie de la Grande Chaumière.

Partly for fun and partly to continue a family tradition, Laurent de Brunhoff decided to write a *Babar* book. Titled *Babar et ce Coquin d'Arthur* ("Babar and That Rascal Arthur"), it was published in 1946. Success was again immediate, and Laurent de Brunhoff went on to write many more *Babar* stories. At the same time he continued with his painting and had his works exhibited in galleries from Paris to New York. He also contributed *car*toons to such publications as *Paris-Match* and *Elle,* and he created the character of Serafina the Giraffe in the 1950s. The *Serafina* books never attained the popularity of the *Babar* series, however. His latest effort, The *One Pig with Horns* (1979), is also a non-Babar book.

Laurent de Brunhoff has traveled to the United States many times to promote his books, and he helped design as well as write the *Babar* animated cartoon special directed by Bill Melendez and first seen on American television in 1968. This was followed by a weekly series on HBO, starting in 1989, and by *Babar: The Movie,* released the same year by New Line Cinema.

M.H.

Laurent de Brunhoff "Babar." ©L. de Brunhoff.

BUBBLE AND SQUEAK (G.B.) Bubble, the Cockney taxi driver, and Squeak, his brand-new baby cab that walked rather than rolled on wheels, were the first postwar "series characters" in British cartoon films. Named after the traditional British dish "bubble and squeak" (a mixture of cooked potato and cooked cabbage fried in a pan), they were created by George Moreno, Jr., during his active service in France as an American GI.

Moreno had worked for the Max and Dave Fleischer Studios before America's entry into World War II, and a chance wartime meeting with a British soldier, Richard A. Smith, led to the two men forming a private company to promote and produce British animated cartoons. They called themselves British Animated Productions, and produced their first seven-minute short in Smith's office in Walthamstow, London. It was called *The Big City* (1947), and it introduced Bubble and Squeak. Rather rough-and-ready in style and technique (perhaps not surprisingly), the animation showed more than a little trace of the rubbery Fleischer school. Moreno wrote, produced, directed and animated, with some assistance from Harold F. Mack.

Fun Fair followed, and Bubble and Squeak visited the holiday fairground on Hampstead Heath and won a golden horn. *The Old Manor House* (1948) was a departure from the series: it introduced Colonel Rat (voice, Jon Pertwee) and his pet monster, Frankie Stein. The colonel also starred in *Loch Ness Legend* (1948). *Home Sweet Home* was the last Bubble and Squeak adventure, and it introduced a "baby car" called Squeaker. By this time B.A.P. cartoons had developed a decided style, but without big studio backing the venture collapsed. After a period drawing strips for the children's weekly *TV Comic (Polly Copter,* etc.), and drawing *Bubble and Squeak Annual* (1950-52), Moreno formed his own company, Moreno Cartoons, to produce animated commercials for television. Talent on the Bubble and Squeak series included: Harold Mack (director), Hugh Gladwish, Pamela French, Jimmie Holt, Fay Thompson (animation), Claude A. Lipscombe (layout) and José Norman (music).

D.G.

BUCCHI, MASSIMO (1941-) Italian cartoonist born in Rome in 1941. He studied at Florence University where he graduated in History of Medieval Art. Then he tried different jobs and also worked as a graphic designer for a couple of industrial companies. In 1976 he became a graphic designer at the nationwide daily *La Repubblica.*

In 1978 he began to contribute political cartoons to the above paper, developing in due course of time a personal, original and unique style. Bucchi applies modern techniques to photography—through a photocopying process he modifies photographs, turning them into images quite similar to a drawing. Then he proceeds to a patchwork of images adding, if necessary, some handmade drawings

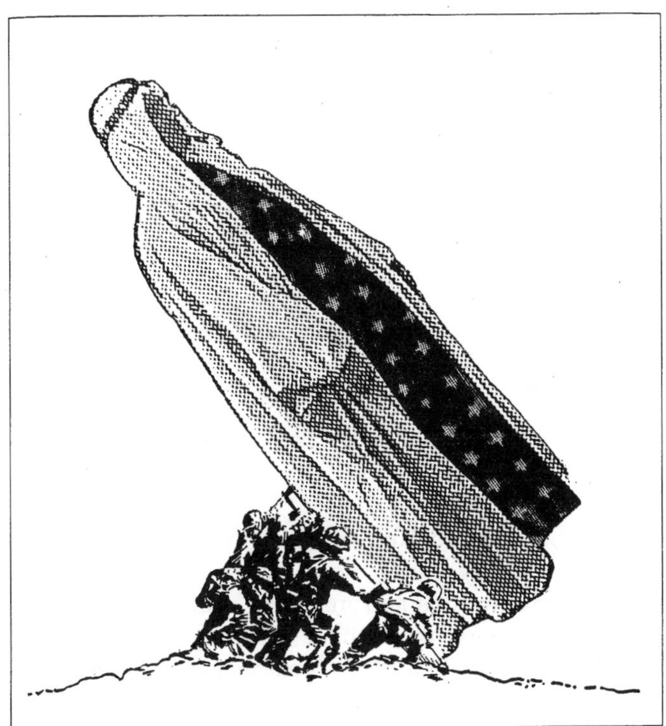

Massimo Bucchi. © Massimo Bucchi.

and usually a typewritten title or remark. Bucchi's cartoons are, graphically, rush and harsh, and express severe satirical judgments on topical issues—mainly political, moral and social ones.

Bucchi has directed *Satyricon*, the weekly humor supplement of the newspaper *La Repubblica* and has also contributed to its literary supplement *Mercurio*.

At the beginning of his career, Bucchi wrote and illustrated two history books for children: *Roma Story* and *Alla Bastiglia*. His cartoons have been partly collected in book format: *Torna a casa lessico* (1987), *Storie di pazzi* (1991), *Partito preso* (1993). He has also written a book, *Mille e non più mille*, illustrated by Vauro. In 1987 and 1991 the artist was awarded the Prize Forte dei Marmi for Political Satire.

G.C.C.

BUDD, CHARLES J. (1859-1926) American cartoonist born in South Schodack, New York, on February 14, 1859. C.J. Budd received art training from the Hudson River Institute, the Pennsylvania Academy of Fine Arts and the Art Students League. Budd entered the art field in Philadelphia in 1885 as a magazine and children's book illustrator. In 1890 he moved to New York, becoming a regular contributor to *Life* magazine in 1894, after winning a contest illustrating quotations. He drew for *Life* until 1917, and briefly for *Harper's Weekly*—through the influence of *Life's* editor E.S. Martin—in 1912 and 1913. In retirement Budd ran a successful business manufacturing artistic gifts. He died in March 1926.

The main contribution of C.J. Budd to cartooning was his innovation of combining photographs and realistic wash drawings, mostly for caricature effects. When he worked in pen and ink, his figures were somewhat stiff, and his style, though fully competent, was never quite polished. His work in wash, however—even without the photographic gimmicks—was self-assured and realistic. His humor cannot be branded any better or worse than many of his fellows'; and like other *Life* artists of his period he dabbled in social commentary.

R.M.

BUGS BUNNY (U.S.) There have been almost as many cartoonists claiming the distinction of having created Bugs Bunny as there were ancient Greek cities vying for the honor of having been Homer's birthplace. *The World Encyclopedia of Comics* (Chelsea House, 1978) unraveled the mystery thus: "The creation of the wise-cracking rabbit (under producer Leon Schlesinger, releasing through Warner Brothers) was done in stages with contributions by many studio employees. The genesis was in a *Porky Pig* film, 'Porky's Hare Hunt,' directed by Ben ('Bugs') Hardaway and Cal Dalton, based on a story by Bob Clampett (1938). The hare, quite unlike the final Bugs, proved popular and warranted another film. 'Hare-um Scare-um' was done by the same directors. . . . Another version appeared in "Presto Change-o," directed by Chuck Jones. In 1939 . . . two more films were assigned: 'Elmer's Candid Camera,' directed by Jones; and `A Wild Hare,' directed by Fred ('Tex') Avery."

In Avery's cartoon the rabbit used for the first time the famous catchphrase "What's up, doc?" and later got his name—Bugs Bunny. More than any other director, Avery was responsible for the development of the Bugs Bunny persona—a feat all the more remarkable in light of the fact that he directed only three more cartoons: "The Heckling Hare," "Tortoise Beats Hare" and "All This and Rabbit Stew." All of Bugs's personality traits were already in evidence: the flippant attitude, the disjointed walk, the jaunty demeanor and the all-pervasive assertion of superiority. A star was born, and it remained for other hands (Avery having left for MGM in 1941) to bring him to full glory.

Bugs Bunny was at his best when resisting the encroachments of some aggressive type, and the animators had fun matching him against each and every character in the Schlesinger\Warner Brothers stable. The bumbling Elmer Fudd had been Bugs's most constant foil ever since "Elmer's Candid Camera," and the "wascally wabbit" (as the exasperated Elmer called Bugs) thwarted his every attempt at shooting him in such gems as "A Wild Hare," "Wabbit Twouble," "Rabbit Seasoning," "Rabbit Fire" and "Duck, Rabbit, Duck." (In the last three, Daffy Duck and Bugs Bunny kept confusing Elmer about just what hunting season it was—duck or rabbit.) Bugs and Fudd, however, were best partnered in two musical en-tries in the series, "Rabbit of Seville" and the irrepressible "What's Opera, Doc?"

Bugs's declared foe, the diminutive, gun-toting and foul-tempered Yosemite Sam, appeared for the first time in "Hare Trigger" (1944), in which he was outsmarted at every turn by the cunning rabbit. He reappeared time and again in countless cartoons, such as "Hare Lift," "Mississippi Hare," "Southern Fried Rabbit," and especially "Rabbitson Crusoe," a glittering little gem featuring Bugs and Yosemite stranded on a desert island in the vicinity of a ravenous shark.

Bugs also contended with lesser fry such as the irascible

"Bugs Bunny." © Warner Brothers.

opera singer of "Long Haired Hare," the feckless mobster of "Bugs and Thugs," the inept vampire of "Transylvania 6-5000" and the supremely silly Tasmanian devil of "Devil May Hare." In 1958 the fearless rabbit finally won an Oscar (for "Knighty Knight Bugs"). Bugs Bunny's most perfect moment, however, had occurred nine years previously when, in the opening sequence of "Frigid Hare," he bounded, with beach towel and sunglasses, upon the icy wastes of the North Pole and incredulously exclaimed, "So, this is Miami Beach?"

Virtually every animator in the Schlesinger and Warners studios worked on *Bugs Bunny;* in addition to that of Avery, the work of Chuck Jones, Friz Freleng, Robert Clampett, Robert McKimson and Frank Tashlin must be singled out. They raised the character of Bugs Bunny to mythical proportions and made the rabbit into the most celebrated cartoon creation next to Mickey Mouse and Donald Duck. Credit for Bugs's extravagant success is also due Mel Blanc, who gave the bunny his inimitable nasal voice and street-wise Brooklyn accent. Among the latter titles mention should be made of *Bugs Bunny's Easter Special* (1978), *Bugs Bunny's Looney Christmas Tales* (1979), *Bugs Bunny: All-American Hero* (1980), *Bugs Bunny/Looney Tunes 50th Anniversary Special* (1986), and *Bugs Bunny's Wild World of Sports* (1989). The cantankerous rabbit has also starred in several theatrical compilations, the latest of which has been the 1990 *Happy Birthday, Bugs.*

The popularity of Bugs Bunny spilled out to other media. In 1941 he started his career in comic books, and the following year a *Bugs Bunny* Sunday page started syndication. Bugs has also been the star of countless commercials, notably those directed by Tex Avery for Kool-Aid, and he still appears on reruns of *The Bugs Bunny Show* and in many TV specials.

M.H.

BUGVILLE LIFE (U.S.) In the pages of adult humor magazines around the turn of the century—in the days when that term did not mean pornography, and as distinct from the humor columns of children's magazines like *St. Nicholas*—animal and insect cartoons were quite common. In *Puck, Judge* and *Life,* interspersed among savage political broadsides and biting social commentary, was a goodly number of purely cute and lightweight gags about outdoor creatures in human situations. That they were simply entertaining takes nothing away from the competence or cleverness of these creations; indeed, some brilliant artwork highlighted this widespread theme, and the public appreciated the material greatly.

Perhaps the foremost exponent of this school was Gus Dirks, and his cartoons and series can serve here as representative. *Bugville Life* was his series for *Judge* in the late 1890s and featured the doings of busy colonies of insects and small animals in real-world situations. The drawings were distinguished by Dirks's remarkable pen work and shadings and were collected in a book (with verses by veteran humorist R.K. Munkittrick) published by *Judge* in 1898. Dirks also drew this type of material for *Puck* and

Life before he was lured away by Hearst to do Sunday comics in 1903.

Dirks was by no means alone, and when he left *Life,* Walt Kuhn was already establishing himself as a consistent delineator of bird life. Kuhn continued his back-of-the-book panel cartoons for *Life* right through his organizational efforts in behalf of the famous Armory Show. He published a book, *A Little Bird Told Me,* in 1908. Imitating Kuhn was "Lang" (Louis Lansing Campbell, according to the best available research), who later drew birds in *Adventures of the Clothesline* for *Puck* in the 1910s. Harrison Cady drew a series of stunningly detailed *Beetleburgh* cartoons for *Life. T.S.* Sullivant, of course, often concentrated on animal subjects, and C. Barnes and Larkin were among a host of others. One of the most prolific was A.Z. Baker (Baker-Baker, who often signed his cartoons with a double *B* monogram). His animals were easily the funniest, rendered in a style of such freedom that they seem out of place in the more rigid turn-of-the-century milieu.

The animal and bug cartoon went out after World War I, when the general mood seemed more sophisticated and/or cynical and talking animals seemed out of place. But in the first two decades of the 20th century, a random sampling of 10 magazine cartoons was bound to include several animal subjects, whether those listed above or Kemble's frogs, Frost's cats and goats, Carl Anderson's pups or E.G. Lutz's mice.

R.M.

BULL, CHARLES LIVINGSTON (1874-1932) American cartoonist and illustrator born in 1874. Charles Livingston Bull is considered the foremost depicter of animals in American illustration. His animals and birds, even in cartoons, were never caricatured or exaggerated; rather cartoonists' shorthand techniques (bold outlines, dropped backgrounds, etc.) were employed for breezy poster effects. His series in *Life* in the 1920s contrast with Sullivant's delineations of fauna but are striking cartoons nonetheless. Bull variously used crayons and wash for his shadings.

No doubt Bull's expertise grew from his taxidermy skills; as a youth he skinned pelts for Ward's Museum in Rochester, New York. Later, when employed by the Smithsonian Institution in Washington, D.C., he attracted the notice of Theodore Roosevelt. The president admired Bull's skills as an artist and taxidermist and, in fact, Bull later mounted many of Roosevelt's bird specimens for the Smithsonian. Like Paul Bransom, another cartoonist-illustrator of animals, Bull learned much from studious observation at the Bronx Zoo. And like Ding Darling, another cartoonist-conservationist, Bull was active in work to preserve dwindling species of birds.

Books: *The Kindred of the Wild* (1902); *The Call of the Wild* by Jack London (1903); *Denizens of the Deep* (1904); *The Race of the Swift* (1905); *Before Adam* by Jack London (1907); *Haunters of the Silences* (1907); *Old Crow Stories* (1917); and many others.

R.M.

Yule-log in Bugville: "Come on Billy. Hurry up and help me carry it. This cigarette will make the best Yule-log ever."

"Bugville Life."

"The Bullwinkle Show." © Jay Ward Productions.

BULLWINKLE SHOW, THE (U.S.) Producer Jay Ward, writer Bill Scott, and directors Bill Hurtz and Peter Burness teamed up to create *Rocky and His Friends,* a television animated series that first aired on NBC in 1958. This was a weird mock-adventure program relating the exploits of resourceful Rocket J. Squirrel (alias Rocky) and dumb Bullwinkle Moose, both of Frostbite Falls, Minnesota, and their unending struggle against sinister Boris Badenov and his scheming female assistant, Natasha Fatale. The show, initially telecast on Saturday mornings, proved so popular with children (and their parents) that the network later rescheduled it for an evening slot, rechristening it The *Bullwinkle Show* (in recognition of the star status that the goofy moose had attained in the meantime).

The Bullwinkle Show was actually made up of several segments, only one of which featured the continuing adventures of Rocky and Bullwinkle. There was in addition a north-of-the-border tale recounting the harebrained exploits of Dudley Do-Right of the Royal Mounted Police as he tried to collar the snarling, top-hatted Snidely Whiplash and to save his girl friend, the blond Nell Fenwick, from the villain's clutches. Another popular segment was "Fractured Fairy Tales," which joyously demolished such traditional tales as "Little Red Riding Hood" and "Sleeping Beauty."

In 1964 the network cancelled *The Bullwinkle Show* and it went into syndication. In the early 1960s, and again in the 1970s, there was a *Bullwinkle* comic book. Al Kilgore, who drew the first comic book version, was also responsible for the short-lived *Bullwinkle* newspaper strip (1962-64).

The Bullwinkle Show was a highly entertaining work which managed to overcome the "limited animation" techniques that have usually proved the bane of TV animated cartoons. Its success was due to clever direction, imaginative plot lines, irreverent dialogue and excellent voice characterizations by such luminaries as William Conrad, Charlie Ruggles, June Foray and Hans Conried. The show again enjoyed a brief run on NBC in 1981-82.

M.H

BURCHARD, FRANZ (1799-1835) German cartoonist and printmaker born at Fellin in what was then Livonia (now the Latvian Soviet Socialist Republic) on February 22, 1799. Franz Burchard worked under the pseudonym "Dörbeck" and is best known by that name.

In 1816 Dörbeck began to study the art of engraving in St. Petersburg, the European capital nearest to his native region, and got a job there working in the Russian government bank as an engraver of legal tender. After the death in 1820 of his first wife, a native of St. Petersburg, he moved to Riga, where he worked as a commercial engraver and portraitist. Marrying again in Riga, he traveled on in 1823 to Berlin, where his chief artistic development took place. In Berlin, Dörbeck continued to engrave portraits, but he also extended his range to engraved and lithographed illustrations for historical and medical books and such works of fiction as *Robinson Crusoe.*

His importance in the history of cartooning rests on commissions he received from the active art-publishing firm of Gropius—which also patronized Schadow and Hosemann—for humorous scenes of everyday life in Berlin. For such Gropius print series as *Berliner Witze* ("Berlin Jokes") and *Berliner Redensarten* ("Berlin Sayings"), Dörbeck did numerous color pen lithographs on such subjects as street and market scenes, domestic servants, small storekeepers and householders, student jollity, trades and occupations, conveyances (for the series *Berliner Fuhrwerke)* and the like. His drawing style, somewhat roughhewn but extremely energetic, was exactly right for this subject matter, the common denominator of which was the glib, wide-awake and never-to-be-bested character of the population of Berlin. Dörbeck's influence in this area on the young Menzel, on Hosemann—and, through him, on Zille—was incalculable. His work is always featured prominently in anthologies of old Berlin humor and in illustrated cultural and social histories of Berlin.

Beginning in 1832, Dörbeck worked on a series completely dedicated to student life and called *Album Academicum.* He died in his native town at the early age of 36, on October 2, 1835.

S.A.

BURCK, JACOB (1904-1982) American cartoonist and Pulitzer Prize winner born in Bialystok, Poland, in 1904. When he was ten, he and his family emigrated to America to join his bricklayer father. He was educated in the Cleveland public schools and attended the Cleveland School of Art. In 1930 Burck studied at the Art Students League under Boardman Robinson and Albert Sterner, whose protégé he became. At this time he aspired to fine arts, but both his mentors were cartoonists, and Burck was a strong partisan whose entry into cartooning was made even easier by the desire for work during the Depression.

He was a radical leftist and worked for the *Daily Worker* and *New Masses.* Whitaker Chambers, in *Witness*, recalls that Burck's 14th Street studio was a hangout for radicals and artists. Shortly after the publication of his anthology of cartoons, *Hunger and Revolt* (with deluxe editions sold in a very bourgeois manner), he was invited to Russia by the Soviets to execute murals. He returned to the United States disillusioned with communism. He was offered a position as political cartoonist for the St. Louis Post-Dispatch in 1937, and a year later he transferred to the Chicago Times (later the Sun-Times). He retired in 1980 and died in May 1982.

"If I should die before I wake."
Jacob Burck, Pulitzer Prize-winning cartoon, 1941. © Chicago Times.

Burck's work, especially the cartoons drawn in his radical prime, is squarely in the tradition of Boardman Robinson, Robert Minor and the original *Masses car*toonists. He obviously had an ax to grind but was more than gifted in his presentations. Stylistically, he was the heir of Robinson, Minor and Fred Ellis. When his radicalism waned, so did much of his punch, although his Pulitzer was well deserved in 1941 for his devastatingly poignant comment on war. Today his artwork is sharply simple and abbreviated, but his ideas and humor are fresh.

R.M.

BURIED TREASURE (U.S.) In the late 1920s a group of prominent New York cartoonists (reportedly including Winsor McCay, George McManus and Bud Fisher) got together and, as a prank, decided to collaborate in the making of one of the few (and possibly the first) pornographic animated cartoons. This short feature came to be known as *Buried Treasure.*

Buried Treasure is less remarkable, however, for its subject matter—the sexual adventures of an extravagantly well-endowed little man by the name of Ever-ready Hardon (sic)—than for the quality and imagination of its animation. The process was characterized by a lusty, outrageous humor—a kind of graphic equivalent of the ribald tales of Petronius and Rabelais. Laughter at Everready's sustained but inept efforts at sexual fulfillment far overwhelms the incongruous and, to some, obscene shenanigans. As Professor Rabkin observes in his study of the stag film, *Dirty Movies: An Illustrated History of the Stag Film,* 1915-1970, *"Buried Treasure* is consistently amusing because it fully exploits the power of animation to delineate a logic photography can only suggest: when men are led by (sex), they have problems as well as pleasures."

An oddity among underground movies, *Buried Treasure* is probably the only film of its kind worth mentioning.

M.H.

BURNESS, PETER (1910-198?) American animator born in Los Angeles, California, on June 16, 1910. In the early 1930s Peter Burness worked for the Harman-Ising animation unit, later switching to the Amédée Van Beuren studio (where the *Little King* cartoons were among his more notable efforts). He finally came to rest in the late 1930s at the Disney studio and later at MGM (where he worked on many of the *Tom and Jerry* cartoons). His work all that time remained largely uncredited and unnoticed.

Burness finally came to prominence in the 1940s as one of the original founders of United Productions of America, grouped around Stephen Bosustow. He worked on a number of early UPA cartoons but gained fame with the Mr. Magoo series, to which he was the most prolific contributor. He directed such Magoo classics as Bungled Bungalow" (1949), "Trouble Indemnity" (1950),. "Captains Outrageous" (1952), "Magoo Goes West" (1953), the hilarious "When Magoo Flew" and the classic "Destination Magoo" (both 1954), "Stagedoor Magoo" (1955) and "Magoo's Puddle Jumper," which earned him an Academy Award in 1956.

When UPA began to falter in the late 1950s, Burness joined the Jay Ward organization, most notably as a director on the witty and very popular *Rocky and His Friends* (later retitled *The Bullwinkle Show*) from 1958 to 1964. In recent years Burness has made a great number of animation commercials as well as a few TV specials. He is widely acknowledged as one of the masters of the "limited animation" technique, which he has perfected to a high degree of sophistication and polish. He died a few years after retiring in the 1980s.

M.H.

Peter Burness, "Destination Magoo." © UPA.

BUSH, CHARLES GREEN (1842-1909) American cartoonist and illustrator born in 1842. C.G. Bush studied fine arts in Paris under Bonnat and followed a dual career in painting and illustrating upon his return to America. American magazine illustration being what it was in the 1860s, and given Bush's famed sense of humor, it was natural that he would turn to the new art of social cartoons. For *Harper's Weekly* he produced a series of complicated, involved double-page cartoons on topics of the day. When the *New York Daily Graphic* was established on March 4, 1873, Bush's cartoons appeared from the first several issues; he was, therefore, a pioneer in the American daily cartoon, along with other *Graphic* artists like C.J. Taylor, W.A. Rogers, E.W. Kemble, Gray-Parker, Livingston Hopkins, Michael Angelo Woolf, A.B. Frost and Walt McDougall.

Bush was one of the earliest and most frequent contributors to *Life* magazine during its first year (1883). By this time—and because of the advent of photolithography—his style was well established and mature. As New York dailies began to use daily political cartoons, he became, with McDougall, a pioneer in that field, drawing for the *New York Telegram* and the *New York Herald.* A series of notable and forceful local cartoons attracted attention in 1895; he evidently relished lambasting corrupt political bosses Thomas Collier Platt, Richard Croker and David Bennett Hill.

Bush's new fame resulted in an offer from Joseph Pulitzer to join the staff of his *New York World.* Here the veteran drew his most sophisticated political cartoons—although stylistically he was just as biting and polished a generation earlier. Bush finished his career with the World and died in New York in 1909. His most amusing cartoons and, regrettably, virtually the only ones for which he is

Charles Bush, 1887.

remembered today, were of Theodore Roosevelt during his presidency. Bush's Roosevelt was always in his Rough Rider costume and was frequently portrayed in keeping with Joseph Pulitzer's Democratic policies.

Bush's style marks him as one of the most talented cartoonists ever to touch pen to paper in America; his current obscurity represents a tragic loss to scholars and fans of the art alike. Perhaps only in the forgotten work of Joe Donahey of a later generation can another sad parallel be found. C.G. Bush was fecund and technically awesome; he was the first cartoonist of his generation to employ conscious physical exaggeration and distortions to his creations—no mean feat when there are absolutely no artistic precedents. In this regard he was definitely the artistic father of A.B. Frost, whom he preceded and later worked side by side with for several years. Frost's artistic gymnastics are well known today, and he inspired many cartoonists himself, but his mature work always resembled that of Bush, whose classical training obviously stood him in good stead: for the best exaggeration is based on a thorough knowledge of anatomy and other fundamentals.

The delightfully wispy lines of Bush's art led the reader's eye through comically distorted scenes. Figures were agile and constantly in motion, the reader's perspective down at the figure's feet but up at the face—all combining for a friendly, zany atmosphere. Bush's world was as consistent and competent as T.S. Sullivant's or George Herriman's, and fully as personal. It is to be hoped that a major reprinting of his work will take place in the near future.

R.M.

BUSHKIN, ALEKSANDR IVANOVICH (1896-1929) Animator born in Kiev, in the Ukraine, Russia, on April 1, 1896. Aleksandr Bushkin showed an early disposition for art and drawing, and in 1919 he graduated from Kiev Art College. In 1922 he founded the first Soviet animation workshop, at the Moscow State Film Studios, under the guidance of Dziga Vertov; the following year he co-directed (with Aleksandr Ivanov) the first Soviet film cartoon, *Soviet Toys,* released in 1924.

For the rest of his short life Bushkin turned out a number of artistically distinguished cartoons, often of a political or didactic nature, including *Yumoreski* ("Humoresques," 1924), a group of three separate political cartoon films; *Sluchay v Tokio* ("Incident in Tokyo," 1924); *Kar'yera Makdonal'da* ("MacDonald's Career"), a satire on the British prime minister, in 1925; and *What the Peasant and Worker Should Know About the Soviet Union,* a flag-waving, morale-building lesson in civics, Soviet style. Bushkin also wrote several newspaper and magazine articles about the craft of animation, and in 1926 he authored a book-length study of the medium, *Tryuki i Mul'tiplikatsiya* ("Trick Films and Animated Cartoons"). His untimely death on June 5, 1929, at age 33, cut short a brilliant and promising career.

M.H.

BUSINO, ORLANDO FRANCIS (1926-) American magazine gag cartoonist born in Binghamton, New York, on October 10, 1926. Orlando Busino wanted to be a cartoonist from the time he started drawing, at about nine years old. As a youth he idolized the drawing in Elzie Segar's *Popeye* and the work from the Walt Disney studios, which he, like most kids, thought was done entirely by Disney himself.

Orlando Busino graduated from high school just at the end of World War II. He entered the United States Army and served from 1945 to 1947. In high school, cartooning for the student newspaper and yearbook had been important to him, and he was able to do some cartooning in the military. He continued his education under the GI bill after his tour of duty, earning a fine arts degree from the State University of Iowa in 1952. While at college he contributed cartoons to the *Daily Iowan.* As the result of high scores achieved in a competitive test for former GI's, Busino was able to continue his studies in art at the School of Visual Arts in New York City. During the day he worked in the advertising department of the Macmillan Company, book publishers.

In 1954 Orlando Busino decided to freelance magazine gag cartoons. "I was very lucky and sold on my first try," he says. He had taken ten cartoons to the *Saturday Evening Post,* and they bought one. Sales to *Colliers'* and *American Magazine* soon followed. His entire freelance career has

Aleksandr Bushkin, "Humoresques."

"You're getting warmer."
Orlando Busino. © Busino.

been with general readership magazines doing mostly family humor. "I draw a big nose and big foot type cartoon and enjoy it," he says. Cartoons about children, animals, men from Mars, married life, doctors and all the standard themes for general readership have consistently received a fresh and humorous treatment from Orlando Busino. *Ladies' Home Journal, Family Circle,* Good *Housekeeping* and other women's magazines have steadily published his work. For seven years he has drawn *Gus,* a monthly panel cartoon about a big white shaggy dog, for *Boys' Life* magazine, the national magazine of the Boy Scouts of America. Both King Features' *Laugh-a-Day* and McNaught Syndicate's *Funny World,* syndicated gag-a-day panels, publish innumerable Orlando Busino cartoons.

Although he regularly sold to *True* and *Argosy* magazines several years ago when they were the leading cartoon market for men's adventure magazines, Busino admits he doesn't seem to think up risqué gags, so he's never submitted work to *Playboy.* Hallmarks of his cartoons are a clean, strong design and outline in the drawing. A light wash or benday dot pattern is used for shading, depending on whether his market is a magazine or newspaper. Unlike some cartoonists, Orlando Busino is a traditionalist who believes the picture has to be funny, and not just the gag line. He has won the National Cartoonists Society's award for Best Magazine Gag Cartoonist three times. As of 1998 he was still active as ever turning out cartoons for the magazine market.

B.C.

BUTE, MARY ELLEN (1914-1983) American animator and film director born in Houston, Texas, at the start of World War I. Mary Ellen Bute began her career in the early 1930s with Lewis Jacobs and then married the cinematographer Ted Nemeth, with whom she made a long series of abstract animated films, starting with the silent *Synchrony* (1934). She later set her films to music. Her most important pictures of the 1930s, all in black and white, are: *Rhythm in Light,* set to Edvard Grieg's "Anitra's Dance" (1936); *Synchrony No. 2,* set to Richard Wagner's "Evening Star" (1937); and *Parabola,* set to Darius Milhaud's *La Création du Monde* (1938).

In 1940 Bute added color to her musical experiments in motion with *Escape,* set to J.S. Bach's Toccata and Fugue; this was followed in 1941 by *Spook Sport,* a film set to Camille Saint-Saens's "Danse Macabre," which Norman McLaren animated. Increasingly Bute turned to live-action film, first documentaries and later features, such as *Finnegan's Wake* and *The Skin of Our Teeth,* only occasionally going back to animation (*Color Rhapsody,* 1958, is one such exception). She died in October 1983.

Mary Ellen Bute used objects as well as cutouts and drawings in her animation films, but her experimentation with light, color and music was later widely transposed to the medium of traditional animation.

M.H.

BUTTERWORTH (1905-1988) Butterworth, who signed himself only with his surname, was a provincial cartoonist with both topical drawings and comic strips to his credit. He worked only in newspapers, and was not known in London or the South until his Manchester-based newspaper, the *Daily Despatch,* was incorporated in the national *News Chronicle,* which took over his strip *The Daily Dees.*

George Godwin Butterworth was born in Westmoor, England, on January 5, 1905. From Stockport Art School he won a scholarship to the Manchester College of Art, and at the early age of 17 was signed on as sporting cartoonist and caricaturist by the *Stockport Express.* Five years later he joined Kemsley Newspapers as a staff cartoonist, from whence he supplied the *Daily Despatch* with sports cartoons signed "Gee Bee," and several Kemsley-owned newspapers with political cartoons: *Evening Chronicle, Empire News,* and *Sunday Chronicle.*

In 1952 he created his first strip, *The Daily Dees* for the *Daily Despatch,* a strip series based on a TV-addicted family. This was later seen in the *News Chronicle,* and when that paper failed, in the *Daily Mail.* It was syndicated to the USA and appeared in the *New York Times* and the *Chicago Tribune.* His one book, *Hitler and His Crazy Gang,* was published around 1940. Butterworth died on October 17, 1988.

D.G.

BUXTON, DUDLEY (189-?-19—?) "They're British, quite British, you know!" was the jovially patriotic catch line to the advertisement for the first Tressograph Cartoons (pro-

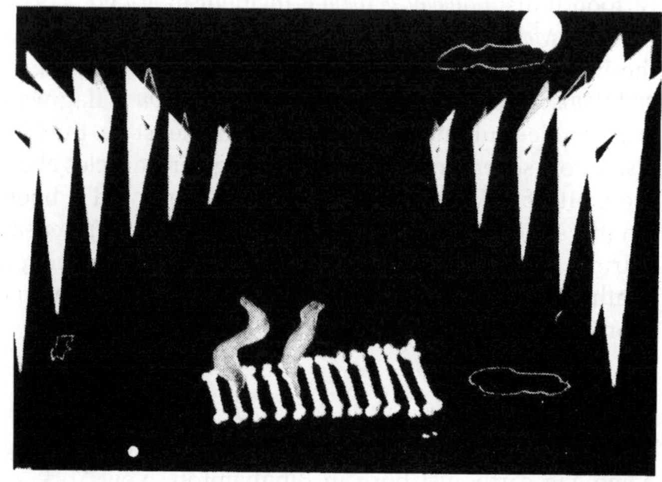

Mary Ellen Bute, "Spook Sport." © Bute.

ducer, H. Tress) in November 1914, "drawn by the eminent lightning cartoonist, Dudley Buxton." Buxton, a familiar signature to humorous cartoons in the pictorial periodicals of the day, produced a series of three *War Cartoons* half-reelers during November 1914, then the following spring joined the Cartoon Film Company at 76 Wardour Street, London (proprietor, J.A. Clozenberg). There he worked in tandem with Anson Dyer, producing alternating editions of a series entitled *John Bull's Animated Sketch Book.* This ended with number 21 in November 1916, despite Buxton's delightful, if unauthorized, use of Charlie Chaplin as his "star"! Buxton's sense of humor often outshone Dyer's, although from time to time his skill shone in his choice of subject, such as the sinking of the German battleship *Blucher* (which preceded Winsor McCay's *Sinking of the Lusitania* by three years).

In 1917 Buxton joined Kine Komedy Kartoons, run by Frank Zeitlin, and *The Devil's Little Joke* was the first of eight short films he produced there. Unlike the *John Bull* series, these were not made up of short cartoon items. Rather they told a story, and one, *Ever Been Had?*, is preserved in the British National Film Archive. It is a humorous, even satirical, story of the Man in the Moon coming down to meet the Sole Surviving Englishman. In between the jokes Buxton creates a superb sequence of science fiction warfare. More famous, however, was Buxton's dramatic reconstruction of real warfare, *The Raid on Zeebrugge* (1918).

After World War I, Buxton's sense of comedy returned, and he created several series of cartoons, all sadly short-lived: *The Cheerio Chums* (1919), *Bucky's Burles*ques (1920), and The *Memoirs of Miffy* (1920), which actually had a daily newspaper strip syndicated to some local English newspapers. One of the Miffy series, *Running a Cinema* (1920), is in the National Film Archive and marks a stage in the evolution of British cartoon filmmaking. Gone is the old cutout system; it is replaced by the American cel technique. Gone, too, are the deliberate jokes and captions, replaced by fast-moving visual gags.

In late 1924 Buxton launched what was to be his last series, *Pongo the Pup.* Six short cartoons were made as items in the magazine film series *Pathé Pictorial,* which alternated with Sid Griffith's established series *Jerry the Troublesome Tyke.* The first was *Pongo Arrives,* followed by *Pongo's Day Out, Pongo Gets a Meal, Pongo at the Rodeo, Pongo Cheers Up the Goat Family* and *Pongo Catches the Crossword,* a cartoon comment on the craze of the day. This series marks the last trace of Buxton on the animation scene. He appears not to have survived the transition to sound.

D.G.

Cc

CABUT, JEAN (1938-) French cartoonist born in Châlons-sur-Marne, in the Champagne region of France, on January 13, 1938. After attending classes for a while at the Estienne art school in Paris, Jean Cabut (who signs simply "Cabu") started his professional career on the daily *L'Union* in Reims in 1953 with gag and editorial drawings. After military service in Algeria (where he worked on the military publication *Le Bled* and during which time he kept sending cartoons to such varied magazines as the racy *Paris-Flirt* and the newsweekly *Paris-Match*) he moved to Paris and in 1960 began his long collaboration with the satirical weekly *Hara-Kiri*.

Left-leaning and even radical in his outlook, Cabu showed himself relentless in his attacks against President De Gaulle and his cabinet ministers, whom he lampooned in cruel caricatures that caught the likeness of the subjects perfectly, bringing to light unflattering traits (stupidity, arrogance, greed, intolerance) that his victims would have preferred to have kept hidden. His favorite target, however, was the military, and his anti-military cartoons earned him a number of lawsuits for "insults to the honor of the army" (he won most of them). He later widened his shooting range to include administrations of all colors and politicians of all stripes, the lot of whom he regarded as dangerous, authoritarian, or simply inept. In the course of his long career Cabu has had his cartoons (humorous as well as political) published not only in *Hara-Kiri* and its sister magazines, *Charlie* and *Charlie-Hebdo*, but also in *Le Rire, Le Pacifiste, Le Monde, Le Nouvel Observateur, Le Canard Enchainé*, and in a multitude of other publications, big and small.

In parallel with his cartooning activities, Cabu has also turned out a number of successful comic strips, notably *Le Grand Duduche* ("The Tall Duduche," 1962-85), about a gangly, somewhat naive college freshman, and *Mon Beauf'* ("My Bro' in Law," created in 1976), which features a typical French right-winger, narrow-minded and bigoted. He has also illustrated books by such diverse authors as Antoine Blondin, Paul Guimard and André Halimi, and has appeared on television talk shows.

Cabu's line, at once sharp and nimble, has made his cartoons easily recognizable. "I have the fault of turning out cartoons that are too militant, too partisan, that end up annoying people," he once declared. Despite this perceived flaw, the artist has kept many unswerving devotees throughout the years and has earned a number of honors and awards (though, predictably, not the Legion of Honor).

M.H.

Jean Cabut ("Cabu") © Cabu.

CADY, WALTER HARRISON (1877-1970) American cartoonist and illustrator born in Gardner, Massachusetts, on June 17, 1877. Harrison Cady received no formal art training, but Parker Perkins, a local marine painter, introduced the youngster to art, and the elder Cady took his son on innumerable hikes, thereby instilling a love of nature in the future cartoonist.

After the death of his father Harrison Cady moved to New York to pursue a career in art; the 19-year-old boy arrived with $19 in his pocket. He made an early sale to *Harper's Monthly* (the subject matter—a gnome, tiger lilies and bugs—was precisely the type with which he was identified throughout his career) and soon was a staffer on *Truth* magazine and a news sketch artist for the *Brooklyn Eagle*. By the late 1890s his work was a regular fixture in the pages of *St. Nicholas* (it was at the staff's suggestion that he removed the "Walter" from his signature), and his cartoons—intricate pen-and-inks as well as pleasant wash drawings—were soon also appearing in the *Saturday Evening Post, Country Gentleman, Ladies' Home Journal* and *Good Housekeeping*.

There were three phases to Cady's career: strips, book illustrations and magazine cartoons. His first work in comics was a jungle strip for the *Philadelphia Press* in 1905, and for 29 years his *Peter Rabbit* strip ran through the Herald-Tribune Syndicate. As an illustrator he achieved his greatest fame—which endures today—for his work on

"Hurrah! The first potato vine is up!"

Harrison Cady.

hundreds of Thornton W. Burgess children's books and newspaper columns. The *Mother West Wind* and *Peter Rabbit* series were two of the umbrella titles under which several generations of children were enchanted, a real reflection of the warm personal friendship between author and artist, and a tribute to their skill at weaving animal fantasy tales. In the magazine field, *Life* was Cady's principal cartoon outlet for two decades into the middle 1920s; editor J.A. Mitchell said approvingly, "I like men who see things that aren't there."

Cady's cartoons were remarkable for their overwhelming detail work. Literally thousands of tiny crosshatch lines composed his invariably large drawings (either full- or double-page cartoons), imparting an almost photographic shading quality when taken as a whole. His subjects fell into two quite disparate categories: pleasant, amusing bug and animal jokes, many of them set in Beetleburgh (the running title for the cartoons with no recurring characters); and vicious anti-Jewish polemics on matters pertaining to immigration, business practices, etc. The latter ran primarily in *Life* from the turn of the century to the mid-1910s, a time when ethnic slurs were the stock-in-trade of many cartoonists.

Meticulous shading and unfettered concept presentation combined to make Cady one of the most interesting cartoonists of his time. As his later work still lives in reprinted Burgess books, so should his early work be rediscovered; his artistic visions were impressive and fiercely personal. The later work was as simplified as the earlier work was detailed. Thin lines and careful shading patterns gave way to thick outlines and broad open areas of white (a change dictated, perhaps, by self-inflicted eyestrain). The colors in some of the illustrations in the Burgess books are among the handsomest and most soothing ever to grace cartoon illustrations.

Cady is remembered also as a distinguished, cultured conversationalist and friend, and a member of many clubs and societies, some of which exhibited his ventures into oils and watercolors. He won the Palmer Memorial Prize from the National Academy and exhibited at the Pennsylvania Academy and the Chicago Art Institute. He had one-man shows at the Salmagundi and Pleiades clubs, as well as at the Macbeth, Kleeman and Currier galleries and the Rockport Art Association. His etchings are in many museum collections as well.

Cady retired from active work in his seventies and died, much honored, on December 9, 1970, at the age of 93. His very special talents and insights have made him immortal. The world of fantasy, the realm of friendly animals, the pastel home of magical happiness, was his domain; he was one of the lucky few who retained the special childhood vision of that world-and the rest of us are the luckier for his charming depictions of it.

R.M.

CAJETAN

See Elfinger, Anton.

CAMPBELL, ELMER SIMMS (1906-1971) American cartoonist born in St. Louis, Missouri, on January 2, 1906. The son of an assistant high school principal, Elmer Campbell was known as Elmer to his friends and as E. Simms Campbell professionally. He began showing an interest in art at about the age of four, and was undoubtedly encouraged by his mother, who herself painted watercolors. When Campbell was 14, his family moved to Chicago, Illinois. He graduated from Englewood High School there and attended the University of Chicago briefly. He knew art would be his career and switched to the Chicago Institute of Fine Art, from which he graduated.

In 1932 and 1933 he lived with his aunt on Edgecombe Avenue in the Harlem section of New York City. He studied at the Art Students League under George Grosz during the day and drew for *College Comics,* a humor magazine, at night. Although extremely talented, Campbell was a black American and as such was no stranger to discrimination in his early efforts to sell his work. In a 1966 interview in *Ebony,* he said, "Oh, I could always draw, but I was a failure as an artist 'til I became a successful dining car waiter."

Campbell was 27 years old when his big break came in the spring of 1933. He got his chance through a combination of talent, luck and the recommendation of famed cartoonist Russell Patterson. A new magazine named *Esquire* was starting up. Arnold Gingrich, one of the founders of *Esquire,* had hoped to use art by Patterson, whose drawings of beautiful women were almost as famous as the Ziegfeld Girls. At the time Gingrich could offer only $100 per featured cartoon, and Patterson declined his offer. However, as Gingrich remembered in his memoir of *Esquire's* early days, "He did have a suggestion; that is, he did—if I didn't 'draw the color line.' I said I didn't."

"But, honey, I haven't got a girl in every port.
I ain't BEEN in every port!"
E. Simms Campbell. © New York Journal-American.

Gingrich needed color cartoons for *Esquire's* debut issue. E. Simms Campbell solved his problem. After visiting Campbell at his aunt's apartment, Arnold Gingrich had an armload of finished color cartoons and rough idea sketches. The debut issue of October 1933 contained 13 color cartoons, a good portion of which were by E. Simms Campbell or were worked up by artists such as John Groth and George Petty from Campbell idea sketches. *Esquire* was an instant success, and Gingrich credits the color cartoons with a significant contribution to that success.

Although dated January 1934, the second issue of *Esquire* appeared on December 5, 1933, the day Prohibition was repealed. It also marked the debut of Esky on the cover of *Esquire.* This popeyed, white-moustached, large-nosed admirer of female beauty was created by E. Simms Campbell. His cartoons also appeared in the old *Life, Judge, Collier's,* the *Saturday Evening Post,* the *New Yorker, Playboy. Cosmopolitan* and *Redbook.* King Features Syndicate distributed his daily panel *Cuties* from about 1943 until his death. The panel featured beautiful women and a gag.

Early in his career a friend had told Campbell that if he specialized in drawing beautiful women, he'd always have work. It was advice he took to heart. Beautiful women were his favorite subjects. One of his most famous creations was a continuing series in *Esquire,* and later *Playboy: Sultan and Harem* cartoons. The sultan, a short, rotund, jovial sort more in love with food and toys than sex, was always surrounded by his harem. The series was published as a full-page color cartoon rich both in the intensity of the bright orange tones Campbell favored and in lush odalisques.

E. Simms Campbell changed from pen and ink to pencil and watercolor with ease. His drawing had a spontaneity that often made the gag secondary. His color cartoons were painted and not just line drawings with color dropped in between the borders. Although he did illustrate such work as black writer Langston Hughes's *Popo and Fifna,* Campbell mostly cartooned the world of high society, nightclubs, expensive wine, women and song. Ironically, many admirers of his work are often surprised to learn he was black.

His work did not elicit a belly laugh as much as a chuckle and the sincere gratitude of male readers who didn't know much about art but knew what they liked. Throughout Campbell's work, the women portrayed in sensuous watercolors and line drawings were usually white. This prompted *Negro Digest* to ask in a 1951 article on Campbell, "Are Black Women Beautiful?" Occasionally, he did draw dark-skinned women, but they were usually Polynesian and not black.

For the last 14 years of his life until shortly before his death, E. Simms Campbell lived in Neerach, Switzerland. The expatriate life in Switzerland proved ideal, as he told *Ebony* in 1966. "Out here in this little off-the-wall village we don't have to prove nothin' to nobody. . . . Nobody bothers us unless we invite them in, and nobody gets mad because we're out here living in their community. Man, I can walk into any joint I want to out here and nobody starts looking as if they're thinking, 'Ugh, there's a nigger in here.'"

E. Simms Campbell left Switzerland after the death of his wife, Vivian, in October 1970. He returned to White Plains, New York, where on January 27, 1971, he died after a brief illness.

B.C.

CANEMAKER, JOHN (1943-) American animator, author and educator born in Waverly, N.Y. on May 28, 1943. While pursuing his studies at Marymount Manhattan College and later at New York University (where he earned a Master of Fine Arts degree), John Canemaker worked as actor, singer and dancer to put himself through college. In the early 1970's he began in earnest a twin career as an animator and an animation educator. He is among that rare breed of artists who can both do and teach.

As an animator Canemaker has produced a number of award-winning cartoons, notably *Confessions of a Stardreamer,* which the artist described as having been animated "to an improvised spoken track in a variety of styles and techniques (including cel, Xerography, and child-like crayon and watercolor sketches)." He is also responsible for some of the more interesting compilations and documentaries devoted to great animators of the past, such as Winsor McCay, Otto Messmer, and Oskar Fischinger. He has contributed animated sequences to a number of entertainment spectacles ranging from Broadway musicals to movie and television dramas. His more personal films have included *Confessions of a Stand-up, Bottom's Dream,* and *John Lennon Sketchbook.*

Canemaker is also a prolific writer about animation, and his contributions in such diverse periodicals as *Connoisseur, Horizon, Variety, Millimeter*, and *Film Comment* cover a wide range of subjects and themes. His 1977 book, *The Animated Raggedy Ann and Andy,* goes well beyond its stated subject into the history of the form and a general discussion of the art of animation. In 1987 he published *Winsor McCay: His Life and Art*, the definitive biography of this great American artist. Other books have included *Felix: The Twisted Tale of the World's Most Famous Cat* (1991), *Before the Animation Begins* (1996), and *Tex Avery: The MGM Years, 1942-1955* (also 1996).

Canemaker has also widely taught and lectured at institutions of higher learning in the U.S. and abroad, and has brought to his lessons a practical knowledge added to a broad understanding of theory and history. He is currently director of film animation at New York University.

M.H.

Robert Cannon, "Madeleine," from Ludwig Bemelman's story. © UPA.

CANFIELD, WILLIAM NEWTON (1920-) American cartoonist born in Orange, New Jersey, on October 8, 1920. "Bil" Canfield studied at the American School of Design in New York in 1940 and 1941 before taking a job as sports cartoonist for the *Morning Telegraph and Racing Form* in New York (1941-46). An admitted follower of the style of Bill Crawford, Canfield secured a job as sports cartoonist on Crawford's paper, the *Newark* (N.J.) *News,* in 1946 and continued in that position, and as staff artist, until Crawford left for the Newspaper Enterprise Association in 1960. In 1972 the *News* folded, and Canfield became editorial cartoonist of the *Newark Star-Ledger.* He also draws editorial cartoons for the *Red Bank* (N.J.) *Register* under his wife's maiden name, Lev. He is now retired.

Canfield's earlier tight style and careful crosshatching and crayon shading have given way to a hurried, informal look that includes shading with broad strokes of the brush over doubletone paper. His cartoons exude movement and emotion and are generally liberal-Democratic in political content.

R.M.

CANNON, ROBERT (1910-1964) American animator born in San Bernardino, California, in 1910. Bob Cannon started his animation career in 1934 as an assistant to Bob Clampett and Chuck Jones at the Leon Schlesinger studio. He began as an in-betweener but later worked as a full-fledged animator on a number of *Porky Pig* cartoons, especially "Porky's Duck Hunt" (1937), which marked the first appearance of Daffy Duck. In the 1940s Cannon moved over to Walt Disney, where he worked on some of the *Mickey* and *Donald* shorts. In 1945 Cannon helped found United Productions of America (UPA) and became its vice-president. He directed some early UPA cartoons, *Fear* and *The Brotherhood of Man* (the latter in collaboration with Stephen Bosustow), in the mid-1940s, at the same time continuing to do animation work for MGM and Disney (his name appears on the credits for Melody Time as late as 1948).

Cannon finally gained fame and recognition in 1949 with the creation of Gerald McBoing Boing, the little boy who could not talk but made noises through his nose. *Gerald McBoing Boing* won the Academy Award in 1950, and Cannon went on turning out more *Gerald* cartoons. In 1952 he created another child character, Christopher Crumpet, who turned into a chicken when he threw a temper tantrum; the *Christopher Crumpet* cartoons were never as popular as his earlier creation, however. Aside from his work on the *McBoing Boing* and *Crumpet* series, Cannon also directed a number of outstanding cartoons, including *Madeleine* (from Ludwig Bemelmans's story) and *Willie the Kid* (both 1952); *Fudget's Budget, Ballet Oop* and *Little Boy with a Big Horn* (all 1954); and *Department of the Navy* (1958). After the breakup of UPA in the late 1950s, Cannon went into commercial work and also taught animation at San Fernando College. He died in Northridge, California, on June 5, 1964.

M.H.

CAO, JOSÉ MARÍA (1862-1918) Argentine cartoonist born in Lugo, Spain, in 1862. José María Cao was apprenticed at age 15 to a manufacturer of porcelain in Gijón, Spain, where he became a designer. In 1884 he went to Madrid to further his art studies. He immigrated to Argentina in 1886 and settled in Buenos Aires. In the years immediately following, under the pseudonym "Democrito II," he collaborated on a number of Argentine magazines as a political cartoonist. His best work was done for *Don Quijote, Caras y Caretas* and *Fray Mocho.*

A great admirer of the French cartoonist Nadar, Cao often resorted to morality plays in comic strip form. His cartoons would tell a little fable (often in verse) in which the regular characters were replaced by well-known personalities in business or government. He also often used black silhouettes on white backgrounds to make his point and contributed many more innovations to the Argentine cartoon scene. He died in Buenos Aires in 1918.

A.M.

CAPTAIN PUGWASH (G.B.) "Captain Pugwash had three particular belongings: (1) His plank (for walking); (2) His compass (for navigating); (3) And a Very Special Box (invariably locked)." Thus was the "bravest, most handsome pirate in the Seven Seas" introduced in the first issue of the weekly comic *Eagle* (April 14, 1950), along with his wife ("who was far more terrifying than Pug-wash"), his ship (*The Black Pig*) and, in due course, Cut-throat Jake (his deadly enemy). Later came the cabin boy Tim, who was smarter than Pugwash and his crew put together. It was Tim, really, who thwarted the entire British navy under Admiral Sir Splycemeigh Maynebrace!

The original strip, taking up two rows on one-third of a page, ran only 19 weeks before it was dropped. But its writer and artist, John Ryan (who continued in *Eagle* with *Harris Tweed, Extra Special Agent*), put the Cap'n into mothballs, reviving him later for a television series. This series of short cartoon films for children, *The Adventures of Captain Pugwash,* was simply drawn and produced in the cutout style of early animation. But good editing and construction prevented it from becoming boring, and the series continues intermittently to this day. Ryan still draws and produces the strip. It reappeared in *Swift* in 1958, then turned up in *Playland* in 1974, and is currently in *Pippin in Playland.*

Books: *Captain Pugwash* (1957); *Pugwash Aloft* (1958); *Pugwash and the Ghost Ship* (1962); *Pugwash in the Pacific* (1973); and *Captain Pugwash Annual* (1975). Other long-running strips by Ryan include *Sir Prancelot, Mary, Mungo and Midge*, and *Lettice Leefe*. His published books exceed 40 and include *The Ark Stories* (1980) and *Jonah a Whale of a Tale* (1992).

D.G.

CARAN D'ACHE
See Poiré, Emmanuel.

CARLOS, J.
See Brito e Cunha, José Carlos de.

CARMICHAEL, ALBERT PETER (1890-1917) American cartoonist born in Albany, New York, on December 13, 1890. Albert P. Carmichael started his cartooning career with the *New York World* when he was not yet 17. Among his co-workers on the World art staff were Gus Mager, Jack Callahan and George McManus, whose style Carmichael greatly admired and endeavored to emulate.

Albert Carmichael. © New York World.

Carmichael contributed a great many cartoons and spot illustrations to the columns of the *World,* as well as a number of panels and comic strips, including *Jay Jones and His Camera, So English* and *Why Be Discontented* (all 1907), *The Adventures of Sonny and Sue* (1908), *Our Funny Language* (a panel dissecting the idiosyncrasies of the English language), *Dr. Spook's Explorations* (1909), *Rosie, the Joy of New York Life* (1911) and a funny takeoff on the vagaries of contemporary life, *Everybody s Doing It!* (1912).

Carmichael is best noted for his continuation of McManus's *The Newlyweds,* which he took over in 1914, and for his sophisticated daily strip, *The High Cost of Loving,* which he began in the same year. He also did a series of editorial cartoons characterized by an imaginative combination of photographic collages and pen drawings. Carmichael died on February 3, 1917, from complications of an appendicitis operation, at the age of 26.

Albert Carmichael's style was characterized by a deft, witty and uncluttered line which he adopted from McManus. His later cartoons show him in greater control of his work, with added individuality and expressiveness. Despite his untimely death, Carmichael remains one of the minor glories of the cartooning world.

M.H.

CARTER, ROBERT (1875-1918) American cartoonist born in Chicago in 1875. Robert Carter began his newspaper career in Chicago, where he chronicled some of the major murder trials of the day as a sketch artist. He attracted the attention of William Randolph Hearst, who brought him to New York around 1910 to work for the *New York American.* There he drew giant half-page cartoons to accompany the editorials of Arthur Brisbane. He later switched to the Progressive *Globe* and then to the *Sun.* In late 1916, he moved to Philadelphia and drew for the *Press* until his untimely death at the age of 44, on February 28, 1918.

Carter was at the forefront of his field during the 1910s, and it was the consensus of his peers and the newspaper profession in general at the time of his death that he was destined to be one of America's great cartoonists. An examination of his work bears out this contention. Carter drew in bold, slashing brushstrokes, yet without the harshness of, say, W.A. Rogers. His knowledge of anatomy and composition made nearly every cartoon a powerful message. He seldom pulled his punches, and his cartoons—supporting Roosevelt, attacking Wilson, furthering the war effort—place his regrettably small body of work squarely in the tradition of Nast, Keppler and Davenport.

R.M.

CARUSO, ENRICO (1873-1921) Italian tenor and American cartoonist born in Naples, Italy, on February 25, 1873. Enrico Caruso began to sing locally at age 11 and debuted in opera in 1894. He sang four seasons in La Scala before touring Europe to great acclaim. He was also a tremendous success in America after debuting at the

Enrico Caruso, self-caricature as Pagliacci. © La Follia.

Metropolitan Opera in New York on November 23, 1904. He made his home in Florence but spent much time in America, becoming, incidentally, one of the first great recording stars.

Caruso was also a talented caricaturist who captured his subjects on menus, envelopes and from memory. His fame as a cartoonist spread until, in 1907, he began contributing weekly caricatures for the Italian-language paper *La Follia di New York—a* schedule he maintained for years, although he declined salary. He died on August 2, 1921.

Caruso had a definite eye for characteristics and for translating a personality to paper. With his fame he had some of the world's best subjects pose willingly, and the informal circumstances of execution were evidenced by the rough media used in drawings. He was less polished as an artist than as a singer but could have achieved fame and respect on the basis of his cartoons alone. He is reported to have been offered a $50,000-a-year contract to draw for the *New York World;* for his work he must be recognized as America's first true caricaturist in the modern sense. A collection of Enrico Caruso's caricatures was published by *La Follia di New York* in 1916 and reprinted by Dover Books in 1977.

R.M.

CASPER (U.S.) Casper, a sprightly little spirit who had come from the netherworld to make friends with humans, was introduced in 1945 in "The Friendly Ghost," produced by Famous Studios, Paramount's animation arm. The cartoon was released under the Noveltoons title reserved for one-shots and features. It proved quite popular, however, and before the end of the 1940s several more Casper cartoons had been released, including "There's Good Boos Tonight" (1948) and "A-Haunting We Will Go" (1949).

The first *Casper* cartoons were directed by old hands I. Sparber and Seymour Kneitel and animated by Otto Messmer and Bill Turner on scripts by Joe Oriolo and Sy Reitt; Frank Gallop provided the voiced-over narration. By the start of the 1950s the series had acquired its permanent cast of characters: Wendy the Good Little Witch, Nightmare the Ghost Horse, the villainous Ghostly Trio, etc. The series rapidly lost whatever charm it had possessed in its beginning, however, and it was strictly aimed at a juvenile audience. It finally folded, along with Famous Studios, in the 1960s.

In the meantime *Casper* had been adapted to the comic book medium, first by Jubilee, then by St. John and finally by Harvey, which made it into a huge success. After Paramount sold the rights to the *Casper* cartoons to Harvey, these were successfully released to television under the Harveytoon banner. A new series of television shorts was produced in the 1990s for the Fox Kids Network. The character also came to the big screen in the 1995 *Casper,* a disastrous live-action-cum-animation movie with Christina Ricci and Bill Pullman, and the voice of Malachi Pearson. This was followed in 1997 by *Casper—House of the Spirits,* a direct-to-video release.

M.H.

CASSELL, JONATHAN H. (ca. 1875-1940) American cartoonist born in Nebraska City, Nebraska, around 1875. John Cassell, as he became known (although he signed his work "Jno. Cassell") was educated at Doane College of Crete, Nebraska (1892-94). He studied art at the Art Institute of Chicago and began drawing cartoons for the *Ram's Horn* in that city; the magazine was a religious publication for which Frank Beard had drawn.

In the 1890s Cassell began freelancing to *Puck, Judge* and *Life* magazines and illustrating for popular monthlies and books. Around 1913, when the *New York World* lost Macauley and Minor as editorial cartoonists, Rollin Kirby

"Casper the Friendly Ghost." © Harveytoons.

and Cassell replaced them on the evening and morning editions, respectively. Though Cassell was eclipsed by Kirby, he was a respectable and forceful cartoonist in his own right. He drew vicious anti-Hughes cartoons in 1916 and generally supported the Democratic cause. When the World went to a single edition, Cassell left and, changing his political allegiance, drew editorial cartoons for the *Brooklyn Eagle.*

Cassell had a handsome crayon line and shaded his drawings neatly. There was much animation in his figures, and he had a way of endowing his targets with squint-eyed, dour expressions. He died in 1940.

R.M.

CASTANYS I BORRÁS, VALENTÍ (1898-1965) Spanish cartoonist born in Barcelona, Spain, in 1898. Valentí Castanys's first cartoons were published throughout the late 1910s and early 1920s in such Catalan humor magazines as *El Sr. Daixonses i la Sra. Dallonses, El Senyor Canons, En Patufet, El Bé Negre* and *La Veu de Catalunya.*

Castanys is best known for his contributions to the magazine *Xut*, which he directed for 15 years (1922-36). During that period he was not only the publication's chief cartoonist and illustrator but one of its most important literary contributors as well. At the same time, he regularly contributed cartoons and comic strips to the illustrated magazine *Papitu* under the name "Eufemio Rodriguez." In addition he founded a humor magazine specializing in film spoofs and in 1937 wrote *Barcelona-Hollywood,* dealing with movies and filmmaking. During the Spanish civil war Castanys went to France and later to Italy. When the war ended in 1939, he returned to Spain, working *as* a cartoonist and comic strip artist and later founding a sports magazine, *El Once.*

From 1925 until the time of his death in Barcelona in 1965, Castanys was one of Spain's most celebrated cartoonists. The fictitious places and characters he created (La Familia Sistacs, Succesors de la Viuda Pasturet, Gafarro en Comandita, Rafeques i Companya, Picamoixons, Masrampinyó, etc.) have become so popular that they are now referred to in everyday conversation. Perhaps the best testimony to Castanys's creative genius as a cartoonist is his *El Pais de Sidral* ("The Land of Sidral"), a science fiction strip based on a utopian country.

J.M.

CATROW, DAVID JOHNSON III (1952-) American cartoonist born in Fort Lee, Virginia, on December 16, 1952. After three years in the Navy and a couple of years at Kent State University, David J. Catrow became a book illustrator in 1978 and, starting in 1984, editorial cartoonist for the *Springfield News-Sun* as well. There, his mostly conservative cartoons have resonated with his southwestern Ohio readers, who appreciate his vigorous graphic style and sense of humor. Now that he is represented by the Copley News Service, he should also gain recognition beyond the state.

Crudely drawn, Catrow's cartoons are immediately recognizable by some of the ugliest faces and bodies in cartoondom along with strong, often biting political position.

'FREEZE! I'VE GOT 3 POUNDS OF LEAN GROUND BEEF AND I'M NOT AFRAID TO USE IT!"

David Catrow. Springfield News-Sun.

These range from a Pentagon news conference on UFO landings at Roswell given by a Martian in an American general's uniform ("Case closed") to USAF Lt. Kelly Flinn just discharged for adultery: "The bad news is you can never have a government job. The good news is you can still be president," her lawyer informs her.

Catrow's social commentary goes from the ridiculous to the hilariously absurd, whether he depicts an ATM depositor whose wallet is being pickpocketed by outrageous bank fees or, following the August 1997 recall of millions of E-coli-infected beef patties, an old woman holds up a bank, yelling "Freeze! I've got 3 pounds of lean ground beef and I'm not afraid to use it!"

In addition, Catrow has illustrated a number of children's books, including several important historical events as part of the "Cornerstones of Freedom" series, such as the trek over the Oregon Trail and the 1890 massacre of Indians at Wounded Knee Creek.

P.H.

CAVALLI, RICHARD (1923-1997) American cartoonist born in New York City in September 1923. Dick Cavalli exhibited strong talents for cartooning during his school days in Brooklyn. Drafted into the army after his graduation from high school, he served three years in the infantry and the air force. Discharged in 1946, he studied art on a GI college bill, first at the School of Industrial Arts, and later at the School of Visual Arts.

Cavalli started freelancing cartoons in the late 1940s with such success that a 1956 *Writer's Digest* article described him as "having risen to the top faster than any other cartoonist in the business." Retitled *Winthrop,* the feature was done by Cavalli until its discontinuance in 1993. After *Winthrop* folded, he went back to humor cartooning and wrote gags for Johnny Hart's *B.C.* He died of heart failure at his home in New Canaan, Conn., on October 16, 1997.

Dick Cavalli is best known for *Winthrop,* but the innumerable gag cartoons which he contributed to *Collier's,* the *Saturday Evening Post* and other magazines were often funnier and certainly more pungent.

M.H.

"I don't understand it. Why didn't he marry both of them?"
Richard Cavalli. © This Week.

CAVANDOLI, OSVALDO (1920-) Italian animator born in Maderno del Garda, Italy, in 1920. Osvaldo Cavandoli is a self-taught artist who started his career in the early 1940s, settling in 1946 at the animation studio of the Pagot brothers. In 1948, along with Nino and Toni Pagot, Osvaldo Piccardo and Carlo Bachini, he completed *I Fratelli Dinamite* ("The Dynamite Brothers"), a feature-length cartoon begun in 1942 (the original drawings for the film had been destroyed in a bombardment).

In the 1950s, after working on theatrical cartoons that were well received critically but disastrous at the box office, Cavandoli devoted himself to the production of advertising cartoons to be shown during film intermissions. In 1970 he directed a number of animated mini-films of a few seconds' duration, such as *L'Amore E la Fine* ("Love Is the End") and *Attenti alle Colombe* ("Beware of Doves"). The critics have recently "discovered" Cavandoli and have showered him with countless awards at Italian and foreign film festivals.

Cavandoli's fame is founded above all on the recent cartoons titled simply *La Linea* ("Line") followed by a numeral (there are to date eight *Line* cartoons). The technique involves running a simple line along the film, shaping it at given intervals into various objects, people or animals.

Osvaldo Cavandoli, "La Linea." © Cavandoli.

The effect is startling and was further enhanced when Cavandoli introduced color. Of the *Line* cartoons, Ralph Stephenson wrote: "They are engaging little comedies, perfectly drawn, full of humor and in a unique style which should be capable of development." The cartoons have been seen on television and have given rise to a series of *Mr. Linea* comic books, in which Cavandoli indulges in linear variations that cannot be shown over the prudish Italian television networks. *La Linea* is a genial, unusual creation that allows its author to confront his one-dimensional hero with all the obstacles surrounding him, thus establishing a man-object rapport-which, as Buster Keaton has taught us, is a permanent love-hate relationship.

In the last 20 years La Linea has become Cavandoli's trademark character. It has been featured in a TV series from 1975 to 1984, was made into several cartoon theatricals, was adapted to comic books, and collected in several book anthologies. The author was invited to exhibit his work at the Italian embassy in Prague in 1986, and was awarded first prize at the Bordighera Humor Salon in 1987.

S.T.

CECCON, SILVIUS PETRUS CLAUDIUS (1937-) Brazilian cartoonist born in Garibaldi, Rio Grande do Sul, Brazil, in 1937. While he was still a child, Claudius Ceccon's parents moved to Rio de Janeiro, where their son received his art education. His first job was doing page layouts for *O Cruzeiro.* In the mid-1950s he started doing spot drawings for *O Cruzeiro,* as well as illustrations to short stories published in the magazine *A Cigarra.*

Claudius (as he is professionally known) began his cartooning career in 1957 on the daily *Jornal do Brasil,* first as a general cartoonist, then as the newspaper's political cartoonist, a position he held from 1961 until 1965. That year Claudius became the regular cartoonist for the magazine *Manchete,* and some of his most pungent cartoons have been published in its pages. Since the end of the military dictatorship in the 1980s, his cartoons have become even more in demand.

A prolific worker, Claudius has also contributed cartoons to most major Brazilian publications *(Diário Carioca, Revista da Semana, Mundo Ilustrado, Senhor, Fairplay, Correio da Manha, O Jornal,* etc.), as well as to foreign publications (the *New York Times, Life, Paris Match* and *Stern,* among others). He has had a number of his cartoons collected in book form, and he has received many awards, both Brazilian and foreign.

A.M.

CEM

See Martin, Charles Edward.

CEMAK

See Giulietti, Leonardo

CESARE, OSCAR EDWARD (1885-1948) American cartoonist born in Linkoping, Sweden, in 1885. Oscar Cesare studied art in Paris, then moved to America at the age of

"When the President kicks Congress he's not kicking his dog; he's kicking his People's dog."
Oscar Cesare. © New York Times.

18 and continued his art studies in Buffalo. He took his first jobs in Chicago and worked for several newspapers, including the *Tribune,* for which he drew dramatic sketches. Moving to New York, Cesare drew editorial cartoons for several papers, including the *World,* the *Sun,* the *Post* (after Munsey bought the *Sun* in 1916 and banished cartoons from its pages), *Harper's Weekly* and the *New York Times.* He also worked for the *Sun* magazine, and it was for the *New* York *Times Magazine* that he did much of his notable work.

For the dailies Cesare drew in a remarkably free and seemingly slap dash style, a whirlwind combination of loose brushstrokes and thickly applied grease crayon; the results looked more like the studies of a fine painter than the finished products of a daily editorial cartoonist. In a day when fellow cartoonists were using crayons to liberate the form from the tight pen-and-ink style, Cesare took things further; his busy cartoons were widely admired as fine examples of composition and rendering. His liberal concepts were translated lucidly, and his work was generally free of captions and labels. For the weeklies he drew in wash and gained much fame with the *Times* as an interviewer-sketcher. His most famous interview was with Lenin in 1922; he also visited General Billy Mitchell, Orville Wright and Benito Mussolini.

Cesare was married briefly in the 1910s to Margaret Porter, the daughter of O. Henry. *One Hundred Cartoons by Cesare,* a collection dealing mostly with war-related issues, was published in 1916 by Small, Maynard. Cesare died at the age of 63 at his home in Stamford, Connecticut. Lamentably, his brilliant work is largely forgotten today.

R.M.

CHAD (G.B.) This familiar cartoon character, almost a symbol, spread like wildfire throughout the British Army during the Second World War. Perhaps because he was so simple to draw, his popularity, always unofficial, was boundless and he appeared on almost any wall or vacant space, peering over a line suggesting the top of a fence or wall, his pendulous nose hanging over, two dots for eyes in a balk head, proclaiming his famous three-word motto, only the third word of which ever changed. This was the phrase, "Wot no..." followed by the name of whatever he was currently complaining about. Thus, there were, "Wot no fags?" (meaning cigarettes), "Wot no women?", "Wot no beer?", and so on.

The simple drawing was apparently based on an electrical symbol, and was claimed to have been created by a cartoonist named George Chatterton, who was in the RAF at the time. Chatterton signed himself 'Chat' for short, and so after the war a new strip appeared every week in the magazine *People's Friend* entitled *Chad by Chat*. A three-panel pantomime series, Chad never spoke, and thus was without his famous wartime catchphrase.

"I was a new recruit in the Air Force in 1938," recalled Chat. "I was asked to design some posters for camp dances and socials. I used Chad as a recurring cartoon on these. Later I was posted from RAF Cardington in Bedfordshire to Farnborough and then to Little Rissington. Thus Chad was turning up on posters at each of these camps. By this time the fellers had picked up the simplicity of the character and he was appearing all over the place." But it was especially the Army that made Chad universal, he remembered. "The first time I ever saw Chad abroad was on a bombed wall in Tobruk. Those guys in the desert were short of just about everything you could think of, and Chad made the perfect anonymous complainer."

After Chad's success as a strip, Chat began to draw for children's comics, and was soon on the front page of the *Wonder* with a western hero, Sheriff Shucks. He died September 29, 1996.

D.G.

CHAM
See Noé, Amédée de.

CHARLES, WILLIAM (1776-1820) American cartoonist born in Edinburgh, Scotland, in 1776. William Charles set himself up in his native city as a printmaker and caricaturist but was chased from the country for the viciousness of his personal attacks and his scatological humor.

He moved to the United States in 1805, adopted the style of James Gillray and worked as a printmaker and caricaturist in New York (until 1814) and Philadelphia (1814 until his death on August 29, 1820). He had ample opportunity during the War of 1812 to mete out revenge to his former countrymen, and the first great sustained series of American cartoons flowed from Charles's pen, savagely attacking the British, their allies, their troops and their king.

Charles also occupies an important place in the history of American humorous illustration. He drew for the *American Magazine of Wit* (1808), illustrated *Pinkerton's Travels* (1810-12) and was one of several artists to illustrate

The Travels of Doctor Syntax. Charles pioneered the use of line stipple and aquatint and during his career worked as a bookseller and stationer as well.

R.M.

CHARLIE BROWN
See Peanuts.

CHAST, ROZ (1954-) One of the most distinctive cartoonists of the 1980s, and one of the few women at the top of her field, Roz Chast depends on neither a quirky graphic style nor a specifically female perspective for her shrewd social and psychological commentaries. Ms. Chast was born in Brooklyn, New York, in 1954, and took Saturday morning classes at the Art Students League in Manhattan while still in high school before going on to the Rhode Island School of Design. After receiving a bachelor of fine arts degree from that prestigious school in 1977, she tried her hand at commercial art, but her somewhat sketchy style brought her little success. Since she had always drawn cartoons for her own amusement, she offered one to New York's alternative newspaper *Christopher Street* on a whim, and sold it for ten dollars. Encouraged by this modest success, as she recalls, she reasoned, "I was going nowhere with the stupid editorial cartoons that I didn't want to do anyway, so I figured, "What do I have to lose at this point?" A few sales to such periodicals as the *Village Voice* and the *National Lampoon* emboldened her to submit her work to the top cartoon market in the country, the *New Yorker*. In April 1978, her first *New Yorker* cartoon appeared.

In 1979 Chast became a staff cartoonist for the *New Yorker*, which gave the magazine first rights to all her work. Of the 40 staff cartoonists under contract to that magazine in 1996, she was the only woman and has consistently been one of the weekly's most regular contributors. She continues to appear occasionally in other periodicals and also does advertising illustrations from time to time. Since 1992 she has illustrated several books, including juvenile titles for which her "wonderfully waggish illustrations" have been widely praised.

Unlike traditional gag cartoons, Chast's *New Yorker* pieces usually do not carry captions but either employ dialogue balloons like comic strips or are simply labeled portraits of her characters. Her people are exaggerated versions of maladjusted types such as "Susan D, the woman without a heyday," or "The Imperfect Hostess," who announces, "We're having DIRT for dinner!....And you're not invited!....and I forgot your name anyway." "The Male Biological Clock" is illustrated by a man reflecting "If I don't learn how to play golf by the time I'm forty-three, I'll never learn." Her keen eye for contemporary angst is dramatized by "The Tournament of Neuroses Parade," which included floats with such labels as "I Never Really Broke Away From My Parents." Her insight into social pretensions and the vacuity of verbal clichés is reflected in her *New Yorker* series "The Bonfire of the Banalities."

Chast has published several collections of her work, beginning with *Unscientific Americans* (1982) and including *Parallel Universe* (1984), *Mondo Boxo* (1987), *The Four Elements* (1988), *Proof of Life on Earth* (1991), and *Childproof* (1997). Of one of her collections, the *Village Voice Literary Supplement* noted, Chast "can be counted on to decode and recontextualize the small talk, inflated claims and petty impulses that make up life on this planet—and to make it a hoot."

D.W.

CHAVAL
See Le Louarn, Yvan.

CHEN HUILING (1916-) Since 1953, Chen, a self-taught cartoonist, has never stopped his cartooning. Before he retired, he worked as art editor of *Children Education* magazine published by Jiangsu Educational Institute. Cartoons are the by-products of his leisure time.

As many others, Chen's cartoons are of both political and societal humor, and most of them are single cartoons. His cartoon "I am Yellow River, too" won the "excellent creation" award in 1982. It was an urgent call for stopping the denudation in China, which has brought much mud into the rivers making them yellowish-looking. In the cartoon, one dragonized river, a symbol of China, is calling another one: "Changjiang, Changjiang (Yangtze River), I am Yellow River," while the other one replies: "Yellow River, Yellow River, I am Yellow River, too" Technically, the images are not fancy or exaggerated but rather quite a simple metaphor, helped by four written Chinese characters saying "denudation of the trees." However, this cartoon added much fame to Chen after it was quoted by a famous scientist at a national meeting for environment protection.

Among other top cartoonists, altogether ten of them, Chen was awarded the highest prize in the Chinese cartoonist profession, the Gold Monkey Award, in 1993. It was the first such honor and recognition gained by cartoonists since the People's Republic of China was founded in 1949.

Interestingly, Chen's four adult sons have all followed their father in cartooning as self-taught artists, although

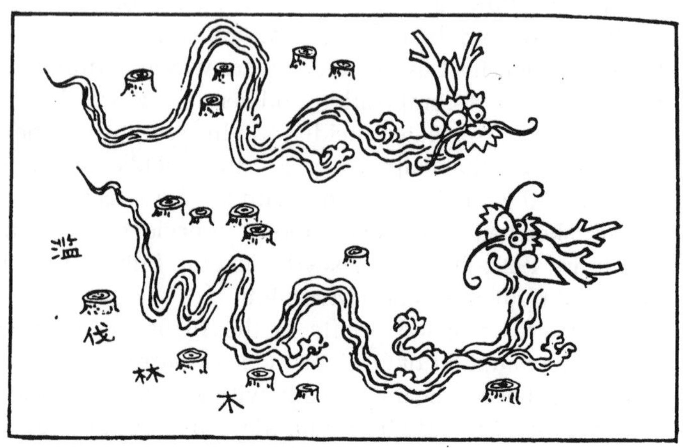

Chen Huiling. © Chen Huiling.

none of their work has achieved such artistic distinction. All of them have been actively publishing cartoons in different print media.

H.Y.L.L.

Chen Shubin. © Chen Shubin.

CHEN SHUBIN (1938-) Many readers did not know Fang Tang, meaning "to be an honest Chinese," was the penname of Chen Shubin, but they became familiar with the style of his cartoons and comics published as special panels in Shanghai's well-established magazines, such as the *World of Cartoons* in Shanghai. Actually Chen is skillful in either political caricatures or societal humor. After the devastating "Cultural Revolution" ended (1966-1976), during which no cartoons were allowed to be created and published, Chen's comic series entitled *New Stories of Old Soldiers* tremendously affected the whole nation. The stories were about the experience of the youth, possibly based upon his own, during those ten years of political turmoil. Since the mid-1980s, his comic series of different topics have appeared in various print media across the country.

Chen's art style in single-cartoon creation is quite different from that in his comics. In contrast to his comics which usually contain dialogues, captions, and written language, most of his cartoons contain no more than just a title. Images in his comics present the influence of those in Japan or Taiwan, which have strongly spread to China in recent years. In comparing Chen's comics and single cartoons, it seems that Chen's comics were created in the afternoon while the artist is an early morning person who usually gets up at three or four A.M. to work in a completely quite environment. However, the meaning of each creation, presented by either sharp satire or mild humor, shows the artists profound understanding of the events recreated in his artwork. Chen's creations easily make readers think deeper after laughter. This has been Chen's creative goal.

Chen's creation has won many prizes at domestic or world competitions. His comics won the second class award in the National Comics Contest in the late 1980s, and he was also awarded in Japan, Italy and Bulgaria. In addition to his comics collection published in the late 1980s, *Chen Shubin's Cartoon Selection* published in 1995, was among the eighteen best-selling cartoon books in China.

H.Y.L.L.

—"The light bulb was invented by our people, Yablochkov and Ldygin"—"Yes, but the Americans invented the idea that Edison invented it!"
Mikhail Cheremnykh. © Krokodil.

CHEREMNYKH, MIKHAIL MIKHAILOVICH (1890-1962) Soviet cartoonist and graphic artist born in Tomsk, Russia, on October 30, 1890. Mikhail Cheremnykh graduated from the Moscow Institute of Painting, Sculpture and Architecture in 1917. He was active during the Russian Revolution and the ensuing civil war. In 1919 he founded the Orkna Rosta ("Windows of the Russian News Agency"), which turned out propaganda posters of current events, and he himself contributed many noted posters of the era.

In 1922 Cheremnykh became one of the founders of the satirical weekly *Krokodil,* to which he contributed innumerable cartoons over the years. During World War II he went back to poster designing and created a number of powerful anti-Nazi images. In addition to his cartooning and poster work, Cheremnykh found time to illustrate books by famous Russian authors, including Saltykov Shchedrin, Krylov and Chekhov. He was also a professor at the Surikov Art Institute in Moscow from 1949 until his death on August 7, 1962.

Cheremnykh was a member of the *USSR Academy of Arts,* and a People's Artist of the Russian Federated Republic. He was the recipient of many honors and awards, including the Stalin Prize in 1942.

M.H.

CHEVALIER, GUILLAUME-SULPICE (1804-1866) French cartoonist, watercolorist and lithographer born in Paris, France, on January 13, 1804. Better known under the pseudonym "Paul Gavarni," Guillaume Chevalier studied at the Conservatoire des Arts et Métiers while selling some of his paintings. His first success came at 20, when his *Etrennes de 1825: Récréatians Diabolico Fantasmagoriques,* a volume of lithographs, was published by Blaisot. In 1829, during a land-surveying tour in southwestern France and the Pyrenees, he painted a landscape, *Cirque de Gavarnie,* which gave him his pseudonym. His drawings, full of elegance and wit, caught the attention of the press magnate of the July Monarchy, Emile de Girardin, who published

—"My dear lady . . . so sweet . . . a little kiss . . . for God's sake."
—"Your father had me already this morning . . . "
Guillaume-Sulpice Chevalier ("Paul Gavarni").

many of Gavarni's fancy-dress costume studies in the newly founded *La Mode* (1830); they appeared as well *in L'Artiste* and *La Silhouette.*

The year 1837 marks an important date for Gavarni because he went to work for *Le Charivari,* where he was allowed to exercise his elegant style and charming irony to the fullest on his favorite subjects—street urchins, bohemians and the foibles and adventures of women, whether sophisticated, low-class or of easy virtue. *Fourberies de Femmes en Matière de Sentiment* ("Women's Deceptions in Matters of the Heart," 1837-40), *La Boîte aux Lettres* ("The Mailbox," 1837-39), *Les Lorettes* (1841-43) and *Le Carnaval* (1846) are the most important series of that period.

After the death of his mother and an unhappy marriage, Gavarni went to England and Scotland (1847-51). where he depicted the plight of the poor with bitter and compelling realism, mainly for the *Illustrated London News.* On his return to France he abandoned his portrayal of dandies to show, in *Masques et Visages* (1852-54), ugly old men and women in their dirty, vulgar getup, and to satirize, often bitingly, the profiteers of the Second Empire. These cartoons have been published in series like *Les Propos de Thomas Vireloque* (1851-53), with its philosophical beggar, *Les Partageuses* (which may be translated as "The Gold Diggers," 1852), *Bohèmes* (1853) and *Histoire de Politiquer* (1853-54).

Although he became famous, Paul Gavarni never overcame the pessimism caused by social and political conditions both in Paris and London. He died in Paris on November 24, 1866, at the age of 62, leaving behind more than twenty-seven hundred lithographs and over five thousand drawings and sketches. Gavarni's art, while not as powerful as Daumier's, was graceful, polished and light and was much praised by Balzac, Delacroix, Baudelaire and Gautier, who called it "as profound and cynical as Swift or Voltaire."

P.H.

CHIAPPORI, ALFREDO (1943-) Italian cartoonist born in Lecca, Italy, in 1943. Alfredo Chiappori studied at the State Art Institute in Fano under the guidance of the sculptor Edgardo Mannucci. After graduation in 1965, he tried his hand at painting but returned to his hometown in 1967, taking up a teaching position at the local high school. It was then that he drew his first political cartoons.

In 1968 Chiappori created *Up il Sovversivo* ("Up the Subversive"), a political comic strip, for the monthly magazine *Linus.* It was collected in book form in 1970, the same year he started contributing political cartoons to the left-wing magazine *Compagni.* In 1972 Chiappori published a book of comics titled *Alfreud,* and the next year he came out with *Vado, l'Arresto e Torno* ("I Go, Arrest Him and Come Back"), in which Up commented on the wave of terrorism that had descended upon Italy. The book established Chiappori as one of the most acute political observers of the Italian scene.

In collaboration with Fortebraccio, a political writer for the Communist daily *L'Unità,* Chiappori authored another book derisively called *Il Belpaese* ("The Fair Country") and started a cartoon column of the same title for the weekly Panorama. In 1975 he published another volume of political comic strips, *Padroni* e *Padrini* ("Bosses and Godfathers"), in collaboration with Oreste del Buono. He also contributes weekly political cartoons to the Rome daily *Paese Sera.* At the same time Chiappori continues to devote a good portion of his talent to painting.

L.S.

CHIES, GIAMPAOLO (1947-) Italian cartoonist born in Bologna, Italy, on January 26, 1947. Giampaolo Chies decided to go into cartooning after finishing his high school studies. He started his career in 1968, drawing *Virus Psik,* a comic strip about a somewhat extravagant woman psychiatrist, on texts by Max Bunker (Luciano Secchi). He then drew a great number of cartoons and illustrations for the monthly magazine *Eureka.*

In 1971 Chies moved to Milan and briefly worked as *an* animator for Gamma Film. Later that year he resumed the *Virus Psik* strip and also created a monthly cartoon panel, *Monodia* ("Monody"), in which he gave free rein to his absurdist humor. In these somewhat disquieting cartoons, strange objects float in the air, mechanical women nurse real-life babies, and robots weep or bleed. The air of eerie unreality is further enhanced by the total absence of captions or dialogue. Chies had his comic-book version of Pinocchio published in 1980. Since that time he has been very active as a comic-book artist for a variety of Italian and European publishers.

L.S.

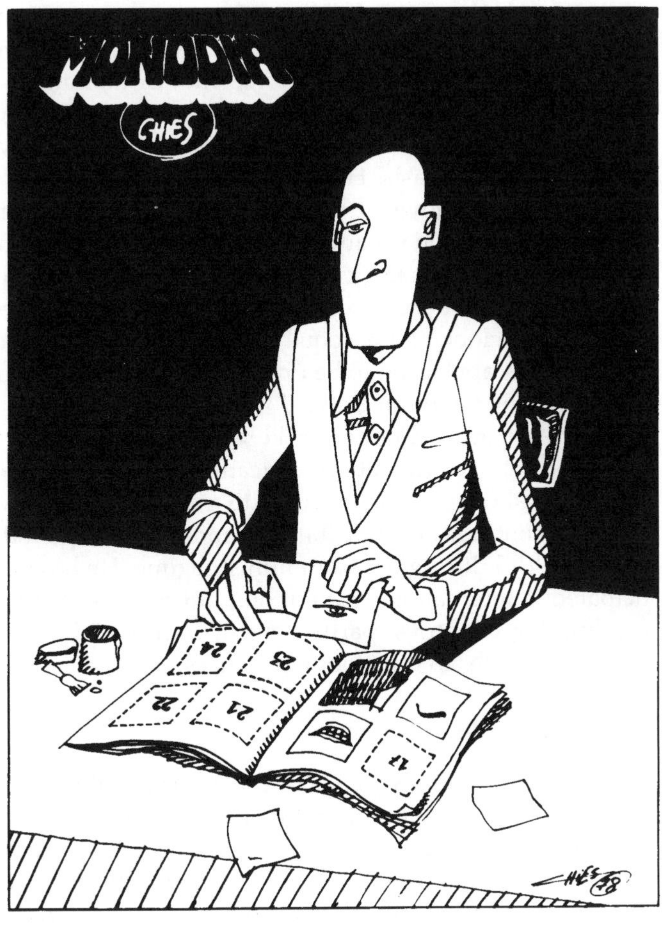

Giampaolo Chies, "Monodia." © Editoriale Corno.

CHILLY WILLY (U.S.) In 1953 Walter Lantz attempted to duplicate the roaring success of his red-crested woodpecker, Woody, with a bird of a different plumage—the black-attired Chilly Willy, a penguin.

Chilly Willy was a sad-faced little creature who lived in the icy wastes near the Pole and whose main occupation in life was the continuous search for food and shelter. Fighting off dumb dogs, moronic polar bears and benumbed humans, the indestructible little penguin would resist all attempts to kick him out of trappers' cabins, Eskimos' igloos and scientists' weather stations. No less dogged in his intent to secure food, Chilly Willy would hijack a boatload of fish or mooch a meal of dog food with the single-mindedness of despair. There was a touch of pathos in the *Chilly Willy* series that one rarely found in other animated cartoons of the period.

As with all his products, Walter Lantz released the *Chilly Willy* cartoons through Universal until production was halted in 1973. Among the directors who worked on the series were Alex Lovy, Jack Hannah, Sid Marcus, Paul J. Smith and especially Tex Avery, who realized two of the best entries in the field, "I'm Cold" and "The Legend of Rockabye Point" (the latter nominated for an Academy Award in 1955).

Chilly Willy can still occasionally be seen on television in *The Woody Woodpecker Show.*

M.H.

CHIP

See Bellew, Frank P.W.

CHIP `N' DALE (U.S.) Chip and Dale were relative newcomers to the Walt Disney menagerie of funny animals. They made their debut in 1946 in a *Pluto* cartoon titled "Squatter's Rights" (nominated for an Academy Award), in which they bedeviled the simpleminded dog.

Chip and Dale were two resourceful chipmunks whose penchant for pranks and larceny often caused them to run afoul of an enraged Donald Duck. In "Donald Applecore," for instance, they laid waste to Donald's apple orchard; in "Chips Ahoy" they commandeered Donald's model boat for a cruise down a park basin; and in "Up a Tree" they turned the tables on lumberjack Donald trying to cut down their tree.

The redoubtable chipmunks never ran out of enemies. Trying to steal eggs, they had to disguise themselves as baby chicks in order to avoid the fury of a mother hen ("Chicken in the Rough"), and they even faced up to Disney's all-purpose cartoon villain, Pegleg Pete, playing a bank robber in "The Lone Chipmunks." While the chipmunks enjoyed the bonds of mutual friendship, they would occasionally have a falling out, as when they vied against each other for the affections of the fickle *chanteuse* Clarice in "Two Chips and a Miss."

"Chilly Willy." © Walter Lantz.

The *Chip 'n' Dale* theatrical shorts were discontinued in the late 1950s. The two irrepressible chipmunks continue to be seen, however, on the Disney TV program in specials *such as* "The Adventures of Chip `n' Dale" and "Mixed Nuts"; there was even a spirited song composed for these occasions ("I'm Chip—I'm Dale"). The *Chip 'n' Dale Rescue*

Chip 'n' Dale in "Up a Tree." © Walt Disney Productions.

Rangers TV series premiered on the Disney Channel in March 1989, before going into syndication later that year.

M.H.

CHŌ, SHINTA
See Suzuki, Shūji.

CHODOROWSKI, ANTONI (1946-) Antoni Chodorowski was born on June 7, 1946, in Chodory, Poland, a town that carried the name of his nobleman family. He graduated from the Academy of Fine Arts and the Polytechnic Institute, both in Warsaw, with emphases in civil engineering and interior design. Yet, as he said, he has never built a bridge or done any interior designing, sustaining himself all his life on freelance cartooning.

Antoni Chodorowski. © Pen Tip International Features.

Chodorowski is noted for his prodigious output, contributing to as many as 20 to 30 magazines and newspapers on a regular basis. He claims his prolific production results from his love of work (which keeps him from thinking about money) and the necessity of raising nine children. Chodorowski's cartoons take a variety of styles and formats; some are very detailed with graceful touches, taking on the look of a Baroque painting, while others are rather crude, appearing to be unfinished. He describes his work as being "without a style."

A versatile artist, Chodorowski seems equally comfortable doing book illustration, caricature, or gag, satirical, and political cartoons. In addition to mainstream publications, he continues to contribute to underground periodicals as he did during the Communist regime. He has participated in international exhibitions, but confines them to neighboring countries, partly "out of courtesy," but also because he hates to travel long distances.

J.A.L.

CHODOWIECKI, DANIEL (1726-1801) German illustrator, printmaker and painter born in Danzig (now Gdańsk, Poland) on October 16, 1726. In his astonishingly fruitful career, Daniel Chodowiecki supplied a wealth of visual imagery and inspiration to his generation and those that followed. His specifically humorous works, although drawn academically and comprising only a part of his total production, entitle him to be considered the father of German cartooning in the 19th and 20th centuries.

Chodowiecki's father, a merchant who also painted miniatures, died when Daniel was 14. Three years later the young man was sent to Berlin to work for an uncle who taught him how to paint miniature portraits on parchment for application to snuffboxes and similar bric-a-brac. By 1754 he and his younger brother, Gottfried, were established enough to set up on their own as painters on enamel. In 1757 Daniel began painting in oils (this proved to be a weaker sideline and dropped out after the 1770s) and, most important, etching. He was eventually to etch over two thousand images on nearly a thousand copper-plates, nine-tenths of this output coming after 1773.

Besides documentary illustration (of human types for the works of the phrenologist Lavater; of trades and occupations for the encyclopedia of the educator Basedow) and illustrations for countless novels and almanacs, Chodowiecki tirelessly depicted the everyday bourgeois world around him with all its small sorrows and joys, its sentimentality and its fun (never boisterous in his pictures, but genuine all the same).

As a careful observer of reality and as the single most prolific delineator of life in Berlin, Chodowiecki is the precursor of such cartoonists as Schadow, Dör-beck, Hosemann and Zille. The gluttony of a Berlin picnic is expressed in a famous 1775 print, "The Pilgrimage to Französisch Buchholz." A series of five prints entitled *The Law-Abiding Citizens of Berlin* concerns a new city ordinance about leashing dogs. Foolish fashions, gossiping servants, ill-matched couples and the like abound in his

Citizens of Berlin well supplied for a picnic.

Daniel Chodowiecki, 1775.

pictures. His images of the *Aeneid* are important examples of the parodies of antiquity that cropped up here and there in that sternly neoclassical period.

Chodowiecki became a member of the Berlin Academy in 1764 and its director in 1797. He-was also a major art collector, owning 146 paintings and some 10,000 prints and drawings. He died in Berlin on July 2, 1801.

S.A.

CHUA, MORGAN (1949-) Born in Singapore, May 3, 1949, of ancestors who hailed from China, Morgan Chua has been a very influential figure in Asian political cartooning, setting the pace with his true-to-life caricature, aggressive satire, and elaborate artistic style.

Chua's first published artwork appeared in a military periodical, *The Pioneer*, while he fulfilled his Singapore Armed Forces duty. For a short time, he was cartoonist for the ill-fated Singapore *Herald*, drawing less-than-flattering caricatures of the country's authoritarian leader Lee Kuan Yew. When Lee closed the *Herald*, Chua joined *The Asian*, a new regional paper published in Hong Kong, but it too failed in 1973 because of financial problems.

Chua's major success was achieved while cartoonist and art editor of the Hong Kong-based *Far Eastern Economic Review*. During his more than 20 years on this weekly magazine, Chua was responsible for a few major redesigns, many colorful covers and inside illustrations, and a regular political cartoon that appeared at the top of the "In Other Words" page. Ronald Searle and Pat Oliphant were heavy influences upon his style; in fact, like Oliphant, he used a tiny animal figure as a sideline observer/commentator of the main message. Chua left the *Review* at about the time Hong Kong reverted to China.

J.A.L.

CHUMY-CHUMEZ
See González Castrillo, José María.

CLAMPETT, ROBERT (1910?-1984) American animator and producer born in San Diego, California, around 1910 (his exact birthdate is a closely guarded secret). Bob Clampett moved in childhood to Hollywood, where he received his schooling. While in high school he drew a comic strip for the *Los Angeles Times*, and after graduation he went on to study at the Otis Art Institute in Los Angeles.

Clampett joined the animation unit of Rudolph Ising and Hugh Harman in 1931. There he worked on the early Looney Tunes and Merrie Melodies that were turned out for distribution by Warner Brothers. When Harman and Ising left Warner, Clampett joined the studio Leon Schlesinger was forming to continue the Warner Brothers cartoons. Clampett received his first directorial assignment in 1936, when he did a cartoon sequence for a Joe E. Brown picture called *When's Your Birthday?* (that same year he also tried in vain to produce a cartoon series of his own based on E.R. Burroughs's John Carter stories).

Clampett's star rose in the following years with a number of imaginative *Porky Pig* cartoons such as "Porky's Badtime Story" and "Porky in Wackyland." He also

Bob Clampett, "Horton Hatches the Egg." © Warner Brothers.

helped assure the solid success of the Bugs Bunny character in such entries as "What's Cookin', Doc?" "Falling Hare" and "Corny Concerto" (featuring Bugs at his most obnoxious during a Johann Strauss recital). In the late 1940s Clampett was one of the trio of directors who propelled the Warner cartoons to unheard-of popularity. In addition to the many *Bugs Bunny, Porky Pig* and *Daffy Duck* shorts he directed, he did such ground-breaking cartoons as *Horton Hatches the Egg* (from a Dr. Seuss story), *Tin Pan Alley Cats* (a wild and raucous musical parody) and the morale-boosting *Russian Rhapsody,* also known as *The Gremlin from the Kremlin.* He also introduced Tweety Pie the canary in the 1942 "A Tale of Two Kitties."

Clampett left Warner in 1946, worked briefly for Columbia and then formed his own studio, turning out animation commercials. In the late 1940s he created the highly successful puppet show *Time for Beany* for television. Beany and his friends, Captain Huffenpuff and Cecil the Seasick Sea Serpent, became favorites of the public and lasted in syndication well into the 1960s. Clampett later took his puppet characters on tour, turned out a few animation commercials, and lectured on college campuses. He has received many awards, including three Emmys and an Annie Award from ASIFA. His work has been studied and analyzed by scholars in the field of animation who recognize him as one of the outstanding craftsmen of the form. He died in Detroit, Mich., on May 2, 1984.

M.H.

CLARK, JAMES ALFRED (1886-19?) American cartoonist and illustrator born in Eustis, Florida, in 1886. James Clark was raised in Springfield, Massachusetts, and studied art at the Connecticut League of Art Students in Hartford. While studying and working on early jobs, he fell under the artistic influence of fellow artist René Vincent, a Frenchman—and friends dubbed Clark with the nickname "René," which stuck.

Clark was in the forefront of the field of illustrators when the markets shifted from the popular monthlies to the weeklies. In the late 1910s he drew for the comic weeklies and appeared frequently in *Judge* in the early 1920s. His cartoons were marked by simplicity of line and masterful spotting. His decorative drawings in *Judge* were often complemented by a single-tone shade of color.

After the mid-1920s the bulk of his work was in advertising, a field which he led in both influence and awards. Here he showed that watercolors were also his domain, although he never abandoned his restrained but striking pen-and-ink work. Clark won many awards from the Art Directors Club and ultimately became president of his advertising agency, Calkins and Holden. The date of his death has not been ascertained.

R.M.

CLARKE, ROBERT JAMES (1926-) American cartoonist and illustrator born in Port Chester, New York, on January 25, 1926. Raised in the neighboring town of Mamaroneck, New York, Bob Clarke was always interested in cartooning as a child and got his first break by winning a high school art contest. The prize was the opportunity to help Robert Ripley on his syndicated comic strip, *Ripley's Believe It or Not!*

During 1943 and 1944, Bob Clarke did research and some spot art and lettering on *Ripley's Believe It or Not!* Upon graduation from high school he immediately enlisted in the army. World War II in Europe was winding down, and Clarke was assigned to Germany and *Stars and Stripes,* the armed forces newspaper, as art editor in 1945. He returned to the United States as a civilian in 1946 but spent the year recovering from illness contracted while in the military. In 1947 he began working for a Madison Avenue advertising agency, and when he left agency work to freelance in 1955, he was an art director at Dancer, Fitzgerald and Sample.

Bob Clarke got his chance to join the *MAD* magazine group of freelance cartoonists as a result of the Bill Gaines and Harvey Kurtzman split in 1955. *MAD* needed some new cartoonists, and the information was passed on to Clarke by his friend from army days and fellow cartoonist Gill Fox. Samples were submitted and accepted. A two-page story entitled "Motorists Beware" was Bob Clarke's first artwork published in *MAD.*

With *MAD* his cartoons have often illustrated parodies of advertising, a natural for him given his years of ad agency experience. Generally he considers himself to be "a troubleshooter," illustrating pieces that don't fit the special talents of other *MAD* artists. Bob Clarke's style emphasizes controlled line drawing and is considerably tighter than many of the other *MAD* artists'. The end result is a sophisticated look based on line rather than wash tones.

Besides his work for *MAD,* Bob Clarke has done straight and humorous illustration for many trade journals such as *Fleet Owner, Electronics* and *Data Communications.* He's done a series of humorous covers for *American Legion* and cartooned for *Fortune* magazine. Clarke has also illustrated four original *MAD* paperback books that do not reprint material previously published: *MADvertizing* by Dick DeBartolo (1972); and *MAD's Turned On Zoo* (1974), *MAD Jumble* (1975) and *More MAD About Sports* (1977), all by

Frank Jacobs. In the 1980s he developed a series of books based on the TV show *The Littles*. He later moved from New York to Seaford, Delaware, whence he still regularly contributes to *MAD*.

B.C.

CLAUDIUS
See Ceccon, Silvius Petrus Claudius.

CLAY, EDWARD WILLIAMS (1799-1857) American cartoonist born in Philadelphia, Pennsylvania, on April 19, 1799. Edward Clay was a midshipman under Commodore Perry in the War of 1812 and later studied law, being admitted to the bar in Philadelphia in 1825. Clay became an etcher, engraver and cartoonist in Philadelphia (1825-36) and New York City (1837 to about 1840), after which he deserted the artist's craft to become a public servant, holding such jobs as clerk of the Delaware orphan's court.

During his career as a cartoonist Clay was one of several artists responsible for introducing the lithograph as a cartooning medium; his most famous cartoon is of a devastated Andrew Jackson in the wake of the Peggy Eaton scandal. "Rats Leaving a Falling House" was judged one of the most effective and professional cartoons of early 19th-century America by several critics.

Clay published volumes of his cartoons and produced *Life in Philadelphia* and *Sketches of Character* (both in 1829). He contributed to Child's *Views of Philadelphia* and was remembered as a merciless caricaturist. While in New York he drew his cartoons for the firm of Henry R. Robinson, a prominent lithographer and printmaker. Clay died on December 31, 1857, in New York City.

R.M.

CLAY, JOHN CECIL (1875-ca. 1930) American cartoonist and illustrator born in Ronceverte, Greenbrier County, West Virginia, on April 2, 1875. John Clay was educated at the Friends School in Washington, D.C., and received art training at the Students League of Washington (1895-96) and New York's Art Students League (1897-98).

Clay, in the late 1890s, became a frequent contributor to *Life* and in 1899 broke into the illustration market with a sale to the *Saturday Evening Post.* Among his books are *In Love's Garden* (1904), *Portraits of Celebrated Actresses* (1905), *Portraits of Celebrated Authors* (1906) and *The Lovers' Mother Goose* (1907).

Perhaps "Vanity" is Clay's most famous cartoon. Originally drawn for *Life,* it shows a high-fashion lady at her dressing mirror; the mirror and its reflection, upon studied observation, give the effect of a human skull. It has been reprinted in the millions and is still sold today, even in Times Square souvenir shops. It is fitting that Clay is remembered by this cartoon, because it is characteristic of his output—he often dealt with society in a moralistic and melancholy way. His renderings were in wash—here he was in the vanguard of the school *Life* nurtured through the 1890s and the early years of this century—and careful pencil shadings. In these techniques he was a master.

R.M.

The principal characters of "Clémentine Chérie." © Jean Bellus.

CLÉMENTINE CHÉRIE (France) Clémentine, the daughter of a middle-aged, middle-class couple, made her debut in the weekly magazine *Jours de France* in the early 1950s. The creation of French cartoonist Jean Bellus, she has had a successful career for more than a dozen years.

A comely, vivacious and charming brunette with a Jean Seberg haircut, Clémentine seems to spend most of her time dancing at parties, gossiping with girl friends, buying things and in general having no graver worries than how to put off an eager beau or catch the eye of an indifferent one. She represents the modern though not fully liberated young woman, and her bald, rotund father and plump mother regard her tolerantly, even permissively, reacting to her adventures in a manner more amused than shocked.

Of the thousands of well-drawn, humorous Clémentine cartoons, often enhanced by color, a few hundred have been issued in albums and translated. The last one, *Vivre avec Son Temps* ("To Live with the Times"), was published in 1967, the year Bellus died.

P.H.

CLERICETTI, GUIDO (1939-) Italian cartoonist and writer for radio and television, born in Milan on September 10, 1939. After graduating in Law at the Catholic University of Milan, he studied at Brera Art School. He contributed regularly humorous cartoons to the illustrated magazine *Epoca* from 1964 to 1974, when he was dismissed since, as a Catholic, he opposed divorce on which that year a referendum was being held. He then moved to the Catholic weekly magazine *Famiglia Cristiana* to which he contributed regularly from 1974 to 1987. He has also produced cartoons for other Catholic periodicals, such as the weekly magazine *Il Sabato* (1978-1988), the daily *Avvenire* and the magazine *Studi cattolici*.

Clericetti has written a tale for children, *Il drago vecchio* (1978), made an animated cartoon, directed the weekly *Il cartone* (1996-1997), and written texts for radio broadcast-

ATTITUDES
HIGH SCHOOL

Guido Clericetti. © Guido Clericetti.

ings and television programs. His humor is as soft as his drawing style in which the eyes of his characters are quite recognizable—they look like two little crosses. His satirical interest lies more in social and moral issues than in political ones. But when his religious convictions are at stake he can assume an ironic attitude towards politics, though his irony has a charming flavor.

Some of his cartoons have been collected in book format: *...e il settimo giorno sorrise* (1965), *Ma tu ci credi all'inferno?* (1969), *Soprappensieri* (1978), *Contraddizionario* (1979), *Clericettario* (1993), *C'era una volta il Medioevo* (1975), *Famiglia e tu: istruzioni per l'uso* (1996) Clericetti has been awarded several prizes: Palma d'oro at Bordighera (1974), Premio Forte dei Marmi for Political Satire (1974), Dattero d'Argento at Bordighera (1978), Premio Scacchiera at Marostica (1989).

G.C.C.

CLOSE TO HOME (U.S.) After working for several years as an engineer, John McPherson, who graduated from Bucknell University in 1983, became a freelance cartoonist in 1990 when he started to contribute to a number of national periodicals. This early success was followed on November 30, 1992 by the daily and later Sunday debut of *Close to Home* in some 50 newspapers. Today, distributed by Universal Press Syndicate, the panel cartoon appears in about 700 papers and magazines.

It is a sassy, quirky depiction of contemporary home and family life, which owes much to Gary Larson for its off-the-wall humor and rudimentary style. Whether McPherson presents a surgeon in his O.R. being slowed down by the billing clerk ("Whoa! Whoa!... You're getting way ahead of the insurance paperwork") or lobsters in shackles being escorted under armed guard to their tank as shocked restaurant diners look on, he likes to use a cluttered scene, the better to emphasize overall absurdity.

Because any situation can and does become fodder for McPherson's satirical grinder, he pokes fun at premarital

MORTAR MIX
2-13
"OK. There are no monsters under your bed! There will never be monsters under your bed again, ever! Now get to sleep."

"Close to Home." © John McPherson.

counseling, Internet romances, blood drives, or chocolate-flavored stamps ("Another marketing success for the Postal Service"). However, hearth, home, and their environs remain his principal targets. Thus, he portrays the clever dunce who brings home D's and F's altered to Fabulous!, Far Out!, or Darn Good! and whose jubilant mother exclaims, "*Another* 'Fantastic'?! Danny, you have *really* turned your grades around! I am so proud of you!", or he presents a modern parenting class in how to dress your baby using a rambunctious piglet as a highly realistic model.

In telling it like it is, McPherson has created a world in which suburbanites and city-dwellers, marrieds and singles, parents and childless couples, all can acknowledge how quirky, and how very funny, life can be. It is no wonder, then, that many of his cartoons have been reprinted in collections and page-a-day calendars.

P.L.H.

COBEAN, SAM (1917-1951) American magazine gag cartoonist born in Gettysburg, Pennsylvania, in 1917. Sam Cobean was raised in Altoona, Pennsylvania, and attended the University of Oklahoma. Following college he worked for the Walt Disney studios and other motion picture companies in Hollywood. He joined the U.S. Army Signal Corps during World War II and while in the army met Charles Addams, already well known as a *New Yorker* magazine cartoonist. The two men became close friends, and Addams encouraged him to submit cartoons to the *New Yorker.* By 1944 Cobean's cartoons were a regular feature there.

Sam Cobean's most famous cartoon image, variations of which extend throughout all his published work, was based on the idea that ever since women began wearing clothes, men have been trying to visualize how women would look without clothes. His X-ray-eyed heroes' thought balloons showed any woman who passed by in the nude. This international masculine pastime was first published in the *New Yorker* in June 1945. Scores of variations on the theme followed. For example, a man passes a woman modeling a dress before a triple mirror in a clothing store. The man's thoughts conjure up four nude views of her—front, back and both sides. In another a man passes by four bathhouses at the beach, and his thoughts show four beautiful unclad women changing into swimsuits. Another recurring theme Cobean used was the young, presumably unwed mother with her child in her arms being turned away from home, dogs, children, artists, models and bars.

Cobean drew easily with economy of line. Besides the *New Yorker,* his cartoons were published in the *Saturday Evening Post* and *Collier's.* His cartoons have a spontaneous, unlabored look to them. Some gray wash and black areas were used in the design, but in general he preferred minimal use of these techniques in favor of simple line drawing.

In 1950 a collection of his *New Yorker* cartoons, *Cobean's Naked Eye,* was published in both hardback and paperback editions. The collection was the cartoon-book best seller of the year. Then, on the night of July 2, 1951, Sam Cobean's brilliant career was tragically ended. The Jaguar sports car he was driving crashed into the rear of another car near Watkins Glen, New York, and Cobean was killed instantly. He was 34.

Shortly after Cobean's death, Charles Addams said, "I hope he knew or at least suspected that he will be long remembered as one of the great comic artists of all time."

Sam Cobean. © Anne M. Cobean.

An anthology, *The Cartoons of Cobean,* was published in 1952. The book was edited by Saul Steinberg, with a foreword by Charles Addams. In 1954, the fledgling *Playboy* magazine also paid posthumous tribute to Sam Cobean's cartoons.

B.C.

Neg Cochran, "The Worry Wart." © NEA.

COCHRAN, NEGLEY (1913-) American cartoonist born in Oak Park, Illinois, on August 27, 1913. After studies at Western Reserve University and the Cleveland Institute of Art, Neg Cochran worked in the advertising office of a Cleveland department store. In 1936 he joined the staff of the Newspaper Enterprise Association (NEA) in Cleveland. (His father, Negley Cochran, was an NEA editor and had discovered many budding cartoonists.) Soon thereafter Cochran started assisting J.R. Williams on the daily *Out Our Way* panel, and especially on the Sunday page, which featured the adventures of the Willett family. Cochran stayed close to Williams's style and made the *Willetts* family strip into an endearing chronicle of domestic life in mid-America.

When Williams died in 1957, Cochran took over the daily *Out Our Way,* which he continued in his typically gentle, unobtrusive manner until his retirement in 1975. A solid, dependable craftsman, Neg Cochran is one of the unsung heroes of the daily newspaper panel, a medium that has remained neglected for too long.

M.H.

COCO, GIUSEPPE (1936-) Italian cartoonist born in Biancavilla near Catania, on May 1, 1936. Since he was 16 and a student at an art school, he contributed regularly to the humorous cartoon magazine *Travaso.* After graduation and a short abstract painting activity, in 1960 he moved to Milan where he became a regular contributor for an increasing number of Italian, European and American

CRISI ENERGETICA

Guiseppe Coco. © *Guiseppe Coco.*

magazines like *Epoca, Europeo, Grazia, Amica, Playmen, Panorama, L'Espresso, L'Avanti, Corriere Medico, Humor Graphic, Playboy, Punch, Saturday Evening Post, Stern, Ele Ola, Paris Match,* etc.

Coco is inclined to smile on social manners and costumes rather than on politics. His style is clear and linear, his situations are sometimes surrealistic but the comic outcome is always guaranteed. Coco's graphic humor is at its best in wordless, self-evident single panels. This accounts for his success at home and abroad, where he is the Italian humorous cartoonist more widely read. Coco has also created a comic strip on the medical profession, *Esculapia,* which is still appearing on various periodicals. A certain amount of his cartoons have been collected in books: *Coco est content* (1968), *I satiri* (1980), *È grave, dottore? (1987), Attenti al sedere* (1988). Some of these titles have also been printed also in France, Germany, Holland, Spain and Portugal.

Coco has also illustrated several advertising campaigns for national products, like Perofil (handkercheif), Vino Turà (wine), Telefonino Sip (cell phone), or for safety at work.

Coco has been awarded several national and international prizes in Montreal; Canada; Bordighera; Italy; Istanbul, Turkey, and elsewhere.

In 1986, Coco returned to Sicily, where he now lives and works.

G.C.C.

COELHO, EDUARDO TEIXEIRA (1919-) Portuguese illustrator and cartoonist born in Angra do Heroísmo, Azores Islands, on January 4, 1919. E.T. Coelho went to Lisbon at the age of 11 to attend a commercial course. He published his first drawings, some short, naive anecdotes, in the weekly *Sempre Fixe* in 1936. He improved rapidly and produced some very good illustrations at the beginning of the 1940s in *Colecção de Aventuras, Senhor Doutor, Engenhocas e Coisas Práticas* and *Filmagem.* Starting in 1943 in the magazine *O Mosquito,* he achieved total mastery in the illustration of novels of historic, modern or fantastic characteristics.

It was also for *O Mosquito* that Coelho drew his first comic strips, among which *Os Guerreiros do Lago Verde, O Grande Rifle Branco, Os Náufragos do Barco Sem Nome, O Feitiço do Homem Branco* and *O Falcão Negro* deserve mention. His masterpieces, however, are *Trilogia das Mouras* ("Trilogy of the Moorish Women"), *O Caminho do Oriente* ("The Far East Path"), *A Lei da Selva* ("The Law of the Jungle") and the comic strip versions of some of Eça de Queiroz's stories. Coelho also had drawings published in daily newspapers (*O Século, Diário* de *Noticias*), magazines (*Portugal Ilustrado, Auditorium*), books (*Caminhos da Terra Santa, Lições de Ginástica Infantil, A Nossa Pátria*), and on the covers of volumes of the *Biblioteca dos Rapazes* and the *Biblioteca das Raparigas.* A great part of his work was also published in the Spanish magazine *Chicos.* For the festivities directed in 1947 by Leitão de Barros to commemorate the 800th anniversary of the reconquest of Lisbon from the Moors, Coelho did the models, sketches and drawings included in the illuminations of the allegoric messages.

Because of the restrictions imposed by the Portuguese press on the expansion of his art, Coelho emigrated in 1953 and worked for publishers in England, France and other countries. The characters he created after that date derive from the Viking era (Ragnar, Bjorni, Eric le Rouge), the Middle Ages (Robin des Bois, Le Furet, Yves le Loup) or other periods (Davy Crockett, Till l'Espiègle, Cartouche, Wango). In Portugal he sometimes signed simply *ETC,* whereas in France he mainly used the pseudonym "Martin Sièvre." Among his most recent works are some chapters of *Histoire de France en Bandes Dessinées* (under the signature Eduardo Coelho) and documentaries about Italian armory. In 1985-86 he realized the monumental *La Mémoire des Celtes* ("Memory of the Celts"). He now resides in Italy.

Coelho's early style—with its thin, sinuous line and long, dynamic figures weaving in a spiral composition—prompted the Spanish artist Emílio Freixas to call him a "poet of line" (in *Lecciones de Dibujo Artístico*). This initially clear and fluent style has gradually become more static and detailed, as can be seen in the work Coelho has done since his departure from Portugal. In 1973 he received the Best Foreign Illustrator award at the Lucca Festival. Coelho, who presently lives in Florence, Italy, is married and has a daughter.

C.P.

COHL, EMILE
See Courtet, Emile.

COLIZZI, GIOACCHINO (1894-198?) Italian cartoonist born near Rome, Italy, in 1894. After completing his studies, Gioacchino Colizzi (better known under the pseudonym "Attalo") joined the State Railway Authority as an accountant for the planning office in Rome. He had always loved to draw as a hobby, and he sent some of his cartoons to the humor and satirical magazine *Serenissimo* in 1920. These were accepted, and Attalo continued to contribute cartoons to the publication until it was suspended by the Fascist authorities in the late 1920s. Colizzi, who did not want to lose his civil service post, then judged it prudent to switch from cartoons to movie posters.

When the humor magazine *Marc' Aurelio* started publication in the 1930s, Attalo was among its first cartoonists. Federico Fellini, who was writing a column for the maga-

Gioacchino Colizzi. © Attalo.

zine at that time, recalls, "Attalo very seldom came to the magazine. . . . The captions were sent to the railway office for him to illustrate." Among the characters made famous by Attalo's cartoons are "the ugly Genoveffa," always chasing after her elusive lover Gastone, and especially "the barfly who told his friends," whose boasts were always deflated in the cartoons. He retired in the 1970s and died in the early 1980s.

The cartoons Attalo has drawn for the pages of *Marc' Aurelio, Marforio, Pasquino, Il Travaso* and others number over ten thousand; the most famous are those on the theme of "the easygoing war" (waged with cork-guns and water pistols). Fellini was inspired by Attalo's depictions of old Rome when he made his movie *Roma,* thus paying a deserved homage to his former co-worker.

S.T.

COLL Y COLL, JOSÉ (1923-1984) Spanish cartoonist born in Barcelona, Spain, in 1923. José Coll graduated from art school and started his career in the 1940s as an illustrator. In 1948 his first cartoons were published in the magazine *La Risa,* followed by more cartoons in most major Spanish publications. Coll's most important work appeared in the comic weekly *TBO,* where, starting in 1953, he had an average of four cartoons or comic strips running in each issue. Since the late 1960s, however, his output has been decreasing. Illness dogged him during most of his later years, but he had the consolation of being rediscovered in the 1980s; and an antholgy of his cartoons, *De Coll a Coll,* was published shortly before his death in 1984.

Coll's characters move with incredible elasticity: they shrink, bend, spring back like rubber dolls, but always retain their verisimilitude. Coll creates a highly personal, original and coherent universe. The "gags" do not arise from the characters themselves, but from the situations in which they are placed, and the cartoons are almost completely silent. Coll is a master of visual and sequential organization, and his success is due to the particular attention he pays to landscapes and backgrounds, his carefully delineated graphics and his respect for perspective, which is unusual among cartoonists.

J.M.

COLLINS, CLIVE (1942-) Clive Collins, one of the top British newspaper and magazine cartoonists and a man very active in the cause of cartoonists, was born at Weston-Super-Mare on February 6, 1942. He studied graphic design at Kingston School of Art from 1958, and worked as an extra in movies for a while.

He began freelancing cartoons to *Punch* from 1964, and became the staff editorial cartoonist on *The Sun,* a daily newspaper, in 1969. He moved to the Sunday paper *People* in 1970 returning to *The Sun* in 1971 to take over the racing tipster cartoon "Lucky Jim" on the death of Gordon "Gog" Hogg. He continued this series to 1985. He was also used as a stand-in cartoonist for Franklin of *The Sun* and "Jak"

"Colonel Heezaliar." © Bray Studios.

of the *Evening Standard*, before finally settling down on the staff of the *Daily Mirror* in 1986.

His other freelance cartoons were drawn for *Reader's Digest*, *Sporting Life*, and for the American magazines *Mad* and *Playboy*. He was elected Chairman of the Cartoonists Club of Great Britain, a post he held from 1990 to 1994. His many awards began with the Glen Grant Cartoonist of the Year in 1979, followed by Knokke-Heist (Belgium) in 1982, Montreal (1984), Skopje (1986), five successive Japanese Awards starting in 1980, and Cartoonist of the Year (CC of GB) (1984, 1985 and 1987). His books include *The Idiot's Guide to Sex* (1991).

D.G.

COLONEL HEEZALIAR (U.S.) John Randolph Bray created *Colonel Heezaliar* in 1914 for Pathé Exchange. The colonel, a short, middle-aged, rotund man, was modeled after the character of Baron Munchausen, and his adventures were a variation on the tall tale; he got himself into all kinds of predicaments from which he escaped by extraordinary means (tying together the tails of a couple of lions or getting out of quicksand by grabbing the feet of overflying geese, for example). The colonel, with his never-ending wild animal hunts in the remotest parts of the globe, is also said to have been a lampoon of Theodore Roosevelt.

"Colonel Heezaliar in Africa" seems to have been the first cartoon in the series. J.R. Bray directed most of the early cartoons in an adequate if somewhat stilted style (the 1916 "Colonel Heezaliar Wins the Pennant" and "Colonel Heezaliar Hobo" are two good examples). In the 1920s Bray left the responsibility for the series to Vernon Stallings, who directed the best-remembered of the cartoons, such as "Colonel Heezaliar and the Ghost," "Colonel Heezaliar Detective" and "Colonel Heezaliar in the African Jungles."

The advent of sound was fatal to the series, which was discontinued in the late 1920s. Its importance lies not only in the fact that *Colonel Heezaliar* was one of the earliest cartoon series ever produced, but also in that it was the first successful American series of animated films based on an original cartoon character.

M.H.

COME ON STEVE! (G.B.) "Come on, Steve!"—the cry of the crowd at prewar racetracks as champion jockey Steve Donoghue rode for yet another win—formed the ready-made title to a weekly strip drawn by Roland Davies. Steve, a cheerful cart horse, began his adventures in the *Sunday Express* on March 6, 1932, and became the first British newspaper strip character to appear in sound cartoon films.

In 1935 Davies taught himself animation from available books, and with a camera that cost him 18 shillings, he set up a small studio in his country kitchen. Seven months later he had a somewhat primitive and jerky silent cartoon, but on the strength of a showing the minor British distributor Butcher's Films agreed to back him for a series in sound. With one or two professional animators and some students from the Ipswich Art School, Davies completed his first sound cartoon, the black-and-white *Steve Steps Out*, in 1936. It was not trade-shown until December of that year, by which time two additional, better cartoons had been completed: *Steve of the River* (a burlesque of the Alexander Korda feature film based on Edgar Wallace's *Sanders of the River)* and *Steve's Treasure Hunt*.

Davies, addressing the Ipswich Rotarians, stated, "A film could be produced in about eight weeks by (the) staff of 43, and . . . except for twelve artists, (the) staff consisted of local boys and girls, practically all products of the Ipswich School of Art."

Steve's Cannon Crackers came in April 1937 and *Steve in Bohemia* and *Steve-Cinderella* in May. The first two films were published as picture-story paperbacks by The Children's Press.

D.G.

CONACHER, JOHN (1876-1947) American cartoonist born in 1876. Around 1907 John Conacher's drawings began to

We're coming to it:—"Oi hear they do be sindin' messages now widout woires er poles. Faith, it's wondherful toimes we're livin' in, Dinnis!"—"It is, Moike, Shure, th' way things is goin' we'll be aboe t' thravel widout lavin'home, wan av thim days."
John Conacher.

appear in *Life;* they were "semi-cartoony" but promised polish because of their controlled lines and grasp of composition and anatomy. By 1912 Conacher was a polished illustrator-type cartoonist, and his work was showcased in *Life* and *Judge.* He never did covers and only occasionally strayed to do straight illustration for the popular monthlies. Unlike fellow cartoonists such as Angus MacDonall who dabbled in washes and sentimental pieces, he remained loyal to pen and ink and to purely humorous cartoons.

His cartoons dealt with absurdities, contradictions and character delineations. His mature style was wonderfully realistic and detailed. Several of Conacher's cartoons were widely circulated, particularly one in *Judge,* a double-page cartoon done after Lindbergh's transatlantic flight in 1927. By the 1930s Conacher had retired from cartooning; the day of the illustrative cartoon was over. Conacher died in Rowayton, Connecticut, on December 14, 1947.

R.M.

"Drunk? . . . Of course I'm not drunk!"
Paul Conrad. © Los Angeles Times.

CONRAD, PAUL FRANCIS (1924-) American cartoonist born in Cedar Rapids, Iowa, on June 27, 1924. Paul Conrad grew up in Ding Darling country and claims that for years he hardly knew there was such a thing as a cartoonist other than Ding. With this influence, after a five-year hitch in the army, he studied art at the University of Iowa and graduated with a B.S. degree in art. Shortly thereafter, in 1950, he joined the *Denver Post* as political cartoonist. His work attracted wide attention for its cleverness and sharp commentaries. He was syndicated weekly by the Hall Syndicate and later by the L.A. Times Syndicate until the *Times* itself picked him up in 1964. He has remained in Los Angeles since.

Conrad has won a gaggle of awards, including Pulitzers in 1964 and 1971; the Sigma Delta Chi awards for 1962, 1969 and 1971; and the Overseas Press Club award in 1969. He has lectured on cartoons and been reprinted widely. He won the Pulitzer Prize for a third time in 1984. He retired in 1993, but continues to draw five cartoons a week for the Los Angeles Times Syndicate.

His style is reminiscent of Ding's but has a striking individuality that especially stands out during the post-Oliphant era. Conrad has even retained, like Herblock, the integrity of the vertical format and crayon rendering. His concepts are among cartooning's most forceful, and his drawings display an amazingly consistent quality. The *Post* and *Times* are both independent Republican papers, but Conrad's views have usually been to their left.

R.M.

CONTES À REBOURS (France) Richard Peyzaret (who was later to sign "F'Murr") started his collaboration with the weekly *Pilote* with *Contes à Rebours* ("Wrong-Way Tales"), a hilarious series of parodies which first appeared, appropriately, on April Fool's Day in 1971.

In these artfully addled tales (usually spread over one or two pages), F'Murr took a resolutely revisionist view of folk stories. Thus the Big Bad Wolf was pictured as the fall guy (fall beast?) in a power play between Red Riding Hood and her eager grandmother, Cinderella was depicted as a sobbing little hypocrite who blamed her poor stepsisters for her own shortcomings, and so on. The artwork, slap dash and falsely naive, provided an appropriate graphic counterpoint to the sardonic commentary.

Contes à Rebours ran only for a short period and was discontinued on December 28, 1972. It is apparent that the series bewildered many of the readers of *Pilote* during its short existence, but it also won F'Murr a small but devoted coterie of fans and admirers. All the tales were later collected into a book published by Editions Minoutchine in Paris. Now considered classics, they have been reprinted time and again, most recently in 1979 and 1993.

M.H.

COONTOWN SKETCHES (U.S.) On July 13, 1899, E.W. Kemble began a regular series of cartoons based on life in an impoverished black rural community for *Life* magazine. The series ultimately came to be called *Coontown Sketches.*

Fully half of Kemble's output at this time consisted of black-oriented cartoons, and his handling was expert, sympathetic and wildly funny. Many of the situations in the cartoons were based on high-society themes or fads of the day transferred to the black milieu. Some were rendered in pen and ink, giving free rein to Kemble's masterful crosshatching, but some were executed in wash—a then-recent innovation for magazine reproduction—and are handsome comic masterpieces.

The *Coontown Sketches* series continued for several years, with the cartoons collected in *Coontown Sketches, Coontown's 400* and *Kemble's Coons.*

R.M.

CORDEIRO, CALISTO (1877-1957) Brazilian cartoonist and painter born in Niteroí, a suburb of Rio de Janeiro,

Brazil, in 1877. Calisto Cordeiro did his first painting at age 13 while working as an apprentice at the Casa de Moeda (the mint) in Rio. In 1898 his first cartoon was published in *O Mercurío* under the pseudonym "Klixto," by which he has since become known.

For over thirty years Klixto contributed cartoons to all major publications in Rio, such as *O Riso, D. Quixote, Carêta, Fon-Fon!, A Caricatura, A Semana Illustrada, Gazeta de Notícias* and *O Cruzeiro.* In the early 1900s he was instrumental in the founding of no less than four magazines: *O Malho, Avança, Degas* and *O Tagarela.*

From 1913 on, Klixto created carnival themes and costumes for one of the carnival associations in Rio. He received a multitude of honors, including the bronze medal (1916) and later the silver medal (1954) of the National Salon of Fine Arts. He was a member of the National Academy of Art, and his works were displayed in many exhibitions throughout Brazil. He was also highly regarded as a painter, poster designer and poet.

Klixto's drawings display an elegance of line that excludes the baroque and the grotesque. He showed a predilection for depicting members of café society, easy women and barflies in ironical but compassionate compositions that often recall the themes dear to Toulouse-Lautrec. He died in São Paulo in 1957.

A.M.

Siegfried Cornelius ("Cosper"). © PIB.

CORNELIUS, SIEGFRIED (1911-) Danish cartoonist of international renown born in Copenhagen, Denmark, on April 20, 1911. The son of opera singer Peter Cornelius, Siegfried ("Cosper") Cornelius debuted as a jazz musician in the 1930s. He later began to draw almost surrealistic cartoons that editors thought too naive and stereotyped. As he could not find a market, he founded the humor magazine *Hudibras* in 1943, together with Asger Jerrild. There, his and other young artists' cartoons—lightly frivolous, sometimes pornographic—settled with the prudery and narrow-mindedness of the middle class by proving that one can be naughty without being dirty.

Cornelius worked closely with Jørgen Mogensen (forming the famous "Moco" signature which combined the first two letters of their surnames) and moved to Nice, where together they drew the comic strip *Alfredo* (*Moco* in the United States). Each cartoonist delivered three of the six weekly strips, but they were almost indistinguishable from each other. Most characteristic of Cornelius, however, is his daily panel *Cosperier*, syndicated to 80 European dailies. Within its limitation of crazy nonsense and sex, *Cosperier* has founded a humorous tradition that is still alive. Also worth mentioning are his Sunday page, *Mr. Mox,* and his one-column panels syndicated under the pen name "Pollux" by PIB, Copenhagen.

Cornelius's humor, which at the outset was based on an untranslatable play on words, is sometimes very tough (for example, a father to his child: "No, I don't know where the little kids come from—and if I knew, I would send you back!").

Cornelius has made countless theater decorations for Copenhagen revues and cabarets and done book covers and magazine illustrations. He and Virgil Partch are kindred souls. He moved to Rome towards the end of 1950 and lived in Venice until 1973. He is now working in Copenhagen.

J.S.

CORNET I PALAU, GAIETÁ (1878-1945) Spanish cartoonist born in Barcelona, Spain, in 1878. Gaietá Cornet studied engineering at the University of Barcelona, but he never

Gaietá Cornet.

pursued an engineering career. His first cartoons were published in *L'Esquella de la Torratxa* at the turn of the century. In 1902 he became the director of *Cu-Cut!*, a magazine gravitating towards the conservative Catalan party, La Lliga Catalana. It was in this magazine that Cornet realized his best work in terms of both quantity of output and quality of draftsmanship. When *Cu-Cut!* ceased publication in 1912, Cornet went on to contribute cartoons to such publications as *En Patufet, Virolet, L'Esquitx,* and most importantly, *La Veu de Catalunya,* where he openly expressed his politically conservative views.

Cornet's drawings are as clear and straightforward as is his humor, based on the life-styles, customs and stereotypes that he found around him. His lines are often moralistic and didactic in tone and intention. He died in Barcelona in 1945.

J.M.

CORREIA DIAS DE ARAÚJO, FERNANDO (1893-1935) Brazilian cartoonist born in Pantoja, Portugal, in 1893. Fernando Correia Dias studied art at the University of Coimbra in Portugal. Starting in 1912, he regularly contributed cartoons to the magazines *A Rajada* (Coimbra), *Aguia* (Porto) and *Illustração Portuguêsa* (Lisbon). In 1914 he went to Rio de Janeiro to organize an exhibition of his works that included not only cartoons and illustrations but also ceramics and caricatural characters carved in wood. The success of his exhibition made Correia Dias decide to stay in Rio, and he soon found himself very much in demand. For the next 20 years he tirelessly contributed cartoons and illustrations to most major Brazilian magazines (*O Pais, Fon-Fon!, D. Quixote, Illustração Brasileira, Revista da Semana, Brazilian American,* etc.) and newspapers (*O Jornal, O Radical, Diário de Notícias, O Globo*).

Correia Dias also illustrated many books by Brazilian authors, as well as a revamped version of *The Arabian Nights*. He was active in newspaper circles and managed a printing plant for a time (1916-17). He died a suicide in Rio de Janeiro in 1935.

A.M.

CORY, J. CAMPBELL (1867-ca. 1925) American cartoonist born in Waukegan, Illinois, on September 11, 1867. J.C. Cory was educated in Waukegan and began cartooning in New York in 1896. His style was breezy, with slashing, thick-and-thin pen strokes held together by beautiful areas of precise, old-fashioned crosshatching; he and Fred Morgan of the *Philadelphia Inquirer* were probably the last great crosshatch political cartoonists. Throughout his career the doctrinaire Democrat drew for many of America's largest newspapers and magazines, including the *New York World* and *Harper's Weekly*.

Cory's significance lies in his enterprising approach to cartooning, however. He was a self-starter, almost a vagabond, who worked in many formats, experimented with the business end and was a pioneer syndicator. As a publisher, he put out the *Great West* monthly in 1907-08 and the *Bee*, an oversized chromolithographed humorous weekly, during the Spanish-American War. In 1912, beginning a practice that was to continue for two decades, he became a paid cartoonist for a political party; the Democrats supplied Cory cartoons to any paper that could use them. Soon afterward, in the early days of large-scale syndication, Cory started a syndicate, distributing his own cartoons and those of others. He ran a correspondence school and published books teaching the elements of cartooning, including *Cory's Hands* and *The Cartoonist's Art*. Active in other spheres as well, Cory was a prospector, miner, champion balloonist, pioneer aviator, big game hunter, sportswriter and athlete.

. . . said the game chick to the old Rooster.
Campbell Cory, 1919.

Cory was responsible for helping many youngsters into professional cartooning careers. Charles Kuhn was one, and Cory's niece, Fanny Y. Cory, was another; just after she had her first work published in *St. Nicholas,* she became a featured contributor to the *Bee*, and her uncle boosted her early work through newspaper syndication as well.

R.M.

COSGROVE-HALL (G.B.) Cosgrove-Hall sounds like a grand English country seat but is in fact a combination of the surnames of two leading animators, Brian Cosgrove and Mark Hall, who started their production company with the partnership of John Hambley of Thames Television. For a studio they converted an old tobacco and confectionary warehouse in Chorlton-cum-Hardy, near Manchester, and with a staff of 6 they made 39 episodes of their first series, *Chorlton and the Wheelies*, tales of a magic land where the inhabitants had wheels instead of feet (1976). By 1984 the company had grown to 70 people and had produced more than 3,000 minutes of animated film, from 5-minute shorts to 75-minute features.

Brian Cosgrove worked in Independent Television for seven years prior to forming the company. His first cartoon series was *The Magic Ball* (1970) which won awards at Venice and other animation festivals. Mark Hall graduated from Manchester College of Art and Design in 1957 and after National Service worked in ITV for 11 years. The two joined forces in 1971, forming a small independent company to make series for children's television. They made the first *Noddy* series based on Enid Blyton's popular books, and in 1975 produced the musical film *Captain Noah and his Floating Zoo*, based on the Flanders/Horowitz show, for Granada TV. It was chosen as the ITV entry for the Prix Italia.

In 1976 Cosgrove-Hall Productions was set up as a subsidiary of Thames TV, the largest commercial television station in the UK, at the suggestion of senior executive John Hambley, Controller of Children's Programmes. Their biggest success in the animated cartoon class was *Dangermouse* (1985), an animal parody of Danger Man and Superman. Feature-length cartoon and puppet films include *The Pied Piper of Hamelin* from Robert Browning's ever-popular poem (British Film Academy Award 1982), *The Talking Parcel* from Gerald Durrell's fantastic novel, *Cinderella* made without dialogue, and the long-running series *Cockleshell Bay*. *The Wind in the Willows* was a puppet series taken from Kenneth Grahame's classic novel for children, and included a 75-minute feature (1983). Unlike all these juvenile films was *Captain Kremmen.* Made as shorts for the *Kenny Everett Show*, these were adapted into an adult-appealing 25-minute film. Combining adult and child appeal was the 65 episode series *Count Duckula* (1987), which burlesqued the Bram Stoker novel, *Dracula.*

The Government cancellation of Thames TV's franchise in 1991 was virtually the end of the studio, although some production continued, frequently American-financed. There was *The Fool of the World and the Flying Ship* (1992) which won a U.S. Emmy Award, and *BFG: The Big Friendly Giant* from Roald Dahl's book, which won the European Prix Jeunesse. Their last major series was *Truckers*, animated models depicting Terry Pratchett's characters. By 1994 the company was down to a staff of 20, a true tragedy of the transience of commercial television.

D.G.

COSPER

See Cornelius, Siegfried.

COSSIO, CARLO (1907-1964) Italian cartoonist and animator born in Udine, Italy, on January 1, 1907. The Cossio family moved to Milan, where the young Carlo grew up and went to school. After first working as a graphic designer, he went into animation with his brother Vittorio in 1928, at the urging of the painter Bruno Munari. From 1928 to 1931 the Cossio brothers produced a number of advertising shorts. In 1932 they released *Zibillo e l'Orso* ("Zibillo and the Bear"), a silent animated short which is a milestone in Italian animation.

In 1937 the Cossio brothers embarked on a grandiose experiment: to produce in full color, on stereoscopic 70-mm film devised by the engineer Gualtiero Gualtierotti, the tale of chivalry *La Secchia Rapita* ("The Stolen Bucket") and H.G. Wells's fantastic novel *The Time Machine.* The

Carlo and Vittorio Cossio, "Zibillo e l'Orso." © Fratelli Cossio.

films did not find a distributor, however, and the two artists returned to their activities as comic strip cartoonists. During World War II, together with Luigi Giobbe, the brothers produced an animated short titled *Pulcinella i Briganti* ("Punch and the Brigands"), which made children's eyes "open in wonder," as one critic wrote. After the success of this cartoon Carlo Cossio made a sequel without his brother, but again in collaboration with Giobbe: *Pulcinella e il Temporale* ("Punch and the Storm"), with music by Derevitzky.

The difficulty of finding a market for animated cartoons in Italy again drove the brothers to the comics, and Carlo Cossio successfully worked for the weeklies *L'Intrepido* and *L'Audace.* In 1954 he went back to animation briefly, designing the titles for the film *Giove in Doppio Petto* ("Jove in a Double-Breasted Suit"). He died of cancer in Milan on August 10, 1964. (For further information about Carlo Cossio's career in the comics, see *The World Encyclopedia of Comics,* Chelsea House, 1976.)

S.T.

COSSIO, VITTORIO (1911-1984) Italian cartoonist and animator, younger brother of Carlo Cossio, born in Udine, Italy, in 1911. Like his brother, Vittorio Cossio grew up in Milan, and like him he started work as a graphic designer. When Carlo decided to devote himself to animation towards the end of the 1920s, Vittorio, who was already a fine draftsman, agreed to join him; the two brothers thus became pioneers of Italian animation.

The Cossio brothers, with Bruno Munari as designer, produced several advertising shorts between 1928 and 1931. On his own Vittorio directed two shorts in 1931, *Tango dell' Amore* and *Tango del Nomade,* based on songs popular at the time. In 1932 the Cossio brothers brought out *Zibillo* e *l'Orso* ("Zibillo and the Bear"), an open imitation of John Foster's and Frank Rufle's *Tom and Jerry* cartoons, but the film and its characters met with utter indifference.

The Cossio brothers then went back to the comics. Vittorio, who had previously collaborated on *Rin-Tin-Tin, Primarosa* and *Il Corriere dei Piccoli,* took over the comic strip *Furio Almirante* in 1941; in 1945 he created *Raff, Pugnio d'Acciao* ("Raff, the Iron-Fisted"), his most notable success in the field. In the meantime he had gone back to animation, producing *Pulcinella* with his brother in 1941. A fire destroyed the Cossio studio in 1943; after that date Vittorio returned to animation only twice: in 1954, when he and his brother designed the titles for the movie *Giove in Doppio Petto* ("Jove in a Double-Breasted Suit"), and in 1958, when he directed, in collaboration with Luciana Pensuti, the Andersen fable *The Magic Flintlock.*

Vittorio Cossio continued his career as a cartoonist, book illustrator, and painter, alos finding time to manage a book publishing company with youthful vigor, until his death in 1984.

S.T.

COTRIM, ALVARO (1904-) Brazilian cartoonist and caricaturist born in Rio de Janeiro, Brazil, in August 1904. After studying art and drawing in high school and college, Alvaro ("Alvarus") Cotrim sent his first cartoons in 1925 to *A Pátria,* which immediately accepted them. From that moment he became one of Brazil's most popular and respected cartoonists.

Alvarus has been justly mentioned as the Brazilian caricaturist par excellence. His style was influenced in the beginning by contemporary European, and especially French, cartoonists, but he soon found himself, and his signature is as distinctive as his cheerful attitude to life. He is famed for his caricatures of personalities in politics and the arts, which appeared from 1927 on in *Para Todos* and *Vamos Ler!* He also drew cartoons for *Diário de Notícias, Diário da Noite* and *A Noite Illustrada.* He later also did political cartoons for publications like *A Manhã, Critica* and *A Granada.*

Alvarus has had his works exhibited in many shows and has received a great many awards and honors. His cartoons have been reprinted in books like *Hoje Tem Espetáculo* ("There Is a Show Today," 1945) and *Alvarus e os Seus Bonecos* ("Alvarus and His Characters," 1954).

A.M.

COUNIHAN, NOEL JACK (1913-) Australian cartoonist and caricaturist born in Melbourne, Australia, in 1913.

Master cartoonists like Honoré Daumier, Olaf Gulbransson, Will Dyson and Ralph Steadman, among others, have demonstrated that satire succeeds totally when expressed from a definite point of view. Noel Jack Counihan in fact works from two uncompromising points of view—as a person he stands for socialism and the cause of the working man, as an artist he pursues the practice and discipline of sound draftsmanship with no shortcuts to drawing.

Today a nationally recognized painter, printmaker and lithographer, Counihan began a career in journalism in 1935 during the Great Depression, when, after seeing an exhibition of Counihan's pencil portraits, the editor of the Melbourne *Argus* commissioned him to draw a weekly caricature for that newspaper. During this dreadful and difficult period his caricatures of prominent national personalities were being published in the *Bulletin,* and his drawings also appeared in the weekly magazine *Table Talk* and the Melbourne *Sun* newspaper.

Noel Counihan, caricature of Australian prime minister Ben Chifley. © Counihan.

The first political cartoons Counihan drew also date from this period. In 1935 he began cartooning for the Communist party newspapers *Worker's Weekly* and *Worker's Voice* and for trade union publications.

In 1943 Counihan started submitting a weekly cartoon for the *Guardian.* His antifascist cartoons and those attacking political corruption and defeatism on the home front were powerful features and continued through the war years until early 1949, when he departed for Europe. His post on the *Guardian* was taken over by the greatly talented and ideologically committed Ambrose Dyson, son of a *Bulletin* cartoonist and nephew of the London *Daily Herald's* world-famous cartoonist, Will Dyson. On his return to Melbourne in 1951, after travel and study in Europe, where his work was published in Prague, Warsaw, Budapest and London, Counihan joined with Ambrose Dyson back on the *Guardian.* He relinquished his feature cartooning in 1958 to again travel and paint full time.

Counihan's development as a cartoonist and caricaturist was influenced by a number of artists, including George Finey, whose astonishingly virile caricatures were featured in *Smith's Weekly.* Early in his career Noel Counihan had also discovered the fine satirists and caricaturists of the celebrated German publication *Simplicissimus* and the dramatically presented full-page cartoons of the American William Gropper in the radical journal *New Masses.* Counihan was later to meet and travel through Poland with Gropper in 1949.

A collection of his *Guardian* work, *60 Caunihan Cartoons,* was published in 1946; in 1974 he was distinguished by the publication of his biography by the Melbourne University Press.

Noel Counihan was among the last of the notable cartoonists to draw for the left-wing press in Australia—a list which included Syd Nicholls, Claude Marquet, Tom ("Tac") Challon, Ambrose Dyson and George Finey. The art of caricature as Will Dyson, David Low and Finey practiced it is gone; there is no longer an outlet for it in Australia today. In recent years, however, the enterprising Australian publisher Lloyd O'Neil commissioned Counihan to prepare two sets of caricatures to highlight two volumes of published reminiscences of Australian celebrities. A selection of these superb caricatures is now in the Ballarat Fine Art Gallery collection. And a magnificent series—comic portraits of Australian authors (in a private collection)—has been bequeathed to the Australian National Library in Canberra.

Art critics, gallery experts and his fellow brush practitioners agree that Counihan's brilliant comic portraiture has established his place for all time in the master class.

V.L.

COURTET, EMILE (1857-1938) French cartoonist and animator born in Paris, France, on January 4, 1857. Emile Courtet was first apprenticed to a jeweler, but he liked drawing, and he made many sketches of his co-workers and, after he was drafted into the army, his fellow soldiers. Back in civilian life in 1878, he became a pupil of the famous cartoonist André Gill. Taking up the *nom-de-plume* "Emile Cohl," he embarked on a successful career as a cartoonist, his work appearing in such leading French magazines of the day as *Le Rire* and *La Vie Parisienne.* In 1885 he added photography to his many endeavors.

Cohl joined the Gaumont movie studios in 1907 as the director of trick films in the manner of George Méliès. His first effort at animation took place in 1908 with a series of cartoon shorts featuring a timid but resilient character known as *le fantôche* (literally, "the puppet"), often drawn in white ink on black backgrounds. His first animated film was *Fantasmagorie,* followed by *Le Cauchemar du Fantôche* ("The Puppet's Nightmare"), *Un Drame Chez les Fantôches* ("A Drama Among the Puppets") and others. In 1908 he also directed *Le Baron de Crac,* an animated version of the adventures of Baron Munchausen.

Emile Courtet ("Emile Cohl"). "Un Drame Chez les Fantôches."

Among Cohl's enormous output from 1908 to 1918, mention should be made of *Les Joyeux Microbes* ("The Jolly Microbes"); *Transfiguration; Castro à New York* and *Le Subway* (both made in the United States); *Metamorphoses; Flambeau Chien Perdu,* about the misadventures of a stray dog; *Bonne Année 1916* ("Happy New Year 1916"); and *Le Tour du Monde en 80 Minutes* ("Around the World in 80 Minutes"), an enchanting spoof of Jules Verne's novel.

From 1912 to 1914, Cohl was in New York working with George McManus on a series of *Snookums* animated cartoons, based on McManus's successful comic strip, *The Newlyweds.* Cohl's last notable work of animation was another adaptation of a popular comic strip, Louis Forton's *Les Aventures des Pieds-Nickelés,* which he realized in 1918 in collaboration with the noted French cartoonist Benjamin Rabier.

Ruined by World War I, Emile Cohl stopped making films in 1918; until 1923 he labored in obscurity on commercial cartoons for theatrical release. Destitute and out of work, he spent the last years of his life in a home for the aged at Orly, near Paris. There, in a freak accident, his long white beard caught fire, and Emile Cohl died of his burns on January 27, 1938.

Cohl left behind him an enormous legacy that has not been adequately assessed to this day. Along with J.S. Blackton and Winsor McCay, he can be regarded as one of the discoverers of the art of animation. In *Animation in the Cinema,* Ralph Stephenson summed up Cohl's achievements in these words: "Cohl had a fertile imagination, and a sharp sense of the comic. . . . The pace of his films never flags and they are packed with the fantastic invention appropriate to the cartoon world. . . . His gags today are as fresh as when he made them."

M.H.

COVARRUBIAS, MIGUEL (1904-1957) Mexican cartoonist, author and artist born in Mexico City, Mexico, in 1904. Miguel Covarrubias's highly stylized caricatures of famous contemporaries earned him an international reputation while still a young man. Covarrubias was born and raised in Mexico City, and his father was a politician well connected in the national government. His family was affluent, and his artistic talents blossomed although he never went to art school. His father's connections got Covarrubias his first job as a draftsman with a federal bureau producing maps. Bored on the job, he began drawing caricatures that he soon sold to Mexico City newspapers. By age 18, Miguel Covarrubias was a syndicated cartoonist in publications from Cuba to Buenos Aires.

His caricatures earned him the patronage of the celebrated poet Juan Tablada. A government grant was arranged for the young Covarrubias to spend six months in New York City studying art. In 1923, he arrived in New York City, but instead of studying art, he immediately began selling his own to *Vanity Fair* and other magazines. Among his most famous caricatures early in his career were the Prince of Wales, Charles Chaplin and John D. Rockefeller, Sr. An anthology of his work, *The Prince of Wales and Other Famous Americans,* was published in 1927. Covarrubias enjoyed the high life of New York City of the 1920s. He frequented the Harlem nightclubs then in

Miguel Covarrubias, caricature of Rudolph Valentino. © Covarrubias.

vogue, and in 1927 a second book, *Negro Drawings,* was published.

The style of his caricatures was distinct. His line was geometric and sculptural in defining mass and features of his subjects. However, for all the stylization, his heavy lines were full of vigor and enthusiasm. His most famous group caricature was done in color for *Vanity Fair* in 1933. It showed an impudent and fanciful version of Franklin D. Roosevelt's first inauguration as president.

Plump, with a dark complexion, Covarrubias lived abroad more than he lived in Mexico. He was the model of the talented, cultured gentleman with financial security. His interests in painting, lithography, anthropology and archaeology eventually overshadowed his interest in drawing caricatures. In 1937 *Island of Bali,* Covarrubias's drawings supplemented by photographs taken by his wife, was published. The next year an edition of *Uncle Tom's Cabin* illustrated by Covarrubias was published. *Mexico South,* a history of the Olmec Indians, was published in 1946.

He returned to Mexico and taught art at the National Anthropological School. He later became director of dance for the National Institute of Fine Arts. But he continued to paint; his panels decorate numerous public buildings in Mexico. *Eagle, Jaguar, and Serpent,* a survey of Indian art of the Americas, was published in 1950 and was his last important book.

On February 2, 1957, at the age of 53, Covarrubias died in Mexico City of septicemia, a kind of blood poisoning. In honor of his accomplishments, his body lay in state at the National Museum of Anthropology and History prior to his funeral.

B.C.

COX, PALMER (1840-1924) American cartoonist and poet born in Granby, Province of Quebec, Canada, on April 28, 1840. As a boy, Palmer Cox worked in a railroad office in California. After it became clear that a trainman's life was not for him, he lived in San Francisco from 1863 to 1875 and cartooned for local publications, including the *Golden Era* and *Alta Californian.*

In 1875 Cox moved to New York City, set up a studio, and began to gain a reputation as an illustrator of children's books and for his animal drawings. He drew for the first issues of *Life,* lending it critically needed quality, along with other nascent talents like E.W. Kemble and Oliver Herford. But Cox's real success came about this time in the pages of *St. Nicholas* magazine, with *The Brownies.* In the poems and cartoons—crammed full of dozens of his little characters—he managed to create a separate world. *The Brownies* was enormously successful and spawned 13 books and a host of merchandising items.

Cox remained a lifelong bachelor, but his studio was filled with portraits of children and he corresponded with many of his young fans. After leaving his New York studio, he returned to rural Quebec and settled in Brownie Castle in Granby—the mountains around which are said to have inspired the Brownie legends. Cox died on July 7, 1924, in his 84th year.

Cox's drawing style, especially for *The Brownies* but throughout all his work, was detailed and precise. It was crosshatched, whether manifesting itself in seriocomic animals or romping Brownie snow scenes. Here was a cartoonist, the reader must conclude, who loved his work and all his characters; there was great humor and warm affection in the smallest detail—which, when Brownies were concerned, often constituted a major point of interest! His originals are about the size of the printed work, so his dedication and working methodology must have been akin to an etcher's. The Brownies, of course, are classic cartoon creations and began a wondrous heritage that continued through the *Kewpies* and *The Teenie Weenies.*

Books: *Squibs of California, or Everyday Life Illustrated* (1875), republished as *Comic Yarns* (1889); *Hans von Pelter's Trip to Gotham* (1876); *How Columbus Found America* (1877); *That Stanley* (1878); *The Brownies, Their Book* (1887); *Queer People* (1888); *Queer People with Wings and Stings* (1888); *Queer People with Paws and Claws* (1888); *Another Brownie Book* (1890); *The Brownies at Home* (1893); *The Brownies Around the World* (1894); *The Brownies Through the Union* (1895); *The Brownies Abroad* (1899); *The Brownies in Fairyland* (1895); *The Brownies in the Philippines* (1904); *The Palmer Cox Brownie Primer* (1906); *Brownie Clown in Brownie Town* (1907); *The Brownies' Latest Adventures* (1910); *The Brownies' Many More Nights* (1913); and The *Brownies and Prince Florimel* (1918). A three-act play based on the Brownies was also produced in 1895.

R.M.

CRANE, FRANK (1856-1917) American cartoonist, cousin of author Stephen Crane, born in Rahway, New Jersey, in 1856. A graduate of the New York Academy of Design, Crane became a staff cartoonist for the *New York World* in the early 1890s, and ultimately its art editor. He then moved to the *Philadelphia Press* in the same capacity, supervising such later greats in the fields of cartooning and illustration as Everrett Shinn, John Sloan, William Glackens, James Preston and F.R. Gruger.

Crane returned to New York as cartoonist for the *Tribune*

Palmer Cox, "The Brownies and the Tide."

and later switched to the *Herald* (as art editor) and to the *Times;* the *Boston Herald* also ran his cartoons and strips. Among his strips were *Willie Westinghouse Edison Smith, Muggsy* and *Uncle Dick's Contraptions.* Crane drew panel cartoons for *Life* around the turn of the century as well. He died at his home in New Rochelle, New York, on October 26, 1917.

Crane's style was broad and humorous, full of animation, technically similar to Walt McDougall's. His cartoons had an appearance that suggested, according to the taste of the observer, either crudity or native humor.

R.M.

CRAWFORD, ARTHUR (1867-1922) American writer and agent born in Montreal, Canada, on July 2, 1867. Arthur Crawford was graduated from the Royal Military College of Kingston, Ontario, in 1883, and began a career on the stage; he acted throughout Canada until 1896. He then moved to New York and, after a feeble attempt at cartooning, hit upon a system that suited his talents and in a major way shaped the course and content of American magazine cartooning for a generation. Crawford became an idea man, providing cartoonists with gags or themes for their drawings. At the same time—a time when cartoon markets were burgeoning and many artists eschewed humbling personal visits to editors' desks—he became an agent of sorts, submitting portfolios of cartoons to the various cartoon markets.

His success is attested by the many cartoonists' signatures followed by the caption "+A.C." giving credit to the originator. Sometimes half the cartoons in an issue of *Puck, Judge* or *Life* would bear Crawford's mark. His fecundity was amazing, and his ideas spanned the "he-she" gags to the single-caption era. He also pioneered the full-page theoretical cartoons later popularized by Gluyas Williams, Forbell and Rea Irvin.

Crawford committed suicide on November 14, 1922. Whether the resultant absence of his enormous influence was responsible for the advent of the new humor of the 1920s and the so-called one-line caption or merely coincided with the new era is probably beside the point. In terms of sheer production, the pen of Arthur Crawford played as large a role in shaping America's conception of humor as any other man's. The years 1900 to 1922 should rightly be called the Crawford era.

R.M.

CRAWFORD, WILL (1869-1944) American cartoonist born in Washington, D.C., in 1869. Will Crawford's first art assignments were for the *Newark* (N.J.) *Call* and then the *New York World.* His first major cartoons appeared in the pages of the old *Life* magazine when he was in his mid-twenties.

In the mid-1890s cartooning styles were relaxing. Crawford, with Sullivant and Hy Mayer, was the first since Frost and Bush to test distortion and exaggeration; most American cartoonists were slavishly sticking to "realism" or copying Gibson.

Crawford was soon drawing full-page cartoons for *Life.* He did series *(Historical Bits* was one—later historical illustrations for *Puck* in the mid-1910s were factual rather than satirical) and complicated genre drawings. Crawford's style was one of marvelously crosshatched understatement. There was motion, but it was arrested. He managed a blend of realism and caricature and spotted his figures in an impressive way that led the reader's eye through the cartoon as a guide would conduct a museum tour. There were seldom solid blacks in his cartoons; thin, spiny lines would combine for crosshatch and shading effects of incredible visual variety.

By the middle of the first decade he was a major fixture in *Puck,* perhaps due in large part to his friendship with Joseph Keppler, Jr. Crawford drew some brilliant double-page spreads in color, although his political attempts were shallow. After Keppler sold his interest in *Puck,* Crawford remained for some time but ultimately left and, in temporary semi-retirement, joined Keppler in the West to live among and work on behalf of Indian tribes—whose welfare and way of life became a consuming interest of the two cartoonists. Crawford died in Nutley, New Jersey, in 1944.

In addition to his numerous cartoons and magazine illustrations, Crawford illustrated many books, where his work can be (and deserves to be) discovered today: *Jack Morgan, A Boy of 1612* (1901); *Pigs Is Pigs* (1907); *The Great American Pie Company (1907); The Mystery* (1907); *Skunny Wundy and Other Indian Tales* (1926); *Paul Bunyan and His Great Blue Ox* (1926); *A Narration of Col. Ethan Allen's Captivity. Containing His Voyages and Travels* (1930); and *Long Remember* (1934), among many others. Whether the illustrations were straight or in cartooning style, the wispy, textured elements of Will Crawford's work were always in evidence.

R.M.

CRAWFORD, WILLIAM H. (1913-1982) American political and sports cartoonist born in Hammond, Indiana, on

"May carry your books?"
William H. Crawford. © NEA.

March 13, 1913. Raised in Germantown, Pennsylvania, Bill Crawford took the W.L. Evans correspondence cartooning course and studied at the Art Institute of Chicago. He was graduated from Ohio State with a fine arts degree after studying sculpture under Hoyt L. Sherman.

Study in Paris followed at l'Académie de la Grande Chaumière, under Lucien Fontanarosa and others, for fine arts and drawing. Returning to the United States, he free-lanced cartoons before taking a job on the art staff of the *Washington Post.* Later he switched to the *Washington Daily News,* where he cartooned for two years in the sports and editorial departments. Harold Talburt, chief political cartoonist of the *News,* informed Crawford of an opening on the *Newark* (N.J.) *News,* which Crawford applied for and won. That was in 1938, and among his assignments was drawing one editorial cartoon a week to relieve Lute Pease. Eventually he took over the full-time political chores—as well as contributing sports cartoons, news features and theatrical caricatures. In 1962, when John Fischetti left the Newspaper Enterprise Association, Crawford moved over under editor Boyd Lewis. For years, as America's most widely circulated editorial cartoonist, he drew six a week, eventually reducing his load to five a week and then two a week; he retired in 1977.

Crawford, originally a liberal Democrat, has an amazing versatility of talents, including photography, the classical viola and especially sculpture. He has done many portrait busts and, on the lighter side, fashioned the National Cartoonists Society Reuben award from a Rube Goldberg sketch. He has illustrated 20 books, won the Best Editorial Cartoonist award three times, and has several Freedoms Foundation and National Headliners Club awards to his credit. He died of pneumonia on January 6, 1982, in Washington, D.C.

Crawford's style displays exceptional verve and competence; all his figures are distorted and exaggerated but technically correct and balanced. He drew on a very large scale, and his prime work shows a feeling of scope and great, arresting composition. His shading, before he switched to Craftint in the 1970s, was with a free and slashing crayon. Crawford's work from the 1930s to the early 1950s was among the strongest produced in America—he is just one of the many outstanding artists who somehow evaded Pulitzer recognition. His work deserves to be anthologized.

R.M.

CRÉATION DU MONDE, LA (France) In 1945 French cartoonist Jean Effel (François Lejeune) started a series of humorous cartoons based on the Book of Genesis. Collectively called *La Création du Monde* ("The Creation of the World"), they depicted God as a bearded and well-meaning old fussbudget who brought forth the sky, stars, water, etc., only after much prodding from his high-spirited retinue of angels. His old adversary, Satan, was always lurking in the shadows, trying to turn each of his creations into a disaster. The cartoons enjoyed incredible success and were later collected into a series of five books, *Le Ciel et la Terre* ("The Sky and Earth"), *Les Plantes et Animaux* ("The Plants and Animals"), *L'Homme* ("Man"), *La Femme* ("Woman") and *Le Roman d'Adam et Eve* ("The Romance of Adam and Eve").

In 1956 Barandov Studio in Prague produced a full-length animated cartoon of *La Création du Monde.* It was directed by Eduard Hofman from a screenplay by noted cartoonist (and former ambassador to France) Adolph Hoffmeister. The film was very successful, both artistically and commercially, and received many awards. In 1974 a sequel, *The Tribulations of Adam and Eve,* also based on Effel's drawings, was produced by the Czech studio.

M.H.

"La Création du Monde." © Jean Effel.

Gib Crockett. © Washington Star-News.

CROCKETT, GIBSON MILTON (1912-) American political cartoonist and painter born in Washington D.C., on September 18, 1912. After graduation from high school, Gib Crockett visited the art department of the *Washington Star* to show his sketches, thereupon beginning a 41-year association with the paper. His only art training—other than what he was to acquire on the job—was an unfinished cartoon correspondence course. His early influences were Dorman H. Smith and Willard Mullin.

He advanced at the *Star* from apprenticeship in spot cartooning, human interest sketches and sports cartoons to editorial and political cartoons. It was in 1948, the year before Clifford Berryman's death, that Crockett began on the editorial page, at first at the rate of one a week, as relief for Jim Berryman.

Crockett is an accomplished painter and a member of several painting societies in the Washington area. He has had exhibitions of his paintings and received a U.S. Treasury medal for war work, as well as Freedoms Foundation awards and a National Headliners award for his cartoons. Crockett, an independent-leaning Republican, draws in the portraiture school of cartooning; he employs likenesses of his subjects rather than the frequent use of caricature itself. His shading medium was usually crayon until, in recent years, he switched to a single-tone wash. For years his work was syndicated by King Features Syndicate. He was art director of the American Publishing Company in Washington, D.C., when he retired in 1985.

R.M.

Dale Cummings. © Winnipeg Free Press

CUMMINGS, DALE (1947-) Canadian cartoonist born in St. Thomas, Ontario, in 1947. After studying animation and illustration at Sheridan College in nearby Oakville, Dale Cummings moved to New York City in the early 1970's, contributing drawings and cartoons to the *New York Times*. Returning to Ontario in 1976, he became one of the most prolific cartoonists in Canada, where he freelanced for the *Toronto Star, Canadian Forum, Maclean's, Canadian Magazine*, and many other periodicals.

In 1982 he became the full-time editorial cartoonist of the *Winnipeg Free Press*. There he found both his stride and his style, winning the National Newspaper Award the very next year. His deceptively simple line hides a clever sense of design: his cartoons are sharp and to the point, augmented by a telling use of captions when needed. Whether he depicts a homeless person asleep on a grate over which a sign proclaims, "Heat vent courtesy of Health and Welfare: do not abuse the privilege"; or when he draws a public lecture hall hung with a banner reading, "Tonight! Canada: Myth or Hoax?," his cartoons are sure to attract contoversy on which Cummings seems to thrive. The back cover of one of his cartoon collections carries the following excerpts from indignant letters to the editor: "Most of the child-like drawings look evil" and "My husband and I and our friends take great exception and disgust to your cartoons."

Nor does he confine himself to Canadian issues; his forays into international affairs are equally meant to draw blood. In one of Cummings's cartoons, former Austrian President (and Nazi member) Kurt Waldheim mutters, "An old war wound," while his body is contorted into the shape of a swastika. Another cartoon depicts President Clinton literally blasting off George Bush and Ross Perot with his saxophone playing. Yet another one shows Ferdinand Marcos with wife Imelda at his side averring, "I would like to go back to the Philippines and live the life of a peasant... Perhaps plant shoes." Cummings skewer these and other world figures with a sharp wit and a slashing pen, tempered by a grudging admiration for their effrontery. As William Dafoe, editorial page editor of the *Free*

Press, observed in his preface to to the cartoonist's *The Best of a Bad Lot*, "A bad lot Dale calls them, but they are a wonderful lot for a cartoonist. Dale Cummings does them all justice."

Cummings's cartoons have appeared in a number of anthologies and have been collected into several books.

M.H.

CUMMINGS, MICHAEL (1919-1997) British political cartoonist of the Beaverbrook newspaper group, brought in to give some serious commentary contrast to the often knockabout comedy of their principal cartoonist, Carl Giles. Michael Cummings was born in Leeds in 1919, the son of A.J. Cummings, a political columnist who became the political editor of the *News Chronicle*. Educated at The Hall, Hampstead, and Gresham's School, Norfolk, he studied art at the Chelsea School of Art for three years before World War II took him into the Air Ministry. As an RAF draftsman he drew airplane parts until his discharge, then resumed his art studies at Chelsea.

His first cartoons, reflecting his political leanings, were published in the left-wing weekly *Tribune* in 1939, and the same magazine took him on in postwar days as an illustrator for the book page. He contributed cartoons of a political nature until 1948, when, at his father's suggestion, he applied for a job on the *Daily Express*. After a trying trial period he made the grade and provided the *Daily* with three cartoons a week, plus one for the *Sunday Express*. He published a book, *These Uproarious Years*, in 1954. He retired in the mid-1980s. He died in October 1997.

D.G.

CURRIER AND IVES (ca. 1834-1898) The Currier and Ives operations—first-under Nathaniel Currier's name and later in partnership with James M. Ives—made many contributions to American culture: popular art was introduced to the masses, lithography was refined under its aegis, the spirit of an age was almost inadvertently but uncompromisingly captured and, certainly not least important, the American appetite for visual humor was given great impetus.

Lithography on stone, a unique medium of Bavarian descent, was new to America when Nathaniel Currier was engaged as an apprentice by one of the pioneering firms in Boston. Currier was only 15 but soon experimented with his own shop—and, later, his own techniques—as his bookkeeper, Ives, handled the business affairs so he could continue to concentrate on themes and art direction.

Of course, Currier and Ives prints were to become synonymous with sentiment, primitive political persuasion and scenes of racetrack, steamboat and railroad Americana, but one of the firm's most successful lines was its humorous portfolios. Much of the humorous work was submitted by Thomas Worth (he never lithographed directly on the stones), but Currier himself had a famous sense of humor and was responsible for many of the concepts and comic prints. Sol Eytinge was another prolific artist. By far the most popular series through the years was Worth's *Darktown* series. Without regular characters, these prints lampooned practically every aspect of black life and were best sellers; they presaged Kemble's *Coontown Sketches* by more than a generation.

"The Bad Man at the Hour of Death," a Currier and Ives lithograph, ca. 1858.

Aside from the purely humorous prints, political cartoons were a Currier and Ives stock-in-trade. They flourished, of course, at every presidential election, although most of the activity in this genre occurred during the Civil War and dealt with Abraham Lincoln. It should be noted that as mere "printmakers to the people," Currier and Ives sometimes issued, simultaneously, prints supporting opposing sides of an issue. Many cartoons were crude, and balloons were frequently employed.

Currier and Ives print portfolios ranged in price from twenty cents to four dollars, although cartoons were always at the cheap end of the scale. Virtually none were lithographed in color; rather, a dozen or so German ladies worked in production-line fashion, adding watercolors to bring the prints to life.

The firm sold its last original lithograph in 1898, after the deaths of Currier and Ives (in 1888 and 1895, respectively). Descendants of the founders and employees struggled for several years until the stock and equipment was liquidated in 1907—even the stones were cleaned and auctioned by the pound. The Currier and Ives phenomenon really lost its vitality in the mid 1870s. Several reasons can be suggested, including the fading novelty of colored prints. But certainly a major factor must have been the rise of illustrated journalism and particularly the advent of colored lithographic cartoons in *Puck* and similar weekly magazines.

R.M.

"I'm going to have to ask you not to cheat."

Tom Curtis. © Milwaukee Sentinel.

CURTIS, TOM (1938-) In 14 years as the editorial cartoonist of the *Milwaukee Sentinel* and a regular contributor to national magazines, Tom Curtis has achieved wide recognition as one of the few conservative voices in the field. Born Thomas Pelham Curtis on June 10, 1938, in New York City, he received a classical education in art. His degree in architecture from Harvard (1960) and studies of art at the Corcoran School in Washington, D.C., and Cardinal Stritch College in Milwaukee are apparent in his painterly approach to cartooning. Curtis is not a conventional caricaturist; his drawings of public figures, whether his point is positive or negative, have rather the character of insightful portraits than the exaggeration and grotesquerie of lampoons.

Curtis made his first major sale to the *National Review* in 1967. He became a staff cartoonist for the *Sentinel* in 1969, and was distributed nationally by the Register and Tribune Syndicate from 1971. At the *Sentinel* he enjoyed full editorial freedom until a change in management moved the paper politically toward the left. Increasingly uncomfortable with the experience of having editorial writers dictate the ideas of his cartoons, he left the paper in 1983 to become art director of PM Advertising in Milwaukee. During his decade and a half with the paper he received numerous honors, including the George Washington Honor Medal from the Freedoms Foundation at Valley Forge in 1970, 1971, 1975, and 1977; the Best Editorial Cartoon Award from the Milwaukee Press Club in 1976, and the Silver Ink Bottle Award from the Association of American Editorial Cartoonists in 1983. He served as president of that association in 1977 and 1978.

Editorial cartoons by Curtis have been used as illustrations in several standard reference books on cartooning, and published collections of his work include *Obadiah and the Decline of the Great Society* (1968), *The Turn of the Decade* (1970), and *Curtis in Profile* (1983).

Although he acknowledged missing the give and take of editorial meetings and "the opportunity to engage in not only art but history," Curtis has had a successful career since leaving a full-time job in editorial cartooning. He continues contributing to the *National Review* and teaches art history at Brookfield Academy, near Milwaukee, but his principal work is conducted in his own art studio. A successful illustrator and studio painter, he has had a notable career in portraiture. Among the more than 200 commissions he has executed are likenesses of such prominent figures as Supreme Court justices Scalia, Thomas, and Rehnquist, economist Milton Friedman, William F. Buckley, Jr., Barry Goldwater, Clare Booth Luce, and Ronald Reagan.

Curtis's powerful compositions are achieved by an artful balance of solid black with clean, crisp lines, matching the power and precision of his ideas. Often shrewdly witty, he never descends to what he dismisses as "drawing jokes." Instead, he employs his medium like a surgical instrument. "An editorial cartoon is like a laser beam," he has observed. "It can cut deep and sharp." In his hands, the pen and brush have often done just that.

D.W.

CUSHING, OTHO (1871-1942) American cartoonist born in Fort McHenry, Maryland, in 1871. Otho Cushing, a descendant of Nicholas Cooke, colonial governor of Rhode Island, received art training from the Boston School of Fine Arts and was graduated with honors. He later studied at the Académie Julian in Paris and then became a professor of drawing at the Massachusetts Institute of Technology. After the turn of the century Cushing returned to Paris to become art editor of the European edition of the *Herald-Tribune.* In late 1906 Cushing submitted his first cartoons to *Life* and upon acceptance also received an offer to join the magazine's staff. He made his mark early when a series satirizing President Theodore Roosevelt in a Ulyssean motif—*The Teddyssey*—created a stir in the press because of its cleverness. It was ultimately reprinted in book form.

Cushing's style was heavily mannered and ultra-formal. Perhaps a third of all his cartoons used Greek gods and goddesses as characters (oftentimes attempting social or political comments in a satiric vein); one has the feeling that *all* his characters were Olympian. His society women didn't wear gowns, they seemed to wear togas. High-society jibes, historical mixups and "socioclassical" departures formed nearly his total subject range.

During World War I, Cushing left *Life.* As a captain in the Army Air Corps he was in charge of camouflaging American airfields on the Western Front. His mentor, J.A. Mitchell of *Life,* must have been proud, as France's fight was as dear to his heart as any of the magazine's crusades through the years. After the war Cushing retired to his home in New Rochelle, New York, where he became a successful watercolorist. He died on October 13, 1942.

R.M.

CYBORG 009 (Japan) Japanese cartoonist Shotarō Ishimori created his successful comic strip *Cyborg 009* in 1964; the feature became so popular that it gave rise to a long-running animated series of television cartoons in 1965 and was adapted to theatrical animation a year later. In this feature-length animated film, closely following the original script, Cyborg 009 and his cybernetic companions fought the Black Ghosts, a host of malevolent characters bent on taking over the world. Helped by their inventor,

Otho Cushing.

"Cyborg 009." © Toei Studio.

Dr. Gillmore, the cyborgs succeeded in thwarting the devilish schemes of the Black Ghosts and their leader, Beagle. The action was swift and suspenseful, and the animation (directed by Yugo Serikawa) well handled.

The whole enterprise was so successful that it inevitably spawned a sequel, *Cyborg 009–Underground Duel.* In this film the cyborgs and their mentor, Dr. Gillmore, fought the second round of their duel against Beagle and his surviving Black Ghosts. After destroying a monster robot that was wreaking havoc on the high seas, Cyborg 009 and his companions finally destroyed the headquarters of the Black Ghosts, thus putting an end to this international band of evildoers. Again the feature was directed by Serikawa; the script, however, was repetitive, and the animation, though done at the Toei Studio, like that of its predecessor, somehow seemed wooden. There were no more *Cyborg 009* features after this second version (1967).

M.H.

CYNICUS

See Anderson, Martin.

Dd

DAFFY DUCK (U.S.) "That darnfool duck," as he was called before he got his official name, first appeared in Tex Avery's 1937 cartoon "Porky's Duck Hunt" as the elusive target of at least three dozen hunters. He returned—as Daffy Duck—in the 1937 "Daffy Duck and Egghead," also directed by Avery, and proved popular enough to be given his own cartoon series by producer Leon Schlesinger, releasing through Warner Brothers. The personality of the insanely active duck was well established early on: that of the supremely confident, albeit totally incompetent, con man whose nefarious schemes invariably backfired on him. In "Daffy Duck in Hollywood" (1938) he played to the hilt the role of a dictatorial movie director, and in "Plane Daffy" (1940), that of a daredevil aviator. In both he ended up getting the boot.

Never were the fast-talking duck's pretensions so promptly deflated as on the numerous occasions that found him confronting the unflappable Bugs Bunny. In cartoon after inspired cartoon ("Beanstalk Bunny," "A Star Is Bored," "The Abominable Snow Rabbit," etc.) Daffy played his most underhanded tricks on Bugs, only to be outwitted at every turn. The last shot usually showed the duck crawling up to the carrot-munching Bugs and uttering the heartfelt apostrophe "You're despicable!" In "Robin Hood Daffy" (possibly the best of the *Daffy Duck* cartoons), Daffy, posing as Robin Hood, vainly tried to persuade a skeptical Porky Pig (as Friar Tuck) to join his band, and decided to join the order instead ("Friar Tuck, meet Friar Duck!"). One of Daffy's best solo efforts came in "Aqua Duck" when, searching for water in the desert, he only came upon useless gold.

In addition to Avery, notable directors of the *Daffy Duck* cartoons have included Frank Tashlin, Chuck Jones, Bob Clampett, Friz Freleng and Bob McKimson. Like the rest of his Warner Brothers compères, Daffy disappeared from theater screens in 1969 but still appears on television on the *Bugs Bunny and Friends* show. He has also been continuously featured in comic books since 1951.

Daffy Duck in "The Wise Quacking Duck." © Warner Brothers.

Like many of his *compères* at Warners, Daffy has starred in a number of television specials, most of them compilations of earlier cartoons. There were *Daffy Duck's Easter Show* (which featured three new cartoons) and *Daffy Duck's Thanks-for-giving Special Show* in 1980, and *Life of the Living Duck* in 1988. The same year he appeared *in Who Framed Roger Rabbit*, playing a piano duet with Donald Duck.

M.H.

DAGGY, A. SMITH (1858-1942) American cartoonist born in 1858. A.S. Daggy is representative of turn-of-the-century magazine cartoonists who handled all genres well. He also had a secret life as a quite respectable painter. Daggy studied fine arts in Paris and at the Pennsylvania Academy of Fine Arts, where he trained under Thomas Eakins and became his close friend. In the 1880s Daggy's cartoons and back-of-the-book drawings began appearing in *Harper's Monthly*, where only the finer and more genteel magazine cartoonists could cross over. In the 1890s his work was a pillar of *Judge*'s cartoon establishment; he had no specialty of themes but rather was a journeyman gagster who vied with the best of his fellows for the apportioned ethnic, rural and household cartoons.

His style ranged gently from the illustrative to the exaggerated (when Sullivant and others introduced big-headed characters to cartooning). One area in which he excelled was visualized puns—the audacity of some is admirable!

Daggy's best friend was the great A.B. Frost, with whom he studied and painted through the years. Daggy's own canvases show a respectable talent for media other than pen and ink. His "straight" artistic activities brought him to the vice-presidency of the Silvermine Guild in Norwalk, Connecticut. He died in Stamford, Connecticut, on June 16, 1942.

R.M.

DALE, ARCHIBALD (1882-1962) Canadian cartoonist born in Dundee, Scotland, on May 31, 1882. Arch Dale began his cartooning career on the Aberdeen *Courier* at age 17. For the next ten years or so he worked on the *Courier*, the Glasgow *News* and finally *Comic Cuts* and *Funny Wonders* in London.

In 1908, Dale left for Canada. He later said that glowing accounts by friends of the rich homesteads in Saskatchewan convinced him to come to Touchwood Hills. After arriving, he came to the conclusion that there are many Scottish settlers on the prairies because Scotsmen like company in their misery and are ready to suppress the truth to get it. After a few months behind the plow, he moved to Winnipeg, Manitoba, and spent two years there, cartooning for the *Free Press* and the *Grain Growers' Guide.* In 1910 a windfall from a real estate boom enabled him to finance a trip back home. He stayed for three years, cartooning for papers in Manchester and London, but returned to Canada in 1913, later stating that he became fed up with the extremes of wealth and poverty in England.

Dale again worked for the *Grain Growers' Guide,* remaining until 1921. During this time, he married Claire Porter (their only child, Julie Dale, was to become head of the Winnipeg *Free Press* art department). In 1921 Dale went to Chicago to work for the Universal Feature and Specialty Company, which syndicated his *Doo Dads.* Here Dale portrayed the humorous experiences of Doc Sawbones, Old Man Grouch and other little people who populated this weekly strip against a surrealistic background. Dale left the United States in 1927, afterwards observing that he had spent most of his time there on streetcars getting to and from work.

Dale's position as a major Canadian political cartoonist dates from his return to the Winnipeg *Free Press* in 1927; he remained there until his retirement in 1954. He began with little knowledge of the political situation in an affluent, inflationary society, but the 1930s provided Dale with many targets for his pen. Prime minister R.B. Bennett, with his top hat, pince-nez and pinstriped suit, embodied the Conservative party image to western farmers hit hard by the Depression. Dale exploited this image and continually pointed out the failings of the Conservatives. Yet Mr. Bennett often wrote to Dale for originals of these cartoons, and once, when an original was lost, Dale drew a copy and sent it to him. Not all of Dale's barbs were reserved for the Conservative party, however. After World War II, the *Free Press* attacked the Liberal party's wheat policy, and Dale drew a cartoon with Minister of Agriculture Gardiner upside down and everyone else right side up. Unfortunately the point was somewhat lost when a printer accidentally put the cartoon in upside down.

Three collections of Dale cartoons were published in Winnipeg: *Five Years with R.B. Bennett* (1935); *$25 a Month, Adventures in Aberhartia* (1938); and *The Left and the Right with Arch Dale of the Winnipeg Free Press* (1945).

Eight years after his retirement, Dale died in a Winnipeg hospital on June 18, 1962.

D.K.

D'ALESSIO, GREGORY (1904-1993) American painter, cartoonist and art teacher born in New York City on September 25, 1904. Gregory d'Alessio worked as an assistant to a commercial artist and as a bank teller on Wall Street prior to the Depression. Fired from his Wall Street job, he began freelancing cartoons, at the same time studying at Pratt Institute and the Art Students League. About 1932 he sold his first cartoon to the *Saturday Evening Post.* This was quickly followed by sales to *Collier's, Esquire,* the *New Yorker* and most of the major cartoon markets of the day. In the 1930s his feature *Twimbly Twins* was published by the *Saturday Evening Post.* After World War II, *Collier's*

Jenö Dallos. © Dallos.

"NOW your seasickness is gone! The cruise is over!"

Gregory d'Alessio. © d'Alessio.

magazine featured his panel *Welcome Home,* about the arrival home of the American troops and the humorous problems that arose.

In 1940 a daily panel, *These Women,* starring the svelte secretary Miss Jones, was syndicated by Publishers Syndicate. The panel was stylish, and d'Alessio's quick brushwork gave it a light, relaxing quality. His magazine cartoons were also mostly brush and ink plus wash to the exclusion of much pen work. But since his magazine work was directed to specific audiences, d'Alessio could be more sophisticated in his humor and art than with *These Women.* A classic *Esquire* cartoon shows a shapely woman in a fur coat and hat walking past two other sophisticated New York women. One woman says to her companion, "There's a mink, from a rat, on a cat."

During World War II, d'Alessio was chairman of the committee on war cartoons of the American Society of Magazine Cartoonists. The committee worked closely with different government agencies in determining how cartooning could help the war effort and morale of the people.

Gregory d'Alessio eventually decided to end his distinguished cartoon career in favor of painting. He has long been associated with the Art Students League in New York City, where he teaches drawing and anatomy. His wife, Hilda Terry, whom he married in 1938, is one of the foremost women cartoonists in America. He published a book of memoirs, Old Troubadour, in 1987. In the 1990s ill health forced him to curtail his activities; he died in 1993.

B.C.

DALLOS, JENÖ (1940-) Hungarian cartoonist born near Budapest, Hungary, in 1940. After studying art in various Budapest schools, Jenö Dallos started contributing cartoons to magazines and newspapers around 1965, rapidly becoming one of the top Hungarian cartoonists. Since 1970 he has been on the staff of *Ludas Matyi,* a satirical weekly magazine with a circulation of over five hundred thousand. In addition to a successful career in his home country, Dallos has had many of his cartoons printed abroad in such publications as *Pardon, Interpress Grafik, Das Magazin* in Germany, and *Punch* and *City* in England. Since the late 1980s, when Hungary broke away from the Communist system, he has been very active in the Western press, turning out drawings for the opinion pages and winning numerous cartoon contests.

Dallos's main concerns are threats to the environment and the endangered future of mankind; he treats his themes in a sparse, linear style not dissimilar to that of Michel Folon and often develops his usually captionless cartoons in a sequential form close to that of the comic strip.

Dallos has been the recipient of a number of international awards, including the special prize at the 1975 Bordighera Humor Salon and the second prize at the 1969 Moscow Cartoon Exhibition.

M.H.

DALRYMPLE, LOUIS (1861-1905) American cartoonist born in Cambridge, Illinois, on January 19, 1861. Louis Dalrymple, educated in public schools, studied art at the Pennsylvania Academy of Fine Arts, where he was gradu-

Louis Dulrymple, 1898.

ated with credit, and at the Art Students League in New York.

In 1886 he submitted drawings to Joseph Keppler, founder and art director of *Puck*, and was engaged as a staff member. The magazine was then in a rebuilding period following the departure of Bernard Gillam and Eugene Zimmerman to *Judge*, and the death of James A. Wales. Nevertheless, Dalrymple's hiring was not out of desperation; although some consider his work crude, he had the flavor of early Opper, Frost and Bush. Dalrymple's work never really transcended the first rough impression it made, but he was prolific and his style was full of native humor. There was much animation in his figures, and he proved a valuable asset to *Puck* for 15 years.

Dalrymple handled lithographic political subjects as well as black-and-white humorous cartoons. In spite of occasional masterpieces, his anatomy could sometimes be awkward and his composition unsure. Just after the turn of the century, when he also dabbled in Sunday comic strips, Dalrymple left *Puck* and drew for its Republican rival, *Judge*. It was a short tenure, however, as he died in 1905.

R.M.

DAME OYAJI (Japan) *Dame Oyaji* (roughly translatable as "No-Good Daddy") is a long-running and hilarious Japanese comic strip that first appeared in the magazine *Shōnen Sunday* in 1970. Created and drawn by Mitsutoshi Furuya, *Dame Oyaji* relies for its humor on role reversals of stereotypes in the Japanese family.

Dame Oyaji, the central figure, has the misfortune to marry Oni Baba ("Demon Hag"). Totally dominated by her, he spends his wretched existence trying to find ways to assert himself and to somehow convince both himself and his two children that he is not completely incompetent. Alas, nobody respects Dame Oyaji; at work he is despised by his superiors and tolerated by his peers, and at home he is a pathetic, persecuted figure. As might be expected, he is tiny in comparison with his wife, who towers over him like a scowling Sherman tank. At the slightest offense Oni Baba is liable to fly into a blind rage and attack her husband with whatever happens to be at hand, be it chair, shovel or meat cleaver. Between moments of pathetic cowering, Dame Oyaji often makes appeals to his children for support, but to his ultimate chagrin they usually remain impartial and impassive bystanders.

In actual Japanese families, the father is usually a rather distant and dominant figure, especially from the viewpoint of children, and as befits a male-oriented society, his word is law (although the women do have their own foolproof methods of getting their own way). *Dame Oyaji*, by successfully parodying this family relationship and the male role in it, has tapped a virtually inexhaustible source of humor for children.

Furuya supposedly derived inspiration for the strip both from his compatriots at work and from his own experience. He was born in Japanese-controlled Manchuria in 1936 and repatriated to Japan after the war; upon graduation from middle school he worked for three years in a clothing store. He has worked as an assistant to Osamu Tezuka and also as a staff member of Fujio Productions, and his drawing style is clearly influenced by Fujio Akatsuka in its use of simple lines with no shading and maximum deformation of facial features. Furuya is well known in Japan for other humorous works such as *Techan* and *Nettarokun*, but *Dame Oyaji* remains his most representative and comical work to date.

Furuya is well known today for many other humorous works, such as *Genten Papa* ("Demerit Dad"), as well as for works that incorporate information such as *Bar Lemon Heart* (about bartending). *Dame Oyaji*, however, remains his masterwork and an all-time classic; in 1979 it won the 29th Shogakukan Manga Award.

F.S.

DAR, SUDHIR (1932-) Sudhir Dar was born in Prayag (now Allahabad), India, in 1932. He earned a masters degree in geography from the University of Allahabad, after which he worked at All-India Radio and assorted other jobs. In 1960, he began a seven-year stint as cartoonist for *The Statesman*, doing a daily front page pocket cartoon called "Out of My Mind." From 1967 until his resignation in anger in 1989, Dar was cartoonist on the *Hindustan Times*. There, he did his first political cartoons and "This Is It," a pocket cartoon voted one of the most popular features of the daily. His career at the *Hindustan Times* was marked by acts of resistance; when editors spiked his work or otherwise curtailed his freedom, he quit drawing political cartoons for varying periods.

Dar's subsequent position on *The Pioneer* has been more satisfying; he said he does six front-page cartoons every week without editorial interference. Influenced by British and American cartoonists during his wartime childhood, Dar has developed a style of drawing that makes his gag and social commentary cartoons universally appealing. Some of his funniest work has been done with a minimum of line, no words, and very clever twists. His cartoons have appeared in newspapers and magazines throughout the world, including *Mad*, *New York Times*, *Die Welt*, *Neue Zurcher Zeitung*, and *Saturday Review*, and have won many awards, most prominent of which is India's Durga Ratan.

J.A.L.

DARCY, THOMAS (1932-) American cartoonist born in Brooklyn, New York, on December 19, 1932. Tom Darcy grew up in Long Island and studied art at the Cartoonists and Illustrators School (later the School of Visual Arts) under Jack Markow and Burne Hogarth. While in art school, he sold his first cartoons—gags to men's magazines—and in 1959 he took a job on the art staff of the Long Island newspaper *Newsday*. Shortly thereafter he worked for the *Phoenix Gazette* for a year, but the liberal attitudes he expressed in his editorial cartoons soon caused difficulties, and he returned to advertising, a field he had worked in briefly after art school.

Starting in 1964, Darcy held a succession of political cartooning jobs that both matured his style and reflected his political drift leftward. The Houston Post published him for just under two years, and in 1966 he switched to the *Philadelphia Bulletin*. Two years later he found a comfortable berth on *Newsday* again; in another two years he was

Tom Darcy. © Newsday.

the possessor of the Pulitzer Prize for editorial cartooning. In 1977 Darcy abandoned editorial cartooning to do a weekly potpourri page of social comment and reportage, "Tom Darcy on Long Island," for the Sunday *Newsday*. "After Nixon, Vietnam and civil rights, what's left to attack?" Darcy asked. "I had too much of the sixties and seventies." His feature was discontinued in the 1990s, and he has now returned to freelancing.

Darcy's later style is reminiscent of Herblock and Conrad but retains its individuality. His lines are bold, and he uses facial expressions and emotions to advantage in depicting his characters. In his political cartooning career Darcy copped three Overseas Press Club awards and a National Headliners award.

R.M.

DARLING, JAY NORWOOD (1876-1962) American cartoonist, twice a Pulitzer Prize winner, born in Norwood, Michigan, on October 21, 1876. Jay Darling first signed himself "Ding" (a contraction) in a Beloit, Wisconsin, school yearbook lampooning faculty members as chorus girls; he was suspended for a year.

In 1900 Ding was a reporter for the *Sioux City* (Iowa) *Journal*. In tracking down a story, he sketched a lawyer who refused to be photographed, and he became a sketch artist for the paper on the strength of its quality. While honeymooning in the West Indies in 1906, Ding was offered a job by wire with the *Des Moines Register and Leader*. He worked there until offered a position with the *New York Globe* and its syndicate. There he drew editorial cartoons and two comic features, *Alonzo Applegate* and *The Iowa Farmer*. An obvious homesickness for Iowa was further manifested in 1913, when he accepted a position with the *New York Tribune*, one of the most prestigious papers in the country: his terms were to be the *Tribune's* regular cartoonist while maintaining residence in Iowa. These arrangements were long-standing, with Ding also doubling as the regular cartoonist of the *Des Moines Register and Tribune*. He was syndicated by the Herald-Tribune Syndicate.

Ding was as famous for his friendships and causes as for

Jay Norwood Darling ("Ding"). © Des Moines Register & Tribune.

his cartoons. He was close to Theodore Roosevelt and especially close to fellow Iowan Herbert Hoover. For years he was the nation's most famous conservationist and promoted wildlife protection in particular. In 1934 he was named chief of the Biological Survey in the Department of Agriculture but resigned soon thereafter, angry over New Deal red tape and frustrated over FDR's evident lack of sincerity in appointing and charging him. He remained active in conservation work, however, serving on committees and designing a wildlife stamp. He won many awards, including the Distinguished Service Medal from the Theodore Roosevelt Memorial Association for appropriating $20 million and setting aside 4.5 million acres during his brief tenure in office.

Ding's first book was a collection of war cartoons published in 1917; he has been anthologized much through the years. *Ding's Half Century* was published in 1962; *As Ding Saw Hoover* in 1954; and *Calvin Coolidge: Cartoons of His Presidency*, wherein he was the featured artist, in 1973. *Palimpsest*, journal of the Iowa State Historical Society, published a superb issue devoted to Ding in March 1972. He wrote text and drew cartoons for *Ding Goes to Russia* in 1932 and wrote *The Cruise of the Baby Bouncer* (about a trailer trip from Des Moines to Miami) in 1937.

Originals by Ding are extremely large; he drew in slashing brushstrokes that, reduced, looked like stiff pen lines. Ding gloried in the traditional conventions of his craft and never really sought to simplify his art; his cartoons are full of crosshatching and labels, are crammed with visual humor and usually seek a chuckle as well as a message. The spirit of his cluttered masterpieces is as important as any transitory object lesson they may illustrate.

His work was sometimes confused with that of Tom Carlisle, who was for awhile his assistant—one of the few instances of an editorial cartoonist employing help on art (Rube Goldberg was another). When a cartoon was wholly Ding's it would contain an x after the signature. Dan Dowling, a Des Moines man with a similar name who succeeded Ding on the *Herald Tribune*, was also confused with him at times.

In his day the great Ding Darling was one of the most influential and most often reprinted cartoonists in America. He died on February 12, 1962.

R.M.

DARROW, WHITNEY, JR. (1909-) American cartoonist born in Princeton, New Jersey, on August 22, 1909. Whitney Darrow, Jr., was initially more interested in writing than in art. During his sophomore year at Princeton University, however, his doodlings in a notebook inspired someone to suggest that he submit some drawings to the school's humor magazine. He did so, they were accepted, and so began his career.

While attending summer classes at the Art Students League in New York and serving as art editor of the *Princeton Tiger*, Darrow refined his approach in matters of style (though he remains to this day, he says, primarily an idea man). He also changed his major from English and history to art and archaeology. Graduating in the midst of the Depression, he decided to try freelance cartooning and had immediate success with submissions to *Judge, Life* and

"At first we thought, "Oh, well, puppy love';
but now we find he's asked her here for a week end."
Whitney Darrow. © Collier's.

College Humor (at fifteen to twenty dollars per sale). As a young cartoonist, Darrow's idol was Peter Arno, and his fondest desire was to have his work represented in the *New Yorker.* He first approached the magazine in 1933, and with his second submission he enjoyed success, selling seven of ten pieces. His first panel appeared in 1934, and he has been one of the most prolific and consistent of the *New Yorker* cartoonists ever since.

Darrow is a keen observer of the world around him and has an infectiously amusing way of conveying his conclusions about what he sees. His humor is of the sort that takes a familiar idea or a cliché and pushes it just beyond the borders of plausibility. The result is seldom without its intended effect—as in the panel where the secretarial-school teacher explicates a demonstration she has arranged for her students: "Notice, class, how Angela circles, always keeping the desk between them." Regarding his brand of humor, Darrow has claimed that the various liberation movements of our time frustrate him in his search for subjects because reality seems to be constantly outstripping fantasy. Most *New Yorker* readers would hardly agree, for Darrow manages to use this predicament to advantage in cartoons like the one of a voluptuously nude female balloon floating above the holiday parade in company with the usual comic and mythic creatures. As it passes by, one onlooker remarks matter-of-factly to another, "I suppose Macy's was bound to fall in line."

The style of Darrow's pencil, charcoal and wash pieces is functional and takes second place to the substance of his work; his ideas are so often self-explanatory that complex or detailed representation is unnecessary. Even so, his renderings are disciplined and pleasing to the eye, and there is a definite if subtle individuality to them. Though his cartoons are less immediately identifiable than those of

Arno or Price or newcomers like Koren and Hamilton, one learns to recognize and appreciate the quiet craftsmanship that supports Darrow's comic inventiveness.

Collections of Darrow's work include *You're Sitting on My Eyelashes* (1943), *Please Pass the Hostess* (1949), *Stop, Miss* (1958) and *Give Up* (1966). He has also illustrated a number of books, including Sam Levenson's *Sex and the Single Child* and Jean Kerr's *Penny Candy*. In addition, since 1981 he has illustrated a number of children's books (*Walter the Homing Pigeon*, and others). In the 1990s he retired to Shelburne, Vermont, whence he still contributes an occasional cartoon for the *New Yorker*.

R.C.

DART, HARRY GRANT (1869-1938) American cartoonist born in Williamsport, Pennsylvania, in 1869. Harry Grant Dart's first job as an artist was making portraits of deceased personalities for the National Crayon Company; thenceforth he was connected with various periodicals. In the mid-1890s he worked briefly for the *Boston Herald*, and in 1898 the *New York World* sent him to Cuba to cover the Spanish-American War as a sketch artist. After the war he joined the *New York World*, rising to the rank of art editor, a working position in which he covered news events and court trials with his staff. Dart later worked for the *New York Recorder* and the *Denver Times*, but he is best remembered for his freelance magazine work, chiefly for *Life* during the first decades of the century, and for *Judge* and *Life* in the late 1920s.

Dart's work, always vast in scope and large in size, was characterized by enormously complex perspective viewpoints or architectural superstructures. For years he was obsessed with fantastic flying machines and consequently drew many aerial shots. His perspectives were always perfect, his drawing precise, his crosshatching exactingly neat, and his figures—there would often be dozens and dozens in a drawing—carefully drawn and funny. Invariably the cartoons took a full page or ran as double spreads.

The cartoonist, a member of the Players and the Society of Illustrators, died in Laconia, New Hampshire, on November 15, 1938. His work deserves rediscovery and republication today.

R.M.

We'll all be happy then.

Harry Grant Dart, 1911.

DAUMIER, HONORÉ (1808-1879) French caricaturist, cartoonist and painter born in Marseilles, France, on February 20, 1808. At age seven Honoré Daumier moved to Paris with his family. There he received a middle-class education, but he liked only to draw, and he was apprenticed to the painter Alexandre Lenoir. Daumier's first original drawing appeared in 1822, and by 1830 he was already publishing lithographs in La Silhouette. In 1831 he served a six-month jail sentence for his cartoon "Gargantua," in which he depicted King Louis-Philippe as a bloated Rabelaisian monster. In 1834 he landed in more trouble after another of his famous political cartoons, "Le Ventre Législatif" ("The Legislative Belly"), in which he castigated the entire legislative branch as one monstrous belly gobbling up the wealth of the nation.

After 1835—the year in which a stern new censorship law was passed in France—Daumier thought it prudent to abandon the more blatant political themes, and he decided to launch a more general attack on the values bred by the capitalist economic system. During that time he produced his most famous series of cartoons—*Les Bons Bourgeois* ("Solid Citizens"), *Les Moeurs Conjugales* ("Matrimonial Mores"), *Philanthropes du Jour* ("Philanthropists of the Day"), *Les Plus Beaux Jours de la Vie* ("The Best Years of Life") and others—in which he mercilessly satirized every aspect and representative of middle-class society: doctors, lawyers, judges, the army, the banks, the stock exchange—the entire structure of bourgeois life.

Daumier's wit found its best expression in two series: *Caricaturana* (1836-38), in which he depicted with obvious relish all types of fakes and charlatans—quack doctors, corrupt politicians, "bought" judges, crooked stock promoters, pandering journalists, phony evange-lists and degenerate nobles; and *Robert Macaire* (from a stage character created by actor-playwright Frédérick Lemaître), a series of over one hundred cartoons detailing the imaginative swindles perpetrated by a suave and dexterous con man.

After 1850 Daumier turned more and more to painting (his masterpiece in this field is considered to be *The Third-Class Carriage*), with only occasional forays into cartooning. Toward the end of the Second Empire, he violently attacked the regime of Napoleon III, and in 1871 he ardently supported the Paris Commune. Daumier died in obscurity on February 11, 1879.

Daumier's fame grew slowly after his death. In 1893 Henry James established Daumier's preeminent position

Honoré Daumier, "Two Barristers."

in modern art in his famous essay "Daumier, Caricaturist." A general reevaluation followed; from relative obscurity during his lifetime, Daumier now rests on a lofty pedestal as the patron saint of cartooning. Best of all, Daumier's incomparable books of cartoons have been kept in print continuously over the last 70 years, not only in his native France, but in the United States and many other countries as well.

M.H.

DAVENPORT, HOMER CALVIN (1867-1912) American cartoonist born near Silverton, Oregon, on March 8, 1867. Homer Davenport had no art training and precious little general education; he worked in his youth as a jockey, railroad fireman and circus clown. He claimed that admiration for Thomas Nast's cartoons led him to secure a job with the *Portland Oregonian,* where his abysmal artistic performance sent him on his way in short order. He had similar experiences at the *San Francisco Chronicle* and several newspapers in Chicago, but his efforts attracted the attention of William Randolph Hearst, who sensed a special quality in Davenport's crude cartoons and offered him a position with the *San Francisco Examiner* in 1892.

What Davenport lacked in draftsmanship he made up for with conceptual force, whether the political venom was his own or was supplied by a Hearst staffer. His cartoons attacking political bossism soon drew statewide attention, and when Hearst moved to New York in 1895 to take over the *Journal,* he brought Davenport along as a linchpin in his drive to agitate the city. Less than a decade later, Davenport drew a series of cartoons unrivaled in

Honoré Daumier, caricature of Victor Hugo.

Wall Street's New Generation
Homer Davenport, 1898.

savagery and effectiveness since the days of Nast in his prime and *Puck*'s Blaine series. Hearst published the cartoons in an extremely large format, and Davenport's work is perhaps the closest a major American cartoonist has come to pure propagandizing and cynical rejection of reasoned advocacy. In 1896 he was paid to bludgeon McKinley; his portrayals of the candidate and his manager, Mark Hanna, as slave-driving murderers competed in irresponsibility with Republican cartoons of William Jennings Bryan as a crazed anarchist—but they did attract attention to the fledgling *Journal,* which was all they were really supposed to do. Hanna's exaggerated corpulence and his suit festooned with dollar signs ("Dollar Mark" was his nickname) were Davenport's contribution to cartoon iconography. Other targets included Republican boss Tom Platt of New York, who tried in vain to pass an anti-cartoon bill (such efforts were not unknown at the turn of the century) because of Davenport's barbs.

Davenport admired Theodore Roosevelt, and in 1904 the cartoonist switched to the Republican *New York Mail,* where he drew his most famous cartoon, *"He's Good Enough for Me,"* Uncle Sam's endorsement of the Rough Rider for reelection. It was widely reprinted as a campaign document. As an advocate, however, Davenport lost his force. He drew less often after 1904, though he returned to the pro-Roosevelt cause during the Bull Moose campaign, just before his death. He turned increasingly to private pursuits, in-cluding the breeding of the only (at that time) pure white Arabian horses in America, a gift of the sultan of Turkey, who made Davenport the Desert Brother of Akmut Haffez, the Great Bedouin. Davenport was the author of *Cartoons by Homer C. Davenport, The Bell of Silverton and Other Short Stories of Oregon* and *The Dollar or the Man?* He died at his home in Morris Plains, New Jersey, on May 2, 1912.

If Nast was a bit stiff as a draftsman, Davenport was a puzzle: anatomy, composition and rendering were unknown elements in his artistic universe. The figures in his drawings are awkward—arms fall to different lengths, heads fit on necks strangely—and backgrounds scribble off into confusion. But Davenport was never embarrassed. Every cartoon was a devastating statement, an attack that riveted attention so forcibly as to render criticism of the drawing superfluous—a rare feat for a bad artist. In spite of his shortcomings as an artist (in justice, it must be said that some of his cartoons were handsome, or at least adequate), Davenport stands as the best proof that artistic competence is but one component of the political cartoonist, and not necessarily the most important.

R.M.

DAVIS, ROY (1921-) It is difficult to decide whether Roy Davis should be entered in this series as a 'Cartoonist' or a 'Comic Artist'; or, indeed, if there were a third volume, a 'Scriptwriter.' His career has not only embraced all three, but even a fourth cartooning field, that of a film animator.

Roy Davis was born in October, 1921, in London, the son of a church verger. Failing the Junior County Scholarship at the age of eleven, he eventually furthered his education at the West Kensington Central School on the Commercial Side, where for four years he studied typing, short-hand and bookkeeping. Granted an interview for a job at Sandersons, a famous firm of furnishers, he had the courage to enquire after an opportunity in their design studio. Given the chance to paint a bowl of flowers as a test piece, he was immediately given a job as a junior artist. Gone for ever was typing, shorthand and the keeping of books!

It is interesting to note that comics, which would form a major part of his latterday career, had no interest for him as a youngster. Instead he admired the humorously weird 'inventions' of W. Heath Robinson, who inspired him to devise his own crazy inventions. 'Fougasse' was another inspiration, but not at Sandersons, where he designed flowers for wallpaper!

On the outbreak of World War Two, Roy joined the R.A.F. Regiment, where he took a commission. He served in Singapore, Java and finally Berlin, although the aftermath of the war took him to India before he was demobilized in 1946. Sandersons took him back on the art staff and asked him to design a bowl of flowers! As this was the first thing he had done for them in 1938, Roy felt more than frustrated, and began to seek work elsewhere. Spotting an advertisement for cartoonists to join the brand new J. Arthur Rank Animation Studio being opened at Moor Hall in Cookham, Berkshire, by the ex-Disney director David Hand, Roy sent in some samples and was immediately taken on as a trainee animator. Excited by the job, he took a one-third price cut from his weekly stipend at

Sandersons, who were paying him six guineas. Failing to make it as a full animator, Roy was tried out in the Story Department. Here he made good, and with character design and gag creation he became a minor force at the studio. Eventually Rank closed the studio, but with great confidence the well-trained cartoonist left animated cartoons for the popular press.

Roy was soon a full-blown freelancer of gag cartoons, contributing to the many publications that were pleased to publish one-off jokes in the postwar period. He drew for the monthly *London Opinion*, the weekly *Punch*, the upper-class society weekly *Tatler*, and the working-class *Daily Mirror* (a series entitled "Laughter at Work"), *Tit Bits* and *Sporting Record*. His unique style, wherein all the characters looked more like toys, or neatly carved puppets, than humans, soon caught the editorial eye. He continued cartooning for many years, and from 1950, Roy began submitting strips to children's comics.

In 1950 Roy began a burlesque serial called *55 B.C.*, a comic history of Britain under the Roman invaders. This ran in *The Sun*, a weekly comic newly taken over by the Amalgamated Press. Other historical epics followed: *Alfred the Great*, *Ethelred the Unready*, and *1066* in *Sun*, *Private Tich* in *Comet*, and *Whacko the Wizard* in *Mickey Mouse Weekly*. The strip closest to his animation background was Roy's lively serial page about *Harold Hare*, a character not of his creation, but one which had many cartoonists throughout the years. From 1960 he worked mainly for *Lion*, a new boys' comic, supplying *Drake Ahoy!*, *The Backwood Boys* and *P.C.1*. For *TV21* he drew *The Boy King* (1969), and had the gall to see his *Lion* series reprinted in *Whizzer & Chips* in the 1970's, without pay!

Leonard Matthews, editor of *Knockout* and other titles, took Roy on as a staff script writer in the early 1960's, where he served the comics for ten years, never using his learned ability as a typist, but always his other learned ability as a gag-man. All his scripts were supplied as pencil roughs, ready for the artists concerned to adapt as they fancied. The volume of characters created and scripts written by Roy is impossible to assess. Even after going freelance again, in his 'retirement,' he produced one script a day! Famous characters he created in this period include 'Sam Snake,' 'Oddball,' 'Joker,' 'Faceache,' 'Gums' (a burlesque of the film *Jaws*), 'Animalad,' 'Shipwreck School,' 'Chalky,' 'Scream Inn,'and dozens more. And he still finds time enough to create three-dimensional comic sculptures out of junk!

D.G.

DAY, CHAUNCEY ADDISON (1907-) American cartoonist born in Chatham, New Jersey, on April 6, 1907. Chauncey ("Chon") Day attended Manlius Military School from 1923 to 1926 and then Lehigh University. His father was a lawyer who felt Chon should become a civil engineer, not a cartoonist. At Lehigh he drew humorous spot art for the *Burr*, the university's humor magazine. As his father wouldn't finance art school, Chon Day was on his own and held a variety of jobs. In 1928 he sold cars, such long-extinct makes as the Hudson and the Essex. He was also a dispatcher for Western Union.

He eventually attended the Art Students League in New York City and there studied under Boardman Robinson and George Bridgman. Day felt he learned quite a bit from Bridgman, but he left the school the day Bridgman took a drawing Day had worked on for two weeks, erased it and sketched in how he said it should look. Day promptly erased Bridgman's drawing and walked out of the class. He began publishing cartoons in 1929, with sales to the *New Yorker*, *Film Fun*, *Ballyhoo*, *Slapstick* and *Hooey*.

"Well, the curse is starting to work. My wife is on her way out here."

Chon Day. © True.

Chon Day's distinctive style gives a sense of open space to his cartoons, which are drawn in a thin, shaky line. He draws with a variety of fountain pens, and his line style began during World War II, when paper was scarce and he got an excellent buy on some thin charcoal paper with a rough finish. Once his initial supply was gone he found #1025 paper by Bee Paper Company the most compatible with his needs. Editors seemed to love the shaky look, and Day stayed with it and refined it. Most of his cartoons have some benday or wash tone to round out the figures or cast a shadow. He has never felt comfortable with strong, heavily inked black areas in his compositions.

Chon Day's cartoons have been published by nearly every major national magazine, from the *New Yorker*, *Saturday Evening Post* and *Look* to *Playboy*. His most famous cartoon feature, *Brother Sebastian*, was created at the request of Gurney Williams when the renowned cartoon editor left *Collier's* to join *Look*. Williams was taking Larry Reynolds's panel *Butch* with him to *Look* and wanted a companion piece. As *Butch* featured two bumbling robbers, a gentle little monk was the perfect foil.

Chon Day's ability to sell the gag with his simple, ordered and well-designed cartoons and the year-in-year-out consistency of his humor have earned him a spot at the pinnacle of the magazine cartoon field. In 1956, 1962 and 1971 he won the National Cartoonists Society's award for

Best Magazine Cartoonist. At 91 years of age he lives in Rhode Island and still draws an occasional cartoon.

B.C.

DAY, CHON
See Day, Chauncey Addison.

DAY, ROBERT JAMES (1900-1985) American cartoonist born in San Bernardino, California, on September 25, 1900. Robert Day studied at the Otis Art Institute in Los Angeles between 1919 and 1927, when he was also employed in the art department of the *Los Angeles Times.* In 1927 he moved to the *Los Angeles Examiner,* and in 1930 he came east to New York, where he joined the staff of the *Herald-Tribune.* As a cartoonist he has been widely represented since the early 1930s in the *New Yorker,* the *Saturday Evening Post, Punch, Look, Saturday Review, This Week* and *Sports Illustrated,* among others. A prolific producer of comic art, he seems less wedded to a particular style than many of his colleagues, using a quick ink line here, a highly detailed wash there. One of his early *New Yorker* pieces—which has become something of a classic because of the gag, Eleanor Roosevelt visiting a coal mine—illustrates Day's mastery. One would be hard put to find a more genuinely gloomy setting—the darkened pit of a mine feebly illumined by head lamps—applied to the purposes of humor.

At his best Day is a very funny man capable of sharp asides about a world he has seen change a great deal since his entry into it at the turn of the century. On the effects of television, for example: a man changing a flat tire in a driving rainstorm explains to his two small children inside the car, "Don't you understand? This is *life,* this is what is happening. We can't switch to another channel." If he has a flaw, it lies in his very productivity. He is certainly one of the most widely published cartoon artists of the century, and it is not surprising that he should occasionally strike a flat note. For the most part, however, his consistency is admirable. Along with Steig, he was the most frequently reproduced artist in the *New Yorker*'s 50th anniversary album, and his cartoons have been exhibited in shows throughout the United States and Europe. He died in February 1985.

"I'll look it up to be sure,
but I'm positive you're not in our free-delivery area."
Robert Day. © Collier's.

Books: *All Out for the Sack Race* (1945); *We Shook the Family Tree* (1946); *Fun Fare* (1949); *Lower Prices Are Coming* (1950); *Stories I Like to Tell* (1952) and *Little Willie* (1953) by Arthur Godfrey; *Any Old Place with You* (1958); *Mad World of Bridge* (1960); *Over the Fence Is Out* (1961); *What Every Bachelor Knows* (1961); *I've Only Got Two Hands and I'm Busy Wringing Them* (1966); and *Rome Wasn't Burnt in a Day* (1972).

R.C.

The Lickin'
"The Days of Real Sport." © New York Tribune.

DAYS OF REAL SPORT, THE (U.S.) A nostalgia-packed, sentiment-filled panel, *The Days of Real Sport* was Clare Briggs's recollection of and paean to his own small-town boyhood. It is difficult to ascertain the exact date of the feature's start, but it seems to have originated in the *New York Tribune* in the early 1910s.

The Days of Real Sport consisted of small vignettes with a constantly expanding cast of characters, the most prominent being Skinnay, who was never seen but whose presence was always made known by some of the other kids ("Oh, Skin-nay!"). Thus Briggs lovingly recalled the small joys and vicissitudes of a young boy growing up, from the paternal licking to the first pair of long pants ("Are they your pa's, ha, ha?"). The panel characters (boys were primarily featured) were depicted as high-spirited and prank-loving but never mean or vicious; there was not one juvenile delinquent in the lot. Each panel had a descriptive subtitle ("The Talking Machine," "The Party," "The Giant Cracker," "Fifteen Years Old," etc.) which immediately set the mood of the piece.

The Days of Real Sport was one of Briggs's most celebrated panels and continued to be reprinted in newspapers around the country long after its creator's death in 1930.

M.H.

Philibert Debucourt, "The Public Promenade," 1792.

DEAN, ABNER
See Epstein, Abner.

DEBUCOURT, PHILIBERT-LOUIS (1755-1832) French caricaturist and engraver born in Paris, France, on February 13, 1755. After studying art with the renowned master Joseph-Marie Vien, Philibert Debucourt was admitted to the Academy in 1782. He first practiced oil painting but then, starting in 1785, took up watercoloring and especially etching.

Debucourt was greatly influenced by William Hogarth's engravings, and he was one of the first artists to introduce the tradition of English caricature and cartooning to the Continent. He often depicted the fads and manias of his times, and since he lived through one of the most troubled periods in French history, his drawings and etchings carry a historic importance at least equal to their artistic quality. He spurned Hogarth's more vulgar proclivities, always preferring the velvet glove of irony to the mailed fist of caricature. Emmanuel Bénézit characterized him as "the engraver of French elegance," but he could also be biting and vigorous, as in his depictions of aristocratic decadence (*La Manie de la Danse* and *La Promenade Publique*) and later of bourgeois smugness. Debucourt's position as one of the founding fathers of French cartooning was later reinforced when he made a number of engravings from sketches by his contemporary Carle Vernet. So great was his fame in these years that his color etchings (described as belonging to "the grotesque genre") were usually sold with an English as well as a French text.

Debucourt died at his country home in Belleville (then a village outside Paris, later incorporated into the city) on September 22, 1832.

M.H.

DECAMPS, ALEXANDRE-GABRIEL (1803-1860) French cartoonist and painter born in Paris, France, on March 3, 1803. Alexandre Decamps studied art with Abel de Pujol,

Charles X as "le pieu monarque."

Alexandre Decamps, 1830.

and early in life he developed a conviction that art should serve socially useful causes. He started his cartooning career on the Parisian magazines of his time and soon became famous for his biting political caricatures of the leaders of the day. His targets included King Charles X, whom he satirized in two famous and savage cartoons, "Charles X, the Pious Monarch" and "The Year of Grace 1830, Fifth of the Glorious Reign," that depicted the king as a decadent, ridiculous and senile figure soon to be engulfed by the winds of revolution.

In the late 1830s Decamps abandoned cartooning in favor of oil painting. He did a number of Oriental compositions which he based on his two-year stay in Turkey in 1827-28, as well as a number of socially conscious paintings (*The Beggars,* which he completed in 1845, is probably his most significant work in this genre).

Alexandre Decamps died in Fontainebleau, near Paris, on August 22, 1860.

M.H.

DECKER, RICHARD (1907-) American cartoonist born in Philadelphia, Pennsylvania, in 1907. Richard Decker studied at the School of Industrial Design in Philadelphia. His work first began appearing in the *New Yorker* in the early 1930s, when he was also a frequent contributor to *Collier's, Life* and the *Saturday Evening Post.* Using watercolors, oils and woodblock prints, Decker specialized in humorous art as opposed to caricature. This choice of media and approach places him in the tradition of great political cartoonists like Nast and Daumier and links him with his older *New Yorker* colleague Garrett Price rather than with the modern gagsters. Yet he remained primarily a gag cartoonist, and unlike his contemporaries Constantin Alajalov and Norman Rockwell, he stuck to a format employing art and caption in a mutually reinforcing context. Occasionally he did simple line drawings in ink, but for the most part he was a painter who thought like a cartoonist.

And a rather funny cartoonist, at that. One especially fine example of Decker's work is a church scene featuring two anything but delicate-looking workers and a priest. The picture reveals that one of the workers has just dropped a hammer from his perch up on a ladder and bounced it off his colleague's head. While the priest looks benevolently on, the injured party remonstrates with his fellow in a most unlikely way: "Gee, Jack! That was very careless of you." This sort of symbiosis between art and humor is characteristic of Decker's output and exemplifies his technique.

Decker's work has been exhibited at the New York Illustrators Show, the Philadelphia Art Alliance, the Philadelphia Academy of Fine Arts and the Salon of American Humorists in New York. Decker's cartoons appeared regularly in the *New Yorker* into the mid 1950s, after which his output somewhat declined. He has not been heard from since the 1980s and is presumably deceased.

R.C.

DEDINI, ELDON LAWRENCE (1921-) American cartoonist born in King City, California, on June 29, 1921. Eldon Dedini grew up in the Salinas Valley region and has lived in California throughout his career, though his submissions have mainly been to magazines with editorial offices in the East. His cartoons have been a most enjoyable feature of national magazines since 1940, when he sold his first to *Esquire.*

Dedini decided to become a cartoonist while in high school. He learned how to submit roughs to magazines and gleaned the names of cartoon editors from a how-to book by Lawrence Lariar. Encouraged by an art teacher at Salinas Junior College, Dedini submitted samples and for experience offered to work for free on the *Salinas Index-Journal* and the *Salinas Morning Post.* With the teacher's help Dedini earned college credits for his editorial cartoons.

In 1942 he won a scholarship to Chouinard Art Institute in Los Angeles, but he deliberately went to school only four days a week so he could continue to freelance magazine cartoons. From 1944 to 1946 he did storyboards for the Disney studio. One day at Disney he received a call from Dave Smart, editor at *Esquire,* who offered to double Dedini's salary if he would work exclusively for *Esquire* as a gag man and featured cartoonist. This arrangement lasted from 1946 to 1950. However, he continued to sell to *Esquire* into the 1960s.

In 1950 he began selling to the *New Yorker,* and in 1960 Hugh Hefner began to publish Dedini cartoons in *Playboy.* The full-page color Dedini cartoon in a wet watercolor style has become a regular *Playboy* feature. Rubenesque nymphs and licentious satyrs, themes Dedini first did for *New Yorker* cartoons, have subsequently blossomed to their full potential in *Playboy.* In addition, he excels in the humorous treatment of historical period pieces. Social and political comment also surfaces in Dedini's work.

Dedini writes almost all of his own gags, and back in his *Esquire* days he wrote many of the gags for other *Esquire* cartoonists such as Paul Webb, Barbara Shermund and E. Simms Campbell. He acknowledges having been influenced in the development of his style by the watercolors of E. Simms Campbell and the work of Peter Arno and Whitney Darrow, Jr.

Dedini's color cartoons are carefully staged. He calls them "productions." However, simplicity of design and gag, usually arrived at through hard work, are hallmarks of his style. The lush, painterly richness of his color work blends perfectly with the ripeness of the female form he draws for his *Playboy* cartoons. With heavy washes running the full range of tone from light gray to black, Dedini keeps this painterly look in his black-and-white cartoons. No matter what his theme, Dedini's work seeks the good strong laugh, not the chuckle. More often than not, he succeeds. Undoubtedly one of the superstars of magazine cartoonists, Dedini is one of a number of top cartoonists such as Dana Fradon, Mort Gerberg, and Joseph Farris, who for some bizarre reason seem to have been purged from the pages of the *New Yorker* since about the mid-1990s. Fortunately for the reading public, *Playboy* recognizes the humor and joy of his artwork that the editors of the *New Yorker* are suddenly blind to.

An anthology of his work, *The Dedini Gallery,* was published in 1961. He is also included in many cartoon anthologies published by *Playboy* and others. In 1958, 1961 and 1964 he was voted Magazine Cartoonist of the Year by the National Cartoonists Society. One more award came his way in the 1990s.

B.C.

DEITCH, GENE (1924-) American animator and producer born in Chicago, Illinois, on August 8, 1924. Gene Deitch's father was a salesman who often took his family along on his travels around the country. Deitch was educated mainly in southern California, and with the encouragement of a teacher he made his first animated cartoon at the age of 13. After graduation from high school in 1942, he was drafted into the U.S. Air Force.

Upon his return to civilian life Deitch joined with the original founders of UPA in 1946. He worked as a layout assistant and in-betweener for Bob Cannon on the "Flight Safety" series (for the U.S. Navy) and also assisted on some of the *Fox and Crow* cartoons and the first *Mr. Magoo*. In 1949 Deitch left to join the Jam Handy Organization in Detroit, where he directed a number of industrial and promotional cartoons. Returning to UPA in 1951, he subsequently became the creative director of its New York studio. During his four-year tenure, Deitch directed the celebrated Bert and Harry Piels commercials, as well as many other advertising films; he also wrote and directed the delightful entertainment cartoon *Howdy Doody and His Magic Hat* (1952).

After a short hiatus drawing a comic strip, *Terr'ble Thompson*, for United Feature Syndicate (1955-56), Deitch returned to animation. As the supervising director for Terrytoons, which had just been taken over by CBS, he oversaw the production of *Tom Terrific, Flebus, Clint Clobber* and *Gaston Le Crayon*, among other cartoons. He also directed (with Al Kouzel) the much-acclaimed *The Juggler of Our Lady* (1957).

Deitch's life took a decisive turn in 1959, when he left for Czechoslovakia to supervise Rembrandt Film's animation studio in Prague. There he directed *Samson Snap and Delilah, Anatole* and the Oscar-winning *Munro*. He also later directed many cartoons for the *Tom and Jerry* series (1960-61), the *Popeye* series (1961-62) and the *Krazy Kat* series (1962-63). He further produced a series of cartoons of his own, *Nudnik*, which Paramount released in the United States from 1963 to 1967. In recent years Deitch has been producing the ambitious "Animated Picture Book" project, adapting children's books to the animation medium. So far he has brought to the screen the works of such author-illustrators as Tomi Ungerer (*The Beast of Monsieur Racine, The Three Robbers*), Pat Hutchins (*Changes, Changes* and *Rosie's Walk*), Crockett Johnson (*Harold's Fairy Tale, A Picture for Harold's Room*), Gail Haley (*A Story—A Story*) and Maurice Sendak (*Where the Wild Things Are*). Later works in this vein include *Strega Nonna* and *Charlie Needs a Cloak* (from Tomi de Paola), *Wings, a Story of Two Chickens* (from James Marshall), and *Sylvester and the Magic Peeble* (after William Steig), among many others, which in total have won over 100 top prizes at children's film festivals.

In 1997 Deitch's memoir, *For the Love of Prague*, was published, recounting the author's three decades of life there under the Communist regime. Deitch was the only American in Prague during those years who was not beholden to the regime. He was able to have an objective view of the realities of life in Czechoslovakia that no other American was allowed to see. He was making his cartoon films for his American clients, building a life with his Czech wife, and flummoxing the Communist Party authorities at the same time. Two of his son, Kim and Simon, are also cartoonists.

M.H.

Gene Deitch, "Where the Wild Things Are," from Maurice Sendak's story. © Weston Woods.

DELANNOY, ARISTIDE (1874-1911) French cartoonist born in Béthune, in northern France, in 1874. After studies

"Army service really changes a man; since I'm back, the only thing I care about is cockfights!"

Aristide Delannoy, 1903.

at the Paris Ecole des Beaux-Arts, Aristide Delannoy started on a career as a socially conscious painter around the turn of the century. His stark, soot-filled landscapes and pictures of begrimed miners were derived from the realistic school of Gustave Courbet. At the same time, his cartoons were published in the leading humor and satire magazines of the day, including *Le Rire, La Guerre Sociale, Les Hommes du Jour* and especially *L'Assiette au Beurre,* where he first appeared in 1901.

Delannoy's cartoons were, like his paintings, strongly tinged with social protest; some of his topics included child labor, police corruption and official malfeasance. In 1908 he was sentenced to one year in prison and a heavy fine for "defamation of the honor of the military." It has been said that Delannoy's imprisonment eventually led to his death in 1911, at the age of 37.

Delannoy drew in a heavy, dark style especially suited to the gloom expressed by his captions; his emaciated, empty-eyed victims and orphans bear a strong similarity to the characters later depicted by Kathe Kollwitz.

M.H.

DEL RÍO, EDUARDO (1934-) Mexican cartoonist born in Zamora, Michoacan, on June 20, 1934. Born to a poor family, Eduardo del Río went to work at the age of 15. He worked as an office boy, bookstore employee, door-to-door salesperson and mortician's assistant. In 1965 he made his debut as a professional cartoonist on the humor magazine *Ja-Ja.* Since that time Eduardo del Rio (who signs "Ríus") has worked for most of the leading magazines and newspapers in Mexico, including *La Prensa, Novedades, Diario de México, Siempre, Politica, La Nacion* and dozens of others.

Eduardo Del Río ("Rius"). © Ja-Ja.

Ríus has also edited a number of humor publications, such as *La Gallina, Marca Diablo, El Mitote Illustrado* and *La Garapata.* It has been with his politically committed and socially conscious comic books, however, that Ríus has finally achieved widespread popularity. These include *Los Supermachos* ("The Supermales"), created in 1965, and *Los Agachados* ("The Stooped Ones"), which has earned Ríus fame and fortune since its inception in 1968.

The most famous political cartoonist in his country, Ríus has tackled national and international problems—government repression, guerrilla warfare, world hunger, corruption and inflation—in a straightforward, almost simplistic way. His leftist convictions strongly permeate all his works, even his comic books. He has received many awards, including first prize at the 1968 Montreal Cartoon Show. Ríus has had several collections of his cartoons published in book form, *Cuba para Principantes* ("Cuba for Beginners"), *La Jóven Alemania* ("Young Germany") and *Pequeño Ríus Illustrado* ("Little Ríus Illustrated") being the most notable. While continuing to contribute cartoons and drawings to Mexican and foreign publications, Rius is also very active promoting the appreciation of the art of cartooning: in 1988, for example, he organized a huge national cartoon exhibition in Cuernavaca.

M.H.

DE MARIA, GUIDO (1932-) Italian cartoonist and animator born in Lama Mocogno, Italy, on December 20, 1932. After graduation from high school, Guido De Maria attended the University of Bologna but soon abandoned his studies to devote himself to cartooning. In the 1950s he became one of the most prolific of Italian cartoonists, and his work appeared in the major Italian newspapers and magazines.

In 1960 De Maria went into advertising and later founded a production studio, Vimderfilm, which brought out a great number of short subjects, in live action as well as in animation. Among his entertainment cartoons was *Salomone, il Pirata Pacioccone* ("Solomon, the Chubby Pirate"), which can still be seen on Italian television. In 1968 he worked on the movie *Flashback,* and in 1969 he left Vimderfilm and moved to Modena, where he worked for a year with Bignardi's studio.

In 1971 he founded a new studio, Playvision, and with Franco Bonvicini ("Bonvi") created *Nick Carter,* a series especially designed for television. In 1972, again for television, he produced the *Gulp, i Fumetti in TV* program and several specials devoted to the comics. From 1972 to 1976 he produced 25 *Nick Carter* shorts, as well as other shorts featuring famous comic characters, among which *Alan Ford e il Gruppo TNT* ("Alan Ford and the TNT Group") was the most successful. Since March 1977, De Maria has been directing *Supergulp, i Fumetti in TV* ("Super-gulp, the Comics on TV"), which is an expanded version of his earlier *Gulp.* De Maria remains an important player on the Italian scene, notably working on the new series of Nick Carter cartoons of the 1980s and 1990s.

L.S.

Michel Demers. © L'Aurore.

DEMERS, MICHEL (1949-) Canadian cartoonist born in Quebec City, Canada, on April 20, 1949. After studies in Quebec and Montreal, Michel Demers had his first cartoon published in the French-language weekly *Sept-Jours;* since that time he has been contributing one cartoon to the magazine every week.

Michel Demers is now busily engaged in a promising and prolific professional career. His political and gag cartoons have appeared in such publications as *Forum, Perspectives* and the daily *Le Jour.* He has also produced several comic strips, the most notable being *Célestin* for *Le Jour*, but none have proved long-lived.

Michel Demers has been influenced, in his graphic style as well as in his choice of themes, by Tomi Ungerer and Jean-Jacques Sempé: his drawings have a dry, sparse look, while his themes lean heavily toward surrealism, social protest and black humor.

M.H.

DEMOCRITO II

See Cao, José María.

DENI

See Denisov, Viktor Nikolayevich.

DENISOV, VIKTOR NIKOLAYEVICH (1893-1946) Soviet cartoonist and poster designer born in Moscow, Russia, on February 24, 1893. After studying art under the noted teacher Nikolay Ulyanov, Viktor Denisov started his cartooning career in 1913 (under the pseudonym "Deni") with contributions to the magazines *Bich, Satirikon, Sontse Rossii,* etc.

After the outbreak of the Russian Revolution in 1917, Deni turned to social and political cartooning. During the ensuing civil war he also devoted his talents to poster painting, first in Kazan and later in Moscow. In 1921 he became the permanent editorial cartoonist for *Pravda,* and he exerted a tremendous influence on the course of Soviet political cartooning. His style, hard-edged and almost realistic, became the official norm for all aspiring cartoonists of the period in the USSR. In addition to his daily cartoons Deni also designed a number of propaganda posters (those he did during World War II are now highly regarded as among the best efforts in the field).

Deni was made an Honorable Art Worker of the Soviet Federated Socialist Republic in 1932. He died in Moscow on August 3, 1946.

M.H.

DEPOND, MOISE (1917-) French cartoonist and animated cartoon director born in western France on October 9, 1917. Moise Depond was taking courses at the Ecole des Beaux-Arts of Tours and also earning a living as a schoolteacher when he saw Saul Steinberg's *All in Line* (1945) and decided to embark on a cartooning career in 1946. Under the pen name "Mose" he has worked mainly for *Paris-Match.*

His drawings, which are more like visual gags, show in a clear, direct and unobstructed style the inescapable absurdity of fate: a man drowning in a puddle or a truck driver crushed to death by a falling rock in a barren desert. Not all his cartoons are so cruel; in one, a cop surrepti-

Moise Depond ("Mose"). © Fernand Hazan.

tiously gives a ten-franc note to a hobo—who is totally flabbergasted.

Mose's drawings have appeared in several albums, among them *Manigances* ("Underhanded Machinations," 1953, with Chaval and François), *Noirs Dessins* ("Black Designs," 1956), *Paris Ma Rue* ("Paris Is My Street," 1964, a 24-page continuous strip) and *Mosaïque* (1971). His artwork has also been exhibited in Prague, Casablanca, Paris and Brussels. In addition to book illustrations (e.g., Swift, Twain, language texts) Mose has created more than fifty animated cartoons, from *Bonjour Paris* for Jean Image (1951-52) to the TV series *Romeo* (1965) to *Animoses* (1973). He retired in the mid-1980s to devote himself to painting and collage techniques.

P.H.

DERGATCHOV, OLEG (1961-) Oleg Dergatchov was born in Rostov-on-Don, Russia, July 18, 1961. He graduated from the Ukrainian Print Academy in Lvov. From 1979 to 1989, he worked as a book illustrator in the Soviet Union, Ukraine, and Moldova, but tired of working with publishers and struck out on his own as a printer. In 1989, Dergatchov established Do Press, a small printing shop in his Lvov home, where he has hand-crafted and published 20 limited edition books. Working on the principle that the words and images should be drawn by the same hand, Dergatchov combines a number of products from his fertile mind to make the books - poems, etchings, drawings, printing.

Oleg Dergatchov. © Oleg Dergatchov.

Jean-Pierre Desclozeaux. © Albin Michel.

Dergatchov works in other fields besides bookmaking, such as graphic arts, caricature, painting, cartooning, drawing, sculpture, and photography. His cartoons have been featured in nine one-man exhibitions and at least 60 group showings all over Europe, Japan, U.S., and Canada. He has been awarded many prizes including the grand prize at both Satyricon (Legnica, Poland) and the International Competition of Humorous Drawings, Anglet, and others in Australia; Belgium, Italy, Germany, Turkey, Poland, Russia, Japan, Macedonia, Slovakia, and Yugoslavia.

Calling his style lyrical surrealism, Dergatchov incorporates aspects of the real, the absurd, and the grotesque into his cartoons, sometimes blurring the distinction between comedy and tragedy, painting and cartooning. His masterful technique is less important to him than the message and aesthetic pleasure he wants to give. Dergatchov has said: "My line is my way, created on paper and extended during my wanderings and journeys. It is not possible to measure the lines of our life or to get to know them. The magic of drawing is akin to the everlasting fascination with the mysterious and the unknown."

J.A.L.

DES

See Asmussen, Andreas.

DESCLOZEAUX, JEAN-PIERRE (1938-) French cartoonist born near Paris, France, in 1938. After finishing his studies, J.-P. Desclozeaux went to work as a commercial artist and industrial designer. In the early 1960s he started sending cartoons to different publications, and he now appears widely in such magazines *as Paris-Match, Le Nouvel Observateur* and *Elle,* as well as in the yearly cartoon exhibitions he has organized since 1966 in Avignon, in southeastern France.

Desclozeaux's cartoons are often cruel and unyielding, and the artist himself is frequently classified as a "black humorist." Yet he can also be dreamlike and even nostalgic, as in his flippant retelling of fairy tales. His satire is pointed, but it aims more at the human condition than at any political or social aspect of society. There are two sides to Desclozeaux's work: the bitterness of his cartoons of a world gone mad (as in his depiction of office workers imprisoned in cabinet drawers), and the lightheartedness of his drawings of circuses, jugglers and clowns. It is no wonder, then, that an essay discussing his work was titled "Tender and Cruel Desclozeaux."

Desclozeaux's cartoons have been anthologized in a number of books, the latest being *L'Oiseau-Moqueur* ("The Mocking-Bird," 1977). From 1980 on he has added numerous new vehicles for his cartoons, including *Le Figaro Littéraire, Playboy,* as well as *L'Anamorfico* in Italy and *Nebelspalter* in Switzerland.

M.H.

DESETA, ENRICO (1908-198?) Italian cartoonist and illustrator born in Catania, Italy, on February 17, 1908. Enrico Deseta's father, a lawyer, moved to Rome with his family when Enrico was still a child. Deseta went to school in Rome, where he developed a talent for drawing; his first drawing was accepted by the satirical weekly *Serenissimo* when he was not yet 15.

In 1930 Deseta joined the staff of *Il Travaso;* in the color pages he drew for this magazine, he already displayed mastery of the humor cartoon with his limpid, wriggly, highly individual line. He reached his height, however, with his collaboration on *Marc' Aurelio,* which began publication in 1938. There he created his famous gallery of neurotic characters, sexually repressed and always on the verge of exploding, drawn with a stylized line that prefigured the work of Johnny Hart or Charles Schulz. Some of these characters have become legendary, such as Bacu the Magician, whose likeness was painted on the fuselages of warplanes, and whose supernatural powers have passed into the Italian language.

In 1937 Deseta formed a small group of Italian cartoonists around the weekly *Argentovivo* in order to compete against the flood of foreign comics. He edited and drew several comic strips for *Argentovivo,* including *Capitan Rosmarino* and *Ludovico.* During the 1940s Deseta contributed short stories to the girls' weekly *La Piccola Italiana,* but his efforts were mainly devoted to the Fascist youth weekly *Il Balilla,* for which he drew cartoons, illustrations and several comic strips; one of these strips, *Re Giorgetto d'Inghilterra* ("King Georgie of England") became famous because of its central character, *Ciurcillone* (Li'l Churchill), who was a favorite with children. Since this defeated the purpose of making Churchill into a hated symbol, Deseta was reprimanded by his boss.

Deseta pursued his activities regardless of historical circumstances. In 1944, along with Federico Fellini, he founded the Funny Face Shop, where the Allied soldiers who had just liberated Rome could have their caricatures drawn by the two cartoonists against the background of the Colosseum or Saint Peter's Basilica. In recent times Deseta has collaborated on *Clown,* where he drew with particular humor a panel titled *La Ballata del Povero Cittadino* ("The Ballad of the Poor Citizen"). Since the collapse in the 1970s of most of the humor magazines, he has devoted most of his time to designing movie posters. Since the collapse in the 1970s of most of the humor magazines, he devoted his time mainly to designing movie posters until his death at the end of the 1980s.

S.T.

DE VERE, ALISON (ca. 1930-) Alison de Vere is one of the leading feminist animators in England. She has won the Grand Prix at Annecy Animation Festival more than once, including *Cafe Bar* (1975) and *Monsieur Pascal* (1979). Her first desire was to become a painter, which she studied at London's Royal Academy of Art. She failed to finish the course, marrying while still a student. She took many kinds of jobs ending up as a paint-and-tracer on Paul Grimault's cel animated film *The King and Mr. Bird.* This was her first experience of animation, and the work changed her life. She won a job at the Halas & Batchelor Studio as a color mixer in 1956, gave birth to a son, but concluded her marriage to artist Karl Weschke.

Television commercials were her next field, plus many instructional films, credit sequences and special effects for features. Meanwhile she began to write poetry for underground magazines and in 1969 she made her first personal film, *Two Faces.* The World Health Organization commissioned her to make a ten-minute film about drug addiction. This used animated silhouettes and was called *False Friends.* She became background supervisor on the famous Beatles musical feature *Yellow Submarine,* under art director Heinz Edelman. Then came along a ten-year stint at the Wyatt-Cattaneo Studio. Here she was given time to make her next two personal films, *Cafe Bar* (1975) and *Mister Pascal* (1979). Even more personal and certainly longer and more perfect in animation was her *Black Dog* (1987), sponsored by the independent commercial station Channel 4 after their animation editor Paul Madden saw her preliminary sequence of three minutes' animation. Inspired by her dreams, she recalls, "The dog itself used to haunt my dreams, which is also where the ship with eyes and the wheel that becomes a child come from." Her style and philosophy are summed up in her comment, "An animator has to be some kind of actor."

D.G.

DEVÉRIA, ACHILLE (1800-1857) French cartoonist, book illustrator and lithographer born in Paris, France, on February 6, 1800. In Paris Achille Devéria studied with Girodet and Laffitte. His lithographs (totalling almost 450) of high-society ladies and their coquettish ways and of the most important personalities of the arts express charming wit, good humor and graceful elegance. The most interesting series of women are *Galerie Fashionable, Le Goût Nouveau* ("The New Taste") and *Les Heures de la Parisienne* ("The Hours of the Parisian Woman," 1840). His portraits of the high priests of French romanticism (Hugo, Balzac, Liszt, Dumas, Delacroix, etc.) are remarkable for the way they capture the very essence of the artists' characters without the caricatural devices found in Nadar and Gill. Using wood engraving, a technique which had then been repopularized, Devéria also illustrated numerous literary works, among them La Fontaine's *Fables* (1826) and Defoe's *Robinson Crusoe* (1836).

Achille Devéria was assistant curator of the Prints

Department of the Imperial Library (now Bibliothèque de France) from 1848 to April 1857, when he was promoted to head of the department. He died that same year on December 23.

P.H.

DEVILMAN (Japan) *Devilman* was created by the Japanese comic book artist Gō Nagai at the request of Toei Dōga ("Toei Animation") in 1972. It was unique in that it appeared simultaneously as a comic strip and as an animated television series. It was inspired by the success of a previous work of Nagai's entitled *Maō Dante* ("Dante, Lord of the Devils"), which first appeared in the comic book *Bokura Magazine.* In both formats, *Devilman* was a stunningly exotic work characterized by powerful images and plenty of action. The plot of the comic strip formed the basis for the movie. Akira Fudō the young hero, learns that the forces of evil as personified by a host of devils are attempting to destroy mankind. The only way he can combat this menace is to become one of them: Akira becomes Devilman and devotes his life to battling hordes of monsters and demons.

The comic strip managed to interweave a bizarre vision of a universe populated by spine-chilling monsters with a fascinating theme of good versus evil. It was graphically violent and at times filled with erotic imagery. The animated version, however, was of necessity aimed at a younger audience, and the plot had to be toned down considerably. At its worst it was a series of endless battles between Devilman, who had seven super-powers, and the innumerable monsters arrayed against him, but the cartoons were in brilliant color (which the comic strip was not), and the images never lost their impact. Nagai relied on illustrated books of flora and fauna as his source of inspiration for the countless monsters he created. Comic relief was provided in the animation by minor characters such as Akira's girl friend's little brother. *Devilman* ran from July 8, 1972, to April 7, 1973, on the NET television network in Japan for 39 episodes. It was produced by Yoshifumi Hatano (who also worked on *Okami Shōnen Ken,* Japan's first animation for television), and the script was written by Masaki Tsuji.

In 1973 Devilman appeared in a full-length animation feature titled *Majinger Z vs. Devilman,* based on a story developed by Nagai and his company, Dynamic Productions. In it Devilman and Majinger Z, another character created by Nagai in his comic strip of the same name (1972), were involved in a series of battles, but the movie lacked the suspense and gripping power of the *Devilman* television series and comic strip. It was produced by Toei Dōga with Junichi Toishi. Koichi Kadota was in charge of animation. The television series has also been remade into two Original Video Animation volumes in 1997, both available in North America in an English-language version.

F.S.

DICKINSON, GEOFFREY (1933-1988) Geoffrey Samuel Dickinson, born in Liverpool, England, on May 5, 1933, sent his first cartoon to *Punch* in 1963, and would serve on its staff until 1984, when he left to become a pocket cartoonist for a national newspaper. After school he attended the Stockport School of Art from 1950 to 1953, then advanced to the Royal Academy Schools until 1957. His intention was to become a landscape painter, but instead he became the art master at Tavistock Boys School in Croydon (1957), then moved to teach art at Selhurst Grove School until 1967.

In 1963 he began to freelance graphics to BBC Television, then began to send cartoons around to various magazines. Two years later he was so far advanced as a cartoonist that he won the 1965 First Prize at the International Periodical Publishers Congress in Rome. This prize was for his color cover for *Punch,* and the award prompted the editor to offer him a staff job as Deputy Art Editor. Two years later he was made a member of the exclusive *Punch* Table, which entitled him to engrave his initials on the ancient board.

Geoff drew two covers for *Time* magazine (1966-1967), and freelanced cartoons to *Reader's Digest, Esquire* and *High Life.* He also left the *Punch* staff in 1984 to join the important daily, *Financial Times,* supplying a regular column-breaker or "pocket cartoon," as they are known in the trade. Geoff died on March 21, 1988. Among the collections of his cartoons, mention should be made of *There's a Lot of It About* (1985) and *Probably Just a Virus* (1986).

D.G.

DING
See Darling, Jay Norwood.

DINGODOSSIERS, LES (France) In 1965 comic writer René Goscinny and gag cartoonist Marcel Gotlib teamed up to produce a weekly panel series entitled *Les Dingodossiers,* which can be loosely translated as "The Goofy Files." The first installment appeared in the May 27 issue of the comic weekly *Pilote.*

As the title implies, these were freewheeling improvisations on a number of unrelated subjects, sometimes takeoffs on current topics, sometimes mock-serious studies of broad fields of interest, sometimes satires on well-known personalities. The similarities to *MAD* magazine were obvious, even down to the breakdown of the panels and the outrageous, pun-riddled captions. Goscinny and Gotlib attacked with relish such features of modern life as the high school newspaper, transistor radios, television news and Polaroid cameras; they slaughtered with vigor such sacred cows as paid vacations, compulsory education and space exploration; and they demolished with verve a variety of accepted ideas, from the desirability of physical exercise to the culturally enriching qualities of foreign travel (in the last one Goscinny and Gotlib had a field day showing tourists returning home from abroad even more prejudiced and parochial than before they left).

After awhile Goscinny tired of the game, or maybe ran out of ideas, and the series folded on November 30, 1967. Many of the *Dingodossiers* were later collected into two books published by Editions Dargaud in the late 1960s.

M.H.

Snail newsboy: "Extree—Extree! All about Washington crossing the Delaware!"

Gus Dirks, 1901.

DINKY DOODLE (U.S.) Dinky Doodle (not to be confused with Terrytoons' later Dinky Duck) arrived on the animation scene in cartoon adventures created by Walter Lantz and produced by the Bray studio from 1924 to 1926.

The *Dinky Doodle* series can be divided into two groups. The first had the title hero, a resourceful little boy, marching bravely into some outlandish adventure or looking for new worlds to conquer ("Dinky Doodle and the Bad Man," "Dinky Doodle in the Army," "Dinky Doodle in the Wild West" and "Dinky Doodle in the Arctic" are good examples of this trend). In the second—and more interesting—group, Dinky confronted some famous personage from legend, folklore or literature. This was the larger category and included such enjoyable little tales as "Pied Piper," "Robinson Crusoe," "Little Red Riding Hood," "The Three Bears" and "Uncle Tom's Cabin." These cartoons proved something of a trend-setter, and the formula was widely imitated in years to come, not only in animated cartoons but in comic strips as well.

All of the *Dinky Doodle* cartoons were written and directed by Walt Lantz, who was then in his twenties, and it can be assumed that the experience thus acquired helped immeasurably when Lantz set up his own animation studio later in the decade.

M.H.

DINOV, TODOR GEORGIEV (1919-) Bulgarian animator and filmmaker born in Alexandropolis, Greece, on July 24, 1919. After showing early talent for art and drawing, Todor Dinov attended the Academy of Art in Sofia, Bulgaria, from which he graduated in 1943 with a major in stage design. He became a member of the Bulgarian Communist Party in 1945 and was sent to study animation in the USSR.

After serving his apprenticeship on different phases of animation, Dinov went back to Bulgaria, where he made his first animated film, *Iunak Marko* ("Marko the Hero"), in 1955. He then brought to the screen *The Little Guardian Angel* (1956), from the humor cartoons of Jean Effel, followed by several more pleasantly drawn and competently handled cartoons. Notable among them are *The Fox Outfoxed* and *In Cannibal Country* (both 1958), *Prometheus* and *The Golden Slippers* (both 1959), *Story of a Twig* (1960), *Duo* (1961), the much-praised *The Lightning Rod* (1962), *The Apple* (1963), a rather ponderous fable called *The Daisy* (1965) and the ambitious but disappointing *Exile from Paradise* (1967). In 1970 Dinov tried unsuccessfully to adopt a more modernistic style with the overly trendy *The Artist and the Girl*. Dinov has also co-directed, with Khris Khristov, the feature film *Iconastasis* (1962). He is now involved mainly in live-action films and documentaries, although he directed a cartoon film, *The Drum*, in 1974.

Todor Dinov is without a doubt the best known of Bulgarian animators. He has received a number of prizes and awards and was declared an Honored Artist of the People's Republic of Bulgaria in 1969.

M.H.

DIRKS, GUS (ca. 1879-1903) American cartoonist born in Chicago, Illinois, around 1879. Gus Dirks was the brother of cartoonist Rudolph Dirks, who was two or three years his senior. After moving to New York in 1895 and meeting with success in the cartooning world, Rudy Dirks induced his brother to move east from Chicago. Gus did so—twice, as it turned out, for his first foray yielded few sales to magazine markets. In the late 1890s, however, he hit his stride in the humorous weeklies. In *Judge* particularly he was an instant success; readers could expect at least two Gus Dirks cartoons an issue, many of them half a page, and in color in special and holiday numbers.

In his cartoons, Dirks dealt exclusively with bug and small animal life; he was a leader in that very popular genre of the times. He utilized confident pen strokes and achieved shading effects with short thick-and-thin lines combining for textures and crosshatch patterns.

The ever-alert William Randolph Hearst noted Dirks's immense popularity around the turn of the century and secured the cartoonist's services for his Sunday supplements. For Hearst Dirks drew *Bugville Life,* a collection of panel gags named after a book of drawings published by *Judge,* with verses by R.K. Munkittrick. Tragically, Dirks's life ended in suicide in 1903. The young genius's feature was continued by Paul Bransom, but the charm and inventiveness that could have delighted another generation or two of readers was sadly absent.

R.M.

DISNEY, WALTER ELIAS (1901-1966) American animator, producer and businessman born in Chicago, Illinois, on December 5, 1901. Walt Disney's father kept moving throughout the Midwest, taking his family with him. Young Walt grew up in a variety of places and became accustomed to hard work at an early age. He sought refuge in drawing and at 14 enrolled in an art class at the Kansas City Art Institute. After briefly serving as an ambulance driver in France in World War I, he returned to the United States in 1919.

Disney then sought employment in Kansas City, where he met Ub Iwerks. The two worked together at the Kansas City Film Ad Company and in their spare time produced a series of short animated films for a movie theater, the Newman Laugh-O-Grams. This experience spurred Disney to form his own company to produce animated cartoons. The Laugh-O-Gram Company lasted until 1923, at which time Disney decided to leave for Los Angeles, where more and bigger opportunities abounded. Soon striking a deal with an independent producer, Margaret Winkler, he produced a series called *Alice in Cartoonland;* in the course of producing these cartoons (which ran from 1924 to 1926), he assembled the nucleus of his animation team, including Ub Iwerks, Hugh Harman and Rudolph Ising. In 1927 Disney embarked on a new animated series, *Oswald the Rabbit*, but it was taken away from him the next year by his scheming distributor, Charles Mintz (who had married Margaret Winkler).

Walt Disney. © Walt Disney Productions.

With the help of Iwerks, Disney then created his most famous character, Mickey Mouse, who debuted late in 1928 in the first sound cartoon, "Steamboat Willie." In 1929, following the success of *Mickey Mouse*, Disney released *Skeleton Dance,* the first of his *Silly Symphonies.* In the course of the 1930s more winning characters were added to the Disney menagerie: Goofy, Pluto and the cantankerous Donald Duck. The Disney cartoons enjoyed tremendous popularity, and Walt, with the help of his brother Roy, decided to consolidate his studio's position in the filmmaking world. In addition to his extensive use of song and color, he took the lead in the production of feature-length animated films.

The first feature was *Snow White and the Seven Dwarfs* (1937), and its success encouraged Disney to venture further into feature filmmaking. *Pinocchio* followed in 1940, and *Fantasia* later that year. In the meantime the spreading effects of World War II had drastically reduced the studio's income, and Disney was among the first to produce films for the U.S. government. At the same time he continued to make entertainment cartoons, including the whimsical *Dumbo* (1941), the almost naturalistic *Bambi* (1942) and two package films, *Saludos Amigos* (1943) and *The Three Caballeros* (1945); in a class by itself was *Victory Through Air Power,* a 1943 animated film advocating long-range bombing, based on a book by Major Alexander de Seversky.

After World War II, feature-length animation became the mainstay of Disney's production as shorts were phased out of movie house showings. From 1946 until the time of Disney's death, the studio produced the following cartoon features: *Make Mine Music* (1946), *Song of the South* (part live action, 1946), *Fun and Fancy Free* (package film, 1947), *Melody Time* (part live action, 1948), *Ichabod and Mr. Toad* (1949), *Cinderella* (1950), *Alice in Wonderland* (1951), *Peter Pan* (1953), *Lady and the Tramp* (1955), *Sleeping Beauty* (1959), *101 Dalmatians* (1961) and *The Sword in the Stone* (1963). *The Jungle Book* (1967) was completed after Disney's death.

Starting in the late 1940s Disney diversified into live-action features and documentary films. His *True-Life Adventure* and *People and Places* won a number of Oscars in their category and were widely popular. Among his best feature films, *Treasure Island* (1950), *20,000 Leagues Under the Sea* (1954), *Davy Crockett* (1955), *The Absent Minded Professor* (1961) and *Mary Poppins* (1964) are particularly noteworthy. The studio also produced the popular TV program *Disneyland* (later renamed *Walt Disney Presents)* for ABC, and its successor, *Walt Disney's Wonderful World*, for NBC. These programs have been broadcast every season since 1954. Other Disney TV series include *The Mickey Mouse Club* and *Zorro*. Disney also built the Disneyland amusement park in California in 1955; another park, Disneyworld in Florida, was well on its way to completion when Disney died in St. Joseph's Hospital, directly across from his studio in Burbank, on December 15, 1966. The empire he built endures, as strong as ever.

No man ever dominated his field as Disney dominated animation. His cartoons were the most popular, the most farsighted and the best crafted of any in the 1930s. He monopolized the Academy Award for animated shorts from the creation of the category in 1932 until 1940 (with many more Oscars afterwards). The awards and distinctions bestowed on Disney numbered more than a thousand at the time of his death, and the U.S. Post Office issued a commemorative stamp in his honor. There have been more articles and studies written on Disney than on any other film personality, with the possible exception of Charlie Chaplin. Notable among the full-length books about the man and his career are R.D. Feild's *The Art of Walt Disney* (1942), Richard Schickel's *The Disney Version* (1968) and Christopher Finch's *The Art of Walt Disney* (1975).

More than 30 years after his death the public fascination with Disney continues unabated. Many TV and film documentaries have been devoted to the man and his work in the last 15 years, along with countless newspaper and magazine articles, and more than a score of full-length books. The most informative of the latter is probably Kathy Merlock Jackson's *Walt Disney: A Bio-bibliography* (1993), which documents hundreds of references on Mickey's creator; while the most provocative is undoubtedly Marc Eliott's *Walt Disney, Hollywood's Dark Prince* (1992), which accuses Disney of having been an FBI informer.

M.H.

DISTELI, MARTIN (1802-1844) Swiss cartoonist and illustrator born at Olten, Switzerland, on May 28, 1802. Martin Disteli's father ran a successful cotton-goods factory, and young Martin had the leisure to gather notions of art technique in a dilettantish way while pursuing loftier philosophical studies in various Swiss and German cities. In 1820 he was jailed in Jena for participation in student demonstrations and decorated his cell with clever parodies of ancient Roman legends. Around 1826 he studied art in Munich for awhile, under the guidance of Peter von Cornelius. His world changed in 1829 when his father's business crumbled and the family became part of the dispossessed petty bourgeoisie of their Swiss canton. Disteli's reaction was that of a fighter for human rights.

His artistic skills now became his means of making a living. At first he drew scenes from Swiss history for liberal publishers in Aarau. Fame, but not ease, came from his illustrations of the *Fables* of Abraham Emanuel Fröhlich, etched in a manner influenced by Grandville and other contemporary Frenchmen. In 1836 Disteli became an art instructor at his old secondary school in Solothurn, but his difficult nature led to many conflicts with the authorities, a situation that was echoed in his bumpy career as an army reserve officer. Unhappy in both his marriage and his extramarital affairs, Disteli at times led the life of a true vagrant.

During the 1830s he contributed to various magazines and almanacs. He did political cartoons for J.J. Reithard's *Republikaner-Kalender* in 1834, and between 1831 and 1839 he was regularly represented in the publication *Alpenrosen*. In 1838 he founded the annual with which his name is most closely linked-the *Schweizerischer Bildkalender* (often called *Disteli-Kalender*, a term that was long used as a designation for satirical almanacs in Germany as well as in Switzerland). This liberal organ reviewed the events of the past year from a progressive point of view and aimed at enlightening the common people politically. Disteli's lithographs struck out at local and national authorities, earning him numerous lawsuits and attacks by conservative politicians and churchmen.

In the last five years of his life he worked on illustrations of the Munchausen tales, the Reinecke Fuchs (Roman de Renard) stories and other cycles about humanized insects and beasts. Most of this work was never published because of Disteli's early death (in Solothurn on March 18, 1844), but the highly interesting drawings are preserved in Swiss public collections.

S.A.

DOBBINS, JAMES J. (1924-   ) American political cartoonist born in Woburn, Massachusetts, on August 12, 1924. His education included navy courses at Cornell and a bachelor's degree from the Massachusetts College of Art in 1951. Jim Dobbins's early interest was sports cartooning, and he was influenced by Willard Mullin and Bob Coyne. He began his career on the weekly *Woburn Press* in 1945-46 and then switched to the *Woburn Daily Times* (1947-49). During the presidential campaign of 1952 and into the next year he was engaged by the *Lowell* (Mass.) *Sun*, and he substituted on the *New York Daily News* in 1953 during C.D. Batchelor's vacation. The *Boston Post* had Dobbins from 1954 to 1956, but then he went to the *Traveler* and *Herald-Traveler* until 1972 and to the *Herald-American* until 1977, when he switched to William Loeb's *Manchester*

Rocky pushing Romney in N.H.

Jim Dobbins. © Boston American.

(N.H.) *Union Leader,* one of the nation's prominent right-wing dailies.

Democrat Dobbins is a Boston institution, and his broad, freewheeling cartoons in crayon and brush show much enthusiasm. A collection of his cartoons, *Dobbins's Diary of the New Frontier,* was published after the death of John F. Kennedy. Among a host of awards Dobbins has received are thirteen Freedoms Foundation honor medals (and two grand prizes), three National Safety Council awards and the Christopher Literary Award. He is the father of ten children—five boys and five girls. Starting in the 1980s he has also illustrated a number of books, has appeared on television, and has been on the lecture circuit doing chalk talks.

R.M.

DOBUZHINSKII, MSTISLAV VALERIANOVICH (1875-1957) Russian cartoonist and graphic artist born in Novgorod, Russia, on August 14, 1875. Mstislav Dobuzhinskii studied art at the St. Petersburg School of Drawing from 1895 to 1897, then in Munich with A. Azbè and S. Hollosy from 1899 to 1901. He started his cartooning career in 1905 with contributions to the antiestablishment magazine *Zhupel* ("The Bogeyman"). His graphic style, heavily influenced by the Jugendstil school, was very distinctive and lent to his cartoons a stark, almost ghostly quality. He also did paintings and designed sets for the theater.

After the Russian Revolution, Dobuzhinskii turned primarily to book illustrations and also taught at the Academy of Art in Petrograd (now Leningrad), starting in 1922. In 1925 he moved to Lithuania and taught at the Kaunas School of Art. At the outbreak of World War II, Dobuzhinskii moved first to London, then emigrated to the United States. He designed sets for numerous Broadway productions and occasionally drew a few cartoons.

Dobuzhinskii died in New York City on November 20, 1957. Despite his self-imposed exile he has not been forgotten in his native land. His works are still being exhibited in several galleries in Leningrad, and a number of articles and monographs on his art and career have recently been published in Moscow.

M.H.

DONAHEY, JAMES HARRISON (1875-1949) American cartoonist born near West Chester, Tuscarawas County, Ohio, on April 8, 1875. J.H. ("Hal") Donahey worked in downstate Ohio as a printer's devil before moving to Cleveland in 1895. He studied drawing and sculpture at the Cleveland School of Art and supported himself by doing little busts of political figures before taking a job as a news sketch artist on the *Cleveland World.* He soon switched to the *Plain Dealer* to do cartoons at $35 a week. His first editorial cartoon appeared in the *Plain Dealer* on January 2, 1900; he subsequently drew a daily cartoon until three weeks before his death on June 1, 1949.

Donahey's only major book, *In Egypt,* an illustrated account of his travels to that still-exotic land, was published in 1915. About the same time he did illustrative reporting of the U.S. Senate for *Cartoons* magazine. Donahey's older brother Vic was a U.S. senator and three-time Ohio governor; his younger brother William was a cartoonist on the *Plain Dealer* and the *Chicago Tribune* who created one of the all-time children's classics of text and art, *The Teenie Weenies.*

The bare facts of Donahey's career mask one of the most remarkable bodies of work in cartooning history. J.H. Donahey was one of the greatest—the most talented, prolific and influential—of American native cartoonists. His drawing style, widely copied, was a combination of mature, sophisticated composition and informal, scratchy, homespun lines. He developed a method of tying all the elements in his cartoons together with a handsome crosshatch "cloud" that would float through the drawing. He worked almost exclusively in pen and ink.

Donahey's major contribution to our heritage was not a stylistic one, competent and individual though his drawing was. His genius lay rather in his method of presentation (searingly powerful but never vicious in political cartoons, a mellow nonexaggeration in caricature) and his choice of themes. Only a portion of his output was political. The rest of his panel cartoons were on subjects of home and hearth, farm and suburbia. He caught everyday events and workaday pursuits, seeming to challenge himself by dealing with even the most mundane habits of his Plain Folks characters. But in the end he succeeded in becoming the premier artist-chronicler of American democracy. His glimpses of American life are warm, sympathetic, tender, sometimes gibing, often tinged with pathos. Donahey's portraits of farmers washing up for dinner, middle-class husbands shopping for Christmas presents, little kids crying over the loss of their dogs, arguably place him ahead of McCutcheon and Briggs in this genre and certainly put him in the front rank of American cartoonists.

Discovering Donahey's lifework is one of the genuine treats awaiting cartoon historians and fans in the future. He never drew outside Cleveland, despite many offers, but his cartoons were reprinted widely; his current obscurity is one of the many ironies of cartooning history. But the body of his work—particularly the homespun material—stands as a textbook example of the genius of the art form of the cartoon: that one man could in such a simple and restricted format completely capture the soul of a people.

R.M.

DONALD DUCK (U.S.) Donald Duck made his debut in a 1934 *Silly Symphony, The Wise Little Hen,* and the first line he uttered was "Who, me? Oh, no! I got a bellyache." His character—cantankerous, ornery and irascible—was established from the first and later developed in such *Mickey Mouse* cartoons as "Orphan's Benefit" and "Mickey's Service Station." The duck's persona owed much to Art Babbit and Dick Huemer, who were responsible for his early incarnation, and to Clarence Nash, who supplied Donald's high-pitched, squawking voice.

Donald came into his own in "The Band Concert" (1935), in which his persistent fife playing constantly disturbs and finally overwhelms Mickey's performance of the *William Tell Overture.* From this point on, Donald was to co-star in most *Mickey Mouse* shorts (often alongside Goofy), contributing much of the slapstick in such classics as "Moose Hunters," "Clock Cleaners" and "Don Donald." The duck's violent and intemperate displays of emotion comically contrasted with Goofy's phlegmatic unconcern and Mickey's stiff-upper-lip determination in these and other cartoons of the period.

Donald Duck in "Donald's Dilemma." © Walt Disney Productions.

By the mid-1930s Donald had risen to unprecedented heights of popularity and was fast eclipsing Mickey as the star of the Walt Disney studios. He made his solo debut in 1937 in "Donald's Ostrich." In 1938 Donald's mischievous nephews, Huey, Dewey and Louie, made their appearance, and many of the subsequent *Donald* shorts revolved around the adversary yet affectionate relationship between the duck and the ducklings. (In addition to the initial "Donald's Nephews," best examples of the trend can be found in "Good Scouts," "Donald's Vacation" and "Fire Chief.")

After the outbreak of World War II Donald, along with other Hollywood stars, was prepared to do his duty for his country, as evidenced by such efforts as "Donald Gets Drafted," "The Vanishing Private" (in which Donald accidentally discovers invisible paint) and, most memorably, "Der Fuehrer's Face," which won a 1942 Academy Award. (Just as notable in this respect is *The Spirit of '43,* a cartoon short made for the Treasury Department and credited with leading millions of Americans to pay their income tax ahead of time.) Donald's most important contribution to U.S. policy came in the "good neighbor" department when the patriotic duck made two well-publicized visits south of the border, first in *Saludos Amigos* (1943), and later in *The Three Caballeros* (1945), where he was teamed with the Brazilian parrot José Carioca and the Mexican rooster Panchito.

After the war Donald retired to a more sedate, middleclass life. In addition to his nephews he found two new adversaries in the persons of the spunky twin chipmunks Chip and Dale ("Chip 'n' Dale," "Trailer Horn," "Up a Tree," etc.). Some of the best cartoons in Donald's later career were directed by Jack Hannah, and their fast pace and inventiveness made them as good as any in the series. Donald was depicted to best advantage in exotic situations, as in "Clown of the Jungle" (where the duck is confronted by the loony araquan bird) and "Frank Duck Brings 'em Back Alive" (in which Donald hunts for wildman Goofy, only to be left stranded in the jungle when

Goofy hotfoots it back to civilization in Donald's motorboat).

The *Donald Duck* series came to an end in the late 1950s, only a few short years after *Mickey Mouse.* Donald can now be seen only in reissues or occasionally on some of the Walt Disney programs on television. During his long career the duck has been featured on every conceivable product, from soap to toy trains. Donald Duck was also portrayed in books, in newspapers (the *Donald Duck* strip started in 1936, first as part of the *Silly Symphonies* feature, then under its own title, and was drawn most memorably by Al Taliaferro), and especially in comic books. Donald's comic book adventures, originated in 1943 under the aegis of Carl Barks, the supreme "duck artist," have contributed in perhaps even greater measure than his screen escapades to the continuing popularity of the silly duck in the silly sailor suit. More recently Donald made a cameo appearance in *Who Framed Roger Rabbit* (1988), in which he played a piano duet with Daffy Duck.

M.H.

DONOVAN, ROBERT (1921-) American cartoonist born in Buffalo, New York, on August 12, 1921. Bob Donovan, whose father was also a cartoonist, went to St. Monica's Parochial School in Buffalo, where he displayed his early talents lettering and illustrating the school newspaper. After graduation from high school in 1939, he worked in a conservation camp near Binghamton, New York, and later as an assembly worker for General Motors. After the start of World War II, he enlisted in the Marine Corps and served in Guadalcanal, Guam and Okinawa from 1942 to 1945. He later joined the staff of the corps newspaper, *The Leatherneck,* where he met fellow cartoonist Fred Lasswell.

After receiving his discharge, Donovan joined Lasswell as an assistant on the *Barney Google and Snuffy Smith* newspaper strip while freelancing a number of cartoons and panels to various publications. In 1950 he joined the staff of the *Danbury* (Conn.) *News-Times,* where he drew a daily panel called *Felty Fedora* about a meek little hat salesman (1950-54). In 1959 Lasswell encouraged Donovan to create his own strip, and this resulted in *Biddie and Bert*, a feature about a retired couple, which the Hall Syndicate distributed from 1960 into the early 1970s. After the feature was dropped, Donovan returned to freelancing sport and editorial cartoons and assisting on *Snuffy Smith.* He retired from Snuffy Smith in 1987, and is now devoting his time to drawing children's books.

M.H.

"Knock it off, you two . . .
this is no time to settle your differences."

Robert Donovan. © Leatherneck Magazine.

DÖRBECK, FRANZ
See Burchard, Franz.

Gustave Doré, "Musical Soirée," 1855.

DORÉ, GUSTAVE (1832-1883) French illustrator, cartoonist and painter born at Strasbourg, France, on January 6, 1832. Gustave Doré came from a wealthy family. At 13 he started to contribute lithographs to newspapers in eastern France. Brought to Charles Philipon's attention, Doré published from 1848 to 1852 a weekly satirical drawing in Philipon's *Le Journal pour Rire.* These drawings, which made gentle fun of French foibles and fashions, were later collected in albums released as *Ces Chinois de Parisiens* ("Those Parisian Characters," 1851), *La Ménagerie Parisienne* ("The Parisian Zoo," 1854) and *Les Différ-ents Publics de Paris* ("The Different Parisian Publics," 1854).

However, it was as a book illustrator that Doré became deservedly famous, starting with *Les Travaux d'Hercule* ("The Labors of Hercules"), which he did when he was 15 years old. Full of verve and irony, the sketches debunk the Hercules myth and already indicate young Gustave's interest in the blacks and whites that became so prevalent in his later works.

In 1854, a turning point in Doré's career and in the history of the comic strip, he published an illustrated version of Rabelais's *Gargantua et Pantagruel* (new edition, 1873) and the *Histoire Pittoresque, Dramatique et Caricaturale de la Sainte Russie.* The first shows the artist's growing delight in the fantastic and menacing world of death and nightmares, probably stemming from his Germanic romantic background; the second is technically a brilliantly executed comic strip that traces the "picturesque, dramatic and caricatural history of Holy Russia," using such devices as white squares of different shapes to reflect uninteresting periods or an enormous black stain to symbolize the reign of Ivan the Terrible.

Of the more than two hundred books he illustrated, the most important and best known are Balzac's *Contes Drolatiques* ("Droll Stories," 1855), *Dante's Inferno* (1861), Cervantes's *Don Quixote* (1863) and the Bible (1866). Most of his illustrations are interpretive and reflect the gloom and horror of his outlook: grotesque and bizarre representations of nature with haunted forests and terrifying storms; an abundance of crows, vultures, wolves, rats and supernatural creatures; dark, gloomy, foreboding medieval towns and streets; men, women and children, tortured, hanged, beheaded.

Gustave Doré died in Paris, a very rich man, on January 23, 1883, leaving behind over ten thousand works.

P.H.

DOSH
See Gardosh, Kariel.

DOTAKON (Japan) *Dotakon* is a humorous work by Hōsuke Fukuchi that began running in the magazine *Manga Sunday* in 1968. It falls into the genre of "salaryman cartoons" because it depicts the everyday life of the typical white-collar worker in Japan. Dotakon, the hero, is the average worker to a tee. He is, in fact, the proverbial cog in the machine, and therein lies the humor of the work. In one classic episode Dotakon, who follows a machinelike pattern in his daily life, arrives at the office at the scheduled time only to discover that the position of his desk has been ever so slightly changed—which, of course, plays havoc with his entire day.

Fukuchi's characters are invariably low-ranking employees who are clumsy, lazy and irresponsible save for their mindless devotion to routine. His drawings depict the frustration and anomie experienced by the mass of employees in a seniority system where there is no danger of being fired, but where there is also little encouragement or recognition of individual achievement. One episode shows workers in an office building exclaiming over the exploits of a young Japanese who sailed solo across the Pacific. In his own little way, Fukuchi's hero tries to match this feat by taking his desk to the top of the office roof and sitting alone.

Hōsuke Fukuchi was born on June 1, 1937, in Gifu Prefecture, Japan. He attended Waseda University, where he was a member of the Waseda Manga Kenkyukai ("Cartoon Study Group") at the same time as Shunji Sonoyama and Sadao Shōji. All three men did similar work. Fukuchi's drawings are deceptively simple, to the point of looking as though they could have been drawn by a child. Like Shōji and Sonoyama, he had no formal art training, which contributed to his unique style. His humor at its best is hilarious; at its worst it is banal. He draws in a variety of formats, from single-panel cartoons to five-page comic strips, and his subjects are often both topical and political. In 1970 the best of *Dotakon* was compiled by Chikuma Shōbō into a volume called *Gendai Manga Fukuchi Hōsuke Zenshu* ("Modern Cartoons: The Collected Works of Hōsuke Fukuchi"), which was also released in two single volumes titled *Dotakon* and *Dotakon Koiyatsure* ("Dotakon Lovesick").

F.S.

DOTY, ROY (1922-) American cartoonist born in Chicago, Illinois, on September 10, 1922. Roy Doty was taken by his parents to Columbus, Ohio, where he grew up and went to school. Drafted in 1942, he worked as an artist on different army projects, and following his honorable discharge in 1946, he began freelancing cartoons in New York City. Soon Doty's work was appearing in all the major publications, from the *Saturday Evening Post* to *Look* and *Collier's*. In the 1950s Doty worked on many advertising campaigns and illustrated a number of books and magazine stories.

In 1968 Doty was asked to produce a Sunday newspaper version of the then-popular *Laugh-In* television show. Working feverishly, he designed a graphic counterpart to the TV program that was as funny as anything on the show. His gags for such subfeatures as "Mod Mod World," "Sock It to Me Time" and "Ask Gran Flanders" were hilarious. Unfortunately *Laugh-In* went off the air a few years later, and Doty's panel expired in 1971.

Since the demise of *Laugh-In* Doty has resumed his work for magazines, trade journals and corporations such as Mobil Oil. He is one of the most prolific cartoonists around today, and his style, deceptively simple and easy, commands much respect in the profession. He is also much in demand as a book illustrator: "Just finished illustrating my 164th book," he averred in 1996, "and starting the 165th." In addition to which he keeps turning out a monthly panel, *Wordless Workshop*, for *The Family Handyman*, a feature he started back in the mid-1950's.

M.H.

DOVNIKOVIĆ, BORIVOJ (1930-) Yugoslav cartoonist and animator born in Osijek, Yugoslavia, in 1930. After studies in his hometown and in Belgrade, Borivoj Dovniković enrolled at the Art Academy in Zagreb in 1949. The following year he began contributing cartoons to the humor magazine *Kerempuh* and sold a number of comic strips to publications such as *Jez, Plavi Vjesnik* and *Glas Slavonije* (for Dovniković's career in the comics see *The World Encyclopedia of Comics,* Chelsea House, 1976).

Dovniković went into animation in the early 1950s as an assistant animator for Duga Film; there he worked notably on *The Big Meeting* (1951), *The Gay Experience* and *The Goal* (both 1952). When Duga Film closed down in 1952, he went back to drawing gag cartoons and comic strips, also continuing to do advertising cartoons. When his unit was absorbed into Zagreb Film, he returned to entertainment animation and was head animator on *The Little Train* (1959) and on a number of *Slucaj . . .* and *Inspektor Masku* series cartoons.

Dovniković made his directorial debut on the *Slucaj . . .*

Borivoj Dovniković, "Maneuvers. © Zagreb Film.

cartoons in 1961. The same year he also directed *Lutkića* ("The Doll"), followed by *Olé Torero!* in 1962. Recognition came to Dovniković with the 1964 *Bez Naslova* ("Without Title"), a witty cartoon in which words spell out the predicament of a meek little Everyman. More inspired cartoons followed: *Ceremony* and *The Story of Fashion* (both 1965), *Curiosity* (1966), *Krek* (1967), *The Strange Bird* (1969) and *The Flower Lovers* (1970).

Unlike many Zagreb cartoonists whose creativity has faltered in the last decade, Dovniković remains prolific and inventive. The 1971 *Maneuvers* was a little masterpiece of sardonic humor, and the 1973 *Second-Class Passenger* proved that the artist had lost nothing of his keen sense of observation and his sensitivity to the little ironies of life. In 1975 he realized a series of eight television cartoons to teach the Croat language; his latest cartoon, *Walking School*, came out in 1978. Like so many of his colleagues from the former Yugoslavia, he has since the 1980s been working mainly for the German market.

Though he started later than some of his colleagues, Dovnikovic soon established himself as one of the masters of the "Zagreb school" of animation. His style is more subtle, less flamboyant than, say, that of Vukotić, and he is thus less well known in the West. But as Ronald Holloway observed in his study *Z Is for Zagreb* (1972), Dovnikovićs "humor is mixed with a fine sense of psychology and keen observation of the human species."

M.H.

DOWLING, DANIEL B. (1906-1993) American political cartoonist born in O'Neil, Nebraska, on November 16, 1906. Dan Dowling was raised in Iowa, where he daily saw the cartoons of Jay Norwood ("Ding") Darling, who started cartooning the year of Dowling's birth and influenced the style of the younger cartoonist immeasurably. (Carey Orr was another influence, but one that must be called ideological and conceptual.)

Dowling studied at the University of California at Berkeley and at the Chicago Academy of Fine Arts before getting a job as a police reporter for a Chicago newspaper. From 1940 to 1942 he was editorial cartoonist for the *Omaha World-Herald*, a job interrupted by World War II. A brief return to Omaha preceded an offer from the *New York Herald-Tribune.* His work was patently derivative of Darling's, and the paper's editor, Geoffrey Parsons, sought out Dowling precisely because Ding, star of the *Trib's* stable, was nearing retirement age. Dowling remained with the New York paper—syndicated by the *Tribune* and its successor agency, Publishers-Hall Syndicate—until 1965, when he switched to the *Kansas City Star.* He cartooned there until his retirement in 1973. He died at his home in California in 1993.

Dowling, a Republican, won several awards during the course of his career, the major ones being the 1960 Sigma Delta Chi and Freedoms Foundation citations. He was the first president of the Association of American Editorial Cartoonists. Besides the similarity to Darling (in style and even in name!), Dowling's trademark was the high dose of humor injected in each cartoon; exaggeration figured prominently in his pen-brush-crayon and benday cartoons.

R.M.

Dan Dowling. © New York Herald-Tribune.

DOYLE, RICHARD (1824-1883) British cartoonist born in 1824. Richard Doyle, the cartoonist who created the classic cover of *Punch* which graced that weekly magazine from 1849 to 1956—a world's record run—was the son of artist John Doyle, who drew cartoons under the signature "H.B." John Doyle encouraged artistic expression in his large family—all seven children had to participate in a weekly Sunday-morning "salon." "Dickie's" first pub-

Richard Doyle, design for the cover of "Punch."

lished work was a burlesque of the Eglinton Tournament, and its publisher, W. Fores of Piccadilly, commissioned him to execute a series of color designs for envelopes (1840). He illustrated his first book, *The Fortunes of Hector O'Halloran,* in 1842, and the following year, at age 18, he joined *Punch. In* March 1849 the first of his famous series *Ye Manners and Customs of Ye Englyshe* appeared, and this led to his experiments in the serial strip form. *The Pleasure Trips of Brown, Jones and Robinson, Part One* ("The Visit to Epsom") appeared in *Punch* on July 6, 1850, and led to a long series of adventures in which Doyle's heroes took the Grand Tour of Europe. Unhappily, his excellent association with *Punch* ended abruptly with an argument arising from that paper's antipapal attitude. Doyle resigned, taking *Brown, Jones and Robinson* with him. He continued to do more book illustration but died of a stroke on December 11, 1883.

Books: *The Eglinton Tournament* (1840); *Jack the Giant Killer* (1842); *The Fairy Ring* (1846); *Rejected Cartoons* (1848); *Fairy Tales from All Nations* (1849); *Book of Ballads* (1849); *Pip's Diary* (1849); *An Overland Journey to the Great Exhibition* (1851); *The Newcomes* (1854); *The Foreign Tour of Brown, Jones and Robinson* (1854); *The Juvenile Calendar* (1855); *Merry Pictures* (1857); *The Scouring of the White House* (1859); *A Bird's Eye View of Society* (1864); *An Old Fairy Tale* (1865); *Fairy Tales* (1868); *The Visiting Justices* (1868); *Puck on Pegasus* (1869); *Christmas Books* (1869); *In Fairyland* (1870); *Piccadilly* (1870); *Snow White and Rosy Red* (1871); *Fortune's Favourite* (1871); *The Enchanted Crow* (1871); *Feast of the Dwarfs* (1871); *Benjamin Disraeli* (1878); *Princess Nobody* (1884); *King of the Golden River* (1884); *A Journal Kept in 1840* (1885); *Comic Histories* (1885); *Scenes from English History* (1886); *Home for the Holidays* (1887); *Early Writings of Thackeray* (1888); *The Fairy Book* (1890); *The Queen and Mr. Punch* (1897); *Sad Story of a Pig* (1901); *Mrs. Caudle's Curtain Lectures* (1902); *The Enchanted Doll* (1903); *Humorous Masterpieces* (1905); and *God's Englishmen* (1948).

D.G.

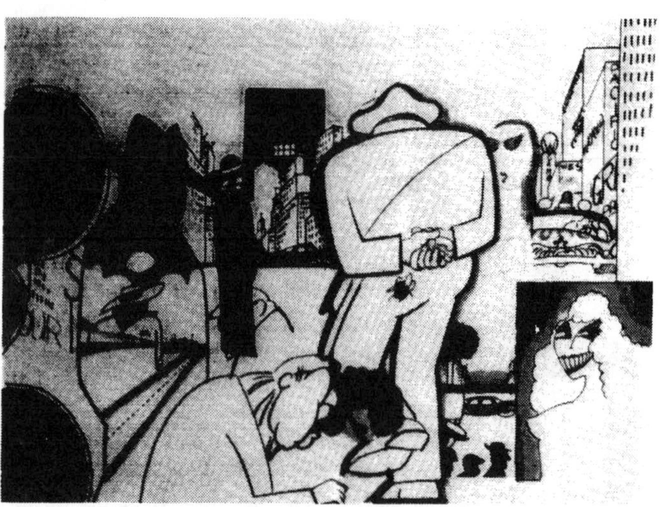

Nedeljko Dragić, "Diary." © Zagreb Film.

DRAGIĆ, NEDELJKO (1936-) Yugoslav cartoonist born in Paklenića, Yugoslavia, in 1936. Nedeljko Dragić studied law in Zagreb, but his love of drawing led him to abandon his studies and devote himself to cartooning. As early as 1953 he had contributed numerous cartoons to Yugoslav publications and had gained a modest reputation as the creator of several "anti-comic strips." In 1964 a collection of his cartoons, *Alphabet for Illiterates,* was published in Belgrade.

It was, however, as an animator that Dragić made his mark. In 1961 he joined Zagreb Studio as a designer on such productions as *The Dreamer, Cupid* and *Rivals*. He was also one of the directors on the *Inspector Mask* series (1962). After a brief hiatus he directed his first independent cartoon, *Elegy* (1965), which he adapted from his newspaper cartoons. There followed the much-awarded *Tamer of Wild Horses* 1966), with which Dragić gained international recognition. Two more cartoons of the period, the ambiguous *Diogenes Perhaps* (1967) and the lyrical *Passing Days* (1969), definitively established him as one of the most innovative and creative talents in animation. Dragić, through his two short, ironical works *Per Aspera and Astra* and *Striptiz* (both 1969), was also responsible for the trend toward the so-called mini-cartoons.

In recent years Dragić has again been a prime mover in the animation field, scripting, designing and directing many award-winning films. Two of the more notable are *Tup Tup* (1972), which won the Melbourne Prize in 1973 and was nominated for an Academy Award, and especially *Diary* (1973). An overwhelming stream of images, both figurative and abstract, *Diary* was described by its creator as "an attempt to animate at 24 frames per second the inexplicable in man." Dragić's most impressive effort to date, it won first prize at the 1974 Zagreb Film Festival. His most notable effort in the last decade and a half has been *The Day I Stopped Smoking* (1982).

M.H.

DREAMY DUD (U.S.) It is reported that Wallace Carlson, after one full year of dogged and solitary effort, brought out a five-minute animated short that so impressed Essanay Studios that they commissioned him to direct a cartoon series for them. That series became *Dreamy Dud,* and the first entry, "Dreamy Dud Lost in the Jungle," was released in June 1915. The series lasted only a year, and Carlson abandoned *Dreamy Dud* in 1916.

Like J.R. Bray's early creation *Colonel Heezaliar,* Carlson's *Dreamy Dud* was built around the tall tale; as his name implies, however, Carlson's titular hero was not a boastful curmudgeon but rather a daydreaming urchin whose imaginary feats of valor and flights of fancy were born out of boredom and loneliness. "Dreamy Dud in Love" is typical in this respect; it shows the little character projecting himself into all kinds of heroic situations in order to win the affections of the haughty girl who spurns him.

Carlson directed more than a score of *Dreamy Dud* cartoons, sending his hero, along with his loyal dog Wag, into wilder and wilder imaginings as the series rolled on. "He Goes Bear Hunting" is a rather conventional hunting story, but "Dreamy Dud Lost at Sea" and especially "Dreamy Dud in King Koo Koo's Kingdom" are little gems of fantasy, inventiveness and humor that cry out to be rediscovered. "Dreamy Dud Sees Charlie Chaplin" perhaps epitomizes the series as the ragamuffin dreams that he finds a dime so he can watch a Charlie Chaplin movie.

M.H.

"Let me know if that falls on you."
Boris Drucker. © Saturday Evening Post.

DROOPY (U.S.) The dog Droopy, the most popular character created by Tex Avery during his tenure at MGM, made his first appearance in a 1943 cartoon entitled "Dumb-Hounded," in which the unflappable police dog thwarted all attempts at escape by a shaggy wolf.

The pattern was repeated in a number of other cartoons, notably "The Shooting of Dan McGoo" (based on a Robert Service poem), "Northwest Hounded Police" and "Drag-Along Droopy," which pitted the sad-faced little dog against his old adversary, the Wolf (not otherwise named). In the 1949 cartoon "Wags to Riches," Avery introduced a new rival for Droopy, the dumb bulldog Spike, who had first appeared in the *Tom and Jerry* cartoons and was later to star in his own series. Spike and Droopy engaged in the most hair-raising competition, from the Canine Olympics ("The Chump Champ") to a circus show ("Dare-Devil Droopy").

After Avery left MGM in 1954, *Droopy* cartoons continued to be produced (often from old drawings stretched to Cinemascope size), but they had become tired and repetitive. When they were discontinued after the studio closed down in 1957, hardly a murmur was heard. The character was revived in the 1990s, however, on Ted Turner's Cartoon Network.

M.H.

DRUCKER, BORIS (1920-) American cartoonist and painter born in Philadelphia, Pennsylvania, on May 22, 1920. Educated in Philadelphia's public schools, Boris Drucker attended the Philadelphia College of Art from 1938 to 1942, graduating with a degree in advertising design. After service in the Army Air Corps (1942-46), he began his career as a freelance artist, selling his first drawing to the *Saturday Evening* Post in 1946. Since that time, his cartoon art has appeared in all the major magazines, including the *New Yorker, Punch, Ladies' Home Journal, Collier's, This Week, Redbook, McCall's, Holiday, True* and *Playboy.*

As a cartoonist, Drucker works mainly in pen and wash and turns out a variety of drawings, from simple inked outlines of minimal detail to elaborate panels representing more complex ideas. A cartoon in the first category, an ink line sketch, simply shows a man standing before a doctor's desk. Nothing more is necessary to underpin the gag: "You can be glad you're having problems, Harkness. A man without problems is usually dead." In a wash of the second category, the caption—"That's Quiet Quiet Baily, our school librarian"—depends heavily for its humor on the drawing, which shows a small boy addressing his father as the latter turns to regard the devastatingly apparent charms of the young woman he's just walked past. Drucker is also capable of some fine representational art, as with the locker room scene in wash that features a number of battered football players being lectured by a disgruntled coach. Rendered in watercolor, it would make a fine cover for some football-season issue of the *New Yorker,* so well does it capture the sense of the moment.

In addition to comic art, Drucker has worked widely in advertising art and animation for such accounts as Bell Telephone, Du Pont, the Insurance Company of North America and Atlantic-Richfield. His work has garnered six gold and ten silver medals at the Philadelphia Art Directors' Shows over the years. He was represented in the Philadelphia Art Alliance's 1971 show, Geometric Paintings by American Artists, and was commissioned in 1975 as the muralist for the Finley Playground in Philadelphia. He wrote and illustrated a children's book, *Henrietta* (1965), and illustrated the volume *How to Play with Your Baby* (1971). A full record of Drucker's published work is on file at the George Arendts Research Library at Syracuse University.

Drucker is a member of the Cartoonists Guild (board of directors, 1971-78) and has served at various times on the boards of the Philadelphia Art Directors' Club and the Philadelphia College of Art, where he also taught advertising art (1960-65).

R.C.

DRUCKER, MORT (1929-) American cartoonist and illustrator born in Brooklyn, New York, on March 29, 1929. A graduate of Erasmus High School in Brooklyn, Mort Drucker was more interested in sports as a young man than in cartooning. Although he did pencil sketches, he was not the high school's cartoonist-in-residence, as so many successful cartoonists have been in their school days.

His first contact with professional cartoonists came shortly after his high school graduation in 1947. Through the help of a family friend, Mort Drucker was hired by Bert Whitman as an assistant to do the backgrounds in Whitman's comic strip *Debbie Dean, Career Girl*. The strip was begun on January 11, 1942, with Debbie Dean as a rich, beautiful debutante turned cub reporter. Debbie later returned to her hometown of Deansburg to become its, and the comics', first woman mayor. The former mayor, her uncle Gunga Dean, was allowed to make a most painful pun by saying, "She's a better man than I, Gunga Dean." *Debbie Dean* was syndicated by the New York Post Syndicate. "The style of the strip was similar to the Milton Caniff style," remembers Mort Drucker. "I only worked for Whitman about six months but it was my first contact with cartooning as a career."

In 1948, Drucker joined National Periodicals and was assigned to make slight corrections on the artwork. He remembers it as on-the-job training. His three years at National Periodicals were Drucker's initiation into the business of cartooning. His own artwork improved, and in 1951 he became a freelance cartoonist. He handled many comic book assignments, including war, romance and teenage stories. He drew the Bob Hope comic book. However, a freelance artist always has to be on the lookout for new work. When Drucker spotted a classified ad seeking two artists for *MAD* magazine, he applied. *MAD* needed new artists in 1956 because the departure of Harvey Kurtzman and several *MAD* cartoonists had created openings on the staff. Although many cartoonists had already been interviewed, the *MAD* editors liked Drucker's samples, and he got the job.

His first assignment for *MAD* was a parody of a cigarette ad. Soon Mort Drucker's art became the standard for *MAD's* movie and television takeoffs. His assignments at *MAD* were consolidated to mostly movie parodies when his freelance advertising art commitments became more demanding. Of all the parodies he's drawn, Mort Drucker says *The Godfather*, Parts I and II, is among his favorites.

Drucker tries to capture the physical attitude of the people he caricatures. Emphasis is placed on the slightly-larger-than-true-proportioned heads and hands of his characters. His so-called *MAD* look presents a page with little white space left. The characters of the parody and details of the background are presented in a finely drawn pen outline with gray wash distinctive to *MAD*. In addition to his work for *MAD*, he has done a syndicated newspaper strip, *Benchley*, in the mid-1980s in collaboration with Jerry Dumas and has illustrated a number of caricatural coloring books.

Mort Drucker has painted several movie posters, including the one for *American Graffiti*. He has also illustrated a number of *Time* magazine covers. However, his most phenomenally successful venture was *The JFK Coloring Book* that he and *MAD* magazine writer Paul Laiken created in 1962. Turned down by almost every publisher in New York City until Kanrom Publishers decided to take a chance on it, *The JFK Coloring Book* appeared on May 8, 1962, and to everyone's surprise quickly climbed onto the *New York Times* best-seller list, selling about two million copies.

B.C.

DRY BONES (Israel) *Dry Bones* is Israel's answer to *Feiffer*. Like its American counterpart, it exhibits a wry, sophisticated, sarcastic and often bitter humor, as well as a disillusioned commentary on the state of the world.

Ya'akov Kirschen, the creator of *Dry Bones*, is a transplanted New Yorker living in Jerusalem. After a career as a cartoonist in the United States, during which time he had drawings published in *Playboy, Esquire* and other magazines, Kirschen decided to emigrate to Israel in 1968. He promptly began drawing what he terms "a radical Zionist comic strip" for underground Jewish newspapers. The feature, *Dry Bones*, was picked up in the early 1970s by the *Jerusalem Post*, in which it currently appears. (The title is derived from Ezekiel.)

Although it has been called "Israel's first comic strip," *Dry Bones* is closer to the conventions of the cartoon, and it does in fact often appear as a single panel. In it Kirschen lampoons everything and everybody from Yasir Arafat to Henry Kissinger, from the United Nations to Israel's own bloated bureaucracy. "Jewish humor is traditionally based on grotesquely desperate situations," Kirschen once declared, "and, lucky for me, we have a desperately grotesque situation. . . ."

Dry Bones cartoons have often been reprinted outside Israel. In 1977 Kirschen's sardonic plan to divest the United States of its "occupied lands" and return it to the frontiers of the 13 original colonies drew an amused comment from President Jimmy Carter. A collection of *Dry Bones* cartoons was published in 1976 by Cherryfield Associates in Tel Aviv.

Kirschen continues to produce *Dry Bones* which has been enjoying growing success in Israel and abroad in the last 15 to 20 years. Some of the cartoons have been reprint-

Albert Dubout, detail from "Jour V." © Dubout.

ed in such publications as the *New York Times* and *Newsweek*; and two anthologies of his work have been published in the U.S.: *Trees...the Green Testament* in 1993, followed in 1996 by *What a Country!*, subtitled *"Dry Bones Looks at Israel."*

M.H.

DUBOUT, ALBERT (1905-1976) French cartoonist, poster designer, illustrator and animated cartoon director born in Marseilles, France, on May 15, 1905. While a student at the Montpellier Ecole des Beaux Arts he started to submit cartoons to various newspapers in 1923, in particular to *L'Echo des Etudiants.* These drawings already had many of the themes and characters that would appear later in Dubout's work: the skinny little fellow, henpecked and terrorized by his big-busted and overbearing wife; Sparadra, the mean and muscular hood with the hang dog look and the unshaven face covered by a Band-Aid (*sparadrap* in French); and especially the crowds of thousands who are shown from very weird angles and whose faces, physiques, dress and gestures are depicted in the most grotesque manner.

After being expelled from art school, Dubout went to Paris at the age of 17 and placed his sketches with small newspapers (*Pêle-Mêle, Gens Qui Rient, Paris-Flirt*) and weeklies (*Le Rire, Le Journal Amusant, Candide).* In 1929, he illustrated his first book, Boileau's *Les Embarras de Paris,* a 17th-century satirical poem on the traffic jams of Paris. This was followed by illustrations for almost a hundred books, among them works of Rabelais (1936-37), Rostand's *Cyrano de Bergerac* (1947), Poe's *The Fall of the House of Usher* (1948), Dumas's *The Three Musketeers* (1968), *The Kama Sutra* (1973) and his favorite, Cervantes's *Don Quixote* (1937-38 and 1951). De-vaux's *La Rue sans Loi* ("The Street Without Law"), for which he did the drawings, was published in *Ici Paris* as a daily comic strip (October 1950-March 1951); it was released in 1951 as a film, and Dubout wrote the scenario and drew the poster.

His own albums include, among others, *Du Bout de la Lorgnette* ("From the Binocular's End," 1937, with a pun on his name), *Dubout . . . en Train* ("Dubout on a Train," 1952), *Corridas* ("Bullfights," 1966) and *Dubout* (1974). In addition to a couple of animated cartoons, *Anatole Fait du Camping* ("Anatole Camps Out") and *Anatole à la Tour de Nesle* ("Anatole in the Tower of Nesle"), which are quite funny but do not have the quality found in American animated shorts, Dubout drew hundreds of publicity posters for restaurants, newspapers, wines, beers and films (e.g., Chaplin's *The Great Dictator).*

Despite his being a shy man, all his drawings show his love for crowds and trains and for "noninvisible mend-ing" jobs: there are overcrowded beaches, free-for-all fights, gigantic assemblies of people (as in the famous VE Day cartoon of 1945, "Jour V"); his trains, especially the one serving the southwestern burgs between Montpellier and Palavas-les-Flots (in 1974, the Palavas city fathers renamed the Rue de la Gare "Rue de la Gare Albert Dubout"), are all antiquated, dilapidated, obsolete, malfunctioning, overcrowded, of course, and literally held together by tape, Band-Aids, knots, patches. Finally, his characters are naturally ugly; the women have warts, chin whiskers, pimples, and men do not fare any better. They have long noses, stupid faces, funny-looking moustaches or long beards which always get caught in something; most of the time, they are proverbial 98-pound weaklings.

This "virtuoso artist" (as the French surrealist poet Philippe Soupault called him), this modern Bruegel or Doré who loved to disguise himself with false moustaches, wigs, pince-nez, beards and baggy pants held up by suspenders, died in Montpellier on June 27, 1976.

P.H.

DUCHAMP, GASTON (1875-1963) French painter, engraver and cartoonist born in Damville, France, on July 31, 1875. Known to posterity as Jacques Villon, Gaston Duchamp was the brother of the well-known painters Suzanne Duchamp and Marcel Duchamp and the sculptor Raymond Duchamp-Villon.

After his high school studies, Villon worked as a clerk in a notary's office in Rouen. Clerking left him unfulfilled, and he went to Paris in 1894. Over the next fifteen years he made his mark as one of the most sought-after cartoonists in the French capital. His work appeared in all the major publications, including *Le Chat Noir, Le Rire, Le Courrier Français, Gil Blas Illustré* and *L'Assiette au Beurre,* where he was featured in the very first issue. So well established was Villon the cartoonist that it is said that the owner of *Le Courrier Français* had his coach and coachman sent to the artist's domicile in order to sign him up for his magazine.

Villon left all this acclaim in 1911 to throw in his lot with the Cubists. He then repudiated his cartooning work as mere "potboiling," but there is no doubt that the discipline he showed in his early drawings, their almost abstract composition and their precise lines, helped form his later artistic idiom. Villon never achieved the celebrity status of other Cubist artists such as Picasso, and he had to struggle all his life. He died, more or less forgotten, in Puteaux, near Paris, on June 9, 1963.

M.H.

Conclusion!
Gaston Duchamp ("Jacques Villon"), 1902.

The Outstretched Hand
Ed Duffy, Pulitzer Prize-winning cartoon, 1940. © Baltimore Sun.

DUFFY, EDMUND (1899-1962) American cartoonist and three-time Pulitzer Prize winner born in Jersey City, New Jersey, in 1899. The son of a policeman, Edmund Duffy studied at the Art Students League from 1914 to 1919 with George Bridgman, John Sloan and Boardman Robinson. His first published work was a page of Armistice Day celebration drawings for the *New York Tribune Sunday Magazine* in 1918; he soon was selling illustrations to the *New York Evening Post* and *Scribner's* magazine. In 1920 he sailed for Europe to study in Paris; he also contributed to the *London Evening News* and mailed back cartoons to the *New York Herald.*

Upon his return to America Duffy drew for *Collier's* and the *Century;* he became a staff cartoonist with the *Brooklyn Eagle* (1922) and then the *New York Leader* (1924), until he was "borrowed" to draw cartoons advocating the presidential candidacy of John W. Davis for the *Baltimore Evening Sun.* He was to remain there for 24 years, gather-

Stoyan Dukov. © Starchel.

ing three Pulitzers as well as a national reputation for liberal policies and devastating presentations. His themes, he said, were "politics, peace, and the poor taxpayer. While on the *Sunpapers* he dabbled in book reviews and reporting (he filed memorable accounts of Will Rogers's funeral in 1935). In 1948 he yearned for semi-retirement and, having turned more conservative, accepted a post as editorial cartoonist for the *Saturday Evening Post,* his first cartoon appearing on January 15, 1949; he remained until 1957, five years before his death.

Duffy's drawing style, always arresting, resembled that of his teacher, Boardman Robinson: heavy brushstrokes, deliberate use of dark shading (and scraping with a razor blade to achieve highlights) and a brutally employed sense of the ridiculous. His compositions were handsomely balanced, and his themes never equivocated. Duffy won the George Washington Honor Medal from the Freedoms Foundation in 1956.

R.M.

DUKOV, STOYAN (1931-) Bulgarian cartoonist and animator born in Sofia, Bulgaria, in 1931. Stoyan Dukov graduated from the Higher Institute of Pictorial Arts in Sofia and started his professional career in 1950 with contributions to Bulgarian newspapers and magazines, notably *Starchel.*

Dukov had become an established print cartoonist when he decided to join Todor Dinov at the fledgling Studio of Animation in Sofia in the mid-1950s. There he worked as an animator for several years before co-directing (with Dinov) his first cartoon, *The Apple,* in 1963. In succeeding

Indignant Anglo-Saxon (to Provincial French Innkeeper, who is bowing his thanks for the final settlement of his exorbitant and much-disputed account): "Oh, oui, Mossoo! pour le matière de ça, je PAYE! Mais just vous regardez ICI, mon Amim! et juste—vous—marquez—mes—MOTS! Je PAYE—MAIS JE METTE LE DANS LA 'TIMES'!"

George Du Maurier, "The Time-Honoured British Threat."

years Dukov directed more animated films, including *Golden Treasure* (1964), *Adventures* (1965) and *Travels in the Cosmos* (with Troyanov, 1966). All these were intended for children, but in 1967 Dukov came out with the adult film *Fortified Houses,* which was hailed as an imaginative experiment in line and composition. After a relapse into routine animated filmmaking, Dukov redeemed himself with *Sisyphus* (1975), a witty burlesque that contains such hilarious moments as Jove getting entangled in his thunderbolts and the Olympians playing practical jokes on Sisyphus—including getting him to lift a heavy boulder up a steep hill, of course. (This cartoon should not be confused with a Hungarian short of the same name and year that was nominated for an Academy Award.) His later films have included *Requiem* (1982), an impassioned plea against intolerance, and *March* (1986), a racy comedy about an itinerant sex shop. Bulgarian film production collapsed in the late 1980s, and Dukov has done little work in animation since that time.

After Dinov, Dukov is the artist most responsible for the remarkable development of Bulgarian animation. He has also maintained his position as a noted gag cartoonist with regular contributions to foreign and Bulgarian publications.

M.H.

DU MAURIER, GEORGE LOUIS PALMELLA BUSSON (1854-1896) British writer and cartoonist born in Paris, France, in 1854. George Du Maurier's youthful years as an art student in Paris's Latin Quarter later provided him with the authentic background for his famous novel *Trilby,* a four-volume romance published in 1894. His first novel, *Peter Ibbetson* (1892), was based on his happy childhood in Paris, but in his last novel, *The Martian* (1897), he wrote about the accident which had lost him the sight of one eye. That tragedy halted his projected career as a portrait painter and resulted in his coming to London as an artist in black and white. His delicate and refined cartoons, virtually illustrations to lengthy captions of high society's conversations, capture the dress and manners of his Victorian age; they were published once a week from 1859 and in *Punch* from 1860.

Du Maurier was elected to the famous Punch Table when the death of John Leech created a vacant chair. His artwork and his jokes, both polite and refined, suited the tastes of his middle-class readers, and he created a gallery of types: Sir Georgius Midas, the newly rich parvenu; Mrs. Ponsonby Tompkins, the social climber; and, of course, his elegant ladies, gowned goddesses who preceded the American Gibson Girls. He died in 1896.

Books: *English Society at Home* (1880); *Society Pictures* (1891); *Peter Ibbetson* (1892); *Trilby* (1894); *In Bohemia* (1896);

Alan Dunn. © Architectural Record Books.

The Martian (1897); *English Society* (1897); *A Legend of Camelot* (1898); *Social Political Satire* (1898); *Pictures by George Du Maurier* (1911); *Satirist of the Victorians* (1913); *George Du Maurier and Others* (1937); *George Du Maurier, His Life and Work* (1948); *Young George Du Maurier* (1951); and *George Du Maurier* (1969).

D.G.

DUNN, ALAN (1900-1974) American magazine gag cartoonist born in Belmar, New Jersey, on August 11, 1900. Alan Dunn studied at Columbia University in 1918-19 and then spent four years at the National Academy of Design. In 1923-24 he studied at the American Academy in Rome.

The most prolific of all the *New Yorker* magazine's cartoonists, Alan Dunn was published 1,915 times by the magazine between August 7, 1926, and May 6, 1974, including 9 published cover drawings. Several more of his cartoons were published posthumously by the *New Yorker.*

Dunn considered himself a social cartoonist "whose pen is no sword but a titillating feather that reminds us constantly that we do not act as we speak or think." He felt that this approach, gentler than the sharp satire of political cartooning, was more effective in enlightening his readers about society's foibles. It was his belief that people were a combination of "true virtue" and "pure human cussedness." Using a distinctive realistic style, Dunn commented on a wide range of topical subjects.

The literary quality of Dunn's cartoons was important to him, and he spurned both gag writers and attempts by editors to change his gag lines. Drawing with charcoal and grease pencil on paper with a pebble finish, Dunn successfully used the medium of many political cartoonists to a much subtler and often more memorable end. His drawings were always vigorous. In his later years they gained a lyrical quality.

A man of tremendous personal style, Dunn worked seated at a card table in the small apartment he shared with his wife, *New Yorker* cartoonist Mary Petty. The couple were self-styled recluses. Alan Dunn was referred to as a "hermit around town" by Harold Ross, the *New Yorker*'s editor for many years. Thin, dapper, with a tiny moustache and deep-set eyes, Dunn also suffered from many phobias. Fear of fire was a major phobia, and the couple's apartment on East 88th Street in New York City was on the ground floor.

Architecture was Dunn's avocation, and he became a regular contributor to the *Architectural Record* beginning in 1936. The changes of architectural styles in New York City and their relationship to people were constant themes of his cartoons. For example, a man is shown picking himself up from the debris of a caved-in apartment wall and addressing a surprised couple seated having breakfast: "Sorry, neighbors. I just happened to lean against it." In another cartoon a small sports car pulls into the garage of a towering apartment building that looms straight up out of the drawing. The passenger says to the driver, "It's good to be home."

His cartoons were published in innumerable *New Yorker* anthologies and in book form under the titles *Rejections* (1931), *Who's Paying for This Cab?* (1945), The *Last Lath* (1947), *East of Fifth* (1948), *Should It Gurgle?* (1956), *Is There Intelligent Life on Earth?* (1960) and *A Portfolio of Social Cartoons—1957-1968* (1968).

In addition to his cartooning, Dunn was a devotee of chess and woodworking. His manuscripts are at Syracuse University. On May 20, 1974, at the age of 73, Alan Dunn died at his home.

B.C.

Relief (coming in): "Couldn't yer wait till yer got out to 'ave yer flamin' wash? Yer know we've got ter sleep in this ruddy water."
Frank Dunne. © Smith's Weekly.

DUNN, ROBERT JOSEPH, JR. (1908-1989) American cartoonist born in Newark, New Jersey, on May 15, 1908. Bob Dunn was educated at St. Benedict's Preparatory School in Newark and St. Anselm's College in Manchester, New Hampshire. He studied at the Art Students League in New York City while selling magazine gags to *Judge* and *Life.* Dunn then went from a job on the art staff of the *Newark Ledger* to a six-month stint with Hearst's International News Service, where he has remained ever since.

In 1932 Dunn became Milt Gross's assistant on his several features and seven years later was taken on by Jimmy Hatlo, with whose creations—*They'll Do It Every Time* and *Little Iodine*—Dunn was to become permanently associated. His own efforts, however, flourished through the years: he invented the "knock-knock" joke (in a million-selling book); wrote several other books, including *I'm Gonna Be a Father* and *One Day in the Army;* and drew his own Sunday cartoon, *Just the Type,* for nearly two decades. Since Jimmy Hatlo's death in 1963 Dunn has signed the Hatlo features, on which he has been assisted through the years by Moyer S. Thompson, Fred Faber, Al Scaduto and Hy Eisman.

Dunn's style is an amalgam of Gross's and Hatlo's: animated, exaggerated, full of characterization and broad humor. *They'll Do It,* of course, relies on readers' contributions, but Dunn's own *Iodine* scripts display a sure mastery of mayhem and zany anarchy—the title character is a one-girl equivalent of the Katzenjammer Kids.

A past president of the National Cartoonists Society, Bob Dunn is in constant demand as one of America's funniest, most entertaining after-dinner speakers and raconteurs. While *Little Iodine* folded in 1986, he continued to produce *They'll Do It Every Time* until the time of his death in his native Newark, on January 31, 1989.

R.M.

DUNNE, LAWRENCE FRANCIS (1898-1937) Australian illustrator and cartoonist born at Boorowa, near Harden, in New South Wales, in 1898. Frank Dunne, who succeeded Cecil Hartt as a portrayer of Digger humor, had been a process engraver before World War I and enlisted in 1915, just after his eighteenth birthday. He served in the Australian Imperial Forces overseas with the First Field Ambulance until 1919. After his war service he progressed from process engraving newspaper blocks into press art and worked on the *Sydney Truth* as an illustrator before joining the staff of *Smith's Weekly.*

Dunne was known to *Smith's* readers as Frank. His strong, vigorous pen drawings, detailed and accurate down to the correct color flashes of the various army units—infantry, Pioneers, and so forth—were, like Cecil Hartt's drawings of Diggers, outstanding for the facial characterization of their subjects. His drawing technique, owing nothing to Phil May, was traditional and realistic, based, like that of Norman Lindsay, on drawing in the round, with light and shadow falling correctly. He blended this technique well with a zesty comic sense that was thoughtfully conceived. With splendid composition and figure placement, Dunne's drawings were almost alive with expressive movement. What could be termed the timing of his humor was faultless; there was never any confusion in his drawings as to who was saying what, nor was the reaction of the listener ever other than fitting. This was a point of subtle concept with Frank Dunne, for these exchanges in comic art are often ignored or more commonly confused.

To many ex-soldiers in the 1930s, Dunne's drawings and humor undoubtedly recalled not the shellfire, suffering and privation, but a nostalgic journey back to a slangy, aitch-dropping world of rum rations, flamin' chats (fleas), affable padres asking silly questions—and getting silly answers—and a certain brazening it out with humor under fire. It was partly this kind of nostalgia that fostered the perpetuation of the Digger spirit; Australians have tended, more than most peoples have, to look back on the "good old days" when soldiers were all mates together. This strain in Australian male life was encouraged not only through the pages of *Smith's Weekly* but also by the soldier organizations.

Frank Dunne, although color-blind to red and green, was a capable landscape painter in oils of the "tonal" school. He had planned an exhibition of his paintings prior to entering a Sydney hospital for elective treatment.

But there Dunne's career was sadly ended by his death following a tonsilectomy in 1937.

A collection of Dunne's *Smith's Weekly* cartoons, *Digger Days,* subtitled *Laughing Through the Great War,* was published in 1931. Priced then at two shillings, (twenty cents), this publication is among the very rarest items of "Australiana" of interest to comic collectors.

V.L.

DUNNING, GEORGE (1920-1978) Canadian animator born in Toronto, Canada, in 1920. George Dunning studied at the Ontario College of Art, then became a freelance illustrator. He later settled in England to produce some of the funniest and most revolutionary cartoon films, including the trend-setting feature *The Yellow Submarine.*

In 1943 he was the third cartoonist to be hired by John Grierson for the animation unit at the National Film Board of Canada. Working under the inspired supervision of Norman McLaren, Dunning made his directorial debut with *Auprès de ma Blonde* (1943), a French-Canadian singalong in the *Chants Populaires* series. A propaganda film, *Grim Pastures* (1944), and an accident prevention cartoon, *Three Blind Mice* (1945), followed before the individuality of Dunning as an artist first emerged in *Cadet Rousselle* (1946). His use of flat, jointed, painted figures was quite new; instead of working with paper cutouts, Dunning made his characters of metal. With Jim McKay, who had helped him on the film, Dunning left the NFB to form a company called Graphic Associates (1949), but he later returned to Canada on a Film Board grant to experiment with an animation technique involving painting on glass.

In 1956 Dunning contracted with the New York animation company United Productions of America to open a production subsidiary in London, England, and make cartoon commercials for the newly established Independent Television. During this period Dunning directed *The Gerald McBoing Boing Show* for U.S. television. When UPA folded their English outpost, Dunning remained to establish his own company, TV Cartoons. Many successful commercials poured from the company for products ranging from Mother's Pride Bread, Golden Wonder Crisps and Start-Rite Shoes to Mentholatum Deep-Heat Rub. Sponsored documentary cartoons include *The Ever Changing Motor Car* (1962) for Ford, *The Adventures of Thud and Blunder* (1964) for the National Coal Board, and *Discovery Penicillin* (1964).

Dunning's association with scriptwriter Stan Hayward began with his first theatrical cartoon for public entertainment, a crazy comedy, *The Wardrobe* (1959). His paint-on-glass experiments bore fruit when *The Flying Man* (1962) took the Grand Prix at the International Animation Festival in Annecy. Two television series for America followed, directed by Dunning's partner, Jack Stokes: *Cool McCool* and *The Beatles* (1967). The latter series, cartoon adventures of the internationally acclaimed singing group from Liverpool, led to the production of *The Yellow Submarine* (1968), an influential cinema feature designed by the German Heinz Edelmann, and an epic of animated pop art. Dunning also produced the only triple-screen cartoon, *Canada Is My Piano* (1967).

Other films by Dunning include *Memory* (1969), *Moon Rock 10* (1970), *Horses of Death* (1972), Plant a Tree and *The Maggott* (both 1973), *Damon the Mower* (1974) and *Teamwork* (1976).

D.G.

DUPRAS, PIERRE (1937-) Canadian cartoonist born in the province of Quebec on June 3, 1937. Showing precocious talent, Pierre Dupras completed his first painting at the age of 12 (he has since exhibited widely). He later drew for his high school paper and for *Quartier Latin,* the publication of the University of Montreal, from which he graduated in 1960.

Pierre Dupras has contributed many cartoons (mostly of a political nature) to such Canadian newspapers as *l'Indépendance, Dimanche-Matin* and *QuébecPresse.* He draws in an old-fashioned, straightforward style, well suited to his rather doctrinal political and social views. His humor is also simple and rather one-dimensional. He has, however, achieved a notoriety that extends well beyond the borders of Quebec and Canada, making him a force to be reckoned with on the Canadian cartooning scene. In the 1980s he ventured into comics production without great success. He has since then returned to editorial and humor cartooning.

His cartoons and comic strips have been reprinted in book form: *Vive le Québec Libre* ("Long Live Free Quebec," 1967), *La Drapolice* (1969), *La Bataille des Chefs* ("The Battle of the Chieftains," 1971) and *Recettes pour Grévistes et Chômeurs* ("Recipes for Striking and Unemployed Workers," 1972) are the most notable. Dupras has also drawn *Les Oraliens,* a series of cartoon shorts for Canadian TV.

M.H.

DYER, ANSON (1876-1962) British cartoonist born in Patcham, Brighton, Sussex, on July 18, 1876. "Britain's Answer to Walt Disney" the press called him, and he was—in every way except success. Ernest Anson-Dyer (he dropped the Ernest and the hyphen) studied at the Brighton School of Art, specializing in ecclesiastical design, then began work in the stained glass studio of C.E. Kempe. He remained in this field for many years, and his windows are said to still decorate many an English church and cathedral.

His bent towards humorous cartooning first showed in his habit of sketching funny animals to amuse his children. On the outbreak of World War I in 1914, Dyer, rejected by the army, tried for an acting job in films. Although turned down because of his excessive height, he met the managing director, and the result was a contract to make his first animated cartoon. *Dicky Dee's Cartoons,* a series of three, were released by the British and Colonial Kinematograph Company through the last three months of 1915. Dyer gave a fascinating account of his early experiences in animation as a lecture to the British Kinematograph Society, published as number 40 in their series under the title *Technique of Film Cartoons* (1936).

Dyer then joined the Cartoon Film Company, and his cartoons alternated with those of Dudley Buxton in the series *John Bull's Animated Sketchbook.* Dyer's first was number 8, and it introduced a caricature of George Robey, the famous music hall comedian. Dyer made eight in the series, then in 1917 joined Kine Komedy Kartoons with Buxton and Ernest H. Mills. His first release for Kine was *The Kaiser's Record* in June, but by October 1918, he had completed ten. With the end of the war, the topical comment cartoon died, and Dyer switched styles to produce his first series of children's cartoons. *Uncle Remus*, based on the Joel Chandler Harris stories, ran for three films through 1919, under the blanket title of *Phillips Philm Phables.*

Dyer then joined the pioneer producer Cecil M. Hepworth at his Walton-on-Thames Studio (having in the interim animated battle scenes for the live-action film *Nelson*), where he produced a series generally called *Cartoon Burlesques.* These were parodies of Shakespeare plays: *The Merchant of Venice, Romeo and Juliet* and *'Amlet* were 1919 releases, followed by *Othello* and *The Taming of the Shrew* (1920). A series of three came next for Hepworth, featuring Bobby the Scout (1922), Dyer's first original character for the screen. Unhappily, Hepworth crashed into bankruptcy and Dyer's career went with him, for awhile. Two titles that were made during this dim period were *Little Red Riding Hood* and *The Three Little Pigs* (1922).

In 1927 he made what was announced as the first full-length animated feature film, *The Story of the Flag*, but Archibald Nettlefold, the producer, decided it would stand a better chance if released in single reel parts. Nettlefold later secured financial backing for Dyer's most ambitious project, a color cartoon studio, and in 1935, amid much local publicity, the "New Competitor for Mickey Mouse" was launched. As Anglia Films, with a studio supervised by Sid Griffiths, Dyer swung into intensive production. The Dunning process, a two-color system, was used, and with Stanley Holloway narrating, *Sam and His Musket* was shown in October 1935. The series of six was released through 1937, and in between came *Carmen* (1936), a musical cartoon of Bizet's opera, *The Lion and Albert* (1937) and *Three Ha'pence a Foot* (1937), both adapted from Marriott Edgar-Stanley Holloway monologues.

Also in 1937 Dyer began the production of commercial cartoons for sponsors: *The King with the Terrible Temper* (released as *The King Who Had Terrible Hiccups*), narrator Sutherland Felce, and *All the Fun of the Air,* both for Bush Radio. In 1938 *Red White and Blue* was produced by Publicity Films for Samuel Hanson's "Red White and Blue Coffee Essence," again with Sutherland Felce narrating.

With World War II (1939), Dyer formed Analysis Films to produce cartoon shorts for the Ministry of Information, the War Office, and the Air Ministry, but the titles have gone unrecorded. After the war (1946), under production manager D.R. Gardiner, he made "Diagram and Technical Films." The J. Arthur Rank renaissance of British cinema provided a new opportunity to produce cartoons for the Saturday matinee programs of the Odeon and Gaumont children's clubs. Squirrel War (April 1947) was another first, a cartoon serial. Three episodes were made (11 minutes; 12 minutes; 10 minutes) from the story by Helen Williams, screenplay by Mary Cathcart Borer and designs by A.A. and W.M. Carter. José Norman, who had provided Dyer's cartoon music before the war, came back for the score. *Who Robbed the Robins* (1947) was the last Analysis Film, running 9 minutes in technicolor. *Fowl Play* (1950) was released as an Apex-Halas and Batchelor Production through Grand National and ran 11 minutes (animator, Harold Whittaker).

For a long life devoted to animated cartoons, Anson Dyer received remarkably little acknowledgment, either during his life or after. He died on February 22, 1962.

D.G.

DYSON, WILLIAM HENRY (1880-1938) British caricaturist and political cartoonist born in Ballarat, Australia, in 1880. "The first major cultural figure since Charles Dickens to champion the working man forthrightly and without reserve," wrote historian Vane Lindesay about Will Dyson in his *Inked-In Image,* a history of Australian cartoons and cartoonists. But Dyson's main political work was done in England.

William Henry Dyson was born into a veritable nursery of cartoonists: his elder brother Ambrose (born in 1876) drew cartoons for the famous weekly the *Sydney Bulletin,* and his friends, the brothers Norman and Daryl Lindsay, were cartoonists on the Melbourne *Punch.* Will Dyson taught himself to draw by emulating his elders and began to get his work published in the *Bulletin* and the *Lone Hand* from the age of 17. In 1903 he took over his brother's weekly stint on the Adelaide *Critic,* where his cartoons were printed in color, the first in Australia. He contributed to C.J. Dennis's weekly *Gadfly* (1906), and drew more caricatures in color for the covers of the *Clarion* (1908). In 1906 he illustrated a book written by another brother, Edward Dyson, called *Fact'ry 'Ands,* but he tended to concentrate more on caricatures. An exhibition of these works opened in Melbourne in May 1909, and the following year he set sail for the broader horizons of Fleet Street, London.

Art holding the Mirror up to Nature
Will Dyson, "The Royal Academy Opens," 1913.

The *Weekly Herald* was the official magazine of the Labour party, and Will Dyson found it a perfect platform for his political cartoons. Still a caricaturist at heart, he drew distorted symbolic figures that, executed in brilliantly bold brushwork, brought a new style to British cartoons. The underdog who was the British working man became a new and dominant figure of latent power; the capitalist lost his comical topper-and-spats image for one of a bloated boss and bully.

With the outbreak in 1914 of World War I, Dyson's art took an even more grotesque turn as his bullies changed nationality to become the German enemy. His newspaper series of *Kultur Cartoons* was reprinted in book form with an introduction by H.G. Wells. In 1915 Dyson was appointed an official war artist and was twice wounded while sketching Australian soldiers in action on the Western Front.

After the war his career was blighted by the death of his wife, Ruby (the sister of childhood friend Norman Lindsay). Dyson returned to Australia in 1925 and was appointed staff cartoonist to the Melbourne *Herald.* In 1930, after a trip to America to exhibit his newly adapted technique of drypoint etching, Dyson returned to London. Here he was appointed cartoonist to the new *Daily Herald,* the first Labour newspaper, and his cartoons were often featured on the entire front page. He died, in harness, in January 1938, age 58.

Books: *Fact'ry 'Ands* (1906); *Syndicalism and the Cooperative Commonwealth* (1913); *Cartoons by Will Dyson* (1913); *Cartoons No. 2* (1914); *Kultur Cartoons* (1915); *War Cartoons* (1916); *Australia at War* (1918); *Poems in Memory of a Wife* (1919); *Drawings by Dyson* (1920); and *An Artist Among the Bankers* (1933).

D.G.

Ee

EFFEL, JEAN
See Lejeune, François.

EFIMOV, BORIS EFIMOVICH (1900-?) Soviet cartoonist born in Kiev, Russia, on September 28, 1900. Boris Efimov, who is largely self-taught, started contributing cartoons to the newspapers *Pravda* and *Izvestia* and to the humor magazine *Krokodil* in 1922. He soon became one of the most popular, as well as one of the most mordant, cartoonists in the USSR. His popularity reached its peak during World War II, when his cartoons helped in no small measure to keep up the morale of the Soviet citizens. He is best noted for his savage depictions of the Nazi leaders, especially Josef Goebbels, whom he never tired of lampooning.

Efimov's style, sparse and to the point, is very close to Western cartooning. His cartoons have been collected in a number of books over the years, including *Political Cartoons from 1924 to 1934* (1935), *Hitler and His Gang* (1943), *International Reporting (1961)* and *Boris Efimov in Izvestia* (1969).

Boris Efimov has been the recipient of many awards and honors, including the State Prize of the USSR in 1950 and 1951, and is a member of the Academy of Arts of Russia. One of the best internationally known Russian cartoonists, Efimov has also had a number of his cartoons reproduced in Western European and American publications. Nothing has been heard from him since the late 1970s, and he is presumably deceased.

M.H.

In search of "dangerous thoughts"—
the Statue of Liberty under investigation.
Boris Efimov. © Krokodil.

EGGELING, VIKING (1880-1925) Swedish animator and artist born in Lund, Sweden, in 1880. Viking Eggeling was fascinated by forms and colors from his earliest age, and in 1897 he went to Paris in order to study art. When World War I broke out, Eggeling went to Switzerland, and he became one of the founders of the Dada movement in Zurich in 1917. In 1919 Eggeling settled in Germany and applied his artistic tenets to the fledgling art of animation.

Working in Berlin, Eggeling explored the relationships between images and time sequences: he carried out his experiments by painting abstract figures or motifs on scrolls or strips of paper, later transferring them to film. It appears that Eggeling made only two independent films before his untimely death at the age of 45: *Horizontal Vertical Orchestra* (1920) and *Diagonal Symphony* (1923). But these films exerted a seminal influence on subsequent avant-garde and abstract animation, inspiring a whole school of German (and later, European and American) animators, starting with Eggeling's friend and collaborator Hans Richter. *Diagonal Symphony* was particularly impressive for its new concepts of rhythm and the movement of images synchronized to sound and music (this years before the first commerical sound cartoon was released).

Viking Eggeling died in Berlin on May 19, 1925; his achievements are now being resurrected.

M.H.

EHRENFRIED, GEORG (1893-1959) German cartoonist and painter born in Berlin, Germany, on July 26, 1893. Georg Ehrenfried, widely known as George Grosz, lost his father when he was seven; his widowed mother cooked for army officers in northeastern Germany. He studied at the Dresden Academy from 1909 to 1912, and by 1910 he was already sending cartoons to the Berlin magazines *Ulk, Lustige Blätter* and *Sporthumor.* He continued his art studies in Berlin in 1912. After a year in Paris (1913) came military service in the war. By 1915 Grosz's personal cartoon style had pretty well crystalized: a jagged, unlovely, expressionistic approach consciously based on toilet and fence graffiti. (Was Grosz, who as a boy had reverently studied and copied the famous cartoonists of the time, perhaps influenced by the intentional imitation of children's art practiced by Adolf Oberländer, the celebrated *Fliegende Blätter* artist?)

By 1915 Grosz had already met the liberal writer and

Ouch! "What a washout! The boy turned out to be a real girl!"
Georg Ehrenfried ("George Grosz"), 1926. © Grosz.

publisher Wieland Herzfelde and his artist brother, who went by the name of John Heartfield. In 1916 the Herzfelde brothers established the left-wing Malik-Verlag, which was to publish Grosz's most significant work up to 1930. The first two *Grosz Albums* appeared in 1917, followed by such masterworks as *Das Gesicht der Herrschenden Klasse* ("The Face of the Ruling Class," 1921), *Ecce Homo* (1922), *Abrechnung Folgt!* ("The Account Will Be Settled!," 1923), Die Gezeichneten ("Marked Men," 1930) and many others. Grosz depicted—with savage relish, unmitigated contempt and a decidedly erotic bias—the militarists, capitalists, profiteers, sensualists, mindless murderers and monsters of his Germany, whom he repeatedly showed alongside exploited workers, handicapped veterans and those wiped out by inflation and hard times. In the eyes of many, these albums make him the greatest of all German cartoonists.

On and off between 1919 and 1924 Grosz worked on the 11 issues of the Herzfeldes' paper *Die Pleite* ("The Bankruptcy"). In the later 1920s he sent a few drawings to *Simplicissimus* and did important innovative stage designs, the most famous being those for Erwin Piscator's production of *The Good Soldier Schweik.*

In 1932 Grosz left Germany for the United States. For a few years he was associated with Maurice Sterne in a private New York art school, but he is better remembered for his 20 years on the staff of the Art Students League (1933-53). *Vanity Fair, Esquire* and *Harper's Bazaar* commissioned drawings from him, but these were chiefly to illustrate weird stories; strong political statements and overtly expressionist methods were not wanted. At the same time, Grosz himself seems to have become weary of his early bitterness and turned increasingly to a genre that had interested him as a young man: nature and landscape studies. These oils and watercolors were generally very finely executed but extremely bland.

In 1959 Grosz returned to West Berlin but died almost at once, on July 6 of that year.

S.A.

ELFINGER, ANTON (1821-1864) Austrian cartoonist born in Vienna, Austria, on January 15, 1821. Like Heinrich Hoffmann, creator of *Struwwelpeter,* Anton Elfinger was a physician by profession, but while the self-taught Hoffmann gained immediate celebrity as a draftsman, the well-trained Elfinger was not generally identified as the cartoonist "Cajetan" until quite recently.

Elfinger, born into an impecunious family of druggists, felt compelled to study medicine (1839-45) rather than devote himself to art, but as a youngster his talent for drawing had been nurtured by instruction from Matthias Ranftl and Leopold Kupelwieser, both of whom had been friends of Moritz von Schwind in the 1820s. Even in his medical work, Elfinger made use of his art training: in the then very progressive dermatological section of the Vienna General Hospital, he did watercolor illustrations of skin diseases that were highly regarded and subsequently published in lithographic portfolios. In 1849 he became official medical illustrator at the hospital and later published several books of anatomical plates.

But while still a medical student, Cajetan (the pseudonym may have been taken from the name of a 17th-century anatomical wax modeler) began contributing humorous drawings to the most widely circulated Viennese magazine, the *Wiener Allgemeine Theater-Zeitung,* which had been edited by the popular playwright Adolf

Anton Elfinger ("Cajetan"), "The Ladies' Rejuvenation Tax," 1850.

Bäuerle since 1806. Between 1841 and 1853, Elfinger drew over a hundred *satyrische Bilder* (generally social satire), theatrical costume studies and devilishly difficult punning rebuses for the *Theater-Zeitung.* Elfinger was also associated with more politically oriented humor magazines, which were necessarily very short-lived in the repressive atmosphere of Vienna at that time. In 1846 he worked on the 6 issues of Otto Bernhard Friedmann's *Kasperl im Frak* ("Punch in a Frock Coat"), and in 1849, the year of the abortive revolution, he edited the 12 issues of *Blitzstrahlen* ("Flashes of Lightning"). He also designed an extremely popular political tarot deck.

After 1849 political satire was out of the question, but Cajetan continued to work at least into the mid 1850s as an illustrator for books and for various popular almanacs, including some edited by the outstanding Viennese humorist Moritz Gottlieb Saphir. Influenced by Grandville, Gavarni and Cham, Cajetan's humorous art is generally heavily shaded and modeled in a supple version of basically academic manner.

Elfinger, whose parents and elder brother had all died young, was himself carried off by a hemorrhage of the lungs on January 19, 1864, a few days after his 43rd birthday.

S.A.

ELIES I BRACONS, FELIU (1878-1948) Spanish cartoonist born in Barcelona, Spain, in 1878. Feliu Elies (who used the pen name "Apa" throughout his career as a cartoonist) began contributing to satirical magazines when he was still a teenager. His cartoons were published in *L'Esquella de la Torratxa, La Campana de Gracia, Cu-Cut* and *En Patufet.* In 1904 he founded the very popular magazine *Papitu,* which he also directed for the first two years of its existence. Later Elies had his cartoons published in most major humor magazines in the country, including *El Poble Catalá, Picarol, La Publicitat, Mirador* and *Iberia.*

During World War I Elies savagely attacked German military power and war policies; his cartoons of this period, which originally appeared in the pages of *Iberia,* were later collected in a book titled *Kameraden.* In addition to his work as a cartoonist, Elies painted, wrote, and was a respected and often feared music critic. He is best known, however, for his acute and satirical cartoons. Public performers were often targets of his wrath and could expect to be caricatured along with politicians and other public figures. He also attacked with special harshness the Catalan political party La Lliga Catalana, as well as other conservative or moderate parties of the period. Feliu Elies died in Barcelona in 1948. (His brother, Lluis Elies, was also a cartoonist.)

J.M.

EMETT, ROWLAND (1906-1990) Cartoonist, builder of fantastic working models and sole proprietor and stationmaster of the Far Tottering and Oyster Creek Railway, born in London, England, on October 22, 1906. Rowland Emett was one of the first British eccentrics to express his eccentricity—an obsession for Victoriana—in his drawings. His police flying squad arrive in horse-drawn chariots, a Mississippi paddleboat crosses the stormy Atlantic

"Of course we are prepared to make one or two small alterations for suitable tenants.
Rowland Emett. © Punch.

to entertain the GIs, and, of course, there is always Nellie, the quaint yet sturdy steam-driven "Puffing Billy."

Emett, of the oft-misprinted surname, was born in 1906, just too late for his beloved Victorian age. Educated at Waverley Grammar School, he studied art at the Birmingham College of Arts and Crafts. His first work was for Siviter Smith, Ltd., a commercial studio in Birmingham where he worked until 1939. During World War II he was a draftsman working on the development of the jet engine.

Emett's first cartoon to be published in *Punch* (1939) was realistic, but he quickly developed his unique brand of fantasy. His technique was seen at its best in the full-color covers and color plates for *Punch* specials and almanacs. His American magazine work includes *Vogue, Life, Harper's Bazaar, Holiday* and *Cosmopolitan.* Much in demand with advertisers, he has designed campaigns for Shell fuel, Abdulla cigarettes and Guinness stout.

In 1951 he designed and built a full-size working version of his cartoon railway for the Festival of Britain Pleasure Gardens at Battersea, London. This led to his equally famous construction, the Guinness clock. His mechanical cartoons have been featured in many window displays and exhibitions in England and abroad, including the British Trade Fair in New York (1960). He was forced to give up cartooning in 1958 due to failing eyesight, although he continued with his zany sculptures. He died on November 13, 1990.

Books: *Anthony and Antimacassar* (1943); *Engines, Aunties and Others* (1943); *Sidings and Suchlike* (1946); *Home Rails Preferred* (1947); *Saturday Slow* (1948); *Buffers End* (1949); *Far Tottering* (1949); *High Tea* (1950); *Peacock Pie* (1951); *Festival Railway Cutout Book* (1951); *The Forgotten Tramcar* (1952); *Nellie Come Home* (1952); *New World for Nellie* (1952); and *Hobby Horses* (1958).

D.G.

EMMWOOD
See Musgrave-Wood, John.

"Just think, Daddy—that phone is still warm from Alvin's voice!"
"Emmy Lou." © United Feature Syndicate.

EMMY LOU (U.S.) Cartoonist Martha (Marty) Links originally produced her newspaper panel dealing with the antics of a teenage girl for the *San Francisco Chronicle.* Syndicated nationally by Consolidated News Features as a daily panel on November 20, 1944, it was titled *Bobby Sox* but was later rechristened *Emmy Lou* after its heroine (the *San Francisco Chronicle* still retains the former title, perhaps for old times' sake).

Emmy Lou was an awkward, gangling, freckle-faced brunette whose days were mostly spent waiting for the phone to ring or in helpless dependence on her mooching, no-good boyfriend Alvin. Emmy Lou and Alvin broke up time and time again (to the unconcealed glee of Emmy Lou's harassed parents), only to make up just as often. When she was not busy dreaming about her love life, Emmy Lou was wont to talk about it in endless (and boring) detail to her long-suffering school friend Taffy. The drawing for the panel, adequate if unoriginal, was from the early 1970's on done mostly by Link's assistant, Ted Martine, while many of the gags were supplied by Jerry Burdsen. At the end of 1979 Link, feeling that Emmy Lou no longer represented the teenagers of the day, retired the feature.

Emmy Lou (which has been distributed by United Feature Syndicate since 1958) is a pleasant, rather innocuous feature. Its longevity may be due, at least in part, to its unabashed attachment to American types and attitudes that belong to the nostalgic past.

M.H.

ENGL, JOSEF BENEDIKT (1867-1907) Austrian-German cartoonist born at Schallmoos, near Salzburg, Austria, on July 2, 1867. Though he was born in Austria (his father was a railroad technician who was transferred from place to place), Josef Engl's whole life and career were bound up with Munich, where he moved as a child. As a cartoonist he was the typical spokesman—never condescending, never severely critical—of the workingmen and peasants in and around the Bavarian capital.

The Candidate for Holy Orders
—"Please let me go, Your Reverence. I must get back to the kitchen, or my goose will burn!"—"Don't worry, Josephine. As long as You're with me, your goose is in God's hands!"
Josef Engl, 1900.

Showing early signs of artistic talent, Engl was apprenticed to a lithographer for two years and in 1885 was able to enter the Munich School of Applied Art (second only to the Academy in prestige). To earn his tuition he did all sorts of commercial artwork, including the production of souvenir plaster statuettes. By 1888 Engl was contributing cartoons to a Munich magazine specializing in satires on the bicycle craze, *Radfahr-Humor* (for which his future *Simplicissimus* colleagues Eduard Thöny and Ferdinand von Reznicek also drew). In 1894 the venerable and beloved *Fliegende Blätter* opened its pages to Engl, who kept up with his art studies at the Academy in the evenings, working under Franz von Stuck. Unfortunately, before his consecration into *Simplicissimus,* Engl suffered an accident—a severe kick by a horse while in military service—that was eventually to shorten his days.

Virtually the only artist from Munich itself on the early staff of *Simplicissimus,* he was with it from its very beginnings in 1896. Much milder in tone and more easygoing in draftsmanship than most of his colleagues on that hard-hitting magazine, Engl soon found his weekly cartoon pushed into the advertising pages, but he made that niche his very own, with a very faithful readership. He was his own gagman and wrote his own captions, which were usually couched in a savory and authentic Bavarian dialect. His celebration of the common man in everyday situations caused him to be compared with the Berlin artist Zille, but Engl lacked Zille's deeper strain and latent reforming zeal.

An album of Engl's *Simplicissimus* work was published under the title *Münchener Humor.* He died in Munich at only 40 on August 25, 1907.

S.A.

ENGELHARDT, THOMAS ALEXANDER (1930-) American cartoonist born in St. Louis, Missouri, on December 29, 1930. Tom Engelhardt studied at Denver University (1950-51), the Ruskin School of Fine Arts at Oxford University (1954-56) and the School of Visual Arts in New York (1957). He freelanced in New York until 1960, when a staff job in the editorial cartooning department of the Newspaper Enterprise Association opened up; Engelhardt drew for the NEA's Cleveland office for nearly two years. In 1962 Bill Mauldin left the *St. Louis Post-Dispatch* for the *Chicago Sun-Times,* and Engelhardt was chosen as the successor to Robert Minor, Dan Fitzpatrick and Mauldin. He continues there today, one of the few cartoonists who still uses (with beautiful mastery) the lithographic crayon. After 35 years at the Dispatch he is still faithful to the view he expressed some 30 years earlier, "Catch the reader's eye with a first-rate picture and there's a much better chance that the message is going to get across."

Engelhardt has said that Fitzpatrick was his idol, but it is obvious that Mauldin's is the style he has adopted through the years. His cartoons are drawn in vertical format, handsome and tightly rendered, with a sense of reserve rather than exaggeration. He is consistently left-wing in his concepts.

R.M.

MOM
DAD
"YOUR MOTHER AND FATHER HAVE TO WORK LATE BUT THEY'D LIKE TO TALK TO YOU ABOUT GUNS AND DRUGS. WILL YOU HOLD FOR A CONFERENCE CALL?"

TRADE YA
7
Mickey Mantle
God

Bob Englehart. © Hartford Courant.

ENGLEHART, ROBERT, JR. (1945-) Editorial cartoonist Bob Englehart combines a broadly humorous graphic style with a keenly critical eye for social injustice and political ineptitude. He acquired a flexible technique, leavening his indignation with genial wit, through a wide range of journalistic experience. "I've worked with a gaggle of editors and have learned how to cope with just about every situation an editor can invent," he reported to *Cartoonist Profiles* in 1982. "I've had my cartoons approved by a committee, a liberal Socialist, two conservative Reaganauts, a closet psychotic, a Victorian patriarch, a nit-picker, and the role model for TV's Lou Grant."

Englehart's adaptability may be the result of extensive and varied experience, but he came to his career equipped with a thorough professional education to prepare him for it. Born in Fort Wayne, Indiana, on November 7, 1945, he attended Chicago's American Academy of Art on a full scholarship, and at the age of 21 he joined the *Chicago American* (later *Chicago Today*) as a cartoonist and illustrator. He remained with that evening paper till it closed in 1972 and then returned to Ft. Wayne with his wife and two children. For the next three years he freelanced, drew cartoons for the Fort Wayne *Journal Gazette,* and ran his own commercial art studio, Englehart & Associates. In 1975 he joined the staff of the Dayton, Ohio *Journal Herald* as political cartoonist. After five years in that post, he was hired by the country's oldest newspaper, the *Hartford Courant,* as the first full-time editorial cartoonist in the paper's long history.

Englehart's work is distributed internationally by the Los Angeles Times-Washington Post News Service and the Copley News Service and has appeared in the *New York Times,* the *Washington Post, Time, Newsweek,* and *Playboy*. It has also been collected into two volumes with appropriately ironic titles: *Never Let the Facts Get in the Way of a Good Cartoon* (1979) and *A Distinguished Panel of Experts* (1985). Among the awards he has earned are several from the Overseas Press Club, the U.N. Population Institute, the John Fischetti Contest, and Planned Parenthood of Connecticut. He was a finalist for the 1979 Pulitzer Prize and in 1989 received the H.L. Mencken Award from the Free Press Association. Original work by Englehart is in the permanent collections of the International Museum of Cartoon Art, the Connecticut Historical Society, the Ohio State University Cartoon Museum, and the Indiana University/Purdue University Fort Wayne Campus Library.

Englehart's professional range extends beyond the newspaper cartoons: in 1972 he illustrated a children's book, *1, 2, 3 I Can Count*; from 1986 to 1991 he and his wife Pat McGrath wrote and produced a "video comic strip for Connecticut Public Television"; and from 1991 through 1995 the creative couple did a sports video comic strip, "Last Row with Englehart and McGrath," every Sunday on ESPN. During the summer of 1992 the cartoonist appeared in person at Caroline's Comedy Club in New York in the political comedy review "Raucous Caucus."

A versatile and perceptive cartoonist, Bob Englehart turns a satiric searchlight on the public scene with finesse and feeling. A growing body of work has earned him a place in the top rank of American political commentators.

D.W.

On a joyous occasion, Kolingen meets his childhood friend Pale Phil, who has embellished his otherwise rather disheveled costume with an almost new hat: "Jumping Jehosophat, Phil! Are your lice swarming since you've given them a new hive?"
Albert Engström, © Søndags-Nisse.

ENGSTRÖM, ALBERT (1869-1940) Swedish painter, cartoonist and author born in Småland, Sweden, in 1869. More than any other, Albert Engström has most fully shown the innermost human characteristics and impact of the Swedish people. In a brilliant way his work has succeeded in laying bare the desires of the country, good or bad, and one common trait throughout is his sympathy and respect for the free individual, and for all human freedom.

Engström studied Greek and Latin at the University of Uppsala. There he learned the importance of the classical languages and developed into a brilliant literary stylist. Few of the world's greatest artists have succeeded to the same extent in combining the drawn and the written into a sublime unity. A director of the Painting School Valand in Göteborg saw his talent and encouraged him to go to Stockholm to pursue a career as a cartoonist. There he worked for the humor magazine *Søndags-Nisse* from 1894 to 1896, until his friends helped him start the magazine *Strix* and the foundation for his art and books was laid. Though a bohemian, he worked steadily and hard and obtained a respected position in all the leading circles.

Engström's characters' ease in relating to each other—whether they are drinking pals, aristocrats, intellectuals or financial wizards—is seen through a razor-sharp eye and an attentive ear. Typical is the situation where the family counsel in a lower-nobility family considers securing a mistress for the oldest, unmarried squire. The grandmother, who with age has become somewhat prejudiced, exclaims, "Might it then at least be a *believing* woman!"

Engström's well-developed instinct for language was always perfect, in dialogue as well as in thought. In Scandinavia he is an institution copied by many but never surpassed. He became a professor at the Academy of Art, one of *De Adotons* ("The Eighteen") honorable doctors, and was the recipient of countless honors and titles. He died in 1940.

J.S.

ENSOR, JAMES (1860-1949) Belgian etcher and painter born in Ostend, Belgium, on April 13, 1860. James Ensor

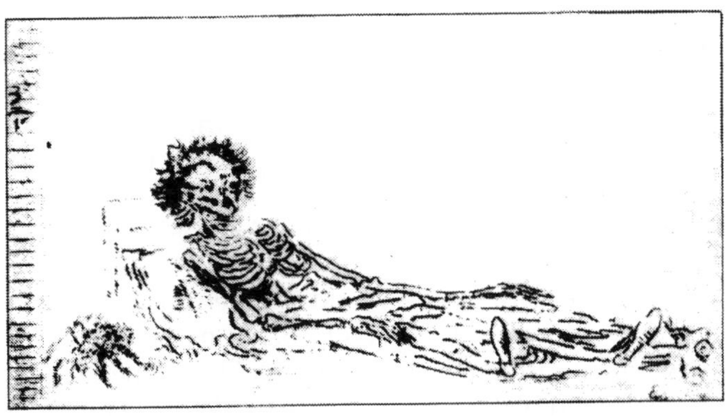

James Ensor, "My Portrait in 1960," 1888.

studied at the Brussels Academy of Fine Arts (1877-79), where he was influenced by French impressionist and intimist artists. He quickly developed an original style that is closer to Flemish expressionism, as in his *Woman Eating Oysters* (1882). A protégé of Félicien Rops, he founded Les XX in 1884 with other painters and sculptors to fight against the philistine backwardness and incomprehension of academic judges, but even this group refused to exhibit Ensor's *Entrance of Christ into Brussels,* and he became more and more bitter about having his work rejected.

Ensor's social and political etchings bitingly satirize the powerful members of middle-class society: gendarmes (1888), judges and lawyers ("The Good Judges," 1894), doctors ("The Bad Physicians," 1895), etc. His work shows a violent, anarchistic power and an unrestrained anger which finds its best expression in the grotesque world of macabre visions, masks, specters. In the fantastic tradition that runs from Bosch to Flora, and using violent colors, grimacing, stupid faces and repulsive skeletons and allegories, James Ensor presents human comedy as it is really performed on the world's stage. Among his most interesting etchings are *Masks in Front of Death* (1888), *Skeletons Warming Themselves Around the Stove* (1889), *The Intrigue* (1890), *Skeletons in the Studio* (1900), *Pierrot and Skeletons* (1907) and especially the morbid, playful and self-deprecating *My Portrait in 1960* (1888).

In December 1898 the French review *La Plume* devoted a special issue to Ensor in conjunction with an exhibition of his work, and this established him as one of the important artists coming out of Belgium. As early as 1895, however, he had more or less given up painting and etching, only occasionally producing a piece or two a year. Indeed, success came belatedly to Ensor, but he was eventually honored with a barony, membership in the Belgian Academy, exhibitions in France, England and Belgium, artworks hanging in French, German, Belgian, American and other galleries and museums, and a commemorative statue in his hometown, where he died on November 19, 1949.

P.H.

EPSTEIN, ABNER (1910-1982) American cartoonist born in New York City in 1910. Known professionally as Abner Dean (a derivation from his mother's first name, Deanna), Abner Epstein attended Dartmouth College in Hanover, New Hampshire, from which he received his B.A. in 1931. He then enrolled in the National Academy of Design and continued his art studies. His first work in the field was freelancing, particularly in advertising and industrial illustration. It was probably in this latter capacity that he designed the industrial folding table for which he holds the patent.

One hesitates to call Dean a gag cartoonist, though one often laughs at the absurd but familiar antics of his simple, naked pen-and-ink figures, usually set against stark, almost lunar landscapes. A strong vein of alienation, however sardonic, runs through all his work, and his (not uncritical) debt to Freudian psychology is at times naively apparent. His captions are frequently "attitude" words or the intellectual and social clichés of modernity, and his capricious realization of them is undeniably unique. An example from one of his anthologies, *It's a Long Way to Heaven* (1945): a man hanging by the neck from a single blasted tree in one of Dean's characteristically barren landscapes scribbles away on his "appeal," his face contorted into a ghastly burlesque of a smile; the caption, "Optimism." As is so often the case with a Dean work, it is as depressing as it is amusing. (A clue to the reaction Dean is seeking in this and his other cartoons in *Heaven* can perhaps be found in the brief introduction to the volume, penned by no less an "angry young man" than Philip Wylie.)

Perhaps the best brief, serious appraisal of this controversial artist's work comes from Clifton Fadiman's introduction to Dean's 1947 anthology *What Am I Doing Here,* published by Simon and Schuster. "The urge to call Dean bats," Fadiman writes, "will be strong; but that is only because we have so large a vested interest in being 'normal' that we panic easily when this investment is threatened."

As an artist Dean has been represented in many of the major magazines, including the *New Yorker,* and has published no less than eight anthologies of his work, bearing such provocative titles as *Come As You Are* (1952), *Cave Drawings for the Future* (1954), *Not Far from the Jungle* (1956) and *Abner Dean's Naked People* (1963). He died in New York City on June 30, 1982.

R.C.

EVANS, RAYMOND OSCAR (1887-1954) American cartoonist born in Columbus, Ohio, on July 15, 1887. Ray O. Evans received his B.A. from Ohio State University in 1910 and became an advertising artist in Columbus. He joined the art staff of the *Columbus Dispatch* in 1910, receiving on-the-job training from Billy Ireland, and drew editorial cartoons for the *Dayton News* in 1912 and 1913. In 1913 he transferred to the *Baltimore American,* a Hearst paper, drawing editorial cartoons until 1920 and freelancing for *Puck* in 1915 and 1916. He drew briefly for the combined *Baltimore News and American* before returning to Columbus in 1922 and remaining there until his death on January 18, 1954.

Evans taught cartooning at the Maryland Institute, created school features in cartoon formats and illustrated for *Better Homes and Gardens* ("The Diary of a Plain Dirt Gardener"). He had an uncluttered style and effectively used the brush and crayon. In his political leanings, he was a Democrat. Evans's son, Ray, Jr., was also a cartoonist.

R.M.

EVE (G.B.) *The Adventures of Eve,* subtitled "An Irresponsible Record of Some Incidents in the Career of a Frivolous Little Lady, To Say Nothing of Adam, Aunt Matilda, Uncle Fred and Tou-Tou," appeared weekly in the *Tatler,* a slightly upper-class glossy magazine. During World War I the *Tatler* was advertised as "the brightest, prettiest, most unique weekly paper in the world," and it brought a delightful touch of decorative humor to an unfunny and undecorative era.

Eve, a decidedly society "sweet young thing," did her best to cope with 1914-18 conditions in her own feminine way. She joined the police with her socialite sisters Evelyn and Evelinda, became a hospital nurse in a cute kilt, stayed on the east coast of England with Uncle Fred and survived a zeppelin raid by hiding under the dining room table, did her bit as a postman in cute boots, and was saved from the seaside tide by a handsome submariner. She also made it from the printed page into films, and a set of 12 silent two-reel comedies was produced by Gaumont in 1918. Eileen Molyneux portrayed Eve, with Pat Somerset as boyfriend Adam and Cecil Morton York as Uncle Fred.

Eve was drawn by "Fish" and "written and designed by Fowl." Fish was, in fact, Miss Fish, one of those rare birds, a woman cartoonist. Her artwork, thin line balanced against solid blacks, is still extremely original and stylish. The cartoons departed from the standard strip technique by dispensing with panels and being laid out over full pages and occasional spreads, with an eye to decorative composition rather than to progression. *The Eve Book* was published in 1917.

D.G.

Ff

FABLES FOR THE TIMES (U.S.) The creation that first brought widespread attention to T.S. Sullivant, *Fables for the Times,* ran in *Life* beginning with the issue of February 13, 1896, with text by H.W. Philips. It was an up-to-date *Aesop's Fables* rendered in slang, with ironic twists and in a generally sarcastic vein. After the tale (usually with animals, in the Aesopian tradition), an *im*moral rather than a moral would follow.

The cartoons were snappy and made social and political points that obviously delighted the readers of *Life,* but their most striking characteristic was the artwork of freshman T.S. Sullivant; he had just begun to explore the visual delights of his singular exaggeration and composition. His line was still delicate, but his formats were bold—qualities rarely surpassed by others, or in his own later work. In several instances the cartoon ran one narrow strip the height of a page. In this series Sullivant staked a claim as a brilliant cartoonist unbound by conventions of format, perspective or rendering. Henceforth he became one of *Life's* heralded attractions.

The popular series ended with the issue of July 30, 1896, and was immediately published in book form by R.H. Russell and Son.

R.M.

"Your Excellency, pardon . . . we're closing up."
Abel Faivre.

FABLIO LE MAGICIEN (France/Hungary/Romania/Bulgaria) *Fablio le Magicien* ("Fablio the Magician") may possibly represent the ultimate in the growing internationalism of animated filmmaking. This 85-minute feature was produced by Edic Films in Paris and animated in the studios of Pannonia Film in Budapest, Animafilm in Bucharest and the Sofia Animation Studio; it was released in 1969.

The program was based on six different fables of La Fontaine. Attila Dugay, a Hungarian, directed no fewer than four of the fables: "The Frog That Wanted to Be As Big As the Ox" (a satire on overreaching), "The Dog and the Wolf" (a backhanded tribute to freedom), "The Lion and the Gnat" (a musical and animal parody on the David and Goliath theme) and "The Tortoise and the Two Ducks" (a twist on the old saw "Curiosity killed the cat"). The program was completed by the Romanian Victor Antonescu's version of the well-known fable "The Grasshopper and the Ant" and the Bulgarian Radka Batcharova's whimsical tale "The Cat and the Old Rat."

"Fablio le Magicien." © EDIC.

The six sketches were linked together by introductory sequences featuring the title character, a little magician who wove elements of poetry, fantasy, and humor into these well-worn tales. Despite some nice pieces of animation (principally by Dugay) and the clever use of color, *Fablio* was not a commercial success, nor was it an unqualified artistic achievement. It is noted here as a noble experiment.

M.H.

FABULOUS WORLD OF JULES VERNE, THE
See Vynález Zkázy.

FAIVRE, ABLE (1867-1945) French caricaturist, cartoonist, poster designer and painter born in Lyons, France, on March 30, 1867. Abel Faivre attended the school of Fine

"Ah! Here it is! 'The Discourse on Method.'"
Jacques Faizant. © Faizant.

Arts before studying at the Ecole des Beaux-Arts in Paris (1886-89). He started his caricaturing career by contributing from 1895 on to *Le Rire,* which became *Le Rire Rouge* during World War I; he also contributed for 37 years to *Le Journal* and for 7 to *Le Figaro,* as well as to other humor magazines, especially *L'Echo de Paris* and *L'Assiette au Beurre.* For *L'Assiette*'s issue of March 22, 1902, Faivre, the son and brother of physicians, drew a biting series of cartoons satirizing doctors. Probably the most famous drawing is the one where a physician dressed in black carries a funeral wreath bearing the inscription "To My Clients" and smilingly declares, "Ils ne l'ont pas volée. . . ."("They richly deserve it").

His cartoons and caricatures make use of many right-wing themes, from anti-Semitism to anti-German revanchist spirit; his "We'll Get Them" (1917) or the French Victory Loan posters (1918) epitomize this genre. He imputes an unrelieved ugliness to his victims, often presenting them in an angry black humor manner. Some of his war sketches were published in the albums 56 Dessins de Guerre ("56 War Cartoons," 1915) and *Jours de Guerre 1915-1919* ("War Days," 1921). On the other hand, his paintings and murals have an agreeable, airy, almost light-hearted pleasantness about them, rather reminiscent of the 18th century. Some received prizes and now hang in museums in Paris and Lyons (for instance, his *Woman with the Fan,* in the Louvre).

Abel Faivre died in Nice on August 14, 1945.

P.H.

FAIZANT, JACQUES (1918-) French cartoonist born in central France on October 30, 1918. After taking a degree in hotel management at the Ecole Hôtelière of Nice and working for several years in the trade, Jacques Faizant abandoned the hotel business to try his hand at animation (1942-45). When this venture failed, he became a cartoonist (1945) and collaborated on all the important weeklies, especially *Jours de France* and *Paris-Match.* Since 1967 he has also drawn political cartoons for *Le Figaro* and *Le Point.*

His drawings have been published in the highly successful albums *Les Vieilles Dames* ("The Old Ladies"), *Histoires de France* ("Histories of France"), *Les Caprices de Marianne* (1969), *C'est Ouvert* ("It's Open," 1970), *Les Vieilles Dames et les Hommes* ("Men and the Old Ladies," 1972) and *Allons-y à Pied* ("Let's Go There on Foot," 1974). He also illustrated his own novels, *Ni d'Eve ni d'Adam* ("Neither from Eve nor from Adam," 1954), *Les Marins* ("The Sailors," 1964), *Les Gros Soucis* ("Big Worries," 1972) and *Albina et 1a Bicyclette* (1976).

Faizant has an uncanny knack for showing the contradictions in our character or behavior, as with the man who, having unmethodically emptied his bookcase and thrown the books pell-mell on the floor, joyfully exclaims, "Ah! Here it is! Descartes's *Discourse on Method!*" or the king who brings the phone to one of his guards and says, "It's for you." His most famous series, however, features "the old ladies," all more or less looking alike, with their hanging jowls, their white buns, their long black dresses showing flashes of petticoat white, their knitting. These little old ladies are not necessarily gentle and sweet. As a matter of fact, they are often mischievous, if not somewhat mean, as in the case of one lady blowing up a paper bag at the very moment another old lady is walking by with an armful of dishes. This kind of humor has helped to make Jacques Faizant's books and cartoons well-deserved successes. In 1987 he was nominated for a seat in the prestigious Académie Française, the first cartoonist to be so honored; and while he narrowly lost, his candidacy brought new prestige to the profession.

P.H.

FALLS, CHARLES BUCKLES (1874-1960) American cartoonist and illustrator born in 1874. Charles Falls was largely responsible for the brighter moments of the last years of *Puck* magazine in the late 1910s. His line drawings graced James Hunecker's "Lively Arts" column and were among the best of Falls's career of decorative brushwork. C.B. Falls was also known as a designer, muralist and portrait painter, and he taught for years at the Art Students League in New York. His early work in *Puck* was signed with a little black square.

His style was impressionistic and full of contrasts and solid blacks. His lush brushstrokes later gave way to a drybrush technique, and his illustrative work for *Puck,*

The way the Kansas druggist toiled behind his prescription case seven years ago was a caution to galley slaves.
Charles Falls.

sometimes running a full page and sometimes with monochromatic shading, was very striking.

Books: *Our Friend the Dog* (1904); *Snow White* (1913); *The ABC Book* (1923), a classic done in woodcuts and still reprinted; *Poems from "Life"* by Oliver Herford (1923); *The Color of a Great City* by Theodore Dreiser (1923); *When Jesus Was Born* (1928); *Two Medieval Tales* by Robert Louis Stevenson (1929, for the Limited Editions Club); and *Reveries of a Bachelor* by Ik. Marvel (1931).

R.M.

FAMILIA SISTACS, LA (Spain) *La Familia Sistacs,* a panel created by the cartoonist Valentí Castanys i Borrás, was first published in the humor magazine *Xut!* prior to the Spanish civil war and was compiled in book form after the war. The panel represented the aspirations of the Spanish middle class trying to ape the manners, mores and rituals of the higher class. At the same time, the Sistacs family embodied many of the wishes, problems and characteristics common to all those who worked hard trying to escape from the cultural limitations of the lower classes.

Castanys showed great interest in customs and traditions springing from regional and subcultural roots. The cultural mix—the melting pot, as it were—that Spain really is under the surface was analyzed with an unjaundiced eye through the Sistacs family. For instance, the language used by Castanys in the feature was half Spanish-Castilian and half Catalan. The cartoonist blended a lively humor into the pathos, however, and *La Familia Sistacs* was one of the most popular features in Spain for over twenty years, until the author's death in 1965.

J.M.

FAMILY CIRCUS, THE (U.S.) The official birthdate of *The Family Circus* is February 19, 1960, the day the Register and Tribune Syndicate started distribution of Bil Keane's popular daily panel. Keane himself feels that the idea for a newspaper panel about family life came to him as early as 1952. The panel's goings-on revolve around an average American family originally made up of Mommy, Daddy, and three children—the eldest son, Billy; his ponytailed sister, Dolly; and Jeffy, the tot of the family. In 1962 a third baby boy, P.J., was added to the household. Barfy the dog rounds out the cast of principals.

Bil Keane draws his daily panel within a circle to accentuate the feeling of closeness and also to symbolize the title by suggesting a circus ring. The Sunday panel is rectangular, but the ring motif is retained around the logo. (A companion panel, *Side Show,* in which the cartoonist illustrates puns submitted by his readers, completes the Sunday feature.) Keane's own wife and family are the models for the panel's family, which may account for the close identification many readers feel with the feature. The happenings are ordinary, everyday incidents only slightly emphasized for humorous effect. "There's a general tendency among people who want to be funny to exaggerate," Keane stated in a 1966 interview. "I do just the opposite. I tone down every idea I get. I also keep my drawing style simple, only the lines necessary. . . . Each cartoon must have life; it should be current and fresh. For instance, the house, the neighborhood, the trappings, the paraphernalia, are kept up-to-date."

Success has amply rewarded Keane's simple cartooning creed. *The Family Circus* is one of today's most popular newspaper panels; it won the National Cartoonists Society Best Syndicated Panel award twice, in 1967 and 1971. Many of the cartoons have been collected into books, the latest being *The Family Circus Treasury,* published by Sheed, Andrews and McMeel in 1977. And in 1978, a TV special, "A Special Valentine with the Family Circus," was aired on NBC.

More honors have come to Keane since 1980. He received the National Cartoonists Society's Reuben Award in 1982. Two more animated specials of *The Family Circus* were broadcast by NBC (in 1980 and 1981), and more collections of the panel have appeared in print. The feature is now distributed by King Features Syndicate, with the cartoonist retaining ownership.

M.H.

"Why CAN'T you play cards with us, Mommy? Grandma always does."
"The Family Circus." © Register and Tribune Syndicate.

Fang Cheng. © Fang Cheng.

FANG CHENG (1918-) Graduated from Wuhan University in 1942, majoring in chemistry, Fang abandoned his profession as a chemist in a research institute to become a cartoonist in 1946 as the chief-editor of the cartoon section in the semi-monthly *Observer* in Shanghai. Since the 1950s, Fang was art editor and later senior editor of the *People's Daily*, Beijing, and to this day has been a member of many professional organizations.

As one of the best established cartoonists in China, Fang has published a great number of cartoons and has been a productive author on theoretical books on cartoon art. His cartoons deal with many topics, including international political satire as well as domestic societal criticism. With a profound knowledge of the Chinese classical literature, his cartoons were often based on those popular historical stories or proverbs. One such example was his "Wu Dalang's Restaurant" made in the 1980s, after the disastrous "Cultural Revolution" ended. It ridiculed some leaders who hated any subordinates who would be more intelligent than themselves. In recent years, with a group of other cartoonists, Fang has been experimenting cartoon making in Chinese traditional brush and ink.

What is worthy of notice is that Fang's late wife, Chen Jinyan (1924-1977), was the first woman cartoonist in the People's Republic of China, as well as a talented comic artist, printer, oil painter, ivory carving handcrafter and sculptor. She worked as an editor for *Beijing Daily* from the 1950s to the 1960s, and transferred to the Beijing Art and Handcraft Research Institute in 1973 until her unexpected death of a heart attack, possibly caused by the years of mental depression and suffering during the "Cultural Revolution." In 1983, Mr. Fang managed to collect as much as he could of her art works to publish the *Selected Art Works of Chen Jinyan*. One of her cartoons was chosen as its cover page, in which Queen Dowager Cizi of the Qing Dynasty was telling a Communist Party leader: "You are really the number one money-spender. I hadn't thought about using glazed tiles for the royal kitchen when I was in charge of my Summer Palace's construction."

H.Y.L.L.

FANTASIA (U.S.) Walt Disney had been planning a musical cartoon film as a vehicle for Mickey Mouse (whose popularity was waning) as far back as 1938. Eventually this project evolved into a full-length feature, considered by most critics as Disney's single most stunning achievement: *Fantasia*, first released at Christmastime 1940.

Intended as a marriage between animation and musical arts, the film was introduced by musicologist Deems Taylor, while the score was conducted by maestro Leopold Stokowski. The program itself consisted of the following pieces: Bach's Toccata and Fugue in G Minor (as adapted for orchestra by Stokowski); excerpts from Tchaikovsky's *Nutcracker* Suite; Paul Dukas's scherzo "The Sorcerer's Apprentice"; Stravinsky's "Rite of Spring"; Beethoven's *Pastoral* Symphony; Ponchielli's "Dance of the Hours" (from his opera *La Gioconda*); and a combination of Moussorgsky's "Night on Bald Mountain" and Gounod's "Ave Maria."

As can be expected from the diversity of the selected pieces, the resulting sequences were of uneven quality, but there were dazzling moments in each of them. Perhaps the most flawlessly realized sequence, from the point of view of pure animation, was "The Sorcerer's Apprentice," in which Mickey played the title character; but "The Dance of the Hours" (with its hilarious cast of animal ballerinas) was not too far behind. Special mention should go to the abstract treatment of the Toccata and Fugue, clearly inspired by the work of Oskar Fischinger (who was called in to help with the sequence); the dinosaur battle in "Rite of Spring" and the delicate color work on the *Nutcracker* must also be cited.

Fantasia drew mixed reviews upon its first release and proved an unmitigated disaster at the box office. Eventually the work was reappraised, and is now regard-

The "Dance of the Mushrooms" sequence of "Fantasia." © Walt Disney Productions.

ed as a forceful and masterly statement of animation art. Thanks to its many reshowings in later years, it also finally managed to turn a profit for Walt Disney Productions.

M.H.

FANTASTIC PLANET

See Planète Sauvage, La.

FAR SIDE, THE (U.S.) Undoubtedly the most unique and trendsetting newspaper panel of recent times, Gary Larson's *The Far Side* was an unlikely candidate for phenomenal success at its onset. The Seattle-based artist sold his offbeat feature *Nature's Way* to the local magazine *Pacific Search* in late 1976 and the *Summer News Review* shortly after. In 1978 the *Seattle Times* began running it weekly in their Saturday edition, yet it was dropped due to numerous reader complaints. Immediately following, the panel was bought by Chronicle Features, where it was initially syndicated in their parent newspaper the *San Francisco Chronicle*, among others. Retitled *The Far Side*, it made its official debut on January 1, 1980, expanding quickly to wider circulation.

The feature was remarkable, as it brought to newspapers the macabre and black humor initiated earlier in periodicals by Charles Addams, B. Kliban and Gahan Wilson. Larson gradually transformed *The Far Side* from a crudely rendered characterization of shock material and recurring role-reversals into a nimble-witted skewer of human foibles, phrases and customs. Considerable emphasis was affectionately pointed at pedantic academics and eccentric devotees of Natural Science, making it a particular favorite with those in that profession. Existing in a cosmos of abnormality, the panel's deadpan characters contrasted by design with their usually absurd situations, rendered in a deceptively simple style. Alongside the cloddish humans, animals, microorganisms, alien monsters, inanimate objects and even the Deity were humorous subjects juxtaposed into any possible context.

"The Far Side." © Gary Larson

In 1982 Andrews and McMeel published the first book collection, leading to a syndication contract with its affiliate Universal Press in 1984. A Sunday version was finally added on May 4, 1986, soon after an unprecedented exhibition of the cartoon began touring natural history and science museums in 1985, while a permanent display is installed at the California Academy of Sciences. The feature has seen adaptation into animation with TV commercials and two 'Tales from the Far Side' specials in 1994 and 1997. A zealous merchandising campaign was created, featuring greeting cards, mugs, calendars and over twenty books, most notably *The Prehistory of the Far Side* retrospective in 1989.

Seen in 1,900 newspapers at its peak, the feature also earned considerable accolade, including two Best Syndicated Panel and Reuben Awards from the National Cartoonists Society and the Max and Moritz Prize by the German International Comics Salon.

The style and intent of Larson's work have spawned a host of imitators, yet none have matched his consistent range of imagination and humor. Canceled by the artist on January 1, 1995, it still appears in reruns internationally, while an unlikely return is an earnest wish from its legion of fans.

B.J.

FARKAS, ANDRÉ (1915-) French cartoonist, poster artist, set designer and painter born in Temesoara, Romania, on November 9, 1915. He studied at the Budapest School of Fine Arts before going to France, where he began his cartooning career in 1944 under the name "André François."

François has contributed cartoons to numerous magazines, in particular to *La Tribune des Nations* (1953-60), *Holiday* and *Sports Illustrated,* and designed covers for the *New Yorker, Punch, Esquire* and *Fortune.* He has also created posters for Kodak, Olivetti, Citroën and Esso, as well as illustrating, among other works, Homer's *Odyssey* and Jarry's *Ubu-Roi* (1958). A collection of his drawings entitled *The Biting Eye* (1960) has been released by Perpetua (Ronald Searle's publishing company). In addition, he has done several animated cartoons for American TV ads, the most interesting being for Jack-in-the-Box drive-in restaurants and the American Gas Association.

Notable among François's own books are: *The Tattoed Sailor,* with an introduction by Walt Kelly (1953); *The Half-Naked Knight* (1958); *Les Larmes de Crocodile* ("Crocodile Tears"), which won the U.S. Best Children's Book Award (1956); and *You Are Ri-di-cu-lous* (1970). Finally, François has designed stage sets for Roland Petit's ballet company (1956), Peter Hall's production of *The Merry Wives of Windsor* (1958) and Gene Kelly's *Pas de Dieux* (1960).

All these works present a modern look at a world which is poetic and absurd, where man does the incongruous with normality and aplomb, where the underlying joke is

André Farkas ("André François"). © Punch.

at once cruel, tender and ingenuous: an engineer drawing at his drafting board with flowers growing out of his head, a woman wearing a witch's mask on her face and having her breakfast, a young boy in the Napoleonic pose, holding a watermelon on his head and standing beside his father, who is eating a watermelon slice. Searle's and Steinberg's influence is apparent in the clarity and beauty of the lines, while Grosz and Klee have undoubtedly played a role in his choice of grotesque themes and characters.

Since 1960, André François has devoted himself mainly to painting, and his figurative canvases have been exhibited in New York (1962) and at the Stedelijk Museum in Amsterdam (1967), the Musée des Arts Décoratifs in Paris (1970), the Chicago Arts Club (1975) and the Galerie Delpire in Paris (1965 and 1976). To his already numerous honors the artist has added in recent years those of Knight of the Legion of Honor (1990) and Doctor honoris causa of London University.

P.H.

FARKAS, YA'AKOV (1923-) The Israeli cartoonist signing himself with the single name Ze'ev is one of the most distinctive pictorial spokesmen for Near Eastern social and political thought. Born Ya'akov Farkas (Ze'ev is the Hebrew translation of the Magyar word *Farkas*, ("wolf") in Budapest, Hungary in 1923, the artist works from a unique position of authority, having been personally involved in all the horrors and triumphs of his adopted country since its establishment. He narrowly survived the Nazi holocaust by his skills as a carpenter when he was impressed into labor for the German army after its occupation of Hungary, and was transferred from Buchenwald to Dachau two days before the inmates of that death camp were liberated at the end of World War II. After a ten-month detention with fellow survivors in Cyprus, he made his way to Palestine in 1947, six months before the state of Israel was declared. Ze'ev served with the Israeli army through the War of Independence and then made his home on a co-operative farm in the newly independent nation, laboring with his fellow pioneers to build a village.

Ze'ev has been devoted to journalism since his early youth; at the age of twelve he produced his own handwritten newspaper every Sunday, and in Cyprus he created a weekly periodical for his fellow detainees, including

Ya'akov Farkas ("Ze'ev"). © Ze'ev.

his own caricatures in each issue. In 1952 he began submitting his drawings to the few journals beginning in Tel Aviv, and by the end of that year became the first to produce a daily political cartoon in Israel. In 1953 he became an illustrator and theatrical cartoonist for the Tel Aviv paper *Ma'ariv*. He was also to become a regular contributor to the short-lived *Dahlil* and the art director of the weekly *Dvar Hashavua*. In 1962 he became the political cartoonist for *Ha'aretz*, Israel's most prestigious newspaper, for which he produced a full page of editorial cartoons as well as a sports cartoon weekly for the next 27 years. Self-taught as an artist, Ze'ev employs a deceptively simple, economical line, conveying his ideas with a minimum of extraneous detail. As independent in thought as he is in graphic style, he has consistently used his pen without fear or favor, sparing United States and Israeli political figures and policies no more than those of the Soviet, Arab, or Nazi foes of his people. Typical of his concise expression of shrewd political insights is his 1968 drawing of Uncle Sam extending a long arm to reach for the moon while with a much shorter one he gropes for peace in Vietnam.

Long recognized as Israel's premier editorial cartoonist, Ze'ev has received numerous international honors, including the Nordau Prize (1965), the Schwimmer Prize for Journalism (1971), the Herzl prize (1973), the Sokolov Prize for Journalism (1981), the Top Hat Prize (1986), and the prestigious Israel Prize for Journalism (1993). His work has been given solo and group exhibition in Tel Aviv, Jerusalem, Haifa, and elsewhere in Israel, as well as in Montreal, Canada, and Budapest, Hungary. Distributed by Cartoonists & Writers Syndicate in New York to over 100 newspapers internationally, his cartoons have been reprinted in such American periodicals as *Time* and the *New York Times*, as well as in *Le Monde* in France, *The Times* (London), *Der Spiegel* in Germany, and the *New Times* in the U.S.S.R. Collections of his work have been published in Hebrew, in Hebrew-English bilingual editions, and in Hungarian.

D.W.

FARMER AL FALFA (U.S.) Paul Terry created his first cartoon series, *Farmer Al Falfa*, in 1916 for the Thomas A. Edison Corporation. The early cartoons were rather crude; they showed an old farmer with white whiskers vainly trying to cope with the various animals around his farm. The 1917 "Farmer Al Falfa's Wayward Pup" is typical in this respect. In 1921 Terry went over to Pathé Exchange, and it was there that the series took its definitive form. Farmer Al Falfa is chiefly remembered today for his epic battles against the hordes of mice that were always invading his property ("Rats in the Garret" is one good example), but he had his troubles with all kinds of animals, as evidenced by such titles as "The Farmer and the Ostrich," "The Farmer and His Cat" and "Farmer Al Falfa's Pet Cat."

After the founding of Terrytoons, *Farmer Al Falfa* became the first series of the fledgling studio, starting in 1932. Under the close supervision of Terry, and with the help of directors Frank Moser, Mannie Davis and George Gordon, the Farmer (as he was simply called) went through a number of entertaining if hardly memorable adventures: "Farmer Al Falfa's Birthday Party," "Farmer Al Falfa's Bedtime Story" (both 1932), "Mice in Council" (1934) and "Farmer Al Falfa's Surprise Package" (1936) are some of the better-known cartoons. In 1936 Terry released "Farmer Al Falfa's Twentieth Anniversary," a compilation of some of the highlights of the series.

The series degenerated rapidly in the 1940s as it became progressively more repetitive and predictable. The title character was later renamed Farmer Gray but appeared only sporadically through the 1950s.

While not a classic by any means, *Farmer Al Falfa* was one of the earliest American cartoon series and one of the longest-running (it was discontinued in the early 1960s). As such, it deserves greater attention than it has hitherto received.

M.H.

FARMER GRAY
See Farmer Al Falfa.

FARRIS, JOSEPH (1924-) American cartoonist, painter and sculptor born in Newark, New Jersey, on May 30, 1924. Joseph Farris was raised in the Danbury, Connecticut, area. When he was 14 or 15 he saw an article in the *Danbury News-Times* saying that Richard Taylor, the famous *New Yorker* and *Esquire* cartoonist, would conduct an art class in neighboring Bethel. That same week *Collier's* magazine had profiled Taylor. Suitably impressed, Joseph Farris joined thirty or forty others in Taylor's art classes.

"You can't raise my property tax anymore. It's yours!"
Joseph Farris, "Farriswheel." © Chicago Tribune-New York News Syndicate

"He gave me the very basics in art, and he wasn't particularly trying to make cartoonists of us," remembers Farris. "I was impressed by the quality of his life-style and with his ability to see things freshly." Farris continued his art lessons with Richard Taylor until he graduated from high school and entered the army during World War II.

He served in the military from 1943 to 1946, and some of his cartoons were published in *Stars and Stripes.* At the end of the war he studied in a three-month school for GI's in Biarritz, France, and then as a civilian studied fine arts for four years at the Whitney School of Art in New Haven, Connecticut. After a year of book and magazine illustration, he began his freelance cartoon career in earnest. One of Farris's first magazine cartoon sales was to a Catholic religious publication, *The Victorian.* Not knowing the nature of the magazine, he accidentally sprinkled some risqué cartoons into the ones he submitted for general readership. *The Victorian's* editors forgave him that sin, and his career was launched.

Joseph Farris considers himself a "social cartoonist," and philosophically he is very much a kindred spirit to cartoonist Alan Dunn. His cartoons are pointed comments on man and society, but with a chuckle. They are drawn with pen and ink in a decorative style that rests on the quality of the line. A regular contributor to the *New Yorker* and many other magazines, he has also been published in *Playboy,* his cartoons having a social comment rather than a sexual gag. He is one of the select cartoonists under contract to the *New Yorker.* From 1971 to 1974 the Chicago Tribune-New York News Syndicate distributed his panel *Farriswheel.* The feature was a daily cartoon with social comment. Now in his seventies he still goes on his merry cartooning way.

Joseph Farris's painting and sculpture represent the "fine-arts side of me completely free of commercialism." While his paintings have a humorous flair, his sculpture is mostly abstract. In 1969 a series of cartoons he had sold to various magazines on the topic of unidentified flying objects was published in a collection called *UFO HoHo.*

B.C.

FATHER CHRISTMAS (G.B.) In an iconoclastic age, it is perhaps to be expected that the traditional image of Jolly Old Santa Claus with his red cloak, white beard and happy "Ho-ho-ho!" would be shattered. But the artist who finally "upped and did it," Raymond Briggs, did it with such unexpected good humor, wit and pleasant drawing that the result is not the destruction of a childhood dream (hence tears), but a humanization of the gentleman of legend (hence chuckling delight). "Happy Blooming Christmas to you, too," grumbles the tired old boy at the end of his busiest day, and as he tucks himself into his lonely cot we sympathize with his aching old bones and wonder, perhaps, if we might not somehow stick a present in his darned old sock.

Raymond Briggs was born in 1934 in Wimbledon, London, and attended the School of Art there from 1949, going on to the Slade School of Fine Art (1955-57). He freelanced as a general illustrator for the BBC, Conde Nast, Oxford University Press, Penguin Books, and many other publishers, specializing in writing and illustrating books for children. His first book, The *Strange House,* was published in 1961, and his *Mother Goose Treasury* (1966), with over eight hundred pictures, was awarded the Kate Greenaway Medal for the best illustrated book of the year.

His first venture into the strip cartoon idiom, *Father Christmas, a* 32-page full-color picture story, was published in 1973. It remains his most successful book, having been translated into 16 languages (including Serbo-Croat). He drew a sequel in 1975, *Father Christmas Goes on Holiday,* and one further adventure of the character for the Christmas 1976 issue of *Ally Sloper* magazine. Briggs achieved great success with the animated cartoon versions of his stories produced for television. These began with *The Snowman* (1982), followed by *Father Christmas, Fungus the Bogeyman,* and the adult cartoon *Where the Wind Blows.* Later books include *Unlucky Wally Twenty Years On* (1989).

D.G.

FAWKES, WALTER ERNEST (1924-) British political cartoonist, comic strip artist and musician born in Ontario, Canada, in 1924. "Trog," the familiar pseudonym that hides Wally Fawkes, is short for Troglodyte, the name of a small jazz band specializing in playing in cellars. Fawkes plays clarinet whenever he can find time, which is less often than he would like, since he draws a daily strip as well as his weekly stint of political cartoons.

Fawkes came to England at the age of seven, in 1931, was educated in Sidcup, then studied art at the Camberwell School of Arts and Crafts. During World War II he drew maps and painted camouflage, but when some of his work in an exhibition caught the eye of Leslie Illingworth, political cartoonist of the *Daily Mail,* Illingworth, recognizing talent, got the young artist a job on the art staff of the *Daily Mail.* From 1945 small spot illustrations began to appear over the Trog signature. At that time the *Mail* also had a healthy book department, and Trog drew cartoons and illustrations for the *Daily Mail Children's Annual* every year. In 1949 he was given the chance to draw a new daily strip for children, *Rufus,* which eventually developed into *Flook.* Originally decorative whimsy, the strip advanced into caricatural satire (see *The World Encyclopedia of Comics,* Chelsea House, 1976). At the same time, Trog's technique pared down overdecorative Victorianism to a clean, bold black and white.

Trog began to draw political cartoons for the weekly *Spectator* in 1959, then moved to another political weekly, *New Statesman,* and then to the Sunday national, the *Observer.* When his mentor Illingworth retired from the *Daily Mail,* Trog was thrilled to take over the spot and drew the paper's principal cartoon from 1968 to 1971, when the *Mail* reduced to tabloid size. Trog then moved to *Punch,* where he draws brilliant full-color covers and the weekly political cartoon. He is sttill active, with books that include *Flook by Trog* (1970), *Flook and the Peasants Revolt* (1975), *The World of Trog* (1975), and *Trog Shots* (1982).

D.G.

F.C.G.

See Gould, Sir Francis Carruthers.

"Felix the Cat." © Pat Sullivan.

FELIX THE CAT (U.S.) The exact birthdate of one of animated cartooning's most celebrated characters, Felix the Cat, has long been a matter of speculation. It varies from one historian of the field to the next, falling somewhere between 1914 and 1925. To compound the confusion, Pat Sullivan, Felix's creator, had a very casual attitude toward copyright regulations, and the first *Felix* cartoons were not copyrighted until 1925. Finally, two live-action comedies featuring another hero named Felix *(Felix Gets in Wrong* and *Felix on the Job)* were released in 1916 by Universal.

Felix's complicated genesis resulted from the collaboration between Sullivan and his talented animator Otto Messmer, whom Sullivan hired in 1916. That same year they developed a black feline character for use as the animal hero of a new series of cartoons. The dry run for the series was released in 1917 after Messmer had left to fight with the American Expeditionary Force in Europe; titled *Tail of Thomas Kat,* it can be considered the first Felix cartoon in all but name (already the cat was using his tail as a removable object to get him out of all kinds of predicaments).

With Messmer back from the war in 1919, the series was launched in earnest. The first entry was the 1920 *Feline Follies,* in which the cat was still called Tom. More titles followed, to the tune of two a month; in these cartoons, released by Educational Films throughout the 1920s, the cat finally acquired the name Felix. Messmer directed most of them, assisted by a team of animators that included at one time or another Al Hurter, Hal Walker and Raoul Barré. Sullivan, meanwhile, spent less and less time in the studio and took less and less interest in the further development of his cartoon series. Though his animators had been working on a sound system as early as 1926, for instance, he vetoed the proposal for sound cartoons as too costly and thus lost his preeminent position in the animation field to Walt Disney.

Felix was by then an established figure. The game little black cat with the soulful eyes not only engaged in the outlandish adventures required of a cartoon hero, braving the elements and fighting hordes of enemies in exotic climes (as in "Eats Are West," "Arabiantics," "Felix the Cat Scoots thru Scotland" and countless others) but also embarked on wild flights of fancy through time and space ("Felix the Cat Trifles with Time," "Felix the Cat in Land o' Fancy," "Felix the Cat in Futuritzy," etc.). Messmer constantly experimented with his character, giving him depth and pathos: the cat was seen as an outsider fighting all odds to win the love of the flighty Phyllis ("Felix the Cat as Roameo," "Two-Lip Time"), to stay ahead of the pack ("A Tale of Two Kitties," "Jack from All Trades") or simply to get a square meal ("Felix the Cat on the Farm," "Scrambled Yeggs").

The success of *Felix the Cat* was enhanced by a catchy song played in movie houses showing the shorts: "Felix kept on walking/Kept on walking still." In 1923 a *Felix* newspaper strip came into being (drawn by Messmer); comic books followed. There were also Felix toys, books, games and other artifacts. By 1930, however, the *Felix* cartoons had come to a halt; still silent in a movie world agog with sound, they could no longer compete. In 1936 Van Beuren tried a comeback with "Felix the Cat and the Goose That Laid the Golden Eggs," but it proved short-lived. Joe Oriolo acquired the title in the 1940s; he successfully revived Felix for television. By 1961, when production was discontinued, he had turned out 260 shorts. Felix proved to have nine lives, however, and in 1994 he made a comeback in a Saturday-morning show aired on CBS. (The credit reads "created by Pat Sullivan and Joe Oriolo"!)

Felix will be remembered for the extraordinary cartoons directed by Messmer in the 1920s. They not only brought the animated cartoon close to technical perfection; they also sometimes approached art in their inspired exploration of the infinite possibilities of motion (translation, dislocation, gyration, etc.). They represent a high-water mark in the history of silent animation.

M.H.

FELLOWS, LAURENCE (1885-1964) American cartoonist and advertising artist born in Ardmore, Pennsylvania, in 1885. Laurence Fellows studied art at the Pennsylvania Academy of Fine Arts, and in England and France. In 1914 he was drawing regularly for *Judge,* sharing spots with the newly sophisticated F.L. Fithian—their subjects were droll society cartoons. Fellows (at one time he signed his work "Felloes") drew large, decorative-type cartoons that usually ran a full page or most of a page and were often tinted in two tones.

Laurence Fellows. © Judge.

Fellows's style must be described as trendy: it was highly mannered and reminiscent of fashion drawings of the day. Heads were small, and everything that could be—clothes, cars, furnishings—was "correct" and thoroughly modern. Lines were thin, and Fellows achieved a handsome balance of open spaces, highlight areas, and pastel shading. This very smart look inspired a school that followed his style into the early 1920s; Ralph Barton and John Held, Jr., were obvious imitators early in their careers.

Fellows, who also drew for *Vanity Fair, Apparel Arts* and *Esquire,* is most remembered for his weekly adver-tisements for Kelly-Springfield tires. They ran full pages and were insipid cartoon gags hiding behind a smart illustration betraying great technical competence as well as a flawless design sense. Fellows died in 1964.

R.M.

FENDERSON, MARK (1873-1944) American cartoonist born in Minneapolis, Minnesota, in 1873. The Fenderson family moved to Temple, Maine, but upon his father's death young Mark was sent by his mother to her brother's school in Billerica, Massachusetts. Here Mark's uncle discerned in the boy a talent for drawing and encouraged his artistic instincts.

Later, Fenderson was to study art in France and Italy before he returned to America as a newspaper sketch artist. In the 1890s his work began appearing in *Life* on a regular basis. In 1894, he got credit, with Walt McDougall in the *New York World,* for the first colored comic strip in an American newspaper: *The Unfortunate Fate of a Well-Intentioned Dog.* The drawing style suggests that Fenderson supplied the idea; collaborations were uncommon in those days, and the young cartoonist might not as yet have graduated from the apprentice stage, especially where a veteran like McDougall was concerned.

Fenderson's own style was breezy and casual. In later years he seldom drew large-scale cartoons, often confining himself to little squibs, perhaps one column by one inch. He drew in loose, heavy pen or a handsome gray wash. One of his most popular pieces was done for *Life:* a dejected rooster musing, "What's the use? Yesterday an egg, tomorrow a feather duster!" *Life* made a print of the cartoon, and it was a big seller for years. Fenderson also drew for *Judge* and in the 1910s for *Puck,* but he gradually retired from cartooning and became an accomplished and famous wood-carver. He also taught art at the special Townsend Harris High School in New York from 1918 to 1941. He died on December 6, 1944.

R.M.

FENWICK, IAN (1915?-1944) One of the most recognizable cartoonists of the 1930s, Ian Fenwick was clearly influenced by the simple styles of *New Yorker* contributors, which made his work stand out in British publications. Biographical details are slight, but he was educated at Winchester College, and his social cartoons began to grace a number of classy publications during the Thirties: *Bystander, Tatler, London Opinion, Men Only, Lilliput, Strand* and *The Humorist.* Heavily influenced by Peter Arno, a trademark was the fact that his characters tended to loom somewhat larger than his framelines.

During the Second World War, Fenwick served as a Major in the Special Air Service Regiment. Being a chum of David Niven, the Hollywood film star who had returned home for his war service, Fenwick met Niven's best pal, Michael Trubshawe. This tall, mustachioed officer, almost a living cartoon himself, became a central character in Fenwick's cartoons, just as he was frequently named in Niven's films, even when he did not appear in a small role. Fenwick was killed in action behind the enemy lines in 1944.

Books: *Pick-Me-Up* (1933), *Songs of a Sub-Man* (1934), *Weepings and Wailings* (1935), *The Bed Books* (1935), *I'm Telling You When and Where to Winter Sport* (1937), *Car Company* (1939), *Enter Trubshawe* (1944).

D.G.

FERNANDES, MILLÔR (1924-) Brazilian cartoonist and playwright born in Rio de Janeiro, Brazil, on August 24, 1924. In 1937, at age 13, Millôr Fernandes (better known as Millôr) started a 25-year-long collaboration with the magazine *O Cruzeiro* as a cartoonist. Under the pseudonym "Emmanuel Vão Gôgo," he contributed cartoons to *O Pif-Paf* (of which he was the founder) and other publications. He was art director of several magazines, including *A Cigarra* and *O Guri* (1940-44), *Detetive* (1940-42) and *Revista do Brasil* (1944-46).

In addition to *O Pif-Paf,* Millôr founded another short-lived magazine, *Voga,* in 1952. He published a book, *Tempo e Contratempo,* in 1956. He is also a talented playwright and the author, among other works, of *Liberdade, Liberdade* (with Flávio Rangel), *Do Tamanho de um Defunto* ("From the Size of a Dead Man"), *Um Elefante no Caos* ("An Elephant into the Chaos") and *O Homem, do Príncipio no Fim* ("Man, from Beginning to End"). Millôr has also translated plays by Shakespeare, Synge and Molière, and has written several teleplays. Among the many awards he has received as a cartoonist are first prize at the 1960 exposition of the Museum of Caricature in Buenos Aires (jointly with Saul Steinberg) and second prize at the 1963 Montreal Salon of Humor. His works have been exhibited in galleries in Rio and elsewhere. During the period of military dictatorship (lasting into the mid-1980s) he was a contributor to the anti-government magazine *O Pasquim,* which earned him a stay in prison. He is currently drawing editorial cartoons for various dailies and magazines, illustrating children's books, and designing posters.

A.M.

FIDDY, ROLAND (1931-) Roland John Fiddy, who signs simply with his surname, was born in Plymouth, Devon, England, on April 17, 1931. He attended Devonport High School, then studied illustration at the Plymouth College of Art from 1946. Called into the RAF for National Service from 1949-1951, he afterwards continued to study art at the West of England College of Art (1952-1953), then became an art teacher in Bristol (1954).

His first cartoon was published in the July 1949 edition of the pocket magazine *Lilliput,* and his first for *Punch* was published in 1952. Apart from magazines including *Everybodys, Weekend, She,* and *Woman's Realm,* he has drawn for most newspapers, including the *Daily Express, Daily Mail, Daily Mirror, Evening Standard,* and *News Chronicle.*

His comic strip began in children's weeklies with *Sir Percy Vere* in the famous *Eagle* (1959), followed by *Private Proon* in *Boys World* (1963) and *Fun with Fiddy* in *Ranger* (1965). Enjoying strip cartoon work, he turned to newspaper strips and created *Tramps* for the *Daily Express* (1976-1985), which also appeared in the Sunday edition. This popular series was followed by *The Paying Guest* in the *Sunday Express* from 1985-1986, and *His Andora* for *Sunday People* from 1986 to 1990.

Fiddy won several international prizes: Belgium (1984), Netherlands (1985), Sofia (1986), Sao Paolo (1987), Yomiur Simbun (1988) and Knokke-Heist (1990).

Books: *Best of Fiddy* (1966), *Tramps in the Kingdom* (1979), *The Crazy World of Love* (1985), *The Crazy World of the Handyman* (1988), *For Better For Worse* (1989), *The Fanatics Guide Series* (1989 onwards).

D.G.

Roland Fiddy. © Roland Fiddy.

FIGURINE PERUGINA, LE (Italy) In 1937 the spaghetti and chocolate manufacturers Perugina-Buitoni hit upon the idea of organizing a competition based upon the collection of a series of one hundred trading cards. Whoever completed one album would receive a prize; whoever completed 150 albums would get a car. The cards were placed in each package of chocolate or spaghetti. To design the cards the company called upon newspaper cartoonist Angelo Bioletto, who dreamed up a humorous gallery of celebrated figures from legend and history: D'Artagnan, Buffalo Bill, Tarzan, Greta Garbo, Shanghai Lil, etc. Bioletto's tongue-in-cheek caricatures proved very popular in their own right. By a strange oversight, however, the card representing "the ferocious Saladin had only limited circulation and caused despair among millions of Italians who could not complete their collections.

After a legal dispute with Perugina, Bioletto designed

Aramis and the Ferocious Saladin, two characters from "le figurine Perugina." © Perugina.

another series of trading cards for a competing chocolate manufacturer. In 1939 he came back to Perugina to draw more cards for them. Entitled *Two Years Later,* this second Perugina series gave rise to a book but was not as profitable as the first, since this time there was a more exact card count. Bioletto was then sent to Paris to design a similar series based on French movie stars for the French subsidiary of Perugina. He had drawn only 15 figures when war broke out between France and Italy in June 1940.

Bioletto went back to drawing cartoons for newspapers. In 1942 he designed the characters of one of the most famous Italian animated cartoons, *La Rosa de Bagdad.* He is now a noted book illustrator, but in the eyes of many he is still remembered chiefly for his creation of the *figurine Perugina.*

S.T.

FILHO, HENRIQUE DE SOUZA (1944-1988) Brazilian cartoonist born in Neves, Minas Gerais, in 1946. Two years later the Filho family moved to Belo Horizonte, the capital of the state, with their three sons, including Henrique, all of whom were hemophilic. In 1962 Henrique started his career as an illustrator for the weekly magazine *Alterosa,* using the pen-name "Henfil" (a contraction of his full name). His brother, Bentinho, was an activist against the military rulers that had taken power in Brazil in 1964. This led Henfil to start drawing political cartoons for the daily *Diàrio de Minas* in 1965; the following year he published his first book of cartoons, *Hiroshima Meu Humor* (a take-off on Alain Resnais's movie *Hiroshima Mon Amour*).

After working at the Minas Gerais branch of Rio de Janeiro's daily *Jornal dos Sports,* he was invited to move to Rio, where he drew a full page of cartoons for the newspaper. In 1969 the weekly satirical magazine *O Pasquim* was formed as a vehicle of opposition to the military dictatorship, with the collaboration of the most important Brazilian cartoonists of the time: Millor Fernandes, Ziraldo, Sérgio Cabral, and Paulo Francis. In its pages

Henrique de Souza Filho ("Henfil"), "Fradinho." © Henfil.

Henfil brought back the character of the anti-clerical Fradinho, which he had created in *Alterosa*, in a feature called *Fradinhos* ("Little Monks"). In 1973 it began as a daily strip, featuring Zeferinho (a cangaceiro), the intellectual goat Orelana and the masochistic bird Grauna in addition to Fradinho, for the *Jornal do Brasil*.

In the meantime his health was deteriorating, and he moved to New York with his family in search of treatment. In the U.S. Henfil tried to work for *Mad, Playboy*, and other publications, without success. Finally Universal Press Syndicate in 1975 accepted to distribute his *Little Monks*. It was greeted with hostility from the start, labeled "sick", and discontinued after a few weeks. Discouraged, the artist went back to Brazil, where he picked up where he had left off. He created new characters, such as the paranoid political militant Ubaldo. He wrote a book about his experiences in the U.S. which was later made into a television documentary, drew a daily editorial panel, and authored a stage play. After the fall of the military regime in 1983 he worked for the democratization of Brazilian society and institutions. Paradoxically, with the return of democracy, his popularity started to wane. *O Pasquim* closed its doors in 1985, and he tried working for the conservative *O Estado de Sao Paulo*. In 1987 he directed a live-action movie, *Deu no New York Times* ("God at the New York Times"), but it flopped.

Henfil died on January 4, 1988, from AIDS, contracted as a result of a blood-contaminated transfusion. As Gabor Geszti wrote for the magazine *WittyWorld*, the "crowd that said farewell to the artist at his funeral was made up of the most representative expressions of Brazilian cultural and political life."

A.d.M.

FINEY, GEORGE (1895-198?) Australian caricaturist and political cartoonist born in Parnell, Auckland, New Zealand, in 1895.

No appraisal of the great draftsmen working for the Australian press would be complete, or just, without reference to another New Zealander who in 1919 came to Sydney. He is George Finey. At 14 Finey sold his drawings to local newspapers in Parnell. Later, during World War I, he served as an underage private with the New Zealand Expeditionary Force; there, having served three and one-half years on active service, he was appointed an official war artist. After the war, Finey decided to take a refresher course at the Regent Street Polytechnic Art School in London. In 1921, after traveling to Australia, he approached Alek Sass, the art editor of *Smith's Weekly*, and was instantly engaged at £9 ($18) a week, a small fortune in those days, and a sum that was increased to £2,000

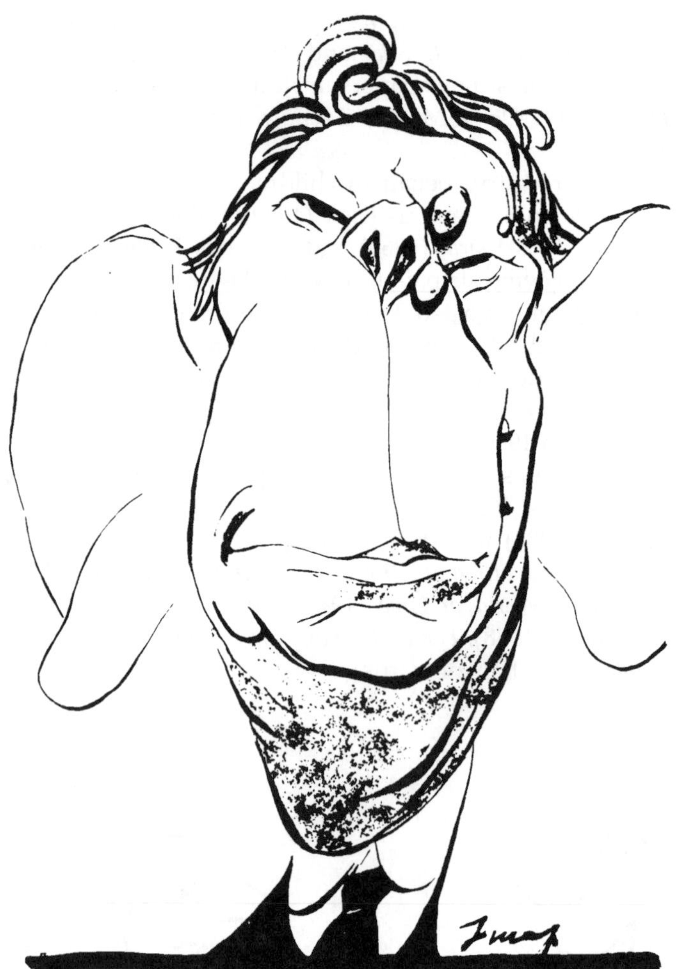

George Finey, caricature of prominent Sydney magistrate. © Smith's Weekly.

($4,000) a year. Although he drew comic jokes in Australia, it was not for that work but for portrait caricatures that Finey became one of the most famous of 20th-century artists working in this field.

The art of caricature did not have the continuity or persistence of tradition in Australia that it did in Europe, although there was something of a local school of caricature that had been distinguished, though at widely spaced intervals, by the likes of Phil May, Will Dyson and David Low. In recent times it has been furthered by the geometrically stylish caricatures of the Adelaide artist Lionel Coventry, by the outstanding comic portraiture of Noel Counihan (both onetime contributors to the *Bulletin*) and by the highly finished work of Tony Rafty, who is striving to keep this art alive in Australia.

Universally, the convention for popular caricature was to draw a big head, in left or right profile, on a little body; Finey's emphasis was on portraiture—stark, powerful and tremendously dramatic. With his approach to the human face, Finey's caricature portraits were fantastic—pushing and punching his subjects' features across the paper with grotesque but controlled draftsmanship. Finey drew big: often his caricature portraits were nearly twice life size. And he worked in many media—with pen and ink, with oil paint and in a medium recently revived by designers, known as collage. For Finey the latter was a method of picturemaking achieved by pasting down colored paper torn from the advertising pages of magazines.

George Finey was by temperament a bohemian. His hatless, sockless, collarless appearance around the Sydney streets, his tremendous generosity, his perversity and scorn for diplomacy were backed by an artistic achievement that made him a legend during his heyday in the period between World Wars I and II. During World War II Finey drew political cartoons for the *Daily Telegraph* and later for the *Tribune,* both Sydney newspapers. In retirement in the 1970s he painted and produced carvings and ceramics; he died in the early 1980s.

V.L.

FISCHER, ANTON OTTO (1882-1962) American cartoonist and painter born in Munich, Bavaria, on February 23, 1882. Anton Fischer was orphaned at age five and sent to the local archepiscopal seminary, where he lived for three years. He ran off to sea at age sixteen and saw quite a bit of adventure on sailing and merchant vessels; memorable to him was sailing around Cape Horn.

Following an interest in art, he enrolled at the Académie Julian in Paris, studying there from 1906 to 1908. Fischer decided to come to the United States after having his money stolen; he was then to settle and ultimately become a citizen upon the entrance of America into World War I. Before entering the cartooning and illustration fields, however, he raced on yachts and taught sailing.

After an initial sale to *Harper's Weekly* and a Jack London illustration assignment for *Everybody's,* he did many cartoons for *Life.* He drew cartoons and covers for years, mostly through the 1910s. The bulk of his cartoon work was in the Angus MacDonnall-Power O'Malley vein—nostalgic and sentimental scenes. As time went on, marine themes dominated his work, and he eventually left cartooning to become a noted marine painter. Even in the 1930s and 1940s, when he frequently illustrated for the *Saturday Evening Post,* much of it was sea-oriented. He did humorous illustrations for the riotous, classic *Glencannon* stories by Guy Kilpatrick and the *Tugboat Annie* stories of Norman Reilly Raine.

During World War II Fischer was active in the Coast Guard as artist laureate, was named a commander in the reserves, and published a book, *Fo'c's'le Days* (1947). He died on March 26, 1962.

R.M.

FISCHETTI, GIOVANNI (1916-1980) American artist born in Brooklyn, New York, on September 27, 1916. John Fischetti lived a childhood of varied experiences, dropping out of Catholic Sunday school to be confirmed as a German Lutheran, and dropping out of high school to travel and seek employment around the country. He took a job for a time operating the elevator in the hotel of Rollin Kirby, his idol, and he spent a year at sea working on a steamer. From 1937 to 1940 Fischetti studied art at the Pratt Institute and then traveled west to seek a job in cartooning. He worked for awhile at the Disney studios until eye-strain forced him to abandon in-betweening. Freelancing in Los Angeles, San Francisco and Chicago followed, including work for *Coronet* and *Esquire.* Just before the war, he became the editorial cartoonist for the *Chicago Sun.*

"Forward!"
Giovanni Fischetti. © Chicago Daily News.

In Europe, during his military service, Fischetti rose to the rank of sergeant and was a staffer on *Stars and Stripes,* where he formed friendships with future cartoonists Gill Fox, Dick Wingert and Curt Swan. Back in America, with his *Sun* job unavailable, he freelanced in various capacities and cartooned for *Coronet, Pageant,* the *Saturday Evening Post* and the *New York Times Magazine.* He also painted color editorial cartoons for *Collier's* and assisted Dick Wingert on *Hubert.* He drew for the *New York Herald-Tribune* before joining the Newspaper Enterprise Association as its editorial cartoonist, succeeding Dorman H. Smith.

The NEA served many hundreds of papers, and during his years there (1951-62) Fischetti was probably the most published editorial cartoonist in America. But editorial strictures and the necessity of keeping everything general enough for an army of editors of various persuasions eventually made him restive. Fischetti accepted an offer to join the *Herald-Tribune* in New York but insisted on his own terms: utter editorial freedom. Having won this much, he went a step further and sought to change the look of his—and hopefully, by example, others' —formats and concept presentation.

Fischetti's style had been solid and somewhat traditional, executed in the vertical format with brush and crayon. He now sought to emulate the European convention of horizontal cartoons and abandon the tired icons of donkeys and Uncle Sams, replacing them with social-commentary themes. Points were scored through wry humor rather than by a cluster of labels, and in this he borrowed the magazine approach. (Indeed, he had been contributing to *Punch* for several years before the thematic inspiration struck.) His cartoons at once became influential and widely reprinted, due as much to the format innovation as to his very real sense of conceptual execution and literate partisanship. And he very clearly paved the way for the "new look" of Oliphant and others several years later.

With the demise of the *Herald-Tribune* in 1966, Fischetti moved to the *Chicago Daily News,* the paper of his syndicate's half-owner, Marshall Field. Within three years he had won a Pulitzer Prize. Other awards include the National Headliners Medal in 1951, the Sigma Delta Chi award in 1956 and 1958 and the National Cartoonists Society editorial award in 1963 and 1964. He was also presented with an honorary doctor of fine arts degree from

Colby College. In 1973, the liberal cartoonist penned an autobiography, *Zinga Zinga Za!,* relating his life story, telling tales of many cartoonist friends (by whom he is beloved), and collecting the best cartoons of his career. He died at his suburban Chicago home in November 1980.

R.M.

FISCHINGER, OSKAR (1900-1967) American animator and painter born in Gelnhausen, Germany, in June 1900. Oskar Fischinger, who always had a talent for drawing, had to quit school in order to help support his impoverished family. He worked as an apprentice in a furniture factory and later designed church organs. Finding his surroundings too constricting, Fischinger moved first to Munich in the early 1920s, and then to Berlin in 1927. While in Berlin he became interested in film and devised the special effects photography for Fritz Lang's 1928 science fiction movie, *Die Frau im Mond.*

In 1930 Fischinger started work on a series of startlingly original film cartoons in which he used abstract forms synchronized to music on the soundtrack. Some of his most famous creations include *Studie No. 8,* to the accompaniment of Paul Dukas's "The Sorcerer's Apprentice," *Hungarian Dance* (on Brahms's music), and *Lieberspiel* ("Love Game"). In 1933 he began experimenting with color, and this gave rise to his best-known work, *Komposition in Blau* ("Composition in Blue"), a delightful kaleidoscope of forms, shapes and patterns moving rhythmically to music.

With the coming to power of the Nazis Fischinger's experimentation was increasingly hampered; his works were branded as decadent, and he finally went to the United States on a contract with Paramount Films in 1936. His credits at Paramount include a number of special effects for films, particularly *Allegretto,* his animated introduction to *The Big Broadcast of 1937.* It was Fischinger who first suggested to Leopold Stokowski the idea for a feature-length animated film on music; this eventually led to Walt Disney's *Fantasia.* Fischinger was hired to work on *Fantasia* (the Toccata and Fugue sequence was based entirely on his designs) but quit after nine months. Fischinger's last work of animation was *Motion Painting,* on a grant from the Guggenheim Foundation.

Oskar Fischinger was a pioneer in the use of abstract design and music in animation. He received many awards for his work, notably at the Venice and Brussels festivals. In the 1940s, however, he decided to abandon animation for painting. He exhibited widely in the United States and abroad; his last painting, fittingly titled *Nirvana,* was completed a few weeks before his death in 1967.

Fischinger's widow, Elfriede Fischinger, is currently at work on a biography of the artist.

M.H.

FISHER, DUDLEY (1890-1951) American cartoonist born in Columbus, Ohio, in 1890. Dudley Fisher entered Ohio State University in 1910, attending classes at the Arts College for a little over a year. Dropping out of college, he went to work in the art department of the *Columbus Dispatch* at the end of 1911. During World War I, he was commissioned a second lieutenant and commanded the 45th Photo Section of the army. While flying over enemy-held territory taking pictures, Fisher acquired his individual bird's-eye-view style of drawing scenes from his war experience.

Returning to the *Dispatch* in 1919, Fisher redesigned the photo department and later that year created *Jolly Jingles,* a two-color daily panel of illustrated verse which eventually developed into a Sunday feature. It was while working on an idea for *Jolly Jingles* in 1937 that Fisher came up with the concept of a Sunday page illustrating in a single panel the doings of a farm family being visited by their big-city relatives. He later developed the feature more fully under the title *Right Around Home,* and in January 1938 King Features started syndicating it nationally. The panel proved so successful that King asked Fisher to do a daily spin-off in comic strip form: this was *Myrtle,* started in 1942.

A diligent sort, Fisher continued to work for the *Dispatch,* drawing his daily and Sunday features at the same time. He died of a heart attack on July 10, 1951, while on a vacation trip in Rockport, Massachusetts. *Right Around Home* and *Myrtle* went on, however, for almost two decades longer.

M.H.

FISHER, HARRISON (1877-1934) American cartoonist and illustrator born in Brooklyn, New York, on July 22, 1877. Harrison Fisher's father, Hugh Antoine Fisher, was a landscape painter who began to instruct his son when he was only six. When the family moved to San Francisco, young Harrison entered the Mark Hopkins Institute of Art and by age 16 was already drawing for the *San Francisco Call* (and later the *Examiner).*

Returning to New York in the late 1890s, Fisher submitted two drawings to *Puck* and soon was hired as a staff artist. His pen-and-ink work showed the same spirit as Charles Gibson's—handsome women and virile men—but it has to be judged mostly on its imitative qualities, as aping Gibson was the major goal of the young artist. It was a fault, however, common to a whole generation of new cartoonists, and Fisher soon distinguished himself.

His style attained a maturity without ever losing its boldness. The "Fisher Girl" became another American favorite, and his pretty heads and striking groups soon graced the pages of the *Saturday Evening Post, Ladies' Home Journal, McClure's* and *Cosmopolitan,* among others. Eventually *Cosmopolitan* hired him exclusively for covers, often rendered in pastels, before he retired to paint portraits and etch. Fisher died on January 19, 1934.

R.M.

FITZPATRICK, DANIEL ROBERT (1891-1969) American Pulitzer Prize-winning cartoonist born in Superior, Wisconsin, on March 5, 1891. Dan Fitzpatrick was educated at public schools in Superior and attended art classes at the Chicago Art Institute. In 1911 he accepted a job on the *Chicago Daily News* drawing editorial cartoons and general art assignments. In two years his forceful cartoons, signed "Fitz," attracted the Pulitzer organization; *New*

Wings over Europe
Daniel Fitzpatrick. © St. Louis Post-Dispatch.

York World-bound Robert Minor's position as chief editorial cartoonist for the *St. Louis Post-Dispatch* was offered to the 21-year-old cartoonist. It was another fateful match, just as with Rollin Kirby at the *World* later the same year. Fitzpatrick was to become a fixture in St. Louis and nationally for the next 45 years. He was widely reprinted and copied and was the recipient of many awards, including Pulitzers in 1926 and 1955.

Fitzpatrick was Minor's heir in another way—the generous utilization of grease crayon as a shading device. When Fitzpatrick began to use it, most cartoonists still shaded with crosshatching. He was to use it more heavily than most, and his cartoons—built on lush brushstrokes—are dark, brooding, powerful statements. The crayon-on-grain also covered minor deficiencies, such as Fitzpatrick's faulty rendering of anatomy; indeed, many cartoons have absolutely no figures in them or have characters occupying a very small proportion of the space. Mood was essential to the typical Fitzpatrick cartoon.

He was fiercely liberal and influenced the styles of many of the succeeding generation of cartoonists, including Ross Lewis and Tom Little. Fitzpatrick drew for *Collier's* in the 1920s and won many distinctions, including the John Frederick Lewis Prize for caricature at the Pennsylvania Academy of Fine Arts in 1924 and the Distinguished Service Journalism Medal from the University of Missouri in 1958. He retired in 1958 and died on May 18, 1969.

R.M.

FLAGG, JAMES MONTGOMERY (1877-1960) American cartoonist and illustrator born in Pelham Manor, New York, on June 18, 1877. Young James Flagg was raised in Brooklyn and Yorkville and displayed an early interest in drawing. He sold his first cartoon to *St. Nicholas* magazine at age 12—it was a group of illustrated Latin axioms, a humorous device common since pre-Civil War days—for $10.

Although Flagg later claimed to be "firmly established" on the staffs of *Life* and *Judge* at the age of 14, his work did not regularly begin appearing until the mid 1890s. Through association with *St. Nick,* he had entrance to the *Century* offices and gained access to the originals of Frost, Abbey, Pyle, Kemble and others, the better to study their work. His first sale, to *Life* for eight dollars, was followed by almost forty years' association with that magazine as well as with its rival, *Judge.*

Flagg's style grew less cartoony as he joined the multitudes seeking to copy Charles Gibson's style—rather awkwardly at first. But he preserved his cartoon discipline for interior work in the magazines (paintings graced the covers); *Nervy Nat* was a colored comic strip with captions instead of balloons that ran in *Judge* for years and was wildly successful, inspiring even the young W.C. Fields as he fashioned his vaudeville tramp character. Also, illustrated puns were common, pictured limericks danced for years through *Life's* pages, and ultimately, of course, Gibson-style society drawings by Flagg were spread over double pages.

Flagg's friendships with J.A. Mitchell, founder and art editor of *Life,* and Grant Hamilton, art editor of *Judge,* stood his career in good stead—Flagg's famous force of personality and grand manner were as much responsible for his popularity as was his artwork. In later years he was the toast of Broadway and Hollywood for his famous impromptu portrait sketches of celebrities. These two-minute drawings were among the best works of his career, certainly as mature and accomplished as any pen-and-inks, covers or posters.

It was as a poster artist that Flagg gained his greatest recognition, particularly for "Uncle Sam Wants You!," a recruiting poster from World War I that first appeared as a cover for *Leslie's Weekly,* which was owned by *Judge.* He also did other posters during both World Wars and conservation posters in the 1930s.

Flagg's artistic influence was great; if he never had the elegance of Gibson, he had an overwhelming sincerity and

James Montgomery Flagg, 1911.

forcefulness in his work. Where Gibson was reserved, Flagg had flair, mirroring his own personality. His men were not only good-looking, but dashing and virile. His women (and *Judge* early touted the "Flagg Girl") were seldom demure but rather handsome and assured.

His social influence was great, too, and many anecdotes in and out of art circles survive. He was a founder of the Dutch Treat Club and a prime figure in the Artists' and Writers' Balls. His many portraits, sketches and program covers for the Lambs attest to his conviviality. He was the friend of actors, presidents and other artists. And his themes and delineations of women were so individual that they became a genre bearing his name. Flagg died in New York on May 27, 1960.

Books: *The Diva's Ruby* (1908); *City People* (1909); *Yours Truly* (1910); *Personality Plus* by Edna Ferber (1914); *I Should Say So* (1914); *His Soul Marches On* (1921); *A Lighter of Flames* by William S. Hart (1923); several small books published by *Life* before 1910, including *Tomfoolery, If, or a Guide to Bad Manners* and *Why They Married;* and his autobiography *Roses and Buckshot* (1946).

R.M.

FLEISCHER, DAVID (1894-1979) American animator and producer, younger brother of Max Fleischer, born in New York City on July 14, 1894. Dave Fleischer exhibited a strong penchant for drawing in his early years, but upon leaving high school, the only job he could find was as a theater usher. Soon afterward, however, he found work at an engraving company and in 1912 became a cutter for Pathé Films.

The Fleischer studio's Ko-Ko the Clown. © Fleischer.

Dave Fleischer's career in animation started in 1915, when he joined his brother Max in the production of the *Out of the Inkwell* cartoons. After a brief stint in the army during World War I, Fleischer went back to animation and in 1919, again with his brother Max, set up Out of the Inkwell Films, later to become Fleischer Studios. From that time on Dave became the titular director of all the Fleischer cartoons (Max being the producer), working on *Betty Boop, Popeye, Gulliver's Travels* and others. His main contribution took the form of the many gags that he was endlessly able to work into the Fleischer cartoons.

In 1942, after a falling out with Paramount (which released the Fleischer films), Dave became the head animator at Columbia Pictures. He produced some of the *Fox and Crow* cartoons, as well as a short-lived *Li'l Abner* series, before leaving in 1944 for Universal. There, among other things, he is reported to have been in on the origin of the *Francis the Talking Mule* series of live-action films. Dave Fleischer retired in 1967 and died in June 1979.

Dave Fleischer's career has been retraced in Leslie Cabarga's *The Fleischer Story* (Nostalgia Press, 1976).

M.H.

FLEISCHER, MAX (1883-1972) American cartoonist and film producer born in Vienna, Austria, on July 19, 1883 (not 1885 or 1888, which have for a long time been the accepted dates). At the age of four Max Fleischer was taken to the United States by his parents, who settled in New York. He attended Evening High School, the Mechanics and Tradesmen's School, the Art Students League (where one of his teachers was George Bridgman) and Cooper Union. Having completed his training, Max Fleischer starting working in 1900 as an errand boy for the *Brooklyn Eagle,* later graduating to the art department. After a few years he left for Boston to take a better-paying job as a retoucher and photoengraver.

Returning to New York in 1914, he became the art editor of *Popular Science Monthly,* where he wrote and illustrated articles on recent inventions. Combining his talent as an artist and his taste for technical innovation, Fleischer developed, in collaboration with his brother, Dave, the "rotoscope," a device for tracing live action into animated footage, thus eliminating many painstaking steps in the animation process. The machine was patented in 1917. (Fleischer's love of science stood him in good stead; in 1923 he produced an animated film called *The Einstein Theory of Relativity.)* With the help of the rotoscope, Max and Dave Fleischer completed their first cartoon, *Out of the Inkwell.* They presented it to J.R. Bray, who commissioned them to do an animated cartoon a month, to be released through Paramount. After the start of World War I, Fleischer also produced a number of technical cartoons for the U.S. Army.

In 1919 Max and Dave Fleischer founded Out of the Inkwell, Inc. They turned out not only *Inkwell* cartoons (which featured the famous Ko-Ko the Clown) but also the celebrated *Screen Songs* series, in which the spectators were urged to "follow the bouncing ball" and sing along. When sound came to film, Fleischer was one of the first to see its possibilities; he produced his *Talkartoons,* introducing Bimbo the Dog and later Betty Boop (1930), who soon became the star of the Fleischer studios. In 1933 Fleischer brought Popeye to the screen, and he soon had two hits on his hands.

A strike by the employees in 1937 briefly threatened the Fleischer studios, leading Max to open his new studio in the more propitious environment of Miami, Florida, in 1938. There he embarked on his most ambitious project, a full-length animated version of *Gulliver's Travels,* completed in 1939. It proved moderately successful, but another feature, *Mr. Bug Goes to Town* (1941) was a dismal flop. This precipitated a conflict between the Fleischer brothers and their distributor, Paramount Pictures, and in 1942 the Fleischers were summarily dismissed by Paramount, which took over their production directly (mainly *Popeye* and *Superman* cartoons).

Max Fleischer remained in animation for some time, producing *Rudolph the Red-Nosed Reindeer* in 1944 and starting his own animation correspondence course in 1951. In 1955 he sued Paramount for title to his old cartoons but lost. In 1958 he went back to the J.R. Bray studio as head of the art department, and in 1961 he produced a new, cheaply done series of *Out of the Inkwell* cartoons. Dispirited and bitter, Max Fleischer retired to the Motion Picture Country Home and Hospital in Woodland, California, where he died, almost completely forgotten, on September 11, 1972.

A full-length study of the Fleischer studios, Leslie Cabarga's *The Fleischer Story,* was published by Nostalgia Press in 1976.

M.H.

FLINTSTONES, THE (U.S.) The Hanna-Barbera studios produced the first animation series ever to be seen on prime-time television. It was called *The Flintstones* and debuted on CBS in the fall of 1960. For this series Hanna and Barbera simply adapted the clichés of 1960s situation comedy to a Stone Age setting, the mythical town of Bedrock.

Reputedly modeled on the tremendously popular *The Honeymooners, The Flintstones* featured the loudmouthed, know-it-all Fred Flintstone (in a variation on the Jackie Gleason character) lording it over gaping, gullible Barney Rubble (a takeoff on the Art Carney role). The "boys" were often in competition with their domineering spouses, the acidulous Wilma Flintstone and the sarcastic Betty Rubble, and they had to concoct all kinds of excuses in order to get out to an evening of bowling or a meeting of the Waterbuffaloes lodge. The stories were carried in an adequate but pedestrian style of limited animation, a far cry from Hanna and Barbera's halcyon days at MGM.

The gags were often supplied by the incongruity of modern appliances in prehistoric times: foot-propelled automobiles, pterodactyl-winged planes, dinosaur-powered cranes and so on. After awhile, however, these inventions began to wear thin. The marital fights that fueled the plots of many of the half-hour episodes also became hackneyed and increasingly repetitive. Two infants were introduced to the series in an attempt to bring new life to it: the mischievous Pebbles (daughter of the Flintstones) and the muscular Bamm-Bamm (son of the Rubbles). Their shenanigans failed to save the show, which mercifully

"The Flintstones." © Hanna-Barbera.

ended in 1964. This was not the end of the Flintstones, however, as they went into wide syndication the next year; Fred Flintstone's famous battle cry, "Yabba Dabba Doo," can still be heard on the *Flintstones and Friends* show broadcast over hundreds of stations.

The *Flintstones* was Hanna and Barbera's most popular and successful creation. It was transposed to the movie screen in the spy-thriller spoof *A Man Called Flintstone* (1965), in which the animation, while expertly handled, still did not amount to much. The Flintstones have enjoyed a long career in newspapers with their own comic strip, drawn by Gene Hazelton and distributed by McNaught Syndicate since 1961; and they also have appeared in comic books without interruption since 1961.

In 1986 CBS aired a nostalgic prime-time special, *The Flintstones 25th Anniversary Celebration,* with old and new animation. Not to be outdone, ABC came up with two specials of its own, both in 1993, *I Yabba-Dabba Do!* and *A Flintstone Family Christmas.* A live-action movie version of *The Flintstones,* starring John Goodman and Elizabeth Perkins, was released in 1994 to generally lukewarm reviews.

M.H.

FLIP THE FROG (U.S.) After leaving Walt Disney in 1930, Ub Iwerks set up his own animation studio; there, the following year, he created his most celebrated series, *Flip the Frog.* In the beginning the series was more than a little reminiscent of the *Mickey Mouse* shorts (to which Iwerks's contribution had been decisive), but it slowly acquired a style and pace of its own. Iwerks had a great talent for drawing and animation, but he lacked a strong story sense, and his plotting tended to meander.

In all, Iwerks made 36 cartoons for Celebrity Pictures (which at one point intended to rename the title character Tony). All of these are scintillating little gems, the more notable (if a choice has to be made) being "The Cuckoo Murder Case" and "Fiddlesticks" (both 1931), "Africa

"Flip the Frog." © Celebrity Pictures.

Squeaks," "Spooks" and "Phoney Express" (all 1932), "Flip's Lunch Room" and "Chinaman's Chance" (both 1933). The last entry in the series was released in 1934.

The *Flip the Frog* cartoons enjoyed only moderate success when they were first released. They are now being rediscovered and shown at animation festivals around the world—a fitting if belated tribute to the brilliant but star-crossed creativity of Ub Iwerks.

M.H.

FLOHRI, EMIL (1869-1938) American cartoonist born in 1869. Emil Flohri joined the staff of *Leslie's Weekly* as an artist at the age of 16 and soon switched to the affiliated *Judge* magazine, where he drew humorous panels in pen and ink before switching to stone. Flohri became an accomplished lithographer, and his political cartoons in color are masterpieces of subtlety. He developed a technique of capturing photographic likenesses and drew many decorative holiday covers for *Judge* as well as specialties like the *Sis Hopkins Joke Book* magazine covers. Around 1910 he took up the brush and executed many of *Judge*'s last colored political cartoons.

Flohri remained in New York through the 1910s, drawing pen-and-ink cartoons and illustrating. In 1920 he moved to California and there painted portraits of silent film stars—a carry-over from similar duties on *Film Fun* magazine, a *Judge* publication, in the 1910s. In the late 1920s he went to work for Walt Disney and remained there for nearly a decade. He died in Van Nuys the day before Christmas, 1938.

Flohri had an amazingly agreeable style, at once comic and realistic. His moods were gentle, and his humor never of the slapstick variety. He was a strong Republican, and his cartoons were very influential in every presidential campaign between 1896 and 1908.

R.M.

FLORA, PAUL (1922-) Austrian cartoonist and illustrator born in Glorenza, Italy (which is called Glurns by Austrians and lies in the much disputed South Tyrol-Alto Adige area), on June 29, 1922. After schooling in Innsbruck, Paul Flora studied from 1942 to 1944 at the Munich Academy under Olaf Gulbrannson, the master of line drawing and a great contributor to *Simplicissimus.* After military service in 1944 and 1945, Flora set up as a freelance artist in Innsbruck. His varied work is published in Germany and Switzerland as well as in Austria, so that he is one of the key artistic figures of the entire German-speaking territory.

During the 1950s Flora built up an unshakable reputation as an intellectual and witty cartoonist with imaginative subject matter and a quizzical, probing line akin to Steinberg's or Thurber's. Among his highly successful albums of that decade were two that punned on his name—*Flora's Fauna* and *Trauerflora* (without the final *a,* this means "mourning crepe" in German)—as well as *Das Musenross* ("The Steed of the Muses"), *Das Schlachtross* ("The War Horse"), *Menschen und Andere Tiere* ("People and Other Animals") and *Vivat Vamp.* In the same years, he was busy illustrating numerous books, including an edition of Wilde's *Canterville Ghost,* a literary anthology by Erich Kästner, H. *Weigel's O Du Mein Osterreich* ("My Austria") and anthologies of ghost and spy stories.

Meanwhile, in 1957, Flora began a secondary career as a political cartoonist for the Hamburg weekly *Die Zeit.* These drawings are more stumpy, sketchy and simple than the bulk of his work and reveal no profound insight into world affairs, but they are genuinely amusing and likable. A collection of 200 of them was published in 1962 with the punning title *Ach du Liebe Zeit!* ("Oh, What Wonderful Times!").

In the 1960s Flora turned to more pretentious albums in which, without an appreciable growth in technique, he concentrated on ominous scenes of empty houses, assassinations of kings in frightening palaces, the seamy side of cities and the like, indulging in a personal mythology made up of such figures as omnipresent scarecrows. Albums in this series include *Der Zahn der Zeit* ("The Tooth of Time," 1961), *Königsdramen* ("Royal Dramas," 1966) and *Veduten und Figuren* ("Views and Figures," 1968), which boasts an appreciative foreword by the major Swiss dramatist Friedrich Dürrenmatt. His list of books has grown longer over the years. His latest book of cartoons was published in 1997 as *Dies und das: Nachrichten und Geschichten* ("This and That: News and Stories").

S.A.

FLUFFY RUFFLES (U.S.) Wallace Morgan's *Fluffy Ruffles,* a verse-captioned, multi-panel Sunday color page about a woman so stunningly lovely and superbly dressed that she proved too disconcerting to susceptible males to hold any job, began in the *New York Herald* just after the turn of the century. It was distributed across the country to a multitude of papers printing *Herald* features and proved to be a nationwide hit by the close of the year. *Fluffy Ruffles* was so winningly drawn by Morgan, and her outfits so stylishly representative, that she was accepted from coast to coast as a weekly symbol of what young American womanhood should emulate and young American manhood should admire.

Fluffy's lightly comic attempts to hold one position after another, each failing because of her devastating effect on men, was the weekly theme of the Morgan feature until its close on January 3, 1909. After 14 months of globe-girdling career pursuits, Fluffy's quest climaxed in her conquest of Paris and receipt of the "freedom of the city" on a silver salver. In the meantime, one thousand stores across the nation had featured "Fluffy Ruffles sales" or singled out particularly attractive gowns and dresses as "Fluffy Ruffles specials"; at least one hit song had been published ("My Irish Fluffy Ruffles" by Will A. Heelan and Albert Gumble, in November 1908); a book collection had seen print; and the heroine's name had entered the language for the next few decades as a synonym for any woman dressed in the height of fashion and dashingly lovely as well.

Morgan moved on, the week after *Fluffy Ruffles*'s close, to start a new but similar weekly feature for the *Herald* called *Cynthianna Blythe*, with verses written by Harry Grant Dart, himself a cartoonist of note. *Cynthianna Blythe* ran until February 1910 and was replaced by a new verse-and-picture weekly feature titled *The Widow Wise*, by a different artist and writer. Morgan then returned to the magazine illustration work which had already gained him national fame.

B.B.

FOGELBERG, OLA (1894-1952) Finnish cartoonist born in Oulunkylä, Finland (then part of the Russian empire), on July 7, 1894. During his relatively short life Ola Fogelberg experienced and depicted in his cartoons all the great and traumatic changes in recent Finnish history: the czarist repression, independence, revolution and civil war, short-lived monarchy, and two world wars.

In the 1910s, after his school years, Fogelberg (alias "Fogeli") devoted himself to cartooning. He studied art and animated film in Paris, Italy, Leipzig and Berlin. He traveled extensively and published a book based on his experiences *(Harhateillä*, 1920). Fogeli's work seems to have been influenced by the Jugendstil movement. He also mentioned the work of the Swedish satirist Albert Engström as one of the most important influences on him.

In the golden era of the humor magazines of the Finnish workers' movement, Fogeli was the most active political cartoonist in the most important magazine, *Kurikka*. In his cartoons he slashed at political trials, prisons, lawlessness, excessive authority, and the rise of fascism. Earlier he had courageously attacked the czar, Rasputin and Kerensky, and in this connection his character, the young maiden Finland" *(Suomineito)* became well known. He also drew portraits of the workers' leaders and scenes of the 1918 civil war.

Most of the time Fogeli worked for the large cooperative chain Elanto, where he was first a commercial artist and then, for a long time, the head of the advertising department. Many of his cartoons and books were meant to advance the ideals of the cooperative movement. He did posters, vignettes, and children's books. His cartoons appeared in such publications as *Elanto, Kuluttajain Lehti* and *Suomen Kuvalehti,* among others.

Ola Fogelberg ("Fogeli"), "Finland and Russia."

Fogeli was an amiable, impulsive and colorful man, and a versatile one—a nationally famous athlete, a family man, an inventor. He was a pioneer of animation in Finland (starting in 1927) as well as a comic strip artist. Fogeli left Elanto in 1944, and during his later years he drew almost exclusively his wonderfully funny comics, notably *Pekka Puupää,* which he had created in 1925. He worked on them even on his deathbed. He died on August 25, 1952, in Helsinki.

J.R.

FOGELI

See Fogelberg, Ola.

FOGHORN LEGHORN (U.S.) During his long tenure at Warner Brothers, Robert McKimson proved himself a skilled and imaginative animation director; yet he contributed only one memorable character to the Warner cartoon menagerie, and that was Foghorn Leghorn, the boisterous rooster who sprang to life in 1946 in a cartoon titled "Walky Talky Hawky."

In this first cartoon, as in many of the later ones, Foghorn was bedeviled by the diminutive Henery Hawk, who kept trying to catch the imposing bird despite their disparity in size ("I'm a chicken hawk and you're a chicken; are you coming with me, or do I have to use force?"). Another thorn in Foghorn's side was the widow Priscilla, who was also forever trying to ensnare the rooster, but for matrimonial purposes. To humor the old hen, Foghorn would take her genius son Egghead on country outings and try to teach him the rudiments of life, only to be shown up by the precocious youngster (in "Crockett Doodle-Doo," for instance, Foghorn tries to teach Egghead the art of building a fire, baiting a trap and catching fish,

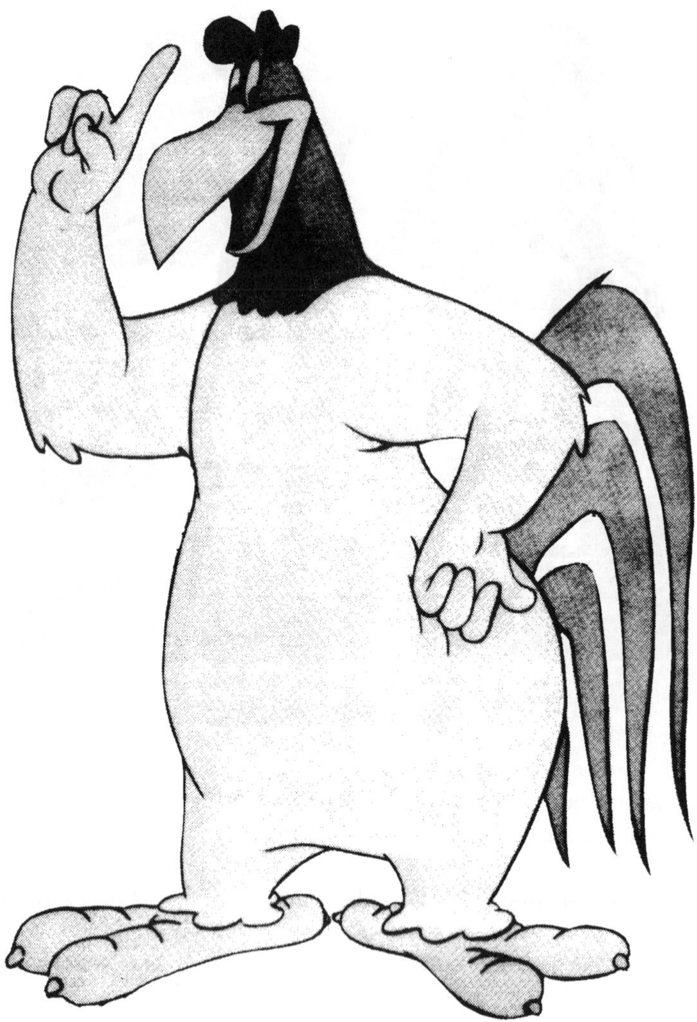

"Foghorn Leghorn." © Warner Brothers.

but he is hopelessly outclassed in every department by his charge).

Foghorn Leghorn is reported to have been inspired by Fred Allen's impersonation of Senator Claghorn. As voiced by Mel Blanc in an irresistible twang, the rooster came through as an overbearing and obnoxious ignoramus who never learns from his mistakes. Never quite as popular as his Warner *compères*, Foghorn Leghorn made his last bow, along with the others, sometime in the 1960s.

M.H.

FOLDES, PETER (1924-1977) Hungarian cartoonist, painter and animator born near Budapest, Hungary, in 1924. Peter Foldes moved to England in 1946 and studied at the Slade School of Art and the Courtauld Institute. In 1951, with a grant from the British Film Institute and in collaboration with his wife, Joan, he realized *Animated Genesis,* a surrealistic work of animation characterized by unpredictable motions and bold patterns (the film was awarded a prize at the 1952 Cannes Festival). *A Short Vision,* on the theme of nuclear devastation, followed in 1954 (it also won a prize, at Venice in 1956). Despite his *succès d'estime,* no work was forthcoming in Britain, and Foldes left for France.

For ten years (1956-66) Foldes devoted himself entirely to painting, moving from abstract to minimal art, and from stabiles to mobiles. His paintings were widely exhibited throughout Europe, in the United States and in South America. Foldes's first love remained animation, however, and he returned to the field in 1966 with *Un Garçon Plein d'Avenir* ("A Lad with a Future"), a fantastic gallery of metamorphoses and transformations. Three more works followed in quick succession: *Un Appétit d'Oiseau* ("Eating Like a Bird"), a ferocious description of the war between the sexes; *Plus Vite* ("Faster"), a fanciful statement about a society gone stark mad; and *Eveil* ("Awakening"), a more sedate short subject.

In the 1970s Foldes's talents blossomed in all directions. He went on painting, tried his hand at a short-lived comic strip, *Lucy* (1974), and directed a number of advertising films. Occasionally he went back to animation: *Daphnis et Chloé, La Faim* ("Hunger," 1974) and *Je, Tu, Elles* ("I, You, They"), which blend animation and live action, are among his most notable later works. At the same time he experimented with computer animation, notably in Canada, and his works became more and more detached from objective reality. He died in Paris in 1977.

Peter Foldes was one of the most fascinating of modern animators. His works have received the highest praise and have been just as vehemently condemned. Lack of consistency always plagued even his best efforts, and his *oeuvre* remains enigmatic and somewhat disappointing.

M.H.

FOLGER, FRANKLIN (1919-) American gag cartoonist born in Westboro, Ohio, on January 28, 1919. Franklin Folger, whose popular newspaper-panel gag feature about suburban housewives, *The Girls,* was widely followed in the 1950s and 1960s, sold his first gag cartoon at 15. He studied at the art academy in Cincinnati, Ohio, for three years in the mid-1930s and continued with gag cartoon

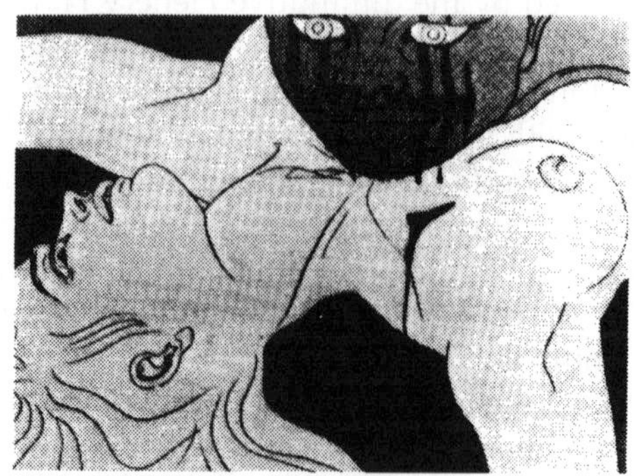

Peter Foldes, "Daphnis et Chloé." © ORTF.

work while sharing a Manhattan studio with fellow cartoonist Stan Stamaty. Folger was drafted in 1942 but returned to civilian cartoon work four years later. He also did advertising art for awhile before he created *The Girls* for the *Christian Science Monitor* of Boston in 1948.

Moving on to the *Cincinnati Enquirer* in 1952, Folger saw his increasingly popular feature (essentially his interpretation of the Helen Hokinson clubwomen types long featured in the *New Yorker)* syndicated nationally in 1953; it continued to be widely syndicated for the next two decades. *The Girls* was distributed by Field Newspaper Syndicate until the early 1980s and has been collected in several books. Folger still lives near Cincinnati, where he contributes cartoons to various magazines.

B.B.

FOLON, JEAN-MICHEL (1934-   ) Belgian cartoonist, illustrator and lithographer born at Uccle-Brussels, Belgium, on March 1, 1934. J.M. Folon attended the Brussels School of Architecture but soon dropped out to move to Paris in search of a career in graphic art. In the early 1950s he contributed many cartoons to *L'Express* and *Le Nouvel Observateur,* two French newsweeklies. His drawings for *Fortune* and the *New Yorker* in the 1960s spread his fame to the United States. In 1965 an exhibition of his works was held at the School of Visual Arts in New York.

Folon, who is also the author of a number of books, perceives the world as dehumanized and desensitized. "We live in the jungle of the cities, signs grow like trees, in the place of trees," he says. His cartoon universe, in which men are dwarfed by the proliferation of panels, signs and symbols, reflects this dark view. It is worthy of note, however, that Folon, himself a successful creator of advertising symbols, is one more contributor to the very alienation he denounces. Folon has largely abandoned cartoons in recent times in favor of lithographs and serigraphs. Since the 1980s he has also extended his activities to include mural painting, animated cartoons and stage design.

One of the most significant graphic artists of our time, Folon is representative of a whole generation of graphic practitioners who hold that multiplicity of clever and imaginative design ideas can make up for paucity of philosophical concepts. It is therefore not surprising that Folon should be most celebrated in New York City, where this view is most prevalent.

M.H.

Jean-Michel Folon, "The Jungle of Cities." © Folon.

"Foolish Questions," 1912.

FOOLISH QUESTIONS (U.S.) Rube Goldberg's earliest separately titled continuing feature to become an individual hit with readers was *Foolish Questions.* This intermittent daily panel was first drawn as a small part of Goldberg's large *New York Evening Mail sports* page cartoon layout in late 1908. Contrived as a mild putdown of the sort of pointless questions anyone can encounter (or ask) about the obvious, *Foolish Questions* had no continuing characters and was essentially patterned on the following format: a goofy-looking person asks another engaged in some visually evident course of action (e.g., smoking a pipe, putting a golf ball, typing) if that is indeed what he is doing ("Hey, are you smoking a pipe . . . putting . . . typing . . . ?"). The second individual, disgusted, makes a sarcastic riposte ("No, I'm frying smelt for dinner . . . kicking a field goal . . . tiptoeing through the tulips . . ."). The gag was funny the first few times, simply on a self-recognition basis, but Goldberg repeated it hundreds of times over the years. He revived it over and over again in later miscellany gag pages, seemingly to inexhaustible reader approbation, with only minor variants and only a vestige of imaginative relevance in the sarcastic responses to the questions.

A very typical *Foolish Questions* exchange from 1908—the second one, reprinted in Peter C. Marzio's *Rube Goldberg* (1973)—runs flatly as follows: Goofy: "Hello, George. Are you going automobiling?" Driver, dressed in full gear of the period, near his car: "No, I'm going out to play a game of checkers." The panels carried multiple-digit numbers for each question, largely to indicate the endless quantity of such inquiries, so that *Foolish Questions No. 308,792* might be followed the next day by *Foolish Questions No. 997,608,* and so on. Not very memorable or amusing in bulk, *Foolish Questions* ran in one form or another in Goldberg's work through his last potpourri page, *Sideshow,* in the late 1930s.

B.B.

FORAIN, JEAN-LOUIS (1852-1931) French cartoonist, lithographer, etcher and painter born in Rheims, France, on October 23, 1852. After one year of studies at the Ecole des Beaux-Arts of Paris, Jean-Louis Forain earned his living as a cartoonist for various minor newspapers and periodicals, mainly *Le Scapin* and *La Cravache Parisienne,* where his first sketches were published in 1876. Taking Parisian life as his inspiration, he attacked, often in sarcastic fashion, the world of politics, high finance, law and the theater in series such as *Les Affaires* ("Business") or *Dans les Coulisses* ("In the Wings"); starting in 1887, these series appeared in the most important publications of the period: *Le Figaro, La Vie Parisienne, Le Rire, Le Journal Amusant.* Later these more than three thousand drawings were collected and released in albums like *Comédie Parisienne* ("Parisian Comedy," 1892), *Les Temps Difficiles* ("Hard Times," 1893) and *Doux Pays* ("Sweet Country," 1897).

In 1889, Forain launched *Le Fifre* in order "to narrate everyday life, to show the silliness of certain sorrows, the sadness of numerous joys, and to record, sometimes harshly, how hypocritically Vice tends to manifest itself in us. This is my goal." This journal was even more ephemeral than *Psst . . . !* (1898-99), which he founded with his friend and fellow cartoonist Caran d'Ache, and which served as a vehicle for his violent attacks on Dreyfus and his supporters. Forain's cartoons were drawn in a caustic and even cruel style further underlined by biting captions, direct and to the point. It is no wonder, then, that Forain has often been called "the Juvenal of the pencil."

In 1879 and 1880 he exhibited some of his paintings alongside the Impressionists, many of whom admired his work (especially Degas, from whom he borrowed the quick-line technique). During World War I he returned to etchings, paintings and lithographs, mainly of religious themes. Many of his drawings, along with Steinlen's, were exhibited at the Arden Gallery of New York in January 1919.

Rich, famous, the host of Parisian high society in his mansion near the Bois de Boulogne, Forain died on July 11, 1931, at the age of 79.

P.H.

FORATTINI, GIORGIO (1932-   ) Italian cartoonist born near Rome, Italy, in 1932. Giorgio Forattini never completed his college studies; instead he went to work in an oil refinery in the 1950s. He then became a salesman for a record company, rising to the position of sales manager. When a flowering of political cartooning took place in Italy in the wake of the 1960s student revolt, Forattini thrust himself to the forefront of the movement. His first drawings appeared in the late 1960s in the daily *Paese Sera* (where he was then working as a graphic designer) and in the weekly *Panorama.* In the 1970s he went over to the daily *La Repubblica* as their regular editorial cartoonist. At present, he also works in Italian television, contributing political and topical cartoons.

Giorgio Forattini. © La Repubblica.

Forattini's favorite targets are the high and mighty in all fields; in recent years he has never lacked for models. An anthology of his cartoons, *Quattro Anni di Storia Italiana* ("Four Years of Italian History"), published by Mondadori, reviews the principal deeds (and misdeeds) of Italian politicians, with a few forays abroad (Nixon and Brezhnev are attacked with particular vehemence). In contrast to many other cartoonists, Forattini prefers to ridicule his targets directly, at times focusing on some physical defect (as in the case of former premier Amintore Fanfani), but never falling into vulgarity. More often he denounces with harshness and irony the faults of the powerful, especially the Christian Democrats.

In a sense, Forattini is the cartoonist who most belongs to the tradition of Scalarini and Galantara; but in contrast to these earlier cartoonists, whose vision of the society they fought against was gloomier and more bitter, Forattini is more cheerful, more flippant, more ironic, breezier. In his cartoons there is always a pinch of optimism and confidence that raises a smile even when reality is darker than the mood of his cartoons.

C.S.

FORBELL, CHARLES H. (1886-1946) American cartoonist born in Brooklyn, New York, in 1886. Charles Forbell received his art training from the Pratt Institute in New

York and then secured a position on the art staff of the *New York World.* Around 1910 he began submitting cartoons to *Life* and *Judge,* almost all in wash and written by Arthur Crawford. They dealt with all subjects but often displayed the technical expertise Forbell had acquired at Pratt. Soon he was to restrict himself to a certain few subjects and exploit them for years.

His series involved individual cartoons, usually full-page, that would have taxed a cartoonist with no technical and mechanical background. They were full-scale perspective drawings, complicated architectural scenes and mazes of balconies, parapets and minarets peopled by scores of animated figures. The major series were *In Ye Goode Old Days for Life,* and *In Ancient Times* and *Ancient Sources of Modern Inventions* for *Judge* in the 1920s. They were busy drawings, but Forbell was always in control.

"My profession is psychological," he once said. "The art—the draftsmanship—this one must have, but it is a tool through which the message is presented to the public." Even so, he in no way slighted the visual factor.

Forbell also drew daily cartoons featuring a little lamb as advertisements for a clothing company (Rogers Peet) for almost thirty years and produced popular cartoons for the Aetna Casualty Company and the Central Savings Bank of New York. He died in Bayside, New York, on April 15, 1946.

R.M.

FORD, NOEL (1943-) Noel Ford was born on December 22, 1942 at Nuneaton, England, educated at King Edward VI Grammar School, and later at the Birmingham College of Arts (1958). As the lead guitarist in a travelling pop music band, he appeared in the television talent show *New Faces.* Meanwhile he worked as a furniture salesman, a laboratory technician and an office clerk. His first professional cartoons were political sketches drawn for the crime novelist, John Creasey, who was trying to stand for a parliamentary election.

Noel tried his hand at writing short stories, before turning full-time freelance cartoonist in February 1975. He was published in *Punch* the following year, and worked for magazines as disparate as *Private Eye* and *Weekend.* In 1979 he began drawing topical and editorial cartoons for the *Daily Star,* and for the *Church Times.* Once again, papers at the opposite ends of the social scale. He also drew some humorous greetings cards, one of which won the award, Best Humorous Card of 1990. In the same year he won the Cartoonist of the Year Award.

Books: *Deadly Humorous* (1984), *Golf Widows* (1988), *Cricket Widows* (1989), *Business Widows* (1990), *Nuts* (1991), *Lineroons* (1992), *The Cannibal Cook Book* (1992), *The Last Wag* (1993), *An Earful of Aliens* (1994).

D.G.

FOUGASSE

See Bird, Cyril Kenneth.

FOURBERIES DE FEMMES (France) The theme of the "cuckolded husband" runs through the entire history of French caricature and cartooning. Gavarni mined this rich vein in a series of drawings published between 1837 and 1840. Entitled *Fourberies de Femmes en Matière de Sentiment* ("Women's Deceptions in Matters of the Heart"), they catalogue a whole array of tricks played by cheating wives on their husbands. In one particularly telling cartoon Gavarni shows a visiting "friend" lounging in an armchair with his fly open and his high hat on; the woman, knitting by the window, spies her husband coming and whispers, "Here he comes! . . . Take off your hat."

"Here he comes! Take off your hat."
"Fourberies de Femmes," 1840.

There was a note of levity in the hundred-odd lithographs Gavarni dedicated to womanhood unrepentant. The cartoonist rarely sided with the husbands, whom he depicted as gross, overbearing, stupid and blind (the lovers usually fared no better). He marveled at the eternal resourcefulness of women more than he sympathized with the eternal plight of husbands. His women, deceiving though they might be, were clearly the most lovable side of the eternal triangle. (Gavarni was probably the French cartoonist most sympathetic to women; he loved to represent them in his drawings, and whatever their rank or status in life, he never ridiculed or castigated them.)

M.H.

FOX, GILBERT THEODORE (1915-) American artist born in Brooklyn, New York, on November 29, 1915. Gill Fox evinced an early interest in art and studied at New York's Textile High School, along with future cartoonists John Stanley and Vincent Alacia. He took life drawing lessons at Washington Irving High School and subscribed to the full Landon Correspondence Course. At Textile, he drew for the school paper, *The Spinning Wheel.*

Fox applied to the Fleischer New York animation studios in 1936 and secured a position as an opaquer working on *Popeye* and *Betty Boop* cartoons. He had risen to the rank of inker by the time of the famous strike that ultimately resulted in the studio's move to Florida—and Fox's loss of a job. For a year he drew movie and sports filler pages for the Chesler comic book studio and freelanced to the Major Nicholson shop; then he joined Busy Arnold's comic book crew (1939-43). *Wun Cloo* was Fox's first sale—it was a two-page strip about a Chinese detective—and he soon graduated from filler pages to the assistant editorship of Quality Comics. Here he drew *Poison Ivy, Cyclone Cupid, Super Snooper,* and *Slap Happy Pappy,* as well as covers for *Plastic Man, Doll Man, Uncle Sam, Black Condor* and other titles.

In 1943 Fox joined the army. For *Blood and Fire,* his stateside divisional paper, he drew a strip called *Bernie Blood* and sports and editorial cartoons. In Europe he worked on maps and codes in a G-2 unit near the Siegfried Line and ultimately was transferred to *Stars and Stripes,* working at various times on four editions of the armed forces newspaper and running the Paris office art staff for two months. Fox rejoined the Arnold crew in 1946 and until 1951 worked on such titles as *Daffy, Torchy* and *Candy.* In 1950, while penciling for Arnold, Fox joined the Johnstone and Cushing advertising agency—the legendary shop that produced comic strip ads for dozens of products. Fox's accounts included Ex-Lax, the Ford Times, Campbell's beans, Smith Brothers, Realemon, and Prestone. At this time he also became associated with *Boys' Life* magazine, ghosting several of their monthly color strips.

Fox's first syndicated feature was *Jeanie,* a comic strip done in collaboration with writer Selma Diamond for the Herald-Tribune Syndicate in 1951 and 1952. Another artist continued the strip for a year while Fox returned to Johnstone and Cushing, although he again created a syndicated feature the following year (*Wilbert,* a one-column panel for General Features, which ran until 1959). *Bumper to Bumper* was a Sunday filler feature for the *New York News* and other papers; approximately twenty-five to thirty ran each year between 1953 and 1963.

On the recommendation of Newspaper Enterprise Association editorial cartoonist John Fischetti, Fox took over the feature *Side Glances* in 1962. He drew a portion of each week's panels, sharing duties with William Galbraith Crawford; he took full charge and began signing the feature with the release of November 12, 1962. Fox remained with *Side Glances* for 20 years; he is currently the cartoonist of the *Connecticut Post.*

For many years Fox has been widely known as the cartoon industry's "man for all styles." He has adapted to any requirement with utter mastery. With *Side Glances,* the oldest continually running and still one of the most popular cartoon panels, Fox has maintained freshness and a unique, slightly bird's-eye view. One of his changes has broadened its appeal: he has expanded topical gags from a couple per month to half of all gags. His fierce Middle America sympathies cause many to identify with the feature and its treatments.

R.M.

FOX AND CROW (U.S.) Following Charles Mintz's death, Frank Tashlin became the head of the animation unit at Columbia in 1940. The following year he brought out "The Fox and the Grapes," a cartoon based on the familiar Aesop fable, introducing the characters Crawford Crow and Fauntleroy Fox, two friendly enemies in the tradition of Tom and Jerry. The cartoon enjoyed enough success to give rise to a *Fox and Crow* series of cartoons, several of which were directed by Tashlin himself before his departure from Columbia in 1943.

"Fox and Crow." © Columbia Pictures.

In a switch from the original fable, the plots revolved around the unceasing efforts of Crow to separate Fox from whatever food, money or material goods he happened to have in his possession at any given moment. The extraordinary lengths to which Crow was prepared to go in order to cheat Fox (concocting the most outrageous schemes or donning the most unlikely disguises) constituted the basis of the stories. The *Fox and Crow* cartoons were ably written and well directed by such veterans as Bob Wickersham, Howard Swift and Art Davis. Some of the post Tashlin entries include "A-Hunting We Will Go"(1943), "Be Patient, Patient" (1944), "Ku-Ku Nuts" (1945), "Foxey Flatfoots" and "Mysto Fox" (both 1946). In 1948 Columbia closed down its animation unit, and *Fox and Crow* was briefly taken over by UPA, only to be abandoned the following year.

Fox and Crow have lasted longer in comic books, where they have enjoyed a long career spanning more than twenty years, from 1945 to 1968.

M.H.

FRADON, DANA (1922-) American cartoonist born in Chicago, Illinois, in 1922. Dana Fradon studied at the Art Institute of Chicago, then moved to New York, there continuing his art education at the prestigious Art Students League. He served in the Army Air Corps from 1942 to 1945, returning after the war to New York to begin work as a freelance illustrator. Besides his work for the *New Yorker,* where he became a regular contributor in the 1950s, he has also appeared in *Look, Saturday Review* and the *Saturday Evening Post.*

As an artist, Fradon does not show the highly individualized style of *New Yorker* colleagues like George Price or

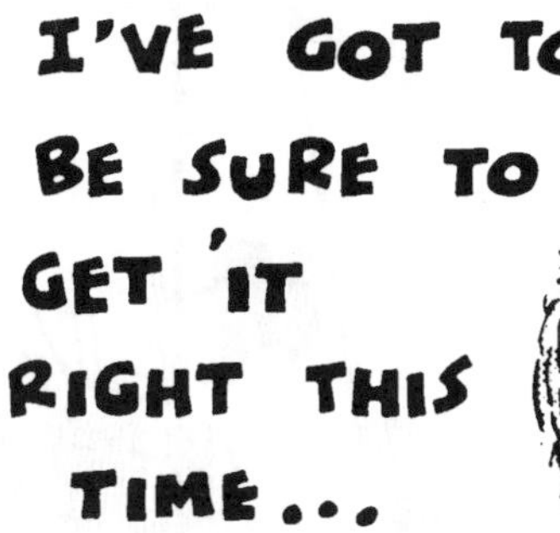

"Frank and Ernest." © NEA.

Charles Addams. He generally avoids portraying physical-action situations in his sparsely populated panels, preferring instead to concentrate on the delivery of sophisticated gag lines through the medium of clean, simply drawn, strong-featured representational figures. His favorite targets include the IRS, television and television's inseparable mate, Madison Avenue. One particularly clever example of his penchant for twitting the tax man portrays two wealthy Romans over a bowl of wine, one complaining to his obviously understanding guest, "I'd hate to tell you how much *I'm* going to have to render unto Caesar this year."

Fradon's success as a cartoonist rested on his ability to be topical without becoming easily dated. Thus, much of his work from as far back as the 1950s remains, upon reacquaintance, as fresh now as it was then. His talent showed no sign of flagging in the 1970s, when he could have a shocked and concerned chemist finding traces of tuna fish in his latest shipment of mercury. He left the *New Yorker* after a dispute with the cartoon editor in the late 1980s. A student of medieval lore, he has devoted most of his time since then to writing and illustrating children's books set in that period of European history.

Besides his voluminous contributions to the best of the mass circulation periodical press, Fradon has also been published in two separate anthologies, *Breaking the Laugh Barrier* (1961) and *My Son the Medicine Man* (1964). His work is represented in the permanent collection of cartoon art in the Library of Congress.

R.C.

FRANÇOIS, ANDRÉ
See Farkas, André.

FRANK AND ERNEST (U.S.) In 1972 cartoonist Bob Thaves started *Frank and Ernest,* a daily panel that occupies the entire space of a comic strip, for NEA Service. The horizontal format—unusual for a panel feature—allowed Thaves to depict the action in the left side of the picture while the right side was taken up by text or dialogue lettered in large, bold print. The experiment proved successful, and a Sunday *Frank and Ernest* feature was later added.

Frank and Ernest are two zany characters hovering on the fringe of normal society. At first they were only two among a large cast, but they stood out to such an extent that the feature was almost entirely given over to them after only a few weeks. The shaggy, tall Frank, who does most of the talking, and the short, awestruck Ernest, who does most of the reacting, are placed by Thaves in the most unusual situations and in settings that may vary from day to day. In the tradition of earlier cartoons, the two are bank tellers one day, door-to-door salesmen the next, and so forth, but they remain basically the same in character. The illogical and the outlandish are the main sources for the gags. In one panel, for instance, Frank looks bemusedly at the drooping beam issuing from his flashlight and mutters somewhat self-consciously, "Maybe the battery is getting weak."

Bob Thaves, an industrial psychologist by profession, manages to keep up with his consulting career while working on the *Frank and Ernest* feature, but he admits it is not easy. The success of his feature has allowed him to devote himself to cartooning full-time in the early 1980's. Since that time *Frank and Ernest* has garnered a number of honors: it was voted Best Syndicated Panel by the National Cartoonists Society in 1983, 1984 and 1986, and received the Mencken Award for Best Cartoon from the Free Press Association in 1985.

M.H.

FRASER, PETER (1888-1950) Born in the Shetland Islands on November 6, 1888, Peter Fraser attended the Central School of Arts and Crafts and also took Percy Bradshaw's Correspondence Course. In 1907 he was working in the city of London, but keen on cartooning, he freelanced in the evenings. *Punch* published his first cartoon in 1912, and by 1941 Peter had over 200 cartoons published in that prime humorous weekly. Other magazines to which he contributed include *The Sketch, The Tatler,* and *Time and Tide.*

Specializing in animals, Peter contributed to a lot of children's books published by many of the pre-war publishers, and collected his cartoons in a number of books. He was also more than sympathetic towards the poor children of the Old Kent Road and Stepney areas of London, where he worked part-time as a missionary worker. Many of his pages in the above-mentioned children's books were in strip cartoon format. From 1938 he began contributing animal strips to the Amalgamated Press's sumptuous new comic for younger readers, *Happy Days*. These were *Jim*

Crow and *Pip the Pup*, both of which were distinguished by his being allowed to sign his name in full, a privilege not normally granted by editors of the period. Peter died on March 5, 1950.

Books: *Funny Animals* (1921), *Tufty Tales* (1932), *Humour in the East End* (1933), *Jack and Jock's Great Discovery* (1944), *Camping Out* (1945), *Moving Day* (1945), *The Blackberry Picnic* (1946), *Binky and the Giant* (1948).

D.G.

FRED

See Aristides, Othon.

FRELENG, ISADORE (1905-1995) American animator and producer born in Kansas City, Missouri, around 1905. Isadore ("Friz") Freleng went to work at the Kansas City Film Ad Company in 1924. Like many alumni of this fabled outfit (which at one time employed Walt Disney), he went on to join Disney's Hollywood studio (in 1927). After a short stint working on Charles Mintz's *Krazy Kat* series in 1929, Freleng joined Hugh Harman and Rudolph Ising in 1930 as an animator on the cartoons they produced for Warner Brothers. Except for a brief period at MGM (1938-40), he remained with Warner until the closing of the studio in 1963.

Freleng first assisted Harman and Ising on their *Bosko* cartoons. After the pair left Warner in 1933, he became a director of animation, notably directing *My Green Fedora* (1935), *The Fella with the Fiddle* (1937) and the first *Porky Pig* cartoon, "I Haven't Got a Hat" (1935). He really hit his stride, however, during his second, longer association with Warner Brothers. He directed a number of memorable *Bugs Bunny* cartoons, from his first, "Hiawatha's Rabbit Hunt" (1941), to the Oscar-winning "Knighty Knight Bugs" (1957), not to mention such glittering gems as "Captain Hareblower," "Rabbitson Crusoe," "Hare Lift," "Bugs Bunny Rides Again," "Fresh Hare," "Hare Splitter" and "Hyde and Hare." He also directed two more Oscar-winners, "Tweety Pie" (1947) and his own creation, "Speedy Gonzales" (1955).

In 1963, in association with David DePatie, Freleng formed DePatie-Freleng. The new company created, among other cartoons, *The Pink Panther* series and took over many of the former Warner cartoon characters. In recent years DePatie-Freleng has concentrated on animated film series for network television. The studio's entries in this field include *The Pink Panther, Baggy Pants* (a cartoon version of the Charlie Chaplin silent movie shorts), *The Nitwits* and animated adaptations of Marvel Comics' horde of comic book superheroes.

Friz Freleng was one of the most prolific and gifted of Warner animators, and his work has earned him an impressive number of awards, including four Oscars. Yet his cartoons have never received as much attention as those of other Warner animators, probably because Freleng has obdurately chosen to remain a private person and has rarely granted interviews. He retired from active animation in the 1980's and died on May 27, 1995, in Los Angeles.

M.H.

Nose-diving Stuka, 1978 Model
Alberto Fremura. © La Nazione.

FREMURA, ALBERTO (1935-) Italian cartoonist born in Leghorn, Italy, in 1935. Alberto Fremura embarked on a cartooning career soon after completing his studies. In the 1960s he started collaborating regularly on *La Nazione* and *Il Resto del Carlino,* two conservative dailies published respectively in Florence and Bologna.

Fremura has virtually never left his native region, Toscania, but his fame has spread beyond its confines, and his talent has put him at the forefront of Italian political cartoonists. He is perhaps Forattini's most forceful antagonist, not so much on the levels of draftsmanship and inventiveness, where the two cartoonists have much in common, but in the political field. While Forattini usually hits at the conservative forces (not forgetting to take a few swipes at the left), Fremura always picks his targets out of left field.

Fremura's polemics are never personal, violent or mean; he is an ironist rather than a satirist and prefers a smile to a grimace. For this reason his cartoons often take the form of a slap on the wrist rather than a whipping on the shoulders (unlike the drawings of Scalarini, for instance). Instead of attacking individuals, Fremura illustrates and denounces emblematic situations in the Italy of the 1970s—as seen, of course, from the vantage point of a conservative. In this respect his cartoons go beyond the urgency of daily concerns; taken together, as in one of the many Fremura cartoon collections from *Pelle e Ossola* ("Skin and Bones") to *Italia Purtroppo* ("Italy Alas"), they provide a bitterly ironic chronicle of modern Italy.

FRIELL, JAMES (1912-) Using the pen-name of "Gabriel" for most of his cartooning career, James Friell was the best-known left-wing press artist who drew exclusively for the

Communist newspaper, the *Daily Worker*. He joined that small circulation paper in 1936, when he was editorially introduced as "Fleet Street's Greatest Discovery Since David Low!"

James Friell was born in Glasgow, Scotland, on March 13, 1912. Leaving school early at the age of 14, he began work in a solicitor's office as the office boy. A self-taught artist, he was given a staff contract with the Glasgow *Evening Times* in 1930, at the age of 18, and was sent in the evening to the Glasgow School of Art. In 1932 he joined the photographic company Kodak in their advertising department, where he worked until he was signed on by the *Daily Worker*.

Now signing himself "Gabriel," he also drew topical cartoons for the *World's Press News*, the journalists' weekly. When the Second World War started in 1939 he joined the Royal Artillery, but was secretly listed by the War Office as a "Dangerous Red," although Russia was at the time Britain's ally. During his service, he helped set up the regular magazine for Army personnel, *Soldier* (from 1944). After the war he returned to the *Daily Worker*, continuing his political cartoons until 1956 when, with the Soviet Union's invasion of Hungary, he turned in his Communist badge, left the paper and moved across to the London *Evening Standard*. Here he abandoned his pen-name and drew under his own name of Friell. Later, during the early years of commercial television in England, he drew cartoons on screen for Thames television's consumer programs.

Books: *Gabriel Cartoons* (1938), *Daily Worker Cartoons* (1944), *Gabriel's Review* (1946), *Water on the Brain* (1979).

D.G.

FRIERS, ROWEL (1920-) Ireland's leading and certainly funniest cartoonist, Rowel Boyd Friers was born in Belfast on April 13, 1920. Leaving school at 15, he was apprenticed to a printer to train as a lithographic artist. By 17 he was designing showcards and posters, whilst studying art in his spare time at the Belfast Municipal College of Art (1935-1943).

In 1940 his printer employer went bankrupt, and Rowle freelanced his first cartoon to the *Portsmouth Evening News*. Soon his cartoons were turning up in local Irish publications, from the *Belfast Telegraph* to the *Irish Times*, and more especially the leading Irish humorous weekly, *Dublin Opinion*. Later came cartoons for London publications, including *Men Only*, *Punch*, *London Opinion*, and *Radio Times*.

His more serious side continued to progress. During World War Two he designed posters for the Ministry of Food, and his water colors, oil paintings and murals led to being elected to the Royal Ulster Academy in 1940, and the Ulster Water Colour Society in 1977. He has designed hundreds of stage sets for the theater, both for drama and operas, and his work has appeared on both Ulster Television and BBC-TV. He was awarded the Medal of the British Empire in 1977.

Books: *Wholly Friers* (1950), *Mainly Spanish* (1951) *Riotous Living* (1971), *Book of Friers* (1973), *Pig in the Parlour* (1974), *The Revolting Irish* (1974), *On the Borderline* (1982), *Trouble Free* (1988), *Friers Country* (1992). He has also illustrated over fifty books written by others, including *Irish Folk Tales* by W.B. Yeats.

D.G.

FRITZ

See Mota, Anísio Oscar da.

FRITZ THE CAT (U.S.) In 1970 Ralph Bakshi and Steve Krantz, who had just started their own animation company, approached underground comic artist Robert Crumb with a proposal to film his famous creation, Fritz the Cat. Crumb first demurred, then relented and sold the rights to *Fritz* for a flat fee (he later claimed to have been misled by his associates). Crumb's protestations notwithstanding, the pair went to work with alacrity, and with Krantz producing and Bakshi directing, *Fritz the Cat* was released as a theatrical feature in 1972.

Bakshi remained faithful to the original, using many of Crumb's drawings and a number of his compositions; many of the original situations were also utilized to good effect (particularly Fritz's continually interrupted orgy in the bathtub, itself reminiscent of the stateroom scene in *A Night at the Opera*). The story line also followed closely the plot of the original stories. Fritz the Cat, a winsome if slightly unsavory feline, went through a number of obligatory "scenes," including barroom brawls, all-night bull sessions in tacky New York flats and a confrontation with cops portrayed as pigs. Fleeing the police, he then moved west, fell in with a group of rather seedy revolutionaries and got involved in "direct action." The final sequence depicted Fritz in a hospital, blown up and dying of his wounds, only to be revived by the sight of his weeping girl friends and engage in a tumultuous sex orgy on the hospital bed—a fitting fade-out to a bawdy movie.

Fritz the Cat caused an instant sensation upon its release. It was the first animated cartoon to receive an "X" rating, a fact which doubtless attracted many spectators who would not otherwise have gone to see an animated film. The feature proved to be a critical as well as a commercial success; in his 1973 study, *The Animated Film*, Ralph Stephenson, for instance, enthused, "Scandalous, irreverent, satiric but pulsing with life, *Fritz the Cat* . . . is a major work."

"Fritz the Cat." © Steve Krantz.

Despite a few weaknesses and some nonartistic sour notes (such as a lawsuit brought in by the disgruntled Crumb), the feature is well on its way to becoming a classic. Prompted by the success of the original film, an obscure outfit brought out a would-be sequel in 1974, *The Nine Lives of Fritz the Cat,* which turned out to be a dismal artistic failure as well as a box-office disaster.

M.H.

FROST, ARTHUR BURDETT (1851-1928) American cartoonist and illustrator born in Philadelphia, Pennsylvania in 1851. Self-taught in art, A.B. Frost grew up in the Philadelphia area at a time when it was perhaps the most fertile city in America for artistic growth and innovation; Edwin Abbey and Howard Pyle were active there, and Frost belonged to several of the drawing and print clubs. In the 1870s he first achieved prominence as the front-page cartoonist for the *New York Graphic,* the nation's first illustrated daily. His first illustrated book, *Out of the Hurly-Burly* by Max Adeler, appeared in 1879.

From that time on, for half a century, Frost was in a position of near-dominance of American illustration and cartooning. He produced strips (mostly for *Harper's Monthly* for years), panel cartoons (occasionally for *Puck* but also for *Life* in the 1880s and especially in the 1920s), editorial cartoons (for the *Graphic* and *Life)* and painted illustrations (for books, *Harper's Weekly* and *Collier's).* Among his scores of book credits are collections of his own works (*The Bull Calf, Stuff and Nonsense, The Golfer's Alphabet, Sports and Games in the Open* and *A Book of Drawings*) and illustrations for others, most notably the series of *Uncle Remus* books by Joel Chandler Harris, who acknowledged Frost's contribution by writing, "The book was mine, but you have made it yours."

Very simply, Frost held sway in just about every possible way. Technically, he made the strip a viable format in which cartoonists could express concepts. Thematically, he introduced broad humor, slapstick and animation in treating rural and suburban subjects. Artistically, he was among the first major artists to use exaggeration as a major element, and he had a photographer's eye for arresting action at the point of greatest tension or movement. Among his followers in these respects were the greatest names in the next two generations of American cartooning: Opper, C.J. Taylor, Sullivant, Kemble, Donahey, Ireland.

"Keep dry!! How can I help it?"

A.B. Frost, 1922.

Frost was an absolute master of anatomy and composition, in total charge of his media—pen and ink for cartoons, a handsome gray wash for illustrations. With the introduction of photoengraving, he became the pathfinder in achieving subtle, almost photographic tones in his reproductions. His magazine work, especially in *Collier's* after the turn of the century, was not only solid illustration, but a perfect, sympathetic mirror of rural, suburban and sporting America. Frost drew with a scratchy, informal line that perfectly suited his subjects. His favorite targets were animals, farmers, rural painters, golfers, prissy clerics, blacks and dandies. In the 1880s and 1920s, his figures were drawn with enormous heads, hands and feet—the better, it must be assumed, to focus on characterization and action.

A.B. Frost died on June 22, 1928. It is difficult to conceive how American cartooning would have developed without his presence. For his reportorial eye and his intrinsic artistic merit, he deserves major recognition today.

R.M.

FRUEH, ALFRED (1880-1968) American caricaturist and cartoonist born in a house on Main Street, Lima, Ohio, in 1880. Alfred Frueh pronounced his surname "free," and usually shortened his first name to Al. This brisk disyllabic name, pronounced "alfree," was as much an exercise in brevity as was his style of caricature.

Frueh was raised to be a farmer but also worked in a brewery prior to taking a job in the art department of the *St. Louis Post-Dispatch.* He stayed with the paper from 1904 to 1908. Fame came to Al Frueh in 1907, when a newspaper caricature of music hall star Fritzi Schneff so enraged her that she canceled a performance in St. Louis.

Frueh traveled to Europe in 1909 and then went to New York City, where he drew for the *New York World* from 1910 to midway through 1912. This was followed by another trip abroad that included his marriage in London in 1913. He returned to caricature for the *New York World* again from 1914 to 1925 and then joined the staff of the fledgling *New Yorker* magazine. The first issue of the *New Yorker* had two Al Frueh cartoons, and he drew the cover of the second issue. It depicted two huge policemen squeezing into a tiny new patrol car. He was 45 years old when the *New Yorker* began, and he was a regular contributor until the advanced age of 82.

He is most famous for his theatrical caricatures covering a period of American theater from 1905 to 1962. Frueh once said that he became interested in caricature while studying in a Lima, Ohio, business school as a young man. He began by turning the Pitman shorthand symbols into caricatures.

Swiftness, economy of line and a sure likeness were hallmarks of Frueh's style. His work relied heavily on first

Alfred Frueh, caricature of Winifred Lenihan as Saint Joan. © Frueh.

impressions, and he preferred to sit in the eighth row on the side aisle in a theater so he could see the actors at close range when they entered on his side of the stage, but also in differing perspectives when they moved across the stage. He did no drawings at the theater, nor did his subjects pose for him. Instead he would return to his Greenwich Village studio and draw his impressions on scraps of brown paper.

Al Frueh didn't consider himself a critic. He stated, "My job was just to draw." He was at his best with the fewest lines creating his caricature. Capturing the physical characteristics of a subject was as important to him as facial caricature. One of his most famous drawings was of George M. Cohan. The face is blank. The entire caricature is based on Cohan's body.

His magazine cartoons for the *New Yorker* included a series on suggested designs for buildings. His classic is a skyscraper in the shape of a beautiful woman's leg. It was his design for a Midwest center for the glorification of the American woman to be built by showman Florenz Ziegfeld. He also drew the decorative heading at the top of Frank Sullivan's annual Christmas poem.

Frueh gained a considerable reputation at the *New Yorker* for being an eccentric. He favored an old-fashioned, wide-brimmed brown fedora, and in slushy winter weather he would appear at the *New Yorker's* offices with unbuckled galoshes and his caricature rolled up in an old newspaper to protect it from the weather. He was a tall, rangy, shy man who made a point of not socializing with his theatrical subjects lest it interfere with the accuracy of his caricature. Al Frueh owned a hundred-acre farm in Sharon, Connecticut, where he planted seven thousand pine trees and forty varieties of grapes, and tried unsuccessfully to hybridize a soft-shelled black walnut. Only in his later years and to please his wife did he allow electricity and some central heating in the farmhouse. He died in the hospital in Sharon after a long illness on September 13, 1968. He was then 88 years old and had created one of the longest continuous records of caricature in the annals of American theater.

B.C.

FÜCHSEL, FRANZ (1927-) Danish cartoonist born in Skærbæk, Denmark, on September 16, 1927. Füchsel, who also draws under the pen name "Skærbæk," became widely known around 1955 when he was part of a team and shared a drawing office with cartoonists Quist and Holbæk. They created a new type of newspaper cartoon and, though having different styles of artwork, they complemented each other extremely well.

Füchsel, who sells his cartoons throughout Europe and frequently is seen in American media, has a "realistic," only slightly caricatured style. He is a master of all cartooning's special effects, from thin-line to broad brushstrokes—and also does full-page illustrations in watercolors and oil. His several tries as a comic strip artist *(Barbarossa)* were without much success.

His humor is often centered around classic topics—desert islands, problems with in-laws, etc.—but he is most outstanding when he takes four drawings and works with an often trivial, everyday topic to present a brand-new

"Hansen, 21 Homecastle Street . . . I suppose this is the place."

Franz Füchsel. © Hendes Verden.

and funny angle. Outside the cartoon columns, his drawings appear as funny illustrations to ads, as eye-catchers in brochures and on book covers. Of late he has branched out into poster design, notably illustrating a series of posters in the 1990s promoting safety on the farm.

J.S.

FURNISS, HARRY (1854-1925) Irish cartoonist, caricaturist, illustrator, author, publisher, lecturer, entertainer and star of silent films born in Wexford, Ireland, on March 26, 1854. Harry Furniss's very productivity has tended to lessen his appreciation in sophisticated circles. The son of a Yorkshireman and a Scotswoman, he was educated at Wesleyan College, St. Stephen's Green, Dublin, where he edited and drew his own magazine, *The Schoolboy's Punch.* He also studied art at the RHA Schools, Dublin, and the Life School of the Hibernian Academy, and at 17 he freelanced his first professional cartoons to *Zozimus,* a satirical weekly.

He came to London two years later, drew for *London Society, Illustrated London News, Cornhill, Graphic,* etc., and sent his first joke to *Punch* in October 1880. At first infuriated with the magazine for having his work redrawn by another artist, he settled his differences with the editor and became a regular contributor for 14 years. His weekly feature, *Essence of Parliament,* often portrayed William Gladstone, a character Furniss made his own thanks to his predilection for the winged collar! In his time with *Punch* Furniss drew 2,600 cartoons, from small thumbnails to the largest ever to appear in the paper (Christmas 1890). In 1884 Furniss's cartoon of a tramp writing to the manufacturer of Pears soap ("Two years ago I used your soap since when I have used no other") became the most famous advertisement of its era. From the ridiculous to the sublime, he also created that Victorian-Edwardian lovely known as the "Furniss Girl."

Furniss's paintings were exhibited in London galleries from 1875, and he fought a long and vociferous feud with the Royal Academy: *Harry Furniss's Royal Academy, An Artistic Joke* (1887) and *Royal Academy Antics* (1890). He created a regular cartoon in 1886, *Our Own Juggins,* for the weekly comic *Illustrated Bits,* and in 1894 he launched his own humorous weekly, *Lika Joko.* His book illustration work began in 1879 with William Makepeace Thackeray's *Ballads* and continued through Lewis Carroll's *Sylvie and Bruno* (1889) and G.E. Farrow's *The Wallypug of Why (1895)* to an 18-volume edition of the works of Charles Dickens (1912), for which he produced 500 full-page pictures. His daughter, Dorothy, was also artistic and often collaborated in his illustration work. Furniss went to New York in 1912 to write and star in a series of short comedy films for the Thomas A. Edison Company, and he wrote up his experiences in a book—which of course he illustrated—*My Lady Cinema* (1914). He died in 1925.

"Shadowing" Members of Parliament
Harry Furniss.

Books: *A River Holiday* (1883); *Talk of the Town* (1885); *Romps at the Seaside* (1885); *Parliamentary Views* (1886); *Romps in Town* (1886); *Romps All the Year Round* (1886); *The Comic Blackstone* (1887); *Travels in the Interior* (1887); *The Incompleat Angler* (1887); *Harry Furniss's Royal Academy* (1887); *How He Did It* (1887); *Pictures at Play* (1888); *MPs in Session* (1889); *Royal Academy Antics* (1890); *Diary of the Salisbury Parliament* (1892); *Flying Visits* (1892); *The Grand Old Mystery Unravelled* (1894); *How's That* (1896); *Pen and Pencil in Parliament* (1897); *Australian Sketches* (1899); *Confessions of a Caricaturist* (1901); *Financial Philosophy (1902); Our Joe* (1903); *Harry Furniss at Home* (1904); *How to Draw in Pen and Ink* (1905); *Harry Furniss's Christmas Annual (1905); Friends Without Faces* (1905); *Poverty Bay* (1905); *My Undiscovered Crimes (1909); My Lady Cinema* (1914); *More About How to Draw* (1915); *Byways and Queerways of Boxing* (1919); *My Bohemian Days* (1919); *Years Without Yawns* (1923); *Some Victorian Women* (1923); *Some Victorian* Men (1924); *Paradise in Piccadilly* (1925); and *The Two Pins Club* (1925).

D.G.

Gg

GABLE, BRIAN (1949-) Canadian cartoonist born in 1949 in Saskatoon, Saskatchewan. After studies at the Universities of Saskatchewan and Toronto, Brian Gable graduated in 1971 with degrees in Fine Arts and Education. He briefly taught art in Brockville, Ontario, before contributing cartoons to the Brockville *Recorder and Times*, starting in 1977. He then worked full-time for the *Regina Leader-Post* before becoming editorial cartoonist for the influential *Globe and Mail* of Toronto in 1988.

Gable's cartoons are characterized more by visual and verbal wit than by vitriol or bite. In one cartoon, for instance, the Canadian ambassador to China reads to his interlocutors from a file named "Human Rights in China," while only a blank speech balloon issues from his lips, prompting one Chinese to whisper to another, "Quiet diplomacy." In another cartoon a writer calling his union gets the following recorded message, "If you are a victim of cultural imperialism, please press 1... eurocentric meritocracy, please press 2... voice appropriation, please press 3..." Gable especially delights in depicting Canada's national mascot (a beaver) in all kinds of dicey situations: hung by his thumbs the better for the taxman to pick his pockets, having a cocked gun put to his head by Quebec's separatist leader Lucien Bouchard, etc. The hapless rodent always displays the same expression, halfway between affront and indignation, a feeling that according to the cartoonist accurately reflects Canada's current national mood.

Gable's drawing style is caricatural but detailed, with halftones and brushstrokes to add perspective, which places him in the tradition of British rather than contemporary American cartooning. He has been the recipient of a number of distinctions, including the National Newspaper Award in 1986 and 1995.

M.H.

Brian Gable. © Globe and Mail.

GABRIEL
See Friell, James.

GALAKTIONOV, STEPAN FILIPPOVICH (1779-1854) Russian cartoonist and graphic artist born in St. Petersburg, Russia, in 1779. Stepan Galaktionov studied at the St. Petersburg Academy of Art from early childhood in 1785 to 1800. He worked mainly in drypoint in combination with etching and later mastered the art of lithography. Primarily a book illustrator and landscape artist, Galaktionov also regularly contributed cartoons on everyday life and St. Petersburg events to several newspapers and almanacs. His familiar scenes of Russian life were depicted with good-natured humor tinged with a touch of pathos. Some of his drawings were later collected in book form.

Galaktionov's drawings of the 1820s are probably among the first genuine Russian cartoons. They are only mildly amusing and rather tame (Galaktionov never touched social or political subjects), but they show a good knowledge of what was happening artistically in France and England at the time. Galaktionov became a professor at his old alma mater in 1817, and he taught there until his death on July 2, 1854.

M.H.

GALANIS, DEMETRIUS EMMANUEL (1882-1966) French cartoonist and painter of Greek origin born in Athens, Greece, on May 22, 1882. Demetrius Galanis published cartoons in Athens newspapers as early as 1897. In 1899 he won a drawing contest sponsored by the Paris daily *Le Journal* and came to Paris to study, first at the Ecole de la Rue Bonaparte, then at the Beaux-Arts. While still a student, he started contributing cartoons to many French publications, such as *Le Rire, Le Sourire, Le Matin, Le Journal du Dimanche* and especially *L'Assiette au Beurre,* where he had several issues devoted entirely to his cartoons.

Galanis went to Germany in 1907 to work for the *Lustige Blätter* but returned to Paris in 1909. At the outbreak of World War 1, he joined the French Foreign Legion and became a French citizen while serving in Corfu. After the war Galanis veered away from cartooning and devoted most of his time to painting (mostly portraits) and to book illustration. He received many honors and awards, was named a professor at the Ecole des Beaux-Arts and taught there from 1945 to 1952. He died in 1966 in his native Greece, to which he had returned some years earlier.

Galanis's work as a cartoonist was vibrant and vital. His affinity with the Fauves and the post-Impressionists is clearly evident, although notably absent from his paintings. While he made his name primarily as an academic

We must go on guillotining because . . . Society must be avenged—by the death of a dumb brute, a madman or an idiot.
Demetrius Galanis, 1907.

artist, Galanis will probably be best remembered as a peerless and innovative cartoonist.

M.H.

GALANTARA, GABRIELE (1865-1937) Italian cartoonist born in the Emilia region of Italy in 1865. After a brief stay in Bologna, where he started his career by contributing cartoons to the magazines *Bononia Ridet* and *La Rana,* Gabriele Galantara moved to Rome in 1890. There, together with Guido Podrecca, he founded the satirical *L'Asino* a few years later. From the first issue, the success of this socialist and anticlerical weekly was due to the incisiveness of Galantara's cartoons (which he signed with the anagram "Rata-Langa"). The political background of these last years of the 19th century—punctuated by scandals, conspiracies, mad colonial adventures and miscellaneous corruption—provided ample grist for Galantara's socialist mill.

In his cartoons (as also in some of his watercolors and oil paintings) Galantara depicted with vigor the growing power of the masses and represented the proletariat smashing the chains forged by the bourgeoisie and the dictatorship and rising to shake the world. Rather than drawing cartoons in the traditional sense, Galantara gave life to the themes of socialist ideology. Unlike Scalarini, he did not limit himself to topical polemics but strove to represent the epochal struggle between the haves and have-nots. Some of his cartoons and caricatures have the impact of Daumier's drawings and remain powerful even today.

Galantara worked for many publications other than *L'Asino,* including the Italian daily *Avanti!* and foreign magazines like the German *Der Wahre Jacob* or the French *L'Assiette au Beurre,* both close in spirit and ideological content to *L'Asino.* Galantara's activity, like that of Scalarini, came to a virtual end in 1926 when the Fascist laws of exception conclusively stifled freedom. Lawsuits, persecutions and jailings punctuated Galantara's last years, and he died in 1937.

Together with Scalarini, Galantara is indisputably Italy's major editorial cartoonist; in a way the two artists complemented each other. While Scalarini, in his *Avanti!* cartoons, denounced the misdeeds of the capitalist world with a violence that hit immediately, Galantara, mainly in *L'Asino,* depicted the grotesque and horrid images of a world dominated by war, dispossession, misery and hunger.

C.S.

Gabriele Galantara ("Rata-Langa"), an ironic comment on the conquest of Tripoli, 1911.

GALLAGHER, GEORGE GATELY (1928-) American cartoonist born in Queens Village, New York, in 1928. George Gately (as he signs his work in order to avoid confusion with his older brother, John Gallagher, also a cartoonist) grew up in Bergenfield, New Jersey, where he received his primary and secondary education. After graduating from high school in 1946, Gately attended Pratt Institute and went to work for an advertising agency, where he remained for 11 years. "One day in the spring of 1957," he later recalled, "I decided to give cartooning a try. About three months later I had my first important sale. I've been doing well ever since."

Gately's gag cartoons appeared in the *Saturday Evening Post, Parade, This Week* and other publications. In 1964 he created *Hapless Harry,* a comic strip about a fat little man always thwarted by chance. Distributed by the Chicago

Tribune-New York News Syndicate, it had only a brief career and disappeared in the late 1960s. After *Hapless Harry* folded, Gately went back to freelancing cartoons and also worked briefly for a greeting card company. In 1973 he came up with *Heathcliff,* a panel cartoon about a self-assertive cat; with the success of this feature (distributed by the McNaught Syndicate) Gately began devoting all his time to the exploits of his rascally feline. He has also provided some scripting for the ABC TV show of the early 1980's, *Heathcliff and Dingbat,* and for *Heathcliff—the Movie,* released in 1985. His panel is now syndicated by Tribune Media Services.

A conscientious craftsman, Gately exhibits a pleasant style and a fine sense of humor. There is nothing wildly original about his drawings, but they instantly strike a familiar, almost homey note that puts his readers at ease.

M.H.

GALLEPPINI, AURELIO (1917-) Italian cartoonist born in Casal di Pari, Italy, on August 28, 1917. Aurelio Galleppini moved to Sardinia, where he paid his way at the School of Architecture by contributing humor cartoons to the magazine *Candido.* Dropping out of school to devote himself entirely to drawing, Galleppini collaborated from 1937 to 1939 on the Napolitan magazine *Modellina* and also illustrated for them the book *Il Segreto del Motore* ("The Secret of the Motor").

Galleppini is best known, however, for his work in the comics field, which he began in 1939 during his military service. He drew the comics *Pino il Mozzo* ("Pino the Cabin Boy") and *Le Perle del Mare d'Oman* ("The Pearls of the Arabian Sea") for the illustrated weekly *Topolino.* Discharged in 1940, Galleppini moved to Florence, where he wrote and drew a number of comic strips for the Nerbini publications. After a recall to service in 1942, he went back to Sardinia the next year, freelancing cartoons, designing advertising posters and teaching drawing. In 1947 he again drew a number of comic strips for the publishers Del Duca and Nerbini, including a highly controversial version of *Mandrake.* Galleppini's main opportunity came in 1948, when he was asked to draw *Tex Willer* (on a scenario by Gianluigi Bonelli), a western strip that became a phenomenal success in Italy and is still among today's top-ranked comic features. His autobiography, *L'arte dell' avventura,* was published in 1989. He died on March 10, 1994.

S.T.

Mrs. Stalin: "Ah, you finally decided to take me to the mountains."
Aurelio Galleppini, 1941. © Galleppini.

Bill Gallo, "Basement Bertha." © Chicago Tribune-New York News Syndicate

GALLO, BILL (1922-) American cartoonist born in New York City on December 28, 1922. Bill Gallo is of Spanish, not Italian, descent, as is often erroneously assumed. He started publishing cartoons while still in high school. In 1942 he joined the Marine Corps and served for more than three years. After an honorable discharge, Gallo attended the Cartoonists and Illustrators School (now the School of Visual Arts) and Columbia University on a GI scholarship. But, as he himself stated, "most of (his) education came from the *New York Daily News.*"

Gallo had joined the *News* even before entering the Marine Corps, and he has remained with the paper to this day. After doing various cartooning and art jobs at the *News,* Gallo became its standby sports cartoonist and later its regular sports illustrator, after Willard Mullin's partial retirement in the late 1960s. In addition Gallo also draws an occasional editorial cartoon, and in the early 1970s he created *Basement Bertha,* a Sunday half-page with a sports theme (Basement Bertha was originally Casey Stengel's most loyal and vociferous fan in Gallo's cartoons about the New York Mets).

Bill Gallo has received many cartooning and sports awards, including several Page One awards and National Cartoonists Society Best Sports Cartoonist awards. He was president of the NCS from 1973 to 1977. One of the last sports cartoonists on staff at an American daily newspaper, he marked in 1991 the 50th anniversary of his association with the *Daily News*.

M.H.

GALLO, VINCENZO (1946-) Italian political cartoonist born in Palermo in 1946 and better known with his art name Vincino. He graduated in architecture at the University of Palermo in 1972 and soon began contributing illustrations and political cartoons to the local newspaper *L'Ora*. When he got engaged in an extreme left movement, he moved to Rome to draw political posters, leaflets and cartoons for the daily *Lotto Continua* (1975-1977) and the satirical magazine *I Quaderni del Sale*.

In 1978 Vincino started with other artists *Il Male*, a satirical weekly which was a radical breakthrough in the tradition of Italian graphic satire. *Il Male* was a totally independent and unofficial information magazine which for almost five years skewered left, center and right political movements, pouring forth images of all kinds: drawings, cartoons, comic strips, photos, photomontages, collages. The quality of the paper and the printing standards were very poor and the images were coarse and often vulgar. In spite of this shabby general look, *Il Male* came out to be quite effective and was the object of many legal complaints.

Vincino's contributions to the magazine were covers, editorial cartoons and comic strip pages sketched with a style which was clumsy but spontaneous, ironical and often gross. More than on sophisticated gags and puns, Vincino's satire is based on a rough description of reality, of its grotesque and tragicomic happenings which make the reader reflect on life and its values.

During the 1980s Vincino started contributing to several satirical periodicals like *Linus, Tango, Cuore*, to the weekly news magazine *Panorama* and to the nationwide daily *Corriere della Sera*. In the 1990s his cartoons have appeared in the satirical magazine *Il clandestino* (1994-1995) and at present they are published in the daily *Il Foglio* and in *Boxer*, a weekly satirical pullout of the daily *Il manifesto*.

Vincino has also illustrated some books and some of his cartoons have been collected in book format: *Il naso del presidente, L'importante è non vincere* (1977), *Fatti e rifatti* (1997). In 1987 he was awarded the Prize Forte dei Marmi for Political Satire.

G.C.C.

Vincenzo Gallo ("Vincino"). © Vincenzo Gallo.

GAMBLE, ED (1943-) The editorial cartoonist of the *Florida Times-Union* in Jacksonville, Floriday, for many years, Ed Gamble has been a voice for social and political responsibility since early childhood. The son of a government official and a newspaper columnist, the nephew of newspaper owners, and the brother of a United Press International reporter, he has been associated with journalism all his life, and fixed his keen eye on a career in the field while still in elementary school in Morristown, Tennessee. His first honor was an award in a city-wide art contest won at the age of nine. He was a regular contributor of cartoons to his high school newspaper, and that of the University of South Florida, from which he graduated with a degree in journalism in 1970.

Gamble served an apprenticeship as a reporter and sports editor for several newspapers before landing his first job as a staff editorial cartoonist in 1972 with the Knoxville, Tennessee, *Banner*. Within a year the Register and Tribune Syndicate (later Cowles Syndicate) signed him on and distributed his cartoons nationally until he transferred to King Features some years later. He remained with the *Banner* until 1980, when he accepted a position with the *Florida Times-Union*.

Gamble has been identified with a conservative stand, but his political position, like that of any good editorial cartoonist, varies with the issue he addresses. An independent spirit, he is an equal opportunity satirist, aiming his barbs without fear or favor at both sides when the occasion seems to call for it, and while his attacks are often cutting, they are seldom without a sense of fun. His shrewd political and social commentary has earned him wide praise in the profession. Among his many honors are the Dragonslayer Award from the U.S. Industrial Council in 1976, Small Business Association Awards in 1978 and 1979, and a Freedoms Foundation George Washington Award, a Tennessee School Bell Award, and a Metro Nashville Teachers Award in 1980. In 1992 he received a Citation for Excellence from the Overseas Press Club, and four years later both the Wilbur Award for Editorial Cartoons from the Religious Public Relations Council and the Sunshine State Award for Best Editorial Cartoons from the Florida Chapter of the Society of Professional Journalists.

Ed Gamble. © Florida Times-Union.

Gamble's cartoons appear regularly in collections. He is represented in *Peek at the Great Society* (1965) and *100 Watts* (1983), a collection lampooning Interior Secretary James Watt, and he has been included in every issue of Charles E. Brooks' *Best Editorial Cartoons of the Year* since 1973. In 1995 a collection of his own work, *You Get Two for the Price of One!*, was published with forewords by two former presidents, Gerald Ford and George Bush.

Gracefully composed and meticulously executed, Gamble's art reflects a sense of design as keen as his eye for the unjust and the absurd in public life. Over more than a quarter century, his shrewd observations have illuminated and focused issues for a wide public of appreciative readers.

D.W.

GAMMIDGE, IAN (1916-) Ian Berwick Gammidge was not only a newspaper cartoonist of an especially zany nature, he was also a leading scriptwriter for several daily newspaper strips of differing characteristics. He was born Ian Berwick Gammidge in Ashtead, Surrey, England, on April 16, 1916. A self-taught cartoonist, he began work as an insurance salesman during the Thirties, and served in the Army during World War II. After demobilization he served in the Territorials, and attended the Saint Martin's School of Art in Charing Cross Road, London, to polish up his drawing.

Ian sold his first cartoon to *Lilliput* in May 1946, and was soon freelancing to such weeklies as *John Bull, Everybodys, The Tatler, London Opinion* and several trade papers. He joined the staff of the *Daily Mirror* in May 1947, taking over the scriptwriting of *The Flutters*, which had been done by Jack Hargreaves (art by Len Gamblin). Later he took over *The Larks* from Brian Cooke, a cartoonist who he had met with luck as a television situation comedy writer, and still later added a third strip to his collection when editorial writer William Connor, who wrote a daily column as "Cassandra", found the work too distracting. This was *Ruggles*, a daily family strip drawn by Steve Dowling.

The *Daily Mirror*'s Sunday edition, then entitled *Sunday Pictorial*, gave Gammidge a chance as a topical cartoonist, and *Gammidge's Bargain Basement* (a pun on the department store of Gamage's of Holborn) began. The *Mirror* then added a new children's strip, *Little Joe* drawn by Bert Felstead as "Fel." Gammidge scripted this, as he did the Saturday gardening strip by Jack Dunkley entitled *Mr. Digwell*. He also became the final writer to work on the world-famous *Jane* strip, created by Norman Pett in the 1930s.

Books: *Little Joe* (1975), *Mr. Digwell's Every Day Gardening Books* (1977), *Life With the Larks* (1978), *The Gardener's Mirror* (1981).

D.G.

GANDY GOOSE (U.S.) Terrytoons' web-footed cartoon character made his first appearance in a 1938 short titled, logically enough, "Gandy the Goose." The definite article was subsequently dropped, and he was simply Gandy Goose in later cartoons.

Gandy was a smart-alecky, street-wise and tough-minded creature who got himself involved in all kinds of scrapes, as in "G-Man Jitters" (1939), for instance, where he helped the FBI bag a gang of criminals. With the coming of World War II Gandy applied his talents to fighting the minions of the Axis (if one can picture a goose having it out with goose-stepping storm troopers!). Some of the cartoons of this period bear such titles as "Lights Out," "Camouflage" and "Somewhere in Egypt." After the war Gandy settled for somewhat more sedate pursuits and conventional situations in cartoons like "Mother Goose Nightmare," "Mexican Baseball" and "Gandy Goose and the Chipper Chipmunk."

Most of the *Gandy Goose* cartoons were directed by the trio of Mannie Davis, Connie Rasinski and Eddie Donnelly. Fairly popular in the 1940s, the series petered out in the 1950s. It should be noted that Gandy Goose had a short and checkered career in comic books from 1953 to 1958.

M.H.

GARBANCITO (Spain) In 1947 Arturo Moreno, who had previously enjoyed a successful career in advertising cartoons, brought out an ambitious 72-minute animated film featuring a game little hero named Garbancito (literally, "little chick-pea" in Spanish). *Garbancito de la Mancha* was the title of the feature; like his literary model, Don Quijote de la Mancha, Garbancito was fired up by tales of chivalry and dreamed of becoming a fearless knight. His wish was granted by his fairy godmother, and Garbancito, with the help of the other children and his goat, Pelegrina, valiantly and victoriously defended his village against the depredations of the ogre Caramanca and the schemes of the evil wizard Pelocha. The success of the feature inevitably gave rise to a sequel. Almost as inevitably, the sequel, *Alegres Vacaciones* ("Happy Holidays"), did not measure up to the original, and the characters romped through the plains and mountains of Spain in what amounted to an unending travelogue.

The two *Garbancito* films brought no innovation to the animation medium and were in fact very much in the tradition of the Disney cartoons. Their importance lies in the fact that they were the first feature-length animated films ever produced in Spain and signaled a revival of Spanish interest in animation after a long period of silence and sterility.

M.H.

GARCÍA-CABRAL, ERNESTO (1890-1968) Mexican cartoonist born in Huatusco, province of Veracruz, Mexico, in 1890. Ernesto García Cabral went to Mexico City in 1907 to study art at the famed San Carlos Academy, from which he graduated two years later. He embarked on a cartooning career in 1910, contributing cartoons to the humor and political magazines *La Tarántula, Multicolor* and *Frivolidades.*

García Cabral received a grant from the Mexican government in 1912 to pursue his studies in Europe. He graduated first in his class from the Colarossi Academy in Paris and thereupon resumed his cartooning career with contributions to the French humor magazines *Le Rire* and *La Vie Parisienne.* When World War I broke out, he chose to remain in Paris, and he expressed his staunch anti-German feelings in cartoons published in the patriotic magazine *La Baïonnette.* In 1917 he was named cultural attaché at the Mexican embassy in Paris; he later served in Madrid and Buenos Aires.

Returning to Mexico City in 1918, García Cabral soon became one of the most popular and sought-after press cartoonists. He contributed countless gag and editorial cartoons to most major Mexican publications and drew a number of comic strips (*El Fifi,* about a frustrated man-about-town, is probably his best-known creation in this domain). He was also a talented mural painter, decorating the Pavilion of Tourism in the city of Toluca, among other projects. He died in Mexico City on August 8, 1968.

M.H.

Ernesto García Cabral, self-caricature.

GARCÍA-JUNCEDA I SUPERVÍA, JOAN (1881-1948) Spanish cartoonist born in Barcelona, Spain, in 1881. Joan García-Junceda (who signed simply Junceda) began to draw at an early age. His first cartoons appeared in 1902 in the newly created humor magazine *Cu-Cut.* His cartoons were radical and often controversial, and he was very sharply criticized for some that appeared in *Cu-Cut* and *Papitu,* another humor publication, to which he began contributing in 1908. (As a result of one Junceda cartoon in *Papitu,* the political party La Lliga Catalana decided to withdraw its financial support from the magazine.) Junceda also contributed cartoons to *L'Estevet, La Tralla, En Patufet, Paginas Viscudes* and other, lesser-known publications. In view of his radical leanings, his 30-year association with *En Patufet* (1904-38), a magazine closely tied to the conservative party, can only be explained by his close friendship with the manager, Folch i Torres. In the 1930s Junceda illustrated a great number of children's stories and is recognized internationally for his work in children's books.

Junceda's career went into eclipse with the coming to power of Generalissimo Franco, and he died at his country home in Blanes, near Barcelona, in 1948. Because of his radical political positions, evaluations of his cartoon work are often prejudiced, and his long association with *En Patufet* leaves him open to charges of hypocrisy. Objectively, however, his clear and subtly critical drawings mark him as an important cartoonist. Junceda's style was personal and often poetic, very much in the Catalan tradition of Josep Lluis Pellicer and Apel. les Mestres.

J.M.

GARDOSH, KARIEL (1921-) Israeli cartoonist born in Budapest, Hungary, in 1921. Kariel Gardosh received his art education first in Budapest and later in Paris, where he started his career as a cartoonist just before the outbreak of World War II. During the war he joined the underground movement, and in 1948 he emigrated to Israel. After contributing a great number of cartoons and illustrations to various Israeli and European publications, Gardosh in 1953 joined the staff of the afternoon newspaper *Ma'ariv,* where his cartoons (signed with his pen name, "Dosh") became instantly popular.

Gardosh created the figure "little Israel," a spunky young boy who soon became the symbol of the country; he used his little character to comment with mordant irony on political, social and economic issues confronting the state of Israel. Gardosh's cartoons have also been published in the English-language *Jerusalem Post* and in the Hungarian-language daily *Lej Kelet,* as well as in many newspapers outside Israel. Gardosh has illustrated books and written short stories and one-act plays, but it is as a cartoonist that he is most famous. His cartoons have been collected several times in book form. *Selihah she-Nizzahnu!* ("So Sorry We Won," 1967) and *Oifla Menazzehim* ("Woe to the Victors," 1969), two volumes dealing with the Six-Day War and its aftermath, are probably the best known. *To Israel with Love* was published in the United States by Sagamore Press in 1960. In 1997 an exhibit commemorating the 50th anniversary of the Little Israel ("Shroolik") character was held in Tel Aviv.

M.H.

GAREL, LEO (1917-) American cartoonist and painter born in New York City on October 8, 1917. Leo Garel studied at the Parsons School and at the Art Students League of New York with George Grosz and Vaclav Vytlactil. A serious painter in the abstract expressionist mode, Garel has gained broad critical acceptance with his watercolors and gouaches of northeastern landscapes and seascapes. His paintings have been widely exhibited, and he has had shows at the Zabriskie Gallery in New York (1957), Mills College (1960), the Cober Gallery in New York (1967), the Berkshire (Mass.) Museum (1967), the Pennsylvania Academy of Fine Art at Philadelphia (1969) and the Montclair (N.J.) Art Museum (1975). His work is also represented in the permanent collections of the Norfolk Museum of Arts and Sciences, the Albany Institute of History and Art, the Santa Fe Museum and the Chase Manhattan Bank Collection. In 1961 he took a first prize for his watercolors at the Albany Institute of History and Art.

Cartooning is apparently of secondary interest to Garel; in fact, he makes no mention of his comic art in his *Who's Who in American Art* biography. Yet during the 1940s and 1950s he was a regular contributor of cartoons to the *Saturday Evening Post*, and probably to other magazines as well. His style as a cartoonist was not particularly distinctive, but his panels were always well planned, and important detail work was never neglected. Drawn with the same broad, quick strokes characteristic of his brushwork, Garel's pen-and-ink caricatures are not only quite "readable" but also show a fair talent for the workable gag line. Thus the retirement ceremony portrayed in a 1950 *Saturday Evening Post* panel. It is arranged in an almost formalistic way, with the boss (standing on a chair and taking the office clock off the wall) and the old retiree in the center, flanked by clusters of employees. "Pearson," the boss is saying, "for years I've noticed you admiring this clock, so I thought it only fitting to present it to you on your retirement." Or the panel in which a cheerfully smiling dentist tells his cringing patient just before starting to drill, "Let me know when it gets excruciating."

Garel seems to have stopped cartooning in the 1950s to devote himself full time to painting, apparently with good success, as has been noted. In this he is rare, for most of those who come to the comic field from the fine arts are eventually diverted into some commercial variation like illustration or ad art. Garel has avoided this route, remaining the abstract watercolorist he always wanted to be. He later switched to watercolor and landscape painting, and his New York cityscapes and views of the Hudson Valley and the Berkshires (many in gouache) gained him a respectable following through the 1980s and 1990s.

R.C.

"Garfield." © United Feature Syndicate.

GARFIELD AND FRIENDS (U.S.) Jim Davis's *Garfield* had been a hit for almost ten years in newspapers when CBS decided to add an animated version of the strip to its Saturday-morning lineup of cartoons. The show, called *Garfield and Friends*, premiered on October 15, 1988, with the author supervising the production.

All the familiar characters from the comic strip are there going through their usual paces. Garfield in his arrogant fat cat persona plays all kinds of underhanded tricks on his favorite foil, Odie the dog, and runs circles around his putative master, the cartoonist Jon Arbuckle. The plots—what there is to them—revolve around the smug feline's love of food and sleep. Although limited, the animation is nicely done, and the series exudes a charm and freshness too often absent from most "kidvid" fare.

The "Friends" promised by the title are Orson the piglet, the four-legged hero of Davis's short-lived *U.S. Acres* comic strip, and his cohorts. These include Roy the rooster, who uses a bugle to wake up the neighborhood; Booker the chick who believes Orson to be his mother; and Orville, Sylvia, Woodrow and Fred, the early worms Booker is constantly (and vainly) trying to catch. These animals cavort in separate segments of the series, and the off-the-wall humor of these small vignettes often makes them funnier than the main feature.

In advance of the regularly-scheduled program, there

had been a number of *Garfield* animation specials, many of which won Emmy Awards, including the first one, *Here Comes Garfield* (1982). Produced by Lee Mendelson and directed by Bill Melendez, the team responsible for the *Peanuts* cartoons, it went on to spawn many sequels. In contrast to the serenity of most of the *Peanuts* shorts, the *Garfield* episodes were filled with action and movement. In one of them the gutsy cat fought against ghosts and goblins; in another adventure he had a run-in with unfriendly natives on a tropical isle. In these specials Garfield often played a variety of tough characters, including Cave Cat, Space Cat, and the no-nonsense private eye Sam Spayed. In all the cartoons the cat's thoughts are voiced by Lorenzo Music, while Thom Hoge and Greg Berger play the other regulars.

M.H.

GASOLINE REGGIE AND HIS AUTO
See Little Johnny and His Teddy Bears.

GATELY, GEORGE
See Gallagher, George Gately.

GAVARNI, PAUL
See Chevalier, Guillaume-Sulpice.

GAVIOLI, GINO (1923-) Italian cartoonist and animator born in Milan, Italy, on May 9, 1923. After completing his studies at the Brera Art Institute in Milan, Gino Gavioli began his cartooning career in 1940, drawing comic strips for the Italian publisher Traini in collaboration with Paolo Piffarerio. He was drafted in 1943 and did not resume his artistic activity until 1948, when he drew *Nonno Bigio* ("Gray-Haired Grandpa") for Edizioni Alpe. In 1952, together with his brother Roberto and Paolo Piffarerio, Gavioli founded Gamma Film, an animated cartoon studio. Most of Gavioli's production was geared to television commercials, and many of the characters he created became popular, including Il Vigile ("The Watchman") and Babbut, Mammut and Figliut, as well as Gregorio, Capitan Trinchetto, Pallina and more recently Taca Banda and Cimabue.

Gino Gavioli, "Puttiferio Goes to War." © Gamma Film.

In 1952 Gavioli also started doing a panel featuring anthropomorphized animals for the magazine *Il Monello*. In 1960 he drew covers and game pages for *Il Corriere dei Piccoli*, and the following year he did cover illustrations and comic features for Il *Giornalino*, a collaboration that continues to this day. He has also written and illustrated several children's books, including *Eroi in Pantofole* ("Heroes in Slippers"), *Mio Nonno Pirata* ("My Pirate Grandfather") and *Le Invenzioni Quasi Tutte* ("Almost All the Inventions"). In the field of theatrical animation Gavioli worked on the 1961 *La Lunga Calza Verde* ("The Long Green Stocking") and directed *Puttiferio Va alla Guerra* ("Puttiferio Goes to War," 1967); he also directed *La Maria d'Oro* (1972) for a German production company. He is now mostly involved in running Gamma Film in collaboration with his his brother Roberto.

L.S.

GAY NINETIES, THE (U.S.) *Life*, by the 1920s, had became one of the freshest of American magazines after the infusion of such talents as Robert Benchley, Robert E. Sherwood, Dorothy Parker, Heywood Broun, Gluyas Williams and John Held, Jr. It also had the best of an older generation in staffers like T.S. Sullivant, E.W. Kemble, A.B. Frost, E.S. Martin and the magazine's new owner, Charles Dana Gibson. But in its role as the respectable leader of American comic papers, it hit an ambiguous snag in the Roaring Twenties. Although it would never get as raucous as the later *College Humor* and *Ballyhoo*, or even *Judge*, it did have to acknowledge the "new morality" and life-style of the 1920s. The new writers (as well as Held and later Russell Patterson) were to reflect the times, but tradition was still honored.

A manifestation of this dichotomy was a *Life* series of black-and-white half-page cartoons, *The Gay Nineties*, debuting in the issue of April 9, 1925. A less reverent publication would have taken off with a mocking tone, as Perelman was about to do in *Judge* and Held in the *New Yorker* with his woodcuts. But the *Life* series, drawn by Richard V. Culter, seldom ridiculed; it was steeped in nostalgia and fondness. Indeed, when an anachronism was noted, it was usually in order to point out how superior the 1890s were to the frenzied, irreverent 1920s. Sometimes no comment was implied, as in the similarity between the novelty of the phonograph and that of the later radio. Culter's chronicles pointed to the fact that far more than 30 chronological years separated him and his subject; in spite of (or perhaps because of) the different atmosphere of the Jazz Age, the series was an enormous hit.

There were no continuing characters save the spirit of the age, which was widely acknowledged as captured perfectly. Culter proved himself a provident researcher rather than an able memorialist—his work relied heavily on books and personal accounts. The series was approved and admired by Gibson, who nevertheless was somewhat embarrassed at finally proving himself a *bona fide* relic: the Nineties were *his* age inseparably.

The cartoons were executed in crayon and sought photographic likeness. Needless to say, all fashions and decoration were historically accurate. Each cartoon was more an archaeological expedition than a knee-slapping gag, but the series was popular enough to inspire several editions of a reprint book (published first in 1927 by Doubleday Doran with an introduction by Gibson). The cartoons in the book included those in *Life* up to December 23, 1926. *Life* devoted a whole issue to the nostalgia craze generated by the series on October 7, 1926; there was a double-page cartoon by Culter for the occasion.

The Gay Nineties, which gave its name to the decade it dissected, ran weekly at its inception and then with varying frequency until its last appearance on March 22, 1928, when it was discontinued due to the untimely death of the artist. Culter had found a formula—and provided succeeding generations with a truthful and sympathetic portrait of an age. The only cartoonists who did it better were Gaar Williams (in *Among the Folks of History*), who managed an infusion of gags, and Clare Briggs, who was overwhelmingly evocative.

R.M.

GAYMANN, PETER (1950-) Peter Gaymann was born in Freiburg im Breisgau in 1950. As a child he was often beset by illness and had to stay in bed. To avoid boredom, he started drawing and copying other drawings. His family, however, had nothing at all to do with art. This did not keep young Gaymann from drawing posters for private parties—once he even conceived a carpet for Corpus Christi Day celebrations. After finishing school in Freiburg, Gaymann had to join the army despite his having registered as a conscientious objector. Following his turn in the army he studied at the College of Social Pedagogics and after graduation worked as a social worker from 1972 to 1976. On the side he still made drawings for all kinds of events. He also painted still lifes and realistic landscapes. At age 26 Gaymann finally discovered that his real talent lay in cartoons. Instead of working on one picture for days on end, he could simply toy around with ideas in cartooning. He became a freelance cartoonist and, to supplement his income, he taught and gave drawing lessons at technical high schools. When he applied to become a student at the Academy of Art in Karlsruhe, however, no one took interest in his talent, so he flunked the entry test.

This did not deter Gaymann (pseudonym P. Gay). Big success finally came in 1985 when Gaymann's first chicken postcards were published. Chickens of all kinds with very "now" gag lines were readily picked up by just about every one. Success helped Gaymann realize a dream. He moved to Rome with his family. Then, one day, on a visit to Germany, he noted that all of a sudden women in the street wore city rucksacks instead of handbags. So he decided that, in order to be able to continue as a cartoonist in touch with the audience he worked for, he had to be close to everyday life. And he moved back to Cologne where he is currently living.

Now themes for his Cart-Huhns (Gaymann's combination of Cartoon and Huhn, "Huhn" being German for "chicken") are all around him. And, after all of those cartoon postcards, books, and parodies, Gaymann has landed an "eggsclusive" (as he puts it by way of pun). He is now a regular contributor to *Gong*, one of the TV guide-type large format magazines. Here, he now has his own gag cartoon page to further and foster his huhn-credible cartooning career of subtly comparing animals and humans with sidesplitting results.

W.F.

GEARY, RICK (1946-) Described by comics critic Dale Luciano as "a true American original," San Diego-based artist Rick Geary commands one of the most gracefully articulate and subtly suggestive styles in contemporary cartooning, straddling the often blurry line between the alternative "New Wave" and the mainstream.

Geary was born in 1946 in Kansas City, Missouri, and attended the University of Kansas, from which he holds a BFA in commercial art (1968) and an MA in film (1971). From 1976 he has supported himself as a freelance advertising artist and illustrator, but from 1977 to 1980 he issued at his own expense a series of 15 imaginative little collections entitled *Rick Geary's Mini-Comix*, each containing a story or a series of related drawings. Elegantly produced, the 15 booklets were issued in 6 sets and earned high praise in cartoon journals.

Geary's clean, crisp visuals have appeared in numerous periodicals, ranging from true underground comix such as *Snarf, Bop, Raw Sex,* and *Alien Worlds,* to *Los Angeles Magazine, San Diego Magazine, Rolling Stone,* and the *New York Times*. His work has appeared frequently in *National Lampoon* and *Heavy Metal,* and from 1985 Copley News Service has syndicated his single-panel newspaper feature *The Perfect Couple*. In 1983 he illustrated Preiss and Sorkin's *Not the Webster's Dictionary,* and several of his pieces were included in Harvey Kurtzman's *Nuts!* I and II (1985). In that year he was commissioned by the Southern California Exposition to do a huge cartoon map of the fair-

Rick Geary. © Rick Geary.

grounds, and Fantagraphics Books issued a retrospective of his work, *At Home with Rick Geary: Collected Stories 1977-85*. In 1991 another anthology, *Housebound with Rick Geary*, appeared under the same imprint. Long associated with the annual San Diego Comics Convention, Geary won its Inkpot Award in 1980.

Geary has never had a wide popular audience as a cartoonist, but his highly individual style has earned the admiration of the profession. An oblique criticism of culture, his collections of fragmentary images are frequently presented in innovative formats and viewed from odd angles, engaging the mind as well as the eye. His themes range from Southern California architecture, television, and computers to human relations and violent crime, but always with a focus on the psychological. Of his story "Murder in the Garage," published in *Voyages* (1985), *The Comics Journal* commented on his "sinister glimpses into the bizarre workings of the human psyche" and applauded his "eerie talent for creating uncomplicated, often banal, images that resonate with ironic meaning."

Since 1978, Geary has been a director of the San Diego International Film Festival, and his devotion to the cinema emerges in both his composition and his eye for the telling detail. He calls himself "a movie junkie" and acknowledges the influence of such film directors as Hitchcock, Welles, Buñuel, and Kurasawa on his work. Like these auteurs, he has followed a personal vision in his creative work. "All I've sought," he noted in *Contemporary Graphic Artists* (1987), "is to convey my own bemused and detached view of life."

D.W.

GÉBÉ
See Blondeau, Georges.

GÉBÉ
See Butterworth, George.

GEISEL, THEODOR SEUSS (1904-1991) American cartoonist, author and publisher born in Springfield, Massachusetts, on March 2, 1904. Theodor ("Dr. Seuss") Geisel went to Dartmouth College and graduated in 1925. His cartoons in the campus humor magazine attracted the attention of Norman Anthony of *Judge*, and soon his *Birdsies and Beasties* page of nonsense was a weekly feature. It consisted of various soberly couched explanations of natural history and animal life—all, of course, absolutely absurd—with the wildest concoctions in the cartoons that illustrated the captions. Soon Dr. Seuss's name was appearing on gags and strips inside the magazine and on color covers. After Anthony switched to *Life* magazine, Dr. Seuss's zany humor was sought there as well; his chores were similar, except that his page was retitled *Life's Zoological Charts*. His other work at this time included cartoons for *Vanity Fair* and *Liberty*, as well as advertising campaigns for insecticides ("Quick, Henry, the Flit!" was a classic series).

As the magazines faded during the Depression years, Dr. Seuss began turning out children's books of a variety that delighted adults with their whimsy and enchanted children with colors, rhymes and comical drawings. During World War II he served with the Army Signal Corps and Educational Division and won, among other distinctions, the Legion of Merit for his film work. In the 1940s his versatility led him to conquer ever more fields; he drew political cartoons for the newspaper *PM* in New York and entered the field of animation, winning Academy Awards in 1946 (Best Documentary Short for *Hitler Lives)*, 1947 (Best Documentary Feature for *Design for Death)* and 1951 (Best Animated Cartoon for the strikingly innovative *Gerald McBoing Boing)*.

As president and publisher of Beginners Books, Dr. Seuss changed the nature of children's books in the 1950s and thereafter with the *Cat in the Hat* series. Once again his charming drawings were combined with clever, amusing, comprehensible phrases and stories—a classic formula for young readers. His work spawned a generation of books, both under his direction and otherwise, featuring large, colorful cartoons, whimsical subjects, simple (often alliterative) phrases and large type. Indeed, he launched a new tradition that later found expression in *Sesame Street* and other modern approaches to children's education.

Lately Dr. Seuss entered the TV world, animating many of his creations and winning awards thereby (Peabody awards for *How the Grinch Stole Christmas* and *Horton Hears a Who;* Critics' Award at the Zagreb festival for *The Lorax*). Among his other credits were honorary degrees from his alma mater (he also studied at Lincoln College, Oxford, England, in 1925-26) and from American International College. He continued his educational work as president of the Beginners Book Division of Random House and publisher of Bright and Early Books. He also designed a line of toys for Mattel and furniture for Sears, Roebuck. He was awarded a honorary doctorate in fine art by Boston University in 1985. He died September 25, 1991, at his home in La Jolla, California.

Dr. Seuss, for all his activities, remains basically a cartoonist, one of the profession's proudest members. His work is always a special mixture of drawings and thoughts, with a unique sense of humor thrown in. His cartoon style has consistently been one of confident but loose pen lines, with a masterful use of composition and color. His animal creations are classics, supremely logical in an inimitably Seussian way. Most of his books are readily available, but the early cartoon work of this genius—nonsense easily the equal of Perelman's—begs republication for audiences who, without regard to generation or background, could not fail to fall in love with it and be enchanted by its humor.

Books: *And to Think That I Saw It on Mulberry Street; The 500 Hats of Bartholomew Cubbins; The Seven Lady Godivas; The King's Stilts; Horton Hatches the Egg; McElligot's Pool; Thidwick the Big-Hearted Moose; Bartholomew and the Ooblick; The Lorax; Marvin K. Mooney, Will You Please Go Now!; Did I Ever Tell You How Lucky You Are?; The Shape of Me and Other Stuf(; There's a Wocket in My Pocket; Great Day for Up; Oh, the Thinks You Can Think!; The Cat's Quizzer; Scrambled Eggs Super; Horton Hears a Who; On Beyond Zebra; If I Ran the Circus; How the Grinch Stole Christmas; The Cat in the Hat; The Cat in the Hat Comes Back; Yertle the Turtle; Happy Birthday; One Fish Two Fish Red Fish Blue Fish; Green Eggs and Ham; The Sneetches and*

Other Stories; Dr. Seuss' Sleep Book; Hop on Pop; Dr. Seuss' ABC Book; Fox in Socks; I Had Trouble in Getting to Solla Sollew; The Cat in the Hat Songbook; The Foot Book; I Can Lick 30 Tigers Today and Other Stories; My Book About Me; I Can Draw It Myself; Mr. Brown Can Moo, Can You?; and many others.

R.M.

GEORGE AND JUNIOR (U.S.) *George and Junior* is one of Tex Avery's less-celebrated cartoon creations, but while it is certainly not on a par with the impeccable *Droopy,* it does have merit. The cartoons featured a duo of uncouth bears and started unobtrusively in 1946 with "Henpecked Hoboes." The heroes of the piece were cartoon parodies of John Steinbeck's George and Lenny characters in *Of Mice and Men;* Avery's George was suitably nasty and short-tempered, and Junior exceedingly big and obtuse.

The pair reappeared in two 1947 cartoons, "Hound Hunters" and "Red Hot Rangers." In the first they proved helpless as dogcatchers, and in the latter they displayed the same ineptitude fighting forest fires. The exchanges between them were quite funny, and Avery's sight gags kept coming at a fast and furious pace. Somehow the characters never caught on with the public, and in 1948, following one last effort, "Half-Pint Pygmy," Avery gave up on the series.

George and Junior are still fondly remembered for George's comic double takes and exasperated efforts at communication with Junior, whose feeble attempts at comprehension were sure to bring some untold disaster to both bears. The cartoons themselves (which Avery directed for MGM) were very hip, but the two characters were too ill-defined and not lovable enough to become popular.

M.H.

GERALD MCBOING BOING (U.S.) Gerald McBoing Boing came into the world in 1949 in an animated cartoon of the same name created for UPA by Robert Cannon from a story by Dr. Seuss. The sad-eyed little boy with the booming voice capable of uttering the weirdest sounds (the squeaking of tires, the clanging of a bell, etc.) became an instant hit with moviegoers. The cartoon won the 1950 Academy Award for shorts, and the *Gerald McBoing Boing* series was on its way.

"Gerald McBoing Boing." © Columbia Pictures.

The cartoons revolved around Gerald's inability to speak human words, and the mishaps and contretemps resulting from his handicap. In "Gerald's Symphony" (1953) the little boy substituted for an entire symphony orchestra when the musicians failed to appear for a radio program; in "How Now, Boing Boing?" (1954) the only way he could converse with his parents was through a scrambler telephone; in "Gerald's Birthday" he caused first panic, then glee among his little companions with his weird sound effects; and in "Gerald McBoing Boing on Planet Moo" he led the inhabitants of an alien planet to believe that all earth people talked like he did.

Most of the *Gerald McBoing Boing* cartoons were directed by Cannon until the late 1950s. DePatie-Freleng, which had bought most of the UPA properties, tried to revive the character in a television series of his own in the mid-1960s, but it lasted only one season. *Gerald McBoing Boing* also had a short comic book run in 1952-53.

M.H.

"I just cancelled your vote!"
David Gerard, "Citizen Smith." © Register and Tribune Syndicate.

GERARD, DAVID (1909-) American cartoonist born in Crawfordsville, Indiana, in 1909. Dave Gerard attended Wabash College, where he edited the school magazine. Graduating in 1931, he went to New York the next year to try a career in cartooning. After two years of unsuccessful efforts he returned to Crawfordsville in 1934. From there he freelanced cartoons to a number of national magazines, including the *Saturday Evening Post* and *Collier's.* He signed a contract with the latter publication in the early 1940s for a weekly full-color cartoon.

In 1949 Gerard created a nationally syndicated panel, *Viewpoint,* for the National Newspaper Syndicate. The feature lasted four years; upon its demise the syndicate asked him to draw a kid strip, *Will-Yum,* which ran daily and Sundays from 1953 to 1967. That year Gerard went over to the Des Moines Register and Tribune Syndicate, for which he created *Citizen Smith,* a daily panel that reflects, in Gerard's own words, a "type of current, relevant humor." It also reflects the artist's interest in politics: Dave Gerard has served two terms on the city council and in 1971 was elected mayor of his hometown. *Citizen Smith* ended its run in 1982, and the cartoonist lives now retired in his native state.

M.H.

GÉRARD, JEAN-IGNACE-ISIDORE (1803-1847) French illustrator and cartoonist born in Nancy, France, on September 15, 1803. The son of a fashionable portrait painter and the grandson of a famous stage actor, Gérard showed talent at an early age in his caricatures of his father's subjects. Moving to Paris at age 20, he took the pseudonym "Grandville," by which he is best known. He soon became one of the contributors to the newly created satirical magazine *Le Charivari,* even before Daumier started drawing for it. Grandville's forte was the depiction of scenes teeming with human characters with animal heads. His 1829 book *Les Métamorphoses du Jour* ("Metamorphoses of the Day"), in which he made systematic use of this device, was a sensation, as was his later *Scènes de la Vie Publique et Privée des Animaux.*

Grandville then took up a whole series of liberal and radical causes, using his pen to mercilessly attack the regime of King Louis-Philippe. At the same time he also illustrated La Fontaine's *Fables,* Swift's *Gulliver's Travels* and Defoe's *Robinson Crusoe,* for which he created a weird menagerie of half-human, half-animal characters.

In the 1840s Grandville suffered a series of personal tragedies—first the death of two young sons, then that of his wife—and these losses embittered him further. He started drawing morbid, nightmarish scenes in such works as *Métamorphoses* and especially in *Un Autre Monde* ("Another World," 1844). When his third son died, it was too much for Grandville to bear, and he himself died a short time later, on March 17, 1847.

Grandville's visionary and hallucinatory art has been much praised by the Surrealists, who claimed him as one of their precursors. In 1857, in a very lucid essay on Gérard and his work, Baudelaire wrote, "There are some superficial minds who are amused by Grandville; as for me I find him terrifying." After a long eclipse, Grandville's artistic reputation is now at its zenith; many of his books have been recently reprinted in France, and a number of his cartoons have appeared regularly in the *New York Review of Books.*

M.H.

GERBERG, MORT (ca. 1930-   ) American cartoonist and author born in Brooklyn, New York, in the 1930s. He is best known for his magazine cartoons and for writing *Cartooning: The Art and the Business,* considered by many one of the best guidebooks especially about magazine cartooning. Mort Gerberg graduated from Brooklyn's Lafayette High School and drew a comic strip for the student newspaper, following the example of a predecessor at Lafayette named Maurice Sendak. He then attended City College of New York majoring in advertising. His cartooning began to flourish on student publications at City College.

Following two years in the U.S. Army, Gerberg worked five years in the newspaper and ad promotion field, before devoting himself to freelance cartooning. He considers himself self-taught as a cartoonist. His influences as a child were the comic strips *Skippy* and *Alley Oop.* As a young man he studied the styles of Charles Saxon and Frank Modell in the *New Yorker.* His first published professional

Ravens as medical students.
Jean-Ignace-Isidore Gérard ("Grandville"), lithograph from "Les Métamorphoses du Jour," 1829.

Hang In There!

Mort Gerberg, "Hang in There." © Chicago Tribune-New York News.

magazine gag cartoons were in the legendary satirical magazine *The Realist* in 1962. He also began to sell regularly to the many magazine gag markets that then existed, such as *Saturday Evening Post*, *Saturday Review*, *Look*, *Harper's*, *Esquire*, and his more risqué cartoons to "men's" magazines such as *Cavalier*.

In 1963 he made his first sale to *Playboy* and in 1965 sold his first cartoon, a full page, to the *New Yorker*. He had reached the top markets for magazine gag cartoons and has remained a cutting edge humorist, both satirical and sexy in their pages ever since. Often topical, Gerberg's take on the first wife being divorced by her corporate exec hubby shows two women talking over coffee. One says, "He didn't exactly ask for a divorce—he offered me an early-retirement package."

Gerberg has written and/or illustrated 37 books for adults and children. These include *Joy in Mudville: The Big Book of Baseball Humor* with Dick Schaap and for children, *More Spaghetti, I Say*, which has sold over 800,000 copies. However, his most important book is *Cartooning: The Art and the Business*, which was re-published in 1989 by William Morrow and recently went into its seventh printing. An earlier edition was entitled *The Arbor House Book of Cartooning* when published in 1983. Gerberg's career also demonstrates that few are given the luxury of exclusively being magazine gag cartoonists anymore. In his basic book on cartooning, he describes truthfully how creative people have to hustle to keep on top.

Beginning in 1975, he joined the faculty at Parsons School of Design, New York City, where he taught cartooning for over 16 years. Gerberg worked in television in New York City at NBC's local news program for several years. There he created two topical cartoons a day drawing/performing on camera, the "Cartoon Views of the News."

Gerberg's personal experience with syndication includes drawing the panels *There Ought To Be A Law* for United Media and *Hang In There*, about financial problems, for Tribune Media Services. The Tribune also syndicated *Koky*, a contemporary family comic strip about a working mom, her husband and kids between 1978-1980. He co-created the strip with gag writer Richard O'Brien. Recognizing the possibilities of computer technology, Gerberg has recently been an information content provider for ABD Multimedia, Prodigy, America Online and on the WorldWide Web's Bookwire, which hosts his *Gerberg's Gallery* site.

Gerberg's sophisticated black and white *Playboy/New Yorker* style cartoons are collected in the following anthologies: *Boys Love Girls, More Or Less*; *Right on, Sister*, about women's liberation; *The All-Jewish Cartoon Collection*; *More All-Jewish Cartoons, Yet*; and *Try It, You'll Like It*.

B.C.

GERTIE (U.S.) Winsor McCay's *Gertie, the Trained Dinosaur* may well be the most famous cartoon short in the entire history of animation. Hundreds of articles and glosses have been written on its inception, its technique, its artistry, its influence—yet there is uncertainty as to the date of its first showing. For a long time it was generally accepted that *Gertie* was released as a vaudeville act in 1909; recent research, however, has led some to settle on 1914 as the likeliest date. This conclusion is based on the actual date of copyright and on various newspaper announcements of *Gertie's* theatrical release. Yet the Museum of Modern Art, in its description of the films in its archives, gives *Gertie's* date of birth as 1909 and flatly states that the 1914 showing was a reissue. Some doubt, therefore, still persists. (To add to the confusion, there are two sets of *Gertie* prints in existence: one of the original one-reel cartoon, and the other with live-action film of McCay, George McManus and other cartoonists added at the beginning and end.)

Gertie was reportedly the result of a bet made between McCay and McManus (and recorded in the prologue of

"Gertie, the Trained Dinosaur," 1914. © Winsor McCay.

the extended *Gertie* print); to win his bet McCay single-handedly turned out the more than ten thousand drawings that went into *Gertie.* The artist then took his creation on the vaudeville circuit, where, dressed as a circus lion tamer, he would order his cartoon dinosaur through her paces, even throwing a ball for her to balance on her nose.

Gertie, the Trained Dinosaur created a sensation with the public and elicited unbounded admiration from fellow cartoonists. It is unquestionably the first work of animation art. Dick Huemer, Isidore Klein and others have described the shock *Gertie* created in the ranks of the cartooning profession when it was first released. The cartoon was such a commercial and critical success that McCay was prompted to follow with *Gertie on Tour* (1916), a two-minute sequel not without charm and invention, but decidedly less spontaneous and exuberant than the original.

It should be noted that McCay's son Robert tried to bring his father's creation to the newspaper pages in the 1940s in a comic strip called *Dino,* but this attempt at resurrection met with little success.

M.H.

GETTERMAN, ORLA (1913-) Danish cartoonist born in Copenhagen, Denmark, in 1913. Orla Getterman, whose pen name is "Get," started out as a cartoonist on a number of minor dailies and weekly magazines. He made a name

Orla Getterman. © PIB.

Giulo Gianini (and Emanuele Luzzati), "The Thieving Magpie." © Gianini-Luzzati.

for himself with his front cover cartoons in the cartoon magazines that mushroomed during the German occupation of Denmark (1940-45). With his clean and realistic, sometimes quite streamlined style of drawing, he is sure to produce eye-catchers, and his strong point is in the one- or two-column panel.

Getterman's international success is *Naboens Helle,* a daily panel that is syndicated to more than one hundred European dailies (in the United States and South America it is distributed under the name of *Ginger* through United Feature Syndicate). A *Ginger* Sunday page was discontinued, however, failing as have many of his attempts at strips (among them *MacMoney.* a daily strip running from 1953 to 1959). In the pantomime drawing, however, his abundant imagination and impact of line always come into their own, as in *Televiews,* a panel syndicated to a substantial number of dailies, now in its 20th year.

Getterman is a frequent supplier to magazine and newspaper humor columns and also an illustrator of crossword puzzles, humorous short stories, etc.

J.S.

GIANINI, GIULO (1927-) Italian cartoonist and animator born in Rome, Italy, in 1927. Giulo Gianini started his career in the 1950s as a movie cameraman. At the same time he indulged his love for drawing by contributing occasional cartoons to Rome newspapers. In the late 1950s this double interest led him into partnership with Emanuele Luzzati to produce animated films. Their collaboration has given birth to a number of quality cartoons, with the better-known Luzzati taking credit as director and Gianini acting as his chief operator and assistant. Starting with *The Paladins of France* in 1960, the films produced by Gianini and Luzzati include *House of Cards* (1962), *The Thieving Magpie* (1964), *The Italian Girl in Algiers* (1968), *Ali Baba* (1970), *Marco Polo* and *Pulcinella* (1973). After the 1979 *Il Flauto Magico* ("The Magic Flute"), the duo went on to make their last film together, *Il Libro* ("The Book") in 1984. Since that time Gianini has done a series of undistinguished cartoons on his own (the most interesting being the 1986 *Cornelius*).

Gianini has also worked on his own, and the films he produced have a more somber, less sunshiny look than the ones done in partnership with Luzzati. *Le Message* (1967) and *Swimmy* (1970) are both based on the disturbing drawings of the Belgian cartoonist Michel Folon, while the 1969 *Federico* is a children's tale more terrifying than entertaining.

S.T.

GIANNELLI, EMILIO (1936-) Italian cartoonist born in Siena on February 25, 1936. He graduated in law at the University of Siena, passed the bar examination and later became the head of the legal department of the Bank Monte dei Paschi di Siena. Now he is the general manager of the Foundation Monte dei Paschi di Siena which holds a share of the same bank.

Since he was a teenager, Giannelli enjoyed drawing cartoons which appeared in school magazines, and later on in local newspapers and also in the house organ of the bank for which he was working. In 1980 Giannelli started to contribute political cartoons for the nationwide daily *La Repubblica* and in 1991 he moved as editorial cartoonist to the first page of the other Italian national daily, *Corriere della Sera,* to which he still collaborates. His cartoons have also been printed in different periods of time in the weekly magazines *Epoca, Panorama, L'Espresso.*

Giannelli's cartoons, mainly devoted to the Italian political scene and based on plays upon words, are drawn with caricatured accuracy and care for details, which make them quite intelligible. He looks at politics as a farce, a comic opera. This accounts for his satirical tone which is never bad-tempered or wicked, but gentle, and it also explains why he likes to dress up Italian politicians in period costumes and set the present Italian political situations in the historical or literary past of the nation. Since the mid-1980s Giannelli's cartoons have been regularly collected in books: *Fratelli d'Italia* (1985), *Scherza coi santi* (1986), *Visti da dietro* (1987), *Contropelo* (1988), *Alla faccia loro* (1989), *Gli inaffondabili* (1990), *Gli uomini che disfecereo l'Italia* (1991), *Senza parole* (1993), *In fondo a destra* (1994), *Servo Vostro* (1995), *Olivolì-Olivolà* (1996), *Il re nudo* (1997), *Cacciaballe* (1997).

Giannelli has received many awards including the Dattero d'Oro (Bordighera, 1985), the Prize Forte dei Marmi for Political Satire (1986) and the Prize Città di Tolentino (1997).

G.C.C.

Gianelli. © Emilio Gianelli.

Charles Dana Gibson, "The Eternal Question," 1903.

GIBSON, CHARLES DANA (1867-1944) American artist born in Roxbury, Massachusetts, on September 14, 1867. With Thomas Nast, Charles Dana Gibson had more impact on American life than any other artist or cartoonist.

Gibson was born into a somewhat prominent family of New England stock and early betrayed artistic talent, producing marvelous cutout silhouettes of realistic human figures and fanciful animals. As a young man he lived in Flushing, Long Island, and aspired to a career in art. His companions, fortunately, provided the contacts and environment for an entry into the cartooning profession: among his friends were Victor and Bernard Gillam, Grant Hamilton and Dan Beard. In Beard's studio Gibson took the entrance examination for the Art Students League, and then entered the school in 1884.

After two years of study, some decidedly poor drawings were rejected by various New York humor magazines, but finally one cartoon—unsigned—was accepted by *Life* and ran in the March 25, 1886, issue. Thereafter Gibson's cartoons appeared with greater frequency (in *Life,* profusely in *Tid-Bits* and *Time* and occasionally in *Puck* into 1887). Seldom does an artist display such a discernible, rapid and qualitative progress in drawing style as Gibson did over those next few years. His drawings were transformed from awkward, tight scribblings to breezy, carefully cross-hatched cartoons; for awhile, however, the figures alternated from anatomical curiosities to obvious swipes from classic and academic poses. He drew, in these early days, as many political as social cartoons.

In 1878 he traveled to England (where he paid a call of homage on George Du Maurier) and France and returned to America with a mature, photographic style that immediately made him the illustrator most sought-after by the popular monthlies. His work was gripping and detailed, breathing life. He had mastered (one of his many tangible and intangible improvements) the art of molding and shaping his figures by means of fluid shading lines; every pen stroke indicated depth and texture as well as shadow.

But Gibson reaffirmed his status as a cartoonist, favoring his cartoons in *Life* over "finer" illustrations (indeed, in later years, when the genteel dubbed him a caricaturist," he rejected the euphemism and proudly called himself a cartoonist). In the early 1890s, when Gibson's society cartoons were attracting widespread notice, *Puck's* Charles Jay Taylor was drawing his *Among the 400* series featuring his beautiful high-bred "Taylor-made Girl"; and Sid Ehrhart's earthy, busty beauties were also appearing in *Puck. Life* responded by bestowing the monicker "Gibson Girl" on its prize artist's creations, and this alliterative fortuity combined with Gibson's "voguishness" to produce a national sensation that spawned many imitators and dictated the fashions and mores of a generation. Beards were suddenly out, due to Gibson's depiction of the "ideal beau." And the American woman became a wasp-waisted, somewhat tousled, haughty, athletic beauty. Gibson's models included the ill-fated but lovely actress Evelyn Nesbit and a close friend, dashing Richard Harding Davis.

As his pen line became firmer, his cartoons became more striking—in characterization if not conception. His cartoons at once reflected and led manners, fashions, morals. They stand today as representations of what Gibson's contemporaries thought, how they acted and reacted and what their very basic social conventions were; many of his themes deal with embarrassing situations and lovers' discussions.

Soon Gibson was one of America's most famous celebrities. The Gibson Girl was merchandised widely, and amid much fanfare her creator signed a $100,000 contract to draw exclusively for *Collier's*, excepting work as he desired for *Life*; Gibson's loyalty to his discoverer was fierce. In 1905, in a shocking move dictated not so much by an aversion to the pen as a desire to conquer new worlds, Gibson announced his retirement as a cartoonist and left America and enormous wealth behind to study and paint in Europe. He returned in 1910 and was persuaded to illustrate a Robert Chambers story; *Life* cartoons resumed a year later. His style now was more sketchy than bold but was softer and dealt with less serious subjects than before, except during the war years when weekly anti-kaiser cartoons by Gibson appeared.

In 1920, after the death of *Life*'s founders, Gibson became owner and editor of the magazine that had originally graced him with his first signs of encouragement. Unfortunately he was a better artist than editor, and although in many ways the early 1920s were *Life*'s best years, his reign ultimately stultified the magazine. Gibson sold out in the early 1930s after a threatened suit by Norman Anthony, hired from *Judge* to pep up *Life's* circulation and fired because he was succeeding in a jazzy way. Gibson returned to the easel and died in retirement at his estate in Maine in 1944.

Gibson illustrated 20 books, most notably *Gallegher* by Richard Harding Davis. He served several terms as president of the Society of Illustrators, and as head of the Division of Pictorial Publicity during World War I, he waged an impressive propaganda campaign. Among his many honors, he was named doctor of fine arts by Syracuse University in 1931. His popular series included *The Education of Mr. Pipp, A Widow and Her Friends* and *Mr. Tagg*. Sixteen collections of his cartoons were published, as well as a larger compilation titled *The Gibson Book* (two volumes, 1906).

Gibson's contribution to American life was enormous, and in the cartoon world his influence can be assessed by the number of imitators in his wake. Some transcended sycophant status (e.g., Flagg, Orson Lowell), but hundreds merely aped Gibson's amazing grasp of his time and his art.

R.M.

GIBSON GIRL, THE (U.S.) The Gibson Girl, never a formal, titled series, was nevertheless one of the most identifiable and avidly followed cartoon creations in history. However, the Girl was not the same character from cartoon to cartoon, except on rare occasions. Rather, Charles Dana Gibson's conception of the ideal American woman was a type. Ultimately the Gibson Girl transcended the comic pages and gave her name to countless real-life imitators.

Gibson's drawings in *Life* in the late 1880s and early 1890s featured handsome men and strong-willed, athletic young women. As Gibson's drawings matured, so did his characterizations and popularity. Soon his cartoons became the arbiter of fashions, coiffures, leisure activities, tonsorial standards and the like. The artist was fortunate to be drawing during the greatest period of ostentation in American high society, but his women were not always members of "the 400." They were to be found in any social position in any cartoon. What made a Gibson Girl was her attitude—a magical blend of authority and winsomeness, the tilt of the hat and arch of an eyebrow. She was liberated but not a suffragist, a post-Victorian phenomenon.

Countless imitators followed in Gibson's path—many aping his style (or trying to), e.g., James Montgomery Flagg, Penrhyn Stanlaws and Howard Chandler Christy. All named their women after themselves and produced series of prints, as Gibson had done; other imitators included R.M. Crosby, Walter Tittle, Rudolph Schabelitz,

Orson Lowell and Gordon Grant. Indeed, a whole generation of "pretty girl" magazine cover artists can be traced to Gibson's inspiration.

Not since the *Yellow Kid* blitz had there been such a flurry of cartoon-inspired merchandising and popularization. In 1901, Marguerite Merrington starred in the two-act *Gibson Play. The Belle of Mayfair* of the 1906 Broadway season had a song singing the Gibson Girl's praises. The first Ziegfeld Follies (1907) contained the hit song "The Gibson Bathing Girl." The Girl's face and endorsement appeared on all types of ladies' fashions; famous Gibson Girl cartoons were burned into a series of Doulton porcelain plates; next to them on tables were Gibson Girl souvenir spoons. A wallpaper pattern with Gibson Girl heads was a popular seller for bachelor apartments. Pyrography, a popular craft at the turn of the century, appropriated her face for designs on pillows, handkerchiefs, chair backs, etc. And an unending series of prints—often limited and signed—was enormously popular.

R.M.

GIERSZ, WITOLD (1927-   ) Polish animator born in Poraj, Poland, in 1927. Witold Giersz studied economics but later switched to art, graduating in 1950. After working as a painter and newspaper cartoonist in the early 1950s, Giersz joined the animation studio of Bielsko-Biala in 1956, directing *The Secret of the Old Castle* that same year. This was followed by *In the Jungle* (1957), *Musical Adventures* (1958) and *The Gnomes in Spring* (1959), all unpretentious and charming little cartoon fantasies.

In 1960 Giersz organized the Warsaw unit of Bielsko-Biala, which was later to become Miniatur Film Studio. There he produced what is probably his best-known cartoon, *The Little Western* (1960), a clever, good-natured parody entirely painted in watercolors. More cartoons followed: *The Treasure of Black Jack* (1961), a spoof of adventure films; *Dinosaurs* (1962); *Red and Black* (1963), an amused look at bullfighting; *Ladies and Gentlemen* (also 1963), a sharp look at the war between the sexes; and *The File* (1966), a dig at bureaucracy. Giersz abandoned his humorous, lighthearted approach to describe the taming of a wild stallion with dramatic graphic effects (*Portrait of a Horse*, 1967), but he soon reverted to his usual levity with *The Intellectual* (1969). In 1968-69 he worked in Yugoslavia, returning to Poland to direct *The Glorious March* (1970). His output in the 1970s has been mixed, alternating between light and serious subjects. Titles of some of his recent films are: *The Stuntman* (1972), *An Indonesian Family* (1973), *The Old Cowboy* (1974) and *Traces* (1975). Since the 1980s he has worked mainly in live-action filmmaking.

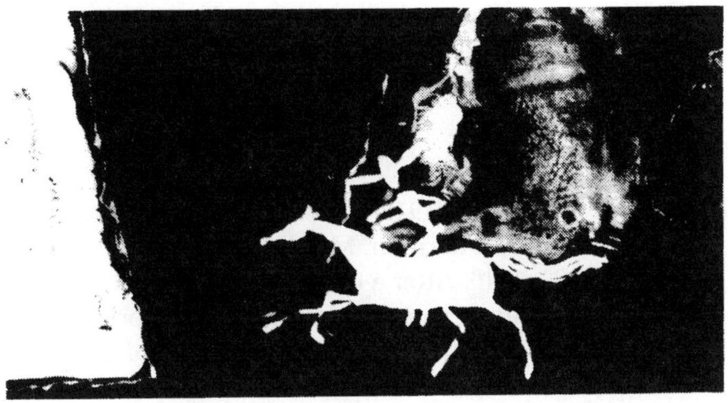

Witold Giersz, "The Little Western." © Miniatur Film.

One of the most talented practitioners of the Polish school of animation, Giersz is a dazzling artist of color, spraying bright splashes of paint on celluloid to obtain dramatic effects. He is also an *auteur* of great wit and perception who uses his medium with a deft touch, never descending to preachment or obviousness.

M.H.

GIL
See Lenoir, Carlos.

"Good evening, Sir Launcelot."

Carl Ronald Giles, 1940. © Reynolds News.

GILES, CARL RONALD (1916-1995) British cartoonist born in Islington, London, on September 29, 1916. Carl Giles, O.B.E., was the last and perhaps most popular of the great British newspaper cartoonists. His education was of the Council School variety that he has immortalized in his cartoons of Chalky and the kids. His family was from ancient East Anglian stock, and the little black grandma of his cartoons was autobiographical. At 14 he left school to become an office boy in Wardour Street film offices, and with his native ability to draw and fib, he talked himself into a job as an animator with an advertising-short film company. When Roland Davies began to produce his newspaper strip *Come On Steve!* as an animated series from a studio in Ipswich, Giles joined him: Giles was the only experienced animator on the team!

Giles's signature to cartoons and strips first began to appear in the Sunday newspaper *Reynolds' News* during World War II (1940). He drew a weekly topical panel and the pantomime strip *Young Ernie.* He joined the Beaverbrook Newspapers in 1943, alternating with Sidney Strube in the *Daily Express* and weekly in the Sunday Express. Here he established his style and regular characters—the Cockney family, the Cockney schoolkids, the wealthy GI's, etc. His sense of humor, present in every drawing, was a new characteristic in the newspaper cartoon and quickly established him at the top of his profession.

Arthur Christiansen, the executive editor of Express Newspapers who "spotted" Giles, wrote in an introduction to one of Giles's annual collections: "Giles does not caricature. He does not fake. He does not invent. He draws real buildings, real pubs, real railway stations. . . . And he draws from the largest and finest selection of models that any artist could wish—the British people." Her Majesty the Queen, awarding Giles the Order of the British Empire in 1959, said: "I might be accused of exaggeration if I said that the Englishman's ability to laugh at himself has won us the British Empire, but I am sure that it has contributed a good deal to keeping it together." In his later years he attained star status with many exhibitions of his works organized in galleries and museums throughout Britain, including a giant retrospective following his death on August 27, 1995.

Books: *Sunday and Daily Express Cartoons* (annually from 1943); *Children* (1955); *The Wit of Prince Philip* (1965); and *Nurses* (1974).

D.G.

GILL, ANDRÉ
See Gosset de Guines, Louis.

GILLAM, BERNARD (1856-1896) American cartoonist and publisher born in Banbury, England, on April 28, 1856. Bernard Gillam moved with his family to the United States in 1866, shortly after the Civil War's end, and settled in New York. He always displayed an inclination toward art, and a perhaps apocryphal story has the famous preacher Henry Ward Beecher encountering the impoverished Gillam in his youth and sponsoring his art training. (If the story is true, Gillam did not respond in kind—or with kindness—as he and fellow cartoonists were later to vilify Beecher mercilessly.) His first job was as a copyist in a lawyer's office, and he studied engraving at the same time.

Gillam sold his first cartoon in 1876 and was soon contributing ideas and cartoons to two of the nation's leading cartoon markets, the Leslie publications and the *New York Graphic.* When James A. Wales left *Puck* magazine to found *Judge* in 1881, Joseph Keppler needed a full-time political cartoonist to balance the social humor in his pages. When he plucked Gillam from *Leslie's* he was following a pattern: Keppler and Opper, another *Puck* mainstay, were alumni of the *Leslie's* shop.

The British-born cartoonist added a new element to the predominantly German *Puck* staff and soon became one of its stars through his powerful cartoons. He is most remembered for his vicious anti-Blaine cartoons in the American presidential campaign of 1884 (such as the Tatooed Man, a concept used by Keppler in similar contexts years before), although Gillam reportedly took little interest in politics (when he did, however, he admitted to Republicanism). He is recorded as actually having voted for Blaine.

In 1886, after Wales made a decided failure of running *Judge* and sold it to entrepreneur William J. Arkell, the latter lured Gillam away from *Puck* with a half-interest in the magazine. Eugene Zimmerman also followed Gillam, and it was rumored that the Republican party itself invested heavily in *Judge* to make it a counterpart to *Puck.* Gillam was now able to give his crusades full range, although the fire of the 1884 campaign never returned (as was true with Keppler). *Judge*'s position was somewhat obscured as it straddled the Harrison Blaine fence, but under Gillam it remained obdurately anti-Cleveland. Gillam died in his prime at Canajoharie, New York, on January 19, 1896.

Bernard Gillam was for a short period the most partisan cartoonist of his day and seemed sure to earn the mantle passed by Nast to Keppler. His fame was great and his cartoons bitingly powerful, but his most famous creations were simple assignments designed in *Puck's* editorial sessions. His cartoons were technically proficient and carefully detailed, and perhaps it was their stiff, mechanical nature that kept them from achieving Keppler's verve and Opper's native humor.

Lest he be judged too harshly, it should be noted that Gillam is in the league with the early giants because his vision was great and his executions bold. He never shied from difficult subjects, artistically or thematically. His stiff, slashing lines and forthright use of color lent a solidity to the art of the cartoon and accomplished the task of every cartoonist—to command attention.

R.M.

GILLAM, F. VICTOR (1858?-1920) American cartoonist, brother of Bernard Gillam, presumably his close contemporary. As Bernard Gillam was graduating from the black-and-white *New York Graphic* to the colored *Puck* in 1883, his brother Victor was assuming major cartooning duties on *Puck*'s Republican rival, *Judge.* Until Bernard's death in 1896, the public was largely in ignorance of their family relationship—even when Bernard switched to *Judge* in 1885; for Victor signed his cartoons "F. Victor" until he was the only cartooning Gillam.

Victor Gillam's style was, like his brother's, a bit harsh, with slashing lines instead of the smoother contours of, say, Grant Hamilton or the later Zim. Practically all his work was done on stone in color. As an idea man, in terms of partisanship and biting advocacy, he was easily the equal and perhaps the superior of his brother. He mercilessly attacked Grover Cleveland and even William McKinley in supporting his own favorite Republicans; he was at the cutting edge of the "Full Dinner Pail" campaign of 1896 and accused perennial Democratic presidential candidate William Jennings Bryan of everything from nihilism to vagrancy and lunacy.

Victor Gillam left *Judge* after the turn of the century, in the latter part of the first decade, and was reported to be drawing in Colorado. His later activities included work in the advertising field, where he created and painted the "His Master's Voice" image for Victor records and record players. He died in 1920.

R.M.

GILLIAM, TERRY V. (1940-) American animator, actor and film director born in Minneapolis, Minnesota, on November 22, 1940. After a college education on the West Coast, Terry Gilliam went to New York and worked as an assistant editor on Harvey Kurtzman's *Help!* (1960), a monthly satire magazine designed as a successor to *MAD.* After the magazine folded, Gilliam moved to Europe, where he set up as a freelance illustrator and cartoonist.

Unable to sustain a steady income, he turned to comedy writing for television and in 1968 sold a couple of short skits to *Do Not Adjust Your Set* (London Weekend). This experimental series attempted to broaden the horizons of juvenile entertainment, and among its team of performers were Eric Idle, Michael Palin and Terry Jones. For Gilliam, it would prove a rendezvous with fate.

An experimental comedy series for adults followed, entitled *We Have Ways of Making You Laugh.* Its scriptwriter, Dick Vosburgh, made a hobby of collecting on tape the inane linking chatter of radio disc jockey Jimmy Young. There seemed to be no way of using this material on television until Gilliam came up with a concept of cutout animation, using clippings of photographs, drawings, lettering and anything visual that came to hand. The resulting sequence was run on the show and proved so hilarious that Gilliam was awarded a regular spot. This led to further animation sequences for the Marty Feldman series *Marty* (1969), which in turn led to a series that proved a watershed in adult television comedy, *Monty Python's Flying Circus.*

Gilliam's reunion on this series with Idle, Palin and Jones, plus John Cleese and Graham Chapman, all as writer-performers, brought a unique, insane, freewheeling humor to television; the stage was set each week by Gilliam's animated title sequence. He also contributed at least one animation sequence per show, always using the technique he had evolved: a combination of cutout ready-made material with original airbrush figure and background art. Not content with supplying the noises and voice-overs, Gilliam began to make bit-part appearances in the body of the show itself: in one famous burlesque he is the bloated figure belching "Beans! Beans!"

Gilliam's animated sequences appeared on the cinema screen for the first time in the Python movie *And Now for Something Completely Different* (1971). He went on to appear in the stage version of *Monty Python,* acted as co-producer on the feature film *Monty Python and the Holy Grail* (1975) and attained a high level of excellence by producing and directing the outrageous live-action fantasy *Jabberwocky* (1976). Later films he directed include *Time Bandits* (1980), *Brazil* (1983), *Adventures of Baron Munchausen* (1989), and *The Fisher King* (1991).

D.G.

GILROY, JOHN (1898-1985) John Thomas Gilroy, a brilliant cartoonist in full colors, was the man behind many of the famous Guinness Irish Stout campaigns from the Thirties to the Fifties. His hilarious characters, including a put-upon zoo keeper (catchphrase: "My Goodness! My Guinness!") and a long-billed toucan ("Just think what 'toucan' do!"), are still remembered in an era when advertising has changed vastly from the old style of comfortable comedy.

Gilroy was born in Newcastle-upon-Tyne on May 30, 1898. His father was a painter, and home encouragement led to study at the King Edward VII School of Art, followed by the Royal Academy of Art in 1919, when he won a travelling scholarship. He became a teacher there, designing advertising posters in his evenings off. In 1925 he joined the staff of the agency S.H. Benson, and began working for Guinness in 1925, a run that would last 43 years. He illustrated the *Mustard Club Recipe Book,* which was written for Colman's Mustard in the Twenties by the young Dorothy L. Sayers. He also drew a number of colored covers for special issues of *Radio Times* in the Thirties. After World War Two he began portrait painting, and his models included Winston Churchill and H.M. Queen Elizabeth. He died on April 11, 1985.

D.G.

GINGER NUTT (G.B.) With his cheery cry "Chipetty-chippety!," Ginger Nutt, a red squirrel, scampered out of his treehouse and into *It's a Lovely Day* (1949). He was off on a fishing expedition despite all the pranks played by his pals Corny Crow, Dusty Mole (with the dark glasses on the end of his nose) and Loopy the Mad March Hare. Ginger Nutt (pun-named after a popular biscuit) was the first and only "star" of the *Animaland* series of animated cartoons produced by ex-Disney aide David Hand for the J. Arthur Rank enterprise Gaumont British Animation (GBA). Previous entries in the series (Ginger's debut came in number 8) had all featured on-off characters, and it was felt that greater audience appeal would be found if a cartoon star could be created.

Ginger was given a girl friend in the second of the series, the first to feature his name in the title: *Ginger Nutt's Bee Bother* (1949). She was Hazel Nutt. The third entry, *Ginger Nutt's Christmas Circus* (1949), was very special, as it rounded up all the *Animaland* characters from earlier cartoons for "guest star" appearances. Cooky Cuckoo was the one-man (one-bird) band, Digger and Dinkum from *The Platypus* were the jugglers, and Zimmy Lion, Oscar Ostrich and Chester Cat all appeared in supporting roles. The last cartoon, the fourth, was also the last GBA release: *Ginger Nutt's Forest Dragon* (1950).

Director for the series was Bert Felstead, with story supervision by Ralph Wright, screenplays by Pete Griffiths, Reg Parlett and R.A.G. "Nobby" Clark, and music by Henry Reed. Animators included Stan Pearsall, Frank Moysey, John Wilson, Bill Hopper; backgrounds were by Betty Hansford and Kay Pearce. Among the merchandising may be mentioned *The Ginger Nutt Gift Book* (1950), a full-color annual adapted from the films, with illustrations by Reg and George Parlett, among other anonymous artists.

D.G.

GIRERD, JEAN-PIERRE (1931-) Canadian cartoonist of French origin born in Algiers, Algeria, on March 6, 1931. Jean-Pierre Girerd attended the Algiers School of Fine Arts from 1952 to 1957 and went to work for the daily *Le Journal d'Alger* at the end of his studies. There he did fashion drawings and courtroom sketches but soon turned to editorial cartooning. In June 1961, toward the end of the Algerian war, Girerd moved to the United States and soon found employment as a cartoonist on the *Minneapolis Star.* In 1964 he decided to settle in Montreal, working as a cartoonist for the newly founded daily *Métro-Express* and freelancing for the weekly publications *Le Petit Journal, Dimanche-Matin* and *Le Travail.* In 1967 he became the edi-

—"We're twelve thousand, eh!"
—"Twelve thousand and twelve, to put your mind at rest!"
Jean-Pierre Girerd. © La Presse.

torial cartoonist of the daily *La Presse,* a position he held until his retirement in 1996.

Girerd has also done gag cartoons and advertising drawings, illustrated a number of books, and contributed cartoons to the weekly news magazines *MacLean's* and *Perspectives.* He is the author of an album of comic strips, *On A Volé la Coupe Stanley* ("The Stanley Cup Has Been Stolen," 1975), and of a collection of political cartoons, *Chien Chaud . . . et les Aut' Dogues!* ("Hot Dog . . . and Other Dogs!," 1970). He won the Grand Prix at the Montreal Salon of Caricature in 1985.

Working with pen gives Girerd's cartoons an impact similar to that of the contemporary French cartoonists. He also uses other techniques, such as charcoal drawing and painting, notably for his caricatures of celebrities. Union bureaucracy, the army and the police are his favorite targets, and his experience of the Algerian war has nurtured in him a profound antimilitaristic sentiment.

S.J.

GITÉ
See Turgeon, Jean.

GIULIETTI, LEONARDO (1949-) Italian cartoonist born in Senigallia on April 25, 1949, of an Italian farmer and a Polish mother whose family name, Cemak, he uses to sign his artwork. He attended the art school and the Academy of Fine Arts. After graduation and some activity in the art field, he began to produce for some important Italian periodicals: the daily *l'Unità* (1982-1988), *Satyricon* (weekly centerfold of the daily *La Repubblica,* 1981 to 1991), and the weekly magazines *Travaso, Epoca* (1988-1990), *Panorama, L'Europeo, Rinascita.*

Two characters recur regularly throughout his work. The first is a middle-aged bald man wearing a dark grey suit—in a way, he is the personification of the middle-class manners and mentality, often sanctimonious. The second character is a teenage girl in a old-fashioned attire with a virginal and innocent outlook who seems the personification of purity and naivety. But when she faces the corruption and harshness of reality, she reveals an unexpected malice which shows through subtle puns and double meanings. This ambiguity of language enables Cemak to denounce the hypocrisy widespread in society and in politics. His wit is sometimes daring but never vulgar, sometimes a bit surrealistic and cold but always elegant and sophisticated like his graphic style.

Cemak has also written and drawn strip cartoons for the magazines *Linus* (1993-1995) and *Comix* (1995-1997), and illustrated some humorous books like *La storia del signor Pensiero* (1988) by Giovanni Scipioni, *Gli ultimi eccentrici* (1990) by Lea Vergine, *L'amore è...* (1992), *Enciclopedia comica del diritto* (1997) by Bruno Gambarotta.

Some of his cartoons have been collected in two books, *Un peccato originale* (1989) and *Homino Sapiens: lo scemo del villaggio globale* (1991), both prefaced by important art critics and academicians. Cemak has been awarded the Prize Forte dei Marmi for Political Satire (1988) and the Prize Palma d'Oro of the Salone dell' Umorismo, Bordighera (1991).

G.C.C.

Leonardo Giulietti ("Cemak"). © Leonardo Giulietti.

Louis Glackens, 1913.

GLACKENS, LOUIS M. (1866-1933) American cartoonist and animator born in Philadelphia, Pennsylvania, in 1866. Louis Glackens was the brother of Ashcan school painter and illustrator Williams Glackens. Around 1890 his work began appearing in *Puck* magazine, occasionally in the back pages; the special World's Fair *Puck* editions produced in Chicago in 1893 stretched the staff a little thin, and Glackens, still a freelancer, appeared more often. By the late 1890s he was a staffer, producing much of the interior art in the weekly. After the turn of the century, Glackens became *Puck*'s most versatile (and therefore arguably its most important) artist. He drew political cartoons in color as well as all manner of black-and-white art, from decorative pieces to straight gags to continuing strips. Thematically, he ranged from ethnic subjects to depictions of old New York in the New Amsterdam days—a favorite genre of his. Among his continuing features was *Hans and His Chums,* a strip about a little German boy and his dachshunds.

Glackens remained with *Puck* almost until it was sold to the Strauss dry-goods concern in 1914; at that time he left to become a pioneer animator. Evidently his many chores on *Puck* taught him speed as well as competence—an animator's natural ally, especially in those early days. Among the studios he worked for was the Barré-Bowers Studio, owned by Bud Fisher, where other magazine alumni turning out *Mutt and Jeff* cartoons each week included Ted Sears and Dick Huemer (*Judge*), Frank Nankivell and Leighton Budd (*Puck*), and Foster M. Follett (*Life*). Glackens also illustrated occasional articles for *Cartoons* magazine during this time. He died in New York in 1933.

Glackens had one of the most agreeable styles in cartooning—understated, not exaggerated, uncluttered, handsomely composed. He used negative space well and in color work let broad patches of pastel shades ease the eye into the cartoon. To add variation, he sometimes gave his work a mannered poster look or used a pseudo-woodcut style, but mostly his figures were drawn half-realistically, half-comically, bigger-than-normal heads being his only concession to comic conventions.

R.M.

GODFREY, ROBERT (1921-) British animator born of British parents in West Maitland, New South Wales, Australia, on January 27, 1921. Bob Godfrey, who has been dubbed "the Wild Man of British Animation," was brought to England at the age of six months; he went to school in Ilford and studied art at the Leyton Art School. His first job was with the Uni-lever organization, where his artistic prowess moved him into the company's advertising agency, Lintas, as a general assistant. After war service in the Royal Marines, he returned to Lintas, then entered animation as a background artist for the Larkins company at Film Producers Guild. He worked on many industrial films, then moved to Talkiestrips, a small company producing filmstrips for industrial sponsors.

Godfrey's first animated cartoon was The *Big Parade (1952),* made with Keith Learner, an associate from Larkins. In 1954 they made *Watch the Birdie,* the first film to reflect the Godfrey sense of humor; with the capers of the camouflage-conscious Uncle Wungle Bird (*Kodachromus panchromaticus*), it echoed the kind of comedy currently popular in the radio *Goon Show.* Made on 16mm film in Godfrey's basement in Tufnell Park at a cost of ten pounds, it won the *Amateur Cine World* Ten Best award. It was the first film of Biographic Cartoons, the company Godfrey formed with Learner and Jeff Hale, and it won them a contract to make commercials for Gillette razor blades. Biographic was enlarged by the enlistment of Nancy Hanna and Vera Linnecar, old colleagues from Larkins, and quickly became the leading independent animation studio.

Continuous production of commercials enabled Godfrey to indulge in an occasional personal production under the imprint of "Biographic 4." His first solo effort, *Polygamous Polonius,* was selected for the Royal Film Performance of 1960. It was the first cartoon to reflect another aspect of Godfrey's humor—a bawdiness linked

Robert Godfrey, "Alf, Bill and Fred." © Biographic Film.

to the great British tradition of the saucy seaside postcard. He continued to mine this vein after leaving Biographic in 1965; *Henry 9 till 5,* in which a dull office clerk fantasizes outrageous sexual activities, was produced by his own company, the Bob Godfrey Movie Emporium. The third chapter of what is regarded as the "Godfrey Trilogy" was *Kama Sutra Rides Again,* an animated manual of unlikely sex positions. It was the first Godfrey cartoon to become financially viable and paved the way to *Great,* his 30-minute musical based on the life and exploits of Isambard Kingdom Brunel, Victorian builder. *Great* won the Academy Award as the Best Animated Film of 1975 and in turn paved the way for Godfrey's first feature-length cartoon, presently in production with the working title *Jumbo.*

Godfrey has also produced two successful animated series for television, *Roobarb* (1974) and *Sky-Lark* (1976), featuring Nutty Noah and Nelly, from Grange Calveley scripts. On the side he finds time to teach animation every week at the West Surrey School of Art and Design. He also ran a course on BBC television, *The Do-It-Yourself Animation Show* (1974), and wrote the accompanying book. Other notable animated films by Godfrey include *One-Man Band* (1965); *Rope Trick* (1967); *Two Off the Cuff* (1969); *Ways and Means* (1970); *The Electron's Tale* (1971); Dear Marjorie Boobs (1976) and *The Key* (1977).

Since the mid-1980s he has devoted more and more of his time to turning out political satires, many in collaboration with Steve Bell, and most attacking Margaret Thatcher. He also continued to produce animation for TV and (very witty) commercial cartoons. In November 1997 he was honored by a retrospective showing of his favorite cartoons at New York University's Tisch School of the Arts. Later films include: *Dear Margery Boobs* (1977), *Safe in the Sea* (1979), *Marx for Beginners* (1979), *Dream Doll* (1979), *Instant Sex* (1980), *Bio Woman* (1981), *Three Knights* (1982), *La Belle France* (1989), *Happy Birthday Switzerland* (1991), *Know Your Europeans* (1994), and the TV series *Bunbury Tales* (1992).

D.G.

GONICK, LARRY (1946-) American cartoonist and author born on August 24, 1946, in San Francisco. Larry Gonick forsook an early love of drawing for a foray into mathematics at Harvard University, where he received both his B.A. and M.A. His first love won out in the end, however, and he later averred, "I dropped out of mathematics graduate school and into cartooning because I wanted to abandon the esoteric for the accessible and popular."

Gonick's efforts at enlightening the masses initially took the form of the comic books he turned out for the Rip Off Press from 1978 to 1985 under the general title *The Cartoon History of the Universe*. These proved reasonably successful and turned into best-sellers when they were reprinted in two trade paperbacks a few years later. Thus encouraged, the author followed up with *The Cartoon Guide to U.S. History* (1987-88). In the meantime he had also penned *The Cartoon Guide to Genetics* (in collaboration with Mark Wheelis), *The Cartoon Guide to Computer Science*, and *The Cartoon Guide to Physics* (with Art Huffman). His latest venture in this vein has been *The Cartoon Guide to (Non) Communication* (1993), which is a revised version of an earlier work he turned out for a Belgian publisher, *New Babelonia.*

In all these endeavors Gonick's method consists in treating his serious subjects with a light, even facetious touch. A chapter of U.S. history is titled "In which happiness is pursued, with a gun," while a chapter dealing with Julius Caesar is called "Caesarian Section." In his overview of the legal institution of slavery in the South, he writes, "Race mixing was illegal—which only proves that not all the laws were enforced 100%." He doesn't even shrink from retelling old corny jokes, like "Where do you find Texas?" "Go west till ya smell it... Go south till ya step in it." Compared to the writing, the drawing is primitive, even crude, and only serves as humorous counterpoint. His works are more like comic treatises with doodles than bona fide cartoon books, but they are very entertaining, as well as highly informative in a light-hearted kind of way. Gonick may have found the key to every educator's dream—making learning fun.

M.H.

GONZÁLEZ, JOSÉ VICTORIANO (1887-1927) Spanish painter, sculptor and cartoonist born in Madrid, Spain, on March 23, 1887. José Victoriano González—known to posterity as "Juan Gris"—showed a disposition for drawing at the earliest age. His parents enrolled him in the Escuela de Artes y Manufacturas in Madrid in hopes that he would choose an engineering career, but he dropped out of school in 1904 and started contributing cartoons to the Madrid humor magazines *Blanco y Negro* and *Madrid Cómico.* In 1906 Juan Gris moved to Paris (he lived in the same building as Picasso in Montmartre) and resumed his

The supernatural child:
—"You don't have a mommy?"
"No, Papa got me with my aunt."
José Victoriano González ("Juan Gris"), 1908.

cartooning career with contributions to such magazines as *Le Cri de Paris, Le Charivari, L'Assiette au Beurre* and *Le Témoin.* His drawing style was straightforward and forceful, and he often chose social themes for his drawings.

Gris met the poet Guillaume Apollinaire, who introduced him to Cubism in 1912. He then completely abandoned cartooning for painting and sculpture. His position in the vanguard of the Cubist and abstract movements is well established and needs no further elaboration here. Gris's health deteriorated after 1923, and he died of uremia in Boulogne, near Paris, on May 11, 1927.

M.H.

GONZÁLEZ CASTRILLO, JOSÉ MARIA (1930-) Spanish cartoonist born in San Sebastian, Spain, in 1930. José María González worked first as a house painter and was then an office clerk for some years. His career as a cartoonist started in 1957, when his work began appearing under the pseudonym "Chumy-Chumez" in *La Codorniz,* the most important satirical magazine of the postwar years. In subsequent years Chumy-Chumez's cartoons were published in all the major Spanish magazines—*Triunfo, La Gaceta Ilustrada, El Hermano Lobo,* etc.—making him one of the most recognized cartoonists in Spain. Chumy-Chumez has received a number of awards, including one at the International Humor Exhibition in Montreal. He has also published several books; one of these, a fictional autobiography in cartoons, has seen print not only in Spain but also in France, Italy, Greece and the United States.

José-María González Castrillo ("Chumy-Chumez"), self-portrait. © González Castrillo.

One of the most creative of Spanish cartoonists, Chumy-Chumez often does collages as well as drawings. His work displays a peculiar humor midway between satire and social criticism, with a lot of crazy inventions thrown in. His cartoons have been called "sub-realistic," and their interpretation is often a matter of vociferous debate. Chumy-Chumez now uses a sun as his trademark, and it has become almost as popular as the cartoons themselves. From 1980 to 1997 he did a weekly series of cartoons for the magazine *Blanco y Negro*. He also worked for the daily *El Independiente*, and he had a number of his cartoons compiled in book form in later years. He is currently writing articles for the magazine *El Golondriz*.

J.M.

GOODRICH DIRT (U.S.) In the second decade of the century animation was flourishing in all parts of the United States. Working in Chicago, Wallace Carlson (who had started in animation as early as 1915) produced a number of series which he released first through Essanay and later through Metro. His most notable creation was Goodrich Dirt, a slightly disreputable character in the tradition of the countless tramps and hoboes made popular by Charlie Chaplin and Happy Hooligan. Goodrich was a scraggly, unkempt and unredeemable bum who stopped at nothing in his pursuit of a square meal or a dishonest buck. *"Lunch Detective"* (1917) is a good example of the early entries in the *Goodrich Dirt* series.

In later cartoons Goodrich was to assume many guises, from railway cop to sheepherder, while remaining true to his unshaven, slovenly self. "Goodrich Dirt, Cowpuncher" (1918), for example, displays the diminutive tramp's underhanded talents in a tale of one-upmanship between rival cowhands. The series unfortunately ended in 1919, when Carlson went on to direct the unsuccessful animated version of *The Gumps.*

The *Goodrich Dirt* series shows that, contrary to commonly accepted belief, silent animation in the United States had achieved a high degree of polish. Carlson's cartoons were excellently drawn, well paced and skillfully animated; even the lack of speech was no hindrance thanks to Carlson's judicious use of word balloons. One of the unsung heroes of early animation, Carlson left the medium in 1923 to devote himself exclusively to comic strip work. (For a complete biography of Wallace A. Carlson, see *The World Encyclopedia of Comics,* Chelsea House, 1976.)

M.H.

GOOFY (U.S.) Goofy developed from a canine character named Dippy Dawg who debuted in the 1932 "Mickey's Revue." Continuing to appear in an increasing number of *Mickey Mouse* cartoons, the character had his name changed to Goofy. Starting in 1935, he went on to co-star alongside Mickey and Donald Duck in some of the funniest shorts produced by the Disney studios in the middle and late 1930s. (The Goof, as he was affectionately called, gave one of his best performances in the 1936 "Moving

Day," but he was also featured in "Mickey's Service Station," "Alpine Climbers," "Moose Hunters" and others, many directed by Art Babbitt.)

By 1939 Walt Disney had decided that Goofy had a following of his own, and he starred him in "Goofy and Wilbur." This was followed by more *Goofy* cartoons, including "Goofy's Glider," "Baggage Buster" and "The Olympic Champ." In 1941 Goofy was put into a demonstration spoof called "How to Ride a Horse," and when the short proved popular, he was placed into more incongruous situations, variously illustrating in his own hapless, ingratiating way "The Art of Skiing," "The Art of Self-Defense," "How to Play Baseball," "How to Swim," "How to Dance" and "How to Play Football."

Goofy's unflappable if discombobulated behavior and his unmistakable voice characterization (built up by Disney staffer Pinto Colvig) provided most of the gags. In the late 1940s he was put into more substantial gag situations, especially in the cartoons produced under the able direction of Jack Kinney. "A Knight for a Day," "Two Gun Goofy" and "Motor Mania" are gems of invention, movement and pacing.

Despite its popularity, the *Goofy* series came to an end in the mid-1950s, when it was decided by studio executives that shorts were no longer economically feasible. Goofy made a comeback in 1992 in the television series *Goof Troop*, seen on the Disney Channel before being broadcast on ABC. An original theatrical feature, *A Goofy Movie*, was released in 1995.

Goofy had his own comic book title published by Nedor (later Standard) Comics from 1943 to 1953, at which time the character was picked up by Dell, which published his adventures until 1962.

M.H.

GOOLD, PAUL (1875-1925) American cartoonist born in Casco Bay, Maine, in 1875. Paul Goold began his cartooning career with the *Portland* (Me.) *Sunday Press and Sunday Times* as an illustrator and cartoonist, after graduating from high school. He later studied at the Yale art school.

From 1899 to 1903 Goold was on the art staff of the *New York Times* before modestly entering the magazine field. He drew mostly for *Life* but also for *Judge*. His work appeared frequently in the 1910s and shared formats and a somewhat similar reserved drawing style with fellow cartoonists A.B. Walker, Donald McKee and Paul Reilly. In the 1920s, though, the others loosened somewhat and Goold seemed a little out of place—at least in the raucous pages of *Judge*. His style was tight, uncomplicated and often static. In addition to cartoons on all subjects, he often drew title and decorative pieces. Goold was killed in a four-story fall from his Carnegie Hall studio in New York City on December 6, 1925.

R.M.

GOREY, EDWARD (1925-) American cartoonist, illustrator, designer and author born February 22, 1925, in Chicago, where his father was a journalist with the Hearst newspapers. Edward Gorey is primarily self-taught in art, although he took a few courses at the Chicago Art Institute. After service in the U.S. Army in 1944-46 he went to Harvard University, graduating with a B.A. in 1950.

Throughout the 1950's Gorey illustrated books and designed book covers. To be closer to publishers he moved to New York City in 1953, and that same year he published his first novel, *The Unstrung Harp*. Other self-illustrated books followed: *The Listing Attic* in 1954, then *The Doubtful Guest* and *The Object Lesson* (both 1957). On the other hand *The Beastly Baby*, which was the first book he had ever written, was repeatedly turned down and was finally published only in 1962 by Gorey himself under his own imprint, Fantod Press.

During the 1960's Gorey turned out a number of offbeat, slightly askew children's books, such as *The Gashlycrumb Times* (1963), *The Insect God* (1963 also), and *The Gilded Bat* (1966). With *Amphigorey* (1972), which the *New York Times* called a "retrospective exhibition" of two decades of work, the artist finally penetrated the collective consciousness of the general public. Two more anthologies followed: *Amphigorey Too* in 1975 and *Amphigorey Also* in 1983.

Among the books he has published in the last two decades, the most notable and/or most representative have been *The Loathsome Couple* (1977), *The Dwindling Party* (a very funny pseudo-mystery, 1982), *The Helpless Doorknob* (1989), *The Betrayed Confidence* (1992), *The Pointless Book* (1993), and *Fighting Acrobats* (1994). In addition he has illustrated books by others, has done watercolor and pen-and-ink drawings, and has contributed illustrations and cartoons to the *New York Times* and other publications.

Gorey has been very active in the theater of late, both as a designer and as a playwright. His elegant, lightly seasoned pastiches range from the 1985 *Tinned Lettuce* to the 1992 *Amphigorey: The Musical*. Christmas has especially appealed to his sardonic wit, with *Blithering Christmas* (1992) and *Stumbling Christmas* (1995). His warped sense of humor made him a natural to design the tongue-in-cheek titles for the crime-and-detection TV series, *Mystery!*, on PBS.

Throughout his career the artist has lived up to his name: his productions are appropriately Edwardian in mood and gory in execution. His is a private universe peopled by sinister aristocrats in cutaway coats and bowler hats, sulfurous vamps with plumed hats and long cigarette-holders, rowdies in striped turtlenecks, and disquieting, too-knowing children. Monstrous creatures pop up at the most unexpected moments, and people disappear without explanation. Weird, ghoulish, macabre, Gothic, and outré are the most common qualifiers applied to the creator's art and imagery, and to his cryptic, finicky texts.

Gorey has been the subject of a number of essays and exegeses, the latest of which is the 1996 book-length study *The World of Edward Gorey* by Clifford Ross and Karen Wilkins.

M.H.

GORIAEV, VITALY NIKOLAYEVICH (1910-) Cartoonist born in Kurgan, in western Siberia, Russia, on April 14, 1910. Vitaly Goriaev studied at the Moscow Higher Institute of Art and Technology and the Moscow Polygraphic Institute from 1929 to 1934. He started cartooning soon after graduation, with contributions to *Krokodil* beginning in 1936 and to *Frontovoi Iumor* from 1942. He is one of the most prolific among Russian cartoonists, having drawn thousands of cartoons on themes ranging from everyday life to international events. Goriaev has also traveled extensively abroad, and his series of cartoons *Americans at Home* (published in 1958) depicts the seamier side of American life.

Goriaev has illustrated a number of books, but his specialty has always been the cartoon, of which he is an acknowledged master. His graphic style, expressive and caricatural, borders on the grotesque. Many of his cartoons have been collected in book form and have earned a number of awards. Goriaev himself was awarded the Order of the Red Star and was made an Honored Art Worker in 1966.

M.H.

GOSSET DE GUINES, LOUIS (1840-1885) French caricaturist, illustrator and painter born in Paris, France, on October 17, 1840. Introduced by Nadar to the publisher Charles Philipon, Louis Gosset de Guines used the pen name "André Gill" for his satirical caricatures for Philipon's *Le Journal Amusant.* His fame spread when, in 1866, he joined the staff of the newly created *La Lune,* subsequently renamed *L'Eclipse.* During his ten-year stay with the magazine, and later for his own *La Lune Rousse* (1876-1879), he contributed a weekly caricature of the most important personalities from the world of arts, letters, politics.

Gill's caricatures of such celebrities as Victor Hugo, Gustave Courbet, Sarah Bernhardt, Richard Wagner and Napoleon III, with their enlarged heads standing on undersized bodies in comic poses and costumes, show immediately all the details of facial expression, dress and profession needed to give a very clear idea of who is being represented. Able to magnify the characteristics and idiosyncrasies of his "victims," Gill nevertheless confined himself to mere prickling fun in order not to wound; he lacks the caustic sharpness of a Daumier or a Grandville even in his political cartoons.

In addition to his cartoon work, Gill illustrated several of Zola's novels (*Nana, L'Assommoir, Le Ventre de Paris*) and exhibited his realistic paintings in various salons. At 40 he went mad and died five years later in a Paris insane asylum, on May 2, 1885.

P.H.

Louis Gosset de Guines ("André Gill"), caricature of Gustave Doré, 1878.

Ray Gotto. © Sporting News.

GOTTO, RAY (1916-) American cartoonist born in Nashville, Tennessee, on August 10, 1916. Ray Gotto once confessed that he was only interested in football and baseball in high school. Dropping out of school, he toured the country "via freight cars and thumbs," as he puts it, before landing a job as an editorial and sports cartoonist for the *Nashville Banner* in the mid-1930s. During World War II he served in the U.S. Navy as an artist on animated and documentary training films.

Back in civilian life in 1945, Gotto created *Ozark Ike,* a noted sports comic strip, for King Features Syndicate. Despite the success of the feature, he left in 1954 due to a contractual dispute with the syndicate and went on to pro-

The coalition between Lord Salisbury and Joseph Chamberlain.
Sir Francis Carruthers Gould, 1895.

duce *Cotton Woods,* another sports strip, for General Features later that same year. Unhappily, *Cotton Woods* folded after a few years, and in the late 1950s Gotto went back to his first love, sports cartooning, with occasional forays into advertising and commercial art. He designed the New York Mets emblem in 1961, and his cartoons and illustrations for the *Sporting News* have been reprinted many times. (His baseball-uniformed Uncle Sam has by now become part of the sport's popular lore.) He retired in 1990, and as he put it in his bio for the 1996 National Cartoonists Society Album, he is "now escaping all dead-lines by hiding out in Florida."

While his comic strip work has been lauded by many (see the entry on *Ozark Ike* in *The World Encyclopedia of Comics,* Chelsea House, 1976), Ray Gotto is best noted as a sports cartoonist. His contributions to the field have been many, and he has earned a number of distinctions from sporting and cartooning organizations throughout the country.

M.H.

GOULD, SIR FRANCIS CARRUTHERS (1844-1925) British cartoonist born in Barnstaple, England, on December 2, 1844. Sir Francis Carruthers Gould, who signed his work with his initials, "F.C.G.," was the first British cartoonist to contribute daily drawings to a newspaper. For more than 20 years he was a member of the London Stock Exchange, and he did not turn to professional cartooning until he was 35. His first published cartoon was printed in the Christmas issue of *Truth* in 1879.

His politically liberal cartoon comments appealed to E.T. Cook, editor of the daily newspaper the *Pall Mall Gazette,* who put Gould on contract in 1888. He began contributing to *Punch* in 1890 and changed newspapers, going to the *Westminster Gazette* in 1893. For this daily he also wrote articles and became the assistant editor. He was knighted in 1906. He was also perhaps the first political cartoonist to develop a "character" out of a living personality: his caricatures of Joseph Chamberlain, complete with distinctive monocle, took on the popular proportions of a fictional creation. Gould reckoned up one hundred different guises in which he had portrayed the prime minister in his cartoons! Outside humorous comment, he is remembered for his landscape drawings of Normandy and Brittany. He died on January 1, 1925.

Books: *ABC of the Stock Exchange* (1880); Ah Chin Chin (1880); *Evaluations in the Sit Tee Desert* (1880); *The United Artist* (1880); *Fairy Tales from Brentano* (1885); *New Fairy Tales* (1888); *New Song of Malden* (1889); *Story of the Home Rule Session* (1893); *Cartoons of the Campaign* (1895); *Who Killed Cock Robin* (1896); *Westminster Cartoons* (1896-1900); *Political Struwelpetter* (1899); *Tales Told in the Zoo* (1900); *Struwelpetter Alphabet* (1900); *Snowflakes and Snowdrops* (1900); *The Khaki Campaign* (1900); *Great Men* (1901); *Indian Fables* (1901); *New Fairy Tales from Brentano* (1902); *Froissart's Modern Chronicles* (1902); *The Westminster Alice* (1902); *Book of Country and Garden* (1903); *Peeps at Parliament* (1903); *FCG, Caricaturist* (1903); *Capture of the Schools* (1903); *Political Caricatures* (1903); *Cartoons in Rhyme and Line* (1904); *John Bull's Adventures* (1904); *Later Peeps at Parliament* (1904); *Golden Treasury* (1906); *Wild Nature in Pictures* (1907); *Nature Verses* (1923); and *Nature Caricatures* (1929).

D.G.

GOURSAT, GEORGES (1863-1934) French caricaturist and writer born in Périgueux, France, on November 23, 1863. Georges Goursat is better known under the pen name "Sem." He gave up his grocery store in his provincial hometown and went to Paris at the turn of the century, quickly becoming the most feared and admired caricaturist of the period.

Sem's first album, *Les Sportsmen* ("The Horse Fanciers"), appeared in 1900 and portrayed members of the aristocratic and snobbish Parisian high society. Thereafter, he published annually a new book of sketches with the fashionable people and resorts of *la Belle Epoque* as subjects, and these albums constitute important graphic documentation of one of France's most fascinating eras. All his faces are reduced to one extreme characteristic feature (nose, eyes, hairdo) and are drawn in profile only; the effect is sometimes witty and daring, sometimes monotonous.

Sem also illustrated Courteline's civil-service satire, *Messieurs les Ronds-de-Cuir* ("Government Bureaucrats"),

(Left, Maurice de Rothschild; right, James de Rothschild): "All the same, he has that English style!"
Georges Goursat ("Sem").

and his own books: *Un Pékin sur le Front* ("A Civilian at the Front," 1917), *Le Grand Monde à l'Envers* ("High Society Inside Out," 1919) and *La Ronde de Nuit* ("Night Watch," 1923). He died in Paris in 1934, a member of the Committee of the Salon of Humorists.

P.H.

GOYA Y LUCIENTES, FRANCISCO DE (1746-1828) Spanish painter born in Fuentetodos, near Zaragoza, Spain, on March 30, 1746. Francisco Goya received a mediocre art education in Zaragoza in his youth, and he traveled to Italy to further his education. In 1775 he was appointed to make carpet designs for the Royal Manufacture of Carpets in Madrid. During the 16 years he worked there, under the reigns of Carlos III and Carlos IV, he had access to the royal art collection. It was at this time that he became familiar with the works of Velázquez and Rembrandt. Throughout his life Goya considered these two artists his masters.

In 1792, as a result of illness, Goya became totally deaf. His deafness and the sadness it brought were strongly reflected in his art. The series of drawings entitled *Los Caprichos,* for instance, was made around this time. In 1808, during the war of independence against Napoleon, Goya painted his most famous subjects, and he also did the renowned and controversial series of engravings *Los Disastros de la Guerra* ("The Disasters of War"). Following the war Goya voluntarily exiled himself to France as the result of difficulties with the new king of Spain, Fernando VII. He died in Bordeaux, France, on April 16, 1828.

Francisco Goya, plate 53 of "Los Caprichos," 1799.

Goya was technically and artistically very much ahead of his time; his bitter and satiric tastes and his strong character made him unpopular among his contemporaries. Nobody, however, denied his extraordinary and self-willed competence as a master of the art of painting. Today, of course, Goya is universally regarded as one of the greatest artists who ever lived. *Los Caprichos* establishes Goya as one of the first cartoonists in the world. Indeed, in the 19th century these strong and satiric drawings were highly influential among cartoonists. In *Los Caprichos* "reason becomes dream" and "dream becomes reason," producing strange monsters capable of criticizing cultural regression and political repression in Spain. In the strong Castilian tradition of Quevedo and Góngora, Goya used black humor to express his own political and cultural views.

J.M.

GRAMATKY, HARDIE (1907-1979) American watercolorist, author and cartoonist born in Dallas, Texas, on April 12, 1907. Hardie Gramatky studied at Stanford University (1926-28) and at the Chouinard Art School in Los Angeles (1928-30) while drawing a little weekly strip, *Captain Kidd, Jr.,* for the *Los Angeles Times.* This science fiction/fantasy strip caught the attention of Charlie Plumb, artist on the popular *Ella Cinders,* who engaged Gramatky as penciler and letterer on the strip for $15 a week—while Plumb himself was collecting about $1,800 a week. Shortly after his ghosting stint, Gramatky was contacted by Walt Disney. In June 1932 he wrote six months' continuity for the *Mickey Mouse* strip and was hired by the studio for chores ranging from storyboarding to animation; by 1936, at the end of his four-year hitch, he was chief animator. Gramatky remembers his first sessions, with only a dozen men including Disney; when he left, the department had risen in numbers to about 250.

The major period of Gramatky's career began in 1936, when he moved to New York. He did reporting-painting jobs for *Fortune* magazine, illustrated many articles and books, and became a top-flight watercolorist, winning dozens of awards and prizes. He was a member of the National Academy and director of the American Watercolor Society. He had numerous shows of his watercolors and is represented in many museums and collections. Gramatky is probably best remembered for his series of *Little Toot* children's books, illustrated by himself; the little tugboat character has become a classic creation. And, in a full circle of sorts, Disney animated the character in 1946.

Hardie Gramatky died on May 1, 1979.

R.M.

GRANDES GUEULES, LES (France) Jean Mulatier (born December 1, 1947, in Paris) and Patrice Ricord (born June 22, 1947, in Cagnes-sur-mer, on the Riviera) met while studying art at the School of Decorative Arts in Paris in the 1960s. After graduation they each went their separate ways but joined up again in 1969 when both began working for the illustrated weekly *Pilote,* where they met Jean-Claude Morchoisne (born September 14, 1944, in Orleans, south of Paris). For almost three decades, the three of them would for all practical purposes function as a team.

They started plying their trade in earnest in December 1970 in a color feature that occupied *Pilote*'s back page and which caricatured national and international celebrities and political figures. Called *Les Grandes Gueules* (which in French can mean either "The Great Mugs" or "The Loud Mouths"), it presented each week an eclectic gallery of loaded portraits ranging from French President Georges Pompidou and Queen Elizabeth to Brigitte Bardot and Robert Redford; most of these caricatures were executed by Morchoisne, Mulatier and Ricord, with an occasional assist from outside cartoonists. Writing for the group, Mulatier in 1987 tersely summed up the artists' professional philosophy thus, "We are explorers of the human face." Each member of the group signed individually, but they succeeded in evolving a collective style that made one undistinguishable from another. The graphic excellence of their caricatures along with their psychological insight made them much admired in France and abroad, especially in the United States where the artists were featured in a 1972 *Esquire* article.

In 1974 the trio left *Pilote* to launch their own publication, *Mormoil*, in which *Les Grandes Gueules* were the main attraction. Following the failure of *Mormoil* a few years later, the group's drawings started appearing everywhere, in *Paris Match*, *Le Nouvel Observateur*, *Lui*, *Le Matin de Paris*, *Esquire*, *Time*, *Der Spiegel*, and others. At the same time collections of their caricatures were published with great success in France in the 1970s and 1980s, beginning with *Les Grandes Gueules* (1979), followed by *Grandes Gueules de France*, *Grandes Gueules par Deux* ("Loud Mouths in Two's"), *Grandes Gueules Superstars*, etc.

The association dissolved in 1987, with each member going his own way. Morchoisne has devoted his time to publishing and advertising, while Mulatier has become a roving photographer. Only Ricord has remained true to his calling, regularly contributing political and theatrical caricatures to the newsweekly *L'Express*.

M.H.

GRANDJOUAN, JULES-FÉLIX (1875-1968) French cartoonist born in Nantes, France, in 1875. Félix Grandjouan started law school in Nantes but then embarked on an artistic career by both writing and illustrating *Nantes la Grise* ("Nantes the Gray City," 1899). He went to Paris a year later and contributed cartoons to the most important satirical (and oftentimes anarchistic) journals of the begin-

The lady: "Excuse me, can you tell me—"
The clerk (roaring): "Ask at window 11."

Jules Grandjouan, 1904.

ning of this century: *Le Rire, Le Sourire, Le Canard Sauvage, Les Temps Nouveaux, L'Assiette au Beurre,* etc.

Grandjouan's 2,000 drawings deal with every political and social problem from granting Algerian independence to more enlightened labor laws, from foreign spies to the Courrières mine disaster. They have a haunting quality about them that conceals the bitterness of a socially committed artist. Grandjouan was also a fervent admirer of Isadora Duncan, whom he met in Paris in 1901. He drew 25 sketches of the American dancer (1912) in addition to illustrating, along with Bourdelle and Clará, her *Ecrits sur la Danse* (1927).

Félix Grandjouan, who was erroneously reported dead of tuberculosis in 1912, actually died in his bed in 1968 at the ripe age of 93.

P.H.

GRANDVILLE
See Gérard, Jean-Ignace-Isidore.

GRAN'POP (G.B.) Gran'pop, an artful and ancient ape, bald of pate with kneecaps to match, ginger-haired with pink patches showing through, was popular with children and adults alike. Indeed, his first appearances were in the very adult magazine *The Sketch,* that glossy weekly which had given birth, in a previous generation, to Bonzo. Lawson Wood, the painter and illustrator who fathered Gran'pop, undoubtedly had G.E. Studdy's popular pup in mind, for Gran'pop followed the trail of success blazed by Bonzo: merchandising via picture postcards, prints, children's books, novelties and, but for the outbreak of World War II, animated cartoons. Wood drew the key drawings for four Gran'pop cartoons and delivered them to the Ub Iwerks Studio in Hollywood, but the films were never made. That they were contracted for is, today, one indication of the worldwide popularity of Wood's cheerful old chimp; since the artist's death, however, the character has virtually disappeared into limbo. All that remains to show for the old ape's years of fame are the battered *Gran'pop's Annuals* and collections of Kensitas cigarette cards (1935) that change hands among nostalgic collectors at ever-increasing prices.

Lawson Wood, one of the finest black-and-white illustrators to excel in watercolor cartoons, was born in Highgate, London, in 1878. His grandfather was L.J. Wood, an architectural artist, and his father was Pinhorn Wood, a landscape painter. Lawson studied art at the Slade School and Heatherley's, with night classes at the Frank Calderon School of Animal Painting. At the age of 18 Wood entered the offices of C. Arthur Pearson, the magazine publisher, swiftly rising to a position of chief artist. The all-round experience as magazine and newspaper illustrator for six years gave him a speed and journalistic sense which, added to his academic training, made his style unique. His main line was poster design, often serious, which he supplemented with humorous cartoon work for weeklies as disparate as the *Graphic* and the colored comic *Puck.* His first "fixation" was on the prehistoric period, and his Stone Age series spanned many years. His first one-man exhibition was held in Sunderland in 1932, where it was remarked: "He is sincere in his work, for he rejoices in making people smile." He died in October 1957.

Books: The Book of *Lawson Wood* (1907); *The Bow Wow Book* (1912); *A Basket of Plums* (1916); *A Box of Crackers* (1916); *Splinters* (1916); *The Art of the Illustrator* (1918); *The Mr. Books* (1916); *The Mr. and Mrs. Books* (1918); *The Mrs. Books* (1920); *Rummy Tales* (1920); *Rummy Tales Painting* Book (1921); *Noo Zoo Tales* (1922); Lawson Wood's *Colour Books* (1925); *Jolly Rhymes* (1926); *The Scot Scotched* (1927); *Lawson Wood's Funny Farm* (1931); *The Old Nursery Rhymes* (1933); *Granpop's Annual* (1935-); *Bedtime Picture Book* (1943); *Granpop's Book of Fun* (1943); *Meddlesome Monkeys* (1946); *Mischief Makers (1946);* and *Popular Granpop* (1946).

D.G.

GRANT, GORDON HOPE (1875-1962) American cartoonist, artist and member of the National Academy born in San Francisco, California, in 1875. Gordon Grant, noted in fine-art circles as a premier marine painter, acquired a love for the sea at an early age. His father, seeking to strengthen racial and ancestral bonds, sent young Gordon to Scotland to attend elementary school; a voyage of almost five months around Cape Horn in a Glasgow sailing vessel seemed to chart the excited Grant's own artistic course.

His art training was received later at the Heatherly and Lambeth school in London. Back in the United States, practical art experience came with jobs as a newspaper artist in San Francisco and New York. These two cities were great cartoon centers, and before long Grant was a regular contributor to humor magazines. Around the turn

Gordon Grant, 1912.

of the century his work became a fixture in *Puck,* and soon thereafter his illustrations adorned the pages of the second-level popular monthlies.

Grant's work for *Puck* was at first an awkward groping for a Gibson affinity—a foible of too many cartoonists of the period. But Grant was able to rise above the throng and develop quite a handsome and distinctive style of his own: crisp, bold pen lines, judicious shading and empathetic characterizations. His "girls" were heralded, justifiably, as much as other artists' characters who followed the Gibson Girl's successes. Grant worked for *Puck* nearly until its change of ownership in 1914. He had graduated to cover art and seldom dealt with politics in his cartoons.

Gordon Grant's cartoon work is today unfortunately obscured by his other achievements—famous illustrations for Booth Tarkington's *Penrod* stories, his painting of the *Constitution* that became the focal point for the restoration of "Old Ironsides," his self-written and self-illustrated books, including *Ships Under Sail* (1941) and *The Secret Voyage* (1943), as well as his representations in many major museums and galleries.

R.M.

GRANT, VERNON (1902-1990) American cartoonist born in Coleridge, Nebraska, on April 26, 1902. Vernon Grant moved with his family to a South Dakota homestead when he was five and to California ten years later. He attended the University of Southern California for two years and received art training at the Otis Art Institute in Los Angeles. Between 1923 and 1928 he also took classes in portraiture at the Chicago Art Institute. It began to dawn on Grant that portraiture was not his calling when teachers and classmates became more excited about the fantasy drawings of gnomes and other creatures that he doodled on the borders of his paintings. He moved back to Los Angeles to do advertising work, with Wrigley, Southern Pacific and Packard autos as accounts. He also taught and had many future Disney staffers in his classes.

In 1932 Grant moved to New York to expand his activities. He immediately became *Judge* magazine's premier cover artist, painted for *Ladies' Home Journal, Liberty* and the *American Legion* magazine, and did ad work for Everready, General Motors, Westinghouse, General Electric, Arrow shirts and Junket rennet, among others. In 1933 his first cartoons apeared in Kellogg's Rice Krispies ads, and his characters—Snap, Crackle and Pop—kept Grant busy for 15 years. They are still used today (by other artists) and are among the most famous images in American advertising. King Features Syndicate was the biggest customer of Grant's career; for many years he did one cartoon cover a month for the Hearst Sunday supplement magazine. He wrote and illustrated two books, *Tinker Tim the Toymaker* and *Mixey Dough the Baker,* both for Whitman. Recently Grant has been active in his South Carolina hometown, has executed paintings and cartoons on commission, and has seen the York County Museum dedicate a gallery to him. He died in July 1990.

Vernon Grant has one of the most unique and agreeable styles in American cartooning. He does very little line work, painting in his broad, flat areas with swatches of color. His characters are cute, big-headed fantasy beings who live in the artist's world of sparse backgrounds and handsome compositions. His special creations rank with the Brownies and the Kewpies in the tradition of fantasy cartoon characters.

R.M.

GRAYSMITH
See Smith, Robert Gray.

GREEN, BERT (1885-1948) American cartoonist and animator born in England in 1885. Bert Green was taken to the United States by his parents when he was a child. After studies in art school he went on to work as a cartoonist on several New York newspapers before being promoted to art department manager on the *Chicago Examiner* in 1914. When Hearst International Film Service was established in 1916, Bert Green became one of its earliest animators and scriptwriters, working notably on *The Katzenjammer Kids.*

After the closing of Hearst's animated film operation in 1918, Green went on to create the comic strip *Kids* for the *Chicago Tribune,* and the feature lasted through the 1920s. He also produced training cartoons for the U.S. Navy through the Vocafilm Corporation during World War I, and he later wrote hundreds of humorous articles and stories for *Liberty,* the *Saturday Evening Post* and others. His satires on Prohibition (illustrated by himself) were later collected in book form under the title *Love Letters of an Interior Decorator.*

During World War II Green served as a member of the U.S. Coast Guard and was assigned to antisubmarine duty. After the war he returned briefly to cartooning. He died after a long illness at the Bronx Veterans Hospital on October 5, 1948. His contributions to the early art of animation deserve recognition.

M.H.

GREEN, WILLIAM ELLIS (1923-) Australian cartoonist born at Essendon, Melbourne, Australia, in 1923.

A visiting cartoonist from England recently remarked in Melbourne how appalled he was at the quantity of work demanded from Australian cartoonists in a week, stating that no cartoonist working in Britain would stand the pace. Among others working in Australian journalism, John Jensen's reference was of course to artists like William Ellis ("Weg") Green of the *Melbourne Herald.* He has been producing, together with other work, 11 joke ideas and drawings every week for 23 years.

Green has a declared disinterest in political cartooning, valuing his independence rather than accepting and expressing the editorial line of a newspaper. He saw one well-known cartoonist destroyed in this way, and that is not for him. His real interest is in social comment: with Weg, humor comes first, but he is adamant about sound drawing.

Weg started with the *Herald* after leaving the army (he served in New Guinea with an army intelligence unit drawing maps and general cartographic work on active service) and after studying drawing at the National Gallery School in Melbourne. Sam Wells, the *Herald's* political cartoonist, recommended Weg to do the leader

"As I was saying when the store closed last night!"
William Ellis Green ("Weg") © Melbourne Herald.

page cartoon while Wells was on holiday. Green's work impressed the staff, and an invitation to join the paper followed during June 1947.

In October 1949, his regular daily feature, *Weg's Day*—a single-column drawing wittily commenting on current news items—appeared on the front page of the *Herald* and has continued to appear daily since that time. Weg was also required to illustrate feature articles, design headings for feature departments and draw caricatures of politicians, sports figures and other personalities.

His popular pocket cartoon had been running for just under four years when, in March 1953, a new feature that made his pen name a household word all over the state of Victoria was introduced into the *Herald* columns. This was the brilliant *Weg's Weekend,* a six-cartoon panel satirizing people and events in the news, at home and abroad, and displayed across the top of a broadsheet page and to a depth of six inches or more. Weg's drawing is broadly comic and wholly original, with only faint echoes of his earlier admiration for the work of William ("Wep") Pidgeon. Drawing with pen, ink and brush, Weg condemns the modern trend of drawing with pentel-type pens, which cannot give sensitivity or quality of line to drawings. He retired in the early 1990s, along with his panel.

The wonderfully funny drawings by William Green are the work of a thoroughly professional artist, a gently mannered and articulate craftsperson concerned for the future of Australian cartoonists, resenting foreign influences and domination in terms of the threat imposed from syndicated material dumped less expensively upon the market. Although Weg has illustrated several books, no collection of his cartoons has been published.

V.L.

GREENING, HARRY CORNELL (1876-ca. 1930) American cartoonist born in Titusville, Pennsylvania, on May 30, 1876. H.C. Greening was educated in drawing techniques at the Art Students League and in 1896 began selling cartoons regularly to the *New York Herald, Life* and *Truth.* He contributed panel cartoons and one-shot strips to Hearst's *American Humorist* Sunday comic section in 1898 and soon was a frequent contributor to *Puck, Judge, Life, Harper's* and *Scribner's.* For *St. Nicholas* he drew the children's series *Prince Red Feather.*

Greening's newspaper work was soon confined to the *New York Herald* again, and there he created such strips as *Percy, Fritz von Blitz* and the classic *Prince Errant.* During World War I he served with the American Expeditionary Force as an artist and returned in the 1920s to draw for the McClure Newspaper Syndicate (a kid strip, *Eb and Flo)* and the *Illustrated Daily News* of Los Angeles. He was the inventor of Sporty Sam and Funnyfishes toys and developed the Wishbone Man Game, which was based on his *Eb and Flo* strip, as was a storybook.

At the height of his productive days, between 1900 and 1910, Greening was among the most published of American panel cartoonists. There was a feeling of humor in his work, and he eschewed the obsession with pretty illustrative techniques. His cartoons were nevertheless handsome—boldly composed and carefully shaded. His *Prince Errant,* designed to replace *Little Nemo* in newspapers, was a masterpiece of whimsy and visual delights.

R.M.

The Labor Question—Both Sides of it
H.C. Greening, ca. 1905.

GRGIĆ, ZLATKO (1931-1988) Yugoslav cartoonist born in Zagreb, Croatia, Yugoslavia, in 1931. Zlatko Grgić studied journalism and law at the University of Zagreb. In 1951 he left his studies to devote himself to cartooning and contributed a number of cartoons to *Kerempuh* and other Yugoslav humor magazines. Turning to animation in 1957, Grgić became an assistant to Nikola Kostelac and worked on *Opening Night* and *Encounter in a Dream.* The following year he was the chief animator on Norbert Neugebauer's *The False Canary* and Dušan Vukotićs *The Great Fear* and *Revenger.*

In 1960 Grgić directed his first animated films for an advertising agency. From 1960 to 1969 he variously assist-

Zlatko Grgić, "Who Are We?" © National Film Board of Canada.

ed and animated for Vukotić, Kristl, Vrbanić, Stalter and Dovniković. Under the supervision of Vukotić, Grgić directed *A Visit from Space* (1964) and *The Devil's Work* (1965), and he co-directed with Stalter two of the most celebrated of Zagreb films, *The Fifth* (1965) and *Scabies* (1969). As an independent director Grgić has realized several entries in the *Inspector Mask* and *Case* series (1961-62), as well as *Little and Big*, the delightful *Inventor of Shoes* (1967) and *Twiddle-Twaddle* (1968). He co-directed with Branko Ramtović *Tolerance* (1967) and *The Suitcase* (1969) and, along with Kolar and Zaninović, produced the popular *Profesor Balthasar* series. In 1970 Grgić also directed the whimsical *Maxi-Cat*.

In recent years Grgić has worked mainly outside of Yugoslavia. One of his more interesting efforts in animation is the 1974 *Who Are We?*, which he directed for the National Film Board of Canada. Zlatko Grgić is one of the most important creators to come out of the famed "Zagreb school"; Ronald Holloway described him as "one of the subtlest poets in the animation business." After co-directing *Dream Doll* with Bob Godfrey in England in 1979, he moved to Canada, where he worked in advertising and taught college courses. He died in Montreal in 1988.

M.H.

GRIFFIN, GEORGE (1943-) American animator born July 18, 1943, in Atlanta, Georgia. Since his father was a cartoonist as well as an architect, George Griffin's artistic inclination may be ascribed to heredity; yet unlike many of his colleagues who discovered an affinity for animation early in childhood, he did not find his calling until after his graduation from Dartmouth in 1967. After he got a job at an animation studio he realized that the assembly-line process of making commercial films did not suit him, and he boldly struck out to make his own films as an independent animator, even starting his own studio, Metropolis Graphics, in 1972.

Beginning with his first effort at animation, *Rapid Transit* in 1969, Griffin's films have tended to display a winning combination of humor, whimsy, absurdity, and self-revelation. *Rapid Transit*, for instance, uses patterns of black beams running along tracks of white paper; his next film that year, *Displacement*, was another exercise in motion and vorticity. It was with his third personal film, *The Candy Machine* (1972), that the artist scored his first critical breakthrough. Using live-action footage later xeroxed and re-photographed, this tale of an old codger fighting a recalcitrant vending machine on a subway platform has been much praised by reviewers and widely exhibited in the United States and abroad.

Ever artistically restless as well as technically experimental, Griffin toyed with hand-drawn animation in *Trikfilm I* and *III* (there is no *Trikfilm II*), explored phallic imagery in *The Club*, and utilized a variety of media to produce *Head*, which is at once an ostensibly objective self-portrait and a meditation on the art of animation. Griffin's most personal statement up to that time (1975), *Head* delighted some critics and baffled others. Perhaps as atonement, the artist went back to his previous manner of witty commentary with *L'Age Door* (a pun on Luis Bunuel's early surreal film, *L'age d'or*, in which a hapless little man tries endlessly to open one door after another in what the artist appropriately termed "an exercise in futilty."

The 1976 *Viewmaster*, based on photographer Edward Muybridge's famous motion studies, is at the same time an ironic take on the "rat race," a display of pure animation, and a homage to the nineteenth-century pioneer, as a number of figures drawn in different styles run endlessly in circles, the center of which is occupied by Muybridge's famous running man. With the 29-minute long *Lineage* (1979), Griffin realized an even more ambitious project and the one in which he further explored the techniques and experiments of the early masters of the medium. Significantly dedicated to pioneer animator Winsor McCay, this strongly autobiographical feature used line drawn directly on film, puppet animation, and live action, among other methods, as the artist struggled with his fascination for animation and the meaning of his own existence.

Griffin's more recent films have included *Ko-Ko* (1988), a visual riff on a jazz theme by Charlie Parker, and *New Fangled* (1992), a pointed satire on the jargon and ethics of the advertising profession. In the 1994 *A Little Routine*,

George Griffin, "The Candy Machine." © Metropolis Graphics.

"the brutal realities of combat in the parent/child war zone" (in Griffin's own words), are unflinchingly rendered.

Griffin's films have been presented at numerous one-man shows and have garnered an impressive number of awards. In addition to his work as an independent filmmaker, he has produced many television spots, published several flipbooks, and taught at a number of institutions of higher learning. The artist's career is best summed up in a 90-minute anthology of his shorts (along with insightful liner notes) which he produced in 1996 and pointedly called *Griffiti*.

M.H.

GRIFFIN, SYDNEY B. (1854-ca. 1910) American cartoonist born on October 15, 1854. Educated in the public schools of Detroit, Michigan, Syd B. Griffin moved to New York in 1888 to become a cartoonist. He took his drawings first to *Puck,* which rejected them, and then to its rival, *Judge,* where he was offered a position on the art staff. Griffin took the trouble to inform *Puck*'s art editor, W.B. Gibson, who replied that Griffin's drawings were refused only because their excellence suggested a lack of originality; Griffin was then offered, and accepted, a position on *Puck*'s art staff. For that great weekly, he drew—badly—occasional lithographed political cartoons but concentrated mainly on pen-and-ink panels. He remained with *Puck* until the mid-1890s, when he lost control of his drawing hand. Training himself to draw with his left hand (a similar task was to confront H.T. Webster and Tad in later years), he contributed to *Judge, Truth* and the early New York newspaper supplements; it was for the *World* that he created *Clarence the Cop* in 1901, later relinquishing it to C.W. Kahles.

In his prime—his "first" career—Griffin had an astonishingly supple line and a style that combined perfectly the animation of A.B. Frost and the sophistication of Charles Dana Gibson. For awhile he threatened to eclipse other *Puck* black-and-whiters like Opper, although his humor was not as evident as Opper's. His themes were largely suburban and rural, and his depictions still come alive on the page, filled with personality and vitality.

R.M.

GRIMAULT, PAUL (1905-1994) French animator born at Neuilly-sur-Seine, a suburb of Paris, France, on March 23, 1905. The son of an archaeologist, Paul Grimault studied art at the Germain-Pilon school, then went to work for the Bon Marché department store. After completion of his military service in 1930, Grimault worked for an advertising agency where he met André Sarrut. In 1936 Grimault and Sarrut founded Les Gémeaux (literally, "The Gemini"), producing animated cartoons for advertisers. In 1939 they released their first theatrical cartoon, *Gô Chez les Oiseaux* ("Gô Among the Birds").

The outbreak of World War II interrupted the collaboration when Grimault was drafted into the army. After demobilization, he went back to animation and in 1942 brought out *Les Passagers de la Grande Ourse* ("The Passengers of the Big Dipper"), again featuring Gô, followed in 1943 by *Le Marchand de Notes* ("The Music-Note Merchant"), in which he created a fantastic character, the Niglo. That same year saw the release of *L'Epouvantail* ("The Scarecrow"), on a script by Jean Aurenche. Grimault's best animated cartoon to date, it related the adventures of a couple of lovebirds pursued by a cruel cat and befriended by a scarecrow that came to life.

The end of the war brought more creations from Les Gémeaux. First there was *Le Voleur de Paratonerres* ("The Lightning-Rod Thief," 1945), in which two moustached cops relentlessly pursue but always fail to catch the young thief (the film won first prize at the 1946 Venice Film Festival). Then came *La Flûte Magique,* on the same story as Mozart's opera (1946), and *Le Petit Soldat* ("The Little Soldier," 1947), a little masterpiece of poetry, humor and fantasy based on Hans Christian Andersen's tale of the toy soldier who goes to war.

Soon thereafter Les Gémeaux started work on their most ambitious project: a feature-length animated cartoon also based on an Andersen story, *La Bergère et le Ramoneur* ("The Shepherdess and the Chimney Sweep"). After many vicissitudes, delays, and even a lawsuit, the film was finally released in 1953 in mutilated form.

Having broken with Sarrut in 1951, Grimault founded his own studio, Les Films Paul Grimault, which produced a number of animated films and documentaries such as *La Faim du Monde* ("World's Hunger," 1958) and *La Demoiselle et le Violoncelliste* ("The Girl and the Cello Player," 1964), a beautiful cartoon short directed by Jean-François Laguionie. In 1973 Grimault returned briefly to directing with the delightful *Le Chien Mélomane* ("The Music-Loving Dog"). In 1980 he finally completed his masterwork, the unabridged version of the Andersen tale, now retitled *Le Roi et l'Oiseau* ("The King and the Bird"). With famed filmmaker Jacques Demy he co-produced in 1988 *La Table Tournante* ("The Whirling Table"), a compilation of some of his best work over the years. He died in Paris in March 1994.

Paul Grimault is the most widely known French animator, and his work has been hailed in many quarters. In 1956 Philippe Collin and Michel Wyn wrote in their study *Le Cinéma d'Animation dans le Monde* that Paul Grimault

Paul Grimault, "Le Petit Soldat." © Les Gémeaux.

created "a new world in the animated cartoon . . . he is the only cartoonist who can be compared to Renoir in his deep feeling for reality, for humanity, for the joy and sadness of our existence."

M.H.

GRIN AND BEAR IT (U.S.) George ("Lichty") Lichtenstein started his hilarious newspaper panel series, *Grin and Bear It,* in March 1932, in the pages of the *Chicago Times*. It has continued to run since that time.

In *Grin and Bear It* Lichty took a hard, satirical, yet amused look at the ways Americans act, talk and fantasize about themselves. Lichty has seen fit to lampoon all subjects and types in his characteristically scratchy, slapdash style: his politicians are as bombastic as any, his generals as bloodthirsty as they come, and his business tycoons as befuddled as they are ruthless. The "common man" does not come off any better: he is pictured as conniving, lazy, lecherous and gullible. The institution of marriage has suffered particularly from Lichty's sarcastic pen: the domineering wife and the helpless husband wage unceasing, if hardly equal, warfare upon each other with blind ferocity. Love, death and taxes are also among Lichty's favorite subjects, and it is to his credit that he has made his readers laugh as hard at the latter two as at the first.

In 1934 *Grin and Bear It* was picked up for syndication by United Feature, which distributed it nationally until 1940. It was then reclaimed by Field Enterprises (which had acquired the *Chicago Times* and consolidated it into the *Sun-Times*). It is now being syndicated by Field Newspaper Syndicate.

Lichty retired from the feature in December 1974, and *Grin and Bear It* is now done by Fred Wagner in a style close to that of Lichty (whose name still appears on the byline). In recent years Ralph Dunnagin has been co-authoring the feature in tandem with Wagner.

M.H.

GRIS, JUAN

See González, José Victoriano.

GROPPER, WILLIAM (1897-1977) American artist and cartoonist born in New York City on December 3, 1897. William Gropper studied art at the National Academy of Design, at the New York School of Fine and Applied Arts and with Robert Henri, George Bellows and Howard Giles. He described his field as "satirical figuration"; his art ranged from biting political cartoons to social-theme murals. Gropper's work first appeared in the *New York Tribune* in 1919 and then in the pages of radical, Socialist and Communist magazines and liberal newspapers and journals; in 1935 he got *Vanity Fair* magazine banned in Japan by drawing a vicious attack on the emperor for its pages.

Gropper consistently utilized a free brush and heavy crayon shading, producing the look of a stone lithograph (indeed, many of his works were actually to be drawn on stone). In this regard he was the technical as well as ideological cousin of Boardman Robinson, Robert Minor and Fred Ellis, among others. On various trips to the Soviet

Another Pact

William Gropper, 1936. © Gropper.

Union he produced many cartoons and was honored with a place in the Museum of Western Art in Moscow. Gropper's cartoons were lucid, hard-hitting and very effective—practically propaganda tracts for his viewpoints.

Among Gropper's books of drawings are *Golden Land, Gropper, The Little Tailor, Twelve Etchings* and *The Shtetl.* He also did book illustrations, including those for *Alley Oop* (about acrobats), *Circus Parade* by Jim Tully and *Reminiscences of a Cowboy* by Frank Harris. His work has been collected by several museums, and he won many awards (especially for his lithographic work) and executed murals throughout America. Gropper died on January 8, 1977.

R.M.

GROSS, SAM (1933-) American cartoonist born in the Bronx, New York, on August 7, 1933. Sam Gross received his B.A. from the City College of New York, specializing in advertising. According to him, his success in the field of cartoon art has been very gradual, but the process has paid off. Today his work appears with regularity in the *New Yorker, Saturday Review, Oui, Cosmopolitan, Ladies' Home Journal, Good Housekeeping,* the *New York Times, Esquire, Audubon* and *TV Guide.* In addition, Gross serves as senior contributing artist on the *National Lampoon,* a position that not only involves him editorially but also indicates the high esteem in which his talent is held at that well-known institution of American humor.

Working in ink (line and washes), Gross creates a manic *comédie humaine* in which certain themes and characters constantly reappear. This recurrence, which seems to be a carefully calculated aspect of Gross's art, can be most fully appreciated in a collection like *I Am Blind and My Dog Is*

Dead (Avon, 1978). From page to page, one encounters fairy-tale figures—the gingerbread house witch, the little match girl, the gingerbread man, blind men, frogs (Gross's frogs are marvelously engaging creatures), cornucopias, snakes, nervous old maids, birds, street vendors and other mendicants, and little Soglovian-style kings—at times interacting with one another, as when a bird asks his mother up in the tree if he may eat the gingerbread man who has followed him home.

Such themes impress themselves subtly on the reader, and the sense of hilarity is heightened by increasing familiarity. In the gingerbread-man drawings, for example, each panel is a masterpiece of inspired lunacy, but cumulatively they are even funnier. Thus, by the time one comes upon the drawing of the gingerbread man running out of a pizzeria while two disgruntled bakers look after him, agreeing from now on to stick to pizza, one's laughter is literally uncontrollable. While this happy penchant for thematic consistency makes Gross especially collectible, it takes nothing away from his ability to be brilliantly funny in a solo context. Thus, Goldilocks walks into a cottage and confronts a sign on the wall: "Occupancy by more than three bears is both dangerous and unlawful," signed by the fire commissioner, "Bruin McMirth." Or a single pigeon ignores the man feeding the rest of the flock at one end of a park bench, instead approaching the wino at the other end to announce, "I'm not very hungry, mister, but I sure could use a drink."

The free linear style Gross has evolved to convey his highly individual humor appears to reflect the influences of both Steinberg and Thurber, though the blending is undeniably and effectively personal. Gross's achievement is especially commendable in light of the fact that he has had no formal art training; for it is the self-taught artist who is often the most derivative. Besides the volume mentioned above, the artist is also responsible for *How Gross* (Dell, 1973). Gross originals are represented in many private collections. He is a member of the Illustrators Guild and of the Cartoonists Guild and has served the latter organization as treasurer (1969-71), vice-president (1972-73) and president (1974-75). In the 1990's he has also involved himself in electronic publishing ventures, including screen savers and advertising.

R.C.

GROSZ, GEORGE
See Ehrenfried, Georg.

GRUEL, HENRI (1923-) French animator and filmmaker born in Mâcon, in the Burgundy region of France, on February 5, 1923. Henri Gruel became interested in animation while in high school, and after a variety of jobs in commercial art, he finally started working in animation with Jean Arcady in 1946, graduating from in-betweener to director in the space of a few years. He first conceived of incorporating children's drawings (as well as some of their idea suggestions) into his cartoons in 1949. His first film using this concept was the charming *Martin et Gaston* (1950). The whimsical *Gitanes et Papillons* ("Gypsy Girls and Butterflies") was also based on children's drawings, but Gruel's treatment was sophisticated and sharply satirical.

In the late 1950s Gruel made a number of cartoons that have since become classics. First came the 1955 *Voyage de Badabou* ("Badabou's Journey"), an utterly enchanting children's film that won the Prix Emile Cohl in 1956, followed in 1958 by the wildly inventive *La Joconde*, a series of Mona Lisa jokes to end all Mona Lisa jokes. That same year Gruel worked with the transplanted Polish animator Jan Lenica on the funny and iconoclastic *Monsieur Tête* (released in 1959). Gruel also made *Un Atome Qui Vous Veut du Bien* ("An Atom Which Means You Well," 1959), about the peaceful uses of atomic energy, and *La Lutte contre le Froid* ("The Fight Against Cold," 1960), two didactic subjects that he treated with unusual wit and humor.

In the 1960s Gruel virtually abandoned the animation medium (with the exception of an occasional advertising film or two) in favor of live action, starting with the 1963 comedy *Le Roi du Village* ("The King of the Village"). He came back to animation, however, as the head of the newly formed Idéfix Studios in 1973. After the studio folded in the late 1970s he went back to producing cartoons for advertising. He retired in the early 1990s.

M.H.

GRUELLE, JOHNNY (1880-1938) American cartoonist and author born in Arcola, Illinois, in 1880. Johnny Gruelle began cartooning in Indianapolis, Indiana, and after the turn of the century drew children's fantasy strips for small syndicates, where he created some of the most wonderful fantasy the comics have ever known. In 1910 he won a $2000 prize offered by the *New York Herald* and had a comic strip, *Mr. Tweedeedle,* accepted; it ran until 1921.

In 1912 he created the *Yapp's Crossing* series for *Judge.* Running weekly, a full page in the front of the magazine, the series concerned the doings of small-town folk during celebrations, holidays, events, etc. The whole town was portrayed from an angled bird's-eye view. With minor recurring characters, the series became immensely popular and spawned imitators (Eugene Zimmerman and Tony Sarg adopted the genre well); it ran in *Judge* until 1923. Gruelle imitated himself and ran the *Yahoo Center* series in *Life* and the *Niles Junction* adventures in *College Humor*.

Gruelle's biggest success was his *Raggedy Ann* series, which included cartoons he illustrated himself. He had specialized in children's stories in such magazines as *Women's World*, but his *Raggedy Ann* stories about dolls and toys that come to life are all-time classics of children's literature. The very conceptions are as brilliant as the cartoons, which are often in color. A whole series of books was produced which continue to be just as popular today, with much ancillary merchandising (particularly the Raggedy Ann doll itself), in the traditions of other children's fantasy classics like *The Wizard of Oz* and *The Brownies.*

Gruelle's son, Worth, became a cartoonist and switched assignments with Harry Neigher on the *Bridgeport.* (Conn.) *Herald* in the 1930s; much of his work consisted in taking old *Yapp's Crossing* drawings and writing local captions and labels. Johnny Gruelle retired from Norwalk,

The war: "Have you heard? In order to help the Russians, Roosevelt had decided to advance the winter."
Giovanni Guareschi, 1942. © Bertoldo.

Connecticut, to Miami Springs, Florida, where he died on January 9, 1938. (His Western comic strip, *Brutus,* which he had started in 1928, died with him.)

R.M.

GUARESCHI, GIOVANNI (1908-1968) Italian cartoonist and writer born in Parma, Italy, on May 1, 1908. The name of Giovanni Guareschi is indissolubly tied to those of Don Camillo and Peppone, respectively the priest and mayor of a fictional Italian village, fighting one another but ultimately the best of friends. In these two characters many have seen a prefiguration of the "historic compromise" between the Christian-Democratic and Communist parties in Italy.

Guareschi the writer was preceded, however, by Guareschi the cartoonist, who started to draw for *Bertoldo* toward the end of the 1920s, and whose cartoons reflected the honest, ribald qualities of Italian comedy. His cartoons were so well appreciated, in fact, that he became the editor in chief of the magazine in 1936, holding that post until 1943. Right after the end of World War II, Guareschi founded *Candido,* one of the most successful of Italian satirical and humorous magazines; he directed it from 1945 on, first with Giovanni Mosca, then by himself. During that time he was sentenced to one year in prison for his attacks on Prime Minister A. De Gasperi. But if Guareschi did not spare the Christian Democrats, his favorite targets remained the Communists, whom he represented in his cartoons as ugly, bullying, ignorant and crude (at the time, Stalin was still alive, and the cult of personality was very much in evidence). In 1950 Guareschi wrote the first of the *Don Camillo* books, and their success led him to do less and less cartooning. The quality of his cartoons declined markedly toward the end of his life. He died in July 1968.

C.S.

GUILLAUME, ALBERT (1873-1942) French cartoonist, painter and poster designer born in Paris, France, on February 14, 1873. The son of a professor of architecture at the Paris Ecole des Beaux-Arts, Albert Guillaume studied art there with Gérôme. Starting in the late 1880s, he contributed satirical drawings (sometimes as many as ten a week) to all the important magazines (*Le Rire, Gil Blas, Le Gaulois, Le Musée des Familles, La Revue Illustrée,* etc.). He also decorated the main dining room of L'Auberge du Grand Cerf in Senlis, 30 miles north of Paris.

His cartoons deal mainly with the frivolous life of chic, sophisticated demimonde women and rich, *bon vivant* men forever engaged in eating, drinking and sexual pursuits. They have done much to capture the fashionable turn-of-the-century world of restaurants, seaside resorts and racetracks, and to perpetuate our image of what is commonly referred to as *la Belle Epoque.* These drawings were published in albums, the most important being *Des Bonshommes* ("Goodnatured Men" 1890-92), *Petites Femmes* ("Little Women," 1891), *Y' A des Dames* ("Ladies Present," 1896) and *Frivoles Femmes* ("Frivolous Women," 1902).

Albert Guillaume, "A Bachelor's Life," 1896.

Albert Guillaume had the sharpness of a born social observer and an eye for detail which uncovered at a glance not only the erotic connotations of a scene but its vulgar aspects as well. He died in Dordogne on August 12, 1942.

P.H.

GULBRANSSON, OLAF (1873-1958) Norwegian-German cartoonist, illustrator and painter born in Oslo (then Kristiania), Norway, on May 26, 1873. Olaf Gulbransson studied at the Oslo applied-art school from 1885 to 1892 and spent some time at the Académie Colarossi in Paris in 1900. By 1892 he was contributing cartoons to the local publications *Tyrihans, Transvikspost* and *Karikaturen*. By the turn of the century he was Norway's most prominent cartoonist, and his 1901 album of celebrity caricatures, *24 Karikaturer* (including Ibsen, the painter Christian Krohg and many others), was already a masterpiece.

In 1902 Albert Langen, who had founded the Munich satirical magazine *Simplicissimus* in 1896, invited Gulbransson to work for him in Munich. (Langen had long had influential connections with the Scandinavian countries, and such artists as Theodore Kittelsen and Ragnvald Blix also worked for *Simplicissimus.)* Gulbransson accepted, spent a little while in Berlin to learn German and then arrived in Bavaria, which was henceforth to be his physical and spiritual home. He clicked right away as a *Simplicissimus* artist and, with certain interruptions, remained on its staff until its demise in the 1940s, continuing to be one of its two or three most influential and admired associates. His style changed gradually, and not without reverses, from a dark, shaded look to an extremely flexible open contour method of great beauty of line. His celebrity caricatures were always a specialty (as early as 1905 a Munich album, *Berühmte Zeitgenossen,* echoed the successful Oslo album of 1901), but his subject matter was extremely varied and generally on the good-natured side.

Olaf Gulbransson, caricature of Isadora Duncan, 1904.

Gulbransson also did extensive book illustration, continuing well into the 1950s. He was especially well known for his illustrations of the works of the Bavarian author Ludwig Thoma and for his own hand-lettered autobiography covering his childhood and young manhood, *Es War Einmal* ("Once upon a Time").

In 1924 he started teaching at the Munich Academy, where he became a full professor of drawing and painting in 1929 and could boast over the years of numerous successful students. From 1922 to 1927 he lived in Oslo, working on the magazine *Tidens Tegn* ("Signs of the Times"). He died on September 18, 1958, at his estate, Schererhof, on the Tegernsee in Bavaria.

S.A.

"Gulliver's Travels." © Paramount Pictures.

GULLIVER'S TRAVELS (U.S.) Flushed with the roaring success of his *Popeye* cartoons (which a 1938 opinion poll found to be more popular than *Mickey Mouse),* Max Fleischer decided to challenge Walt Disney on his own ground with a full-length animated feature to be produced in the new Fleischer studios in Miami, Florida. Fleischer chose Jonathan Swift's *Gulliver's Travels* as the source for his artistic venture, and after much discussion, it was decided to limit the film to Gulliver's first journey to the kingdom of Lilliput. After much ballyhoo and fanfare, the film finally opened in December 1939.

The Fleischers' *Gulliver* was a mixed bag. Swift's original story had been changed and sugared down to such an extent that only the bare essentials remained. A number of characters were added to the plot, including Prince David and Princess Glory of the feuding kingdoms of Lilliput and Blefuscu, the three comical spies—Sneak, Snoop and Snitch—and Gabby, the cowardly crier of Lilliput who nearly stole the show (Gabby went on to star in his own cartoon series). There were some nice bits of animation (Gulliver being tied up by the tiny Lilliputians, the royal feast in Gulliver's honor, and the slapstick shenanigans of the three spies), but on the whole *Gulliver's Travels* proved something of a disappointment.

Practically the whole studio staff had worked on the picture. Dave Fleischer received his usual credit for direction, but a host of "directors of animation" shared the honors, including such stalwarts as Seymour Kneitel, Willard Bowsky, Grim Natwick, Roland Crandall and Orestes Calpini. Ted Husing, "famous CBS announcer," supplied the voice for Gulliver, while the prince and princess spoke and sang through the voices of Lanny Ross and Jessica Dragonette.

M.H.

GURNEY, ERIC (ca. 1920-1992) American cartoonist and author born in Winnipeg, Manitoba, Canada, around 1920. As a boy, Eric Gurney moved with his family to Saskatoon, Saskatchewan, and then to Toronto, where he attended school. After graduating from Central Technical School, he attended night classes at the Ontario College of Art and in 1938 went to California to work at the Disney studios. Over a 10-year period Gurney garnered credits on 20 films, working in various animation departments. In 1948 he moved to the East Coast, where he established himself as a major cartoon-style advertising artist (for such clients as Texaco, Ethyl Gas and Southern Railways) and illustrator (for *Collier's*, the *Saturday Evening Post*, *Look*, *Life*, *Reader's Digest* and *Outdoor Life*, among others).

It was as a book illustrator, however, that Gurney hit his stride. He had a genius for depicting cartoon animals, and his works were consistent best sellers and award winners. Nobody in cartoon history has surpassed his sympathetic portrayals of dogs, cats and birds. His style was one of exacting detail and crosshatching, combined with genuinely funny characterizations and expressions on his subjects. His use of color was handsome, and he steadfastly refused to "humanize" his animals à la Snoopy or the major animated characters. He devoted his efforts in later years to writing and illustrating children's books until his death in 1992.

His books include *How to Live with a Neurotic Dog*, *How to Live with a Calculating Cat*, *How to Live with a Pampered Pet*, *Gilbert*, *Eric Gurney's Pop-Up Book of Dogs*, *Eric Gurney's Pop-Up Book of Cats*, *Impossible Dogs and Troublesome Cats*, *The King, the Mice and the Cheese* and *The Return of the Calculating Cat*. Several of the books were written by his late wife, Nancy, and the last-named by Nancy Provo. Gurney has illustrated several animal cartoon calendars as well.

R.M.

GUSTAVINO
See Rosso, Gustavo.

Hh

HAAS, LEO (1901-198?) Czechoslovakian cartoonist and painter born in Opava, Bohemia, in 1901. Leo Haas studied art in Vienna and Berlin; in 1925 he became the manager of a lithographic printing house in his hometown. He became noted for his paintings and for the many cartoons he contributed to the leading Czech magazines of the 1920s and 1930s.

After the Nazi takeover of Czechoslovakia in 1938, Haas was sent to the Theresienstadt (Terezin) concentration camp. There, in a number of drawings that he managed to hide, he made a visual record of the horror surrounding him. Having next survived Auschwitz, he returned to Terezin at the end of World War II; his drawings, published in a book called The Artists of Terezin, evoked an immediate worldwide response. Settling in Prague, Haas became one of the leading political cartoonists of his country before leaving for East Germany in 1955. He died in the late 1980s.

Leo Haas held a number of exhibits of his cartoons, and his works hang in museums in Prague and East Berlin. (Haas inspired the character of Karl Weiss in Gerald Green's teleplay *Holocaust.)*

M.H.

"Hadashi no Gen." © *Manga.*

HADASHI NO GEN (Japan) *Hadashi no Gen* ("Barefoot Gen") is for very special reasons one of the most moving "comics" ever created. It is the semiautobiographical story of the author and artist, Keiji Nakazawa, and his experiences as a child during and after one of history's greatest tragedies—the atom bombing of Hiroshima.

Little Gen Nakaoka, the hero, is in the second grade in 1945. Because of his father's opposition to a war still being bitterly contested, Gen's entire family is subjected to ostracism and persecution. Despite hunger and injustice the Nakaoka's survive—until 8:15 a.m., August 6, 1945. At that instant the world is transformed into a raging inferno the likes of which have never been seen. Gen and his mother survive, but his father, sister and brother are killed (as Nakazawa's were). From that point on, a bitter struggle for existence commences, a struggle against starvation, radiation sickness and social breakdown. In a situation guaranteed to bring out the ugliest aspects of man and society, little Gen serves as an example of compassion, perseverance and the will to live.

Hadashi no Gen was an attempt by Keiji Nakazawa to convey some sense of the horror he experienced to a generation that knows nothing of war, let alone atomic holocaust. It was originally serialized in 1973 in the weekly comic book *Shōnen Jump* (which then had a circulation of one million), but it has since been compiled and published in several four-volume editions, with over six hundred thousand volumes sold. Despite its length (over twelve hundred pages), it won instant popularity and was made into a two-part movie of the same name. Furthermore, *Hadashi no Gen* was the first Japanese comic book of its kind to be translated into English for distribution overseas. In 1977 Project Gen, a volunteer group, was established with the express goal of conveying Gen's message to the world, and translation is being done by Dadakai (the Neo Dada group). In 1982 Educomics in San Francisco published part of the story in American comic book style under the title *Gen of Hiroshima*—marking the first time a Japanese comic had appeared translated in American format. Later the series was issued by New Society Press and eventually by Penguin Books. Subsequently, *Gen* has been published in several formats in English, and translated into languages as diverse as Swedish, Tagalog, German, and even Esperanto. At least two feature-length animated films based on the story have also been made, in 1983 and 1986 respectively.

F.S.

HADDAD, HABIB (1945-   ) Lebanese cartoonist born in 1945 in Tripoli, in northern Lebanon. The son of a barber, Habib Haddad showed an early love of drawing, and he sold his early efforts to Lebanese newpapers in 1965. His first editorial cartoons, however, appeared some years later in the Kuwaiti newspaper *Al Ambra* and in the Lebanese magazine *Horoscope*. These in turn led to his first one-man show in 1972. The outbreak of the civil war in the

Habib Haddad. © Habib Haddad.

mid-1970's cut short his rocketing career and caused him to leave Lebanon for France, where he worked for a number of Arabic-language publications headquartered in Europe (notably the London-based Arabic daily *Al Hayat*) as well as French magazines.

Haddad's drawings reflect the influence of some of his models, particularly Don Martin's offbeat humor and Pat Oliphant's acute perception of the political scene. While many of his political cartoons are—perhaps not surprisingly—anti-Israeli (he once depicted Israeli Prime Minister Menachim Begin waist-deep in a mound of skulls), he can also sharply criticize his fellow Arabs, notably Yasser Arafat whom he has pictured as a vacillating buffoon on more than once occasion. A favorite target for bitter denunciation has been the Arab world's lack of democratic freedom (his self-portrait as an artist wearing handcuffs for spectacles and wistfully gazing at a fountain pen in a bird-cage is very revealing in this respect). Away from the politics of the Middle East, Haddad often displays a more humorous facet of his talent, as in his cartoon depicting a gigantic "mad cow" clinging to the Parliament Tower in London while trying to fend off biplanes of all nations shooting at her from all angles.

Haddad has received a number of honors and awards for his work and was voted Best Cartoonist in the Arab World in 1991.

M.H.

HAGIO, MOTO (1949-) Japanese cartoonist born in Ōmuta, Fukuoka Prefecture, Japan, in 1949. Moto Hagio is one of the most popular, prolific and talented comic book artists in Japan today. She exhibited a passion for comic books from a very early age, actively drawing them herself. After reading Osamu Tezuka's *Shinsen Gumi*, she became convinced that comics were her future and formed an association with friends of a similar persuasion in her junior year in high school. Upon graduation, Hagio began attending design school. During one winter vacation in Tokyo, she approached a publisher with samples of her work, and this resulted in *Bianca* and *Yuki no Ko* ("Snow Child").

With *Ruru to Mimi* ("Lulu and Mimi"), a humorous work that appeared in a girls' comic in 1969, Hagio began her professional career. Two years later, *Juichigatsu no Gimnajium* ("November Gymnasium"), a tale of two identical twins in a German boarding school for boys, caused her popularity to soar. This was followed by works such as *Juichini Iru!* ("Eleven People Are Here!") and *Pō no Ichizoku* ("Pō's Family"), which won her the 21st Shogakkan cartoon award for 1976. *Juichini Iru!* was a science fiction work that ran in girls' comics to great acclaim. *Pō no Ichizoku*, a humanistic portrayal of a vampire, was influenced by Ryoko Ikeda's classic *Berusaiyu no Bara* ("The Rose of Versailles"), particularly in its dramatic layout. Hagio also crossed over into boys' comics with *Hyaku Oku no Hiru to Sen Oku no Yoru* ("Ten Billion Days and One Hundred Billion Nights").

Moto Hagio is an extraordinarily prolific and successful writer. Seven years after her debut with *Ruru to Mimi* she had turned out sixty-eight works, and a special collection that appeared in *Putchi Komik* in November 1977 was sold out the moment it appeared in the bookstores. Hagio's strength, and the source of her popularity, lies in her draftsmanship and plots. Her drawings tend to be very realistic and almost three-dimensional relative to the fashion-design style so popular in Japanese girls' comics, and her stories are quick to capture and hold the reader with their skillfully unfolding plots and unexpected climaxes. She is, moreover, at home in almost every genre, whether gag strips, science fiction or historical romance. Ironically, nearly all her works feature foreign Caucasian children as subjects, a trend very evident in young girls' comics in Japan, but one she seems to take to an extreme. Nonetheless, her fan mail is enormous, and drawing comics is her true passion. In that field she has added, among other works, the science-fictional *Marginal* (1985-87) and the social drama *Zankoku no kami ga shirai shiru* ("A Cruel God Reigns," 1992 to present) to her list.

F.S.

HAHN, ALBERT (1877-1918) Dutch editorial cartoonist born in Groningen, the Netherlands, on March 17, 1877. Like Jan Holswilder a generation earlier, the short-lived Albert Hahn fought ill health (he spent years in the hospital as a boy and suffered from frequent periods of exhaustion) to become a major artistic force of his time. Hahn, a workingman's son turned imaginative and subtle political cartoonist, was said to have created the aesthetic embodiment of the social idealism inherent in the Dutch labor movement during its first period of heroic combat.

From 1890 to 1896 Hahn attended the Academie Minerva in his native Groningen and then continued his studies in the two main art schools of Amsterdam until 1901. After a period as a commercial artist designing bookplates and posters, Hahn joined the staff of the Amsterdam socialist paper *Het Volk* in 1902. For years he was the sole or principal artist of its Sunday supplement. *Het Volk* was only equipped to print black-and-white line art, and Hahn soon became a master of simplification of form and of striking, somewhat ornamental composition, with great originality of visual concepts.

Hahn and *Het Volk* were anticapitalist and anticlerical, so that Dr. Abraham Kuyper, head of the Calvinist political party, was one of their main targets. The titles of a number of the albums in which Hahn's cartoons were collected allude to Kuyper's career: *Van de Dorpspastorie naar het Torentje* ("From the Village Parish to the Tower"), *In*

Abraham's Schoot ("In Abraham's Bosom") and *Onder Zwart Regime* ("Under a Black-Clad Regime"). One of Hahn's most famous single cartoons was "The Wooden Sentry," which depicted Kuyper as a toy soldier guarding a safe (the wealth of the country) on top of which the crown and other regalia reposed. Other publications in which Hahn's work appeared besides *Het Volk* were *Der Notenkraker, De Ware Jacob*, and *De Hollandsche Revue.*

Hahn's cartoons during World War I were outspokenly anti-German (Holland was neutral, but it was hard for many Dutch to disregard the unethical invasion of neighboring Belgium). Although his work never became a cause célèbre like Raemakers's, he lashed out against "Hun brutality," the sinking of the *Lusitania* and the defacing of Rheims Cathedral (another of his masterpieces shows the cathedral rebuilt after the war as a montage of bombs and ammunition).

Hahn died in Amsterdam at the age of 41 on August 3, 1918.

S.A.

HAITZINGER, HORST (1939-) Horst Haitzinger, son of a policeman, was born June 19, 1939, in Eferding in Upper Austria. He had always wanted to become an artist, and therefore, after public school he became a student of the Kustgewerbeschule, a school of graphic design in Linz, from 1953 to 1957. This was followed by twelve semesters at the Academy of Arts in Munich, Germany, where Haitzinger studied painting and graphics and decided he wanted to stay in Munich.

In 1958 Haitzinger's first political cartoons were published in the satiric magazine *Simplicissimus.* What initially was just a gig to finance his studies soon turned into a lifelong career of political and editorial cartooning. The editors of *Simplicissimus* made Haitzinger a regular contributor. When Haitzinger finished his studies at the Academy of Arts, he started working as a freelance painter and political cartoonist with a very distinctive, flashy style.

Horst Haitzinger. © tx.

Haitzinger became known to a larger audience when his political cartoons started appearing in the Munich newspaper, *tz,* ever since it was launched in September 18, 1968. ("tz" allegedly is not an abbreviation of any word, not even of "**T**ages**z**eitung" (daily news). So maybe it was picked simply from the middle of Hai**tz**inger's name.) Haitzinger's cartoons for *tz* were often quoted in other papers and magazines like *Der Spiegel* and *Quick.* In fact, Haitzinger also started contributing original cartoons to those magazines and to various newspapers while still staying with *tz,* the newspaper which probably had given his career the biggest kick. Haitzinger has contributed to newspapers and magazines in Germany, Austria, Switzerland, the United States and England. According to *Der Spiegel,* Haitzinger is probably the best known editorial cartoonist of the German-language countries.

Ever since 1972 Haitzinger's best political cartoons of the year were compiled for book publication. The cartoonist has also come up with a number of book projects for which he has painted cartoons along a thematic line like *Archetypen* ("Archetypes", 1979) or *Deutschland Deutschland* (1991). Besides cartooning, Haitzinger has continued painting oils along the lines of phantastic realism. Both Haitzinger's paintings and his political cartoons have not only been widely published, they have also been put on exhibition in various cities of Germany and other countries. Horst Haitzinger lives and works in Munich, Germany.

W.F

HAJDU, EMERIC (1911-1989) French animated cartoon director and producer born in Budapest, Hungary, on January 26, 1911. Emeric Hajdu studied at the School of Decorative Art in Budapest and later in Berlin before arriving in Paris in 1932. There he worked as a commercial artist until he went to London for an apprenticeship in animation with John Halas (1936-37).

In 1944, back in Paris and using the name "Jean Image," he directed his first short animated cartoon, *Les Noirs Jouent et Gagnent* ("Black Plays and Wins," 1944). Two years later *Rhapsodie de Saturne* ("Saturn Rhapsody") was produced by his own studios and screened officially at the Cannes Film Festival (1947). Thereafter, there was a series of prize-winning animated cartoons starting with *Jeannot l'Intrépide* ("Johnny the Giant Killer"), his first feature, with the animation done by Boutin, Klein and Breuil. The film, which won the Grand Prize for Children's Film at the Venice Festival in 1951, relates the many adventures of little Johnny in his fight against a mean and frightening ogre. *François S'Evade* ("François Escapes") was awarded a prize at the Mar del Plata Festival in Argentina in 1959. *Aladin et la Lampe Magique* ("Aladdin and the Magic Lamp"), a 1969 feature film, was presented in 1970 at the Mamaia Film Festival in Romania and at children's film festivals in Gijón, Spain, and Tehran, Iran. Although it took him only seven months to direct, *Aladin* is by far his best animated work to date. The script adaptation by Image and his wife is excellent, as is the animation of Boutin, Breuil, Lehideux

Emeric Hajdu ("Jean Image"), "Aladdin and the Magic Lamp." © Image.

and Xavier, and the colors and psychedelic backgrounds are absolutely stunning. His latest feature-length venture, *Pluk, Naufragé de l'Espace* ("Pluk in Cosmos"), was released in 1974. It is in the epic tradition of interplanetary travels from Jules Verne to Star Wars.

Jean Image, who has been called the French Walt Disney but is probably closer to being the French Hanna-Barbera, has also directed and/or produced five animated television series: *Les Aventures de Joë* ("Joe's Adventures," 1960-62); *Picolo et Picolette* (1963-64); *Kiri le Clown* (1966-69), actually a puppet series; *Au Clair de Lune* ("In the Moonlight," 1971-72); and *Arago X 001* (1972-73). In addition, he has directed scores of industrial and special events shorts, many of which have won prizes (e.g., *Rhodialine Emballage,* 1957 Cannes Film Festival; *La Petite Reine,* 1958 Cortina d'Ampezzo Film Festival). He died in Paris on October 21, 1989.

P.H.

HAKUJADEN (Japan) *Hakujaden* ("Legend of a White Snake") is a classic of Japanese animation. Produced in 1958 by the newly created animation department of the Toei film company, it was Japan's first technicolor animation feature and also the first film of its kind designed for export.

Hakujaden is a love story based on an ancient Chinese classic. The plot revolves around a young Chinese boy, Kyosen, who has a little pet snake. Scolded by his parents, he reluctantly and tearfully abandons it. After he has grown up, a beautiful girl appears, and she and Kyosen fall in love. The girl is, of course, the spirit of the snake. Many trials and tribulations ensue, threatening to thwart the love of the two young people, and considerable dramatic action results from the confrontation between the snake girl and Hokai, a priest who is opposed to their union. Finally, however, the snake girl becomes a true human on the condition that she renounce her supernatural powers, and she and Kyosen sail off into happiness.

Taiji Yabushita wrote the screenplay and directed the film, and such well-known figures as Yasuji Mori, Akira Kaikuhara and Masao Kumagawa worked on the animation. Overall production took more than a year and required 214,154 drawings. The result was an animated feature film that was acclaimed not only in Japan but abroad and received several awards, including a special mention at the 1959 Venice International Children's Animation Festival. In the years since its release, *Hakujaden* has served as an inspiration to an entire generation of young animators in Japan.

F.S.

HALAS, JOHN (1912-1995) British animator born in Budapest, Hungary, on April 16, 1912.

Animation in Great Britain may never have produced a character to equal Mickey Mouse, but Halas and Batchelor Cartoons is universally acknowledged as the British equivalent of Walt Disney. The company holds a record of continuous production second only to the Disney studio's, dating back over forty years to the chance meeting of John Halas and Joy Batchelor at British Animated Films in 1938.

John Halas freelanced on French magazines in Paris (1930), then returned to Budapest to work for George Pal on the first Hungarian animated cartoons—advertising shorts made in the cutout technique. In 1933 he studied at The Studio, a private graphic design school run by Alexander Bortnyik and László Moholy-Nagy as a split-off from the German Bauhaus. Two years later he established the first Hungarian studio devoted to animation, but it produced only films advertising cigarettes and liquor. However, one of his color cartoons was seen in London, which led to an invitation to come to England and join British Animated Films, a commercial company run by photographers Gabriel Denes and Trigg and the financier Weisbach. Here, on the short *Music Man,* Halas met Joy Batchelor.

Halas and Batchelor as a company really got under way in 1942, when the Ministry of Information contracted them to produce entertaining animated propaganda shorts. *Filling the Gap* and *Dustbin Parade,* both in 1942, led the way to a series of four cartoons featuring a regular character, Abu *(Abu's Dungeon,* etc., 1943), but these were not seen by British audiences, as they were made for showing overseas. Special commissions began to flow in, and for the Admiralty they made their first feature-length cartoon, the documentary *Handling Ships* (1945). Another similar feature-length instructional, *Water for Fire Fighting* (1948), was made for the Home Office. A new series character, Charley, was created for the Central Office of Information, and six cartoons were made, beginning with *Charley's New Town (1947).*

After the war, in 1949, came the company's first cartoon for children, an old sea shanty set to animation, *Heave Away My Johnny.* Commercial sponsorship played an increasing role in their output, ranging from *Flu-ing Squad* for Aspro aspirin tablets (1951) to *As Old as the Hills* (1950) and other serious shorts for the Anglo-Iranian Oil Company. For the Festival of Britain in 1951, Halas and Batchelor produced a set of four unusual and artistic shorts, the *Poet and Painter* series, which combined the work of famous artists (Mervyn Peake in *Spring and Winter,* Henry Moore in *The Pythoness*) with that of famous poets (Thomas Nashe's *The Time of Pestilence*), singers (Peter Pears) and speakers (Michael Redgrave, Eric

John Halas, "Animal Farm." © *Halas & Batchelor.*

Portman). In 1952 came the first British cartoon in 3-D, *The Owl and the Pussycat,* from Edward Lear's poem.

The year 1953 brought another sponsored feature for the Admiralty, *Coastal Navigation,* with their first "proper" cartoon feature following in 1954. This was *Animal Farm,* an adaptation of the fantasy novel by George Orwell, made for the American producer Louis De Rochemont. The styling of the animals in the currently acceptable Disney mold spoiled for some the satire of the story. Animated sequences for the giant screen of *Cinerama Holiday* (1955) were the next challenge for the little company, and in 1956 came the first of several entertainment shorts for the cinema, *The World of Little Ig.* This was made with television in mind, and shortly the studio embarked on *Habatales* (1959), a series for the new medium, and *Foo-Foo* (1960), an animated series for the international TV market that used no words. Then came *Snip and Snap,* a children's series featuring animated paper sculpture. A live-action feature followed, *The Monster of Highgate Ponds* (1961), made for the Children's Film Foundation. In 1963 came another experiment, animated sequences made in "living screen" technique for a traveling show, *Is There Intelligent Life on Earth?*

Dodo, the Kid from Outer Space (1965) was the first Halas and Batchelor series for color television, and it led to commissions for *The Lone Ranger* (1967), *Popeye* (1968), *Tomfoolery* (1970), *The Jackson Five* (1971), *The Osmond Brothers* (1972), *The Count of Monte Cristo* (1973), *The Addams Family* (1973) and *The Partridge Family* (1974)—a tremendous output, but one which was, unfortunately for a British studio, geared entirely to the United States. More to English tastes, perhaps, was their second feature-length cartoon, *Ruddigore* (1966), which Joy Batchelor directed from the Gilbert and Sullivan operetta. Unhappily, it was no box-office beater. More successful were their cartoons adapted from the drawings of Gerald Hoffnung, especially *The Hoffnung Symphony Orchestra (1965).* The studio returned to safer, sponsored ground with such efforts as *Cars of the Future* for British Petroleum (1969). Currently, with around one thousand television commercials to their credit, Halas and Batchelor are into both computer animation and entertainment, having completed a television special for Germany based on Wilhelm Busch's immortal comic strip, *Max und Moritz* (1977). He alas died on January 21, 1995.

Books by John Halas: *How to Cartoon* (1951); *The Technique of Film Animation* (1959); *Design in Motion* (1961); *Art in Movement* (1970); *Computer Animation* (1974); and *Visual Scripting* (1976).

D.G.

HALL, HELGE (1907-) Danish cartoonist whose pen name is Hall, born in Hellerup, Denmark, in 1907. Hall debuted in 1925-26 as a cartoonist in the magazines *Ude og Hjemme, Hjemmet* and the Copenhagen morning paper *Berlingske Tidende.* In 1927, he had his first job as a theater set piece decorator and as a stage drawer in Copenhagen cabarets (Tivoli and Lorry) along with "Storm P." (Robert Petersen) and others. His first strip, *Hilarius Petersens Radio-Oplevelser,* appeared in the daily *Politiken*'s radio supplement.

Hall immigrated to the United States in 1928 and tried in vain to sell cartoons to American newspapers. He got a job in a Minnesota music hall, worked at a tile factory and decorated a synagogue in Los Angeles. He returned to Denmark in 1929 as a freelance cartoonist, making panels and features with varied life-spans. In 1947 he originated the biggest Danish success within family strips, *Hans og Grete,* which was syndicated in 1960 by PIB, Copenhagen, to over one hundred client papers. The strip is still going strong and in Scandinavia has a greater readership than, for example, *Blondie.*

Undoubtedly Europe's most industrious cartoonist, Hall has for several decades delivered two daily strips and five to six cartoons *per day,* besides countless book covers and book illustrations. He has been a board member of Danske Bladtegnere (Danish newspaper cartoonists' guild) for many years until his retirement in the early 1980s.

J.S.

HAMILTON, GRANT (1862-ca. 1920) American cartoonist and editor born in Youngstown, Ohio, on August 16, 1862. Grant Hamilton was graduated from Yale in 1880 and resided for awhile thereafter near Flushing, New York, where he and a group of other young cartoonists formed the Nereus Boat Club to race on the Harlem River; among the members were the Gillam brothers, Dan Beard and Charles Dana Gibson. Hamilton began to contribute to *Judge* magazine in 1881, upon its establishment as one of several magazines around the nation in hopeful competition with *Puck.*

Judge soon relied heavily on Hamilton for its political and social cartoons, and when the magazine changed hands in 1886, he was one of the very few staffers retained. He eventually became art editor of *Judge* and, after a merger, of *Leslie's Weekly.* James Montgomery Flagg was one of many cartoonists who had fond memories of the big, genial Hamilton as the man who really held the magazine together, outlasting and out-shining text editors who came and went. Hamilton could sense when to give talents like Flagg complete freedom.

Hamilton contributed his own art for years—fortunately for his readers and later cognoscenti—except for the period during the election of 1904 when he drew anti-Republican cartoons for the rival *Puck.* Otherwise, he was

The Spanish brute adds mutiliation to murder.
Grant Hamilton, 1898.

a strong Republican throughout his career. His work gradually disappeared from *Judge*'s pages in the 1910s.

Hamilton's art is a happily polished style glowing with technical competence and anatomical soundness. His exaggerations were slight, and during his mature years he never fell prey to the overkill school of cross-hatching; breezy and rounded pen lines combined with gentle crayon shading in his color work for a comfortable, genial visual feeling. Thematically, he pioneered, no later than Opper, the new cartoon genre of light social comment in the format of casual vignettes and observations. In the late 1880s and early 1890s the back page of *Judge* was his, and he filled it with airy examinations of the fads, fashions and mores of his time. The works of Hamilton and Opper deserve special republication; theirs were superb talents that mirrored their times—a gift peculiarly the cartoonist's in many happy instances. And Hamilton's overall work merits discovery for its substantial contributions to the cartoonist's art.

R.M.

HAMILTON, WILLIAM (1939-) American cartoonist and playwright born in Palo Alto, California, on June 2, 1939. William Hamilton attended Yale University, receiving a B.A. in English in 1962. After a two-year hitch in the army (1963-65), he became a staff cartoonist for the *New Yorker* on the strength of his first submissions—a feat somewhat akin to batting .400 as a rookie.

Hamilton claims no formal training in art, and there is no evidence that he has been influenced by any of the major artists working in the field. An unusually delicate ink line makes his work immediately identifiable. His close-up renderings of features have more the quality of preliminary portrait sketches than of caricature, and various faces clearly recur in his cartoons, suggesting that he works from life, probably using friends or family members as models.

His humor also tends to be of a rather personal stamp—very much New York, corporate and Ivy League in setting, and dedicated to the deflation of intellectual pretension and cliché. It may not be everyone's sort of humor, but those familiar with the rather hermetic environment he satirizes will laugh (or wince) at his thrusts. Especially keen are his frequent variations upon the theme of the cocktail party—surely one of civilization's more persistent forms of self-inflicted torture. The drink is innocuous, the food familiar, and the topics of conversation hopelessly predictable. No wonder the heroine of one panel inquires plaintively of her mate as they emerge from one of these get-togethers, "Why are our new friends always just like our old friends?" Why, indeed?

In addition to his work for the *New Yorker,* Hamilton's cartoons are syndicated to 30 newspapers by the Universal Press Syndicate. Collections of his work include *Anti-Social Register* (1974), *Terribly Nice People* (1975), *Husbands, Wives and Live Togethers* (1976), *Money Should Be Fun* (1976) and *Introducing William Hamilton* (1977). He is also the author of two plays, *Save Grand Central* (1976) and *Plymouth Rock* (1977), and a member of the Dramatists' Guild and the Screenwriters' Guild. While continuing to draw gag cartoons, Hamilton since the early 1990s has been doing a weekly business cartoon panel, *Keeping Up,* for Chronicle Features.

A final and rather surprising note: this consummate New Yorker lives in California.

R.C.

HANCOCK, MALCOLM (1936-1992) American cartoonist born in Erie, Colorado, on May 20, 1936. After graduating from the University of Denver in 1958, Malcolm Hancock (who signs "Mal") broke into cartooning with features for the George Matthew Adams service, beginning with *Nibbles,* and with initial sales to the *Saturday Evening Post* and *Playboy.* He went on to contribute to most major American publications, including *The New Yorker, Saturday*

"Cleared with the state, cleared with the county, cleared with the zoning boys, the building boys, the historical society, the ecology groups, and now the little old lady changes her mind about selling the farm."
William Hamilton. © Thomas Y. Crowell.

Review, TV Guide, the *New York Times, National Review, Evergreen Review, Changing Times* and *Cosmopolitan.* Hancock, a paraplegic who sought diversion in drawing, is also the creator of two newspaper panels, the short-lived *Polly,* about a four-year-old child of nature, and *Fenwick,* about a contemporary Everyman confronted by a mad world. *Fenwick* was syndicated for a number of years by Chronicle Features.

Hancock's style is straightforward, and his line pleasantly simple; his affection for somewhat outlandish situations sometimes results in strained humor, but his cartoons are genuinely droll and warm most of the time. Several collections of Hancock's cartoons have been published, notably *How Can You Stand It Out There* (1968), *The Name of the Game* (1969), and *Gifford, You're a Very Stupid Elephant* (1980). He died at his home in Montana in 1992.

M.H.

HANEL, WALTER (1930-) Walter Hanel was born in Teplitz Schonau, Czechoslovakia, on September 14, 1930. He moved to Germany with his father (his mother having died when he was eight) in 1942 and lived through the Allied bombing of Dresden. He credits his witnessing of wartime killing as playing a role in his decision to become a political cartoonist. His interest in art was there from early childhood, but it was not until he was 20 that he started to study the subject. He had been working as a painter in an automobile plant when a friend suggested that he get some training.

In his early art career, Hanel worked for advertising agencies. In 1965, he started doing political cartoons which made him famous throughout Europe in the intervening three decades. Although he works as a freelancer, he has contracts to do political cartoons on a regular basis for *Frankfurter Allgemeine Zietung, Kolner Stadt-Anzeiger, Rheinischer Merkur/Christ Und Welt,* and *Der Spiegel.* Twenty regional newspapers of Germany and others worldwide reprint the cartoons through arrangements with *Frankfurter Allgemeine Zietung.* For the past 15 years, he has spent half of his work weeks doing illustrations, characterized by very subdued colors and a fine line "so delicate it cannot be reproduced."

Hanel describes his style as a very careful, slow process, and compares himself to a hen sitting for long hours to hatch an idea. He calls himself a realist cartoonist who tries to connect with the common folks with his philosophical messages.

More than 20 volumes of Hanel's cartoons and illustrations have been published, and his work has appeared in at least 100 other anthologies and in exhibitions throughout Germany, Poland, Belgium, France, and Italy.

J.A.L.

HANNA, WILLIAM DENBY (1910-) American animator and producer born in Melrose, New Mexico, on July 14, 1910. William Hanna studied to become a structural engineer but had to drop out of college with the onset of the Depression. A talent for drawing led him to join the Harman-Ising animation studio in 1930; there he worked for seven years in the story and layout departments.

Walter Hanel. © Wienand Verlag.

When the MGM animation unit was established in 1937, Hanna became one of its first staff members and directed many of the *Captain and the Kids* cartoons in 1938-39, together with William Allen. In 1938 he and Joe Barbera were teamed for the first time on a short titled *Gallopin' Gals;* the association became permanent the next year when the duo directed the first of the *Tom and Jerry* cartoons, "Puss Gets the Boot." Over the next 18 years Hanna and Barbera directed more than 200 *Tom and Jerry* shorts, winning great popularity and a number of Oscars along the way. For a brief period following Fred Quimby's retirement in 1956, they were also in charge of production.

In 1957 Hanna and Barbera struck out on their own and formed Hanna-Barbera Productions with a view to producing cartoon films for television as well as for theatrical release. The success of their early television series, *Huckleberry Hound* and *Yogi Bear,* helped establish them in the field, but their theatrical venture, *Loopy de Loop,* fizzled out. In the early 1960s the phenomenal success of *The Flintstones* boosted the studio to the top of the TV cartoon field; Hanna-Barbera Productions was sold to Taft Communications in 1966 for a reported $26 million, with Hanna and Barbera remaining at the head of the company.

Hanna-Barbera has been churning out animation material at an increasing pace as television has provided a greater and greater market for their product. Among the more than 100 cartoon series and specials produced by Hanna-Barbera in the 20 years of the studio's existence, there are very few that are commendable or even watchable. Some of the series titles are *Atom Ant, Magilla Gorilla, The Perils of Penelope Pitstop, Quickdraw McGraw, Ruff and Ready, Augie Doggie and Doggie Daddy* (an imitation of the earlier *Spike and Tyke* MGM cartoons), *Dastardly and Mutley* and *Birdman;* the specials include *Alice in Wonderland, Jack and the Beanstalk, Cyrano de Bergerac* and *Charlotte's Web.*

Hanna-Barbera has been called "the poor man's Disney," but even that appellation is probably too charitable. There is no artistic reason why Hanna and Barbera, who proved themselves very talented craftsmen during their halcyon days at MGM, could not have used limited animation to better effect than they have in all their days as independent producers. Jay Ward and others have proved that TV animation need not be as dreadful an exercise as Hanna-Barbera made it. On November 24, 1977, CBS aired a special called *The Happy World of Hanna-Barbera*, in which their current production was contrasted with their earlier work at MGM—the worst condemnation that could possibly have been imagined.

The 1980's and 1990's have been a period of intense activity for the studio. They continued to be major players in the field of animation for television, not only with their already existing series, but also with such new entries as *Captain Caveman, Richie Rich,* the highly successful *The Smurfs*, even *The Bible*. Among the TV specials they produced in that period mention should be made of *The Secret World of Og* (1983), *The Amazing Bunjee Venture* (1984), and an almost unlimited number of *Smurfs* and *Flintstones* featurettes. They also reentered the theatrical feature field with a vengeance, notably producing such cartoon films as *Heidi's Song* (based on Johanna Spyri's novel, 1982) *The Jetsons* (1990), and the critically acclaimed (for a change) *Once Upon a Forest* (1993).

M.H.

A married man looking for his rights in the lawbook.
Edmund Harburger, caricature.

HANS AND HIS CHUMS (U.S.) *Puck* throughout its history utilized the series concept far less than its rivals for reasons that are not clear; one of the primary functions of a series (as newspapers were to learn in the early days of strips) is to build readership. Suspense, anticipation, character identification all combine for a more loyal, if not a larger, circle of devotees.

In any event, *Puck* did dabble in the genre occasionally, usually with happy results. One such instance was with *Hans and His Chums,* a long-running series throughout the first decade of the 20th century, by Louis Glackens. The series revolved around a little Dutch boy, three obedient and mannered dachshunds, and one mischievous dachshund, Dachel. The latter would always involve the rest of the party in some trouble or slapstick misadventure—and of course a rebuke followed in the last panel. The lesson was heeded only until the next week.

Glackens was at that time heralded by *Puck* as its delineator of historical periods; many of his cartoons were set in New Amsterdam or during the American Revolution. For *Hans and His Chums,* the setting was obviously Germany sometime in the past, and this may have been a calculated effort to retain the magazine's German readership (the German-language edition of *Puck,* which predated the English version, was dropped in this period). The series usually ran in color on the back page, though it was occasionally in interior black and white. Verses often accompanied the cartoons. They were drawn in Glackens's marvelously economical cartoon style and colored handsomely in pastel shades.

R.M.

HARBURGER, EDMUND (1846-1906) German cartoonist, illustrator and painter born in Eichstätt, Bavaria, on April 4, 1846. Edmund Harburger grew up in Mainz and, still an adolescent, painted frescoes on a public building there. In 1866 he moved to Munich, where he attended the Technische Hochschule and the Academy. Soon he found work doing book illustrations (some of them were for the publisher J. Scholz in Mainz) and political cartoons for *Die Gartenlaube,* a magazine that is chiefly remembered today as having offered the blandest family fare, but that was somewhat more diversified and adventurous in its early years.

By 1870 Harburger was on the staff of Munich's most important art and humor magazine, Braun and Schneider's *Fliegende Blätter,* where he was to remain for 36 years and produce some 1,500 drawings. Harburger was a masterly delineator of Bavarian types from all classes of the population: professors and students, peasants and proletarians, the arch-conservative beerhall barflies, small householders, musicians, women and children.

Having made a careful study of the 17th-century Netherlandish masters, especially Teniers and Ostade—and having observed all kinds of urban and rural settings during his own travels (including trips to the Tyrol in 1871 and to Venice in 1876-78)—Harburger specialized in placing his humorous figures (themselves very little distorted) in interiors rich in realistic and characteristic details and painterly charm. Indeed, Harburger's constant (and admired) work in oils—genre scenes, still lifes and portraits—had a great effect on his cartoon style; his drawings were done in soft pencil or charcoal and were carefully modeled and shaded. The editors of the *Fliegende Blätter* in this period were happiest when their artists had academic training and made obvious use of it. Harburger apparently suffered very little from the doubts, ambitions and personality clashes that made Wilhelm Busch break away from the *Fliegende Blätter* and made Hermann Schlittgen wish that he had done so when offered the chance.

In the late 1870s, his future certain, Harburger designed his own house in Munich. He worked there successfully up until the time of his death on November 5, 1906.

S.A.

HARCA
See Sanchis Aguado, Julio.

HARDAWAY, JOSEPH BENSON (1891-1957) American cartoonist born near Kansas City, Missouri, in 1891. Joseph Benson (Ben) Hardaway started his career as a cartoonist for the *Kansas City Star* around 1910. During World War I he was the top sergeant in Captain Harry Truman's 129th Field Artillery. After the war Hardaway resumed his cartooning career on various midwestern newspapers, finally deciding to move west and into animation at the end of the 1920s.

In the early 1930s Hardaway was among the first group of artists working on the Merrie Melodies and Looney Tunes produced by Leon Schlesinger; as a scriptwriter he earned the nickname "Bugs" because of the outrageousness of his plot lines. His moment of fame came in 1938 when he co-directed (with Cal Dalton) "Porky's Hare Hunt," in which there appeared for the first time a wisecracking rabbit of whom more was to be heard. In 1940 the rabbit, officially named Bugs Bunny in reference to Hardaway, became the star of the studio—ironically, since 1940 was also the year Hardaway decided to leave Schlesinger for Walter Lantz.

At the Lantz studios Hardaway worked variously as animator, writer and director on many of the *Woody Woodpecker* cartoons. In the early 1950s he left Lantz to write stories for Temple-Toons Productions in Los Angeles. He died at his home in North Hollywood on February 5, 1957.

Bugs Hardaway deserves to be remembered here, if only for his contribution to the Bugs Bunny character.

M.H.

HARDING, NELSON (1877-1944) American Pulitzer Prize-winning cartoonist born in Brooklyn, New York, in 1877. Nelson Harding was educated at the Greenwich Academy in Connecticut and studied art at the Art Students League, the Chase School and the New York School of Design. In 1895 he was apprenticed to an architect but quit in 1898 to serve with the Rough Riders under Theodore Roosevelt at San Juan Hill. He was a lithographer from 1899 to 1907 and then freelanced as an illustrator for a few months before joining the *Brooklyn Eagle* as its staff cartoonist in 1908. He remained with the *Eagle* for 21 years.

Harding's ideas were always well conceived, but his drawings seemed to betray an even more painstaking execution. Indeed, throughout his career Harding's style was stiff, almost awkward. The anatomy was always rudimentary, caricature limited, and attempts at loose shading belabored and mechanical. But Harding's concepts were clever and forceful; his skill and overall excellence were reflected in his two Pulitzers (1927 and 1928) and in the fact that Hearst lured him away in 1929 to draw for the *New York Journal.*

A collection of his cartoons, *The Political Campaign of 1912 in Cartoons,* was published by the *Eagle* in 1912. For years he wrote and illustrated the front-page column "Here and Now" in the *Eagle.* He retired in 1943 and died on December 30, 1944.

R.M.

HARDY, DUDLEY (1866-1922) British cartoonist, oil painter and poster designer born "with a brush in my mouth" in Sheffield, England, in 1866. Son of a marine painter, Dudley Hardy grew up in an artistic atmosphere and was sent to Germany to study art at the age of 15. His studies took him through several European schools, resulting in an almost unique versatility.

His first success came at the age of 22 when his oil painting Sans Asile ("Without Home"), a scene of tramps dossing in Trafalgar Square, was exhibited throughout Europe. The "poster boom" in Britain, which came in the last decade of the 19th century and followed the established French school of poster art, found its leading practitioner in Dudley Hardy. His striking design for the first issue of *Today,* a weekly magazine edited by Anglophile and humorist Jerome K. Jerome, had an enormous impact on both the advertising industry and the public. Hardy's image of a contemporary young woman on the move became known as "The Yellow Girl" and was extremely influential in its striking simplicity and use of bold, flat colors.

With cartoonist contemporaries Tom Browne and Phil May, Hardy formed the London Sketch Club, where weekly two-hour drawing sessions were held in an atmosphere of friendly competition. The stimulating experience of these regular get-togethers was seminal in its influence on British commercial art; out of the contact came a regular flow of new styles, techniques and ideas. Hardy's cartoons appeared in all the latest illustrated papers, alongside those of his fellow club members: *The Pictorial World, Black and White,* the *Sketch,* the *Lady's Pictorial* and, of course, *Punch.*

In 1902 Hardy joined the swelling ranks of the postcard artists, painting several series of cartoons for the Davidson Brothers, publishers. These were sets of pictorial puns illustrating "Proverbs" (his first series), "Book Titles," "Song Titles" and cards that formed a set, after the format of a comic strip: "Mr. Smith's Tramp Abroad" and "Little Billy's Love Affair." Other postcards reproduced his posters for the Egyptian Mail Steamship Company, the Royal Naval Tournament and others, including a set of six poster girls, glamorous, healthy young Victorians for which Hardy will always be remembered.

D.G.

HARMAN, HUGH (1903-1982) American animator born in Pagosa Springs, Colorado, in 1903. Hugh Harman studied at Westport High School and at the Art Institute in Kansas City. In the early 1920s he went to work for the Kansas City Film Ad Agency, where his older brother, Fred (the creator of *Red Ryder*) had also worked, and where he was soon joined by his younger brother, Walker. There he met Rudolph Ising, with whom he was to form a lifelong friendship, as well as Ub Iwerks and Walt Disney. He then became a member of the original Disney team that turned out the Laugh-O-Gram cartoons from 1921 to 1923.

In 1926 Harman joined the fledgling Disney studio in Los Angeles. He worked on the last of the *Alice in Cartoonland* cartoons and on the new *Oswald the Rabbit* series. When Charles Mintz, Disney's distributor and the owner of the *Oswald* name, took the series away from Disney in 1928, he hired Harman and Ising to produce it for him. The following year Harman and Ising decided to form a partnership and become independent producers. They produced the first Looney Tunes cartoons in 1930 for Leon Schlesinger, for release through Warner Brothers, followed the next year by the Merrie Melodies. Their most famous cartoon character at that time was Bosko, a little black boy, whom they took with them when they left Schlesinger to become independent producers for MGM in 1933. Their cartoons were called Happy Harmonies and included such memorable shorts as Hey Hey Fever (1935) and *The Old Mill Pond* (1936), in addition to the *Bosko* series. In 1938 they produced *Merbabies* for the overworked Disney (he reportedly never even set foot in the Harman-Ising studio). That same year they also joined the newly formed MGM animation studio as producers and went their separate professional ways.

At MGM Harman produced a number of outstanding cartoons, including the antiwar *Peace on Earth* (1939), which was nominated for a Nobel Prize, the haunting *Lonesome Stranger* (1940) and the raucous *Alley Cat* (1941). He also formed Hugh Harman Productions later that year and produced instructional, educational and patriotic cartoons for the U.S. government, including *Gonorrhea* (on the dangers of promiscuity, 1943), *Message to Women* (1945) and *Easy Does It* (1947). In the late 1940s Harman made a few unsuccessful cartoons for TV. Dispirited, he then went into advertising work and soon dropped out of public view. In his waning years he lived in retirement near Los Angeles, in close proximity to his old friend and partner Ising. He died in November 1982.

One of the more interesting of ex-Disney animators, Harman has received a number of awards and honors. He was nominated several times for an Oscar, though he never won. His animation work was simple, direct and handsome and is badly in need of critical rediscovery.

M.H.

HARRINGTON, OLIVER WENDELL (1912-1995) The son of an African-American laborer and a Jewish-Hungarian immigrant, Oliver Wendell ("Ollie") Harrington was born in Valhalla, N.Y., and educated in the South Bronx public schools. One of his teachers, who felt black people belonged "in the trash basket," sparked his fury and an early desire to caricature the hated schoolmarm in cartoons which he drew in the margins of his notebooks. "Each drawing," he later wrote, "lifted my wounded spirits a little higher."

"Jackson, it's my duty to tell you that the last culled guy who won in this town got moldered in his dressin' room. Okay now boys, make it a clean fight!"

Ollie Harrington. © Oliver Harrington

Harrington started contributing cartoons to black newspapers in New York in the early 1930's. Moving to Harlem, he became one of the leading figures in the Harlem Renaissance, along with Langston Hughes and Romare Bearden. It was in 1935, for the *Amsterdam News*, that he created his best-remembered character, a pudgy, feisty, proud black man named Bootsy who starred in a series of weekly panels titled *Dark Laughter*, which were later widely syndicated and reprinted in the black press.

In order to further his artistic skills, Harrington took courses at Yale University, from which he graduated in 1939, and at the National Academy of Design. In 1940 he created a war adventure strip, *Jive Gray*, with a black soldier as its hero, for the *Pittsburgh Courier*, and he later went with the troops to North Africa and Europe as a war correspondent. He kept up his political activities along with his professional career throughout the war and afterwards, actively militating in favor of civil rights and in opposition to segregation. These activities brought upon him the ire of the McCarthyites, and he was forced to leave the country, going first to Paris, then to East Germany, where he took up permanent residence in 1961 and later married a German woman.

Throughout the Cold War period, Harrington continued to send from Europe articles and cartoons to black and liberal publications in the States; in 1968 he became the editorial cartoonist for the *Daily World*, the organ of the Communist Party U.S.A. He also contributed to a number of European periodicals, working notably for the German

Das Magazine and *Eulenspiegel*. These cartoons displayed an incisive, often bitter bite in ringing denunciations of what the author perceived to be American racism, militarism, and third-world exploitation.

At the time of the German reunification, Harrington was still living in Berlin, where he died on November 2, 1995. He had lived long enough to see two anthologies of his works published in the United States: *Why I Left America*, a collection of essays, and *Dark Laughter: The Satiric Art of Oliver W. Harrington*, a selection of his cartoons.

M.H.

HARTT, CECIL LAURENCE (1884-1930) Australian cartoonist and Digger humorist born in Prahran, near Melbourne, Australia, in 1884.

The Australian newspaper the *Bulletin* is rightly credited with the emergence of the first era of Australian graphic humor, when from 1880 up to the period of World War I cartoons and joke drawings began to develop and acquire a distinctive national character. The second development in this field is recognized as the *Smith's Weekly* era—a period that started when this weekly paper was founded in 1919. *Smith's*, which was primarily an illustrated broadsheet newspaper carrying whole pages smothered with joke drawings and political cartoons, quickly established in its pages a department devoted to fostering the *Digger* (returned soldier) spirit, under the title *Unofficial History of the AIF* (Australian Imperial Forces). Up until it ceased publication in 1950, *Smith's Weekly* continued this page, featuring jokes, anecdotes, cartoon strips and cartoon drawings of army humor—the latter significant and important because they lasted for over a quarter of a century of Australian graphic humor.

Many writers have observed the characteristics of the Australian soldier, but it was the artists of the now defunct *Smith's Weekly* who did most to establish the Digger as a folk type, depicting him as resourceful, casual in speech and attitude, by turns modest and boastful, and rebellious to all forms of military authority and red tape. Two of the artists who gave the Digger page of *Smith's Weekly* its special character and its popularity were Cecil Hartt and Frank Dunne.

First swaggie: "Why do yer make it a point of goin' ter Bourke every couple of years?"
Second swaggie: "Well, I get all me letters addressed there!"

Cecil Hartt. © Smith's Weekly.

Cecil Hartt, himself a soldier, twice wounded at Gallipoli, was the first Digger artist of note. However, very little is known of his early art training, although for a period he did take lessons with Alek Sass, a popular cartoonist for the Melbourne *Punch* who conducted a school in Melbourne before he too joined *Smith's Weekly* in its infancy.

Around 1908, Hartt was freelancing, contributing to *Comments*, a weekly news magazine edited by Grant Hervey, and to Randolph Bedford's *Clarion*. Before Hartt joined the 18th Battalion AIF at the outbreak of World War I, his joke drawings were appearing with some regularity in the *Bulletin*. Like Phil May, Hartt had a fondness and sympathy for the city tramps and down-and-outs, subjects he drew in a fine, finished style of pen drawing.

Cecil Hartt's first Digger humor was drawn in London, where he was invalided in 1916, for publication in his *Humorosities* (1917), a collection of soldier humor and war cartoons. The observations in these drawings are outstanding for their humor and for their character portraits of Australian soldiers. Through his drawings, Hartt revealed a true but kindly record of easygoing, fussless men expressing a sardonic reaction to life in the trenches, on recreational leave, in the training camps and on a spree.

After his discharge from the army, Hartt joined *Smith's Weekly* in 1919, where for 11 years he perpetuated the Digger legend with his joke drawings, his city-tramp and occasional "backblocks" themes. He was known as an utterly tolerant and uncritical person, kind and good-hearted; standing just six feet tall, he fit the popular conception of the lean Australian.

The news of his tragic death on May 21, 1930, came to his public and friends as a great shock. He had been found dead, with a wound in the head and a shotgun beside him, on a mountain near Moruya, in New South Wales. In a tribute, the famous Australian cartoonist Stan Cross said: "He was nearest of all his contemporaries to the Australian tradition, as far as humorous art can expound it, and we practitioners, as well as Australian comic art in the abstract, owe him a lot."

Two collections of Cecil Hartt's soldier humor were published: *Humorosities* (London, 1917) and *Diggerettes* (Sydney, 1919).

V.L.

HARVEY, ALICE (1905-198?) American cartoonist born around 1905. Biographical details about Alice Harvey are hard to come by. She began contributing to the *New Yorker* shortly after its foundation in 1925. Of the original trio of major women artists working for the *New Yorker*—the others being Helen Hokinson and Barbara Shermund—Harvey's association with the magazine was the shortest.

For a time Harvey shared a studio (and a famous neighbor, E.L. Masters) with Hokinson back in Chicago's

—"Do you like Kipling?"
—"Why, I don't know. How do you kipple?"

Alice Harvey. © Life.

Montgomery Ward Towers, where they worked as fashion illustrators, principally for Marshall Field. In the early 1920s, both left the Windy City for New York, applying upon arrival for jobs in the comic art department of the Hearst-owned *New York Mirror.* Both were hired on the spot by the editor, Arthur Brisbane, at the princely sum of $100 per week. When Hokinson's humor proved too sophisticated for the mass market, she left the Mirror and resumed her art studies, eventually catching on in the *New Yorker* as a regular contributor. Soon after (and perhaps by her intervention), Alice Harvey too joined the magazine's regular staff. Harvey worked as an illustrator and occasional cartoonist until, as Dale Kramer reports somewhat vaguely in *Ross and the New Yorker,* marriage and children pushed her art career into the background. In any case, after the mid-1930s, there was no further evidence of her work in the pages of the magazine. She reportedly died in the late 1980s.

Purely as an illustrator, Harvey was perhaps the most noteworthy of the three contemporaries. Her figures were always clean and rakishly executed (in pen and ink or charcoal), and she had a way of expressing actions and facial expressions that was at times quite striking. The frightened-timid-bewildered face of a young flapper lost in the bustle of her first cruise-ship embarkation (in a December 1930 drawing) is a fine example of this ability. Unfortunately, her eye and ear for amusing situations fell far short of Hokinson's or Shermund's, which probably explains her relatively infrequent appearances as a cartoonist. Still, when it came to rendering the gracefully unfettered femininity of the faintly naughty, style-conscious Jazz Age, there was no other artist, male or female, on the *New Yorker* staff who could carry it off with greater aplomb.

R.C.

HASSALL, JOHN (1868-1948) British cartoonist born in Walmer, Kent, England, on May 21, 1868. "Skegness Is So Bracing": one of the most famous posters in British history. The Jolly Fisherman (as he is known) dancing over the sunny sands of the seaside resort is still seen at railway stations; it is the oldest poster in the business. John Hassall drew it in 1909 and was paid 12 guineas (then 50 dollars) outright.

Hassall was educated at Newton Abbot College, Devon, and at Heidelberg (his father was a paralyzed army lieutenant). Failing his entry into Sandringham Military College, Hassall went to be a farmer in Minnedosa, Canada. From there he mailed a series of sketches to the London *Daily Graphic,* and "A Manitoba Surprise Party" was published on February 26, 1890. Encouraged, he decided to concentrate on art and studied both in Antwerp, Holland, and at the Académie Julian, Paris. Back in London, however, he found himself unable to earn a living as a classical painter, and in 1894 he answered an advertisement of the color printers David Allen and Sons seeking poster designers. Hassall quickly developed a distinctive style inspired by the famous French school of poster design. He used a bold black outline, cartoon fashion, with equally bold flat colors and almost always a sense of humor. Borwicks baking powder ("Let Me Help You to Rise") and Veritas gas mantles ("Dismayed But Not Dismantled") are typical of his work and contrast comically with his dramatic theater posters ("The Only Way," etc.).

Hassall rose speedily to fame, and he was elected to the Royal Institute of Painters in Watercolours in 1901. He shortly opened the John Hassall School and taught many artists of the younger generation, particularly the cartoonists. His first book illustration work was for A Cockney in Arcadia (1899). Despite his great output and popularity, by May 1939 he was awarded a civil list pension of £110 per annum, and his bank account stood at four shillings and fourpence. "People don't want my work nowadays. They say I am old-fashioned," he said, yet the government commissioned him for one last poster on air raid precautions. They didn't pay him. But not everyone forgot Hassall; on his death in 1948, the Skegness Corporation sent a wreath in the shape of his "Jolly Fisherman."

Books: A *Cockney in Arcadia* (1899); *Primeval Scenes* (1899); *Two Wellworn Shoe Stories* (1899); *Active Army Alphabet* (1899); Oh My Darling Clementine (1900); *By the Way Ballads* (1901); *A Moral Alphabet* (1901); Six and Twenty Boys (1902); *Grimm's Fairy Tales* (1902); *Pantomime ABC* (1902); *ABC of Everyday People* (1902); *People* (1903); *Absurd Ditties* (1903); *Round the World ABC* (1904); *The Old Nursery Stories* (1904); *The Twins* (1904); *All the Best Nursery Rhymes* (1905); The Magic Shop (1905); *Ruff and Reddy* (1905); *Paris Not to Mention Monte Carlo* (1906); *The Happy Annual* (1907); *Good Queen Bess* (1907); *Sport and Play* (1907); Through the *Wood (1907); Book of John Hassall (1907); The Princess and the Dragon* (1908); *Little Robin Hood* (1909); *Potted Brains* (1909); *Mother Goose's Nursery Rhymes* (1909); *Miss Manners* (1909); *Tales and Talks* (1909); *The Doll's Diary* (1909); *Friday and Saturday* (1910); *One Hundred Years Hence* (1911); *Tommy Lobb* (1912); *The Sleeping Beauty* (1912); *Love and a Cottage* (1913); *A Day in Tangier* (1913); *Children's Party Book* (1914); *Keep Smiling* (1914); *The Wookey Hole* (1914); *Ye Berlin Tapestrie* (1915); *Peter Pan Painting Book* (1915); *With Love from Daddy* (1918); *Hassall ABC* (1918); *Blackie's Popular Fairy Tales* (1921); *Blackie's Popular Nursery Rhymes* (1921); *Wembley Leaflets* (1925); *The*

Twins (1927); *Humours of Bridge* (1928); *Our Diary* (1928); *Robinson Crusoe* (1930); and *Blackie's Popular Nursery Stories* (1931).

D.G.

HAUGHTON, WILFRED H. (1893-197?) British cartoonist born in West Norwood, London, England, on December 12, 1893. The first cartoonist to be permitted to draw Mickey Mouse in the United Kingdom was Wilfred Haughton. He was educated at Salters Hill Board School, then Alleyns School, Dulwich. His father was a compositor, but a printers' strike prevented the boy from entering the trade. He became a clerk in commerce and on the outbreak of World War I joined the Kings Royal Rifle Corps. After service in Salonika, he was invalided out and was eventually granted a two-year art course at the Regent Street Polytechnic (1919-20).

He began freelancing cartoons to *Passing Show, London Mail* and other humor magazines of the period, and in 1921, with a fellow student, set up Meccart Studios. This two-man outfit specialized in creating and designing novelties and paper gimmicks for use in advertising, then marketing them and manufacturing them in conjunction with a small printer, Lydall and Son of Dulwich. The novelties met with immediate success and were mainly purchased by the Amalagamated Press as giveaways and inserts for their children's comic papers. Unfortunately, a bad business partner caused the collapse of the budding studio.

Haughton then met W.H. Cornelius of 23 Paper Street, Clerkenwell, London, a novelty supplier of cheap children's toys to small shops and market stalls. Cornelius signed Haughton as a freelance novelty creator, sending him on periodic trips to Nuremberg, Germany, to supervise the manufacture of his designs. Cornelius had already exploited the cartoon character Felix the Cat to good advantage in silent film days. When Mickey Mouse was opened up for exploitation by Walt Disney's London representative, William Levy, Cornelius obtained the contract through Haughton's ability to draw the new character. Haughton then designed toys, books and novelties, such as color transfers, featuring Mickey, and made trips to Germany to arrange for their manufacture. Dean and Son, publishers of children's books, approached Levy for the rights to produce The *Mickey Mouse Annual*, and Levy in turn passed the artwork on to Haughton. Haughton drew the entire *Annual* (128 pages plus color plates) within two months and continued to draw the *Annual* from 1931 through to the forties. Many of his *Annual* strips were syndicated abroad, throughout Europe, and appeared as serials in comic papers.

Haughton also drew other Mickey Mouse books, and when Ub Iwerks left Disney to produce his *Flip the Frog* series, Haughton drew the only edition of *Flip the Frog Annual* (1932). In 1936 Levy and the Walt Disney-Mickey Mouse Ltd. operation produced the first comic weekly printed in photogravure, *Mickey Mouse Weekly,* through Odhams Press. Haughton was given the front cover and painted a large tabloid adventure of the Disney characters every week for the first three years. Meanwhile, his connections had provided further opportunities, and for the Sunday newspaper *The People,* he created and drew the strip *Eb and Flo,* about two blacks whose "Cheery Coons Club" feature ran from October 30, 1932, to World War II. They also appeared in *Eb and Flo Annual* (1937?) and in *Mickey Mouse Weekly,* and in his "spare time," Haughton also drew the daily strip *Bobby Bear* in the *Daily Herald* from 1932, plus the colorful Christmas *Bobby Bear Annual.*

Haughton experimented with animation for films, devising a system of pliable rubber puppets built on wire framework, but unhappily a series of business disasters put an end to his ambitions as an animation producer. For some years he lived on his old-age pension in South Africa, actively ambitious to create a successful children's puppet series for television. He died in the late 1970s.

D.G.

HAYASHI, SEICHI (1945-) Japanese animator, cartoonist, comic book artist, illustrator and film director born in Japanese-controlled Manchuria in March 1945. Soon after the end of the war, Seichi Hayashi's father and older sister died, and he and his mother were repatriated to Japan, where he entered school in the Tokyo area. Hayashi reportedly hated school from the start and spent much of his time drawing cartoons. After graduating from middle school, he watched as many movies as he could for half a year and then found work in the animation department of the Toei film company. At 16 he became an assistant to Sadao Tsukioka, creator of *Ōkami Shōnen Ken* ("Ken the Wolf Boy"), Japan's first TV animation. With his talent, and because of the demand for animators that existed at the time, he quickly took on more and more responsibility. At 20 Hayashi quit Toei to help Tsukioka, who was by then doing independent animation, and ever since he has been freelancing actively as a true dilettante in animation, cartoons and illustration.

Hayashi made his debut as a comic book artist in 1966 with *Azuma to Musuko to Kuenai Tamashi* ("Japan, the Son, and the Inedible Spirit"), which appeared in *Garo,* the forum for many a new artist in Japan. He was heavily influenced by Yoshiharu Tsuge in the confessional form his work took. He next turned out a series of popular strips, also running in *Garo,* such as *Kyodai na Uo* ("Giant Fish"), *Aka Tombo* ("Red Dragonfly"), *Hana no Uta* ("Poems of Flowers") and *Aka Iro no Ereji* ("Red Elegy"). *Aka Iro no Ereji* appears to be a semiautobiographical work portraying his days at Toei and the dilemma he faced when caught between his job and union activities. Hayashi also did some animation, independently producing a work entitled *Kage* ("Shadow") in 1968, and the following year doing *10 Gatsu 13 Nichi Satsujin* ("October 13 Murder").

Hayashi's work is almost psychedelic in its evocation of moods. His women characters are unique in that they tend to be frail but erotic women of the world rather than the voluptuous middle-class beauties so often depicted by other artists. He concentrates on the development of a lyrical aesthetic in all the mediums he works in, and plot is generally secondary. Today, Hayashi is best known as an illustrator rather than a cartoonist, although he recently created a story titled *Guppii wa Shinanai* ("Guppies Don't Die") for the magazine *Garo,* and it was reprinted in book form in 1996. Whatever Hayashi does, he does well: he has won a string of awards for his films, television commercial

"If you won't play my way I'll take my ball and go home."

Hugh Haynie. © Courier-Journal.

work, and illustrated books. Posters by him, in his immediately identifiable style, can be seen in train stations and public places throughout Japan.

F.S.

HAYNIE, HUGH SMITH (1927-) American cartoonist born in Reedville, Virginia, on February 6, 1927. Hugh Haynie was educated at the College of William and Mary, from which he received a B.A. in 1950. He also holds an L.H.D. from the University of Louisville (1968). He began his career on the *Richmond Times-Dispatch* in 1952 as a staff artist and editorial cartoonist. Fired soon thereafter, he secured a similar position with the *Greensboro Daily News* in North Carolina (1953-58), with a six-month stint for the *Atlanta Journal* in the middle (1955-56). Since 1958 Haynie has been the political cartoonist of the *Louisville Courier-Journal.* He retired on October 1, 1995.

Haynie is in the forefront of contemporary American political cartooning on two counts: his ideas—consistently liberal—are cleverly conceived and designed, and his drawing style is one of the most individualistic in the field. It is stylized (some would say too mannered and labored) and rendered carefully in pen and brush with a wide variety of shading media. Shadows and wrinkles are meticulously laid in, and backgrounds often disappear in borderlines to make a stylized whole of the drawing. Haynie's effective cartoons are distributed widely by the Los Angeles Times Syndicate.

R.M.

HAYWARD, STANLEY (1930-) British cartoon scriptwriter born in London, England, on October 30, 1930. The leading and most prolific writer of scripts for animated cartoons in England, Stan Hayward was educated at Dartford Technical College. He joined the merchant navy at 16 and two years later jumped ship in Australia. There he studied chemistry and music, returning to London in 1952 to play electric guitar in the "coffee bar skiffle" boom. Then the navy caught up with him, making him serve another two years, during which he began to try his hand as a writer. In 1956 he contributed gags to the BBC radio *Goon Show* series, and in 1958 he entered the animation industry as a writer for the new TV Cartoons company formed by George Dunning, Dick Williams and Bill Sewell.

Hayward's first solo commercial was for Courage beer. His first entertainment cartoon, *The Wardrobe,* was made by the same company in 1960; it was described as "an exercise in surrealist humor that uses sounds and images forced against the viewer's logical interpretation." It set the style and pace for all subsequent Hayward cartoons; he himself describes this as variations on the theme of "the little man trying to make sense of the world. He knows what he wants, but doesn't know what it is when he gets it." *The Ever-Changing Motor Car* followed; it was a longer film sponsored by Ford, as was *Power Train,* a deliberate departure from the didactic type of film so common at the time (1961).

During 1962, his most successful year, Hayward scripted *The Flying Man,* George Dunning's unique exercise in painted animation; *The Apple,* drawn in black and white but shot in color; *Love Me Love Me Love Me,* in which Richard Williams drew directly onto cels with wax crayons; and *The Rise and Fall of Emily Sprod,* his first association with breezy Bob Godfrey, using a free-style mix of cutouts, live action and animation. A fallow period followed, with Hayward working for awhile as ghost writer on Peter Maddocks's *Daily Express* strip *Hector Cringe,* and *Saints and Sinners,* a strip for the Glasgow *Evening Citizen.* Then Hayward changed direction and became a skin diver. Meanwhile his cartoons were shown at the Annecy Animation Festival, and in consequence the National Film Board of Canada offered him a year's contract. Little came of this on screen, and in 1964 Hayward returned to London, writing *Alf, Bill and Fred* for Godfrey and a number of scripts and loop films for Halas and Batchelor. For this studio he also wrote *Flow Diagrams* and *The Question* (1967), *Topology* and *Linear Programming* (1969) and *What Is a Computer* (1971). He was well able to answer the latter question because he had won his own computer in a contest run by *New Scientist* magazine!

Comedy films continued to spice the line of industrial and educational cartoons: *Whatever Happened to Uncle Fred* and *The Rope Trick* (both Godfrey, 1967), *Two Off the Cuff* (Godfrey, 1968), *The Trendsetter* (Biographic, *1969), Henry 9 till 5* (Godfrey, 1970), *I Love You, Package Deal* and *Fairy*

Story (all Wyatt-Cattaneo, 1970), *I'm Glad You Asked That Question* (Biographic, 1971), *Kama Sutra Rides Again* (Godfrey, 1971), *Way Out* and *When I'm Rich.* The last two cinema cartoons were made in 1975 and 1977 by New Fields Animation, a company Hayward owns with Ted Rockley and Derek Phillips. It represents Hayward's third attempt to go independent. Computer Studio, started in 1970, collapsed, and Video Animation (1973), which made titles for BBC TV shows, was sold to EMI. Hayward's first book, *Scriptwriting for Animation,* was published in 1977. Later films include *Switched On* (1975), *Mathematician* (1976), *When I Am Rich* (1977), *Henry's Cat* (TV series, 1983), and *Lily* (1995).

D.G.

HAZEL (U.S.) The *Saturday Evening Post* added a new star to its list of luminaries in the autumn of 1943: Hazel, the sarcastic, assertive and take-charge maid of the Baxter household. She joined other classic characters like Henry and Little Lulu who had run weekly in the *Post.* Cartoonist Ted Key had been running the maid character in the Sunday supplement *This Week* and in *Collier's* before the *Post* offered a contract and a regular spot in the magazine in return for ownership.

Even during the war Key maintained weekly output, and after the war many movie, Broadway and TV offers were considered. In the 1950s Hazel came to television, played by Shirley Booth, and gathered an accumulated total of 22.5 Nielsen average points and an average 36.4 share of its audience potential. In four years on NBC it was sponsored by Ford Motor; one year on CBS was sponsored by Procter and Gamble. The half-hour comedy episodes are still syndicated. Key also produced several animated Hazel cartoons for commercials.

In 1969 the *Saturday Evening Post* folded, and Hazel lost her familiar back-page berth. But King Features immediately picked up the panel, and it is now one of the most successful of newspaper panels, appearing six days a week; the revived *Post* also runs the feature again. Key has regained rights to his character.

"Hazel." © Saturday Evening Post.

The cast includes Hazel the maid (by circumstances and character the *de facto* head of the household), George and Dorothy Baxter, and their son Harold and adopted daughter Katie. The large dog Smilie and cat Mostly (she's mostly Siamese) round out the regular cast. The kids' friends, who fight a constant battle with the maid for prerogatives, and the Baxters' guests, who never fail to be shocked by some statement or action of Hazel's, provide variety in the lively and unpredictable panel. It is to Key's great credit that what is essentially a single-situation premise in a single-panel format has succeeded so well, and so interestingly, for more than fifty years.

The many *Hazel* anthologies include *Hazel, Here's Hazel, If You Like Hazel, Hazel Rides Again, All Hazel, The Hazel Jubilee, Hazel Time, Life With Hazel, Hazel Power, Right On, Hazel* and *Ms. Hazel.*

R.M.

HE WEI (1934-) As one of the best cartoonists, He has published thousands of cartoons since the early 1950s. A member of the Man ethnic group, He has been working as editor at the *Worker's Daily* in Beijing. He is one of the pioneer cartoonists experimenting with cartoons made in brush and ink as were the traditional Chinese paintings. With such uncommon cartooning, He and his colleagues are trying to prove successfully that cartoons are, and should be, regarded as a branch of the school of fine art. His works have won many awards nationally and internationally: in 1983 and 1985 he won "Beijing Best Arts Awards"; in 1986 "The Best Editorial Caricature"; in 1987 and 1988 he won prizes in Japan; and in 1988 he was awarded the medal of "Promotion of the Nation" by the State Council of China.

He studied fine art in the well-known Lu Xun Art Institute in Shenyang between 1950 and 1951, but was teaching art in a high school in Heilongjiang Province as early as 1949. After the People's Republic of China was founded, he came to Beijing and worked as art editor in the *Worker's Daily,* a nationally distributed newspaper, from 1953 to the present. He has been a member of several professional organizations, including Chinese Artist Association, Chinese Cartoon Art Commission, Chinese Press Cartoon Research Society, and Beijing Art and Calligraphy Study. He has been included in several *Who's Whos*, such as *Contemporary Chinese* (Shanghai, 1991), *Dictionary of the Man Minority* (Liaoning, 1990), *World Cartoon Encyclopedia* (Taiwan, 1988), *Chinese Artist Dictionary* (Shanghai, 1987), and *Directory of International Biography* (Cambridge, England, 1992).

As well as some other top Chinese cartoonists, He has a good knowledge of Chinese classical literature and folklore, which he has applied to both his satirical caricature and humorous cartoons. One of his interests is to find humor and problems in ordinary life, and present them via the Chinese traditional style of brush-and-ink. His recently published *He Wei Brush-and-Ink Cartoons* selected mainly such works. While enjoying his strong colorful brushworks, readers also learn the deep meaning in each cartoon's satirical humor.

"You'll be glad to know
Heathcliff got down off the roof all by himself."

"Heathcliff." © *McNaught Syndicate.*

In He's collection, published in 1994, he selected his most outstanding brush-and-ink cartoons. On the cover page, a big-bellied Buddha is laughing with his mouth wide open. In the traditional way of Chinese painting, a poem accompanies the painting which says: "A big bully can contain whatever difficulty matters in the world; and a laughing mouth opens often to laugh at all the laughable people in the universe." Such a philosophy may be good medicine for all to enjoy life better.

H.Y.L.L.

HEATHCLIFF (U.S.) *Heathcliff* is a newspaper panel created by George Gately (brother of noted cartoonist John Gallagher) for the McNaught Syndicate; it made its debut on September 3, 1973.

Heathcliff is the quintessential fat cat. Smug, self-assured and underhanded, he stops at nothing to get what he regards as his just desserts: a better than square meal, the easiest chair in the house and complete sway over the neighborhood pets. The elderly couple who happen to be Heathcliff's owners do not stand a chance when they try to thwart the schemes of the crafty feline. Always ready to lend a paw when he is least needed, Heathcliff can turn tough on occasion; and even the neighborhood dogs keep a prudent distance when the cocky striped cat ambles down the street.

In a field overrun on all sides by cartoon cats, it is to Gately's credit that he has been able to create a highly individualized, original character. With his sly mien and roguish demeanor, Heathcliff stands out sharply as a worthy successor to such comic strip cats as Felix and Spooky. Gately's drawing style is deceptively easy and pleasingly cartoony, making *Heathcliff* one of the most refreshing gag panels to come along in some time.

So far *Heathcliff* has spawned over 40 paperback collections. Two animated cartoon programs aired on ABC in 1980 and 1981; and in 1985 there came *Heathcliff the Movie*, along with a comic-book series published by Marvel. Of late *Heathcliff* (now syndicated by Tribune Media Services) has been largely done by Gately's brother, John Gallagher.

M.H.

HECKLE AND JECKLE (U.S.) Heckle and Jeckle burst onto the screen in 1946 in Paul Terry's "The Talking Magpies." They were two identical-looking rascally birds who delighted in playing pranks on all and sundry. Their anarchistic personalities and fast talk carried them to extremes of aggression and outrageousness.

The best *Heckle and Jeckle* cartoons were those produced in the 1940s, when the two birds were at the height of their

"Heckle and Jeckle." © *CBS Films.*

diabolical inventiveness. In "The Uninvited Pests" they crashed a party and made mincemeat of the hosts and other guests; in "McDougal's Rest Farm" they turned a bucolic oasis of quiet and peace into a madhouse; in "The Stowaways" they wreaked havoc on the crew and passengers of an ocean liner. The two magpies were at their best (or worst) in "In Again, Out Again," during which they repeatedly tried to escape from jail, and in "Magpie Madness," where the animators simply let the birds run amuck without any semblance of rhyme or reason. As the 1950s rolled in, the magpies' mischief became more and more mindless and repetitious. Their personalities were toned down after CBS took over the series, and they simply became filler material on the televised *Mighty Mouse Show.* The two birds again played second bananas to the super-rodent in the 1979-1980 *The New Adventures of Mighty Mouse and Heckle and Jeckle,* an animated series produced for CBS by Filmation.

Among the directors who worked on the *Heckle and Jeckle* cartoons, mention should be made of such Terrytoons stalwarts as Connie Rasinski, Mannie Davis and Eddie Donnelly. Heckle and Jeckle have been featured in comic books since the late 1940s, and there have also been Heckle and Jeckle toys and puzzles.

M.H.

HEINE, THOMAS THEODOR (1867-1948) German cartoonist, illustrator and painter born in Leipzig, Germany, on February 28, 1867. The son of a chemist and manufacturer of rubber products, T.T. Heine got into trouble with his biting cartoons while still a gymnasium student. After art study at the Düsseldorf Academy, he finally settled in Munich in 1889, painting and submitting cartoons to the *Fliegende Blätter* and, from early 1896, to *Jugend.* He also did posters, commercial art and book illustration, as he was to continue doing through the years.

When the publisher Albert Langen founded the magazine *Simplicissimus,* Heine became one of the charter members and remained on its staff with minor interruptions until 1933, doing about twenty-five hundred drawings for it. He quickly stood out as the most versatile and ingenious artist on the magazine, working brilliantly in either line or color, in either painterly modeling or contour, and parodying anyone else's style with ease. The painter Lovis Corinth said that as an artist Heine could do anything he set his mind to, and the old Berlin master Max Liebermann called him the greatest German draftsman.

All this skill and genius were at the service of an aggressive intelligence that oddly mingled reforming zeal with a penchant for cruelty and sadism. Not well liked personally even by his colleagues, Heine became anathema to the Wilhelmine establishment and even served a jail sentence in 1898.

Though all social folly was his fodder and his means of expression were protean, several visual themes recurred obsessively in his art—especially dogs (he frequently interpreted human society in terms of the interactions of various canine breeds, and he invented a pugnacious bulldog as an emblem for *Simplicissimus*) and a very personal brand of devil, obese and bestial, mingling in all human affairs as a tempter or an avenger.

A rich man of Munich returns to patronize the arts.

T.T. Heine, 1925. © Simplicissimus.

Heine's album publications included *Bilder aus dem Familienleben* ("Scenes from Family Life") and *Torheiten* ("Follies"). He wrote and illustrated a book of cynical modern fairy tales—*Die Märchen* (1935)—and a very thickly veiled autobiographical novel—*Ich Warte auf Wunder* ("I'm Waiting for Miracles," 1945).

In 1933 Heine, who was Jewish, could no longer remain in Germany, and years of wandering lay ahead for the elderly man; he went to Prague, Brno, Oslo and finally, in 1942, to Stockholm. Heine became a Swedish subject and drew for the *Göteborgs Handelsoch Sjöfartstidning.* He died in Stockholm on January 26, 1948.

S.A.

HELL (U.S.) Art Young, an atheist by trade, had a lifelong fascination with the infernal region, largely for its possibilities as a comic device and as contemplated last stop for the devils—capitalists, bores, salesmen, quack doctors—who plagued him on this side of the Styx. *Hell* is the generic title for four separate cartoon series appearing over a 47-year period.

Not content to let Homer, Virgil, Dante, Milton and hellfire preachers monopolize speculations about Hell—and Botticelli, Dürer, Bruegel, Callot, Flaxman, Blake and Doré record its physical aspects—the young Young began the chronicle *Hell Up to Date* in 1887. In a book published by Schulte, the Chicago cartoonist averred that the entrance to the region was located in that city. The book, which sold fairly well in the Midwest, carried the subtitle "The reckless journey of R. Palasco Drant, special correspondent, through the infernal regions, as recorded by himself: with illustrations by Art Young." The title of the deluxe edition was softened to *Hades Up to Date.*

Snapshots in Hades was later a long-running feature in *Life,* and Young drew a similar, untitled series concurrently in *Puck.* It featured the fates that awaited the malevolent and greedy. Here the captions and concepts were somewhat more developed than in the published collection. For the fledgling *Cosmopolitan* under John Brisben Walker, Young drew *Hiprah Hunt's Journey Through the Inferno,* about a descendant of New England witch-burners, in May, June, July and August of 1900. Only the first installment carried text, and the series of cartoons was collected in book form in 1901 by C. Zimmerman publishers under the title *Through Hell with Hiprah Hunt.* In this treatment Hell was populated by bad poets and refurnished with modern improvements. "I wanted a democratic Hell," Young wrote, "and modern efficiency."

These series were produced in the years of Art Young's conversion from political orthodoxy to socialism. By 1933 he was a Communist, and the cartoon-and-text series *Art Young's Inferno* was by far his bitterest indictment of life, the system, hypocrisy as he saw it and human nature in general. As a matter of fact, it was probably the most consistently sardonic material of his career, including sustained periods on the *Masses* and the *New Masses.* Here, in line drawings and wash, he excoriated drug and alcohol addicts, radio programs, patriotism, inherited wealth, apathy, subways, Sunday comics, graft, slang, cheerful people, comfort stations, travelogues, country clubs and courage. There was actually little political substance in Young's work, but he injected as much cynicism and vitriol—and basic truth—as Ambrose Bierce at his most caustic. Characteristically, this last visit to Hell (published privately in 1934 by Delphic Studios) featured the self-caricatured Young as the tourist.

R.M.

HELL UP TO DATE
See Hell.

HENFIL
See Filho, Henrique de Souza.

HENGELER, ADOLF (1863-after 1923) German cartoonist and painter born at Kempten in Allgäu, southern Germany, on February 11, 1863. Adolf Hengeler was one of the foremost contributors to the venerable Munich humor magazine *Fliegende Blätter* in the late 19th century. The son of an estate steward, at the age of 15 he was apprenticed to a lithographer. In 1881 he began attending the Munich Arts and Crafts School, moving on to the Academy in 1885. The year before, he had already begun his association with the famous magazine, which was to publish some 4,000 Hengeler drawings in the next 20 years.

His style was direct and hearty, using a juicy and sinuous line that might or might not be accompanied by washes. His subject matter included witty studies of German life in the earlier half of the century (the cozy and smug Biedermeier period); animal fables, with insects a specialty; travesties of ancient and medieval history; peasant and genre scenes; and a series of intricate machines that prefigured those of Rube Goldberg (one contraption replaces an entire tavern, serving the customer food and drink, playing cards with him and then bouncing him when he grows unruly). These drawings appeared as separate panels or as illustrations for droll verses, or they formed little wordless (or laconic) picture stories in the manner of the Russian-French cartoonist Caran d'Ache. A large number of Hengeler's *Fliegende Blätter* pieces were gathered into a *Hengeler-Album* by the magazine's publishers (the firm of Braun and Schneider) in 1904.

All through his years as a cartoonist Hengeler had been painting secretly for his own satisfaction; about 1899, unfortunately, he decided to share these works with the world, and for at least the next two decades he concentrated on idylls and archaic romantic scenes that were diluted Spitzweg and deluded homage to the Munich academicians. He also painted frescoes on houses in Murnau and in the main chamber of the town hall in Freising.

During World War I, Hengeler kept a pictorial diary containing symbolic representations of "the attack of our (Germany's) enemies on Germany's people and property," as an art critic put it (as late as 1923!). On the occasion of his 60th birthday, in 1923, Hengeler published an album of imaginative colored crayon drawings that combine some of the best elements of his double career as cartoonist and painter. With their real charm and humor, their touch of mystery and their great freedom of execution, these form a very likable close to his oeuvre.

S.A.

HENG KIM SONG (1963-) Heng Kim Song was born in Singapore on June 7, 1963. After graduating with a diploma in business studies from Ngee Ann Polytechnic in 1983, Heng put his drawing skills to use, contributing political cartoons to the Chinese newspaper, *Lianhe Zaobao.*

OLLIE HARRINGTON
"Jackson, it's my duty to tell you that the last culled guy who won in this town got moldered in his dressin' room. Okay now boys, make it a clean fight!"

Heng Kim Song. © Cartoonists and Writers Syndicate.

Maurice Henry. © Henry

Since 1984, he has been a mainstay at the daily, drawing on a commission basis three political cartoons weekly. For awhile in the mid-1980s, the government-controlled daily, *Straits Times,* also published many of his works.

Because cartooning in Singapore has not been popular and lucrative enough to build a reputation and earn a living, Heng has published many of his cartoons abroad and, since 1986, has worked as designer at Giftrend Designs and Productions. Represented by Cartoonists and Writers Syndicate in New York, Heng is one of the most frequently published of that agency's cartoonists, his works appearing in the *International Herald Tribune, New York Times, Newsweek, Asahi Shimbun,* and others. The Hong Kong-based *Asiaweek,* which depends upon freelance cartoons, carries a greater proportion of cartoons by Heng then by any other artist.

Working in an authoritarian state such as Singapore, Heng has had to labor under strict libel laws and government guidance that are both repressive and ludicrous, yet he has been able to get in his digs at the political and social system. His style is made up of filled-in details and liberal uses of shading and cross-hatching.

J.A.L.

HENRY, MAURICE (1907-1984) French cartoonist and animated cartoon director born in northern France on December 29, 1907. After studies at the Paris Law School Maurice Henry became a journalist and art critic for various dailies. One in particular, Le Petit Journal, published his first sketch in 1932. Since then, Henry has drawn close to 30,000 cartoons for over 160 newspapers and magazines, chiefly for *L'Oeuvre, Le Canard Enchaîné, L'Express* and *Carrefour.*

Much of his artwork has been reedited in albums: *Les Mystères de L'Olympe* ("Olympus Mysteries," 1945), *Les Métamorphoses du Vide* ("Metamorphoses of Emptiness," 1955), *Kopfkissenbuch* ("Pillow Book," 1956), *A Bout Portant* ("Point-Blank," 1958), *Les 32 Positions de l'Androgyne* ("The 32 Positions of Androgynous Man," 1961), *Hors Mesures* ("Beyond Bounds," 1969), etc. In addition, two collections of his *dessins* ("drawings") covering the decades between 1930 and 1970 were published in 1960 and 1970. He was a gagman and adaptor for the movie *Les Aventures des Pieds-Nickelés* and has also done several animated cartoons, the most interesting a short explaining the workings and advantages of the Marshall Plan (1948).

His characters, whether humans or humanized animals, all have big, wide-open eyes that make them look constantly surprised, empty-headed and even deranged. The subjects he treats most often come from mythology, religion (as in the drawing of Christ with the cross, calling for a porter), prison life and especially—in the surrealist tradition Henry belongs to—the oneiric world (as in the cartoon where the husband is sleeping in a parked Venetian gondola while his wife, lying in a regular bed, is asking him to "let me climb in your dream").

Maurice Henry was a regular exhibitor at the Salon de Mai and other art galleries. He died in 1984.

P.H.

HERBLOCK
See Block, Herbert Lawrence.

HERFORD, OLIVER (1863-1935) American cartoonist, poet and epigrammist born in Sheffield, England, in December 1863. Oliver Herford's father, a minister, was transferred to a parish in Boston when his son was young, and the future cartoonist grew up with a foot in both societies. He was educated at Lancaster College in England and Antioch College in Ohio, and received art training at the Slade School in London and the Académie Julian in Paris.

Herford sold his first cartoon to the *Century* magazine, where only the more respectable cartoonists appeared, and soon became a regular contributor to *Life* and *Punch* in England. At first his cartoons were formal and realistically rendered. By the 1890s he had loosened to a trademark wispiness—breezy and very economical lines always resting on a solid foundation of anatomy and composition. Throughout his life his cartoons were droll, urbane and sophisticated.

The cartoonist himself became as famous as his pen-and-ink (and wash) creations. He was followed slavishly for epigrams and *bons mots,* and with his monocle he was the very essence of an aloof but pointed outlook on life. William Dean Howells called Herford the Charles Lamb of

Oliver Herford. © Life.

his day. In his sense of presence and wit he was the American Oscar Wilde.

Many notable and classic cartoons (as well as verses for *Life* and the *Century)* were supplemented by a series of books that retain their cleverness today. Most remembered are: *Behind Time* (1886);*Artful Antics* (1888); *Pen and Inklings* (1893);*An Alphabet of Celebrities* (1899);*A Child's Primer of Natural History* (1899); *Overheard in a Garden* (1900); *The Cynic's Calendar* (1902), with many sequels on this theme; *The Rubaiyat of a Persian Kitten* (1904); *Two in a Zoo* (1904); *A Little Book of Bores* (1906); *The Peter Pan Alphabet* (1907); *Confessions of a Caricaturist* (1917); *Poems From "Life"* (1923); and *Excuse It, Please* (1930).

Herford also wrote a column, *Pen and Inklings,* for the *Saturday Evening Post* under Norman Hapgood, and a column for the *March of Events* section of the Hearst newspapers, all the while entertaining an acerbic and quite public aversion for the publisher (Hearst, as always, recognized genius and recruited well). Herford wrote four successful plays: *The Devil, The Florist Shop, The Love Cure* and *Con and Co.* He died, much honored and missed, on July 5, 1935.

R.M.

HERMAN AND KATNIP (U.S.) The success of MGM's *Tom and Jerry* cartoons prompted every other American animation studio to produce its own cat-and-mouse series. Famous Studios/Paramount came up with Katnip, a slow-witted feline perpetually at war with the mischievous mouse Herman. The duo devoted most of their energies to unmotivated pranks, mindless chases and moronic exploits. The *Herman and Katnip* cartoons were like scaled-down versions of *Tom and Jerry,* minus the wit, the pace and the inventiveness.

The series started in 1951 with such entries as "Cat Tamale" and "Cat-Choo"; it plodded along all through the 1950s on such frolicsome titles as "Drinks on the Mouse" (1953), "Bicep Built for Two" (1955), "Cat in the Act" (1957) and "Katnip's Big Day" (1959); and it ended ingloriously

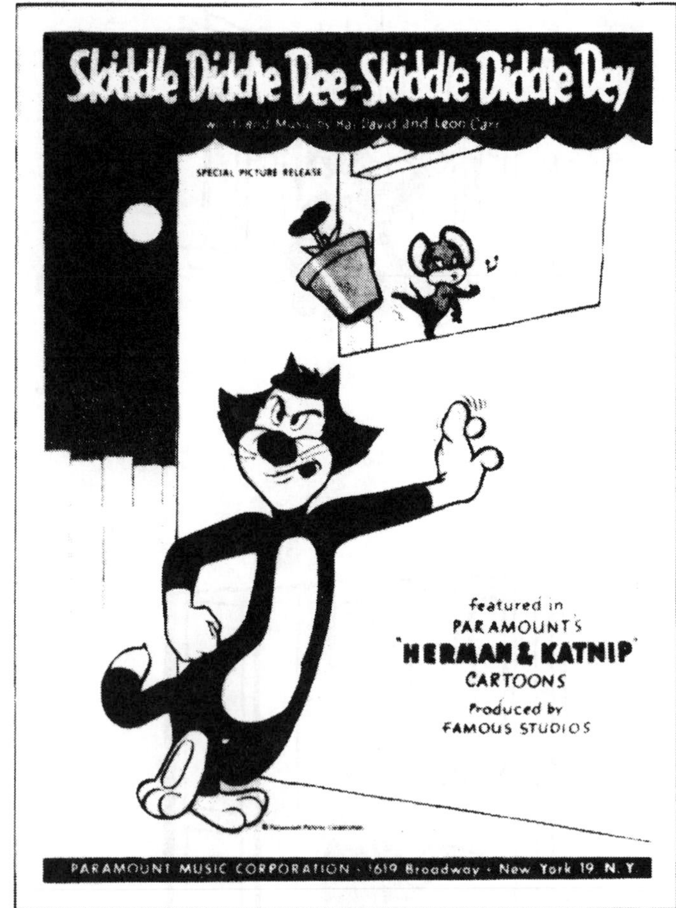

"Herman and Katnip" © Paramount Pictures.

in the early 1960s. The *Herman and Katnip* cartoons were of deplorable quality in terms of both story and animation, and it is therefore saddening to find among the names associated with the series those of Seymour Kneitel, I. Sparber and Bill Tytla, all of whom had proved capable of better things.

M.H.

HEROLD, DON (1889-1966) American cartoonist, author and advertiser born in Bloomfield, Indiana, on July 9, 1889. Don Herold graduated from high school in 1907, from the Chicago Art Institute in 1908 and from Indiana University in 1913.

Herold drew newspaper cartoons in Los Angeles for a year before returning to Indianapolis to manage the Hollenbeck Press. From Indiana around 1919 he free-lanced stories to *Harper's, Collier's* and the *American* magazine, and articles and cartoons to *Judge.* With the advent of the 1920s his work became popular, appearing in *Life* and the cartoon columns of popular weeklies. His advertising copy and drawings ran frequently, and he established a successful advertising agency in New York. The agency and articles for *Scribner's* occupied the rest of his career, as did a constant stream of books, until his death in 1966.

Herold's style was a totally original and fresh statement of simplicity: flowing, economical lines, characters barely more than stick figures, virtual elimination of backgrounds. In ads his work was in the spirit of Fish and Soglow; Herold was among the first to break the grip of the Gibson school on magazine cartooning. His concepts

—"Your public will ban your pictures when they hear how you treat me." —"I provide them with recreation; I don't see why they should care how I get mine."

Don Herold. © Tribune Syndicate.

were fresh and irreverent, and his material is still funny today.

Books: *So Humane!* (1923); *Bigger and Better* (1925); *There Ought to Be a Law* (1926); *Our Companionate Goldfish* (1927); *Strange Bedfellows* (1930); *Doing Europe—and Vice Versa* (1931); *Typographical Handbook (1946); Love That Golf* (1952); *Drunks Are Driving Me to Drink* (1953); *The Happy Hypochondrise* (1962); and *Humor in Advertising* (1963).

R.M.

HERR PIEPMEYER (Germany) The year 1848 was one of revolutions throughout Europe. The various German states won numerous civil liberties but not liberty in general; republican movements were defeated and unification of Germany was not achieved, largely because of the almost total incompetence of the constituent assembly that met for several months in Frankfurt am Main beginning in May 1848, with delegates coming from all over Germany.

Nevertheless, that assembly had one important result: no event in German history since the Reformation had inspired satires and caricatures to such an extent! Many of the delegates themselves wielded the pen for this purpose. One of them, Johann Hermann Detmold of Hanover, wrote the scenario and text of a work that would become a classic of humorous art thanks to the drawings provided by Adolf Schrödter, who had already made a mark as a humorous artist in Berlin and Düsseldorf and who would later be active in Karlsruhe for many years.

Published in six issues in Frankfurt in 1849, the 49 lithographs (each containing several panels) that comprise *Thaten und Meinungen des Herrn Piepmeyer, Abgeordneten zur Constituierenden Nationalversammlung zu Frankfurt a/Main* ("Deeds and Opinions of Mr. Piepmeyer, Delegate to the National Constituent Assembly at Frankfurt am Main") tell a continuous story. Totally ignorant but inordinately ambitious, Piepmeyer (this proper name occurs in *Münchhausen,* a novel by the humorous writer Immermann, and may also have referred to an actual person named Mittermaier) promises everything to his local electors, no matter what their political persuasion, and is

Herr Piepmeyer practicing oratory.

"Herr Piepmeyer."

unanimously chosen as delegate to Frankfurt. Once there, he changes political sides frequently according to the pressure of events (he is always on the side of the majority) and in pursuance of an unscrupulous journalist's advice. He practices orations and appropriate attitudes in front of his mirror but never gets to make an important speech at the assembly. One bit of advice given by the journalist leads to a lot of fruitless research on Piepmeyer's part: a unified Germany, he is convinced, needs a single national beverage that will combine the attractions of the beer, wine and brandy that are now preferred by various segments of the population.

The self-taught cartoonist A. von Boddien was apparently involved in the creation of *Herr Piepmeyer* at the very outset of the project, but the major credit belongs to Adolf Schrödter.

S.A.

HERZMANOVSKY-ORLANDO, FRITZ VON (1877-1954) Austrian writer and cartoonist born in Vienna, Austria, in 1877. Although he enjoyed a long life, Fritz von Herzmanovsky's fame, to the extent that it exists, is a matter of the last twenty-odd years since his death. His complete literary works, eccentric humorous stories and plays, have been published, and some of the plays have been produced in Munich and Vienna in their difficult local dialect. His legacy as a draftsman, not much more substantial, has been portrayed by certain Austrian art critics and historians, particularly Werner Hofmann, as a small but inalienable exemplification of true Viennese style.

Apparently a leisured member of a family associated with the highest level of the imperial civil service, Herzmanovsky studied architecture at the Vienna Polytechnic (Technische Hochschule) and traveled extensively. He enjoyed the friendship of two other important eccentrics of the decaying Austro-Hungarian empire: the writer Gustav Meyrink, whose famous stories of the German and Jewish elements of Prague include Der Golem, and the superb cartoonist Alfred Kubin, whose stylistic influence on Herzmanovsky the artist was definitive. Other visual influences pointed out by Hofmann are

Fritz von Herzmanovsky-Orlando, "The Neighbors," 1909.

the earliest graphics of Paul Klee, with their uncanny elongated figures; Franz Kalka's drawings; the early cartoon style of Lyonel Feininger; the drawings Jules Pascin did for *Simplicissimus;* and the visionary works of James Ensor.

Herzmanovsky provided 24 illustrations for his own satirical novel *Der Gaulschreck im Rosennetz* ("The Cabhorse-Frightener in the Net of Roses"), about a Viennese civil servant in the Biedermeier period—his only piece of writing published in book form within his lifetime (1928). These spindly line drawings are slightly diluted Kubin; the characters have the same eerie aimlessness, and the settings have the same linear importance in the overall composition. The novel was greatly appreciated by Hugo von Hofmannsthal. Herzmanovsky also did a number of works in crayon and pastel (satires, odd metamorphoses, personifications of death, etc.) that have been exhibited in Vienna; Hofmann sees strong traces of cabaret and operetta, as well as a preoccupation with court ceremony, in this artistic output.

It remains to be seen whether Herzmanovsky's glory will extend beyond the boundaries of his homeland. At any rate, he is now familiar to a much larger audience than the tiny band of connoisseurs who knew of his work while he was alive. This "Sunday painter of the grotesque," who died at Merano in the Tyrol in 1954, has been called "the last genius of baroque Old Austrian humor."

S.A.

HESS, DAVID (1770-1843) Swiss cartoonist and printmaker born in Zurich, Switzerland, on November 29, 1770. Most of the classic German-speaking political cartoonists through the years have used their art on behalf of liberal and advanced views. The case of the important Swiss artist David Hess reminds us that the gods do not bestow all the talent on one side of the fence. This army officer of aristocratic, *ancien régime* views, who lived during the French Revolution, Napoleonic Wars and the days of the early socialists, was influenced in his opinions by the official British position on these matters, and was influenced in his art by the great British caricaturists Rowlandson and Gillray. Not only did Hess's cartoons reflect the drastic action, oddly shaped bodies and intense play of "physiognomy" characteristic of these Englishmen; he even signed some of his pieces "Gillray, junior."

From 1787 to 1795 Hess was in one of the Swiss regiments that served the traditional government of Holland, but in the latter year French might drove out the stadholder, and a puppet République des Provinces-Unies, or "Batavian Republic," was established. Hess's regiment was disbanded without pay. This situation inspired his most famous series, *Hollandia Regenerata,* 20 drawings that were etched by none other than James Gillray himself and published in London in the summer of 1796. These drawings heap abuse on the various public agencies set up on the French revolutionary model by the Batavian Republic: the members of the welfare committee are shown gorging themselves while the populace starves, the fraternity committee is engaged in a hostile free-for-all, and so on down the line.

The year 1801 was a fertile one for Hess; among several other successful works, he produced his second most important series, the six plates comprising *Der Scharringelhof, or Die Positionen* (published under the pseudonym Daniel Hildebrandt). In this series two men—the owner of a townhouse and a guest—take leave of each other with endless exaggerated ceremony, an orgy of bowing and scraping; no doubt they are meant to be uppity bourgeois enriched by the wars and foolishly aping their "betters." It is hard not to be reminded of the Alphonse and Gaston of a century later (or, for that matter, of a famous early cartoon by Paul Klee), especially since *Der Scharringelhof* has some of the elements of a comic strip: the leave-taking continues through the series from within the house through different rooms to the exterior; in the next-to-last plate, the viewer can tell that the departing guest, lost to the world in his fatuous courtesy, is almost certainly going to trip over a stone and fall—and in the last plate ("panel") he does so!

Other celebrated Hess items are his satirical drawing on the phrenology fad (1808) and his book about his trip to Baden, the *Badenfahrt* (1818). He also wrote poems, stories, satires and biographies. He died in Zurich on April 11, 1843. His son Ludwig Adolf Hess (1800-1826), who drew landscapes and figures, also did some cartoons.

S.A.

HESSE, DON (1918-) American cartoonist born in Belleville, Illinois, on February 20, 1918. Don Hesse studied at the St. Louis School of Fine Arts at Washington University and joined the *Belleville* (Ill.) *Daily News-Democrat* as an artist-photographer in 1935; he remained until 1940. In 1946 he joined the *St. Louis Globe-Democrat* art staff and has worked there ever since, becoming chief political cartoonist in 1951. He was syndicated for years by the McNaught Syndicate and is now distributed by the Los Angeles Times Syndicate; it is possible that he is the most published political cartoonist in America, as the

Step by step—Where are we going?

Don Hesse.

Hesse cartoon is picked up by hundreds of rural papers as well as by big-city dailies. He is now retired.

Hesse may also be the strongest defender of conservative positions in American cartooning. His cartoons are consistently simple, direct, lucid and attractively presented statements. He draws with a brush and continues to effectively employ grained paper, which he judiciously shades with crayon. He has won many Freedoms Foundation and National Headliners awards.

R.M.

HETTIGODA, WINNIE (1953-) Winnie Hettigoda has been one of Sri Lanka's staunchest defenders of press freedom. His strong convictions that the political cartoonist, and journalists in general, should not be hampered in any way by government has resulted in threats to his life, loss of newspaper jobs, libel suits, and housing discrimination.

Born in the turbulent southern part of Sri Lanka, Hettigoda began his newspaper cartooning as a letterer on the daily *Divaina* in 1981, after graduating with a Bachelor of Fine Arts degree from the Institute of Aesthetic Studies of the Kelaniya Campus, Colombo. He soon advanced to illustrator and in 1983, began drawing a regular political cartoon for *Divaina*. In 1986, he received a scholarship to study art at the University of Baroda in India, where he earned a masters degree. Upon his return in 1988, Hettigoda rejoined *Divaina*.

In the 1990s, Hettigoda decided that there were other audiences for cartoons besides those who read newspapers, at which point he launched a touring exhibition of his work. At one such exhibition at the University of Colombo, a small politically-charged fracas erupted, resulting in Hettigoda removing his cartoons for safety sake. After the incident was reported in the media, *Divaina*'s parent company claimed the bad publicity was potentially damaging and asked Hettigoda to resign.

In 1991, he was approached by the publisher of Prabhat periodicals to help start a new paper, *Lakdiva*. This he did and his political cartoons, featuring his popular "Maraputhra" character, again appeared on a regular basis. But, in 1993, Hettigoda and the entire editorial staff of *Lakdiva* resigned when the publisher abandoned an agreed upon policy not to use advertising, and simultaneously, brought out a sex-oriented sister periodical. Hettigoda organized another touring exhibition of his political cartoons, raising money to start still another paper, *Hiru* ("Sun"), launched that year. He continued to draw a social commentary panel, *Bus Halt*, which features seven Sri Lankans discussing a current topic while waiting for the bus.

J.A.L.

HICKS, WOLFGANG (1909-1983) German editorial cartoonist born in Hamburg, Germany, in 1909. Wolfgang Hicks attended schools in Hamburg and Hanover but had no special art training beyond the ordinary drawing classes of these institutions. His earliest work was published in the *Hamburger Fremdenblatt* in 1928. It was not until the early 1930s that he entered the field of political cartooning, and then it was for a publication called *Echo der Woche* that abruptly ceased to exist in 1933. For the rest of the 1930s he drew advertising and other nonpolitical cartoons for the *Hamburger Anzeiger*, the *Hamburger Illustrierte*, *Koralle* and the *Berliner Illustrierte*.

During World War II, Hicks served in the navy and did front-line reportage while continuing to draw for magazines. It was in the new West German republic established after the war that he found the place he continued to occupy with such distinction, as senior editorial cartoonist for the two chief Hamburg news periodicals. Hicks joined the staff of *Die Zeit* when the paper was founded in 1946 and stayed there until 1957, when he switched over to *Die Welt*. He died in Bonn on March 23, 1983.

There can hardly have been an anthology of German cartoons that has not included a generous sampling of Hicks's ingenious drawings, with their strongly personal style. Thus, for instance, he was amply represented in the two major omnibus volumes chronicling Adenauer's career: *Konrod Sprach die Frau Mama* ("Konrad,' Said Mother," 1955) and *Konrad Bleibst Du Jetzt zu Haus?* ("Konrad, Are You Going to Stay Home Now?," 1963). But Hicks has also had at least one album completely devoted to his own cartoons for *Die Welt*, the 1966 volume *Das War's* ("That Was It").

Hicks drew in a very fluid and rounded pen style (sometimes with sharper lines over a softer base) characterized by the prominence of certain especially thick lines singling out a principal figure or object. As with most of his colleagues, his viewpoint was independent and liberal.

S.A.

Draper Hill. © Commercial Appeal.

HILDE
See Weber, Hilde.

HILDEBRANDT, DANIEL
See Hess, David.

HILL, DRAPER (1935-) American cartoonist and historian born in Boston, Massachusetts, on July 1, 1935. Draper Hill graduated from Harvard magna cum laude in 1957, having written a thesis on Joseph Keppler, the cartoonist who founded *Puck* magazine. Hill decided on a cartooning career, and a visit with the legendary David Low in London cemented his enthusiasm.

Hill's staff work on the *Patriot Ledger* of Quincy, Massachusetts, evolved from obituary assignments to spot illustrating to editorial cartooning. In 1959 he received a Fulbright Fellowship to study political cartooning in London. A matured historian's perspective and several books on Gillray (the most notable being *Gillray the Caricaturist*) resulted. Hill drew political cartoons for the *Worcester* (Mass.) *Telegram* between 1964 and 1971, at which time he switched to Memphis to assume the post of *Commercial Appeal* editorial cartoonist Cal Alley, who had recently died. In 1976 he moved to the *Detroit News*, succeeding Art Poinier. He still wields his pen there after 20 years; he has also written cogent articles on cartoons and cartooning for the specialized press in the last two decades.

Draper Hill's drawing style is one of the most singular in American cartooning. Interestingly, though he is a student of 18th- and 19th-century cartoonists, his work bears little resemblance to that of his mentors, Gillray and Keppler, except in terms of conceptual originality and effectiveness. Hill draws with a wide, loose brush, and his broad strokes are then shaded with doubletones. His caricatures are simple, as are the backgrounds and nonessentials in his handsome, liberal-oriented cartoons.

R.M.

HIPRAH HUNT'S JOURNEY THROUGH THE INFERNO
See Hell.

HIROKANE, KENSHI (1947-) Japanese animator, cartoonist and comic book artist. Born on September 9, 1947 in Iwakuni City, Yamaguchi Prefecture. Interested in art since early childhood, Kenshi Hirokane enrolled in Waseda University (Tokyo) and he joined the Manga Club. After graduating, he joined Matsushita Electric Co. (Osaka). As a member of the Publicity Department for four years, he designed countless posters, catalogues, neon signs, etc. He resigned from Matsushita and went to Tokyo to become a cartoonist. In 1974 his *Kaze Kaoru*, a short love story about a girl with a speech impediment, was published. His debut as a professional cartoonist came in 1976 with *Asano Hikari no nakade* (In the Morning Sun).

What made Hirokane a household name was *Kacho Shima Kosaku* ("Section Chief Kosaku Shima"), a series in the weekly magazine *Morning* which started in 1983 and lasted until 1992. Reflecting his experience as an office worker at Matsushita, Hirokane pumped life into a young man working for a major electric company: Shima's struggle for survival, his romance with a working girl in another company, etc. Hirokane also sent Shima to the company's overseas branches (in Manila, Jakarta, etc.) to resolve conflicts with local employees. All are portrayed with the gripping realism of one who well knew the inside story of a Japanese company. *Kacho Shima Kosaku* became a feature film, a television series and drama special, and is compiled in 17 volumes which are still selling well. Because he is regarded as one of the best Japanese "businessman comics," Hirokane has been asked to give lectures at big companies as part of their freshman orientation programs.

Among Hirokane's other popular works are *Ningen Kosaten* ("Human Scramble") and *Hello, Harinezumi* ("Hello, Hedgehog"). Both started in 1980, and were also very successful. *Ningen Kosatsuen* deals with various aspects of modern life, and sold more than four million of its 23 volumes. Widely read, Hirokane even received fan letters from prison inmates. These two pieces were made into feature films as well.

Another well-received and recent series is, *Tsogare Ryusei-gun* ("Twilight Shooting Stars"). Fully aware of the fact that the original manga generation is now middle-aged or older, the series includes love stories of middle-aged or senior characters.

Hirokane's comics are characterized by realism, well-constructed plots, lively characters (all results of his careful research) and almost cinematic angles and layout, reflecting his study of such film masters as Ozu, Kurosawa and Mizoguchi. Needless to say, Hirokane's works are extremely popular in Asian countries.

As for his private life, he is married to popular comic book artist Saimon Fumi, who used to be his assistant. They live in Tokyo and are blessed with two children.

K.O.

HIRSCHFELD, ALBERT (1903-) American caricaturist and writer born in St. Louis, Missouri, on July 21, 1903. Al Hirschfeld studied at the National Academy and the Art Students League in New York City, the County Council in London and the Académie Julian in Paris. He also traveled extensively in France, Italy, Spain and North Africa in the years following World War I.

Albert Hirschfeld, caricature of Geraldine Fitzgerald. © New York Times.

Hirschfeld contributed his first caricatures to the *New York Times* in 1925. He became theater correspondent for the *New York Herald-Tribune* in Moscow in 1927-28 and the following year became the theater caricaturist of the *New York Times,* a position he holds to this day. A peripatetic soul, Hirschfeld has traveled around the world almost without cease, either on assignment for such publications as *Holiday* and *Life,* or on U.S. government-sponsored tours.

Hirschfeld has been married twice. The name of his daughter by his second marriage, Nina, has become well-known among the artist's many admirers, as he is wont to slip it into every one of his caricatures. In the course of his long career Hirschfeld has depicted the greats and the near-greats of the artistic and political worlds with an uncanny eye and an unflinching pen. His works have been exhibited in galleries throughout the world and have earned him countless awards and distinctions from organizations and governments.

Though best known for his caricatures, Hirschfeld has also authored a number of books: *Manhattan Oases* (with Gordon Kahn, 1932); *Harlem by Hirschfeld* (1941); *Broadway Scrapbook* (with Brooks Atkinson, 1947); *Show Business Is No Business* (1951); *The American Theater* (1961); *Rhythm* (1970); and *The World of Hirschfeld* are the most notable. The artist was the subject of a monograph, Lloyd Goodrich's perceptive analysis in *The World of Hirschfeld,* which provides a lucid comment on the art of the famed caricaturist. Now well into his nineties, Hirschfeld still draws his theatrical caricatures every week. In 1991 and again in 1994 he designed a number of stamps for the U.S. Postal Service depicting Broadway celebrities and Hollywood stars of the silent era. His book of memoirs, *Hirschfeld: Art and Recollections from Eight Decades,* was published to rave reviews in 1995.

M.H.

HISTORIC AFFINITIES (U.S.) Otho Cushing found an outlet for his individual, classically inspired style in the series *Historic Affinities* for *Life* in 1911. Throughout his career, he frequently cast contemporary political and social notables in Greek or Roman settings, but *Historic Affinities,* wherein the ancients and moderns meet, was his cleverest and most popular series. Purely humorous on the surface, it made telling critical points.

Beginning on February 2, 1911, the following encounters—or misalliances—were portrayed: Dr. Parkhurst and Catherine II; Anthony Comstock and Sappho; Dr. Cook and Queen Isabella; Andrew Carnegie and Queen Boadicea; Mrs. Leslie Carter and Michelangelo; Dante and Lillian Russell; Richelieu and Maude Adams; Uncle Joe Cannon and Mary Stuart; Hetty Green and Lucullus; Catherine de Medici and John D. Rockefeller; Launcelot-Drew and Julia-Guinevere-Arthur; Augustus and Emma Goldman; Sir Galahad and Sarah Bernhardt; Queen Elizabeth and President Taft; J.P. Morgan and Helen of Troy; and Jack London and Madame de Sévigné.

The popularity of *Historic Affinities,* which ran half a page in black and white, led to a contract for Cushing to illustrate auto advertisements with a motif of classical settings for the modern vehicles.

R.M.

HODGINS, RICHARD HENRY, JR. (1931-) American cartoonist born in Binghamton, New York, on May 9, 1931. At the age of 12, Dick Hodgins moved with his family to New York City, where he made his first cartooning sale—a dollar for a sports page filler—to the *New York Mirror.* He studied at the Cartoonists and Illustrators School (later the School of Visual Arts), received art instruction from his father, a professional cartoonist, and took the Kuhn correspondence course. Hodgins cartooned and did illustra-

Dick Hodgins. © New York Daily News.

tions for filmstrips before and after army service in Japan (1949). During his hitch he edited the base newspaper and contributed to *Pacific Stars and Stripes;* at this time he also sold gags in America by mail (mostly to Crestwood publications). Upon his discharge, he took on many national advertising accounts.

Between 1956 and 1969 Hodgins was a staff artist with the Associated Press in New York, doing feature art and substituting for editorial cartoonist John Milt Morris. During the last two years of that hitch he also drew occasional editorial cartoons for the *New York News* under the name "Dick Henry." Thereafter Hodgins switched to the *News* and worked under his own name as backup cartoonist for Warren King. He also became a full-time ghost for Hank Ketcham, working on the *Half Hitch* comic strip for King Features and on its 1975 reincarnation, *Poopsy,* for Field. He now assists Dik Browne with various art chores on *Hägar the Horrible* and its spin-offs and handles numerous national advertising accounts. Hodgins has served the National Cartoonists Society for years in various capacities, most recently as editor of its magazine, and he won the 1979 Silver T-Square award for his services. He also drew for the Smith Service package for weekly newspapers, run by Al Smith.

Hodgins has a versatile style, ranging from the somewhat stiff renderings of his Associated Press days to his contemporary supple look of lush crosshatch shadings and format innovations. His work has always been marked by a feeling for humor and solid composition. His artwork on the *Half Hitch* strip was just about its only redeeming feature, especially on Sunday pages rich with detail and handsome colors. Since 1990 he has been responsible for the artwork on *Hagar the Horrible.*

(Hodgins's father, Dick Hodgins, Sr., was born on July 13, 1905, and was a cartoonist for General Electric publications before drawing editorial cartoons for the *Orlando Sentinel-Star* in Florida; he retired in 1970 after cartooning there for 13 years. He was curator of the Cartoon Museum in Orlando until his death in the late 1980s.

R.M.

HOFF, SYD (1912-) American cartoonist and author born in New York City on September 4, 1912. Syd Hoff was educated in the public schools of the city but dropped out before finishing high school. He reports that he started drawing at the age of four and planned on becoming a "serious" artist all through his youth. To this end, he spent a term at the National Academy of Design, but at age 16 he sold his first cartoon. Thereafter, he says, his interest in serious art faded. An incredibly prolific artist, Hoff has been a *New Yorker* staff cartoonist since 1939 and has contributed to virtually every major mass-circulation periodical of his time, from *Look* and the *Saturday Evening Post* to *Playboy.*

Hoff works in a variety of media, including watercolors, crayon, washes and ink. His dumpling-shaped, round-nosed, wisecracking characters are often stock types, obviously drawn from the New York City Jewish neighborhoods in which he grew up—the aggressive wife, the mother with the marriageable daughter, the ambitious girl, the *ganef,* the small merchant—but they are universally accessible, even while remaining immediately recognizable as his creations. Of course, no one boasting 61 titles in his *Who's Who* entry is going to hit the mark every time, and in truth, Hoff registers his full share of misses. But he is frequently and insightfully funny, too. Consider the dean of a college looking over the record of a dreamy-eyed new coed and blandly asking, "Is there anyone besides

hoff
"I've given you a home, cloths, luxury. Now what do you want?"

Syd Hoff. © Collier's.

Elvis Presley we can notify in case of emergency?" Or the hippie-radical artist to the model who's just walked into his studio: "In this picture I want to capture the surge of jet power in the second industrial revolution. Take off your clothes."

Besides the many collections of his cartoons—including *Oops, Wrong Party* (1950), *Twixt the Cup and the Lipton* (1962) and *How to Run a Country* (1963)—Hoff has written and illustrated numerous children's books, illustrated books by other authors—Paul Gallico's *How to Name a Boy,* for example—and written or compiled three volumes about cartooning: *It's Fun Learning Cartooning* (1956), *How to Draw Cartoons* (1975) and *Editorial and Political Cartooning* (1976).

In a field boasting so many original and inventive artists, Hoff's sheer good nature and love of what he is doing is perhaps more important than critical evaluation of his work. These qualities are apparent in his drawings—even the most ingenuous of them—and in his writings about cartooning, directed particularly to young people. There can be few professions more deserving of a boost than those concerned with making people smile—and Syd Hoff has certainly done more than his share in this regard. Seemingly oblivious to the changes in children's book content in the past 20 years, he has continued to turn out endearingly old-fashioned tales, such as *Barney's Horse* (1987), *Mrs. Brice's Mice* (1988), *Captain Cat* (1991), *Bernard on his Own* (1996), and the *Barney and the Dinosaur* series.

R.C.

HOFFMANN, ERNST THEODOR AMADEUS (1776-1822) German writer, composer and cartoonist born in Königsberg, East Prussia (now Kaliningrad, USSR), on January 24, 1776. E.T.A. Hoffmann (born Ernst Theodor Wilhelm Hoffmann) was astoundingly versatile, successful in all his artistic fields of endeavor; he is of course best remembered today for his "tales," fanciful stories in which modern critics have discovered realism and social and political awareness. His graphic output, however, even if it is only a small part of his total activity, is at the core of his work. Essentially a visually oriented man who had thought of becoming a professional painter (in Warsaw he did important murals), Hoffmann was continually inspired in his writing by works of art (Callot especially) and used graphic art to establish the scenes and characters of his stories and novels.

E.T.A. Hoffmann, "Fantastic Figures in the Manner of Callot," ca. 1810.

Born into a family of jurists, Hoffmann too studied law, and between 1800 and 1806 he practiced as a judge in East Prussian cities that are now part of Poland: Posen (Poznań), Plock and Warsaw. In 1806 the invading French armies caused the collapse of this German realm, and Hoffmann began freelancing: in Berlin in 1807 and 1808; in Bamberg from 1808 to 1813 as music director, composer and stage designer for the local theater (it was here that he wrote his first tales, as well as music criticism that has earned him the title of "founder of modern musical aesthetics"); and in Dresden and Leipzig in 1813. In 1814-15 Prussia was reconstituted, and Hoffmann settled in Berlin, where he wrote the bulk of his stories and also served efficiently and courageously as a court aide. He died in Berlin on June 25, 1822.

Although Hoffmann worked as a cartoonist throughout his career, the following high points can be cited. It was his bold caricatures of his government superiors in Posen that got him fined and transferred to the remote and dreary Plock in 1802. In Berlin in 1808, he drew three caricatures of actors published as *Groteske Gestalten nach Darstellungen auf dem Nationaltheater zu Berlin* ("Grotesque Figures After Performances at the Berlin National Theater"). In Leipzig in 1813 he drew several anti-Napoleonic cartoons for local print publishers (these are pleasant but much more formal and constrained than his private caricatures). Lastly, in Berlin between 1814 and 1822 he constantly drew illustrations and covers for his own stories, as well as street scenes and portraits of himself, of friends and chance acquaintances encountered at his favorite wine shop, Lutter and Wegner's, which he did so much to immortalize.

S.A.

HOFFMANN, HEINRICH (1809-1894) German cartoonist born in Frankfurt am Main, Hesse, on June 13, 1809. Heinrich Hoffmann was the creator of *Struwwelpeter,* perhaps the most influential of all German works of humorous art, and surely the most popular, along with Busch's *Max und Moritz.* Ironically, he was never more than an amateur as a draftsman and versifier. Hoffmann was by profession a practicing physician, a teacher of anatomy and, from 1851 to 1888, Frankfurt's leading doctor for mental diseases. He was an enlightened, if conservative, citizen with many interests; his club life brought him into contact with various intellectuals, and he had turned his hand to writing even before his great comic creation.

In 1842 he published a volume of poetry and in 1843 a clever verse play, *Die Mondzügler* ("The Colonizers of the Moon"), a satire on Hegelian philosophy and on aspects of German society that offended the author. It was at

Christmastime in 1844 that, dissatisfied with the dry and pedagogic children's books then available, he wrote and illustrated the original manuscript of *Struwwelpeter* for his three-year-old son. Published by a personal friend in 1845, these cautionary tales of disobedient and careless children started to sell like hotcakes. As German editions followed one another rapidly and the translations piled up (even into Latin and Esperanto!), Hoffmann found himself the world's most popular children's author (see the entry "Struwwelpeter").

Further children's books by Hoffmann, all with the primitive draftsmanship and often limping verse of *Struwwelpeter* but never equaling that volume's appeal, included: *König Nussknacker und der Arme Reinhold* ("King Nutcracker and Poor Reinhold," 1851), Hoffmann's own favorite, a story with characters based on actual folk toys; *Bastion, der Faulpelz* ("Bastian the Lazybones," 1854); *Im Himmel und auf der Erde* ("In Heaven and on Earth," 1857); and *Prinz Grünewald und Perlenfein mit Ihrem Lieben Eselein* ("Prince Greenwood and Pearlfine with Their Dear Little Donkey," 1871). Similar material he had composed for his family was gathered into a posthumous volume, *Besuch bei Frau Sonne* ("Visit to Mrs. Sun," 1924). Like *Struwwelpeter,* a number of these later books feature the same type of bloodthirsty violence that is found in many folktales and that Hoffmann bequeathed to Busch, Dirks and many others; too wildly exaggerated to be taken seriously by any normal child, this kind of extreme slapstick has often been impugned by hypersensitive 20th-century education teachers.

The revolution year of 1848 and the years immediately following led to some further adult satirical writing by Hoffmann, particularly the very witty, though antirepublican, *Handbüchlein für Wühler oder Kurzgefasste Anleitung in Wenigen Tagen ein Volksmann zu Werden* ("Little Handbook for Agitators, or Brief Guide to Becoming a Man of the People in a Few Days," 1848), which he signed "Peter Struwwel, Demagog" and illustrated with a title vignette.

Hoffmann died in Frankfurt on September 20, 1894. Some time earlier he had added his wife's maiden name, Donner, to the end of his own surname, so that he is now known to pedants and librarians as Heinrich Hoffmann-Donner.

S.A.

HOFFMEISTER, ADOLF (1902-1973) Czech cartoonist, writer and diplomat born in Prague, Bohemia (then part of the Hapsburg empire, now in Czechoslovakia), on August 15, 1902. Adolf Hoffmeister displayed remarkable talents as a writer and artist while still in high school and had his first book published at the age of 17. After he graduated from Charles University in Prague in 1925, he went to work as a writer, editor and cartoonist on several Czech magazines. When Hitler came to power in Germany and started laying claim to the Czech Sudetenland, Hoffmeister ridiculed him in savage cartoons that were reprinted all over Europe.

After the 1938 Munich agreements, Hoffmeister spent several months in solitary confinement. He went into exile in France and worked for the Czech resistance movement there; when the Germans invaded France in 1940, he was put into a concentration camp. He then escaped to Casablanca, was interned by the Vichy regime, and escaped from there to Spain, only to be interned again by the Franco government. In January 1941 he made his final escape, to the United States from Spain via Havana. A book reflecting his experiences, *Animals Are in Cages,* was published in New York at the end of 1941. (Adolf Hoffmeister is reported to have inspired the character played by Paul Henreid in the movie *Casablanca.)* Settling in New York City, Hoffmeister worked as a cartoonist and poster designer and edited the Czech programs of Voice of America.

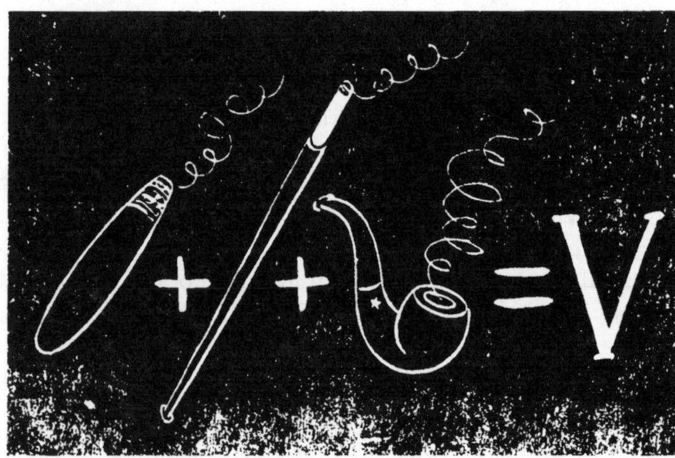

Adolph Hoffmeister's famous "V-cartoon." © Hoffmeister.

In 1944, at the behest of President Beneš, Hoffmeister returned to Czechoslovakia. He was appointed delegate to the United Nations in 1945 and from 1948 to 1951 served as ambassador to France, and later to China. Hoffmeister never stopped drawing, however; he was officially declared "national artist" in 1950, and his graphic works were widely exhibited in Prague, Paris, Brussels, Venice, London, New York and other places.

Hoffmeister supported Alexander Dubček in his unsuccessful attempt to bring democracy to Czechoslovakia in the mid-1960s. After Czechoslovakia's occupation by the Russian army in 1968, he went into disgrace. He was allowed neither to publish nor to exhibit, and his cartoons (many of them classics) were expunged from official anthologies. Hoffmeister died in Prague of a heart attack on July 25, 1973.

M.H.

HOFFNUNG, GERARD (1925-1959) British cartoonist, writer, musician, speaker and eccentric, born in Berlin, Germany, on March 22, 1925. To those who saw him and heard him it is impossible to think Gerard Hoffnung has been gone for so long. His rise to fame was meteoric, and his memory continues to delight through reprintings of his books, recordings of his broadcasts and speeches, and restagings of his extraordinary tongue-in-cheek music festivals that rocked London in the 1950s.

Gerard Hoffnung, so superbly British, was a student at the Highgate and Harrow School of Arts and Crafts under J.G. Platt, and then served as art master at Stanford School (1945) and assistant art master at Harrow (1948). In between, in 1947, he worked as a staff artist on the London

Gerard Hoffnung. © Punch.

Evening News, contributing funny little "spot" drawings and column-breakers that livened the tabloid pages of the time. In 1950 he went to New York to draw for the Cowles chain of magazines, returning to England the following year to freelance in art and his main hobby, music. He drew for *Punch, Lilliput* and other weeklies, illustrated books for children, and became a regular radio broadcaster for the BBC, delivering superb and lengthy anecdotes in a rich, fruity voice. In 1956 he created the Hoffnung Music Festival, which became a regular and hilarious treat at the Royal Festival Hall, a kind of upper-crust Spike Jones show. It became the Hoffnung Interplanetary Music Festival for 1958 and 1959.

He died quite suddenly in 1959, at the age of 34: everyone thought him a much older man. His cartoons, much collected, are eternally witty, and the John Halas-Joy Batchelor animation studios converted a number of his little books and sequences into a technicolor *Tales from Hoffnung,* which remains among that studio's best work.

Books: *The Right Playmate* (1952); *The Maestro* (1953); *The Hoffnung Symphony Orchestra* (1954); *The Isle of Cats* (1955); *The Hoffnung Music Festival* (1956); *The Hoffnung Companion to Music* (1957); *Hoffnung's Musical Chairs* (1958); *Ho Ho Hoffnung* (1959); *Hoffnung's Acoustics* (1959); *Birds, Bees and Storks* (1960); *O Rare Hoffnung* (1960); *Hoffnung's Little Ones* (1961); *Hoffnung's Constant Readers* (1962); and *The Boy and the Magic* (1964).

D.G.

HOFMAN, EDUARD (1914-1987) Czechoslovakian animator born near Prague, Czechoslovakia, in 1914. Eduard Hofman was trained as an architect but started working in animation as early as 1943. He joined the Barandov studio as an administrator in 1945, but under the influence of Jirí Trnka, he acquired a taste as well as a talent for animation. He refined his newfound skills on educational cartoons before venturing into entertainment animation. Hofman's first theatrical film, *All Aboard,* was released in 1947, followed the next year by *The Angel's Cloak,* a delightful tale of a magic cloak that had the power of changing evil into good.

In the 1950s Hofman became one of the most prolific of Czech animators, with countless shorts to his credit; *ABC* (1950), *The Golden Apples* (1952), *Where Is Misha?* (1954) and *The Fox* (1955) are among the more notable. From 1950 to

"I'll never feel as safe again as I did with Mr. Coolidge."

Helen Hokinson. © Collier's.

1954 Hofman also directed the hilarious *Dog and Cat* series. In 1956 he released his masterwork, *The Creation of the World,* a feature film based on the work of French cartoonist Jean Effel. Other cartoons by Hofman include *Tale of the Dog* (1959), *My Twelve Daddies* (1960), *The Postman's Story* (1961) and *The Ladder* (1964), all of which received awards or nominations. Since the mid-1960s Hofman has devoted his talents to turning out routine cartoons for children and for television, although he did make a second animated feature, *The Tribulations of Adam and Eve* (1974), also inspired by Effel. Hofman's films in the 1980s were hurried and over-intellectualized. He died in Prague in 1987.

M.H.

HOKINSON, HELEN ELNA (1893-1949) American cartoonist born in Mendota, Illinois, in 1893. The daughter of a farm-equipment salesman, Helen Hokinson was of Swedish descent, and until her father's time the family name had been spelled Haakonson. Her first recognition as an artist came when her surreptitious sketches of the teachers at Mendota High School were found by the teachers themselves in a mislaid sketchbook.

Helen Hokinson studied fashion illustration for five years at Chicago's Academy of Fine Arts. She then went to the Parsons School of Design in New York City, where her studies with Howard Gile were based on Hambridge's theory of dynamic symmetry. Her drawings had a natural humorous flavor, and with fellow artist and cartoonist Alice Harvey she sold a comic strip to the *New York Daily Mirror.* This strip, *Sylvia in the Big City,* had a short run.

In 1925, at the encouragement of friends at the Parsons School of Design, she submitted a drawing to the brand-new *New Yorker* magazine. Much to her surprise the *New Yorker* purchased it. The cartoon appeared without caption or signature on page one of the July 4, 1925, issue, in the middle of *"The Talk of the Town"* column. It was a rear view of a plump woman in floppy hat and sensible shoes who had climbed a railing to wave bon voyage at a pier. Most of her early work for the *New Yorker* was captionless.

Helen Hokinson's most famous cartoon characters were her so-called Hokinson Girls. These amiable but vague clubwomen were duly noted by the *New York Times* as being the inspiration for a cult which avidly followed her cartoons in the *New Yorker* and considered her characters as "the emblem of clubwomen the country over." (The concept of the clubwoman series was created in 1933 by James Reid Parker, a *New Yorker* writer who from 1931 to 1949 was Hokinson's silent partner and gag writer for her cartoons.)

Hokinson's style depended on a simple line drawing painted in gray wash to give it depth and form. She loved to roam New York City with her pocket-sized sketchbook, making drawings in soft pencil. Flower shows and department stores proved especially fruitful in researching real-life Hokinson Girls. They were depicted on incessant shopping sprees, tangling traffic, molesting flowers, cajoling maids and generally indulging themselves to pass the time. Mature women, they were more weighty physically than intellectually. A typical cartoon shows two Hokinson Girls seated in a Schrafft's restaurant for lunch. One says, "Sometimes I think Schrafft's doesn't care about calories." Helen Hokinson's aim was to poke fun at these American matrons without wounding. However, in light of the women's movement and general female consciousness-raising of the 1960s, to be a Hokinson Girl today would be considered an insult by most women.

Hokinson herself never married, and as early as 1929 she divided her time between a New York City apartment and a cottage in Wilton, Connecticut. James Reid Parker remembered that her youthful flair for colorful blouses and scarves gave way to more conservative fashions as she aged. Her interests ranged from Shakespeare, backgammon and French Impressionists to Gilbert and Sullivan, wildflowers and Connecticut's back country. One of her last projects was a play about women in which her Hokinson Girls would be funny but would not be ridiculed.

The play was never finished. On November 1, 1949, Helen Hokinson, en route from New York City to Washington, D.C., for a speaking engagement, was killed when a P-38 fighter recently sold to the Bolivian air force split the aircraft in which she was traveling. All 55 people aboard were killed in the worst American civil aircraft disaster up to that time.

Helen Hokinson's cartoons were published in a number of collections, both before and after her death. They are *So You're Going to Buy a Book* (1931), *My Best Girls* (1941), *When Were You Built* (1948), *The Ladies, God Bless 'Em* (1950), *There Are Ladies Present* (1952), and *The Hokinson Festival,* with a memoir by James Reid Parker (1956). She also drew a cartoon panel featuring men, entitled *The Dear Man,* that was published for a time in the *Ladies' Home Journal.* She illustrated three books by Emily Kimbrough and a poetry book entitled *Garden Clubs and Spades* by Laurence McKinney.

B.C.

Color in Cartoons

Although the print cartoon is generally considered a pen-and-ink medium (as it largely is), color has also played a role in its development. The plates of 18th-century cartoonists were hand-colored, often by the artists themselves; in the 19th century chromolithography became the vogue. Modern-day printing and reproducing methods make it easier than ever to publish color cartoons. Color, though not unimportant, is not essential: it can enhance a composition or bring out some telling detail, and of course it adds to our aesthetic enjoyment; but it seldom contributes to the main point of the cartoon, which is one of the reasons it is so rarely used in editorial cartoons.

In animation cartoons, on the other hand, color adds immeasurably to the basic appeal of movement. As in print cartoons, color in the early animation films was done by hand, painted on the cels; only in the 1930s was a color film stock of sufficient reliability and fidelity perfected. Since then, color in animation has come into widespread use: color sets the scene, etches the characters in sharper detail, and rhythmically accompanies the action. Without color the animated cartoon would lose some of its attributes of fantasy and poetry. Indeed, present-day animation is the product of its three basic elements: motion, form and color.

The illustrations in this section have been selected on the basis of representativeness, as well as on purely aesthetic grounds.

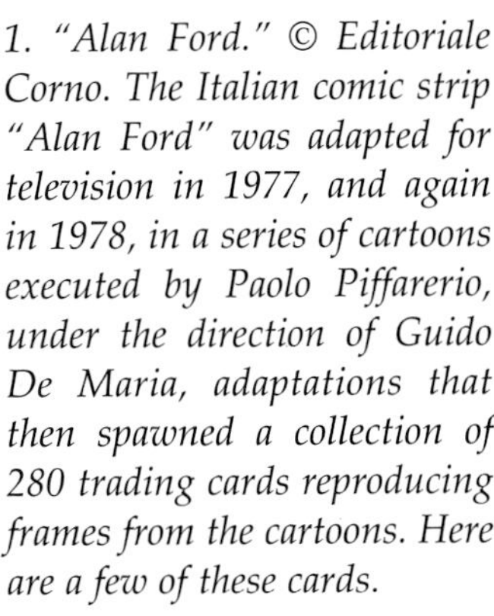

1. "Alan Ford." © Editoriale Corno. The Italian comic strip "Alan Ford" was adapted for television in 1977, and again in 1978, in a series of cartoons executed by Paolo Piffarerio, under the direction of Guido De Maria, adaptations that then spawned a collection of 280 trading cards reproducing frames from the cartoons. Here are a few of these cards.

1

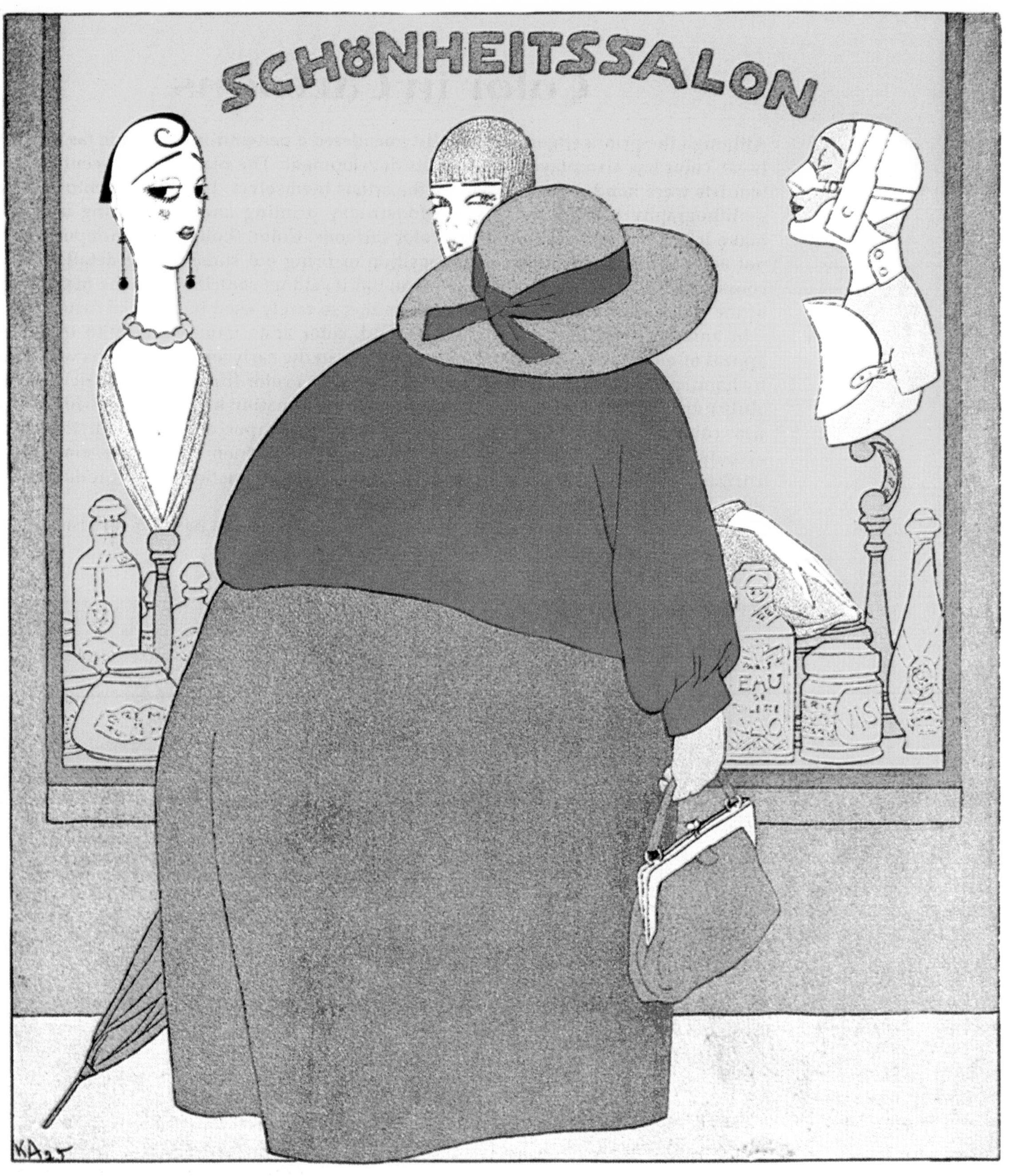

How Can I Stay Young and Beautiful? "We women are spared nothing!"

2. Karl Arnold. © Simplicissimus. Arnold began his long association with "Simplicissimus" in 1907. In the course of his work for the magazine, his style shifted from strong dependence on shading and hatching to reliance on pure linear contours, as in this example dating from 1925. Arnold was also a keen observer of Munich life and of its smug bourgeoisie.

3. Lev Atamanov, "The Golden Antelope." Atamanov is one of the pioneers of Soviet animation. In 1949 he was appointed head of the All-Union Cartoon Film Studios in Moscow, and as such he has been the man most responsible for the current state of Soviet animation. "The Golden Antelope" (1954) is one of Atamanov's best efforts, and a fairly well-crafted feature.

4. Anselmo Ballester, "Rita Hayworth as Gilda." © Columbia Pictures. Ballester's drawings are not just figures on publicity posters but are really portraits, barely caricatured and charged with evocative expression. This poster, representing a scene from "Gilda," is one of the artist's most famous interpretations.

3

BARTAK
Prague
CZECHOSLOVAKIA

5

6

Some of the Reasons Why Money Is Scarce in the United States

7

5. Miroslav Bartak. © M. Bartak. Bartak is best noted for his immediately funny cartoons, drawn in a simple style, with few or no words, on easily recognized themes.

6. Frank Beard, cartoon for "Judge." Beard was one of the most prolific cartoonists working for American humor magazines during the second half of the 19th century. For "Judge" he drew some very striking, handsome and sophisticated lithographic cartoons, of which this is one.

7. "Beauty and the Beast." © Walt Disney Company. The first animated feature ever nominated for a Best Picture Academy Award, "Beauty and the Beast" contains dazzling sequences of animation.

8. "Believe It or Not!" © King Features Syndicate. Originally started as a sports feature by Robert Ripley in 1918, "Believe It or Not!" was soon venturing as far afield as geology, history, botany and numismatics. The first feature of its kind, "Believe It or Not!" has enjoyed tremendous popularity for over half a century, presenting "facts" that dwell heavily on the bizarre, the absurd, the incredible and the outlandish.

Ripley's Believe It or Not!
THE MOST GENEROUS TIP IN ALL HISTORY
THE CHAULAKHI A GROUP OF BUILDINGS THAT COST $194,000 TO BUILD WAS GIVEN BY KING WAJID ALI SHAH OF OUDH, INDIA TO HIS BARBER
Lucknow, India - 1847
A CROCODILE KILLED IN ZULULAND HAD 32 ALUMINUM DOG LICENSES IN ITS STOMACH
1942
WHITE MAN'S MAGIC
THE TRIBAL DRUMS OF THE BAYAKA TRIBE OF THE CONGO RESEMBLE AN OLD-FASHIONED WALL TELEPHONE
THE SHAPE WAS COPIED FROM AN EXHIBIT IN A MUSEUM
A RING
PURCHASED FOR 10 CENTS IN A 5 AND 10-CENT STORE BY MISS VELMA JOHNSON WAS FOUND TO CONTAIN A GENUINE DIAMOND
Sanford, N.C.
TWIN CYPRESSES
SHAPED BY JOSEPH SARTOR
Gilroy, Calif.
THE MAN WHO RODE HIS HORSE OFF A MOUNTAIN PEAK
ETTORE FIERAMOSCA
of Italy
PLUNGED HIS HORSE INTO THE ADRIATIC FROM A HEIGHT OF 690 FEET
—AND ESCAPED UNHARMED
FIERAMOSCA MADE THE JUMP FROM A CRAG OF MONTE SANT'ANGELO
Copr. 1954, King Features Syndicate, Inc., World rights reserved.

This is the average foreigner's idea of a typical street-scene in Paris, —

and in London,

and in Amsterdam, —

and in Madrid, —

and in New York, —

whereas, as a matter of fact, a typical street-scene in any one of them is very much like this.

BIZARRO
BY PIRARO

Almost without exception, the silverback controls the remote, surfing the channels endlessly in spite of the disapproval of the rest of the troop.
PIRARO
WWW.VDGI.COM/BIZARRO
©DAN PIRARO·1997 Dist. by Universal Press Synd.
6-1

10

11

9. C.K. Bird ("Fougasse"). © Fougasse. Fougasse, as he signed himself, evolved one of the most individual and recognizable styles in England. His handwritten lettering, as exemplified in this multi-panel cartoon of the 1930s, also became extremely well known.

10. "Bizarro." © Dan Piraro. Piraro has described his feature, which is variously inspired by Salvador Dali and "Mad" magazine, as being "bizarre, surreal explanations for everyday events." As such it has certainly lived up to its billing.

11. Don Bluth, "An American Tail." © Amblin Productions. An animal allegory set in Czarist Russia, this is probably Bluth's best-known work of animation.

12. Milan Blažeković, "Gorilla Dance." © Zagreb Film. One of the most famous practitioners of the fabled "Zagreb school" of animation. Blažeković taught himself cartooning. He directed some of the wittiest of the Zagreb cartoons, of which "Gorilla Dance" is probably the best known.

12

13

14

13. *Valentina and Zenayeda Brumberg, "Fedya Zaytsev." A sister team of Soviet animators, the Brumbergs have been among the most prolific film cartoonists in Russia. They have often dealt with fairy tales and other material directed at children. "Fedya Zaytsev" is one of their most enchanting features, and it has received many awards in Russia and in the West.*

14. *Bugs Bunny and his cartoon companions, as drawn by Chuck Jones. © Warner Brothers. The nonchalant rabbit with the Brooklyn accent is one of the most celebrated creations in animated cartoons. Along with his stablemates, Daffy Duck, Porky Pig and others, he was the protagonist of some of the fastest and wittiest cartoons ever produced by an American studio.*

CUTIES by E. Simms Campbell

"YES, HE'S HERE.. BUT HE'S BUSY RIGHT NOW. COULD YOU CALL BACK?"

16

15. E. Simms Campbell, "Cuties." © King Features Syndicate. Campbell specialized in drawings of beautiful women. In the panel "Cuties," which he drew from 1943 to the time of his death in 1971, the gag was secondary to the depiction of the gorgeous creatures promised by the title. Color greatly added to the appeal of Campbell's basic premise.

16. Chen Shubin. © Chen Shubin. Chen is one of the most representative of contemporary Chinese cartoonists. He is skilled in both political caricature and social commentary.

17

17. "Close to Home." © John McPherson. McPherson's panel is a sassy, quirky depiction of contemporary home and family life, generously sprinkled with off-the-wall humor.

18. Clive Collins. © Clive Collins. This is a good example of the very British humor of Clive Collins, one of the top newspaper and magazine cartoonists in the United Kingdom.

19. Miguel Covarrubias, caricature of Mussolini, 1928. © Life. The style of Covarrubias's caricatures was very distinct. He used a geometric and sculptural line to define the mass and features of his subjects. For all their stylization, however, his heavy renderings were full of vigor and enthusiasm. Covarrubias's most important work was done in the United States in the 1920s and 1930s.

Clive Collins/England

18

The Photographer: "Now—SMILE!"

20 Something in a Name. Mr. Horse-fly: "Hang it all! Just 'cause my name is Horse-fly that fool poet insists on using me as a horse."

20. Gus Dirks, drawing for "Judge." In his cartoons Dirks dealt exclusively with insect and small animal life; he was a leader in that very popular turn-of-the-century genre. He utilized confident pen strokes and achieved shading effects with short lines combining to give his cartoons texture and pattern.

21. "Donald Duck." © Walt Disney Productions. Created in 1934, Donald rapidly rose to unprecedented heights of popularity and was soon eclipsing Mickey Mouse as the star of the Walt Disney studios. His character—cantankerous, ornery and irascible—was established from the first and was further developed in scores of movie cartoons from the 1930s to the 1950s.

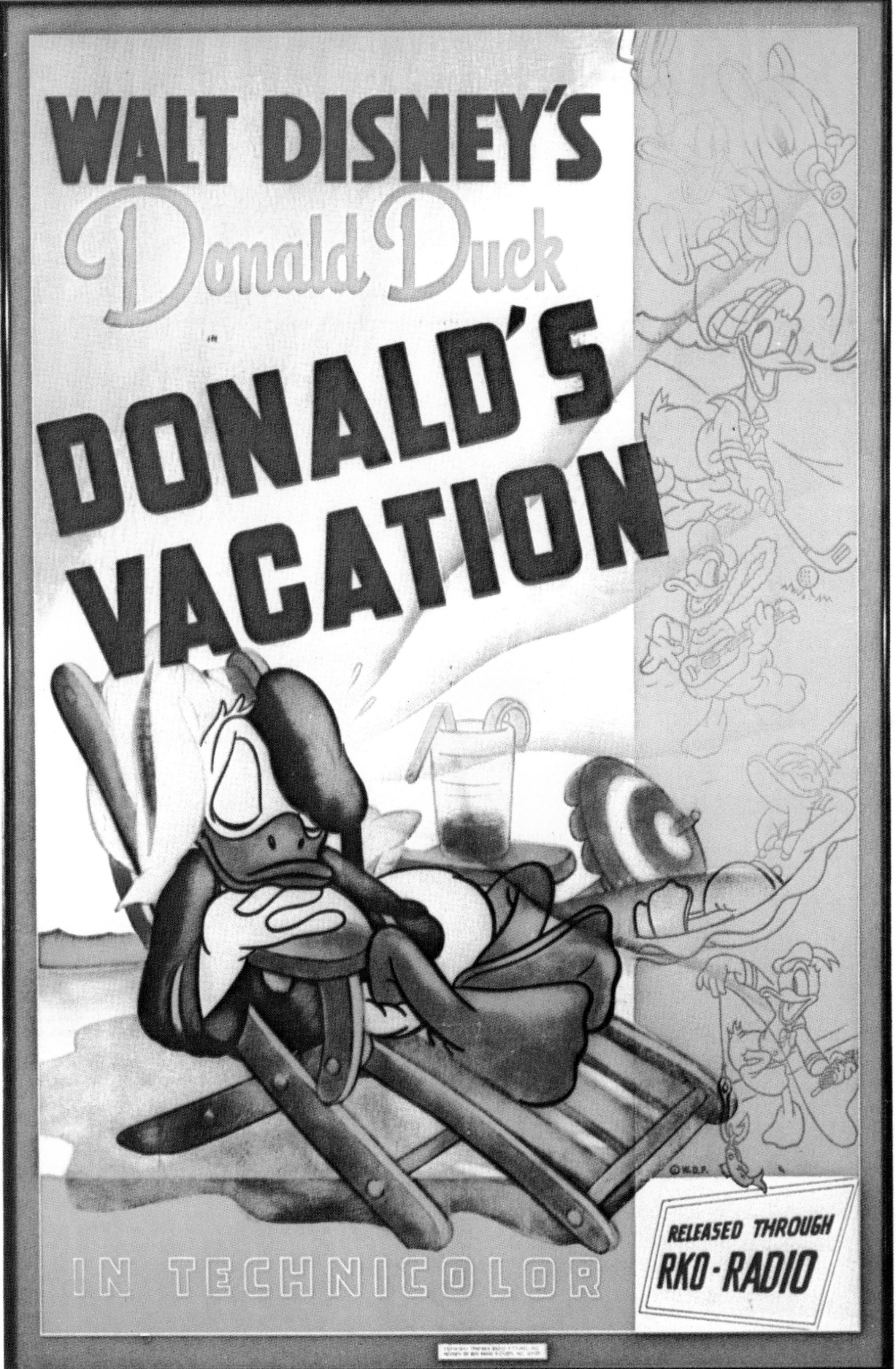
WALT DISNEY'S
Donald Duck
IN
DONALD'S VACATION
© W.D.P.
IN TECHNICOLOR
RELEASED THROUGH
RKO-RADIO

WHAT IS AN "ARYAN"?
HE IS HANDSOME
AS GOEBBELS

22. Boris Efimov, World War II poster. Efimov is one of the most popular cartoonists in Russia, as well as one of the most mordant. His popularity reached its peak during World War II; he is best noted for his savage depictions of the Nazi leaders, especially Josef Goebbels, whom he never tired of lampooning.

23. Abel Faivre, cartoon for "L'Assiette au Beurre." Faivre, a son and brother of physicians, liked to draw biting cartoons satirizing doctors. The most famous of these were executed for a special issue of "L'Assiette au Beurre" (1902) in which Faivre gave free rein to his sardonic humor.

24. "Fantasia." © Walt Disney Productions. "Fantasia," a full-length animated feature, is considered by most critics to be Disney's single most stunning achievement. Intended as a marriage between animation and the musical arts, the film is a forceful and masterly statement blending music, rhythm, movement and color in one cohesive work.

23

24

25

26

25. James Montgomery Flagg, caricature of Theodore Roosevelt. Although Flagg gained his greatest notability as a poster artist, he had earlier made his mark as a distinguished and forceful cartoonist for "Judge" and "Life." Flagg displayed an overwhelming sincerity in his work and had a flair for showmanship.

26. "Fluffy Ruffles." Wallace Morgan's "Fluffy Ruffles" was a verse-captioned, multi-panel Sunday page about a woman so stunningly beautiful that she proved too disconcerting to susceptible males to hold a job. It began in 1907. Fluffy Ruffles was so winningly drawn, and her outfits so stylish, that she was accepted from coast to coast as a weekly symbol of what young American womanhood should emulate.

27

27. Peter Foldes, "Je, Tu, Elles." © ORTF. Peter Foldes was one of the most fascinating of modern animators. His works have received the highest praise and have been just as vehemently criticized. This is a frame from "Je, Tu, Elles," one of his last works, which blended animation and live action.

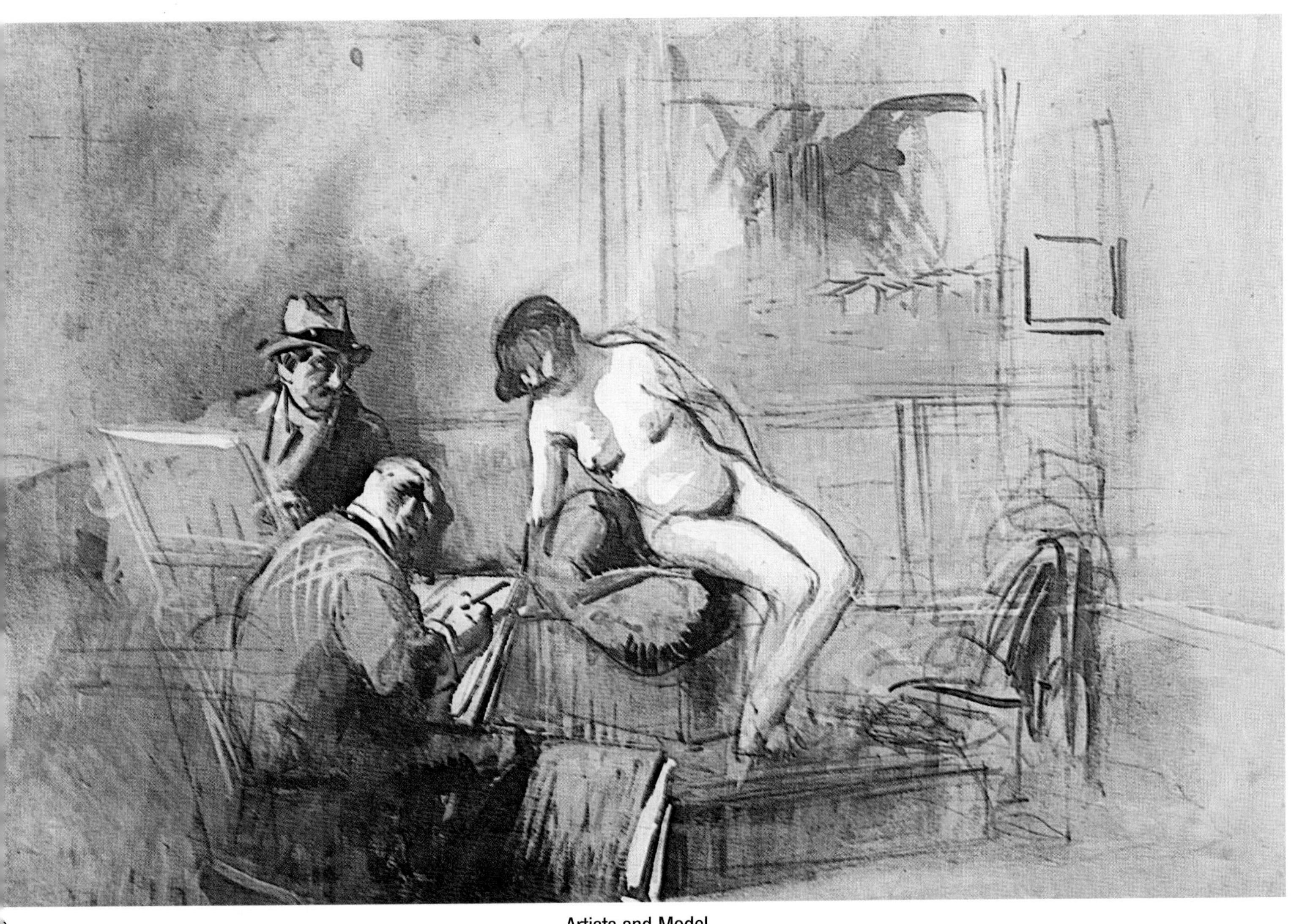

Artists and Model

28. Jean-Louis Forain, painting. Forain's cartoons were drawn in a caustic and even cruel style that earned him the nickname "Juvenal of the pencil." He was also a talented painter who, in 1879 and 1880, exhibited some of his canvases alongside those of the Impressionists, many of whom admired his work.

RIFORMA TRIBUTAR
LEGISLAZIONE SOCIALE
DIVORZIO
MIGLIORAMENTI PEL MEZZOGIORNO
ECC. ECC.

29

30

29. Gabriele Galantara, cartoon for "L'Asino." Along with Guido Podrecca, Galantara founded the satirical weekly "L'Asino" in Rome in the late 1890s. The success of this socialist and anti-clerical publication was due to the incisiveness of Galantara's cartoons, which he signed with the anagram "Rata-Langa."

30. Giulo Gianini, "Ali Baba." © Gianini/Luzzati. The duo Giulo Gianini and Emanuele Luzzati have made some of the most enchanting cartoons in Italy. They have often dwelt on legends and folktales, as in this example.

31. Theodore Geisel ("Dr. Seuss"), cover illustration for "Judge." © Judge. Better known for his children's books, Dr. Seuss is also a cartoonist of long standing. He started drawing cartoons and covers for "Judge" in the mid-1920s. His depictions of natural history and animal life, accompanied by soberly couched explanations, were totally absurd.

32. Bernard Gillam, cartoon for "Puck." One of the stars of "Puck," Gillam is most remembered for his vicious anti-Blaine cartoons during the American presidential campaign of 1884—of which this is one good example. Gillam's cartoons were technically proficient and carefully detailed; in his time he was regarded as one of the giants of his profession.

Judge
JANUARY 3, 1931
PRICE 15 CENTS
January
1

HE instituted the ordeal—can he stand it himself?

Uncle Sam: "We have heard from Mr. Cleveland. Now then, Mr. Blaine, YOU made this issue; it is your turn to step up and—TELL THE TRUTH!"

Judge

December 28, 1918
Price 10 Cents

Drawn by John B. Gruelle

Christmas Eve at Yapp's Crossing

34

33. John B. Gruelle, cover for "Judge." © Judge. Johnny Gruelle's biggest success came with his "Raggedy Ann" stories, illustrated with his own cartoons. Before that, however, he had created the "Yapp's Crossing" series, which ran weekly on the cover of "Judge" magazine; this is a fine example.

34. Seichi Hayashi. © Hayashi. This Japanese artist's work is almost psychedelic in its evocation of moods. His women characters are unique in that they tend to be frail but erotic women of the world, as in this example.

35

35. He Wei. © He Wei. He Wei considers his cartoons to be part of the Chinese fine art tradition, and this example shows his skill in this domain.

36

36. John and Faith Hubley, "Everybody Rides the Carousel." © The Hubley Studio. Faith and John Hubley closely collaborated on a number of award-winning cartoon films, of which this is one of the most notable.

CELEBRITY PRODUCTIONS, INC. Presents a
P. A. POWERS
COMICOLOR
CARTOON
ALADDIN and
the WONDERFUL LAMP
in CINECOLOR
by UB IWERKS

38

37. Up Iwerks, "Aladdin and the Wonderful Lamp." © Celebrity Productions. After years of working with Walt Disney, Iwerks set up his own studio in the 1930s. There he produced the enchanting "Flip the Frog" cartoons, as well as a number of "Comicolor Cartoons" based on fairy tales and popular stories; "Aladdin" is an example of Iwerk's work in this vein.

38. "Jungle Tatei." © Mushi Productions. Japanese cartoonist Osamu Tezuka himself adapted his long-running comic strip, "Jungle Tatei," for animation. "Jungle Tatei" also bears the distinction of having been the first color animated cartoon shown on Japanese TV.

39

39. *Kevin Kallaugher ("Kal"). © Kal. Kallaugher (who signs "Kal") wields a trenchant, even wicked pen. His style accords well with his motto that "the editorial cartoonist's job is not to make you laugh but to make you think."*

40. *Joseph Keppler, cartoon for "Puck." Keppler, a German born immigrant, founded the famed humor magazine "Puck" in the 1870s in New York. He also contributed many political cartoons to the magazine, often laid out with a heavy hand.*

A Harmless Explosion

41

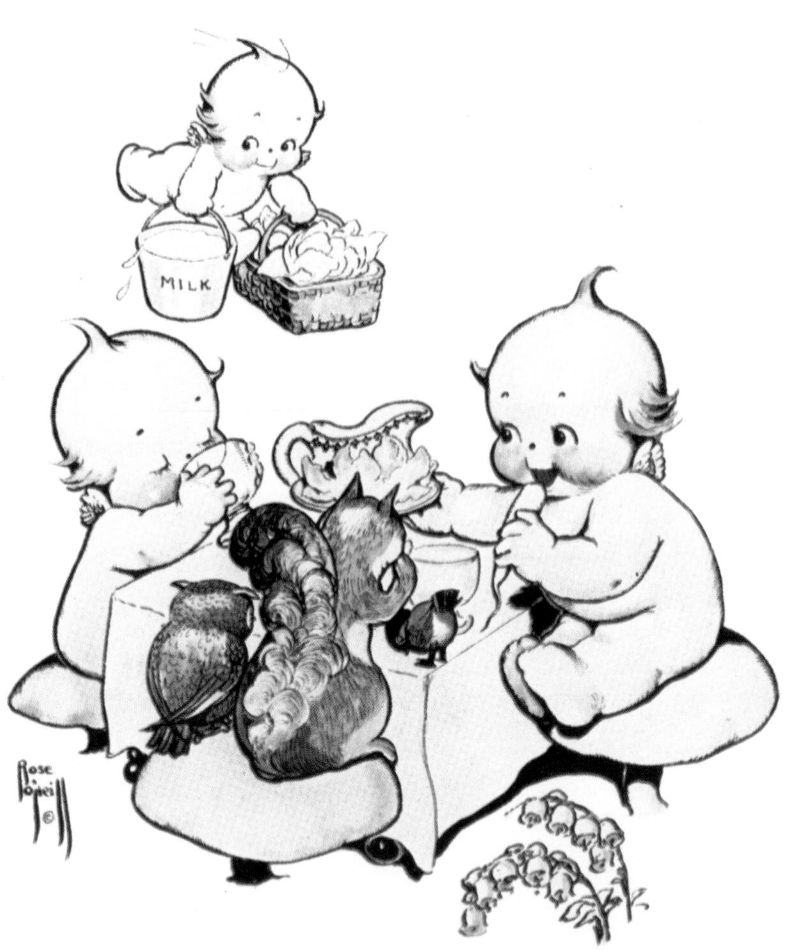

41. "The Kewpie Korner." © Rosie O'Neill. The "kewpies," Rose O'Neill's famed elfin cupids, appeared in a variety of newspapers and magazines from 1905 to 1918. "The Kewpie Korner" was essentially a work of intense visual charm, with little wit or humor.

42. "King of the Hill." © Fox Network. Cartoonist Mike Judge's latest animated sitcom, "King of the Hill" is an unusually perceptive satire on lower-middle class Texas culture.

42

JOHN RICE FOR TV GUIDE

43

43. Renzo Kinoshita, "Made in Japan." © Lotus Productions. Kinoshita is one of the most prolific Japanese animators. His animation short, "Made in Japan," parodies the commercialism of modern Japan. It won the Grand Prix at the 1972 International Animation Festival, held in the United States.

44. Hidezo Kondo, caricature of Franklin Roosevelt. © Manga. Kondo drew his famous (or infamous) color cover portraits of the "evil demons" Churchill, Roosevelt and Stalin during World War II. He often painted their faces green to give them an appropriately ghoulish appearance, and sometimes, as in this example, he added fangs.

眼で見る時局雑誌
漫画
二月號
30セ

ИЗ ПЕТЛИ, ИЗ ЭТОЙ ЕМУ НЕ УЙТИ!

СОГЛАШЕНИЕ

ДОГОВОР

МЕЖДУ СССР

АНГЛИЕЙ и США

45

46

47

45. *Kukryniksy, "The Big Three Will Tie the Enemy in Knots." Kukryniksy is the collective signature of three Soviet cartoonist: Mikhail Kupryanov, Porfiry Krylov and Nikolay Sokolov. The trio's anti-German posters and cartoons are justly famous for their incisive style and visual impact.*

46. *"Land Before Time." © Sullivan-Bluth. The 1988 "Land Before Time" was Steven Spielberg's attempt at bringing back the dinosaurs (in animated form) well ahead of "Jurassic Park."*

47. *Jan Lenica, "Ubu-Roi." © Lux Film. The Polish-born Lenica is unquestionably one of the most famous and representative of today's animators. His films are pessimistic explorations of a decadent world, full of foreboding, terror and absurdity, portrayed with a high sense of drama and punctuated with a steady stream of jarring images.*

48. *Albert Levering, Christmas page for "Puck." Levering was one of the mainstays of "Puck" magazine, to which he contributed large topical drawings around the turn of the century. This multi-panel page is a good example of his draftsmanship.*

Ye GOOD OLD THANKSGIVING TIME
Ye Good old Cheer From Ye Good Old Folks
Ye Good Old Dinner with Ye Good Old Jokes
Ye Good Old Voices In Ye Good Old Airs
Ye Same Old Quarrels And Ye Same Old Flares
DRAWN BY ALBERT LEVERING
Then With Clearing Skies, Come Ye Fond Good Byes

49

50

49. *Sandro Lodolo, humorous drawing. © Lodolo. While best known as an animator (chiefly for Italian television), Lodolo is also a noted cartoonist whose works are often exhibited in galleries.*

50. *George Luks, political cartoon. Better remembered as a fine artist, Luks also contributed many cartoons to turn-of-the-century humor magazines. His style, at first awkwardly stiff, later became pleasantly free in execution. His cartoons were often reproduced in chromolithography.*

51. *"Mr. Magoo." © UPA. The nearsighted Mr. Magoo was created by John Hubley in 1949. He was a bald-headed, crotchety old gent who got himself involved in all kinds of misadventures due to his sight impairment. The "Magoo" cartoons proved so popular that the character was starred in a 1959 feature-length film, "1001 Arabian Nights."*

52

52. Mickey Mouse as the Sorcerer's Apprentice in a scene from "Fantasia." © Walt Disney Productions. Mickey Mouse is inarguably the most universally recognized cartoon character ever created. Actually, it is fair to say that Mickey must be regarded not as a cartoon character but as a genuine cultural phenomenon of the first magnitude.

53

53. Camilla Mickwitz, "Jason." © Mickwitz. A cartoonist of international renown, Mickwitz has written and directed many animated cartoons, most of them for the Finnish Broadcasting Company. "Jason" won the prize for Best Children's Animation at the 1975 Hollywood Festival of World Television.

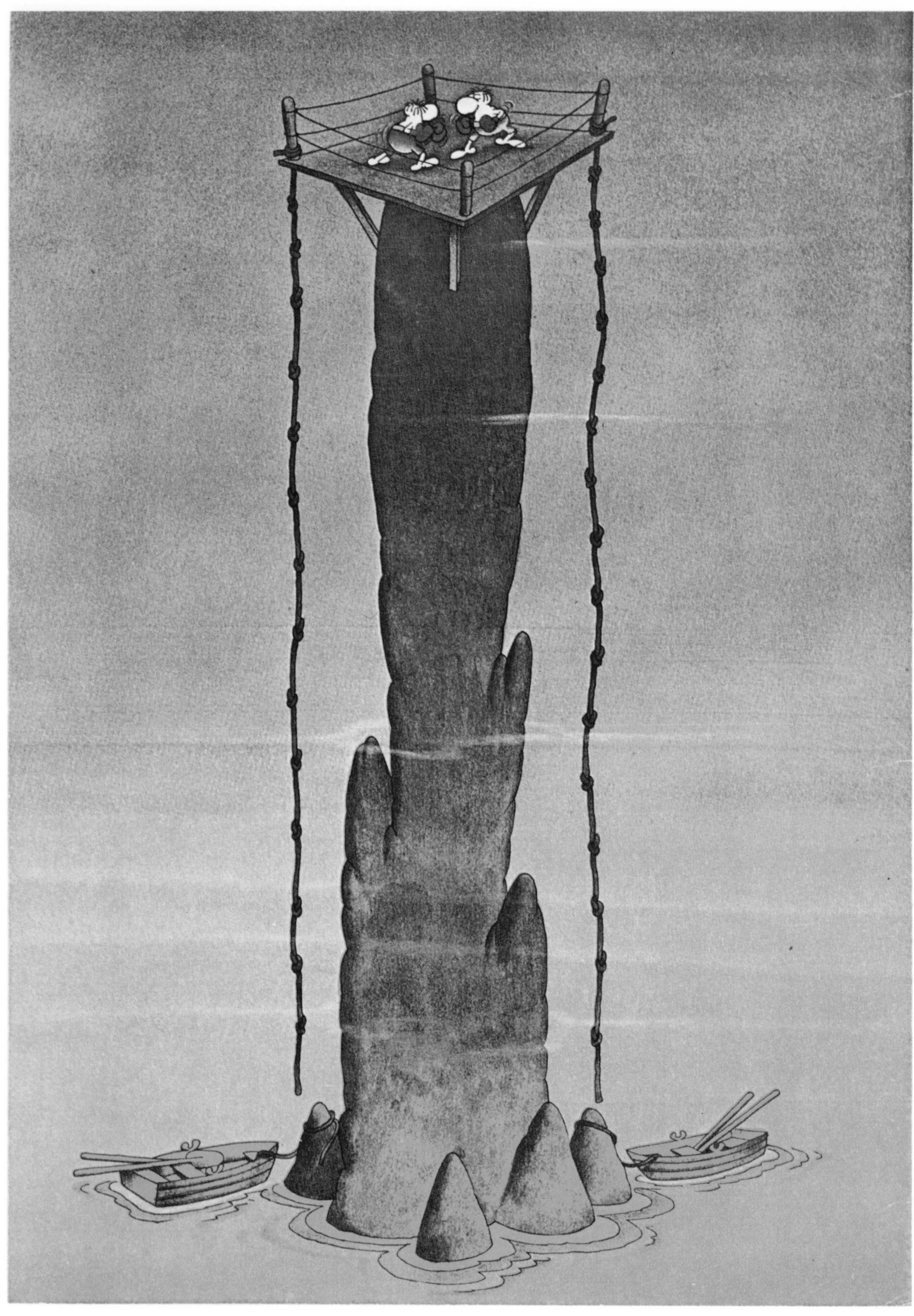

55

54. Guillermo Mordillo. © Mordillo. The Argentine-born Mordillo is one of the most popular of modern-day cartoonists. His humor rests heavily on the unusual, the incongruous and the unexpected; his cartoons, usually captionless (as in this example), are minutely detailed.

55. "The Mouse and His Child." © Wolf/Swenson. This 1978 full-length animation feature was directed by Fred Wolf and Chuck Swenson in a sometimes grim style very different from that of the Disney or Hanna-Barbera animal cartoons. While not always successful, the feature signals a rejuvenation of the American theatrical cartoon.

56

56. Saseo Ono. © Tokyo Puck. *Ono was a forceful Japanese cartoonist whose covers for "Tokyo Puck" were often a grim reflection of the times, as in this example from the 1930s. It was drawn for an issue documenting the plight of the workers of Tokyo's famed Ginza district (including cooks and prostitutes) during the Depression.*

57. Tomás Padró, political cartoon. The Spanish cartoonist Padró received his greatest recognition for the color cartoons he drew for the magazine "La Flaca" in the 1870s. These cartoons testify to his keen political insight and his outstanding artistic abilities, as in this example showing government censorship clipping the wings of a free press.

The Press

58

58. Mstislav Pashchenko, "The Unusual Match." The Soviet animator Pashchenko brought out his most interesting cartoon film, "The Unusual Match," in 1955. This animated short, depicting a soccer match played by wood figures, was well drawn, well designed, and very witty, and it received much acclaim in the Soviet Union and abroad.

59. Bruno Paul, cartoon for "Simplicissimus." Paul's contributions to "Simplicissimus" from 1896 to 1907 are among the most beautiful work ever published in that magazine. Paul used large, flat color areas, arresting angles of vision and fascinating negative spaces, always creating a masterly overall composition.

LIBERTÉ
ORDEN

61

60. Josep Lluis Pellicer. Pellicer's cartoons have strong political overtones. While most were geared toward social struggles in his native Catalonia, he could also take a more international perspective, as in this caricature of the French emperor Napoleon III.

61. "La Planète Sauvage." © Films Armorial. Released as "The Fantastic Planet" in the United States, this animated feature film was produced by Roland Topor and René Laloux. Using a thinly disguised science fiction parable, Laloux and Topor managed to tell an arresting story, visually gripping and narratively suspenseful.

62

62. "The Pink Panther." © DePatie-Freleng. Veteran cartoonist Friz Freleng was assigned to animate the credits for a 1964 movie comedy, "The Pink Panther," and came up with a rose-colored feline of rascally instincts and silent demeanor. His creation was as big a success as the film that inspired it, and there was soon a series of "Pink Panther" animated shorts.

63. "Pluggers." © Tribune Media Services. "Pluggers" is the latest cartoon creation of three-time Pulitzer Prize-winner Jeff MacNelly. Written with the contributions of its readers, and currently drawn by editorial cartoonist Gary Brookins, the panel is a huge critical and popular success.

64. Vladimir Polkovnikov, "Grayneck." Polkovnikov is a solid craftsman whose warm humor and pleasing style are very popular in Russia. "Grayneck," a charming tale about a wild duck, is his most memorable cartoon.

© Tribune Media Services, Inc. / Pluggers, Inc.
All rights reserved.
FLOYD'S BAIT AND AEROSPACE SYSTEMS
You're a plugger if your life depends on anything made by the lowest bidder.

63

64

65

ROBOTECH
ART I
STARBLAZE EDITIONS
The official guide to the Robotech universe—
Macross, Southern Cross and Mospeda!

66

65. Paul Revere, "The Boston Massacre." Revere was primarily a silversmith, but his versatility was amazing; among other things, he engraved some of the earliest American cartoons. "The Boston Massacre," a precursor of the political cartoons of succeeding generations, was drawn, engraved and hand-colored in 1770.

66. "Robotech." © Tatsunoko Productions. An amalgam of Japanese anime techniques and American plot development, "Robotech" was turned into a long-running sci-fi saga on American television.

67. Heath Robinson, "A Christmas Deed of Kindness." © Hutchinson's Magazine. Robinson was a noted book illustrator, but he also contributed many humorous drawings to magazines. His style, however, was always more illustrative than "cartoony."

W HEATH ROBINSON

佐伯俊男画

69

68. Toshio Saeki. © Saeki. Saeki is generally regarded as an avant-garde cartoonist who draws bizarre, beautifully graphic pictures. He is particularly known for his somewhat surreal depiction of demonlike figures that appear to have materialized from another world to crack our civilized veneer.

69. Julio Sanchis Aguado ("Harca"). © Harca. As "Harca," Sanchis has been one of the most prolific Spanish cartoonists in recent times, having freelanced cartoons to almost every newspaper in Spain.

("If you want a beano its a fair old treat!")
'APPY 'AMPSTEAD
BY THE
UNDERGROUND
HUMOURS OF LONDON Nº 7

71

70. *Tony Sarg, poster for the London underground railway. Born in Guatemala, Sarg finally adopted America as his home. He entered the advertising field in England in the early years of this century. He specialized in bird's-eye views of congregations of people, as in this example.*

71. *"Senya Ichi no Monogatari." © Mushi Productions. This feature-length animated film (released in English as "A Thousand and One Nights") was produced by Osamu Tezuka. It is a surprisingly beautiful, erotic and at times hilarious cartoon with outstanding color artwork and composition.*

72. *A "Silly Symphonies" cartoon, "Flowers and Trees." © Walt Disney Productions. "Silly Symphonies" is the collective title of a series of inspired cartoon shorts produced by Disney from 1929 through the 1930s. The 1932 "Flowers and Trees" was the first animated cartoon entirely filmed in color. It created a sensation upon its release and later earned the first Academy Award in its category.*

72

73

73. "The Simpsons." © Twentieth Century Fox Film Corporation. One of the most critically and popularly acclaimed TV cartoon shows in decades, "The Simpsons" not only satirizes every known TV sitcom cliché but also offers a snide commentary on contemporary American society.

74. Maurice Sinet ("Siné"). © Lui. Siné, who has been compared to Jules Feiffer and Virgil Partch, is the uncontested leader of the new generation of French cartoonists. He is noted both for his acerbic sophistication and for his zany puns, as in this example, which adapts the subtleties of horse racing's "triple play" to the games of love.

74

75

75. "The Smurfs." © Hanna-Barbera Productions/Sepp Inter S.A. "The Smurfs" was that rarety—a popular Saturday-morning cartoon show based on a foreign (in this case Belgian) comic strip.

76 Good Friends All!

76. "Snow White and the Seven Dwarfs." © Walt Disney Productions. "Snow White" was the first commercially successful feature-length animated film. Its scenes were enchanting, often dazzling, and its animation all but flawless. The story was further enhanced by the masterful use of color.

77

77. "Speed Bump." © Creators Syndicate. Funny and off-beat, "Speed Bump" is the latest entry in the crowded field of oddball panel features.

78. Uli Stein. © U. Stein. One of the most entertaining cartoonists currently working in Germany, Stein possesses a graphic style that is deceptively simple but highly effective. This very lack of apparent sophistication is what has made his cartoons highly popular with the readers.

79. T.S. Sullivant. Sullivant did his best work for "Judge" from 1900 to 1903. His was a wonderworld of funny animals, bizarre realities and outrageous character types. Beneath all his visual fun and playful tampering with reality lay an absolutely stunning perception of things as they should be.

80. Joe Szabo. © Joe Szabo. While he is better known as the editor and publisher of WittyWorld, the international cartoon magazine, Hungarian-born Szabo is also a cartoonist of talent.

78

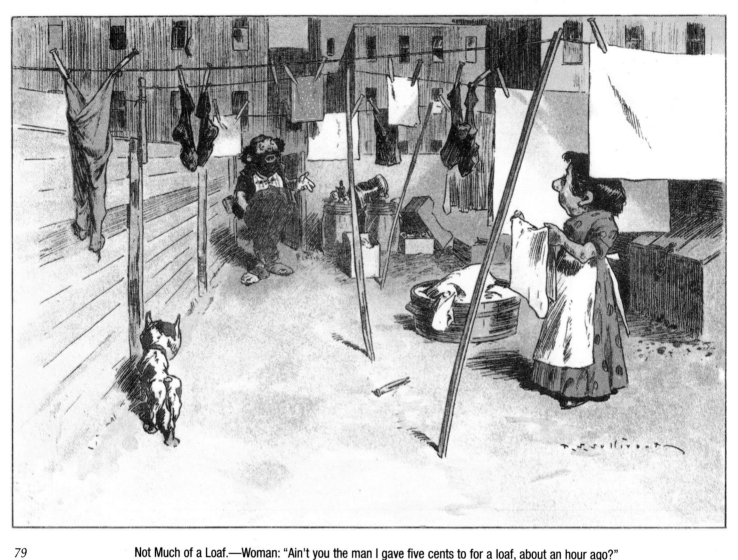

79 Not Much of a Loaf.—Woman: "Ain't you the man I gave five cents to for a loaf, about an hour ago?" —Tramp: "Why, certainly, mum! How long do you t'ink a feller kin loaf on a nickel?"

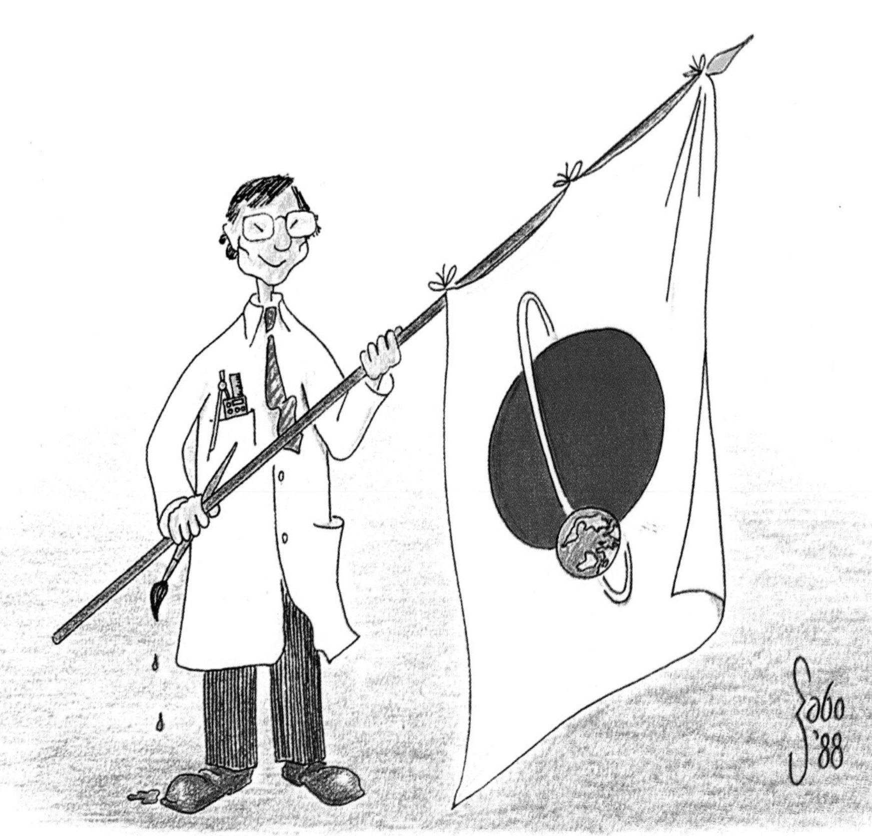

Collier's
DECEMBER 12, 1942
TEN CENTS
DECEMBER 7, 1941

82

81. Arthur Szyk. © Collier's. A prolific and talented cartoonist, illustrator and miniaturist, Szyk is probably best noted for the striking covers he did for "Collier's," chiefly on war themes. This savage depiction of the Japanese sneak attack on Pearl Harbor is a classic.

82. Hideo Takeda, "Monmon." © Takeda. In this series of full-color serigraphs, Takeda dwells with irreverent humor on irezumi, *a Japanese style of body tattooing; the artist literally transforms the tattooed man into an object devoured by his tattoos.*

83. Eduard Thöny. © Simplicissimus. One of the great veterans of the German satirical magazine "Simplicissimus," Thöny was on its staff from its first year to its last (1896-1944). His drawing style, always impressive, was quite academic at the outset, became more fluid and alert with the years, but never partook of an outright cartoon quality. This 1926 drawing is an excellent example of his work.

84. "Tintin et le Temple du Soleil." © Belvision. In the years after World War II, Hergé's Tintin was inarguably the most popular comic character in Europe. To capitalize on this popularity, the Belvision animation studio in Brussels released a full-length animated cartoon starring Tintin in 1969. (The cartoon is known as "Prisoners of the Sun" in its English version.)

83 Nudism! "The only stimulating thing about this review is the audience—there the women aren't completely undressed."

84

85

86

87

88 His Majesty Edward VII, King of England, Emperor of India; the Thunderbolt of War

85. "Tom and Jerry." © MGM. The inseparable duo of Tom Cat and Jerry Mouse was created in 1939 by that no less inseparable duo of animators, Bill Hanna and Joe Barbera. The "Tom and Jerry" cartoons were instantly popular and earned no fewer than seven Oscars from 1943 to 1952.

86. Roland Topor. © Topor. Topor is at the forefront of French and international cartooning. He is a master of black humor and portrays the most far-out and disturbing images in a deceptively classical style. The transformation of the human form is one of Topor's most recurrent and most typical themes.

87. "The Two Types." © Eighth Army News. John Philpin Jones gave birth to the Two Types (under the pseudonym "Jon") in the course of World War II. The Two Types had no name; they were both officers of the British Eighth Army and fought all the way to victory—not, however, without a great many hilarious mishaps in the meantime.

88. Jean Veber, caricature of Edward VII. Although Veber never achieved great artistic stature, he had several succès de scandale. A special series of cartoons that he did in 1901 on the Boer War was banned by the French government. Here he depicts the English king as a bloated drunkard to whom the people of the Transvaal had to pay homage.

89. Sam Viviano, cover for WittyWorld. © Sam Viviano. Viviano is best noted for his lively caricatures, of which this is a good example.

WittyWorld

WINTER SPRING 1989
6/7

International Cartoon Magazine

$13.60

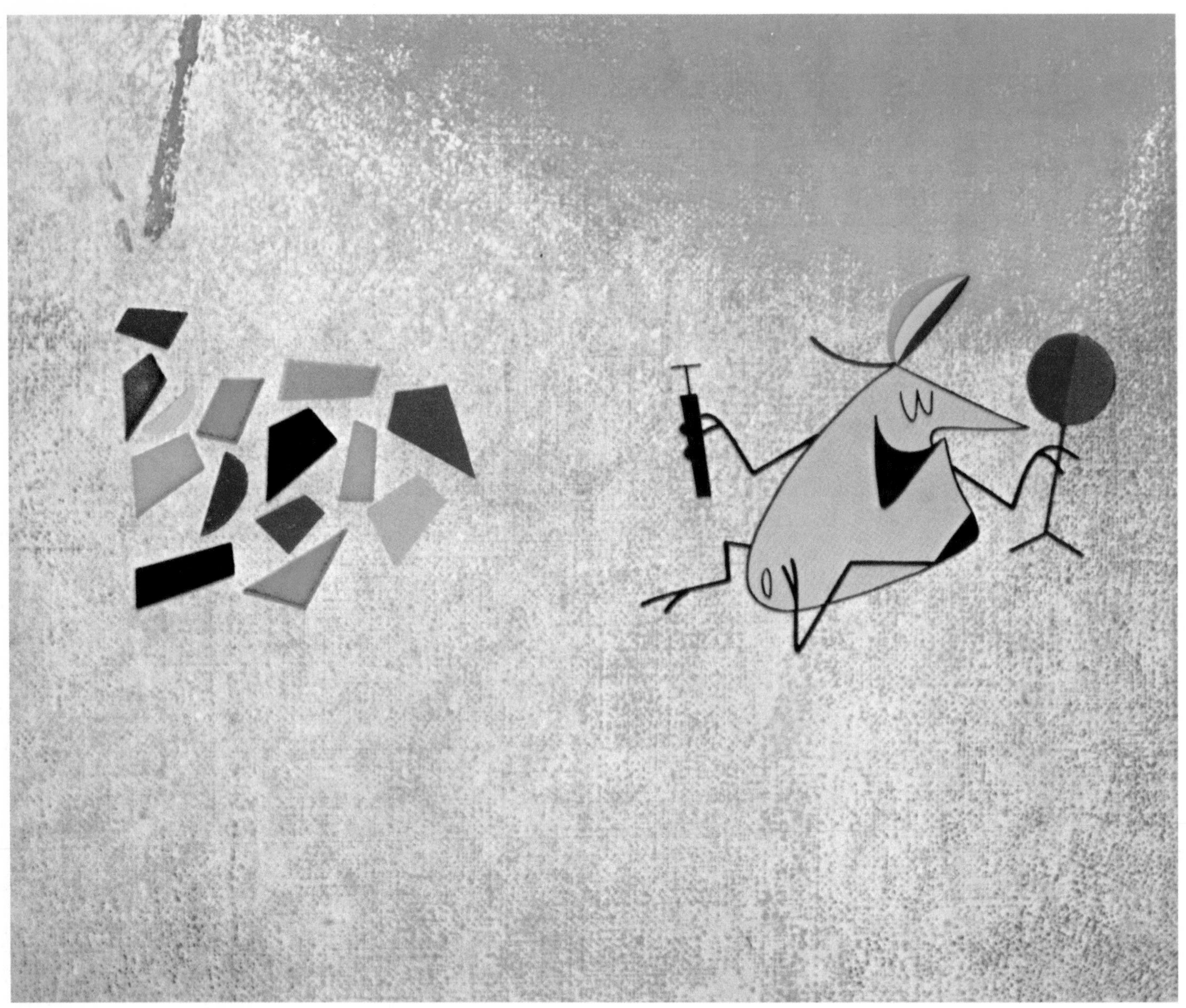

90

90. Dušan Vukotić. "Ersatz." © Zagreb Film. The major figure in Yugoslav animation, Vukotić has directed a great number of enchanting and award-winning films. This is a frame from "Ersatz," which won the Academy Award in 1961.

91. James Wales, cover cartoon for "Puck." Wales was a competent pen-and-ink artist who had a faculty for forceful presentation of ideas. He was never fully comfortable with the lithographic stone, but he did manage to produce some effective color drawings, as in this example.

VOL. IX.-No. 224.
JUNE 22, 1881.
Price, 10 Cents.
"What fools these Mortals be!"
MIDSUMMER-NIGHTS DREAM.
Puck
PUBLISHED BY
KEPPLER & SCHWARZMANN.
NEW YORK
TRADE MARK REGISTERED 1878.
OFFICE No. 21 - 23 WARREN ST.
"ENTERED AT THE POST OFFICE AT NEW YORK, AND ADMITTED FOR TRANSMISSION THROUGH THE MAILS AT SECOND CLASS RATES."
HISTORY OF TREASON BY AN EX-TRAITOR
SECESSION CEMETERY
1861
DEAD ISSUES
EMANCIPATION PROCLAMATION
A. LINCOLN
WITH CHARITY FOR ALL WITH MALICE TOWARD NONE
HISTORY OF TREASON PROFITS
T.A. Wales

92

Sentimental People, No. 7: "So, Mother dear, I'm going now—important appointment at the club—in case you die, don't forget to turn off the lamp first."—"The good boy, he thinks of everything."

92. Rudolf Wilke, drawing for "Simplicissimus." Wilke's style was a highly personal blend of patterned composition and a proto-expressionist treatment of the human figure. He was internationally acclaimed in his lifetime as one of the most powerful talents in German cartooning.

93. Rowland Wilson, advertising cartoon. © New England Life. Wilson is famous for his witty advertising cartoons. This New England Life series of over forty ads gained him national recognition.

"My insurance company? New England Life, of course. Why?"

94

94. *"Yellow Submarine."© King Features Syndicate & Subafilms. The first animated cartoon to cash in on the Beatles craze, "Yellow Submarine" was produced by George Dunning; German designer Heinz Edelmann contributed the artwork. The film is best remembered for its wild experimentation with color and form, and for some of the best songs the Beatles ever wrote.*

95. *Zhan Tong. © Zhan Tong. From the 1950s to the 1990s Zhan has been one of the most versatile as well as one of the most respected illustrators and cartoonists in China. He has successfully worked in such different media as children's book illustration, film animation, and newspaper cartooning.*

95

96

96. "Ziggy." © Universal Press Syndicate. Ziggy is a little fellow with no particular status in life—and no particular talents either. In short, he is a modern-day Everyman completely overwhelmed by our mass civilization. Created by Tom Wilson, Ziggy is a very endearing character who becomes embroiled in countless hilarious contretemps.

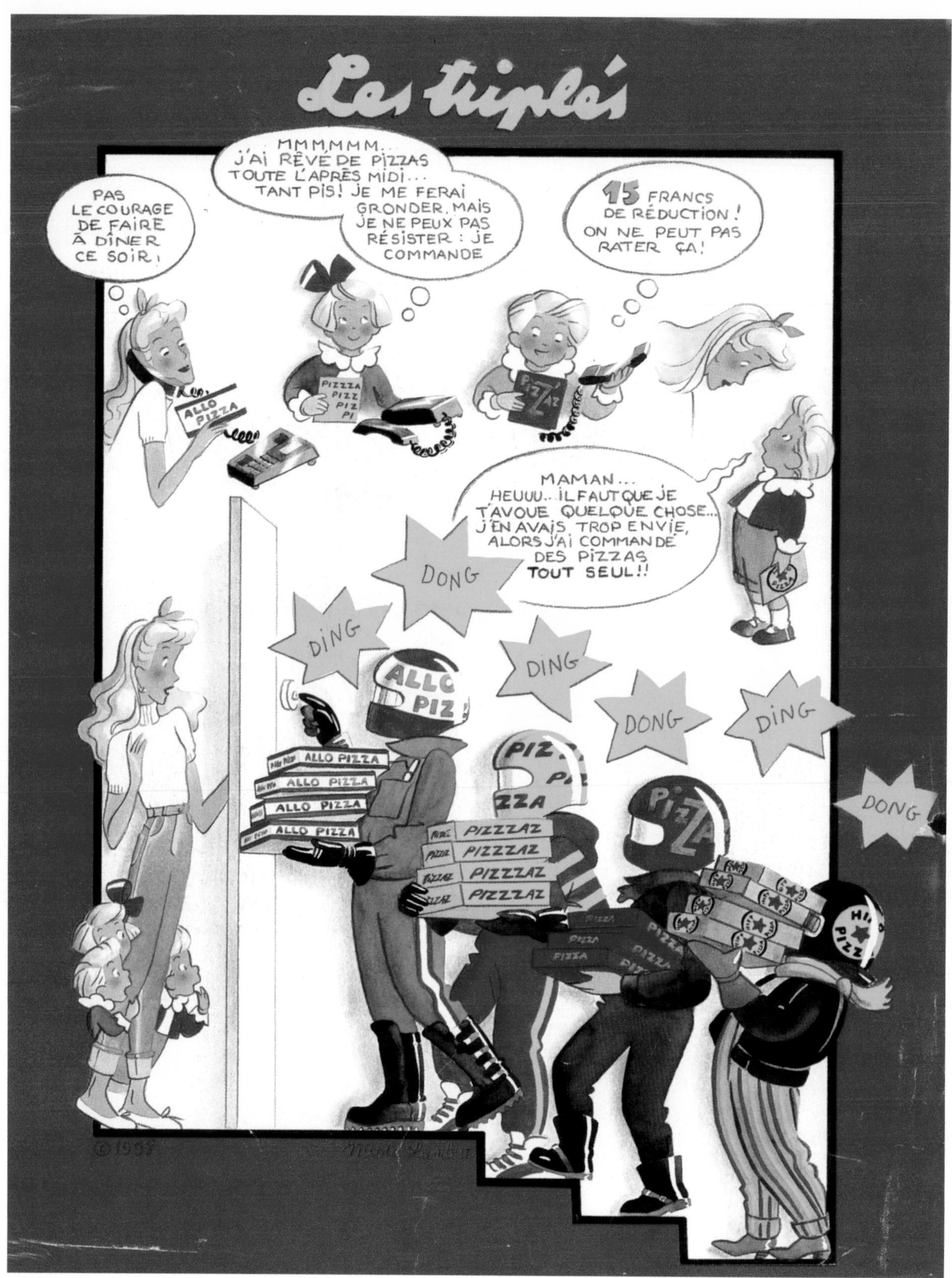

97

97. *"Les Triplés." Published as a full page color feature in the French weekly "Madame Figaro" magazine, "Les Triplés" was created by Nicole Lambert in 1983.*

Brad Holland. © New York Times.

HOLCK, POUL (1939-) Danish cartoonist born in Copenhagen, Denmark, on September 30, 1939. Holck's specialty is innocent sophistication, and in his drawing style he shows the simple and the wonderful, knowing that there is something ugly in everything beautiful. Since his debut he has worked as a house cartoonist at the daily *Politiken,* where he, at a fixed spot that he shares with two or three others, gives his comments on topical events several times a week. He also illustrates articles and editorials.

Poul Holck. © Holck.

Holck often appears on television as an illustrating political commentator. Here, too, the curls and the chins appear, always displayed with kindness and tact. His well-developed sense of motion comes across whether his cartoons are animated or printed on paper. On his way to world fame, he won first prize at the 13th International Salon of Caricature in Montreal in 1976, with participants coming from 57 countries. In the last two decades his worldwide reputation has grown by leaps and bounds, and he is often included in international cartoon anthologies.

J.S.

HOLLAND, BRAD (1943-) American cartoonist and illustrator born in Fremont, Ohio, in 1944. Brad Holland is one of the youngest of the prominent artist-illustrators in the modern graphic art tradition of the Push Pin Studio school. He grew up in Fort Sumter, Arkansas, a relatively isolated rural community, and his peculiar artistic development owes much to this environment. Driven by an inner need to express himself in a graphic style, yet cut off from all sources of artistic inspiration save Norman Rockwell magazine covers and Walt Disney comics, Holland developed a very personal approach to expression.

His first attempts at drawing, he recalls, were pornographic cartoons over which he would labor, only to tear them up lest his mother find them. By the age of 13, he was drawing cartoons and sending them to various magazines, without success. Undaunted, Holland left Arkansas at the age of 17, determined upon a career in art, notwithstanding his lack of formal education. He moved to Chicago, where his first job as an "artist" was in a tattoo parlor; this was followed by a job with Hallmark Cards, which Holland recalls as no more "artistic" than the tattoo parlor. There he received a small salary because of his lack of formal training and worked in a separate room in the art department because his stuff was so "weird." In keeping with his reputation, he founded during this period the Asylum Press, through which he and a group of friends printed "eccentric projects."

When he moved to New York City, however, everything began to come together for Brad Holland. With his alien style now fixed, he was able to refine it in the hothouse artistic environment of the city in the 1960s—the lively underground press, the more serious pop and op movements, the downtown gallery scene and finally the museums. With this refinement came some commercial success, notably in the *Playboy* "Ribald Classic" series. But his most striking work haunted the pages of the underground press organs—black-and-white illustrations unequivocally stating his own (and the underground movement's) opposition to the established order. By 1971 the relevance of his work had triumphed over its weirdness, and he was hired as a staff artist by the *New York Times*, where his work has become a staple of the Op-Ed Page.

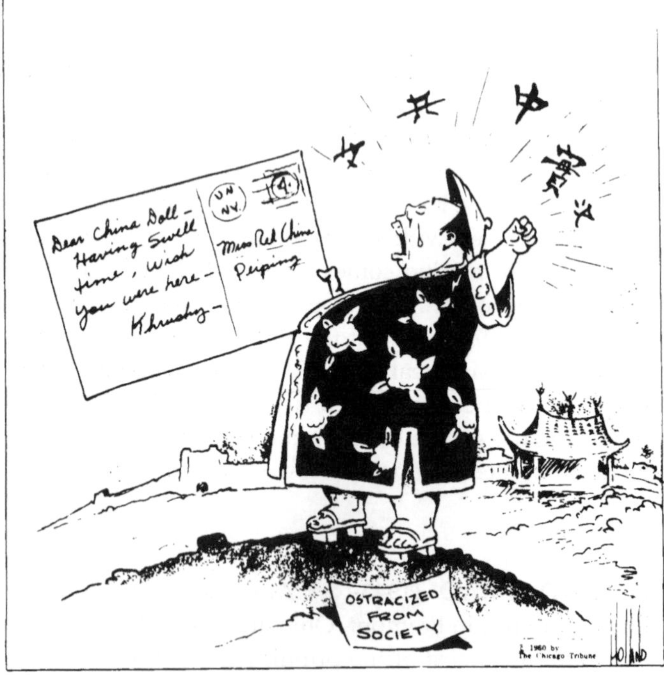

The girl he left behind

Ed Holland. © Chicago Tribune.

His work does not readily lend itself to description, though the title of a 1975 Paris exhibition of the work of Holland and his fellow *Times* artists perhaps comes close: "Beyond Illustration." It has a peculiar quality of depth reminiscent of grotesque china figurines—alienated Hummels, perhaps—and an impact that is frequently anything but benign.

In keeping with the visibility the *Times* connection has gained him, Holland's work has become fashionable. Besides appearing in other outlets like *Intellectual Digest*, he has received increasing numbers of commissions to illustrate books. A collection of his work has also been published under the title *Human Scandals* (Crowell, 1977). This book is worth looking at, not only as art but as documentary evidence of the strange and wonderful visions that isolated, eccentric development can sometimes promote and as a testimony to innate human creativity. In this respect, Holland's achievement perhaps provides the best antidote to the bleak view of humanity frequently represented in his work. Since 1980 he has continued his highly regarded career as an illustrator, poster and stage designer, and lately art director, winning more professional awards in the process.

R.C.

HOLLAND, DANIEL E. (1918-) American cartoonist born in Guthrie, Kentucky, on February 2, 1918. Daniel ("Ed") Holland was educated at David Lipscomb College (1936-38) and the Chicago Academy of Fine Arts (1938-39). The man who was to become the last of the *Chicago Tribune*'s classic-style cartoonists followed his immediate predecessors, Carey Orr and Joe Parrish, from Nashville to Chicago. Holland went from the *Nashville Banner* (1939-41) to the *Chicago Tribune* (1945-50) to the *Washington Times-Herald* (1950 until its merger with the *Post* in 1954) and back to the *Chicago Tribune.* He shared duties until 1972 and was then chief editorial cartoonist until his retirement in 1975.

Stylistically, Holland belonged to the Billy Ireland school of photographic likenesses amidst unexaggerated but simplified cartoon figures. He seldom used crayon shading, relying on handsome crosshatching rendered in a supple line. Many of his cartoons ran in color on the *Trib*'s front page. Holland was probably the last major American cartoonist to receive such a regular place of honor, and also the last of a distinguished line of fierce, old-school conservatives. His pleasant style formed an amiable link with the earlier look of American political cartoons. He won many Freedom Foundation citations and taught for years at the Chicago Academy of Fine Arts.

R.M.

HOLLEY, LEE (1933-) American cartoonist born in Phoenix, Arizona, on April 20, 1933. Lee Holley displayed a love of cartooning at an early age, and he started selling his cartoons at the age of 15. He attended Chouinard Art School in Los Angeles, and in 1954 he joined the Warner Brothers animation studio, where for three years he worked on *Bugs Bunny, Road Runner* and *Daffy Duck* cartoons, as well as on a number of *Porky Pig* comic books. In

"What's your second choice for a career if you can't be a bunny?"

Lee Holley, "Ponytail." © *King Features Syndicate.*

1957 he became assistant to Hank Ketcham, helping him draw the *Dennis the Menace* Sunday feature.

All the while Lee Holley kept submitting cartoon ideas to syndicates, and in 1960 he finally succeeded in selling a teenage panel to King Features. Called *Ponytail,* it is now running daily and Sundays. Drawn in a seemingly slap dash but effective manner, it tells of the everyday trials and tribulations of the title heroine and her teenage cohorts. While the theme is neither new nor startlingly original, Holley has been able to impart to it an impish charm that redeems its more obvious and hackneyed situations. After his panel was discontinued in the early 1980s, he went back to freelancing gag cartoons.

M.H.

HOLLREISER, LEN (1923-) American cartoonist born in Brooklyn, New York, on September 16, "the year Casey Stengel beat the Yankees twice in the World Series with home runs," which, according to the record books, turns out to be 1923. Soon after graduation from high school in 1941, Len Hollreiser embarked on a fledgling cartooning career that was nipped in the bud by his induction into the army. After demobilization in 1945, he worked briefly for comic books and magazines. In 1947 he met Willard Mullin and on his recommendation was hired as the sports cartoonist for the *New York Herald-Tribune.*

In 1953 Hollreiser created for the Chicago Tribune New York News Syndicate *Looking Back in Sports,* a cartoon panel of sports history that was followed a few years later by *This Day in Sports,* a daily installment of vignettes retracing some sports event of the past. The panel ran for years, but in 1975, partly due to deteriorating eyesight, Hollreiser was forced to drop it.

Hollreiser was one of the few remaining syndicated sports cartoonists. His style, heavily inspired by Mullin's, is by turns realistic, with heavy shading and accurate body placement, and cartoony, with whimsical figures popping out in odd situations. After working for Lockheed Aircraft into the late 1980s, he is now retired, although still drawing an occasional cartoon for local and charitable organizations.

M.H.

HOLSWILDER, JAN (1850-1890) Dutch cartoonist, painter and printmaker born in Leiden, the Netherlands, on November 17, 1850. Despite the weak health that shortened his life—only the last 10 of his 40 years could be devoted to cartoons and caricatures—Jan Holswilder gained the reputation of having freed Dutch humorous drawing from a blight of allegory and amateurism, and of having been the first Dutch political cartoonist to reflect in his work the advanced level that fine art had reached in his time.

In 1878 Holswilder moved permanently to The Hague, and his intimate knowledge of life in the Dutch capital was to be of paramount importance in his production. After art study at the Academy there and a period of ordinary clerical jobs, he worked for some time in a lithographic printshop, where he acquired essential technical know-how. His first important published cartoon work was an 1880 series called *Haagsche Penkrassen* ("Pen Sketches of The Hague"). In 1882 he began drawing for the magazine *Uilenspiegel.* The decisive move in his career occurred in 1885, when he became the chief draftsman for the new semimonthly *De Lantaarn* (named after a lively Dutch paper of the era of the French Revolution).

The new *Lantaarn* was an aggressively liberal and anticlerical publication that had its hands full in the 1880s (as did the *Uilenspiegel*) combatting two powerful parties that seriously threatened the separation between church and state: the Calvinist group led by Kuyper and the Catholic group led by Schaepman. Holswilder's long, careful acquaintance with Hague affairs made him a natural as a chronicler of daily infighting in Parliament; he knew all the deputies, and his was essentially an art based on reality and direct observation. While working for *De Lantaarn,* he changed his basic cartoon technique from his earlier lithographlike charcoal drawing on rough paper to straight pen work in a sketchy, impressionistic manner. He was also known for his caricatures of the politically prominent, some of which were published in Netscher's book *Uit Ons Parlement* ("From Our Parliament").

Holswilder was also a painter, etcher and lithographer who produced portraits, landscapes and figure studies. He died in The Hague on August 20, 1890.

S.A.

HOLTROP, BERNARD WILLEM (1941-) French cartoonist born in Ermelo, the Netherlands, on April 2, 1941. Holtrop started contributing satirical cartoons under his

Willem Holtrop ("Willem"). © Willem.

middle name, Willem, to a number of anti-establishment publications in 1967. The next year he moved to Paris and took part in the worker and student rebellion of May 1968, providing vitriolic cartoons for the notorious weekly *L'Enrage* ("The Rabid One"), the organ of the more radical of the protesters.

Willem later worked for the left-wing *Hara-Kiri* (self-styled as "one mean and dumb journal") and for its sister publication *Charlie-Hebdo*. His cartoon attacks on the Gaullist regime proved so ferocious and telling that the authorities tried to have him deported. To forestall any further such attempt, he took up French citizenship in the early 1970's.

Willem became the political cartoonist for the Parisian daily *Liberation* in 1981, coinciding with the coming to power of the Socialist Party. At first he was a lukewarm supporter of the new regime, but turned against the government once again when he felt the Socialists had betrayed their mandate. Since that time he has been a thorn in the side of whatever party happened to be in power in France, whether from the left or the right. His cartoons, all the more effective for being served by an elegant, supple line, are extremely influential and they have been anthologized in numerous collections.

Concurrently with his work as a political satirist, Willem has also turned out a number of comic strips, usually on social and political issues. His most noted work in this domain is *Euromania* (1992), wherein he attacked the values and goals of the European Union.

M.H.

HONDA, KINKICHIRO (1850-1921) Japanese artist and cartoonist born in Edo (now Tokyo), Japan, in 1850. Kinkichiro Honda was one of the typical progressive artists of the Meiji period (1868-1912). In 1863 he traveled to Hiroshima to undergo military training based on British methods of instruction. The exposure to Western-style education stimulated young Honda to take an interest in the English language, and in 1868 he enrolled in the school of Western learning that Fumio Nomura had founded after his return from studies in England. Nomura had taken an interest in the humor magazines he saw during his travels abroad, and it was no doubt his teacher's interest in cartoons that prompted Honda to travel to Tokyo four years later and begin a career as an illustrator and cartoonist.

In March 1877, Fumio Nomura founded the *Marumaru Chinbun,* one of the historic humor magazines of the Meiji era, and Honda joined his former teacher to draw the back cover for every issue. His first illustration showed three *Punch*-style characters with somewhat comic expressions, the *Marumaru Chinbun* logo and a horse and a deer at the top of the page (the words horse and deer read together in Japanese are pronounced *baka,* a common expression meaning "stupid" or "foolish"). In the years that followed, Honda produced many satirical cartoons on human rights, civil liberties and other political affairs. He was fond of atrocious puns, a characteristic that reveals his classical upbringing; like many of the early cartoonists, Honda was heavily influenced by the light, farcical *haikai* and *haiku* literary traditions. Bad puns were a legacy of these earlier literary forms, and Honda and others transmitted them to the modern cartoon. One such example was a Honda cartoon entitled "Minken Tohai," which could be interpreted as "Colleague of Human Rights" or "Howling Dog of the People." Of course, Honda completed the pun by drawing a huge dog howling over some government officials and thus produced a humorous statement on the growing demand for human rights.

Honda's contributions as an artist are significant not only for their historical value but also for the techniques by which they were produced. Honda worked in a printshop in Tokyo that was owned by a foreign printer, and he used the shop's lead-plate presses to produce copies of much better quality than the wood-block prints that had been common until then. Honda eventually gave up drawing for the *Marumaru Chinbun,* turning his pen over to Kiyochiku Kobayashi. He spent his final years drawing and designing traditional Japanese gardens. He also published several books on the art of garden making. He died in 1921.

J.C.

HONOBONO-KUN (Japan) *Honobono-Kun* was a four-frame cartoon in the traditional Japanese format that first appeared in the *Tokyo Shimbun* ("Tokyo Newspaper") in 1956. It was drawn by Kimihiko Tsukuda. The hero of this piece was a three- or four-year-old little boy called Honobono (meaning "glimmer" or "hope") who was usually accompanied by his dog. For reasons never really clarified, he had no mother, but this created a format for a warm bond with his round-faced father. The daily chores that they performed together were often a central theme, and part of *Honobono-kun's* popularity may have stemmed from the fact that most Japanese children feel very distant from their fathers. The thought of a home where a father is not only a "friend" but also performs household chores was both appealing and amusing.

Honobono-kun was very simply drawn, and as a result the overall subtle sentimentality of the work was further increased. Moreover, it tended to concentrate on the little things that happen in ordinary, everyday existence and therefore had a particularly broad appeal. A unique characteristic of *Honobono-kun* was its "silent" or "pantomime" technique (Tsukuda was apparently greatly influenced in this respect by Erich Ohser, a German cartoonist who, among other things, wrote *Vater und Sohn* under the name of E.O. Plauen.) The resulting atmosphere of *Honobono-kun* is one of wistful solitude. Later, *Honobono Ojisan,* a slightly altered version starring the father, ran in *Asahi Shimbun* ("Asahi News"), but it did utilize some words.

Tsukuda, the artist, is also known for his *Aisubekya Tsura* ("Face That Should Be Loved"), *Dorobo Shinshi* ("Gentleman Thief") and *Honobono Kazoku* ("Honobono Family").

F.S.

HOOK, GEOFFREY RAYNOR (1928-) Australian political cartoonist born in Hobart, Tasmania, in December 1928.

Since World War II a significant factor in the style of Australian political cartooning has been the filtered influence of the drawing and presentation initiated by William ("Wep") Pidgeon during the 1940s. In theme, the "grand manner" approach, the sort previously drawn with allegorical or symbolic figures labeled "Nationhood" soberly indicating rising suns labeled "Health-Wealth-Prosperity," has completely disappeared. One of the present-day press cartoonists to favor humor above moral posturing is the Melbourne *Sun-News Pictorial*'s Geoffrey ("Jeff") Hook. Jeff has the distinction of being the first political cartoonist to work for the *Sun* since it was founded in 1922.

Hook joined the art staff of this morning paper in April 1964 as a layout artist, and during this period, keen to be a cartoonist, he fed cartoon ideas to the editor, who eventually asked Jeff to produce one finished cartoon a week, then two, then five a week plus a football cartoon for the *Sporting Globe,* another of the *Herald* group weekly newspapers. In this early period of his career he assisted with feature page layouts as well!

Jeff took a night-school commercial art course at the Hobart Technical School while working as a public servant. He secured a job with the Hobart *Mercury* as a press artist in 1959, coming to Melbourne five years later. Politically, Jeff has stated that he prefers no party but remains permanently in opposition to all, believing that this is the way the man in the street is most of the time.

His cartoons, drawn with bold lines, with their first-class portrait caricature of personalities in politics, are compulsively readable and display well on the tabloid page of the *Sun.* And, as in the old *Cole's Funny Picture Book* puzzle-drawings—"Here is the pig, here is the horse, and here is his dog. Where is the farmer?"—or as with the Souter cat or Emile Mercier's gravy cans, Jeff hides away in his cartoons his personal pun, a small fishhook, the discovery of which gives *Sun* readers a feeling of triumphant satisfaction. He retired in 1993.

None of Jeff's cartoons have been published as a collection, but he has illustrated a number of books displaying in another context his fine comic skill.

V.L.

Family of Man!

Jeff Hook. © Melbourne Sun-News Pictorial.

HOOVER, ELLISON (1890-1955) American cartoonist born in Cleveland, Ohio, in 1890. Ellison Hoover studied art at the Art Students League in New York before landing a staff position with the *New York World.* He later worked for the *New York Evening News* and the *New York Herald-Tribune.*

In the 1910s and 1920s Hoover frequently drew for *Judge* and *Life;* his fat little German-Americans attracted some attention amid the fervid anti-German hysteria preceding and during World War I, and one character, Otto, later starred in a short-lived strip for the *Herald-Tribune.* As depicted by Hoover, however, these characters were so ridiculous as to undermine the intended venom of the drawings. In the 1920s much of his work consisted of full-page drawings on speculative themes such as "Visiting — City by One Who Has Never Been There," and other series in this genre, which was really handled better by Gluyas Williams, Forbell and Rea Irvin. Hoover also frequently lampooned the art form of the comic strip, viciously accusing it of low humor, monotony and an absence of talent.

Hoover had a chance to set the world straight when he inherited the comic strip *Mr. and Mrs.* upon the death of Clare Briggs. He failed miserably. His work was an insult to Clare Briggs's genius, and for years the strip reflected low humor, monotony and an absence of talent—in spite of the fact that the otherwise clever comic writer Arthur H. Folwell contributed gags. Aside from his poor imitation of Briggs, Hoover's style was sterile and empty. His full pages are curiously unbalanced, and white spaces dominate instead of framing the points of interest. His shading was always done with methodical parallel lines that, if nothing else, indicate dedication.

Hoover died in his New York apartment on March 17, 1955.

R.M.

HOPPIN, AUGUSTUS (1828-1896) American cartoonist, illustrator and lawyer born in Providence, Rhode Island, on April 13, 1828. Augustus Hoppin graduated from Brown University in 1848 and the Harvard Law School in 1850, when he was also admitted to the Rhode Island bar. The growing (or creeping) sophistication of wood-cut engraving, however, and the increasing tribe of native American humorists, combined to lure Hoppin away from law and toward drawing. His drawings appeared in many monthly magazines and in a long list of humorous books, including *The Potiphar Papers* (1853), *The Autocrat of the Breakfast Table* (1858), *Hay Fever* (1873), *A Fashionable Sufferer* (1883), *Two Compton Boys* (1885) and *Married for Fun* (1885). He also authored romances anonymously. Whether he contributed to the later humor magazines is doubtful; his work is often mistaken for that of Livingston Hopkins.

But in the very early comic sheets and in the humor columns of the early monthlies his work is omnipresent. As late as 1872 he was producing three daily cartoons for the four-page sheet *Jubilee Days.* To Hoppin must go a large share of the credit for priming the American public for the panel cartoon. He was essentially an illustrator who devoted his career to funny subjects, but as such he paved the way for the new profession of magazine cartooning. He died in Flushing, New York, on April 1, 1896.

R.M.

HORRABIN, JAMES FRANCIS (1884-1962) British strip cartoonist and illustrator born in Sheffield, England, on November 1, 1884. James Francis ("Frank") Horrabin, one of the most prolific strip cartoonists and illustrators of his time, studied historic ornament at the Sheffield School of Art and designed flower show prize cups for his father's silverplate works before joining the art department of the *Sheffield Telegraph* in 1906. On that provincial newspaper he provided a daily topical strip in the format popularized by W.K. Haselden in the *Daily Mirror.* He quickly rose to art editor and went to London in 1911 to take up the same position on the *Daily News.*

It was the time of the Balkan Wars, and Horrabin, a keen geographer, began to supply his paper with maps of the war. Popular, topical cartography would become a major sideline to his cartoon activities, and he map-illustrated the progress of both world wars in newspapers and books and on television. His "serious side" took him into lecturing on geography at the London Labour College, and thence to the editorship of *The Plebs,* the monthly Labour magazine, and finally into Parliament itself: he campaigned for and was elected Labour member of Parliament for Peterborough (1929-31).

Frank Horrabin's first daily strip, *Adventures of the Noah Family Including Japhet,* began as a single panel in the *Daily News* on June 13, 1919. This was later known as *Japhet and Happy,* and still later as *The Arkubs.* It transferred to the *News Chronicle* in 1930 and continued until after the war. Many annual volumes of this popular children's strip were published from 1920 to the 1950s. For the same publisher's evening newspaper, the *Star,* Horrabin created *Dot and Carrie.* This office strip about two typists began on November 18, 1922, and ran to March 1, 1962, when it was ended on Horrabin's death.

Besides running both daily strips, Horrabin drew many book illustrations and was a regular on prewar television, with *Newsmap* shows and "Lightning Cartoon" appearances. Horrabin is largely forgotten today, except by nostalgic collectors of his *Japhet and Happy Annuals,* but a *Dot and Carrie* supplement was reprinted as a pullout to the revived *Ally Sloper* magazine in January 1977.

Books: *Some Adventures of the Noah Family* (1920); *The Noahs on Holiday* (1921); *More About the Noahs* (1922); *Mr. Noah* (1922); *Japhet and Fido* (1922); *Dot and Carrie* (1923); *Economic Geography* (1923); *Outline of Economic Geography* (1923); *The Japhet Book* (1924); *Dot and Carrie and Adolphus* (1924); *Working Class Education* (1924); *Dot and Carrie Not Forgetting Adolphus* (1925); *About Japhet* (1926); *Japhet and Co.* (1927); *The Workers History of Great Britain* (1927); *Japhet and the Arkubs* (1928); *Short History of the British Empire* (1929); *Japhet and the Arkubs at Sea* (1929); *Japhet and Co. on Arkub Island* (1930); *The Japhet and Happy Book* (1931); *Socialism in Pictures and Figures* (1933); *Japhet and Happy Annual* (1933-51?); *Atlas of Great Events* (1934); *Atlas of European History* (1935); *The Japhet Holiday Book* (1936-40); *How Empires Grow* (1935); *The Opening Up of the World* (1936); *Atlas of Europe* (1937); *Plebs Atlas* (1938); *Atlas*

History of the Second World War (1940-46); *Geography of the War* (1940); *Outline of Political Geography* (1942); *Youth Service in an English County* (1945); *Atlas of the USSR* (1945); *Land of the Soviets* (1946); *Search for Peace* (1949); *The Japhet and Happy Painting Book* (1949); and *Atlas of Africa* (1960).

D.G.

HOSEMANN, THEODOR (1807-1875) German cartoonist, illustrator, painter and printmaker born in Brandenburg, Prussia (just west of Berlin), on September 24, 1807. The most complete published catalogue of Theodor Hosemann's works included over a hundred oils and watercolors and over five hundred graphics, of which about four hundred are illustrations for books, magazines and almanacs, about seventy-five are individual prints and about a hundred are commercial and occasional works (menus, greeting cards, calendars). Among this large production, humorous drawings are prominent.

Hosemann came from an old family that had furnished Prussia with many pastors and many soldiers. His father was an officer stationed in Brandenburg at the time of Theodor's birth. The boy spent an unsettled childhood because of the Napoleonic Wars. In 1816 the family, now impoverished, made their home in Düsseldorf. At the age of 12 Theodor began working in a lithographic printshop.

Scenes from the lives of domestic servants.

Theodor Hosemann.

He worked as a commercial artist from 1822 to 1828 and also studied at the Düsseldorf Academy under such masters as Peter von Cornelius and the younger Schadow. There he met the cartoonist Schrödter, who had followed Schadow down from Berlin. Hosemann maintained relations with the artistic circles of Düsseldorf even after he left that city and later contributed to the important art and humor magazine *Düsseldorfer Monatshefte.*

In 1828 the partners that Hosemann worked for, Arnz and Winckelmann, split up, and Hosemann accepted Winckelmann's offer to come along to Berlin and illustrate a line of children's books—a major innovation for Germany at that time. Once in Berlin, Hosemann also did work for such publishers as Meyer and Hofmann, Julius Springer and G. Reimer. Among the authors whose works he illustrated, aside from the many children's books he did, were Eugène Sue (very famous pictures for *The Mysteries of Paris*), E.T.A. Hoffmann and "Munchausen." A great deal of work was also done for clubs and private festivities.

Last but not least, there was the publishing firm of Gropius, which commissioned numerous witty lithographs about Berlin everday life of the same sort that the elder Schadow and Dörbeck did. It is this aspect of Hosemann's production that is best remembered and most often reproduced today, and that was later of the greatest importance to his pupil Heinrich Zille. Hosemann became known as "the Gavarni of Berlin." Besides the individual prints, his albums and books in this area included *Buntes Berlin* ("Colorful Berlin") and *Berlin Wie Es Ist—und Trinkt* ("Berlin As It Is—and Drinks," with a pun on *isst,* "eats"), with text by the famous humorist Adolf Glassbrenner.

Hosemann began painting about 1840. He continued working until his death in Berlin on October 15, 1875, but his style did not materially develop after 1840. In 1857 he began teaching at the Berlin Academy and became a member in 1860.

S.A.

HOWIE, ROBERT LANGFORD (1933-) American cartoonist born in Jackson, Mississippi, on April 8, 1933. Bob Howie was educated in Jackson public schools and attended the University of Southern Mississippi and Tulane University, from which he was graduated in 1955 with a degree in journalism.

While in high school, Howie contributed sports cartoons to the *Jackson Clarion-Ledger,* and in college to the *New Orleans Item.* Since 1955 he has been the sports and editorial cartoonist for the *Jackson Daily News.* His early influences were Karl Hubenthal, L.D. Warren and Willard Mullin; the conservative-Democratic cartoonist has won three Freedoms Foundation awards.

His ideas are strongly Southern and forthright; although he draws a number of general-theme editorial cartoons, his political subjects are biting. His style is a stiff, uncluttered brush rendering with crayon shading.

R.M.

HUA JUNWU (1915-) Hua started his cartooning in 1933 when he was a high school student, although he never studied art in any art schools. Hua was known as a productive political cartoonist since the mid-1940s when the Civil War broke out in China. His cartoons were positively received and greatly encouraged the soldiers in the Communist army fighting in the front against the Guomindang (the Nationalist Forces). From the early 1950s after the People's Republic of China was founded, Hua was appointed by the Party for the leading position in the National Chinese Artist Association, which was under the Party's control. Between the late 1950s and early 1960s, cartoon creation in China was influenced strongly by the political attitudes of the Chinese government toward domestic affairs and international relations alike. The capitalist Western countries were regarded as the main enemies, and domestically, Mao's "class struggle" was the dominating philosophy in the nation. Anyone who would stray from these fixed paths would be risking his/her life to be criticized as "anti-Socialist System" or "anti-Communist Party". Under such circumstances, it was worthy of mentioning that Hua was the only one in that period who dared to publish numerous so-called "interior satire" cartoons, aiming at the red-tape and bureaucracy at the local government level and bad behavior in society. For the "incorrect" creations, Hua was the only lucky one who was not labeled and demoted as "Rightest" as were many others.

In his *Scientific Division of Labor* (1962), Hua ridiculed the anti-productive decisions of the leadership. And his *Wasting People's Youth* (1961) attacked some of the leaders' long, pointless speeches at the frequently held political meetings. These two and many other similar Hua cartoons reflected common situations in China in those years under Mao.

H.Y.L.L.

Huang Yuanlin. © Huang Yuanlin.

HUANG YUANLIN (1940-) Chinese cartoonist born in Sichuan province in 1940. Huang Yuanlin enrolled in the Chinese Art Academy in 1960. Since graduation in 1965, he has worked as a researcher at the Fine Art Research Office, and has been editor at *On Art History* and the *Chinese Art Journal*. In addition to his works of criticism on cartoons and cartooning, he has been busy creating his own cartoons and participating in cartoon exhibitions.

Huang's name is often linked with that of Bi Keguan with whom he has co-written the authoritative *History of Chinese Cartoons*. Their cartoons, published jointly or separately, have often been seen in the same print media and exhibitions. Furthermore both artists are living in Beijing, where they have been working at the same Fine Art Research Office and Chinese Arts Research Institute.

H.Y.L.L.

HUARD, CHARLES (1875-1965) French cartoonist, illustrator and etcher born in Paris, France, in 1875. Charles Huard studied at the Ecole des Beaux-Arts in Paris for one year. He contributed drawings satirizing the foibles of Parisian life and the vanities of provincials to many French and foreign humor journals, especially *Le Rire, Le Journal Amusant, La Baïonnette, Scribner's Magazine* and *Punch*. Some of these cartoons were published as albums, the most important and amusing being *Paris, Province, Etranger* ("Paris, Provinces, Abroad," 1906). Huard also traveled extensively in Europe and the United States, bringing back a series of sketches on New York (1906), Berlin (1907), London (1908), etc. In addition, he illustrated many of the important books of the 19th and early 20th centuries: Clemenceau's *Figures de Vendée* ("Vendean Figures," 1903), Flaubert's *Bouvard and Pécuchet* (1904) and Balzac's *The Human Comedy* (1912-40), Huard's best work. Finally, his impressionist etchings, although they do not have the satirical bite of his cartoons, present interesting country street scenes set mainly in Normandy (124 on the small fishing port of Granville alone). They were exhibited in 1915 at the Panama-Pacific International Exposition in San Francisco, California.

Charles Huard was a strong draftsman who very ably used the graphic contrast between slender men all in black and fat women all in white, between well-delineated fig-

Solution to Nothing

Karl Hubenthal. © Los Angeles Examiner.

ures and bare background outlines. He died near Dijon on March 30, 1965, at the age of 90.

P.H.

HUBENTHAL, KARL (1917-) American political cartoonist, illustrator and sports cartoonist born in Beemer, Nebraska, on May 1, 1917. Karl Hubenthal was raised in California, graduating from Hollywood High School and Chouinard Art School in Los Angeles. Early in his artistic career Hubenthal worked with George Herriman, Will Gould and Willard Mullin, each of whom influenced his development. His first job was with the art department of the *Los Angeles Herald-Express* from 1935 until his induction into the Marines in 1942. During the war he was on the staff of *Leatherneck* magazine.

In 1945 Hubenthal achieved his art-school goal of being a successful advertising artist and commercial illustrator; he worked in both New York and Los Angeles. But in 1949 William Randolph Hearst, in the twilight of a long career of discovering and developing cartoon talent, recognized some of Hubenthal's commercial work and remembered his cartoons on the old *Herald-Express.* Hubenthal became the sports cartoonist for the *Los Angeles Examiner* until 1955 and has been chief editorial and political cartoonist with the *Examiner*—later the *Herald-Examiner*—since then. He retired in 1982 and now devotes his time to painting and running his own art gallery in Laguna Beach, Calif.

A Republican, Hubenthal has won a roomful of awards, including the National Headliners award, the Helms Foundation medal for sports, 21 Freedoms Foundation awards, 3 National Cartoonists Society Best Editorial Cartoonist awards, one NCS sports cartoon award and others. He was on the board of governors of the NCS and is a past president of both the Society of Illustrators and the Association of American Editorial Cartoonists.

Hubenthal's cartoons display amazing command of composition, anatomy and his media—brush and crayon or toned shading. His work is handsome and easy to look at; Hubenthal can make a hard-hitting point or elicit a chuckle with equal ease.

R.M.

HUBLEY, FAITH (1924-) American animator born in New York City on September 16, 1924. After attending the Actor's Lab in California, Faith Chestman variously worked as film editor, script supervisor, and music editor in Hollywood, where she met renowned animator John Hubley. Here is how she recounted the meeting to John D. Ford in *The American Animated Cartoon*: "We met... in 1946 or 47. I was editing a film called *Human Growth* on sex education (I think it was the first) produced by Eddie Albert, directed by Irving Lerner, and UPA did the animation... When John started to work on *Finian's Rainbow*—an animated feature that never got made—I was hired as his assistant. We were married shortly after that and we continued working separately, some together."

The Hubleys started their own animation studio in 1955 and soon produced a number of critically praised and award-winning films, from the cheerful *Adventures of an* * to the grim *Eggs*, about an unpromising future when a couple needs a permit to have a child. Most of the Hubleys' films are optimistic in outlook, however, and are much admired for their poetic and lyrical mood. John Hubley died in 1977 during the filming of *A Doonesbury Special* (the couple's last project together) and Faith com-

W.O.W. (1975) by Faith Hubley was made to commemorate the International Women's Year. (Courtesy Faith Hubley)

Faith Hubley, "W.O.W.." © Hubley Studio.

pleted the picture with Garry Trudeau, the creator of the Doonesbury newspaper strip on which the film is based. (For more details refer to the entry for Hubley, John.)

Since her husband's death, Faith Hubley has carried on alone and her animated films have continued to enchant audiences and critics alike. She has produced on the average a film a year for the last 20 years. Her first solo pictures have included most notably *Whither Weather* (1977), *Step by Step* (1978), *The Big Bang and Other Creation Myths* (1979), and *Enter Life* (1982). Her 1985 production, *The Cosmic Eye,* was her first feature-length animated film and brought her additional fame. Among her later animation films mention should be made of *Time of the Angels* (1987), *Yes We Can*, which received an Honorable Mention at the Cannes Film Festival in 1989; *Who Am I?* (1989), *Amazonia* (1990), *Cloudland* (1993), based on myths from Australian aborigines; and *Rainbows of Hawaii* (1995). Every one of these films has reflected the artist's unique, other-worldly vision; she declared to an interviewer in 1993 that "her true home is a dreamworld."

Faith Hubley received an honorary doctorate from Hofstra University in 1995; and her paintings have been exhibited in galleries in New York, California, and Europe.

M.H.

HUBLEY, JOHN (1914-1977) American cartoonist and producer born in Marlette, Wisconsin, in 1914. A graduate of the Art Center of Los Angeles, John Hubley started his cartooning career with Walt Disney in 1934. Working his way up from cel painter and in-betweener, he rose to become an art director on *Pinocchio* (1940), the "Rite of Spring" segment of *Fantasia* (1940) and *Bambi* (1941). That same year Hubley's career with Disney came to an end in the aftermath of the celebrated animators' strike.

Hubley worked on several army cartoons during World War II (including the famous *Flathatting* for the U.S. Navy in 1945) and was one of the founders of United Productions of America (UPA) that same year. As a director at UPA he was responsible for some of the most acclaimed cartoon films of the postwar era, such as *Robin Hoodlum (1948), The Magic Fluke* and *Punchy de Leon* (both 1949) and *Rooty Toot Toot* (1952). He also directed some of the more memorable *Mr. Magoo* cartoons, including the first one, "Ragtime Bear," in 1949.

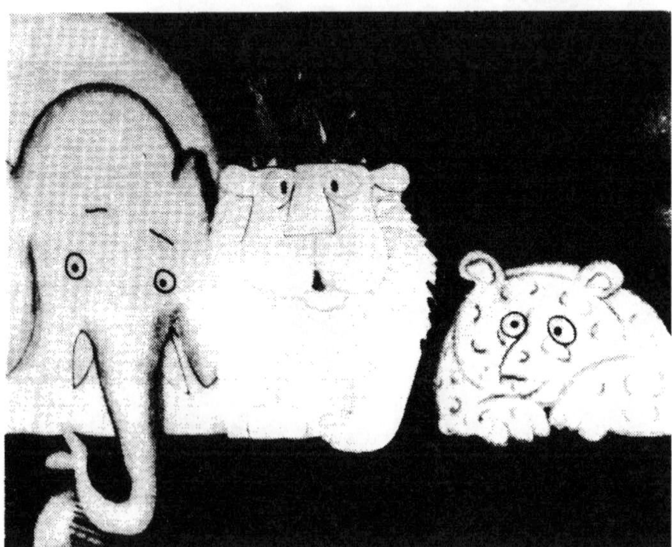

John Hubley, "Of Stars and Men." © Hubley Studio.

Hubley left UPA in 1953, and in 1955 he founded his own company in collaboration with his wife, Faith, a former film editor and script supervisor; it was called Storyboard, Inc. Working closely with his family (his children have often contributed to story lines and have voiced some of the characters), Hubley produced *Adventures of an Asterisk* in 1956, followed by *The Tender Game, Harlem Wednesday* and *A Date with Dizzy* (all 1958). These were gentle, cheerful works, as were *Seven Lively Arts* (1959) and the Oscar-winning *Moonbird,* as well as *Children of the Sun,* produced for UNICEF. It is, however, with his later, less rosy works that Hubley gained worldwide fame and recognition. Most notable among these are *The Hole,* a story about a nuclear holocaust, and the Oscar-winner of 1962; the military fable *The Hat* (1963); and the 1971 *Eggs.* Hubley occasionally went back to his earlier, gayer mood, as with the delightful *Of Stars and Men* (1963), the swinging *Herb Alpert and the Tijuana Brass* (1966 Academy Award winner), and the whimsical *Windy Day* (1968).

Hubley also directed many commercials. His last completed film was a 1976 television special, *Everybody Rides the Carousel,* based on the works of psychoanalyst Erik H. Erikson. John Hubley died shortly thereafter, on February 21, 1977, during heart surgery at the Yale-New Haven Hospital. At the time of his death he had been working on an animated version of Garry Trudeau's *Doonesbury;* the film was completed by his wife and aired on television in November 1977.

John Hubley stands as one of the greats of cartoon animation. His work is personal, original and highly innovative. Many articles have been written about Hubley and his films, and he was the recipient of countless honors. He was nominated for an Academy Award no fewer than eleven times, and he won on three different occasions.

M.H.

HUDON, NORMAND (1929-1997) French-Canadian cartoonist, painter and television personality born in Montreal, Quebec, on June 5, 1929. After finishing high school in 1947, Normand Hudon attended the Montreal School of Fine Arts. While still in school, he contributed illustrations to several newspapers (*La Presse* as early as 1945, *La Patrie* and *Le Petit Journal* in 1948-49). In 1949 Hudon left for Paris, where he briefly studied art and drawing with Fernand Léger. Back in Montreal in 1951, he succeeded the following year to Robert La Palme's position as editorial cartoonist for *Le Devoir,* at the same time collaborating on the political weekly *L'Autorité du Peuple.* When La Palme, also back from Paris, reclaimed his cartooning job later in 1952, Hudon embarked on a television career that eventually made him famous.

The decade between 1955 and 1965 proved to be highly productive for Hudon. He held a very successful showing of his cartoons in 1955 and in 1958 mounted a one-man show of his paintings that met with critical praise as well as public acclaim. He also did two murals for Expo '67, as well as many posters. During this period Hudon was omnipresent in the Montreal press, as a political cartoonist upon his return to *Le Devoir* in 1959 and as a social car-

Normand Hudon, caricature of René Lévesque, 1961. © Hudon.

icaturist. He also published a number of his cartoons in book form: *J'Ai Mauvaise Mine* ("I'm Not Looking Well," gag cartoons, 1954), *La Tête la Première* ("Head First," caricatures, 1958),*A la Potence* ("To the Gallows," political cartoons, 1961), *Un Bill 60 du Tonnerre* ("A Dynamite Bill 60," 1964) and *Parlez-Moi d'Humour* (1965).

Hudon's importance as a political cartoonist is best perceived in *A la Potence.* This collection reproduces all his cartoons for *Le Devoir,* including those that were censored. With drawings of extreme simplicity and fierce partisanship, Hudon attacked Maurice Duplessis, then prime minister of Quebec, whom he pictured either as a ravenous wolf or as a sick old man sunk in an armchair, on the back of which a vulture was perched. Hudon is regarded today, along with René Lévesque—who was then a journalist—as one of the engineers of the "quiet revolution," the political awakening of Quebec that started in 1960. In this respect Hudon's work for *Le Devoir* may be more historically significant than the cartoons he has been publishing regularly in the mass-circulation daily *La Presse* ever since 1961. He died of cancer at his home in Montreal on January 8, 1997.

S.J.

HUEMER, RICHARD (1898-1979) American animator born in Brooklyn, New York, on January 2, 1898. Dick Huemer went to school in Brooklyn and the Bronx and developed an early love for drawing. After graduating from high school in 1915, he attended the Art Students League in New York City, studying with George Bridgman for about a year. He also contributed cartoons to *Judge.*

Huemer started in the animation field in 1916 as an animator on the *Mutt and Jeff* cartoons. In the early 1920s he joined Max and Dave Fleischer and soon became their top animator. At the Fleischer studios, Huemer worked on many of the *Out of the Inkwell* and *Ko-Ko the Clown* cartoons and created the character Bimbo the dog. He left the studio in 1928 and briefly drew a newspaper strip, *Good Time Guy,* which was syndicated by the Metropolitan Newspaper Service and lasted for about a year. Like so many other East Coast cartoonists, Huemer then left for California, where he joined the animation staff of Charles Mintz in 1930, directing many of the *Scrappy* and *Toby the Pup* cartoons. In 1933 he moved over to the Disney studio, where he did animation work on a number of *Silly Symphonies* (*Lullaby Land, The Tortoise and the Hare, The Wise Little Hen,* etc.) and *Mickey Mouse* cartoons (most notably "The Band Concert").

Huemer stopped doing actual animation work in 1938 ("I'd really had it," he declared simply in a 1969 interview). After directing a couple of shorts, he found his niche as a story director, working on many of the studio's most ambitious projects (*Fantasia, Dumbo, Saludos Amigos, Make Mine Music, Alice in Wonderland*). During World War II he wrote many of the instruction and propaganda shorts produced by the studio. After a short stint in the early 1950s as an independent producer, Huemer went back to Disney in 1953, working on the Oscar-winning *Toot, Whistle, Plunk and Boom.* He also later collaborated on many of Disney's television programs. After retiring in the 1970s he occasionally acted as a consultant on animated film production and animated cartoon retrospectives. He died on November 30, 1979.

M.H.

HUICI, ALBERTO (1929-) Mexican cartoonist born in Mexico City on March 10, 1929. Alberto Huici exhibited a love of drawing at an early age, and he sold his first cartoon in 1945, while still going to school. From then on he

Alberto Huici. © Ja-Ja.

Etta Hulme. © Fort Worth Telegram-NEA.

worked as a freelancer, contributing a number of cartoons to various Mexican newspapers and publications.

In 1952 Huici went to Los Angeles and tried to break into the U.S. market. While submitting contributions to various magazines (most of which sent back rejection slips), he worked as gas station attendant, dishwasher and garbage collector in order to support himself. Coming to New York in 1954, Huici again was turned down more often than not, and he went back to Mexico City the following year. With the experience he had acquired in the United States, he soon rose to the top of his profession, having his gag cartoons regularly published in the humor magazine *Ja-Ja,* and his political cartoons distributed by Editorial Excelsior. He also occasionally contributes cartoons to Los Angeles and New York publications. Now nearing 70, Huici is still active on the Mexican cartoon scene.

Huici's style is simple, almost stark, with weird characters cavorting in strange surroundings. His humor is mostly visual, and he uses captions sparingly. His cartoons have earned awards in the United States, Europe, and Central and South America, as well as in his native Mexico.

M.H.

HULME, ETTA (1923-) The award-winning editorial cartoonist of *The Fort Worth Star-Telegram,* Etta Hulme is one of the pioneer women editorial cartoonists. Since 1978, her cartoons have been nationally syndicated in the U.S. by Newspaper Enterprise Association.

Born in Sommerville, Texas, on December 22, 1923, Etta Hulme grew up around her family's grocery store where she could observe the human condition and had wrapping paper to draw on. After graduating from the University of Texas with a BFA degree, she took a job drawing animation at Disney Studios in California. After two years she returned to Texas where she freelanced cartoons and illustrations in the Dallas area. While on a trip to study lithography at the Art Institute of Chicago, she briefly drew a children's comic book, *Red Rabbit.*

She married in 1952 and moved to Germany with her husband who was then in the army. Upon returning to Texas, her first editorial cartoon was published in 1954 in the *Texas Observer* of Austin. For 13 years she and her husband, a chemical engineer, raised a family and moved between Austin, Houston, Corpus Christi, Shreveport (LA), Odessa and finally back to the Dallas area.

Hulme's editorial cartoons first appeared in *The Fort Worth Star-Telegram* in 1972. She now draws five a week, working at home in a six-sided gazebo style studio. Hulme works in brush-and-ink on Coquille board. She likes the texture it gives her work with grease pencil added. According to Hulme, "I'm more often labeled liberal than anything else, but I've been accused of being various things. I am most comfortable letting the cartoons speak for themselves."

She is a past president of the American Association of Editorial Cartoonists.

B.C.

HUMAN COOK BOOK, THE (U.S.) One of James Montgomery Flagg's last magazine cartoon series before he engaged in full-time cover and illustration work, *The Human Cook Book* closely followed in format his earlier series. It featured tableaux of characters with exaggerated heads and had humorous rhymes underneath; this series, which began in *Life* on February 11, 1911, and continued through 28 treatments, proved to be among Flagg's cleverest work.

In the series Flagg poked satirically at the pretensions of individual types and professions. His witty and quite wise observations on human nature and sham were all executed in the form of kitchen recipes, and Chef Flagg served up a consistently engaging fare. Typical of the subjects are two captions: a Sweetheart—"Take a Peach and remove both her parents / Add a suggestion of Dough / Garnish with bonbons and flowers / And turn the gas rather low"; and the Actor—"To one slice of Ham add assortment of rolls Steep the head in mash notes till it swells / Garnish with onions, tomatoes and beets / Or with eggs—from afar—in the shells."

Other targets included the Straphanger, the Policeman, the Editor, the Orchestra Leader, the Telephone Operator, the Vaudevillian, the Chauffeur and the Suffragette. The cartoons ran two or three to an issue and were unfortunately not collected in book form as were other series from earlier in the decade.

R.M.

HUMBERT, ALBERT (1835-1886) French cartoonist and illustrator born in eastern France on February 24, 1835. After an unsuccessful attempt at painting, Albert Humbert turned to full-time cartooning and collaborated on the most important satirical papers of the second half of the 19th century: *La Lune, Le Journal Amusant, L'Eclipse,* etc. In 1868, he launched his own humor and satirical journal, the antimilitarist and anticlerical *La Lanterne de Boquillon* (first titled *Le Reverbère de Deux Sous*), which became immediately popular and ran for 18 years (1868-86).

Humbert also wrote and illustrated (sometimes under the pen name "Onésime Boquillon") novels narrating the endless vicissitudes faced by the character he had created, a simple, average Frenchman portrayed in various life situations. The most noteworthy of these are *Le Plébiscite de Boquillon* ("Boquillon's Plebiscite," 1870), *L'Art de Ne Pas Payer Ses Dettes* ("The Art of Not Paying One's Debts," 1874), *Vie et Aventures d'Onésime Boquillon* ("The Life and Adventures of Onésime Boquillon," 1876) and *Lettre du Soldat Onésime Boquillon* ("Letter from Private Onésime Boquillon," 1877). In addition, he was the author of non-Boquillon comic novels and of several comedies (written with his brother).

He died in Paris in 1886.

P.H.

HUMOR AND SATIRE (China) During the ten-year long "Cultural Revolution" (1966-76) cartoons were banned and branded "poisonous weeds" against the people and the socialist system. After this depressing period ended, Chinese cartooning underwent a resurgence. helped in no small measure by cartoon journals springing up all over the land. The first one and still the most notable is *Humor and Satire,* the comic supplement of the *People's Daily* which came to life early in 1979, and was followed by many more publications in the same mode.

Ying Tao, himself a cartoonist of high repute and the chief editor of *Humor and Satire* since its inception, has kept the publication on top of the competition with a roster of cartoonists that have included the most respected names in the profession. The journal has included among its staff Jian Fan (born 1924), Miao Di (born 1925) and Jiang Yousheng (born 1921); all three are now retired. Xia Quingquan (born 1946) and Xu Fengfei (born 1949) are the current members of the editorial staff. Each one of these artists has contributed innumerable cartoons to the publication. In addition to publishing cartoons in its pages, *Humor and Satire,* as the most established professional journal in China, has organized contests and other cartoon-related events for professionals in China as well as those abroad.

True to its name, *Humor and Satire* has published gag cartoons and running cartoon series as well as editorial cartoons excoriating local officials and hidebound bureaucrats. It is probably one of the most open as well as one of the most outspoken publications of its kind in China.

H.Y.L.L.

HUMORS OF HISTORY (G.B.) "History," says the learned Herr Niemand, "is the consolidation of doubtful traditions into undoubted facts. Such are the histories of dry-as-dust historians; but Mr. Moreland, in his pictorial past, is on surer ground. All his events are founded on fact, and all his details are stranger than fiction." This excerpt from the preface to one of the many collected editions of *Humors of History* indicates the style of Arthur Moreland's once-famous, long-forgotten series: classic incidents of history brought up-to-date and given an anachronistic topical twist.

Beginning with the cartoon entitled "Ages, B.C.: Prehistoric London" (depicting dinosaurs snorting on the banks of the Fleet River at Blackfriars "where now L.C.C. Tramcars attempt to arrive and depart") and concluding with "The Present Day" ("remarkable for great activity in financial circles"—a cigar-puffing City gent outside the offices of the Brique d'Or Syndicate), *Humors of History* was perhaps the first regular "series cartoon" in British newspapers. It began in the *Morning Leader* in 1898 and wound up in the *Daily News* some 160 cartoons later. There were many paperback and hardback editions of the series, including one in full color (1905).

Of the artist, Arthur Moreland, little is known save that to judge from his book list, he continued to work as an illustrator into the thirties.

Books: *Humors of History* (1898, 1903, 1905, 1913, 1915, 1918, 1920, 1921, 1923); *Gentle Golfer* (1905); *History of the Hun* (1917); *The Comic History of Sport* (1924); *More*

Humours of History (1925); *The Difficulties of Dr. Daguerre* (1927); *Dickens in London* (1928); *Lays from Lancashire* (1930); and *Dickens Landmarks in London* (1931).

D.G.

HUNGERFORD, CYRUS COTTON (ca. 1890-1983) American cartoonist born in Manilla, Indiana, around 1890. Cy Hungerford began his cartooning career for the *Wheeling* (W. Va.) *Register* in 1907. In 1912 he switched to the *Pittsburgh* (Pa.) *Sun,* where he claims the engraving method was still chalk-plate (he was succeeded on the *Register* by Terry Gilkison).

Between 1915 and 1926, Hungerford drew *Snoodles,* a syndicated comic strip for kids. Warm, sympathetic and zany—akin to Payne's *S'Matter, Pop?*—the strip was a minor classic and a personal favorite of colleague John McCutcheon, who nicknamed his son Shaw (now an editorial cartoonist) after the title character. In 1927 Hungerford switched from the *Sun* to the *Pittsburgh Post-Gazette,* where he drew editorial cartoons for an incredible 50 years, until his retirement in 1977. He traveled abroad as a reporter-cartoonist in 1923, 1937, 1947, 1948 and 1953, and he received a National Headliners award in 1947 and a Freedoms Foundation award in 1953. He died in 1983.

Hungerford's style hardly varied at all from the first day of his career to the last. He worked in simple, bold pen and brush lines, never used shading, and relied on streamlined caricature rather than gross exaggeration. A pleasant, uncluttered atmosphere and a genial outlook pervaded every Hungerford cartoon. He was, needless to say, a Pittsburgh institution.

R.M.

Jud Hurd, "Ticker Toons." © *United Feature Syndicate.*

HURD, EARL (ca. 1880-ca. 1950) American animator born around 1880. Earl Hurd is one of the most important figures in early animation, and possibly the most shadowy. Very little is known of his background before he burst onto the animation scene in 1913, developing with J.R. Bray the process of drawing on celluloid.

In 1914 Bray and Hurd formalized their partnership and formed the Bray-Hurd Processing Company, which lasted into the 1920s. In 1915 Hurd created his cartoon series *Bobby Bumps,* which was released through Bray. On this series he honed his animation skills to a fine point and brought out some of the best-crafted cartoons up to that time. In 1923 Hurd left Bray and went into independent production, setting up Earl Hurd Productions. Under the overall name Pen and Ink Vaudeville, he made such cartoons as *Artist's Model, Hoboken Nightingale, Bone yard Blues, Two Cats and a Bird* and *He Who Gets Socked,* as well as a few *Bobby Bumps* cartoons; he also seems to have produced several live-action comedy shorts. At any rate, he was not successful, and his studio closed down in 1925.

After an absence of almost ten years, Hurd surfaced again in the mid-1930s at the studio of Charles Mintz before going on, like so many others, to Walt Disney. At Disney he worked on a number of shorts and received credits for story adaptation on *Snow White* and as a character designer on the "Dance of the Hours" segment of *Fantasia.* Hurd left the Disney studio in the late 1940s and is reported to have died on the West Coast in the 1950s.

Earl Hurd was not only a technical innovator (as Dick Huemer put it, he "invented things") but also a master of the art of animation. It is to be hoped that more information will come to light as his achievements are rediscovered.)

M.H.

HURD, JUSTIN (1912-) American cartoonist and publisher born in Cleveland, Ohio, on November 12, 1912. Justin ("Jud") Hurd showed a love of and talent for drawing at an early age, but he graduated from Western Reserve University in 1934 with a degree in economics. During his college years, however, he was the art editor of the college magazine, *The Red Cat,* to which he contributed numerous cartoons. After a year of classes at the Chicago Academy of Fine Arts, Hurd got his first professional job, as an in-betweener, at the Charles Mintz animation studio (1935-36). For two years (1936-38) Hurd drew a feature about movie celebrities, *Just Hurd in Hollywood,* for the Central Press Association, but he felt homesick in Los Angeles and returned to Cleveland and a job in the Newspaper Enterprise Association's art department drawing weekly political cartoons (Herblock was doing the dailies during that same time).

Hurd spent four years with the Signal Intelligence Section of the U.S. Army in World War II; his duties included the drawing of a daily panel, *Crypto Chris,* about the pitfalls of operating codes and ciphers. Demobilized in 1946, Hurd opened an industrial art studio in Cleveland and ran it until 1959, when he decided to move east. In 1959 he also started *Ticker Toons,* a daily financial panel that he first syndicated himself before United Feature Syndicate picked it up (it ran until 1969). In collaboration with Michael Petti, M.D., he created a medical panel in 1961, *Health Capsules,* also for United Feature.

Jud Hurd is best known, however, for his founding and editing of *Cartoonist Profiles,* a unique professional magazine exclusively devoted to comics and cartoons. Since its first appearance in 1969, the publication has featured innumerable articles, vignettes and reminiscences about all aspects of cartooning, thus providing an invaluable record for scholars and students in the field of graphic art. In 1993 he wrote an engaging book, *To Cartooning,* based on his lifelong experiences in the field.

M.H.

HURD, NATHANIEL (1730-1777) American cartoonist and silversmith born in Boston, Massachusetts, on February 13, 1730. One of the first American cartoonists and visual propagandists, Nathaniel Hurd was in the Paul Revere school—a metalsmith who dabbled in cartooning and caricaturing. He was trained by his father to engrave on silver and gold; he experimented with engraving on copper—which later became a standard medium—and mainly confined himself to working on bookplates. Among Hurd's most famous drawings was an editoral cartoon produced as a handbill, dealing with the subject of counterfeiters.

Hurd, whose portrait by John Singleton Copley hangs in the Cleveland Museum of Art, died on December 17, 1777.

R.M.

HÜRLIMANN, ERNST (1921-) Ernst Hürlimann was born November 15, 1921, in Oberstaufen in the Swabian Allgäu region of Bavaria. Early on he showed an interest in painting. This he pursued after graduating from school by studying architecture at the technical universities of Munich, Germany, and Zürich, Switzerland. Hürlimann's familiy, incidentally, is of Swiss descent.

Hürlimann settled down in Munich in 1939 and, since 1947, has been working as an architect. Also in 1947, Hürlimann became one of the regular cartoon contributors to the then new *Süddeutsche Zeitung*. He has worked for them ever since, besides being successful at his chosen profession as an architect.

Ernst Hürlimann has come up with a very simple yet highly effective cartooning style which allows him to depict all human follies. While he did not shy away from political cartoons, he basically depicts everyday situations

Ernst Hurlimann. © Suddeutscher Verlag.

in a very funny way, and many of his cartoons parody the Munich way of life.

Hürlimann's style is noted for the crisp lines and for many rotund, neckless characters with very thin extremities. The cartoonist claims that his being left-handed was no hindrance to his becoming a cartoonist, but influenced the seeming simplicity of his drawings. Hürlimann also was a television regular. Like his colleague, political cartoonist Ernst Maria Lang, Ernst Hürlimann has made hundreds of television appearances drawing live on camera his cartoon comments on everyday life.

Munich is graced by a number of Hürlimann's architectural works, and his cartoons are just about everywhere since many public service ads and posters used by the city of Munich have been created and drawn by him.

Noted art critic Joachim Kaiser once commented that "Hürlimann is worrying over the little people, their hurt optimism, their self-assured pessimism, their Munich and all-German grumpiness." Thanks to a number of book reprints, to several art awards, and to *Süddeutsche Zeitung*'s being a national paper, Hürlimann, a Munich cartoon phenomenon, is known—and imitated—in all of Germany.

W.F.

HUSBAND, WILLIAM ANTHONY (1950-) William Anthony Husband was born in Blackpool, Lancashire, on 28 August 1950. Self-taught, his style is extremely loose and untraditional, and he mixes strips with panel cartoons easily. His early jobs included printing for an advertising agency, window dressing and repairing jewellery. in his spare time he freelanced cartoons to the *Daily Mirror* and *Weekend* magazine, turning full-time in 1984. The following year he helped found and edit the unusual weekly comic for children called *Oink,* an experiment in new styles and satirical humor. He followed this failure with a pop music cartoon feature for the *Daily Star* and football cartoons for *Shoot. Punch* and *Private Eye* followed, and the strips *The Yobs* (1986) and *Mr. Clean* (*Sunday Times* supplement). Gag cartoons of his were published in such disparate magazines as *Playboy* (US) and *Readers Digest.* Other activities include co-writing the television series *Round the Bend* using caricature puppets built by Spitting Image, and giant cartoons projected during the unusual stage play *Save the Human.* He also drew 100 different cartoons for the greetings card series "Rhino's Revenge" for Camden Graphics. Awarded Joke Cartoonist of the Year by the Cartoonist Club of Great Britain, 1985, 1986 and 1987, plus Strip Cartoonist of the Year, 1988.

His many books include *Use Your Head* (1984), *Bye Bye Cruel World* (1985), *Animal Husbandry* (1986), *The Greatest Story Never Told* (1988) and *Environmental Madness* (1990).

D.G.

HYDE, WILLIAM HENRY (1858-1943) American cartoonist and painter born in New York City on January 29, 1858. W.H. Hyde graduated from Columbia in 1877 with an A.B. degree and studied painting in Paris with Boulanger, Lefebvre, Doucet and Harrison. His cartoons began appearing in the earliest issues of *Life* in 1883 (he was an exception to the Harvard corps at work there) and continued into the 1890s. His pen-and-ink work was among the smartest to appear in the weekly's pages—especially in the awkward early years—and was marked by supple lines, confident crosshatch shading and a reserved, dignified sense of composition. His subject was almost always society folk.

A member of the National Academy, Hyde died in Albany, New York, on February 7, 1943.

R.M.

Ii

Clodhoppers: "Good-for-nothings! On my rye straw!"

Henri-Gabriel Ibels, 1901.

IBAÑEZ, FRANCISCO (1935-) Spanish cartoonist born near Madrid, Spain, in 1935. Francisco Ibañez never finished his high school studies but went to work as a clerk in a Madrid bank in the early 1950s. He is a self-taught artist, and his love of drawing led him to send contributions to the various Spanish magazines of the day. His first cartoons were published in the humor magazine *La Risa* in 1954. Ibañez's work was a sharp contrast to the sorry state of Spanish cartooning during the Franco regime. His drawings were crisp and neat, and his humor was brisk and cheerful, marking him as an obvious disciple of the classic cartoonists of Spain. He was also a keen observer with an eye for the telling line or detail.

In 1957 Ibañez joined the Editorial Brughera publishing house and scored a hit the next year with an original comic strip, *Mortadelo y Filemón,* about a pair of outrageous private eyes; the strip became the most successful Spanish comic feature of the 1960s. The artist has been in such demand since then that he has a tendency to repeat himself, with the same stories and situations cropping up again and again. Ibañez, however, keeps his cartoons filled with the same crazy dynamism, and it can be said that he is a baroque artist who has been able to keep up with the realities of his time, always at full speed. After Bruguera went out of business in the mid-1980s, Ibanez formed his own studio where he continues to turn out *Mortadelo y Filemon* with the help of a number of assistants.

J.M.

IBELS, HENRI-GABRIEL (1867-1936) French cartoonist, painter and writer born in Paris, France, on November 30, 1867. Henri-Gabriel Ibels was largely self-taught and studied art mainly from nature. He was noted, from the age of 17, for the freshness and spontaneity of his landscape paintings. He exhibited widely, and in 1893 he coauthored with Toulouse-Lautrec an album of lithographs, *Le Café-Concert.*

Ibels is best remembered today as a political and editorial cartoonist. In 1899 he founded a short-lived magazine, *Le Sifflet,* in which he expressed through his drawings his strong sense of outrage at the injustice meted out to Captain Dreyfus in the course of what has been called "the Dreyfus affair." After his magazine folded, Ibels went to work for various satirical magazines, notably for *L'Assiette au Beurre,* in which his cartoons appeared regularly from the first issue (1901) until 1910. Ibels's drawings, full of verve, often undercut his sometimes bitter captions.

After World War I Ibels devoted himself mainly to painting and lithographing. He taught art in a number of Paris schools and had several of his plays produced on the stage. He was also active in lobbying for artists' rights. Ibels died in February 1936; during his lifetime he had received many honors, including the Legion of Honor, bestowed upon him in 1913.

M.H.

IF THEY SHOULD COME BACK TO EARTH (U.S.) Winsor McCay, who had drawn a series of strong anti-imperialist cartoons for *Life* following the Spanish-American War, returned in 1900 to do a series that, while perhaps not wholly original, was certainly the first strong link in a chain of similar themes explored by such artists as Otho Cushing, Harry Grant Dart, Charles Forbell and R.B. Fuller through the late 1920s.

If They Should Come Back to Earth featured historical figures in modern settings. The series began in the issue of September 20, 1900, and ran through November 8 of the same year. The large single-panel cartoons included Eve shopping for clothes, Ben Franklin besieged by newsboys, Nero watching firemen, Meissonier crowded by photographers, William Penn at a prizefight, Sir Walter Raleigh among tobacco fiends, Shakespeare nosed out by the Theatrical Syndicate and James Watt contemplating a horizon of smokestacks.

The cartoons were all executed in wash and typically were crowded with figures and architectural fancies. An important series that has gone unrecorded by McCay scholars, the cartoons were signed "Winsor Mc," as was most of his work for *Life.* This cartoon series was evidently submitted by mail from Cincinnati, and it preceded by more than two years his seminal newspaper cartoon series *Tales of the Jungle Imps by Felix Fiddle,* drawn for the *Cincinnati Commercial Tribune* beginning on January 18, 1903.

R.M.

ILLE, EDUARD (1823-1900) German cartoonist, illustrator, painter and writer born in Munich, Bavaria, on May 17, 1823. In 1842, Eduard Ille entered the Munich Academy, where he studied under the major painters Schnorr von Carolsfeld and Moritz von Schwind (himself a humorous artist on occasion). It became clear that Ille would never be a master of the grandiose religious painting style then so much in demand, and he turned to illustration in the 1850s. Among the magazines to which he contributed were *Punsch* (edited by M. Schleich) and the *Illustrirte Zeitung* (edited by J.J. Weber). He also did drawings for fairy-tale writer Ludwig Bechstein's 1853 volume *Deutsches Sagenbuch* ("Book of German Legends").

Eventually Ille was drawn into the orbit of Munich's principal publishers of humorous and popular art, Braun and Schneider. First he worked for their *Hauschronik,* then for their *Münchener Bilderbogen* (with a total contribution of some sixty items) and at last for their flagship publication, the celebrated *Fliegende Blätter.* In 1863 Ille became one of the editors, playing a big part in the magazine's continuing success and remaining with it until his death.

Largely because of his thorough academic training, Ille was a master of historical styles; it was he who illustrated the *Fliegende Blätter* poems (by L. Eichrodt) that gave the period of German cultural history from about 1815 to 1848 its lasting designation, "Biedermeier." With uncanny skill (and, no doubt, great personal satisfaction) he parodied the style of various 19th-century academic painters—not only his own teachers, Schnorr and Schwind, but also Peter von Cornelius, Kaulbach, Overbeck and Piloty. In another genre, Ille produced drawings of humanized animals that recalled those of the French artist Grandville.

Among Ille's separately published volumes were several children's books (illustrations of Grimm tales and of his own stories, books with movable figures and so on). He also continued to illustrate serious works and wrote poems, poetic dramas and opera librettos. Other artistic activities included puppet designs and two projects for the eccentric king, Ludwig II of Bavaria: a watercolor cycle on German legend and history, and in the 1870s, wall paintings (on cloth)—about the lives of the poets Walther von der Vogelweide and Hans Sachs—for the king's dressing room in the castle of Neuschwanstein.

Ille died in Munich on December 17, 1900.

S.A.

ILLINGWORTH, LESLIE GILBERT (1902-1979) British newspaper cartoonist, humorous artist and book illustrator born in Barry, South Wales, in 1902. Leslie Illingworth had a Yorkshire father and a Scottish mother: this perhaps explains why his artwork is so "typically" British! He left school in Cardiff with a scholarship to the Royal College of Art but gave up his studies after six months to become a cartoonist for the provincial daily the *Western Mail* in 1920. Illingworth was 18 years old, and his weekly wage was £6. In 1926, his first humorous drawing was published in *Punch,* and in 1927, after touring the United States, he returned home to become a freelance cartoonist.

His drawings, including excellent full-color, full-page cartoons in *Punch Almanac* and the "summer specials," established him as a top cartoonist, although he supplemented his humor work by illustrating magazine stories, articles and books. In 1939, he won the coveted position of *Daily Mail* cartoonist after the retirement of Percy ("Poy") Fearon, and he held this exacting job through the reigns of no fewer than nine editors! He retired from the *Mail* in 1968 but has been busy ever since. He was drawing a weekly cartoon for the Sunday paper *News of the World.* He died on December 20, 1979.

When Illingworth (as he always signs his drawings) was asked to describe his work, he replied that it gave people "symbols to think with." In fact, Illingworth broke away

"I'm the Guy." © *Rube Goldberg.*

from the old-style symbolic cartoons. Although he physically inherited the symbol technique when substituting for, then taking over from, Sir Bernard Partridge in *Punch* (1945), his sheer excellence of drawing and draftsmanship enabled him to do without the labels and symbols beloved by the earlier cartoonists.

D.G.

IMAGE, JEAN
See Hajdu, Emeric.

IMPRESSIONS BY ONE WHO HAS NEVER BEEN THERE (U.S.) In the late 1910s and early 1920s Ellison Hoover became a favorite cartoonist of *Life*'s editors, and presumably of its readers. He was a cartoonist' who constantly mocked newspaper comics, yet he was destined to draw *Mr. and Mrs.* after Clare Briggs's death; he strove to emulate the compositions of Rea Irvin and Gluyas Williams but was for the most part doomed to produce empty, unbalanced full-page line drawings. His *Intimate Glimpses of American Generals of Industry,* for instance, was not original; neither was Gluyas Williams's *Industrial Crises,* which was contemporaneous but far superior. If Hoover was a deficient wit, he was nevertheless respected as an advocate—Benchley was one who lauded him as a satirist.

In *Impressions by One Who Has Never Been There,* Hoover transcended his limitations and his frequent editorializing and produced a very funny series of double-page black-and-white cartoons for *Life.* Here was a travelogue by reputation, a Cook's tour of stereotypes. Hoover collected every chestnut and mistaken impression about famous cities and drew bird's-eye views of them, exercising a consistent disregard for geography, history and logic. Hence, New York had Cohan giving his regards to Broadway, a tiger inside Tammany Hall and a flat bush in Brooklyn; Dublin was full of Blarney stones, begobs and begorras and signs indicating a long way to Tipperary.

It was great fun and is still fresh reading today. Held worked a similar theme with his woodcut-style maps, but not as well, which demonstrates that Hoover could indeed originate a successful format. Some of the cartoons in this series were collected in *Cartoons from Life* by Hoover, published by Simon and Schuster in 1925.

R.M.

I'M THE GUY (U.S.) One of Rube Goldberg's many intermittent continuing panel gag features, published daily in the 1910s as part of his nationally distributed *New York Evening Mail* sports page potpourri, *I'm the Guy* was a particularly memorable hit with Goldberg readers when it was introduced early in 1911. It ran for many months thereafter and appeared across the country in lapel-button reproductions by the tens of thousands. With no continuing feature characters, *I'm the Guy* was basically a one-line gag panel in which individuals of wildly differing appearance proclaimed to other startled individuals, at the rate of one per panel, that each was the guy who had made some fundamental contribution to a general term, as in the following examples (all considered hilarious at the time): "I'm the guy that put the germ in Germans"; "I'm the guy that put the saint in St. Louis"; "I'm the guy that put the gum in gumption"; "I'm the guy that put the ham in Hamburg"; "I'm the guy that put the wish in wishbone"; and so on.

The little feature caught on so much that a songwriter named Berg Grant wrote the lyrics to a 1912 song called "I'm the Guy" that was popular for over a year and was an early phonograph record hit. (Oddly, however, Grant's lyrics paid no attention to the structure of Goldberg's gag line and went their own way on the same theme—without any more wit or point, however.) Eventually dropped by Goldberg after a few years, *I'm the Guy* continued in word-of-mouth use for some time afterward on the same low-brow level as "twenty-three skidoo" and similar catch-phrases of the imitative and unimaginative.

B.B.

IN THE BLEACHERS (U.S.) After graduating from Ohio State and receiving his master's degree in journalism from the University of Oregon, J.D. Steve Moore went to work as sports editor for the *Maui News* in Hawaii. It was there that he created a panel cartoon titled *In the Bleachers* in June 1985, which was then syndicated by Tribune Media Services in early September.

Inspired by artists at *Mad* magazine and by B. Kliban, Charles Addams, and especially Gary Larson, Moore presents universal stupidities through a skewed view of the sport-and-leisure activity world and its human or animal

"In the Bleachers." © Universal Press Syndicate.

denizens in an uncommitted sort of way—from the bleachers so to speak. His characters are of the ugly, weirdly coiffed, misshapen variety (and this includes fish, reptiles, and mammals, too), and are easily recognizable by their protruding eyes with a dot in the middle—the better to convey one single emotion. The cartoon's humor is right on target, and the situations depicted are hilarious. Such is the case with the May 12, 1997, panel showing a long line of women outside the ladies' room and a man yelling, "I am the architect who designed this stadium!" The caption simply reads: "Death wish."

Naturally, Moore also makes fun of our popular culture and celebrities. In one drawing, for example, Obi-Wan Kenobi, now a sports agent, has brainwashed an NFL recruiter into paying ten million dollars to his overweight, stupid-looking quarterback, while in another, a horrified scientist, observing a television viewer in the lab, exclaims to his assistant, "Aaaah! I've lost all signs of brain activity! Turn off the Dick Vitale basketball commentary!"

Distributed since 1995 by Universal Press Syndicate, *In the Bleachers* is being made into an animated sitcom for Viacom/Paramount, probably to debut in the 1999-2000 TV season.

P.H.

INDEPENDENT NEW PARTY
See Tattooed Man, The.

INDOOR/OUTDOOR SPORTS (U.S.) As a diversion from his coverage of sports events in the *New York Journal*, Thomas Aloysius Dorgan ("Tad") conceived his *Indoor Sports* panel around 1910 and began discoursing with unmitigated glee on such unathletic pursuits as poker, crap shooting and betting on football scores. Later Tad

"Indoor Sports." © King Features Syndicate.

added *Outdoor Sports* to his lineup of newspaper features, alternating the new panel with *Indoor Sports.* In the 1920s the two became almost indistinguishable in theme, as Tad had by that time moved away from sports into the field of social and psychological observation. Only the setting justified the use of either the "indoor" or "outdoor" label.

Tad's slice-of-life cartoons were quite amusing and often insightful. He joyously deflated the pretensions of small-town hucksters, would-be financiers and self-appointed experts. He had as fine an ear for language as he had an eye for observation, and the dialogue he put in the mouths of his bums, mountebanks and social climbers was accurate and excruciatingly funny. Tad also started the trend of having various matchstick figures cavort in a corner of the panel and comment (sometimes in song) on the action.

Tad died in 1929, but his *Indoor/Outdoor Sports* panel survived him for a long time in countless reprintings in the *Journal* and in newspapers across the country.

M.H.

INOUE, YŌSUKE (1931-) Japanese cartoonist and illustrator born in Akasaka, Tokyo, Japan, on March 7, 1931. After graduating from the Western art department of the Musashino Art University, Yōsuke Inoue joined the Dokuritsu Mangaha ("Independent Cartoonists Faction") in 1952 and actively contributed cartoons to its magazine, *Gamma.* When *Gamma* folded and the Dokuritsu Mangaha dissolved, Inoue sought other outlets and joined the now famous and influential Manga Shudan ("Cartoonists Group") in 1964. The same year, he began holding exhibitions of his paintings and cartoons, as he continues to do today. Exhibition titles include Eroticism (1966), Yōsuke Inoue (1969) and Nonsense (1974). In 1965 his *Kaiki Nonsense Manga Sakuhin* ("Strange Nonsense Cartoons") won the eleventh Bunshun award for cartoons, and in 1970 he received the fourth Tokyo Illustrators Club prize.

Yōsuke Inoue is often referred to as an avant-garde cartoonist, and the subjects he chooses indeed lend themselves to this description. Often they are nonsensical, Kafkaesque sketches like "Ippon Michi" ("One-way Street"), which appeared in the magazine *Bunshun Manga Dokuhon* in April 1967. It depicted two bored and tired-looking little men approaching each other from opposite directions on a narrow bridge and then actually walking through each other, much to their mutual surprise. Inoue is comfortable in nearly all media, working skillfully in oils, prints, or pen and ink, with terse, single-panel cartoons or multi-panel cartoons covering several pages. His simple, wiggly line sketches are often accompanied by a humorous narrative as surreal as the subject they treat, and they frequently have erotic overtones.

Among the books written by Inoue, *Sado no Tamago* ("Sado's Egg," 1963), *Hakorui Zukan* ("The Picture Book of Boxes," 1964) and Inoue *Yōsuke Tan-pen Gekigashū* ("Yōsuke Inoue's Collection of Short Comics") are representative. He is also active as an illustrator of picture books such as *Dare ga Pai o Tabeni Kita* ("Who Came to Eat the Pie?"), and he formerly taught cartooning at the Tokyo Design College. Lately he has become an illustrator of children's books and of the popular form known as *e-hon* (artistic picture books for children also prized by adults).

"The Inspector Returns Home," from the "Inspektor Masku" series. © Zagreb Film.

Some of his representative works in this field include *Furimukeba Neko* ("Turn Around and There Were Cats") and *Getsuyo no Jidosha* ("Moon-night Car"). Among the numerous awards he has won mention should be made of the 1994 Kodansha Culture Prize for *e-hon.* In 1997 over eighty books authored or illustrated by Inoue were in print.

F.S.

INSPEKTOR MASKU (Yugoslavia) In 1959 Vatroslav Mimica wrote and directed, and Aleksandar Marks designed, a witty confection blending object and cartoon animation, *Inspektor Se Vratio Kući* ("The Inspector Comes Home"). Produced by the famed Zagreb Film studio, the cartoon, which depicted a day in the life of an inept police inspector, won first prize at Oberhausen. It proved so popular that it gave birth to *Inspektor Masku* ("Inspector Mask"), a series named for the hero, which started production in 1962.

In the series the inspector appeared in the guise of various objects in order to track down a clever band of crooks. There were chases, fights and various kinds of violence, but the attempt at emulating the fast pace and breathless action of American cartoons was not successful. *Inspektor Masku* was discontinued in 1963, after 13 entries in the series had been completed.

Virtually every hand at Zagreb Film worked on the series. Most notable were Boris Kolar ("Citizen IM5"), Nikola Kostelać ("The Rape of Miss Universe") and Ivo Urbanic ("El Cactusito").

M.H.

INVENTIONS OF PROFESSOR LUCIFER G. BUTTS, THE (U.S.) Rube Goldberg started drawing crazy and impractical "inventions" for the delight of his readers soon after he went to work as a cartoonist for the *New York Evening Mail* in 1907. These developed some time later into a regular feature whose complete title, *The Inventions of Professor Lucifer G. Butts,* was as ludicrous as the crackpot contraptions purportedly invented by Goldberg's alter ego, Professor Lucifer Gorgonzola Butts, A.K.

Professor Butts perfected such ingenious devices as a painless tooth-extractor, an automatic typewriter eraser,

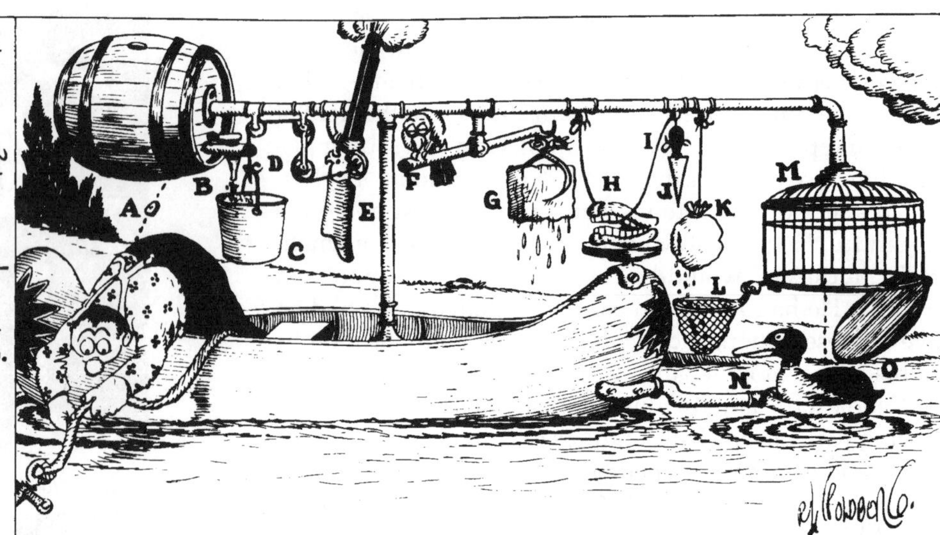

PROFESSOR BUTTS TRIES TO FIX A LEAK IN THE BOILER AND WHEN HE IS RESCUED FROM DROWNING HE COUGHS UP AN IDEA FOR AN OUTBOARD MOTOR THAT REQUIRES NO FUEL.
AS YOU REACH FOR ANCHOR, BUTTON (A) SNAPS LOOSE AND HITS SPIGOT (B) CAUSING BEER TO RUN INTO PAIL (C). WEIGHT PULLS CORD (D) FIRING SHOT GUN (E). REPORT FRIGHTENS SEA GULL (F) WHICH FLIES AWAY AND CAUSES ICE (G) TO LOWER IN FRONT OF FALSE TEETH (H). AS TEETH CHATTER FROM COLD THEY BITE CORD (I) IN HALF ALLOWING POINTED TOOL (J) TO DROP AND RIP BAG OF CORN (K). CORN FALLS INTO NET (L). WEIGHT CAUSES IT TO SNAP LATCH OPENING FLOOR OF CAGE (M) AND DROPPING DUCK INTO SHAFTS (N). AS DUCK (O) TRIES TO REACH CORN IT SWIMS AND CAUSES CANOE TO MOVE AHEAD.
IF THE FALSE TEETH KEEP ON CHATTERING YOU CAN LET THEM CHEW YOUR GUM TO GIVE YOUR OWN JAWS A REST.

"The Inventions of Professor Lucifer G. Butts." © Rube Goldberg.

and a moth exterminator, all with a generous helping of pulleys, electric fans, bellows and sundry household items arrayed in the most bewildering system imaginable. In later years Goldberg averred that the inspiration for Professor Butts and his inventions had come to him during his college days at the University of California, but it is more likely that he was influenced, at least in part, by Clare Dwiggins's panel *School Days.*

The Inventions (which were later syndicated through King Features) ran for decades, until Goldberg finally tired of the feature in the mid-1930s. He revived it, however, in 1939 for the Register and Tribune Syndicate, which distributed it until 1948.

Of all Goldberg's creations, *The Inventions* is the one that most contributed to his fame. Even after he had abandoned drawing them on a regular basis, he continued to throw in an "invention" or two, usually on some burning issue of the time, for a magazine or on a TV program. The "inventions" also earned him an entry in the dictionary as an adjective (a "Rube Goldberg" contraption is synonymous with an implausibly complicated device).

M.H.

IONICUS
See Armitage, Joseph.

IRELAND, WILLIAM A. (1880-1935) American cartoonist born in Chillicothe, Ohio, on January 8, 1880. Educated in public schools, Billy Ireland secured his first cartooning job with the *Chicago Daily News* in 1897. The next year he switched to the *Chicago News-Advertiser* and in 1899 returned to Columbus, Ohio, near his birthplace, to draw for the *Columbus Evening Dispatch.*

Ireland's style was highly cartoony in its appearance but technically very competent. He had a sure sense of composition and anatomy and drew with a self-confident hand. His shading was never overdone; economy of line was a watchword but not a fetish. Almost all of his political cartoons were partisan (he was a Democrat) but exceedingly good-natured. His neat, bold cartoons gave rise to a whole school, beginning with Carey Orr in Tennessee. When Orr moved to Chicago, the style lived on in him and his successors on the *Tribune,* Parrish and Holland.

Except perhaps for Joe Donahey of the *Cleveland Plain Dealer,* Ireland was the most democratic of American cartoonists. He stayed close to home up to the time of his death in 1935 and had no pretensions to greatness or fame. It is said that the *New York Herald-Tribune* offered him a blank check to draw in New York; he refused, saying, "My object isn't to break into New York—it is to break back to Chillicothe." The *Trib* settled for Ding Darling.

Ireland seldom left his part of Ohio; he was reprinted widely but not syndicated. His weekly full-page color collection of observations, *The Passing Show,* is remembered by many as a minor masterpiece. And one of his great contributions was the kindly advice and guidance he gave to local youngsters interested in cartooning, two of whom were Noel Sickles and Milton Caniff, who revere Ireland's memory today. Generally, he is all but forgotten, and he deserves to be reprinted in a major collection.

R.M.

IRONIMUS
See Peichl, Gustav.

IRVIN, REA (1881-1972) American cartoonist and editor born in San Francisco, California, on August 26, 1881. Rea Irvin was educated at the Mark Hopkins Institute of Art and worked on the art staffs of several newspapers, including the *Honolulu Advertiser,* before becoming an actor in 1903. This career was short-lived, however, and Irvin moved to New York and began contributing to *Life* magazine. He soon became a major fixture there, doing covers and many interior cartoons, and his influence was widespread. It was a coup for Harold Ross in 1925 to lure Irvin to the fledgling *New Yorker,* where he served as art editor. In 1951, after the death of Ross, Irvin quarreled with the founder's successors and left the publication. He continued to paint and draw cartoons for his own outlets,

Bill Ireland, "The Passing Show," 1932. © Columbia Journal-Dispatch.

"Sure, if it's dramin' I am, I'll never touch anither drop, but if it's the real ting, I'd loike a big drink right now!"

Rea Irvin. © Life.

attended functions of the Players and the Dutch Treat Club, and finally moved to the Virgin Islands, where he died at the age of 90 on May 28, 1972.

It is hard to fully appreciate Irvin's enormous impact on American cartooning. His simplified, posterlike drawings were almost revolutionary and inspired a generation of imitators. His composition was flawlessly attractive, and his figures, for all their animation and exaggeration, were anatomically sound. He used broad brushstrokes and flat shaded areas. For *Life* and *Collier's* he illustrated Wallace Irwin's *Letters of a Japanese Schoolboy.* He drew many series of full-pagers for *Life,* illustrated many books, created the cover design for the *New Yorker,* and helped shape that magazine's formidable approach to cartooning, certainly one of the major forces in American graphic arts.

R.M.

ISING, RUDOLPH (1903-1992) American animator born in Kansas City, Missouri, in 1903. Rudolph (or Rudolf) Ising went to work at the Kansas City Film Ad Company soon after graduating from high school. From 1921 to 1923 he helped Walt Disney in the production of his Laugh-O-Grams cartoons and joined Disney in Los Angeles in 1926. Ising was one of the first members of the Disney staff and worked on *Alice in Cartoonland* and later on *Oswald the Rabbit.* In 1928, in collaboration with Hugh Harman, he produced the *Oswald* cartoons for Charles Mintz, Disney's former distributor.

In 1929 Ising and Harman formed a partnership (Harman-Ising); they first produced cartoons for Leon Schlesinger for release through Warner Brothers, then became independent producers for MGM in 1933. The partners' best-known creation was *Bosko,* a series that continued throughout the 1930s. They also produced the Happy Harmonies cartoons for MGM. Their collaboration came to an end in 1938, when Harman and Ising became producers on the newly formed MGM animation unit (their friendship remained unaffected). Ising produced the 1940 *Milky Way,* the first animated short ever to break the Disney monopoly on Oscars. He also created the *Barney Bear* series, starting with "The Bear That Couldn't Sleep" (1939), and directed a number of entries in the series between 1939 and 1942.

Ising left MGM in 1942 (his last cartoon, *Bah Wilderness,* was released the following year) to join the Hal Roach studio, where he was in charge of animation and training films for the U.S. Air Force. After World War II Ising drifted out of the animation field and variously worked in advertising and industrial promotion. He lived in retirement in the Los Angeles area, near his longtime associate Hugh Harman. He died of heart failure in July 1992.

Ising's name is indissolubly tied to that of Harman; they made many memorable cartoons together. Like Harman, Ising was a remarkable animator and skilled designer. In addition to his Oscar, he received several other honors, including an exhibitors' award.

M.H.

ISLAM, NAZRUL (1949-) Born in Satkira (now Bangladesh), on March 3, 1949, Nazrul Islam started his cartooning career at his country's birth in the early 1970's. A 1972 graduate of the Dhaka College of Arts and Crafts, he began freelancing political cartoons for the daily, *Ganokantho*, the same year, while employed as a graphic artist for the Bangladesh Tourism Corporation. From 1974-76, Nazrul did cartoons for *Bicitra Weekly Visitor*, one of the very few periodicals that encouraged artists; in more recent years, his political cartoons have appeared in the *Weekly Robbar*. Most of his work now is done for non-government agencies; since the dawn of the 1990's, he has been a staff artist at the Bangladesh Environmental Lawyers Association.

Nazrul has participated in festivals and exhibitions in France, Canada, Turkey, Japan, and Bangladesh. He uses a sparcity of line and prefers wordless cartoons as aids of understanding for Bangladesh's large illiterate population.

J.A.L.

IT'S AGAINST THE LAW (U.S.) Humorist Dick Hyman reportedly got his idea of collecting some of the ludicrous laws still on the books from an Alabama judge. Be that as it may, Hyman's first compilation of silly statutes appeared in the *New York Mirror* in 1933. A few months later it was picked up by Hearst's *American Magazine,* which ran it as a monthly cartoon panel drawn by Otto Soglow starting in 1934.

"It's Against the Law." © The Reader's Digest Association.

The feature was exactly what its title implied—a depiction of some of the more harebrained prohibitions spelled out by states and municipalities across the United States. "A Colorado law forbids the serving of food in a room used for any other purpose," one caption read, while Soglow's cartoon depicted a hotel servant lugging breakfast to a moustached gentleman taking a leisurely bath in his tub; "Gloversville, New York, prohibits women wrestlers appearing in the city," said another, under a cartoon of a brawny female about to throw her opponent over the ropes as two cops show up at ringside. The feature was funny not so much because of the captions, which became monotonous after awhile, as for the loony Soglow cartoons depicting befuddled humans and mixed-up animals in an endless and hilarious gallery of incongruities.

The feature folded along with the *American Magazine* in 1956. Some of the texts were later run as filler material (minus the cartoons) in the *Reader's Digest*. The Reader's Digest Association published an *It's Against the Law* booklet (this time adding some of Soglow's cartoons) in 1971, with great success.

M.H.

IVANOV, ALEKSANDR VASILYEVICH (1899-1959) Animator and filmmaker born in eastern Russia on June 5, 1899. Aleksandr Ivanov studied at the Tambov Teachers Institute and then went on to attend the Tambov Art Studios. Upon graduation in 1921, he became a cartoonist for such satirical publications as *Gudak* and *Rabochaya Moskva.* In 1924, in collaboration with A. Bushkin, he produced the first Soviet animated cartoon, *Soviet Toys,* under the supervision of Dziga Vertov.

From the mid-1920s on, Ivanov became one of the Soviet Union's most distinguished animators. In 1927, in collaboration with H. Voinov, he made *The Cockroach,* a frightening allegory about a giant cockroach conquering the world. This was followed by a number of delightful films, mostly for children: *Vor* ("The Thief," 1935), *The Popular Favorite* (1937), *The Magic Flute* (an enchanting retelling of

Aleksandr Ivanov, "The Cockroach."

Ivan Ivanov-Vano, "Tales of Czar Duranda."

the Mozart opera, 1938) and *Okhotnik Fyodor* ("Fyodor the Hunter," 1939) are the most notable among his pre-World War II production. After turning out propaganda films during the war, Ivanov returned to entertainment animation with his 1947 fable *The Fox and the Thrush.* In 1948 he released two impressive works, *Kvartet* ("Quartet," a musical cartoon) and the sometimes bitter *Champion.* More films followed, usually on nature themes, and with an often somber outlook: *Zay i Chik* ("Zay and Chick," 1952), *In the Depths of the Forest* (1954), *The Forest Story* (1956) and *The Sorceress* (1957).

Concurrently with his animation career, lvanov was also a political cartoonist and poster designer of some repute. He received a number of awards for his films, including first prize at the 1958 Moscow Film Festival. Aleksandr Ivanov died in Moscow on March 13, 1959.

M.H.

IVANOV-VANO, IVAN PETROVICH (1900-1987) Animator and filmmaker born in Moscow, Russia, on February 8, 1900. Ivan Ivanov-Vano graduated from the State Higher Art and Technical School in 1923, and he started his long and prolific career in animation the next year as an assistant director. In 1927 he directed his first film, *Senka the African,* the dream adventures of a little boy, followed by *Katok* ("The Skating Rink," 1929), an enchanting exercise in white line on black background in a manner reminiscent of Emile Cohl, *Black and White* (1932), *Tales of Czar Duranda* (1934) and *The Three Musketeers* (1938), to cite only his most notable achievements.

World War II interrupted Ivanov-Vano's career when, along with other Soviet moviemakers, he was called upon to produce propaganda films. In 1945 he went back to animation with the much-awarded *A Winter's Tale.* Since that time Ivanov-Vano turned out animated cartoons by the score, most of them screen versions of Russian classics and folktales, notably *The Little Hunchbacked Horse* (1948), *Wild Geese* (1950), *The Snow Maiden* (1952) and *Seasons of the Year* (1969). Of somewhat greater interest are his puppet film, *The Mechanical Flea* (1964), and especially a medium-length cartoon film, *The Battle of Kerzhenets* (1971), which received first prize at the 1972 Zagreb Festival.

In addition to his career as a filmmaker, Ivanov-Vano taught since 1939 at the All-Union State Institute of Cinematography (as a full professor since 1952) and wrote a number of books on the subject of animation. Ivanov-Vano was named a People's Artist in 1969 and received a host of honors in Russia, including the coveted State Prize in 1970. He died in May 1987.

M.H.

IVEY, JAMES BURNETT (1925-) American editorial cartoonist born in Chattanooga, Tennessee, on April 19, 1925. Jim Ivey received his formal education at George Washington University and the University of Louisville, and his art training at the National Art School in Washington, D.C. (1948-50), as well as from the Landon Correspondence School.

Ivey started his cartooning career on the *Washington Star* (1950-53), moving from there to the *St. Petersburg* (Fla.) *Times* (1953-59) and the *San Francisco Examiner* (1959-66). After a short interlude as a freelance cartoonist, he joined the staff of the *Orlando Sentinel* in 1970, contributing many political and editorial cartoons, as well as a great number of topical graphic comments on local issues. In 1977 he went back to freelancing again. Ivey is also the author of a syndicated panel, *Thoughts of Man,* in which he illustrates in a woodcut style quotes from some of the famous men in history. (The feature ended in 1981).

THOUGHTS OF MAN

Ignorance is less remote from the truth than prejudice.

—Denis Diderot

Jim Ivey. © Chicago Tribune-New York News Syndicate.

Jim Ivey's strong points are a humorous approach, a good sense of caricature, variety in the physical shapes of his cartoons (often in keeping with the particular theme) and a loose, modernistic line. In 1964 the *National Observer,* commenting on Ivey's work, said, "He's imaginative, always prowling for a fresh approach. His cartoons often appear without a caption, reflecting his belief that 'cartooning is a graphic and not a verbal art.'"

Jim Ivey is also a noted scholar of the cartoon field. In 1959 he was granted a Reid Fellowship to observe political cartooning in Europe: his conclusion that European cartoonists were, in style and approach, far ahead of their colleagues in the United States was met with controversy but paved the way for radical changes in American cartooning. Ivey has written many articles for cartoon and comic art magazines, has been the editor of his own fanzine, *Cartoon,* and is now the coeditor of *Cartoonews.* He is also the founder and curator of the Cartoon Museum in Orlando. *Cartoon* ceased publication in 1980, but Ivey continues to pursue his activities in the field: in 1979 he was awarded the Silver T-Square for outstanding service to the profession.

M.H.

IWERKS, UBBE (1901-1971) American cartoonist and animator born in Kansas City on March 24, 1901. Ubbe ("Ub") Iwerks displayed an early talent for drawing and caricature. He dropped out of school to work at various odd jobs in commercial art shops in and around Kansas City; it was in one of these shops that he first met Walt Disney in 1920. An informal partnership developed between the two young men: they worked together again at the Kansas City Film Ad Company and, for a brief period, as independent producers in Kansas City. Later, after Disney had become established in Los Angeles, he sent for Ub Iwerks, and Iwerks joined his studio in 1926.

Iwerks's greatest contribution to the art of animation came the following year when he designed and developed the character of Mickey Mouse (his work on "Plane Crazy" was especially decisive). He also defined (and refined) the concept of the early *Silly Symphonies.* In 1930 a contractual dispute led Iwerks to leave Disney and strike out on his own. Setting up his own studio, he produced the enchanting *Flip the Frog* cartoons for Celebrity Pictures,

Ub Iwerks, "Summertime." © Celebrity Pictures.

which released them through MGM. These enjoyed moderate success, as did Iwerks's companion series, *Willie Whopper,* and a number of so-called "Comicolor Cartoons" based on popular stories (*Don Quixote, Aladdin and His Magic Lamp,* etc.).

In the mid- and late 1930s Iwerks worked as an independent producer, turning out *Porky Pig* cartoons for Warner Brothers, *Color Rhapsodies* for Columbia, and a number of commercial cartoons. In 1940 Iwerks returned to the Disney studios and worked mostly in the technical and development departments. (His perfecting of the multiplane camera was his most notable achievement in this field.)

For over 25 years Iwerks thus lived in obscurity until he was suddenly "discovered" at the Montreal International Animation Festival in 1967 and found himself acclaimed as "the creator of Mickey Mouse." Many international awards and distinctions followed—a fitting, if belated, tribute to a man and an artist whose unique contributions to the art of animation put him on a par with the giants of the field.

Ub Iwerks died on July 8, 1971.

M.H.

Jj

JACKSON, RAYMOND (1927-1997) British cartoonist born in London, England, in 1927.

"Homo-electrical-sapiens Britannicus 1970" was the caption to a cartoon that almost closed the London *Evening Standard* for good. The picture was of a boneheaded British "bolshy" trade unionist, and the signature was "Jak." The cartoonist behind the pen name is Raymond Jackson, the son of a tailor. Jackson attended Clipstone Road School during World War II, then studied at Willesden School of Art before being called into the army. At first a driver, he transferred to the Education Corps, where he taught conscripts to paint. On demobilization he joined a publishing house art staff, where one of his jobs was retouching the pubic hairs on photographs for a naturist magazine called *Health and Strength.* Discharged when the magazine collapsed, he worked for awhile in an advertising agency, freelancing gag cartoons to *Lilliput* and *Punch.*

He applied to the *London Evening Standard* when they advertised for a visualizer and won the job of spot illustrator instead. He supplied thumbnail sketches to illustrate the television page. Then came a chance to draw a large cartoon for the Saturday edition, and finally, one year after the death of "Vicky" (Victor Weisz), the *Standard's* famous cartoonist, he inherited the vacant space on the Diary Page. Jak has supplied a cartoon a day since, in a style not dissimilar to that of Carl Giles of the *Daily Express*: bold art, amusing characters, humorous ideas. In 1972, he signed a 20-year contract with the newspaper and is perhaps the highest paid cartoonist in Fleet Street. His motto: "Never explain, never complain." A collection, *Jak,* has appeared annually since 1968. He was voted Social Cartoonist of the Year in 1985, and died in 1997.

D.G.

JACOVITTI, BENITO (1923-1997) Italian cartoonist born in Termoli, in the Abruzze region of Italy, on March 19, 1923. When he was 16, Benito Jacovitti started drawing stories for *Il Vittorioso,* a Catholic children's weekly magazine. From that time until 1967, when *Il Vittorioso* closed down, he gave life to hundreds of different characters in scores of comic strips (for Jacovitti's career in the comics, see *The World Encyclopedia of Comics,* Chelsea House, 1976). His burlesque and parodistic talents found their best expression, however, in the single-panel cartoons and color pages he drew during the same period. In these outsized cartoons (some as big as an entire newspaper page), Jacovitti gave free rein to his volcanic fantasy: surrealistic, crazy vignettes and pointed satires, gigantic wives and diminutive husbands, black humor and ingenuous irony, all colliding, intertwining and becoming lost in an immense caricatural panorama of demented proportions.

"Your money or your life . . . um . . . um . . . I mean . . . tarinlalle-tarinlalla. . . ."

Benito Jacovitti. © Jac.

Jacovitti also drew cartoons for a number of humor magazines (such as *Il Travaso)* and for daily newspapers (such as *Il Giornale d'Italia,* for which he has recently been commenting on the day's major events); but he has not been able to give to his editorial cartoons the biting and sometimes mean tone of other cartoonists. His best efforts in the cartooning field (although in a somewhat looser key) remain his large panels, particularly those he drew in the course of the 1960s. Since 1980 Jacovitti added even more magazines to his roster, including *La Domenica del Corriere, La Notte, Linus, L'Europeo,* and *Intervallo.* In 1982, in collaboration with Marcello Marchesi, he adapted the *Kama Sutra* in cartoon form. He died in Rome on December 3, 1997.

C.S.

JAGO, MIK (1938-) A pioneer in the cartoon industry of Israel, Jago, who signs his work simply "Mik," arrived in that country as a volunteer to the army in 1967 and remained to become one of the most prominent members of its graphic art community. Born Miki Jago in Mousehole, Cornwall, Great Britain, he obtained a traditional art education. He graduated from Kingston on Thames Art College with a degree in fine art and sculpture in 1957, and served as a commercial graphic artist during his early days in Israel while he tried to establish himself as a cartoonist. In a short time, however, his cartoons and

Mik Jago ("Mik"). © Mik.

illustrations began appearing in both Hebrew and English-language Israeli periodicals and in reprints elsewhere. His gag and editorial cartoons have been published in magazines and newspapers in more than 25 countries in Europe, the Middle East, and the New World. From 1987 to 1989 he drew and wrote a daily comic strip, *Bad News*, for the British weekly *Early Times*. Like his editorial cartoons, the feature balanced humor with genial but perceptive political commentary.

Calling on a wide cultural background that embraces both Europe and the Near East, Jago transcends regional boundaries in work that views both the political and the human situation with insight and wit. His expressive line and balanced compositions are in the classic tradition of cartooning, and he makes his points, whether political or comedic, with a minimum of detail. Shrewd in conception and deft in execution, his visual metaphors are invariably memorable.

After a dozen years in Tel Aviv, Jago took up residence in a kibbutz on the Golan Heights, where he participates fully in community activity while producing cartoon and illustration art and lecturing widely on cartooning and caricature. His work has been exhibited widely in Israel, receiving solo shows throughout the country as well as in Belgium, Holland, France, Italy, the former Yugoslavia, Poland, Norway, and Canada and has earned him awards in Israel, Italy, and Yugoslavia. An active worker in and for his profession, he was a co-founder of the Israel Cartoonists Association and served as the Israel Editor of the international cartoon magazine *WittyWorld* while continuing to provide work for many of his country's national newspapers.

Jago has also been a productive illustrator of books. The volumes he has illustrated include *With a Smile* (1976), *The Moon Is Granpa* (1978), *Passages* (1985), and *I Tied a Golden Ribbon* (1982), all published in Hebrew. His own work has been collected in several volumes in Israel, including *Look at Life with Jago* (1969) and *Tzioneh Derech* (1992).

D.W.

JAGUARIBE, SERGIO DE MAGALHÃES GOMES (1932-) Brazilian cartoonist born in Rio de Janeiro, Brazil, on February 29, 1932. Largely self-taught as an artist, Jaguar (as he is best known) saw his first cartoon published in *Manchete* in 1957. His career took off dramatically the next year, when he started contributing cartoons to the magazines *Pif-Paf, Revista da Semana, Senhor* and *Revista Civilização Brazileira,* as well as to the daily newspapers *Ultima Hora* and *Tribuna da Imprensa.* In the 1960s he started working for *Correio da Manhã* and *Pasquim.* Jaguar also collaborates regularly on the Swiss magazine *Graphis.*

Jaguar has received several awards, notably at the Bordighera and Montreal cartoon festivals. His cartoon anthology, *Atila, Você é Bárbaro* ("Attila, to Yell Is Barbaric"), was published in 1968. In 1960 he opened (along with the designers Glauco Rodrigues and Beatriz Feitler) an internationally renowned studio of commercial art, Studio G in Rio. He has a very striking graphic style, very modern in approach, with bold strokes and ambiguous lines. He also often utilizes collages and montages in his cartoons.

A.M.

JAK
See Jackson, Raymond.

JÁNOS VITEZ (Hungary) In recent years every country, it seems, has tried to come up with at least one feature-length animated cartoon. *János Vitez* ("John the Hero") is Hungary's most notable entry in this category.

Based on Sandor Petöfi's epic tale, *Childe John,* the film was directed by Marcell Jankovics, produced by Pannonia Film in Budapest, and released in 1973 in commemoration of the 150th anniversary of Petöfi's birth. It tells of the tribulations of Jancsi, the orphan shepherd boy, and his sweetheart, Ileska, victimized by her vicious foster mother. Jancsi sets out to conquer the world, coming back as Childe John, the boy hero; fighting dragons and witches,

"János Vitez." © Pannonia Film.

he finally arrives on the Isle of the Fairies, where he is reunited with Ileska.

The story was handled with great fidelity to the original tale, without losing its dynamic thrust. The battle scenes were particularly well rendered by a team of animators that included József Nepp, Bela Ternovsky and Jankovics himself. The result was a pleasant, entertaining cartoon, well crafted and without stylistic surprises.

M.H.

JEFF
See Hook, Geoffrey Raynor.

JERRY THE TROUBLESOME TYKE (G.B.) "Jerry the Cardiff Film Star," the *South Wales Echo* proudly announced him in May 1925, and two months later, in July, *Jerry the Troublesome Tyke* made his cinematic debut. He appeared as the tail-end item in *Pathé Pictorial* number 382, in the position previously occupied by Felix the Cat. This British magazine film had lost the rights to the American animated animal after a dispute with Pat Sullivan, who wanted his films released as separate cartoons, not as serialized items in a compilation. The cartoon item had for years been a popular part of the *Pathé Pictorial,* and the Wardour Street company was delighted when a Welsh cinema projectionist sent them a reel of his homemade cartoons.

Sid Griffiths, a Cardiff man, was sent for and promptly commissioned to produce a regular series for the *Pictorial.* A dog was selected as hero, to contrast with the dispossessed cat, and the series ran for two years, with one adventure every other week. Typical titles were: *In and Out of Wembley* (a topical trip to the annual exhibition), *Treasure Island Travel, One Exciting Nightmare* and *Ten Little Jerry Boys.*

Griffiths was aided with the series by Brian White, ex-animator on the *Bonzo* series. After *Jerry* was discontinued, Griffiths and White remained in partnership, making cartoon filmlets for Superads (1929), including a sequence for use in a stage production starring Jack Hylton and his band, called *Tiptoe Through the Tulips* (1930). With the coming of sound, Griffiths and White formed the Comedy Cartoon Sound Films Company and made *Topical Breezes* (1930), starring "Hite and Mite." In 1933 they produced *Colonel Capers* and *Down on the Farm,* two cartoons based on the artwork of H.M. Bateman (see *The World Encyclopedia of Comics,* Chelsea House, 1976). These were made in the Raycol Color Process, a system doomed to failure by the necessity for special apparatus affixed to the cinema projector. In 1935 Griffiths joined Anson Dyer to work on the ambitious *Sam* series, while White became a successful strip cartoonist with his *Nipper.* Griffiths died on November 11, 1967, forgotten except by his former colleagues.

D.G.

JETSONS, THE (U.S.) Encouraged by the success of their animated series *The Flintstones,* Hanna-Barbera developed *The Jetsons,* which debuted on ABC in 1962. While the Flintstones were a typical suburban family that happened

"The Jetsons." © Hanna-Barbera Productions.

to live in the Stone Age, the Jetsons were a typical suburban family of the future. The formula was otherwise the same and never varied from the time-honored clichés of television situation comedy: George and Jane Jetson, their children Judy and Elroy, and the family dog Astro found themselves week after week in some kind of trouble or predicament, such as the family rocketship being stolen or the children wrecking the astro-set. The drawings were undistinguished, and the limited animation was especially disappointing in view of the almost unlimited opportunities provided by the futuristic setting.

Despite these drawbacks *The Jetsons* was fairly successful. After its run on ABC, it was picked up for syndication by CBS, and in 1971 NBC in turn programmed the series on its Saturday morning schedule. *The Jetsons* was also adapted into comic books from 1963 to 1973. In 1985 and 1987 new animated episodes were produced for syndication; and in 1990 a feature-length film, *Jetsons: The Movie* was released.

M.H.

JOB
See Onfroy de Bréville, Jacques.

JOHN CITIZEN (G.B.) The first national hero to win the approval of the British public, John Citizen differed significantly from his predecessor, John Bull. The contrast would in itself provide sufficient material for a book. Where the big, bold, bluff Bull, human counterpart of "The Roast Beef of Old England," was the personification of Olde England (he was created in 1712 by John Arbuthnot, pamphleteer), the bespectacled, wing-collared, umbrellaed Citizen represented the new backbone of the nation, 20th-century style: meek, mild and middle-class. The long-suffering, tax-paying John C. made a typical appearance on a dark day during World War I. His mouth was spread into a false grin by a glove-stretcher, and the caption was "Smile, Damn You, Smile!"

John Citizen was created by a cartoonist named Percy Fearon, who signed himself "Poy," and was one of many cartoon symbols he originated. These characters, who

Two of John Citizen's "colleagues," Dilly and Dally, the procrastinating bureaucrats.

came and went regularly in newspaper cartoons, included Dilly and Dally, the procrastinating bureaucrats, Dux and Drakes, the cheerful dispensers of public funds, Cuthbert the Whitehall Rabbit, and Dora, the dreary old biddy who personified DORA, the dreaded Defense of the Realm Act (1914).

Percy Arthur ("Poy") Fearon was born in Shanghai, China, in 1874. He studied art in New York, where the locals pronounced his name as "Poicy"—hence the pseudonym. He began drawing daily political cartoons for British newspapers in 1905 and produced 10,000 during the ensuing 34 years. His main work was for the *London Evening News* (1913-35) and *Daily Mail* (1935-38). He died in November 1948, leaving behind an immortal gallery of pleasantly drawn characters.

Books: *Poy's War Cartoons* (1915); *Dilly and Dally* (1919); *100 Poy Cartoons* (1920); and *How to Draw Newspaper Cartoons* (1930).

D.G.

JOHNSON, HERBERT (1878-1946) American artist born in Sutton, Nebraska, on October 30, 1878. Herbert Johnson studied at the University of Nebraska and at Columbia University. Around 1903 he created several comic strips for boiler-plate syndicates and shortly thereafter became a frequent contributor to *Life,* specializing in equestrian cartoons.

Johnson held editorial and cartooning positions on the *Denver Republican* (1896) and the *Kansas City Journal* (1897-99) before freelancing in New York (1903-05) and accepting a position with the *Philadelphia North American* during the years of political insurgency. He was head of the Sunday art department (1906-09) and was also a cartoonist (1908-12). Van Valkenburg's *North American* was a Progressive paper, and Johnson was to retain the Theodore Roosevelt creed throughout his life.

By 1912 Johnson's cartoons had attracted the attention of his Philadelphia neighbors, the Curtis family and George Horace Lorimer of the *Saturday Evening Post.* He was offered a job as regular cartoonist and art editor of the prestigious weekly; he accepted (though relinquishing the latter post in 1915) and drew editorial cartoons, often several per issue, until 1941.

He continually upheld Republicanism and was most effective in fighting the New Deal. Indeed, Johnson graphically portrayed some of the most telling arguments against FDR's brand of government controls and finance capitalism. After his initial devotion to the pen-and-ink style of drawing—at which he excelled—he adopted for the *Post* a very breezy, casual brush-and-wash look that lent an air of informality to his work. His cartoons were mostly in a horizontal format and were full of animation, action and cartoon conventions, including his version of the Common People used by Opper and Shoemaker.

The bulk of Herbert Johnson's work deserves to be resurrected as a fine portrayal of his times. One collection was published in his lifetime, *Cartoons by Herbert Johnson* (1936). He died in 1946.

R.M.

JOHNSTON, DAVID CLAYPOOL (1799-1865) American cartoonist and actor born in Philadelphia, Pennsylvania, in March 1799. From the first, like later cartoonists Joseph

D.C. Johnston, ca. 1834.

"Are you kids comin' out f'r y'r bath or do I send these ferrets in after y'r?"

Eric Jolliffe. © Sydney Sun.

Keppler and Bill Mauldin, Johnston divided his attention between acting and drawing. In 1815 he was apprenticed to Philadelphia engraver Francis Kearny, but six years later he made his acting debut as Henry in the play *Speed the Plow;* he was to act full time in Boston and Philadelphia from 1821 to 1826.

He worked in both lithography and woodcuts with simplicity of style and economy of labels. As an artist he was enterprising: he painted (exhibiting at the Boston Atheneum and the National Academy of Design), made prints and illustrated books, including *Fanny Kemble's Journal* (1835) and Joseph C. Neal's *Charcoal Sketches* (1838). As a cartoonist he was widely circulated in broadsides and handbills—his attacks on Jackson were famous—and published annual collections of his works as *Scraps* for years. He also wrote and illustrated in cartoons *The House That Jeff Built* (1863), a satire on Jefferson Davis.

Johnston died in Dorchester, Massachusetts, on November 8, 1865.

R.M.

JOLLIFFE, ERIC (1907-) Australian cartoonist born in Portsmouth, England, in January 1907. Eric Jolliffe, one of a family of 12 who came to Australia in 1914, went outback to work when he was 15. Returning to the city at age 21, he enrolled in an art course at Sydney Technical College. For years he freelanced cartoons while window-cleaning for a living. Eventually, in the late 1930s, he became a regular contributor to the *Bulletin* and launched his outback farmer character, Saltbush Bill, in the weekly magazine *Pix.* This feature, together with his *Witchetty's Tribe* (outback humor about an aborigine tribe) and his comic strip *Sandy Blight* (starring a typical struggling farmer) was later drawn for the Sydney *Sun* and the weekend *Sun-Herald.* Jolliffe's cartoons, drawn with watercolor washes in monotone, are renowned for their authentic "bush furniture" and background details: a broken wagon wheel, an old weathered barn, a pig trough fashioned from a large log, rabbit traps—anything that appeals is interesting.

Jolliffe's annual outback wanderings, which he spends sketching, photographing and collecting bush paraphernalia, last from three to four months. It is on these trips that he paints his wash studies, which are fine tonal exercises of outback farm buildings and portraits of aborigines. In December 1987 Jolliffe published his 120th cartoon collection. He retired shortly thereafter.

V.L.

JONES, CHARLES (1912-) American animator and producer born in Spokane, Washington, on September 21, 1912. Chuck Jones grew up in Los Angeles, where he received his art education at the Chouinard Institute. In the early 1930s he joined the Leon Schlesinger studios as an animator, working for such directors as Friz Freleng, Bob Clampett and Tex Avery. He graduated to director sta-

Chuck Jones. © Warner Brothers.

tus in the late 1930s (one of the first cartoons he directed was the 1938 "Presto-Change-O," featuring Bugs Bunny in one of his early incarnations).

Chuck Jones's talents came to full fruition in the 1940s and 1950s, when he contributed some of the most imaginative cartoons ever produced by the Schlesinger/Warner Brothers studios. "What's Opera, Doc?," "Mississippi Hare," "Frigid Hare" in the *Bugs Bunny* series; "Duck Amok," "Duck Dodgers in the 24fi Century," "Robin Hood Daffy" among the *Daffy Duck* cartoons; and the *Tweety and Sylvester* entry "Birds Anonymous"—these are but a few of his classics. In collaboration with Michael Maltese he created the characters of Pépé le Pew, the romantically inclined skunk, and of Wile E. Coyote and his nemesis, the Road Runner. During World War II Jones directed the campaign film *Hell-Bent for Election* for Stephen Bosustow and helped create the *Private Snafu* series of cartoons for the U.S. Army.

In 1966 Jones joined the MGM studio as head of its animation department. While there, he briefly took over the *Tom and Jerry* series after Hanna and Barbera had left and Gene Deitch had failed. In 1970 he was appointed vice-president in charge of children's programming for ABC-TV and created the Saturday morning program *The Curiosity Shop*. He then founded his own company, Chuck Jones Enterprises, and in recent years he has been directing and producing a number of memorable TV specials, including *Rikki-Tikki-Tavi* (adapted from Rudyard Kipling), *Horton Hears a Who, The Grinch Who Stole Christmas* (both from Dr. Seuss stories) and *The Pogo Special Birthday Special* (based on the Walt Kelly comic strip). Jones has also gone back occasionally to his old Warner characters—Bugs Bunny, Daffy Duck, *et al.*—featuring them in such TV specials as the Saint-Saens-inspired *The Carnival of Animals* (1976) and the Twain-derived *A Connecticut Rabbit in King Arthur's Court* (1978). In addition he has produced a full-length animated cartoon, *The Phantom Tollbooth* (1969). Chuck Jones's latest venture, a kid strip called *Crawford,* started syndication in 1978.

Now in his mid-eighties Jones has, in his own words, "enjoyed more than 60 years in animation and is still hard at work , having recently signed a new contract with Warner Bros. to create animated short subjects for theatrical release using many of the classic Warner Bros. characters." He has been the subject of two book-length studies, and in 1996 he was awarded an honorary Oscar as well as a Honorary Life Membership Award from the Directors Guild of America.

Once called by scriptwriter Heck Allen "an intellectual in a non-intellectual business," Jones nonetheless managed to win four Oscars; he was also executive producer on a fifth Oscar winner, *A Christmas Carol* (1972). One of the most respected names in the animation field, Jones has lectured extensively on university campuses in the United States and abroad.

M.H.

JONSSON, JOE (1890-1963) Australian cartoonist born in Halmstad, Sweden, in 1890. In the distinctiveness of its technique and in its extremely deceptive drawing style, the work of *Smith's Weekly* cartoonist Joe Jonsson was truly unique. Compared with the subtle draftsmanship of Norman Lindsay or the elegant, mannered drawing of

Missus: "What made you buy a whole barrel of beer?"
Husband: "There are rumors that we're going out on strike."

Joe Jonsson. © Smith's Weekly.

George Molnar, Jonsson's drawings looked as if they had been drawn with a toothbrush instead of with a pen. Yet his brilliant pen drawings were outstanding for their distinction, skill and humor: they were drawn with tremendous dash and zest.

Jonsson, "a bletty Swede," as he termed himself, left his family's farm for the sea at age 18, sailing before the mast for nine years and arriving in Australia in 1917. Before he became a professional comic artist with *Smith's Weekly* in 1924, Jonsson worked at a variety of jobs: timber cutter in Queensland and high rigger on Sydney's wheat silos at White Bay. Then when he decided to become an artist, he studied at the Watkin Art School, where he was so successful he became an art instructor within a year. Then followed a period as a commercial artist prior to his joining *Smith's Weekly*, where he remained until it ceased publication in 1950. In that year, Jonsson was engaged by Sir Keith Murdoch of the Melbourne *Herald* and produced weekly, until his death, his popular, nationally syndicated comic strip *Uncle Joe's Horse, Radish*, featuring an outlandish racehorse that was the answer to the punter's dream.

Joe Jonsson's humor fitted *Smith's Weekly* perfectly. It was tough, sometimes cynical and always uninhibited. Older readers of *Smith's* will recall his wonderful comic strip *Oigle*, with a small boy prankster and Gran'pa, a fatefully incompatible pair. His drawings and rollicking humor about burglars, cardsharps, turf punters, jockeys and "blottos" (drunks) were a continuation in theme of the work of the early *Bulletin* artists Alf Vincent and Ambrose Dyson. No comic artist in Australia has drawn as many jokes around the theme of drunks and drinking as Jonsson. His many comic drawings on this social activity in Australia have continued since the time of the Rum Corps through the era of the gold field sly-grog shanties to the present. (In 1961 Australia occupied second place on the list of the world's top beer-drinking nations, leaving Australians with a rather frothy tradition.) Appropriately, a large, fellow-brush wake was held in Sydney to pay tribute to "the gentle Swede" following his funeral in March 1963.

V.L.

JOYNER, SAMUEL (1924-) A pioneer cartoonist and illustrator of African-American parentage, Samuel Joyner was born in Philadelphia in 1924 and received rudimentary art instruction, first at the Free Graphic Sketch Club in South Philadelphia and later at South Philadelphia High School. There he was told by his art teacher that, despite his talent, he would be unable to find any art job from the white Establishment in 1939 America. Surmounting initial discouragement, he decided to continue with his art education while at the same time working for the Post Office.

After service in the U.S. Army, he went on to study on a G.I. bill at the Philadelphia Museum School of Industrial Art, from which he graduated in 1948. "This really was the start of my professional career," he later declared. He sold cartoons to the *Philadelphia Inquirer* and worked as a staff illustrator and advertising cartoonist for a large department store. In the racial climate of the 1950's he could not find the outlet his talents warranted. "At some firms, as soon as I opened the door and the receptionist saw my art portfolio, I was told that the art director was away, or not available." Thus barred from the more lucrative white art market, Joyner freelanced illustrations and editorial cartoons to African-American weeklies like the *Texas Houston Sun*, the *Georgia Metro Courier*, and the *Philadelphia Tribune* from 1947 until the mid-1990's, while teaching art at a technical school in Philadelphia and running a print shop during most of these years.

It is a tribute to Joyner's determination that he never lost his love of cartooning and a testimony to his talent that he succeeded at it despite long odds. Yet his experience did not leave him cynical or bitter. "At the present time," he wrote in 1992, "I thank God I still have enough energy and skill to meet several deadlines." In an age of unbridled recrimination, such a modest claim comes as a refreshing as well as an inspirational statement.

M.H.

JUCH, ERNST (1838-1909) Austrian cartoonist, painter and sculptor (of German birth) born in Gotha, then capital of Saxe-Coburg-Gotha, on April 25, 1838. At the turn of the century the eminent historian of humorous art Eduard Fuchs considered Ernst Juch far and away the best cartoonist in Austria. Nor was Juch merely a brilliant comet: he was on the staff of the Vienna *Figaro* from 1869 (not long after it was founded) almost until his death in Vienna on October 5, 1909.

Juch's father, a painter, died when the boy was very young. Ernst was then slated to become a designer of

The politician Thuns trampling on the Austrian constitution.

Ernst Juch, 1898.

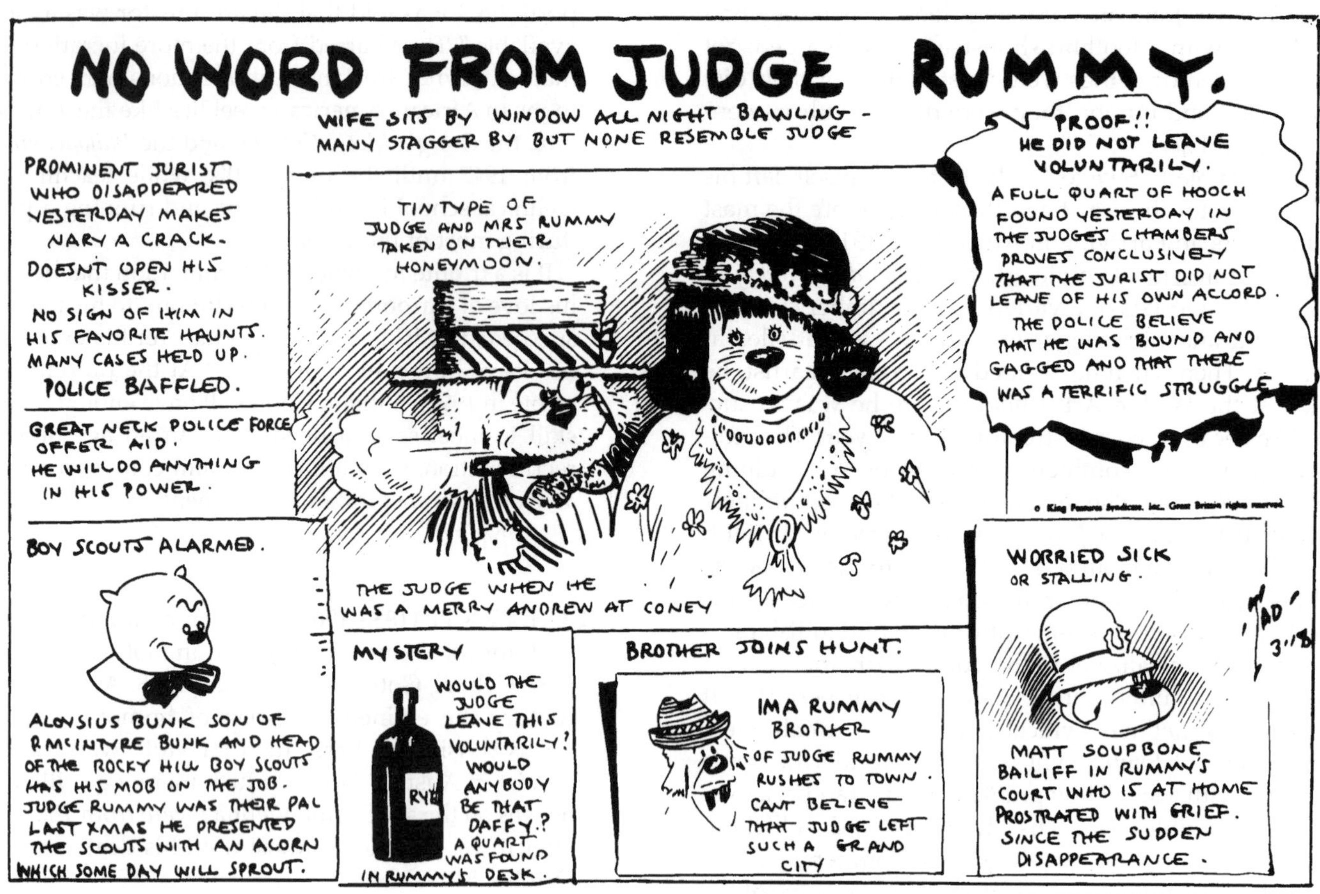

"Judge Rummy," 1921. © King Features Syndicate.

porcelain statuettes and was apprenticed to a local sculptor. As a journeyman he wandered to Passau, and from there to Vienna, where he settled in 1859. He did some sculpture and designs for metal objects, but his drawings soon brought him more fame and money. His first published cartoons appeared in the weekly *Der G'rade Michel* in 1864. Then, five years later, came the *Figaro*.

When Juch became an artist for that publication (at first alongside Leopold Müller, who was soon invited to teach at the Academy, leaving Juch in sole possession of the field), the *Figaro* was edited by the outstanding author of Austrian folk plays Ludwig Anzengruber, with whom the artist formed a close friendship. Not only did Juch illustrate Anzengruber's almanac *Der Wiener Bote* with storytelling pictures, but he did numerous private drawings for "Die Anzengrube," the club to which both men belonged. Juch was also known for the ingenious watercolor postcards he sent his friends. Among the books he illustrated were the *Krebsbüchlein des Figaro* ("The Figaro's Crab—or Remaindered—Book," 1881) and J. Bendel's *Allerlei Weisen und Märlein* ("All Sorts of Tunes and Tales," 1892).

The special feature of Juch's cartoon style was its intentionally distorted anatomy, with certain parts of the body strongly emphasized to the detriment of others. His people's faces were small but very clearly drawn and recognizable. He was famed as an unsentimental but also good-natured observer of Viennese life.

Shortly before his death, Juch transferred from the *Figaro* to its rival, *Kikeriki*. After he died, it was learned that he had indulged in meritorious private experiments in painting that he had withheld from public view.

S.A.

JUDGE RUMMY (U.S.) A funny animal character created by Tad Dorgan for his daily Hearst sports page space in 1910, Judge Rummy was a dog of no apparent breed whom Dorgan usually portrayed in judicial black presiding over his courtroom. Originally drawn for the *New York Evening Journal* at Dorgan's sports department desk, the often unnamed *Judge Rummy* strip was published nationwide in a number of Hearst afternoon dailies and ran intermittently as a Dorgan feature until the cartoonist's death more than twenty years later. Although it was never printed or designed as a Sunday color page, it often appeared in Hearst Sunday sports sections in its weekday format.

Initially an occasional three-, four- or six-panel gag strip (in which Judge Rummy was floored by a riposte from one of the culprits brought before him or capped a felon's gag with one of his own), few of which had anything whatever to do with sports, the all-dog character feature developed considerable continuity when the Judge became a principal figure in Dorgan's long-running and popular narrative of the 1910s, *Silk Hat Harry's Divorce Suit*. During its run *Judge Rummy* was seldom seen as a separate title. Revived after the explosive climax of the *Suit* strip, *Judge Rummy* continued as an irregular gag feature between panels of Dorgan's *Indoor Sports* and *Outdoor Sports* features until a few weeks after Dorgan's death on May 2, 1929.

Judge Rummy was one of the Dorgan animal characters involved in a curious experiment by the cartoonist late in the 1910s. Dorgan arranged an onstage metamorphosis of his dog figures, such as Rummy, Silk Hat Harry, Curlock Holmes and others, into human equivalents. This was apparently met with widespread protests, for Dorgan hurriedly returned his characters to their original canine state.

Basically a rather simple hit-or-miss gag strip, very simply drawn, *Judge Rummy was* nevertheless an enormously popular strip with Hearst metropolitan readers; it was reprinted for years, with other Dorgan material, in Hearst papers after Dorgan's death.

B.B.

JUMP, EDWARD (ca. 1838-1883) American cartoonist born in France, probably in 1838. E. Jump traveled the world with his sketchbook and lived in various parts of Europe and in Australia before arriving in the United States. It is reported that he first settled in San Francisco as a commercial artist designing whiskey labels before moving to Washington, D.C., as a portrait specialist demanding high commissions.

He was active in New York, Montreal, Cincinnati, St. Louis and Chicago as a freelance artist. It was in New York that he executed most of his work—or rather, New York was his base once he became the leading staff artist on *Leslie's Weekly* in the 1870s. In 1867 he had illustrated the book *Beyond the Mississippi* by A.D. Richardson and thereby established a reputation for western subjects. One notable *Leslie's* series was a Jump sketchbook report of activities in Leadville, Colorado, published between February and June, 1879.

As an important *Leslie's* staffer, Jump also contributed to the Leslie humor publications; there, along with Frank Beard, he was one of Opper's teachers, and he also came to know the elder Bellew and Keppler. Jump was an able caricaturist and also freely contributed to *Wild Oats,* the *Graphic* and minor imitations of *Puck,* into 1882.

E. Jump died a suicide in Chicago on April 21, 1883.

R.M.

JUNCEDA

See García-Junceda i Supervía, Joan.

JUNGLE TATEI (Japan) *Jungle Tatei* ("Jungle Emperor") was Japan's first color animation series for television and was produced by Osamu Tezuka's Mushi Productions in 1965. It was based on the comic strip of the same name, also by Tezuka, which ran for years in the magazine *Manga Shōnen* from 1950 on and was briefly revived again in 1964 by Kodansha in a magazine called *Disneyland.* When *Jungle Tatei* finished its television run in September 1966, it was followed by *Shin Jungle Tatei: Susume Leo!* ("New Jungle Emperor: Go Ahead Leo!"), which ran from October 1966 to March 1967.

The animated versions of *Jungle Tatei* closely followed the original comic in depicting the life of Leo the white lion and his efforts to reconcile the animals in Africa with the men who encroached upon their domain. Leo was no ordinary lion; he could talk to humans when the need arose, and he devoted himself to attempting to organize the animal kingdom into a civilization that could withstand the human threat. He was brilliant, strong and fast, but at the same time he was gentle and had a sense of humor.

"Jungle Tatei." © Mushi Productions.

In the first series Leo's age was equivalent to that of a third-grade child, but viewers had a chance to watch him gradually mature, and in *Susume Leo!* he assumed his final form, complete with throaty roar and flowing mane. Supporting characters also changed. In the first series Leo's father, Panja, and his mother, Raga, both appeared, but Panja died battling humans and Raga was captured. As Leo matured, he too took a wife named Raiya, and they produced two cubs. Numerous other animals also appeared, such as Bubu, an evil lion who competed with Leo for spheres of influence; Koko, a parrot; Tommy, a Thomson's gazelle; and Mandy the Mandrill. Bubu was assisted by a variety of villains, including two comical hyenas.

The animated versions of *Jungle Tatei,* like the comic strip, were a spectacular success—full of brilliant color and action, and incorporating Tezuka's favorite themes of idealism, perseverance and the vitality of life. Humor, tragedy, love and drama were skillfully woven into the main theme and its subplots. The first series, which ran in 52 episodes of 23 minutes each, won a host of awards, including one from the 1967 International Children's Film Festival in Venice. Some of the best talents in animation in Japan were used on both, with Masaki Tsuji writing most of the scripts, and people like Shinji Nagashima and Sadao Tsukioka directing some of the episodes. Eichi Yamamoto served as chief director and producer, and brilliant music was composed by Tomita.

In the United States the first series ran on NBC television in 1965 under the title *Kimba the White Lion;* it was produced by Fred Ladd. The second series, in which Leo appeared as a grown lion, ran on Canadian television in French with the title *Le Roi Leo.*

In 1994 *Jungle Tatei* received unexpected coverage in the U.S. and Japanese media when Disney's *The Lion King* was widely believed to have borrowed heavily from the late Osamu Tezuka's work without giving him credit. In 1997, in a delicious bit of irony, Tezuka's company created its own full-length theatrical animated feature of *Jungle Tatei,* thereby allowing theatergoers in Japan to make their own comparisons.

F.S.

JÜRGENSEN, FRITZ (1818-1863) Danish cartoonist born in Copenhagen, Denmark, in 1818. Considered to be Denmark's first real cartoonist, Fritz Jürgensen was also a watchmaker. His father was watchmaker to the royal court and "General Inspector for the Public Measuring of Time," and he encouraged his son to enter the profession. But in 1835, before Jürgensen started as an apprentice, he made a trip to Italy, and then another extensive trip to Switzerland on behalf of the watchmaker profession. There he blossomed as a letter and diary writer, two occupations that, together with his drawings, were to become main parts of his life.

In 1842, 24 years old, he married his cousin and childhood sweetheart, Lise, and succeeded his father as court watchmaker. His first 48 drawings, *Gysse-bogen,* are from this period and are dedicated to his nephew, who was called Gysse. A year later his wife died in childbirth, and Jürgensen sold his watchmaker business, led somewhat of an idler's life, practiced music and was a treasured party guest, not least because of the many drawings he left with the families he visited.

Jürgensen's gallery of characters is the Copenhagen citizenry, their narrow-mindedness, human weaknesses and vanity. It has often been said that his drawings are dilettantish and competently amateurish in style. On the other hand, the naiveté—as it was later in James Thurber's drawings—is a charming addition to his witty captions. For example, an office clerk who practices his speech in front of an empty chair says: "You know too much about the business, sir, not to be aware how much our work load has increased. But to ask for a raise for all the employees would be too forward. I *only* wish it for myself." But he was no merry soul, which his diaries and drawings also show. He was a student of Søren Kierkegaard and talked about "the state of things in Denmark: mediocracy, dullness, philistinism. Ideals are lost, forgotten, and mediocracy has complacently moved up to take the seat of honor." The fact that Jürgensen's production first and foremost was a historical picture of society does not eliminate the possibility that later times and other countries can identify similar traits. His humor was ironic and bitter, though filled with empathy.

His melancholy was interrupted by momentary bouts of merriment, and a contemporary painter appropriately likened him to the cuckoo in the clock, coming out to call and right away withdrawing in silence. On an artistically lower level he is related to Honoré Daumier and has to a great degree inspired succeeding generations of Scandinavian cartoonists. In 1854 he had a violent hemorrhage, and in the following years he suffered from fevers, coughs and headaches. He drank heavily, and in the spring of 1863 he died from tuberculosis.

J.S.

JÜSP

See Spahr, Jürg.

Kk

KALLAUGHER, KEVIN (1955-) Known internationally by his signature KAL, editorial cartoonist Kevin Kallaugher is one of the few members of his profession who stand comfortably with a foot on each side of the Atlantic. Providing a daily cartoon for the *The Baltimore Sun* and three a week for *The Economist* in London, he is also a regular contributor to *Business Central Europe* in Vienna, the *International Herald Tribune* and *Le Monde* in Paris, *Der Spiegel* in Berlin, *Pravda* and *Krokodil* in Moscow, and national papers in Japan, Australia, and India.

Kallaugher began his career in art modestly. After graduating, with honors, from Harvard in 1977, he played and coached for a basketball team in England, supplementing his income by working in a sports goods shop and doing caricatures on the pier at Brighton. When his team failed, he took his sketchpad to Trafalgar Square in London and drew tourists until he found a regular job as the first resident caricaturist on the staff of *The Economist* in 1978. During the next ten years his work was to appear in more than 180 papers worldwide. In 1988 he became the editorial cartoonist of *The Baltimore Sun* without diminishing his output for his many affiliations in Europe. His trenchant visual commentary has earned him numerous awards, including Feature Cartoonist of the Year from the Cartoonist Club of Great Britain in 1981, Best Editorial Cartoon at the WittyWorld International Cartoon Festival in Budapest in 1990, and a Grafica Internazionale Award from the Italian Satire Festival in 1996. Collections of his cartoons include *Drawn from the Economist* (1988), *KALtoons* (1992), and *Kal Draws a Crowd* (1997). His art has received solo exhibitions in London, New York, Baltimore, and Washington, and he has served as President of the Association of American Editorial Cartoonists in 1993-1994.

Kevin Kallaugher ("Kal"). © Cartoonist and Writers Syndicate.

Commanding a masterful style, Kallaugher stands among the premier caricaturists of the century. Defining caricature as "part portrait/part poison," he employs his graphic gift as a weapon, with great finesse on a wide range of subjects. Although he commands an unusually international perspective, his work for the *Sun* addresses local and national issues with equal insight and with equal objectivity. He is nobody's man but his own, and is given free reign. As Joe Stern, the *Sun*'s editor, has written, "He does not suffer much editorial supervision, and he does not get it. When you have a genius on the premises, you don't mess with him."

Kallaugher's powerful pen is seldom wielded to amuse. Although it is hard to repress a smile at his wickedly drawn public figures—Perot as a sinister vulture watching Clinton and Bush pacing off for a duel, a gross Saddam Hussein toasting marshmallows in the flames following the Gulf War—the artist's goal is clearly a serious one. "When I look for a subject to comment on, the question I ask myself is not, 'what is funny today?' but 'what is important today?,'" he has written. "That's because the editorial cartoonist's job is not to make you laugh but to make you think."

D.W.

KAMLER, PIOTR (1936-) Polish animator born in Warsaw, Poland, in 1936. After completing his art studies in Warsaw, Piotr K,amler went to France in the late 1950s. He started animation work in 1960 for the research department of the French television system. His first films were abstract compositions such as the 1960 *Etude* and *Conte* ("Tale"), *Composition* and *Structures* (both 1961) and *Lignes et Points* ("Lines and Dots," 1963). He then moved to less abstract if equally cryptic themes with the 1964 *Meurtre* ("Murder") and the 1965 *Prière Enfance* ("Childhood Prayer"). The same year he also directed *La Planète Verte* ("The Green Planet"), a science fiction tale entirely drawn

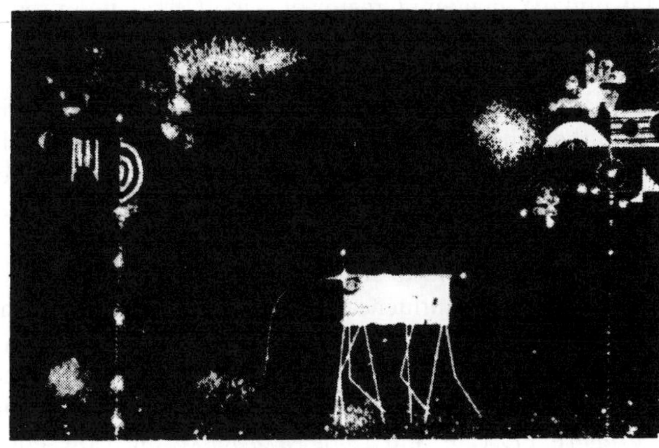

Piotr Kamler, "L'Araignéléphant." © Cinéastes Associés.

on a green background, with extraordinary visual effects reinforced by a narrative written by Jacques Sternberg. In 1968 he came out with the no less extraordinary *L'Araignéléphant* (which can be translated "The Spiderlephant"), about a monstrous creature on the loose. The 1970 *Délicieuse Catastrophe,* which seems to be a parable of the mating ritual, reinforced Kamler's position as one of the most intriguing of contemporary animators.

Kamler's production in recent years has somewhat declined in quantity, but its quality remains high. *Coeur de Secours* ("Spare Heart," 1972*)* is an ironic mirroring of the modern quest for fulfillment, and *Les Pas* ("Steps," 1975) is an outstanding abstract film that appears to recapitulate the whole of Kamler's discourse. A recipient of many awards and prizes (at Annecy, Zagreb and elsewhere), Kamler has been the subject of a number of studies in France and abroad. After many trials and tribulations he finally completed his first feature film, *Chronopolis,* in 1982. A science-fiction picture with social and political undertones, it won a number of awards.

M.H.

KAMOGAWA, TSUBAME (1956-) Japanese cartoonist born in Fukuoka Prefecture, Japan, in 1956. Tsubame Kamogawa, one of the youngest and most eccentric Japanese cartoonists, began drawing cartoons soon after learning how to hold a pencil and thereupon resolved to make it his career. In what was a dramatic act of courage given Japan's highly competitive school system, Kamogawa reportedly submitted a completely blank test paper during his high school entrance examination (compulsory education extends only to the ninth grade in Japan). The reverse side was filled with cartoons. In 1974, at age 17, he dropped out of high school and began working as an assistant to Baron Yoshimoto, the creator of numerous popular comic strips, but supposedly was told that his drawings resembled those of a first-grader. This served only to strengthen his resolve to make it on his own, and after ten rebellious, grueling months he quit.

After an initial period of hardship, Kamogawa began having his works accepted by various magazines, and in 1977 he came out with *Macaroni Hōrenso* (roughly, "Macaroni-Spinach Apartment") in the weekly magazine *Shōnen Champion. Macaroni Hōrenso* became an immediate success and represented a type of humor totally different from that of Fujio Akatsuka (creator of *Tensai Bakabon*) or Tatsuhiko Yamagami (creator of *Gakki Dekka),* two prominent gag strip artists who had been pioneers in their own right. The stars of *Macaroni Hōrenso* are 41-year-old Kindo, 25-year-old Hisakata and 16-year-old Soji, an unlikely trio all in their first year of high school. Their antics can only be described as bizarre, for there is almost no plot whatsoever, the humor deriving from endless outrageous situations and the intersplicing of multiple levels of reality.

Kamogawa refers to his style as "rock-beat"; as other artists have been influenced by jazz or classical music, he draws his inspiration from rock 'n' roll, which he plays constantly as he works. The result is an unprecedented sense of speed in all of his cartoons and comics—as in *Purupuru Propellor* and *Dora Neko Rokku* (also presently running in *Shōnen Champion*)—and frame transitions that border on the surreal. Kamogawa's drawing style is simple to the point of appearing amateurish, and it remains to be seen whether he will have the staying power and flexibility required to survive in Japan's quickly changing market. At present, however, he is riding on a crest of popularity. Unfortunately tastes in the gag manga market in Japan change constantly, and even Kamogawa has never been able to replicate his former success. In 1996 he was even included in Ohizumi Mitsunari's book titled fittingly *Kieta Mangaka,* or "Manga Artists Who Have Disappeared." Nonetheless his work will always remain as an icon of late 1970s humor in Japan.

F.S.

KANEVSKII, AMINADAV MOISEEVICH (1898-1983) Cartoonist and illustrator born in Elizavetgrad (now Kirovgrad) in the Ukraine on March 29, 1898. From 1924 to 1930 Aminadav Kanevskii attended the State Higher Art and Technical Studios and the Higher Art and Technical Institute, where he studied under P. Pavlinov, N. Kupreianov and D.S. Moor, among other leading Soviet graphic artists of the time.

Kanevskii started on his professional career with illustrations for children's books, mostly of a humorous nature. His illustrations for A.L. and P.N. Barto's *The Crybaby* (1934) and Saltykov-Shchedrin's *The Pompadour and the Lady Pompadours* (1935) were particularly well received. At the same time, Kanevskii also did cartoons. In 1936 he became one of the regular contributors to *Krokodil,* for which he drew over the years a number of memorable cartoons, some of a political nature, but most on comical situations derived from everyday Soviet life. In addition to his cartooning career Kanevskii developed his interest in caricature with illustrations for Vladimir Mayakovsky's *Satirical Poems* (1964) and for a number of Nikolai Gogol's novels and stories.

Kanevskii was the recipient of many Soviet distinctions for his work, including the Order of the Red Banner of Labor. He became a corresponding member of the Academy of Science of the USSR in 1962 and was named People's Artist of the USSR in 1973. A book-length study of Kanevskii's work was published by Iuri Khalamenski in Moscow in 1961. He retired in the late 1970s and died in 1983.

M.H.

KAPTEN GROGG (Sweden) The first two decades of this century were a period of intense research and experimentation in the field of animated cartooning all over the world. One of the early pioneers was the Swede Gustav Victor Bergdahl, who created a character called Kapten Grogg in 1915. (The character was apparently inspired by C.W. Kahles's panel The Yarns of Captain Fibb, then published in Sweden). Bergdahl was a newspaper cartoonist who had been greatly impressed by the work of Winsor McCay (contrary to what has been asserted by some historians, he never actually worked for McCay but only decided to follow in his footsteps).

Kapten Grogg (whose name can be loosely translated as "Captain Brandy") was a cheerful, hard-drinking sea dog

"Kapten Grogg." © Victor Bergdahl.

whose adventures took place all around the globe. He first appeared in "Grogg's Underbara Resa" ("Grogg's Wonderful Voyage"). This proved successful enough to allow Bergdahl to launch a full-fledged *Kapten Grogg* cartoon series. The irrepressible old salt next went around the world in an airship ("Kapten Grogg's Balloon Trip," 1917); later he got married to a nagging harridan ("Kapten Grogg's Wedding," 1918). Other notable entries in the series include the 1917 "Kapten Grogg at the North Pole," the 1920 "Kapten Grogg at Sea" and the 1922 "Kapten Grogg Puts on Weight." This last put an end to the *Kapten Grogg* series, which seems to have disappeared in the early 1920s, after a run of 13 cartoons.

Kapten Grogg was a remarkable achievement and is one of the few animated cartoon series originating in Europe during the silent era that can bear comparison with the best of the American production of the period.

M.H.

KARI

See Suomalainen, Kari Yrjänä.

KASHEM, KAZI ABUL (1913-) Kazi Abul Kashem was born May 7, 1913, in Matulal, Jessore District, India. During his long career, he has had the distinction of being a pioneer cartoonist in three countries, two of which, Pakistan and Bangladesh, evolved from India.

Fascinated with pictures and cartoons as a schoolboy, he was admitted to the Calcutta Art School in 1928 but did not finish because of financial difficulties. His first job was as a low-salaried worker in a commercial art studio. In 1930, at age 17, Kashem became Calcutta's first Moslem cartoonist, much to the chagrin of family and the larger society, since drawing figures was contrary to his religion's beliefs. From the beginning, Kashem applied literary verses, many of which he wrote, as captions to his cartoons, and attacked social and political problems, particularly British colonialism.

In the 1930s, he also created a comic strip for the newspaper *Nabajug*, while still submitting work to *Azad*, *Saugat*, and other dailies. After 1937, he worked as an art designer in the government's Department of Industries. His fame spread as he drew attention to the Muslim League government and social-economic inequalities.

From 1945 to 1948, Kashem was the main cartoonist working on one of India's earliest animation films, *Shabash* ("Bravo"), but shortly after, he left his native land to live in partitioned East Pakistan. All leading East Pakistani newspapers, including *Ittefaq*, *Mohammedi*, and *Bicitra*, sought his political cartoons, usually signed with his pen-name, "Dopeaza."

All this work was on a freelance basis until 1964, when he became head artist at the British publishing company, Franklin Book. Kashem continued drawing cartoons after Bangladesh split from Pakistan, maintaining his national reputation as a fine artist and writer of juvenile literature. His work philosophy is a simple one—"When the Bangladeshi masses are enraged about a subject, so am I as a cartoonist."

J.A.L.

KATCHOR, BEN (1951-) The graphic work of Ben Katchor occupies a shadowy area between the mainstream and the underground comic strip. His lyrical and multilayered vision of the urban landscape, "Julius Knipie, Real Estate Photographer," has been praised by the *New Yorker* (April 17, 1995) as "doing for the comics what Marcel Proust did for the novel," and has been compared elsewhere to the work of Kafka, Joyce, and Borges.

Born in Brooklyn, New York, in 1951, Katchor took classes at the Brooklyn Museum Art School and the Art Students League before graduating from Brooklyn College with a degree in painting and art history. He spent a decade running a small graphic design company, familiarizing himself not only with all aspects of print production but with a wide range of often bizarre small businesses of the city. He drew for fanzines during his teens and was a frequent contributor to the avant-garde comic magazine, *Raw*, from its second issue, in 1980. Katchor also edited and published his own cartoon journal, *Picture Story*, which presented the work of such innovative cartoonists as Peter Blegvad and Mark Beyer, but it found little support and appeared only twice, in 1978 and in 1986.

Katchor's following is based on "Julius Knipie," a series he began in the independent paper *New York Press* in 1988. Described as "fragmentary nocturnal epiphanies from the mean streets of [Katchor's] own version of New York," these eight-panel vignettes provide their hero's reflections on the life of a generic city and the curious occupations it supports—"an unhappy young man with a bleak future in the ornamental toothbrush business," a manure futures broker, a breeder of pedigreed cockroaches. The headlines glimpsed on abandoned newspapers include "Cowboy Lifeguard Breaks Up Chihuahua Love Nest" and "Unread Books Blamed for Collapse of Continental Shelf." The strip appeared weekly in the *New York Press* until 1994, when it transferred to the *Village Voice* for a year. After a six-month hiatus, it reappeared in the New York weekly, *Forward*, in 1995, and has since then also been a feature of about a dozen other independent papers around the country. During the 1990s Katchor has published other features in *Esquire*, the *New Yorker*, and *Metropolis*, and from 1992 to

1993 he produced a continuity strip called "The Jew of New York" for the *Forward*.

"Julius Kniple" was collected in *Cheap Novelties: The Pleasures of Urban Decay*, published in 1991. A second, larger collection appeared as *Julius Kniple, Real Estate Photographer* in 1996, and a third, as well as an expanded version of *The Jew of New York*, are scheduled for book publication in 1998. In 1995-96, an audio adaptation of the strip was presented on National Public Radio in 16 monthly episodes. Although his audience has remained small, Katchor has earned a devoted following. In 1990 he was one of the first artists to win a Swann Foundation Award for Excellence in Cartoon, Caricature and Comic-Strip Art, and he received a Guggenheim Fellowship in 1995-96. He teaches at the School of Visual Arts and has lectured widely, and his original art has been exhibited in the United States and France.

D.W.

KATZENJAMMER KIDS, THE (U.S.) At the time that W.R. Hearst founded International Film Service in 1916 with the express purpose of bringing to the screen the comics that were syndicated in his newspapers, no comic strip had been so enduring and successful as *The Katzenjammer Kids*, created by Rudolph Dirks in 1897. It was therefore fitting that the two terrible twins be the heroes of the first series of cartoon films produced by the service. (*Happy Hooligan, Silk Hat Harry, Jiggs and Maggie, Krazy Kat,* and others were to follow.)

In 1916 Dirks had already left Hearst and gone on to create a new version of the strip (first called *Hans and Fritz,* it was later rechristened *The Captain and the Kids*), but he was still credited, along with Bert Green, for the story lines. The animation—rather crude and primitive but lovable in its simplicity—was done by John Foster and Walter Lantz, under the direction of Gregory La Cava. Due to the rise in anti-German feelings, the series was discontinued in 1918, and the studio closed soon afterward. (Later, Bray Studios revived the *Katzenjammer* cartoons for a few years.)

Hans and Fritz, der Captain, die Mama and the other protagonists came to life again in a series of animated cartoons released by MGM under the title *The Captain and the Kids.* Based on Dirks's revived strip, 14 cartoons were produced in 1938 and 1939, from "Blue Monday" to "The Winning Ticket," under the direction of Robert Allen and William Hanna (of later Hanna-Barbera fame).

The Katzenjammers again appeared in an undistinguished series of animated shorts produced for television by King Features Syndicate in the 1960s. The Katzies are currently featured in a number of amusing TV commercials.

M.H.

KAULBACH, WILHELM VON (1805-1874) German painter, illustrator and cartoonist born at Arolsen, not far from Kassel, in Hesse, on October 15, 1805. Though contemporary and even later writers condemned certain satirical works by Wilhelm von Kaulbach as sordid betrayals of his serious artistic principles, a careful analysis of his career points to a deep-seated dichotomy between his urge to storm Mount Olympus and an equally strong need to hurl down abuse from his lofty peak. His childhood and youth were impoverished, nomadic and unhappy. As an adolescent he studied with his father, a noted goldsmith. When he entered the Düsseldorf Academy in 1822, the historical painter and influential teacher Peter von Cornelius became his protector. It was clear that Kaulbach could paint the kind of allegorical frescoes and grandiose religious pictures so much in demand at the time.

He lived and worked in Munich from 1826 on, not counting a couple of long trips to Italy, the first in 1835, the year of his famous realistic print *Das Narrenhaus* ("The Madhouse")—which throughout the 19th century was generally considered one of his humorous works! By 1837 Kaulbach had become a Bavarian court painter. By the early 1840s his graphic wit was already widely appreciated, and the Stuttgart publisher Cotta commissioned what was to be Kaulbach's most famous set of satirical illustrations, those for Goethe's *Reineke Fuchs,* a retelling of the medieval animal epic. In drawing these humanized animals, Kaulbach was directly influenced by the work of the French illustrator Grandville, but he achieved a notable personal creation all the same. *Reineke Fuchs* was published in 1846 with copper-engraved illustrations, and in 1857 with wood-engraved versions.

In the years of revolutionary troubles, 1848 and 1849, Kaulbach drew some political cartoons (one shows a royal snowman melting); he has been tentatively credited with salacious depictions of Lola Montez, the royal mistress who caused the abdication of Bavarian king Ludwig I. The greatest scandal in Kaulbach's career occurred in 1850. Having already executed numerous frescoes, and having been named director of the Munich Academy in 1849, Kaulbach nevertheless could not resist poking fun at old colleagues and masters in his frescoes in the Neue

Wilhelm von Kaulbach, illustration for Goethe's "Reineke Fuchs," 1857.

Pinakothek depicting the furtherance of art and culture in the reign of Ludwig I.

Other humorous works include the *Kinderfibel* ("Children's Primer"), delightful drawings he made for his own children in 1852; a lengthy series of *Dance of Death* sketches dating from the 1850s to about 1870, including both generalized victims (as in traditional series in this genre) and specific historical characters; and witty drawings found in sketchbooks of his last years, the early 1870s. He is also said to have done lewd versions of his own successful coffee-table books portraying characters and scenes in works by Goethe, Schiller and Shakespeare.

Other artists in Kaulbach's immediate family included his brother Karl, his son Hermann and especially his nephew Friedrich August von Kaulbach, also a cartoonist. Wilhelm von Kaulbach died in Munich on April 7, 1874.

S.A.

KAWAMOTO, KIHACHIRO (1925-) Japanese cartoonist and puppet animator born in Shibuya, Tokyo, on January 11, 1925. After graduating from Yokohama University with a degree in architecture, Kihachiro Kawamoto began working as an assistant art designer for Toho Motion Picture Company but quit in 1949 to begin freelancing. Kawamoto quickly established himself as an expert puppet maker, and in 1953 he made two one-minute black-and-white commercial animated puppet films with Tadahito Mochinaga, a former graphic animator and one of the founding fathers of Japanese puppet animation. In 1956 Kawamoto again worked with Mochinaga to create an 11-minute color puppet animation film called *Beer Mukashi Mukashi* ("A History of Beer") for a beer company. By this time Kawamoto was in charge of both puppet making and animation.

In 1959, having gained considerable experience and training with Mochinaga, Kawamoto established Shiba Productions with Tadasu Iizawa, a director and playwright who had also worked with Mochinaga. Shiba Productions specialized primarily in animated commercial films for television, and Kawamoto's abiding interest in puppets led him to quit, leave Japan in 1962 and study for two years in Czechoslovakia under the world-famous puppet animator Jiří Trnka. Returning to Japan in 1964, Kawamoto soon began refining his skills, and in 1968 his *Hana Ori* ("Breaking Branches Is Forbidden"), a 14-minute color puppet animation film, won him the silver prize at the Mamaia International Animated Film Festival in Romania. Since 1968 Kawamoto's independently produced films have regularly won awards internationally and in Japan. Notable among them are *Oni* ("The Demon," 1972), which employed beautiful backgrounds modeled after Japanese lacquerwork and won both the coveted Ofuji award in Japan and a special mention at the Annecy International Animated Film Festival; *Shijin no Shōgai* ("A Poet's Life," 1974), a cutout animation film based on a story by the novelist Kobo Abe; and *Dojōji* ("Dojō Temple," 1967), which garnered awards not only in Japan but also at animated film festivals in Annecy and Melbourne.

Most recently, Kawamoto has been working on a 20-minute puppet animation film titled *Kataku* ("House of Flames"), but he also creates puppets for television programs and commercial advertising. Moreover, he regularly works with his colleague Tadanari Okamoto, also an animated filmmaker, to produce highly popular puppet shows (that include animation) annually in Japan.

"Now let out the clutch and step on the gas!"

William Keane. © This Week.

Kawamoto has probably received his widest public recognition from his work on the puppet dramas shown in 1993 on NHK (Japan Broadcasting Corporation), which featured traditional tales such as *Sangokushi* ("The Three Kingdoms") and *Heike Monogatari* ("The Tale of Heike"). Reflecting the level of his achievement and the esteem in which he is now held nationally, he has won Imperial medals of honor for his contributions to culture, including the Medal with Purple Ribbon in 1988 and the prestigious Order of the Rising Sun, Gold Ray with Rosette in 1995.

F.S.

KEANE, BIL (1922-) American cartoonist born William Keane near Philadelphia, Pennsylvania, in 1922. Keane, like many other future cartoonists, showed an early talent for drawing, and his inclination was encouraged by his parents. While attending Northeast Catholic High School in Philadelphia, he contributed cartoons to the school newspaper. After graduation from high school in 1940, he became an errand boy for the *Philadelphia Bulletin.*

Drafted into the army in 1941, Keane worked on *Yank* magazine, then was sent to Australia (where he met his future wife) and later drew cartoons for U.S. savings bonds and GI insurance. When the war ended, Keane was a staff member of the army newspaper *Stars and Stripes,* where his first panel series, *At Ease with the Japanese,* appeared.

Discharged in 1946, Keane rejoined the *Bulletin* as staff artist while continuing to freelance cartoons to such publications as the *Saturday Evening Post* and *This Week.* In addition to spot cartoons for the *Bulletin,* Keane also drew *Silly Philly,* a gag panel with a homegrown flavor, and in 1954 he launched his successful *Channel Chuckles* cartoon series. This amused look at television was later picked up by the Register and Tribune Syndicate for national distribution. Keane followed up in 1960 with his best-known creation, *The Family Circus,* an endearing domestic panel, also syndicated by the Register and Tribune.

In 1959 the Keane family moved from Philadelphia to Arizona, where, Bil Keane claimed, "I draw *The Family Circus* and *Channel Chuckles* between tennis games." Keane finally gave up *Channel Chuckles* and concentrated on *The Family Circus.* He had his name legally changed to Bil (with one "l") Keane. He served as president of the National Cartoonists Society in 1981-83. In addition to his daily and Sunday feature, he has illustrated a number of books, notably Erma Bombeck's *Just Wait Till You Have Children of Your Own.*

M.H.

KEEFE, MICHAEL (1946-) American cartoonist born in Santa Rosa, California, on November 6, 1946. While pursuing mathematics studies at the University of Missouri, where he earned bachelor's and master's degrees and successfully completed his courses for the doctorate (he never wrote the dissertation), Mike Keefe contributed numerous cartoons to various campus publications during the heyday of Watergate. After he began teaching at Penn Valley Community College in Kansas City, however, he was faced with a shrinking job market; therefore, in 1975, he submitted a portfolio of political cartoons to Bill Sanders of the *Milwaukee Journal,* who recommended him for the position left vacant by Pat Oliphant at the *Denver Post*. He was hired that same year and has been there ever since.

Keefe is an equal opportunity satirist who enjoys exposing the double-talk hypocrisies of spinmeisters, Democrats or Republicans, on the right or left hand of God. One cartoon shows a smiling Yassir Arafat exclaiming, "But I *am* cracking down on Hamas... Every time there's a suicide bombing... that's one less radical!" In another, "according to Clinton spokesperson Rosemary Woods," no illegal fundraising activities took place in the White House, whereas a November 6, 1996 drawing presents a dour Bob Dole holding a copy of the *Chicago Tribune* with the headline "Dole Defeats Dole" in a famous reprise of President Truman's 1948 victory picture.

Mike Keefe. © Denver Post.

Keefe relies on his readers' knowledge of historical and cultural icons to convey his humor (for example, Rodin saws his passionately kissing couple apart and places a checkerboard between them so as not to lose his NEA support). He synthesizes the many elements of an issue, without preaching, and appeals to the readers' thoughtful reactions to oftentimes absurd behaviors, whether from environmentalists concerned over "global static" now that people drive electric cars, the panhandler with "no home page on the web," or a blossoming ski safety industry that in the wake of the accidental deaths of Michael Kennedy and Sonny Bono is aggressively marketing tree feelers, air bags, helmets, roll bars, and drag chutes.

For nine months in 1992, Keefe drew "Penpoint," a series of political cartoons for KMGH, the *Post*'s sister television station. In order to gain better creative control, he founded dePIXion studios, not only to distribute his newspaper cartoons but also "Talking Heads," his weekly animated caricatures (not limited to politics), which debuted in 1995 on *InToon with the News* on America OnLine. In addition, he and *Pittsburgh Post-Gazette* editorial cartoonist Tim Menees launched a couple of short-lived comic strips in the late 1980's entitled *Cooper* and *Iota*. Finally, besides writing and illustrating *The 10 Speed Commandments* (1987), an irreverent guide to the complete sport of cycling, or simply illustrating such informative booklets as *A Consumer's Guide to Water Conservation* (1993), Keefe has reprinted a number of his cartoons. Particular mention should be made of *Running Awry* (1979) and *Keefe-Kebab* (1984).

Close to caricature, with figures sketchy or having one or two distinguishing features, Keefe's cartoons have a subdued quality that acquires its potency in their captions, props, and/or characters' words-within-balloons. His work, which appears regularly in newsmagazines and in over 200 newspapers, including *The New York Times, The Washington Post*, and *USA Today*, has received awards from the National Headliners Club and the Society of Professional Journalists (both in 1986).

A former John S. Knight Journalism Fellow at Stanford University, Mike Keefe was also President of the Association of American Editorial Cartoonists.

P.H.

KEENE, CHARLES (1823-1891) British comic artist born in Hornsey, London, in 1823. Considered by David Low to be "the greatest of the British comic artists" (he made a distinction between caricaturists, cartoonists and comic artists), Charles Keene was "supreme in catching Nature in her humorous moments." Low also considered Keene an artist's artist, appreciated by his peers rather than his public, which was more amused by the often extensive captions beneath the cartoons. These gags were usually supplied to the cartoonist rather than created by him, but

A soft answer, &c. Stout lady passenger (wincing—he had trod on her best corn): "phew!—Clumsy—" Polite old gent: "Very sorry, my dear Madam, but if you had a foot large enough to be seen such an accident couldn't occur!"

Charles Keene, ca. 1880.

his pictures were all his own. Although working in a period when woodblocks were the style, Keene managed a certain fluidity and lightness about his line work. He drew on scraps of paper with slivers of pointed wood dipped into homemade inks of various colors, which made the task of his translators into wood a difficult one.

Keene was educated at a local London boarding school, then at Ipswich Grammar. He was apprenticed to an architect in 1840 and five years later began to contribute topical sketches to the *Illustrated London News.* His humorous drawings began to appear in *Punch* from 1851 and continued in that weekly to 1890. He died in 1891.

Books: *Voyage of the Constance* (1860); *Ewan Harrington* (1860); *Sea Kings and Naval Heroes* (1861); *Eyebright* (1862); *Cambridge Grisette* (1862); *Tracks for Tourists* (1864); *Legends of Number Nip* (1864); *Mrs. Caudle's Curtain Lectures* (1866); *Our People* (1881); *Robert, Diary of a Waiter* (1885); *Life and Letters* (1892); *Work of Charles Keene* (1897); *21 Etchings* (1903); *Pictures by Charles Keene* (1909); *Charles Keene, The Artist's Artist* (1934); *Charles Keene* (1935); *Charles Keene* (1947); and *Drawings by Charles Keene* (1952).

D.G.

KEMBLE, EDWARD WINSOR (1861-1933) American cartoonist and illustrator born in Sacramento, California, on January 18, 1861. E.W. Kemble's father was the founder and publisher of the *Alta Californian* newspaper but moved to New York when his son was young to take a job as an inspector with the Bureau of Indian Affairs. In 1875 young Kemble was enrolled at a boarding school in Philadelphia, then a hotbed of artistic activity (the likes of A.B. Frost, E.A. Abbey and Howard Pyle had made their first connections there). Kemble returned to New York infused with a yearning to draw and took a job with Western Union, peddling sketches on the side.

In 1880 four of Kemble's sketches were bought by Charles Parsons of the Harper's organization, and *Harper's Bazaar* ran Kemble's first cartoons in September and October of that year. Soon his career was in full swing. He became the major (front-page) political cartoonist for the *New York Graphic* while receiving his only formal artistic training at the Art Students League, taking classes alongside Frederick Remington. In 1883 *Life* magazine was founded, and Kemble was a frequent contributor to early issues of this black-and-white weekly. (Kemble, by the way, was to draw more cartoons for *Life* than for any other publication throughout his career.) His lively cartoons, some of the magazine's most mature work, attracted the attention of Mark Twain, who engaged Kemble to illustrate *Huckleberry Finn.* The marriage, of course, was a happy one; the cartoonist's line and the writer's prose were perfectly suited and led to further collaborations.

Kemble was a staff political cartoonist for *Collier's Weekly* (1903-07) and *Harper's Weekly* (1907-12) before returning to *Collier's*, *Leslie's Weekly* and *Judge* in the late 1910s. In his capacity as political analyst he accompanied Colonel George Harvey to Princeton, New Jersey, on the fateful visit that cemented Harvey's support of the somewhat obscure college president Woodrow Wilson for the U.S. presidency. Kemble also drew for *Puck* and the Hearst papers over the years. In the decade between 1896 and

"If I can only manage to skin out and go home without fussing with those other brats, I'll be thankful."

E.W. Kemble.

1905 he drew various Sunday strips and colored panels and was an active advertising artist and book illustrator. In the early and mid-1920s, the last years of his professional life, he returned almost exclusively to the pages of *Life*. Kemble died on September 19, 1933.

For all his fine illustrative and political work, E.W. Kemble is best remembered—and justifiably so—for his specialty, cartoons of the Negro. He is perhaps cartooning's supreme delineator of the Afro-American, and his characterizations were often sympathetic. While his treatments were usually comic, Kemble took care to study the real urban and rural environs and living conditions of blacks. His caricatures were never absurdly exaggerated, although every convention—wild dress, chicken stealing, etc.—was thematically exploited to the fullest. Kemble produced many sensitive, almost photographic portraits of blacks.

It is practically impossible to overestimate the influence and popularity of E.W. Kemble. Like A.B. Frost, his technical cousin, he brought a stunning vitality to cartooning and illustration, and his stylistic imitators—at least those who inherited the freedom and animation of his drawings—were many. Kemble drew with a scratchy, loose pen line that in later years gave way to an economical use of thick emphasis lines. Almost every figure he drew was alive with emotion, tension, anticipation, surprise. Kemble had a photographic gift for arresting action and motion, again like Frost; his cartoons featured characters in midair, writhing, dancing, jumping, running, laughing uproariously. In his illustrations, often sophisticated reportorial assignments on social themes, Kemble employed a classical, attractive crosshatch. Like his talented compatriots Frost, Bush and Taylor, Kemble the cartoonist is woefully neglected today and deserves to be rediscovered as an accomplished observer and penman.

Among the books Kemble illustrated are: *Huckleberry Finn, Pudd'nhead Wilson* and *The Library of Humor* by Mark Twain; *Uncle Tom's Cabin; Knickerbocker's History of New York; On the Plantation; Uncle Remus; Col. Carter of Cartersville; Samantha on the Race Question;* and *Phoenixiana.* His own books include the *Thompson Street Poker Club* anthology for *Life; Blackberries; Kemble's Coons; Rosemary; Virginia Creeper; Billy-Goat and Other Comicalities; Comical Coons; A Coon Alphabet; Coon Calendar; Kemble's Sketchbook; Coontown's 400; A Pickaninny Calendar; The Gold Dust Twins;* and others.

R.M.

KENDRICK, CHARLES (1841-1914) American artist born in London, England, in 1841. Charles Kendrick first achieved prominence as a principal artist on the *Illustrated London News.* Around 1870, when the journal sought to establish a Canadian edition, Kendrick went to Montreal.

In 1871 Kendrick moved to Brooklyn and attached himself to the Leslie publications. His facile pen work appeared occasionally in *Puck* after 1877 and frequently in the heavily illustrated *New York Graphic.* He was a major factor in the early respectability and success of *Life,* to which he contributed regularly for several years, beginning with the second issue (January 11, 1883).

In the 1870s Kendrick's theatrical caricatures were popular, and he continued personality themes in the *Graphic, Chic* (a *Puck* imitation) and *Life,* where he was its first major (and exclusively) political cartoonist. For *Life* throughout 1883 he illustrated the weekly *Biographettes.* He contributed to the *New York Herald* and to the major monthlies and for years taught at his Manhattan studio.

Kendrick was an important and polished pen-and-ink artist when photoengraving was introduced. His style was the illustrator's, but he seldom left the realm of political cartooning or humorous sketching. Realism and a dimensional and evocative method of shading were his trademarks; he influenced many cartoonists and illustrators, among them True Williams, an obvious follower. Kendrick died at his home in Brooklyn after an illness of three months on June 16, 1914.

R.M.

KEPPLER, JOSEPH (1837-1894) American artist and publisher born in Kieligenstadt, Austria, on February 1, 1837. Joseph Keppler's father, probably a descendant of astronomer Johannes Kepler, was a participant in the 1848 political upheavals and was obliged to flee to the United States, settling in Missouri. His family remained in Austria, and young Joseph enrolled in the K.K. Akademie der Bildern Kunste to study art. When a hoped-for scholarship to study in Italy failed to materialize, the impulsive and romantic Keppler joined a theatrical troupe departing for that country.

Keppler became a moderately successful stage performer and, resettling in Vienna, divided his time between acting and drawing (for such papers as *Kikeriki*). Within a year and a half he joined his father in America and pursued the same activities, with the same success. On August 28, 1869, Keppler launched his first publishing venture, a weekly satirical sheet in German called *Die Vehme,* of which he was the principal cartoonist. The magazine was short-lived (ceasing publication on August 20, 1870) but has the distinction of being the first American humorous journal with lithographic cartoons.

The following March Keppler introduced *Puck* magazine, a German-language weekly that aimed for national circulation. Though his cartoon-and-light-text journal lasted only a year and a half, it brought Keppler's work to the attention of publishing entrepreneur Frank Leslie, who invited Keppler to join the staff of his magazines in New York. Keppler excelled at *Leslie's,* produced some outstanding cartoons, made a large circle of acquaintances and nurtured his dream of running his own cartoon magazine.

In September 1876, the New York *Puck* debuted; it was a quarto in German containing front-, back-, and center-page cartoons by Keppler, and it was run by Keppler and Adolph Schwarzmann, late the business manager of the Leslie publications. The new company was persuaded to issue an English-language edition, introduced on March 14, 1877. Color was soon added to the lithographed cartoons (the interior cartoons were reproduced by photoengraving), and slowly *Puck* became a newsstand eye-catcher, a political force and a breeding ground for cartoonists and humorous writers.

In every presidential election thereafter until his death, the brilliant Keppler contributed at least one symbol, one cartoon icon, to political history. He is variously credited with creating the Tattooed Man, Uncle Sam's Whiskers (during his *Leslie's* days), the figure of the Independent New Party and the Grandfather's Hat of Benjamin Harrison. His powerful support for Grover Cleveland gained Keppler additional respect and, incidentally, a lifelong friendship with the new president.

Except during two trips to Europe, Keppler was very active in assuming art assignments and the management of his magazine, which had become one of the most influential of all American journals. He had surpassed Nast as the premier American cartoonist. Shortly after overseeing an impressive display—the erection of the *Puck* Pavilion at the Chicago World's Fair and the issuance of the *World's Fair Puck*—Keppler died, on February 19, 1894.

The influence of Joseph Keppler on American cartooning can hardly be overstated. Granted that he was indebted to Nast and that they were both potent forces in national politics, Keppler's directing a national magazine gave him additional influence, while Nast was often at odds with his own management. Moreover, Keppler tutored a generation of cartoonists and inspired more imitators than Nast ever did. The point would be academic and slightly irrelevant but for the fact that Keppler should be given more credit; his work deserves major republication.

Keppler worked nearly exclusively on stone. His art always retained a German flavor: a reliance on allegory and the avoidance of extreme exaggeration. He frequently alluded to Shakespeare and Wagner, and was content to depict his subjects in a style approximating portraiture, relying on the concept for the ridicule or satirical point. Keppler's fine arts background served him well in composing and executing cartoons, the backgrounds and incidental props of which were flawlessly drawn.

He was a devastating partisan—after 1884 consistently Democratic—and filled his dramatic work with invective, liberal advocacies and succinct political sermons. After 1881, when he was bolstered by enough other cartoonists on *Puck,* he virtually abandoned social satire to concentrate on political subjects. His favorite causes were civil service reform, women's suffrage and Grover Cleveland; among his dislikes were the tariff, radical labor unions, the Catholic church, Prohibition and politicians like Grant, Robeson, Blaine, Logan, Hill and the high-tariff and Tammany Democrats.

R.M.

KEPPLER, UDO J. (1872-1956) American cartoonist, publisher and Indian rights activist born in St. Louis, Missouri, on April 4, 1872. Udo Keppler, who signed his cartoons "Joseph Keppler, Jr." after the death of his father, was educated at the Gymnasium of Heilbronn, Germany, the Columbia Institute of New York and the Academy of Arts in Munich. He began drawing for his father's weekly cartoon magazine, *Puck,* in 1891, signing his little illustrations and black-and-white panel cartoons "U.J.K." Soon, however, he was drawing full spreads in color, and he assumed leadership of the art staff after his father's death in 1894.

Udo J. Keppler, 1908.

For *Puck* he drew some notable cartoons—his talent would have found him a berth on any art staff—but after 1908 his interest seemed to diminish. The cartoons became less detailed and less frequent. In 1914, as majority stockholder in *Puck,* he sold the magazine to the Nathan Strauss interests. "Kep" continued to draw intermittently into the late 1910s, even doing full-page cartoons for *Leslie's* and *Judge*—once his magazine's hated rivals. Much of the reason for his waning interest lay in his awareness of American Indian problems, and he, like cartoonist Will Crawford, devoted much time to Indian history, lore and welfare. (For his concern and informed efforts, Theodore Roosevelt had once offered Keppler the commissionership of the Bureau of Indian Affairs.) Udo Keppler died in 1956.

Keppler the younger composed in broad strokes and with bold concepts. He was as strong an idea man as his father but simplified his own work to a radical degree, for the most part eschewing labels and allegories. He used massive, powerful, muscular, almost classical figures when he could, but he generally let the concept carry the cartoon. He was a strong Democrat, although he refused to support William Jennings Bryan.

R.M.

KEWPIE KORNER, THE (U.S.) An undated daily package panel feature, Rose O'Neill's *Kewpie Korner* was introduced into most subscribing newspapers in December, 1917, on varying dates, at the same time that her companion Sunday page was introduced. The Sunday page, with no regular running title, featured continuity adventures involving the famed elfin cupids that O'Neill had nicknamed "Kewpies" in their first magazine appearance in 1905. On the other hand, the daily feature was initially a one-column, single-panel drawing in which one or sometimes two Kewpies would make a short statement of witty philosophy that was printed beneath the panel. In early 1918, the daily panel was increased to a two-column width and proportionate height, and the Kewpie figures became involved in more elaborate action, although the lower gag line was retained.

Essentially a work of intense visual charm—the Kewpie image was extraordinarily popular as limned by O'Neill and was featured in hundreds of toys, games and other artifacts—*The Kewpie Korner* had no intrinsic merit beyond its cheerful presence on the newspaper page during a grim war, and its captions had no great wit or humor of their own. Now ferociously collected by hundreds of elderly Kewpie addicts around the country (when they can find copies), *The Kewpie Korner* was folded by a bored and war-distracted O'Neill little more than a year after its highly popular introduction, leaving most papers in late December 1918.

B.B.

KEY, THEODORE (1912-) American artist and writer born in Fresno, California, on August 25, 1912. Ted Key graduated in 1933 with a degree in art from the University of California at Berkeley, where he was editorial cartoonist and art editor of the Daily Californian and associate editor of the campus humor magazine, The Pelican. While in college he sold a gag cartoon to Life, and upon graduation he moved to New York; in his first week there he sold cartoons to Judge, the New Yorker and Collier's. In the late 1930s, when he was associate editor of Judge, he sold to all major markets and was possibly the most published gag cartoonist in America for several years.

Key scored a hit with a strong-willed maid character who appeared in his gags for *Collier's, This Week* and the *Saturday Evening Post* in 1943; by autumn of that year the *Post* had contracted for sole rights. Two and a half years as a master sergeant in the Army Signal Corps did not interrupt Key's new success; he submitted roughs and did one finish a week of *Hazel* throughout World War II. After the war Key was offered a position with the J. Walter Thompson Advertising Agency, where he had done some writing previously, but he decided to cartoon full time instead. *Hazel* became a bigger success, leading to a flock of reprint books and movie, radio and stage offers before a five-year TV series was produced, with Shirley Booth in the title role. When the *Post* folded in 1969, Key turned the panel into a daily feature for King Features.

Key has been active in other media. For ten years he did the *Diz and Liz* double-page feature for *Jack and Jill* magazine. He also draws a series of widely used industrial posters and has illustrated books for other authors. He wrote a radio play (*The Clinic,* on NBC, which was collected in *Best Broadcasts of 1939-40*) and three screenplays for Disney (*Million Dollar Duck,* starring Dean Jones and Sandy Duncan; *Gus,* starring Ed Asner, Don Knotts, Tim Conway, Tom Bosley and the L.A. Rams; *The Cat from Outer Space,* starring McLean Stevenson, Sandy Duncan, Ken Berry, Hans Conried and Henry Morgan). *Million Dollar Duck* and *Gus* were adapted into serialized comic strips in King Features' *Disney Treasury of Family Classics.* In addition to 11 *Hazel* anthologies, the amazingly prolific Key has produced *Phyllis* (a classic among children's books), *So'm I, Fasten Your Seat Belts, The Biggest Dog in the World* (a movie version of which has appeared in Britain), *Diz and Liz* and *Squirrels in the Feeding Station.* Still distributed by King Features, the panel about "the lovable live-in maid" (as the syndicate calls her) is still going strong after more than a half-century.

Key's productivity speaks for itself. Recently his gag production has received an assist from his son Peter, who also writes for other cartoonists. His drawing style reveals a breezy brushstroke, with details expertly reduced to the minimum. Characterization and facial attitudes are the strongest elements of his work. His books and some magazine work reveal an attractive use of color. Key's brother-in-law, incidentally, is cartoonist Fritz Wilkinson.

R.M.

Theodore Key. © This Week.

KHITRUK, FYODOR (1917-) Animator born in Moscow on May 1, 1917. Fyodor Khitruk joined Soyuzmult'film, the giant Soviet animation studio, in 1938 as an animator. After being drafted into the Soviet army during World War II, he returned to animation in 1947. For some fifteen years Khitruk was content merely to work as an animator on other directors' films (notably Lev Atamanov's and Ivanov-Vano's). In 1962 he finally came out with a work of his own, *Story of a Crime,* an acidulous fable with undertones of social criticism that went unnoticed in the Soviet Union. This was followed by the mischievous *Toptychka* ("Teddy Bear," 1964) and the enchanting *The Lion's Holiday* (1965). Khitruk scored again with *Othello 67* (1967) and especially with *Film, Film, Film* (1968), a very amusing satire on filmmakers and filmmaking.

In 1970 Khitruk went to East Germany to direct, in collaboration with Katia and Klaus Georgi, a German-Russian co-production. Titled *A Young Man Named Engels,*

Fyodor Khitruk, "Film Film Film."

it was a 20-minute cartoon based on the drawings of Marxist theoretician (and would-be cartoonist) Friedrich Engels. In recent years Khitruk seems to have abandoned his earlier, more optimistic attitude in favor of a somber, almost despairing outlook, as evidenced in *The Island* (1973), which concludes on a note of utter alienation. His last film was *The Lion and the Bull* (1983), an anti-war fable. He retired shortly thereafter.

Khitruk is unquestionably the most exciting of the contemporary Soviet animators. His works have been widely shown and honored around the world, notably at the Zagreb and Mamaia festivals.

M.H.

KHODATAEV, NIKOLAY (1892-1979) Painter and animator born in Russia on May 9, 1892. Nikolay Khodataev graduated from the Moscow Institute of Painting in 1917. After working in posters and oils, he joined the first Soviet studio of animation in 1924. His best-known film cartoon, *Mezhplanetnaia Revolutsiia* ("Interplanetary Revolution"), was produced the next year. A spoof of Yakov Protazanov's 1924 science fiction film *Aelita*, it was also an incredible feat of animation, depicting all kinds of space vehicles and futuristic weapons years ahead of *Buck Rogers*. Khodataev effectively directed the film, though the credits list him only as an animator, along with Yuri Merkulov and Zenon Komissarenko. In 1925 he also made *China in Flames*.

In the late 1920s Khodataev worked mainly with his sister Olga (*The Ten Rules of Cooperation* and *The Embezzlement*, both done in 1928) and with the Brumbergs (notably on *The Young Samoyed* in 1928). He also experimented with mixing live action and animation in such works as *The Terrible Vavila* and *Auntie Trova*. His solo efforts include *The Happy North* and *Eureka* (both 1930), *The Crocodile in Geneva* (a satire on the League of Nations, 1932), *The Music Box* (a satire on czarist militarism, 1933), *The Career of Fyalkin* and *Organchik* (both 1935). In 1935 Khodataev left animation for painting, although he is reported by Western sources to have made one more cartoon, the 1938 *Little Muck*. He died in Moscow on December 27, 1979.

Khodataev's sister, Olga Khodataeva (1894-1968), was also a distinguished animator. In addition to the films she made with her brother, her directorial credits include *Happy Life* (1932, with the Brumbergs), *Return of the Sun* (1937), *The Boy with the Stick* (1938), *The Clouded Sun* (1943, with Ivanov-Vano), *A Song about Chapaev* (1944, with Pyotr Nosov), *Tale of the Old Bludgeon* (1949), *The Miracle Mill* (1950), *Tale of the Taiga* (1951), and two cartoons co-directed by Leonid Aristov, *The Brave Little Deer* (1957), which received an award at the Edinburgh Festival, and *The Little Golden Feathers* (1960).

M.H.

KIJOWICZ, MIROSLAW (1929-   ) Polish animator born in Leningrad, the Soviet Union, in 1929. Miroslaw Kijowicz graduated from Warsaw University in 1955 and from the Warsaw Academy of Fine Arts in 1961. After making several amateur and experimental films, he joined the Bielsko-Biala animation studio in 1960, directing his first short, *Arlekin*, that same year. Then, in rapid succession, came *The Story of a Dragon* (1962), *The Town* (1963), *Cabaret* and *Portraits* (1964), *The Smile* and *The Flag* (1965); the last is regarded as one of Kijowicz's best works.

In 1966 Kijowicz took a job with the newly formed Miniatur Film Studios; *Rondo* and *Cages* were the first cartoons he produced there. In 1967 he followed with *Laterna Magica* ("The Magic Lantern"), an utterly charming little fable poking gentle fun at universal human weaknesses. *Miniatures* and *The Blue Ball*, both made in 1968, were further explorations of the familiar and commonplace. Kijowicz later became more ambitious with such projects as *Panopticum* (1969), *Science Fiction* and *Variations* (both 1970) and *Pandora* (1973), but he occasionally returned to his earlier, lighter style, as in the 1969 version of *Arlekin* and the 1972 *Magnolia*. His recent efforts have been a mixed bag that includes such works as *Welder, The Hand, Manhattan* and *The Inspection*. Even more recently he has realized *A-B* (a study in authoritarianism, 1979) and *On the Train* (a study in conformity, 1984). Little has been heard from him in the 1990s.

Kijowicz has won a number of awards in Poland and elsewhere. His most familiar trademark is the lighthearted

Nikolay Khodataev, "Mezhplanetnaia Revolutsia."

satire that has characterized his more successful films. He himself has described his cartoons as "short aphoristic films addressed to mental activity."

M.H.

KILVERT, B.S. CORY (1879-1946) American cartoonist and illustrator born in Hamilton, Ontario, Canada, on April 14, 1879. The son of Francis Edwin Kilvert, member of Parliament, B. Cory Kilvert moved to New York in 1900 to study at the Art Students League. He soon became a regular contributor to *Life,* where he drew one of the most popular cartoons in that magazine's history—"Hers," a depiction of a young country boy pining over a pair of little girl's panties hanging on a washline. It originally appeared as a cover and was reissued for many years afterwards as a print. Kilvert continued to draw for *Life* into the 1920s, was a staff artist for the *New York World* and illustrated many children's books. He died on March 29, 1946.

Although Kilvert often drew with a scratchy, busy pen line, it was exactly the opposite style—flat, heavily outlined, open-spaced—that made his career. It produced a striking posterlike result with broad areas of pastel color and could be described as the technique of Edward Penfield translated to cartoons. In Kilvert's hands, it was employed to good effect.

R.M.

KING OF THE HILL (U.S.) The unusually perceptive satire of a caricature of lower middle-class Texas culture, *King of the Hill* is cartoonist Mike Judge's latest animated sitcom. Co-created with *Simpsons* writer Glen Daniels, it debuted on the Fox network in January of 1997. Set in the fictious town of Arlen, Texas, the program is cast with bubba types who are really into their power tools. Patriarch Hank Hill is an earnest and straightforward father and proud propane salesman, an articulate everyman who can't seem to loosen up. Equally monotone and narrowly honed is his wife Peg, a substitute teacher at portly son Bobby's middle school. Sheltered and generally obedient, the impressionable boy's awkward interface with his more progressive environment is initiative for much of the subtle comedy and modern charm. Niece Luanne rounds out the immediate family; a wannabe-free spirit and student of the local beauty academy, with an unruly mother that has been incarcerated.

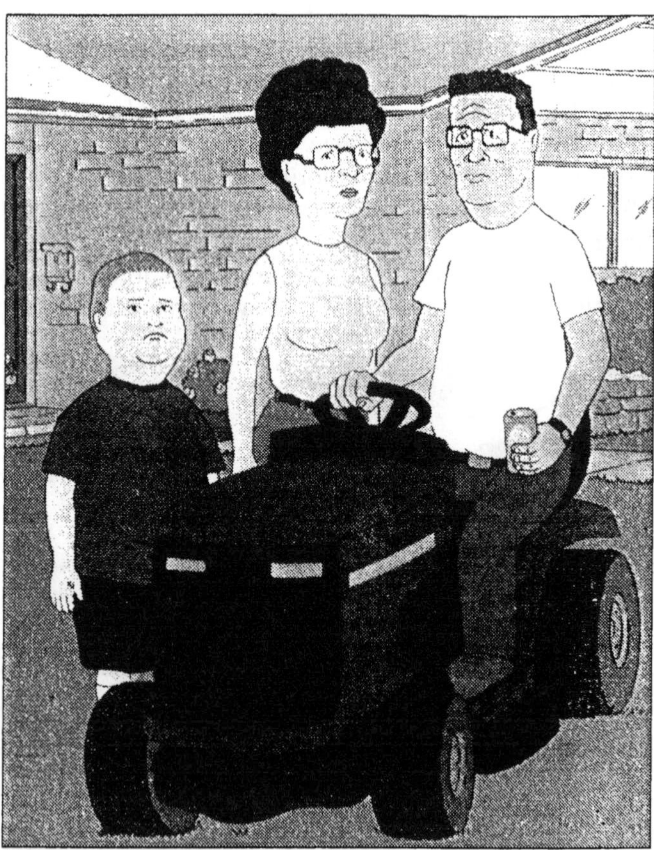

"King of the Hill." © Fox Network.

The neighborhood provides unique, somewhat affable sidekicks Bill, a sympathetic divorced laborer, Dale, an exterminator fixated on cars and conspiracy theories and the undeciperhable mumbler Boomhauer, voiced by Judge himself. The languid pace and dim-witted milieu thus created provide a comfortable framework, allowing the audience a familiarity with the players and their not-so contrived situations. Brilliantly dry in its no-nonsense delivery, the crew at Judgemental Films have added a notably fresh new family to television's redefined culture. We can expect a length run of the sardonically skewered vision of low-rent suburbia nad prevailing family consciousness in their world of tract homes and monster truck shows.

B.J.

KINOSHITA, RENZO (1936-1997) Japanese animator born in Osaka, Japan, on September 3, 1936. As a young boy in the early postwar period, Renzo Kinoshita was an avid fan of the comic books then popular, such as those created by Osamu Tezuka and Fukujiro Yokoi. Graduating from high school in 1956 (after majoring in electronics), Kinoshita became increasingly interested in animation and was particularly impressed by Walt Disney's *Fantasia.* In 1958 he joined a commercial film production company called Ikko, in Osaka, and became a protégé of Tsunoyama Kimura, himself a former disciple of the famous Kenzo Masaoka. Kimura's influence was a determining factor in Kinoshita's decision to pursue a career in animation.

Kinoshita worked on the front line of animation in Japan; one of his strengths was the experience he had gained by working both independently and for a broad range of production companies. He first began working independently in 1963 as Puppe Productions, primarily subcontracting for television commercials. At the request of Tokyo Movie he worked on such TV hits as *Obake no Q Tarō,* and in 1966, on invitation from Osamu Tezuka's Mushi Productions, he moved to Tokyo, where he participated in the creation of such classics as *Tetsuwan Atom* ("Astro Boy"). In 1968 Kinoshita finally left Mushi Productions and two years later created his own company, Lotus Studio, which is supported mainly by the production of television commercials but also collaborates on animated television series and produces independent shorts. Kinoshita's wife, Sayoko, whom he met while working at Mushi Productions, is an artist in her own right and assists in productions.

Kinoshita was extremely prolific and had garnered many awards in Japan and internationally for his animated television commercials, animated series and independent works. Among his most outstanding achievements in animation for television are *Subarashi Sekai Ryoko* ("Wonderful World Journey") for NTV in 1967; *Geba Geba 90 Pun,* a 90-minute comedy with animation spliced into live-action shots; and *Curricula Machine,* a 1976 Japanese version of *Sesame Street.* It was with his independent, experimental productions, however, that Kinoshita and Lotus Studio have made a lasting name for themselves internationally. *Made in Japan,* a short parodying the commercialism of Japan, won the Grand Prix award in the 1972 USA International Animation Festival, and in 1977 *Japonese,* another film satirizing modern Japan, won the honorary prize at the international film festival in Leipzig, East Germany. Most recently, Kinoshita completed *Pika Don* (1979), perhaps the first attempt to deal with the sensitive subject of Hiroshima in a medium such as animation. *Pika Don* is a nine-minute color short that Kinoshita conceived after viewing paintings drawn by survivors of the explosion in Hiroshima. The experience moved Kinoshita to create a film that would not only appeal to the world but could also be used as an educational tool to further the cause of peace.

Through his versatility and breadth of perspective, Renzo Kinoshita established himself as one of the more talented animators in Japan. However, as is often the case, his most imaginative creations have at times received more acclaim internationally than at home. The challenge confronting Kinoshita, as well as other artists, was to achieve international appeal without alienating the Japanese audience. After 1985, Kinoshita worked hard as an executive of ASIFA to introduce foreign experimental animation into Japan and to introduce Japanese animation overseas. He was responsible for the establishment of the ASIFA-authorized International Animation Festival held in Hiroshima. He passed away in January, 1997.

F.S.

KIRBY, ROLLIN (1875-1952) American cartoonist and three-time recipient of the Pulitzer Prize, born in Galva, Illinois, on September 4, 1875. Around the turn of the century Rollin Kirby traveled to Philadelphia and New York to work as a freelance illustrator. During the next ten years his work appeared frequently in the pages of *Collier's, McClure's, Harper's* and the *American Magazine;* cartoons ran in *Life* starting around 1909. In this early period his style closely resembled those of his very good friend John Sloan and other nascent Ash-can artists like Everett Shinn and William Glackens. Other lifelong friendships formed by Kirby in New York at that time were with humorists Don Marquis and Franklin P. Adams.

In 1911 Kirby secured a job as editorial cartoonist through Adams with the latter's paper, the *New York Mail.* In 1913 he switched to the *New York Sun,* only to be fired in a dispute a couple of weeks later. But another newspaper dispute across Park Row—as Charles Macauley left the *New York World*—provided an opening for Kirby.

It was with the *World* that Kirby was to become one of the most influential and republished of American editorial cartoonists. He adopted a gentle crayon style that contrasted with his devastating and withering advocacies and attacks. His background as an illustrator served his style well, as its refined appearance never tilted toward caricature but relied on virtual portraiture—his concepts did all the ridiculing. Anatomy was correct in all his work. Kirby used a pencil rather than brush or pen for his outlining, and the careful engraving that was standard for his day captured all the details in reproduction. It is doubtful that today's offset mills could do his originals justice.

"Has anybody seen an elephant?"

Rollin Kirby, 1930. © New York World.

Kirby's most famous contribution to cartoon iconography was Mr. Dry, a figure representing Prohibition (and, generously, all the other "anti" crusades of the 1920s) which bore an almost exact resemblance to a figure employed for the same function by Joseph Keppler in *Puck* a generation earlier. The character was clad in a dour frock coat and tall, black hat. He reminded one of a mortician, and some other cartoonists who borrowed the figure strapped a black armband on him.

The cartoonist's glory days were on the *New York World* in the 1920s; he won three Pulitzer Prizes in the decade and his policies happily coincided with those of the liberal journal. What many newspapermen have called the greatest staff in American journalism was jolted by the sale of the *World* in 1931; Kirby remained, unhappy and uneasy, with the new *World-Telegram* and *Sun* until a dispute with Scripps-Howard in 1939 caused him to switch over to the *New York Post,* a liberal bastion. In 1942 he semi-retired to do occasional work for the *New York Times Magazine* and for *Look* magazine.

Kirby published two anthologies of his works, *Highlights: A Cartoon History of the 1920s* (1931) and *Political Cartoons: 1930-1942* (1942). He frequently wrote and published verse and magazine articles and penned a pair of one-act comedies, *Spin of the Wheel* (1937) and *As the Limb Is Bent (1938).* Kirby, a scholar of his craft, wrote the entry on cartoons for the 14th edition of the *Encyclopedia Britannica.* He died on May 10, 1952.

R.M.

KITTELSEN, THEODOR (1857-1914) Norwegian artist born in Oslo, Norway, on April 23, 1857. Theodor Kittelsen was an artist whose drawings of trolls are legendary in Scandinavia. As an illustrator of Norwegian folktales, he found a style completely his own. His trolls, living in the woods and rambling in the rocky Norwegian mountains, almost seemed to resemble the richly varied gods from mythology. In his animal illustrations (especially in the series *Do Animals Have a Soul?*) he seemed to be a forerunner of Walt Disney; his insects and frogs seemed to become everyday people one could meet on street corners, in buses and shops. One almost looked for their antennae or webbed feet.

Another of Kittelsen's specialties was satirical drawing for dailies that weren't afraid to express an opinion. In his childlike way he made these drawings into great human poems where the grotesque was natural. Many consider him to be Norway's greatest graphic artist.

J.S.

KLEIN, ISIDORE (1897-1986) American cartoonist and animator born in Newark, New Jersey, on October 12, 1897. Isidore Klein got interested in art during his high school days in Newark and later attended the National Academy of Design in New York. He started his animation career in 1918, working at Hearst's International Film Service on such series as *The Katzenjammer Kids* and *Krazy Kat.* When IFS closed down a few months later, Klein joined the Mutt and Jeff Studio, writing and animating a number of *Mutt and Jeff* shorts.

Isidore Klein, "Tick Tock." © Klein.

In 1925 Klein strayed from the animation field and freelanced cartoons to all major American publications, including the *Saturday Evening Post, Collier's, Judge* and the fledgling *New Yorker.* When animated cartoons began to talk, Klein decided it was time to return to the fold, and in 1934 he went to work with Amédée Van Beuren. Moving to Hollywood the following year, he joined Charles Mintz and worked on the *Scrappy* and *Barney Google* series. In 1936, like so many other animators, he went over to the Disney studio, where he animated and wrote stories for such short subjects as *Wynken, Blynken and Nod* and *Woodland Café.* Klein came back to New York in 1939 and joined Terrytoons, working on *Farmer Al Falfa* and later *Mighty Mouse.* From there he went to Famous Studios/Paramount in the late 1940s, and his handiwork can be seen in a number of *Casper* and *Little Lulu* cartoons.

In the 1960s Klein resumed his freelance activities, doing animation for television, producing commercials and directing animated shorts (one of these, *Tick Tock,* won a special citation at the 1967 Montreal Exposition). He retired in the 1970's, but continued to write, often cogently, about animation, sharing his reminiscences of the field's pioneer days with the readers of specialized magazines. Early in the 1980's he moved into a nursing home in New York City, where he died on January 30, 1986.

M.H.

KLEY, HEINRICH (1863-1945) German cartoonist and painter born in Karlsruhe, Baden, on April 15, 1863. Possessor of a dazzling pen technique and unbounded visual imagination, Heinrich Kley was perhaps the most successful of the many draftsmen who have humanized animals or created animal-human hybrids. His purely human figure studies, with their strongly erotic emphasis, are also breathtaking. Moreover, none of this is harmless fun, but biting social satire. And when some of his cartoons, such as those done for *Simplicissimus* from 1908 to 1919, are viewed in the light of contemporary events, they prove to be scathing political statements as well.

Much has been made of the dichotomy in Kley's output; his style as a painter was quite different. He studied at the Karlsruhe Academy from 1880 to 1885, and for a brief time in Munich. In the late 1880s, back in Karlsruhe, he did some illustration but soon became a painter of genre scenes, interiors, portraits and still lifes. In 1893 he completed a series of murals in the Baden-Baden post office. Around the turn of the century he began to specialize in paintings of industrial subjects and was hailed for his canvas *Crucible Smelting at the Krupp Steelworks.* He also did architectural views. It was his move to Munich in 1908 that seems to have released the cartoonist within him, for he was soon supplying the two great local magazines, *Simplicissimus* and *Jugend,* with his remarkable pen drawings, which were gradually anthologized in the albums *Skizzenbuch I* (1909), *Skizzenbuch II* (1910), *Leut' und Viecher* ("People and Animals," *1912)* and *Sammel-Album* ("Omnibus Album," 1923).

Yet an interesting catalogue of an exhibition at a Viennese art gallery in March 1912 (preserved in the New

Heinrich Kley, "Tango," 1914.

York Public Library) demonstrates that there was no definitive break in Kley's production, and that the painter-cartoonist split was not schizophrenic, since that exhibition (shared with two other artists) included a large number of landscapes and scenic watercolors alongside a generous helping of his satirical pen works.

Kley also illustrated several books by authors both ancient and modern. The date of his death in Munich has been called into doubt but is generally given as February 8, 1945.

S.A.

KLIBAN, BERNARD (1935-1990) American cartoonist born January 1, 1935, in Norwalk, Connecticut. Bernard ("Hap") Kliban studied art at Pratt Institute in Brooklyn and Cooper Union in Manhattan, but didn't graduate from either institution. He worked for a time as a mailman, but contributed a few cartoons to some local publications. He moved to the San Francisco Bay area in 1959 and supported himself by doing various jobs before hooking up with *Playboy* in 1974, when his cartoon career took off in earnest.

His association with *Playboy* led to B. Kliban (as he signed his work) getting his first cartoon book, *Cat*, published in 1975. The work proved an instant hit, sold over 800,000 copies, and eventually gave rise to a fifty million dollar industry. Kliban's cats appeared on coffee mugs, calendars, T-shirts, beach towels, greeting cards, tea pots, and every other appurtenance known to man and beast. This unprecedented bonanza also brought out a host of copycats (pun intended) who rushed out to produce their own cartoon cat books (most of them failed). Queried in 1977 about the clamoring success of his book, the author replied, "I find it amazing to be making money at what I like doing... So much success is just perseverance."

Defining cats as "one hell of a nice animal, frequently mistaken for a meat loaf," Kliban went on to spin humorous tales of feline mischief and mystery in cartoons that were as hilarious as they were perplexing. One drawing showed a minstrel cat twanging a guitar and singing this ditty: "Love to eat them mousies. Mousies what I love to eat. Bite their little heads off... Nibble on their tiny feet." On the other hand a cook flapping a cat in his frying pan went on like this: "My cat is fat/ so now I'll dine/ and eat all up/ that cat of mine." There were cats in basketball shoes, cats in polo gear, felonious cats being paw-printed, even a "Cat in Fat Hat on Mat," along with tongue-in-cheek lessons on "how to draw a cat" (or "quat," as was the cartoonist's favored spelling).

More cartoon books followed, all sporting outlandish titles and all of them bestsellers, such as *Never Eat Anything Bigger than Your Head* (1976), *Whack Your Porcupine* (1977), *Two Guys Fooling Around with the Moon* (1982), and *Luminous Animals* (1983). In those there were drawings about animals other than cats (porcupines came in a close second) and even about humans. In one of the latter a farmer came home and found his wife in bed with a porker, exclaiming in disgust, "Not *that* pig!" Kliban particularly delighted in skewering all the self-appointed sages proliferating under the California sun. To a truth-seeker who had trekked all the way to his mountaintop, a guru offered this terse advice, "Grow in accordance with your inner directives, asshole," while a Zen master instructed his disciples this way, "The road to enlightenment is long and difficult, which is why I asked you to bring sandwiches and a change of clothing."

Bernard Kliban, self-caricature.

After his death in a San Francisco hospital on August 12, 1990, following heart surgery, Kliban was eulogized in *Time* magazine as an "ailurophilic art-school dropout." He has remained a strong presence in the field. All his books are kept in print, and a new anthology of his cartoons, *CatDreams*, was published in 1997.

M.H.

KLIXTO
See Cordeiro, Calisto.

KNIGHT, BENJAMIN THACKSTON (1895-1977) American cartoonist born in Dillsboro, North Carolina, on April 4, 1895. Benjamin ("Tack") Knight's first cartoon was published in the local *Waynesville Enterprise* when he was 14. In 1913 he moved to San Francisco and studied art at the Mark Hopkins Institute; the next year he became sports cartoonist for the *Oakland Tribune*, an activity interrupted by service in the navy during World War I. After the war Knight began his intermittent lifelong career as a teacher of cartooning (as newcomers to the field often did in the 1910s and 1920s). He published *Tack's Cartoon Tips* in 1923, and for years he operated a correspondence school. He also ghosted for Gene Byrnes on the *Reg'lar Fellers* comic strip (his style was virtually indistinguishable from Byrnes's) before relinquishing those duties to G. Burr Inwood and creating his own strips.

Knight drew *My Big Brudder* and *Peaches* for the very earliest Dell comic book formats in the early 1930s, and *Little Folks* with top-strip *Baby Sister* for the Chicago Tribune Syndicate shortly thereafter. He introduced two kid strips at the same time, and after a poll of readers Knight's strips were retained at the expense of Tom McNamara's *Teddy, Jack and Mary*. Knight also dabbled in animation at the Disney story department in 1935 and at Fleischer in 1939-40. In 1974 he won the Silver T-Square award from the National Cartoonists Society and the Good Guy award from the Northern California Cartoon and Humor Association, on whose advisory board he served. Tack Knight died in San Francisco in 1977.

Knight's style, as noted, was a virtual carbon copy of Gene Byrnes's. He likewise specialized in the kid cartoon and had a flair for capturing the happiness, playfulness, innocent scheming and inquiring confusion of children. His drawings, like object lessons from his cartooning course, were always lively and full of animation.

R.M.

KNOTT, JOHN FRANCIS (1878-1963) American cartoonist born in Austria on December 7, 1878. John Knott studied at the Holmes School of Illustration in Chicago and at the Royal Academy of Art in Munich. In 1905 he secured a position with the *Dallas* (Tex.) *News* as editorial cartoonist. His cartoons were simple, uncluttered affairs with spotted shading areas, some rendered in crayon, others in brush. In 1936 he received an honorary mention from the Pulitzer Prize committee and in 1939 the National Headliners Club award. He died on February 16, 1963, in Dallas.

John Knott is often confused by researchers with Jean Knott, Hearst cartoonist of the 1920s who drew the panel *Penny Ante* in the style of Thomas Aloysius Dorgan ("Tad").

R.M.

KÖHLER, HANNS ERICH (1905-1983) German cartoonist and printmaker born in Tetschen, Sudetenland (now Děčín, Czechoslovakia), on April 17, 1905. Hanns Köhler studied at the Applied Art schools in Dresden and Vienna and at the Vienna Graphische Lehr und Versuchsanstalt. He began drawing political cartoons in 1935, and from 1942 to 1945 he directed the professional class in illustration and commercial art at the then-existing German school of fine arts in Prague. Since the end of World War II, his excellent political (and social) cartoons have appeared in a host of German newspapers and magazines: the *Deutsche Zeitung* in Cologne and Stuttgart, the *Nürnberger Nachrichten* in Nuremberg, the *Kölner Stadt-Anzeiger* in Cologne, the *Frankfurter Allgemeine Zeitung, Die Zeit* in Hamburg and the reincarnation of *Simplicissimus* in Munich.

Köhler's work has been reprinted in numerous anthologies of German political cartoons, such as the two anti-Adenauer omnibus volumes *Konrad Sprach die Frau Mama* ("'Konrad,' Said Mother," 1955) and *Konrad Bleibst du Jetzt zu Haus?* ("Konrad, Are You Going to Stay Home Now?," 1963, cover drawing by Köhler). He has also been represented by albums of his own. The 1959 volume *Wer Hätte Das von Uns Gedacht?* ("Who Would Have Thought That of Us?"), published on the occasion of the tenth anniversary of the German Federal Republic, contained a large selection from the two thousand drawings Köhler had done during that ten-year period. The 1969 book *Nun Lacht Mal Schön* ("Smile, Please") covered the first twenty years of the Bundesrepublik Deutschland and included a number of items that had already appeared in the 1959 volume.

In his work Köhler has cried out against militarism and rearmament, the division of Germany, the opportunistic nature of German political leadership (in his interpretation), the weakness of the UN as a peacekeeping force, the emergence of neo-Nazis in Germany and the vulgarity of everyday life and thought at home and abroad.

Köhler has also done book illustration: for example, an edition of *Don Quixote* in 1952. His home is in Herrsching, on the Ammersee in Bavaria. He died at his home on November 7, 1983. That same year the last of the books he had written and illustrated was published.

S.A.

KOLAR, BORIS (1933-) Yugoslav cartoonist and animator born in Zagreb, Croatia, Yugoslavia, in 1933. Boris Kolar exhibited a fondness for caricature from his earliest years. After his high school studies he became a cartoonist for the humor magazine *Kerempuh*. His first encounter with animation came in 1955, when he started working for advertising film cartoons. From 1956 to 1960 he worked variously as an animator, background designer and chief designer for Vukotić, Kostelac and Ranitovic (among the

Boris Kolar, "The Monster and You." © Zagreb Film.

cartoons he animated, mention should be made of the celebrated *Concerto for Submachine Gun*).

Kolar's work as a director has included *The Boy and the Ball* (1960), *Boomerang* (1962), *Woof-Woof* (1964), *Discoverer* (1967) and *Dialogue* (1968). Kolar has also directed several cartoons in the *Inspector Mask* and *Profesor Balthasar* series. For the National Film Board of Canada he produced *Specialists* (1969), and in 1964 he made *The Monster and You* for the World Health Organization. Kolar's most notable effort in recent years, *Utopia* (1974), is the story of a meek little man slowly being crowded out and crushed by the material objects surrounding him—a brilliant parable of modern life and paranoia.

A typical representative of the "Zagreb school," Boris Kolar is noted for his wit and invention. His cartoons have been awarded prizes in festivals around the world.

M.H.

KONDO, HIDEZO (1908-1979) Japanese political cartoonist born in Nagano Prefecture, Japan, on February 15, 1908. Hidezo Kondo is one of the elder statesmen of Japanese cartooning, and his career parallels the various transitions and developments in the field. He has a reputation as one of the foremost political cartoonists in Japan, particularly in the field of caricature.

Kondo began as a cartoonist with the *Third Tokyo Puck*, a humor and cartoon magazine edited by Kenichiro Shimada. Shimada was a high-spirited social critic whose outspokenness no doubt had great influence on Kondo's growth as a political cartoonist. In the late 1920s, Kondo actively produced a number of single-panel political cartoons, many in the proletarian genre, that criticized the Japanese government's treatment of labor unions. Later, Kondo became involved in another form of Japanese cartoon art called *nansensu manga* ("nonsense cartoons"), which had grown out of the "new art movement" inspired by Dadaism and the artistic and political experimentation of the early 1920s. Kondo joined the production staff of *Manga Man* ("Cartoon Man") in September 1929 and produced a number of artistic cartoons in the *ero* ("erotic") and *guro* ("grotesque") styles of the nonsense genre. This innovative publication introduced some American cartoons and comics and also included pages done in full color. The magazine was short-lived, however, because the government closed it down for political reasons in 1931.

In an attempt to fight the pervasive conservatism of the cartoon world in Japan and gain exposure for lesser-known cartoonists, Kondo, along with 17 other young artists, formed the Shin Mangaha Shudan ("New Cartoonists' Group") in 1932. They had some success in placing new cartoons in newspapers and magazines that had formerly printed only "ready-made" cartoons of the most conservative kinds, but the growth of militarism and the resultant censorship dashed any hope of maintaining an artistically free cartoon organization.

In 1938 Kondo made his first concession to the demands of the military government and began producing propaganda cartoons for the publication *Manga Jōhō* ("Cartoon Report"). In 1939, the Shin Mangaha Shudan became the Shin Nippon Mangaka Kyokai ("New Japan Cartoonists' Association") and began producing *Manga* ("Cartoon"), a wartime propaganda magazine. In it, Kondo drew his most memorable political cartoons, most famous among them the color cover portraits of the "evil demons" Churchill, Roosevelt and Stalin. At times, Kondo painted their faces green to give them an appropriately ghoulish appearance, and a particularly effective touch was the addition of fangs to the portraits of these Allied leaders. Kondo was eventually sent to Borneo, where he spent the rest of the war as a military correspondent and drew more propaganda cartoons for distribution on the battlefront.

After the end of the war, Kondo drew political cartoons for *Van* (1946) and created many one-panel cartoons depicting the severity of postwar life in the black markets and bombed-out cities. In 1948 he revived *Manga* and did the cover drawings for each issue; as during the war, these were portraits of political leaders—minus the fangs this time. In 1951 Kondo covered the San Francisco Peace Conference for the *Yomiuri News*, and he was a poilitical artist for the Yomiuri firm until his death on March 23, 1979.

J.C.

KOREN, EDWARD B. (1935-) American cartoonist born in New York City on December 13, 1935. Ed Koren received his B.A. from Columbia College in 1957 and went on to study art under S.W. Hayter at Atelier 17 in Paris. Upon his return to New York, he enrolled at the Pratt Institute, receiving a master's degree in 1964. Since entering the highly competitive field of illustration and cartooning, he has developed a graphic style that has earned him serious consideration as an artist of wit and originality. Reviewing the *New Yorker*'s 50th anniversary cartoon album in 1975, *New York Times* art critic Hilton Kramer found in Koren's work a quality that promises to rank him, alone among the newer contributors, with Steinberg and Thurber.

Like the most inventive of his fellow cartoonists, Koren must be considered from the point of view not only of style but also of substance; he has forged a highly personalized mode of representation that he uses to convey his special brand of humor. His pen-and-ink drawings are almost stubborn in their unwillingness to display a fine, unbroken line. (Calvin Trillin, in fact, quotes a *New Yorker* colleague as likening Koren's work to a barbershop floor just before closing time.) The vaguely or overtly reptilian cast of his woolly characters may be inexplicable but somehow does not strike one as inappropriate. Koren has obviously seen something in his fellow man that most of us only sense and incorporated that perception into his work.

Koren's humor finds inspiration along a broad spectrum, from the topical (dropouts, Spock-saturated parents, hip intellectuals) to the lunatic (smooth-talking bulls, pistol-packing carrots and indeterminate crocodilian creatures). Those familiar with the Upper West Side academic scene in New York in the 1960s will find his renderings of it especially amusing (hip critics speaking of graffiti-spattered busses in highly technical "art-ese" and pronouncing them master-works, or a cocktail party guest announcing, "I used to be a management consultant but now I'm into making up songs and poems"). But alongside this socially acute cartoonist is also a Koren who can send all the animals boarding the ark through a metal detector or have a pet-store owner go out of business by simply throwing open the door of his shop and standing aside, smiling as the liberated birds and beasts stream happily into the street.

In the light of his relative youth, the extent of Koren's recognition as a force in the world of graphic art is impressive. His work can be found in the permanent collections of the Fogg Art Museum in Cambridge, the Rhode Island School of Design, Princeton University Museum, the U.S. Information Agency and the Swann Collection of Cartoons and Caricatures. Exhibitions of his art have been mounted for the Exposition Dessins d'Humeur at Avignon, France (1973), the Biennial Illustration Exposition at Bratislava, Czechoslovakia (1973), the Art from the *New York Times* show organized by the New York Society of Illustrators (1975) and the Terry Dinfass Gallery (1975-77). Koren received a Guggenheim Fellowship in 1970-71, a third prize at the Bratislava competition, designation by the *New York Times* as one of the ten best children's book illustrators of 1973 and the Prix d'Humeur at the Avignon Exposition. He is a member of the Authors' Guild, the Society of American Graphic Artists and the Cartoonists' Guild. He has published collections of his work under the titles *The People Maybe* (1974), *Do You Want to Talk About It?* (1977) and *Dragons Hate to Be Discrete* (1978). Some of his more recent cartoon books have been *Well, There's Your Problem* (1980), *Small Ensembles*(1983), *What About Me?* (1990), and *Quality Time* (1993).

R.C.

KRAZY KAT (U.S.) George Herriman's immortal creation has been a perennial of the animated film, appearing in no fewer than five separate series from the 1910s to the 1960s.

The first series was initiated by Hearst's International Film Service in 1916. Gregory La Cava was in charge of production, and Herriman himself supervised the proceedings. Despite all this attention, Krazy Kat, Ignatz Mouse and the other denizens of Coconino County failed to achieve popular success, and the series (which consisted of one-minute shorts usually running at the end of Hearst's weekly newsreels) was discontinued in 1917.

"Krazy Kat." © International Film Service.

The J.R. Bray studios then took over the title and produced a series of cartoon films that rank as the best and the most faithful to the style and spirit of Herriman's *Krazy Kat*. Begun in 1919, they lasted into the early 1920s.

Bill Nolan, who along with Bert Green, Frank Moser and Leon Searl had directed the first *Krazy Kat*, now produced a fresh batch of *Krazy Kat* cartoons from 1926 to 1928 for the Winkler Picture Corporation. Nolan's Kat bore no resemblance to its comic strip counterpart, except in name.

In the 1930s *Krazy Kat* was again adapted to animation, this time by Charles Mintz for Columbia (1936-39). Bill Nolan was one of the directors, but it was an exercise in mediocrity.

King Features Syndicate directly produced a new series of cartoons featuring Krazy Kat in 1963, this time for television. While the title character again looked like the newspaper strip Krazy, the series lacked Herriman's wit and poetry, and it lasted only one season.

M.H.

KRISTL, VLADIMIR (1923-) Yugoslav painter, animator and film director born in Zagreb, Yugoslavia, in 1923. Vlado Kristl graduated from the School of Fine Arts in Zagreb and started painting in the mid-1940s. He became one of the first cartoonists on the staff of the humor magazine *Kerempuh* and also dabbled in animation for Duga Film in the early 1950s. Kristl went into self-imposed exile in 1953, working in Europe and South America. He returned to Zagreb in 1959 and joined Zagreb Film that same year. In 1960, along with Ivo Urbanić he directed his first animated film, the brilliant, black-humored *La Peau de Chagrin*, about a gambler who sells his soul to the devil (the script was adapted from a Balzac story).

In 1961 Kristl produced single-handedly the much-praised and much-awarded *Don Quixote*, a fascinating adaptation of Cervantes's tale. After the success of this cartoon, however, disputes arose between the artist and the studio, and Kristl departed again, later that year, for West Germany. Since then he has chiefly directed live-action features such as the hermetic *The Dam* (1964), only

Vladimir Kristl, "La Peau de Chagrin." © Zagreb Film.

occasionally venturing into animation, as with *Prometheus* (1964) and *Das Land des Uberflusses* ("The Land of Plenty," 1967).

M.H.

KRYLOV, PORFIRY
See Kukryniksy.

KUBIN, ALFRED (1877-1959) Austrian graphic artist and cartoonist born in what was then Leitmeritz, Bohemia, in the Hapsburg empire (now Litoměřice, Czechoslovakia), on April 10, 1877. For a man whose artistic capital lay in the realm of the uncanny and the namelessly terrifying, Alfred Kubin had auspicious beginnings: the early death of his mother, the hostility of his father (an ex-army officer turned civil servant), a suicide attempt, a nervous breakdown while in military service, the sudden death of his fiancée. By 1906 he had purchased Schloss Zwickledt, a remote country house in Upper Austria that was to be his home until he died there on August 20, 1959.

Bureaucrats

Alfred Kubin, 1926. © Simplicissimus.

His art studies were equally choppy. As a boy he was apprenticed to an uncle who practiced landscape photography; he spent some time at a commercial art school in Salzburg; in Munich, where he arrived in 1898, he attended the Academy and a private art school. His style seems to have been chiefly derived from close observation (sometimes amounting to psychic "inspiration") of such great masters of the fantastic and macabre as Goya, Klinger, Rops, Redon, Ensor and Munch.

Kubin's weird drawings were soon appreciated by the public. The pivotal year in his development, the year in which he wrote and illustrated the unique autobiographical novel *Die Andere Seite* ("The Other Side"), was 1908-09. From 1912 through the 1920s he contributed numerous drawings to the Munich satirical magazine *Simplicissimus* (some of these come as close to being garden-variety "cartoons" as Kubin's work ever got) and a few to *Jugend.* The thousands of drawings in his total production included illustrations for a host of books by himself and by authors such as Poe, Nerval, Dostoevsky, E.T.A. Hoffmann, Hans Christian Andersen and Strindberg. Kubin worked tirelessly into the 1950s.

His mature drawing style is nervous and scratchy, the sheets often being covered with a compulsive network of lines. Every linear element of his landscapes and interiors contributes to the obsessive or hallucinatory quality of the whole configuration. His dramatis personae include murderers, misfits, eccentrics, outcasts, charlatans and animated skeletons; the farms and buildings he draws are often ramshackle; death, pain and shame are always just around the corner. But a fine-honed wit and subtle irony constantly restore balance to Kubin's view of the world, reminding us that there is also humor, grim though it may be.

Kubin, of course, is one of the most highly esteemed 20th-century graphic artists. There is a Kubin-Archiv in Hamburg and a Kubin-Kabinett in Linz.

S.A.

KUBOTA, BEISEN (1852-1906) Japanese cartoonist born in Kyoto, Japan, in 1852. Beisen Kubota's real name was Mitsuhiro Kubota, but he preferred to draw under his pen name, which translates "rice hermit." He studied art in Kyoto and pursued a career as a traditional artist until 1893, when he made his way to Tokyo and contributed cartoons to the *Kokumin Shimbun* ("People's News"). His cartoons, appearing in a section of the newspaper called "Saiankoku no Tokyo" ("Blackest Tokyo"), captured the lives of the lower classes of Japan's largest city. They were stark, literal statements of the sufferings of those who worked in the ditches, cheap kitchens and bars of Tokyo. The most popular of these drawings have been frequently republished and are considered valuable exposés of Japanese society before the Sino-Japanese war of 1894-95.

Later in 1893 Kubota paid his own way to the Columbian Exposition in Chicago, where he made sketches of what he saw and sent them back to Japan to be published in the *Kokumin Shimbun*. The outbreak of the Sino-Japanese war found Kubota back in Japan, and in May 1894 he traveled to what is now Korea as an army artist. There he made sketches of battle scenes and life at the front. Though many of these glorify the courageous Japanese soldier, they also capture accurately the stench, suffering and death found on the battlefield. Many of his works from *Beisen Jugungahō* ("Army Illustrator Beisen's Drawings") powerfully convey the tribulations of the native populace during the conflict.

Kubota's style owes more to the brush than to the pen. His lines are thick and full, and the message of his cartoons is direct and immediate. Dying horses, poverty and despair are frequent themes in his work. His vitality waned toward the turn of the century, and he produced little after the Sino-Japanese war. He died an unknown in 1906, leaving a son who, like his father, worked as an illustrator of the military conflicts before and after the turn of the century.

J.C.

KUEKES, EDWARD D. (1901-1987) American Pulitzer Prize-winning cartoonist born in Pittsburgh, Pennsylvania, on February 2, 1901. Displaying an early interest in cartoons, especially in the work of Gaar Williams, Ding Darling and Billy Ireland, Ed Kuekes attended, after Baldwin-Wallace College, the Chicago Academy of Fine Arts and the Cleveland School of Art for his artistic training.

His first job was as an artist for the Art Engraving and Color Type Company of Cleveland, and in January 1922 he joined the art department of the *Cleveland Plain Dealer.* He remained in the art department and was the regular cartoonist for the following 17 years.

In 1953, he won the Pulitzer Prize for a comment ("Aftermath") on a Korean War casualty old enough to die but too young to vote. Other honors include three Freedoms Foundation medals (one presented by General Eisenhower in 1949) and an honorary doctor of humane letters degree from his alma mater, Baldwin-Wallace College. He died on January 13, 1987, in Oklahoma City.

Kuekes drew in a lush pen and brush style and occasionally used crayon instead of crosshatches for shading. During his career he also worked on two syndicated features, *Alice in Wonderland* and *Do You Believe*, collected in comic book form by the United Feature group.

R.M.

KUHN, CHARLES HARRIS (1892-1989) American cartoonist born in Prairie City, Illinois, on March 20, 1892. Charles ("Doc") Kuhn was raised in Bushnell, Illinois, and subscribed by mail to the Landon Cartooning Course, which he failed to complete (as did, curiously, many otherwise avid aspirants).

In 1910 Kuhn's first cartoon appeared in the *Message*, a socialist magazine published in Girard, Kansas. Other sales followed: to *Hope* magazine (for 50 cents!), to the *Addressographer,* a house organ, and to the *Galesburg Mail* in Illinois. In 1913, seeking further training, Kuhn enrolled in the Chicago Academy of Fine Arts cartoon school, then in its infancy. At the time, Carl N. Werntz was director, and

Aftermath

Edward Kuekes, 1953 Pulitzer Prize-winning cartoon. © Cleveland Plain Dealer.

The Stranger at Our Gate

Charles Kuhn, 1942.

among his teachers were the local cartoonist Frank King and an unknown, though talented, Will DeBeck.

Around 1915 a chance inquiry at the *Chicago Journal* led to a position as cartoonist alongside J. Campbell Cory, who became Kuhn's mentor. They were later to collaborate on a few cartoons, and Kuhn recalls constantly correcting Cory's misspelling. With America's entry into World War I, Kuhn served in the navy, and during the postwar depression he took a job in a plow factory. Through Cory, Kuhn then secured a job in Denver as cartoonist for the *Rocky Mountain News,* where he remained for more than two years.

On January 3, 1922, Kuhn received a letter from Gaar Williams of the *Indianapolis News* stating his intention to switch to the *Chicago Tribune* and to recommend Kuhn for his job. This was high honor indeed, as Williams was one of the most respected American political and editorial cartoonists, and one of the most imitated—not least by Kuhn himself. Kuhn was to draw the daily editorial cartoon for the *News* for the next 25 years. Though he followed Williams's style, his work was individual and competent. He seldom used crayon, and he showed a seasoned mastery of the pen and the crosshatch technique. There was much native humor in his work; he deliberately eschewed the savage comment.

During World War II Kuhn conceived the idea of gift boxes or family "CARE packages" for servicemen and profited greatly until cardboard supplies became scarce; then others adopted the idea. He also published several cartoon courses which are remembered today by many professional cartoonists as their starting points.

In 1947, for the Richardson Feature Service of Indianapolis (which had recently flopped with a revived *Little Nemo*), Kuhn created several comic features, including one about a tomboyish, mischievous old lady who was a friend to the neighborhood boys. Duke Richardson syndicated *Grandma* for a year and a half before King Features picked up the strip and enlarged its client list. *Grandma* enjoyed a genteel and popular run until 1969; it was a friendly, old-fashioned strip in the Kuhn style and introduced the innovation of a black-and-white Sunday panel for children to color. When his strip ended, Kuhn retired to Florida where he died in January 1989.

R.M.

KUHN, WALT (1877-1949) American cartoonist and painter born in New York City on October 27, 1877. Walt Kuhn was educated in private schools and received art training in Germany, France, Holland, Italy and Spain. His first job was as a cartoonist for a San Francisco newspaper at five dollars a week. Freelance sales of cartoons to the *New York Sun* brought him back to New York.

There, just after the turn of the century, he frequently contributed to *Life.* His specialty was little bird cartoons, and his small drawings seemed to fill the spot left by Gus Dirks, who had taken his Bugville cartoons to Hearst at that time. Kuhn's cartoons were small and often served a second function as fillers between blocks of text or ad copy. They were immensely popular, and *Life* printed a collection in a book entitled *A Little Bird Told Me.* The art was crisp, clean and jovial.

Low life high up. Weary Warbler: "I just asked the lady up in the house for a hand-out, and she gave me a worm that wasn't fit to eat."

Walt Kuhn, 1903.

It should be noted, too, that although Kuhn gradually left the ranks of cartooning after 1910, his style was continued for another decade. Little bird character cartoons continued to appear, signed "Lang" (Louis Lansing Campbell); they were very close to Kuhn's work. Campbell was later to become a major illustrator of the Howard Garis *Uncle Wiggly* stories.

Kuhn sold his first serious painting in 1907, when he was 30. But in five years he was well on his way to becoming one of the great American painters, the career for which he is, of course, most noted. He was secretary of the 1913 Armory Show, fronting for a group of artists whose work was too modern for the National Academy. Fellow cartoonists John Sloan, Gus Mager and Rudolph Dirks (whom he taught to paint) also exhibited in this landmark show.

Although he was later to aver that "art can't be taught," Kuhn was a respected teacher for years, beginning at the New York School of Art in 1908 and 1909 and running through courses at the Art Students League in 1926 and 1927. His work now hangs in many galleries and museums. He wrote, designed and produced stage plays in pantomime and satirical ballets; his activities even led him to paint railroad club car murals. Kuhn, with other cartoonists and painters, was also active in the artists' community in Ogunquit, Maine. He died on July 13, 1949.

R.M.

KUKRYNIKSY (Russia) Kukryniksy is the collective signature of a team of three cartoonists: Mikhail Kupryanov

The fascist Lie-Gun

Kukryniksy, 1942.

(born in 1903 in Teyuschi), Porfiry Krylov (born in 1902 in Tula) and Nikolay Sokolov (born in 1903 in Moscow). The three met while attending the Moscow Institute of Higher Arts and Techniques, and they started working together on cartoons for the students' wall newspaper in 1924.

Deciding to stay together after graduation, they adopted their soon-to-be famous pen name (made up of the first syllables of their names). The first professional cartoons they signed were for the youth magazine *Komsomolskaya;* in 1933 they started to contribute cartoons to *Pravda* on a regular basis. Kukryniksy drew a number of anti-Franco cartoons and posters during the Spanish civil war, and the anti-German posters and drawings they produced during World War II are justly famous for their incisive style and visual impact. They are best remembered for their series of savage cartoons lampooning Goebbels and Hitler.

Kukryniksy is the best-known signature in the history of Soviet cartooning. The team has had a great number of exhibits throughout the former Soviet Union, and their cartoons have been reproduced in countless books. They received the Stalin Prize no less than five times (in 1942, 1947, 1949, 1950 and 1951) and were awarded the coveted Lenin Prize in 1955; they are also full members of the Soviet Academy of Arts. After several personel shakeups and due to changed political circumstances the group disbanded in the late 1980s.

M.H.

KUPKA, FRANTIŠEK (1871-1957) Czechoslovakian cartoonist and painter born in Opočno, Bohemia, on September 22, 1871. František Kupka studied art in Prague and Vienna before settling in Paris in 1894. There he started his career with fashion drawings for department stores and various magazines. In 1899 he exhibited his first humorous drawings.

Kupka had his art studio in Montmartre and designed several posters for Montmartre cabarets. His first cartoons were published in the humor magazines *La Plume* and *Cocorico* in 1900. He also contributed to most humor and satirical magazines of the time, including *Le Rire, Le Canard Sauvage* and *La Vie en Rose,* as well as to the anarchistic publications *Les Temps Nouveaux* and *Le Cri de Paris.* His most notable cartoons, however, were done for *L'Assiette au Beurre,* starting with the first issue of the magazine in 1901 and continuing until 1906. His drawings and captions were so savage that they had to be toned down even for such an outspoken publication as *L'Assiette*!

In 1907 Kupka began phasing out his cartoon work, and in 1910 he devoted himself almost exclusively to painting, doing occasional book illustrations. He started the Abstract-Creation group and is now regarded as one of the founding figures of the nonrepresentational school. He died in Puteaux, near Paris, on June 21, 1957.

M.H.

KUPRIANOV, MIKHAIL
See Kukryniksy.

KURI, YŌJI (1928-) Japanese cartoonist, animator and filmmaker born in Fukui Prefecture, Japan, on April 9, 1928. Yōji Kuri first started working in the prefectural tax office, but in 1956 he changed direction and entered the art department of Bunka Gakuin. When he graduated, his cartoons were already appearing in *Chisei,* the supplement to the *Nihon Shimbun Times.* After independently publishing the *Kuri Yōji Mangasha* ("Collected Cartoons of Yōji Kuri"), he won the Bungei Shunju cartoon award for 1958.

In animation Kuri attracted worldwide attention when his three-minute-long *Ningen Dobutsuen* ("Human Zoo")

The Foundations of the European Balance of Power

František Kupka, 1904.

received an award at the 1963 Venice Film Festival. This was followed by a string of international awards for his experimental animation in films such as *Love* (1963), *Za Botan* ("The Button," 1964), *Samurai* (1965) and *AOS* (1967), which all garnered prizes in film festivals in Italy and Germany. *Ningen to Sekai* ("Man and the World") was awarded a silver medal at the Montreal World Exposition Film Festival of 1967. More recently, Kuri made *Froito no Ki* ("The Freudian Tree," 1973), *Jinko Bakuhatsu* ("Population Explosion," 1975), *Shinka* ("Evolution," 1976) and the cartoon short *Shōmetsu ("Extinction,"* 1977). Between 1964 and 1985 he probably gained his broadest exposure with the mini-animation pieces he created for the late-night adult TV show *11 PM*; 317 were produced overall.

Ironically, because of the lack of Japanese theaters showing experimental or avant-garde films, Kuri has in many respects been more widely recognized outside Japan. His works range from pure animation to montages of photographs and animation to films with no animation at all. Two of his recurrent themes are atomic explosions and weak men being chased by strong women. The former is used to good effect in his *Za Botan,* where a couple visiting a horrendously developed industrial complex press the doorbell, only to have everything transformed into ashes. In *Atchi wa Kotchi* ("There Is Here"), an excellent experimental film made in 1962, Kuri combines animation and photography with an avant-garde seriocomic theme of strange devolution occurring after a missile is fired. Kuri is a prolific animator and cartoonist and has solidly established himself as a master of surreal comedy. He holds exhibitions of his work regularly. These take place not only in Japan but in other places as well, including New York and Paris. In recognition of his contributions he has been awarded medals of honor such as the prestigious Medal with Dark Blue Ribbon in 1983, and the Medal with Purple Ribbon in 1992.

Yōji Kuri, "The Human Zoo." © Kuri.

F.S.

Ll

LA CAVA, GREGORY (1892-1949) American cartoonist and filmmaker born in Towanda, Pennsylvania, in 1892. Gregory La Cava started his career as a newspaper cartoonist for W.R. Hearst, then in 1916 joined the newly created International Film Service devoted to the animation of Hearst-syndicated comic strips. La Cava was the titular head of the studio, producing the *Krazy Kat, Happy Hooligan, Maggie and Jiggs, Silk Hat Harry* and *Katzenjammer Kids* cartoon series. What later came to be called "the La Cava touch" was already in evidence in these animated films, which abounded in witty gags. One has only to compare the La Cava-produced *Krazy Kat* cartoons with the later, sorry bunch of cartoons of the same title to see the difference in style and humor.

These gifts of slapstick and humor were to serve La Cava well when he moved into live-action films in the early 1920s. La Cava directed several W.C. Fields comedies, including the memorable *Running Wild* (1927). Later he turned out some of the most enjoyable movie comedies of the sound era: *She Married Her Boss* (1935), *My Man Godfrey* (1936), *Stage Door* (1937) and *Unfinished Business* (1941), to name but a few.

Gregory La Cava died in Los Angeles on March 1, 1949.

M.H.

LADD, FRED
See Laderman, Fred.

LADERMAN, FRED (1927-   ) American animator and producer born in Toledo, Ohio, in 1927. Fred Laderman went to Scott High School in Toledo, later attending the School of Radio Production at Ohio State University, from which he graduated with honors in 1949. In 1950 he went to work at WFDR, a leading radio station in the New York area, moving in the mid-1950s to the position of vice-president and general manager of Radio and TV Packages, a production company. While there, he was responsible for bringing to television such programs as *The Greatest Fights of the Century* and the noted animal life series *Jungle;* he also produced over four hundred one-minute animated cartoons, *Cartoon Classics.*

Attracted by the medium of animation, Laderman began in 1960 to bring to American TV, in collaboration with Universal Pictures, such noted animation series as *Astro-Boy, The Big World of Little Adam, Kimba the White Lion* and *Gigantor,* as well as the feature-length *Pinocchio in Outer Space.* In addition to being the producer in charge, Laderman also doubled as writer-director on these films (under his own name as well as under the pen name "Fred Ladd").

Giuseppe Laganà, "L'Om Salbadgh." © Corona Films.

Laderman was the co-producer as well as the writer-director of the animated film *Journey Back to Oz* (1972), which was shown on ABC-TV and in theaters abroad. This production featured the voices of such acting luminaries as Liza Minelli, Milton Berle, Danny Thomas and Mickey Rooney. Laderman is currently the writer-director of *The Children's Film Festival* shown on CBS-TV and of *The Greatest Tales,* an animation series based on fairy tales, legends and fables from the entire world. In the early 1980s he moved to Los Angeles, where he worked at Filmation and other studios. He is now retired, although he does occasional consulting work.

M.H.

LAGANÀ, GIUSEPPE (1944-   ) Italian cartoonist and animator born in Milan, Italy, on July 28, 1944. After finishing his high school studies, Giuseppe Laganà attended the Brera Art Academy. Graduating in the mid-1960s, he worked as a cartoonist for magazines and started his animation career directing commercial shorts along with Paolo Piffarerio and Gino Gavioli for Gamma Film in Milan.

Laganà worked on two of Bruno Bozzetto's full-length animated films, *West and Soda* (1965) and *VIP, Mio Fratello Superuomo* (1968), and was the art director on two sequences of Bozzetto's animated musical, *Allegro Non Troppo* (1976). He directed independently two animated films, *Preghiera nella Notte* ("Prayer in the Night," 1972) and *L'Om Salbadgh* (a 1975 film about a lost child raised in the wild), which were well received in various international festivals. Laganà has also pursued a career as a children's book illustrator and as a cartoonist for a number of magazines, including *Playboy.* From 1970 to 1972 he drew a comic strip, *Orlando,* for the cartoon magazine *Eureka.* His most notable films of the last 20 or so years have been the 1982 *Pixnocchio* (the first Italian full-length animated picture done entirely on computer), and *Orpheus* (1986), featuring (among others) a convent of nuns dancing to Offenbach's music.

L.S.

LAGATTA, JOHN (1894-1976) American artist born in Naples, Italy, in 1894. John LaGatta grew up in America, studying art at the New York School of Fine and Applied Art under Kenneth Hayes Miller and Frank Alvah Parsons. His early advertising work showed the influence of the French illustrator Drian, but it was under the artistic influence of Coles Phillips that LaGatta hit his stride. Although he eventually liberated himself from this stylistic sycophancy, it was while drawing and painting "fadeaway" cartoons that LaGatta made his first major sales. He executed pieces for *Life* in the early 1910s, mostly covers with gag captions. It was a major market to break, but the young cartoonist showed a real flair for design, composition and color.

In the 1930s and 1940s LaGatta became a major fiction and advertising illustrator. With Jon Whitcomb, Gilbert Bundy and Bradshaw Crandall, he was hailed as the era's chronicler of the American Girl. In his later years LaGatta taught at the Art Center School in Los Angeles, California. He died in 1976.

R.M.

LALOUX, RENÉ (1929-) French painter and cartoonist born in Paris, France, in July 1929. At the age of 13 René Laloux learned to draw at school, but he was largely self-taught. After World War II, while doing many odd jobs in order to support himself, he studied painting. From 1955 to 1959 he directed an art studio and also produced several shows with the inmates of a mental home at Cour-Cheverny. In 1960, he produced his first animated cartoon, *Les Dents du Singe* ("The Monkey's Teeth"), also with the help of patients. The story of a wicked wizard and of the monkeys who outwit him, *Les Dents du Singe* was awarded the Prix Emile Cohl for animation.

A few years later Laloux met fellow cartoonist Roland Topor, and together they realized *Les Temps Morts* ("Dead Times," 1964), followed the next year by *Les Escargots* ("The Snails"), a weird and disturbing tale of a mad gardener who grows giant lettuce and of the giant snails that destroy everything in their path in order to eat them. After a short interlude devoted to painting (with shows in Paris and Brussels), Laloux, again in collaboration with Topor, started in 1969 on his most ambitious project to date, a feature-length cartoon based on a science fiction novel by Stefan Wul, *La Planète Sauvage* ("The Wild Planet"). It was awarded a special prize at the 1973 film festival in Cannes. He followed this up in 1981 with a second science-fiction feature, *Les Maitres du Temps* ("The Time Masters"), in collaboration with noted French comic-strip artist Jean Giraud ("Moebius"); and in 1987 he released in partnership with another comic-strip artist, Philippe Caza, *How Wong-Fo Was Saved*, based on an ancient Chinese folktale.

A man of many talents (he is also a screen and song writer), René Laloux is probably the most gifted artist of the new French school of animation. He has received many awards for his work in animation at festivals throughout Europe.

M.H.

René Laloux, "Les Temps Morts." © Laloux.

LAN JIAN'AN (1926-1997) Chinese cartoonist born in 1926. Lan Jian'an started to publish cartoons while still in high school, and in the 1950s he edited a publication called *East European Cartoon Collection*, and he was the editor of the international section of *Cartoon Monthly* between 1953 and 1960. From 1964 until the time of his death, Lan worked at the *Beijing Monthly* turning out cartoons and illustrations on world affairs. In addition to his cartoons on international issues, Lan was also known for introducing the work of numerous foreign cartoonists to Chinese readers in the many publications he authored. He has exerted a

人尽其才，物尽其用 蓝建安 Lan Jianan Making the best use of every talent and everything

Lan Jian'an. © Lan Jian'an.

great influence on the course of Chinese cartooning, an influence that continues after his death in 1997.

Lan's concentration on international cartoon research was quite different from the focus of his two equally famous colleagues, Bi Keguan and Huang Yuanlin. As a matter of fact many Chinese cartoonists have not only produced cartoons but have also written articles of cartoon research, either from personal experience or from the study of other artists' work. Bi Keguan, Huang Yuanlin and Lan Jian'an are only the most outstanding contributors to the field, which is why they are included in this encyclopedia.

H.Y.L.L.

LANCASTER, SIR OSBERT (1908-1986) British cartoonist born in London, England, on August 4, 1908.

"You will notice that the line with which he draws his shrewdly observed people is almost juvenile in its deliberation and simplicity. But the artlessness of the style only serves to add pungency to the wit of a very grown-up mind." Thus wrote cartoonist and critic Percy V. Bradshaw in his chapter on Osbert Lancaster in *Lines of Laughter* (1946).

Lancaster's line is still artless, his wit still pungent, almost forty years since the day he invented the "pocket cartoon." Inspired by the French habit of single-column cartoons in newspapers, Lancaster persuaded the editor of the prewar *Daily Express* to allow him to institute the form in England. At first his column-breakers were an added attraction to the William Hickey page, a gossip column written pseudonymously by Tom Driberg, M.P. With the contracting newspapers of the war years, Lancaster's single-column cartoons became instantly more practicable and found their way onto the front page. They were also imitated by every other newspaper, and the small one-off daily cartoon remains a permanent feature of the British press. Only Lancaster's continues the title, *Pocket Cartoon,* and only Lancaster established a permanent cast of recurring characters, the leader of which is the redoubtable Lady Maudie Littlehampton.

Osbert Lancaster was educated at Charterhouse and Lincoln College, Oxford (1926-30); he took an honors degree in English literature and sat several law examinations. He studied art at the Byam Shaw School (1925-26) and at the Slade School of Art (1931-32), where he took stage design under Victor Polunin. He went to work for *Architectural Review* and was encouraged to write and illustrate a series of articles that treated the topic humorously. In his first book, *Progress at Pelvis Bay* (1936), he further explored this vein, giving a solemn account of "this well-known plague spot and eyesore" in a style of tongue-in-cheek humor he would make his own. Meanwhile, he did posters for London Transport, book jackets and a large mural in a hotel in Blandford.

Roman Drayneflete
Osbert Lancaster, from "There'll Always Be a Drayneflete." © Lancaster.

January 1, 1939, saw the first of his *Daily Express* cartoons, which continued with but one break from 1944 to 1946, when he was first secretary with the British embassy at Athens, Greece. On his return to England he joined the editorial board of the *Architectural Review,* designed sets and costumes for the ballet *Pineapple Poll* (the first of many such stage designs for the Royal Ballet) and did similar work for the Glyndebourne Opera. He was made Commander of the British Empire in 1953 and knighted in 1975. He died in London on July 27, 1986.

Books: *Progress at Pelvis Bay* (1936); *Our Sovereigns* (1936); *Pillar to Post* (1938); *Homes Sweet Homes* (1939); *Pocket Cartoons* (1940); *New Pocket Cartoons* (1941); *Further Pocket Cartoons* (1942); *25 Caricatures* (1943); *More Pocket Cartoons* (1943); *As-sorted Sizes* (1944); *Osbert Lancaster Cartoons* (1945); *Clerical Landscape with Figures* (1947); *More and More Productions* (1948); *Saracen's Head* (1948); *A Pocketful of Cartoons* (1949); *Drayneflect Revealed* (1949); *Facades and Faces* (1950); *Lady Littlehampton and Friends* (1952); *All Done from Memory* (1953); *Studies from Life* (1954); *Tableaux Vivants* (1955); *Private Views* (1956); *The Year of the Comedy* (1957); *Etudes* (1958); *Here of All Places* (1959); *Signs of the Times* (1961); *Studies from Life* (1961); *In Laws and Outlaws* (1962); *The Water Beetle* (1962); *All's Well That Ends Well* (1963); *Mixed Notices* (1963); *The Penguin Osbert Lancaster* (1964); *Graffiti* (1964); *The Law and the Profits* (1965); *Parkinson's Law* (1965); *A Few Quick Tricks* (1965); *With an Eye to the Future* (1967); *Temporary Diversions* (1968); *Sailing to Byzantium* (1969); *Fasten Your Safety Belts* (1970); *Signs of the Times* (1971); *Meaningful Confrontations* (1971); *Theatre in the Flat* (1972); and *The Littlehampton Bequest* (1973).

D.G.

LAND BEFORE TIME (U.S.) Steven Spielberg had dinosaurs on the brain well before he made *Jurassic Park,* as evidence by this 1988 animated feature, which he wrote and produced in association with George Lucas of *Star Wars* fame. Don Bluth, a defector from the Disney studios and in the 1980's and 1990's, the only animator talented enough (and gutsy enough) to stand up to the Mouse Factory, directed the film, which was released by MGM/UA.

The hero of the piece was a young brontosaurus named Littlefoot that had been orphaned when his herd had been attacked by a Tyrannosaurus Rex. He then went in search of the mythical Great Valley, "where all can live in peace," in the company of representatives of other species (an anatosaurus, a pterodactyl, a stegosaurus, and a triceratops): for the benefit of those viewers who didn't get the symbolism in the first place the animals were all painted different colors. After many a peril and mishap they all reached their destination safely.

Despite Spielberg's gift for sanctimony and the imitativeness of some of the sequences (reminiscent of *Bambi* and *Fantasia*), the story was genuinely engaging. It was helped in no small measure by Bluth's handling of the animation, especially in the more dramatic moment involving earthquakes, volcano eruptions, and stampedes by monstrous pachycephalosauri. The main weakness resided in the depiction of the animals, who never emerged as fully realized personalities. Opening on the same weekend as Disney's *Oliver and Company*, *Land Before Time* outgrossed Disney's animated feature by almost two to one, an unprecedented feat and one not to be repeated for a long time to come. (Bluth and Spielberg went their separate ways after the film's release.)

For the record let us mention another animated opus produced by Spielberg's Amblin Entertainment, the 1993 *We're Back! A Dinosaur's Story*. Derivative and uninspired, it was panned by the critics and ignored by the public, and quickly sank into the sands of time. Let us further mention that in 1993 and 1995 Universal Cartoon Studio released *The Land Before Time II* and *III* directly for the home video market. Aside from the names of the characters, it bore no relation to the original production.

M.H.

John Lane. © NEA.

LANDGRAF, KEN (1950-) American cartoonist and artist born in November, 1950, in Sheboygan, Wisconsin. After seeing service in Vietnam, Ken Landgraf in 1971 moved to New York City; he studied cartooning and animation at the School of Visual Arts where his teachers included Will Eisner and Harvey Kurtzman. While going to school he also worked as an assistant to comic-book artists Rich Buckler, Gil Kane, and Howard Nostrand.

After graduation in the mid-1970s he began working for DC Comics, drawing for some of their best known titles, such as *Superman*, *Hawkman*, *Nightwing*, and *Flamebird*. Later switching to Marvel, he drew some of the earliest *Wolverine* stories. At the end of the decade and into the 1980s he produced two comic-book titles of his own, *Starfighter* and *Rock Comics* (an early attempt at tying together the superhero and rock-and-roll motifs).

Later into the decade Landgraf branched out into storyboarding for both live-action and animation films, as well as for TV series and for industrial and promotional films. In 1986 he did the storyboards for *Adventures of the Galaxy Rangers*, one of the first cartoon shows to use computer animation in addition to conventional cel animation. His credits in the last dozen or so years have included work on *The Cosby Mysteries*, *Law and Order* (television), *Another Kiss* and *Teddy Bear Habit* (film). A versatile and solid craftsman, Landgraf has elevated storyboarding into one of the component branches of the cartooning arts.

M.H.

LANE, JOHN RICHARD (1932-) American editorial and political cartoonist born in Jefferson City, Missouri, on August 12, 1932. John Lane's father, Ralph Lane, was a backbone of the Newspaper Enterprise Association (NEA) art staff for years; he was a gag cartoonist in the twenties and thirties, assisted Roy Crane on *Buz Sawyer* and created his own strip, *Vic Flint*, for NEA. Ironically, when *Vic Flint* folded (under the title *The Good Guys*) it was John Lane who was then its artist. The younger Lane received all his cartoon training and most of his art training from his father, except for two years at the Cleveland Institute of Art.

While yet in his early twenties, John Lane joined NEA as art director, assuming a wide range of duties. Among these were graphics and editorial cartoons. When NEA's chief political cartoonist, Bill Crawford, went into semiretirement in 1974, Lane filled the void and assumed full duties three years later. His style is trendy and illustrative, a handsome holdover from his graphics days. He uses only pen and ink, with no crayon shading but some very effective crosshatching and linework.

As a political cartoonist serving a presold client list of hundreds of papers, the NEA artist has traditionally trod the middle of the political road—a complaint of John Fischetti during his tenure. Lane, however, seems to have moved slightly to the left. Now no longer with NEA, he is still active freelancing cartoons and illustrations.

R.M.

LANG, ERNST MARIA (1916-) German architect and editorial cartoonist born in Oberammergau, Germany, on December 8, 1916. Ernst Lang is from the celebrated family of folk artists (potters and sculptors) whose members have so often played major roles (including Christ) in the recurring Passion plays of their Bavarian village. Like Peichl ("Ironimus") in Vienna, Lang in Munich combines the career of leading architect—he is an expert in modern town planning—with that of political cartoonist. He has also been head of an applied-art and architecture school in Munich.

Lang studied architecture in the Bavarian capital, served as an army engineer in World War II, and set up as a free-lance architect in 1949. In 1947 his skill as a cartoonist was discovered by the Munich *Süddeutsche Zeitung,* to which he contributed for many years. From 1954 on, he also appeared on Bavarian television.

Lang's first album, *Politische Drehbühne* ("Political Revolving Stage"), consisted of cartoons he had done for the *Süddeutsche Zeitung* between 1947 and 1949. These still lacked the imagination and freedom of pen work that were to come. Fortunately, the heavy, unrelieved black backgrounds and the excessive reliance on standard national and allegorical symbols merely marked a passing phase.

Lang's political verses done for television (each poem illustrated with several small pictures) were the basis of his 1959 album *Die Zwerge Gehn in Volle Deckung* ("The Dwarfs Take Cover"). The title is the same as that of one of the poems inside, about the spirit of the dead Stalin suddenly reawakening during the Hungarian events of 1956 while his puny successors scurry to safety. But the cover illustration shows Adenauer as a giant among his fellow German politicians, so that the title applies to local politics as well. Adenauer would continue to be one of Lang's main targets.

Korsaren und Korsette ("Corsairs and Corsets," 1960), a review of recent European politics, is largely anti-Adenauer, although De Gaulle and others come in for their share of abuse. By this time, Lang's contours were much freer, and his cartoon style thoroughly pliable and capable of clever parodies.

Deutschland, Ich Muss Dich Lassen ("Germany, I Must Leave You," 1963) is completely devoted to Adenauer. Not only is the chancellor's entire political career reviewed sarcastically, but Adenauer-like figures are traced through all of world history in an unflattering attempt to analyze the old man's character. Lang is generally referred to as a calm South German "laughing observer" of the world scene, but in books like this one, his bite can be pretty savage. Now in his eighties he is still active creating political cartoons for *Suddeutsche Zeitung*. Age has not mellowed his acerbic comments on the follies of politics and society.

S.A.

LANTZ, WALTER (1900-1994) American animator born in New Rochelle, New York, on April 27, 1900. Walter Lantz started his animation career in 1916 at Hearst's International Film Service, under the supervision of Gregory La Cava. There he animated and later directed a number of *Katzenjammer Kids, Krazy Kat* and *Happy Hooligan* cartoons. After the closing of International Film Service in 1918, Lantz joined the studio of John Randolph Bray, who had acquired the animation rights to many of the Hearst characters. At Bray, Lantz worked notably on *Colonel Heezaliar* and *Dinky Doodle,* but his talents for management led him to various production positions.

In the late 1920s Lantz set up his own studio, releasing through Universal; one of his first assignments, starting in 1929, was to continue the *Oswald the Rabbit* cartoon series, which Universal had just acquired from Charles Mintz. Oswald became the standard-bearer of the Lantz studio and was later joined by Winchester the Tortoise, Li'l Eight-Ball (a black boy) and Andy Panda. Lantz finally got his first solid success with Woody Woodpecker, who made his appearance in 1941. The *Woody Woodpecker* cartoons were to remain Lantz's only popular series, despite his attempts at producing various other characters, such as Homer Pigeon, Inspector Willoughby and Chilly Willy, the penguin created by Tex Avery. Lantz's studio was one of the last to close its doors (in 1973); he continued to produce the *Woody Woodpecker* show as well as an occasional special for television until his retirement in the late 1980's. He died in March 1994.

Walter Lantz, "Andy Panda." © Walt Lantz Productions.

It cannot be said that Walter Lantz ever set high standards of excellence for his staff (Tex Avery once characterized the studio's animation work as "crappy"), but he was resilient and resourceful, and his studio outlasted most of the more artistic units. Among the directors who worked on the Lantz cartoons, mention should be made of Bill Nolan, Dick Lundy, Shamus Culhane, Sid Marcus, Paul J. Smith, Jack Hannah and of course Tex Avery.

M.H.

LA PALME, ROBERT (1908-1997) Canadian cartoonist born in Montreal, Canada, on April 14, 1908. In 1918 young Robert La Palme followed his family to Alberta, where his father became a farmer. Returning with his family to

Jacques Laplaine ("Lap"), "Le petit Présideng." © Le Canard Enchainé.

Montreal in 1925, he applied to the Ecole des Beaux-Arts but was turned down.

In spite of his lack of formal art training, La Palme has enjoyed a long and fruitful career in cartooning. In 1930 he incorporated elements of cubism into his cartoons, thus becoming one of the forerunners of modern art in Canada. In 1934 he became editorial cartoonist of the intellectual daily newspaper *L'Ordre,* while contributing drawings to such publications as the *Philadelphia Ledger, The Nation,* and *Stage* magazine. After a short stint at the Ottawa daily *Le Droit,* La Palme settled in Quebec City in 1937 as the editorial cartoonist of *Le Journal.* Back in Montreal in 1943, he successively worked for *Le Canada* (1943-50), *Le Devoir* (1950-59) and *La Presse.*

In addition to his work as a cartoonist, La Palme has been a librarian at the Quebec Beaux-Arts School and has taught at Laval University in Quebec City. His murals entitled *The History of War* have earned him many awards. He has been active in Canadian television and has worked for the stage as a set designer. In 1968 he founded in Montreal the International Pavilion of Humor, of which he remained the curator until it closed its doors in 1991.

Robert La Palme has received many awards, including the Order of Canada for his contributions to Canadian art and a gold medal at the 1967 International Poster Exhibition in Tokyo. He died of heart failure at Longueuil Hospital in Montreal on June 19, 1997.

M.H.

LAPLAINE, JACQUES (1921-1987) French cartoonist born in Joigny, near Paris, in 1921. Self-taught in art, Jacques Laplaine sold a few gag cartoons to local newspapers before settling in Paris after World War II, working for such publications as *Ce Soir* and the humorous *L'Os Libre.* He joined the staff of the fabled satirical weekly *Le Canard Enchainé* in 1946 and was to remain there for the next four decades.

Signing simply "J. Lap," he chronicled the political scene of the times with gently satirical cartoons, giving his victims a nudge rather than a kick, in contrast to the more ferocious thrusts of many of *Le Canard*'s cartoonists (and writers). His unsophisticated, almost primitive style, his heavy, wavy line, and his subdued humor became instantly (and endearingly) recognizable, making his drawings into staples of the publication. In its pages he created in 1951 *Le Petit Présideng* ("The Little Presideng"), a weekly strip in the mold of Otto Soglow's *The Little King,* in which he lightly mocked French President Vincent Auriol, his short stature, his homey habits, and his southern expansiveness.

Called "a large man with a big heart" by one of his colleagues, Lap was greatly respected in his profession and even among the members of the political class he lampooned but never savaged. His cartoons were widely syndicated to French regional newspapers, and many exhibitions of his works were held throughout France and abroad.

In addition to his work for *Le Canard,* Lap also turned out a great number of humor and editorial cartoons for a host of publications, including *Paris-Presse, Paris Match, Arts, Le Monde et la Vie, Combat,* and the British *News Chronicle.* In the late 1940s and early 1950s he created several short-lived daily newspaper comics (including the winsome *M. Cloche,* about a happy-go-lucky drifter), and he also produced a number of animated cartoons. He retired in 1986 and died the following year at his suburban

R.K. Laxman, self-portrait with his "common man." © Times of India.

home of Jouy, near Paris. His cartoons are still widely reprinted in almost all anthologies devoted to the turbulent years of the French Fourth and Fifth Republics.

M.H.

LAXMAN, R.K. (1920-) R.K. Laxman was born in Mysore, India in 1920. His hopes to attend an art school were dashed first by his mother, who wanted him to obtain a bachelor's degree, which he did in philosophy, economics, and politics, and later by the J.J. School of Arts in Bombay, which turned down his application on the basis of a lack of talent.

Meanwhile, he had already been illustrating the short stories of his famous novelist brother, R.K. Narayan, for *The Hindu*, from the time he entered his teens. While in college, he started doing political cartoons for *Swarjya Magazine*; he worked briefly as cartoonist for the *Free Press* upon graduation.

In 1947, Laxman joined the *Times of India*, where he has remained for half a century, drawing political cartoons and a front page pocket cartoon, "They Said It." In the latter, he includes every day his unobtrusive "Common Man," a bespectacled, balding, and bewhiskered fellow clad in a long striped coat and *dhoti*; always a mute bystander, the "Common Man" has come to represent the silent majority of India.

A cartoonist with sharp and sure lines and a piercing wit, Laxman is also known for his writing ability. He has written three novels, many stories and essays, and a television serial, "Wagle Ki Duniya." His cartoons have also been published in a series of paperback books.

In 1984, Laxman received the prestigious Asia-wide Magsaysay Award for Journalism, Literature and Creative Communication Arts; he has also been awarded India's Padma Bhushan, Durga Ratan Award, and an honorary doctorate.

J.A.L.

Charles Léandre, caricature of the notorious anti-Semite M.E. Drumont, ca. 1890.

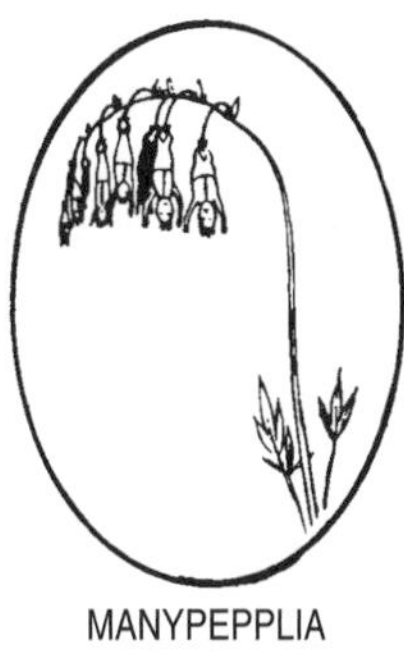

Edward Lear, from "Nonsense Botany."

LÉANDRE, CHARLES (1862-1934) French caricaturist, cartoonist, lithographer and poster designer born in Normandy, France, on July 23, 1862. Charles Léandre studied with Bin and Cabanel at the Ecole des Beaux-Arts in Paris (1878-84). He later joined the ranks of cartoonists at *Le Chat Noir,* contributing as well to *Le Gaulois, Le Rire, Le Journal Amusant* and *L'Assiette au Beurre.* While his caricatures of personalities in politics, arts and literature have a satirical bite (especially the ferocious caricatures of an enormous Queen Victoria sitting on poor, "weak" Kruger, or a curly-bearded Edouard Drumont, the vitriolic anti-Semitic politician and writer, shown devouring Jewish heads), most of his cartoons deal with various social problems, from backroom abortions to prostitution. Some of these drawings, reminiscent of André Gill's style, were released as albums: *Paris et la Province* (1898) and *Le Musée des Souverains* ("The Museum of Sovereigns," 1900).

In addition to posters for various singers and actors (Xavier Privas, 1899; Cécile Sorel, 1901; Yvette Guilbert, 1902), lithographs attacking "war idiocies," and book illustrations (especially for Rostand's *Cyrano de Bergerac,* 1902), he also published his delicate yet powerful sketches dealing with life in and around La Nouvelle Athènes, a Montmartre bistro, under the title *Nocturnes* (1896).

A member of the so-called Montmartre school, Charles Léandre died in Paris in 1934.

P.H.

LEAR, EDWARD (1812-1888) British humorist, natural history artist and illustrator born in Highgate Village, London, England, on May 12, 1812.

The Jumblies (who went to sea in a sieve), the Pobble (who has no toes), the Dong (with the luminous nose), the Owl and the Pussy Cat (who went to sea in a beautiful pea-green boat), the Quangle-Wangle, Mr. and Mrs. Discobbulus . . . the list is almost as eternal as the characters themselves, who live on and on, rediscovered by generation after generation of children who respond instantly to the ageless insanity of Edward Lear, the man who "invented Nonsense." Their latest incarnation was in *Tomfoolery*, perhaps the most original television cartoon series ever, produced by Rankin-Bass in 1971—Although purists would undoubtedly prefer the very Victorian but still appealing original images of the author's own illustrated text.

Edward Lear was one of 21 children of a bankrupted stockbroker. A sickly child, he was educated mainly by his older sister. At 15 he began to earn a living drawing and coloring for medical research. In 1831 he was commissioned by the London Zoological Society to make colored drawings of the parrots in the Regents Park Zoo, a job that took a year and was published as the first colored book on birds in England. Lear's reputation as a natural history artist was made, and for some years his career was soberly pictorial.

Inspired by the form of the limerick, he created many of his own and eventually published them as *The Book of Nonsense* (1846), illustrating each verse. It was a great success, and nonsense verses and pictures became a popular second string to his career as a serious painter—a life which not only took him to foreign parts but raised him to the position of art master to Queen Victoria. The last years of his life saw a return of the ill health that had beset his childhood; he lived in Italy, where he died at San Remo on January 29, 1888, and was mourned by his constant companion, Foss (a cat).

Books: *Illustrations of the Family of Psittacidae* (1832); *Views in Rome* (1841); *A Book of Nonsense by Derry Down Derry* (1846); *Illustrated Excursions in Italy* (1846); *Gleanings from the Menagerie at Knowsley Hall* (1846); *Journal of a Landscape Painter in Albania* (1851); *. . . in Southern Calabria* (1852); *. . . in Corsica* (1870); *Nonsense Songs* (1871); *More Nonsense* (1872); *Edward Lear's London Journal* (1873); *Laughable Lyrics* (1877); *Nonsense Songs and Stories* (1888); *Nonsense Botany* (1889); *Nonsense Drolleries* (1889); *Nonsense Birthday Book* (1894); *Queery Leary Nonsense* (1911); *Edward Lear Coloured Bird Book* (1912); *Nonsense Poetry Book* (1924); *Edward Lear* (1927); *Lear Omnibus* (1938); *Picture Tales for Little Folk* (1938); *Lear in Sicily* (1938); *The Book of Lear* (1939); *Edward Lear's Nonsense Omnibus* (1943); *Complete Nonsense of Edward Lear* (1947); *Tea pots and Quails* (1953); *Lear's Corfu* (1965); *Penned and Illustrated by Edward Lear* (1965).

D.G.

LEASON, PERCIVAL ALEXANDER (1889-1959) Australian painter, illustrator and cartoonist born in Kaniva, Victoria, Australia, in 1889. Not every artist distinguishes himself by becoming a household name on a national scale. Percy Leason, though, is known throughout Australia for his wonderfully funny drawings of events disturbing the placid life in the fictitious country town of Wiregrass.

Hard Luck:—"Is it true that you have races here to-morrow?" —"Yeh; but you're too late to enter him—entries closed yesterday." *Percy Leason, 1923. © The Bulletin.*

Percival Alexander Leason was born and brought up on a wheat farm at Kaniva in Victoria's Wimmera district. From boyhood he practiced drawing the animals, birds, trees and other subjects he found around the farm. "Then something happened," he once wrote, "that nearly put an end to my interest in art. I went to an art school." Twice a week he traveled on the steam engine of the local train to the nearby town of Nhill for these lessons. "And the town's name represents what I learned there," he added.

On an impulse, Leason came to Melbourne armed with some published clippings of work he had submitted to a children's column of a Melbourne newspaper. This led to his being apprenticed for five years as a lithographer with a big city printer. After taking some Melbourne Art Gallery night classes, he freelanced, then moved to Sydney in 1917, still working as a commercial artist, this time with the well-known studio of Smith and Julius. Two years later, as a *Bulletin* artist, he was drawing his nationally popular studies of country people reacting to civilization's progress.

Leason's draftsmanship was faultless; he always drew with a pen, using very fine nibs with etching-like precision. Notable for its accuracy of detail, his draftsmanship showed, like that of Norman Lindsay and David Low, a profound respect for the traditional grammar of drawing. Leason's pen illustrations to the *Selected Poems of Henry Lawson* (1918) are examples of the astonishing technical skill he always brought to his comic art. It was not only Leason's tremendous draftsmanship that was outstanding but also the composition and figure grouping of his comic drawings. For example, in his *Bulletin* drawing "The Finish of the Old Buffers' Race," he drew over ninety people in beautifully arranged groups, plus three old cars, two buggies, two hitched horses, a couple of bicycles, sundry trees—and a dog. It is a typical Leason drawing, one that is, in terms of journalism, breathtaking for its concept, painstaking execution and sheer drawing skill. His drawings, like those of Norman Lindsay, are sure and precise, with no alterations or "chinese-white" corrections.

Leason was lured to Melbourne *Punch* from the *Bulletin* in 1924, and plans were also in hand to attract Will Dyson back to Australia to work for this weekly magazine. With Leason as chief cartoonist, many of Australia's finest black-and-white artists contributed to Melbourne *Punch* in its one year of ownership by the Melbourne *Herald* and *Weekly Times* group. These artists included Will Dyson, Jim Bancks, Hugh McCrae, D.H. Souter, Emile Mercier, Unk White and Mick Armstrong, who was later to earn a strong reputation with his political cartoons for the Melbourne *Argus*. It was no fault of the *Punch* artists that this 69-year-old publication foundered. In December 1925, Melbourne *Punch* was "incorporated" in *Table Talk*, a society gossip magazine also published by the *Herald* group in Melbourne. Percy Leason and Will Dyson, as staff artists, worked out their contracts on *Table Talk*, which in turn ceased publication in 1937. Dyson returned to London in 1930, while Leason renewed his association with the *Bulletin*.

For many years, Leason had been passionately interested in the tonal painting theories of Max Meldrum. After a short holiday in America in 1937, he settled there with his family in 1939 and eventually became successful as an illustrator for *Collier's* magazine, the *Saturday Evening Post* and other periodicals, and as an art director and teacher of painting. He surprised the scientific world with his original research and theories on the Cro-Magnon cave artists, believing that they were the first artists to go directly to nature and suggesting that the seeming action and movement in their cave paintings was achieved by their study of dead, not living, animals.

Percy Leason died in New York at age 70 in September 1959.

V.L.

LEBEDEV, ALEKSANDR IGNATEVICH (1830-1898) Russian illustrator and cartoonist born in St. Petersburg, Russia, in 1830. Aleksandr Lebedev studied at the St. Petersburg Academy of Arts under the reputed teacher P.V. Basin from 1849 to 1857.

Lebedev became one of Russia's first and finest cartoonists in the late 1850s with contributions to the humor magazine *Vesel'chak* ("Merry Man") and *Iskra* ("The Spark," not to be confused with the later Marxist newspaper of the same title, of which Lenin was an editor). Lebedev pursued his cartooning career into the 1890s with his lusty depictions of St. Petersburg life and society. He also authored several albums of lithographs, of which the gently satirical *Fallen but Dear Creatures* (1862) is probably the best known, and he illustrated works by Nikolai Nekrasov and Saltykov-Shchedrin, among others.

Lebedev can be said to have been a forerunner of the Soviet school of social cartooning in many of his more iconoclastic cartoons; but he was first and foremost an entertainer whose politically pointed drawings (for which he was much praised in Soviet publications) do not seem to have bothered the czarist authorities. He died peacefully in St. Petersburg on April 16, 1898.

M.H.

LEECH, JOHN (1817-1864) British illustrator and cartoonist born in London, England, on August 29, 1817.

"The world's first cartoonist" is a title that may well belong to John Leech: he drew the first graphic satire ever to be called a cartoon. In 1843 an exhibition of cartoons proper (the rough designs for frescoes) was held in London: a competition for proposed designs for the walls of the Houses of Parliament. *Punch,* the illustrated satirical weekly, declared it would hold its own exhibition within its pages, "to be called *Punch*'s Cartoons." This announcement appeared on July 1, 1843, and then on July 15 "Cartoon No. 1: Substance and Shadow," drawn by John Leech, was introduced. It was a convenient term and quickly caught on for the weekly full-page topical or political drawing which *Punch* and its contemporaries regularly featured.

Youth: "You needn't be afraid Ma'am. Stand behind me!"
John Leech, 1860.

John Leech was born at the London Coffee House, Ludgate Hill, where his father was a vintner. At age 7 he attended Charterhouse, where the drawing master was Mr. Burgess. At 16 he went to study medicine at St. Bartholomew's, where he executed excellent anatomical drawings. At 18 he drew his first humorous sketches for *Bell's Life in London.* "Etchings and Sketchings by A. Pen" (1835) was his first publication—four quarto sheets sold at two shillings plain, three shillings colored. He became a full-time illustrator from 1838, and his first popular success was a burlesque of Rowland Hill's Penny Post design. He took over the illustration of Charles Dickens's *The Pickwick Papers* upon the sudden death of Robert Seymour. His first *Punch* drawing appeared in the fourth issue (August 7, 1841) and in the next 23 years he executed over four thousand cartoons and illustrations for the periodicals *Illustrated London News,* Jerrold's *Illustrated Magazine, Once a Week,* Bentley's *Miscellany, The Month* and *The Field,* and for books by Charles Dickens (*A Christmas Carol, The Chimes, Cricket on the Hearth*) and R.S. Surtees (the *Jorrocks* series).

Leech was also one of the first British cartoonists to work in the comic strip format: his *Mr. Briggs* began in *Punch* on February 24, 1849. Leech more than fulfilled the prophecy made by the sculptor Flaxman when Leech was seven years old: "Let his genius follow his own bent and he will astonish the world." Leech died quite young, at age 47, on October 29, 1864.

Books: *Etchings and Sketchings* (1835); *Comic English Grammar* (1840); *Comic Latin Grammar* (1840); *Fiddle Faddle Fashion Book* (1840); *Colin Clink* (1841); *Portraits of Children of the Mobility* (1841); *Written Caricatures* (1841); *Hector O'Halloran* (1842); *Jack the Giant Killer* (1843); *Whimsicalities* (1844); *Follies of the Year* (1844); *Comic Nursery Tales* (1844); *Punch's Snapdragons* (1845); *Comic History of England* (1847); *Struggles of Christopher Tadpole* (1848); *Mr. Sponge's Sporting Tour* (1848); *Rising Generation* (1848); *Book of Ballads* (1849); *Young Troublesome* (1850); *Comic History of Rome* (1851); *Handley Cross* (1854); *Pictures from Life and Character* (1854); *The Militiaman at Home and Abroad* (1857); *Encyclopedia of Rural Sports* (1858); *Ask Mamma* (1858); *Little Town in Ireland* (1859); *Paul Prendergast* (1859); *Mr. Briggs and His Doings* (1860); *Punch on Pegasus* (1861); *Early Pencillings for Punch* (1864); *Later Pencillings for Punch* (1865); *Carols of Cockaygne* (1869); *The Right Hon. John Bright* (1878); *Disraeli Cartoons* (1878); *Right Hon. William Gladstone Cartoons* (1878); *Fun for Everybody* (1879); *John Leech Artist and Humorist* (1883); *Adventures of Mr. Ledbury* (1886); *John Leech: His Life and Work* (1891); *Plain or Ringlets* (1892); *Mrs. Caudle* (1902); and *Pleasures of Mr. Briggs* (1906).

D.G.

Fernand Léger, "Ballet Mécanique." © Léger.

LÉGER, FERNAND (1881-1955) French painter born in Argentan, France, on February 4, 1881. After an apprenticeship as an architect's assistant (1897-99), Fernand Léger came to Paris in 1900. He studied at the Ecole des Beaux-Arts and the Académie Julian. Striking up friendships with André Salmon, Max Jacob and Guillaume Apollinaire, he became one of the most important pioneers and leaders in the modern art movement; along with Juan Gris and Pablo Picasso, he is now regarded as one of the founders of the Cubist movement. From 1918 until the time of his death at his summer home near Paris on August 15, 1955, Léger went on painting oils, watercolors, stage sets, posters and murals. Exhibitions of his works were held throughout the world, and he received countless honors, awards and distinctions during his lifetime.

Fernand Léger belongs to the history of cartoons because of one work, *Ballet Mécanique,* an animated cartoon of extraordinary style and versatility that has been called the "ultimate poem of motion." Léger worked on it all through 1923, and it was released the following year. Painted directly on celluloid, the film presents disjointed figures (including that of Charlie Chaplin) in balletic movement, drawing apart, getting together, whirling, jumping, multiplying, in an ever-changing pattern of forms and compositions. This seminal work has exerted tremendous influence on contemporary animators such as Hans Richter, Viking Eggeling and Alexandre Alexeieff; its impact on the history of experimental animation was enormous and continues to be felt.

M.H.

LEGER, PETER (1924-1991) German editorial cartoonist born in Brno, Czechoslovakia, on May 4, 1924. Peter Leger is descended from a long line of sculptors and stonecutters. His father was a painter, teacher and museum director in Brno. The German invasion of Czechoslovakia and World War II destroyed young Leger's chances of a normal art education. After the war he felt compelled to place his art in the service of a political commitment. He edited a magazine and slowly developed his cartoon style. Since 1947 he has been a freelance political cartoonist.

In the early 1950s his work appeared in the *Hannoversche Presse* (he lives near Hanover and has been connected with several local publications). Since at least as early as 1954, he has published frequently in the organ of the Social Democratic party, *Vorwärts* (located successively during those years in Hanover, Cologne and Bonn). Other newspapers and magazines that run his drawings are the *Süddeutsche Zeitung* (Munich), the *Hannoversche Allgemeine Zeitung,* the *EG-Magazin* (Bonn), the *Wirtschafts-Kurier* (Munich) and the central house organs of several labor unions: metalworking; chemicals, paper and ceramics; public services, transport and commerce; and printing and paper. His work has also appeared in several anthologies of political cartoons lampooning Adenauer, Erhard and Brandt, and in numerous textbooks, where they are valued for their usefulness in making history come alive.

Leger's style is basically ruggedly linear, with skillful use of strong black areas on occasion. It is a true cartoon idiom with no overtones of the academy. Without acknowledging any specific artistic influence, Leger gratefully points to Daumier and Thomas Theodor Heine as political thinkers in the field of art who have inspired him.

His artistic aim is to bring a touch of humanity to the area of political commentary. As a humorist, he recognizes the pitiful smallness of every human being, no matter how highly placed, and tries to restore the proper sense of proportion to epoch-making current events. Prizing his independence, he never accepts directives from the publications he works for.

Leger has also written and illustrated articles on politics, has lectured, and for a long time played a leading role in a journalists' labor union. He died in November 1991.

S.A.

LEJEUNE, FRANÇOIS (1908-1982) French cartoonist, poster designer and illustrator born in Paris, France, on February 12, 1908. François Lejeune (better known as "Jean Effel") started his cartooning career in 1933 contributing leftist political drawings to various newspapers and magazines, especially to *France-Soir, L'Express, Le Rire* and *Le Canard Enchaîné.* Most of these have been published in albums, notably *Colonel de la Rogue* (1936), *Jours sans Alboches* ("Days Without Dirty Krauts," 1945), *Toujours Occupés* ("Always Occupied, 1947-55," 1955), *De la Mollarchie a l'Empire Mongaulle* ("From Molletgarchy to the Mongaullian Empire," 1959) and *De la Debré á la Pompidour* (1964). He has also illustrated several books, the most beautiful being La Fontaine's *Fables.*

It was in 1943 that Effel hit upon the idea of using little angels as the supporting cast in *Turelune le Cornepipeux* ("Turelune the Bagpipe Player"), the story of a friendly hobo gone to heaven to look for his little bird. From *Turelune* he developed in 1945 the likable characters of the Good Lord, Adam and Eve in Eden, the cherubs and the animals, who became an instant and worldwide success in *La Création du Monde* ("The Creation of the World," 1951), translated into 16 languages. It explains how God, bored with looking into the void, created the world, and how the Devil was always meddling in and sabotaging his work. Other series in this lighthearted look at the Old Testament include *Le Dioble et Son Train* ("The Devil and His Train,"

"Fakes, from A to Z . . ."
François Lejeune ("Jean Effel"). © Lejeune.

1951), *La Vie Naïve d'Adam et Eve,* ("The Naive Life of Adam and Eve," 1956), *Le Roman d'Adam et Eve* ("The Romance of Adam and Eve," 1956-60), *La Genèse Ingénue* ("In the Beginning," 1966) and *Il Créa l'Homme et la Femme* ("He Made Man and Woman," 1967).

Effel's poetic and gentle world full of angels, flowers, birds, the zest and clarity of his line and the very optimism of his irony appealed to animated cartoon directors. Alain Resnais did a TV short based on his drawings (1948), and the Czech Eduard Hofman directed *The Creation of the World* (1956) with the right mix of tenderness and humor.

Jean Effel, who has drawn close to fifteen thousand pieces and published more than a hundred books (including the amusing novel *Plog,* 1970), has exhibited his art all over Europe and received numerous awards. He was a life member of the Academy of Humor. He died in 1982.

P.H.

LE LOUARN, YVAN (1915-1968) French cartoonist, engraver, illustrator and animated cartoon director born in Bordeaux, France, on February 10, 1915. After studies at the Bordeaux Ecole des Beaux-Arts, Yvan Le Louarn settled in Paris, where he began a cartooning career under the pen name "Chaval." His drawings have appeared in many magazines (e. g., *Punch, Paris-Match, Le Rire*) and since 1946 especially in *Le Figaro* and *Le Figaro Littéraire.*

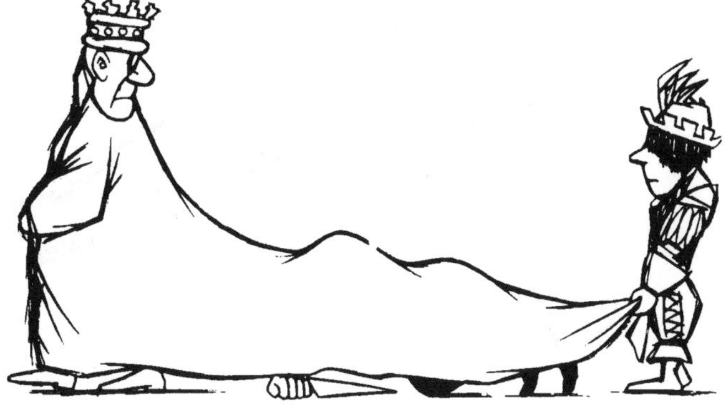

Yvan Le Louarn ("Chaval"). © Paris-Match.

Most of his cartoons have been published in albums: *99 Dessins sans Paroles* ("99 Drawings Without Words," 1955), *C'est la Vie: The Best Cartoons of Chaval* (1957), *Les Gros Chiens* ("Big Dogs," 1962), *L'Homme* ("Man, 1970), etc. In addition, Chaval has illustrated numerous books, including Nietzsche's *Beyond Good and Evil* (1955), Swift's *Directions to Servants* and Flaubert's *Dictionary of Accepted Ideas* (1958), and directed several animated cartoons, one of which, *Les Oiseaux Sont des Cons* ("Birds Are Assholes"), won the Emile Cohl Prize in 1965.

Chaval's drawings reveal a certain influence from some of the early 20th-century French cartoonists and from the American Peter Arno, but his style and themes are all his own. Master of the pun and the aphorism, Chaval shows us a world that is both strange and ambiguous, halfway between fear and comedy, as in his series *A Chacun Son Jouet* ("To Each His Toy"), where we see a bullfighter pulling a toy bull on wheels, an African explorer with a globe, a Russian officer with an ICBM on which a dog is relieving himself. His figures all have rather stupid, cowlike faces and a perplexed look, as if they were not sure who and what they are. They are drawn in very thick and very black charcoal lines, as though to stress the ineradicableness both of their blank stupidity and of the sheer absurdity of the world.

No longer able to bear life's petty demands and disillusionments, Chaval committed suicide on January 22, 1968.

P.H.

LEMAY, ARTHUR (1900-1944) French-Canadian cartoonist born in Nicolet, Quebec, on June 5, 1900. Like Russell Patterson before him, Arthur Lemay was given his start by the Montreal daily *La Patrie.* In 1920 Lemay began his cartooning career with the paper with a series of sports pan-

Union worker, which do you prefer?
Freedom?. . . . . . Slavery?
Arthur Lemay, World War II propaganda cartoon. © Canadian Information Office.

els. He was then asked to take over *Les Aventures de Timothée,* a Sunday strip created by Albéric Bourgeois, which Lemay guided for five years (1920-25), turning it into a burlesque comedy.

In 1922 Lemay went to Paris, studying at the Académie Julian and the Ecole des Beaux-Arts. He financed his studies and his rambles through Europe with the money he received for *Timothée,* which he continued by mail from Europe. Returning to Montreal in 1924, he abandoned *Timothée* the next year (the strip being continued by Maurice Gagnon) to devote himself almost exclusively to political cartooning. This new career was punctuated by Lemay's publication in 1929 of his album *Les Mille Têtes* ("The Thousand Heads"), a series of portraits of Canadian politicians. His graphic style, a little heavy at times, was a hybrid of realism, comic strip techniques and a penchant for lengthy commentary that he had inherited from cartoonists of the 19th century such as Hector Berthelot.

During the 1930s Lemay contributed illustrations to magazines like *La Revue Moderne* and in 1933 published two books: *Trois-Pistoles,* in which he illustrated the landscapes of the St. Lawrence River, and *Noir et Blanc* ("Black and White"), a series of political portraits. He also worked for *L'Illustration* (1930-41), drawing the faces of generations of prizefighters and hockey players. At the outbreak of World War II, Lemay offered his services to the Information Bureau in Time of War located at Ottawa. He also continued to draw two pages of editorial cartoons a week for *La Patrie, Le Monde Comme Il Va* ("As the World Goes") and *La Semaine Illustrée* ("The Week in Illustration"). The tense atmosphere of the times is reflected in Lemay's cartoons as well as in his two cartoon books published by the Information Service, *Album de Guerre* ("War Album") and *Que Préfères-Tu?* ("What Do You Prefer?"). These are typical war propaganda in which the expressionistic imagery competes with the Manicheanism of the captions.

In 1940-41 Lemay stayed in Quebec, where he painted a mural for the planned 1942 New York Universal Exposition. He also contributed cartoons to the *New York News* around the same time. On January 20, 1944, Lemay suddenly died. A retrospective of his work was organized by the International Pavilion of Humor of Montreal in 1976.

S.J.

LEMMI, LEMMO (1884-1926) Brazilian cartoonist of Italian origin born in São Paulo, Brazil, in 1884. The son of the Italian sculptor Ernesto Lemmi, Lemmo Lemmi studied art at the University of Pisa in Italy. Coming back to São Paulo after his studies, he started his cartooning career in 1908 with contributions to the Rio publication *O Malho,* under the pseudonym "Voltolino." Starting in 1911, he collaborated on the São Paulo publications *O Pirralho* (from the inception of the magazine), *Pasquim Coloniale* and *O Saci.* He is best known, however, for his cartoon depictions of the exuberant São Paulo life in *D. Quixote* (from 1919) and for his satires on Brazilian society in *O Parafuso,* under the pseudonym "Cam." He also illustrated children's books and newspaper articles.

Lemmi was one of the most original Brazilian cartoonists, with a zestful style, an eccentric line and an eye for color. His brilliant career was cut short when he died in a car accident in 1926, at age 42.

A.M.

LENICA, JAN (1928-) Polish animator born in Poznań, Poland, on January 4, 1928. Jan Lenica studied music and architecture in college but later turned to art. In 1950 he became one of the founders of the Polish school of poster design with his famous movie posters. He also wrote and illustrated children's books and worked as an exhibition designer.

Lenica's involvement with the animation medium began in 1957, when he produced the experimental *Once upon a Time* in collaboration with Walerian Borowczyk. Two more collaborative efforts followed: *Love Requited* (1957) and the sinister, allegorical *Dom* ("House," 1958). Later that year Lenica left for France, where he directed the slyly subversive *Monsieur Tête* ("Mister Head") in collaboration with Henri Gruel. Lenica continued his pessimistic exploration of a decadent world with *Janko the Musician,* the claustrophobic and surreal *Labyrinth* (1962), the despairing *Rhinoceros* (inspired by Ionesco's play) and the unsettling *A* (1964).

In 1963 Lenica moved to West Germany, where he brought to fruition his most ambitious project, *Adam II,* a feature-length film completed in 1969. A nightmarish, frightening, but also strangely affecting work, it projects the disturbing image of a controlled, computerized universe in which man is but one of many cogs. *Adam II* remains Lenica's most eloquent statement and is his masterpiece to date. In 1976 Lenica brought out his long-awaited *Ubu-Roi,* an animated version of Alfred Jarry's black comedy; although it had its moments, it proved a disappointment to Lenica's many admirers because of its many overlong stretches and stilted dialogue. He directed

Jan Lenica, "Ubu-Roi." © Lux Film.

a sequel to *Ubu Roi, Ubu et la Grande Gigouille,* based on two other plays by Jarry, in 1979. Since that time he has been mainly working in live-action moviemaking.

M.H.

LENOIR, CARLOS (1878-1906) Brazilian cartoonist and caricaturist of French origin born in 1878. Little information on Carlos Lenoir's early years exists, but it seems that he was born in southern Brazil, to which his parents had emigrated in the 1870s. He worked in the Rio de Janeiro central post office at the turn of the century. In 1903 his first cartoon was published in the magazine *A Avenida;* he used the pseudonym "Gil Vaz," which he later shortened simply to "Gil." After this first success, Gil left his post office job and embarked on a prolific cartooning career; his works appeared in most Rio publications, such as *O Molho, O Teatro, Figuras e Figurões, A Comédia, Gazeta de Noticias* and especially *O Tico-Tico,* of which he was one of the founders in 1905.

Gil was one of the most popular caricaturists of the time, and his elegant line was particularly well suited to the depiction (only slightly exaggerated) of theater actors and theater scenes. His cartoons in *O Tico-Tico* were among the most beloved features of the magazine. In the midst of all the acclaim, Gil's life was tragically cut short by illness, and he died in 1906, at age 28.

A.M.

LE POITEVIN, EUGÈNE (1806-1870) French painter, cartoonist, lithographer and illustrator born in Paris, France, on July 31, 1806. After studying with Le Prince at the Paris Ecole des Beaux-Arts, Eugène Le Poitevin started contributing light and naughty cartoons to *La Revue des Peintres* and *La Caricature.* It is, however, for the very amusing series of devils represented in all kinds of postures and situations (some actually obscene) that Le Poitevin is rightly famous. His *Charges et Décharges Diaboliques* ("Diabolical Charges and Discharges") and especially his *Diableries* ("Deviltries")—like those of Grandville but less wittily—poke fun at would-be poets, virginal maidens and middle-class housewives who are all quite literally bedeviled.

In addition to painting battle scenes and seascapes, Le Poitevin illustrated several books, among which are *Boccaccio's Decameron* (1845) and Rousseau's *The New Héloïse* (1846). He died in Paris on August 6, 1870, and was later rediscovered by the Surrealists.

P.H.

LEVERING, ALBERT (1869-1929) American cartoonist born in Hope, Indiana, in 1869. Albert Levering studied architecture with his father and art in Munich, Germany. After his training, he became an architect, working for eight years before transforming his architect's table into a cartoonist's drawing board.

Levering displayed great talent and real native humor; he worked successively for the *Minneapolis Times,* the *Chicago Tribune* and the *New York American.* In New York, he became a mainstay of *Puck's* art staff just after the turn of the century and formed his happiest association with John Kendrick Bangs during the latter's editorship. Levering illustrated a long-running Bangs *Alice in Wonderland* spoof and contributed large topical drawings; at the same time he drew for *Life* and *Harper's Weekly.* For a time Levering was also engaged on the staff of the *Sunday Tribune* in New York.

His drawing style, perhaps due to his architectural background, had a remarkable fullness and solidity of line. Often he would draw involved scenes and crosshatch quite precisely, although there never was a stifling rigidity to his work. Figures were animated and very competently drawn; overall, his drawings (Levering worked almost exclusively in pen and ink) commanded respect.

Albert Levering died on April 14, 1929.

R.M.

LEVINE, DAVID (1926-   ) American cartoonist and caricaturist born in Brooklyn, New York, on December 12, 1926. In his discipline, he was the most influential artist of the post-Hirschfeld era.

David Levine was educated at P.S. 241, Junior High 210 in Brooklyn, Erasmus High School, Tyler School of Fine Arts at Temple University and the Hans Hoffman Eighth Street School of Painting in Manhattan. His influences include cartoonists in the 19th-century English and French satirical traditions, 19th-century paintings and Japanese prints.

The field of caricature (and much of illustration) was revolutionized when Levine's spots and caricatures began

David Levine, caricature of Lyndon Johnson. © New York Review of Books.

appearing in the *New York Review of Books* in the early 1960s. They were devastatingly accurate and incisive—which alone would have assured Levine a niche in cartooning history—but in addition, his medium was the pen, his technique the old-fashioned crosshatch style full of shadings, nuances, blemishes and loose hairs. He reveled in fine pen lines and orchestrated his elaborate shadings to give an interpretation capturing the essence of the subject.

When Levine had established himself, the army of imitators—these, even the talented ones, comprise the bulk of a "school" in any field of cartooning and all the arts—switched from aping Hirschfeld to copying Levine's techniques, just as, contemporaneously, political cartooning was switching from the "Herblock school" to the "Oliphant school."

Levine, whose work has been collected several times, and who is a contributing editor both to *Esquire* and *New York* magazines, is a member of the National Academy and was a Guggenheim Fellow. He has received the Tiffany Award for his paintings and was the recipient of Long Island University's George Polk Award, among others. He is an active member of the Association of American Editorial Cartoonists. In 1978 an exhaustive collection of his works, *The Arts of David Levine,* was published by Knopf in New York.

After 35 years of drawing political and literary caricatures, D. Levine (as he signs his work) has become the most admired and imitated caricaturist in the U.S. In a 1988 interview he described the caricaturist's function this way: "To convey one's feelings and attitudes towards his fellow creatures, as shaped by a world view and expressed through distortion." In addition to being a world-renowned caricaturist he is also a painter of repute, whose works have been exhibited in galleries in New York City, Washington, D.C., Oxford, England, and many other places.

R.M.

LEWIS, ROSS A. (1902-198?) American Pulitzer Prize-winning political cartoonist born in Metamora, Michigan, on November 9, 1902. R.A. Lewis was educated at the University of Wisconsin at Milwaukee, the Layton School of Art, and the Art Students League in New York. He cites the two greatest influences on his work as two instructors at the League: Boardman Robinson and Thomas Hart Benton.

Lewis joined the *Milwaukee Journal* in 1925 as an illustrator and staff artist, after teaching two years at his alma mater, the Layton School. He began to draw editorial cartoons in 1932 after Ding Darling, whom the paper bought as a syndicated cartoonist, declared for Hoover, an advocacy the *Journal* was reluctant to join. Lewis remained the chief political cartoonist, and in 1935, his third year in this position, he was awarded the Pulitzer Prize for his editorial cartoon on industrial strikes and violence. He retired in 1967 after 35 years with the *Journal.* He died in the 1980s.

The style of Lewis's art is reminiscent of Daniel Fitzpatrick and similar to that of Tom Little and other disciples of the crayon. What appears to be a breezy, quick crayon rendering is actually a stylized, careful blend of crayon, brush, thin pen lines and straight lead pencil. It is a style wonderfully suited to newspaper reproduction.

R.M.

LEYDEN, JOCK (1909-) South African cartoonist born in Scotland in 1909. Leyden came to South Africa after the First World War and began his career as a lithographer for a Durban printing company in 1926. While there, in his own words he "spent more time drawing caricatures of the printing house staff," and these were soon noticed by the yachting correspondent of the *Natal Advertiser*. In 1927 he started drawing caricatures of yachting and other sports personalities for the *Advertiser* (which later became the Durban *Daily News*), while at the same time contributing drawings and sketches to British publications.

In 1936 Leyden became editorial cartoonist for the *Sunday Tribune*, and a few years later he rejoined the *Daily News* whose staff cartoonist he was to remain for more than 50 years. During World War II he supported the Allied cause at a time when many nationalist elements were actively pro-Nazi; and his cartoons were part of the Touring Commonwealth Cartoonists Exhibition in 1943-44. In 1948, when the apartheid laws were proclaimed in South Africa, the *News* became one of the main pillars of opposition to the separation policy, and Leyden's cartoons lent strong support to this liberal stance. "I feel a responsibility to bash at" apartheid, he declared. "I don't know what else I can do."

During most of those years, South Africa's then-president, P.W. Botha, was his most constant target. In one of his cartoons Leyden depicted him as Nero fiddling the apartheid tune while the South African economy was going up in blazes. In another one he showed him trying to stay ahead of an avalanche labeled "economic sanctions" his policies had unleashed. These and others of his cartoons earned him the enmity of the government and threats of censorship.

Leyden's cartoons have been anthologized in more than 15 collections to date. He has exhibted at various cartoon festivals in England, Italy, Belgium, Canada, and elsewhere. In 1981 he received the South African Cartoonist of

Jock Leyden. © Durban Daily News.

the Year Award; and in the early 1990's he had the satisfaction of seeing the policies of apartheid come to an end.

In 1992, following a triple-bypass operation, Leyden retired from his editorial position, although he still contributes an occasional cartoon or two for the *News*.

M.H.

LICHTENSTEIN, GEORGE MAURICE (1905-1983) American cartoonist born in Chicago, Illinois, in 1905. George Lichtenstein showed an early talent for drawing and sold his first cartoon to *Judge* at the age of 16. After enrolling at the Chicago Art Institute, Lichtenstein reputedly got dismissed in 1924 for drawing moustaches on some of the portraits hanging in the school's gallery. The following year he entered the University of Michigan, from which he graduated in 1929. During his college years he edited the *Michigan Gargoyle* and won first prize in the 1928 *College Humor* contest.

In 1929 the *Chicago Times* came into existence, and "Lichty" (as the artist was now known) joined its staff from the beginning, mainly drawing sport cartoons and spot illustrations. In 1930 he created the short-lived *Sammy Squirt,* a gag strip about a soda jerk. Lichty was to prove more successful in 1932 with his panel *Grin and Bear It,* which won immediate recognition and national syndication two years later. In addition to *Grin and Bear It* (which he drew for over forty years, relinquishing it in 1974 to Fred Wagner), Lichty has contributed innumerable cartoons to virtually every magazine in the United States. He was also the author of a satirical anti-Soviet panel, *Is Party Line, Comrade,* which ran during the 1950s and 1960s. He died July 18, 1983, on his apple ranch in northern California.

Lichty's style is a winning amalgam of loose penmanship, slapdash composition and broad humor. He works hard and fast ("I can finish a week's work within two days," he once asserted) with almost no wasted motion or redundance of line. Lichtenstein has received countless honors for his work and is a four-time winner of the National Cartoonists Society's Best Newspaper Panel award.

M.H.

"Vandalism, maybe? . . . On the other hand it could be a wedding anniversary!"

George Lichtenstein ("Lichty"), "Grin and Bear It." © Field Enterprises, Inc.

LICHTY
See Lichtenstein, George Maurice.

LIFE'S LIKE THAT (U.S.) Fred Neher's daily gag panel, *Life's Like That,* made its debut on October 1, 1934, followed by a Sunday version on October 7. Both were distributed by Bell Syndicate.

Although the panel does contain the usual family—Ollie and Mollie, the middle-aged parents, teenage daughter Shelley Ann and prankster son Will-Yum, not to mention the family dog Pardner and the goldfish Golde—it is not, strictly speaking, a domestic feature. The goings-on center around the neighborhood and touch on topical subjects, although there is no scarcity of family situations. Just as J.R. Williams did before him, Neher liked to run sub-features such as "Will-Yum," "Us Moderns," "Hi-Teens," "Mrs. Pip's Diary" (so named for the neighborhood gossip) and "Some Punkins" (which refers to the neighborhood siren). The artist kept his gags simple and unaffected, with a view to not offending any of his readers. "I think people have enough grief in their lives without getting more of it on the comic pages," he once asserted. "They come there to be entertained and lifted, not depressed."

"He's been doing the same thing for 40 years but now he calls it 'Golden Age.'"

"Life's Like That." © Bell-McClure Syndicate.

Life's Like That was taken over by United Feature Syndicate when Bell-McClure (successor of Bell Syndicate) went out of business in 1970. It was discontinued on August 20, 1977, upon Fred Neher's retirement.

M.H.

LIMA, VASCO MACHADO DE AZEVEDO (1886?-1973) Brazilian cartoonist born in Porto, Portugal, on September 6, 1886 (some sources say 1883). Vasco Lima emigrated to Rio de Janeiro around the turn of the century and studied drawing with João Batista da Costa. His first cartoons were published in the Rio daily *Gazeta de Notícias* in 1903. Starting in 1905, he contributed innumerable cartoons and caricatures to such publications as *A Tribuna* (until 1912), *O Malho, A Avenida, O Tico-Tico, Fon-Fon!, Figuras e Figurões* and *A Noite.*

Lima was called in to direct the children's weekly *O Fafâzinho* in 1907. In 1911 he started publishing his monthly (later weekly) *Album de Caricaturas,* which lasted until 1913; he drew all the cartoons of every issue under the pen name "Hugo Lea." Lima's fame as a cartoonist was probably unequaled during his lifetime, and it led to his editorship of *A Noite Ilustrada, Carioca* and *Vamos Ler* in the 1930s and 1940s. Toward the end of his long career Lima abandoned cartooning in favor of watercolors, which he exhibited in a number of group shows in Brazilian galleries. He died on August 7, 1973.

Lima's style was precise, direct and much imitated. His draftsmanship was superb, but his humor sometimes veered toward the macabre. The comic strips he drew in the 1910s and 1920s are now regarded as classics by Brazilian historians.

A.M.

LIMMROTH, MANFRED (1928-) German cartoonist and author born in Kassel, Germany, in 1928. He is also a clever collagist whose love-hate relationship with the mass-produced wood-engraved illustrations of the late 19th century recalls that of Max Ernst and other great exponents of collage.

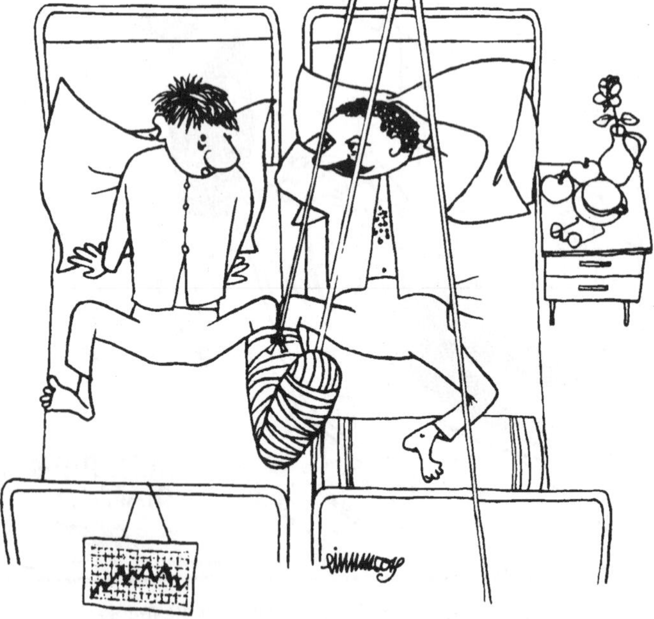

"I guess we both belong to the same group hospitalization plan." *Manfred Limmroth. © Neue Illustrierte.*

Limmroth studied art at the Kassel Academy and in Zurich in the early to mid-1950s, and later worked for *Die* Welt and *Kristall* (both in Hamburg). He illustrated books, did industrial ads (good preparation for his later parodies!) and worked on stage sets and costumes. His best work appeared in his albums of the late 1950s and the 1960s, published in Hanover.

In 1961 he published *Führer durch Deutschland und Umgebung* ("Guide to Germany and Vicinity"), based on a series that had run in *Kristall* that year. These incisive pen drawings touch devastatingly on many social and moral ills of the times: fancy cars that don't work, the destruction of the countryside in the course of army maneuvers, the leveling influence of modern curtain-wall architecture on all large German cities, the pollution of the water supply, etc. The 1963 album *Als Oma Noch ein Backfisch War* ("When Grandma Was Still a Teenager") is an anthology of representative late 19th-century magazine articles and illustrations.

Träum Schön! ("Sweet Dreams!," 1964) consists chiefly of fake ads for incredible products and services (plastic dandruff, roof polish, vicarious book reading, and so on) that appeared alongside real ads in a monthly magazine and fooled many readers with their specific instructions involving real places and mailing addresses. Here again, Limmroth's attack is on the false values of contemporary bourgeois society. His principal artistic vehicle is the wickedly misleading collage.

Other noteworthy Limmroth albums include *Das Güldene Schatzkästlein* ("Ye Golden Treasure Chest"), a handbook of old and new kitsch; *Rathgeber in Allen Lebenslagen* ("Counselor in All Life Situations"), which also uses old wood engravings; and *Liebe am Samstag* ("Love on Saturday"), a five-act play with prologue told in pictures. As of 1998 he has drawn well over 3000 cartoons, published numerous books, and received several art awards.

S.A.

LINDA, CURT (1928-) Curt Linda, born April 23, 1928 in Budweis, Bohemia, came to work for the Bavaria Film studios situated on the outskirts of Munich as a director and scriptwriter for dubbing movies into the German language. Always having had an interest in animated cartoons, he went to Yugoslavia in 1960 for a year of studying the theory and practice of producing animated cartoons. Back in Munich again, he founded his own studio for the production of animated cartoons in 1962. At first he came up with a number of shorts, then moved on to animated feature films when he started producing *Die Konferenz der Tiere* ("The Animal Conference") based on Erich Kästner's novel of the same title. Among his other animated feature films are the prestigious *Shalom Pharao* (1979 - 1982), the adaptation of the children's book *Das kleine Gespenst* ("The Little Ghost", 1990), the ghost story *Harold and the Ghosts* (1994) and *Die Zauberflöte* ("The Magic Flute", 1996-1997) loosely based on the Mozart opera.

During the 1970's Linda worked almost exclusively for television. Most notable among his TV productions are 53 episodes of *Stories from History,* a series of multi-part parodies of heroes like Hercules or the Nibelungs. Also of note are Linda's entries in the pan-European production of *Fairy Tales from Many Nations* and his parodies of opera, *Opera presto,* in which he whittled down 13 operas to their funnybone. He also made a series of animated adaptations of the Dutch comic strip *Suske en Wiske.*

Linda is an obsessive worker convinced that there are stories you can tell only or tell better in the animated format. He has created a drawing style for his cartoons that includes crosshatching instead of sharp shadows. Linda definitely is not and does not aim to be a German Disney. He is Curt Linda with all the advantages and disadvantages that may bring. And he also is an outspoken representative of the cartooning profession. Therefore, in 1978 he founded the German chapter of ASIFA, the international federation of animators, which has since lent more of a sense of unity to German animated cartoonists, who up to then had all gone their separate ways.

Owning a small studio may lead to occasional frustrations, but Linda nevertheless loves the job he created for himself practically out of nowhere.

W.F.

LINDSAY, NORMAN ALFRED WILLIAMS (1879-1969)
Australian cartoonist born in Creswick, Victoria, in 1879.

In the three decades preceding 1900, black-and-white art was seriously regarded as one of the most difficult of all media, and admirable work was produced on the Continent and in England and America. In this medium, the finest penman Australia ever produced was Norman Lindsay.

Equipped. —Bung: "Hey, Dave! ye've left yer whip behind."
—Dave (too lazy to walk back): "That's all right, Bill.
I'll call f'r't comin' back. I got me langwidge."
Norman Lindsay, 1907.

Lindsay first came into national prominence in 1901, at the age of 21, when at the invitation of its editor, J.F. Archibald, he joined the *Bulletin* staff as an artist. The offer came as a result of an outstanding series of pen drawings illustrating the *Decameron* of Boccaccio, which were exhibited in Sydney and reviewed by A.G. Stevens on the famous Red Page of the *Bulletin.* What was remarkable for an artist so young, and self-taught at that, was that these pen drawings were recognized as the finest of their kind yet produced in Australia. (Pen drawing was an art peculiar to the 19th century and came about through the replacement of wood, steel and copper engraving by the new photoengraving techniques of reproduction.)

Norman Lindsay started his career in journalism when he was 16 years of age. From Creswick, a little township near Ballarat in Victoria, he joined his brother, Lionel, to share a studio in Melbourne. He was engaged on his first press work for the *Hawklett,* a Melbourne publication devoted to illustrating crime and the doubtful and seamy side of life. Later, at 19, he worked on lithographic posters. Then followed a period as art editor for the short-lived magazine the *Rambler.* After his appointment to the *Bulletin* staff Lindsay moved on to Sydney to become within a few years an internationally known pen draftsman. Before he had served 12 months, he was given the distinction of drawing a full-page cartoon every week, although before his association with the *Bulletin,* Lindsay had never had any drawings published in that journal and only one in the now extinct Melbourne *Punch.*

As much of the immediate past and present of Australia at that time was rural, much of Norman Lindsay's black-and-white humor dealt with bush types and rural situations. His early joke drawings did much to establish what is today in Australia a legendary outback pattern that originated with the graphic humorists, including Lindsay, George Lambert, Alf Vincent, Frank Mahony, Fred Leist, Benjamin Minns and Ambrose Dyson. Indeed, the whiskers, the waistcoats and the bowyangs of present-day Australian rural comic strips and joke drawings are direct legacies from artists like Lindsay.

But Lindsay's emphasis was not entirely on "backblocks" humor. Lindsay, like Phil May and other artists before him, also drew inspiration from the city. His characters—the larrikins, city tramps, the rabbit-ohs, slum urchins, his "Saturdee" boys and Jiggerty Janes—were all subjects for his superb observation and good-natured ridicule.

Even with journalism's pressures, Lindsay's skill was such that his drawings were never altered or corrected with process-white paint or paste-on patches, expedient devices found repeatedly in the drawings of many artists working under deadlines. Unlike most artists, he never inked in black masses on his drawings. Dark areas were built up with individual strokes and lines to a state perfect in tonal balance—truly a form of pen painting.

Norman Lindsay has produced many thousands of items for the press, but of all his published work—strip jokes, humorous illustrations, joke drawings, political and war cartoons—it is his frolicsome animals that have brought him the most admiration, praise and fame. These drawings of native bears, wombats and bandicoots—and, of course, the animal characters of *The Magic Pudding* (1918), a fantasy Lindsay wrote and illustrated—have, because of the many reprints since 1918, made his name a household word in Australia for the last 50 years.

V.L.

LIONAR, THOMAS A. (1956-1989) Born in Belinyu, Bangka, Indonesia, on December 6, 1956, Thomas A. Lionar developed an interest in drawing as a child, reading, clipping, and copying cartoons and comics found in foreign magazines his father brought home. After high school graduation in 1975, Lionar worked at an educational institute in Sungaliat, Bangka, and freelanced as a cartoonist on the side. In 1988, he began to work on the editorial staff of the daily *Suara Pembaruan*.

Originally, Lionar drew gag cartoons but, over the years, found he was more interested in political cartoons and caricature. These won him three Adinegoro trophies, including one first prize, for best Indonesian political cartoon and a prize for caricature from the journalists' association. As a freelance cartoonist, his works appeared in many places, including *Kompas, Sinar Harapan, Mutiara, Intisari,* and *Gadis*.

In the eyes of many of his colleagues, Lionar was the country's best cartoonists, his works appealing because of their exquisite details, colorful shading, and comical representations. The latter were important to Lionar as he related in an interview shortly before his death from tuberculosis in May 1989: "In my opinion, it is not right when a cartoon or caricature always criticizes, attacks, or offends. The cartoon world is a playful one. A cartoon drawing should not be regarded seriously with a furrowed brow, not be viewed as being able to change a situation. The world will not cease to turn because of a cartoon."

J.A.L.

LION KING, THE (U.S.) The Disney studio realized a long-cherished project when they released *The Lion King* in June 1994. It had begun life years earlier as "King of the Jungle," when a team was sent to Africa to study jungle life in general and lion behavior more particularly. The plot deals with young Simba (Swahili for "lion"), son of King Musafa of the Pride lands, who is tricked by his uncle Scar into believing he has killed his father. Fleeing into exile, Simba is succored by the free-spirited Pumbaa, a warthog, and the wisecracking Timon, his meerkat companion. As he grows into adulthood he is sought out by his childhood friend Nala, the lioness, who persuades him to return to his native land and reclaim his birthright; this he does, defeating Scar and his pack of hyenas that had enslaved the tribe of lions.

Directed by Roger Allers and Rob Minkoff, the film was filled with spectacular incidents and almost non-stop action that included a wildebeest stampede, a flight along treacherous jungle paths, and the climactic fight between Simba and Scar supported by his hyena acolytes. There were moments of levity supplied mosly by the hijinks of Timon and Pumbaa, along with a number of catchy tunes composed by Elton John and Tim Rice (one of them, "Can You Feel the Love Tonight?," won the Academy Award for Best Song).

Upon the film's release there were protests on both sides of the Pacific Ocean accusing Disney of having borrowed the theme and many plot elements from the late Osaku Tezuma's *Jungle Emperor*; Tezuma's family, however, declined to join in the protests.

With *The Lion King* Disney topped a winning streak that had started five years earlier with *The Little Mermaid*. While not as financially successful as *Aladdin*, it did very good business and was extremely well received critically. An animated television series, *The Lion King's Timon & Pumbaa*, based on Simba's animal companions, started airing on CBS in 1995, and a stage version of *The Lion King* opened on Broadway in October 1997.

M.H.

LITTLE AUDREY (U.S.) Inspired by the success of their *Little Lulu* cartoons, Famous Studios/Paramount cast around for yet another comic book girl to bring to the animation screen and came up with Little Audrey. The red-haired, freckle-faced moppet was first seen in the 1949 "The Lost Dream" (written by Isidore Klein and Bill Turner), which proved a fair success with its intended

"Little Audrey." © Paramount Pictures.

juvenile audience. A number of additional *Little Audrey* cartoons, each more forgettable than the last, came out in the 1950s: "Audrey the Rainmaker" (1951) and "Little Audrey Riding Hood" (1955) are typical of the series as a whole in their cloying cuteness.

Little Audrey and her young companions were put through their paces in conventional situations involving homegrown villains and unthreatening menaces. The cartoons were rather professionally directed (by the likes of Dave Tendlar, Ralph Bakshi and John Gentiella) but hurriedly animated, and they were always a waste of otherwise creditable talent. They deserve to be mentioned here as a glaring example of the pitiful state into which American animation had fallen in the 1950s. (It should be noted, however, that *Little Audrey*, who has starred in her own comic book since 1948, has desultorily continued her career in that medium till 1993.)

M.H.

LITTLE BIRD TOLD ME, A
See Kuhn, Walt.

LITTLE JOHNNY AND HIS TEDDY BEARS (U.S.) The versatile John Randolph Bray conquered one more world—the magazines—with several cartoon series for *Judge* just after the turn of the century. Among these was *Little Johnny and His Teddy Bears*, which obviously capitalized on the great popular affection for President Theodore Roosevelt and on the new rage among children, the "Teddy bear." (Another cartoon series, *The Roosevelt Bears*, by Seymour Eaton and R.K. Culver, ran through many books and cards and is avidly collected even today.)

Bray's series concerned itself with the pranks and pratfalls of Johnny, a little boy in a Buster Brown suit, and his friends, six stuffed, animated bears. Episodes ran to six panels, usually in color on the back page, with the tale often told in verse. Bray's artwork was funny and uncluttered, and it showed a great instinct for narration and sequence—which served him well in his later endeavors. (Bray's series did not confine themselves to children's subjects; in 1910, for instance, he lampooned the automobile craze in *Gasoline Reggie and His Auto*.)

Little Johnny was enormously popular, running with great frequency between 1903 and 1907. In 1907 it was collected in a color reprint book published by *Judge*.

R.M.

LITTLE KING, THE (U.S.) *The Little King* is the best known of all the cartoon series produced by the Van Beuren studio in New York. Based on Otto Soglow's famous *New Yorker* character, it started its short run (all the Van Beuren series had a short run) in 1933. The first director on the series was Jim Tyer, and some of the cartoons he released the first year include "Pals," "The Fatal Note" and "Marching Along. "In 1934 Tyer, while remaining chief animator on the series, was replaced as director by George Stallings. Notable among Stallings's efforts are "Cactus King," "Art for Art's Sake" (a funny satire on abstract art), "Jolly Good Felons," "Sultan Pepper" (in which the king matched wits with a visiting potentate) and "A Royal Good Time," perhaps the best cartoon in the series, a wild flight of fancy into the world of clowns and carnivals.

The Little King was quite successful, commercially as well as artistically. Audiences seemed ready to accept the antics of the always silent monarch, while the purely visual humor of the cartoons (there was little dialogue) had an almost surrealistic tinge. The series was discontinued at the end of 1934, reportedly because of a contractual dispute with King Features Syndicate, which had acquired the rights to Soglow's creation earlier that year. In 1936 Max Fleischer tried to bring back the character in a *Betty Boop* cartoon titled, logically enough, "Betty Boop and the Little King," but the effort was not successful, and no further cartoons were attempted.

M.H.

LITTLE LULU (U.S.) Based on the popular series of cartoons done by Marjorie ("Marge") Henderson for the *Saturday Evening Post*, the *Little Lulu* animated shorts started production in 1944, under the aegis of Famous Studios/Paramount. "Lulu at the Zoo," "Lulu in Hollywood" and "Lulu Gets the Birdie" are some of the early titles. Unlike their magazine (and later comic book) counterparts, the *Little Lulu* cartoons did not contain any attempt at adult humor or symbolism but remained strictly at a child's level. The protagonists, the wise little girl Lulu, her boy companion Tubby and the other kids, went through a series of quite innocuous escapades. The drawing and direction were just as literal, and the series was aimed at a very juvenile audience; its quality steadily declined, and it disappeared from theaters in the 1960s, although it continues to be seen on television. A new, original *Lulu* show debuted in 1996 on HBO, with Tracey Ullman providing the moppet's voice.

The *Little Lulu* cartoons of the 1940s are the only ones that are still bearable today, notably "Musicalulu" (1946), "Loose in the Caboose" and "Super Lulu" (1947), and "Dog Show Off" (1948). Isadore Sparber, Seymour Kneitel and Vladimir Tytla were among the directors on the series; many of the stories were written by Otto Messmer.

M.H.

LITTLE MERMAID, THE (U.S.) Walt Disney had intended to make an animated feature based on Hans Christian Andersen's tale as early as 1939; he even commissioned the noted illustrator Kay Nielsen to develop sketches for the planned production. The war intervened, however, and the project was shelved. It took a full half-century for the film to finally make it to the movie screen (with a credit given to Nielsen). Released in 1989, *The Little Mermaid* also marked the studio's return to the genre they always did best—the musical fairy tale.

The plot was an embellishment on the original story. The little mermaid was Ariel, daughter of King Triton, who, to her father's everlasting indignation, fell in love with a human, Prince Eric. Together Ariel and Eric would thwart the evil designs of Ursula, the sea witch who intended to get Eric for herself and to take over Triton's kingdom. In contrast to the ending of the original tale, the lovers in the movie got married and presumably lived happily ever

"Little Lulu." © Harveytoons.

after. As is usually the case in this kind of production, the two romantic leads were upstaged by a secondary character, the court composer, a Jamaican crab named Horatio Thelonius Ignatius Crustaceous Sebastian, who not only got the best lines but also had the best song (the Oscar-winning "Under the Sea").

Jointly written and directed by John Musker and Ron Clements, the film displayed stunning animation on land and at sea, and dazzling special effects. Its success at the box-office prompted CBS to air a weekly *Little Mermaid* cartoon show, starting in 1992.

M.H.

LITTLE ROQUEFORT (U.S.) In the wake of the phenomenal success enjoyed by Tom and Jerry at MGM, Terrytoons (which could already boast Mighty Mouse) came up with yet another rodent, Little Roquefort. Unlike Mighty, however, Little Roquefort used his wits in order to defeat Percy, the villainous feline who was forever lying in wait for him. The fun and games started in 1950 with "Cat Happy" and continued through such forgettable entries as "Flop Secret," "Good Mousekeeping," "Mouse Menace" and "No Sleep for Percy." The *Little Roquefort* cartoons never enjoyed the popularity of the MGM cat-and-mouse adventures, and they disappeared from the screen in the late 1950s.

Paul Terry's able, if unimaginative, stable of directors and animators worked in turns on *Little Roquefort*, with Eddie Donnelly, Connie Rasinski and Mannie Davis the most prominently featured.

M.H.

LITTLE, THOMAS (1898-1972) American artist born in Snatch, Tennessee, in 1898. Tom Little was raised in Nashville and followed his artistic inclinations by studying art at that city's Watkins Institute (1912-15) and at the Montgomery Bell Academy (1917-18). After much doodling and freelance drawing for merchants' windows, Little landed a newspaper job at age 18—but as a reporter, not a cartoonist.

On the *Nashville Tennessean,* as reporter and police reporter, he developed his interest in cartooning through informal tutoring by Carey Orr, who was about to leave the *Tennessean* for the *Chicago Tribune.* (Little's stylistic mentor, however, was to be Dan Fitzpatrick, who had just left Chicago for the *Post-Dispatch* in St. Louis, replacing Bob Minor.) Wartime service in the army (the marines rejected the five-foot-two volunteer as underweight) interrupted his service for the Nashville paper, as did a year in New York (1923-24), where he drew comic strips and was a reporter for the *Herald-Tribune* and its syndicate.

Because of his mother's illness, however, he returned to Nashville. Back at his old desk, he advanced to city editor and in 1934 began drawing editorial cartoons. (After a dispute with the publisher in 1937, he was relieved of desk duties and drew exclusively.) Immediately Little became one of the nation's most influential and republished cartoonists. A fierce liberal Democrat, he produced cartoons of an artistic style and venom closely resembling Fitzpatrick's work. He was a master of composition, and his concepts were no less forceful than their renderings.

In 1934 Little also began *Sunflower Street,* a syndicated cartoon panel as homely and gentle as his political cartoons were powerful. Originally scripted by Tom Sims, this King Features oversize panel chronicled the doings of rural blacks—not their stereotyped predicaments, but their everyday concerns. The comfortable pen-and-ink feature was killed in 1949 due to fear of racially inspired criticism.

Little's editorial work was rendered in brush and crayon on a grained but not patterned paper. In 1948 he won the National Headliners Club award, and in 1957 the Pulitzer Prize. He died on June 20, 1972.

R.M.

LODOLO, SANDRO (1929-) Italian cartoonist and animator born in Udine, Italy, in 1929. After finishing high

Tom Little. © Nashville Tennessean.

school, Sandro Lodolo moved to Rome in 1950 and attended the Italian Center for Film Training; there he studied (and later taught) the art of animation. After a short stint drawing comics, Lodolo secured a job as a graphic artist for the Italian television network in 1957. Three years of drawing weather maps and diagrams of soccer games prompted him to open his own advertising studio. In 1965 Lodolo renewed his contacts with Italian TV (which in the meantime had discovered animation) and subsequently did more than three hundred animated credits for a number of televised programs. In 1966-67 he animated the titles of three feature films, and since 1968 he has also done a number of animated commercials.

In the early 1970s, at the request of Luciano Pinelli, producer of the TV program *Gli Eroe di Cartone* ("The Cartoon Heroes"), Lodolo decided to experiment with the still animation of comic strips. The film treatment of *Krazy Kat* and *Little Nemo* (with disappearance of the balloons, dissolves, zooms, etc.) proved successful and paved the way for the *Gulp, Fumetti in TV* ("Gulp, Comics in TV") series. The Lodolo studio is currently working on an ambitious project: the television reading of Alex Raymond's *Flash Gordon.*

S.T.

LÖFVING, HJALMAR EDVARD (1896-1968) Finnish cartoonist born on January 26, 1896. After five years of high school, Hjalmar Löfving studied for three more years at the Helsinki University of Arts; he began his long career in the 1910s, at the same time as did other "golden era" cartoonists like Ola Fogelberg and Toivo Vikstedt. His famous cartoon characters ridiculed right-wing fanatics and idealized left-wing youths, but he was also able to satirize the Communists when the need arose.

Known principally as a political cartoonist—and during this period he was probably at his best—Löfving later became a typical children's artist. His works could be seen in publications like *Kurikka, Piiska, Suomen Sosiaaldemokraatti, Elanto, Lipas* and *Koitto* (a temperance movement publication that was read in all the schools in Finland). He published several children's books (such as the educative *Oletko Nähnyt?* in 1938) and, beginning in 1916, had his cartoons exhibited at various shows.

Löfving's strong, hard-edged style is very easy to recognize; it sometimes resembles the art of Chester Gould in its economy of line and exaggeration of facial features. Perhaps the most amazing aspect of Löfving's career was his ability to change his views effortlessly according to the wishes of his employers: he drew for socialist as well as for nonsocialist magazines. He never had a permanent job but remained a freelancer throughout his life.

In the 1960s Löfving was a regular guest on television's *Niksulan TV,* where he told and drew fairy tales as "Uncle Pim-Pom." His comic strips were also very popular, and the innumerable riddles, puzzles and "hidden pictures" which he designed and drew made him the indisputable master of the genre. A short animated cartoon he made in 1927 may have been the first ever produced in Finland.

Hjalmar Löfving died on January 29, 1968, in Helsinki.

J.R.

LONDON LAUGHS (G.B.) *London Laughs,* a daily cartoon gag about London and Londoners featured in the London *Evening News* for 32 years, was not, in fact, drawn by a Londoner! Joe Lee, who depicted the familiar sights of the city (both in its landscape and its population), was a Yorkshireman.

The first *London Laughs* was published in the *Evening News* on May 14, 1934, submitted from a slum tenement in Battersea. The artist, who signed it simply "Lee," was given a month's trial—and continued the panel to its final appearance in July 1966! During World War II the title was changed to *Smiling Through,* and although the theme of the jokes became more topical, the spirit remained the same: the Londoner who laughed whatever the world (or Hitler) might throw at him.

The characters in *London Laughs* (the title was restored after the war) ranged through many familiar types without ever developing into regular "heroes." There were the cheeky Cockney urchins with their ready retorts, the cheery Cockney bus conductors with their equally ready cracks, the Cockney charwomen, the middle-class mums, the upper-class ladies and toppered gents, crusty colonels, wide-boy "spivs," bobbies, taxi drivers, Billingsgate fish porters and, of course, during the war, the Yankee GI's. All were drawn with Lee's flowing line and eye for detail. A book, *London Laughs, 1934-1951,* was published in 1951.

Joe Lee, who simultaneously provided the northern newspapers of the Allied Group with a parallel daily cartoon, was retired on pension in 1966. However, he soon found himself unable to remain idle and began freelancing political cartoons to the *Eastern Daily Press.* Then he took up comic strips. In 1933 he had drawn *Pin Money Myrtle* for the *Daily Mail,* but this time he turned to children's comic weeklies. He took over a number of established characters in *Wham,* including *The Spooks of St. Luke's,* and then drew *Angel Face and Dare Devil* in *Whizzer* and *Chips* (1969). He died in 1974.

D.G.

LONDON, ROBERT KEITH (1950-) Born in New York City in 1950, Robert Keith London was raised in the Queens borough of the city. He attended Adelphi University in the metro area for several years before leaving to become a freelance cartoonist.

"Bobby" London, who began drawing cartoons and inventing his own characters at age four, had only given college a try to satisfy his physician father's wish he have a fallback career. It didn't take. The lure of cartooning and popular culture of the late 1960s were much more interesting, and so he headed to the west coast.

In 1970, London met Dan O'Neil, Ted Richards, Shary Flenniken, and Gary Hallgren at a rock festival in Oregon. They soon formed an art studio/residence called the Air Pirates located on Harrison Street in San Francisco near the Oakland Bay Bridge. Underground comix were the rage and the Air Pirates were in the middle of it. San Francisco was the west coast center for publishing underground comix. While London is often still referred to as an underground cartoonist, that segment of his career ended in 1972.

Bobby London, "Dirty Duck." © Bobby London.

However, his first published works were in the underground comix mode. *Annie Rat* and a hippie character, *Merton,* were his first published professional work. They appeared in the *Rat Subterranean News*, a New York City underground newspaper.

The Air Pirates, who were together from 1970-1972, created a comix book by the same name which featured a triple x-rated parody of early Mickey Mouse. Disney sued them and they became underground comix celebrities as a result. However, being sued by Disney is a difficult situation at best.

Between 1972-1977, London's career turned away from the underground to mainline publications as diverse as the *New York Times*, *National Lampoon* and *Playboy*. While he drew for *Time*'s Op-ed page and *Sunday Book Review,* he took his character *Dirty Duck,* which began in underground comix, to *Lampoon* and *Playboy*. *Dirty Duck* is considered by many a homage to *Krazy Kat*. London, while acknowledging stylistic influences, feels it is his own creation. The raucous, lascivious, cigar-chomping Dirty Duck proved a gander always ready for a goose, or a busty woman. The legal problems over the *Disney* v. *Air Pirates* suit continued during this period. London could have settled in 1975 but was talked out of it. He eventually did settle in 1978.

His work with *Dirty Duck* and other characters were a regular feature in *Playboy* until the mid-1980s. His freelance spot art career flourished also until about that time, when all of a sudden art directors seemed to decide he was still an "underground cartoonist" and they wanted a new look.

It's ironic that Disney came to London's rescue. Disney considered the Air Pirates' suit just protection of their trademarked characters. They hired London as a concept artist in the Disney New York City licensing office. He worked there from 1984-1985, until he took over writing and drawing the daily *Popeye* comic strip for King Features. London had grown up reading *Popeye* as drawn by Bela "Bill" Zaboly and written by Tom Sims. In 1959, Bud Sagendorf took over the dailies. London's opportunity to do *Popeye* came when Sagendorf wished to cutback to the Sundays only.

Circulation of *Popeye* in newspapers was less than 50 papers in the United States, a bit more worldwide. However, *Popeye,* just like *Betty Boop,* is a powerful licensing moneymaker. King Features wanted to not only keep it in newspapers but to put a new and more contemporary life back into *Popeye*. Between 1986-July 1992, the *Popeye* dailies were the best they'd been in years. London's style and that used in *Popeye* were a natural mesh. The *Popeye* dailies ceased being a yawn and took a walk on the wild side. St. Martin's Press published an anthology of London's *Popeye* with the title *Mondo Popeye*. However, in July 1992, King Features suddenly fired London.

In London's continuity, Olive Oyl, Popeye's "sweet patootie", had become a beanpole-thin couch potato addicted to a cable TV home shopping show. She orders a baby Bluto doll. It arrives in a box and she doesn't like the doll. The arrival in a box was London's tribute to the 1933 arrival of Swee'pea, Popeye's "adoptid infink" who also arrived on Popeye's doorstep in a box. As Popeye and Olive Oyl discuss sending the baby Bluto back, two clergymen hear the conversation. They misunderstand and think Olive wants an abortion. London's point of view was considered pro-choice.

When the perceived crisis hit King Features, the sequence had already gone through King's editorial division, been approved, drawn, reproduced, and mailed to clients. King asked for the repros back. One small Chicago daily declined to do so. The crisis grew totally out of proportion. King put out a statement quoted in the July 25, 1992 *Editor & Publisher*, "The subject matter of some recent *Popeye* strips was felt to be inappropriate for inclusion in what is a family, humor-based strip." London was fired, although King Features had approved and originally distributed the material. King immediately began distributing re-runs of London's *Popeye* dailies. When the five-and-a-half years of London's re-runs were used up, they began to recycle and continue to publish re-runs of Sagendorf's *Popeye*.

Leo Longanesi. © Longanesi.

London's public persona, which carried over from the *Disney* vs. *Air Pirates* suit as one of the bad boys of cartooning, received an undeserved boost from the *Popeye* flap. He returned to freelancing and his first love of developing new characters. *Dirty Duck* lives on and an animated version is on the drawing board. London's work is also reappearing in *Playboy*.

B.C.

LONGANESI, LEO (1905-1957) Italian cartoonist, journalist and writer born in Bagnacavallo, Romagna, Italy, in 1905. Leo Longanesi's cartoon work, while significant, was only one aspect of his career. He was a talented man who published many books of cartoons and was at the same time a serious, perceptive essayist. His cartoons constitute a lucid running commentary on the events and personages of Italy in the Fascist and Christian Democratic periods.

While he was solidly conservative, Longanesi never espoused the cause of Fascism and conformity. His cartoons and drawings for a myriad of books and publications large and small were often ruthless depictions of the poverty and narrow-mindedness afflicting a world that pretended to renovate itself through rhetoric. Lacking the raw, disruptive force of, say Grosz's cartoons, Longanesi's drawings did their work' more quietly—like pebbles thrown into a stagnant pond. The resultant waves have spread slowly, as has his fame as the premier Italian cartoonist of the period immediately before and after World War II (in which, significantly enough, he did not take part). No postwar Italian cartoonist has been left untouched by his spirit of humor and satire, whether in drawings or captions. Longanesi died in Milan in 1957.

C.S.

LOOPY DE LOOP (U.S.) Although Hanna-Barbera Productions is best known for television animation, it also made a number of theatrical shorts, chief among them the *Loopy de Loop* series, which premiered in December 1959 with "Wolf Hounded." Loopy's character was established early on as that of an uncommonly peaceful wolf whose good intentions, sadly misunderstood by the humans with whom he came into contact, led him into all kinds of trouble. The cartoons stuck closely to this pattern in such entries as "Life with Loopy," "Tale of a Wolf," "Do-Good Wolf" (all 1960) and "Happy Go Loopy" (1961).

Realizing that their series rested on one joke endlessly repeated from cartoon to cartoon, Hanna and Barbera tried to conjure up a fitting *compère* for their ill-starred wolf in the form of a bumbling, befuddled bear. The duo endured countless rounds of catastrophe and mayhem in such forgettable cartoons as "Bearly Able" (1962), "Bear Up," "Bear Hug," "Trouble Bruin" (all 1963) and "Bear Knuckles" (1964). In spite of all these efforts *Loopy de Loop* failed to catch on, and in 1965 Columbia Pictures, which released the cartoons, persuaded Hanna and Barbera to discontinue the series.

M.H.

LORD, MARY GRACE (1955-) One of the few women who have not only survived but flourished in a male-dom-

"Loopy de Loop." © Hanna-Barbera Productions.

inated profession, M.G. Lord has maintained a distinctive personal presence since she began drawing political cartoons. Lord established her identity early; lording it over her high school senior class in La Jolla, California (where she was born on November 18, 1955) as class president and editor of the school paper. She is credited with inventing a new major at Yale—a compound of politics, graphic arts, and letters—and before graduating (cum laude) in 1977, she rounded out her preparation for a career in journalism by serving a summer apprenticeship as a reporting intern with the *Wall Street Journal*. Then she spent ten frustrating months in 1977-78 with the art department of the *Chicago Tribune*, which she describes as devoted mainly to making coffee for the senior political cartoonists. However suppressed her talents were at the *Tribune*, however, she soon attracted the attention of an editor at the Long Island paper *Newsday*, for which she became an illustrator and, in 1978, the staff editorial cartoonist. In 1984 she was signed up for national distribution by the Los Angeles Times Syndicate.

In 1982, Little, Brown published Lord's first collection, *Mean Sheets*, to which her former instructor, the Pulitzer Prize-winning cartoonist Bill Mauldin, contributed an

M.G. Lord. © M.G. Lord.

introduction. Mauldin noted of the caustic Lord that it was not so much anger that makes a good political cartoonists as the capacity for outrage. *Mean Sheets* established Lord as one of the most articulately outraged critics of the public scene. Charged with being abrasive, she has remained undaunted, calling such criticism "water off the back of a very morally committed duck." In fact, however, the churlishness of her wit has become Lord's defining characteristic. *Ms.* magazine, which suggests that "M.G." might stand for Merciless Graphics, quoted her in 1983 as stating unequivocally, "I like drawing vicious pictures of people; I like to be obnoxious." Typical is her portrait of a vacant-faced Ronald Reagan with bats flying out of a window in his forehead, or her description of Senator Jesse Helms as "viscerally loathsome." Garry Trudeau, another of her instructors at Yale, has said of her, "M.G. Lord takes no prisoners!"

Employing a sparse line with no pretensions to pictorial elegance, Lord makes her point with content rather than with graphic style. Increasingly she has turned from the visual image to the written word, following her volume of cartoons with a collection of cynical urban fables called *Prig Tales* a few years later and, in 1995, a searching analysis of the historical and cultural significance of Mattel's popular doll Barbie. *Forever Barbie: The Unauthorized Biography of a Real Doll*, an examination of what the icon reveals of our society's gender stereotypes, was described by a critic in *Booklist* as "better than most biographies of real people." In her perceptive critical prose as in her shrewd visual metaphors, M.G. Lord's idiosyncratic personal outlook has remained constant, and has continued to justify fellow-cartoonist Jules Feiffer's characterization of her as "smart, tough, funny, and original."

D.W.

LORENZ, LEE S. (1933-) American cartoonist, editor and cornet player born in Hackensack, New Jersey, on October 17, 1933. Lee Lorenz attended the Carnegie Institute of Technology in Pittsburgh in 1950-51 but transferred to the Pratt Institute in Brooklyn, receiving his B.F.A. in 1954. He then freelanced as a commercial artist, animator and cartoonist until 1958, when he became a staff cartoonist for the *New Yorker*. In 1973 he was appointed art editor, and in this capacity he has introduced *New Yorker* readers to the work of such fresh talents as Sam Gross, Lou Myers, Bill Woodman and Jack Ziegler.

As a cartoonist, Lorenz is an excellent stylist who works mainly in what appears to be pen and wash. His panels are identifiable by a firm, broad, unbroken line that suggests Peter Arno without being imitative. The wit that infuses his drawings is in the sophisticated *New Yorker* tradition, singling out for particular attention the corporate world, political philosophies and social clichés, all spiced with liberal dashes of lunacy. A good example is the panel featuring a parade of animals, each with a picket sign bearing a popular cliché. Thus a flirtatious duck holds a placard reading "Lord love a duck," while a stubborn-looking horse follows with "You can lead a horse to water, but you can't make him drink." Bringing up the rear is a tiny beetle whose sign is left to the reader's imagination.

Separately published collections of Lorenz's work include *Here It Comes* (1968), *The Upside Down King* (1970) and *Now Look What You've Done* (1977). He is also the illustrator of a volume entitled *The Teddy Bear Habit* (1966). He has served as president of the Cartoonists' Guild and as a member of the board of directors of the Museum of Cartoon Art. Besides his artwork, Lorenz claims to blow a pretty mean cornet—something he has been doing professionally since 1955. He is also the author of several children's adventure books, including *Big Gus and Little Gus* and *Hugo and the Space Dog*, which won the New Jersey Authors Award in 1983. He stepped down from his position as the *New Yorker's* cartoon editor in 1991, but continues to contribute drawings to the magazine.

R.C.

LOVE IS... (U.S.) Although it began syndication with Los Angeles Times Syndicate in 1971 and is technically a United States strip, *Love Is...* was created by Kim Casali, a New Zealander who married an Italian national and lived most of her adult life in England.

Love Is... is all about emotion. It is a simple six-day-a-week panel that is cute, romantic, and universally understood. While hugely successful and published in over 60 countries, *Love Is...* has received little respect from cartoon historians. The reason is possibly its unabashed exuberant sentimentality.

Kim Casali met her husband to be, Roberto, during a ski trip in California. A self-proclaimed total romantic, she began drawing love notes with the boy and girl who became featured stars of *Love Is....* The dark-haired boy was Roberto, the girl, herself. Considering the lack of drawing ability of many cartoonists published today, Kim Casali's statement, "I'm not a cartoonist, I'm a doodler, but I am a person who feels very deeply," seems overly self-deprecating.

The girl-boy duo nude in wide-eyed innocence have always been nicely drawn in strong black line with well thought out if minimal settings. They have been shown with cars, motor scooters, computers, in restaurants, airplanes, sailing, virtually any setting.

The simple caption is always a continuation of the strip's title *Love Is.... Love Is...* believing in family values;....someone very huggable;...sailing into a rosy future; or...when you're the star. Always upbeat, *Love Is...* has over its history, generated a full licensing program and many reprint books. At the tenth anniversary of the panel in 1981, Casali

"Love is . . . " © Los Angeles Times Syndicate.

noted how she'd write the strip while listening to romantic music sung by Tom Jones, Shirley Bassey, and Neil Diamond.

As her years on the strip passed, Casali noted how as "a mature woman in love with life as well as love," her cartoons were written to be slightly more sophisticated and include some double entendre. When Kim Casali died in June 1997, at the age of 55, one of her three sons, Stefano Casali, took over creative duties on *Love Is....*

Although her creation was often ridiculed for being too simple, too cute, too sweet, Kim Casali knew her work was far more than doodles. Incredibly successful, she wrote in *Cartoonist PROfiles* in 1981. "The key in this business of course is to find something new and different. Look at me - it was so simple I'm amazed no one thought of it before me." Asked if she had a favorite among her many panels, Casali responded, *Love Is...* never asking for more than you are prepared to give."

B.C.

LOW, SIR DAVID (1891-1963) British cartoonist born in Dunedin, New Zealand, on April 7, 1891. "Low," as he signed all his cartoons, was probably the most important, popular and influential cartoonist working in British newspapers in the first half of the 20th century. His swift-seeming, bold brushwork, individual and unmistakable, concealed fine draftsmanship and instantly conveyed the artist's strong opinions.

David Alexander Cecil Low was educated at the Boys' High School, Christchurch. Inspired to draw by imported British comics, he copied Tom Browne and other early masters of simplified black-and-white cartooning and had his first sketch published in the *Christchurch Spectator* in 1902, at age 11. He contributed cartoons to the *Canterbury Times* and by age 20 was cartoonist for the *Sydney Bulletin* (1911).

After World War I he emigrated to England, arriving in London in 1919. He quickly found a regular spot in the evening newspaper the *Star* and drew for that paper from

THE SCUM OF THE EARTH, I BELIEVE
THE BLOODY ASSASSIN OF THE WORKERS I PRESUME?

Rendezvous.

David Low. © London Evening Standard.

1919 to 1927. He moved to the *Evening Standard* on a unique contract with its quirky proprietor, the Canadian Lord Beaverbrook. Low was allowed carte blanche to draw whatever he wished, despite the politics and opinions of its owner! He stayed with the *Standard* for 23 years, moving in 1950 to the Labour newspaper the *Daily Herald.* In 1953 he moved again, this time to the *Manchester Guardian,* where he stayed for a decade. Low was made an honorary doctor of law by the universities of New Brunswick and Frederickstown, Canada (1958), and the University of Leicester (1961). He was knighted in 1962 and died on September 19, 1963.

Low created many characters, perhaps none so famous or memorable as Colonel Blimp, who became part of the language. Others include the T.U.C. Horse and the characters of the strip *Hit and Muss on Their Axis.* Winston Churchill said of Low, "He is the greatest of our modern cartoonists because of the vividness of his political conceptions and because he possesses what few cartoonists have, a grand technique of draughtsmanship."

Books: *Low's Annual* (1908); *Caricatures* (1915); *The Billy Book* (1918); *Old Seed on New Ground* (1920); *Man* (1921); *Lloyd George and Co.* (1922); *Low and I* (1923); *Low and I Holiday Book* (1925); *Lions and Lambs* (1928); *The Best of Low* (1930); *Low's Russian Sketchbook* (1932); *Portfolio of Caricatures* (1933); *The New Rake's Progress* (1934); *Low and Terry* (1934); *Ye Madde Designer* (1935); *Political Parade* (1936); *Low Again* (1938); *Cartoon History of Our Times* (1939); *Europe Since Versailles* (1939); *Europe at War* (1940); *The Flying Visit* (1940); *Low on the War* (1941); *Low's War Cartoons* (1941); *British Cartoonists* (1942); *The World at War* (1942); *C'est la Guerre* (1943); *The Years of Wrath* (1949); *Low Company* (1952); *Low Visibility* (1953); *Low's Autobiography* (1956); and *The Fearful Fifties* (1960).

D.G.

LOWELL, ORSON BYRON (1871-1956) American illustrator and cartoonist born in Wyoming, Iowa, on December 22, 1871. Orson Lowell was educated in the Chicago public schools and attended the Chicago Art Institute between 1887 and 1893, after which he went to New York to pursue a career in cartooning and illustration.

His first jobs, reversing a typical pattern, were in illustration work rather than cartooning. His early work was very handsome, if derivative, and was rendered in thin pen lines and careful shading; he seemed to like the interplay of shadows and light and composed well. When he cracked the cartoon market, his style was bolder but, once again, derivative. Lowell's early inspiration seems to have been penman Pyle, whereas his later cartoon work was obviously garnered from Charles Dana Gibson. Lowell was a little less awkward than the horde of other imitators, but he must still be classed an imitator. J.M. Flagg was too, achieving about the same independence: drawings "in the Gibson style" and with Gibson's themes. But Lowell kept his striking sense of composition and managed to gain a name for himself.

From 1907 to 1915 he was under exclusive contract to *Life*—no mean feat—and was lured away by *Judge* with an exclusive contract from 1915 until that magazine shed its classy pretensions in 1923; Lowell's grandiose society drawings were suddenly out of place. They were out of place in almost all cartoon markets, sadly, but Lowell worked successively (and successfully) for the Ericson Advertising Agency (1921-29), *American Girl* magazine (1935-45), the George Matthews Adams Service (1937-38) and the *Churchman* (1943-46).

Lowell died on February 9, 1956.

R.M.

LUCKOVICH, MICHAEL E. (1960-) Mike Luckovich is an editorial cartoonist who has always thrived on controversy. As a freshman in a Catholic high school, the Seattle-born artist enjoyed caricaturing the nuns and priests on the faculty, and he began making graphic comments on school issues when he moved to Eugene, Oregon, in his sophomore year. By the next term, one of his cartoons so outraged his teachers that they banned the school paper from the classrooms. "It taught me a lot about the power I had to affect people," he told *Cartoonist Profiles* in 1989.

Born January 28, 1960, Luckovich attended the University of Washington, where he majored in political science and did a regular cartoon for the school's daily paper. When he graduated in 1982, he tried to get a job with his pen. Some 300 résumés netted him nothing, however, and he settled for what he describes as "one of the world's worst occupations"—selling life insurance. At last in 1984 he answered an ad in *Editor & Publisher* that brought him work drawing for the Greenville, South Carolina *News*. The next year he moved up to the much larger *New Orleans Times-Picayune*, where in 1986 he was a finalist for the Pulitzer Prize. In 1989 he became the staff cartoonist for *The Atlanta* (Georgia) *Journal/Constitution* and accepted an offer from Creators Syndicate. In 1996 a collection of his cartoons, *Lotsa Luckovich*, was published by Pocket Books, Inc., and by the following year his syndicate reported distribution of his work to about 150 papers nationwide. Nineteen ninety-seven marked his tenth consecutive year as the most frequently reprinted cartoonist in *Newsweek*.

Mike Luckovich. © Creators Syndicate.

Luckovich's "power to affect people" has been confirmed by numerous professional honors. In 1990 and 1994 he won prizes from the Overseas Press Club. In 1992 he received a National Headliner Award, and 1994 brought him the Robert F. Kennedy Award for "cartoons that reflect positively on the disadvantaged." The next year his career was crowned with the Pulitzer Prize.

Acknowledging the influence of *Mad* magazine's Mort Drucker, Luckovich commands a fluid line and employs powerful compositions that balance masses of black or gray with clean, empty backgrounds. His easy command of his medium—he inks his images directly on the page without relying on penciled sketches—give his work a breezy, assured look, and his droll caricature provides a striking contrast with his often biting commentary.

Luckovich continues to evoke strong reactions, and he considers that a mark of success. "If I don't get mail," he reports, "I feel I'm being bland." A Luckovich cartoon attacking Georgia Representative Newt Gingrich in 1994 so angered the future Speaker of the House that he barred *Journal-Constitution* reporters from his campaign events—a slight nuisance to the staff of his paper, but a personal triumph for the artist. "Cartooning is therapy for me," he explains. "I can channel my frustrations at the political process, the neglect of the environment, the silliness of the world's leaders, or whatever, into a cartoon. I'm idealistic enough to believe that I can make a difference."

D.W.

"Lucky Luke." © Belvision/Dargaud Films.

LUCKY LUKE (Belgium/France) In 1946 Morris (Maurice de Bevère) created the parodic western strip *Lucky Luke;* when he became burdened with work, he asked René Goscinny to help him out as a scriptwriter. *Lucky Luke* soon became very popular, and it was inevitable that it would be adapted into a full-length animated feature.

In 1971 Belvision, in association with Dargaud-Films, released *Lucky Luke* as a theatrical feature. Goscinny was listed as the director of the film, but it had in fact been supervised by Henri Gruel. The adaptation and dialogue were signed by Morris, Goscinny and Pierre Tchernia. The action, hewing close to the original conception, centered around Lucky Luke, "a poor, lonesome cowboy" mounted on his faithful stallion, Jolly Jumper. In the course of the film the hero rid the little settlement known as Daisy Town of the dreaded menace of the brothers Dalton. The action was fast, and the animation, while spotty at times, adequate and high-spirited.

The success of *Lucky Luke* led to a sequel produced by the newly created Studios Idéfix under the direction of Gruel. A number of mishaps (including Goscinny's death in 1977) slowed down the filming, and the feature, titled *La Ballade des Dalton* ("The Ballad of the Daltons"), was only released in 1978. It again pitted the protagonist against the four comic-opera outlaws, the Daltons. In some ways (its handling of color, its dream sequences) it was superior to the original, and it was fairly successful. Since 1990 a number of cartoon shorts have been turned out by Morris's studio, Lucky Productions.

M.H.

LUKS, GEORGE BENJAMIN (1867-1933) American cartoonist and painter born in Williamsport, Pennsylvania, on August 13, 1867. George Luks was educated in art at the Pennsylvania Academy of Fine Arts, at the Düsseldorf Academy in Germany, and in salons of Paris and London. In 1895 and 1896 he served as a war correspondent and artist in Cuba for the *Philadelphia Bulletin.* He then switched to the *New York World,* where he succeeded R.F. Outcault on *The Yellow Kid* comic strip, approximating the latter's style and perpetuating the emerging journalistic war between the proprietors of the *World* and *Journal.*

Luks was one of the organizers of the 1913 Armory Show that provoked so much turmoil in the art world, and his role in American arts as a member of the Ashcan school is well documented. He won many prizes for his canvases, including the Temple Gold Medal of the Pennsylvania Academy of Fine Arts, the Logan Medal of the Chicago Art Institute, the Hudnut Water Color Prize, the Corcoran Gallery of Art prize and the gold medal of the Philadelphia Locust Club.

Luks's cartooning work in the weekly humor magazines led to his famous stint on *The Yellow Kid* and established the reputation that led to a career in oils. In this sense he joined his fellows John Sloan, Reginald Marsh and Walt Kuhn, who also began as cartoonists and became painters. Luks's chief contributions were to the weekly magazine *Truth,* which had the format of *Puck,* eschewed politics, often colored its cartoons in chromolithography and was decidedly racy in its appeal. Luks was a major fixture and frequently contributed humorous strip-format cartoons for the back page. His style—before he copied Outcault—was at first awkwardly stiff and later pleasantly free in execution. Luks died in New York City in 1933 as a result of a barroom brawl.

R.M.

LUNARI, ENZO (1937-) Italian cartoonist born in Milan, Italy, on January 2, 1937. Enzo Lunari graduated from the School of Political Sciences of the University of Pavia in 1961 but could not find a job in his field. After working as a salesman for a chinaware company, he decided to try his hand at cartooning; his first cartoons were accepted by the monthly *Linus* in 1965.

Lunari's career falls into three periods, each devoted to a cycle or a character but connected to the others by an overall theme. The first phase began in 1965 with *Girighiz,* a comic strip with cavemen as protagonists along the lines of Johnny Hart's *B.C.* Lunari's aim, however, was political and satirical; he attacked bad government, conformism and the opportunism of the people in power. He followed suit with *Fra' Salmastro da Venegono,* in which the adventures of an imaginary 13th-century friar provided the vehicle for a lively satire on the mores of contemporary society. Finally Lunari invented Sodomate, a land of fantasy not unlike the Italy of the 1970s. Here the clever Berlingua (a transparent allusion to Italian Communist party chief Enrico Berlinguer) tries with every means at his disposal to join (or perhaps to replace) the wretched leaders of the country.

Lunari has drawn these and other comic strips, as well as political cartoons, for publications such as *Tempo* and *Mondo Domani.* Since the early 1980's his work has also appeared in such Italian publications as *Panorama, L'Europeo,* and *La Stampa,* as well as in a number of foreign periodicals.

C.S.

LUNATICS I HAVE MET (U.S.) *Lunatics That I Have Met* (the *That* was soon dropped) was among the first of Rube Goldberg's famous newspaper panels. It started on the sports page of the *New York Evening Mail* in 1907. Goldberg would caricature a type—"the physical culture maniac," "the gasoline nut," "the golf nut," "the show fiend"—in a series of panels that depicted those "lunatics" in the most ludicrous situations imaginable. (One showing a "balloonatic" suspended precariously over Manhattan rooftops and exclaiming, "That must be Australia in the near distance," is a classic; it might have inspired the title and the general feeling of Buster Keaton's 1923 film *Balloonatics.*)

Goldberg even ran short signed articles to accompany the graphic descriptions of his "loons," with titles such as

Enzo Lunari, "Fra Salmastro." © Lunari.

"Is Ballooning a Mania?" or "Golf Bug Harmless." He soon grew tired of this endless enumeration of human lunacies, however, and he dropped the feature only a few years after its inception.

M.H.

LURIE, RANAN (1932-) Israeli cartoonist born in 1932 to a sixth-generation Israeli family whose members were among the first settlers in the country. Ranan Lurie studied fine arts in Jerusalem and Paris. He drew political cartoons for the Israeli press as early as 1948 and established his reputation quickly. By the time he was 30, he was regarded as Israel's national cartoonist, reflecting the views of the majority of his fellow citizens.

In 1968 Lurie was contracted by *Life* magazine to draw a weekly editorial cartoon, and he moved to the United States, settling in New York City. In addition to his cartoons for *Life* (which he drew until the magazine folded in 1973), he has contributed to *Paris-Match,* the *Wall Street Journal* and the *New York Times,* among others. His daily political cartoon panel, *Lurie's Opinion,* was syndicated for a long time by United Feature Syndicate and is now distributed by King Features. Lurie has illustrated books and stories, and two collections of his cartoons have been published by Quadrangle Books: *Nixon Rated Cartoons* (1973) and *Pardon Me, Mr. President* (1975).

"Lunatics I Have Met." © Rube Goldberg.

Via Dolorosa
Ranan Lurie, "Lurie's Opinion." © United Feature Syndicate.

Lurie is a veteran of two Middle East wars (1948 and 1967), and his U.S. residency has not dampened his patriotism. His style, caricatural and even outré, and his captions, direct and unabashedly partisan, have won him as many detractors as admirers. He is an influence to be reckoned with, however, in the fiercely competitive world of political cartooning.

Lurie is a Senior Adjunct Fellow at the Center for Strategic and International Studies. He has taught and lectured on "the philosophy of political cartooning" at major American, European and Australian universities. Some of the more recent collections of his cartoons have been *Lurie's Almanac* (1983) and *Ranan's Line* (1986).

Lurie is also the editor-in-chief of *Cartoon News,* billed as "the current events educational monthly." His cartoons are syndicated all around the world by his own Cartoonews Inc. The 1997 *Guiness Book of World Records* lists him as "the most widely syndicated political cartoonist in the world today."

M.H

LUZZATI, EMANUELE (1921-) Italian cartoonist, painter and designer born in Genoa, Italy, in 1921. Emanuele Luzzati graduated from art school during World War II and tried to support himself by cartooning after the war. He then went into designing theater sets, becoming one of the most respected names in the profession.

In the late 1950s Luzzati struck up a partnership with Giulio Gianini that resulted in the production of a number of highly regarded film cartoons. The first was the 1960 *I*

Emanuele Luzzati (and Giulio Gianini), "I Paladini di Francia." *© Gianini/Luzzati Production.*

Paladini of Francia ("Paladins of France"), a medieval ballad featuring cutout characters on a background of violent and contrasting colors. The style of the cartoon, coarse and childlike, suggested a Georges Rouault painting; it became the hallmark of their subsequent efforts, from *Costello di Carte* ("House of Cards," 1962) to *La Gazza Ladro* ("The Thieving Magpie," 1964), in which Rossini's crescendos add a vivifying touch to the graphic universe. *L'Italiana in Algieri* ("The Italian Girl in Algiers," 1968), which again makes use of Rossini's music, blends rhythm, invention and feeling in a joyous burst of movement. In the 1970 *Ali Baba,* Luzzati further accentuated the innocent look of his world through the use of "cheap" materials such as silver and gold foil and crayons.

Luzzati and Gianini animated the fabulous travels of Marco Polo for Italian television in 1972 and then made *Pulcinella* (1973), which can be seen as a summing up of Luzzati's work. It is a fervent homage to the theater but also a fusion of all the elements dear to the artist: fable, naive painting, classical music. The poetic tales imagined by Luzzati and Gianini are peopled by kings and sultans, harem girls and dragons, knights, battles and love scenes, as seen through the eyes of a child, but with the irony of a cultured adult. Again in collaboration with Gianini he realized in 1978 *Il Flauto Magico* ("The Magic Fulte"), a 50-minute feature based on Mozart's opera. His most notable theatrical film in recent years has been the 1984 *Il Libro* ("The Book"). He is now principally working for the stage.

Luzzati is also a talented painter and has recently taken up book illustration as well, with felicitous results.

S.T.

LYE, LEN (1901-1980) New Zealand animator and filmmaker born in Christchurch, New Zealand, in 1901. Len Lye studied at Wellington Technical College and at the Canterbury College of Fine Arts. Disappointed with traditional art, he set out for Samoa to study Polynesian art. He made his first recorded animated film, *Tusalava,* in 1928. In the 1930s he worked for the General Post Office organization in Great Britain, collaborating with John Grierson on a number of films, such as *North or Northwest.*

In 1935 Lye made his major contribution to animation art with *The Colour Box.* The images were painted directly on the film, thereby avoiding the photographic process—a technique Lye pioneered, although he did not invent it. (There are several claimants to this innovation, including Hans Richter, Man Ray and Marcel Duchamp.) Lye followed with two works that combined animation and live action: *Rainbow Dance* (1936) and *Trade Tattoo* (1937). In the meantime he had also produced a puppet film, *Birth of a Robot* (1935).

J. Norman Lynd, "Vignettes of Life." © Ledger Syndicate.

During World War II Lye made only one cartoon, *Musical Poster* (1941). He worked mainly on documentaries such as *Kill or Be Killed,* a cold-blooded account of the techniques of street fighting, and the much more entertaining *Swinging the Lambeth Walk.* After the war Lye moved to the United States, where he collaborated with Ian Hugo on the 1952 *Bells of Atlantis.* Since then Lye has increasingly turned to abstraction; his later works of animation include *Colour Cry* (1955), *Free Radicals* (1957), *Rotational Harmonic* (1961) and *Steel Fountain* (1963). In his last years he had been working in computer animation and turning out sculptures that make their own music. He died in Providence, R.I., in May 1980.

M.H.

LYND, J. NORMAN (1878-1943) American cartoonist born in Northwood, Logan County, Ohio, in 1878. J. Norman Lynd, the son of a Presbyterian minister, spent most of his youth in London and North Ireland, where he was educated. Shortly after his return to New York in 1907, he secured a job on the art staff of the *New York Herald.* There he became primarily a news artist and sports cartoonist, working with cub reporter John Wheeler and drawing in the style of the *Herald*'s soon-to-depart star, Winsor McCay. He remained with the *Herald* until it merged with the *Tribune* in 1924. In the meantime Lynd established himself as one of the most versatile illustrators and cartoonists in magazines; he illustrated humorous fiction for the second-string monthlies and graced the pages of *Puck* and *Life* with his captioned gags.

Beginning on November 20, 1927, Lynd drew the Sunday feature *Vignettes of Life* for the Ledger Syndicate in the style of C.D. Mitchell (his predecessor, whose feature had been called *Follies of the Passing Show*) and Frank Godwin; it contained approximately half a dozen gags on a central theme. The concept was not new (*Puck* had done the trick in the 1880s, and W.E. Hill and Joe McGurk, among others, had worked it for newspapers), but Lynd brought a special look and flavor to the genre. In 1938 Lynd was lured away by Hearst and drew an identical page called *Family Portraits* for King Features. When he died at his home in Lynbrook, Long Island, on November 8, 1943, *Family Portraits* died with him. The *Ledger,* however, had continued *Vignettes of Life* with W. Kemp Starrett, whose style approximated Lynd's.

J. Norman Lynd had one of the most handsome pen lines in cartooning. In his mature work he managed to retain the disciplined crosshatch technique of the early years while infusing an arresting verve both to characters and compositions. His style zeroed in on personality so well that readers were able to recognize character types—a prerequisite for the type of feature Lynd drew. A collection of his work, *Vignettes of Life,* was published by Reilly and Lee in 1930, with a foreword by Charles Dana Gibson.

R.M.

Mm

MACAULEY, CHARLES (1871-1934) American Pulitzer Prize-winning cartoonist born in Canton, Ohio, on March 29, 1871. In 1891 the young Macauley won a $50 cartoon prize from the *Cleveland Press* and on the strength of this secured a position on the art staff of the *Canton Repository* the following year. Through the 1890s he was to draw for the *World, Plain Dealer* and *Leader* (all Cleveland newspapers), *Puck, Life* and *Judge* (freelance) and the *New York Herald* for a short stint. In 1899 he joined the staff of the *Philadelphia Inquirer* as editorial cartoonist; he remained there two years.

From 1901 to 1904 he produced his *Fantasmaland* books and was then hired to succeed the retiring Charles Green Bush on the old *New York World.* There he achieved great fame and was transformed into a fierce partisan. During his career on the Democratic *World,* he contributed heavily to cartoon iconography: Roosevelt's Big Stick, the Camel as the symbol for the Prohibitionists, the Hippo for the wets and the Gold Dust Twins (Taft and Roosevelt) for the campaign of 1912.

In the reform tide that swept John Puroy Mitchell into the mayoralty of New York City, Macauley was active and publicly visible as his campaign finance manager. Pulitzer frowned on such activity, and Macauley was fired—later to sue for his uncollected salary and win. When he finally left the *World* in 1914, he freelanced, comfortably finding temporary berths in Philadelphia and with the *New York Globe* doing war cartoons. He also tried his hand at playwriting; he wrote *The Optimistic Spectator* and several photoplays.

In 1927 Macauley was afflicted with tuberculosis of the spine and endured painful operations, but he bounced back to succeed Nelson Harding on the *Brooklyn Eagle* in 1929. Within five weeks of assuming that position, he drew the cartoon that was to win him the Pulitzer Prize. Two years later he left to draw for the *New York Mirror.*

Macauley's style was bold and occasionally awkward in the way that Davenport's was; like Davenport, he drew with both pen and bludgeon. He stayed loyal to the pen-and-crosshatch technique and was one of its prime exponents; in substance he was primarily a political cartoonist, never dabbling (in his newspaper work) in subjects of the home, hearth or seasons as his fellows often did. In his later years he became a Republican, although he supported Smith in 1928. He died on November 24, 1934.

His published fiction includes *The Red Tavern, Whom the Gods Would Destroy, Keeping the Faith* and *The Man Across the Street.* Macauley was a president of the New York Press Club and a member of the Author's Club.

R.M.

Charles Macaulay, ca. 1910. © New York World.

MACAYA, LUIS FERNANDO (1888-1953) Argentine cartoonist and painter born in Barcelona, Spain, on April 22, 1888. Luis Macaya started his artistic career in 1905 at the Workers' Atheneum and Free Workshop of the Artistic Group, founded in Barcelona by Picasso and Gallardo. In 1908 he traveled to France, Belgium and Germany to further his art studies, settling in Argentina in 1911.

Macaya's first job as a cartoonist was for the newly founded magazine *Crítica* (for which he designed the masthead, among other things). Soon he found himself in great demand, and in subsequent years he worked for most major publications in Argentina. His cartoons, elegant and sharply drawn, appeared in *Caras y Caretas* (1912-32), *Fray Mocho* (1912-20), *Plus Ultra* (1912-29), *La Nación* (1928-32), *El Hogar* (1932-53), *Leoplán* (1938), and *Argentina* (1949-50), among others. Macaya was also a noted landscape painter and held many exhibitions throughout Argentina. In 1925 he was awarded first prize at the Salon Nacional.

Luis Fernando Macaya died in Buenos Aires on January 25, 1953. His son, Luis Macaya (born in 1913), is also a cartoonist.

A.M.

Mino Maccari. © Il Mondo.

MACCARI, MINO (1898-198?) Italian cartoonist, engraver and teacher born in Siena, Italy, on November 24, 1898. Mino Maccari attended the University of Siena, graduating in 1919 with a doctorate in law. As an artist he was self-taught, and he started drawing cartoons soon after his graduation.

Maccari was closely associated with *Il Selvaggio,* the magazine that best reflected Italian life between the two world wars. Like Leo Longanesi—whom he resembles in his style of drawing—Maccari expressed his fundamental anti-Fascism principally in his cartoons, which convey a sense of revolt not so much against the regime itself as against its bad taste, fake underpinnings and the grotesqueness it promoted in the field of culture. His cartoons were in part inspired by Grosz's work but had a particularly Italian slant; while the German artist's drawings were black and dramatic, Maccari's were simply ironic and bizarre. (The regime felt so little threatened by his cartoons that he was named a professor at the Rome Academy of Fine Arts in 1938.)

In the post-World War II period Maccari collaborated on a number of cultural and political publications (*L'Espresso, Il Mondo,* etc.), producing cartoons and comments that sometimes earned him virulent attacks from one political party or another. Cartooning is only one of Maccari's talents—he has also done many engravings and lithographs—but it is the one by which he will be best remembered. He was one of the most important cartoonists of contemporary Italy. He died in the 1980s.

C.S.

McCARTHY, FRED (1918-) American cartoonist born in Boston, Massachusetts, on September 5, 1918. Fred McCarthy was educated at Boston College and took the vows of the Franciscan order, becoming Father McCarthy, and drawing all the while. He was art editor of school papers (drawing sports and spot cartoons) and of the *Friar* magazine (1953-57). In 1953 he created *Brother Juniper,* a panel about a Franciscan, and by 1957 it had been collected in book form. The next year it was syndicated as a newspaper panel.

McCarthy received permission from Rome to leave the order and has since continued *Brother Juniper* as a layman.

Fred McCarthy ("Fr. Mac"), "Brother Juniper." © Publishers Syndicate.

He has lectured on the subject of humor and cartoons at more than fifty colleges, including Yale, MIT, Georgia and Georgia Tech, and he even taught a course on Jewish humor at the University of Miami in Florida! He is now retired and lives in Florida.

McCarthy's style is charming and deceptively simple (it should be noted that because of time pressures, Len Reno ghosted the art for years). His concepts, like Juniper's personality, exude Franciscan warmth.

R.M.

McCAY, WINSOR (1869-1934) American cartoonist, animator and graphic artist born in Spring Lake, Michigan, on September 26, 1869 (some sources say 1871, but 1869 seems more probable in light of McCay's early career and his own comments on the matter). Largely self-taught, Winsor McCay established himself as one of the masters of the emerging medium of the comic strip, principally with his celebrated Little Nemo (for full information on McCay's career in the comics, see The World Encyclopedia of Comics, Chelsea House, 1976).

McCay was already a successful newspaper comic strip artist when he decided around 1907 to go into animation. In 1909 he completed the drawings for his first cartoon film, *Little Nemo,* which was then photographed by Walter Austin under the direction of J.S. Blackton. Blackton's company, Vitagraph, released it in 1911. The cartoon was based closely on McCay's strip and included all its familiar characters: Little Nemo himself, the Princess, the mischief-maker Flip, Impy the cannibal and others. The success of *Little Nemo* prompted McCay to make a second cartoon, *The Story of a Mosquito* (also known as *How a Mosquito Operates*), released in 1912. In the meantime he

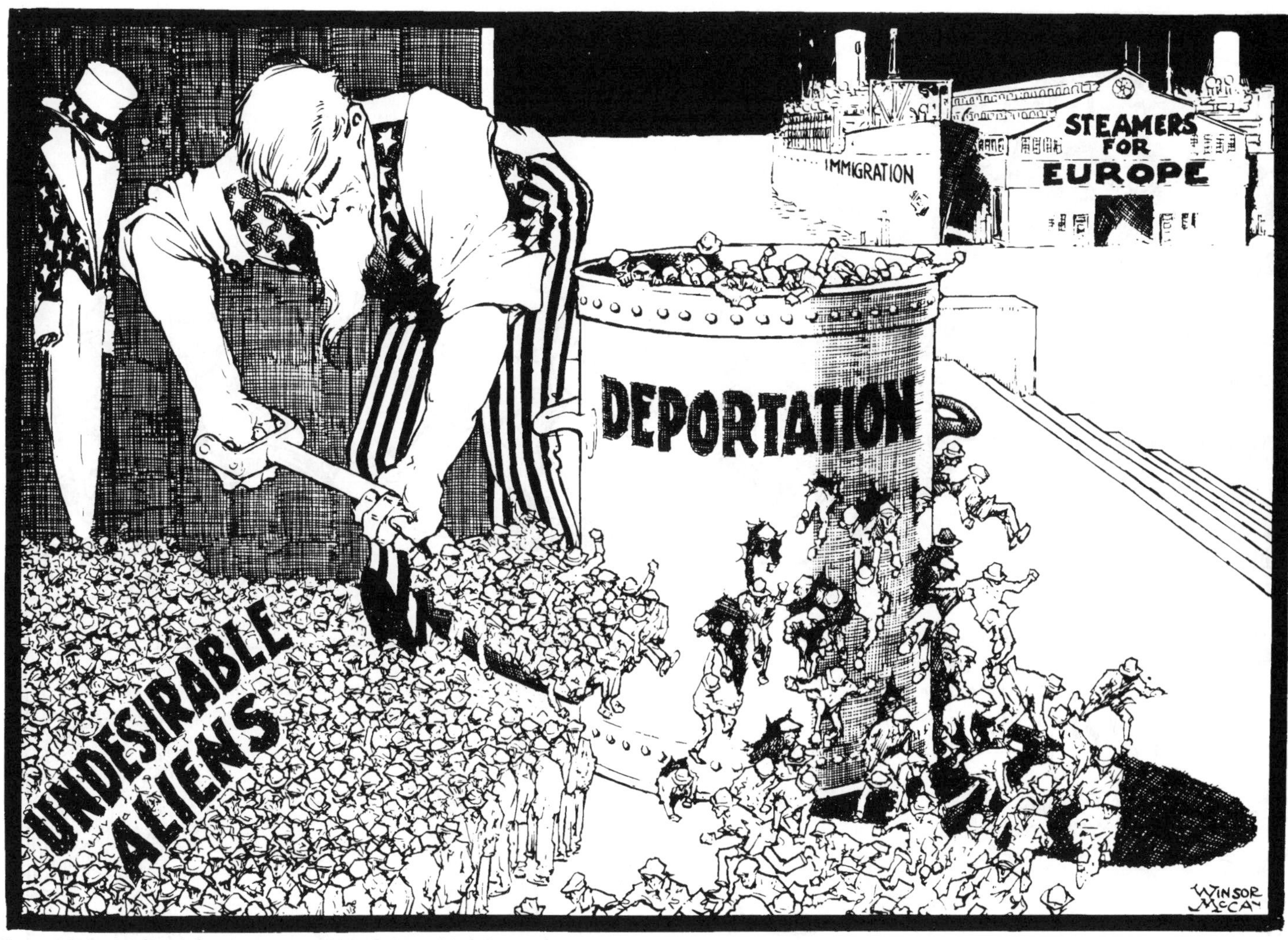

Winsor McCay, editorial cartoon, ca. 1920. © New York Journal.

had started work on *Gertie, the Trained Dinosaur,* which was first released theatrically in 1914 (although it may have been shown on the vaudeville circuit earlier). Arguably the most famous animated cartoon ever made, and certainly one of the most influential, *Gertie* can be said to have established the animated cartoon as an original art form.

McCay then went to work on his most ambitious project, an animated version of the sinking by a German submarine of the British liner *Lusitania. The Sinking of the Lusitania,* a nine-minute featurette, was released in 1918 (it was later expanded to twenty minutes by the addition of live and stock footage). This longest of McCay's cartoons had been preceded by less ambitious efforts, usually two or three minutes in duration, such as *The Centaurs* and *Gertie on Tour* (both 1916), *Flip's Circus* and *The Pet* (1917-18). McCay later made *Bug Vaudeville,* and in 1920 *The Flying House* (which is credited by some to his son, Robert McCay). The last three cartoons were released as a package in 1921 under the title *The Adventures of a Rarebit Eater.*

McCay abandoned animation in the early 1920s, dissatisfied, it is said, with the direction the medium was taking and its increasing commercialism. In addition to his comic strips and early magazine cartoons, he also did editorial cartoons of a conservative bent for the Hearst newspapers. They are much admired today for their draftsmanship and composition, but as means of persuasion they are rather flat and unmoving; while they would have been a credit to a lesser artist, they are dwarfed by McCay's towering achievements in animation and the comics.

Winsor McCay died on July 26, 1934. His fame, already great during his lifetime, has now grown to mythic proportions. As a master of three different cartoon idioms, he deserves the title *primus inter pares,* the first among his peers in the history of American cartoons.

M.H.

McCUTCHEON, JOHN TINNEY (1870-1949) American cartoonist, writer and war correspondent born near South Raub, Indiana, on May 6, 1870. A graduate of Purdue in 1889, McCutcheon published his first cartoons in Chicago, where he had been brought by fellow Hoosier George Ade, for the *Chicago Morning News* (later *Record* and *Record-Herald).* In 1903 he transferred to the *Chicago Tribune,* from which he retired, ill, in 1946.

McCutcheon's first political cartoon was published in 1896; he had previously done newspaper fillers and illustrations. In 1897 he left on the first of many memorable trips around the world with typewriter and drawing board. This particular trip was on the revenue cutter *McCulloch,* which was to join Admiral Dewey at Manila Bay. He soon was a war correspondent on other battlefields in the Spanish-American War, the Filipino insurrection, the Boer War, the abortive Vera Cruz raids, and World War I, where he was with the Belgian and German

Trying to "square it" with the peerless leader.

John Tinney McCutcheon, 1912. © Chicago Tribune

Remarkable view for a city tenement.

Angus MacDonall, 1924. © Judge.

armies, was arrested as a spy and was the first newspaperman to fly over the trenches. He witnessed battles in France, Salonica and the Balkans. On a trip to Africa in 1910, he joined up with an expedition of his good friend Theodore Roosevelt. He was the first newsman to cross the Gobi Desert in an automobile. (His party, finding themselves stranded, rigged up a sail to propel themselves to civilization!) In 1906 the *Tribune* sent him on a trip to the Crimea, the Caucasus, Persia, Russia, Chinese Turkestan and Siberia.

Matching the glamour he attracted with these exploits was McCutcheon's skill and fame as an editorial cartoonist. From his early cartooning days he was referred to as "the dean of American editorial cartooning," and he was certainly the primary exponent (rivaled only by Ireland and Donahey) of the Midwest school: utter mastery of technique and media, gentle political gibes and a strong dose of homey and sentimental subjects. His early fame, in fact, was based on the nation's acceptance of his *Bird Center* cartoons, doings of rural folk that led the thematic way for Dwig, Briggs, Webster and an army of later cartoonists. One of his best series was *A Boy in Springtime* (and . . . *Summertime),* each presenting heavily evocative and nostalgic statements. His political cartoons, however, were strong and partisan. A lifelong admirer of Theodore Roosevelt, he was at home on the *Chicago Tribune,* one of America's most Progressive newspapers. He was the major American cartoonist to support the Bull Moose candidacy in 1912 and was honest enough to admit a change of heart in the 1930s, after initially supporting the New Deal.

Among his famous cartoons is the classic "Injun Summer," which he drew in 1907 and the *Tribune* has printed annually since 1912 (in color since 1934). It is marked by sentiment, the wisdom of age and the wonderment of childhood. His Pulitzer Prize cartoon for 1932 is typical McCutcheon; it is untouched by severe partisanship or personal attack. He was a truly sage commentator as well as a consummate cartoonist.

McCutcheon was the brother of novelist George Barr McCutcheon, and two of his sons have followed in his footsteps: Shaw is a political cartoonist and John, Jr., is editorial page editor of the *Chicago Tribune.* Two honorary degrees were awarded the revered McCutcheon, an L.H.D. from Purdue in 1926 and an LL.D. from Notre Dame in 1931. He died at his home near Chicago on June 10, 1949.

Books: *Stories of Filipino Warfare* (1900); *The Cartoons That Made Prince Henry Famous* (1902); *TR in Cartoons* (1903); *Cartoons by McCutcheon* (1903); *Bird Center Cartoons* (1904); *The Mysterious Stranger and Other Cartoons* (1905); *Congressman Pumphrey* (1907); *In Africa* (1910); *Dawson III, Fortune Hunter* (1912); *The Restless Age* (1919); *An Heir at Large* (1922); *Crossed Wires* (1925); *Master of the World* (1928); and his 1950 autobiography, *Drawn from Memory.*

R.M.

MacDONALL, ANGUS (1876-1927) American cartoonist and illustrator born in St. Louis, Missouri, in 1876. Angus MacDonall moved east and was one of the first illustrators to settle in Westport, Connecticut, and establish it as an artists' community. His work began appearing regularly in the popular weeklies and monthlies in the early 1900s.

The bulk of his work was cartooning and light illustration; he readily became a fixture in *Life* magazine. At first a penman in the inevitable (for the time) Gibson style, MacDonall hit his stride when he discovered the pencil as his medium for finished work. Soon he was regularly appearing in all the humor magazines and kept busy doing mood illustrations for magazine fiction. Upon his untimely death at the age of 51, his work was an advertised main attraction in *Judge* magazine.

MacDonall's work was characterized by two things: the subtle and beautiful use of pencil shadings, and the consistent use of haunting, sentimental and nostalgic themes. Occasionally he touched on social issues—even then to evoke compassion rather than to incite anger—and he seldom aimed for the funny bone. His special world was that of memories, wistful love and shared dreams; the handsome and impressive body of his work deserves reprinting.

R.M.

McGILL, DONALD FRASER GOULD (1875-1962) British comic postcard cartoonist born at Blackheath, London, England, on January 28, 1875. "King of the Seaside Postcard," Donald McGill was the seventh of nine children. This descendant of an ancient Scottish family was educated at Blackheath Proprietary School, where he lost a foot after an accident during a rugby match at the age of 17. He entered the drawing office of a naval architect and began to contribute painted postcard cartoons to publisher Joseph Asher in 1905.

"The Pictorial Postcard Company have discovered a promising young humour-artist, Donald McGill by name, in the confident expectation that comic cards of his designing will soon become widely popular." This was the announcement in the *Picture Postcard Magazine* in December 1905. The confident expectation was realized: his most famous card, showing a small child at prayers, "Please Lord, excuse me while I kick Fido!," sold two million copies. McGill was paid six shillings (then worth a little over a dollar) for each card he produced, which included the full copyright. Working full time, he continued to create cards at the rate of ten a week.

When Asher was interned as an alien during World War I, McGill transferred to Hudson Brothers (1914) and then to the Inter-Art Company of Red Lion Square *(Comique Series)* from 1920 to 1932. Asher returned to postcard production in 1932 under the name of D. Custance (an office employee), and McGill returned to him to produce The New *Donald McGill Comics.* This series ran from 1932 to 1962, the year of McGill's death. He retired officially in 1939 and on the death of Asher joined the board of the company as director in charge of postcard design.

An article by George Orwell, the left-wing essayist, entitled "The Art of Donald McGill," in *Horizon* (February 1941), was the first critical attention paid to McGill's work. While casting doubts on McGill's existence ("He is apparently a trade name"), Orwell wrote, "McGill is a clever draughtsman with a real caricaturist's touch in the drawing of faces, but the special value of his postcards is that they are so completely typical. They represent, as it were, the norm of the comic postcard." McGill's gallery of grotesques—bloated women in skin-tight swimming costumes, equally balloonlike men ("I can't see my little Willie"), drunks, henpecks, courting couples, soldiers ("How long is your furlough?"), Scotsmen in kilts ("I thought it was a cat and I stroked his sporran")—is immortal, a permanent part of the British seaside way of life.

McGill died on October 13, 1962, at age 87. His postcards, perhaps 500 a year for 50 years, sold millions: he left exactly £735. A book, *Wish You Were Here,* was published in 1966.

D.G.

MACHAMER, THOMAS JEFFERSON (1899-1961) American cartoonist born in Holdredge, Nebraska, in 1899. Jefferson Machamer graduated from Nebraska University and got his first job on the art staff of the *Kansas City Star.* Sales of spot gag cartoons to *Cartoons Magazine* in the late 1910s whetted his appetite for Big Apple markets, and he moved to New York. After a stint with the *Tribune* he joined the staff of *Judge* around 1924 and became one of that weekly's major contributors. For *Judge* he did countless boy-girl cartoons, color covers and *Laughs from the Shows* (illustrated lines from Broadway hits), and drew the spots for the *High Hat* feature, a gossipy review of New York's speakeasies. When Norman Anthony left for *Life* in the late 1920s, Machamer began writing *High Hat* in addition. He later contributed to *College Humor.*

As the magazine market declined, Machamer scored variously with newspaper strips and panels: *Petting Patty* for Hearst; *Gags and Gals,* also for Hearst, beginning in 1937; and *The Baffles* (about a small-town family in Hollywood) for the *Los Angeles Times* in the early 1940s. He

"Gosh, men are changeable!
Only last week I was crazy about Freddie."

Jefferson Machamer. © Collier's.

was the author of several revues and conducted a correspondence school in cartooning from his home in Santa Monica, California until his death on August 15, 1961.

Machamer had an individualistic drawing style that varied little from the 1920s to the 1960s. His lack of art training was obvious, but he never shied from any subject or depiction. He drew in slashing, harsh brushstrokes and stereotyped his characters: men were wistful, bewildered and henpecked; women were assertive, dominant and racy (and in fact trod a thin line between the sexy and the grotesque).

R.M.

McKAY, DOROTHY (1904-1974) American cartoonist and illustrator born in San Francisco, California, in 1904. Dorothy McKay studied art at both the California School of Art and the Art Students League in New York City. The former Dorothy Jones, she was the wife of artist and illustrator Donald W. McKay. The couple lived in Greenwich Village, New York City.

Her cartoons, covers and illustrations appeared regularly in *Life, College Humor,* the *New Yorker, Ballyhoo* and *Forum* magazines. Then, as she said, "*Esquire* began to corral my time—from the second issue on." It might seem strange that a woman was a popular and regular contributing cartoonist to a magazine such as *Esquire,* which was noted for its risqué gags. However, Dorothy McKay was not unique. Barbara Shermund, another alumna of the *New Yorker*'s pages, had a career with many parallels.

Dorothy McKay worked in a fluid style that at times resembled the wash work of cartoonist Eldon Dedini. However, she also enjoyed crowding her cartoons with many characters and objects. The result was a look of controlled clutter that was right for her type of sophisticated humor. One *Esquire* cartoon showed a flock of rich and portly stage-door Johnnies waiting for a bubble dancer to emerge. The figures are packed into the space of the cartoon. On second look, one of the Johns emerges as a court official holding a subpoena for the dancer.

"How does it feel to be the first pedestrian I every hit?"
Dorothy McKay. © Collier's.

President Franklin D. Roosevelt was so enamored of one Dorothy McKay cartoon that he hung the original in the White House. It showed a little boy in front of a well-to-do suburban home, writing in chalk on the sidewalk while his sister looks at him with disapproval. The caption read, "Johnny just wrote a bad word." The word on the sidewalk was "Roosevelt."

Dorothy McKay died in New York City on June 3, 1974. She is best remembered for her witty *Esquire* cartoons.

B.C.

McLAREN, NORMAN (1914-1987) British animator born in Stirling, Scotland, on April 11, 1914. One of the true artists in animation, Norman McLaren took the drawing-direct-on-film technique originated by Len Lye and, by refining and continually experimenting, made it all his own. The son of a house painter, he was fascinated from the age of nine by the inventiveness of American animated cartoons. He later founded a film society at the Glasgow School of Art, where he was studying interior design. He scraped the emulsion from a 300-foot reel of old film and, using clear inks, painted a changing design onto the celluloid. The result, McLaren's first animated abstract, was unfortunately lost to posterity when the art school projector chewed it to shreds. Undeterred, he went on to make *Camera Makes Whoopee* (1935), blending cartoons with animated models and objects. Shown at the Amateur Film Festival in Glasgow, the film impressed John Grierson, who invited the student to join his General Post Office film unit in London. Before he did so, McLaren joined an antiwar movement and made *Hell Unlimited* (1936), an impressionistic documentary, with sculptor Helen Biggar. He also visited Spain and filmed some of the events of the civil war with Ivor Montagu (*Peace and Plenty,* 1936).

Joining the GPO film unit, McLaren was trained by Alberto Cavalcanti and Evelyn Spice, makers of documentary films. He made four short films, including *Book Bargain* (1937), a documentary on the telephone directory, and *Love on the Wing* (1938), a plug for the new airmail service which he drew directly onto film. After a short spell with Film Centre, an outfit making sponsored documentaries (here he made *The Obedient Flame*), McLaren went to New York at the outbreak of World War II. On commission from the Guggenheim Museum he drew the film *Stars and Stripes* (1939), this time doing his own soundtrack as well. A few advertising films for Caravelle followed; then came a second invitation from John Grierson, the so-called father of the documentary. Grierson had been made Canadian film commissioner, and he wanted McLaren to start an animation unit at the newly formed National Film Board of Canada. McLaren's first films for the NFB followed his British pattern: *Mail Early for Christmas* (1941), etc. Then he supervised a series of song cartoons, *Chants Populaires* (1944), which used several animation techniques to illustrate favorite French-Canadian songs. *Begone Dull Care* (1949) introduced a new style of hand-drawn film: McLaren ignored the frame lines and used the celluloid strip itself as a continuous canvas.

For the 1951 Festival of Britain McLaren made two short stereoscopic cartoons in three-dimensional sound, *Around Is Around* and *Now Is the Time,* which proved that the 3-D

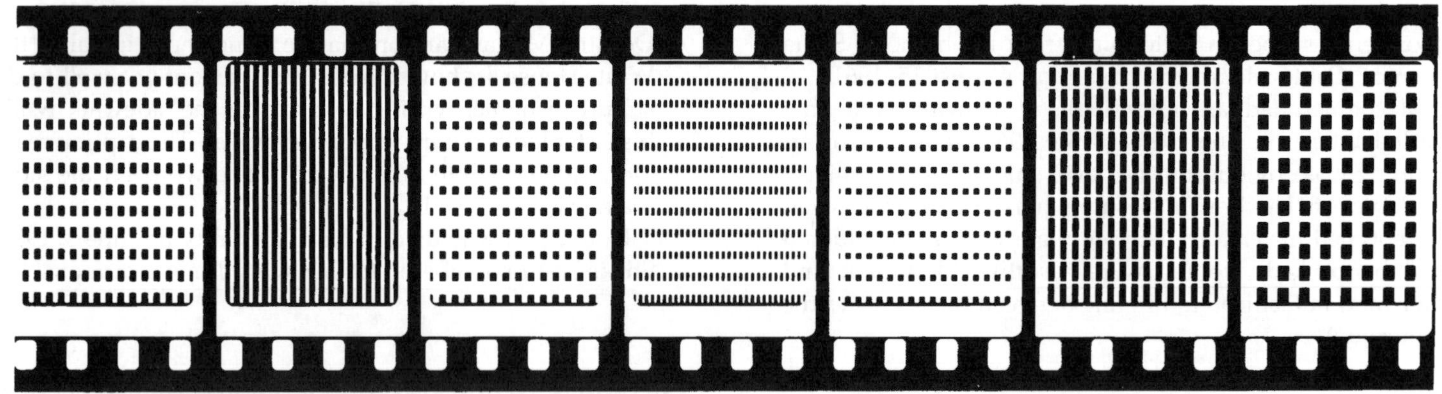

Norman McLaren, seven successive frames of visual material, based on sound track images. © National Film Board of Canada.

technique is ideal for animation. Unfortunately McLaren's experiments were not studied by the film industry, whose few stereoscopic shorts in the 1950s lacked both inspiration and impact. McLaren continued to experiment and in 1952 made *Neighbors,* the first effective use of the pixillation technique (the use of live actors as animated objects). After setting up animation schools in China (1949) and India (1953) for UNESCO, McLaren experimented further with his attempt to visualize music. *Rhythmetic* (1956) was a sophisticated use of cutout animation, *Canon* (1964) a complex mix of almost every known animation technique, and *Pas de Deux* (1967) a stroboscopic short of overlapping images. Now far removed from the commercial entertainment field, McLaren has taken animation into the realm of pure personal art. His last completed work was the ballet *Narcissus* (1983). He died of a heart attack at his home near Montreal on January 27, 1987.

Among McLaren's other films, mention should be made of the following: *Dollar Dance* (1943), *Alouette* (1944), *Hoppity Pop* (1946), *A Phantasy* (1952), *Serenal* (1959), *Mosaic* (1965), *Spheres* (1969), *Synchromy* (1971) and *Ballet Adagio* (1972).

D.G.

MacNELLY, JEFFREY KENNETH (1947-) American artist born in New York on September 17, 1947. Jeff MacNelly came from an artistic family and had his first cartoon published in *Lawrence Life,* the yearbook of Lawrence School in Hewlett, Long Island. Later scholastic markets included the *Mirror* literary magazine at Phillips Academy and the *Daily Tar Heel,* campus newspaper at the University of North Carolina. During his last two years of college he contributed to the *Chapel Hill Weekly*.

On December 1, 1970, MacNelly began drawing political cartoons for the *Richmond* (Va.) *News Leader* and won a Pulitzer Prize for his work during his first full year behind the drawing board. Since then he has won other awards and begun drawing cartoon features. *We Hold These Truths* is a realistically illustrated panel dealing with American history; it is written by his close friend and editor Ross Mackenzie and distributed by United Feature. *Shoe,* a zany comic strip about a colony of birds with all-too-human neuroses, is packaged and edited by Neal Freeman and syndicated by Tribune-News, which also handles his editorial cartoons.

MacNelly is clearly the premier American editorial cartoonist of his generation. He began working in the vein of Oliphant but soon transcended any influences and developed a distinctly individual style. His level of achievement—salient points presented in arresting compositions—is consistently excellent. A cartoonist of conservative political leanings, MacNelly is reprinted widely and has eschewed offers to join larger newspaper staffs across the nation; he prefers to remain in Richmond. His first anthology—*MacNelly* published by Westover in 1972—clearly demonstrated his technique of couching a devastating political observation in an invariably hilarious format. More recent books include *The Best of MacNelly* and *Shoe.* He left the *News-Leader* in June 1981, and since March 1982 he has been drawing editorial cartoons for the *Chicago Tribune*.

R.M.

Jeff MacNelly. © New York Daily News.

MACPHERSON, DUNCAN IAN (1924-1993) Canadian editorial cartoonist born in Toronto, Ontario, on September 20, 1924. Duncan Macpherson began sketching as a youth. While in the Royal Canadian Air Force in England during World War II, he started art training. On release from service in 1946, he enrolled at Boston Museum School of Art, and on graduation in 1948 he took a two-year course at Ontario College of Art. Macpherson then freelanced for about ten years. His work appeared in a variety of publications ranging from the *Christian Science Monitor* to Eaton's mail order catalogues. He illustrated several series in the Montreal *Standard* and *Maclean's.*

Moolah Be Praised
Duncan Macpherson. © Toronto Star.

In 1958 Macpherson joined the Toronto *Star* on the urging of editor Pierre Berton. From there his cartoons have been printed in numerous other Canadian papers and over a hundred different newspapers around the world. Since 1959 he has won the National Newspaper Award six times. His work has also been honored with a 1966 Royal Canadian Academy Medal for distinguished work in the visual arts and the 1971 Molson Prize from the Canada Council for contributing to the arts in Canada. Yearly collections of his editorial cartoons have been published since 1961. He has illustrated several books, including one of his own titled *Macpherson's Canada.*

Macpherson is almost universally recognized as the foremost editorial cartoonist in Canada. His illustrative skills are given a large space at the top of the *Star*'s editorial page. In preparation for drawing, Macpherson makes extensive research use of the library and fills his cartoons with props and costumes when needed. Many times his knowledge of magic tricks and circuses has been put to use in his cartoons. His detailed drawings have been exhibited in various places, from art galleries to university campuses. Edmund Wilson, writing in the *New Yorker,* compared Macpherson to James Gillray and stated that his cartoons "may be fascinating quite independently of our interest or knowledge of the happenings they commemorate. Macpherson is a Gillray reduced in scale, a more scaring and grotesque Lewis Carroll."

With his artwork, Macpherson provides a remarkable commentary on events and individuals. His cartoons reveal weakness and flaws in ways almost everyone can understand and appreciate. His typical Canadian is a tattered, chinless fellow who is usually in some pathetic and humorous situation. John Diefenbaker, prime minister when Macpherson started at the *Star*, said, "He is a great cartoonist with an infinite capacity to get to the heart of things. I like a cartoon that is devastating without wounding."

Macpherson isn't known deeply by many of his colleagues. He has been seen both as a rough character and as compassionate beyond measure. He is about six feet two and weighs about two hundred thirty pounds. One friend characterizes him as a combination of Mary Poppins, Mark Twain and Attila the Hun. He died of pancreatic cancer on May 5, 1993.

D.K.

MADDOCKS, PETER (1929-) British writer, cartoonist, animator and one-man syndicate, born in Birmingham on April 1, 1929 ("All Fools' Day," as he is pleased to point out). Peter Maddocks attended the Moseley School of Art from age 11, until he ran away to sea with the merchant marine at 15. Five years later he returned to dry land and set up a small business as a poster writer and designer for a small chain of cinemas, his first professional artwork. He wrote a trial strip, *Shame of the West,* which was drawn by a friend, cartoonist Terry ("Larry") Parkes, and together they tried their luck with the London newspapers. Nobody was interested, however, so Maddocks began to write strip scripts for the Amalgamated Press *Cowboy Comics* ("Kit Carson") and *Thriller Comics* ("The Saint," from the books by Leslie Charteris). He began to contribute cartoon gags to the "Cartoon Sketch" page in the *Daily Sketch.* Editor Julian Phipps liked his style, which was then close to that of "Trog," and gave him a 12-month contract for a daily gag cartoon.

Much attracted by the strip format, Maddocks then adapted the radio series *The Goon Show* as a daily, but this failed to interest editors. A strip in the same style of humor but with an original character did catch the interest of the *Daily Express,* however, and *Four D Jones,* signed for ten weeks, ran for ten years! The central character was a cowboy who used a time hoop to travel through 4-D (the fourth dimension) to sundry adventures in various worlds. This strip was followed by *Horatio Cringe,* about a dimwitted detective, which appeared in the Glasgow *Evening Citizen.* In 1966, Maddocks became sports cartoonist on the London *Evening Standard* and founded the British Cartoonists' Association. Other of his strips include *A Leg at Each Corner* (*Sunday Telegraph,* 1968) and the political strip *No. 10* (*Sunday Express,* 1971), which changes central characters with every general election!

Maddocks's style has become extremely simple, perhaps out of necessity, because he is extremely prolific. He is currently drawing *Slightly Maddocks* daily in the *Evening News* (since 1971), *Useless Eustace* in the *Daily Mirror* (since 1974 when he took the character over from Jack Greenall) and *The Zanies,* a three-gags-a-day strip that he himself has syndicated since 1970. In addition he draws a full-color three-page folio of permissive gags for *Mayfair* each month and designs and storyboards cartoon commercials for German television, for Credo (a deodorant), Neocid (a fly spray) and Jumbo (a washing powder), to name but a few. His children's comic work includes *The Bouncers* in *Swift* (1959), *Slowcoach* in *Whizzer and Chips* (1970) and *Penny Crayon* in *Lindy* (1975). His books are *The British Elephant Book* (1967) and *No. 10* (1973). Since the 1980s Maddocks has been heavily involved in animation, easily adapting his simplistic style to television demands. His series include *The Family Ness, Jumbo and the Jet Set,* and *Penny Crayon.* Later books range from children's titles to the educational *So You Want To Be a Cartoonist* (1985) and the extremely adult *Condomanic* (1987).

D.G.

Antonio Madrigal. © Antonio Madrigal Collizo

MADRIGAL COLLIZO, ANTONIO (1940-) Spanish cartoonist born into a conservative family in Melilla, an African colony of Spain, on August 20, 1940. After graduating from law school, Antonio Madrigal studied journalism, but what he really loved was the art of painting—and humor. So, from the age of 15, he devoted most of his time to cartooning.

Madrigal began his career in 1955 working for the most popular magazines of the time, *Don José* and *La Codorniz*, both of which were the only publications printing humor cartoons critical of the Franco dictatorship. Along with other artists such as Alvaro de la Iglesia, he succeeded in publishing a lot of satirical work in the pages of *La Codorniz*, which since 1941 had been very close to the Franco regime.

In the 1960s his family moved to Segovia, in metropolitan Spain, and Madrigal began contributing to almost every publication in the country with cartoons that were both functional and spontaneous on the one hand, and somewhat highbrow on the other. Those cartoons won him many honors, awards, and prizes from all parts of Spain in the 1970s and 1980s. In the meantime he also did storyboards for animated cartoons and painted posters. Several exhibitions of his paintings took place over the years. In 1994 he was named Honorary Professor of Humor by the University of Alcala, and in 1997 he received the coveted Humor Prize from the Readers Circle in Madrid.

Madrigal currently contributes a daily cartoon to *El Adelantado* of Segovia (an anthology of his work for the paper was published in 1996) and also works for the important *Diario 16* newspaper.

F.T.J.

MAL

See Hancock, Malcolm.

MANCA, GIOVANNI (1889-1984) Italian cartoonist born in Milan, Italy, in 1889. After World War I, he devoted his talents to drawing cartoons and stories for boys' magazines.

Giovanni Manca. © Il Travaso.

In 1930, in the comic weekly *Il Corriere dei Piccoli, Manca* created one of the most famous of Italian comic strips, *Pier Cloruro de' Lambicchi,* featuring a bald scientist always full of inventions and optimism in a period that did not lend itself to optimism. The protagonist has been engaging in his slightly harebrained adventures ever since. After World War II Manca produced two more humor strips, *Macarietto* and the more unusual *Tamarindo,* in which a breezy confidence man went around the world in the company of such strange associates as the Earl and Sister Cipolla.

Manca has continued to draw gag cartoons over the years and has also illustrated a number of books, including a *Pinocchio* in which his caricatural sense of humor was given free rein. He was still lving in Milan and active as ever well into his eighties. He died at age 95 in 1984.

C.S.

MANFREDI, MANFREDO (1934-) Italian animator and filmmaker born in Palermo, Italy, in 1934. After studying art (he is a painter of great luminosity), Manfredo Manfredi settled in Rome. Starting in 1960, he produced the animated credits for a number of TV programs and also made animated commercials. In 1965, in collaboration with Guido Gomas, Manfredi produced two entertainment shorts: *L'Albero* ("The Tree"), which deals with ecological issues, and *Ballata per un Pezzo da Novanta* ("Ballad for a Heavyweight"), which uses the rhythms of a vibrant popular ballad for an ironical investigation into the world of meat markets infiltrated by the Mafia. Manfredi's *Terun* (1967) is a tale of an immigrant from the Italian south and the prejudices he encounters. In 1969 *K.O.*, an exposé of boxing, was enthusiastically received by the critics. In *Rotocalco* ("Rotogravure," 1970) Manfredi projects the fears, illusions and oppressions of modern man as layouts for a rotogravure press.

In recent times Manfredi has leaned heavily towards the fantastic. In this genre he made *Il Muro* ("The Wall"), *Ritorno nel Futuro* ("Return to the Future," in collaboration with the Romanian Sabin Bălașa) and *The Cat* (in collaboration with the Yugoslav Zlatko Bourek), all released in 1971 and 1972. Manfredi also directed the 1973 *Sotteraneo* ("Underground"), which depicts the terrifying journey of a subway traveler, and the recent *Dedalo* ("Daedalus"), which was nominated for an Academy Award. In a different vein, he was the chief animator on the poetic *Il Giro del Mondo degli Inamorati di Peynet* ("Around the World with

Manfredo Manfredi, "Terun." © Manfredi.

Peynet's Lovers," 1974). Manfredi's wife, Maria Grazia Hay, has also directed a number of animated cartoons, such as *Homo Sapiens* and *La Costola d'Adamo* ("Adam's Rib"). One of the most respected names in Italian animation, he is now devoting most of his time developing the new generation of Italian animators.

S.T.

MANNELLI, RICCARDO (1955-) Italian cartoonist, illustrator and etcher, born in Pistoia in 1955. While a student, he began to draw a comic strip adventure, *I draghi*, printed in the series Fantapocket, but his first humorous and satirical drawings were published in the fortnightly magazine *Help* (1976 and 1978) and in *I Quaderni del Sale* (1976). Afterwards he contributed to the satirical periodicals *Il Male* (1978), *Cane Caldo* (1979), to the comics monthlies *Linus* (1978), *Alter Alter* (1979), *Il Mago* (1979), to the political daily paper *Lotto Continua* (1979-1980) and to *Tramezzino* (humor supplement of the daily *Paese sera*, 1979-1980).

Riccardo Manelli. © Riccardo Manelli.

During the 1980s Mannelli revived a kind of graphic journalism which was in use before the printing of photographs in the papers. He visited different places and law courts (where photographers were not admitted) to sketch the settings and the protagonists of social happenings and celebrated criminal trials. Later on these graphic reports were printed along with the artist's spicy commentary.

In the same decade Mannelli's artwork—which included illustrations, portraits, caricatures, comic strip stories, cartoons and graphic reports—became a feature of satirical supplements and magazines such as *Satyricon* (1980-1983 and 1989), *Tango* (1986), *Zut* (1987), *Mercurio* (weekly culture supplement of the daily *La Repubblica*, 1989-1991), in the news magazine *L'Europeo* (1983-1989), in the dailies *Il manifesto* (1984-1985), *Paese sera* (1986), *Il Messaggero*, *La Repubblica* (1989). Mannelli's comic strip stories were published in the French comics and humor magazine *L'Echo des Savanes* (1983-1984) and in the monthly *ComicArt* (1986-1988 and 1992-1993).

During this decade he has contributed to the satirical magazines *Cuore* (1990 and 1993-1994), *Il clandestino* (1994-1995) and since 1997 to *Boxer* (a satirical pullout of the daily *Il manifesto*). Mannelli is a superb draftsman who can express himself with realistic, grotesque and caricatured outcomes. His powerful graphic style plunges the reader into a large variety of social environments that he pictures, showing little mercy for mankind. His artwork stems from direct experience that he reworks according to his pessimistic attitude.

Part of his production has been printed or reprinted in book format: *Chilometri di chili* (1984), *Nicaragua* (1985), *Mannelli: appunti, cronache, reportages, saldi di fine secolo* (1990), *Carni scelte* (1994). He is also the author of portfolios including serigraphs and etchings: *Susanna* (1991), *Eva* (1992), and *Pornografiche* (1994).

G.C.C.

MANNING, REGINALD (1905-1986) American cartoonist born in Kansas City, Missouri, on April 5, 1905. Reg Manning moved to Phoenix, Arizona, in 1919 and studied art in high school. Three days after graduation he secured a position with the Arizona *Republic*, starting work on May 1, 1926. He was to hang his hat at that office for the next 50 years.

Manning began as a photographer and spot artist. Soon he was drawing both a weekly full-page review of the news (in the Billy Ireland format) called *The Big Parade* and daily editorial cartoons. *The Parade* was given up in 1948 so Manning could devote more time to his editorial cartoons, and three years later he won a Pulitzer for "Hats," one of the most strikingly simple cartoons ever chosen by that committee.

A Phoenix institution, Manning is famed for his good humor, his many speaking engagements and a series of books produced through the years. Titles include *A Cartoon Guide to Arizona* (1938), *What Kinda Cactus Issat?* (1941), *From Tee to Cup* (1954) *and What Is Arizona Really Like?* (1968). The Republic and Gazette Syndicate distributed Manning's work until 1945, when McNaught assumed syndication.

Don't look so glum.
Reg Manning. © Phoenix Republic and Gazette Syndicate.

Reg Manning was for years one of American cartooning's most prominent conservative voices and won numerous awards. Manning retired in 1976—Bill Mauldin was the principal guest at the retirement dinner—and devoted himself to sculpture with as much success as he enjoyed at the drawing board until his death in Scottsdale, Arizona, on March 10, 1986.

R.M.

MARAMOTTI, DANILO (1949-) Italian cartoonist born in Savona on May 17, 1949. After graduating from the local art school he began contributing the comic strip *La signora a cavallo* to the monthly *Horror*. Between 1973 and 1975 he wrote and drew some adventure comic strips for kids, printed in the series Liber Pocket. Then he taught drawing at an art school and abandoned comics for an unsuccessful ceramic workshop.

In 1981 he went back to comics with a story printed in the magazine *Frigidaire*. Since then his contribution to cartoon and comic strip art has been rapidly increasing. He has signed adventure comic strips such as *Bad Cat, Mister Loco, Laura Lover, Rocky Rude,* which were printed in important comics magazines like *Alter, Tic, Corto Maltese* (1986-1993), *Linus* (since 1988), and *Comix* (1995-1996). Along with these adventurous comics, Maramotti has brought out satirical and humorous comics and cartoons which appeared in the weeklies *Cuore* (1989-1996), *Tuttolibri* (pull out of the daily *La Stampa*), *Boxer* (since 1997), *Vivi Milano* (pull out of the daily *Corriere della Sera,* since 1997), in the magazine *Notizie Verdi* (since 1994) and in the daily *Il Messaggero* (1995-1996). Maramotti's well-delineated figures are drawn with a heavy and roundish graphic sign which reminds one very much of Wilson McCoy's style. His style, basically realistic but with a natural flair for caricature, allows him to succeed in mastering both adventurous and comical stories. When he deals with adventure, he likes to develop criminal and exotic subjects in a slightly grotesque style; when he deals with satire, his attention is focused on Italian politics and manners of which he makes fun from a liberal and progressive point of view. It is worth signalling Maramotti's literary single panel cartoon, which he uses to "review" with an ironic gag the outcoming best-sellers.

Maramotti has also illustrated some advertising campaigns and has worked shortly in the animation field.

The comic strip, *Bad Cat*, was reprinted in book format in 1994. In that same year, the artist was awarded the Prize Forte dei Marmi for Political Satire.

G.C.C.

Danilo Maramotti. © Danilo Maramotti.

MARANHÃO, PERICLES (1924-1961) Brazilian cartoonist born in the state of Pernambuco, Brazil, in 1924. Pericles Maranhão studied art in Recife and moved to Rio de Janeiro in 1943. He started his career in cartooning later the same year with As *Aventuras de Oliveira Trapalhão,* a strip he created for the comic book publishers Diários Associados and signed with his first name only. Pericles joined the humor magazine *A Cigara* in 1944 as a staff artist, a position he retained for the next eight years. In 1952 he created the popular panel *O Amigo da Onca* ("The Two-Bit Friend") for the daily newspaper *O Cruzeiro.*

Pericles was a gifted and funny artist who endowed his characters with much humor and humanity. Despite the sunny disposition he displayed in his cartoons, his outlook on life was dark, and he finally committed suicide in 1961. *O Amigo da Onça* was taken over by Carlos Estevão de Souza and remains as a reminder of Pericles's talent.

A.M.

MARCKS, MARIE (1922-) Marie Marcks, one of the very few notable female cartoonists, was born August 25, 1922, in Berlin where she also grew up. She learned how to draw from her mother who headed a private art school. Marie Marcks studied architecture from 1942 to 1944 in Berlin and Stuttgart, but broke off her studies to marry. Since

Marie Marcks. © Marie Marcks.

1948 she has been living in Heidelberg. She was married twice and has five children.

After the war she started working for the American Army as a graphic designer for a magazine, designing posters and comics. From the mid-1950s she turned to conceptualizing exhibitions, among them exhibitions for the German state of Baden-Württemberg, for car exhibitions, for the German pavilion at the World Exposition in Brussels, or for "Atoms for Peace" in Geneva.

Eventually her political cartoons became sought after as she did not shy away from touchy themes, including ecology or suburban madness (which harken back to her erstwhile studies in architecture). Her cartoons have appeared regularly in *Süddeutsche Zeitung* since 1965. They have also been featured in *Die Zeit*, in the social democrat *Vorwärts*, in the satiric magazine *titanic* and in other renowned publications. The cartoons of Marie Marcks' deft lines have also been featured on posters and have graced the pages of many books, besides the well over 20 collections of her own cartoons.

Marie Marcks also produced a number of films on cybernetics and city life. So far two volumes of her autobiographical notes have been published as well.

W.F.

MARCUS, JERRY (1924-) American cartoonist born in Brooklyn, New York, on June 27, 1924. Jerry Marcus grew up in Brooklyn and attended Samuel J. Tilden High School. A skinny kid, he was turned down by the U.S. Navy for being underweight when he tried to enlist in 1943. He joined the merchant marine instead. In 1943 he completed three or four trips to England across North Atlantic convoy routes. During these trips he served aboard tankers loaded with high-octane gasoline. In 1944 Marcus was able to enlist in the U.S. Navy and serve the rest of World War II as a Seabee in the Philippines. While stationed on the island of Calicoan off the tip of Samar, he started a makeshift military newspaper called the *Coral Zephyr.*

Once again a civilian, Jerry Marcus used the GI bill to attend the Cartoonists and Illustrators School in New York City, now known as the School of Visual Arts. He began submitting magazine cartoons and in 1947 made his first professional sale to *Argosy.* A year later he sold to the *Saturday Evening Post, Collier's* and *American* magazines. During the 1950s and early 1960s cartoons by Jerry Marcus were standards in most of the national general readership magazines. He was one of the cartoonists on contract to the *Saturday Evening Post.* The contract assured him of four sales a month to the *Post.* Many of his sports cartoons appeared in *Sports Illustrated.*

Marcus draws everything from kids to pets to suburbia to the classic man-stranded-on-a-desert-island. His drawing style is loose but not sketchy. Sometimes editors would decide they liked his roughs and publish them instead of requesting that more finished drawings be done. Numerous Jerry Marcus cartoons have been published in cartoon anthologies, and presidents Eisenhower and Kennedy both asked for, and received, original Marcus cartoons.

In the early 1960s, he set becoming a cartoonist for the *New Yorker* as a goal. However, after he'd been published five times in the *New Yorker,* the demands of his then-new syndicated comic strip *Trudy* kept him from submitting cartoons regularly. *Trudy* began in March 1963. A daily panel and Sunday page syndicated by King Features

"You may already be a winner!"

Jerry Marcus. © Good Housekeeping.

Syndicate, *Trudy* stars the young suburban housewife personified. Termed by the syndicate "a humorous sendup of marriage, parenthood and nosy next-door neighbors," it is still going strong at century's end.

Recently, Marcus has begun to freelance magazine cartoons as well as doing his *Trudy* strip. *Good Housekeeping, Ladies' Home Journal* and the gag-a-day panels syndicated by King Features and McNaught syndicates have proven ready markets for his cartoons.

A member of the Screen Actors Guild, Jerry Marcus has been an extra in a number of films and acted in television. In 1963 a book of his magazine cartoons entitled *Just Married* was published. A collection of *Trudy* cartoons entitled *Hang in There Trudy* was published in 1975.

B.C.

MARGUERITA
See Bornstein, Marguerita.

MARGULIES, JIMMY (1951-) Being the son of a graphic designer and a fashion illustrator and holding a B.F.A. from Carnegie-Mellon University made a career in art an obvious choice for the New York-born Jimmy Margulies. But it was his combination of social engagement and ironic humor that led him to that of an editorial cartoonist. His work has always maintained a delicate balance between wit and outrage, avoiding the extremes of heavy-handed editorialization and pure gag-writing. "I prefer to reflect the inherent ridiculousness of a particular situation," he has observed, "[but] I like to strike deeper than just a joke."

After graduating from college in 1973, Margulies made some sales to Rothco Cartoons, which distributed his work to such publications as the *New York Post*, the *Boston Herald-American*, *U.S. News and World Report*, and *Newsweek*. In 1978 Suburban Features, a division of Newspaper Enterprise Association, began distributing some of Margulies' editorial cartoons nationally while he worked as a staff artist for CETA in New York, and during the next few years his work appeared frequently in the Bergan, N.J. *Record*, the *Army Times*, and the Virginia and Maryland *Journals*. In 1984 Margulies was appointed editorial cartoonist with the *Houston* (Texas) *Post*.

Since June, 1975, when he won a National Cartoonists Association-Johnson Wax contest, Margulies has earned many honors, including awards from the Freedoms Foundation at Valley Forge (1980, 1981-82); the National Newspaper Association and the Virginia Press Association (1982, 1983, 1984); the International Salon of Cartoons, Montreal, Canada (1985); the Population Institute, Washington, D.C. (the Hemisphere Award and the Global Media Award), (1985); the Fischetti Editorial Cartoon Contest (1991, 1993), the New York State Bar Association (the John Peter Zenger Award), and the National Press Foundation (1993). In 1990, *Ultra* magazine included him in its list of "Texans Who Made the Eighties," and in 1996 he received the National Headliner Award for editorial cartooning. An original drawing by Margulies is part of the permanent collections of the Lyndon B. Johnson Library at the University of Texas.

In 1990, Margulies left the *Post* for the Bergan *Record*. His work was distributed nationally by United Feature Syndicate from 1985 and has been handled by King Features since 1991. King also distributes two Margulies caricatures a week, and the artist himself syndicates his state-oriented cartoons to other newspapers in New Jersey.

Margulies' work has been included regularly in the anthologies *Best Editorial Cartoons of the Year* since 1975 and has also appeared in such collections as *100 Watts: The James Watt Memorial Cartoon Collection* (1983), lampooning the then secretary of the interior, and *ReaganComics*, doing the same to the former president. In 1988, his first independent collection, *My Husband Is Not a Wimp: Margulies Cartoons from the Houston Post*, was published.

A combination of vigorous graphic style, clearly defined message, and good-natured humor have made Jimmy Margulies one of the nation's most respected and popular editorial cartoonists, with both his colleagues and the newspaper-reading public.

D.W.

Jimmy Margulies. © Houston Post.

Javier Mariscal. © Javier Mariscal.

MARISCAL, JAVIER ERRANDO (1950-) The most charismatic of the neo-cultural money-seekers of the 1970s, Javier Errando Mariscal was born in Valencia on February 9, 1950. He liked to draw in his childhood in a somewhat naif style, and this later helped him to be published along with some of his friends, but without much success. Soon he began frequenting political and well-connected social circles, and he made a reputation as a designer for snobbish clients.

In 1973 he saw his first professional publication, called *El Rollo Enmascarado* ("The Masked Drag Queen"). It was a parody of The Phantom and not much artistically, but it got him some needed publicity. He also drew comics for diverse underground magazines, did catalogue covers, and had his first successful comic story, *A Valencia*, published in 1975. This led him a few years later to relocate to Barcelona in search of greater fame and more money.

Mariscal then began working as a cartoonist for the Spanish editions of *Playboy* and *Penthouse*, among other magazines. His reputation grew by leaps and bounds, and in 1992 he finally got his big break, when he was asked to draw the mascot for the Olympic Games held that year in Barcelona. He came up with "Cobi," which he averred to be a dog, though nobody could make head or tail of it. Since then he has devoted most of his time promoting himself, designing shoes, furniture and textiles, and illustrating two books: *!Yo me escape!* ("I Have Escaped!") and *El supervivant de l'ordinador* ("The Surviver of the Computer"), both in 1995. Occasionally he also does some cartooning.

F.T.J.

MARKOW, JACK (1905-1983) American cartoonist born in London, England, on January 23, 1905. Jack Markow moved to New York at the age of two and later studied at the Art Students League under Boardman Robinson and Walter Jack Duncan (1922-29). There have been very few cartoon markets in which Markow's work has not appeared between the 1920s and the 1970s. His gags are almost always based on simple premises, and he draws with a loose, free brush line, usually using crayon shading. His style is one of deceptive simplicity; technical accuracy and flawless composition are hallmarks of his work.

It is possible that Markow will be remembered more for his instructional work in the cartooning field than for his output on paper. He taught for years at the School of Visual Arts, training a generation of magazine cartoonists. He was cartoon editor of *Argosy* between 1951 and 1953, and for many years he wrote a column on cartooning for *Writer's Digest*, providing invaluable tips and advice. He frequently contributes pointers and reminiscences to *Cartoonist PROfiles* magazine.

Markow's books include *Drawing and Selling Cartoons, Drawing Funny Pictures, Drawing Comic Strips* and *The Cartoonist's and Gag Writer's Handbook,* which many professionals still turn to for masterful instruction on their craft. Markow is also a noted painter and lithographer, with works in the collections of the Metropolitan Museum, the Library of Congress, the Brooklyn Museum, the Corcoran Gallery and the Whitney Museum of Modern Art. He died in 1983.

R.M.

MARKS, ALEKSANDAR (1922-) Yugoslav cartoonist and animator born in Cazma, Yugoslavia, in 1922. After graduation from the Zagreb Academy of Art, Aleksandar Marks worked as a cartoonist for *Kerempuh* and also did book illustration. He joined Duga Film as an animator in 1951 and later made advertising films. In 1955 he designed Yugoslavia's first color cartoon, *Little Red Riding Hood.*

Marks joined Zagreb Film immediately upon its formation in 1956. Until 1960 he served merely as a designer on others' cartoons (*Cowboy Jimmy, On a Meadow, At the Photographer's* and *Typhus* are some of the films on which he worked). In 1960, in collaboration with Vladimir Jutriša, he started directing as well as designing. The most important Marks-Jutriša films include: *The White Avenger,* a sequel to *Cowboy Jimmy* (1962); *Metamorphosis* (1964); *The Kind-Hearted Ant* (1965); *The Fly,* a much-awarded cartoon about a fly growing to gigantic proportions (1966);

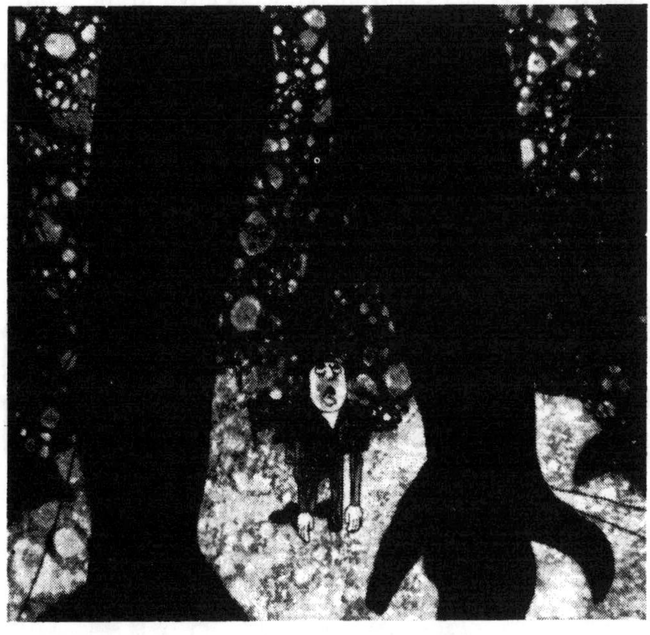

Aleksandar Marks, "The Fly." © Zagreb Film.

Sisyphus (1967—either by coincidence or design there have been two other cartoons on the theme of Sisyphus, one by the Hungarian Marcell Jankovics, the other by the Bulgarian Stoyan Dukov); and *In the Spider's Web* (1970). Marks has also collaborated on the multiphased *Man the Polluter* (1975), and he independently directed the charming little cartoon fable *Cowhand Marko* in 1976. After doing *Obsession* (again with Jutrisa) in 1983, he seems to have faded away following his partner's death in 1984.

Marks stands apart from other Zagreb animators in his insistence on aesthetic and literary elements and in his affinity to the Surrealists, the Bauhaus and other modern art movements. His cartoons have received many awards and much acclaim over the years.

M.H.

MARLETTE, DOUGLAS N. (1949-) American political cartoonist born in Greensboro, North Carolina, on December 12, 1949. Doug Marlette is an alumnus of Florida State University, class of 1971, where he majored in philosophy and minored in art. He also took the Famous Cartoonists correspondence course. Shortly after graduation, in January 1972, Marlette started work as the chief editorial cartoonist of the *Charlotte* (N.C.) *Observer.* The liberal cartoonist garnered instant recognition, winning an Overseas Press Club citation, having his cartoons reprinted widely and being syndicated by King Features Syndicate. In addition to his work as a political cartoonist, he created *Kudzu*, a newspaper strip, in 1981. He won the Pulitzer Prize in 1988.

Marlette draws in the contemporary mode—horizontal format and single-tone shading—but easily manages to distinguish himself and his style. His compositions are surpassed only by those of MacNelly and Oliphant, among his contemporaries. They are masterpieces of planning, crowded but never busy. He has a distinctive wavy-line approach to the art and a consistently devastating delivery of ideas. In short, Marlette is one of the foremost American cartoonists of his time, keeping the great tradition of clever jibes and indictments alive in the political cartooning format.

R.M.

Douglas Marlette. © King Features Syndicate.

MARTIN, CHARLES EDWARD (1910-1995) American cartoonist and painter born in Chelsea, Massachusetts, on January 12, 1910. C.E. Martin was apparently a self-taught artist (available biographical information offers nothing on his educational background). His first reported success was as a painting supervisor in the teaching division of the Work Projects Administration between 1933 and 1937. In 1937 he was hired as a staff artist by the *New Yorker* and has continued in that capacity ever since. Besides cartoons, he has painted over one hundred fifty covers for the magazine under the signature "CEM." Between 1939 and 1941, he was also a staff cartoonist for the magazine *PM.* Over the years he has contributed cartoons, illustrations and cover art to such publications as the *New York Times, Saturday Review, Time, Saturday Evening Post, Life, Look* and *Playboy.*

An accomplished painter, as his wonderful *New Yorker* covers prove, Martin usually works in watercolors, oils or acrylics. His cartoons for the *New Yorker* are generally more elaborate than the line drawings or washes normally associated with cartoon art, and he seems to have become Peter Arno's successor as the magazine's main contributor of full-page comic paintings. If a rule of thumb for most cartoonists is "Gag first and representation second," with Martin it is more often the reverse. His gags do not usually depend upon visual shorthand but upon full, detailed and vibrant panoramas—renderings in which no element, from focal point to background, fails to receive the painter's careful attention. He likes to set his cartoons and cover art in colorful landscapes, and even when he works in ink lines, his concern with minute detail is an identifying trait.

Martin has had numerous exhibitions of his work, including one-man shows at the Rockland Foundation (1951), the Ruth White Gallery in New York City (1955-60), the Brooklyn Museum (1954-65) and the Graham Gallery (1973); he is represented in the permanent collections of the Metropolitan Museum in New York, the Museum of the City of New York, the Library of Congress and Syracuse University. He has taught watercolors as a member of the faculty at the Brooklyn Museum School of Art (1963-65) and was a member of the Cartoonists' Guild (past president) and the Society of Magazine Cartoonists. He died on June 18, 1995, in Portland, Maine.

R.C.

MARTIN, DON (1931-) American cartoonist born in Paterson, New Jersey, in 1931. Don Martin went to the Industrial Art School in Newark, New Jersey, and later to the Pennsylvania Academy of Fine Arts in Philadelphia. In 1953 he moved to New York City and started doing illustrations for magazines and greeting cards.

In 1954 Martin contributed his first drawings to *MAD* magazine, joining its regular staff the next year. Since that time he has become one of the most popular of the magazine's cartoonists, billed as "*MAD*'s maddest artist." Martin's humor is often of the ghoulish variety, and he delights in depicting men squashed by falling safes, split open by buzz saws or literally having their brains blown out. His characters are usually unredeemable louts or ugly harridans. Most of Martin's cartoons (often in comic strip

C.E. Martin ("CEM"). © This Week.

form) have been reprinted either in *MAD* anthologies or as paperbacks. Martin also draws occasionally for other national magazines, and he has designed a few television cartoons. In 1987 he severed his long association with *MAD*, and went over to the rival *Cracked* humor magazine. He has also become a vocal and effective supporter of creators' rights.

M.H.

MARTIN, HENRY (1925-) American cartoonist born in Louisville, Kentucky, on July 15, 1925. Henry Martin was educated at Princeton University and received his bachelor's degree in 1948. Two years of training at the American Academy of Art followed. Besides regular appearances in the *New Yorker,* he has also contributed to *Punch, Ladies' Home Journal, Saturday Review, Good Housekeeping, Gourmet* and *Audubon.* In addition, he has created a syndicated daily panel feature for the Chicago Tribune-New York News Syndicate entitled Good *News/Bad News.* Separately published collections of his work include *Good News/Bad News* (Scribner's), *Yak! Yak! Blah! Blah!* (Scribner's) and *All Those in Favor* (American Management Association).

Martin's specialty as a cartoonist is the world of business. He has apparently studied it well or been part of it and so is frequently encountered peeking into offices and boardrooms or following the executive home after a busy day's work. Working in India ink and wash, Martin renders his ideas with a sharp, unbroken line. His is a bold technique, but it is in substance rather than style that Martin makes his most individualistic statements. He has an ear for the cliché and an eye for the absurd in his gentle satires on the mores of the corporate and advertising communities—which is not to say that he cannot find a fresh twist on an idea as overworked as the desert island or advert with great charm to the days of our Neanderthal ancestors. He also, as befits a Princeton man, has a way with "old grad" humor.

Many examples of Martin's "funny business" have appeared in the *New Yorker.* In one cartoon, he shares with us the contentment of the vacationing businessman who discovers a newsstand advertising the *New York Times* minus the financial section. In another, two executives learn, as a fellow sails toward them from the floor below, that "kicked upstairs" is not after all an empty figure of speech. Finally, in an age when one finds the strangest things advertised on television, we see the shock of a viewer who beholds on his screen "the old bum you often see panhandling on the corner of 43rd Street and Sixth Avenue. As we approach the Christmas Season, I hope you won't forget me. Just mail your dollars today to 'Bum-Christmas' in care of this station." His *Good News/Bad News* panel was discontinued at the end of the 1980s; but he continues to draw book illustrations and contributes cartoons to various publications.

Martin belongs to the National Cartoonists Society and holds a Deuxième Prix from the Salon International de la Caricature, Montreal. His work is represented in the Swann, David E. Lilienthal and IBM collections, all housed in the Princeton library.

R.C.

MASAOKA, KENZO (1898-1988) Japanese animator, artist, musician and composer born in Osaka, Japan, in 1898. After receiving an education in art, Kenzō Masaoka joined Makino Eiga ("Makino Films") in 1925 and was ostensibly involved in art direction. In reality he functioned as a jack-of-all-trades, doing everything from creating props to acting. He appeared as an actor in the 1928 film *Hitojichi* ("Hostage").

In 1927 he independently made a children's film entitled *Umi no Gyūden* ("Sea Palace"), utilizing his broad experience to write the script and do the filming and virtually everything else. This work achieved quick recognition and was purchased by Nikkatsu Films for distribution. Two years later Masaoka became the superintendent of the technical section of Nikkatsu's educational film department. When this folded in 1930 he began creating his own animation, first producing a two-reel silent film entitled *Nansensu Monogatari—Saru ga Shima* ("Shipwreck Story—Monkey Island," with the word *nansensu,* also meaning "nonsense," being a double entendre). It tells the story of a baby shipwrecked on an island inhabited by monkeys. He is raised by them until his superior intelligence causes them to drive him away, in a new twist on Kipling. The film used clever paper cutouts on celluloid to create animation.

By 1932 Masaoka had not only made a sequel but had also created his own animation studio in Kyoto. At the same time, he wrote *Manga Eiga no Shōrai* ("The Future of Animated Films"). He was particularly impressed with Mickey Mouse and intrigued by the possibilities of music and animation, interests that led to *Chikara to Onna to Yo no Naka* ("Strength, Women, and the Ways of the World"). The first talkie animation in Japan, it was produced in 1933 for Shōchiku Urata. Its story revolved around humorous fighting among a husband, his typist and his wife. Following this success, Masaoka made *Gyangu to Odoriko* ("The Gang and the Dancer," 1934), concentrating in particular on music and timing. Then he produced works such as *Kaitei Ryokō* ("Traveling at the Bottom of the Ocean," 1935), *Mori no Yosei* ("Forest Fairies," 1935) and *Benkei tai Ushikawa* ("Benkei vs. Ushikawa," 1939). The last was unique in that it was created and drawn around prerecorded music.

In the interim Masaoko had created his own institute for the study of animation, which was incorporated into the animation department of Shochiku Films in 1941. Two years later Masaoka produced what remains his most representative work: *Kumo to Chūrippu* ("Spider and Tulip"), based on a story by Michiko Yokoyama about a spider, a tulip and a ladybug. It is a balletlike visualization of music using excellent black-and-white contrast and is regarded today as a classic of Japanese animation.

Kenzo Masaoka left an indelible mark on Japanese animation as a pioneer in the use of sound and especially music. In the postwar period he has continued to do animation-related work. He suffered a stroke in 1983 and passed away five years later.

F.S.

MATSUSHITA, KIKUO (1917-) Japanese cartoonist born in Tokyo, Japan, on September 11, 1917. Kikuo Matsushita is best known in Japan as the illustrator of the series *Tokyo Mukashi Mukashi* ("Once upon a Time in Tokyo") and for his numerous appearances on television as an amateur carpenter. Matsushita, while considering everything he does to be part of his career as a cartoonist, is one of Japan's true dilettantes.

Matsushita began his art career after graduating from the Taiheiyo Gajuku (an art school), but at the start of World War II he was drafted into the press corps of the Imperial Japanese Navy and sent to Java, Indonesia. During this time he produced a piece of cartoon reportage titled *Senzen no Kangofu-san* ("Front-Line Nurse"). With the end of hostilities, Matsushita returned to Japan, destitute like everyone else. In order to make a living he hit upon the idea of drawing cartoon portraits of U.S. soldiers as they arrived in the port of Yokohama. In exchange he received chewing gum, chocolate and cigarettes, which he then sold on the black market or bartered. This turned out to be so lucrative an enterprise that he turned it into a business with other cartoonist friends.

As conditions improved in Japan, Matsushita began drawing cartoons regularly for a variety of magazines and eventually formed the YY Club with fellow cartoonists such as Koichi Yoshizaki and Naruo Morita. The YY Club was established to promote the sale of cartoonists' work, but musicians and other artists were also entitled to join. By 1955, Matsushita's cartoons were running regularly in magazines such as *Manga Times* and *Manga Dokuhon* (an example of his work during that period, *Nishiki Hebi,* depicted a boa constrictor run over by a car, his back having been squished into a brocade pattern). It was not until Matsushita illustrated *Tokyo Mukashi Mukashi* in the *Asahi Shinbun* that he gained much of a following, however, and his popularity further increased with several cartoon/narrative series he did for a variety of women's magazines.

Kikuo Matsushita holds strong views on what it means to be a cartoonist. Whether he is on television hosting a show on amateur carpentry (he was formerly director of the amateur carpenters' association of Japan) or building models for an amusement park he views his activities as "cartooning." In 1997 he was an adviser to the Gendai Suiboku Kyokai (Modern Japanese Brush-ink Painting Association).

F.S.

MATSUYAMA, FUMIO (1902-1982) Japanese political cartoonist born in Nagana Prefecture, Japan, on May 18, 1902. Fumio Matsuyama's career has been distinguished by the consistency of his political viewpoint during periods of change in which other cartoonists have done radical turnabouts. He is an inheritor of the tradition of the late Masamu Yanase, Japan's foremost proletarian cartoonist, and like him has devoted his talents to the support of leftist and antiestablishment causes. Matsuyama was an early member of Nihon Mangaka Renmei ("Japan Cartoonists Federation") and in 1926 became an assistant first to Sakō Shishido, then to Masamu Yanase, successive editors of the federation's short-lived publication, *Humor.* His orientation was determined when he participated in the proletarian art movement and drew cartoons for such magazines as *Rōdō Manga* ("Labor Cartoons") and *Nōmin Manga* ("Peasant Cartoons"), both highly critical of the government of the time.

As the 1930s dawned in Japan, the increasingly rightist government became more and more wary of its critics and made moves to silence them, but Matsuyama was unable to compromise as others quickly did. As a member of the Communist party he was a conspicuous target, and in 1932 he was arrested along with his mentor, Yanase, and spent over three years in prison. In spite of repression, however, Matsuyama continued his opposition to the government. Save when he was actually in jail, he drew cartoons attacking the militarists in magazines that would still consent to publish them, such as *Tokyo Puck* and later *Karikare;* but he was often forced to use a pseudonym. In 1936 an exhibition of his work was confiscated by the police, and as war actually erupted and Japan became united behind the fascist cause, Matsuyama effectively found himself with no outlet for his work. With the end of the war, however, Japan entered a new era of freedom of expression, and in 1945 Matsuyama began working for the revived Communist newspaper, *Akahata* ("Red Flag"). Two years later he helped found *Kumanbachi,* a leftist magazine dedicated to carrying on the tradition of Masamu Yanase, and began drawing cartoons ever more critical of the U.S. occupation.

Fumio Matsuyama consistently was the gadfly of Japan's establishment. Whether it was been the militarists, the U.S. occupation authorities or the present conservative government, he satirized them all in countless cartoons that were usually heavily ideological. Among his numerous published works are *Chōjūgiga,* a collection of 30 color political cartoons published over the years (1963), and *Manga de Miru Sengoshi* ("A Postwar History in Cartoons," 1967). He died in 1982..

F.S

MATTICCHIO, FRANCO (1957-) Italian cartoonist born in Varese on March 13, 1957. After attending a school of art, he started contributing to the nationwide daily *Corriere della Sera* (1978-1980) and to the magazines *Salve* (1980-1994), *Linus* (1985-1996), *Moda* (1988-1994), *King*

Franco Matticchio. © Franco Matticchio.

(1988 & 1995), *Il Grifo* (1991-1994), *TVRadiocorriere* (1994-1995), *Anna* (1995-1996), *L'Indice* (since 1986), *Linea d'Ombra* (since 1985), *Internazionale* (since 1997), and *Mano* (since 1988).

Matticchio is not a prolific author, but his cartoons, characterized by total absence of captions and dialogue, are superb examples of graphic invention. It is not easy to classify his humor, which does not make the observer smile, but simply puzzles him. At first sight his cartoons look naive, nonsensical or not perfectly understandable, but if you pause to go deep into them, they show they can communicate a lot of meaning, though they are a bit disquieting. One could label Matticchio's humor as pensive humor. Some of his cartoons have been collected in book format: *Nella foresta di cartone* (1994), *Viaggio in USA* (1996), *Sogni e disegni* (1997). He has also written and drawn the comic strip *Sensa senso* which was printed in book format in 1994 and translated into French in early 1998.

The artist was awarded the first prize at the New York exhibition "Cartoonist Against Drug Abuse" (1988), sponsored by the United Nations, and the first prize for a spot in favor of the environment at the Annecy Animation Festival.

G.C.C.

MAULDIN, WILLIAM HENRY (1921-) American author and Pulitzer Prize-winning cartoonist born in Mountain Park, New Mexico, on October 29, 1921. Bill Mauldin grew up on a ranch near Phoenix. He showed an interest in drawing at the age of 3, executed rodeo posters at the age of 12, and made his first sale ($10) while taking a correspondence course from the Chicago Art Institute.

In September 1940 Mauldin moved from the Arizona National Guard to the 45th Division. He saw early combat in Sicily and then through Italy, France and Germany. On the *Mediterranean Stars and Stripes* he was to create out of the spot drawings, cartoons and illustrations produced on the field two classic figures of American cartooning, Willie and Joe. They became the images of the quintessential soldiers—much to the consternation of spit-and-polishers like General George S. Patton—and personified doggedness, a resigned heroism and cynicism. Willie and Joe were classic partners, with vivid if low-key personalities and complementary roles.

Mauldin's cartoons were popular enough to be syndicated stateside—one won the Pulitzer Prize for 1944—and were continued after the war as a syndicated panel, less and less featuring the civilian Willie and Joe, and increasingly becoming political cartoons. His viewpoint was well to the left, and escalating political pressure was among the reasons he left cartooning around 1947.

For the next decade Mauldin engaged in an incredible variety of pursuits: running for Congress, acting in motion pictures, flying his private plane around the country, covering the Korean War for *Collier's,* writing many articles. In 1958 his plane was grounded near St. Louis, and while visiting the legendary Daniel Fitzpatrick, Mauldin learned of the latter's wish to retire. (Mauldin had recently substituted for vacationing Herblock, and the ink was again starting to flow in his veins.) He soon assumed duties at the *Post-Dispatch* and within a year had another Pulitzer to his credit. In 1962 he switched to the *Chicago Sun-Times,* where he remains, appearing through syndication in about three hundred other papers. Due to an injury to his hand he retired from cartooning in 1992, but continues to write.

Mauldin frequently uses a humorous panel as the format for his editorial punch. He can be devastatingly direct and has always displayed a masterful talent for succinctness. His drawing suggests a man totally in command of his subject and media; his caricatures are never wild exaggerations, and sound anatomy underlies his figures. In recent years some of his cartoons have been reduced to the barest minimums, with benday shading instead of crayon. This development is simply a function of his working arrangement; the fact that he lives in his native New Mexico and sends his cartoons to Chicago via wire dictates the severest economies of detail.

"Just gimme a coupla asprin. I already got a Purple Heart."
Bill Mauldin. © Mauldin.

Mauldin has won many honors besides his Pulitzers: the Sigma Delta Chi award in 1964, several National Cartoonists Society category awards and one Reuben; and honorary degrees from Connecticut Wesleyan (M.A., 1946), Albion College (LL.D., 1970), and Lincoln College (L.H.D., 1970). In 1977 Field Newspaper Syndicate arranged to syndicate thrice-weekly columns of Mauldin's observations and drawings.

In addition to articles in *Life,* the *Saturday Evening Post, Sports Illustrated,* the Atlantic Monthly, the *New Republic* and other magazines, Maul din has many books to his credit: *Sicily Sketch Book* (1943); *Mud, Mules and Mountains* (1944); *This Damn Tree Leaks* (1945); *Up Front* (1945); *Star Spangled Banter* (1946); *Back Home* (1947); *A Sort of Saga* (1949); *Bill Mauldin's Army* (1951); *Bill Mauldin in Korea* (1952); *What's Got Your Back Up?* (1961); *I've Decided I Want My Seat Back* (1965); and *The Brass Ring* (1971). *Up Front* and *A Sort of Saga* have been reissued.

R.M.

MAY, OLE (1873-ca. 1920) American cartoonist born in Pleasanton, Iowa, on June 24, 1873. Ole May began his cartooning career in the early 1890s for newspapers in Los Angeles and Houston; later he drew human interest and editorial cartoons for the *Washington* Post and also pursued a lifelong interest by playing in the Marine Corps band. May followed Charlie Payne into Pittsburgh to draw editorial cartoons for the *Gazette Times* (preceding Billy DeBeck on the staff) before he joined the *Cleveland Leader*.

Cleveland in the 1910s was blessed with a flock of talented cartoonists, among them two of the nation's best: May and Joe Donahey. The two were alike in style and treatment. Both relied on a masterful, feathery use of the crosshatch, which gave their drawings balance and an ethereal air when needed. Figures were soundly but comically drawn. Most important, both artists showed a strong preference for sentimental themes. Boyhood, courtship, family holidays—all were handled warmly and evocatively. While Donahey had the greater fame and dwelt more on home themes, May was the more effective partisan (Republican). His ideas were clear and free of labels, making him one of the first political cartoonists to so liberate himself. His artwork was crisp, animated and arresting.

Ole May, influential during his career, gave life to the symbol of Cleveland, Uncle Mose. He was forced to retire in late 1916 because of his health and died shortly thereafter in Long Branch, New Jersey.

R.M.

MAY, PHILIP WILLIAM (1864-1903) British cartoonist born in New Wortley, Leeds, on April 22, 1864. The creator of the modern, simplified school of cartooning, and the most influential cartoonist of his period, Phil May was the seventh of the eight children of the former Sarah Jane McCarthy of Dublin, Ireland, and Philip May, who worked in the drawing office of George Stephenson. His father died when Phil was nine, but the boy clearly inherited his talent.

Educated at St. George's School (1872-75), then at Oxford Place School (1876) and Park Lane Board School (1877), May learned to draw by copying cartoons from the humorous magazines *Fun* and *Puck,* and won first prize in a drawing competition, for which he received a T-square and a drawing board. His first job was in a solicitor's office, then for an estate agent, then as the timekeeper in an iron foundry. Fascinated by show business, he helped Fred Fox mix his paints for the scenery at the Grand Theatre, Leeds, and in the evenings sketched portraits of the traveling actors for a shilling a time. For six years he worked behind and in front of the scenes, meanwhile contributing his first professional sketches to the local comic papers the *Yorkshire Gossip* and the *Busy Bee.* In 1884, he began to contribute theatrical caricatures to *Society* and drew 178 for the special Christmas number, *Seven Ages of Society.* The following year found his drawings appearing in *St. Stephen's Review,* and when that weekly turned into an illustrated paper, he joined the staff at £8 a week.

His caricatures in the *Penny Illustrated Paper* (1885) caught the eye of W.H. Traill, who offered him a three-year contract as staff cartoonist of the Sydney *Bulletin.* May accepted and journeyed to Australia, arriving November 11, 1885, and returning to London in 1888, having earned the then-astounding salary of £1,000 per annum. He returned with a brand-new style, for England. The *Bulletin* was printed by the new photo-process engraving method that gave its cartoonists a new freedom of line impossible in England, where the line block system still ruled. May continued to contribute to the *Bulletin* until 1894, and his influence on succeeding Australian artists was as immense as it quickly became back home in London.

May joined the *Daily Graphic,* the first illustrated national newspaper, on November 12, 1890, and in 1893 was sent on a world tour for that paper. He also drew for the weekly *Graphic,* which appeared in color at Christmas. By now he was a master of rapid caricature, and his cartoons captured the common life of the London streets and gutters to perfection, appearing in almost every weekly magazine: *Pick-Me-Up* (1891), *Pall Mall, Black and White,* the *Sketch* (all 1892), and the *English Illustrated* (1893). His first *Punch* cartoon appeared on October 14, 1893. May died somewhat suddenly and sadly on August 5, 1903, of tuberculosis and cirrhosis of the liver, at age 39. But his artistic legacy was enormous.

Lumpenproletariat
Phil May, illustration from "Guttersnipes," 1896.

Books: *The Parson and the Painter* (1891); *Phil May's Winter Annual* (1892, 13 editions); *Phil May's Summer Annual* (1892, 3 editions); *Fun, Frolic and Fancy* (1894); *Phil May's Sketchbook* (1895); *The Comet Crash* (1895); *Guttersnipes* (1896); *Isn't It Wonderful* (1896); *Mayville* (1896); *Graphic Pictures* (1897); *Phil May's ABC* (1897); *Zig Zag Guide* (1897); *Songs and the Singers* (1897); *Book of the Bazaar* (1898); 50 *Hitherto Unpublished Pen and Ink Sketches* (1899); *Phil May's Album* (1899); *East London* (1901); *Sketches from Punch* (1903); *A Phil May Picture Book* (1903); *A Phil May Medley* (1903); *Littledown Castle* (1903); *Phil May in Australia* (1904); *Phil May Folio* (1904); *Humorous Masterpieces* (1907); *Pictures by Phil May* (1907); *Humorists of the Pencil* (1908); *Phil May* (1932); and *Phil May* (1948).

D.G.

MAYER, HENRY (1868-1954) American cartoonist born in Worms am Rhein, Germany, in 1868. Hy Mayer moved to America when he was 18 but carried the germ of the free-spirited German cartooning fecundity that flowered there 20 years later. He was versatile, prolific and a jovial leader, at the turn of the century, of the rebellion in American cartooning against tight, disciplined, crosshatched illustration-type cartoons; with him were A.Z. Baker ("Baker-Baker"), Gustave Verbeck, Leighton Budd and Art Young.

His first major work appeared in Life in the mid 1890s. It was loose, unorthodox and slightly distorted and bespoke a gay spirit. Soon his work was also running in *Puck* and *Judge* and in the minor humor journals. At the same time he was contributing to foreign humor magazines, including *Fliegende Blätter* of Munich, Punch, *Pall Mall, Black and White* and *Pick-Me-Up in England*, and *Le Rire* and *Figaro Illustré* in France. His first book, *The Autobiography of a Monkey* (1896), was followed by many others for children and adults. He joined many other strip and magazine cartoonists (like McCay and Louis Glackens) in the animation field and produced more than fifty Travelaughs.

When the ship rolls and your berth becomes uncomfortable, take your pillow and sleep on the wall.
Hy Mayer, ca. 1910.

When Puck magazine was sold to the Nathan Strauss family in 1914, Mayer, long a fixture, became editor, and his own cosmopolitan flair began that weekly's shift towards a more international, sophisticated appeal. From 1904 to 1914, moreover, he drew the weekly *Impressions of the Passing Show*—light commentary—for the *New York Times.* (These were the joyful days when the *Times* did not eschew cartoons; besides Mayer, through the years Ed Marcus and the great Oscar Cesare drew for its pages.) In all, Mayer was a popular cartoonist, writer and versifier, influential in spirit if not style among his colleagues. He was a public figure conspicuous at benefits and shows.

Hy Mayer's style stands up well under scrutiny many years later. His slap dash approach was engaging, and he playfully teased the readers' perceptions with pixieish alterations of perspective. He was fully competent enough to constantly experiment with formats, borders and colors, and he stands as one of the few American cartoonists before World War I to test the waters of the unconventional, as was being done in his native land so splendidly in the pages of *Jugend* and *Simplicissimus.*

R.M.

MAZINGER Z / GREAT MAZINGER / UFO ROBO GRANDIZER (Japan) Just as American's *Superman* was the seminal costumed superhero that created a new genre, Japan's *Mazinger Z* was the seminal giant robot series which has spawned hundreds of imitators over the past 25 years.

Go Nagai began cartooning at the age of 20 in 1965, and exploded prolifically in Japan's comic-book industry. He became a leader in a young radical group of cartoonists analogous to the underground comix movement in America, specializing in humor and action with shock-value demonic violence and sexual innuendoes. In 1970, Nagai and his brothers started their own studio, Dynamic Productions. They began calculatedly designing comic book concepts that would have high merchandising appeal with TV programmers and their sponsors. Nagai's three landmark series, *Devilman, Mazinger Z,* and *Cutey Honey* all debuted as TV animated series from Toei Animation in 1972 and 1973. All were popular, but *Mazinger Z* was the mega-hit.

There had been SF adventure comic books and animation with giant robots before. But Nagai's stroke of genius was twofold: (1) to make the giant robot a vehicle with a human pilot. This increased popularity by giving boys a young hero with whom to identify; a cross between a SF version of a knight in super-armor and a pilot in a fighter plane; (2) to make the robot complex, with a large variety of detachable limbs, weapons, and support equipment. The toy manufacturers who sponsored the TV animation loved Nagai.

Mazinger Z debuted on December 3, 1972 and ran for 92 weekly episodes to September 1, 1974. It segued directly into *Great Mazinger* on September 8, for 56 more episodes to September 28, 1975. The trilogy's conclusion was *UFO Robo Grandizer*, 74 episodes from October 5, 1975 to February 27, 1977. By that time Nagai had already created

"Mazinger Z." © Go Nagai.

several independent giant robot TV cartoon series such as *Getta Robo* (*Combino Robot*, the first transforming robot), 1974-75, 51 episodes; *Kotetsu Jeeg* (Steel Jeeg), 1975-76, 46 episodes; and *Gloizer X*, 1976-77, 36 episodes, with many more to come.

The casts changed but the formula remained the same. A heroic teenager (Koji Kabuto in *Mazinger Z*; Tetsuya Tsurugi in *Great Mazinger)* is the son or grandson of a scientist who has built a giant robot to help mankind. *Grandizer*'s hero is Duke Freid, prince of the planet Freid, who escapes to Earth in the Grandizer super-robot after his world's destruction by the evil Vegans. An army of grotesque villains kill the father and try to seize the robot to use to conquer Earth. The villains may be called mad scientists or space aliens, but they are thinly disguised demonic monsters; their leader in *Mazinger Z* is forthrightly named Dr. Hell. The hero is supported by the friendly scientists of a Science Research Institute who keep his robot repaired. (Duke Freid poses as Daisuke Umon, adopted son of the head of the Interstellar Science Research Institute, as he fights in his Grandizer robot, with Koji Kabuto's help, to keep Earth free of the Vegan Dread Stellar Empire.) The evil army's commanders, who maneuver for power among themselves, unleash a new monster-robot in each episode; giving this genre the satiric nickname of "monster of the week series". The battles have elements of martial-arts contests, with the fighters calling out the name of their next attack: "Rocket Punch!" "Light Power Beam!" The monster-robots grow in strength, increasing the suspense that each new adversary may be the one that will finally defeat the hero and his robot.

The French distribution of *Grandizer*, retitled *Goldorak*, made world news for several weeks in 1978 by achieving a 100% TV share despite complaints of excessive violence. Nagai returned to this series in the 1980s with a new TV program, *God Mazinger* (April 15-September 30, 1984; 23 episodes); and with a graphic art novel consisting of paintings rather than line-art cartoons, titled simply *Mazinger* (1988).

F.P.

MECHAM, WILLIAM (1853-1902) British cartoonist, caricaturist and "chalk talker" on the music hall stage, born in 1853. Mecham, whose pen name was Tom Merry, was also the first British cartoonist to appear in a film. More, he was the first professional performer of any kind to be filmed in Britain.

"Tom Merry" was a familiar signature to readers of the many Victorian humor weeklies to which he contributed his social cartoons and contemporary caricatures. Merry was fond of the stage, and his caricatures of popular comedians and other theatrical notables may have led to his appearance at the music halls as a "lightning cartoonist." It was as a stage performer that he appeared in his films, four of which were photographed by the pioneer producer-director Birt Acres toward the end of 1895. In one brief fragment preserved by the National Film Archive in London, the moustachioed Merry may be seen to dash in front of the camera and swiftly flick off a quick caricature of the German emperor Wilhelm. The other personalities he chose to caricature in his series were Lord Salisbury, William Gladstone and Prince Bismarck. They were evidently well-rehearsed regulars from his stage presentation, as their likenesses had to be completed within 40 feet of film (40 seconds running time), which was all the primitive motion picture cameras would permit. The films formed part of the program projected by R.W. Paul at his initial theatrograph performance at the Alhambra Theatre in London on March 25, 1896. Several of the newspaper reviewers mentioned Merry's cartoons, but he made no more appearances before the cinematograph camera.

His final work was to illustrate *The History of Canvey Island*, a small book by Augustus A. Daly. Inside, a dedication reads: "In memoriam of William Mecham, artist, cartoonist, and caricaturist, better known to the British public by his professional sobriquet, Tom Merry, who died suddenly at Benfleet Station (adjoining Canvey Island), Essex, on Thursday, August 21st, 1902, aged 49 years.

D.G.

MEGGENDORFER, LOTHAR (1847-1925) German cartoonist, illustrator and author born in Munich, Bavaria, on November 6, 1847. Though he never rose to great artistic heights, Lothar Meggendorfer served the German public long and well in a variety of ways. Since he was a native of Munich, where the humor magazine *Fliegende Blätter* was published, it was natural that he should be a steady contributor for many years. His specialty was a proto-comic-strip genre: a humorous incident or contretemps depicted in a series of several small drawings with no or very little text. These picture stories of Meggendorfer's

Lothar Meggendorfer, caricature of Napoleon retreating from Russia, 1813.

were very similar to those of Caran d'Ache in France, but much less incisive and inventive. He also contributed over sixty drawings to the *Münchener Bilderbogen*.

In the late 1880s Meggendorfer began editing a weekly humor magazine of his own; its title varied somewhat over the years, but it is generally referred to as the *Meggendorfer Blätter*. It had a comfortable existence, finding and holding on to its own level of relatively undemanding readership. Only in 1928, three years after its founder's death, was it swallowed up by the *Fliegende Blätter*, which was then more than eighty years old. Printed partly in color and partly in black and white, the *Meggendorfer Blätter* had a steady cadre of mildly skillful and mildly enjoyable cartoonists, none offering a serious challenge to Meggendorfer himself, who, far from hogging the magazine, usually appeared discreetly on black-and-white inner or back pages.

In 1906 Meggendorfer was one of a few German (or German-based) cartoonists whose services were sought by the *Chicago Tribune* in an effort to raise the level of its Sunday comic pages at a period of strong competition. The real prize garnered by the *Tribune*, however, was not Meggendorfer but the American-born Lyonel Feininger, who contributed his pioneering strips *The Kin-der Kids* and *Wee Willie Winkie's World* for several months.

Perhaps the most exciting aspect of Meggendorfer's production was the vast number of children's books he wrote and illustrated. In turn, by far the most interesting of these were many kinds of toy books—books with movable figures, three-part segmented transformation pictures, pop-ups and ingenious variations on wheels, wires and slats. These books, which sold over a million copies, were done for two publishers: Braun and Schneider of Munich, who published the *Fliegende Blätter* and the *Münchener Bilderbogen*, and J. F. Schreiber of Esslingen (near Stuttgart), who published the *Meggendorfer Blätter*. The Braun and Schneider archive of Meggendorfiana was destroyed in World War II, but Schreiber's survived, and in New York in 1975 a dealer offered for sale, as a single lot, hundreds of preparatory drawings, hand-colored guides to the printers and the production files on over sixty titles.

S.A.

MENZEL, ADOLPH VON (1815-1905) German painter and graphic artist born in Breslau, Prussia (now Wroclaw, Poland), on December 8, 1815. Like Chodowiecki, whose role as universal delineator of life in Germany (especially Berlin) he continued through the 19th century and into the early 20th, Adolph von Menzel had a basic fund of humor that repeatedly surfaced in his works although he was not a professional humorist.

Menzel's father had been head of a girls' school but then became a lithographic printer, and young Menzel was his aide. They moved to Berlin in 1830. When the older man died in 1832, Adolph, mainly self-taught, continued to do commercial art for printers and art dealers, especially Sachse. It was in this decade that most of Menzel's specifically humorous items were done—both original and reproductive (after Adolf Schrödter, for instance). These include several witty Berlin (and Leipzig) scenes of the sort Dörbeck, Schadow, Hosemann and Schrödter had done, New Year's greetings adapted to members of various professions and social classes, music covers illustrated with everyday scenes, party souvenirs, pictures for children and the like. (Even much later in life Menzel was officially called upon to create elaborately illustrated and calligraphed testimonial certificates and diplomas.)

Having proved his merit in "higher" things with illustrations of Luther's life (1833) and a lithographic series based on a Goethe poem about the misfortunes of artists (1834), Menzel quickly became the foremost German illustrator, as well as a major painter and printmaker. The outstanding masterpiece of his earlier life—and his best-remembered work—was his group of 400 illustrations engraved on wood for Kugler's life of Frederick the Great (completed in 1842). This led to a long preoccupation with Frederick's period and with military iconography. Among the Frederick the Great spinoffs were the illustrations for that monarch's own writings (completed in 1849); Menzel's ingenious work in connection with the king's satirical pieces forms another major facet of the artist's humorous production.

As time went on, Menzel was drawn more and more into the highest official circles of the German capital and was knighted in 1898. In addition, he occupied himself with brilliant technical experiments in printmaking and

Nante becomes a minister.

Adolph von Menzel, illustration for the title page of a Berlin magazine.

did important paintings in an impressionist vein as early as the 1840s and 1850s (in 1875 his canvas depicting an iron foundry was a pioneering subject). Still, Menzel never stopped producing fresh, carefully observed drawings—thousands of them—of everything about him. Many of these, such as his picture of people arising stiffly after an uncomfortable night on a train (1877), reveal the wit that never deserted the grand old man. Menzel died in Berlin at the age of 90 on February 9, 1905.

S.A.

MERCIER, EMILE ALFRED (1901-198?) Australian humorist and cartoonist born in Noumea, New Caledonia, in 1901.

It was the graphic humorists of Sydney who were first to set a postwar Australian trend in humor satirically critical of social attitudes. The artists who took the lead in this direction were Emile Mercier of the Sydney Sun and George Molnar of the Sydney *Morning Herald,* both of whom must be acknowledged as the two major black-and-white humorists to work in Australia in recent times. Although in approach and drawing style Molnar and Mercier appear to be light- years apart, they nevertheless represent both sides of the social coin, with Molnar satirizing the urban tastes and attitudes of the opulent "gracious living" section of society and Mercier "having a go" not only at high life, as in the past, but at low life, too—and with an approach that is not just humorous. The significant difference lies in a break from the traditional "we're a lot of dags," style that characterized to some extent the humor of an earlier generation and that still typifies much humorous writing and minor works on Australian slang today.

Emile Mercier's view of humor is wide, with a graphic style in the broad historical comic tradition. But Mercier's comment does not contain much that is international in appeal; like that of the early *Bulletin* artists it is specifically a humor that reflects national life, with all the indigenous characteristics unique to Australia.

"No, I'm not in the mood to swear yet —just wait until I get real mad!"
Emile Mercier. © Sydney Sun.

The best humor has always been expressed from a definite point of view; Emile Mercier's is quite clear. It emerges, for example, in a background detail such as a poster on a wall with the wording "Drink Flor de Florita—the Gravy of the Grape! A Symphony in Every Sip!" From his standpoint Emile Mercier presents the typical face of Australian cities—the fly-spotted cafés, noisy pub bars and crowded public transport, the racecourses, back alleys, and people of the city—tired waitresses, rough-and-ready taxi drivers, policemen, barmaids, disc jockeys and tax officials. His comment is unique in Australian graphic satire for its range of social documentation and a wit that is discriminating, responsible and perceptive.

Mercier contributed his joke drawings to the *Bulletin, Smith's Weekly* and Melbourne *Punch* in the 1920s. Recognition eventually came, and with it popularity, resulting in full-time work as a comic artist. When the humorous writer Lennie Lower rejoined *Smith's Weekly* in 1940, Emile Mercier was one of the artists selected to illustrate his pieces for the paper. Joe Jonsson took over the illustration of this feature when, during World War II, Mercier was engaged by *Truth* as a political cartoonist. Then, during the war, followed a period drawing political cartoons for the Sydney *Daily Mirror.* From that period until 1967, when he retired, Mercier's brilliance delighted not only the readers of the Sydney Sun but his fellow graphic humorists all over Australia. He died sometime in the 1980s.

Emile Mercier's pen drawings are often crammed with fun and rollicking detail—something of a triumph considering that his original drawings were never larger than 7 by 5 inches, a size regrettably conditioned by their rather miserable editorial reduction. It is also a triumph for Mercier that during his 40 years or so of drawing he has survived editorial buffeting and resisted the ephemeral fads and fashions of comic art and humor, preserving a sanity in his draftsmanship and satire, and revealing, without preaching, what sort of people Australians are.

V.L.

MERRY, TOM
See Mecham, William.

MESSMER, OTTO (1894-1983) American cartoonist and animator born in Union City, New Jersey, in 1894. The son of a machinist, Otto Messmer studied at the Thomas School of Art. His first published cartoons were gags in the *Fun* supplement of the *New York World* and in *Life* magazine (1914). Around this time, fascinated by the nascent animation field, Messmer made a one-minute test cartoon for Universal called *Motor Matt and His Fliv.* At the studios he met Hy Mayer, who was then doing newsreel cartoons, and the two collaborated on The *Travels of Teddy.* After doing advertising for Auerbach's chocolates, Messmer joined the Pat Sullivan Studios in 1916.

Pat Sullivan had learned animation with Gregory La Cava at the Barré studio. He was a former newspaper strip cartoonist who had inherited his friend Billy Marriner's

Otto Messmer, "Felix the Cat." © King Features Syndicate.

features and also animated some of them. As a studio head, he encouraged the greatest possible creative and personal freedom in his staff. Thus, he would often let his artists do practically anything they chose, and if the film sold, the studio would get half the proceeds. Under this system, before serving in World War I, Messmer created *Fearless Freddy* and *20,000 Laughs Under the Sea,* for which he drew every frame. In France the prolific Messmer, a member of the Signal Corps, won an award for his designs in the Victory Carnival.

Back in America, Messmer drew Charlie Chaplin cartoons and worked with Earl Hurd, Frank Moser and John Terry on *Silly Hoots* (a pun on "silhouettes") for the Paramount Screen Magazine. When Paramount fell behind schedule, they subcontracted the work to Sullivan, who ultimately let Messmer handle it freelance. From there, Messmer's own ideas, the running series *Feline Follies* (or *Frolics)* and probably some other obscure antecedents led to the official birth of Felix the Cat in 1920. Messmer has recalled his formula for success—a sharp, solid, defined black area, a premise with the logic of a child's dreams and fancies, and the exploitation of animation's potential for absurd visual gags—but what really established Felix as an instant classic was Messmer's incredible creativity and childlike imagination. The cat was a huge success and must be recognized not only as a great personal achievement for Messmer but as the prototype for hundreds of other children's fantasy creations, including Disney's.

In 1923 Messmer began drawing a *Felix* Sunday page (which he never signed until the 1940s); earlier a daily strip had begun in the *London Illustrated News* (of all papers), which had asked King Features to arrange with Sullivan for a newspaper version of Felix. (King later assumed the copyright and now owns Messmer's creation.) When Paramount left the picture, the *Felix* cartoons were first syndicated by Margaret Winkler, then by Sullivan's lawyer with the backing of Educational Films; soon the studio was producing one short every ten days. Working with Messmer were Bill Nolan, George Stallings, Bert Gillette and Raoul Barré. Sullivan, who resisted the transition to sound, died in 1933, and so, for awhile, did the animated Felix.

Messmer declined offers to work for other studios. Instead he continued on the strip (until 1954), also working with Douglas Leigh on the development of animated electric signs (1939-40), on the *Felix* comic book for *Toby Press* and on storyboards for *Popeye, Little Lulu, Snuffy Smith* and other animated cartoons (1944-45). After failing to interest Sam Buckwalt of Famous Studios/Paramount in reviving *Felix,* Messmer went back into advertising. He retired at the age of 80. In 1967, with a festival in Montreal, he began to receive the recognition he had seldom had previously. Since then, museum shows, retrospectives, interviews, articles and awards have made up for lost time. He died at his home in Teaneck, N.J., on October 28, 1983.

Messmer is one of the most remarkable men in cartooning. Though others reaped the financial rewards and, until recently, the credit for his creation, modesty has prevented him from regretting the virtual anonymity in which he worked. He could develop sophisticated story lines with impressive speed; he could draw almost as fast and for years did prodigious amounts of animation and strip work simultaneously; and most importantly, he never lost the child's touch so precious to anyone in the business of creating fantasy. His perspective was a manifestation of genius, the genius that overwhelms by sheer simplicity. "Nowadays, kids don't dream about the moon—they know," he has said. "Then, all was magic. All we had was a pencil and paper. We didn't want to duplicate life; a photo would've done that. Felix was always a cat, but with a boy's wonder about the world. That, and visual tricks, and we had it."

R.M.

MESTRES I OÑO, APEL.LES (1854-1936) Spanish cartoonist born in Barcelona, Spain, in 1854. Apel.les Mestres had his first cartoons published in 1880 in the weekly satirical magazines *L'Esguella de Ia Torratxa* and *La Campana de Gracia.* Later his works appeared in magazines like *Pel i Ploma, La Publicidad, El Liberal, L'Avenc* and *La Mainada,* to name but a few of the Catalan and national publications to which he contributed.

Throughout his life Mestres participated in a wide variety of artistic endeavors: literature, newspaper writing (notably in *La Campana de Gracia*), children's stories, theater, painting, poetry and music. His involvement with music grew after 1912, when he lost vision in one eye; after 1920, when he became totally blind, he devoted himself exclusively to music. He was a close friend of the famous Spanish composer Enrique Granados.

Apel.les Mestres produced more than forty thousand cartoons in his lifetime. He frequently expressed his political views in cartoons, sometimes using children as a means of ridiculing the "infantile" behavior of adults and politicians. His cartoons kept in close touch with the sentiments of the common people. Every day the entire country enjoyed Mestres's drawings, his earthy humor and witty criticisms. Because he sought to impart moral values through his cartoons, Mestres often sounds a bit didactic, albeit never pompous. He achieved an impact through the use of naturalistic techniques reflecting the true character of the Spanish people. Mestres died on July 19, 1936, the day following the start of the Spanish civil war.

J.M.

Mi Gu. © Mi Gu.

MI GU (1918-1986) It has been an unanimous opinion among the Chinese cartoonists that the history of Chinese contemporary cartoon development would not be a complete one if it does not include Mi Gu. Mi became well-known in cartooning from the 1940s. Although his major was Western painting when he studied in Shanghai Art College between 1935 and 1937, he began his cartooning in 1943 by publishing in some major journals in Shanghai, such as *Masses*, *United Evening News*, and *Xinmin Evening*. Between 1947 and 1949 he lived in Hong Kong, where he was active with cartoons that were published with *Chinese Business News*, *Chinese Digest* (English), and *Wenhui News*, etc.

After the PRC (People's Republic of China) was founded, Mi continued his cartoon creations and publications in Shanghai, which were re-published by foreign journals in France, the USA, and then the Soviet Union. Between 1950 and 1956, Mi published more than a thousand cartoons and illustrations, of which the topics were mainly international affairs. One of his major successes was the color *Cartoon Monthly*, the only professional cartoon journal in China then, which was edited by Mi and published first in Shanghai, from 1950 (then continued in Beijing from 1956) till 1960. For many cartoonists, many of whom are well-known now, this pioneer cartoon monthly was not just a journal to be published in, but a cultivating garden for improving their skills in cartooning. Mi paid a great deal of attention to those beginners and kept communication with them regarding the issues of how to create a better cartoon. Such areas included helpful suggestions in either redesigning the total image, or changing the drawing partially, or retitling the cartoon in order to highlight the concept, and so on.

Mi's humor in his cartoons was obvious through his keen exaggeration expressed often in a simple background, images usually drawn by fountain pen. His cartoons seldom had more written language than the titles, and his superb imagination transcended the meaningful sense in each creation.

During the "Cultural Revolution" that began in 1966, Mi, as well as the other cartoonists in the country, was forbidden to make any cartoons, since almost every kind of arts was wrongly criticized as "against the socialist system." To detour his physical and mental sufferings from such man-made "class struggle", Mi could only make ducks with clay, then paint them in brush and ink. He humorously called his family room "the hall of a thousand ducks." His self-amusement was forced to stop when he was totally paralyzed in 1978, a result of high blood pressure, till his death eight years later.

Mi's cartoons were included in almost every cartoon collection as well as in *Mi Gu Cartoon Collections*, which were published in the 1980s and 1990s. Mi's name and his artistic works will be remembered as long as history remains.

H.Y.L.L.

MICKEY MOUSE (U.S.) Legend has it that Walt Disney created his most famous character during a 1927 train ride back to Hollywood from New York, where he had just lost his *Oswald the Rabbit* series to Charles Mintz. He wanted to name the little creature Mortimer but was talked out of it either by his wife or by one of his distributors (according to which source one is willing to listen to). Thus was *Mickey Mouse* born.

Setting out to work with his usual alacrity, Disney laid down his concept of "The Mouse." "He had to be simple," Disney later declared, adding, "His head was a circle with an oblong circle for a snout. The ears were also circles so they could be drawn the same, no matter how he turned his head. His body was like a pear and he had a long tail. His legs were pipestems and we stuck them in big shoes to give him the look of a kid wearing his father's shoes."

Retaining overall direction, Disney turned over the actual drawing to his talented assistant, Ub Iwerks. Soon one Mickey short, "Plane Crazy," was completed; another, "Gallopin' Gaucho," was on the boards when the success of *The Jazz Singer* and other early talkies convinced Disney that the future was with sound. Temporarily leaving the first two Mickey cartoons aside, Disney and Iwerks busied themselves with a third short, "Steamboat Willie," which Disney took to New York. There, with the help of a pickup band, a crudely devised score of his own invention and a couple of sound effects men, he recorded the synchronized

Mickey Mouse in "Steamboat Willie." © Walt Disney Productions.

sound track (doing the Mickey Mouse voice himself, as he did for over twenty years). On September 19, 1928, "Steamboat Willie" opened at the Colony Theater in New York, and it was an instant success.

The sound versions of "Plane Crazy" and "Gallopin' Gaucho" followed the next year, along with "Karnival Kid," "The Jazz Fool!" (a spoof of *The Jazz Singer*) and "The Opry House." Mickey was now an established star, and scores of Mickey Mouse cartoons poured out of the Disney studio. It would be impossible to list them all, but among the most popular or noteworthy are: "Mickey's Follies," "The Chain Gang," "Mickey's Choo-Choo" (in which Disney indulged his love of trains), "Mickey's Birthday Party," "Mickey's Nightmare" (which the Disney organization later withdrew from circulation as being too gruesome), "Mickey's Revue," "Mickey's Gala Premiere" (in which Mickey, fittingly enough, played host to other Hollywood stars), "Gulliver Mickey," "Orphans' Benefit" and "The Band Concert" (probably Mickey's most beloved adventure and the first one in Technicolor). All were released from 1930 to 1935.

In these cartoons Mickey assumed any role (alpine climber, explorer, cowboy, etc.) and traveled everywhere (to Arabia, the Sahara, the South Seas, by plane, boat and on horseback). His popularity was extraordinary; George Bernard Shaw praised him to the skies, and Soviet filmmaker S.M. Eisenstein proclaimed him "America's most original contribution to culture." British novelist E.M. Forster wrote what was to become the ultimate Mickey Mouse tribute in *Arbinger Harvest:* "Mickey's great moments are moments of heroism, and when he carries Minnie out of the harem as a pot-plant or rescues her as she falls in foam, herself its fairest flower, he reaches heights impossible for the entrepreneur."

Minnie Mouse had been in the cartoons from the first, as had her villainous pursuer, Pegleg Pete. Clarabelle Cow and Horace Horsecollar were two other early stalwarts. Pluto appeared in 1930 and Goofy only came on the scene in 1932. The last two characters became very popular in their own right, but their success was nothing compared to that of the cantankerous Donald Duck, who edged out Mickey himself in popularity soon after his birth in 1934.

By the late 1930s Mickey was largely confined to the role of master of ceremonies. Disney tried to revive his popularity by casting him as the Sorcerer's Apprentice in *Fantasia* (1940) and giving him a role in another of his package features, *Fun and Fancy Free* (1947), to no avail. The Mouse's later appearances became rare, and he practically disappeared in the mid-1950s when the Disney studio stopped making theater shorts. It took 30 years for Mickey to make his comeback in the movies. In the 1983 *Mickey's Christmas Carol* he played the role of Bob Cratchit (with Scrooge McDuck as Ebenezer Scrooge and Goofy as Marley's ghost). He was also starred in *Runaway Brain* (1995), on a double bill with the live-action feature *A Kid in King Arthur's Court.*

In the meantime, however, Mickey had assumed mythical proportions. He was adapted to comic strip form in 1930, and to comic books a little later. His likeness appeared on toys, watches, school tablets, soap and every conceivable product—not to mention the heads of countless enthusiastic "Mousketeers" who faithfully donned their Mickey ears and followed his career on TV. His name assured the success of scores of children's newspapers (*Topolino* in Italy, *Le Journal de Mickey* in France, *Mickey Mouse Weekly* in England, to name a few). It is only fair to say that Mickey must be regarded not as a cartoon character (as successful as he may have been in this respect), but as a genuine cultural phenomenon of the first magnitude.

M.H.

MICKWITZ, CAMILLA (1937-) Finnish animator and cartoonist born in Helsinki, Finland, on September 22, 1937. Aside from another woman—Tove Jansson—Camilla Mickwitz is probably the Finnish cartoonist best known internationally. She studied from 1955 to 1958 at the Helsinki University of Arts and worked in advertising before becoming a freelance artist in 1966. She now works on films, books and illustrations for the large newspaper *Helsingin Sanomat.*

A mother of three, Mickwitz often touches on human relations, and by depicting authentic family and social life, she obviously aims to provide models for children and adults alike. Her figures are simple and cuddly, and the spirit and colors in her works are warm and vibrant. Critics regard her as an important counterweight to commercial mass culture.

Mickwitz has created an animated cartoon series for TV, *Ollaan Yhdessä* ("Let's Be Together"), as well as 13 other animated cartoons, many of which she also wrote herself, and most of which were produced by the Finnish Broadcasting Company. Her books include *Pikku Kanin Hassu Päivä* ("The Crazy Day of the Little Rabbit," 1972, in collaboration), *Jason* (1975), *Jasonin Kesä* ("Jason's Summer," 1976) and *Jason Ia Vihainen Viivi* ("Jason and Angry Vivian," 1977). Her film *Jasonin Kesä* won the prize for best children's animation at the 1975 Hollywood Festival of World Television. *Ollaan Yhdessä* received a government award and the first Peace Culture prize given by the Finnish Peace Committee in 1976. Her books have been honored in Finland and abroad for both their content and their artwork, and her illustrations have been exhibited throughout the world.

J.R.

MIGHTY MOUSE (U.S.) The first cartoon in the *Mighty Mouse* series, "The Mouse of Tomorrow," was released in 1942. Conceived and created by Isidore Klein for Paul Terry's Terrytoons studios, it was a parody of Superman, "the man of tomorrow," and the principal character was called Supermouse in the first three cartoons (which included the witty "Super- mouse in Pandora's Box"). The hero was later rechristened Mighty Mouse (despite objections from Walt Disney) and gained fame under this new name.

The early cartoons were fast-paced and unpredictable, gently spoofing the contemporary *Superman* animated shorts. "Faster than a bullet, stronger than a bull," the announcer would intone at the beginning of each cartoon, "it's Supermouse!" One of the best entries was "Down with Cats" (1942), in which Mighty Mouse defeated horde upon horde of murderous felines. *Mighty Mouse* soon

Mighty Mouse. © Paul Terry.

turned into Terrytoons' most profitable series, and the studio ground out scores of films that continued to be well received by a juvenile public despite tedious repetition.

In 1955 Paul Terry sold all his properties to the Columbia Broadcasting System; CBS promptly turned out a *Mighty Mouse* television program which met with astounding success. The producers shrewdly mixed old *Mighty Mouse* films with newly minted cartoons. If anything, the new production was wittier and more entertaining than most of the old series. Very often Mighty Mouse was involved in continuing adventures pitting him against the top-hatted villain, Oil-Can Harry the cat; the object of their rival ardor was the pert Pearl Pureheart. A narrator would imperturbably detail the proceedings while fights, duels, forest fires, floods and every imaginable peril took place on the screen. This spoofing of film serials was often sung by the principals, mock-opera style, with a love duo ("You are my sweetheart," "You are my love") by Mighty Mouse and Pearl at the close.

The *Mighty Mouse* TV program came to an end in the early 1960s, but it can still be seen in syndication. Among the directors who worked on *Mighty Mouse,* mention should be made of Conrad (Connie) Rasinski, Art Bartsch, Dave Tendlar and Eddie Donnelly. A *Mighty Mouse* comic book was also released with varying success from 1946 to 1962.

The character was revived twice for broadcast on CBS-TV, first in the 1979-80 season with *The New Adventures of Mighty Mouse and Heckle and Jeckle,* produced by Filmation, and later in 1987 with *Mighty Mouse: The New Adventures,* under Ralph Bakshi's peppery direction. The show ended in controversy the next year, when it was rumored that the super-rodent was shown to sniff cocaine to gain his powers (Bakshi denied the accusation).

M.H.

MIK
See Jago, Mik.

MILER, ZDENĚK (1921-) Czech animator born in Kladno, Bohemia, Czechoslovakia, on February 21, 1921. Zdeněk Miler first attended the School of Design, then studied at the School of Industrial Arts, both in Prague. In 1941 he started as an animator at the Zlfn (now Gottwaldov) studios. At the end of World War II he moved to Prague, where he became one of Eduard Hofman's scriptwriters.

Miler directed his first cartoons, *The Millionaire Who Stole the Sun* and *Red Riding Hood,* in 1948. *The Millionaire* is a tale of greed and cruelty, with the protagonist coming to grief at the end. Miler, however, decided to travel in the direction of his other cartoon, a retelling of the familiar fairy tale; and, with the exception of *The Red Stain* (an allegory of evil made in 1963), all of his work has been aimed at children. *Brigáda* (1950), *Who's Strongest?* (1952) and *The Poppy Pie* (1953) are nice, rather conventional fables. Miler has also created a winsome animal character, the Mole, who has appeared in a series of lively and unpretentious little cartoons ("How the Mole Got His Trousers," "The Mole and the Motorcar," etc.).

In 1958 the Czechoslovakian government awarded Miler a silver medal for his work, which remains largely unseen outside Czechoslovakia.

M.H.

MILLER, FRANK (1925-1983) American cartoonist born in Kansas City, Missouri, in 1925. Frank Miller is the son of a longtime staff artist of the *Kansas City Star,* the spawning ground of many artists, from C.D. Batchelor to Edward McGeehan. But it was Star political cartoonist S.J. Ray whose style influenced the younger Miller most. He studied drawing and painting at the University of Kansas and then continued his art training at the Kansas City Art Institute. His first job was with the *Star,* and he switched to the *Des Moines Register* in 1954, inheriting Ding Darling's mantle. In 1963 Miller's cartoons brought the Pulitzer Prize to Iowa once again. He died of a heart attack on February 17, 1983.

Miller renders his cartoons in a supple, almost old- fashioned pen line, often with handsome and elaborate crosshatching. He spots his blacks well and lays them in with a wet brush.

R.M.

Vatroslav Mimica, "Typhus." © Zagreb Film.

MILLÔR
See Fernandes, Millôr.

MIMICA, VATROSLAV (1923-) Yugoslav animator and filmmaker born in Omiš, Yugoslavia, on June 25, 1923. Vatroslav Mimica fought the Nazis as a partisan during World War II. After the war he became a literary critic before going into film. He started his animation career in 1957 as a scriptwriter for Zagreb Film, notably writing the scenario of *Cowboy Jimmy.* Although not a draftsman himself, he directed many of the most celebrated Zagreb cartoons, often with Aleksandar Marks as his designer. These include *At the Photographer's* and the mixed animation short *The Inspector Comes Home* (both 1959); *Spring Tunes* and *Low Midnight* (1960), which he only scripted; the almost despairing *Perpetuum and Mobile, Ltd.* (1961); and the equally somber *Everyday Chronicle* (1962). The 1963 *Typhus,* a haunting evocation of partisan warfare told through the medium of animated linocuts, marked the last collaboration between Mimica and Marks.

Mimica then returned to live-action filmmaking and became one of the more celebrated of the new wave of Yugoslav movie directors (*Prometheus from the Island of Viševica, Monday or Tuesday* and *Kaya, I'll Kill You* are some of his best-known feature films). He occasionally returned to animation, writing the scripts for *The Fly* and *Tamer of Wild Horses.* Mimica is justly regarded as one of the founders of the Zagreb school, and his cartoons have earned many awards in such places as Bergamo, Venice, Oberhausen, Cork and Edinburgh.

M.H.

MINGO, NORMAN (1896-1980) American cartoonist and illustrator born in Chicago, Illinois, on January 25, 1896. Norman Mingo is best known for his cover paintings of Alfred E. Neuman for *MAD* magazine and *MAD* paperback books.

Always interested in art, Mingo won a children's art contest and received art materials and a course from the Scranton Correspondence School. During high school he worked for Hart, Schaffner and Marx, manufacturers of men's clothing, drawing model cards. He was so successful with his art that he dropped out of high school and worked full time for a year before returning to complete his diploma requirements. World War I interrupted his career, and he served three years in the U.S. Navy. Following World War I, Norman Mingo studied art at the Academy of Fine Arts and Art Institute in Chicago. Other art training came at the Cleveland School of Art and the Art Students League in New York.

The 1920s were the great years of advertising art. Mingo organized and was president of the art studio Mingo, Brink and Jipson, Inc. The firm had its headquarters in the Wrigley Building in Chicago and had offices in Detroit, Michigan, and Cleveland and Toledo, Ohio. "I'll never forget our first month's gross billing was $35,000 for artwork produced," said Norman Mingo. The firm lasted from 1923 to 1931, when it fell victim to the Depression. Its clients included Studebaker Corporation and Packard Motors. It was responsible for hundreds of full-page and double-page illustrations in the *Saturday Evening Post.* Work from the studio can be easily identified by a distinctive pine tree logo used to sign the art.

Norman Mingo was one of the lucky ones in the Depression. After his studio folded he moved to New York City and made the rounds with his portfolio. Based on his previous work, he quickly was selected by Lucky Strike cigarettes to illustrate testimonials about its product by famous people of the day. While in New York City, he organized the Guild Artists Bureau, Inc., which existed from 1939 to 1941 as a sales outlet for the Artists Guild of New York.

"I was married, with kids, and too old for World War II, but I was able to serve with the U.S. Coast Guard Auxiliary and participate in the USO Hospital program, where I would do portraits of wounded servicemen," said Mingo.

In 1953, after years of successfully freelancing advertising art, Norman Mingo opened his own silk screening studio. Financially the studio proved a disaster. "I answered two ads from the classified section of the *New York Times,*" he remembered. "This was in 1956. First I went to Dancer, Fitzgerald, Sample, Inc., a Madison Avenue ad agency, where I was hired as an illustrator and titular head of the bullpen. Then the same day I visited Bill Gaines at *MAD,* also on Madison Avenue."

Bill Gaines, *MAD's* publisher, had been searching for an artist to paint Alfred E. Neuman, the magazine's mascot. At the time all *MAD's* artists were pen-and-ink men not skilled in painting. In 1956, at the age of 60, Norman Mingo painted the first full-color portrait of Alfred E. Neuman. It was published on the cover of *MAD,* number 30, December 1956. After awhile the work load of the ad agency and *MAD* became too great, and Norman Mingo left *MAD,* to be replaced by Kelly Freas as cover artist. However, in 1963 he was contacted by John Putnam, *MAD's* art director, and has been with the publication since then.

· Norman Mingo did not take credit for any cover ideas. His ability was "to bring Alfred to life." An experienced master of illustration, he devoted his attention to composition, color relationships and technique. "I'm essentially concerned with mass and am not a line man," he has stat-

"Largo," a mini-cartoon. © Zagreb Film.

ed. Now in semi-retirement, Norman Mingo was the most prolific *MAD* cover artist until the mid-1970s. He died in 1980.

B.C.

MINI-CARTOONS (Yugoslavia) In 1969 the artists at Zagreb Film decided to produce a number of one- minute animated cartoons to serve as introductions to their work and as a showcase for new talent. These mini-cartoons (as they promptly came to be called) proved tremendously popular and have been a staple of Zagreb Film production ever since.

Among the most popular—or most gifted—of the mini-cartoon practitioners have been Zvonimir Lonćarić (*Dialogue, C'Est la Vie*), Ante Zarnnović (*Ab Ovo*), Dušan Vukotić (*Time*, one of the most successful "minis" ever produced) and Zlatko Pavlinić (*Conditio Sine Qua Non, Miserere, Happy End, The Goal*). But the most prolific of all was Milan Blažeković, who has created more than fifty of these films; among the wittiest or most memorable are two "gorilla joke" cartoons, *Maternity Hospital* and *Flight 54321*, as well as the unpredictable *Icarus I, The Apple* and *A Chair.*

Some of the mini-cartoons centering around the same theme were later released as a series within a series. The most popular of these compilations has been *Largo,* built upon the theme of a man stranded on a desert island. The mini-cartoons, singly or *en bloc,* are still going strong, and they are a special favorite of public-television program directors with a minute or two of time to fill.

M.H.

MINOR, ROBERT (1884-1952) American cartoonist and political organizer born in San Antonio, Texas, on July 15, 1884. The son of a judge, Robert Minor attended public schools and became a sign painter in 1898. He was later employed as a carpenter and then as a cartoonist. He drew for the *San Antonio Gazette*, the *St. Louis Post-Dispatch,* the *New York World* and the *New York Call.* In 1915 he was a European war correspondent for the Newspaper Enterprise Association and, returning to the United States, became a lecturer on antiwar subjects.

In 1919 Minor was one of the founders of the U.S. Communist party and remained a tireless worker in its organization; he ran for governor of New York (1932) and for the Senate (1936) on its ticket, was for awhile acting secretary-general of the party and constantly drew for its organ, the *Daily Worker.* Minor died at his home in Croton-on-Hudson, New York, on November 26, 1952.

Army Medical Examiner: "At last a perfect soldier."

Robert Minor, 1916. © The Masses.

Minor's employment record serves to trace the change and extent of his convictions. He left the most influential daily in New York to draw for its puny Socialist rival and later shunned all establishment journals (unlike his fellow traveler Art Young) to draw only for Communist organs. Throughout his career his cartoons were marked by stunningly forthright presentations—though many may find his politics offensive, this cannot diminish the acknowledgment Minor's work deserves.

As important as his presentation of ideas was, his artwork is equally deserving of recognition. He drew at first in a rounded, pleasant style that foreshadowed a stark simplicity. He pioneered the use of the crayon and, in philosophical and representational terms, inspired a generation of outstanding political cartoonists—perhaps the most important school and certainly the one most neglected by historians— including Fitzpatrick, Burck, Fred Ellis, Ross Lewis, Tom Little, Edmund Duffy, Boardman Robinson and others.

R.M.

MR. MAGOO (U.S.) John Hubley created the nearsighted Mr. Magoo, in collaboration with Robert Cannon, for UPA in 1949; the first Mr. Magoo cartoon was "Ragtime Bear," directed by Hubley himself.

Mr. Quincy Magoo, a bald-headed, crotchety old gent, got himself involved in all kinds of harebrained misadventures due to his sight impediment, which he steadfast-

Mr. Magoo in "Magoo Beats the Heat." © *UPA.*

ly refused to acknowledge. Mistaking dynamite sticks for candles, grizzly bears for visiting matrons and opium dens for his club lounge, he blissfully wandered from one hair-raising situation to the next without ever losing his composure. Piles of merchandise would go up in smoke behind him, passenger boats would sink in his wake, and entire buildings would collapse after his passage, but Magoo would imperturbably continue on his path of destruction, only muttering to himself in self-congratulatory tones, "Aha, Magoo, m'boy, you've done it again!" (Magoo's ripe, gravelly voice characterization was done by Jim Backus). Unlike most other cartoons of the period, Mr. Magoo's humor rested not on the expression but on the expectation of violence. In the end nothing untoward ever happened to the fussing, cantankerous, but essentially lovable Magoo, and even his unintended victims got away relatively unscathed.

Many UPA directors worked on the *Mr. Magoo* series. John Hubley did "Fuddy Duddy Buddy" the same year as "Ragtime Bear"; Peter Burness, the most prolific of them all, directed "Bungled Bungalow" and "Trouble Indemnity" (both 1950), "Captains Outrageous" (1952), "Magoo Goes West" (1953), "Destination Magoo" (1954), "Stage Door Magoo" (1955) and the Academy Award-winning (in 1954 and 1956, respectively) "When Magoo Flew" and "Magoo's Puddle Jumper." Bob Cannon and Rudy Larriva also worked on the series.

Mr. Magoo proved popular enough to be starred in a feature-length film, *1001 Arabian Nights* (1959), which proved a failure at the box office. In the mid 1960s UPA produced a *Mr. Magoo* TV series as well as several specials which were a long way below their former standards. The character was then sold to DePatie-Freleng, which released a made-for-television version starting in 1977. Saperstein Productions packaged a *Mr. Magoo* comic strip (Chicago Tribune Syndicate) in the late 1960s. After almost two decades of absence, Mr. Magoo made his reappearance at Christmastime 1997 in a live-action movie starring Leslie Nielsen in the role of the near-sighted curmudgeon. Despite protests from advocates for the disabled, the film fared well at the box-office (though not with the critics).

M.H.

MR. MEN, THE (G.B.) "Today looks very much like a tickling day!" said Mr. Tickle, and off he went to town to see who he might tickle with his Extraordinary Long Arms. He tickled a teacher who was trying to control his class, he tickled a policeman who was on traffic duty, and he tickled thousands of little children and their parents who had bought the colorful, pocket-sized book for twenty pence. *Mr. Tickle* was the funniest, and most funnily drawn, children's book in a long time, and before 1971 had closed, he had been joined by *Mr. Greedy, Mr. Happy, Mr. Nosey, Mr. Sneeze* and *Mr. Bump.* The *Mr. Book* series was immediately recognizable: square, white, with a big cartoon character drawn in bold black, filled in with a bright color. And each Mr. Man, although basically no more than a simple circle with dot eyes, arms, legs and an occasional nose, had a different and instantly obvious characteristic, made clear by his name. The year 1972 brought a new battalion or Mr. Men, each as funny as the last: *Mr. Messy, Mr. Topsy-Turvy, Mr. Silly, Mr. Uppity, Mr. Small, Mr. Daydream* and *Mr. Snow.* There would be more, many more.

The Mr. Men were created by Roger Hargreaves (born in 1935), an advertising copywriter with very limited drawing ability. He was drawing them (and still does) with a felt-tip pen to amuse his four children long before the publisher Fabbri took them on. With his advertising background, Hargreaves was able to bring promotional techniques to his brainchildren, and through an outfit called Copyright Promotions, the most successful merchandizing campaign in British cartoon book publishing was launched. The Mr. Men began to appear in every conceivable shape and form, from cereal packet stickers to sticking plasters, duvet covers and toiletries—and, of course, toys. The Mr. Men moved into television via an animated cartoon series of five-minute films, narrated by the popular character actor Arthur Lowe. They moved into children's comics as a full-page color strip, and from December 1, 1976, they have appeared daily in a newspaper strip in the *Daily Mirror,* replacing Bert Felstead's *Little Joe.*

The TV series is syndicated through 22 countries, the books translated into dozens of languages (over 6 million copies sold), and there are currently 26 *Mr. Men,* apart from such specials as *The Mr. Men on Holiday* (1976) and *The Mr. Men Gift Book* (1975). Hargreaves has had less success with his other series, *John Mouse* (1973) and *Hippo Potto and Mouse* (1976). He had better luck with *The Little Misses* (1986), a feminist equivalent to the *Mr. Men.* He died in 1988, but all his series remain popular on television.

D.G.

MR. PIPP (U.S.) Accurately described by Fairfax Downey as the most popular of the Gibson creations after the Gibson Girl herself, Mr. Pipp utterly dispelled whatever doubt may have lingered in 1890s America that Charles Dana Gibson was the premier American social cartoonist and illustrator of his day.

In *The Education of Mr. Pipp,* the title character, a wispy little henpecked paterfamilias with white sideburns, embarks on a European trip, complete with baggage and wife and daughters, to acquire a "liberal education." In upper-class America of the day (the series began in the issue of *Life* for September 8, 1898), "doing the Continent" on an extended vacation was obligatory. The series, intended only for a half-dozen glimpses but extended to 37 weeks by public enthusiasm, chronicled Pipp's seasick voyage, his attempts to steer his two pretty daughters away from foreign mashers, his wife's shopping sprees, breaking the bank at Monte Carlo, the ultimate double wedding of his daughters to two handsome Gibson men—and a glimpse into grandfatherhood.

The series of double-page cartoons was enormously popular. A book published by R.H. Russell appeared immediately after the magazine run, and deluxe editions cost $25. In 1905, six years after the series' end, the character was still so popular as to inspire a play which ran for one season in New York and another on the road, and was eventually transformed into a motion picture. When *Life* in the 1920s sought revitalization, *Mr. Pipp* was resurrected in a newly drawn series pointing up the contrasts between an older generation and the Jazz Age, but the novelty and flavor were gone; Pipp was a sorry shade of his former self.

The first *Pipp* series was drawn with slashing and confident strokes and bold composition. It ushered in the finest few years of Gibson's first pen-and-ink period and was as consistently humorous as anything Gibson was ever able to achieve.

R.M.

MITCHELL, JOHN AMES (1845-1918) American cartoonist and publisher born in New York City on January 17, 1845. J.A. Mitchell graduated from the Phillips Academy and studied architecture at the Laurence Scientific School at Harvard from 1867 to 1870. Interrupted by a short period of work in Boston, Mitchell studied in France, principally at l'Ecole des Beaux-Arts in Paris. Although he studied painting, his primary interest was in black-and-white line work; before he returned to America in 1880, his etchings appeared in *L'Art.*

It was while illustrating *The Summer School of Philosophy at Mount Desert* (1882) that Mitchell conceived the idea of founding a national humor and cartoon magazine, not along the lines of *Puck* (which was then all the rage and had spawned an army of imitators), but modeled after the *Harvard Lampoon.* Assisted by old Lampoon staffers and founders, the magazine, *Life,* debuted on January 4, 1883. It was smaller in size than *Puck,* was only black and white, and aimed at a sophisticated audience.

In the early months Mitchell was *Life's* chief cartoonist, but with succeeding issues editorial duties took more of his time; he was to remain the art editor until his death. *Life* was a success, and its pages served as a platform for many of Mitchell's pet crusades: Sunday museum openings, antivivisection, a fresh-air farm for underprivileged urban children. When World War I loomed, he and editor E.S. Martin made *Life* a powerful friend of the Allies. He died on June 29, 1918, before his final desire—the American rescue of France—was accomplished.

Mitchell's cartooning style was competent and assured. He designed the *Life* logo of a cupid dispelling gloom that was used into the 1920s and became a cartoon symbol similar to and as familiar as Puck. His stylistic and thematic preoccupations are vitally important to his role as a cartoonist. As a devotee of line work at a time when photoengraving was being perfected and everyone was trying to duplicate *Puck's* lithography, he ushered in, through Life's standards, the great era of pen and ink in cartooning and illustration. Moreover, Mitchell's own cartoons dealt nearly exclusively with society subjects, establishing a heretofore unexplored area for American cartoonists—and lending sophistication to American cartoon magazines. Mitchell was also responsible for the discovery and tutoring of many cartoonists, not the least of whom was Charles Dana Gibson. He was called "the General" by his staff, two generations of which appreciated his kindly advice and counsel.

Mitchell was a prolific writer of fiction who usually concerned himself with either sentimental or socially conscious themes; he was an armchair socialist. He drew title page cartoons or decorations for some of his books, which include *Amos Judd* (1895), *The Pines of Lory* (1901) and *The Silent War* (1906), his three most notable successes; and *A Romance of the Moon* (1889), *The Last American* (1889), *Life's Fairy Tales* (1892), *That First Affair* (1896), *Gloria Victis* (1897) and *Pandora's Box* (1911).

R.M.

MITELBERG, LOUIS (1919-) French caricaturist, cartoonist and illustrator born near Warsaw, Poland, on January 29, 1919. Louis ("Tim") Mitelberg studied architecture at the Paris Ecole des Beaux-Arts in 1938 and at the outbreak of World War II joined De Gaulle's Free French forces in London, working as an anti-Nazi caricaturist.

After the war, Tim drew first for *L'Action* (1945-52), then for *L'Humanité* (1952-57) and since 1957 for *L'Express.* His political sketches have also appeared in *Newsweek, Time* and *Le Monde,* and occasionally on the Op-Ed page of the *New York Times,* to which he has contributed caricatures of Thieu, Kissinger, Brezhnev, Qaddafi, etc., and a funny depiction of Fisher and Spas sky as toddlers in diapers using chess pieces for building blocks. Tim is also rightly famous for taking great paintings and updating them, as in Cézanne's *The Card Players,* featuring De Gaulle and Khrushchev, or Rembrandt's *Night Watch* guards being assisted by giant computers.

Many of his sketches have been released as albums: *Dessins* ("Drawings," 1953), *Pouvoir Civil* ("Civil Power,"

Louis Mitelberg ("Tim"). © Paris-Match.

1961), *L'Autocaricature* (1974), plus a fine book on De Gaulle, *Une Certaine Ide'e de la France, 1958-1969* ("A Certain Idea of France," 1969). In addition, he drew a weekly strip for the Zurich *Weltwoche, Leben mit Bengo* ("Life with Bengo"), which came out in book form in 1967 as *Junger Hund, Was Nun?* ("Young Dog, What Now?").

As might be expected, Tim has received several prizes, among them the coveted award of the International Caricature Show in Montreal (1967). In 1984 a retrospective of his works was organized at the Museum of Decorative Arts in Paris. He retired in the mid-1990s, covered with awards and honors.

P.H.

MITSUHASHI, CHIKAKO (1941-) Japanese cartoonist born in Ibaraki Prefecture, Japan, in 1941. Chikako Mitsuhashi was fascinated by cartoons as an elementary student, and from the third grade on she regularly amused her classmates by drawing cartoons in notebooks on virtually any subject—even while sitting in the front row of the class under the teacher s watchful gaze. From the start she was heavily influenced by Machiko Hasegawa, the creator of *Sazaesan.*

In high school her cartooning aspirations began to gel. Upon graduation she held a variety of jobs, including work as an animator and an apprenticeship to a designer; the noted cartoon critic Ippei Ito was apparently her mentor. Based on her nostalgic memories of high school, she created a work entitled *Chisana Koi no Monogotori* ("A Little Love Story"), hoping that it would fill the gap between children's comics and those meant for adults. Convinced that it would find a readership, she took the work to a magazine called *Utsukushii Jūdai* ("Beautiful Teenage") and was nonetheless surprised when it was accepted. Since first appearing in 1962, *Chisana Koi no Monogatari* has been a phenomenal success, with over twelve collections subsequently appearing and sales numbering in the millions. It follows the traditional Japanese cartoon format of four frames, in which the shy love of a high school girl for Sari, her boyfriend, is depicted with sweet reserve. The drawings are extremely simple, and the low-key theme has vast appeal among schoolgirls in Japan.

Other works by Mitsuhashi include *Keiko to Mātchin* ("Keiko and Mātchin"), *Tonori no Ken* ("Neighbor Ken"), *Kata Omoi Kara no Shuppatsu* ("Starting from a One-Sided Love") and *Hatsukoi no Ririan* ("First Love Lillian"), appearing in magazines such as *Koitchi Kōsu* ("Freshman Course"). In addition to her work as a cartoonist, Chikako Mitsuhashi is married and is the mother of two boys. She is also well known for her comic strip *Haai, Akko desu* ("It's me, Akko") which ran during the 1980s in the prestigious *Asahi* newspaper. The strip and *Chisana Koi no Monogatari* have been animated for television. Mitsuhashi has also published a wide variety of essays, poems, and collections of her illustrations. In addition to cartooning she likes bowling and haiku.

F.S.

MIYAO, SHIGEO (1902-1982) Japanese cartoonist born in Tokyo, Japan, on July 24, 1902. After studying under the famous cartoonist Ippei Okamoto, Shigeo Miyao began working as a regular for the newspaper *Tokyo Maiyū Shimbun,* where he drew political and social commentary cartoons. Since most other cartoonists were doing the same thing, however, he decided to try something new. In 1922, after clearing the idea with his newspaper, Miyao began drawing *Manga Taro,* a work for children. This six-panel piece took the form of pictures with a narrative, and it ran for over two hundred episodes. It appealed to children but also found an adult following and helped boost the overall sales of the paper. Later, *Manga Taro* was compiled into a book, most copies of which were destroyed in the 1923 earthquake that demolished Tokyo.

In 1924, undaunted, Miyao created *Dango Kushizuke Manyû ki,* the story of a super-samurai boy who travels throughout Japan battling rogues, monsters and assorted villains. The characters all had amusing names, usually puns on names of food, and this contributed to their popularity. With this further success, Miyao firmly established himself as a pioneer in children's cartoons and comic strips. He then began drawing comics for the magazine *Shōnen Kurabu,* starting with *Hanao Bokosuke* (similar to *Dango Kushisuke Manyūki)* and the classic *Songoku. Songoku* appeared in 14 episodes, and when it was published in book form it utilized word balloons rather than a straight narrative. It was an amusing, easy-to-understand rendition of the Chinese classic *Saiyuki,* which has often been a theme in Japanese literature (Osamu Tezuka and Toei Doga each made an animated version). Songoku, the hero, is a semi-supernatural monkey who journeys to India from China to obtain sacred Buddhist scriptures.

Following Songoku, Shigeo Miyao created a string of other children's comics for *Shōnen Kurabu,* such as *Issun Taro* ("One-Inch Taro"), *Manga no Matsuri* ("Cartoon Festival") and *Karutobi Karusuke* (a pun on the name of a *ninja* character in Japanese literature, Saru Tobi Sasuke). Miyao's characters were generally very independent, in keeping with the prevailing mood of Japan in the late 1920s, a period in which democracy and individualism flourished. In 1934 Miyao formed a children's cartoonists' association known as Dōshin Mangadan. During the war he saw action on the southern front while serving in the Imperial Navy. He continued to draw literary cartoons for magazines in the postwar period but also pursued an active interest in *Edo Kobanashi,* or humorous stories from the Edo period of Japan (1600-1867), publishing several books on the subject. He died in 1982.

F.S.

MŁODNICKA, MAŁGORZATA (194?-) Małgorzata Młodnicka was born in Lvov, Ukraine, during a World War II air raid. After the war, her family was moved to Poland, first to Katowice, then to Wroclaw in 1966, where she received her diploma from the Higher School of Fine Arts.

Młodnicka started doing cartoons in early childhood and by fourth form, was expelled from school for doing Lenin's caricature. She started her professional career during her academy days, submitting caricatures to various newspapers and magazines upon request. She has had individual exhibitions in Wroclaw, Warsaw, and Legnica, all in Poland, and has won prizes for her cartoons on four occasions at Satyrykon.

Her caricatures, exhibiting her accurate eye and quick decision, are sophisticated and serious portrayals of people and their retinue of experiences. Polish critic Zdislaw Smektala said that the "guys in her drawing are... pictograms of feelings... sad, angry or downhearted." He called her a "Crumb [Robert] in skirt and lycra tights."

J.A.L.

MODELL, FRANK B. (1917-) American cartoonist born in Philadelphia, Pennsylvania, on September 6, 1917. Frank Modell studied at the Philadelphia College af Art. His first success as a cartoonist came with the old *Saturday Evening Post.* He became a New Yorker regular in the 1940s and remains so to this day. He is also a frequent contributor to *Playboy,* and his work has been published in a volume entitled *Stop Trying to Cheer Me Up* (Dodd, Mead).

As an artist, Modell will use "anything that makes a mark," and his technique varies accordingly. In the course of his long career, his early unbroken-line formalism gradually gave way to the freer quick-study techniques that are more characteristic of his current work—a shift mirrored in the alteration of his signature from "F.B. Modell" to today's simply scrawled "Modell." Given his lack of snobbery about media, it is tempting to speculate that the felt-tip in part explains his stylistic evolution, being more adaptable to sketch techniques than the formal ink-line and wash methods of most other artists of his generation. But this is not to underestimate Modell's capacity for adaptation in general, as anyone surveying the range of his humor will attest. It is in his breadth of imagination that his individual character is most pronounced.

Modell is the quintessential gag cartoonist. In his best work one can clearly see the connection between everyday life and its humorous exaggeration—and marvel that one had never seen it before. This, of course, is the genius of the cartoon humorist. Thus, one of Modell's early *New Yorker* pieces shows a man opening a jam-packed medicine cabinet to test the net installed beneath it for the purpose of catching falling items.

Modell ranges far and wide to find material for his studies. Unlike many of his colleagues, he seems to have no favorite themes and can have as much fun with alienated Cadillac owners as with Bowery bums. His Puritan confined to stocks and fending off an importunate insurance salesman is just as amusing as the cranky waitress in a greasy spoon demanding whether a certain customer intends to eat his entire breakfast with his nose in a newspaper. In almost every case, Modell touches a responsive chord, awakening that laughter which comes as much from sympathetic recognition as from an appreciation of absurdity for its own sake. In the last decade and a half he has devoted much of his time writing children's books that have included to date *Look Out, It's April Fool's Day* (1985), *Ice Cream Soup* (1988), and *Mr. Hacker* (1993).

Modell is a member of the Cartoonists' Guild and the holder of, as he puts it, "some minor award" for animated storyboards done for *Sesame Street.*

R.C.

"Now, let's see—did you tell me to keep my eyes shut and my mouth open, or my eyes open and my mouth shut?"
"Modest Maidens." © King Features Syndicate.

MODEST MAIDENS (U.S.) In 1930 cartoonist Don Flowers created a daily panel called *Modest Maidens* for Associated Press. Although some of his gags were quite amusing, what is best remembered about *Modest Maidens* is the loving way in which Flowers handled his female characters. They were long-legged, sophisticated, almost unattainable creatures, in the spirit of the time. Whether they were office workers or socialites, they exuded optimism, joie de *vivre* and charm, and even their more scatterbrained moments did not detract from their lovable character. Coulton Waugh commented in his study The *Comics,* "The Flowers girls have a real rhythm running through them," and it was indeed a sense of graceful rhythm that gave *Modest Maidens* its peculiar vivacity.

When Associated Press decided in the early 1940s to produce a color section, *Modest Maidens* became one of its chief attractions. Flowers, however, did not stay with AP much longer, leaving in 1945 to create Glamor Girls for King Features Syndicate. Modest Maidens passed into the hands of Jay Alan, who did a creditable job of continuation. Without Flowers's flourishes, however, the feature steadily lost readership, and it was dropped in the late 1950s.

M.H.

MOGENSEN, JØRGEN (1922-) Danish cartoonist, lithographic artist and sculptor born in Hillerød, Denmark, in 1922. Jørgen Mogensen, married to cartoonist Gerda Nystad, is one of Europe's most intelligent cartoonists, although his specialty today is the comic strip.

He made his debut, as did so many other cartoonists of his generation, in the monthly humor magazine *Hudibras* and was an editor and a contributor of several hundred

Jørgen Mogensen. © PIB.

gag cartoons from 1946. *The Magic Artist* (1947) was his original and surprising renewal of the comic strip tradition, a surrealistic play with concepts. He made a name for himself with the internationally syndicated comic strip *Poeten og Lillemor* (1948), on which three films were based, and with the pantomime strip *Alfredo,* on which he collaborates with Siegfried Cornelius under the joint signature "Moco." Especially well known is his daily panel *Esmeralda* (also called *Lullabelle*), one-column cartoons about a lovely, not-so-dumb blonde, syndicated through PIB, Copenhagen, to about fifty newspapers and magazines.

Mogensen has also done some sculpting and has had numerous exhibitions, as well as doing some writing. But his forceful, elegant drawing style and at times completely unsurpassed sense of humor have secured him a leading position among European humorists.

J.S.

MOHASSESS, ARDESHIR (1938-) Iranian cartoonist born at Rasht, in the province of Guilan, north of Tehran, Iran, on September 9, 1938. Ardeshir Mohassess displayed an early talent for drawing and caricature but instead chose political science as his major at the University of Tehran, from which he graduated in 1952. Soon afterward he began drawing for Iranian newspapers and magazines, then went on to contribute to such international publications as *Jeune Afrique* and the *New York Times,* where his work has often appeared on the Op-Ed page. He now lives in New York City.

Ceremonies to inaugurate a district drinking-water system in Iran. *Ardeshir Mohassess. © Mohassess.*

Mohassess's drawings are often disturbing and sometimes even horrifying. He is obsessed with death, inhumanity and violence. His drawing style is stark and somber, in keeping with his subjects. His most frequent themes are some of the more intractable problems of the world: famine, oppression, torture, the dehumanization of modern society and the despair of the disenfranchised of the earth.

Ardeshir Mohassess has been the recipient of a number of international awards; some of his drawings and collages have been collected in book form, and he has had many showings of his work, including one at the Graham Gallery in New York City in 1975. He left Iran after the 1979 revolution, and has now become a permanent resident of New York City, whence he continues to produce editorial cartoons, illustrations, and posters.

A collection of Mohassess's cartoons, Puppets, was published in 1977 by Carolyn Bean Associates of San Francisco.

M.H.

MOISAN, ROLAND (1907-1987) French cartoonist born in Reims, in the Champagne region of France, in 1907. Roland Moisan showed early aptitudes for drawing, and as a child he drew First World War battle-scenes in which the French were always victorious. He put himself through studies at the School of Decorative Arts in Paris working in the mailroom of a large department store. After seeing military service he had his first cartoons published in the humor magazine *Le Pele-Mele* in 1927. From then on his career took flight, and he contributed to such diverse publications as *Le Journal Amusant, L'Assiette au Beurre, Paris-Midi* (a daily newspaper), *Le Rire,* and *Le Merle,* with both gag and editorial cartoons.

During the occupation of France by the Germans in World War II, Moisan restricted himself to drawing only humor cartoons, but he returned to editorial cartooning after the liberation of France in 1944. His long collaboration with the satirical *Le Canard Enchainé* started in 1957 and lasted until his death. It was in the pages of *Le Canard* that he became famous with his weekly feature, "La Cour" ("The Court") in which, on texts by André Ribaud, he depicted General De Gaulle as the King of France, his cabinet ministers as servile courtiers, and the French people as helpless peasants subjected to high taxes and arbitrary edicts (his drawing may have played a part in the student and worker rebellion of May 1968). Even after De Gaulle's resignation in 1969, he never relented in his attacks against the right-wing governments that succeeded him. As Jean Egen commented in 1978, "Moisan brings his pencil to white heat, digs it into the rumps of the princes who govern us. That's what gives them those twisted mugs, those painful grimaces, those dreadfully contorted attitudes." At the same time the artist continued to draw gag cartoons for humor magazines without missing a beat.

Moisan also sporadically drew (in alternance with three other cartoonists) a comic strip, *Zoé,* for the daily *Le Parisien,* in 1949-64. Two anthologies of his political car-

Stu Moldrem, "Sportrait." © Seattle Post-Intelligencer.

toons, *10 Ans d'Histoire en 100 Dessins* ("10 Years of History in 100 Drawings") and *Il a été une Fois* ("Once Upon a Time") were published, in 1968 and 1971 respectively. He died of cancer in 1987.

M.H.

MOLDREM, STUART (1925-) American cartoonist born in Centralia, Washington, in 1925. Stu Moldrem started drawing while in grade school in Bellingham, Washington, and by his own admission hasn't stopped since. He received his formal art education at the Los Angeles Art Center School, at the Lukits Academy of Fine Arts in Los Angeles and later at the Derbyshire School of Fine Arts in Seattle.

After serving two years in the army at the end of World War II (during which time he was sports artist for the Pacific edition of *Stars and Stripes* in Tokyo), Moldrem went back to Seattle and did cartoons for various newspapers. In 1949 he started *Sportrait*, a sports feature for the *Seattle Post-Intelligencer* that still runs regularly. Moldrem's depiction of sports personalities and his dynamic drawing of athletes in action have earned him a respected position among sports cartoonists and sports enthusiasts across the country. He fell victim in the 1980s to the fate that had befallen most newspapers sports cartoonists, and has recycled himself in the 1990s into book illustration.

M.H.

MOLINÉ I MUNS, MANUEL (1833-1901) Spanish cartoonist born in Barcelona, Spain, in 1833. Manuel Moliné studied art with a view to becoming a painter. He soon turned to drawing, however, and his first cartoons appeared in 1859 in the newly founded magazine *El Canan Rayado.*

Moliné was an extremely able and extraordinarily popular cartoonist whose success can be attributed to the fact that his cartoons were straightforward and could be easily understood by everyone. They appeared in most major publications of the day, such as *Un Tros de Paper*, *La Flaca* and *La Mosca Roja*, but his most important work appeared in the magazines *La Campana de Gracia* and *L'Esquella de 1a Torratxa*. To commemorate the 20th anniversary of continuous collaboration between the publication and Moliné, *L'Esquella de 1a Torratxa* dedicated its entire May 3, 1901, issue to him.In all his works Moliné bitterly satirized the privileges of the Spanish upper classes and attacked, often with passion, the aristocracy, the clergy and the military. He died in Barcelona late in 1901.

J.M.

MOLNAR, GEORGE (1910-) Australian cartoonist born in Nagyvarad, Hungary, in April 1910.

International appeal (if not international demand) is a trend in present-day Australian comic art. Much of the coniic art produced in Australia today has no indigenous character, idiom or flavor; a large proportion of it would be at home in the New Yorker or, with suitably translated captions, in Paris Soir. In short, it is a humor with no national identity.

What distinguishes the work of George Molnar as socially significant is its documentary value. Character revelation is the core of Molnar's humor, although his satirical comment usually is aimed at a specific social level (as was that of America's Gluyas Williams), introducing a world of academics, professional and business executives, high society and those occupying the "rooms at the top." Nevertheless, it is humor that spurns all suggestion of syndication-circuit gags of the sort popularized by the *Saturday Evening Post*, which for decades has set an inter-

Manuel Moliné satire on the military and the clergy, 1882.

"Nothing interesting to say . . . let's join the ladies."
George Molnar, "Insubstantial Pageant." © Sydney Morning Herald.

national editorial standard for jokes, not about character, but about men as business creatures, car buyers or meek underlings to overbearing bosses or wives. The *London Times* has said of Molnar: "Mr. Molnar is far and away the best cartoonist-in a country where the tradition of black-and-white illustration is very strong." Molnar has added to the Australian achievement in this field an outlook that is fresh, sophisticated, refined in content and aesthetic in form.

Although born in Hungary, Molnar came to Australia in 1939 and, as an associate professor, has been lecturing in architecture at Sydney University since 1945, the year he commenced drawing political cartoons for the *Sydney Daily Telegraph*. Molnar's self- taught cartooning style was developed over the six years he was with that paper, but in 1952, he joined the *Sydney Morning Herald*, where his *Insubstantial Pageant* became a unique feature of sharp, penetrating satire, preeminent in postwar Australian journalism.

From the 1950s onward, Australians have witnessed a period of national prosperity and expansion in both domestic and foreign matters. This is evidenced in urban growth, which in turn has reflected international tastes and trends in art and entertainment, new conventions like the bistro, the vanities of dress and fashion and styles of civic and domestic architecture. Molnar examines such social conformities and their effects on the opulent Australian. He is a masterful interpreter of the contemporary environment and those who live in it. His wit, intelligence and flair for social satire are complemented by a graphic style that is tranquil and orderly, drawn with fine lines linking carefully balanced black areas in a manner aesthetic yet free of gimmicks and mystique.

Since his first collection, *Statues*, was published twenty years ago, he has had five other books produced: *Insubstantial Pageant*; *Postcards*; *Molnar At Large*; *Molnar, 1970-76*; and a fine collection of his recent work, *Moral Tales*.

V.L.

MONDO PLYMPTON (U.S.) Animator Bill Plympton (born in Oregon City, Oregon, on April 30, 1946) is best known for his outrageous spots on MTV and as the animator in the comedy *The Edge* (broadcast on Fox-TV in 1992-93), in which his spoofs of established television shows brought vituperations and threats of lawsuits against the network. In 1997 he wrapped up his career to date in a full-length feature which he called, appropriately enough, *Mondo Plympton*, touted by the movie's distributor as "guaranteed to turn your head inside out."

The 80-minute film constitutes a virtual travelogue of the cartoonist's art (or perhaps of his mind). "Welcome to the incredibly strange animation of Bill Plympton," he intones at the opening, then proceeds to present (in words and song) the sum of his artistic world, from the 1983 Cold War and Reaganomics (the spoofing "Boom Town") to excerpts from his next project ("sure to offend everyone"), a feature to be called *I Married a Strange Person*, which came out in 1998.

In these cartoons, hand-drawn in colored pencils, the artist harks back to an earlier, more innocent era of animation. These vignettes are far from innocent, however, with their prominent references to sex (there is a short lovingly depicting all the varieties of shapes and names associated with the female breast) and frequent displays of gore (in one segment two antagonists go at it with reckless abandon, gleefully dismembering and disemboweling each

Sketches for "Mondo Plympton." © Bill Plympton.

other). All these affronts are as hilarious as they are disturbing and decisively demonstrate that animated cartoons are no longer the exclusive province of children.

At one point in the film Plympton, directly addressing the spectators, tells them of his adventures and tribulations with the Disney organization: It is safe to assume that the artist, with his attacks on work, success, family and country and in his frank portrayals of sex and the uglier facts of life, would like to be regarded as the anti-Disney.

M.H.

MONNIER, HENRI BONAVENTURE (1805-1877) French cartoonist and satirist born in Paris, France, on June 8, 1805. Henri Monnier, the son of a government employee, dropped out of high school at the age of 16 and went to work in a notary's office, which he left a short while later to become a clerk in the Ministry of Justice. But a desk job was not to Monnier's liking, and he started studying art, first with Anne-Louis Girodet, then with the noted academic painter Antoine-Jean, Baron Gros. There his inordinate penchant for practical jokes soon got him into trouble.

After a try at doing a few sketches and lithographs in 1827, Monnier started his career in earnest the next year, illustrating La Fontaine's *Fables* and especially Béranger's *Chansons,* for which his irreverent style was perfectly suited. Monnier revealed his true talent for satire in a series of ferocious drawings in which he pitilessly lampooned the bourgeoisie and its way of life: *Les Grisettes* ("The Working Girls"), Moeurs *Administratives* ("Administrative Mores") and others asserted his formidable powers of observation and irony in the early 1830s. At the same time he took up writing, collaborating with Emile Augier and Henri Leroux on a couple of farces, *Les Compatriotes* ("Fellow Countrymen") and *Les Mendiants* ("The Beggars").

Henri Monnier, project of a monument to Monsieur Prudhomme (etching by Champfleury).

From the late 1830s on, Monnier became obsessed with the mediocrity, pettiness and servility of middle-class life, which he castigated through his most famous creation, Joseph Prudhomme, the prototype of the hateful bourgeois and everything he stood for. In countless cartoons, comedies and novels he mercilessly attacked the pretensions, follies and stupidities of his age, with Prudhomme as his spokesman; Monnier identified with his creation to such an extent that he played the part on stage, and he even dressed like Prudhomme in private life. The most significant works in which Joseph Prudhomme appears are *Grandeur et Décadence de Joseph Prudhomme* ("Greatness and Decadence of Joseph Prudhomme," 1853), *Mémoires de Joseph Prudhomme* (1857) and *Joseph Prudhomme, Chef de Brigands* ("Joseph Prudhomme, Brigand Chief").

Henri Monnier died in Paris on January 3, 1877.

M.H.

MOOR, D.S.
See Orlov, Dimitry Stakhiyevich.

MOORES, RICHARD ARNOLD (1909-1986) American cartoonist born in Lincoln, Nebraska, on December 12, 1909. Dick Moores was educated in the public schools of Lincoln, Omaha (where his family moved when he was nine) and Fort Wayne, Indiana, where he moved in 1926. He attended the Fort Wayne Art School and held various local jobs, working as a sign painter, a clerk in a Piggly Wiggly store and an usher (later manager) at the Emboyd vaudeville theater.

In 1930 Moores attended the Chicago Academy of Fine Arts, seeking instruction in illustration. Further study at the Chouinard School in Los Angeles preceded service as Chester Gould's second assistant on the young *Dick Tracy* strip; Moores contributed balanced layouts and handsome, textured shading that later emerged in his own derivative strip, *Jim Hardy,* launched in June 1936. This detective strip became a western, *Windy and Paddles,* and ended in October 1942.

Moores then went to work for the Disney studios and assisted Floyd Gottfredson and Frank Reilly on various strips. He inked *Mickey Mouse* dailies and drew the *Uncle Remus* page, occasionally worked on the *Classic Tales* syndicated feature, contributed to Western comic book titles (1942-56) and did much of the artwork for Disney merchandising during his tenure. In 1956, on the suggestion of Bill Perry, Moores became Frank King's assistant on *Gasoline Alley,* assuming the duties of story blocking and then more of the artwork until he became a full ghost. In 1963 he received credit and on King's death in 1969 took full control of the strip.

Seldom in the cartooning world has an inheritor sparkled on an old property as Moores has done on *Gasoline Alley*. In a certain sense it is a different strip-the story lines are more humorous and rely on eccentric personalities-but the strong characterizations remain, as does the family saga aspect. Moores's main contribution is the stunning visual effect he achieves; he eschews panel borders, mixes up textures and tones (almost all drawn by hand, not mechanically) and depicts the most unusual angles in the comics. Most views are from the ground level up (it is strange that a man more than six feet tall, as Moores is, can see the world from under tabletops and carriage bottoms). In all, it is an exciting strip to behold.

Moores was awarded the National Cartoonists Society's Reuben in 1975. Among his many other credits is his pioneering work with animation and comics on television. In the early 1950s Telecomics, coordinated by Moores, ran for a season on the NBC network flagshipped by KLAS. This series translated strips to video primarily via panning and tracking. The first strip, appropriately, was Jim Hardy. He died in Asheville, N.C., on April 22, 1986.

R.M.

MOPSY (U.S.) Fresh from her success with *Flapper Fanny,* Gladys Parker created *Mopsy* as a daily panel for King Features Syndicate in 1936, later adding a Sunday page. Mopsy, a pert, tousle-haired brunette modeled after Parker herself, liked to play dumb for the countless solicitous males who were always around her, but she displayed a fine sense of realism and practicality on many an occasion. In her efforts to cope with suitors, female rivals and the myriad aggravations of daily living, she was sometimes exasperated, sometimes dejected, but always smiling through at the end. Though perpetuating many stereotypes of women (the ritual visits to the beauty shop, the backbiting, the fussing with physical appearances that was so large a part of Mopsy's life), Parker also used her feature to deflate male pretensions. Mopsy prospered mightily through the 1940s, so much so that Newsweek ran a piece on the panel and its creator in March 1949. Its popularity declined after the 1950s, however, and it did not long survive Parker's death in 1966. A fresh, funny, ingratiating feature, Mopsy is recalled with affection by its many former readers. A Mopsy comic book was issued by St. John from 1948 to 1953.

M.H.

"Mopsy." © Associated Newspapers.

Guillermo Mordillo. © Mordillo.

MORDILLO, GUILLERMO (1932-) Argentine cartoonist born in Buenos Aires, Argentina, on August 4, 1932. Guillermo Mordillo displayed an early flair for cartooning and drawing. He embarked on an artistic career as soon as he got out of high school in 1950, doing illustrations of fairy tales for an Argentine publisher. Between 1952 and 1955 he also tried his hand at animation and comic strip drawing, without much success. Leaving Argentina for Peru in 1955, Mordillo worked at the McCann-Erickson advertising agency in Lima for the next five years; during that time he also illustrated books of fables and fairy tales. He moved to New York in 1960 and first worked for a greeting card company, then for Famous Studios /Paramount, where he animated sequences of *Popeye* and *Little Lulu* cartoons.

Mordillo made his final (and, as it turned out, successful) move in 1963. He went to Paris and, after a few years with another greeting card company, managed to get his cartoons published in the mass-circulation magazines *Paris-Match* and *Lui*. Soon Mordillo established himself as one of the major talents in cartooning, winning acclaim and international recognition. His cartoons have been published in major periodicals in France, Germany, Italy,

Japan, the United States and other countries. He has also produced several animated cartoons for French and German television and has written a number of original humor books (*Le Galion, Crazy Cowboy,* etc.). Mordillo has won an impressive number of awards around the world, and in 1977 he was voted Cartoonist of the Year at the Montreal International Salon of Cartoons. His cartoons have been collected in a number of books, among them *The Collected Cartoons of Mordillo, Cartoons Opus I* and *Crazy Crazy*. He moved to Ibiza, Spain, in the late 1970s, and produced several animated cartoons for Spanish TV. From the mid-1980s on he has concentrated on the German market where his cartoons and illustrations are most prized.

Mordillo's humor rests heavily on the unusual, the incongruous and the unexpected; his cartoons, usually captionless, are incredibly busy and detailed. As Serge Jongué of the Pavilion of Humor in Montreal has noted: If we had to describe Mordillo we would say that he is clear to excess. In the themes he deals with, the situations, characters or epic happenings all are ultra-familiar cultural stereotypes." It is this clarity and familiarity that give Mordillo's humor such universal appeal.

M.H.

MOREL-RETZ, LOUIS-PIERRE (1825-1899) French painter and cartoonist born at Dijon, France, on June 3, 1825. Louis Morel-Retz pursued a career as a painter, exhibiting his canvases in various art shows. At the same time, using the pen name "Stop," he also contributed cartoons on the political and social life of the Second Empire, from the Crimean and Franco-Prussian wars to the many scandals prevalent during the Third Republic. Most of his drawings originally appeared in Le *Charivari, L'Illustration* and *Le Journal Amusant* and were released in albums, among which are *Bêtes et Gens* ("Animals and People," 1876), Ces Messieurs ("These Gentlemen," 1877) and *Nos Excellences* ("Our Excellencies," 1878). They present an unashamedly nationalistic view of France and her military might. He also wrote light comedies that were very successful.Morel-Retz died in his birthplace on September 5, 1899.

P.H.

MORGAN, MATTHEW (1839-1890) American and British cartoonist born in London, England, on April 27, 1839. Matt Morgan covered the Austro-Italian war in 1859 as a war correspondent and sketch artist for the *Illustrated London News.* For the magazine *Fun* (1862-67) he cartooned and lampooned many subjects, paying particular attention to the American Civil War. In 1867 he founded, and was chief cartoonist for, *Tomahawk,* and in 1870 he emigrated to the United States.

Soon after Morgan's arrival in New York, he was engaged by Frank Leslie to serve Leslie's papers as an answer to *Harper's Weekly's* Thomas Nast. For Leslie's Weekly Morgan savagely attacked U.S. Grant—one of Nast's idols—and generally upheld a Democratic political point of view in his cartoons, many of which ran over two large pages.

In 1880, having left Leslie's (and with his counterpart's influence on the wane), Morgan founded several of his own enterprises, including the Morgan Art Pottery Company; he also managed the Strobridge Lithographic Company of Cincinnati. Drawn back to the publishing world, Morgan became art editor of Collier's in 1888, serving until his death in New York City on June 2, 1890, with only a brief respite in 1889 to paint backdrops for Buffalo Bill's Wild West Show.

Morgan was an effective partisan whose style was cleaner and more solid than Nast's. He had a firmer grasp of anatomy and executed his shadings in a handsome fashion, but he lacked Nast's native talent for concept and visualization—no derogation, since hardly any cartoonist since has matched Nast in those departments. Morgan must be considered the last great woodcut-era cartoonist.

R.M.

MORGAN, WALLACE (1873-1948) American cartoonist and illustrator born in New York City on July 11, 1873. Wallace Morgan was graduated from the Albany, New York, high school and spent six years at the Academy of Design Art in New York City. He joined the staff of the *New York Herald* and *Telegram,* where he was to spend ten years as a sketch artist. There he created *Fluffy Ruffles,* a weekly color comic about pretty women; *Fluffy* was the first such in the comics, and the feature was newspapers answer to the Gibson Girl. Morgan's other duties included news and courtroom sketches and a stint ghosting *Buster Brown* after Outcault left for the *Journal.*

At age 40 Morgan abandoned "pretty girl" art; the field was indeed glutted, although he excelled. He concentrated on magazine illustrations and shone with Julian Street's *Abroad at Home* series in *Collier*'s. Soon thereafter World War I broke out, and Morgan was commissioned an American Expeditionary Force captain and an official artist; his visual records of Chateau Thierry and Belleau Wood are outstanding. After the war he again immersed himself in illustration and did his best work for comic stories such as the *Jeeves* series by P.G. Wodehouse. He contributed frequently to Life in the early 1920s, as well.

Morgan's style was quick and sketchy—a legacy from his sketch-artist days (fellow newspaper artists William Glackens and Everett Shinn acquired similar styles). His tool was the brush, and the quick staccato lines gave the appearance of pen work. Later he used washes and crayon shadings to good advantage. It is said that he never used models and threw away a drawing rather than make corrections.

Morgan was a member of many clubs and an intimate of the great personalities of his day. He was an honorary president of the Society of Illustrators for the two years preceding his death and was president from 1929 to 1936, a long term. He was also an honorary member of the Art Students League, a rare tribute. The year before his death he was named to the National Academy and was honored by the National Institute of Arts and Letters. Morgan was active until his death on April 24, 1948; he was contributing regularly to the *New Yorker, Collier's* and the *New York Times Magazine.*

R.M.

MORI, YASUJI (1925-1992) Japanese animator and director born in Taiwan, then a Japanese colony, on January 28, 1925. After returning to Japan at age 18, Yasuji Mori saw his first animated film, *Kumo* to Chūrippu ("Spider and Tulip"), a classic in Japanese animation created by Kenzo Masaoka. It moved him deeply. Several years later, after graduating from the Department of Architecture at the Tokyo University of Arts, Mori himself resolved to become an animator and went to the Nihon Dōga company, where Masaoka was working on Torachan to *Hanayome* ("Little Tora and the Bride"). He was hired after being cautioned about the hard life of the profession, and thereupon began his training at age 24. In addition to learning from Masaoka, he was also taught by Nihon Dōga's top animator, Masao Kumagawa.

In 1956 Mori created his first animated cartoon, *Kuroi Kikori to Shiroi Kikori* ("The Black and White Woodcutters"), with Taiji Yabushita in charge of direction. The same year Nihon Dōga was incorporated as the animation department of the Toei company, where Mori continued to work until March 1973. One of Toei's first productions was Mori's *Koneko no Rakugaki* ("Kitten's Doodlings," 1957). The next year, Mori was one of the front-line animators whose talents were used by Toei for its first feature-length cartoon designed for export, Hakujaden ("Legend of a White Snake").

Mori later turned increasingly to directing, and in this capacity he worked on such films as *Nagagutsu o Haita Neko* ("Puss in Boots," 1969) and *Nagagutsu Sanjushi* ("Three Braves in Boots," 1972). In 1973 Mori finally left Toei and began working as animation director for Nihon Animation on cartoons aimed at television audiences, such as *Yamanezumi Rocky-Chack* ("Rocky-Chack the Mountain Mouse," 1973) and *Kuma no Ko Jakki* ("Jack the Bear Cub," 1977). He has also written several children's books. Mori is at his finest, however, when gently depicting subjects of beauty. To this day, *Koneko no Rakugaki* remains one of his best and most representative works. He proved a major influence on many people in the front lines of the Japanese animation industry of today. He passed away of illness in 1992.

F.S.

Jim Morin. © Miami Herald.

MORIN, JAMES (1953-) The editorial cartoonist Jim Morin once identified his political affiliation as "conservative liberal, liberal conservative," and this ability to achieve a balanced view, deeply engaged but without shrillness, pervades the artist's work.

The son of an attorney, Morin was born in 1953 in Washington, D.C., and raised in Boston, where he began drawing at the age of seven. His formal education reflects the professional status of his family: he attended the Suffield Academy in Connecticut from 1967 to 1971 and went on to the University of Syracuse, from whose College of Art he graduated with a Bachelor of Fine Arts degree in 1976. During his junior year at Syracuse, he went to England for a six-month course at the John Cass School of Art in London.

A traditional education in "fine art" has not been wasted on Morin, who feels that "the better draughtsman you are, the better cartoonist you'll be," but from the beginning he was drawn to the genre of political cartooning. In 1974-75 he served as editorial cartoonist for the *Daily Orange*, his university's student newspaper, and when he graduated he canvassed the nation's press looking for work in the field. After what he estimates 400 letters, he found a place as a staff artist with the Beaumont, Texas *Enterprise and Journal* in 1976. There he did spot caricatures, illustrated editorials and news features, made maps and diagrams, designed page layouts, and drew editorial cartoons. It was a great training ground, he recalls, giving him the opportunity to develop his own style and direction as a cartoonist, but it was too good to last. The next year the paper's publisher dismissed his editor for being too independent-minded, and Morin left the paper.

After what he calls "a mercifully brief stay" of a year-and-a-half at the *Richmond* (Virginia) *Times-Dispatch*, he was hired by the *Miami* (Florida) *Herald* in December, 1978. Since February, 1985, his cartoons have been distributed nationally by King Features Syndicate and have been reprinted in a variety of magazines, including *Time*, *Newsweek*, and *U.S. News and World Report*.

In 1982 Morin demonstrated his skill as a caricaturist with *Famous Cats*, a collection of witty drawings of celebrities in feline guise, and in 1985 he published *Jim Morin's Guide to Birds*, a volume of watercolors done in the same whimsical vein. His first collection of editorial cartoons, *Line of Fire*, appeared in 1990. Described by one critic as "a welcome and long overdue addition to the social and political history of the last decade," it established Morin's position in the first rank of American editorial cartoonists. Winner of an Overseas Press Club Award in 1979, an OPC Citation for Excellence in 1981, a Mencken, and a Fischetti, Morin confirmed that status when he received the Pulitzer Prize in 1996.

Jim Morin believes that "a prerequisite for good editorial cartoon ideas is outrage. The more pissed off you are the better." He has turned his wrath on many of the social and political ills of our time, exposing hypocrisy and corruption with his own distinctive style and wit.

D.W.

MORRIS, WILLIAM CHARLES (1874-1940) American cartoonist born in Salt Lake City, Utah, on March 6, 1874. William Morris attended public schools and received no art training; he worked as a gold miner, clerk, teamster and sign painter before landing a job as sketch artist and cartoonist for the *Spokane* (Wash.) *Spokesman-Review* in 1904. There he remained until 1913, when he moved to New York and freelanced; Morris worked for *Puck*, *Harper's Weekly*, the *Independent*, the *Evening Mail* (each of which he saw in their dying days), the Tribune and the George Matthew Adams Service, which syndicated his cartoons widely. He was hired by the Republican National Committee in 1936 to draw propaganda cartoons for use by any papers wishing to print them. Morris died on April 5, 1940.

Morris had an easy, cartoony style that was pleasing to the eye and generally precluded any fierce partisanship, since it could not be presented believably. He seems to have been a gun for hire, as his political convictions changed as often and as simply as he changed employers over the years. His books include *Spokesman-Review Cartoons* (1908), *The Spokane Book* (1913) and *One Hundred Men of Rockland County* (1929).

R.M.

MOSCA, GIOVANNI (1908-) Italian cartoonist born in Rome, Italy, in 1908. Giovanni Mosca studied art in Rome and started on a cartooning career in the early 1930s. His humor, then somewhat surreal and a bit light-headed, was best represented in Bertoldo, a breeding ground for Italian cartoonists of the time. In its pages, practically impersonating himself with the little man in top hat and tails who appeared in almost all his cartoons, he subtly sniped at Mussolini's regime. After World War II Mosca spent many years with *Il Corriere d'In formazione of Milan*, to which he contributed a daily editorial cartoon. He is now the regular political and editorial cartoonist of the conservative Rome daily *Il Tempo*. His draftsmanship is faultless and his captions precise, although his humor is often old-fashioned and founded on puns.

One of the reasons for Mosca's popularity is his consistency. In the 1930s he reflected middle-class distaste for

The conservation of the plants and flower beds is entrusted to the education of the citizens. "It breaks me up, sir, we are so short of manure that we have to substitute civic education for it."
Giovanni Mosca. © Mosca.

the Fascist regime, and since then, without changing his position at all, he has come to represent a nostalgic and conservative viewpoint. His cartoons of recent years express regret and longing for a past that some still regard as a happier time; he draws the present with one eye always on the past.

C.S.

MOSE
See Depond, Moise.

MOSER, FRANK (1886-1964) American cartoonist and animator born in Oketo, Kansas, in 1886. Frank Moser studied at the Art Students League and the Academy of Design in New York. He got his first cartooning job on the *Des Moines Register and Leader* in 1909 and later worked for several Hearst newspapers. Moving to Hastings-on-Hudson, New York, in 1916, Moser became one of the chief animators of the newly created International Film Service (he is listed as co-director, with George Herriman, of the *Krazy Kat* cartoons, but he directed many of the other series as well). In 1929 Frank Moser and Paul Terry established Moser and Terry, which produced the Terrytoon cartoons. Moser worked on the *Farmer Al Falfa* series, among others. In 1936 he sold his interest to Terry, who later suppressed any mention of his former partner.

In his later years Moser painted landscapes and exhibited in galleries in New York City and Westchester. He was

Frank Moser, "Happy Hooligan--Doing His Bit." © International Film Service.

the first treasurer of the Hudson Valley Art Association and later became its historian. Moser died in Dobbs Ferry Hospital on October 1, 1964. His contribution to animated cartoons, which appears as considerable as it is neglected, is now being evaluated in a new light.

M.H.

MOSHER, CHRISTOPHER TERRY (1942-) Canadian caricaturist and illustrator born in Ottawa, Ontario, on November 11, 1942. Christopher Mosher grew up in Toronto, Ontario. He attended several schools, including the Ontario College of Art in Toronto and the Ecole des Beaux-Arts in Quebec City. Serious painting was his goal, and when he drew caricatures of tourists he signed himself "Aislin" (Gaelic for "dream"), preserving his own name for his serious work. After graduation in 1966, when he began to be paid for his caricatures, they became his serious work.

Mosher's work began appearing in various types of publications, such as underground newspapers, university papers and the Montreal Star, where he was staff artist from 1969 to 1971. Winning a Canada Council grant in 1971 enabled him to take a sabbatical and study cartooning in Europe. Afterward he joined the staff of the *Montreal Gazette*. His work has appeared on the covers of *Time-Canada* and *Maclean's* and in *Harper's*, the *New York Times*, *Punch* and many other publications. Mosher is also a founding member of an editorial cooperative that publishes the Last Post. He has received several awards, including one from the International Salon of Caricature in 1970 and the National Newspaper Award in 1977. He was inducted into the Canadian News Hall of Fame in 1985.

Several collections of Mosher's caricatures have been published, and he has also done some book illustration work. In 1975 he produced *The Hecklers*, a 60-minute television documentary on Canadian political cartooning. He co-authored a book on the same subject published in 1979.

Mosher has been described as "bracingly cruel" and "evenhandedly malicious." He calls himself a caricaturist rather than a cartoonist, and his work "an attack on a person, a public figure, a celebrity. A caricaturist creates images that aren't there." His victims are of all philosophies, races, creeds and colors. "I really don't believe in anything," Mosher says. His personal life has been stormy in the past, and Mosher once said that he figured he'd be "burned out" in ten years. As he wrote in a foreword to one of his books, "I would like to extend my gratitude to a Quebec City plainclothesman who worked me over somewhat back in 1963. Without his help I'm quite sure that I would be selling shirts in Eaton's today and liking it." While this earlier image of Mosher may change, much of his work remains quite unconventional.

D.K.

MOTA, ANÍSIO OSCAR DA (1891-1969) Brazilian cartoonist and sculptor born in Rio de Janeiro, Brazil, in 1891. Working under the pseudonym "Fritz," Oscar da Mota had his first cartoon published in the humor magazine *O Malho* in 1910. In 1913 he became the regular caricaturist on the satirical publication *Figuras e Figurões*. As a cartoonist, he was most prolific between 1915 and 1940, when he contributed to many Brazilian publications (*Jornal do Brasil, D. Quixote, A Manhã, Para Todos, A Notícia, Diário da Noite, O Globo* and others); he also collaborated on the Buenos Aires daily *La Prensa*. In 1925 Fritz created the famous character Pirolito for the humor magazine *O Tico-Tico*, and he drew Pirolito as a weekly feature until 1930.

Mota also did a number of monumental sculptures, such as the bronze statue dedicated to "The Little Newsboy" (1933) and two groups for the National Library in Rio de Janeiro. He died in Rio on February 3, 1969, and his passing drew affectionate notices and heartfelt tributes from newspapers throughout Brazil.

A.M.

MOUNTAIN BOYS, THE (U.S.) A classic American cartoon feature of the hillbilly genre, *The Mountain Boys* was created by Paul Webb in 1934. That same year, on August 20, another hillbilly clan, Al Capp's Yokums of *Li'l Abner* fame, also gained national prominence. However, Paul Webb's characters were published twice in the *Saturday Evening* Post prior to the appearance of *Li'l Abner.*

The Mountain Boys was most closely associated with Esquire magazine. It was published as a regular monthly full-page color cartoon feature. Webb's "utterly shiftless" hillbillies first appeared in the October 1934 *Esquire* at a time when the magazine was a quarterly. *The Mountain Boys* appeared in *Esquire* until the early 1960s, when the editorial direction of the magazine changed. Luke, Jake, Willie, Maw and Paw, and the rest of the clan still appear annually in a *Mountain Boys* calendar that has been published by Brown and Bigelow Company in St. Paul, Minnesota, since about 1940. The calendars have always contained 12 previously unpublished *Mountain Boys* cartoons.

The feature came to *Esquire* by a fluke. Webb had initially hoped to sell The Mountain Boys as a series to the *Saturday Evening Post*. However, the *Post* rejected the idea. Then, unexpectedly, Webb received word from Richard McCallister, a gag writer and *New Yorker* cartoonist, that he was associate cartoon editor at *Esquire*, then brand-new.

"Ears ain't big enuf to be one of ourn—Must belong to Lem Hawkins. I heerd him say he was short one t'other day."
"The Mountain Boys." © Esquire.

McCallister requested that Webb, for whom he had done gag writing, submit some cartoons. As soon as it began publication, *The Mountain Boys* soared in popularity.

Initially the cartoon was published in black and white, but soon *Esquire* began to publish The *Mountain Boys* in color. Webb's style was loose both in black and white and in color. He used everything from charcoal to watercolors and gouache on the feature. The cartoons have a distinctly primitive spontaneity. Colors were not laid in meticulously but with an ease and casualness that is in keeping with the mood of the characters.

The Boys themselves were tall, scraggly, unwashed and usually in a state of activity verging on torpor. They were not just lazy: they were the laziest, most no-account hillbillies in America. They were the epitome of cracker-barrel humor. In their most typical pose, they slouched against a cabin, rifle and jug of moonshine whiskey at the ready. In one cartoon a clan patriarch looks at a bedraggled youngster and says, "Ef yew be one o' Lem Hopkins' kids, git on home-ef yer one o' mine get on into th' house." *The Mountain Boys* sometimes went for the belly laugh, but just as often it created a humorous acknowledgment that, as Paul Webb says, "There's some lazier than I—and more worthless."

B.C.

MOUSE AND HIS CHILD, THE (U.S.) Animator Fred Wolf, who in collaboration with Teru Murakami produced a number of intriguing shorts, directed his first full-length animation feature with a new associate, Chuck Swenson. The result of their efforts, *The Mouse and His Child,* was released in 1978. Adapted by Carol MonPere from Russell Hoban's novel, the film recounts the adventures of a pair of wind-up toys, a mouse and his son linked arm in arm. In their wanderings through the outside world, they encounter all kinds of weird creatures, from Euterpe the stage-struck bird to a white-gloved frog (voiced respectively by Cloris Leachman and Andy Devine). They also run afoul of Manny the Rat (whose voice is superbly modulated by Peter Ustinov) and flee the gloom-drenched tenements and mean streets of the city before finally finding peace with the world in acceptance of their condition.

The Mouse and His Child is a witty and at times thoughtful film. The fact that its heroes are mice further accentuates its stylistic and thematic departures from the animation standards of Disney or Hanna-Barbera (whose mice, whether Mickeys or Jerrys, were never so grimly depicted). While not always successful, the feature signals a possible rejuvenation of the American theatrical cartoon scene.

M.H.

MRÓZ, DANIEL (1917-   ) Polish cartoonist, illustrator and poster designer born in Kraków, Poland, on February 3, 1917. Daniel Mróz, the son of a respected Polish journalist and newspaper editor, attended the Kraków School of Arts and Crafts, but his education was interrupted by the outbreak of World War II in 1939. During the German occupation (1939-45) he tookavariety of odd jobs. Mróz resumed his studies in 1947 at the Kraków Academy of Arts, graduating in 1952.

Mróz started his career as a cartoonist in 1951, when he became a regular contributor to the illustrated weekly *Przekrój*; he also drew for other Polish publications and soon became one of the best-known Polish cartoonists.

His drawings, full of eerie humor and strange happenings, often dispense with captions. In 1953 Mróz began illustrating books and has since done more than fifty by Polish and foreign authors. In recent times he has become one of the leading poster designers in Poland, and his work in this field has been widely exhibited at home and abroad.

Mróz has been the recipient of a number of honors for his work in the fields of cartooning, illustration and poster design. In 1959 a monograph on the artist written by Jan Kwiatkowski appeared in Warsaw. His cartoons have frequently been reprinted in the West.

M.H.

MUKUCHI BOSHI (Japan) *Mukuchi Boshi* (which can be translated both as "Silent Mr. Bo" and "Silent Hat") was a collection of fantasy cartoons for children created by Takashi Yanase and published in 1977. It was compiled from a series, *Boshi,* that first appeared in the weekly magazine *Shūkan Asahi* in 1967 and was immensely popular.

Boshi, or "Mr. Bo," was an amusingly drawn little fellow

Willard Mullin. © United Feature Syndicate.

who always wore his hat so far down on his head that his face was invisible—hence the title. He lived in a fantasy world: he could fly, dive into the ocean and swing from the clouds without ever having to worry about his hat coming off. He often traveled in a bigger hat that served as something like a flying saucer. Although Boshi had what amounted to superpowers in his fantasy, he was nonetheless subject to the unexpected. On trying to capture a dragonfly, for example, he might suddenly be swept away by one bigger than himself; when fishing in a pond, he might have his line cut by a mermaid in hiding with a pair of scissors. *Mukuchi Boshi* was a completely silent work, but Boshi, the star, was expressive enough to convey everything the artist attempted. It was a gentle work that appealed to the entire family, and therein lay its broad popularity.

Mukuchi Boshi had its origins in a 1967 contest sponsored by the magazine *Shūkan Asahi,* which offered a prize of nearly $30,000 for the best cartoon submitted. Takashi Yanase, already a professional, entered and won hands down. Yanase was born in Kōchi Prefecture on February 6, 1919. He is extremely versatile and prolific, functioning not only as a cartoonist but also as a poet, animator and song lyricist. Most of his work is for small children, and lie is particularly well known for animated films such as *Yasashii Raion* ("The Gentle Lion") and *Chisana Jumbo* ("Little Jumbo"). Most of his written works are published by SANRIO, a Japanese company that specializes in mass marketing books and toys for small children. In the late 1980s and the 1990s Yanase has had an extraordinary hit with *Anpan Man* ("Sweet Bean-Cake Man"), which has been animated and heavily merchandised.

F.S.

MULLIN, WILLARD HARLAN (1902-1978) American cartoonist born on a farm near Columbus, Ohio, in 1902. Willard Mullin grew up in Los Angeles, where he worked as a letterer in a sign shop after finishing high school in 1920. In 1923 he went to work for the *Los Angeles Herald,* first doing spot illustrations and later turning to sports cartooning.

After a short stint on papers in San Antonio and Fort Worth, Texas, Mullin went to New York in 1934; the next year he replaced Pete Llanuza as sports cartoonist for the *World-Telegram.* Some time later he created the immortal "Bums," who soon became the trademark of the Brooklyn Dodgers. When the Dodgers moved to Los Angeles in 1958, Mullin put sport shirts, berets and sunglasses on his bums but kept them as seedy and contentious as before. In 1966 the World-Telegram closed, and Mullin went on to freelance cartoons for a variety of publications. In addition to his cartoon work, Mullin drew illustrations for magazines (*Look, Life,* the *Saturday Evening Post, Time* and *Newsweek,* among others) and books (the most notable being the 1944 edition of Menke's *Encyclopedia of Sports*). Mullin's love of his craft and of his subjects shone through in all his cartoons: under the surface roughness lurked a strong undercurrent of affection and optimism.

"I'm not an artist," he once said with typical modesty, "I'm a cartoonist." Mullin received many awards during his career; when he retired in 1971, he was hailed as "the sports cartoonist of the century" and a retrospective exhibition of his works was organized in New York City. On December 21, 1978, he died of cancer in Corpus Christi, Texas.

M.H.

MUNTANYOLA I PUIG, JOAQUIM (1914-) Spanish cartoonist born in Barcelona, Spain, in 1914. Joaquim Muntanyola has been one of the most popular cartoonists in Spain since 1931, when he began his career at the age of 17. Throughout the 1930s he worked for three magazines, each very different in nature: *En Patufet,* a middle-class Catalan publication with a strong didactic character; *TBO,* a children's comic magazine with a broad-based audience throughout Spain; and *Bé Negre,* a politically radical magazine. Since the end of the Spanish civil war (1939) Muntanyola has been involved in a variety of activities. His cartoons appear regularly in most of the major newspapers and magazines in Spain, and he continues to contribute to *TBO.* Aside from his cartoons, he has written extensively, often under assumed names; his writings include books, newspaper articles and reviews. He has also illustrated 15 books. His last book was *Tito el Deportista* ("Titus the Sportsman," 1990). He is now happily retired, as he says, "thanks to my good health."

Muntanyola is first and foremost a cartoonist, and his cartoons, filled with unpredictable humor, have a broad following. Their themes draw not only on topical occurrences but also on the traditions established by earlier Spanish cartoonists. Muntanyola's most important creations are the comic strips *Don Felipe, Don Cristobal y Angelina* and *Josechu*. *Don Felipe* began shortly after the civil war and later became popular in South America. *Josechu* still appears after more than twenty-five years of weekiy installments in *TBO*. All three comics reflect in humorous form the anxieties and yearnings of the Spanish middle class.

J.M.

MUSGRAVE-WOOD, JOHN (1915-) British cartoonist and caricaturist born in Leeds, England, in 1915. John Musgrave-Wood (who works under the nationally recognized signature "Emmwood") served in the merchant marine and then with the Chindits in Burma and took his art training at the Goldsmiths' College of Art with a view to becoming a portrait painter. Humor, however, reared its smiling head, and his special ability as a caricaturist combined with a love for show business and won him a post as the theatrical cartoonist for the glossy weekly the Tatler.

While playing a round of golf with a friend, he was interrnpted by a telephone call from the acting editor of the *Sunday Express:* would he come to their Fleet Street office immediately and execute an urgent caricature for the next edition's show business page? He went (in golf gear) and stayed two years as the newspaper's show-biz cartoonist (1953). In 1955 he was lured to the Beaverbrook Press's London daily, the *Evening Standard,* to produce a regular political caricature for the Diary Page. Then, in 1957, he changed publishers, going to the *Daily Mail,* becoming the principal staff cartoonist and allowing "Trog" (Wally Fawkes) more time with his daily Flook strip. When the Mail went to tabloid size in 1971, Emmwood began to alternate his cartoons with newcomer Stan ("Mac") McMurtry.

He retired in 1975, after an 18-year run with the Mail, leaving that newspaper the emptier for want of his excellent, bold and critical line work. He now lives in France.

D.G.

MUSICAL PAINTBOX (G.B.) "*Musical Paintbox* Colour Cartoons created by David Hand. A revolution in animation technique—a screen Sketch Book Fantasy introducing the British countryside in music and picture." These were the words that introduced Great Britain's new animated cartoon series to the film trade in the two-page color advertisement in the *Daily Film Renter*, December 13, 1948.

Musical Paintbox was the second-string series to *Animaland,* which had been created to challenge the power of the Walt Disney cartoons and those from other American studios that had hitherto dominated the "Full Supporting Programme" segment of British cinema programming. With all the wealth of millionaire flour and movie maker J. Arthur Rank behind him, David Hand was hired away from Disney to set up an animation studio in England. Gaumont British Animation, operating from Moor Hall, Cookham in Berkshire, began production in 1947 with short commercials for theatrical release and sing-song shorts for the Saturday morning children's clubs. The first *Musical Paintbox* cartoon was called *The Thames* (1948), and it set the pattern for the series: a wander through a selected area of the English countryside using several techniques, from a blending of still paintings and drawings to short sequences of somewhat limited animation, accompanied by narration in dialect and snatches of music and song. The whole was, frankly, a device to produce a rapid sequence of releases which would alternate with the more complicated productions of *Animaland.*

Director for the entire series was C. Henry Stringer, with Ralph Wright as story supervisor. The second release was *Wales* (1949), followed by *Somerset* (1949) and, with slightly more appealing titling, *A Fantasy on Ireland, A Yorkshire Ditty, Sketches of Scotland, Cornwall, Canterbury Road, Devon Whey* and the final entry, *A Fantasy on London Life* (all released in 1949). Scripts were by Nicholas Spargo, Graeme Phillips and R.A.G. Clarke; artists (not always animators) included Norman Abbey, Deryck Foster, Peter Jay, Brian Ward, Alan Gray, Brian O'Hanlon, John Woodward and John Worsley; music throughout was by Henry Reed. Narrators and singers included John Laurie, Bernard Miles and Ian Wallace.

D.G.

MUSSINO, ATTILIO (1878-1954) Italian cartoonist and illustrator born in Turin, Italy, in 1878. While still a high school student, Attilio Mussino had his first cartoons published in satirical magazines such as *La Luna* and *Il Fischietto*. Inspired in equal parts by Giuseppe Scalarini's heavy line and by Winsor McCay's oneiric compositions, Mussino (who signed himself "Attilio") developed a style of clarity, grace and "D'Annunzio-like aestheticism," as Antonio Faeti once defined it.

Attilio Mussino, illustration for "Pinocchio." © Mussino.

Mussino collaborated from the very first issue (1909) on *Il Corriere dei Piccoli,*for which he created a number of comic strips. The most famous, *Bilbolbul*, was about a little black boy who took figures of speech literally (sprouting wings on his feet, being all at sixes and sevens, etc.), with humorous but slightly sinister results. Other Mussino comic strips include *Schizzo, Doroteae Salmone* and *La Torre del Mago 2000*.

Mussino's masterpiece, however, remains his illustration of Carlo Collodi's Pinocchio, which received the Gold Medal at the 1913 International Exposition. A triumph of the zincography process, the drawings prefigure the *Pinocchio* animated by Disney. Mussino later illustrated several *Pinocchio* sequels, as well as innumerable children's classics, including *Tom Sawyer, Huckleberry Finn, Gulliver's Travels*, and *Grimm and Andersen fables*. After World War II Mussino devoted himself exclusively to books. The hundreds of books he illustrated have enriched the lives of generations of readers, but Mussino died in utter poverty in 1954.

S.T.

MUTT AND JEFF (U.S.) In 1916 pioneer cartoonist Raoul Barré and promoter Tom Bowers set up an animation unit under the name Barré-Bowers to produce *Mutt and Jeff* cartoons for Bud Fisher (who was the actual owner of the studio). In the weekly cartoons they turned out, the tall, smart-alecky Mutt and the put-upon shrimp Jeff had all kinds of adventures, being brush salesmen one week, African explorers the next (early titles include "In the Submarine," "Jeff's Toothache" and "House Painters"). It is said that during the filming of one of these cartoons a studio animator accidentally hit upon the repeal of the law of gravity as a source of gags. Soon the characters were swimming in mid-air, walking on ceilings and falling skyward, much to the amazement of their audiences. Most of the early cartoons in the series were scripted by Bowers and directed by Barré.

The advent of World War I brought a sense of purpose to the cartoons, which became increasingly bellicose. In "William Hohenzollern, Sausage-Maker," for instance, Mutt and Jeff captured the kaiser single-handedly. It is reported that one of the cartoons—depicting the duo as poilus playing jokes on their superior officers—was banned by the French censorship authorities.

"Mutt and Jeff." © Aedita de Beaumont.

In the meantime the relationship between the two partners had steadily deteriorated, coming to a head in 1918 when Barré accused Bowers of swindling; the break became final in 1919. For this and other reasons, Fisher decided to take personal charge of the operation, renaming it simply Mutt and Jeff Studio. *Mutt and Jeff* continued to come out well into the mid-1920s, produced by the studio and by outside contractors (including Paul Terry and Bowers himself). Some of the later entries include "Adventure Shop," "A Trip to Mars" and "Three Raisins and a Cake of Yeast." All these *Mutt and Jeff* cartoons had a tentative air about them, as if waiting for the coming of sound. Withal they were quite entertaining and enjoyed a fair success in the 1920s, second only to *Felix the Cat*. In the early 1930s Walter Lantz tried to revive the series, but by then the characters were no longer in tune with the times, and the attempt lasted little over a year.

The *Mutt and Jeff* cartoons were a proving ground for a host of animators. In addition to Barré and Bowers, the cartoonists who worked on the series at one time or another include Dick Friel (who was the top animator at the studio), Burt Gillett, Al Hurter, Dick Huemer, Isidore Klein, Ted Sears, Frank Sherman, Mannie Davis, George Stallings and Ben Harrison.

M.H.

MY GOD (G.B.) The little man, benign and bearded, sits on a cloud. Another cloud floats by bearing the placard God Is Love. "That's one of my favourite advertisements," he muses with a small smile. Mel Calman's God is a very personal (and personable) creation—so personal, in fact, that He might be a mirror image. Benign and bearded (beaming, too), Calman turns out cartoons that are simple in style, chucklesome in content, yet deep enough under the dashed-down scratches to conceal much thought.

My God appeared as a weekly panel cartoon, column size, in the *Sunday Times* through 1969 and was collected into a paperback reprint in 1970. This comparatively short run of cartoons represents Calman's best work, although others may prefer his experimental comic strip *Couples*, which succeeded My God in the *Sunday Times* and ran for a year. This double- barreled strip about love, life and strife in marriage attempted to show both the surface and the subconscious at the same time.

Mel Calman was born in Hackney, London, in 1931, the son of a timber merchant from Odessa. Educated at Perse School, Cambridge, he attended St. Martin's School of Art and studied illustration at the Goldsmiths' College of Art. At the age of 13 he picked up a book by James Thurber, whose simplicity of style immediately intrigued him. From that moment on he wanted to become a cartoonist.

Calman worked in advertising agencies and publishing houses and first drew his thumbnail style of cartoon for the *Daily Express*. He switched to Sunday publication with the *Sunday Telegraph, Observer* and *Sunday Times*. In 1972, Calman opened a gallery for the exhibition and sale of original cartoons: The Workshop, 83 Lambs Conduit Street, London. He has appeared on television in *Quick on the Draw* and made the animated cartoon *Arrows*. He started drawing daily "pocket cartoons" for the front page of the Times in 1979, and these earned him international fame. He died February 10, 1994, at age 62.

Books: *Bed-Sit* (1963); *Boxes* (1964); *Calman and* Women (1967); *The Penguin Mel Calman* (1968); *Through the Telephone Directory* (1969); *My God* (1970); *Couples* (1972); and *This Pestered Isle* (1973).

D.G.

MYERS, LOUIS (1915-) Cartoonist and illustrator Lou Myers has established a unique place for himself in the art world with his fluid, deliberately crude graphic style and his often no less crude wit. His work ranges from self-illustrated children's books to raunchy gag cartoons in such "adult" publications as *Playboy*, and its presence in magazines as diverse as *Oui*, *National Lampoon*, *Mother Jones*, *Rolling Stone*, the *New Yorker*, the *New York Times*, and *Time* reflects the scope of his creative vision.

Myers was born in Paris on April 17, 1915, to Jewish parents en route from Poland and spent his childhood in the Bronx acquiring the tough spirit and oblique irony of the big city. He served in the U.S. Navy for three years during and after World War II, working as a base illustrator, and studied on the G.I. Bill at Columbia University, New York University, the New School for Social Research in New York, and at the Ecole des Beaux-Arts in Paris. He has otherwise been spared the constraints of institutional affiliation, having expressed his anarchic spirit as a freelance since 1950. A chronic dissenter, he has published widely in journals like *New Masses* and was the house illustrator for the satirical magazine *Monocle*. His engagement in political and social issues took a more concrete form when he sought the office of Bronx assemblyman with the American Labor Party, helped organize the Society of Illustrators' "Artists Against the War" show in 1972, and created an award-winning contribution to the First National Anti-Apartheid Poster Show for the American Committee on Africa in 1982.

Described by Richard Ellman as "the eeriest, vulgarest, cleverest cartoonist now cutting us to pieces," Myers has concentrated on the dark side of the human experience, turning the searchlight of his biting wit on some of the most powerful themes in contemporary life. Religion, politics, psychoanalysis, race, militarism, and sex—often provocatively conflated—are the subjects of many of his jarring visual metaphors. Like James Thurber and Saul Steinberg, both acknowledged favorites of his, Myers freely crosses conceptual boundaries, anthropomorphizing the inanimate and depersonalizing the human.

As a freelance artist, Myers has provided illustrations for Columbia Pictures and 20th Century-Fox and has added his distinctive artwork to numerous books of fiction and humor since he illustrated Oscar Lebeck's *Clementine* in 1950. He has also been an author in his own right. Besides *Tutti Frutti* (1967), *Ha Ha Hyenas* (1971), and *In Plenty of Time* (1972), all written and drawn for children, he has been a frequent contributor of fictionalized reminiscences to the *New Yorker*, where he and Thurber are the only contributors to have published both art and prose. His autobiographical novel *When Life Falls It Falls Upside Down* (1990), and a *Bildungsroman* about growing up in the Bronx, was praised for its clear-eyed observations and its successful blend of humor and pathos. However it is on his collections of trenchant cartoons, including *A Psychiatric Glossary* (1962), *Group Therapy* (1965), and *Absent and Accounted For* (1980), that his reputation as a creative artist is likely to rest.

D.W.

MYRTLE
See Right Around Home.

Nn

NADAR
See Tournachon, Gaspard-Félix.

NAGAHARA, SHISUI (1864-1930) Japanese cartoonist and artist born in Gifu Prefecture in 1864. Son of a samurai family, Shisui Nagahara first made his name as a student of the famous Western oil painter Shōtarō Koyama, but in the mid-1890s he turned to pen and ink to create many cartoons of stinging social and political satire. In 1893 he produced the cartoon magazine *Tobae*. There he introduced such works as *Fūfu* ("The Married Couple"), an earthy cartoon which symbolized the suffering of the lower classes: a man and woman struggle on a muddy road to push a cart carrying their possessions. Typical of Nagahara's early works, this cartoon showed the artist's sympathy for the common people.

In January 1896, Nagahara began to draw the back cover illustrations for the literary magazine *Mezamashigusa* ("Awakening Grass"), published by the famous novelist Ogai Mori. Nagahara continued to do the artwork for this publication until 1902, a span of approximately five years. *Mezamashigusa* provided Nagahara with a highly prestigious intellectual outlet for his political and satirical cartoons, but his drawings remained straightforward, unaffected attacks on the ridiculousness that could be found in a society trying too hard to modernize too fast.

One of Nagahara's most famous techniques was the "split frame," in which he contrasted two pictures or situations to produce a comic result. One such cartoon shows a woman washing rice in a river, and in the accompanying frame, a stack of chamber pots that have obviously just been washed a little farther upstream. Another famous example is Nagahara's drawing of people watching monkeys and monkeys watching people. Nagahara's cartoons were always simple, and his satire clear and to the point. The qualities most obvious in his work were wit, humor, charm and an unending sympathy with the human plight.

Nagahara himself lived a very quiet life. In the 1890s he became an employee of the Tokyo Imperial University's science department, where he drew illustrations for reference books on plants. In 1898 he became an instructor of Western art at Tokyo Bijutsu Gakko (now Geijutsu Daigaku, or Tokyo University of Art), where he taught until his death in 1930.

J.C.

NAKAMURA, FUSETSU (1868-1943) Japanese artist, cartoonist and calligrapher born in Nagano Prefecture in 1868. Fusetsu Nakamura was born into a wealthy family under the name Kintaro Nakamura. He studied art under Shōtarō Koyama and Kakoto Asai before starting his career as an illustrator and drawer of *sagashi-e* ("puzzle pictures," or pictures which have other pictures cleverly concealed within them). In 1893, along with another famous contemporary, Beisen Kubota, Nakamura drew cartoons of the lower classes for the "Saiankoku no Tokyo" ("Blackest Tokyo") section of the socialist newspaper *Kokumin Shimbun* ("People's News"). His works reflected the concern for the masses of the socialist movement of the late 1880s. Typical cartoons included "A View of the Caverns of Poor People," "Steel Workers" and "Farmers." His drawings also appeared in such literary magazines of the time as *Taiyo* ("The Sun"), published in 1895, and *Hototogisu* ("Nightingale"), published in 1897.

Nakamura called his cartoons *haiga*, an allusion to the literary arts of *haiku* and *haikai*. In using this term to describe his work, he attempted to dissociate it from the cartoons found in the *Punch*-style humor magazines that had grown so popular since the start of the Meiji period (1868-1912). Whether his style actually differed from that of the popular cartoons of the period is difficult to tell, but Nakamura was nevertheless a bridge between the arts of premodern Japan and the turbulent era of self-expression that followed Japan's entry into the modern world. Indeed, Nakamura was representative of the early cartoonists who patterned their work after the light, flippant verses of the *haikai* poets of the Edo period. A collection of his art, *Fusetsu Haiga* ("Drawings of Fusetsu"), even included famous words of the Chinese philosophers Laotse and Confucius, quoted in such a way that they seemed to be praising Nakamura's cartoons. Such frivolity was certainly not part of the modern tradition, but Nakamura also traveled to France, where he studied Western painting, and he is credited with having established an association for the appreciation of Western art, the Taiheiyō Gakai. He became a staff cartoonist for the Nihon Shimbun ("Japan Newspaper") in 1898, evidence that he was concerned with contemporary events as well as traditional literary pastimes.

Nakamura's cartoons reflect his classical upbringing. His brushstrokes closely resemble the simple doodlings the early 19th century poets drew next to their poems (a style frequently encountered in the early Meiji period). Nakamura's significance lies in his transitional role during the early development of the Japanese political cartoon. His simple brush drawings became important visual statements about the socialist movement and the tensions of modernization. Nakamura, however, eventually turned to calligraphy. He built a museum dedicated to the art of Japanese and Chinese writing and spent his later years perfecting his skills as a calligrapher. He died in 1943.

J.C.

NANBU, SHŌTARO (1918-1976) Japanese cartoonist born in Osaka, Japan, on November 23, 1918. As a cartoonist Shōtaro Nanbu was unique in that he never left his home city to move to Tokyo, the capital, as virtually all Japanese artists do. After graduating from a technical school in Osaka, he began working for an architectural firm as a draftsman, but he lost his job when World War II ended. Unemployed and at a loss for what to do, Nanbu turned to cartooning and produced a little piece apparently based on his life at that time. He approached the editor of the newspaper *Osaka Shimbun* without much confidence and was surprised when his work was actually accepted.

This break resulted in *Yaneura 3chan,* a strip depicting the humorous life of 3chan, or Sanchan *(san* in Japanese means "three"), which began running in the *Osaka Shimbun* in January 1946. *Yaneura 3chan* was one of the first newspaper cartoons to appear after the end of the war, and it gained instant popularity with its humorous depiction of the problems most people were then experiencing. Living in a room above a barbershop (hence the title of the piece), 3chan was unemployed and disheveled but tried to conduct himself with as much class as possible. Japan in 1946, however, was a land of charred ruins, innumerable thieves, food rationing and constant power blackouts. When 3chan went to the public baths all his clothes were stolen; he bought books in braille so he could read during the blackouts; and he never lost a chance to eat a morsel of food or make a few yen.

As Japan gradually rose from the ashes of defeat, *Yaneura 3chan* declined in popularity, and in 1950 it finally stopped appearing. Nanbu apparently had a nervous breakdown around this time, claiming than he could no longer draw a straight line (although his works were characterized by their humorous wriggly lines). Then, in September 1966, *Yaneura 3chan* was revived in the evening edition of the *Asahi Shimbun,* but it disappeared suddenly after a month, to be replaced by Susumu Nemoto's *Kurichan.* Shōtaro Nanbu virtually vanished from the public eye after 1966. He continued to draw cartoons locally in Osaka but never turned out anything that ranked with *Yaneura 3chan*. On November 5, 1976, he finally died, and his funeral was widely attended by Osaka cartoonists, who saw in him a local example of a greatness all of them hoped to attain.

F.S.

NANKIVELL, FRANK ARTHUR (1869-1959) American artist born in Maldon, Victoria, Australia, in 1869. Frank Nankivell studied art at Wesley College, Melbourne, and intended to study further in Paris. He sailed for France at age 21 but ran out of funds in Japan. There he cartooned for a living; from 1891 to 1894 he was on the staff of the English-language *Box of Curios.* He made the acquaintance of young Rakuten Kitazawa, taught him editorial cartooning and brought him on the staff as its only Oriental. Kitazawa later became the father of Japanese comic art and the founder of *Tokyo Puck* (presumably named after the New York Puck, of which Nankivell was by then staff member), whose title became the generic term for "cartoon magazine" in Japanese. Nankivell left Japan in 1894 to study art in San Francisco; there he published *Chic,* a

New Year, 1905: "Cleaning House."

Frank Nankivell. © Puck.

Puck imitation, and drew for the *Call,* the *Examiner* and the *Chronicle*. In 1896 he moved to New York and joined the staff of Puck, where he remained until 1909 (except for some intermittent work for Hearst). It is reported that during the Depression Nankivell worked in the Graphic Arts Division of the Federal Arts Project.

If Nankivell was influenced by his stay in the Orient, he seldom manifested it in his later work. A cartoonist whose style reflected the latest art trends, he was among the organizers of the 1913 Armory Show. Nankivell never shied from his subject, and this integrity of purpose in concepts and execution was devoted mainly to social subjects or to state and local political issues. He died on July 4, 1959.

R.M.

NAST, THOMAS (1840-1902) American cartoonist born in Landau, Bavaria, on September 27, 1840. Thomas Nast came to America with his family in 1846, entered the Academy of Design and immediately sought employment as an artist with *Frank Leslie's Illustrated Newspaper.* The lad of 15 was hired and began drawing news sketches and cartoons on wood. In 1859 he switched to the *New York Illustrated News,* which sent him abroad; while drawing for that paper (and for the *Illustrated London News),* he became a very biased artist-reporter, traveling with his hero Garibaldi in Italian campaigns.

Shortly after his return to America in 1861, Nast was engaged by *Harper's Weekly*. His bold signature soon became as distinctive as his themes and presentations; Nast was an instant institution. Politically he was a reformer. During the Civil War he was so effective as a Northern partisan that Lincoln called him "our best

Thomas Nast, political cartoon of the 1880s.

recruiting sergeant." In the realm of social subjects, he depicted family life and introduced the now-accepted image of Santa Claus through hundreds of sympathetic cartoons.

Nast's reputation spread after the Civil War. He was a Republican and vigorously defended his friend Ulysses S. Grant; otherwise he was generally a liberal. His greatest influence—indeed, the greatest influence ever achieved by any American political cartoonist—came during the crusade against the corrupt New York political machine known as the Tweed Ring. It culminated in an 1871 series of cartoons that have seldom been equalled in savagery and effectiveness. Almost every member of Tammany Hall was voted out of office, hounded by the law or, like William Marcy Tweed himself, forced to flee the country. It would be presumptuous—even redundant, since every high school civics class studies Nast's campaign—to attempt to fully chronicle the great Tweed cartoons. Among the most famous, however, are "The Tammany Tiger Let Loose-What Are You Going to Do About It? Twas Him" and "Let Us Prey; A Group of Vultures Waiting for the Storm to Pass Over."Nast did not temper his venom after the Ring's dissolution. In 1872 President Grant was challenged by Horace Greeley, the Democratic and Liberal Republican presidential candidate. The cartoonist ripped into the eccentric reformer with such vitriol that Greeley's death just after the campaign was attributed as much to Nast as to Greeley's loss of the election and the death of his wife a month before. The first of Nast's several books, *The Fight in Dame Europa's School*, appeared about this time, as did a succession of annual *Nast's Almanacs.*

Nast, at the time the most powerful influence on public opinion in all of journalism, worked smoothly with Fletcher Harper and George William Curtis of *Harper's.* In the early 1880s, however, the paper became more Mugwump, and Nast more conservative. In addition, friction of a purely personal nature arose. Perhaps inevitably, Nast's cartoons grew a bit stale, and the public seemed to tire of them. Also, *Puck* was leading the field of political cartooning with weekly masterpieces in full color, stealing some of Nast's glamour and novelty appeal. All these factors made for increasing strain between Nast and *Harper's*.

In 1886 he severed his connection with *Harper's*—an action that led to a decline in influence for both Nast and the paper—and formed an association with the struggling *New York Graphic,* flagship paper in a syndicate of Democrat-financed organs. In the pages of the *Graphic,* Nast used his pen on Grover Cleveland's behalf during the campaign of 1888. Thereafter his powers as an artist and partisan—and with them his influence—waned. The rest of his career was a sad succession of short stints on minor papers, erratic chalk-talk lectures and soured business investments. It wasn't just that the public had tired of him; his talents had deteriorated markedly, and his material was embarrassingly bad—an all the more tragic state of affairs for a man still under 50 years of age.

After the *Graphic,* Nast drew for *Time, America, Once-A-Week,* the *Illustrated American,* the *Chicago Inter-Ocean*, the *New York Gazette* and others. His own paper, *Nast's Weekly*, was a dream come true, but it prospered only while it was a fully subsidized organ of the Republican party. Nast's career ended with a charity appointment by Theodore Roosevelt, another of his heroes, as consul to Guayaquil, Ecuador, where he died on November 7, 1902.

The twilight years of his cartooning service cannot detract from the incalculable importance of Nast in his prime. Very simply, he defined the form of the political cartoon for future generations and set the boundaries of taste, judgment and fairness. That he recognized very few boundaries makes his work and legacy all the more significant. Nast made the political cartoonist in America a force to be reckoned with and removed the cloak of anonymity from his profession. He was the first to fully utilize cartoon icons and himself invented many such symbols, like the Republican elephant. Every political cartoonist since the 1870s has been in Nast's debt, consciously or otherwise; in format, themes, symbols, invective and many other ways the traditions are largely his.

Nast's drawing skills, strangely enough, were not outstanding. Although he could and did produce some stunning graphic masterpieces, most of what he drew was stylistically and artistically unimpressive. In his prime, of course, Nast never drew more than sketches that were transferred by another hand to the wood block for engraving; it is probable that more talented artists improved his work. Little matter, really, for it was his concepts and compositions that were most important, not their execution. And his compositions were devastatingly powerful. Technically, his cartoons were loaded with crosshatch shading and sometimes dozens of labels. Even in decline he was a pioneer—his *InterOcean* cartoons (1892-93) were among the first in newspaper color anywhere.

It is a rare and fascinating thing in any of the arts when a pioneer not only defines a form but also, in the estimation of succeeding generations, remains its foremost exponent. In the field of political cartoons, many have occasionally matched the brilliance of Thomas Nast, but none have surpassed him.

R.M.

NASU, RYŌSUKE (1913-1989) Japanese political cartoonist born in Kumamoto Prefecture on the island of Kyushu, Japan, on April 16, 1913. Ryōsuke Nasu is well known in Japan today as the political cartoonist for the *Mainichi* newspaper. His style is characterized by a very direct approach that emphasizes the intrinsic ugliness of politics.

Nasu graduated from Taihei Bijutsu Gakko (the Pacific Art School) but did not attract much attention until he began drawing cartoons for the magazine *Manga* around 1939. At the time, *Manga* was the publication of a cartoonists' group that supported the national policy of militarism, and Hidezo Kondo was its main driving force. With the start of the war with the United States, Nasu's cartoons, as well as those of other *Manga* artists, began to fiercely attack the Allies. Nasu was also hired by the propaganda section of the military general staff to create cartoons that would demoralize enemy troops. These generally relied on portraying the Allies as aggressors and appealing to a Pan-Asian sense of solidarity among the native peoples of Southeast Asia.

After the end of World War II, Nasu continued writing for *Manga* (which was revived, but not necessarily in support of the government this time) and began drawing for the *Mainichi* newspaper, where he remains today. He also submitted cartoons regularly to *Manga Dokuhon* and to *Report*, an exposé magazine that was popular after the war. His work, however, is not confined to caricatures of politicians and policies, for around 1954 he also created a children's work, *Shoboten Mura no Abareuma*, which appeared in *Gekkan Kodomo Manga*.

In 1959 Nasu published a collection of his political cartoons from the Mainichi titled *Yoshida kara Kishi e:Seiji Manga Jyūnen* ("Ten Years of Political Cartoons: From Yoshida to Kishi"). It consisted primarily of works critical of the ruling Liberal Democratic party from the time of Prime Minister Yoshida to that of Kishi. On the other side of the political spectrum, however, Nasu also contributed to Hidezō Kondō's *Anpō ga Wakaru* ("I Understand the Security Treaty," 1969). This collection of cartoons supporting the then highly controversial U.S.-Japan Security Treaty was a major boost in the arm to the ruling but beleaguered Liberal Democratic party (which eventually bought a majority of the books). Nasu's cartoons characterized the Soviet Union as a huge bear gazing hungrily at Japan's northern territories, depicted as a little fish.

Those who are not killed in battle: At the attack on Port Arthur, a Japanese colonel whose regiment was decimated gave the order to retreat. The next day he was shot by a firing squad.

Bernard Naudin, 1904.

Nasu passed away in 1989, and in the same year construction began in his home town on a museum for his work.

F.S.

NAUDIN, BERNARD (1876-1946) French cartoonist and etcher born in Chateauroux, France on November 11, 1876. Bernard Naudin received art lessons first from his father, who was an amateur draftsman and sculptor, then from Bonnat at the Paris Ecole des Beaux-Arts. He gave music lessons until he started contributing to *Le Cri de Paris,* whose success stemmed largely from his drawings.

He then worked for *L'Assiette au Beurre* (1904-09), where cartoons such as those attacking the penal system or life in the Foreign Legion announced many of the themes later to be found in *La Vierge au Galvaudeux* ("The Virgin with the Tramp," 1917) and *Les Afflige's* ("The Afflicted"), moving etchings of the downtrodden masses. Naudin is also famous for his depictions of military scenes witnessed on World War I battlefronts, especially *Dessins pour le Bulletin des Armees de 1a Republique* ("Drawings for the Bulletin of the Armies of the Republic," 1916), *Croquis de Campagne* ("Campaign Sketches," 1915) and *La Guerre, Madame* ("The War, Madam," 1918).

In addition to etching portraits of Beethoven and Chopin, publishing a collection of his work (1916-20) and illustrating his own novels, he illustrated Poe's "The Gold Bug" (1929), Villon's "Testaments" and Diderot's *Rameau's Nephew (1922),* among others. All these show most noticeably the influence of Rembrandt and Goya. Bernard Naudin died in a Paris suburb on March 7, 1946.

P.H.

NAVARRO, OSVALDO (1893-1965) Brazilian cartoonist born in Andrade Pinto, in the state of Rio de Janeiro, Brazil, in 1893. When Osvaldo Navarro was a child, his family moved to the town of Barbacena, Minas Geraés, and it was there that he completed his art studies. From Barbacena he sent his first cartoon to the Rio publication Caréta in 1913, thus initiating a long and fruitful collaboration with this magazine.

In 1917 Navarro moved to Rio. Signing simply "Osvaldo," he contributed to such publications as *RioJornal, D. Quixote, Razão* and *A Rajada*. For the pages of *A Rajada* he drew the famous character Jeca Tatu, on texts supplied by the writer José Monteiro Lobato. He also did caricatures for *Alterosa,* a magazine published in Belo Horizonte. He returned to Barbacena in 1928 and died there in 1965.

A.M.

NED AND HIS NEDDY (Australia) Without question the most liked cartoon of its kind, Ken Maynard's *Ned and His Neddy* occupies almost a full page in the *Australasian Post.* Ned is a bush horseman, and "neddy" is old-time slang for a horse. The two title characters are never involved in the action of the cartoon but are simply observers of the robust humor that has been consistently excellent year after year—the more admirable because Australian cartoonists have to create their own jokes and do not employ gag writers to feed them comic ideas. Most of the fun in the cartoon takes place inside, outside or near the "Ettamogah" pub. And, in a sense echoing Percy Leason's "Wiregrass" drawings of the 1930s, Maynard crams his Ettamogah landscape with random groups of figures and incidental but fitting detail.

Since the start of the panel in January 1959, a strange cockatoo-parrot has been flying around the skies of Maynard's cartoons, shod in large lace-up farm boots. The artist has made this curious creature his personal trademark, prompting the inevitable question from many readers: "Why the boots?" To this question the shy, soft-spoken Maynard invariably answers: Because the tin roofs of the outback houses are too hot to land on barefoot!" The feature was discontinued in the 1990s.

Ken Maynard was born at Albury on the Murray River in June 1928. At the age of 21 he raced with the Albury-Wodonga Cycle Club and won a 50-mile senior state championship. For 20 years Maynard was a uniformed traffic policeman in Melbourne, but bad health forced his retirement from the force. He is a self-taught cartoonist, and his pen-and-ink drawings, which take from eight to ten hours to complete, have been published in trade magazines, in the newspapers the Argus and Truth, on T-shirts and in a book of his Ettamogah cartoons published a few years ago.

V.L.

NEHREBECKI, WLADYSLAW (1923-1978) Polish animator born in Boryslaw, Poland, in 1923. Wladyslaw Nehrebecki began his career as an illustrator after World War II, soon switching to cartooning. He became one of Poland's first postwar animators, starting at the animated film studio of Bielsko-Biala in the early 1950s. He made his directorial debut in 1952 with an unpretentious little fable, *The Woodpecker Told the Owl*. Later films include: *The Adventures of Gucio the Penguin*, a 1953 exercise that predates Tex Avery's *Chilly Willy; The Gossipy Duck* (1954); and two cartoons featuring a mild-mannered savant, *Professor Filutek in the Park* and *The Strange Dream of Professor Filutek* (1955-56).

In 1958 Nehrebecki produced his much-awarded *Myszka i Kotek* ("Cat and Mouse"), in which he used a simple line drawn on film to depict the adventures of his title characters; the technique was to set a trend in animated film-making. He then made a series of cutout and puppet films, the most notable being the 1959 *Tournament*. Between 1960 and 1963, he went back to cartoon animation, producing such films as *The Little Chimney Sweep, The Helicopter, The Crossbow* and *Beyond the Forest, Beyond the Woods.*

In 1963 Nehrebecki directed *The Two Knights*. The success of these cartoon adventures of a mischievous pair of boys, Lolek and Bolek, led to a television series that began in 1964. From then on Nehrebecki devoted most of his efforts to TV animation, working not only on *Bolek i Lolek* but on other series as well (*The Adventures of the Little Blue Knight, Our Grandpa, The Kidnapping of Baltazar Sabka* and others). He occasionally directed an independent cartoon, such as the 1966 *Vendetta*, but since 1973 he has been busy turning out the unprecedentedly popular *Bolek i Lolek* cartoons (including a full-length compilation feature, *Bolek and Lolek Around the World*, released in 1975). He died in Warsaw in 1978.

One of the most prolific of Polish animators, Nehrebecki has yielded to the common temptations of glibness and repetitiveness. Though his *Bolek i Lolek* and other TV cartoons are fresh and often entertaining, Nehrebecki will be remembered for his earlier, more innovative films. In this connection it is interesting to note that the artist's many awards (at Cork, Oberhausen, Bergamo and other places) were received for his pre-1970 works.

M.H.

NELAN, CHARLES (1854-1904) American artist born in Akron, Ohio, on April 10, 1854. Talent and ambition led the young Charles Nelan to parlay his grocery clerkship into a perpetual life class; he retained the job long enough to save money for a trip to New York, where his art samples proved sufficient to gain him entry to the National Academy School. After a year, he earned the Elliot medal there. But money to sustain his art studies ran out, and Nelan returned to Akron and grocery clerking for six years. In 1888 he secured a position as cartoonist for the *Cleveland Press* and was soon picked up by the other papers of the Scripps-McRae League, thus becoming probably the first syndicated newspaper editorial cartoonist. At this time, he was famous largely in the Midwest.

In 1897 he was lured to the *New York Herald* to replace the great Charles Green Bush, who was switching to the World after scoring some outstanding hits with his cartoons. The Spanish-American War broke out shortly after Nelan's arrival in New York, and he gained greater fame because of a series of clever and sage comments on the war and America's "Manifest Destiny." In 1899 he was offered a huge contract by the *Philadelphia North American* to be its daily cartoonist. He accepted the post and remained there until his death at Clay Springs, Georgia, on December 7, 1904.

"The boy stood on the burning deck."
Charles Nelan, 1898.

Charles Nelan paved the way for the daily editorial cartoonists in America and proved that partisanship was a salable commodity. His drawing style was a bit stiff (it was asserted after his death that his wife always had to rescue him from a bugaboo by drawing female figures herself) but was always forceful, not unlike that of Homer Davenport. And like Davenport, Bernard Gillam, Robert Carter and others, Nelan proved that a hired penman could shift his own preferences yet remain an amazingly effective advocate. Nelan published one anthology, *Cartoons of Our War with Spain* (Stokes, 1898).

R.M.

NELL BRINKLEY NARRATIVE PAGES (U.S.) A series of continued full-color graphic narratives, drawn and captioned weekly by Nell Brinkley for the front cover of the *Hearst American Weekly* newspaper magazine-supplement over some twenty years, the "Nell Brinkley Narrative Pages" (they had no formal continuing title in themselves) ran an average of ten weeks per story. They typically consisted of one full-page drawing each week (although there were sometimes subsidiary drawings on the page) and emphasized the sprightlier sides of young romance, superbly limned in Brinkley's intricate webs of line work.

The first narrative was titled *"Golden-Eyes" and Her Hero, "Bill"* and ran from March 31, 1918, to May 5, 1918, for six episodes. It dealt lightly with an American enlistee in World War I, his betrothed and her pet collie, Uncle Sam. A sequel picture-story called *"Golden-Eyes" and Her Hero, "Bill," Over There* ran from September 15, 1918, to

A Nell Brinkley page, 1925. © International Feature Service.

February 23, 1919, for 15 episodes (it didn't appear every week, but ran irregularly) and was much wilder and woolier than the first story, involving battle and bloodshed on the Western Front for all characters (Golden-Eyes was a nurse, Uncle Sam a war dog, etc.).

This war-inspired series was popular with *American Weekly* readers, and on November 7, 1920, a third narrative began. *Kathleen and the Great Secret* continued weekly for 18 episodes until March 13, 1921, and again involved two young lovers in worldwide adventures, from camel's back to cockpit. It was followed by Brinkley's best-liked serial, *Betty and Billy—and Their Love Through the Ages*, which began on December 18, 1921, and continued for 23 episodes to June 4, 1922. It told of the reincarnation of the hero and heroine against successive, colorful historical backgrounds, from caveman culture to the 1920s.

Other serials appeared at greater intervals as Brinkley's daily newspaper and magazine work for Hearst increased. Eventually, in the late 1920s, they moved onto the cover of the Saturday magazine section of the Hearst newspapers, the *Home* magazine, where her last narrative pages appeared, named for such starry-eyed flappers as "Dimples," "Pretty Polly" and "Sunny Sue."

Intensely followed, collected and often even framed by her devoted and largely female readers from 1900 through the 1930s, Brinkley's color narrative pages are still visually striking and fascinating when encountered in the pages of old bound volumes of the Hearst papers. They have considerable value as period prints.

B.B.

NEPP, JÓZSEF (1934-) Hungarian animator born in Budapest, Hungary, on June 23, 1934. József Nepp graduated from the Budapest Academy of Fine Arts in 1957 and immediately went to work in animation, introducing the popular *Gustavus* series of cartoons in the late 1950s. Nepp then concentrated on more adult subjects, which he treated with great economy of line, sense of humor and timing. *Passion* (1961) is a winking look at a *ménage-à-trois,* and *Wish Whatever You Want* (1962) is a lighthearted fantasy, as is *From Tomorrow* On (1963). The 1966 *Five Minutes of Murder* is a black comedy that shows Nepp at his most imaginative, depicting with deadpan earnestness the ingenious lengths to which his characters will go to dispatch one another.

József Nepp, "Evolu." © Pannonia Film.

Nepp's output has somewhat diminished recently. He directed *Don't Imitate the Mouse* in 1967 and scripted *Modern Sports Coaching,* a satire on the teeth-grinding techniques of contemporary athletic training, in 1972. With the exception of the winsome but slight *Portrait* (1974), little has been heard from Nepp in the last few years.

M.H.

NERVY NAT (U.S.) Nearly forgotten today, *Nervy Nat* was the cartoon series that firmly established James Montgomery Flagg as a major figure in American graphic humor. Further, it contributed greatly to the emergence of

"Nervy Nat." © Judge.

the comic strip and the tramp as her—a development that, ironically, was otherwise taking place in newspapers, the media arch-rivals of magazines such as *Judge,* where *Nervy Nat* held sway between 1903 and 1907.

Flagg depicted a ne'er-do-well tramp not as innocent as Happy Hooligan or even Chaplin—in various escapades with railroad police, rich bankers, flirting nurses and the like. It has been reported that W.C. Fields modeled his Tramp Juggler outfit and character after Nat, and their bulbous noses, if nothing else, tend to confirm this. Nat also used hopelessly flowery language. The drawing style was loose and cartoony; Flagg had not yet fallen prey to the slavish attempt to appropriate Gibson's line techniques, a failing that characterized his pen-and-ink illustrations throughout much of his career. *Nervy Nat* appeared in both color and black and white in either 6 or 12 panels per episode, with text under each. The series was numbered, was enormously popular and was reprinted in book form by *Judge.*

In 1907 Flagg left *Judge* to join *Life* exclusively as cartoonist (although he expanded his illustration assignments). *Judge* continued *Nervy Nat* in a second series, drawn with remarkable approximation to the Flagg style by Arthur Lewis; Nat was a bit taller and thinner, but all the trappings of Flagg's delightful cartooning remained. Flagg's work on the series merits republication and fresh appreciation; it is a classic of comic characterization, deflated sham and freewheeling inventiveness.

Nervy Nat was adapted to animation in 1916 by Pat Sullivan.

R.M.

NEWELL, PETER (1862-1924) American cartoonist and children's novelty author born Sheaf Hersey in McDonough County, Illinois, on March 5, 1862. Peter Newell was raised on the family farm in Bushnell, Illinois, and left home at about 17 years of age. Determined to draw, he entered the Art Students League in New York. His drawings appeared in the mid-1890s in children's magazines and the comic weeklies, particularly Judge. His first sale was to *Harper's Bazaar,* the first magazine in which he had seen cartoons. He sent a drawing and inquired whether it indicated talent; the editor replied that he discerned no talent, but he sent a check in payment for the accepted cartoon.

For *Judge* Newell specialized in novelty drawings and visual tricks—upside-down cartoons, etc. This was his forte in books, too, and he was more of a success in the field of humorous illustrated children's books (with huge adult readerships). They employed novel devices like die cuts, slanted pages, camouflaged objects, etc. Notable among them were: *Topsys and Turveys* (1893); *Topsys and Turveys No. 2* (1894); *A Shadow Show* (1896); Peter Newell's *Pictures and Rhymes* (1898); *Alice in Wonderland* (1901); *The Hole Book* (1908); *Jungle Jangle* (1909); *The Slant Book* (1910); and *The Rocket Book* (1912). Several of his books have recently been reprinted by Dover.

Most of Newell's creative period was spent in the artists' colony at Leonia, New Jersey. He was always active with his cartoons, books, and magazine illustrations and even drew a handsome fantasy comic strip, *Polly Sleepyhead,* about 1905. His work stands as a monument to a dazzling imagination and creative fecundity. Newell died at his home in Little Neck, New York, on January 15, 1924.

R.M.

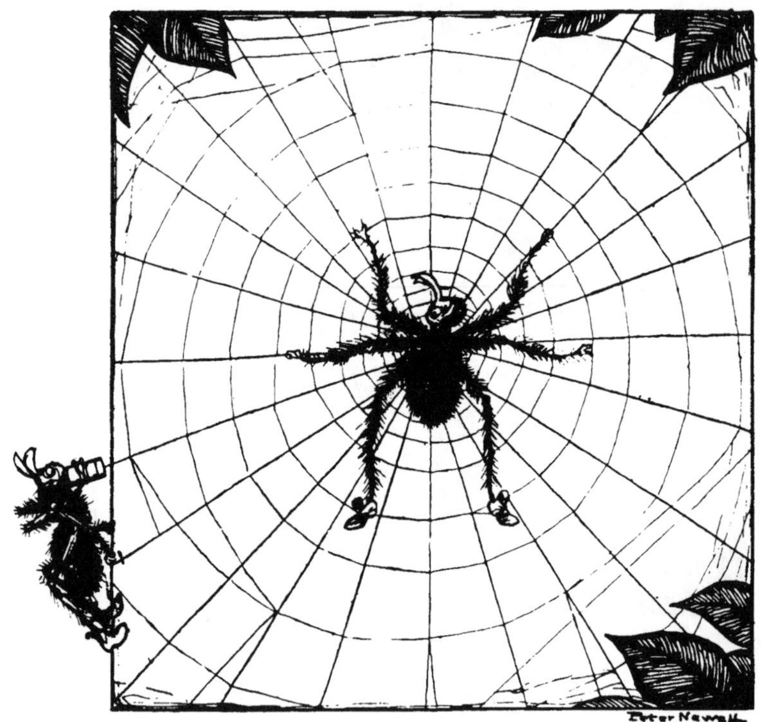

Peter Newell, 1903.

NOBLE, JOE (1894-197?) British animator, writer and director born in Manchester, England, on Christmas Day, 1894. Joe (born Charles) Noble was the son of a notable equine artist, Charles Noble. Joe won a scholarship from a "sixpence-a-week" school and studied art at All Saints School of Art, Manchester. He went to work as his father's assistant in the studio of David Allanand Sons, the leading poster designers and printers of the theatrical profession, where his father was chief artist. Joe designed his first solo poster in 1910, advertising *Ragtime,* a show starring Maud Tiffany. He then came down to London to join E.P. Kinsella, a top poster man of the period, but found himself fascinated by the animated cartoons from America that were becoming the rage: *The Animated Grouch Chasers* by Raoul Barré and *Colonel Heezaliar.* After he served his time in the army, 1919 found him working for the *Daily Cinema News,* designing the "art titles" for the newsreel series. He graduated to title designing for J. Stuart Blackton, the Vitagraph producer (and ex-cartoonist) who was making a picture in London called *The Gypsy Cavalier,* starring Georges Carpentier.

Noble's first brush with animation came in 1920, when he joined Kine Komedy Kartoons at 66 Shaftesbury Avenue (upstairs from the *Daily Cinema News* office). There he assisted Dudley Buxton and the visiting American animator Vet Anderson, learning the rudiments of the trade. Then he moved to Brentford to work for Broda-Jenkins, animating key sketches by two newspaper cartoonists, Tom Titt and W.D. Ford. Tom Aitken, an American war correspondent working for the theatrical agency of Edelstein and Burns, promoted an animated cartoon of Tom Webster's Tishy, the racehorse that crossed her legs! Noble took over the animation from Ford and worked with Margie Hutchinson (ex-Kine Komedy Kartoons) as a tracer to complete the film by Tuesday, December 12, 1922—the night of a royal performance for King George V and Queen Mary at the London Hippodrome.

In 1923 Noble became production manager for Visual Education, Ltd., animating diagram films on a variety of subjects, and in 1924 he rejoined Dudley Buxton for a series called Bongo, which failed to materialize. Tom Webster reentered the animation stakes in 1925, and Noble worked with the ace American animator Dick Friel on the *Alf and* Steve series (a horse and his jockey). Then Noble and Webster produced animation sequences for a unique musical revue at the Criterion Theatre, Piccadilly, entitled Cartoons.

Sammy and Sausage, Noble's first solo series (with Brian White assisting), was made for regular inclusion in the Pathe' Pictorial and *Eve's Film Review,* both "magazine film" series issued by Pathe' Pictures during 1926-27. In 1928 he began production on the first British sound cartoon, *Orace the Armonious Ound,* using a lip-synchronizing system of his own devising. Produced at the Wembley Studio of British Sound Films, the short was shown in January 1929. Also at Wembley, Noble made the first British animated commercial with sound, *Mr. York of York, Yorks,* for Rowntree's chocolate. Live-action sequences were directed by Bertram Phillips, and the character of Mr. York was created by cartoonist Alfred Leete. In 1933 he joined Brian White and Sid Griffiths on their Raycol color cartoons, based on H.M. Bateman drawings. But most of Noble's work was done for Pathé, for whom he not only supplied animation inserts as required for stories in their *Pathé Pictorial* series but also wrote and directed innumerable live-action sequences and stories. He left Pathé in 1945 to work on naval training films for the Directorate of Naval Training. Apart from a number of animated advertisements, his last important work was animating the fantasy sequences on the British Federation Pictures feature Mr. H.C. Andersen (1950). He died in the late 1970s.

D.G.

NOÉ, AMÉDÉE (1819-1879) French caricaturist born in Paris, France, on January 26, 1819. Having failed his entrance exam to the Ecole Polytechnique, Count de Noé went to work for a short time at the Finance Ministry. He then embarked on his cartooning career (1839), taking the name of Noah's son Cham (Noé is Noah in French).

Cham's most important albums are *La Bourse Illustrée* ("The Illustrated Stock Exchange"), *Nouvelles Leçons de Puérilité Civile* ("New Lessons for Children's Behavior"), *Histoire Comique de l'Assemblée Nationale* ("Comic History of the National Assembly") and *Promenades à l'Exposition* ("Walking Through the Exhibition Halls"). In these and in his 30-year contributions to *Le Charivari,* Cham chronicled with comic verve and exaggeration French pomposity and foibles, especially during the Second Empire. However, even in his jingoistic and unflattering portrayals of the invading Prussian soldiers, he was never biting or cruel; he was indeed a caricaturist for whom wit, not meanness,

The cravat is just as irksome to women as the crinoline is to men.
Amédée de Noé ("Cham").

was the basis of both his art and his captions.

In the 1850s and 1860s Cham also wrote many year-end theatrical reviews that are full of unbridled, madcap silliness and fun. Although forgotten today, he died at his Paris home on September 6, 1879, a very famous man.

P.H.

NOGGIN THE NOG (G.B.) "In the lands of the North, where the black rocks stand guard against the cold sea, in the dark night that is very long, the Men of the Northlands sit by their great log fires and they tell a tale. They tell of a Prince and how he built a long ship and sailed beyond the black ice at the Edge of the World to bring home his bride from the Land of the Midnight Sun."

Thus begins The *Saga of Noggin the Nog,* son of Knut, king of the Nogs, and Queen Grunhilda. His epic journey takes him to the Land of the Nooks to woo and wed Princess Nooka before his kingdom falls prey to his wicked uncle, Nogbad the Bad. Guided by the great bird Graculus, aided by Arup, king of the Walruses, and beset by many an adventure, Noggin's mission was accomplished to the delight of his people and the joy of millions of children who watched the oft-repeated series on BBC television.

The *Saga of Noggin the Nog* was created, written and narrated by Oliver Postgate, while the drawings, so vital to the success of the series, were by Peter Firmin. Produced by their own Smallfilms Company for BBC, with music by Vernon Elliott, the series was made in 1968 and is the only children's series filmed in black and white that is still regularly shown during school holidays. A number of books and strips were "spun off," and the saga is currently available in a series of ten colored paperbacks published by Kaye and Ward, beginning with King of the Nogs.

D.G.

NOGUÉS I CASES, XAVIER (1873-1941) Spanish cartoonist and illustrator born in Barcelona, Spain, in 1873. Xavier Nogués's first cartoons appeared in 1908 in the weekly

Papitu, under the pen name "Babel" (the use of biblical pseudonyms was typical of the magazine). In 1912 Nogués was named director of the humor magazine *Picarol*, and in 1914 he joined the staff of the literary *Revista Nova*. Later he contributed cartoons and illustrations to most major Spanish publications. Nogués was a respected illustrator as well as a popular cartoonist. He illustrated some very successful children's books and a number of humorous books. In addition, he was a painter of some repute and produced artworks in wood and glass. He died in Barcelona in 1941.

Nogués is now regarded as one of the most important of Spanish cartoonists. His drawings are extraordinary for their ability to evoke the Spain of the first decades of this century. In them, day-to-day Spanish life seems to unfold before our eyes. Nogués seldom allowed any social or political event to escape his keen critical eye and his elegant but biting pen.

J.M.

NON SEQUITUR (1992-) "Non Sequitur" means "It does not follow," but Wiley Miller's popular panel feature of that name follows a growing tradition in the cartoon industry. Like Gary Larson's *The Far Side* and the work of Gahan Wilson before it, *Non Sequitur* views the world from an oblique angle of vision, playing on the absurdity of both the human situation and the language. Ranging from outrageous puns to black humor, the series finds topics for skewed humor in everything from the homeless to mankind's place in the cosmos.

Wylie Miller, who signs his work with his first name, began his career as a political cartoonist with the Greensboro, N.C., *News and Record* in 1976. In 1982 he left political cartooning to do a comic strip, *Fenton*, which ran successfully until 1985, when he was lured back to the editorial fold with a job for the *San Francisco Examiner*. In 1991 he won the Robert F. Kennedy Journalism Award, and in February of the next year began *Non Sequitur*.

The feature was innovative in several ways. A single panel, it often varied the square format by taking the horizontal shape of a strip and it diversifies layout to include multi-panel strips and labeled single panels with dialogue in balloons. It makes fun of comic-book superheroes (one is shown sitting in a squalid apartment while his wife nags, "Accept money from a grateful metropolis? O, Nooooo... not Mr. Ethical-Crime-Fighter-with-Nothing-in-the-Bank," to demonstrate "The Real Reason Superheroes Never Marry"). It delivers revisionist history (a Native American reports to his chief, as Columbus's ships enter the harbor, "I've discovered Europeans!" presented as "Further Evidence That History Is a Matter of Perspective"). And it finds its themes from a sophisticated range of contemporary preoccupations including business, religion, psychology, lawyers, (a favorite target), doctors, and computers.

Miller left editorial cartooning once again in 1992 to give his full time to *Non Sequitur*. The feature was soon picked up by the Washington Post Writers Group, which reports that it is distributed to 400 newspapers in 20 countries. Much admired for graphic elegance, it has won numerous awards. It was named the Comic Strip of the Year by the National Cartoonist Society in 1992 and the Comic Panel of the year in 1995—the only strip to win NCS awards in two divisions. Also in 1995 it was the youngest strip to be voted among the top ten in an *Editor & Publisher* survey, and the next year it was the youngest strip to rank in the top 20 in a survey of comics usage by the largest 100 newspapers in the country.

Two *Non Sequitur* collections have appeared: *Dead Lawyers and Other Pleasant Thoughts* in 1993 and *Non Sequitur Survival Guide for the Nineties* in 1995, and the content of the strip continues to expand. In 1996 it introduced its first recurring character, Homer, whose adventures in various re-incarnations have further enlarged the intellectual range of this literate and ingenious feature.

D.W.

NORRIS, LEONARD MATHESON (1913-) Canadian editorial cartoonist born in London, England, on December 1, 1913. Len Norris was educated in England, in Port Arthur, Ontario, and at the Ontario College of Art in Toronto. From 1938 to 1940 he was employed as an advertising agency art director. During World War II he served as a captain in the Royal Canadian Electrical and Mechanical Engineers and as editor-writer-illustrator for the Canadian army technical magazine *Cam*. From 1945 to 1950 he was an art director for the Maclean-Hunter Publishing Company, then joining the staff of the Vancouver *Sun* in January 1950; he remains with that newspaper at present.

Norris reintroduced to the Western Hemisphere one of the dominant cartooning genres of England and the Continent: the nonpolitical, illustrative, news interpretation cartoon. In England its prime exponent was Carl Giles, and in the United States John Fischetti was later to utilize, and Oliphant to appropriate, the format. Norris carried the form to heights never surpassed. His sarcastic, incisive comments are drawn (usually horizontally and sometimes on his paper's front page) in a wildly funny brush and shading manner. A typical cartoon might contain a dozen visual diversions-adjuncts to the cartoon's telling comment rather than distractions.

Norris is one of the most influential cartoonists in the

"Our careful check of the records reveals that the job of prime minister is currently filled."

Len Norris. © The Vancouver Sun.

world, both within his profession and with the public at large. His annual reprint books have sold over a quarter-million copies a year for the last 25 years. Norris has freelanced extensively in a style vaguely reminiscent of Searle's, working on magazine illustration and even children's books.

He was awarded the military M.B.E. in 1945 and has received the National Newspaper Award for cartooning as well as several Art Directors' Club awards. He was granted an honorary doctor of laws degree by Windsor University in 1973 and was elected to the Royal Canadian Academy of Arts in 1974. He was the subject of a National Film Board documentary, Len Norris, Cartoonist, in 1984; he received the City of Vancouver Merit medal in 1991 and the Hutchinson Lifetime Achievement Award in 1992. He retired in 1995.

His goal, he once stated, is to "interpret the news as it affects ordinary people like me." With his lunatic shots at reality and devastating humor, he is more consistently on the mark than many who strive for weighty analysis.

R.M.

NOVELLI, ENRICO (1876-1943) Italian cartoonist, writer and illustrator born in Pisa, Italy, on June 5, 1876. Enrico Novelli, son of the famous actor Ermete Novelli, wrote his first novel, *Viaggio Sottoterra* ("Journey Underground") at age 14. In 1894 he moved to Milan, working as a newspaperman on *La Sera.* Toward the end of the century he transferred to Rome, where he founded (with others) the satirical publications *Pupazzetto* and *Il Travaso.* Novelli covered World War I as war correspondent; he later worked in the cinema and in 1919 started a puppet theater that toured all of Europe. From 1927 to 1942 he was the director of the daily *Il Nuovo Giornale,* and he died in Florence in December 1943. Novelli is probably better known under the pseudonym "Yambo" as a writer and illustrator of children's stories. He created hundreds of stories and comic strips, from *Ciufettino* to *Capitan Fanfara,* thoroughly traversing the "archipelago of fantasy'—the title of one of his books but also an apt characterization of his artistic activity. In a style that bears comparison with Albert Robida's, Yambo presented a grotesque and deformed vision of our mechanized world. Instead of demystifying his subjects, however, he preferred giving free rein to his fantasy, thereby mocking the seriousness and high pretensions of scientists and engineers.

C.S.

The "tri-carr" driven madly by James.
Enrico Novelli ("Yambo"), illustration for "King of the Worlds." © *Novelli.*

NOVELLO, GIUSEPPE (1897-1981) Italian cartoonist, painter and illustrator born in Codogno, Italy, on July 7, 1897. Giuseppe Novello's law studies at the University of Pavia were interrupted by World War I, and he did not receive his doctorate until 1920. Like other multitalented personalities such as Leo Longanesi and Mino Maccari, Novello is best known for his cartoons, a career he took up in 1923, after three years of study at the Milan School of Fine Arts.

Novello freelanced cartoons and illustrations for a great many publications in the period between the two world wars; his most notable work was done for the *Gazzetta del Popolo* in Turin (1932-38). Many of his cartoons, especially those of the 1920s and 1930s, were reprinted in book form. Titles include: La Guerra E Bella ma Scomoda ("War Is Beautiful but Inconvenient"), an illustrated chronicle of his experiences during World War I, drawn on texts by Paolo Monelli; *Il Sign ore di Buona Famiglia* ("The Well-Born Gentleman," 1934), a kind of humorous epic, grotesque and somewhat bitter, of a middle-class Italian hiding under a cloak of conformity and resignation; *Che Cosa Dirà la Gente?* ("What Will People Say?," 1937); and *Dunque Dicevamo* ("...As I Was Saying...," 1950), in which he resumed the discourse on the middle class that had been interrupted by World War II.

After World War II Novello became a regular contributor to *La Stampa* of Turin with cartoons and illustrations commenting on people and events in the news. He also worked in 1955-56 for the Swiss magazine *Nebelspalter.* Notable among the books of cartoons he published during this period are *Sempre Più Difficile* ("Harder and Harder") and *Resti fra Noi* ("Stay Among *Us").* He died in the 1980s.

Novello is a talented painter who has exhibited widely and received many awards, but it is as a cartoonist that he will be best remembered. His cartoons are devoid of poison and of rage; they reflect, in the words of Paolo Monelli, "the poetry of lowliness, of misfortune, of lack of money, the awkward joys and squalid duties of the meek." But there is a kind of humane and affectionate complicity between the artist and the world he satirizes, because in the last analysis Novello belongs to bourgeois society, in

"Nudnik" model sheet. © Rembrandt Films.

which he proposes no radical changes and with which he wants no definitive break.

C.S.

NUDNIK (U.S./Czechoslovakia) Nudnik is probably the only original cartoon series written and directed by an American producer in an Eastern European studio for distribution in the United States. Working in Prague, Gene Deitch brought out these delightful shorts, which Paramount released theatrically from 1963 to 1967.

Nudnik was an impish, unpredictable little boy whose attempts at exploring the world around him often led to trouble, if not disaster. The cartoons were animated in a winsome and economical style that made full use of the technique of limited drawing. The stories were full of charm, and though they did not display the frantic pace of American animation, they never flagged. In addition to the first cartoon, which was nominated for an Oscar in 1964, some of the most notable entries were "Nudnik on the Roof," "Home Sweet Nudnik," "Good Night, Sweet Nudnik" and the anthology cartoon "I Remember Nudnik."

Deitch once confided that Nudnik was his favorite and most personal character. The series might have matured and achieved success had it been given a chance (only 13 cartoons were made), but it came at a time when theatrical cartoons were being drastically curtailed, and it did not survive.

M.H.

NURIA, POMPEIA (1931-) Spanish cartoonist born in Barcelona, Spain, in 1931. The daughter and granddaughter of distinguished Catalan artists, Pompeia Nuria studied at the Massana School of Art. After graduation she embarked on a career that was interrupted by marriage and the birth of five children. Her first cartoons finally appeared in 1967, in a book called *Maternasis* published by Pierre Tisné in Paris; it was signed simply "9" and dealt with pregnancy and labor. In 1970 she published *Y Fueron Felices Comiendo Perdices* ("And They Lived Happily Ever After"), a book about the feminine condition, followed by *Pels Segles dels Segles* ("Forever and Ever," 1971), with text in Catalan, about the parallelism between religion and drugs. In 1972 came *La Educaci6n de Palmira* on a text by Manuel Vazquez Montalban, and in 1975 Mujercitas ("Little Women").

Nuria started working for magazines with her successful *Metamoifosis* series of cartoons, which appeared in *Triunfo* in 1968 and was later reprinted in several foreign magazines. She has also worked for many other publications, including *Sabado Gráfico, Cuadernos para el Diálogo* and *Cuadernos de Pedagogía,* and for the daily newspapers *El Correo Cotalán, Avui* and the now defunct *Diario Femenino.* Her work now appears in the magazine *Por Favor*, where she draws a full page of cartoons, *Nosotros las Mujeres Objeto/ras* ("We the Women Object/ors"), and in the new feminist magazine *Opcíon.*

Nuria's professional leitmotif is the struggle for the intellectual, physical and social emancipation of women. The subtlety of her cartoons is her trademark; there is no trace of anger or resentment in her work. This perhaps explains why Pompeia Nuria is not only the best known of all Spanish women and feminist cartoonists, but the most popular as well. After more than 30 years in the field of cartooning, mostly on women issues, Nuria has become an even more important voice in feminist circles.

J.M.

NYDEGGER, WERNER (1945-) Werner Nydegger, born November 18, 1945 in Zürich, Switzerland, got a very legitimate artistic education at the Kunstgewerbeschule in Basel in northern Switzerland. Immediately after graduating from art school in 1966, he opened a studio as a freelance graphic designer and cartoonist in Olten, Switzerland, the city he had spent his youth in. Nydegger became prominently known in Switzerland when his cartoons started appearing in 1971 in such renowned news-

Werner Nydegger, first published cartoon. © Cartoons & Comics.

papers as *Weltwoche, Bilanz* and *Schweizer Illustrierte.* His first published cartoon (May 7, 1971) depicted a camel looking somewhat astonished at his hump which had a surprising similarity to the Matterhorn.

Nydegger's cartoons which display a quiet sarcasm with a streak of black humor were so well received by the public—and the editors—that numerous other papers and magazines asked for his contributions, among them German publications like *Der Spiegel, Quick, Stern, Pardon* or the German edition of *Playboy.* He also created cartoons for display on television and as posters.

A first selection of Nydegger's cartoons appeared in 1979. Other collections of his work as well as original cartoon book projects were published. The first of a line of original books was a two volume satiric history of the world, *Das Neueste von Gestern.* ("The Latest News from Yesteryear").

Werner Nydegger is one of the best known Swiss cartoonists. His style is fluid, his humor fresh and sometimes black.

W.F.

NYSTAD, GERDA (1926?-) Denmark's leading female cartoonist, born in Copenhagen, Gerda Nystad made her debut in 1948 with socially satirical cartoons in the daily paper *Social Demokraten.* Later magazine illustrations and cartoons were published in *Bilen Bab, Prik,* etc.

With her sensitive drawing style and bubbling imagination, she actually seems to make roses spring out of women's dresses. Her biting captions, which seem to be in strong contrast to her poetic drawings, add to the general impression of high artistic quality. *Eva's Diary,* which for more than ten years has been published in the biweekly magazine *Eva,* contains social comments on the changing whims of the times. Married to cartoonist Jørgen Mogensen, Nystad has illustrated several book covers and books (among them, *The Arabian Nights*). She also does a weekly fourcolumn cartoon on the editorial page of the *Berlingske Tidende Week-end.*

J.S.

Gerda Nystad. © Nystad.

Oo

O.A.
See Andersson, Oskar.

OBAKE NO Q TARŌ (Japan) *Obake no Q Tarō* ("Q Tarō the Ghost") was both a comic strip and an animated television series created by Fujiko Fujio. The main character, Q Tarō, became a media star of unprecedented popularity in Japan, spawning not only a host of imitators but also an endless array of children's toys, songs and fashions. Q Tarō was a genial and lovable ghost somewhat reminiscent of his American cousin, Casper the Friendly Ghost. Unlike Casper, however, he lived in the house of a human `family with two children named Shōta and Shinji, and this format provided for a variety of comical situations and was ultimately responsible for his popularity. Q Tarō was certainly a ghost, but he was also very human in his emotions and overall character. He functioned almost as a mischievous pet of the family's children.

Q Tarō made his debut in February 1964 in the weekly comic book *Shōnen Sunday,* but it took several months before his character and final form emerged. By 1965, however, he had become a true star, appearing widely in such Shōgakukan-affiliated children's publications as *Mebae, Yoiko* and *Yōchien.* Although *Shōnen Sunday* ceased to carry the strip after the end of 1966, Q Taro had in the interim materialized in the more powerful medium of television, where he amused Japanese children from 1965 to 1976. The animated version of Q Taro was produced by Toei and Studio Zero and directed by Daisaku Shirakawa, with the voice of Machiko Soga used to great effect in the title role.

Obake no Q Tarō's greatest asset was the lovable character of Q Taro and the excellent differentiation and development of supporting figures such as Shōta and his friends. In the late 1960s Q Tarō was in fact the darling of the children of Japan, and his picture was everywhere. Ironically, when the comic book version first appeared in 1964, it was at one point cancelled for three months due to what appeared to be lack of interest. After an overwhelming protest from Q Tarō's fans, however, it was promptly reinstated.

Obake no Q Taro's creator, Fujiko Fujio, is really two persons, Moto Abiko and Hiroshi Fujimoto, who worked as a duo a la Ellery Queen. They were born in 1934 and 1933 respectively, and worked together professionally from 1954, when they created *Tenshi no Tamachan* ("Tama the Little Angel"). As two artists working under one name for two decades, they seemed inseparable and extraordinarily successful, putting out such classics as *Parmany* (1967), *Doraemon* (1971), and *Suzuke Roboketto,* which won the Shogakukan award for comics. But they may have been too close together to sustain the relationship: in the mid-1980s they split up, and like a couple going through a divorce, they had to split up the copyrights on their works. Abiko took the name "Fujiko Fujio (A)" and the rights to works he had done most of the work on. Fujimoto took the name "Fujiko F. Fujio" and the rights to *Doraemon* and other classics he had authored. But *Obake no Q Tarō* was one of the big exceptions and a work they continued to share. Tragically, Fujimoto passed away in 1996, at the age of 62.

F.S.

OGAWA, SHIMPEI (1887-1924) Japanese cartoonist born in Hiki, Saitama, Japan, in 1887. Shimpei Ogawa was adopted by his uncle, a judge, at an early age, but what might have been a very comfortable life came to an end when his foster father died. Forced to eke out a living on their own, Ogawa and his mother took up residence in a temple, and Ogawa began working as a clerk in the Nihonbashi district of Tokyo. It was during this time that he made his first attempt at cartooning; adopting the pen name "Hyōe," he began drawing pen-and-ink caricatures of the Tokyo populace.

Ogawa eventually responded to an advertisement for aspiring cartoonists and joined Rakuten Kitazawa, one of the major figures in the early development of Japanese cartoons. His first assignment was to draw for the popular humor magazine Tokyo Puck. Later, Ogawa became a cartoonist for the *Yamato* newspaper, where he remained for ten years. During that time, he produced such works as *Engei Gahō* ("Sketches of Plays") and did cover panels for magazines like *Onna no Sekai* ("The World of Women").

Ogawa's cartoons are filled with soft, delicate lines, and they give his drawings a suppleness that belies their sharp humor and sarcasm. Much of his work has been praised for its human qualities; even the most cutting cartoons Ogawa produced seem to retain a mellowness that suggests that the artist is not as tough a social critic as he would have his audience believe.

Later in his career Ogawa again teamed up with Kitazawa to produce the *Jiji Manga,* a Sunday cartoon paper for the *Jiji Shinpō* ("Times Newspaper"). Kitazawa did most of the artwork, and Ogawa acted as editor. Ogawa eventually developed the cartoon section into an eight-page color spread. He also used the paper to advertise for new talent and thus opened the door for young cartoonists to enter the industry in the same manner he had.

In the spring of 1924 Ogawa collaborated with Kitazawa on a special issue of the *Jiji Manga* called the *Jisesō*("Times"). This publication was perhaps the most significant work of Ogawa's career, since it combined his editorial and cartooning talents and contained material which was not only humorous and satirical but also literary and political. However, on April 10 of the same year, at age 37, Ogawa died from a lung ailment. The 208th issue of the *Jiji Manga* reported that Ogawa's last words were an admonition to his young co-workers to produce more and better cartoons.

J.C.

OGAWA, USEN (1868-1938) Japanese cartoonist born in Ibaraki Prefecture, Japan, in 1868. Usen Ogawa's real name was Shigeyoshi Ogawa, but he later changed it to demonstrate his concern for the masses (usen translates "potato money," an aptly proletarian-sounding alias). Ogawa was born in the year that marks Japan's entry into the modern world, and his art reflects the powerful changes that accompanied his nation's attempts at rapid modernization.

Ogawa became one of the major cartoonists on the staff of the *Heimin Shimbun* ("Common People's News"), a socialist newspaper founded in November 1903. He was heavily influenced by the wave of socialist ideology that had begun to sweep over Japan at the end of the 19th century and used this publication to display his antiwar, socialist-inspired attitudes. The Russo-Japanese War (1904-05) was being hotly debated when Ogawa became popular, and he expressed his opposition to it by producing cartoons that are now considered classics of proletarian art. They include drawings of itinerant workers, bean sellers, coal workers-the poor working- class people of Japan who supplied the labor for Japan's modernization. The *Heimin Shimbun* was forced to close down its operations on January 29, 1905, after publishing only 34 issues, but it had remained long enough for Ogawa to become a major spokesman for socialist causes. His drawing of battlefields littered with dead horses and skulls of fallen soldiers no doubt made as great an impact on the masses as it did on the government officials who suppressed the publication.

After the closing of the *Heimin Shimbun,* Ogawa moved to its successor, the bi-monthly Chokugen ("Plain Talk"), which began in September 1905. He also contributed proletarian cartoons to other socialist publications, such as *Himuchi* ("The Whip of Fire") and *Hikari* ("Light"). The government soon closed all of these papers, but Ogawa never lacked an outlet for his cartoons. On January 15, 1907, the *Heimin Shimbun* was brought back to life under the name *Nikkan Heimin Shimbun* ("Daily Common People's News"), and again Ogawa produced cartoons depicting the plight of the poor and oppressed. Many of his cartoons from this period show a more sarcastic and satirical tone.

In 1908 Ogawa collected 150 of his drawings and published an anthology called *Kusashiru Manga* ("The Grass Sap Cartoons"). This anthology reveals another side of Ogawa: the literary man with a classical heritage. Many of the selections had appeared in such literary magazines as *Hototogisu* ("Nightingale") and *Ibaraki,* both of which were forums for the most famous Japanese novelists of the period. Ogawa also revealed his classical leanings by organizing the short essays and poems he included in the collection into sections corresponding to the four seasons—an ancient practice in Japanese literature. In fact, even some of his proletarian cartoons bore ancient Chinese proverbs as captions. One such cartoon, which denounced the evils of materialism, proclaimed in classical Japanese, "Possessions eventually become nothing more than stolen property."

After 1910, as the political climate became more tense and arrests, killings and imprisonment of socialist sympathizers more common, Ogawa withdrew from politics and spent his remaining years writing poetry and drawing water nymphs. He died in 1938.

J.C.

"This year it's a judo boom."

Kenji Ogihara. © Manga Sunday.

OGIWARA, KENJI (1921-1990) Japanese cartoonist born in Yokohama, Japan, on October 10, 1921. Raised in a neighborhood of professional artisans, Kenji Ogiwara too seems to have developed a craftsman's pride in his work. After graduating from elementary school, he attended a technical school at night, and since he loved to draw, he also found time to study art. Shortly thereafter Ogiwara began contributing cartoons to magazines such as *Oru Yomimono* and *Modern Nippon.* In 1939, at the urging of Tamotsu Nagai (also a cartoonist), he joined a cartoonists' association then known as the Manga Tot- sugekitai ("Cartoon Attack Squad") and began his career as a professional. He was 18 years old.

In 1942 Ogiwara was drafted into the Imperial Japanese Army press corps and sent to the front, first in Burma and later in China. Surviving the war, he joined the Manga Shudan ("Cartoonists' Group") and was soon attracting attention with his *Nihon Igai Shi* ("The Real History of Japan," 1948). This work represented not only his postwar debut but also a pioneering effort at demystifying Japanese history through gentle parody. In humorously reminding people that even the emperor was human, and in making fun of old taboos, *Nih on Igai Shi* helped the Japanese people reformulate their self-image in the wake of the psychological devastation of defeat. Other works followed, such as *Hana* Sakeru Bushido (1953), *Kurarisan* (1957) and *Ninlutsu Bushidō* (1959).

With the possible exception of *Kurari-san,* Ogiwara's works tend to be a humorous mix of past and present. One of his favorite techniques is to put samurai and historical personages in a modern environment replete with telephones and bars. He most frequently works with a one-page, eight-panel layout, but he is also expert at single-panel cartoons. In Oo! *Wa ga Shison* ("Oh! Our Descendants"), which ran in the magazine *Manga Dokuhon* in 1969, Ogiwara skillfully employed the "then and now" technique, an excellent example being the two- panel page entitled "Rakujo Mae no Bushō to sono Shison" ("The General Before the Fall of His Castle, and His Descendants"). The top panel shows a samurai general calmly playing a flute before dying, his castle having been captured and enemy arrows having turned the ground around him into a veritable pincushion. The bottom panel illustrates the 20th-century version of a similar situation: a man sits smoking a cigarette in his little house in the midst of Tokyo while a freeway construction crew waits to demolish it. A sign by his door proclaims, "No Relocation!"

Kenji Ogiwara received the sixth Bunshun award for cartoons in 1960. Other representative works by him include *Ada* Uchi *Document* ("Document for Revenge") and *Ogiwara* no *Shakai Gihyō* ("Ogiwara's Comical Commentary on Society"). He passed away in 1990.

F.S.

OHMAN, JACK (1960-) Political cartoonist for the Portland *Oregonian* since 1983, Jack Ohman has been involved in both politics and cartooning since his undergraduate days at the University of Minnesota. While a student, he served as an aide to a Minnesota congressional candidate and a bus driver for Walter Mondale and Jimmy Carter motorcades, and still found time to contribute cartoons regularly to his school paper, the *Minnesota Daily*. His perceptive commentary and finished graphic style won him a job with the *Columbus Dispatch* in 1981, and, two months later, distribution by Tribune Media Services when Jeff McNelly briefly gave up political cartooning to concentrate on his strip, *Shoe*. At 20 Ohman was the youngest cartoonist ever to be nationally syndicated and commanded the second largest readership in the country. After brief stints with the *Dispatch* and the *Detroit Free Press*, he took a post with the *Oregonian*.

In April 1994, Ohman joined the select ranks of "double-dippers," cartoonists who create both editorial cartoons and humor features. His *Mixed Media*, distributed by TMS to nearly 100 papers, is a daily panel in strip format, wittily lampooning popular culture. Their ironically skewed versions of television, the press, movies, and popular music are often based on outrageous puns: a talking mule discussing Immanuel Kant is identified as "Mr. Higher Ed," a sinister masked figure singing a country song as "Garth Vader." "Doing both a comic strip and a political cartoon is a little like being a commodities broker and an emergency-room surgeon at the same time," he has written, "the money is great, but the stress can be absolutely unmanageable." Nevertheless, his breezy style of humor enables him to juggle the two careers with seeming ease.

Ohman's editorial cartoons have brought him numerous honors. Described by *People* magazine as "probably the most uncompromising, the most wicked and the most pointedly funny" pictorial comments on today's op-ed pages, they also appear regularly in *Time, Newsweek, U. S. News and World Report, Business Week*, and *The Economist*. They have earned a National Mark of Excellence Award from the Society of Professional Journalists and an Exceptional Merit Award from the National Women's Political Caucus. His editorial cartoons have been published in two collections, *Back to the '80s* (1986) and *Drawing Conclusions* (1987). Books inspired by his leisure-time activities include *Fear of Fly Fishing* (1988), *Fishing Bass-Ackwards* (1991), and *Why Johnny Can't Putt* (1994).

Ohman commands a graceful style, balancing his compositions with a natural sense of design and capturing the features of public figures with a sharp eye for caricature, but his graphic accomplishments are of little importance to him. "Style," he has written, "is secondary to the message. Either a cartoonist can draw well, or he can draw passably enough to get his point across. . . . A political cartoonist is most effective when he or she can get writing and drawing together." A nationally successful cartoonist since he left his teens, the prolific Jack Ohman fully meets that high standard.

D.W.

OKAMOTO, TADANARI (1932-1990) Japanese cartoon and puppet animator and director born in Osaka, Japan, on January 11, 1932. After graduating from the University of Osaka with a degree in law in 1955, Tadanari Okamoto made a dramatic change in direction. A growing interest in film, and animation in particular, led him to enter the film department of Nihon University, from which he then graduated in 1961. In the spring of the same year, Okamoto joined MOM productions, headed by Tadahito Mochinaga, and worked primarily in puppet animation on order from U.S. companies. Mochinaga, one of the pioneers of puppet animation in Japan, provided Okamoto with the valuable experience and training he needed, and when Okamoto left MOM to establish his own company, ECHO, he began producing unique works that were immediately well received. His debut piece, *Fushigi na Kusuri* ("Strange Medicine," 1965), won him the Ōfuji award and set a level of quality that he has consistently maintained.

Notable among his many award-winning creations are *Home My Home (1970)*, a four-minute short that won another Ōfuji award; *Hana to Mogura* ("The Flower and the Mole," 1970), which won a silver medal at the Venice International Children's Film Festival; and *Namu Ichi Byosokusai* ("The Happy Weakling"), which won an award at the Tehran International Film Festival in 1973. Okamoto works successfully in a variety of media, using puppets, folded paper, reliefs and cartoons. His originality in using new techniques has helped expand the concept of puppet animation in Japan so that it is now regarded not simply as a vehicle for education but as a broader art form. He often deals with Japanese folktales and frequently makes excellent use of traditional Japanese music, as in *Mochi Mochi no Ki* (1971). He died in 1990, and in 1991 he posthumously received the Mainichi Film Competition Special Award.

In addition to his many independent productions, Okamoto also created puppet animation and cartoon ani-

"Well if you knows a better 'ole, go to it."
"Old Bill." © The Bellman.

mation for television programs and commercials. Since 1972, moreover, he had been actively doing a popular annual show with his colleague Kihachiro Kawamoto in which new and old works are presented along with a live puppet show.

F.S.

OLD BILL (G.B.) "If you knows of a better 'ole, go to it!" was the most famous phrase of World War I, the caption of its most famous cartoon. It was growled by one walruswhiskered Tommy to another as shells shattered around them, and it was drawn by Captain Bruce Bairnsfather, a soldier who captured the truth about war in ink, wash and wit. His first effort, a sandbagged trench exploding atop a pale-faced group of soldiers ("Where did that one go?"), was actually scribbled in a trench in 1915 during the second battle of Ypres. It was redrawn in a nearby farmhouse and posted off at a brother subaltern's suggestion to the *Bystander,* a slightly upper-class weekly published in London, merely because the size of the sketch suited that magazine's page!

Wounded, Bairnsfather awoke in a Boulogne hospital to see his cartoon in print. Evacuated to the army hospital in Denmark Hill, London, he spent his convalescence sketching more of the same, all of which ran in the *Bystander* as *Fragments from France*. Gradually the characters of Old Bill, his pals Alf and Bert, and his wife Maggie were developed, and Bairnsfather found his cartoons a national craze. They were republished as a part work, published again in book form; he did them as a play, as a silent film and as a talkie. There were short stories, novels, comic strips in the *Daily Graphic* (1921) and *Passing Show's* comic section (*Old Bill and Bert,* 1934), a film called *Old Bill and Son for World War II* (starring Morland Graham and John Mills) and a new strip, *Young Bill,* in *Illustrated* (1940). The bandwagon seemed never-ending. But end it did, for the humor of World War II was of a different kind, and Old Bill found himself out of date. Bairnsfather, born in 1888, died on September 29, 1959.

Books: Fragments from France (1916); *Bairnsfather* (1916); *Back to Blighty* (1917); *Bullets and Billets* (1917); *For France* (1917); *Somme Battle Stories* (1917); *From Mud to Mirth* (1919); *The Bairnsfather Case* (1920); *The Better `Ole* (1924); *Carry On Sergeant* (1927); *Collected Drawings* (1931); *Laughing Through the Orient* (1933); *Wide Canvas* (1939); *Old Bill Stands By* (1939); *Old Bill Does It Again* (1940); *and Old Bill and Son* (1940).

D.G.

OLIPHANT, PATRICK (1935-) American cartoonist born in South Australia on July 24, 1935. At the age of 18 Pat Oliphant became a copy boy on the *Adelaide Advertiser* and then rose to staff artist and chief editorial cartoonist; he was deemed to have such promise that his employers sent him on a round-the-world four-month study trip in 1959. Five years later, in the midst of the 1964 presidential campaign, the perspicacious editors at the Denver Post, having just lost Paul Conrad to the Los Angeles Times, invited Oliphant to America to cartoon for their pages. In 1976 he switched to the Washington Star. His cartoons during all those years were syndicated by the Los Angeles Times Syndicate.

In the interim, beginning immediately upon his arrival in the United States, Oliphant became the most influential American political cartoonist of his generation. In three areas he was slavishly imitated: his approach (the use of gag-cartoon formats and the virtual elimination of labels and icons save for Uncle Sam); his media (brush and chemically sensitive shaded paper); and his format (always the horizontal cartoon, and sometimes a multipanel gag situation). His influence in each area was as pervasive and revolutionary as was the use of crayon, stark themes and vertical formats in the 1910s.

Oliphant has granted many importunate interviews in which he seems to claim credit for complete originality. Students, however, can easily see that Fischetti, in America, pioneered his forms and approach years before, and that there are strong elements of Searle, Giles, Norris and many others in his cartoons; even his mascot-novel in the late 20th century-was a universal convention years ago for editorial cartoonists. The point is that Oliphant is genius enough to have synthesized several great traditions in his unique way. And a claim to total originality would be justified in reference not to his craftsmanship but to each day's individual cartoon—unfailingly brilliant and incisive. He is among the world's—and cartoon history's—preeminent editorial cartoonists.

His drawings almost always convey a sense of mood, whether of a zany bureaucratic orgy or of a desperate scene of starving Third World natives caught in big-nation power struggles. He is generally left of center and in one respect is definitely not a conservative: he is liberal with his concepts, sometimes embodying several in one cartoon. Indeed, many readers seek the comments of his mas-

"One thing I've found out about oil . . . it's intoxicating."
Pat Oliphant. © Los Angeles Times Syndicate.

cot penguin before looking at the main cartoon. Oliphant won the Pulitzer Prize and the Sigma Delta Chi award in 1967 and has twice won the National Cartoonists Society Reuben.

R.M.

After the *Washington Star* ceased publication in 1981, Oliphant went into wide national and international syndication (his cartoons are currently distributed by Universal Press Syndicate). In addition his cartoon anthologies (coming out once every year on average) have been steady sellers year after year; they include *Ban the Book!* (1982), *...But Seriously, Folks* (1983), *Between a Rock and a Hard Place* (1986), *Nothing Basically Wrong* (1988), *Off to the Revolution* (1995), and *So That's Where They Come From!* (1997). He has been the subject of a number of studies and essays, and the National Portrait Gallery organized a retrospective exhibition od his works, "Oliphant's Presidents: Twenty-Five Years of Caricature," in 1990.

M.H.

O'MALLEY, M. POWER (1880-ca. 1930) American cartoonist born in Waterford, Ireland, in 1880. Power O'Malley immigrated to America with his family at the age of six. He studied at the Artisan Institute in New York and continued his painting studies at the National Academy of Design, where he won the Cannon Prize for drawing, the Baldwin Prize for etching, and other distinctions. After the turn of the century O'Malley began submitting pen-and-ink drawings to the popular monthlies and humorous weeklies. *Life* soon became his primary outlet, and since the magazine was just beginning to utilize halftone painted cartoons in a major way, O'Malley's training with the brush stood him in good stead. Into the 1920s his cartoons in *Life* (and illustrations in lesser fiction magazines) graced full pages, center spreads and covers.

O'Malley worked in gray washes and oil colors (for covers and certain double-page cartoons). His style was one of realism, and his themes, like those of fellow cartoonist-in-paints Angus MacDonall, were often wistful, sentimental and gently humorous.

R.M.

OMOITSUKI FUJIN (Japan) *Omoitsuki Fujin* was a Japanese newspaper cartoon drawn by Fusato Hirai that began in 1938 and was popular during the early years of World War II. The title translates as "The Idea Woman," and that was precisely the theme of the cartoon—the introduction of clever time—and money-saving practices that were most likely intended as helpful hints to aid the war effort. The main character was a housewife who, clad in her white apron, found uses for otherwise old and seemingly functionless items. Each cartoon introduced a new idea such as using an old, beat-up thermos to keep a baby's formula warm for emergencies or using old rags to stuff new quilts.

From the perspective of our age of electronic conveniences, the "clever ideas" of *Omoitsuki Fujin* seem rather laughable, but as an indicator of the social consciousness of prewar Japan, this cartoon takes on added significance. Not only were readers eager to learn how they might make their yen go further in an age of depression, but they were also strongly encouraged to economize in the home so that the money and energy they saved could be collectively used for the goals of Imperial Japan. In a sense, *Omoitsuki Fujin* is a good example of an early wartime propaganda cartoon. During the years in which it ran, most of the newspaper cartoons in Japan became propaganda tools of the military government. Three years after the appearance of *Omoitsuki Fujin,* Koshi Ota, one of the founders of a popular, outspoken cartoon humor magazine called *Karikare,* was imprisoned for "harboring subversive thoughts." *Omoitsuki Fujin,* therefore, represents a state of mind that was encouraged and eventually demanded by the wartime Japanese authorities.

J.C.

ONFROY DE BRÉVILLE, JACQUES (1858-1931) French cartoonist and illustrator born in eastern France on November 25, 1858. While serving in the army, Onfroy de Bréville developed an eye for detail in depicting uniforms and weapons, a talent he used not only in his early military paintings but in his cartoons also. Under the pen name "Job," he contributed from 1892 on to most of the important humor journals, principally to *L'Illustration, La Vie Militaire, La Caricature, Scribner's Magazine* and *Pick-Me-Up* (London). He also illustrated his own books, amusing works titled *Mémoires de César Chabrac* (1892) and *Les Epées de France* ("Swords of France"), as well as other writers' novels dealing with war, history, military life: *Histoire d'un Bonnet a' Poil* ("History of a Bearskin," 1893), *Le Grand Napoléon des Petits Enfants* ("The Great Napoleon of Little Children," 1893), *L'Epopée du Costume Militaire Francais* ("The Epic of French Military Uniform," 1898), *Bonaparte (1910)* and *Washington the Man of Action* (1914). In addition, he designed costumes and weapons for the theater. He died in Paris in September 1931. Job's sketches, well-drawn and full of verve, capture with good-natured irony human foibles both in and out of the army.

P.H.

ONO, SASEO (1905-1954) Japanese cartoonist born in Yokohama, Japan, in 1905. Saseo Ono is best remembered today for his skill at rendering the female form in his uniquely erotic sketches. From an early age he entertained

Saseo Ono, *cover for "Bakusho."* © *Tokyo Puck.*

himself and his friends with drawings both erotic and humorous. He graduated from the prestigious Ueno Art School in Tokyo in 1930 and thereafter regularly submitted his works to *Tokyo Puck*. At the time this magazine was edited by Kenichiro Shimada and had theunique distinction of uniting what would normally be considered two irreconcilable genres—proletarian and erotic art. While the socialist-leaning faction was led by such artists as Masamu Yanase, Fumio Matsuyama and Keiichi Suyama, Ono soon took command over the latter group with the help of his mentor, Oten Shimokawa.

Ono's women were typified by the Japanese "flapper" girls of the time. Western fashions were the rage among the more social young people, who were referred to as *moga-mobo*, a derivation from the English words "modern girl" and "modern boy." Ono's work depicted this somewhat decadent/progressive group in the cafe's, bars and theaters of Tokyo. His cartoons rarely contained much in the way of a direct social statement or catchy ideas; rather, they were subtle illustrations of the society he loved. There were exceptions, however, such as "Mannequin Byo" ("Mannequin Disease"), which appeared as the back cover illustration for *Tokyo Puck* in 1936. It showed a starving young former college student working in a women's lingerie store, a humorous parody of the thousands of college graduates then unable to find work to their liking.

In 1941 Ono became a correspondent for the Imperial Army, as did many of his cartoonist compatriots. He was sent to Java, where he drew for the propaganda campaign then in progress. At the end of the war he became a P.O.W. of the Allies and was repatriated to Japan until 1946; he soon resumed his work, concentrating ever more on depicting sensual women. Ironically, at a time when most Japanese were having trouble finding enough to eat, Ono's women became increasingly full-bodied and voluptuous—almost Western in their proportions. This indirectly contributed to Ono's popularity, and he soon became widely known by the familiar term *Ono-chan*. He joined the new Manga Shōdan ("Cartoonists' Group"), and in 1951 he acted as judge, along with Hidezo Kondo and Kon Shimizu, for the popular Nikaten exhibit held in Tokyo. His own work, "Carnival," was also greatly acclaimed at this time.

In real life Saseo Ono was apparently something of a character. Not only was he a true connoisseur of the female form, but according to one source, he was also quite a dandy, insisting that all his clothes be made by a favorite tailor who could create the Chicago gangster look he preferred. On February 1, 1954, Ono suddenly (but somehow fittingly) collapsed on his way to an appearance by Marilyn Monroe at Tokyo's famous Nichigeki Theater. His loss came as a shock to the many cartoonists and fans who loved and admired him. Today, however, his tradition is carried on by Koh Kojima in the cartooning field, and also by his son, Kosei Ono, who is presently one of Japan's foremost comics and film critics, specializing in the introduction of American comics into Japan.

During his four-year stay in Java, Ono had a major influence on young Indonesian artists. A book of his sketches and essays was published in April 1945, four months before Japan's surrender, and it is a lively documentary of Java and its people in the 1940s. Today, some of Indonesian art historians reportedly regard Ono as one of the inspirations for their nation's postwar modern art. Well-known Indonesian artists influenced by Ono are said to include Affandi S. Sujojono and Henk Ngantung. In 1998 Ono's Java sketchbook ("The Wartime Java Sketch Art of Saseo Ono") was scheduled to be reprinted in a bilingual and Indonesian edition.

F.S.

OPATHA, SHERIDEN CHANDRASEKRA (1935-) Born in Sri Lanka, S.C. Opatha has had a stellar career in political, strip, gag, and commercial cartooning. After receiving his diploma from the College of Fine Art, he joined the Times of Ceylon Group in the early 1960s, serving first as an illustrator on the *Times* and then as political cartoonist for the *Ceylon Daily Mirror*.

After 19 years, he switched to the Associated Newspapers of Ceylon Group, where he has drawn a daily pocket cartoon, *Laugh It Off*, for the *Daily News* and until 1994, a daily political cartoon and a thrice weekly comic strip for the *Daily Observer*. In 1994, Opatha moved to the *Sunday Leader*. The strip's namesake character, "Silva," also appears as a sideline observer in many of Opatha's political cartoons, considered especially hard hitting on issues such as international politics, poverty, environment, terrorism, Third World, U.S. policies, and the Sri Lankan opposition. The latter stemmed from the fact that for years, Opatha worked for newspapers owned by the government.

Additionally, Opatha draws a "Smile a While" cartoon page for Singapore's Sunday *Straits Times* and a weekly "Through the Eyes of a Cartoonist." He derives much of his livelihood from ownership of Pack Ads, an advertising agency of ten artists, over whom he served as chief artist and art director. Opatha cartoons have graced the pages of periodicals, including *Playboy,* in India, Greece, West Germany, and France.

Opatha's work is bold in content and style, leaving little to the imagination as he depicts governmental foes in harsh, dark, and sinister lines. Those who have felt the penetrating thrust of Opatha's pen have retaliated in different ways; former Prime Minister S. Bandaranaike tried to have him arrested for a 1977 election campaign cartoon booklet that smeared her, while others have threatened his life.

J.A.L.

OPISSO Y SALA, RICARD (1880-1966) Spanish cartoonist born in Tarragona, Spain, in 1880. Ricard Opisso had his first cartoons published in the magazine *Luz* in 1898. As a young man he went to live in Paris and at the turn of the century contributed cartoons to the French magazines *Le Rire, Frou-Frou* and *Fantasio.* Later Opisso moved to Barcelona, where he was highly productive. He created many comic strips for *Els 4 Gats, Papitu* and the children's newspapers *Joventut, El Senyor Canons* and *TBO.* His single-panel cartoons appeared mainly in Cu-Cut (1902-12), Xut! (1922-36) and *L'Esquella de la Torratxa* (until 1939). In *L'Esquella* de 1a Torratxa he published his famous cartoons depicting large gatherings of people with distinct personalities making a wide variety of commentaries.

Opisso was one of the most internationally renowned 20th-century Spanish cartoonists. His drawings of crowd-packed scenes are particularly well known. He was also noted for the masterful use of color in his drawings. He died in Barcelona in 1966.

J.M.

OPITZ, GEORG EMANUEL (1775-1841) German painter, draftsman and printmaker born in Prague, Bohemia (then part of the Hapsburg empire, now in Czechoslovakia), in 1775.

In the late 18th and early 19th centuries, German humorous art was chiefly in the hands of universal draftsmen who included humor as one aspect of their wide-spread illustrative activities; Chodowiecki, Voltz and Opitz (also spelled Opiz) are the important representative examples.

After art study in Dresden with Giovanni Battista Casanova (a younger brother of the famous adventurer), Georg Opitz worked as a portraitist. About 1801, he wandered to Vienna, where he started gaining a reputation for his characteristic scenes of folk life; humor was always an element in print series of this kind. His gift for observation and his readiness to record all that met his eye resulted in paintings, prints and drawings of Paris when he accompanied the duchess of Courland there in 1814, upon the (first) capture of Napoleon; outstanding among these Paris productions were two large etchings, one depicting the removal of Napoleon's statue from the column in the Place Vendôme, the other showing Cossacks encamped on the Champs-Elysées.

Opitz spent some time in Heidelberg and Altenburg, too, before finally settling down in Leipzig in 1820 to become the city's artistic chronicler. In that European crossroads, periodically enlivened by the great trade fair (*Leipziger Messe*), Opitz created what has been called "one of the most amusing and instructive cultural documents of Leipzig in the Biedermeier period." In addition to specific scenes of the fair, Opitz drew street cries of Leipzig; a series of German national and military costumes; scenes of the revolutionary activities of 1830 (waves of unrest shook Europe after Charles X was driven from the French throne during the "three glorious days" of July); such eternally popular print-series subjects as the "times of day"; theatrical and other genre scenes; and numerous views of many other European cities and resorts (such as Carlsbad).

Opitz worked up these scenes mainly in watercolor; they were marketed as aquatints or as contour etchings (also available with hand coloring). Sold at the fair, these eventually reached every corner of Europe, exerting a great influence on the image-mad bourgeoisie and the artists who were then rushing to supply that market. Opitz is said to have drawn some three thousand sheets, but the specific subjects of only about one tenth of these can be reconstructed today. He died in Leipzig on July 12, 1841.

S.A.

OPS
See Rábago, Andrés.

OREHEK, DON (1928-) American magazine gag cartoonist born in Brooklyn, New York, on August 9, 1928. The son of a former Austrian cavalry officer, Don Orehek served a tour of duty in the U.S. Navy after high school, and while in the service, he created the comic strip Cyphers for navy newspapers. In 1950, while a student at the School of Visual Arts in New York City, he sold his first cartoon professionally. From 1952 to 1956 he worked for Crestwood Publica tions in New York City. Crestwood published a series of inexpensive newsprint magazines featuring gag cartoons.

Don Orehek became a full-time freelance cartoonist in 1956 and has since become best known for his fluid illustrative style featuring beautiful women and risque' gags. His work is regularly published in *Playboy, Playgirl, Cosmopolitan, Penthouse* and other similar magazines. However, Orehek is a skilled master of magazine cartoons for general readership. *The Saturday Evening Post, Readers' Digest, Ladies' Home Journal* and the *Saturday Review* have often published his cartoons. He is also a regular contributor to *Cracked,* a teenage humor magazine. He has won the National Cartoonists Society's Best Magazine Cartoonist award four times.

Even as a child, Orehek preferred magazine cartooning to comic strips and comic books. His work is more strongly influenced by classical illustration techniques than by anything else. His drawing was considerably tighter in the 1950s and blossomed in the 1960s into the flowing pen lines that are his trademark. Two elements of his style are the use of action in the drawing to promote the gag in the punch line, and the use of detail to qualify the characters

"Remember 'Its a Long Way to Tipperary'?
Well, it's a long way back too!"
Don Orehek. © Saturday Review.

of the people in his cartoons. The combination of quick fluid lines, action and detail gives Don Orehek's cartoons a distinctive look.

Gags in a historical setting are a favorite Orehek device. He also favors gags about doctors, lawyers and other professionals. For the past decade he has been showing his humorous watercolor paintings at the Washington Square Outdoor Art Exhibit in New York City. Don Orehek has illustrated two cartoon paperback books, *101 Pickle Jokes* and *Yankee Doodle Dandies.* With the ever shrinking market for magazine gag cartoons, he has sought other outlets. He has illustrated 35 paperback "101" joke books on a variety of topics for Scholastic Books. He has expanded the amount of work he draws for *Cracked* magazine, especially his "Shut-Ups" feature. Caricature for corporations has also become an Orehek staple.

B.C.

ORLOV, DIMITRY STAKHIYEVICH (1883-1946) Cartoonist and poster designer born in Novocherkassk, Russia, a city near the river Don, on November 3, 1883. Dimitry Orlov finished his high school studies in Rostov, then went to study art at the University of Moscow. He began drawing political cartoons for antigovernment publications such as Budel'nik at the time of the abortive 1905 revolution. After the 1917 revolution he emerged as one of the leading poster artists of the period. He also contributed cartoons to Orkna ROSTA (the Soviet organization responsible for putting up displays in telegraph-office windows all around Russia) as well as to the Krasnoarmeyets newspaper. It was around this time that he took up the pseudonym "D.S. Moor," under which he was to become famous.

D.S. Moor made his mark in the 1920s and 1930s, contributing widely acclaimed cartoons to all the leading Soviet publications, from Pravda and *Izvestia* to the humor magazines *Krokodil* and *Bezbozhnik u Stanka.* During World War II he went back to designing posters with strongly anti-Nazi and anti-Italian themes. D.S. Moor also did a number of book and magazine illustrations. He was made an Honorable Worker of the RSFSR (Russian Republic) in 1932 and also garnered a great many other honors. He died in Moscow on October 24, 1946.

M.H.

ORLOWSKI, ALEKSANDER (1777-1832) Polish cartoonist and painter born in Warsaw, Poland, on March 9, 1777. Aleksander Orlowski was born into a noble, if impoverished, Polish family. At the age of 16 he took part in the 1793 uprising against the Third Partition of Poland, and he painted and sketched some of the battle scenes in Raclawice and Warsaw. He then took up formal art studies with the noted painter J.P. Noblin. In addition to a number of fine paintings, Orlowski did a great many humorous sketches and cartoons directed against Prussia (which was then the occupying power). Some of these cartoons roused the ire of the Prussian authorities, and the artist found it prudent to move to Russia in 1802.

Settling in St. Petersburg, Orlowski soon became a successful artist, turning out innumerable genre, heroic and romantic paintings attuned to the temper of the times. His fame spread so rapidly that he was named a member of the Russian Academy of Arts in 1809. He also did caricatures of leading personalities and cartoons full of robust humor. These were not only published in Russian magazines and almanacs but were also reprinted in the rest of Europe, and they alone assured Orlowski's enduring fame. The latest edition of *The Great Soviet Encyclopedia* characterizes his work thus: "Orlowski's precisely drawn cartoon-portraits and caricatures have earned him recognition as one of the founders of the satirical genre in Russia." Orlowski died in St. Petersburg on March 13, 1832.

M.H.

ORR, CAREY (1890-1967) American artist born in Ada, Oklahoma, in 1890. The first 13 years of Carey Orr's life were spent on his grandparents' farm, where a tramp cartoonist one day inspired him to a career with the pen. His lumberjack father then took him to Spokane, Washington, where he attended high school and worked for a time at a lumber mill. Although he was receiving instruction in engineering, it was professional baseball that next loomed large in his life. Playing for a Canadian team, he earned enough money to pursue his first love, cartooning. He enrolled at the Chicago Academy of Fine Arts.

His only other instruction was through the W.L. Evans Cartoon Correspondence Course, which he took at his home in Hillyard, Washington, and valued highly.

Soon, in 1911, Orr secured a cartooning job with Hearst's

Carey Orr. © Chicago Tribune.

Chicago Examiner and the next year succeeded Charles Sykes on the *Nashville Tennessean.* Here he matured and drew handsome, clever cartoons that attracted national attention. As the South's premier cartoonist, he was widely reprinted, and in 1915 several papers, including the *St. Louis Post-Dispatch,* attempted to lure him away. Orr signed a much-publicized two-year renewal with the *Tennessean*, but at the end of that contract he accepted an offer from the *Chicago Tribune*, joining John McCutcheon and Frank King (and freeing King, incidentally, for general, non-editorial cartoon work). There he remained for 46 years.

Carey Orr became one of America's most potent conservative and patriotic cartoon voices; he was anti-interventionist concerning foreign war and opposed the New Deal as a threat to freedom. His cartoons, reminiscent of the Billy Ireland style and relying on realism rather than broad caricature, often appeared on the front page of the *Tribune,* almost always in color beginning on March 5, 1932.

In the 1910s his *Tiny Trib*, an elongated panel dealing with topics in the news, was a signal success, and the concept was adopted by other papers (which replaced the *Tribune*'s logo with theirs). For years Orr taught cartooning at the Chicago Academy and put a whole generation of successful cartoonists in his debt; his niece, Martha Orr, created the pioneer soap-opera comic strip *Apple Mary*. Orr won a Pulitzer Prize in 1961—an honor long overdue—and died in 1967.

R.M.

ORR, CECIL (1909-1965) Scottish cartoonist Cecil Edward Orr was born in Glasgow, Scotland, on September 29, 1909. His father was a fish and poultry merchant, and the boy was educated at Greenock High School. At the early age of 11 he began to draw posters for local shops and cinemas, and produced and illustrated a school magazine. He studied at the Glasgow School of Art and had his first professional artwork published in *Collins Boys Annual*. At 18 he joined Associated Scottish Newspapers, where he would work on the staff from 1928 to 1941. He was both illustrator and cartoonist, and is especially remembered for his contributions to the Chum Club, run by the *Daily Record*, and illustrated the *Chum Club Annual* (1937). In 1940 he compiled the weekly comic section for the same publisher's *Sunday Mail,* drawing his own strip, *Susie and Sambo*.

Cecil served in the RAF during World War II, after which he became noticeable for his show-business caricatures and cartoons, including dozens of illustrations featuring Lupino Lane, the famous comedian, in Lane's book, *How To Be A Comedian* (1945). In 1952 he began to draw for children's comics, starting with *Stormalong* in *Mickey Mouse, The Rolling Stones* in *Swift*, but especially *Bessie Bunter*, sister of the world-famous Billy Bunter, which began in *School Friend* (1963) and continued in *June* (1965). He died on August 23, 1965.

D.G.

ORTIFUS
See Ortiz Fuster, Antonio

ORTIZ FUSTER, ANTONIO (1948-) Spanish cartoonist born in Valencia on March 15, 1948. After studies at the Conservatory of Music (in 1969-77 he was a member of the rock group Control with which he recorded three CD's) and in art school, Antonio Ortiz started drawing humor cartoons for the daily *Diario de Valencia* in 1980 before branching out into comics. His strip *Invasor el Ultimo* ("Invader the Last"), a humorous treatment of Valencian history, appeared in 1984 in the major daily *Diario Levante*. Afterwards he devoted his talents (under the pseudonym "Ortifus") to editorial cartooning with his personal vision of national and world affairs and a keen sense of humor and satire mixed with social criticism. In the beginning he was influenced by Brant Parker but later developed his own loose but very descriptive style.

In addition to cartoons Ortifus has also done illustrations for books and magazines and has occasionally worked in animation. He is also a terrific piano player and rocker, but unfortunately his cartooning workload has forced him to abandon music.

Many of Ortifus's cartoons and illustrations have been published in book form, starting with *Invasor el Ultimo*. His weekly cartoons, "La semana de Ortifus," were com-

Antonio Ortiz ("Ortifus"). © Ortifus.

piled in *129 semanas y media* (*129 Weeks and a Half*, 1991) and in *De todo hay en las vinetas del Senor* (*You Can find Everything in the Lord's Cartoons*, 1992). In 1990 the local Council published his *Consejos practicos par ir por la vida con sumo cuidado* (*Practical Advice on How to Go Through Life with Great Care*), all in color and full of double meanings not comprehended by the sponsors.

Ortifus is known for his professional courtesy and his willingness to lend his talents to amateur publications without asking for anything in return.

F.T.J.

OSRIN, RAYMOND H. (1928-) American political cartoonist born in Brooklyn, New York, on October 5, 1928. Ray Osrin studied at the High School of Industrial Art in New York and at the Art Students League. His early influences were the strip cartoonists Milton Caniff and Frank Robbins and political cartoonists Herblock, Paul Conrad and many others.

From 1945 to 1957, Osrin served in various capacities in the art field as a comic book inker and as an illustrator. He worked in television animation in 1957 and 1958 and was a newspaper staff artist thereafter until 1966, when he succeeded Ed Kuekes as chief political cartoonist of the Cleveland *Plain Dealer*.

The politically Democratic-independent Osrin has altered his drawing style through the years, but he stands head and shoulders above the gaggle of horizontal- format, tone-shading artists by virtue of his concepts; he is one of the most forceful political cartoonists drawing in the United States today. Osrin's awards have included the 1970 National Headliners Award, several Freedoms Foundation citations, and awards for his freelance advertising work. After more than a quarter-century at the *Plain Dealer* he showed a certain lassitude as expressed in this 1987 advice to would-be cartoonists: "I would advise any young person to go into other work—McDonald's franchise, shoe store, plumbing, auto mechanic, carpenter, etc. But not law." He retired in the early 1990s.

R.M.

Raymond Osrin. © The Plain Dealer.

OSVALDO
See Navarro, Osvaldo.

"Oswald the Rabbit." © Walter Lantz.

OSWALD THE RABBIT (U.S.) In 1927, with the encouragement of his distributor, Charles Mintz, Walt Disney created a new character to replace the played-out Alice in Cartoonland series. They settled on a rabbit, and legend has it that Mintz picked a name for it out of a hat. Such was the birth of Oswald the Lucky Rabbit. With the help of his small team of animators (Ub Iwerks, Hugh Harman and Rudolph Ising prominent among them), Disney developed the floppy-eared rabbit into a well-rounded personality. With his propensity for getting into situations which he then helped solve, Oswald prefigured Mickey Mouse.

The cartoon series (released by Mintz through Universal) was popular enough to attract merchandising tie-ins, so it came as a shock to Disney when Mintz tried in 1928 to force him into accepting a smaller return for his shorts. Having been turned down by Disney, Mintz, who owned rights to the character, set out to produce *Oswald the Rabbit* cartoons (the "Lucky" having been dropped in the meantime) independently, with the help of Rudolph Ising and Hugh Harman, whom he had lured away from Disney. Within a year they had both left Mintz to strike out on their own (thus fulfilling a Disney prophecy, by the way).

Oswald the Rabbit was then farmed out to Walter Lantz; the *1929* "Amateur Nite" started the new series, which did not prove overly successful. Under Lantz's direction Oswald became sprightlier and cuddlier but did not succeed in establishing a strong personality. He seems to have disappeared in the 1940s (in comic.books, however, he lasted until 1962).

Oswald was Disney's first effort at full-fledged animation. The lessons (both artistic and commercial) that he learned with the "lucky rabbit" were to serve him well in later years, especially in the making, developing and marketing of Mickey Mouse.

M.H.

OUTDOOR SPORTS
See Indoor / Outdoor Sports.

OUT OF THE INKWELL (U.S.) Max Fleischer conceived the idea for *Out of the Inkwell* in 1915, but it took him one year before his first cartoon short was released in 1916. Fleischer had used a conventional movie camera, which necessitated a separate drawing for each frame: only with the invention of the rotoscope camera (which he patented in 1917) could Fleischer produce his cartoons in sizable quantities.

The concept of the series was simple: the opening shots showed Max Fleischer (in live action) trying to think up an idea for his next cartoon; then a character in a clown costume would pop up from the inkwell (in animation) and get involved in all kinds of pranks before going back into the inkwell. "We used the title *Out of the Inkwell* for want of a better one," Fleischer later admitted. "The pictures were done in pen and ink. In addition there are so many things that can come out of an inkwell."

"Out of the Inkwell." © Max Fleischer.

W.W. Denslow's illustration for "The Wonderful Wizard of Oz," 1900.

Fleischer produced his first cartoons at the J.R. Bray studios for release through Paramount. In 1919 he left Bray to set up *Out of the Inkwell* Films with his brother Dave. The little clown became so popular that in 1923 the Fleischers finally decided to bestow a name upon him: he was christened Ko-Ko the Clown. Later Ko-Ko was given a dog companion by the name of Bimbo, and the frolicsome pair became known as the Inkwell Imps.

While the *Out of the Inkwell* gags were often crude and the animation (done by Dave Fleischer and Dick Huemer) now seems rudimentary, the series enjoyed tremendous success in the 1920s. It became even more of a hit when Max introduced the famous bouncing ball to coax the audience into singing along with the cartoon characters to the accompaniment of the movie-house organ. (The first such "song cartune" was released in 1924, to the music and lyrics of Gus Kahn and Ted Fiorito's "Oh, Mabel.")When sound came to the movies, the Fleischers discontinued Out of the Inkwell (the last cartoon in the series, "Chemical Ko-Ko," appeared in 1929). Ko-Ko's career ended there, for all practical purposes, but Bimbo continued well into the 1930s, first in the Talkartoons series, then as Betty Boop's companion.

In 1961, at the urging of one of his former animators, Hal Seegar, Max did a new series of cheaply produced *Out of the Inkwell* cartoons for television.

M.H.

OZ (U.S.) L. Frank Baum wrote *The Wonderful Wizard of Oz* in 1900. The book met with such success that it gave rise to scores of additional *Oz* stories written by Baum himself and by his successors; these in turn were adapted to the stage, comic strips, puppet shows, live-action films and animation. The first animated version of *The Wizard of Oz* was reportedly produced in 1933 by Ted Eshbaugh; due to legal difficulties, however, it was never released. An animated cartoon series, *Tales of the Wizard of Oz,* was effectively produced by Videocraft in 1960-61 and syndicated for Saturday morning telecast. In 1964 NBC-TV broadcast another Videocraft effort, *Return to Oz,* one of the most inept cartoon films ever made.

On a higher technical and artistic level, Filmation brought out *Journey back to Oz,* which was released in 1972 in Britain and Australia, but not until 1974 in the United States; it was well directed by Hal Sutherland from a screenplay by Fred Ladd and Norman Prescott. The voices were done by an all-star cast including Liza Minelli (Dorothy), Mickey Rooney (Scarecrow), Danny Thomas (Tin Man) and Milton Berle (Cowardly Lion); Margaret Hamilton, who played the Wicked Witch in the celebrated 1939 movie version, was Mem in this one. An animated version of *The Wizard of Oz* came out in Italy in the early 1980s. In 1985 the Walt Disney studio produced *Return to Oz,* a live-action *cum* animation film starring Fairuza Balk and Nicol Williamson, with Will Vinton in charge of animation.

M.H.

Pp

PACKER, FRED LITTLE (1886-1956) American cartoonist and Pulitzer Prize winner born in Hollywood, California, on January 4, 1886. Packer was educated in the public schools of Los Angeles and attended the Los Angeles School of Design (1902-03) and the Chicago Art Institute (1904-05).

Packer's whole career as a newspaper cartoonist was spent in the employ of William Randolph Hearst. In 1906 and 1907 he drew for the *Los Angeles Examiner* and then switched to the *San Francisco Morning Call* (1907-13); after a merger he served as art director of the *San Francisco Call-Post* until 1918. Advertising work lured Packer to New York in 1919, and he worked for the agencies until 1932, when he rejoined Hearst on the *New York Journal* and *American Weekly*; the following year he switched to the Hearst tabloid, the *New York Mirror*, where he remained until his death on December 8, 1956.

It was for the *Mirror*, in 1952, that Packer won his Pulitzer. Other awards included three successive Newspaper Guild Page One awards and several Freedoms Foundation citations.

R.M.

PADRÓ I PEDRET, TOMÁS (1840-1877) Spanish cartoonist born in Barcelona, Spain, in 1840. During his short lifetime Tomás Padró established himself as the most popular and creative cartoonist in Spain. From 1858 to 1877 he contributed to *El Tiburon* (1858-65), *Lo Xanquet* (1865-74), *Un Tros de Paper* (1865-66), *Lo Noy de la Mare* (1866-67), *La Risotada* (1869-73) and *La Madeja Politica* (1873-76). All these publications were humor magazines unique for their time. Though short-lived, they had a significant cultural impact throughout Spain. (*La Risotada*, the most important of them, underwent a series of name changes, and its entire history is not fully clear to this day. It is known, however, that *La Risotada, La Flaca, La Risa* and *La Carcalada* were all basically the same magazine.) Padró received his greatest recognition for the color cartoons he drew for *La Flaca* toward the end of his life. These cartoons testify to his keen political insight and his outstanding artistic abilities.

Not only was Padró an excellent draftsman, but he was also a good painter, and several of his works are on permanent display at the Museum of Modern Art in Barcelona. At the end of his short life he was a professor at the School of Arts in Barcelona, where he died in 1877. In the opinion of some of the most respected critics of Spanish cartooning, Tomás Padró belongs in the ranks of the great European draftsmen of the second half of the 19th century.

J.M.

Tomás Padró., 1866.

PAGE, GROVER (1886-1951) American cartoonist born in 1886. Grover Page was one of the few genuine innovators of formats and media in the editorial cartooning discipline. He took his first job at age 18 in the art department of the *Baltimore Sun*, and he later studied at the Art Institute of Chicago. He led the small animation cartooning community in Atlanta before joining the *Louisville Courier-Journal* in 1918; there he remained for more than 30 years, until he died of pneumonia on August 5, 1951.

Grover Page, while a master of the solid pen-and-crayon technique of the time, sought to expand the visual parameters of the editorial cartoonist's art. He sometimes rendered his daily barbs via wood blocks, wood engravings and linoleum blocks. Though he did not initiate any trends or schools (sometimes his concepts suffered from the visual unorthodoxy), Page stands as one of the freshest innovators in a field where "innovation" usually refers to switching from a vertical to a horizontal format or from crayon shading to Craftone.

R.M.

PAGOT, NINO (1908-1972) Italian cartoonist and animator born in Venice, Italy, in 1908. Nino Pagot never received formal art training; as a matter of fact, he worked first as a train engineer and later as a skilled mechanic in Milan,

Consultation

Grover Page, 1938. © Courier-Journal.

where he had moved with his parents during World War I. Toward the middle of the 1930s Pagot started contributing cartoons and illustrations to various publications, such as *Attorno al Fuoco* (a Boy Scout paper), *Il Corrierino and Il Balilla.* In the early 1940s, for *Il Corriere dei Piccoli,* he created his first comic strips, *Casimiro Centimetri* and *Poldo e Paola,* in the style of the Disney stories. He also drew a series of cartoons that were published on the front page of the humor magazine *Bertoldo.* In these years of fierce nationalism he signed his name "Pagotto."

Like most other Italian cartoonists of the time, Pagot was entranced by Walt Disney's animated cartoons, and with his brother, Toni, he founded the Pagot animation studio in 1942. He started production on a color film, *I Fratelli Dinamite* ("The Dynamite Brothers"), but it remained unfinished after the studio was destroyed in a bombardment. Pagot then returned to magazine work, but after World War II he decided to go back to animation in collaboration with his brother (who had just been released from a POW camp). In 1947 the brothers released their first theatrical cartoon, *Lalla, Piccola Lalla* ("Lalla, Little Lalla"), and in 1948 they finally completed *I Fratelli Dinamite.* The film was a financial disaster, and had it not been for the advertising work they were doing at the time, the Pagot studio would not have survived.

From then on Pagot devoted himself exclusively to the production of advertising films and animated commercials for television. He created a number of original characters to advertise a variety of products on Italian TV, and he also used under license American characters such as the Flintstones, Speedy Gonzales and Sylvester. Nino Pagot died in Milan in 1972 without having been able to make a comeback in theatrical animation, a project which he himself had termed "a dream hard to achieve" in a 1968 interview.

S.T.

PAL, GEORGE (1908-1980) American animator and producer born in Ceglad, Hungary, in 1908. After graduation from college, George Pal moved first to Holland, where he made several puppet films, including *Aladdin* or the *Magic Lamp, Sindbad the Sailor* (1934) and *The Space Ship* (1935). He next went to Britain and, working for Horlicks, did *On Parade* (1936), *What Ho She Bumps* (1937) and *Sky Pirates (1938).*

After the outbreak of World War II Pal emigrated to the United States. There he produced his famous Puppettoons series of cartoons, featuring a cocky little hero called Jasper; "Jasper Goes Hunting," "Jasper's Minstrels" and "Jasper's Close Shave" are some of the titles. Pal also created special effects for many science fiction films, including *Destination Moon* (1950), *When Worlds Collide* (1951), *War of the Worlds* (1953) and *Conquest of Space* (1955). Later he produced and directed his own films, such as *The Time Machine* (1960) and *The Wonderful World of the Brothers Grimm* (1962).

Although not a cartoonist in the strict sense, George Pal contributed many innovations that were later incorporated into the animated cartooning canon, and in recognition of which he received a special Oscar in 1943. (Pal was also the recipient of five Academy Awards for special effects, in 1950, 1951, 1953, 1959 and 1969.) He died in May 1980.

M.H.

PAPROCKI, THOMAS (1901-1973) American cartoonist born in Rochester, New York, in 1901. Thomas Paprocki went to New York City at the time of World War I. There he attended art classes at night while working during the day for an advertising agency. He had always exhibited a flair for caricature and a love of sports, which eventually led him into a long career as a sports cartoonist. After several false starts, Paprocki joined the staff of the Associated Press in 1930 as their regular sports cartoonist. His cartoons, signed "Pap," were published in newspapers from coast to coast, and he soon found himself so popular that

Nino and Toni Pagot, credits for "Africa Addio." © Pagot Studio.

Thomas Paprocki ("Pap"). © AP Newsfeatures.

AP asked him to write a sports column to be syndicated along with his daily cartoons. Both enjoyed great success and earned Pap a number of awards.

Paprocki retired in 1965; he died of a heart attack on January 4, 1973, while being taken to a hospital in Atlantic City, New Jersey. Along with Willard Mullin, Paprocki represented the best of a dying breed of nationally syndicated sports cartoonists. His cartoons were full of verve and dash; his figures (helmeted quarterbacks, lithe prizefighters, elegant tennis players) moved with ease and grace across the page. The *New York Times* obituary writer called him "the most famous sports cartoonist of this century."

M.H.

PARK JAE DONG (1952-) Park Jae Dong was born on December 20, 1952, in Ulsan, South Korea. He received a bachelors degree in fine arts and a masters in art education from the elite Seoul National University.

Park's entry into cartooning was rather late, coming after he had taught high school for six years. When the progressive *Hankyoreh Shinmun* was started in 1987, he became the daily's cartoonist. During his decade of employment there, Park was unique among political cartoonists, favoring the one-panel format over the more popular four-panel. He usually drew a one-panel political cartoon ("Hankyoreh Canvas") five days weekly and a full cartoon story on Wednesdays. About 85 percent of them dealt critically with Korean issues. He was temporarily dismissed from *Hankyoreh Shinmun* during the country's economic downturn of 1997-1998.

Park entered cartooning to raise peoples' social consciousness level, believing that political cartoons were the eye of newspapers— "the eye that watches the strong, sees the humane world." *Hankyoreh Shinmun* was attractive to him because of its commitment to stay autonomous, and its ownership by 60,000 Koreans who bought into it. Park called them "people looking after democracy with progressive thoughts," and said what they stood for characterized his own cartoons.

At times, Park moved beyond the drawing table to achieve his ends, especially in regards to the Koreanization of cartoons issue. He helped set up demonstrations, exhibits, and workshops/symposia to denounce Japanese comic art influences and promote indigenous comic art forms; some of this activity emanated from Uri Manwha Hyophoe (Our Cartoon Association), a group in which he was heavily involved. Other projects Park worked on were the professionalization and training of cartoonists, his efforts to influence cartoonists to be more liberal in content and style, and the production of animation shorts.

Park is a meticulous draughtsman who conveys views in bold, visual allegories. He has a great following among young people and intellectuals, mainly because he does not pull his punches and because he works hard to represent the common person's positions.

J.A.L.

PARK, NICHOLAS (1958-) Nicholas Park, the Oscar-honored British animator/director/writer of the world-popular *Wallace and Gromit* series of clay model films, was born in Preston, Lancashire, on December 6, 1958. His mother was a tailor and his father an architectural photographer. He first showed artistic talent as a child by making models from squeezy-bottles, and at 7 years he learned to knit, making a mat for his father. He created his first original cartoon character when he was 11, a cider-drinking rat called Walter. He used the corners of his school books to make animated flicker "films" of Walter. At the age of 13 he made his first attempt at animated films using his father's ciné camera which had single-frame exposing. He made a puppet of Walter out of his mother's bobbins, and a worm out of plasticine. The film was called *Walter Goes Fishing* (1971).

Nick Park's first proper animated film, *Archie's Concrete Nightmare* (1973), was shown on BBC television, the story of a castle in distress. He joined Sheffield Art School at 18 taking a course in Communication Arts, but felt that animation would not be taken seriously. At 22, he studied animation at the National Film School in Beaconsfield. Here he started work on what would become the first Wallace and Gromit film, *A Grand Day Out*.

In 1985 Nick joined the small provincial animation company, Aardman Animations, where he would animate and direct numerous projects including pop music promos, title sequences, and inserts for BBC Children's Television. Films included *Sledgehammer* (1986), *War Story* (1989), *State of the Art* (1990), *Eye for Sound* (1992), and *Creature Comforts*. This was one of a series made by Aardman for Channel 4 Television, cartoons which were animated to prerecorded impromptu speech taken during interviews with unsuspecting ordinary folk. It won the Oscar for Best Short Animated Film of 1990.

A Grand Day Out was finally completed in 1989, star-

OFF THE LEASH By W.B. Park
3-8
Being a gazelle, Robert
felt tremendous pressure
to appear graceful.

W.B. Park, "Off the Leash." © W.B. Park.

ring the simple Northern inventor Wallace and his devoted dog Gromit. Made in plasticine, better known as claymation, the 25-minute film won the British Film Academy Award for 1990 and was nominated for an Oscar. The huge success internationally for the film brought a sequel, *The Wrong Trousers* (1993) which won the 1994 Oscar, and a third film, *A Close Shave* in 1995. The characters have been thoroughly commercialized, more than any other characters in British animation history, and in 1997 a handsome book reprinting the complete storyboard for *A Close Shave* was published by the BBC.

D.G.

PARK, WILLIAM BRYAN (1936-) American cartoonist and illustrator born in Sanford, Florida, on June 12, 1936. After studies at the University of Florida, from which he received his B.A. in 1959, and at the School of Visual Arts in New York City, W.B. Park worked briefly as an assistant art director for McGraw-Hill in New York, and later for Tucker Wayne Advertising in Atlanta. In 1963 he definitively settled back in his native Florida and founded the Park-Art Studio; since that time he has enjoyed a successful career as a freelance humor writer, cartoonist and illustrator.

His gag cartoons and his illustrations have appeared in publications as diverse as the *New Yorker*, *Holiday*, *Look*, *Intellectual Digest*, and *Litigation*, the organ of the American Bar Association. He has also contributed illustrations and/or articles to the *Smithsonian Magazine*, *Fortune*, *Reader's Digest*, and to many of Florida's top daily newspapers. He has also written and illustrated a number of children's books, including *The Pig in the Floppy Black Hat*, *Jonathan's Friends*, and *The Costume Party*.

It is perhaps for his daily cartoon panel, *Off the Leash*, that Park is best known. Starting distribution in 1985 with United Feature Syndicate, it showcased the antics of an unruly canine modeled on the artist's own pet companion, a bulldog named Larry. Centered at first on the main character's shenanigans, it later turned into an animal feature of decidedly absurdist humor (the various animals were seen going to parties, playing strip poker, etc.). Dissatisfied with the smallish circulation of his panel, Park switched to Creators Syndicate, to no avail: *Off the Leash* was discontinued in 1996.

Called by Richard Calhoun in *Contemporary Graphic Artists* one of the "few top flight graphic artists," Park has received a great many awards from professional societies, and his work has been exhibited in galleries around the

Gladys Parker, "Flapper Fanny." © NEA.

world. For the record he lists as his best assignment: "the Kentucky Derby for *Sports Illustrated*."

M.H.

PARKER, GLADYS (1905?-1966) American cartoonist born in Tonawanda, New York, about 1905. Gladys Parker sold her first cartoons to magazines while she was still in high school and in 1927 moved to New York City. Later she went to work for the short-lived *New York Graphic;* when the *Graphic* folded in 1932, she then joined the staff of the Scripps-Howard chain of newspapers as a cartoonist. Around that same time she took over the *Flapper Fanny* newspaper strip from Ethel Hays, who had created it for the Newspaper Enterprise Association (another Scripps-Howard concern) in 1924.

Her work on *Flapper Fanny* led to Parker's own creation, *Mopsy,* which Associated Newspapers started releasing in 1936 as a daily panel, and later as a Sunday feature as well. Like *Flapper Fanny, Mopsy* was mainly concerned with the slightly harebrained activities of an attractive bachelor girl. In addition to her well-known work on *Flapper Fanny* and *Mopsy,* Parker drew two little-known features, *Gay and Her Gang* in the early 1930s and *GI Jane* for the armed forces during World War II. Parker also found time to write (starting in 1958) a daily advice column, *Dear Gals and Guys,* that appeared in the *Los Angeles Herald-Express.*

Parker died from lung cancer at Glendale Community Hospital in California on April 28, 1966, and her daily and Sunday feature died with her.

M.H.

PARRISH, JOSEPH (1905-198?) American cartoonist born in Summertown, Tennessee, in 1905. In the early 1920s the young Joe Parrish began drawing political cartoons for the *Nashville Banner,* filling not only the professional shoes of earlier Nashville cartoonists Bill Sykes and Carey Orr, but their stylistic ones as well; his cartoons were filled with animation and relied on likenesses instead of caricature. Parrish stayed with the *Banner* for four years and then switched to the *Nashville* Tennessean, where he remained for another seven. In 1936, on the suggestion of Carey Orr, he moved to the Chicago Tribune. Parrish retired in 1972, but he continues to draw his long-running Sunday feature, *Nature Notes,* for the *Tribune.* He died in the 1980s.

Parrish is an accomplished member of what must be called the Billy Ireland school of political cartooning. He drew with little mechanical or crayon shading, instead using handsome, crisp pen lines and crosshatching. His likenesses were almost photographic, and his situational cartoons aimed for the funny bone without sacrificing their political point. His front-page, full-color *Tribune* cartoons in support of Senator McCarthy's campaign to expose Communist subversion stand as some of America's strongest cartooning work. His part in the doomed crusade to keep America from entering World War II was also notable.

R.M.

PARRISH, MAXFIELD FREDERICK (1870-1966) American illustrator and cartoonist born in Philadelphia,

I don't know art—

Joseph Parrish. © Chicago Tribune.

Pennsylvania, on July 25, 1870. Maxfield Parrish was educated at Haverford College (1888-91) and at the Pennsylvania College of Fine Arts; he later studied with Howard Pyle, as did so many fine illustrators of two generations. His first major sale was a cover for *Harper's Weekly* in 1895, and sales to *Life* and *Scribner's* (humorous and classical motifs, respectively) soon followed. For the next two decades, Parrish's work appeared frequently in *Collier's, St. Nicholas,* the *Century* and the *Ladies' Home Journal.* In the early 1920s he frequently drew and painted for *Life;* his humorous covers, especially for holiday issues, are perhaps the most representative work of Parrish's entire career; they abound with good humor, exacting draftsmanship and the boldest combinations of colors.

Parrish also became a popular book illustrator, with dozens of titles to his credit; among the best remembered are *The King of Hearts,* Eugene Field's *Poems of Childhood,* Kenneth Grahame's *Dream Days* and *The Golden Age.* As a muralist his commissions were many; *Old King Cole,* an outstanding example, now hangs in the Saint Regis Hotel in New York. His many advertising accounts included Edison Mazda lamps, Fisk tires and Jell-O. Over the decades he produced numerous calendar illustrations, reproductions of which still sell today.

Parrish's individualistic utilization of photographic detail and sentimental or classical themes blended elements of the styles of artists as diverse as the PreRaphaelites and Dali. He gave his name to the pure "Maxfield Parrish blue" he used; he indeed had a unique color sense and a consistent approach to the structure of tonal representation. His "gimmicks'—spotted sunlight, golds against blues, blues against oranges, wrinkled checkerboard patterns—functioned to set his moods and not, as might be expected, to annoyingly divert the eye from the focal point of his painting. It was this integration, the obvious clash of internal elements ultimately combining for a total mood and unified image, that made Parrish an illustrator of significance. And with his pretentious themes of classical grandeur and his enormous, fantasy-

"I took a thorn out of his paw a few years back."

Virgil Partch ("VIP"). © True.

filled landscapes, it was his humor, (as manifested in his *Life* cartoon-paintings, for example) that kept his work in perspective.

The recipient of many awards and honorary degrees, Maxfield Parrish died at his home in Plainfield, New Hampshire, on March 30, 1966.

R.M.

PARTCH, VIRGIL FRANKLIN II (1916-1984) American cartoonist born on Saint Paul's Island, Alaska, on October 17, 1916. Virgil Partch (or "VIP," as he signs himself) was educated at the University of Arizona and the Chouinard Art Institute in California. After completing his art education, he spent some time working in the extracurricular art department at the Disney studios. He soon turned successfully to freelance cartooning, and since then his work has appeared regularly in outlets like the *New Yorker*, *Look*, the *Saturday Evening Post*, *This Week* and *True*. He also developed a syndicated strip feature called *Big George* in 1960.

Partch is primarily a black humorist with a boldly sardonic bite. His ink-line characters are strongly reminiscent of those mysterious statues found on the Easter Islands. His panels are not of the "busy" type, for he generally focuses on the main action, with a minimum of attention to the background. In his humor, he seems fascinated by the fool-particularly the literal-minded fool. Thus the man who takes seriously the suggestion that he "dig up" a date for a party, or the husband who is told by a smiling gigolo type with two rather obvious breast-high indentations on his shirtfront that his big-busted wife is a "gifted conversationalist." He also makes use of the absurd, the mildly libidinal and the sight gag, and he is fond of setting his scenes in deserts and on desert islands.

While not especially original either in style or in range of humor, Partch's work is immediately identifiable and avoids the anonymity that befalls so many cartoonists. He has enjoyed a long and successful career because of his ability to be consistently amusing in a darkish vein—no small achievement in so prolific an artist. Among the more recent collections of his cartoons are *VIP Tosses a Party*, *New Faces on the Barroom Floor* (1961) and *VIP's Quips* (1975). In 1964 his work was honored with a first prize at the Brussels Cartoon Exhibition. In addition to *Big George*, Partch began a new comic strip, The *Captain's Gig*, in 1977. He died on August 10, 1984, in a car crash near Los Angeles.

R.C.

PARTRIDGE, SIR BERNARD (1861-1945) British cartoonist born in London, England, on October 11, 1861. The last of the great "classical cartoonists" to grace the full-page plates of Punch, J. Bernard Partridge was the son of Professor Richard Partridge, president of the Royal College of Surgeons. The boy was educated at Stonyhurst Catholic College and matriculated at London University in 1878. He studied painting and stained glass window design at West London School of Art. He also had a spell on the London stage as an actor. Under the name of Bernard Gould he appeared in the premiere performance of George Bernard Shaw's *Arms and the Man.*

Partridge exhibited his oils and watercolors at the Royal Academy and had his first cartoon published in *Moonshine*. Publication in *Judy, Society* and *London* Pictorial followed, and he illustrated *Stageland,* Jerome K. Jerome's series in Playgoer. His first Punch drawing was published in 1891, and he joined the staff the following year, retiring in 1945 after 54 years! He took over the *Cartoon Junior* when Sambourne moved into Tenniel's spot in January 1901, then moved into Sambourne's spot when that artist died in 1910. He continued to draw the weekly cartoon, following the traditional style of his predecessors, until 1945. Knighted in 1925, he died on August 9, 1945.

Bluff and Iron.—The old Chancellor: "Not my methods exactly, but you seem to have nearly the same success."

Bernard Partridge, 1938. © Punch.

Books: *Stageland* (1889); *Voces Populi* (1890); *Travelling Companions* (1892); *My Flirtations* (1892); *Man from Blankley's* (1893); *Mr. Punch's Pocket Ibsen* (1893); *Proverbs in Porcelain* (1893); *The Kitchen Maid* (1896); *Puppets at Large* (1897); *Babboo Jabberlee* (1897); *Tinted Venus* (1898); *Papers from Punch* (1898); *Wee Folk Good Folk* (1899); *Bayard from Bengal* (1902); *Rabbi Ben Ezra* (1915); *Punch Drawings* (1921); *Fifty Years with Punch* (1946); and *Bernard Partridge and Punch* (1952).

D.G.

PASCIN, JULES
See Pinkas, Julius.

PASHCHENKO, MSTISLAV (1901-1958) Animator born in Russia on April 1, 1901. Mstislav Pashchenko graduated from an art school in Petrograd in 1922. He worked as a poster designer and book illustrator before joining the animation studio in Leningrad in 1933, first as an assistant animator, later as an animator. The first cartoon he directed was the 1939 *Dzhyabzha.* Like many other filmmakers, Pashchenko turned out propaganda material during World War II. In 1946 he joined Soyuzmult'film, the same year directing *The Titmouse* in collaboration with Aleksandr Ivanov. His 1947 *Little Song of Happiness* earned a bronze medal at the Venice Biennial. It was followed by a number of pleasant and unpretentious cartoons, such as *Mashenka's Concert* (1949), *Where the Pine Trees Grow* (1950), *Forest Travelers* (1951) and *The Disobedient Kitten* (1953).

In 1955 Pashchenko brought out his most interesting cartoon film, *The Unusual Match;* its protagonists were the wood figures used in the popular European game of table soccer. In this cartoon, however, they came to life and played a real soccer match against the opposition, also made up of wood players. The film was well drawn, well designed and very witty; it received much acclaim in the Soviet Union and abroad. Pashchenko's later films were not on a par with *Match.* They were usually collaborations (notably with Boris Dyozhkin and Dmitri Babichenko) and include *Old Acquaintances* (1956) and *Greetings to Friends* (1957). Pashchenko died in Moscow on October 22, 1958.

Mstislav Pashchenko.

One of the more talented of Russian animation directors (albeit almost unknown in the United States), Pashchenko won many awards at Venice, Durban, Karlovy-Vary, Kraków and Damascus.

M.H.

PASSACANTANDO, STELIO (1927-) Italian animator born in Rome, Italy, in 1927. Stelio Passacantando graduated from the Rome Academy of Fine Arts and, after a brief interlude as a set designer, became interested in film animation. In 1954 he founded an animation school (the first of its kind in Italy) under the auspices of the Italian Ministry of Labor. Around this time he also worked on *Le Avventure di Rompicollo,* an animated film that was never commercially released. In the early 1960s Passacantando moved to England, joining the National Film Board and collaborating on advertising and entertainment cartoons for the BBC, alongside such animators as George Dunning, Dick Williams and Grant Munro. He also worked with American cartoonists on several animated telefilms, including *The Adventures of Mr. Hero.*

After his return to Italy in 1964, Passacantando worked simultaneously on a number of shorts and on audiovisual material for companies in Rome, London and New York. In 1968 he did several shorts for the promotion of highway safety with the famous duo Gianini Luzzati. In 1974 Passacantando worked on the animated feature *Il Giro del Mon do degli Inamorati di Peynet* ("Around the World with Peynet's Lovers"). Using material culled from turn-of-the-century prints and cartoons, he produced a long series of *Chronicles of Another Age* (1974-76), as well as many other programs for Italian TV. For German TV he directed in 1974 *Orphi und Eura,* an animated film based on Dino Buzzati's *Poema a Fumetti* ("Poem in Comic Strip Form"). Passacantando currently manages Studio Margutta 42, an animation unit, and contributes to the television series *Oggi, Tanto Tempo Fa* ("Today, So Long Ago"). In 1984 he produced an animated feature, *Il generale all'inferno* ("The General in Hell"), based on a poem by Chilean writer Pablo Neruda; but in recent years he has become better known as a painter.

S.T.

PATTERSON, ROBERT (1895-1981) American cartoonist and illustrator born in Chicago, Illinois, on November 13, 1895. Raised in Toledo, Ohio, Bob Patterson studied at the Toledo Art Museum and later at the Chicago Art Institute, where his teachers included John Norton. His early work was in advertising, and he drew cuts for Sears-Roebuck catalogs. With Russell Patterson (no relation), he opened the Patterson Studios, doing cartoons and illustrations; Russell also conducted a correspondence cartooning course. (Later, Russell's brother married Bob's sister, keeping the name in the family.)

In the mid-1920s Bob Patterson moved to New York, where he drew for Al Dorne's Kent Studios, doing advertising work, and for the Rahl Studio, illustrating stories for major magazines. In 1924 Norman Anthony, the new editor of Judge, invited Patterson to draw cartoons, and so began the weekly feature *Laughs from the Shows.* Gags from (or loosely attributed to) Broadway shows, illustrated by three to seven pen, ink and wash drawings, comprised the page. Jefferson Machamer took over *Laughs from the Shows* when Judge offered Patterson a dream assignment: to travel in Europe and send back weekly cartoons from fashionable hotels and watering holes. *Betty Goes Abroad,* with a kind of a diary or picture-postcard format, was the result. In 1926 and 1927 it appeared as a weekly series of very handsome and trendy wash drawings illustrating witty captions; most of the locales were in France.

Betty ended in 1927, and Patterson found himself stranded in a Paris filled with colorful American expatriates like Hemingway (for whom he was often mistaken) and with many prospects for fashion drawing assignments. He hooked up with *Vogue of Paris* and *Le Jardin des Modes,* both Condé-Nast publications; he continued to work for the publisher after his return to the United States around 1930. Before leaving Paris, Patterson exhibited at the Salon de Printemps and studied at the Grande Chaumière and the Académie Julian. In America, he continued to cartoon (for *College Humor*), illustrate (for *Good Housekeeping, Redbook, McCall's, Ladies' Home Journal,* the *American* and *Cosmopolitan*) and do book illustrations ranging from pen-and-ink cartoons to lush paintings in oil. In 1964 he became an instructor at the Famous Artists School; in between private commissions, book illustration and recent cartoon submissions to magazines, he continued to teach until his death in 1981.

Patterson's cartoon style was very much in the spirit of the times, and the quality of his line as well as the profusion of gray wash tones paid quiet and attractive homage to Ralph Barton. He composed his drawings beautifully and achieved an effective mixture of realistic and fashion styles with cartoon conventions.

Books: Julia Ward Howe, Girl of Old New York; Harriet Beecher Stowe, Connecticut Girl; john Audubon, Boy Naturalist; Robert Fulton, Boy Craftsman; Barbie, Midge and Ken; Barbie's Secret; Barbie in Television; Living in Our Country and Other Lands; On Our Way; A Brother the Size of Me; You Will Go to the Moon; Jokes for Children; and *The Wizard of Oz to Read Aloud.*

R.M.

Jealousy in a Bavarian Beer Garden

Bruno Paul, 1897.

PATUFET, EN (Spain) This cartoon series was created by Antoni Muntanyola i Carné (1883-1954) and gave its name to the magazine *En Patufet,* which began publication in 1904.

En Patufet was a child who symbolized the new cultural, regional and moralistic attitudes of La Lliga Catalana, a powerful political party founded at the turn of the century. The captions expressed many of the party's ideological positions. Thus, *En Patufet* is a historical document of great importance because it reflected the social changes and revolutionary movements that endlessly gripped Spain between the two world wars. At the same time, *En Patufet* was a very popular cartoon series (or a very unpopular one for those who did not share its political views). It disappeared, along with its magazine namesake, in 1938.

J.M.

PAUL, BRUNO (1874-1968) German architect, designer, educator and cartoonist born at Seifhennersdorf in der Lausitz, Silesia, on January 19, 1874. The son of a master carpenter, Bruno Paul studied at the Dresden School of Applied Art from 1886 to 1894 and then at the Munich Academy from 1894 to 1907. His work for *Jugend,* and especially for *Simplicissimus,* falls almost completely within this Munich period (when he was also doing painting and book illustration). He was already an established figure in the art world when the publisher Albert Langen invited him to work on the new *Simplicissimus* (first published 1896), and Paul helped choose the artistic cadre for the magazine.

It has been said that Langen enlisted Paul's aid chiefly for prestige and to acquire a solid artistic "front" behind which he could more safely attack the establishment. Be that as it may, the drawings Paul contributed for some ten years are just about the most beautiful ever published in *Simplicissimus,* though not the most savage or avant-garde. In a personal application of postimpressionist and art nouveau patterning, Paul used large, flat color areas, arresting angles of vision and fascinating negative spaces, always creating a masterly overall composition. His subject matter was folly in general, but he betrayed a special weakness for the Munich proletariat and peasantry.

In 1907 the kaiser, delighted with Paul's decorations for the triumphal opening of a museum, named him director of the art school of the Berlin Museum of Applied Art (Paul was also co-founder of the United Workshops for Art in Manufacture), and his Berlin career began. After working in several educational institutions, he was head of the United Government Schools for Fine and Applied Art from 1924 to 1932. In these years he was a prominent architect, designing office and medical buildings, villas and ships, doing interior decoration and furniture design, arranging exhibitions and creating all kinds of commercial graphics, as well as teaching. (His architectural endeavors had begun about 1900 with a personal reinterpretation of earlier German styles.)

In 1933 he resigned from his official position and retired to Diisseldoff. After the fall of the Third Reich he was once more in the public eye and was honored by the Bundesrepublik. He moved back to Berlin, where he died on August 17, 1968.

S.A.

PAYNE, EUGENE GRAY (1919-) American cartoonist born in Charlotte, North Carolina, in 1919. Eugene Payne, whose mother was an accomplished watercolorist, was educated at Syracuse University. He majored in fine arts and for years was a commercial artist and portraitist. As a political cartoonist he freelanced to his hometown Charlotte Observer and worked part-time (with Chuck Brooks) for the *Birmingham News* in Alabama. He joined the staff of the Observer full-time in 1958. Payne won the Pulitzer Prize in 1968, and in the early 1970s he turned to the nascent field of political cartooning on television; his work appeared on station WSOC in Charlotte. In August 1978 he returned to the *Observer.* He is now retired.

Payne's style keeps alive the tradition of Fitzpatrick, Tom Little and Ross Lewis. His supple brush and reserved, lush crayon shading are obviously heightened by his fine arts background; his composition and especially his command of anatomy are sophisticated and striking.

R.M.

PEANUTS (U.S.) In 1965 Lee Mendelson approached Charles Schulz, the creator of the highly successful Peanuts comic strip, with a project for adapting his characters to TV animation. Schulz accepted, and the first Peanuts special, "A Charlie Brown Christmas," was aired on the CBS network on December 9, 1965.

Many more specials followed, usually timed for holidays or special occasions; thus, the Peanuts crew variously celebrated Christmas, Easter, Halloween, Thanksgiving and even Arbor Day. Some of the most notable among the 30-minute specials (which numbered almost 20 by 1978) are "It's the Great Pumpkin, Charlie Brown" (1966), "You're in Love, Charlie Brown" (1967), "He's Your Dog, Charlie Brown" (1968), "It Was a Great Summer, Charlie Brown (1969), "A Charlie Brown Thanksgiving" (1973) and "You're the Greatest, Charlie Brown" (1979). In addition National General Pictures has produced full-length *Peanuts* cartoons for theatrical release, starting with *A Boy Named Charlie Brown* in 1969, followed by *Snoopy, Come Home* (1972) and *Race for Your Life, Charlie Brown* (1977). These films were also telecast on CBS-TV. The latest theatrical release to date has been the *1980 Bon Voyage, Charlie Brown (and Don't Come Back.)* In contrast the television specials are being broadcast and rebroadcast every year.

The whole Peanuts clan usually takes part in the goings-on: the wishy-washy (by his own admission) Charlie Brown, the willful Lucy, the rough-and-ready Peppermint Patty, Linus the intellectual, Pig Pen the slob and, of course, Snoopy are some of the principals. (More often than not the beagle steals the show from his two-legged companions.) Although not on the same level of observation and insight as the newspaper strip, the stories and dialogue, written by Schulz himself, are pithy, literate and sometimes poignant. The director of the specials, Bill Melendez, shows what can be done with the techniques of limited animation, and his work is, in terms of artistry and taste, miles ahead of most of the made-for-television cartoon shows. Charlie has been variously voiced by Peter Robbins, Todd Barbee and Chad Webber; Robin Kohn, Pamela Ferdyn, Sally Dryer and Tracy Stratford have supplied the voices for Lucy; while Linus has been played by Stephen Shea and Chris Shea.

"A Boy Named Charlie Brown," a "Peanuts" TV special. © United Feature Syndicate.

The *Peanuts* specials have drawn high ratings from the start and have been shown in countless reruns; they have also—and justifiably so—garnered an impressive number of Emmy awards.

M.H.

PEASE, LUCIUS CURTIS (1869-1963) American cartoonist, editor and Pulitzer Prize winner born in Winnemucka, Nevada, on March 27, 1869. Lucius ("Lute") Pease was orphaned at the age of five and raised by relatives in Charlotte, Vermont. In 1887 he was graduated from the Franklin Academy in Malone, New York, and returned to the West; he worked as a ranchhand, lived in the Oklahoma Territory before the land rush, worked as a teamster, spent five years prospecting for gold in the Yukon, chopped wood and ran a bunkhouse. In between these activities, in 1895, Pease held a job as a reporter-artist on the Portland Oregonian, with more sketches demanded after he depicted a murder-suicide he witnessed. But his activities in the Alaskan Territory attracted the attention of President Theodore Roosevelt, who appointed Pease U.S.

Lute Pease. © Newark Evening News.

commissioner in northwest Alaska; he was seeking a further appointment as a reindeer official when the Oregonian beckoned again with an offer to become the paper's chief editorial cartoonist.

Pease temporarily left the drawing board in 1906 to become editor of the *Pacific Monthly;* in his six years there he raised the circulation from 40,000 to 100,000 by such perspicacious actions as accepting fiction by a writer named Jack London, who had been rejected elsewhere. The magazine was sold to Sunset in 1912, after which Pease traveled east with the intent of establishing a syndicate. Instead, the *Newark* (N.J.) *Evening News* showed its own perspicacity and offered him the job of political cartoonist. He accepted and remained with the paper until 1952.

Lute Pease drew in a native American style, uninhibited and lanky. In spirit his drawings were relatives of Dwig's, and his Democratic politics were definite but never vicious. An accomplished painter, Pease wrote one book, *Sourdough Bread,* and drew a comic strip for the *News,* Powder Pete, about an old adventurer and his young friend; each creation reflected his experiences in the Klondike. He died in 1963.

R.M.

PEDERNEIRAS, RAUL PARANHOS (1874-1953) Brazilian cartoonist, writer and teacher horn in Rio de Janeiro, Brazil, in 1874. In 1898, after graduating with a degree in law, Raul Pederneiras embarked on a cartooning career (using only his first name) at the daily *O Mercurio* in Rio. At the turn of the century, Raul was collaborating (as cartoonist or writer, or both) on such publications as *D. Quixote* and *Jornal do Brasil.* He was also one of the founders of the humor magazines *O Tagarela* and *O Malho.* Pederneiras was a professor of anatomy at the National School of Fine Arts from 1918 to 1938; he then taught international law at the University of Brazil Law School. He also held many exhibitions and one-man shows. As a playwright, Pederneiras wrote *Berliques o Berloques* (1908), a satire of Rio society in the early years of the century. He died in Rio in 1953.

Raul was a humorist, not a satirist, and he aimed at eliciting smiles rather than guffaws with his cartoons.

His style was elegant and a little mannered; his draftsmanship was impeccable, but his drawings lacked spontaneity. Collections of his cartoons include *Liqoes de Caricatura* ("Lessons in Cartooning," 1928) and *Cenas de Vida Carioca* ("Scenes of Rio Life," two volumes, 1924 and 1935).

A.M.

PEDROSA, AMILDE (1920-) Brazilian cartoonist born in Acre, in westernmost Brazil, in 1920. Amilde Pedrosa studied art in Manaus, and in 1940 he started his cartooning career there under the pseudonym "Appe" (the phonetic rendering of his initials in Portuguese). In 1946 he moved to Rio de Janeiro and soon was contributing cartoons to such publications as *A Manha, Vanguarda, Didrio da Noite* and O *Jornal.* Pedrosa achieved fame with his political and editorial cartoons, which have been published in the newspaper *O Cruzeiro* since 1953. He retired at the end of the 1980s.

Pedrosa's drawing style is very sparse, caricatural and exaggerated to the point of absurdity. He gets his message across swiftly and pungently. He is today one of Brazil's most admired editorial cartoonists.

A.M.

PEICHL, GUSTAV (1928-) Austrian editorial cartoonist, architect and printmaker born in Vienna, Austria, on March 18, 1928. It is an open secret that the internationally acclaimed architect Gustav Peichl and the brilliant editorial cartoonist "Ironimus" are one and the same man. He studied at the Vienna Academy from 1949 to 1953 and then set up as a freelance architect and industrial design-

Gustav Peichl ("Ironimus"). © Osterreichische Illustrierte.

er. In this capacity he has done town planning and has designed residences, schools, a convent, airplane interiors, medical buildings and exposition pavilions, including Austria's building (a modernistic mountain lodge) at the New York World's Fair of 1964-65. Awards have been plentiful for Peichl's architectural innovations. Since 1973 he has taught a master class in architecture at the Vienna Academy.

It was not until 1955, however, that Ironimus began his incredible second career, during which he has contributed eagerly awaited cartoons to *Die Presse* in Vienna, the *Siiddeutsche Zeitung* in Munich and *Weltwoche* in Zurich. Employing a tight, wiry contour line something like Saul Steinberg's or Paul Flora's but quite personal, and displaying great ability as a humorous portraitist, Ironimus relentlessly covers all local, European and world events with enormous insight and sophisticated wit.

Also a printmaker, Ironimus has had political and other works (drawings and prints) acquired by such museums as the Albertina in Vienna and the Museum of Modern Art in New York. In a perceptive essay on Peichl-Ironimus, Walter Koschatzky, director of the Albertina, considers the influence of the architect on the cartoonist and finds it not only in the cartoonist's ability to abstract "signs" from reality and render them in terms of line but also in his exceptional organizational and compositional prowess.

Books: Julius, ein Kanzler in der Karikatur ("Julius, a Chancellor Caricatured," 1958); *No Smoking* (1958); *Helden* ("Heroes," 1959); *Made in Austria* (1960); *Die Sechziger Jahre* ("The Sixties," 1970); *Mein Osterreich* ("My Austria," 1975); and *Weltcircus* ("World Circus,"a 1977 anthology of 22 years of political cartoons).

As an architect Peichl has conceived many official and private buildings. Some of his more recent commissions include a school in Vienna (1996), a department store in Dusseldorf (1997), and a sound studio for Austrian television (also in 1997). He is currently involved in the revamping of the Munchner Kammerspiele, a Munich theater, costs being estimated at 147 million deutschmarks. Peichl has also kept busy cartooning and publishing his cartoons. He is a member of the Art Senate of Austria, of the Academy of Arts in Berlin, and an honorary member of the Union of German Architects, of the Royal Institute of British Architects and of the American Institute of Architects (since 1996). He has received numerous awards both as architect and as cartoonist.

W.F.

PELLEGRINI, CARLO (1838-1889) British caricaturist born in Italy in 1838. *Vanity Fair,* the high-class magazine that subtitled itself "A Weekly Show of Political, Social and Literary Wares, was only three months old when its editor, Thomas Gibson Bowles, announced that from January 30, 1869, each issue would contain "A Full Page Cartoon of an Entirely Novel Character, Printed in Chromo-Lithography." To celebrate the event, the price of the magazine was increased to sixpence. The first cartoon, a caricature portrait in color, was of Benjamin Disraeli. It accompanied a biographical piece signed "Jehu Junior," and was itself signed "Singe." The third cartoon of the series, which had already become a collector's item among the educated public, was by the same artist but bore a different signature, "Ape." And "Ape" remained for the rest of the series' run (although the cartoonist was in fact known to his friends and associates as "Pelican").

Carlo Pellegrini, who brought a new kind of caricature to British journalism, traced his maternal ancestry back to the Medicis. As a young man born into a wealthy and landed family, he was a leader of Neapolitan society and fought with Garibaldi at Volturno and Capua. When his inheritance evaporated, Pellegrini went to London. He arrived, penniless but talented, in November 1864. A great success in London society, he studied his fashionable company, drawing them from memory once he was home at his studio.

He died of a lung complaint in 1889; in memoriam *Vanity Fair* published a caricature of Ape, drawn by confrere Arthur J. Marks.

D.G.

PELLICER I FEÑÉ, JOSEP LLUIS (1842-1901) Spanish cartoonist and painter born in Barcelona, Spain, in 1842. Josep Lluis Pellicer studied architecture at the University of Barcelona and was highly respected for his artistic abilities. Following the completion of his studies, he worked briefly with the Catalan painter Marti Alsina and then went to Rome (1864). Pellicer's first cartoons appeared in *Lo Xanguet* (1865-74) under the pseudonym Nyapus." Starting in the early 1870s, his work was published by *L'Esquella de 1a Torratxa* and *La Campana de Gracia.* Concurrently with his career as a cartoonist, Pellicer made a name for himself as a painter. At the time of his death in 1901 he was the director of museums in Barcelona.

Pellicer's cartoons have strong political overtones; they were particularly geared toward the struggles of the socialist parties in Catalonia. As the president of the International Association of Socialist Workers, Pellicer had firsthand knowledge of the social and political climate of Spain. His cartoons show akeen awareness of the ideological complexities of his times. Pellicer's cartoons—a felicitous blend of artistic excellence and topical relevance—were unfortunately often marred by moralistic preaching.

J.M.

PENNES, JEAN (1894-1982) French cartoonist and caricaturist born in Paris, France, on June 3, 1894. After World War I, Jean Pennes collaborated on several satirical and humor magazines (Le Rire, Le Sourire, *Candide,* etc.), and after World War II, on *Le Figaro* (1945-67), using the pen name "J. Sennep."

His cartoons cover all the important political events, figures and scandals of the last 50 years, as the titles of some of his albums indicate: *Cartel et Cie* (1926), *Au Bout du Quai* ("At the End of the Platform," 1929), Livre de Comptes de Stavisky ("Stavisky's Bookkeeping Ledgers," 1934), *"Dans l'Honneur et la Dignité"* ("In Honor and Dignity," 1944), *De Vincent a' René* ("From President Vincent to President René," 1954), *Le Tour du Monde en 80 Visas* ("Around the World in 80 Visas," 1959). He has also illustrated several books, among which Histoire de *France, 1918-1938* ("History of France," 1938) is definitely the best. He died

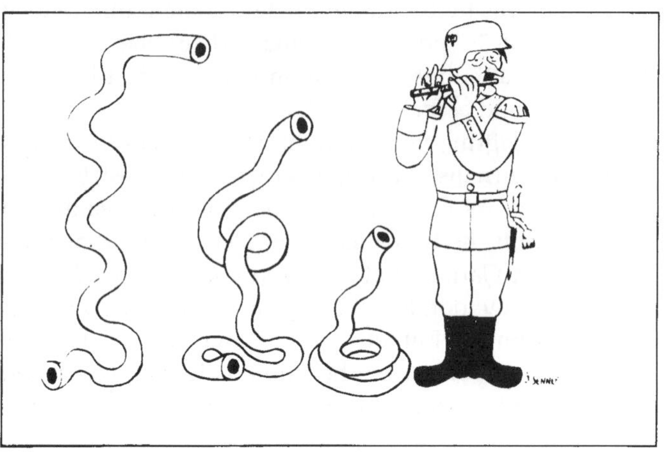

Macaroni Charmer

Jean Pennes ("Sennep"). © Pennes.

in 1982 at his home in Saint-Germain-en-Laye, near Paris.

Sennep's drawings capture with an economy of line the essence of a situation or personality, often reducing it to an absurd extreme. In his "Au Travail" ("To Work"), the workers, the tools, the dog and the factories are idle, folding their hands, legs, handles, tail, chimney stacks and even a moustache in idleness. Another Sennep cartoon shows infant Hitler with a swastika tattooed on his buttock and a moustache under his nose, sucking on Krupp baby bottles that look ominously like bombs and making a toast to scurrying politicos: "To Your Health, My Little Dad- dies!"

P.H.

PEOPLE WE CAN DO WITHOUT
See Advice to the Mentally Feeble.

PÉPÉ LE PEW (U.S.) Chuck Jones and his chief story writer, Michael Maltese, created the character Pépé le Pew the Gallic skunk in 1944. Pépé was a flamboyant, dashing and always amorous creature whose French accent and suave demeanor were more than a little inspired by Charles Boyer's role as Pépé le Moko in the 1938 movie *Algiers;* he first appeared in "The Odor-able Kitty," directed by Jones.

The basic premise of the Pépé le Pew cartoons never varied: a hapless cat (of whatever gender) would accidentally have a white stripe painted on its back, thus becoming the object of Pépé's unrestrained ardor; "Who Scent You?" is one among many good examples. Pépé's very French élan and his knowing asides ("Ah, ah, she is playing hard to get, that little coquette," he would whisper to the audience after being bashed on the head with a baseball bat by one of his intended victims) made him a favorite with the public. Pépé's foil was often the panic-stricken Sylvester, and one of their encounters led to an Oscar ("For Scent-imental Reasons," 1949). Chuck Jones directed all the Pépé le Pew cartoons until the 1960s, when Warner Brothers closed its animation studio.

M.H.

PERELMAN, SIDNEY JOSEPH (1904-1979) American cartoonist and author born in Brooklyn, New York, on February 1, 1904. While a student at Brown University, S.J. Perelman drew for the campus humor magazine and contributed to Judge as early as May 1923; his first original cartoon for the weekly appeared on August 22, 1925 (earlier drawings having been reprints). He was one of Norman Anthony's many discoveries, and a highly irrepressible one; his cartoons, and later his articles, were fully in keeping with the zany atmosphere of what can be called the prototype of *MAD* magazine. If anything, Perelman's material was loaded with even more puns, more nonsensical non sequiturs, more campy irreverence, than that of his fellows.

In 1929 Perelman switched to *College Humor,* remaining for a year. He also worked in motion pictures, writing for the Marx Brothers, among others (he later did the screenplay for Around the World in *Eighty Days,* for which he won the 1956 Academy Award and the New York Film Critics Award). In 1931 he began an association with the *New Yorker* magazine that continued until his death on October 17, 1979. He also wrote sketches for such Broadway revues as *The Third Little Show* and *Work a Little Faster.*

Perelman's drawing style was for the most part a libel on old woodcuts; indeed, much of his early work lampooned sentimental prints and sappy Victorian prose. Usually the cartoons had little to do with their captions (e.g., two men running into an office: "Doctor! I've got Bright's Disease and he's got mine!"). Then Perelman would follow up with several pun-filled approximations

Pépé' le Pew. © Warner Brothers.

The score is forty LOVE, said Frank meaningly.

S.J. Perelman, 1928. © Judge.

of moldy vaudeville routines, often in Jazz Age slang. It was great fun and reads just as freshly today. The drawings were in pen and ink, and the later ones were toned with wash. Perelman also executed color covers for judge. It has been reported that Perelman declined to reprint his early material, but many who know his work from *Judge* and *College Humor* consider it—especially the cartoons—as amusing as any of his later work and look forward to its republication.

Books: *Dawn Ginsburgh's Revenge* (1929); *Parlor, Bedroom and Bath* (a play, 1930); *All Good Americans* (1934); *Strictly from Hunger* (1937); *Look Who's Talking* (1940); *The Night Before Christmas* (1941); *The Dream Department* (1943); *A Touch of Venus* (a play, with Ogden Nash, (1943); *Crazy Like a Fox* (1944); *Keep It Crisp* (1946); *Acres and Pains* (1947); *The Best of S.J. Perelman* (1947); *Westward Ha* (1948); *Listen to the Mocking Bird* (1949); The *Swiss Family Perelman* (1950); *The Ill-Tempered Clavichord* (1953); *Perelman's Home Companion* (1955); *The Road to Milltown* (1957); *The Most of S.J. Perelman* (1958); *The Rising Gorge* (1961); *The Beauty Part* (a plav, 1963); *Chicken Inspector No. 23* (1966); *Baby, It's Cold Inside* (1970); and *Vinegar Puss* (1975).

R.M.

PERICH ESCALA, JAIME (1941-1995) Spanish cartoonist born in Barcelona, Spain, in 1941. After completing his art studies, Jaime Perich decided to turn to cartooning as a career. His first cartoons appeared in the daily press in 1966; *Solidaridad Nacional, El Correo Cataldn* and *Tele/Express* were the newspapers that gave the fledgling cartoonist his forum. Later in the 1960s, as he became more and more recognized, Perich contributed cartoons to most major Spanish magazines, including *Fotogramas, Gaceta Ilustrada, Triunfo, La Codorniz, Hermano Lobo, Cuadernos para el Didlogo, Oriflama, Canigd, Tele-stel* and *Arreu*. He also works for the political magazine *Opinion* and for the humor weekly *Por Favor*, of which he is the coeditor. Perich's daily cartoons are now mainly published in *La Vanguardia* and *La* Voz de *Galicia.*

Perich's *Autopista*, published in 1969, started the current boom in gag cartoons in Spain, and it has consistently been on the best-seller list since it first appeared. Perich is one of the two or three best cartoonists in Spain today, and he has contributed to making the cartoon a major medium of communication there.

Books: Perich-Match; Autopista ("Freeway"); *Setze Fetges* ("Sixteen Livers"); *Los Tres Pies del Gato* ("The Cat's Three Feet"); *Erase una Vez* ("Once upon a Time"); *Perichistorias; Diccionario; Didlogo entre el Poder y el No Poder* ("Dialogue Between Power and Powerlessness"); and *Noticias del 50 Canal* ("News from the 5th Channel," an allusion to the fact that there are only four channels on Spanish television). He died in Mataro, nea Barcelona, on February 1, 1995. Among his latest books were: *Perichmania* (1989), *Lo mejor de Perich* ("The Best of Perich," 1993), *Los gatos de Perich* ("Perich's Cats," 1995), and *Asi lo vio todo el Perich* ("As Perich Sees It," also 1995).

J.M.

PERICLES

See Maranhão, Pericles.

PERICOLI, TULLIO (1936-) Italian cartoonist and artist born in Colli del Tronto, Italy, in 1936. After dropping out of law school, Tullio Pericoli freelanced cartoons to a number of provincial newspapers; in 1962 he became a contract cartoonist for the Milanese daily *Il Giorno*. There he drew illustrations for short stories, cartoons commenting upon the paper's editorials and articles, and comic strips for the literary page satirizing the phobias and manias of literary types. At the same time he pursued a career as a sculptor and painter, and freelanced editorial cartoons to a number of news magazines. His meeting with the writer Emanuele Pirella resulted in two comic strips published in the monthly *Linus: Identikit* , a sort of round-the-world journey with the high and mighty, and *Il Dottor Rigolo*, a further exploration of contemporary themes.

In 1973 Pericoli started contributing to the literary page of *Il Corriere della Sera* with an interesting conceit: a book review in comic strip form. Recently *Il Corriere* has also been publishing Pericoli's weekly panel, *Tutti da Fulvia Sabato Sera* ("Everybody Come to Fulvia's Saturday Night"), a lighthearted spoof of literary salons. Since 1976, for *L'Espresso, Pericoli* and *Pirella* have done a weekly panel called *Cronache del Palazzo* ("Chronicles from the Palace"), in which they purport to disclose the mind-boggling conversations of Italian politicians. From 1980 on he devoted himself increasingly to caricature, and to book and magazine illustration. His works are on permanent display in the modern art museums of Parma and Alessandria.

Books: *Contessa*, Cos'é *Mai 1a Vita* ("Countess, Life Was Never Thus," a cheerful dissection of classic poems); *I Ricchi* ("The Rich," with text by Franco Crepax); *I Mostri* ("The Monsters," with text by Luigi Pintor); *Id enti kit* (with Pirella); *Il Centro-Sinistra Biodegradato* ("The Biodegraded Center-Left," also with Pirella); and *Fogli di Via* ("Travel Diary").

L.S.

PETERS, MIKE (1943-) American editorial cartoonist born in St. Louis, Missouri, on October 9, 1943. Mike Peters attended Washington University in St. Louis and received a bachelor of fine arts degree. Following the inspiration of his acknowledged idol, Bill Mauldin, Peters won awards in 1962, 1964 and 1965 as Best Collegiate Cartoonist for his work on the Washington University *Student Life.*

As he'd done before college (on the Kirkwood-Webster *Advertiser),* Peters joined a newspaper art staff upon graduation, moving to the *Chicago Daily News.* Under the generous tutelage of the Marshall Field cartoonists John Fischetti and, especially, Bill Mauldin, Peters developed into a political cartoonist and occasionally filled in with his cartoons on the editorial page. In 1968 he switched to the *Dayton Daily News* as its political cartoonist; he remains there today. Peters, whose work is distributed by United Feature Syndicate, won the 1975 Sigma Delta Chi award. He won the Pulitzer Prize in 1981. Since 1984 he has been producing the *Mother Goose and Grimm* newspaper strip.

Peters's style is an amalgam of several prevalent contemporary styles, although his own variations have given birth to a separate school. In spite of what some critics call the conformity of his art in terms of media and format, Peters's work shines for its zaniness, clever conceptions and individualistic compositions. *Night of the Living Fred,* an animated television series based on an idea and sketches by Peters, and featuring the Deadmans, a lovable family of zombies, premiered on the Fox network in February, 1998.

R.M.

PETERSEN, CARL OLOF (1881-1939) Swedish-German cartoonist, printmaker, painter and author born in Malmö, Sweden, on September 19, 1881. As a young man Carl Petersen worked for four years as a clerk in Kristianstad (northeast of Malmö); while on that job he did clandestine caricatures of the most prominent townspeople. In 1903 he moved to Germany, where he spent most of his life thereafter. He studied art in Munich and Karlsruhe and settled in Dachau. (Before acquiring quite a different reputation under the Third Reich, this small town outside Munich had long been famed as a picturesque rural retreat.)

Mike Peters. © Dayton Daily News.

While the 20th century was still in its first decade, Petersen began drawing for the two chief Munich art magazines, *Jugend* and *Simplicissimus.* His great specialty was animal drawing, and many of his cartoons featured dogs, chickens and other creatures endowed with human personality traits. The foibles that Petersen castigated were of a social rather than a political nature-greed, drunkenness, etc. The energetic line of *Jugendstil* (art nouveau) was combined in his drawings with a great sense of composition and surface textures.

Petersen, who always invented his own gags for his magazine work, also wrote and illustrated a number of children's books with animal heroes; these volumes were extremely popular and enjoyed very large printings. Among the best known were *Tripp, Trapp, Troll* (the story of three Newfoundland dogs) and two books about birds, *Putiputs Abenteuer* ("The Adventures of Putiput") and *Bei Tante Gruh* ("At Aunt Gruh's").

Another literary work was his unusual autobiography in lexicon form, *Mein Lebens-Lexikon,* published in 1934.

As a fine-art printmaker (strongly influenced by one of his teachers, the artist Emil Orlik), Petersen helped reintroduce the woodcut into Sweden as early as 1905 (Vallotton, Gauguin and others had already restored this medium to glory in France). In 1912 Petersen was cofounder of the Swedish Society for Original Wood- cuts. In this medium too, animal subjects were among his favorites. He also did stage sets for the Munich Kammerspiele.

By the 1930s Petersen was devoting himself almost exclusively to painting landscapes and still lifes. As apolitical as he was, he nevertheless began to feel uncomfortable in the uncanny atmosphere of Hitler's Bavaria, and he planned to return to his native country. His move was not yet accomplished when he died in Ulricehamn (about fifty miles inland from Göteborg) on October 18, 1939.

SA.

PETERSEN, ROBERT STORM (1882-1949) Danish cartoonist, painter, actor and author born in Copenhagen in 1882. Robert ("Storm P.") Petersen made his stage debut at 21 in a small part in *Madame sans Gêne* at the Casino theater in Copenhagen. He had no ambition for big parts, but fulfilled his special talent in the Copenhagen cabaret. He had an ability to listen to life's small nuances and reproduce them in a surprising way. This was later reflected in his newspaper cartoons, among them *Fluer* ("Flies"). For example, two men are sitting on a couch, and one says, "What do you think of the world situation?" The other responds, "I don't know—I've got something in my eye."

This strong social tendency, which was expressed in his earliest paintings and drawings (e.g., "Social Legislation," with the man who cuts off the tail of his dog and feeds it to the dog), was later taken over by a more general philosophy and nonsense humor. No other Danish cartoonist has been able to release all the aspects of humor to such an extent. A satirist of society, gag writer, comics manufactur-

Storm Petersen. © Petersen.

er (*The Three Little Men*, A Strange Man and *Peter and Ping*), at times too industrious, he let himself be inspired by leading international artists, although he was always himself first. Thus Rube Goldberg, whom Storm P. admired immensely, became unknowingly the inspiration for many of *Storm P.'s Inventions,* ingenious laybrinthlike machines whose function was trifling compared with the trouble of constructing them.

Full of poetic humor in its pictorial effects, Petersen's work was an outstanding example of the utilization of national and personal humorous perception. In his countless tramp drawings he used the clown suit in a sublime union of the classical and the romantic in the human being. In his thousands of short stories, he usually concentrated on crazy humor and situational comedy. However, untranslatable as he is, he obtained only a limited following in the other Scandinavian countries. In Germany he is thought of as a student of Wilhelm Busch, who says: *"Humor ist, wenn man trotzdem lacht."* ("Humor is when one laughs in spite of.") What releases the laughter is the short-circuit of the thought.

An attempt to build up a career in the United States in 1919-20 failed, possibly because of language problems. Petersen's influence on later cartoonists has known no geographic bounds, however, and he is still an inspiration, almost thirty years after his death in 1949.

J.S.

PETERSON, ROY (1936-) Canadian cartoonist born in Winnipeg, Manitoba, on September 14, 1936. From childhood in Winnipeg to the present in Vancouver, British Columbia, Roy Peterson has had one goal in life—to be a cartoonist. He took Saturday morning art classes during most of his school years; after high school graduation he continued with night school while working in advertising and display. His cartooning career began when his gag work appeared in magazines in the United States, Canada and the United Kingdom. In 1962 he left commercial art to devote himself full time to freelance cartooning. In the same year, he became a regular contributor to the *Vancouver Sun*, where he shares the editorial cartoon work with Len Norris and illustrates the op-ed page.

Peterson's cartoons have been seen on the covers of *Time-Canada, Maclean's, Weekend Magazine* and *Saturday Night*. He has done numerous book covers and illustrated various articles. A series of books—*Frog Fables and Beaver Tales, The Day of the Glorious Revolution and Blood, Sweat* and *Bears*—illustrated by Peterson and written by Stanley Burke began appearing in 1973. These "children's" books were filled with political satire and brilliantly enhanced by the Peterson cartoon illustrations on alternate pages. They became Canadian best sellers. Peterson wrote and illustrated *The Canadian ABC,* a true children's book that was released in the fall of 1977. In addition two collections of his cartoons, *The World According to Roy Peterson* and *Drawn and Quartered,* were published in the 1980's. In 1982 he became the first Canadian to be elected president of the Association of American Editorial Cartoonists.

Peterson has been recognized with several awards, including two National Newspaper Awards and first place in the 1973 International Salon of Cartoons in Montreal. His work tends toward caricature and political satire. Cartoonists, he feels, are perverted idealists, which means that they will be critical when matters are not as they should be. His work is very personal, and he would never want to be in a position of simply illustrating the views of a publication. His cartoons represent his thoughts and feelings on a subject or individual every bit as much as do the words of a columnist. Peterson is in the position of being able to do what he has always wanted to do.

D.K.

PETRESCU, AUREL (1897-1948) Romanian animator and filmmaker born in Bucharest, Romania, on August 30, 1897. After desultory art studies in various Bucharest schools, Aurel Petrescu started his career as a graphic artist and designer at the end of World War I. His interests shortly shifted to animation, and in 1920 he brought out the first Romanian animated cartoon, *Păcală in Luna.* The character Păcală, a shrewd country type, became popular enough with Romanian moviegoers for Petrescu to come out with several more cartoons, such as *Păcală Amorezat* ("Păcală in Love," 1924) and *Păcală si Tendala 1a Buchuresti* ("Păcală Goes to Bucharest," 1925).

Petrescu's greatest output of animated films came in 1927, when he released successively *Proverbe Illustrate, Femeia* ("Women") and *Capete, Figuri Politici* ("Political Heads and Figures"). The following year, however, Petrescu abruptly left the animation field to become a director of documentaries, and later a cameraman and director of feature films. He never returned to animation, of which he had unquestionably been the pioneer in Romania. He died in Bucharest on April 30, 1948.

M.H.

"We had this funny feeling they were too big for transitors."
Bruce Petty. © The Australian.

PETTY, BRUCE LESLIE (1929-) Australian cartoonist born in Doncaster, near Melbourne, Australia, in November 1929. The random lines of Australian-born Bruce Petty's cheerful drawings were known to readers of the London *Punch*, the *New Yorker* and *Esquire* long before they were seen in the pages of Australian publications.

As a young student, Petty had some art training at the Royal Melbourne Technical College (it now has university status). He worked in advertising in London and traveled around the world—he once crossed Guatemala on a motorbike and worked in a room used by James Thurber at the *New Yorker* office—before returning to Australia and joining Sydney's *Daily Mirror* as political cartoonist in 1961.

In 1965, Petty joined the *Australian*, where his cartoons were widely featured. A lot of his best work was published there; of particular note were those cartoons commenting on the folly of the Australian and United States military involvement in Vietnam. But, following new ownership and a subsequent decline in standards and readership, Petty resigned from the *Australian* to join the *Melbourne Age* in 1976. On this respected broadsheet newspaper Petty has opened his shoulders across nine columns—some sixteen inches—drawing a four-panel satirical weekly comment on events, developing his theme in the form of an updated comic strip. He marked his twenty years of working for the Age in 1996 with a special cartoon.

Machinery and constructions are among Bruce Petty's passionate interests. Enormous, cumbersome, highly involved machines, often foot-pedaled by a small, straining figure, are the basis for many cartoons pointing up the clanking, chain-driven inefficiency of this or that element of the establishment. Filmmaking is another of his interests. A comically articulated machine was built to Petty's design for his film *The Money Game*, made for the Australian Broadcasting Commission's national television network. Petty's graphic style is wonderfully suited to contemporary animated films—a medium he is developing in Australia with outstanding success. To date he has made seven short films, three of them animated *(Australian History; Art; Leisure)*, three of them live *(Big Hand for Everyone; Money Game; Kazzan International)*, and one a combination live and animated *(Hearts and Minds)*. Of these, his animated *Australian History* was a 1972 award winner in an experimental section and won an international award in the world-famous Zagreb cartoon festival in 1973. The Melbourne Film Festival, another festival with international standing, awarded Petty's color cartoon film Leisure the Grand Prix for the best short film out of 130 entries. He marked his twenty years of working for the *Age* in 1996 with a special cartoon.

Penguin Books has published two Bruce Petty titles. His other books, superbly produced and printed, are *Australian Artist in Southeast Asia* and *Petty's Australia Fair* He made an additional animation/live-action film, *The Movie*, in 1986.

V.L.

PETTY, MARY (1899-1976) American cartoonist born in Hampton, New Jersey, on April 29, 1899. Mary Petty was educated at Horace Mann School. While dating her future husband, established *New Yorker* cartoonist Alan Dunn, she was encouraged by him to draw cartoons professionally. Her first *New Yorker* cartoon was published in the issue for October 22, 1927. This triumph was followed on December 8, 1927, by her marriage to Dunn. Later, when Mary Petty had gained fame as one of America's foremost cartoonists, her husband would jokingly refer to her as "my student." Her cartoons were featured continually in the *New Yorker* from 1927 through 1966.

Mary Petty's cartoons are famous for their commentary on the foibles of the upper class. Her style of drawing was linear and combined strong design with a witty attention to detail. When she depicted aristocratic drawing rooms, every detail was perfect, from the oriental rug to the portraits of prior generations.

The people in her cartoons are invariably stiff- necked, self-centered, rich and very serious about themselves. It is through their tribal rites observed that Mary Petty finds her humor and strikes with a lightning-quick jab that is possibly lost on those not familiar with the tribe. For example, a group of very proper gentlemen is enjoying brandy and cigars in a paneled library. Gazing at a sword mounted over the blazing fire, the host says perfectly seriously, "I used it just twice—once at San Juan Hill and once at the Wintermute-Van Nostrand wedding."

However, it was with her skinny, tough-as-nails, slightly eccentric dowagers that Petty created especially unique cartoon characters. One dowager tells her butler, "Here, Pompey, take these meat balls back to the kitchen and tell Lola to step them up with a little shooting sherry." Another tells her husband, who has just given her a kiss on the forehead, "Peabody! Are you completely mad!"

An anthology of her work, *This Petty Pace*, was published in 1945 with a preface by James Thurber. Thurber noted that when she first began selling to the *New Yorker*, Mary Petty was too shy to come to the magazine's editorial offices and would conduct all her business by mail. He also noted that, to his knowledge, from 1927 until the publication of the anthology, only two of her cartoons were not her own idea.

If high society was her theme, it was certainly not her life-style. For over 30 years, she and her husband shared a three-room ground-floor apartment on East 88th Street in New York City. She would work at a drawing table in the bedroom while he drew in the living room. During her career, 271 cartoons were published by the *New Yorker*, including 38 covers.

Her last published cartoon was the cover for the May 19, 1966, issue. The same light and brittle quality she achieved with crayon and pebbleboard in her cartoons shone forth in her watercolor covers.

Mary Petty died on March 6, 1976, at the Pine Rest Nursing Home, Paramus, New Jersey. She survived Alan Dunn by two years but had been an invalid for some time. Before his death, Dunn told *Cartoonist Profiles* magazine that he attributed his wife's poor health to the effects of having been mugged in the streets of New York and that he believed she had never fully recovered.

B.C.

PEYNET, RAYMOND (1908-) French cartoonist, illustrator, and poster and set designer born in Paris, France, on November 16, 1908. Raymond Peynet studied at the School of Applied Arts in Paris and became a professional cartoonist in 1936, contributing to such pre-World War II journals as *Le Journal, Le Rire* and *The Boulevardier*. He now contributes to most of the French humor magazines.

All his drawings show a pair of pleasant-looking, naive lovers surrounded by chirping birds, the young man dressed in a black suit and wearing a bowler, the young lady in a formal suit and wearing a flowered hat. Although the characters have a certain cute charm, they are, if sweet, rather uninteresting and monotonous. Most of these cartoons have been published in book form in France, and in the United States by Grosset and Dunlap in their Lover's Library Collection: *The Lover's Pocketbook* (1954), *The Lover's Bedside Book, The Lover's Weekend Book* and *The Lover's Keepsake* (all in 1964), and *On Parle d'Amour a' Peynet-Ville* ("They Talk of Love in Peynet-Ville," 1961), *Avec les Yeux de l'Amour* ("With Eyes of Love," 1967), *Comme je T'Aime* ("How I Love You," 1971) and others. In addition, Peynet has designed stage sets for *Love's Labour's Lost* and Victor Massé's comic opera *Les Noces de jeannette*, illustrated books, (e.g., Labiche's *The Italian Straw Hat* and Musset's *On Ne Badine Pas avec l'Amour*) and done decorations for Rosenthal china. He retired to the south of France in the late 1980s.

Raymond Peynet. © Peynet.

A World Tour Made by Peynet's *"Lovers"* (1974), a cartoon directed by Cesare Perfetto and animated by Manfredo Manfredi, was based on the characters and drawings of Raymond Peynet. Two years in the making, the film relates the imaginary travels of the two lovers, who encounter only pleasant adventures and finally return to Paris, where everything is beautiful because love reigns supreme. The sole original aspect of this feature is the presentation of the various countries' landscapes and cities through the use of famous paintings. The book Le Tour du Monde des *Amoureux* de Peynet was translated in 1955 as *The Lovers' Travelogue*.

P.H.

"Phenakistoscope." © Taku Furukawa.

PHENAKISTOSCOPE (Japan) *Phenakistoscope* is the English title of *Ugokiban*, a four-minute Japanese experimental animated film that won the special judges' prize at the 1975 Annecy International Animation Festival. This 35 mm color work was directed, illustrated and animated by Taku Furukawa; it made use of changing, repetitive images in concentrically organized circles. *Phenakistoscope* used three media: cartoons, illustration and animation; it was based on a pioneering concept invented by Joseph Plateau, a Belgian, in 1832. Plateau's device essentially consisted of slightly changing images mounted consecutively on a circular panel or band, with slits between each each image. When held in front of a mirror and spun while the viewer looked through the slits, it produced a stroboscopic effect and a sensation of movement. Using a similar technique and then filming it, Furukawa was able to create an illusion of constantly changing patterns-crowd scenes, people running, trees, abstracts.

Phenakistoscope is representative of the more creative trends in Japanese animation and is typical of the style of Taku Furukawa. Furukawa was born on September 25,

1941, in Mie Prefecture. He has won several prizes internationally, and he generally works with graphic animation to produce entirely novel films. Other works by Furukawa include *Beautiful Planet* (1973) and *Nice to See You* (1976). Some of his more recent works of the 1980s and 1990s have included *New York Trip* and *Play Jazz*.

F.S.

PHILIPON, CHARLES (1806-1862) French cartoonist and publisher born in Lyons, France, on April 19, 1806. Charles Philipon (or Philippon) went to Paris in the early 1820s to study art and was for a time a pupil of the famous painter Antoine Gros. He soon abandoned painting in favor of cartooning, however, and became renowned for his pear-shaped caricatures of King LouisPhilippe, of which he turned out endless variations, and which eventually led to a short term in prison.

Tired of being rejected by most of the humor magazines of the day, which were afraid of his reputation as an agitator, Philipon founded *La Caricature* in 1830. This publication served as the focal point for opposition to the regime until it was ordered to close down in 1835. In 1832 Philipon had launched a sister publication, *Le Charivari,* which survived all political vicissitudes and became the standard of excellence in cartooning for most of the century (Punch, for instance, styled itself at its inception "the London *Charivari").* All the important figures in French cartooning appeared in the pages of *Le Charivari;* in 1848, when Philipon brought out a collection of over a thousand cartoons from the magazine, it included every major and not-so-major name in the field. Philipon's seminal influence spread further with his founding of additional magazines: *Le Robert-Macaire* (in partnership with Daumier), *Le Journal pour Rire* (which later became *Le Journal Amusant* and lasted into the 20th century) and others. His energy was boundless, as was his passion for reform. Henry James called him "a little, bilious, bristling, ingenious, insistent man, the breath of whose nostrils was opposition." Charles Philipon died in Paris on January 25, 1862.

M.H.

The Pears
Charles Philipon, caricature of King Louis-Philippe, 1832.

PHILLIPS, CLARENCE COLES (1880-1927) American cartoonist and illustrator born in Springfield, Ohio, in October 1880. C. Coles Phillips (as he often signed his work, also using "Coles Phillips") enrolled at Kenyon College in 1901 and studied there for three years, during which he contributed drawings to the school newspaper and to the yearbook, *The Reveille.*

Phillips moved to New York in 1904 to study art, supporting himself by taking a job with the American Radiator Company, which fired him for drawing a caricature of the firm's president. Coincidentally, a fellow worker who had also been fired (for gleefully exhibiting the sketch) had dinner that very evening with J.A. Mitchell, editor of *Life,* who was both amused by the tale and impressed by the drawing. Phillips sold his first drawing to *Life* three years later, after ignoring Mitchell's invitation to show his portfolio—inexplicable behavior for someone as desperate to break into the field as Phillips was at the time. In any event, after studying at the Chase School of Art and the Free School and running a fledgling advertising agency, Phillips sold his first submission to *Life,* which was published as a double-page center spread—a great honor for a newcomer—on April 11, 1907. Soon he became a frequent designer of covers.

Contrary to the scenario invented by Phillips's biographer Michael Schau *(All-American Girl,* Watson-Guptill, 1978), it was no sudden competitive campaign for four-color covers in *Life* that inspired the gimmick that was to make Phillips's reputation and career; Mitchell had been using full-color paintings for some time on an occasional basis. Rather, it was one of those fortuitous convergences of artist's talent, commercial appeal and public receptivity that seem to dot the history of cartooning and illustration. Phillips's gimmick-first utilized in a cover on May 21, 1908 (again contrary to Schau) and presaged by his cover of February 20 and Henry Hutt's of March 26—was the "fadeaway" look, wherein certain elements of the figures, usually the clothes, blend with the background.

Within the year, *Life's* new artist was appearing frequently, and the magazine soon issued a Coles Phillips calendar, as it was to do for a decade. Phillips began painting covers for other popular monthlies and weeklies like the *Women's Home Companion,* the *Ladies' Home Journal, McCall's, Good Housekeeping* and later *Liberty, Collier's* and the *Saturday Evening Post.* Advertising commissions came rapidly, and Phillips achieved his greatest recognition and exposure through his campaigns for Oneida silver, Norwich pharmaceuticals and Holeproof hosiery. Among the books he illustrated were Michael Thwaite's *Wife and Cords of Vanity* (1909), *The Fascinating Mrs. Halton* (1910), *The Dim Lantern* (1923) and *Peacock Feathers* (1924); collections of his own work appeared under the titles *A Gallery of Girls* by Coles Phillips (1911) and *A Young Man's Fancy* (1912). Phillips died of a kidney ailment on June 13, 1927.

Although he belonged to the realm of illustration and advertising, Phillips's first and last published works were cartoons for *Life.* He painted rather than drew and was a primary link in the transition from the Charles Dana Gibson pen-and-ink school. Almost all his cartoons featured handsome figures in posed scenes, with awkward or vacuous puns as captions-a convention that held sway into the 1930s. His compositions were bold, and his fade-away look both mirrored and defined fashions for a generation; his technique forced an emphasis on form and flow as well as demanding attention to style. Phillips and his gimmick spawned a host of imitators, including the young John LaGatta.

R.M.

PICKERING, LAWRENCE DAVID (1942-) Australian cartoonist born at Greensborough, Australia, in October 1942.

Opportunity is often an accident of history; but it can be given a prod. When Larry Pickering came to cartooning at the age of 30, he had worked for the Victorian Railways and been a proofreader for the Melbourne Herald, a biscuit packer, panel beater, truck driver and contract cattle-musterer—everything, in fact, but the ship's cat. He seized his opportunity when working on the morning *Canberra Times* as a proofreader, by first drawing, then pasting daily cartoons on the wall of the men's toilet in hopes that the editor would see them. He did, and Pickering was asked to draw an occasional cartoon. This arrangement very soon changed to that of producing a daily cartoon.

Australian journalism, used to the irreverent and often sly cartoon, now witnessed the product of a mind with a remarkable grasp of political situations and absurdities, presented with unusually ambitious draftsmanship and with a streak of cruel, devastating wit as well. "To me," Pickering has said, "politics isn't about moving motions and second readings, it's about people. Put 126 people together in one Parliament House and you get incredible inter-reactions so often you can watch Parliament and relate it directly to school. There are the big boys and little boys, the name calling and naughty tricks, gangs in the playground lobbying, 'you be on my side and be my friend or I'll tell on you,' those who do homework and those who don't, bullies and dunces . . . oh, it's beautiful to watch."

Pickering left home (his parents belonged to the Christadelphian sect) and the Caulfield Technical College to work for the railways when he was 14. He continued schooling at night but had no art training whatsoever. During his term with the *Canberra Times* he unsuccessfully stood for Parliament as a Liberal party (anti-Socialist) candidate in 1974. From Canberra, Pickering went east to work on the *Sydney Morning Herald* and the *National Times.* In 1976 he joined the *Australian* after studying animation and cartoon techniques in the United States, England and Europe under a Churchill scholarship. Pickering has won the national Walkley Award for his cartoons four years running (1971, 1972, 1973 and 1974). His work has been published overseas in the *London Times*, the *London Daily Express* and newspapers in Southeast Asia.

Books: Best of Pickering (1973); *Pickering's Year* (1974); *Pickering's Year* (1975); and *Pickering's Best* (1976).

V.L.

PIDGEON, WILLIAM EDWIN (1909-) Australian painter, illustrator and cartoonist born in Paddington, Sydney, in 1909.

By the end of World War II, Australian urban and city-life humor was characterized by a pronounced comic cynicism expressing marital discontent, a focus that had been, of course, the very core of *Smith's Weekly's* domestic humor. Not surprisingly, this universal comic theme spilled over into the humor of other publications, including the *Australian Women's Weekly*, where this domestic cynicism typified William Edwin ("Wep") Pidgeon's *In and Out of Society*, a comic strip ambiguous enough in title to span and incorporate a broad, classless humor.

This humor is not to be taken too seriously, except that it does underline inherited traits of a past all- male society without yearning for it. Rather the humor acknowledges a resigned "You can't win!" attitude where, paradoxically, a once male-dominated pattern of life has become a wife-dominated one. The extremely comic style of Wep's drawing belies anyserious intent. It is a style so refreshingly comic and original, so modern in approach, that Wep has influenced the work of many of today's humorous artists, as Phil May did with his approach to style at the end of the last century.

A million or so Australians over the age of 40 remember the wit of the most famous and popular team in comic journalism—Lennie Lower, the writer, and Wep, his illustrator—two superb humorists who without doubt did much in the late 1930s to make the *Australian Women's* Weekly the magazine with the highest circulation in Australia. Today, almost as many Australians recognize Wep's comic drawings for Culotta's *They're a Weird Mob*, one of the many books enterprising publishers have invited him to illustrate.

Although he had very little formal art training, William

William Edwin Pidgeon ("Wep"), 1934. © The Australian Women's Weekly.

Edwin Pidgeon has also achieved distinction in the field of fine art. Today a nationally known painter, three times winner of the Archibald Prize for portrait painting (1958, 1961 and 1969), Wep started his career in 1925, at the age of 16, as a cadet artist with the Sydney *Evening News.* As a result of combinations, takeovers and the Depression of the 1930s (which put several newspapers out of business), Wep's experience drawing for the Australian press has been wide and varied; he has worked in Sydney with the *Daily Guardian,* the *Sun,* the *World* (with Alex Gurney and the political cartoonist Will Mahony), and the *Australian Women's Weekly* (where he made up the original dummy for this magazine), and as a political cartoonist for the Sydney *Daily Telegraph* during and since World War II.

Wep, with his stylistic drawings of extraordinary zest and movement, broke away from the tradition of tonal draftsmanship, although his style is lineally descended from that of Phil May. Modern, fresh and entirely original, Wep's two-dimensional caricature set a precedent in the comic art genre, an approach that still dominates this field of Australian journalism.

It is many years since Wep retired from newspaper work. He has continued to illustrate books, interpreting with pointed satire the urban social scene in Australia today-a new trend in comic art that reflects in theme the prosperity of a free-spending consumer society.

V.L.

PIEROTTI, JOHN (1911-1987) American political and sports cartoonist born in New York City on July 26, 1911. John Pierotti studied at the Art Students League, Cooper Union and the Mechanics Art Institute. His early influences were Rollin Kirby and the great but largely forgotten political and sports cartoonist Pete Llanuza.

"Who ran the country?"

John Pierotti. © New York Post.

Pierotti began his career as sports cartoonist for the *Washington Post* in 1933, after receiving staff artist training on the *New York World Telegram* and *Sun*. In the 1940s, he drew sports and political cartoons for New York's two radical newspapers, *PM* and the *Star.* In 1950, he became political and sports cartoonist for the *New York Post,* where he remained until he was retired in 1977. Twice Pierotti attempted comic strips with King Features Syndicate, and he drew a sports panel for United Feature, *Pier-Oddities.*

A Democrat, he has won nine Page One awards for his political cartoons. Other awards include six Silurian awards, the California Publishers' Editorial Award for 1955 and the National Cartoonists Society Best Editorial Cartoonist award for 1975. He is a past president of the NCS. In the last years of his life he drew for the *Atlantic City Press.* He died in Drexel Hill, Penn., on May 6, 1987.

Pierotti's style is one of exaggerated simplicity. He draws in a vertical format and shades with crayon.

R.M.

PIFFARERIO, PAOLO (1924-) Italian cartoonist and animator born in Milan, Italy, on August 27, 1924. During World War II Paolo Piffarerio attended the Brera Art Institute in Milan, supporting himself by drawing comic strips for the publisher Alberto Traini. After his graduation in 1948, Piffarerio drew comics for Editore Torelli, in particular creating *Ridolini,* a humor strip that he did until 1953. That same year he joined Gamma Film, one of the most important animation studios in Italy, where he worked alongside the Gavioli brothers and Giulio Cingoli on a number of shorts.

With the rebirth of activity in the comics field, Piffarerio again returned to drawing comics, mostly for Editoriale Corno; his strips included *Maschera Nera* (1962), *El Grin go* (1965), *Milord* (1968) and *Fouché, un Uomo nella Revoluzione* ("Fouché, a Man of the Revolution," 1973). Since 1975 Piffarerio has been drawing the successful *Alan Ford* comic strip. Starting in the 1980s he has been active mostly as an illustrator of history books and of such classic novels as Alexandre Dumas's *The Man in the Iron Mask* and Alessandro Manzoni's *The Betrothed.*

M.G.P.

PILLAI, K. SHANKAR (1902-1989) The father of Indian cartooning, K. Shankar Pillai (Shankar), was born in Kayamkulam, Kerala, India, on July 31, 1902. He graduated in physics from a Trivandrum college in 1927, after which he started to study law in Bombay. His interest in cartooning took over, however, and for 14 years, beginning in 1932, he was staff cartoonist for the *Hindustan Times.* Shankar's cartoons were noted for their fairness; it was said that his work was above malice, cheapness, and vulgarity. Such characteristics endeared him to his readers and to those whose noses he tweaked, including national leaders such as Mahatma Gandhi, Jawaharlal Nehru, and Indira Gandhi.

In 1948, Shankar found his true niche when he started *Shankar's Weekly*, one of India's first satire magazines. The

RESIDENZA PARIGINA DEL GENERALE LAFAYETTE.
TOUCHE'!
GENERALE, IL MINISTRO DEGLI AFFARI ESTERI MONTMORIN CHIEDE DI ESSERE RICEVUTO.

Paolo Piffarerio, "Fouche', un Uomo nella Revoluzione." © Editoriole Corno.

training ground for the country's senior cartoonists, such as Abu, Vijayan, Yesudasan, Kutty, and Ranga, *Shankar's Weekly* castigated all aspects of Indian political and social life, abiding by its credo, "everything laughable will be laughed at." When Shankar closed the magazine in 1975, there was a storm of protest. Prime Minister Indira Gandhi even offered financial aid to keep it afloat, but Shankar remained steadfast, preferring to let the magazine die a natural death, rather than become institutionalized.

Alongside his cartooning and publishing efforts, Shankar also carried out a number of projects built around his love for children. In 1949, he established an annual drawing and painting competition that eventually attracted 150,000 entries from more than 100 countries. He also created the Children's Book Trust, which has published more then 700 books since its opening in 1957, and the International Doll Museum, located in New Delhi.

Shankar received many top honors from the governments of India and other countries. He died on December 26, 1989.

J.A.L.

PILOT OFFICER PRUNE (G.B.) What Bruce Bairnsfather's popular cartoon hero, Old Bill, was to the First World War, so was Bill Hooper's Royal Air Force cartoon hero, Pilot Officer Percy Prune, to the Second. But while Old Bill was the epitome of the grumbling private soldier, Prune was the classic idiot officer, smiling with superiority while making every blunder in the book. Prune gave the erks (as the lowest ranks were known in the RAF) a legal chance to laugh at the lower order of officer, as he descended by parachute upside-down, or posed vacantly, hands deep in pockets, for the slogan, "Take *Tee Emm* regularly—it prevents that Thinking Feeling!" This clever variation on the popular advertising slogan of the war period ("Bovril Prevents that Sinking Feeling") was the work of Squadron Leader Anthony Armstrong Willis, the former "A.A.," the leading humorous writer of *Punch*, who had been given the wartime job of editing *Tee Emm*. This was the monthly magazine of the RAF, originally and boringly christened *Training Memorandum*, a tedious title quickly adapted by A.A.

P.O. Prune had first appeared in a booklet drawn and published by William John Hooper, in his early days as a pilot in 54 Squadron, Fighter Command. It illustrated in a cartoony way lessons learned by fliers in the Battle of Britain, and was rather whimsically entitled *Forget-Me-Nots for Fighters*. A.A. saw the book and realized that here was the artist to illustrate his new magazine. Soon Prune was popping up all over the pages and in specially designed posters made to punch home the RAF's safety regulation. Hooper, now signing his work 'Raff,' polished and improved his originally amateurish style, and in 1941 he and A.A. combined their wits to produce the first of many Prune books. In *Prune's Progress*, A.A. introduced their hero to the civilian public with these words: "Prune is the fool, the boob, the poop, the mug, the mutt, the butt, the clot, and the affable dimwit. He is willing, but wet. He is one in a thousand. Nay, rather one in a million—which is lucky for the Royal Air Force!"

Prune's fame spread, through the books and the posters, until he even achieved an entry in the RAF Telephone Directory under Prune, P, Pilot Officer, Special Duties Branch. Even marshall of the Royal Air Force Lord Tedder rang him once! And after the war, found among the Luftwaffe papers in Berlin, was a citation recommending Prune for the Iron Cross, "for having destroyed so many Allied aircraft." It was signed Hermann Goering!

After the war, the demobilized Hooper became a pioneer in television animation, writing, drawing, narrating and moving cutouts to illustrate his stories about *Willy the Pup*. This led to a factual strip in the *Knockout Comic*, which in turn led to a daily strip in the evening newspaper, *The Star*. Later, in the nostalgia period that blossomed long after the end of WWII, he painted a portrait of Prune for the National Portrait Gallery. ('Raff' Hooper was born in

1916 and died in 1996.)

BOOKS: *Behind the Spitfires* (1941); *Plonk's Party of A.T.C.* (1942); *Prune's Progress* (1942); *Nice Types* (1943); *More Nice Types* (1944); *Whiskers Will Not Be Worn* (1945); *Goodbye Nice Types* (1946); *Sappers at War* (1949); *Odd Facts of Life* (1965); *The Passing of Pilot Officer Prune* (1975); *Clangers* (1970); *The Birds and Beasts of London Town* (1972); *Pilot Officer Prune's Picture Parade* (1991); *The Life and Times of Pilot Officer Prune* (1991).

D.G.

PINCAS, JULIUS (1885-1930) American artist born in Vidin, Bulgaria, on March 31, 1885. The son of a Jewish businessman of Spanish descent, Julius Pincas (better known as "Jules Pascin") grew up in Bucharest. He exhibited early artistic talent, as well as a precocious attraction to sexual activities, in a series of drawings he did while still in his early teens. In 1900 Pascin went to Vienna, where he pursued art studies lackadaisically. He then moved to Munich and began contributing cartoons to the humor magazines *Simplicissimus* and *Lustige Blätter* as early as 1902. He continued to send drawings to Simplicissimus even after his move (in 1905) to Paris, where he studied for a time with Matisse.

At the outbreak of World War I, Pascin went to the United States, traveling extensively through the South, and from there to Cuba; during that period he painted many portraits, landscapes and familiar scenes. Back in Paris in 1921, he turned to illustration for books by Pierre MacOrlan, Tristan Derême and André Salmon. In 1925 he returned to the United States (he became an American citizen about that time), but a few years later he again went to Paris for the final phase of his short and tragic life. Plagued by ill health, bedeviled by a host of marital and sexual problems, obsessed with the loss of creative power, Jules Pascin committed suicide in June 1930, at the age of 45, in Paris.

Among Colleagues: "Well, girls, have you heard that Albert of Monaco is going to be honored with a monument? He's the first in our line of business."
Julius Pincas ("Jules Pascin"), 1907. © Simplicissimus.

Pascin is best noted for his paintings and drawings of Parisian low life, but his cartoons, with their emphasis on bordellos, prostitutes and other dregs of society, are equally representative of his morbid and debilitating view of life; their bite and blackness are often unbearable. Many of Pascin's drawings can be found in *Pascin: 101 Drawings,* published by Dover.

M.H.

PINK PANTHER, THE (U.S.) One of the first assignments of the newly formed DePatie-Freleng Enterprises was to animate the credits for Blake Edwards's 1964 movie comedy, *The Pink Panther.* Inspired by the film title (though not by its main character, the bumbling Inspector Clouseau), veteran cartoonist Friz Freleng came up with a rose-colored feline of silent demeanor and rascally instincts who moved in front of the camera with the same cool, detached aplomb that Edwards was displaying in back of it.

The Pink Panther proved a hit, and so did its animal namesake—so much so that there was soon a series of *Pink Panther* animated shorts released through United Artists. In these cartoons the cunning Pink Panther matched wits with his adversaries (mainly humans); the graceful, silent motion of the panther (who never spoke a line) was in marked contrast to the turmoil he left in his wake. The *Pink Panther* cartoons are amusing, albeit a trifle repetitive: two of the best are "The Pink Phink," the 1964 Academy Award winner, and "The Pink Blueprint" (1966), a very funny takeoff on modern architecture and building practices. Later the series often spoofed well-known movie or comic strip characters ("Super Pink," "Pink Valiant," "Pink Finger," *etc.).* There were also a number of TV specials, including *Olympinks* (1980), *Pink at First Sight* (1981), and *Pink of Baghdad* (also 1981), the last entry in the series.

In 1969 The *Pink Panther* was transferred to television (while continuing to be shown in theaters), and the show can still be seen today on NBC; in 1971 it was adapted to comic book form by Gold Key. The success of the cartoon character also led to his adoption as the mascot and running title of further Inspector Clouseau comedies, such as *The Return of the Pink Panther* and The *Pink Panther Strikes* Back.

M.H.

PINOCCHIO (U.S.) First released in February 1940, *Pinocchio* was Walt Disney's second full-length animated feature.

Adapted from Carlo Collodi's famous tale, the movie tells of the little wooden puppet Pinocchio, given life by the Blue Fairy, and of his subsequent adventures and misadventures. Guided by his conscience in the guise of Jiminy Cricket, Pinocchio crosses swords with the villains

"Pinocchio." © Walt Disney Productions.

J. Worthington Foulfellow, the fox, and Gideon, his cat companion, and with the puppet master Stromboli, before rescuing his foster father Gepetto from the stomach of the gigantic whale Monstro, thereby gaining definitive human stature.

The action (shot entirely on the multiplane camera perfected by Ub Iwerks) moves at a brisk, eventful pace. Both animation and backgrounds are memorably handled by such luminaries as Ward Kimball, Art Babbitt, Bill Tytla and Al Hurter, and there is a profusion of imaginative layouts. Two hit tunes, "Give a Little Whistle" and "When You Wish upon a Star," composed by Leigh Harline, with lyrics by Ned Washington, came out of the film. Despite initial ecstatic reviews, Pinocchio did not fare too well at the box office, but it finally managed to recoup its costs.

While Pinocchio is technically far more accomplished than *Snow White,* it does not have its charm and spontaneity. Despite Christopher Finch's glowing assertion that "it is Disney's masterpiece," it must be granted only secondary rank in the Walt Disney canon.

It should be noted in passing that Pinocchio has always proved a favorite with animators: several cartoon versions of the tale have been filmed, including a 1940 Italian effort and a 1965 full-length Belgian feature titled *Pinocchio* in *Outer Space,* in which the puppet travels to Mars to track down Astro, a flying whale that is threatening Earth with destruction. In 1987 Filmation brought out a theatrical animated feature, *Pinocchio and the Emperor of the Night*, which turned out to be a critical and box-office disaster.

M.H.

PINSCHEWER, JULIUS (1883-1961) German animator and producer born in Posen, Prussia (now Poznań, Poland), in 1883. Little is known about Julius Pinschewer's early years. He appeared on the animation scene in Berlin in 1911 with an experimental short, Die Suppe. The following year he animated two more cartoons, *The Bottle* and *The Sewing Box,* using objects as foils. After World War I he was again active in animation, making commercial cartoons for Muratti cigarettes and Daimler cars. He also produced two theatrical shorts, *The Chinese Nightingale* (from Hans Christian Andersen's tale) and the opera-inspired Carmen (both 1928).

In the wake of Hitler's rise to power, Pinschewer emigrated to Switzerland, settling in Berne in 1934.

There he made hundreds of shorts, most of them cartoons. In addition to his enormous output of commercial, educational and industrial films, he made some notable entertainment cartoons, among them *Spiel des Wellen* ("The Play of the Waves"), produced in 1944; the 1946 *Pleines Voiles* ("Full Sail"); and the satirical *King-Koal (1948).* Pinschewer also made a pilot film for a prospective series based on the popular Swiss comic strip Globi, but it was never released commercially.

Julius Pinschewer died in Berne in 1961. His work as an early pioneer in animation deserves further scrutiny.

M.H.

PINTO, ZIRALDO ALVES (1932-) Brazilian cartoonist born in Caratinga, in the state of Minas Geraes, Brazil, in 1932. Ziraldo Pinto was brought up in Rio de Janeiro and had his first cartoon published at the age of 17 in the humor magazine *A Cigarra.* Returning to his home state in 1950, Ziraldo (as he signs his works) collaborated for the next six years on the local publications *Fôlha de Minas and Binômio.* Upon his return to Rio in 1956, Ziraldo embarked on a national and international cartooning career that included contributions to *Fôlha de São Paulo, O Pasquim, Fotos y Fatos, Fairplay, Jornal dos Sports, Jornal do Brasil* and *Correio da Manha* in his country; as well as *MAD* (U.S.),

Ziraldo Alves Pinto, a parody of Superman. © Pinto.

Penthouse (England), *Planète and Plexus* (France).

Ziraldo created a comic strip feature, Pererê, which was published in book form by *O Cruzeiro* from 1960 to 1964. Pererê denounced under the cover of allegory many of the injustices and inequities afflicting Brazil; it enjoyed great popularity but was suppressed after the present military regime took over. He is also the author of *Supermae* ("Supermom"), a wild parody of Superman that has been appearing in *Jornal do Brasil* since March 1968. In 1969 two original books of cartoons by Ziraldo were published: *Flicts,* a parody of modern life, and *Jeremias, o Bom* ("Jeremy the Good"), a satire on space travel. More books followed in the 1970s. Since the end of the military regime in the mid-1980s he has returned to political cartooning with great effectiveness.

Ziraldo is most famous abroad for his spoofs of movie and comic book heroes (Humphrey Bogart, John Wayne, Superman, Dick Tracy, etc.), whose images he delights in deflating. His brother, Zelio Alves Pinto, is also a noted cartoonist, as is Zelio's wife, Cecilia, professionally known as "Cica."

A.M.

PINTOFF, ERNEST (1931-) American animator and filmmaker born in Watertown, Connecticut, on December 15, 1931. Ernest Pintoff was taken to New York as a child and later attended the University of Syracuse, where he received a degree in fine arts in 1953 and taught for three more years. In 1956 he went to work for UPA as an animator; he stayed with the studio for only one year but had time to work on a number of memorable creations such as The Wounded Bird and Blues Pattern. In 1957 he joined Terrytoons, for which he created Flebus, a series about a diminutive but feisty character.

Pintoff rose to fame, however, as an independent animator. In 1960 he made *The Violinist,* about a scruffy street fiddler. This was followed by *The Interview,* a 1961 cartoon depicting the desperate attempts at communication between a hip jazz musician and a square interviewer. *The Critic* (1962), a hilarious jab at abstract expressionism, won the 1963 Academy Award. *The Old Man and the Flower* (also 1962) was the last cartoon that Pintoff directed. Since then he has devoted himself almost entirely to the production of commercial and theatrical cartoons, and he has occasionally directed a few live-action films, such as *Harvey Middleman, Fireman* (1965), *Dynamite Chicken* (1971) and the 1978 made-for-TV movie *Human Feelings.* His last film credit to date is *St. Helens* (1981). Since that time he has devoted himself almost exclusively to advertising and the stage.

M.H.

Ernest Pintoff, "Flebus." © Terrytoons.

PLANÈTE SAUVAGE, LA (France) In 1972 René Laloux and Roland Topor brought out one of the most ambitious animated films ever produced, *La Planète Sauvage* ("The Wild Planet," released as *Fantastic Planet* in the United States). Based on a 1957 science fiction novel by Stefan Wul, *Oms en Série,* it had taken over three years to produce.

On the planet Ygam, somewhere in a distant galaxy, the 40-foot-tall, blue-skinned, red-eyed Drags are the rulers; they devote their time to such pursuits as meditation and the higher forms of leisure. The Oms (a pun on the French word *homme,* meaning "man") are their pets, and the Drags carefully control their numbers by killing off any excess population. Under the leadership of Terr, the pampered pet of the Drag leader's daughter, the Oms revolt and, not without many struggles and vicissitudes, force the giants to recognize them as equals after they have stolen the Drags' "energy source."

Under this thinly disguised parable, Laloux and Topor have managed to tell an arresting story, visually gripping and narratively suspenseful. The film received the Special Critics' Award at the 1973 Cannes Film Festival, the first feature-length animated cartoon to be so honored.

M.H.

"La Planète Sauvage." © Films Armorial.

PLANTUREUX, JEAN (1951-) French cartoonist born in Paris in 1951. While in high school Jean Plantureux sold his first cartoon to a labor union periodical. He later attended medical school in Paris but dropped out after one year. He then went on to the St. Luc art school in Brussels but dropped out of that one too. While working as a department store sales clerk, he kept sending out drawings to a number of publications, finally having some of his cartoons accepted as early as 1972 by the prestigious daily newspaper *Le Monde*, with which he has remained to this day.

The fledgling cartoonist quickly established himself as one of the newspaper's stars and a readers' favorite. His drawings (which bear the familiar abbreviation of his name, "Plantu") are casually sketched out but show a good sense of design and a sharp point; best of all they are funny. *Le Monde*'s management must have come to share this sentiment eventually, for Plantu's cartoons have regularly appeared on the daily's front page since 1985. In his work for *Le Monde* the cartoonist has commented mainly on national and international affairs, showing for example French President Valéry Giscard d'Estaing in his chauffeur-driven limousine exhorting the long line of "downsized" people in front of the unemployment office to go back to work; French Prime Minister Edouard Balladur, in a sedan chair carried by four of his cabinet ministers, throwing nickels and dimes at the populace; or Generalissimo Franco in the last days of his dictatorship shooting at his opponents from his half-closed coffin. In his editorial cartoons he has showed himself to be an equal-opportunity gadfly. The Communists, who had earlier applauded Plantu's attacks on the politicians of the right, were up in arms after the cartoonist had lampooned French Communist Party bigwig André Lajoinie in a series of biting 1989 caricatures criticizing his stand on reforms in the Soviet Union.

Plantu's cartoons have also appeared in most other major French publications, including *L'Express*, *Science et Vie*, *Témoignage Chrétien*, and *Le Point*. Those are usually less openly political and more generally editorial. A strong advocate for the protection of the environment, he has expressed his commitment in many of his cartoons, notably in the much-awarded drawing of a young environmentalist trying to stop the bulldozing of a tree whose foliage is shaped like the Earth's globe. Plantu has also tried his hand at gag cartooning, but his efforts in that field don't generally have the bite and pungency of his editorial cartoons.

The recipient of many awards in France and abroad, Plantu has also had his drawings exhibited at numerous shows throughout Europe and the Middle East. Since 1978 he has published an annual collection of his cartoons, the first of which, in ironic reference to the squirming politicians he so gleefully skewered, was called *Pauvres Chéris* ("Poor Darlings"), while the latest (1997) bears a title that humorously reflects *Le Monde*'s editorial policy: *Pas de Photos—Rien que des Dessins* ("No Photographs—Only Drawings").

M.H.

PLASHKE, PAUL ALBERT (1880-1954) American cartoonist born in Berlin, Germany, on February 2, 1880. Paul Plashke's family brought him to America at the age of four, and he was educated at Stevens Preparatory School in Hoboken, New Jersey, Cooper Institute and the Art Students League.

At the age of 17 Plashke joined the staff of the *New York World*, where he remained for two years drawing decorations, and then joined the art staff of the *Louisville* (Ky.) *Times.* He served as chief editorial cartoonist for the *Louisville Courier-Journal* from 1913 to 1936, and before his retirement to landscape painting he briefly cartooned for the *Chicago Record Herald* (1937). As a painter he was exhibited in the National Academy and the Pennsylvania Academy of Fine Arts, among others. He died on February 12, 1954.

Plashke, a Democrat, was seldom vitriolic in his approach to political subjects; his attitude was typified by his mascot, a little animal whose tail helped form the P of the artist's signature. Plashke usually drew in line rather than in crayon and should be remembered for his amiability rather than for his partisanship.

R.M.

PLATEAU, JOSEPH-ANTOINE-FERDINAND (1801- 1883) Belgian inventor, scientist and animator born in Brussels, Belgium, in 1801. Joseph Plateau, who suffered from poor eyesight from infancy, became interested in the problems of visual perception early in his life. In 1828 he published his first essay on light and how objects are perceived by the human eye. Using the optical phenomenon of the persistence of vision, he tried to create the illusion of motion

Re-christened
Paul Plashke, ca. 1918. © Louisville Times.

through a series of drawings inked on strips of paper.

In 1832 Plateau devised a machine which he called "phénakistiscope" or "fantascope," and which he described in these words: "The device consists basically of a cardboard disc with a number of little openings toward its periphery and painted figures on one of its faces. When an observer facing a mirror rotates the disc around its center while looking with one eye through the openings, the figures, as reflected in the mirror, instead of becoming indistinct, as would be the case if they were looked at in any other way, seem on the contrary to cease participating in the rotation of the circle, but become animated and execute movements of their own." The phénakistiscope probably represents the first step toward animation as it is practiced today.

Plateau became completely blind in 1843, but despite his sightlessness, he pursued his work with the help of assistants. In 1849 he explored the use of photography instead of drawing as a more realistic means to obtain animation. Plateau held a chair in physics at the University of Ghent in Belgium, where he died in 1883.

While Plateau's experiments did not lead, in the end, to any meaningful application, he deserves to be recorded as an important pioneer in the science of animation.

M.H.

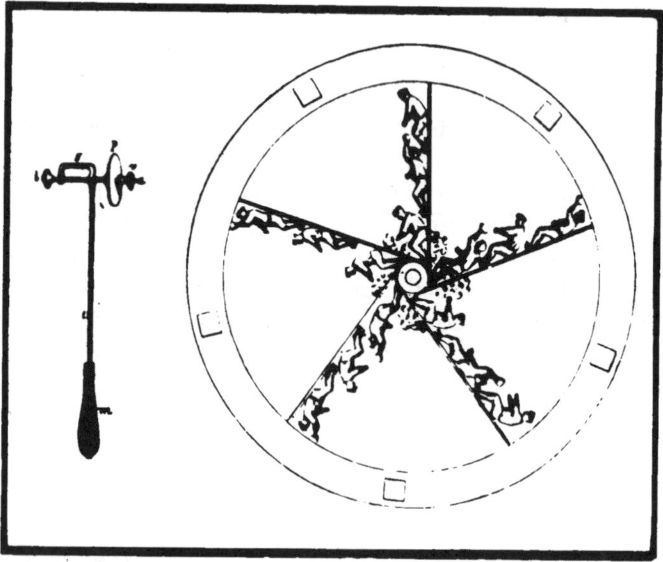

Joseph Plateau's phenakistiscope (two different models).

PLUGGERS (U.S.) When Tribune Media Services launched *Pluggers* on January 3, 1933, its creator Jeff MacNelly wrote, "It's a feature that will address that unheralded, underappreciated segment of society that all too often gets the short straw. Pluggers aren't just victims, however. They're copers. Life happens to them. They are the pieces-picker-uppers, the keep-on-truckers, the hangers-in-there."

MacNelly, the three-time Pulitzer Prize winning editorial cartoonist, creator of the comic strip *Shoe,* and double National Cartoon Society Reuben Award Winner (1978 and 1979), had discovered a new niche audience. *Pluggers* are the people the world depends on. The folks who actually do their jobs. They're whimsical survivors who understand that life does go on—so they make the best of it.

To visually represent pluggers, MacNelly drew on the entire animal kingdom for his cast of characters. The debut panel showed a bear punching into work. The caption read, "If you've ever punched a time clock, chances are you're a plugger." *Pluggers* was drawn in pen and ink with extensive crosshatching in the fine line style MacNelly uses in both his editorial cartoons and *Shoe.*

The panel was an immediate success with readers and their response transformed the strip into one of the comics pages only true interactive cartoons. *Pluggers* now features a reader "Pluggerism" and credits for the writer and his/her hometown each day. Editors are also given the option of loading *Pluggers* into their newspaper Web site or linking to the *Pluggers'* Web site for even greater interactivity.

For example, Phillip Guy of Deatsville, Alabama, wrote

"Pluggers." © Tribune Media Services.

a plugger's seven-course meal is six mini-donuts and coffee. Jim Bock of Irwin, Pennsylvania, who contributed a plugger's romantic overture, is saying to his wife, "Honey, do you need any help with the dishes." The popularity of *Pluggers* quickly resulted in a Sunday page being added to the feature.

With three editorial cartoons a week and two features published each and every day, MacNelly had an extremely full schedule. His son Jake joined the creative team on *Pluggers*. Tragically, Jake was killed in a rock climbing accident in 1996. At MacNelly's request, Gary Brookins, an editorial cartoonist for the *Richmond Times-Dispatch* was chosen to take over *Pluggers* beginning February 10, 1997.

Brookins' editorial cartoons are syndicated as part of a King Features package. His satirical panel *Muddle America*, created with fellow *Times-Dispatch* editorial cartoonist Bob Gorrell debuted into national syndication in December 1997 with Creators Syndicate.

Under Brookins and with readers' contributions writing the gags, *Pluggers* has acquired a much less cynical flavor than it began with. For example, a plugger's facelift is a tight ponytail hairdo. The cast of wonderful animal characters persists with only Brookins' broader pen line differing from MacNelly's art style.

B.C.

PLUTO (U.S.) Pluto made an appearance as "Mickey Mouse's pup" as early as 1930, in "Pioneer Days." His role was small, but by the following year he had grown in stature in such Mickey shorts as "The Moose Hunt" and "Fishin' Around," and soon he had cartoons built around his own earnest but bumbling endeavors. "Playful Pluto," "Pluto's Judgment Day," and especially "Mother Pluto"—in which the gullible dog tries to hatch an egg—are good examples. Unlike other Disney animals, Pluto was not humanized but remained a frisky, if somewhat befuddled, canine. He finally made it to star status in 1937 with his own Pluto series, starting with the hilarious "Pluto's Quintpuplets."

Pluto's personality was further refined and developed in such productions as Pluto's Dream House," "Bone Trouble" and most noticeably "Lend a Paw," which received an Academy Award. When World War II rolled

Pluto in "Pueblo Pluto." © Walt Disney Productions.

along, the eager dog lent his dubious talents to the armed forces in cartoons like "The Army Mascot" (1942) and "Private Pluto" (1943). As the decade wore on, more and more of the *Pluto* shorts were assigned to Charles Nichols, whose easy, gentle style made Pluto into an even more likable character. However, if "Bone Bandit" (1947) is memorable for the scenes in which Pluto battles a rascally gopher for possession of a bone, too many others ("Mail Dog," "Pluto's Fledgling," "Camp Dog") are simply cutesy and repetitive.

Pluto has always occupied a special niche in the Disney menagerie. Above all else he remained Mickey's loyal companion and never strayed far from his master, with whom he teamed up again and again over the years (as in the 1949 "Pueblo Pluto" and the 1952 "Pluto's Christmas Tree," among many others). It is symptomatic that Mickey Mouse and Pluto made their final screen appearance together in the 1953 "The Simple Things," a piece of deep longing for a cinematic and sociological past irretrievably lost—at once an epiphany and a farewell. A nostalgic tribute was paid the guileless canine in *Pluto and His Friends*, a television show that aired in 1982.

Pluto appeared in newspaper strips (usually with Mickey), and he was occasionally featured in comic books published by Dell and Gold Key.

M.H.

POCCI, FRANZ VON (1803-1876) German cartoonist, illustrator and author born in Munich, Bavaria, on March 7, 1803. Although extravagantly dubbed "the Hogarth of Bavaria," Count Pocci was never more than an amateur either in his drawing or in his versifying and composing of ditties—but such an industrious and charming amateur that no record of German humorous art would be complete without him.

Pocci's father was an official at the Bavarian court, and the artist too rose over the years from one gilded court sinecure to another: master of ceremonies (1830), director of musical activities (1847), principal chamberlain (1864), and so on. It was his mother who was an amateur painter and who no doubt turned his thoughts in the direction of graphics. Pocci studied art and law in a desultory manner; when he was about thirty, he was ready to shine forth as an illustrator of books.

The number of works containing his pictures (and often his text) from the 1830s to the 1870s is staggering, but they all share a fondness for simple, folklike verse, music and pictures. A large proportion of these books was meant for children: ABCs, nursery rhymes, fairy tales, etc. Other albums were collections of old and new soldiers' songs, student songs and the like. Pocci also wrote children's plays, puppet plays and books of verse.

Among the periodicals to which Pocci contributed his drawings, with their stiff, stumpy but cheerful little figures, were two short-lived ventures edited by his famous friend Guido Görres, the *Festkalender* (1834-35) and the *Deutsches Hausbuch* (1846-47). More significant was Pocci's work for the two chief periodical publications of the great Munich firm Braun and Schneider. For the *Fliegende Blätter* Pocci drew the adventures of the *Staatshämorrhaidarius*, a dowdy bureaucrat whose years of dusty service had gained him little more than piles; he was featured in the magazine from its first to its thirty-eighth volume. For the *Münchener Bilderbogen,* between 1849 and 1862, Pocci created art for children: alphabets, multiplication tables and silhouettes.

Club activities formed a major part of intellectual life in Munich at that time, and Pocci was an avid clubman. For his favorite among these societies, Old England, Pocci drew hundreds of topical and personal pictures definitely not meant for publication during his lifetime. After viewing any sizable amount of his lovable kiddie pictures, it is a relief to turn to these adult works, which are not more technically proficient but are much more imaginative and refreshingly diabolical.

Pocci died in Munich on May 7, 1876.

S.A.

POIRÉ, EMMANUEL (1859-1909) French cartoonist and watercolorist born in Moscow, Russia, in 1859. At 20 Emmanuel Poiré went to Paris to enlist in the French army and started to draw army scenes and uniforms for *La Chranique Parisienne* under the name "Caran d'Ache" ("pencil" in Russian).

Sketches of military life, with its particular pomp and activities, showed Caran d'Ache's dry and powerful humor and became his trademark in newspapers like *Le Tout Paris, Le Rire, La Caricature* and *La Vie Militaire.* His most famous series is probably *Histoire de Marlborough* ("The Story of Marlborough," 1885). It is full of lively and colorful depictions of all types of soldiers and officers, resplendent in their uniforms, doing battle perched high on their horses, courageously charging artillery pieces.

In 1886 and thereafter, Caran d'Ache contributed drawings *(histoires sans parole,* or "stories without words") to Salis's journal *Le Chat Noir.* For the nightclub of the same name, he created sets and shadow shows—*1809* and *Epopée* ("Epic")—dealing with Napoleonic exploits (his grandfather had participated in Napoleon's Russian campaign); these were full of wit and technical artistry—he cut his characters out of sheets of zinc. Indeed, many of Caran d'Ache's cartoons have this shadow-show characteristic—an all-black figure against an all-white background.

For *Le Figaro's* Monday edition he published weekly drawings that were collected and released in albums in 1889; among these, the most interesting are *La Comédie du Jour sous 1a République Athénienne* ("The Comedy of the Day in the Athenian Republic") and *Physiologies Parisiennes* ("Parisian Physiologies"). Other series, especially *Voyages de M. Carnot* and *Carnet de Chêques* ("Checkbook"), satirize current events like President Carnot's travels or the Panama Canal scandal. During the Dreyfus Affair, he founded with Jean-Louis Forain the short-lived nationalist review *Psst . . . !,* to which he contributed many anti-Dreyfus sketches. Although Caran d'Ache denied any German influence, his art shows the same absurd situations and distortions, the same daring and precise simplicity of line, as Busch's and Oberlander's, for example-precisely the qualities that later surfaced in early animated cartoons.

Caran d'Ache died in Paris on February 26, 1909.

P.H.

Emmanuel Poiré ("Caran d'Ache"), caricature of the Dreyfusard press.

POJAR, BRETISLAV (1923-) Czech animator born in Suffice, Czechoslovakia, in 1923. After studies in art school, Bretislav Pojar started working as an animator on Jiſí Trnka's films in 1948. His credits as an animator include *The Emperor's Nightingale, Old Czech Legends* and *A Midsummer Night's Dream.*

Pojar soon branched out on his own with films that skillfully mixed cartoon, cutout and puppet animation. His first picture, *The Gingerbread Cottage,* attracted little notice when it was released in 1951. It was followed by the better-received *One Too Many* (1953), about a motorcyclist who takes "one more for the road" with fatal results; then came *Spejbl on the Track* (1955) and the utterly charming *The Little Umbrella* (1957). In 1958 Pojar realized his most lyrical work, *The Lion and the Song,* a sophisticated illustration of the old saying "Music hath charms to soothe the savage beast."

Among Pojar's more notable works in later years are *Bombomania* and the very funny *How to Furnish an Apartment* (both 1959), his paper sculpture trilogy about cats (*Cat Talk, Cat Painting* and Cat School, all 1960) and the weird and cartoony *The Orator* (1962), not to mention his children's feature, *It's Hard to Recognize a Princess* (1966). Among his latter films mention should be made of the award-winning *Bum* ("Boom"), about the arms race, and its sequel, *Kdyby* ("If"), about the economic consequences of same. Since the fall of Communism in the late 1980s, he has been working mostly for the West.

M.H.

POLKOVNIKOV, VLADIMIR (1906-198?) Animator born in Russia on June 10, 1906. Vladimir Polkovnikov graduated from the Visual Technical Institute in Moscow in 1930 and started working as an animator the next year, first at a newsreel studio and later on technical films.

When Soyuzmult'film was formed in 1936, Polkovnikov joined the animation staff, graduating to director status in 1940. Through the 1940s and early 1950s (with the exception of a stint at the military studios from 1943 to 1946) he co-directed a number of cartoons with Leonid Amalrik; these included *Limpopo* (1940), *Barmaley* (1941) and the much-awarded *Grayneck* (1948). In 1956, with Snezhko-Blotskaya, Polkovnikov directed *The Bewitched Boy,* a delightful tale reminiscent of the early Disney cartoons, and one of the Soviet Union's all-time best, according to the Soviet *Encyclopedia of Film.* There followed The *Rain's Coming Soon,* adapted from a Vietnamese story, and a winner at *Venice* (1959); *The Cockroach,* a remake of the earlier Ivanov film (1963); and *Narguiz* (1965), a cartoon based on a popular Indian actor. *One, Two Friendship* (1967) marked the last meritorious effort by Polkovnikov, who also turned out some of the more routine children's cartoons in the Soviet Union. He retired in 1972 and died sometime in the 1980s.

Polkovnikov is a solid, craftsmanlike animator whose warm humor and pleasing style are very popular in Russia. His cartoons are always watchable, though seldom memorable.

M.H.

POOCH THE PUP (U.S.) Pooch the Pup was an early Walter Lantz creation. He started his career in 1932 as a pale imitation of Mickey Mouse. Pooch went to great lengths in pursuit of kidnappers (or, more properly, dognappers), bank robbers and assorted animal miscreants. He traveled to Arabia and was shanghaied aboard a ghost ship headed for nowhere in particular.

The plots seemed (and probably were) lifted from some of the Mickey Mouse stories. Early entries included "Terrible Troubadour," "Pooch the Pup?, Athlete," "Cats and Dogs" and "Nature's Workshop.

After a few of these cartoons, Lantz and his chief animation director, Bill Nolan, had the idea of using the Pooch the Pup series to spoof current theatrical films. In this vein "The Crowd Snores" and especially "King Klunk" were quite successful and amusing. These mild parodies failed, however, to revive popular interest in the series, and the Pooch the Pup shorts were unceremoniously dropped from Lantz's production line in the mid-1930s. (In the 1980s an unrelated *Pooch the Pup* comic strip, drawn by Peter Wells, ran monthly in *Scholastic* magazine.)

M.H.

POPESCU-GOPO, ION (1923-1989) Romanian animator, illustrator and filmmaker born in Bucharest, Romania, on May 1, 1923. The son of a painter, Ion Popescu-Gopo was initiated into the secrets of drawing and perspective by his father; at 14 he sold his first drawing to a magazine. In 1938 he completed his first animated cartoon, *Loboda the Mean.* During World War II Popescu-Gopo was drafted into the topographical service of the army; discharged in 1943, he attended the School of Sculpture in Bucharest, from which he graduated in 1947. He then worked as a newspaper editor and illustrated a number of children's books.

When the Romanian government decided in 1950 to create a national animation studio, Popescu-Gopo was called in, and with the help of his father, he produced *The Naughty Duckling,* the first Romanian animated cartoon in color and with sound, strongly inspired by Disney. Other films in the same vein followed, notably *The Bee and the Dove* and *Two Rabbits.* In 1955, during a brief visit to the United States, he finally got to meet Walt Disney, who gave him some fatherly advice. Returning to Romania, Popescu-Gopo then directed *A Short History,* which won the Golden Palm at the 1957 Cannes Film Festival. Like so many other animators, Popescu-Gopo went into live-action films but never quite relinquished his interest in animation. *Seven Arts* and *Homo Sapiens* (both 1958) and *Hullo, Hullo* (1963) are the best known of his later cartoons. Since 1969 he has been working for the World Health Organization in Geneva, where he heads the cinema and television section. In 1982 he produced *Quo Vadis Homo Sapiens,* an anthology of his film shorts reworked into a smooth-flowing animated feature. He remained active as the chairman of the Romanian Filmmakers Association until the time of his death in Bucharest in 1989.

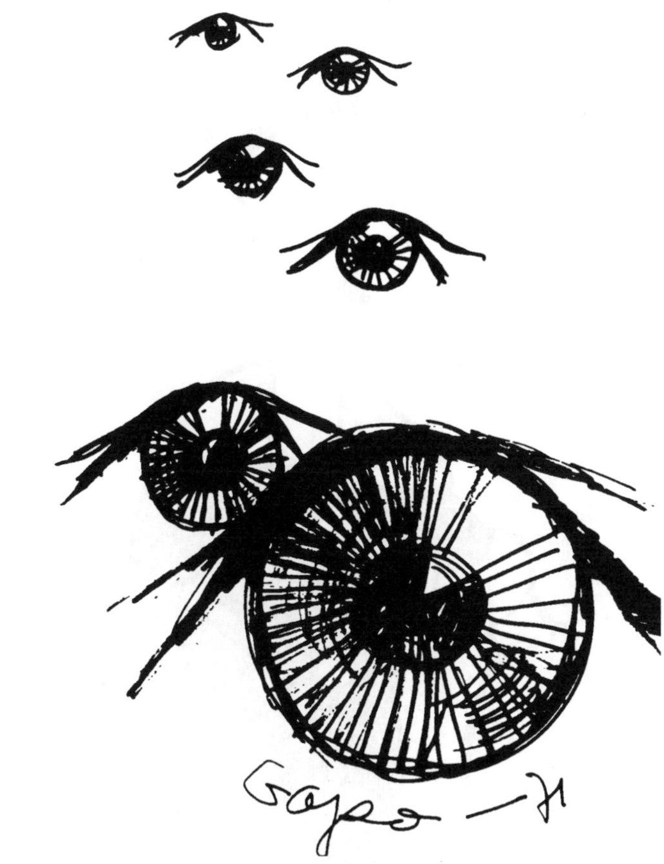

Ion Popescu-Gopo, animation sketches. © Popescu-Gopo.

Ion Popescu-Gopo has received more than fifty international awards over the years. He is also the author of the ten-second animated introductions that traditionally open the Mamaia Animation Festival.

M.H.

POPEYE THE SAILOR (U.S.) E.C. Segar created Popeye the Sailor as a supporting character in his Thimble Theater comic strip in January 1929. Popeye met with such instant success that he soon became the star of the strip. The Fleischer brothers, Max and Dave, then approached King Features Syndicate, the owners, with an offer to adapt the character to the animated film medium. Work on the cartoons began in 1932, with the first one, "Poyeye the Sailor," being released as part of the *Betty Boop* series on July 14, 1933.

This first cartoon was a tremendous hit, and thereafter

"Popeye the Sailor." © *King Features Syndicate.*

Popeye starred in his own series, beginning with "I Yam What I Yam" (September 1933). Cartoon after rollicking cartoon came in quick succession, each one with greater success than the last. If the spirit of the Popeye films remained true to Segar's bumptious creation, there was, however, an impoverishment of themes. In most of the Fleischer cartoons the one-eyed sailor and his bearded rival Bluto would vie for the attentions of the ungracious Olive Oyl. Bluto would always manage to dispose of Popeye in some under- handed manner, only to have the indomitable sailor spring back to victory, thanks to the timely ingestion of his fabled can of spinach. The theme was repeated over and over again, the most memorable variations upon it being "The Man on the Flying Trapeze" (1934), "Learn Polikeness" (1938) and "What-No Spinach?" (1936). Popeye, however, was often at his best when confronted with adversaries other than Bluto, such as the tribe of hostile Indians in "Big Chief Ugh-Amugh-Ugh" or the murderous crew of mutineers in "Mutiny Ain't Nice" (both 1938).

Other protagonists from the Thimble Theater also appeared in the cartoons. Wimpy, the intellectual moocher, made only a pitifully few number of appearances (his best role was in the 1934 "Let's You and Him Fight"), but Swee' Pea, Popeye's adopted "infink," was prominently featured in such cartoons as "Li'l Swee' Pea" (1936) and "Lost and Foundry" (1937). Even Poop-Deck Pappy (Popeye's scrappy father), Alice the Goon and Eugene the Jeep popped up in the cartoons. In the 1940s Fleischer added the quartet of Pipeye, Peepeye, Pupeye and Poopeye (purportedly Popeye's nephews) to the cast of characters, in obvious imitation of Mickey Mouse and Donald Duck, who were also plagued by mischievous nephews.

In 1936 Fleischer began experimenting with color and longer cartoons (two reels): his first feature was "Popeye the Sailor Meets Sindbad the Sailor." It was a roaring success, and two more Popeye two-reelers subsequently appeared: "Popeye the Sailor Meets Ali Baba and His Forty Thieves" and "Aladdin and His Wonderful Lamp" (1937 and 1939, respectively). In 1942 the Fleischers became involved in a bitter dispute with their distributors, Paramount Pictures, and had to abandon the studio. By that time more than a hundred Popeye cartoons had been produced.

Dave Fleischer was the titular director on this first series of Popeye films. Among the many talented artists who worked on the cartoons, mention should be made of Seymour Kneitel, Willard Bowsky, Roland Crandall, Dave Tendlar, Orestes Calpini, Abner Kneitel and Grim Natwick. Mae Questal gave Olive her voice, and Bluto was impersonated by Gus Wickie; Popeye's characteristic gravelly voice was supplied first by William Costello and later by Jack Mercer.After the departure of Max and Dave Fleischer, Famous Studios (an arm of Paramount) continued to produce Popeye cartoons with enough success to last them into the late 1950s. They had become repetitive and witless, however-a far cry from the Fleischers' Popeye, who at one point had rivaled even Mickey Mouse in popularity. King Features Syndicate brought the character down further with a disastrous series of Popeye cartoons produced for television in the 1960s. Coinciding with two television specials at the end of the 1970s, *The Popeye Show* and *The Popeye Valentine Special*, and the 1980 live-action *Popeye* movie, CBS aired *The Popeye Hour* in 1978-81 (changed to *The Popeye and Olive Show* for 1981-82), with some success. The later *Popeye and Son* program, however, proved disappointing and lasted only for one season (1987-88).

M.H.

PORGES, PAUL PETER (1927-) American cartoonist and writer born in Vienna, Austria, on February 7, 1927. Paul Porges is the only cartoonist to regularly contribute cartoons simultaneously to both the *New Yorker* and *Mad* magazines.

In 1939, a year after Austria was annexed by Nazi Germany and just prior to the outbreak of World War II, Porges left home at the age of 12. He had been selected as one of 180 children from Germany and Austria who had been "adopted" by Baron de Rothschild of France. He spent the war years in France fleeing the Germans and in 1944 fled illegally into Switzerland and safety. His elementary schooling was completed in France, and then he was accepted at the Ecole des Beaux-Arts in Geneva, Switzerland, where he studied fine art from 1944 to 1947. He then emigrated to the United States, where he finally rejoined his parents, both survivors of German concentration camps, and his brother, who had served with the U.S. Army in the war.

In America he found himself a 20-year-old unemployed artist, so he took a variety of jobs, including a 6-month stint as an interpreter with the Ringling Brothers-Barnum and Bailey Circus. "Uncle Sam" soon took care of his employment problem, and in 1950 Paul Peter Porges was drafted into the army. It was in the army as a military cartoonist that his interest in cartooning as a career blossomed. His work was published in *Stars and Stripes* and the *Army Times*. Before his two years of duty were completed, he'd sold his first magazine gag outside the military market to *Successful Farming* magazine. Sales to *American Legion* soon followed.

Upon rejoining civilian life, Porges used the GI bill to study during 1953 and 1954 at the Cartoonists and Illustrators School, now known as the School of Visual Arts, in New York City. About 1954 he began selling cartoons to the *Saturday Evening Post*. He was one of the most successful cartoonists selling to the *Post* in the late 1950s and became one of their contract cartoonists. This assured him of an income for the duration of the contract, a rare luxury for a freelancer. Porges's cartoons began appearing in *Playboy* in 1956, the second year of the magazine's existence. In the 1960s he began to sell to the *New Yorker*.

"I was always very adaptable to the needs of the magazines with my style," says Porges. "The *Saturday Evening Post* style of the 1950s is what I call the Cedar Rapids School of Cartooning. Though dated today, it was a very popular style using pen and brush. Its greatest failing was it had no great expression. Everybody's cartoons looked the same." His own style has developed to be much more fluid and loose than it was in the 1950s.

However, the decline of the magazine cartoon market in the 1960s had a devastating effect on his freelance income. His work for *Mad* magazine began in this period, born out of that great inspirational force, survival. In the mid-1990s he left *Mad* due to a contractual dispute but continues to freelance humor cartoons and illustrations to other periodicals.

Though he once used gag writers during the heyday of magazine cartooning, he now writes his own material. *A Mad Look at the Tennis Set*, written and drawn by Paul Peter Porges, consists of 12 cartoons, all sight gags about tennis without captions, published by *Mad* as a two- page feature. The artwork drawn for *Mad* by Porges is as sophisticated in form and style as his cartoons in the *New Yorker* or *Playboy*.

Paul Peter Porges now considers himself not only a cartoonist but a "graphic raconteur." Feature and travel articles written and illustrated by him have recently begun to be published by the *New York Times* and *Signature* magazine. He also teaches a course on graphic humor and cartoons at the School of Visual Arts in New York City.

B.C.

PORKY PIG (U.S.) The first popular character to emerge from the Looney Tunes-Merrie Melodies group of cartoons, Porky Pig made his debut in "I Haven't Got a Hat" (1935), directed by Friz Freleng. The early Porky was a big, tough character who went through a string of crackbrained adventures in such cartoons as "Porky in Wackyland," "Porky the Wrestler" and "Picador Porky." Porky was particularly inept as a hunter, and in "Porky's

Porky Pig. © Warner Brothers.

Duck Hunt" (1937) and "Porky's Hare Hunt" (1938) he was outwitted by the characters who would evolve into Daffy Duck and Bugs Bunny.

By 1940 Porky had achieved definitive characterization as a rather prissy and gullible sort, and he was usually relegated to playing second fiddle to Bugs Bunny and especially to Daffy Duck in such wild parodies as "The Scarlet Pumpernickel" and "Rocket Squad." He also acquired a girl friend, Petunia (created by Frank Tashlin), and for the most part went on to lead a respectable, middle-class life, in contrast to his rowdy stablemates.

The Porky *Pig* cartoons were directed with much effectiveness by Tex Avery, Friz Freleng, Ub Iwerks, Frank Tashlin and Chuck Jones. Porky's distinctive stutter (at first that of a real stutterer) was provided by the man with a thousand voices, Mel Blanc. While not as popular as some of his cohorts at Warner Brothers, Porky Pig proved marketable enough to be on such items as school tablets, books and towels, and he was featured in comic books from the 1940s on. In recent years the stuttering pig has starred in several TV specials of his own, and in one full-length theatrical movie compilation, *Porky Pig in Hollywood* (1986).

M.H.

PORTÉE DE CHATS (France) Siné's *Portée de Chats* ("Litter of Cats") is an amusing series of 93 punny sketches using the word chat as their starting point. First published in the humor magazine *Bizarre,* these cartoons were subsequently reissued in book form in 1957. Like many modern drawings, they rely more on comic situations or characters than on the caption, which is here used to stress the wordplay already expressed in the cartoon's clear line. Any word or expression with chat in it is acceptable, from *chat a' neuf queues* ("cat-o'-nine-tails") to *chat* rade ("charade"), but the most amusing cartoons are those poking fun at fellow artists: chat *gall* represents a cat with an angel's wings, chat *s'Addams* is a cat with the typically morose face of Addams characters, chat plin shows a cat wearing a black moustache, a bowler hat and black shoes, with the tail stretched like a cane, all emblematic of Charlie Chaplin's little tramp.

This very popular collection was followed by another album entitled Je Ne Pense *Qu'a' Chat* ("I Think Only About Pussy"), published in 1968. Siné's cats are the obvious forerunners of such modern American cartoon creations as B. Kliban's Cat. His latest work in this vein is simply called *Le Chat* (1982).

P.H.

POSTGATE, OLIVER (ca. 1935-) Oliver Postgate, the shy, retiring, quiet genius behind the whole history of British television animation, is a name known but a person unknown to millions of British children who began viewing the morning and afternoon "nursery age" transmissions for the littlest, youngest viewers back in 1958. Postgate at that time was the lowest of the low in TV studio staff, an assistant stage-manager busier fetching coffee than really working on productions. Children's television was a minor segment of the newly formed Independent Television companies of the Fifties, and having no titular chief of programming, Postgate went to the Head of Light Entertainment at Associated Rediffusion, the large London company for which he worked. He had an idea for a short series of visual stories about a mouse born to be king. A-R had recently acquired a new animation system using sliding magnets to move small objects, and Postgate was promptly assigned the task of designing, writing, producing and animating *Alexander the Mouse*—live! To help him he found artist Peter Firmin, who became his lifetime partner. The pair were paid thirty pounds per show between them.

Disillusioned by the difficulties of animating live, Postgate determined to work on film in the future, and with a second-hand 16mm camera, made 6 black-and-white cartoon films called *The Journey of Master Ho,* the adventures of a Chinese boy and his water buffalo. It was shot in his bedroom. A-R bought the series, and thus encouraged, Postgate and Firmin began work on a new series set in the wilds of Wales and starring an old engine-driver and his even older steam train. This became their first cult hit, *Ivor the Engine,* which would eventually run to 32 shows, be remade in color with extra stories (40 shows) and is still re-running on satellite and cable today (1998).

Noggin the Nog was an even greater success, being their first made for the BBC. It spanned several series including new stories in color. *The Pingwings* (1960) marked a return to A-R, and a return to puppetry after the artwork of Noggin. Stuffed toy penguins starred, filmed against a natural background. After 18 of these, Postgate and Firmin devised *The Pogles,* later retitled *Pogles Wood,* 32 puppet stories starring Mr. and Mrs. Pogle, a pair of jolly goblins who again inhabited natural surroundings. Their first productions to begin in the age of TV color was the series *The Clangers* (1968), which took their imaginations into the future for the first time. The puppet heroes were pink knitted mice who lived and squeaked on a peculiar planet. In 1973 came *Bagpuss,* a wonderfully fat and floppy cat with pink stripes who co-starred with Firmin's seven-year old daughter Emmy. Only 13 episodes were made, but the BBC showed them 27 times, and the films are today a regular feature on children's cable channels. Thirteen episodes of *What-a-Mess* (1978) were built around writer Frank Muir's series of children's books starring soppy, floppy dog; Muir also narrated. Rumer Godden's book *The Dolls House* was turned into the series *Tottie* in 1982, and in 1985 the company, known as Smallfilms, made their last series *Pinny's House,* which starred a Dutch Doll and her Sailor Doll friend.

D.G.

POULBOT, FRANCISQUE (1879-1946) French cartoonist and illustrator born in Saint-Denis, a working-class suburb of Paris, France, in 1879. If Willette, Caran d'Ache and Steinlen are the artists of the adult world of Montmartre nightclubs and theaters, Francisque Poulbot is undeniably the lyrical draftsman and spokesman of the street urchins in their ragged clothes with patches at the knees, always getting into some scrape. While they are headstrong, aggressive, smart-alecky, growing up too fast in their miserably poor streets and tenements, they also retain a

"I'll give a nickel to the one who kisses me."
Francisque Poulbot, comment on child molesters, 1907.

pathetic gentleness and innocence visible in their eyes and mouths.

Most of Poulbot's work appeared in *Le Rire* and *Le Sourire*, but he also designed posters and illustrated books, such as *Des Gosses et des Bonshommes* ("Kids and Little Men," 1917), Le Massacre des *Innocents* ("The Massacre of the Innocents," 1918) and *Les Gosses dans les Ruines* ("Kids Among the Ruins," 1919). It is no wonder, then, that the word poulbot has entered the French language to mean a wise and mischievous child of the street.

Poulbot died in Paris on September 16, 1946. In 1979 the French government issued a postage stamp in his honor.

P.H.

PRAMONO (PRAMONO R. PRAMOEDJO) (1942-) Pramono was born in Magelang, Indonesia, in 1942, graduated from both the Fakultas Hukum Gagah Mada Jogya (1960) and Akademi Seni Rupa Indonesia (1963). For a few years, he was a designer at the National Museum, after which he joined the daily *Sinar Harapan* as an illustrator. He has worked on that newspaper (now called *Suara Pembaruan*) for more than 30 years, serving as painter, reporter, and cartoonist.

Besides creating political cartoons under the strict guidelines laid down by the government and *Suara Pembaruan*, Pramono also freelances as a caricaturist, sketching for a fee visitors to Jakarta's Taman Impian (Dream Park). In the late 1980s, he was instrumental in organizing Indonesia's well-structured hierarchy of cartoonist associations, including the umbrella group, Pakarti (Indonesian Cartoonists Association), of which he was the first chairman.

J.A.L.

PREETORIUS, EMIL (1883-1973) German art historian, illustrator, designer and cartoonist born in Mainz, Germany, on June 21, 1883. Like Menzel, Stuck, Slevogt, Bruno Paul and others, Emil Preetorius can be considered a cartoonist only for the early part of an exceptionally distinguished career, but in this short time he set standards of excellence that were remembered and emulated by later German practitioners.

Preetorius studied the natural sciences, art history and law (his father was a district attorney). Despite some courses at the Munich Arts and Crafts School, he was basically self-taught as a draftsman. From 1907 to 1910 he illustrated several German and foreign classics, specializing in such imaginative or picaresque authors as Chamisso, Eichendorff and Lesage.

It was about the same time that he contributed a number of cartoons to the Munich art and humor magazines *Jugend* and *Simplicissimus*. The subject matter included pedantic teachers, collusion between brothelkeepers and the police, ineffectual literary aesthetes, bluestockings of the Munich artistic bohemia, poets and swindlers. He used two main styles, quite distinct from one another: a pure black-and-white pen style with sharp, steady contours and large areas of solid black, creating vivid negative spaces; and a style characterized by pale, very wavy lines and a variety of light washes. He sometimes used most arresting points of view and vertiginous perspective.In 1909 Preetorius began designing books for S. Fischer and other major publishers. His covers, title pages and other book decorations quickly became famous. Like his many posters, bookplates, catalogues and other commercial graphics, his book designs often reflected his basic good humor, so that there was no sharp break between the various facets of his work.

From about 1910 until the outbreak of World War I, Preetorius was connected with innovative schools of applied art in Munich. Later (1928) he began teaching at the Munich Academy, of which he eventually became president. Subsequent artistic activities, although highly significant, leave cartooning farther behind and may be summarized swiftly. In 1923 Preetorius entered the field of stage design, in which his most celebrated contributions were his Wagner productions at Bayreuth between 1931 and 1939. He was also a major collector of art, particularly Far Eastern. About 1960 he donated his famous collection to the city of Munich. Theoretical writing and lectures on stage design and art history occupied much of his later life. He died full of years and honors early in 1973.

S.A.

PREHISTORIC PEEPS (G.B.) The curious rockpiles of Stonehenge make ideal wickets for cavemen to play cricket with, though lumbering dinosaurs are omnipresent hazards. Both appear in "A cricket match: How's that, umpire?," one of the weekly series entitled *Prehistoric Peeps* that cartoonist E.T. Reed produced for Punch during the last decade of the 19th century. It was a time when dinosaurs and Darwinism were in the air, and Reed's comical panels portraying contemporary capers in a prehistoric setting touched a popular chord. They sparked off many imitations, from Lawson Wood's pictorial epics to

Stafford Baker's *Stone Age Peeps* in *Puck* (1904), and they may be seen as the forerunner of the popular comic strip saga of the 1940s *Stonehenge Kit the Ancient Brit* in *Knockout*. They may even have inspired Frederick Opper's *Our Antediluvian Ancestors.*

Edward Tennyson Reed was born in 1860, the son of Sir Edward Reed, member of Parliament for Cardiff, Wales. He was educated at Harrow School, and his first drawing was published in *Society* (1888). Punch published his work in 1889 and invited him to join the staff in 1890. Five years later he created his *Prehistoric Peeps* cartoons, which were published in book form in 1896. A second series, *Unrecorded History,* was ingenious but less of a popular success.

Books: Prehistoric Peeps (1896); *Tails with a Twist* (1898); *Mr. Punch's Animal Land* (1898); *Mr. Punch's Book of Arms* (1899); *Mr. Punch's Holiday Book* (1901); *Mr. Punch's Prehistoric Peeps* (1902); *Diary of the Unionist Parliament (1901); Adventures of Picklock Holes* (1901); *The Balfourian Parliament* (1906); *The Unlucky Family (1907); Beauties of Home Rule* (1914); *De Mortuis* (1914); *Quite So Stories (1918); An Epitome of Law Cases* (1922); and *E.T. Reed, a Memoir* (1957).

D.G.

PRICE, GARRETT (1896-1979) American cartoonist and illustrator born in Bucyrus, Kansas, in 1896. Garrett Price attended the University of Wyoming and the Art Institute of Chicago. In 1916 he got his first job as an artist, illustrating news stories for the *Chicago* Tribune. (In those days, the existing technology was not advanced enough to provide actual news photographs.) The illustration of written news accounts naturally called for a realistic style, so it is not surprising that Price developed as he did-into a graphic artist and illustrator who also happened to draw cartoons, and who assisted leading strip artists, including Harold Gray and Sidney Smith. After leaving the Tribune and coming to New York City, he became an illustrator for *Harper's Bazaar, Scribner's, Stage, Collier's* and *College Humor.* But it was at the *New Yorker* that Price really gained his reputation as a cover artist-and the covers of that magazine have always, since Rea Irvin's first in 1925, been taken very seriously.

Garrett Price. © Holiday Magazine.

Working in crayon, washes, pen and ink, and watercolors, Price was also an excellent comic artist whose cartoons appeared in the *New Yorker* and *Esquire*, among others. Whether realistic or in the simpler ink-line style, they conveyed a timeless humor, as illustrated by two panels dating from the late 1940s. In the first, a simple ink-line drawing, a bearded psychiatrist leans intently across his desk to inquire of his patient, "These dreams of yours wherein you find great tubs of money, Mr. Croy—can you describe the spot a little more exactly?" In the second, a detailed ink-line piece in the illustrator's style, two 17th-century Englishmen smoke a pipe of peace with the Indians as one of them informs the other brightly, "Don't worry. If it turns out that tobacco is harmful, we can always quit."

Besides cover art, fiction magazine illustration and cartoons, Price also ventured for a time into the field of comic strip art with the feature White Boy for the Chicago Tribune (1933-36). This strip is described in the World Encyclopedia of Comics (Chelsea House, 1976) as "curious, stunningly drawn, often wildly imaginative" though suffering from the usual syndicate insistence upon juvenile appeal, which "seems to have been a burden for the sophisticated New Yorker cartoonist and fiction magazine illustrator." Price has been represented in the New Yorker albums, and his work is on exhibit in a number of American museums. He died on April 8, 1979.

R.C.

PRICE, GEORGE (1901-1995) American cartoonist born in Coytesville, New Jersey, in 1901. After attending local schools and high school in Fort Lee, New Jersey, George Price crossed the Hudson to seek his fortune as a graphic artist in the bustling metropolis of New York. His art education appears to have been much more practical than academic, largely acquired during the 1920s when Price worked in all areas of graphic art, including advertising, printmaking and lithography. As a freelance artist, he also achieved during the same period something of a reputation as an illustrator of books. From 1926 on, Price was a regular contributor to the *New* Yorker—no mean feat considering the eccentricities of the irascible founding editor, Harold Ross—and today remains one of the last, if not the last, practicing artist of Ross's original cadre of cartoonists and illustrators (which included such luminaries as Thurber, Arno, Soglow, Irvin, Hokinson, Dunn and Rea).

Price's technique is highly individual, and his work immediately recognizable. Bold lines and minimal use of shading characterize his drawings, which are always vigorous and attention-grabbing; Price never resorts to cheap devices. His specialty, if he can be said to have one (all his characterizations—from love-sick lovebirds to mares who've been told they resemble Katharine Hepburn—are of uniform excellence), is the terrible-tempered old man of power. Price's ability to convey a sense of wholly unreasonable and stubborn power never ceases to amaze. He must have studied editor Ross well.

Price's success and longevity in a field where freshness

"Twelve years you studied in Vienna, doctor, and all you can advise is scattering peanut shells?"

George Price. © This Week.

is everything are fairly won and justly deserved; in his more than fifty years of cartooning, he has not failed to grow as an artist and as an observer of a continually changing society. His eye for situations and his ear for cliche's remain no less keen in 1979 than they were in 1926 (indeed, they are even keener); and his appreciation of the absurd (which he stubbornly retained even during the Ross years, when absurdism was taboo) has not weakened one whit since his singularly appropriate Depression gag series about a man floating halfway between his bed and the ceiling. (One could follow this evolving crisis from issue to issue until, all the more obvious solutions having been exhausted, his wife simply shot him down, illustrating Price's characteristic preference for the direct approach.) Over the course of his long career, he contributed more than 1,200 drawings to *The New Yorker*. Happily, collections of Price's work are abundant, ranging from *Good Humor Man* (1940) to *The World of George Price* (1988). George Price died in January 1995 at his home in Englewood, New Jersey.

R.C.

PRIVATE SNAFU (U.S.) During World War II many filmmakers, scriptwriters and cartoonists were enlisted in the effort to explain army procedures to the multitudes of civilians newly in uniform. The *Private Snafu* animated cartoon series produced by the Leon Schlesinger studio was one such effort.

The idea of creating a hapless buck private who would explain the dos and don'ts of military life to the new draftees is credited to none other than Frank Capra, then a colonel in charge of the army's film operation; and the concept was further developed by none other than Theodor Geisel ("Dr. Seuss"). *Snafu* is an acronym for the well-known army catchphrase "situation normal, all fouled up," and Snafu himself was a little man always getting into trouble. He was abetted in his misguided efforts by two buddies, Privates Tarfu ("things are really fouled up") and Fubar ("fouled up beyond all repair"), but in the end he always saw the light with the help of Technical Fairy First Class. The famous question "What's the matter, Snafu?" was a takeoff on Bugs Bunny's "What's up, Doc?" —which is not surprising, considering that Mel Blanc provided the voices of both Bugs and Snafu.

The first cartoon in the *Private Snafu* series appeared in 1943. The cartoons were among the most popular features of the *Army-Navy Screen Magazine*, and they lasted until 1946. Chuck Jones was one of the directors on the Snafu series, and veteran comic book editor Harold Straubing wrote most of the scripts. Other Snafu directors include Frank Tashlin and Bob Clampett.

M.H.

"Private Snafu." © Warner Brothers.

The Queen: "Most satisfactory my lord! Our country need fear no invader with such marksmen and with citizen soldiers so trained to defend it."

John Proctor, cover illustration for "Funny Folks," 1875.

PROCTOR, JOHN (1826-188-?) Scottish cartoonist and illustrator born in Edinburgh, Scotland, in 1836. John Proctor was apprenticed to a brutal local tradesman and then allowed by his father to become the pupil of an engraver, where for six years he learned the trade of steel and copper engraving. He freelanced drawings to Scottish publishers before coming to London in 1859.In London he became an illustrator of topical events for the *Illustrated London News,* then was engaged as a staff artist by Cassell and Company, publishers for whom he provided book and magazine illustrations. He drew humorous and topical cartoons for the many weekly comic magazines of the period, including *Judy* and *Moonshine* (for which he worked nine years).

Transferring to the Red Lion Square publishing concern of James Henderson and Son, Proctor produced a long series of fantastic illustrations for the serial stories Giant Land and Tim Pippin, written by "Roland Quiz" (Richard Quittenton). These ran in *Young Folks Weekly Budget* through the 1870s and were republished as books. The drawings were signed "Puck," perhaps so as not to conflict with the huge full-page topical cartoons he drew under his own name on the front page of Funny Folks (1874), the first British comic. He also contributed to *Will o' the Wisp* and *Fun.* Of his work he said, "I am not a caricaturist. I wish I were. I am a cartoonist." He died in the 1880s.

Books: Bright Thoughts for Little Ones (1866); *Off Land's End* (1867); *Legend of Phyllis* (1872); *Book of Bowling Games* (1873); *Old Jewels Reset* (1873); *Tramps in the Tyrol* (1874); *Tim Pippin* (1874); *Giant Land* (1874); *Billiard Book* (1877); *Harty the Wanderer* (1879); *and The Young Buglers* (1880).

D.G.

PROFESOR BALTHASAR (Yugoslavia) In 1967 Zlatko Grgićs *Inventor of Shoes* introduced Profesor Balthasar, an eccentric but kindhearted inventor who was always ready with help for a friend in need. The cartoon and the character both proved so popular that they soon gave rise to a long-running series, starting in 1968 with "Flying Fabian," on which Grgić, Boris Kolar and Ante Zaninović worked collectively.

Each of these cartoons is built around the same theme, that of human solidarity. To help various of his friends (or even strangers) Profesor Balthasar comes up with the most outlandish inventions since Rube Goldberg. Since the beginning of the series the professor has successively designed (among other contraptions): a flying streetcar ("Flying Fabian"), a traveling machine ("Maestro Koko") and bouncing suspenders ("The Rise and Fall of Horatio"), not to mention an eight-armed sweater for octopuses ("Knitting Pretty").

Profesor Balthasar in "Maestro Koko." © Zogreb Film.

The series, later done mainly by Zaninović and Kolar, was very popular in Europe, especially in Germany where it became a staple of television in the late 1970s. Due to the changing political climate, however, and dissension within the Zagreb unit it came to an end in the 1980s.

M.H.

PTUSHKO, ALEKSANDER (1900-1973) Animator and filmmaker born in Kiev, the Ukraine, Russia, in 1900. After studies at the Architecture Institute in Kiev, Aleksander Ptushko started his career as a puppet animator and special effects man on such films as *Aerograd.* In 1935 he directed the science fiction puppet film *Novii Gulliver* ("The New Gulliver") and worked also on the popular *Dog and Cat* series of animated cartoons. He followed these early efforts with *The Fisherman and the Little Fish (1937),* a charming cartoon film based on a popular folktale, and *The Golden Key* (1939), a puppet film of real warmth and originality.

After a hiatus due to World War II (during which he was called upon to make propaganda films) Ptushko made a comeback in 1946 with the stunning *The Stone Flower,* a puppet film that was voted best color film at the Cannes Festival. Like many other animators, Ptushko turned increasingly to live action with such movies as *Sadko's Round-the-World Journey* (a winner at the 1953 Venice Festival), *Ilya Mouranetz (1956), Kalevala (1958), Scarlet Sails* (1959) and *Czar Zoltan* (1965). He died in Moscow on March 6, 1973.

Aleksander Ptushko was one of the leading animators when Soviet animation had not been overcome with sterility and witlessness.

M.H.

PUGHE, J.S. (1870-1909) American cartoonist born in Dolgelly, Wales, in 1870. Little is known about the early life of J.S. Pughe, but in his short career he produced a large body of impressive work and influenced many of his contemporaries. His drawings, which began appearing in *Puck* just before the turn of the century (he never drew for *Puck*'s rivals, *Judge* and *Life)* were striking in their freshness and vitality; like the work of Albert Levering and L.M. Glackens, they represented a refreshing departure from the prevailing, stiff crosshatch pen-and-ink look.

Pughe's subjects in his black-and-white panels ranged from ethnic and farmer gags to animal jokes. Limited to such themes, he nevertheless turned out a wide array of clever cartoons drawn in crisp lines, often shaded with spackle. His characters were animated, lively, humorous, and frequently drawn with oversized heads—a technique Pughe explored with T.S. Sullivant. His Puck cartoons were virtually all interior black-and-whites and after 1900 were almost never political. Pughe, who could have left us with so many more brilliant cartoons, died tragically young in 1909; he was only 38.

R.M.

P.V.B.
See Bradshaw, Percival Vanner.

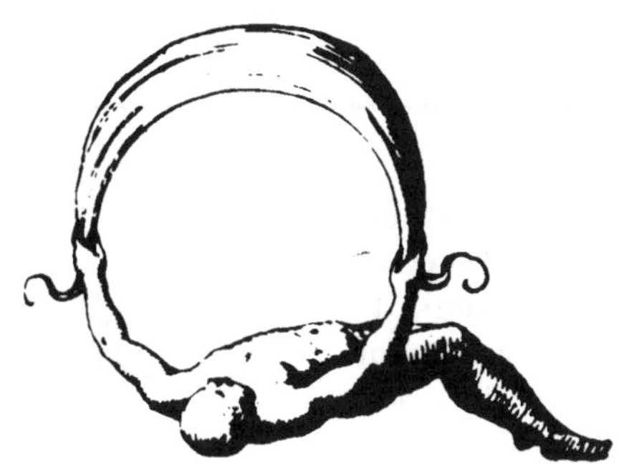

Qq

QUEZADA CALDERON, ABEL (1920-) Mexican cartoonist and businessman born in Monterrey, Mexico, on December 13, 1920. Abel Quezada always exhibited a love for drawing, and he taught himself cartooning while pursuing engineering studies at the University of Mexico. After graduating in 1943, he went to New York for several years and worked as a copywriter at an advertising agency. Returning to Mexico in the mid-1940s, he then went into business, becoming the president of a small well-drilling firm, Perforadores Mexicanos de Petroleo. Quezada's love of cartooning never left him, however, and in 1957, after several unsuccessful tries, he became a daily cartoonist on the newspaper Excelsior while continuing to run his business. Quezada recently gave up his position in the firm to devote himself entirely to cartooning. His work has appeared in the Spanish edition of *Life* and in the *New York Times Magazine,* among other publications.

Quezada's spokesman in the daily *Excelsior* cartoons is a potbellied, moustachioed Mexican Everyman by the name of Charro Matfas; this feisty character sports a huge sombrero on which are printed pointed comments that mercilessly needle government officials, lazy bureaucrats and shady operators. In the 35 years since his creation, Charro has become something of a celebrity; his sayings have been collected in book form, and the cartoons have been endlessly reprinted, bringing fame and fortune to their author. "I couldn't make a centavo writing, I couldn't make a centavo drawing," Quezada once averred, "but when I draw and write together, I do all right." Quezada has won many awards for cartooning in Mexico and abroad. A collection of his cartoons, *The Best of Impossible Worlds*, was published by Prentice Hall in 1963.

M.H.

THE QUIGMANS
by Buddy Hickerson
SEPT.
Z
10-13
hickerson
"You're darn lucky this is casual day, Quigman!"

"The Quigmans." © Los Angeles Times Syndicate.

QUIGMANS, THE (U.S.) One of the most distinctive examples of the alternative cartoon style of the 1980s—occupying a middle ground between the fading underground and the mainstream—Charles "Buddy" Hickerson's feature *The Quigmans* was launched in late 1984 by the Los Angeles Times Syndicate. Grotesquely drawn and bizarre in concept, the quirky panels appear in a reported 50-some papers ranging from Alaska to the London *Times* Sunday magazine and periodicals in Paris and Perth, Australia.

With a degree in art from North Texas State University, Buddy Hickerson began his career in art drawing caricatures at Six Flags Over Texas and as a staff illustrator with the *Denver Post*. Fired after two years for putting cities in wrong places on weather maps, he approached the syndicate with a portfolio of panels in the emerging fashion of Gary Larson's *The Far Side* and it was accepted at once. Influenced by children's art and German expressionism, Hickerson confesses, "I tend to veer away from the traditional comic style." Co-written from 1984 to 1993 by Mike Stanfill, who describes Hickerson's graphic style as "New Wave Primitive," the feature debuted with a panel captioned "Encumbered with a low self-image, Bob took a job as a speed bump."

The Quigman household is populated with characters who look like unbaked cookies. Bob Quigman is a sort of nightmarish version of Ziggy who suffers elevator lag and likes to sit and reminisce about all the good times other people had. "At the beach," one caption notes, "women would dress Bob with their eyes." His dim occasional girlfriend is Francine LaBeef, who answers his calls with "You called at a bad time, Bob . . . The '90s." The sleazy Moe is warmly described as "a nasty, scheming overbearing, irresponsible, cruel snake-in-the-grass." A believer in equality, he treats all women like trash; in a restaurant with an overweight woman, he tactfully informs the waiter, "And my bovine date probably desires a salt lick." Jowles, an amorphous dog who has been described as "a seedy and slightly psychotic Snoopy," completes the regular cast.

Accused of tastelessness and sexism for its frequent reliance on fat-jokes and its misogynistic portrayal of women, and occasionally dropped from papers in response to indignant letters from readers, *The Quigmans* is, not surprisingly, popular on college campuses and has developed something of a cult following. Hickerson has successfully marketed his characters to greeting card companies, as well as to manufacturers of coffee mugs, T-shirts, calendars, and the like, and produces a successful clip-art CD-ROM. The feature has been collected into two volumes, *The Quigmans* (1990) and *The Quigmans: Love Connection* (1992).

Considered "a wickedly funny commentary on the human soul" by some, *The Quigmans* is not for all audiences. Its focus on the grotesque offends as many as it amuses, but Hickerson is unabashed by the criticism he receives. "I wanted to do tacky characters because I find them the greatest source of humor," he reported in 1985. "And there is humor in pain. If I made everyone funny and nice, I'd end up with a traditional strip, and there are too many of those now."

D.W.

QUIMBY, FRED (1886-1965) American producer born in Washington State in 1886. Fred Quimby never finished his high school studies. He took part in different carnival shows in the western states, became interested in the emerging medium of film and acted as an agent for several movie companies. In 1918 he designed, built and ran a movie house, the Iris Theater, in Missoula, Montana. In 1920 Quimby transferred to New York City as the general manager of Pathé distribution and rose to the position of producer the next year. In 1924 he went to Fox, where he became the manager for short subjects; he moved over to Metro in the same capacity in 1927.

Quimby's greatest opportunity came in 1937, when he was asked by MGM to supervise the construction of their new animation unit at Culver City; he was to head the cartoon studio until his retirement in 1956. At MGM he produced the cartoon films of Tex Avery, Bill Hanna and Joe Barbera, among others; his main claim to fame is the Tom and Jerry series, which he nurtured. Although not an animator and hardly an artist, he must be given some credit for MGM's golden age of animation, a period which roughly coincided with his reign as the head of the short subject department.

Fred Quimby died in Santa Monica, California, in 1965.

M.H.

QUIST, HANS (1922-) Danish cartoonist born in Faaborg, Denmark, on December 7, 1922. Hans Quist started out as an apprentice in a sportswear shop, finding out after three years that this was not for him. He tried out his luck as a cartoonist and tennis player in his spare time and was most successful with the latter. Then, in 1950, he managed to get his first cartoon in print. Today he can "look back in anger" at some dull years as a sporting goods salesperson until in 1953 he was able to support himself through his cartoons.

Hans Quist. © PIB.

His drawing style leans toward the absurd, and though one cannot exactly call him a student of Virgil Partch and Cosper Cornelius, it is their artistic effects he has especially adapted into his own highly personal way of expressing himself. His world is one of domineering women and small, cowed, half-bald men with fat stomachs, as well as horrible little boys in short pants and sailor caps with the inscription *Pax.* His first comics character, Skrækkelige Olfert, had his debut in the weekly magazine *Hjemmet* in 1955.

Gradually he won fame and popularity in the Scandinavian countries, in Germany and throughout Europe. With his immense productivity, he is today seen often in the dailies and in magazines. Quist cartoons can regularly be found in several competing newspapers in the same town (in Copenhagen, for example, *Ekstra Bladet* and B.T., in Stockholm Expressen and *Aftonbladet*-the editors seem to have decided to overlook copyright infringements).

He is an illustrator of numerous books on crazy humor, practical jokes, etc., and he publishes an annual album of Skrækkelige Olfert, his favorite comic character, who is seen in a daily strip as well as in thousands of panels.

J.S.

Rr

RAB, PAUL (1898-1933) French cartoonist, poster artist and costume designer born in Paris on August 25, 1898. Under the more phonetic name "Pol" Rab, he contributed sketches to numerous newspapers and magazines of the era between the wars, when his anecdotal subjects and art deco style were much appreciated by public and critics alike. Rab was most famous for telling the adventures of two dogs, Ric, the white fox terrier, and Rac, the little black scottie, who viewed life and people from their special vantage point. These cartoons were published in several collections, of which two of the more amusing are *Ric et Rac, les Célèbres Chiens Modernes* ("Ric and Rac, the Famous Modern Dogs," 1927) and *Pas pour les Jeunes Filles* ("Not for Young Ladies," 1930).

From 1919 until his premature death in February 1933, he was a regular exhibitor at the Salon des Humoristes.

P.H.

RÁBAGO, ANDRÉS (1947-) Spanish cartoonist born in Madrid, Spain, in 1947. Better known under his pseudonym, "OPS," Andrés Rábago is one of the most prolific among the younger generation of Spanish cartoonists. Since 1965 he has had cartoons published in the daily newspapers *Informaciones* and *Pueblo* and in the national magazines *España Económica, Cuadernos para el Diálogo, Triunfo, El Cárabo, La Estafete Literaria, Criba, La Codorniz* and *Hermano Lobo*. He has also contributed to the foreign magazines Pardon (Germany) and Eureka (Italy). His published books include *Los Hombres y las Moscas* ("Men and Flies"), *Mitos, Ritos y Delitos* ("Myths, Rites and Trespasses"), *Ovillos* de *Baba* ("Tangles of Dung") and *La Cebada al Rabo* (literally "The Barley by the Tail," an expression signifying misspent effort). Rábago also made a short cartoon film, *Edad del Silencio* ("Age of Silence"). He dropped his "Ops" pseudonym in the 1990s in favor of "El Roto" ("The Broken-Down One"). After working for a while for the newspaper *El Indepediente*, he now draws a cartoon daily for the Barcelona newspaper *El Pais*.

The OPS cartoons are directly connected to Goya's "Black Spain" on the one hand, and to the aesthetics of surrealism on the other-but only to its aesthetics, because OPS's humor does not spring from the irrational but from real features of our society: avarice, false morality, hypocrisy, crime, insensitivity. OPS's cartoons create in their readers a sense of discomfort and unease; they are the most overtly black and cruel in Spanish publications today.

J.M.

RABIER, BENJAMIN ARMAND (1869-1939) French cartoonist and animator born in La Roche-sur-Yon, in western

Andrés Rábago ("Ops"). © Quipos.

France, on December 30, 1869. Benjamin Rabier never completed high school, and he was largely self- taught. After holding a variety of jobs, he moved on to Paris before the end of the 1880s; there he worked as an employee of the Central Market (les Halles) for many years before making his mark as a cartoonist and illustrator. Rabier had been freelancing cartoons for some time (for instance, *Tintin Lutin*, a picture story about an elf, dates back to 1891), but his real success came in 1904 with *Caramel, Histoire* d'un *Singe* ("Caramel, the Story of a Monkey"), wherein he hit upon the far from novel idea of using animals as the protagonists of his picture stories. Rabier went on from there, adding a host of animals, savage and domestic, to his menagerie. His most popular character was Gédéon, a comic duck who predated Donald by a good twenty years.

Parallel with his work as a print cartoonist, Rabier also became interested in animation. He began collaborating with Emile Cohl after the latter's return from the United States in 1914, notably on *Flambeau, Chien Perdu* and *Les Fiançailles de Flambeau,* and he co-produced *Les* Aventures des *Pieds-Nickelés* with Cohl in 1918. In the 1920s he directed a number of animated films based on his popular animal characters, among them Les *Animaux* de *Benjamin Rabier* and *La* Queue en Trompette ("The Turned-Up Tail"). These films were amusing but did not win any additional fame for Rabier, who quit the animation field with the coming of sound. He died in Faverolle, in central France, on October 10, 1939, a few weeks after the outbreak of World War II; his passing went largely unnoticed.

M.H.

RAEMAEKERS, LOUIS (1869-1956) Dutch editorial cartoonist born in Roermond, the Netherlands, on April 6, 1869. After art study in Amsterdam, Brussels and Paris, Louis Raemaekers taught art at various Dutch schools during the 1890s. His earliest work was in the manner of the Swiss-born Parisian socialist artist Steinlen. His personal style developed slowly while he worked for Het *Algemeen Handelsblad* in Amsterdam and blossomed when he moved to *De Telegraaf.* Cornelis Veth, the historian of Dutch humorous art, asserts that Raemaekers attained the highest imaginative level of any Dutch cartoonist up to that time in his work for De Telegraaf. His caricatures of politicians were especially noteworthy and were collected in several volumes, including *De Heeren in den Haag* ("The Gentlemen in The Hague," 1910).

Raemaekers was one of the very few political cartoonists who have made history in a way, as well as commenting upon it. The one facet of his career that is universally remembered—but quite divergently evaluated—is his all-out artistic attack on the Germans and his outspoken support of the Entente during World War I. Since Holland was officially neutral, there were severe diplomatic protests from Germany, and a price was put on Raemaekers's head there. The cartoonist was tried in Dutch courts for imperiling the neutrality and safety of the nation and was acquitted. The Allied governments showered decorations on him, and his war cartoons, which appeared at home between 1914 and 1917 in seven volumes with the ironical title *Het Toppunt der Beschaving* ("The Pinnacle of Civilization"), were extensively republished in various book and pamphlet packages in all the Allied countries. Reproductions were sold for war charities and for military fund raising. The style of these drawings was quite realistic and heavily pathetic, so that aesthetic historians deplored them as an opportunistic betrayal of finer artistic efforts achieved earlier by the cartoonist.

Louis Raemaekers. © Raemaekers.

The pressure on Raemaekers caused by his wartime activities finally led to his leaving Holland. During a large part of his life he lived and worked in several other countries, including France, Belgium, England and the United States, where he arrived in 1940 at a moment when the new European conflagration failed to spare his native land. He returned to Holland after World War II and died in Scheveningen on July 25, 1956.

S.A.

RAFFET, AUGUSTE (1804-1860) French lithographer, illustrator and cartoonist born in Paris, France, on March 2, 1804. Auguste Raffet studied first with Cabanel, then with Charlet and finally with Gros (1829). Although unsuccessful in the Rome Prize competition, Raffet was already well known for his popular and faithful renditions of army scenes, which helped to preserve the Napoleonic legend. Among these, "Les Adieux de Ia Garnison" ("The Garrison's Farewell"), "La Revue Nocturne" ("The Nocturnal Review"), "Lutzen" and "Mon Empereur, C'est Ia Plus Cuite"("My Emperor, It's the Best One") are the most famous. He also contributed to *La Caricature* political and anticlerical cartoons that were at once bitter and irreverent. In addition, he illustrated the works of Chateaubriand (1831) and Walter Scott (1830-1832), and Thiers's *Histoire de la Révolution Française* (1834), and he published beautifully crafted sketches based on his travels in the Balkans, Spain and Great Britain (1837 and 1849).

Whether Raffet was imagining his battles and uniforms (he was too young for the imperial era, and he never went to Algeria) or was an actual eyewitness (as in Italy), his drawings give an accurate and detailed account of military formations and of the grandeur and misery of war, especially "Le Combat d'Oued-Allez" ("The Fight at Oued-Allez"), "La Prise de Constantine" ("The Taking of Constantine") and the series entitled *Expéditions* et Siège de *Rome* (1850-1859).

Auguste Raffet died of pneumonia in Genoa, Italy, on February 11, 1860. In the course of his career he produced more than 2,000 lithographs, of which 250 were published posthumously by his son under the title Notes et Croquis de *Raffet* ("Notes and Sketches," 1878).

P.H.

RAMBERG, JOHANN HEINRICH (1763-1840) German cartoonist, printmaker and painter born in Hanover, capital of the electorate of Hanover, on July 22, 1763. Johann Ramberg may be considered the first professional German cartoonist of modern times. He was a fine draftsman who consciously used his comic genius to produce humorous drawings for profit, and whose dashing pen style made the fun inherent in the technique as opposed to the reserved academicism of most of his German contemporaries.

Ramberg started drawing as a small child, encouraged by his father, an amateur artist who was by profession a commissioner of war and councillor of state at the electoral court of Hanover (which was then also furnishing kings to England). Soon outstripping his father in skill and in real observation of life, Ramberg junior was called a "young Raphael" by the philosopher and art critic Lichtenberg. In 1780 some of his pictures, probably his series of Harz landscapes, caught the fancy of George III, who summoned him to London for free instruction at the Academy under Benjamin West.

In the English capital, Ramberg learned how to paint ceremoniously, but it was his numerous cartoons that were really appreciated. Between 1783 and 1788 he produced a number of popular prints that are strikingly like Gillray's, though less eccentrically free in draftsmanship (Ramberg never scrupled, even in later years, to lift ideas from his great English colleagues); one famous Ramberg series was that on the Dutch war of 1787. King George, subject to fits of depression before he became altogether mad, often had Ramberg visit him to improvise sketches on given subjects.In 1788 Ramberg was sent back home with a commission for a Hanover theater curtain that he completed the following year before setting out on a subsidized four-year tour of Europe (especially Italy). On returning to Hanover in 1793, he was appointed as court painter, but even then book illustrations and prints remained his chief occupation. After the death of Chodowiecki he was the acknowledged master of German almanac illustration, working on texts by numerous great classical and early romantic authors (although Ramberg's drawing style always remained basically rococo in its elegance and aloofness).

Between 1825 and 1828 Ramberg worked on four important cycles of humorous prints: Reineke *Fuchs* ("Reynard the Fox"), *Tyll Eulenspiegel, Das* Leben Strunks des *Emporkömmlings* ("The Life of Strunk the Social Climber") and The *Iliad Serious and Comic,* a then-scandalous parody of the Flaxman manner and the sacrosanct neoclassical subject matter. Other series and individual works featured accidents on horseback and in carriages; a group of high commissioners of roads, water supply, etc., who are depicted as incompetent and totally swamped by their responsibilities; gamblers, soldiers, eccentrics; a blue stocking neglecting her home and family (in 1802!); and much, much more.

In his last years, because his manner had not "progressed," Ramberg was often derided as a back number, but his accomplishment in German humorous art cannot be overlooked. He died in Hanover on July 6, 1840.

S.A.

RAMIREZ, MICHAEL PATRICK (1961-) Editorial cartoonist Mike Ramirez considers himself a man with a mission, using expert caricature and grotesque exaggeration in the service of his social and political message. Although his wittily drawn statements are often irresistibly funny, the humor is always subordinate to the content. The

Mike Ramirez. © Copley News Service

bewildered voter precariously poised between a collapsed "Clinton Bridge to the Future" and a demolished "Dole Bridge to the Past" in his October 1, 1996, cartoon raises a smile, but the grim point is deftly made.

Born in Tokyo on May 11, 1961, of a Japanese mother and a Spanish-Mexican father, Ramirez was raised in Germany, Belgium, and France before attending the University of California, and the breadth of his cultural background is evident in the unbounded perspective he brings to his art. He wrote for his college newspaper, *The New University*, but the first cartoon he did for it received a much greater response. "That's where I learned that one picture really is worth a thousand words," he reports. From the beginning, he revealed an independent spirit; his cartoons on student candidates drew the ire of the Student Assembly at U.C. with a demand for an apology. "I didn't apologize," he recalls, and, as the Memphis, Tennessee, *Commercial Appeal* reports, "Ramirez hasn't apologized since, in a career filled with cartoons that have evoked howls of protest and cheers of agreement."

Ramirez began selling his work to such local California papers as *The Costa Mesa News* and the San Clemente *Daily Sun/Post* through the Sutton News Group in 1979, and from 1982 Baker Communications/Palos Verdes Peninsula News distributed his cartoons, but he hadn't yet made up his mind to make a career of it. After earning a B.A. in fine art and studio painting in 1984, he took a job as vice-president of Global Travel Express, Inc., but kept his hand in cartooning. In January, 1989, the Copley News Service syndicated his work, a rare honor for a cartoonist not affiliated with a daily newspaper, and the next year he joined the staff of the *Sun/Post*. In March of 1990, he became the editorial cartoonist of the Memphis *Commercial Appeal*.

His shrewd insights and biting wit, embodied in masterfully composed drawings, were not long in attaining a wide audience. By 1995 Copley reported distributing Ramirez's cartoons to more than 540 publications worldwide. His work appears frequently in the *New York Times*, the *Washington Post*, the *Los Angeles Times*, and *Time* magazine, and he produces a regular Monday feature for *USA Today*. In 1994, the youthful cartoonist received the Pulitzer Prize, and other honors soon followed: a Green Eyeshade Award in 1995 and another, along with the H.L. Mencken and the Sigma Delta Chi Awards in 1996.

Ramirez is usually identified as a conservative in his political stance, but has never been clearly classifiable along party lines. "I like to think that I take each issue and weigh it on its own merits," he has stated, and the range of his targets fully confirms the claim. His cartoons strike out at corruption, hypocrisy, and incompetence in public life wherever he finds it, and often with deadly aim.

D.W.

RANMA 1/2 (Japan) *Ranma 1/2* (phonetically *Ranma Nibun no Ichi*, translated as *Ranma One-Half* or *Ranma Half-and-Half*) is the third major work of Rumiko Takahashi, Japan's most prominent woman comic-book creator. Takahashi virtually created the genre of teen fantasy-comedy with her *Urusei Yatsura* at age 21 in 1979 in *Shonen Sunday*, a weekly cartoon magazine. *Urusei Yatsura* ran to 34 volumes through 1982, spun off a 1981-1986 TV cartoon series, six animated theatrical features and several Original Anime Videos, and made Takahashi a millionaire; as well as spawning numerous imitators. Her second major series was the more traditional human-interest comedy *Maison Ikkoku* (1981-1987), which delighted fans of soap opera but disappointed those young adults who enjoyed her unique blend of futuristic science fiction and ancient Japanese mythology crashing in upon teen adolescent angst and social life.

"Ranma 1/2." © Rumiko Takahashi.

The teens got their wish when Takahashi began serializing *Ranma 1/2* in *Shonen Sunday* in 1987. Soun Tendo, owner of the Anything-Goes School of Martial Arts training hall (dojo), tells his three teenage daughters that they are about to receive guests: his boyhood best friend, Genma Saotome, and his son, Ranma. The adults plan that Ranma will wed one of Tendo's daughters to unite the families and inherit the dojo. But a giant panda and a cute young girl arrive during a rainstorm. It transpires that the Saotomes had been learning Chinese martial arts in a remote valley of ten thousand cursed tiny springs. Whoever falls into one of the springs is transformed into whatever had first drowned in that spring. Soaking in hot water breaks the spell, but being doused with cold water brings it on again. Mr. Saotome is the giant panda, and fifteen-year-old Ranma—a budding macho stud in his normal form—is the sweet young girl.

Ranma 1/2 is a zany fantasy-comedy of double lives and embarrassment caused by gender switching. At the same time it brings a unique and sympathetic focus onto the emotional confusion of adolescent sexual development. Ranma is matched by the others with Tendo's youngest daughter, tomboyish Akane who considers herself her father's martial-arts successor. Ranma is determined to treat his off-and-on feminine transformations as a minor inconvenience. But as the serial progresses and adolescence kicks in, Ranma finds his abrupt switching between male and female hormones and the emotions they engender harder to ignore than his physical appearance. Akane, also developing from a tomboy into a young woman, can't decide whether to consider Ranma a martial-arts rival, a potential boyfriend, a freak, or a girl-pal. The cast grows as Ranma enters Akane's high school, and discovers that gender-switching can both create and help solve the problems of teen social life. Then other characters begin showing up who also have fallen into one of those cursed springs. It becomes a game to guess which new cast members will turn out to be one of the "changelings" and what they will transform into.

Ranma 1/2 was serialized from 1987 to 1996, and collected into 38 volumes. Sales exceeded those of *Urusei Yatsura*. *Shonen Sunday*'s reader polls showed that the main fans of both are fifteen-years-old, and that boys prefer *Urusei Yatsura* while girls prefer *Ranma 1/2*. The weekly half-hour TV cartoon adaptation ran for 161 episodes, from April 15, 1989 to September 25, 1992 (with a month break from mid-September to mid-October 1989). There were 2 animated theatrical features, 12 Original Anime Videos, and 2 music videos. In America, the animation is available only on video. Takahashi repeatedly expresses her bewilderment in interviews that *Urusei Yatsura* and *Ranma 1/2* are so popular internationally, because both are so filled with Japanese cultural, mythological, and historical references that are generally unknown outside that country.

F.P.

RAUCH, HANS-GEORG (1939-1994) German cartoonist born in Berlin, Germany, in 1939. Hans-Georg Rauch, who studied art in Hamburg, gained worldwide repute while still in his twenties for intellectual pen cartoons that recall the work of Steinberg (his only acknowledged "master") and Flora. He covers large surfaces of paper with meticulous networks of lines, starting off with an apparently "purposeless" linear construction, then seizing a (or the) subject that it may (or must) represent and completing the drawing along the lines of its established subject matter.

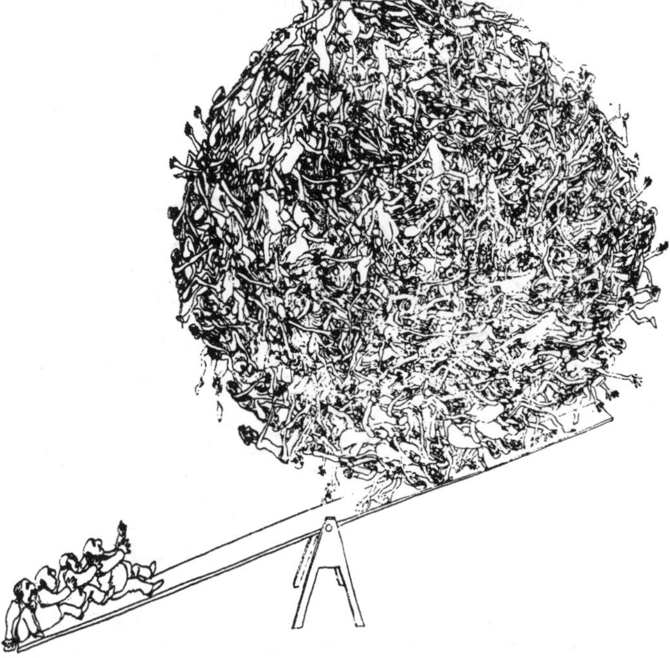

Hans-Georg Rauch. © Rauch.

Architecture has always been a major inspiration to Rauch. He sees in it the ideas and ideals of various periods of human history preserved in stone. Indeed, many of his drawings, when not specifically depicting buildings, are like strange blueprints that have become animated and have burgeoned forth in all directions. His subject matter is human folly and the painful absurdity of the universe. For instance, he will draw a house that is a famed tourist attraction, in which the cluster of obtuse visitors forms a sort of rot or blight on the structure; or a retired general in full uniform watering a garden of ruins; or a city, seen in sharp perspective, about to be dynamited by a single individual; or a complexly detailed cityscape being knitted—or unraveled? —by a calm needlewoman who might be a 20th-century version of the Greek Fates; or a house of the baroque period left standing between characterless skyscrapers, with the people scurrying madly in the street in front of it assuming the shapes of baroque architectural swirls and swags.

Rauch's drawings have appeared in France, England, Holland, Belgium and Switzerland as well as in Germany. In 1968 he took a trip to the United States, establishing contacts that have made him the most widely published there of all living German cartoonists. His work has been seen in *Look, Holiday, Venture, Lithopinion, Town and Country, Travel and Leisure, Harper's, Sports Illustrated* and the Op-Ed page of the *New York Times.*

Since 1969 Rauch has put together several albums, some of which have been picked up by New York publishers. In 1975 Macmillan brought out *En Masse,* and a year later Scribner's published *Double-Barreled Attack.* Rauch's latest volume (as of this writing) is *Schlachtlinien* (published by Scribner's in 1977 as *Battle Lines),* in which he concentrates on the single theme of militarism and its baleful aftermath, in drawings that are rather less structured than in the past and flow more loosely over the pages. This gifted and internationally recognized cartoonist died December 23, 1994, at the age of 55.

S.A.

RAVEN-HILL, LEONARD (1867-1942) British cartoonist born at Bath, England, on March 10, 1867. Leonard Raven-Hill, who appears both with and without a hyphen, is regarded as the natural successor to Charles Keene. His classic cartoon is the one of the fat lady trying to get through the door of a small horsebus. The driver advises, "Try zideways, Mrs. Jones, try zideways!" To which Mrs. Jones replies, "Lar bless 'ee, John, I ain't got no zideways!" Raven-Hill's cartoons catch well the social scene of his period, but although light of touch, his drawings are too overloaded with hatchwork to stand out from his contemporaries'.

Raven-Hill attended Bristol Grammar School and Devon County School prior to his art education. This he received at the Bristol Art School, Lambeth, and the Paris Académie under Bouguereau (1885-87). He exhibited at the Paris Salon in 1887 and the Royal Academy in 1889. He began to freelance a few jokes at this time and appeared regularly in the slightly saucy *Pick-Me-Up*, which appointed him art editor in 1890. In 1893 he started his own comic paper, the *Butterfly*, which ran for a few issues only, but he

Carrier: "Try zideways, Mrs. Jones, try zideways!"
Mrs. Jones: "Lar' bless 'ee, John, I ain't got no zideways!"
Leonard Raven-Hill, 1900.

revived it again in 1899. He joined *Punch* in 1896 and remained on the staff of that weekly until 1935, when failing eyesight hastened his retirement. He died on the Isle of Wight on March 31, 1942.

Books: The Promenaders (1894); *The Pottle Papers* (1898); *East London* (1901); *Our Batallion* (1902); *London Sketchbook* (1903); *Raven Hill's London Sketchbook* (1906); *The South Bound Car* (1907); *Cornish Saints and Sinners* (1906); and *The Happy Vanners* (1911).

D.G.

RAY, SILVEY JACKSON (1891-1970) American cartoonist born near Marceline, Missouri, on March 15, 1891. S.j. Ray studied drawing at the Art Students League in New York in 1919 and 1920. Ray was an illustrator and advertising artist for the *Kansas City Journal* (1913-15) and served on the art staff of the Kansas City Star between 1915 and 1931 (with time out for study), before becoming the paper's regular editorial cartoonist in 1931.

The recipient of many awards, the conservative Ray had a drawing style fairly consistent with the *Chicago Tribune* school of political cartoonists: realistic likenesses, exaggerated action, handsome pen-line rendering. He was especially effective as an opponent of war intervention in the late 1930s and early 1940s, and he saw his cartoons reprinted often during his career. S.J. Ray died in February 1970.

R.M.

RAYNAUD, CLAUDE (1918-1983) French cartoonist born in central France on August 10, 1918. Claude Raynaud started drawing professionally in 1945 and has since contributed thousands of drawings to daily newspapers as well as to magazines that publish graphic humor. His two most important albums are probably *L'Amore E Bello* ("Love Is Beautiful," 1962) and En *Suivant le Crayon de Raynaud* ("Following Raynaud's Pencil," 1965). His work, which has won awards several times (Bordighera, 1960 and 1962; Brussels, 1969, etc.), is irreverently deflating and shows a wacky sense of the ridiculous.

Claude Raynaud's professional activities have also been extensive: since 1952 he has been secretary for France of the International Humorist Association, founding member (with Elsa Maxwell) of Humor for Peace, founder of and judge for the Jean Bellus Prize and member of the French Comic Strip award committee. He died in 1983 in Creteil, near Paris. His son, Olivier Raynaud, is also a cartoonist.

P.H.

REA, GARDNER (1892-1966) American cartoonist born in Ironton, Ohio, on August 12, 1892. As a youth Gardner Rea showed a talent for cartooning and was already freelancing at the age of 15. His first work in *Life, Judge* and *Puck* appeared shortly after 1910. He was educated locally and received a B.A. degree from Ohio State University in 1914. Upon graduation, Rea took the position of theater critic for the *Ohio State Journal* and continued in that capacity until 1916. In World War I he served with the chemical warfare service. In the 1920s his work appeared frequently in *Life, Judge* and the *New Yorker* (from the very first issue, in the case of the latter).

For many years, Rea's style was tightly executed, supple of line and extremely decorative. In the mid 1920s, however, all that remained was the strong (and unerring) sense of design; Rea's work became a constant study of contrasts between white spaces and dark accent areas. His lines, though wiggly, were sure and numerous. Rea's lush brush had given way to a playful but disciplined use of thin pen lines. Economy became his watchword.

For years Rea was one of the most prolific cartoonists in the magazine field. His work spanned the period from *Puck* through the *New Yorker* and *Collier's* and the cheap Dell publications to *Playboy.* He had two anthologies of his cartoons published: *The Gentleman Says It's Pixies* (1944) and Gardner Rea's *Sideshow* (1945). He died on December 27, 1966.

R.M.

RECTANGLE, THE (U.S.) The first nationally distributed general newspaper Sunday gag page, Frank King's *Rectangle,* created in 1916 for the *Chicago Tribune,* was also

"May I have the evening off, sir, or will you be wanting me to listen to your comments on Mr. Truman's advice to the nation?"
Gardner Rea. © Saturday Evening Post.

the birthplace of King's later lifetime work, *Gasoline Alley.* From its inception it was hugely popular with the Tribune reading public across five states in the Midwest, and it was picked up by a number of other newspapers from coast to coast during World War I. Run by the *Tribune* in black and white on the first page of its Sunday theater section, the *Rectangle* feature (the name of which, strictly speaking, referred only to the large rectangular panel at the top of each weekly page) contained several separate one-panel gags on topical themes. There were also occasional one-shot comic narratives in several small panels, sometimes focusing briefly on recurring characters of various kinds: a World War I doughboy in boot camp, etc. Much of this work seems as fresh and lively today as it did at the time of its original publication, and King's vibrant, evocative lines are visually enchanting.

A simple, tentative look at an emerging social phenomenon of the late 1910s—the American urban and suburban back alley, with its converted stables now housing the middle class's new family staple, a car of recent vintage, where husbands fraternize as they work endlessly on their cantankerous machines—King's first "Gasoline Alley" panel appeared in *The Rectangle* on November 24, 1918, without noticeable fanfare. But the public obviously liked it, with its homey familiarity and fresh treatment of a new theme. When King decided to push for a daily strip in the Tribune after the close of the war (at the time, the *Tribune* was running just one strip, The Gumps), it was the "Gasoline Alley" series in the Sunday Rectangle (where Walt Wallet and other regulars of the later strip had already recognizably emerged) that he decided to develop. Its instant popularity did away with *The Rectangle* in 1919, and King continued with the new and hugely popular strip.

B.B.

REHSE, GEORGE WASHINGTON (1868-ca.-1930) American cartoonist born in Hastings, Minnesota, on September 2, 1868. George Rehse was educated in Minneapolis public schools and was self-taught in art, a profession he entered in 1895 when he joined the *Penny Press* as a staff artist. He remained in St. Paul and succeeded to the Globe and the *Pioneer Press* before joining Pulitzer's *New York World* as staff artist, assignment cartoonist and editorial cartoonist.

For Pulitzer, Rehse contributed cartoons in all sorts of styles before settling on his own, one of reserved delineation—virtually no action—and slightly awkward anatomy and composition. He used a gentle shading technique when crayon became the vogue.

Rehse occupies a couple of prominent "in-between" roles; after the resignation of Charles Macauley he seemed slated to become the World's chief editorial cartoonist-until Rollin Kirby firmly assumed his duties (although he and Kirby split top spots on the morning and evening papers for awhile); and he was one of many cartoonists who filled in on the daily *Metropolitan Movies* panel before it became Denys Wortman's own.

R.M.

"My husband has intimated in an offhand way that a five dollar briar pipe would be an acceptable Christmas gift, but the 25¢ ones look about the same, so you may give me twenty of the latter; then he can have a nice fresh one often."
George Rehse, "Metropolitan Movies." © New York World.

REID, ALBERT TURNER (1873-1955) American cartoonist and publisher born in Concordia, Kansas, on August 12, 1873. Albert T. Reid was educated locally, at the University of Kansas, and in New York at the New York School of Art and the Art Students League. His first cartooning job was with the *Kansas City Star* (1897-99), whence he moved to successive one-year stints on the *Chicago Record* and the *New York Herald.*

After the turn of the century Reid freelanced to *Judge, McClure's,* the *Saturday Evening Post,* the *American* and other magazines for about fifteen years; during that time and for years thereafter he operated his own syndicate, distributing Reid cartoons to many local and rural papers around America. In addition, he founded and published a newspaper (the *Leavenworth Post,* 1905-23) and a magazine (the *Kansas Farmer,* 1908-16), and he headed various press associations and an insurance company. Reid stayed active as an artist all his life, designing medals, painting murals and of course continuing his editorial cartoons. He died on November 26, 1955, bequeathing the Albert T. Reid Cartoon Museum to the School of Journalism at the University of Kansas.

Because of his other pursuits, and because his material was syndicated mostly to small-town papers, Reid is a largely forgotten figure in cartooning today. His mastery of the pen was overwhelming, and he had an unerring sense of design and caricature; if he had a fault, it was that his work looked almost too slick-like advertising art rather than political cartoons.

R.M.

The March of Modern Improvement

G.S. Reinhart, 1871.

REILLY, PAUL (ca. 1880-1944) American cartoonist born in Pittsburgh, Pennsylvania, around 1880. For years Paul Reilly was one of the most published of the magazine cartoonists. Reilly joined the staff of *Life* magazine in 1913 and soon was appearing in *Puck* and *Judge* as well. He never handled political subjects, and only during World War I did he touch on international affairs. Generally his subjects were domestic, meaning household; he was one of the first magazine cartoonists to concentrate on family and suburban themes, a major genre of cartooning and comics since his day. Reilly was best at exasperated characters, usually men beset by bills, Prohibition or other annoyances.

His drawing style was very simple; his line grew more confident in the 1920s, but backgrounds were almost always nonexistent. In the 1920s and 1930s he expanded his markets to *College Humor* and *Bal*lyhoo.

Reilly's wife was the detective mystery writer Helen Reilly, and he was a brother-in-law of radio personality John Kieran. He eventually left cartooning to do portraits and landscape painting in Westport, Connecticut, and died at Norwalk Hospital on May 14, 1944.

R.M.

REINHART, CHARLES STANLEY (1844-1896) American illustrator, painter and cartoonist born in Pittsburgh, Pennsylvania, on May 16, 1844. C.S. Reinhart *served* with the Army of the Potomac in the Civil War and then studied art at the Atelier Suisse in Paris (1867) and at the Royal Academy of Munich (1868-70). He returned to the United States to draw exclusively for the Harper Brothers publications. In 1877, after seven years with Harper's, he left to freelance, and his work appeared in the magazines of Scribner's and Appleton, among others. Later he became a painter, and his work was exhibited and sold throughout the world; he specialized in genre subjects and won many distinctions, including the first gold medal and silver medal at the Paris Exposition of 1889. At Harper's, Reinhart was part of the tradition that stretched from Nast and Homer to Abbey and Frost; these men all began as troupers who later decided between cartooning and illustration. But Reinhart, who often drew back-of-the-book cartoons and humorous illustrations, was the first penman of note who did independent illustrations, that is, not depictions of news events.

His style was one of unassuming solidity; his lines were not crude or slashing like other contemporaries', and the figures in his drawings were handsome, well proportioned and carefully shaded. Reinhart, especially with the advent of photomechanical reproduction of ink drawings, was very influential among the younger generation of cartoonists and illustrators. He died in New York on August 30, 1896.

R.M.

Lotte *Reiniger, animation sketches.* © *Reiniger.*

REINIGER, LOTTE (1899-1981) German animator and filmmaker born in Berlin, Germany, on June 2, 1899. Lotte Reiniger is the pioneer, and virtually the only practitioner, of the silhouette film, which adapts the age-old technique of Chinese shadows to animation. She has created films with articulated cardboard, tin or paper cutouts photographed frame by frame. Her first shadow film, *Die Rattefárger von Hameln* ("The Pied Piper of Hamelin"), was made for the Berlin Institut fur Kulturforschung in 1917. More short subjects followed after the end of World War I: *Das Ornament des Verliebten Herzen* ("The Ornament of the Lovestruck Heart," 1919), *Der Fliegende Koffer* and *Der Stern von Bethlehem* ("The Flying Coffer" and "The Star of Bethlehem," both 1921), *Cinderella, Sleeping Beauty* (both 1922), etc.

In 1923, working with her husband, the film director Karl Koch, Reiniger embarked on her most ambitious project-the making of a feature-length silhouette film. *Die* Abenteuer des *Prinzen Achmed* was finally completed in 1926, and it proved to be a very charming and poetic film. In 1927 she made *The Chinese Nightingale* (from Andersen's tale) and *Dr. Doolittle and His Animals;* the latter gave rise to a Dr. Doolittle series that Reiniger produced over the next couple of years. Film followed film, with the added attraction of a musical soundtrack: Zehn Minuten Mozart (1930), *Harlekin* (1931), *Sissi* (1932), *Carmen* (made in Italy in 1933), The *Stolen Heart* (1934), *Kalif Storch, Galathea, Pa pa geno* (all 1935), Silhouetten and *Puss in* Boots (both 1936) are the most notable in a production almost unprecedented in its number and variety.

In 1936 Reiniger went to England, where she made more silhouette films, including the enchanting *Mary's Birthday* and the 1937 *Daughter,* with music by Benjamin Britten. At the start of World War II she and her husband went to Italy, where she co-authored the script for *Una Signora dell'Ovest*. She went back to Berlin in 1944 to make *Die Goldene Gans* ("The Goose That Lays the Golden Eggs"). In 1949 she returned to England, where most of her old films were remade under her direction for British television, often with color added. She also operated a live shadow theater and occasionally worked for television. *Aucassin and Nicolette* (1975), her last film to date, was made for the National Film Board of Canada.

In recent years Lotte Reiniger has put her long experience to good use by holding lectures and workshops on shadow animation on campuses throughout Western Europe and North America. She has also written a book about her craft, *Shadow Theaters* and *Shadow Films* (Watson-Guptill, 1970). She died in Dettenhausen (then West Germany), on June 19, 1981.

M.H.

REISER, JEAN-MARC (1941-1983) French cartoonist born at Rehon, in eastern France, on April 13, 1941. J.M. Reiser was taken to Paris as a child; after completing his high school studies at the Lycée Arago, he briefly worked as an errand boy (like Daumier, as Reiser is fond of reminding people). He became one of the first collaborators on the satirical weekly *Hara-Kiri* in the early 1960s, and he soon proved himself one of the most acute observers (and dissectors) of the modern scene. His cartoons were filled with aggressive, ugly, smug and wrongheaded people whose stupidity was expressed in well-worn clichés enclosed in word balloons (Reiser seldom uses captions). His attacks on prominent personalities (notably French presidents De Gaulle and Pompidou) put him in direct conflict with the authorities (again like Daumier).

From the middle 1960s to the early 1970s Reiser also worked for the comic weekly *Pilote*. His caustic comments on current events and his continued sniping at established authority were a welcome relief from the rather staid contents of the rest of the paper. In recent years Reiser has been working exclusively for *Hara-Kiri* and its companion publications, *Charlie* and *Charlie Hebdo.* He is also the author of a few unsuccessful comic strips and has had several books of his cartoons published. After *Charlie Hebdo* folded in 1981, he went to work for the weekly *Le Nouvel Observateur*. Like too many other humorists he took his own life, on November 5, 1983, in Paris.

Reiser is regarded as one of the most representative cartoonists of his generation. His aggressive, sloppy drawing

"Anyway, when things get too bad, I'll take a pick and dig myself a nice big atomic shelter in my garden."
J.M. Reiser. © *Hara-Kiri.*

style and his cynical observations are much admired and imitated by countless aspiring cartoonists who duplicate his vulgarity without being able to match his talent.

M.H.

REITHERMAN, WOLFGANG (1909-1985) American animator and animation producer born in Munich, Germany, on June 26, 1909. Wolfgang ("Woolie") Reitherman was brought to America by his parents at age two and became a U.S. citizen in 1919. After studies at Pasadena Junior College (1927-28) and at the Chouinard Art Institute in Los Angeles in 1930-31, he joined Walt Disney's company in 1933 during the great expansion of the studio. As is the wont in the profession, he started as an in-betweener on some of the Mickey Mouse and Goofy shorts. He then went into feature animation, working on Disney's first feature-length cartoon, *Snow White and the Seven Dwarfs* (1937), where he received his first screen credit (he animated the mirror sequence). He next was one of the artists animating Jiminy Cricket in *Pinocchio* (1940), but he did perhaps his best work animating the "Rite of Spring" sequence in *Fantasia* in 1940. The next year he completed the "El Gaucho Goofy" segment of *Saludos Amigos* before enlisting into the U.S. armed forces.

After serving with the Air Force in World War II (during which he was decorated with the Air Medal with oak leaf cluster) he returned to Disney in 1946. He was promptly put to work as animation supervisor of the "How to" Goofy shorts ("How to Be a Detective," "How to Ride a Horse," etc.) Of Reitherman's contribution to these cartoons, Frank Thomas and Ollie Johnston wrote in *Disney Animation*: "The Goofy that Woolie animated communicated with the audience in a way that only Woolie could have done it—this was a new type of animation." After working on *Cinderella, The Adventures of Ichabod and Mr. Toad*, and *Sleeping Beauty*, among others, he was the first animator to be given overall direction of an entire feature film with the 1963 *The Sword in the Stone* (in which his son Robert provided the voice of the young Arthur).

After Walt Disney's death in 1966, he became the head of the animated feature department at a difficult time (there had been talk of shutting down the entire unit). He brought *The Jungle Book* to completion in 1967 (another one of his sons, Bruce, voiced Mowgli). Next came *The Aristocats* (1970) and *Robin Hood* (1973). Both of them did well commercially (albeit not critically), and in 1977 the success of *The Rescuers* helped to definitively reestablish the animation studio as a viable concern.

In 1980, at age 70, Reitherman could retire a winner (years earlier he had received an Oscar for the 1968 *Winnie the Pooh and the Blustery Day*, a charming featurette he had directed). His remaining years were spent teaching and lecturing on animation; he died in a car accident in Burbank, California, on May 22, 1985.

Woolie Reitherman was one of the "Nine Old Men," so dubbed because they had spent their entire professional careers with the Disney organization. Unlike many of his fellow animators, he was less interested in character than in entertainment and in communicating with the audience (usually through gags and caricature). As he once declared, "The art of animation lends itself least to real people, and most to caricatures and illusions of a person."

M.H.

REJAB HAD (1939-) Born in Titi Timbul, Penang, on August 23, 1939, Rejab Had has played a significant leadership role in various stages of comic art development in Malaysia. In fact, he is known as *penghulu* (chief) to other cartoonists and fans.

Rejab's formal education ended in 1954 when he left Form V (eleventh grade), but he continued to learn about his favorite topic, drawing, from his association with cartoonist Rashid Din. His first published cartoon appeared in a cinema magazine in 1958, the same year he enlisted in the army. Eventually, his army duties revolved around his artistic abilities; he made instructional materials that included cartoons.

In 1973, Rejab was responsible for organizing the first union of cartoonists and *Ha Hu Hum*, a cartoonists' magazine he edited, but both had short lives. During his last six months in the military, he was given on-the-job training as a cartoonist for *Gila-Gila* ("mad crazy"), the first of a string of humor magazines that revolutionized cartooning in the country. He officially joined *Gila-Gila*'s staff upon retirement from the army in 1979.

Rejab has played a pivotal role in *Gila-Gila*'s tremendous success (the second largest periodical in circulation in Malaysia), holding together and inspiring a team of cartoonists while recruiting and training new talent to Creative Enterprise, publisher of the magazine. In 1987, he started the Gila-Gila School for Cartoonists, a once-a-week workshop which he instructs.

His own work appears in *Gila-Gila*, where he has a regular feature, *Hai KP* ("Hey Chief"), and in anthologies. Rejab's style of humor and drawing, according to anthropologist Ron Provencher, an authority on Malay cartooning, is "the most traditionally Malay" of all cartoonists. Hailing from a village himself, Rejab makes ample use of familiar Malay settings, mannerisms, dress, and language, accurately depicting the traditional Malay villager's concepts of the order of things and of time.

J.A.L.

REN AND STIMPY (U.S.) While attending Canada's Sheridan College in the late 1970s, the young animator John Kricfalusi creaated many assorted cartoon characters for his amusement, including the now famous *Ren and Stimpy*. A decade later, television network Nickelodeon was seeking new animatin properties artistically driven by cartoonists and recognized Kricfalusi's extraordinary work on *The New Adventures of Mighty Mouse* with Ralph Bakshi. John's original concept of shorts featuring various characters introduced by a live host was dropped in favor of a well-developed dog and cat team, Ren and Stimpy. The hyperactive chihuahua with an attitude and the silly, overfed cat instantly acquired a cult status upon their series launch on August 11, 1991. The pilot, *Bighouse Blues*, immediately displayed Spümco studio's command of solid personality animation and hilarious slapstick, coupled with satire and adult theme.

"Ren and Stempy." © Nickelodeon.

The fertile visions of Kricfalusi, art director Bill Wray and storymen Bob Camp and Jim Smith drove the loonic, madcap characters to insanity in outer space, had them revere "Yak Shaving Day" and maintain a collection of "Nosegoblins" stuck underneath a piano bench. Unfortunately, despite the collected talent and promise, friction between John and Nickelodeon over creative control and missed deadlines prompted Kricfalusi's departure after the second season.

Most production then shifted to Carbunkle Cartoons, and although well handled by the remaining staff, the obsessive emphasis on toilet humor and grosser effect significantly lowered expectation of the series. Once enough episodes for syndication were achieved, *Ren and Stimpy* was cancelled with the fall 1996 season. Comic books and a brief flood of merchandising accompanied the series during its peak, in addition to two Primetime Emmy Award nominations.

B.J.

REVERE, PAUL (1735-1818) American cartoonist, silversmith and patriot born in Boston on January 1, 1735. Paul Revere was primarily a silversmith, but his versatility was amazing: he experimented with transferring silverwork techniques to copperplate; he engraved some of the earliest American cartoons; his activities as revolutionist, propagandist and patriot are well documented; he manufactured gunpowder, discovered the process for rolling sheet copper and invented artificial dental devices.

The Able Doctor: America swallowing the bitter draught.
Paul Revere, 1774.

Revere executed engravings for the *Royal American Magazine* and later engraved his own versions of Franklin's classic "Join or Die" cartoon for the *Massachusetts Spy*, or *Thomas's* Boston Journal in 1774. His cartoon "The Boston Massacre," drawn, engraved and hand-colored in 1770, was a precursor of many political cartoons for generations to come. It had little regard for truth (the "massacre" happened not at all as Revere pictured it), was hardly original (in fact, it was copied from a sketch by John Singleton Copley's stepbrother) and was devastatingly effective (becoming a major linchpin in the independence crusade). Other Revere cartoons included "A Warm Place—Hell" and a simple representation of martyred patriots' coffins (for the Gazette), which introduced the coffin as a lasting cartoon icon.As a cartoonist, Revere was a strong "concept man" and an adequate copyist. As an artist and craftsman, his later credits include designing and printing the first Continental money, and designing the official seals of both the Continental Congress and the state of Massachusetts. He died on May 10, 1818.

R.M.

REYNAUD, ÉMILE (1844-1918) French artist and inventor born in Montreuil, France, on December 8, 1844. Emile Reynaud showed a disposition for art and had a curious mind: these proclivities combined in a series of drawings he made forecasting technical developments in ballistics and aerodynamics. He became attracted to photography around 1870 and contributed a number of innovations to the field.

Reynaud is best noted, however, as the most important figure in the prehistory of animation. He developed an apparatus, the praxinoscope, which was an elaboration on the old principle of the peep show and used a clever arrangement of mirrors. The first praxinoscope is said to have been made out of a tin can. In 1882 Reynaud combined his praxinoscope with a projector, and he produced animated cartoons drawn and colored by hand, first on strips of paper, then on celluloid, starting in 1888. In 1892 he felt confident enough to open his own theater, the Théatre Optique, where he showed programs made up of such features as a circus show called *Clown* et Ses *Chiens* ("Clown and His Dogs") and a love story in pantomime, *Pauvre Pierrot* ("Poor Pierrot"). These early efforts were accompanied by special music and ingenious sound effects.

In the meantime, however, the movie camera had been developed and refined; the future belonged to artists like J.S. Blackton and Emile Cohl, who had adapted their skills to the new medium of film. Bitter and financially ruined, Reynaud threw his praxinoscope and all his cartoons into the Seine. He died, a forgotten and broken man, in a sanitarium at Ivry, near Paris, on January 8, 1918. In recent years, however, Emile Reynaud has been rediscovered. Some of his miraculously recovered cartoons were shown to great acclaim at the Annecy Animated Film Festival. Georges Sadoul called his work "spirited, perfect and lasting," while Ralph Stephenson wrote that Reynaud "not

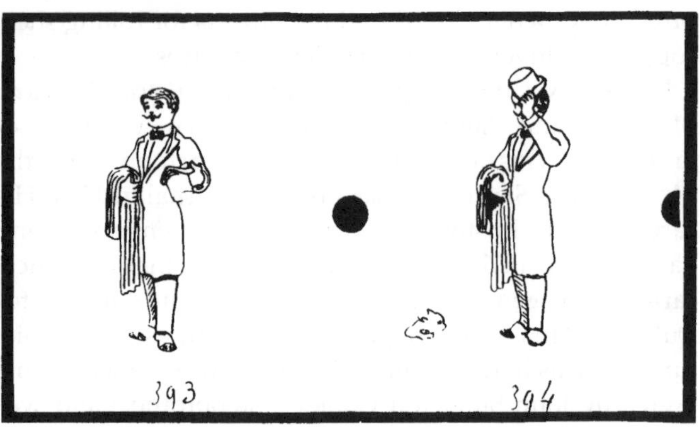

Émile Reynaud, "Réve au Coin du Feu," 1892.

only developed a technique, he originated a genre and was the first to develop the animated film (indeed the cinema, if by *cinema* we mean movement, not photography) into a spectacle."

M.H.

REYNOLDS, FRANK (1876-1953) British cartoonist and painter born in London on February 13, 1876.

There is a rough, harsh quality to the cartoons of Frank Reynolds that makes his work easily identifiable amongst that of his contemporaries in the pages of *Punch.* His career was long enough to make him appear both a modernist and "old hat," according to which end of the shelf you take the volumes from. He studied at Heatherley's School of Art, and as a painter in both oils and watercolors, he exhibited often and was elected R.I. in 1903. A frequent contributor to the *Illustrated London News* and the *Sketch,* he joined the staff of *Punch* in 1919 and was made art editor the following year; he held the job until 1930.

"Fougasse" (Cyril Bird), writing of Reynolds, considered him the forerunner of freestyle cartooning: "He played an important part in the transition from the comparatively tight, naturalistic drawing of the beginning of the century to the freer and more fluid and very much less documentary styles that followed." Reynolds, a left-handed artist, died on April 18, 1953.

Books: *By the Way Ballads* (1901); *The Smiths of Surbiton* (1906); *Frank Reynolds R.I.* (1907); *Pictures of Pain* (1908); *Pickwick Papers* (1910); *David Copperfield* (1911); *Old Curiosity Shop* (1913); *Frank Reynolds and His Work* (1918); *Punch Pictures* (1922); *Frank Reynolds Golf Book* (1932); *Hamish McDuff* (1937); *Off to the Pictures* (1937); and *Humorous Drawing for the Press* (1947).

D.G.

—Motorist: "Will this road take me to Honiton?"
—Boy: "I doan't know."
—Motorist: "Does it go through Chard?" —Boy:"I doan't know."
—Motorist: "You don't seem to know much, do you?"
—Boy: "Noa—but I ain't LOST!"

Frank Reynolds, 1930. © Punch.

"Make him tell me where he hid my burglar tools!"

Larry Reynolds, "Butch." © Look.

REYNOLDS, LARRY (1912-) American cartoonist born in Mount Vernon, New York, on February 12, 1912. Larry Reynolds went into advertising and illustration work after graduating from high school. He sold his first cartoon to Collier's in 1932. His work subsequently appeared in most major publications of the time, including the *New Yorker,* the *Saturday Evening Post* and the New York daily *PM.*

Reynolds was drafted into the army during World War II and subsequently created his famous weekly panel, *Butch,* for *Look* magazine (his first cartoons there were signed "Cpl. Larry Reynolds"). Butch was a burly but lovable burglar who always helped little old ladies across the street, kept apologizing to intended victims and generally made a mockery of the profession of robbery, much to the disgust of his diminutive accomplice, Slug. *Butch* was Reynolds's most enduring feature, lasting until the demise of *Look* in 1971.

In recent years Reynolds has been freelancing with mixed success. He prefers to use wash for his cartoons, and his style is clear and airy. His humor, soft in tone and with malice toward none, has made him a favorite of many.

M.H.

The Colonel's Lady: "Head high and not so nervous, my boy. I'm talking to you now not as a superior, but as a friend."
Ferdinand von Reznicek, 1903.

REZNICEK, FERDINAND VON (1868-1909) Austrian cartoonist and illustrator born in Sievering, outside Vienna, Austria, on June 16, 1868. Ferdinand von Reznicek, an Austrian baron and cavalry officer, was one of the most characteristic contributors to the Munich satirical magazine *Simplicissimus* in its opening years. His early death (on May 11, 1909), together with the death of the brilliant cartoonist Rudolf Wilke in November 1908 and of the founder-publisher Albert Langen in April 1909, in great measure put a close to the glorious first phase of that magazine's long history. Before joining the staff of *Simplicissimus,* Reznicek had already contributed cartoons to three other important magazines based in Munich: *Radfahr-Humor* (a publication devoted to the bicycle-riding fad), the time-honored *Fliegende Bläffer* and *Jugend,* which began publishing three months before *Simplicissimus* in 1896.

Many contemporary and later observers have called Reznicek the most truly popular artist who ever worked for *Simplicissimus* (he did about a thousand drawings for the magazine). His specialties were love and Carnival (the famous Munich *Fasching).* He was the delineator par excellence of the infamous sexual mores of pre-World War I high life in the great Central European capitals. His work is a visual equivalent of such literary pieces as Schnitzler's *Affairs of Anatol* and *Hands Around,* featuring the kept woman and the streetwalker, the casting couch, the secret apartment for ecstatic afternoons, the playboys of all ages, nightclubs, the prurient morals investigators, rivers of champagne and senseless carousing. Reznicek's own life, however, was reportedly quiet and industrious.

His albums included *Der Tanz* ("The Dance," 1906), *Galante* Welt ("Amorous World," 1907), Verliebte Leute ("People in Love," 1909), *Sie* ("She") and Unter *Vier Augen* ("In Private"). He also illustrated stories about Carnival time and works by the popular author and cabaret manager Ernst von Wolzogen.

Reznicek's draftsmanship, though sometimes running the risk of sweetness and facility, was certainly dashing and varied, at times displaying bold chiaroscuro effects or a pure art nouveau swirling division of the picture area or an inventive use of contrasting surface textures.

S.A.

RIBAS, WALBERCY (1943-) Brazilian animator born in Fazenda Guatapara, a cattle ranch in the province of Sao Paulo, 1943. The son of a moviehouse manager, Ribas was fascinated by film at an early age, and he built a homemade movie camera by the time he was 10. At age 13 he went to work as an office boy in the nearby city of Sao Paulo, while studying layout and design in art school at the same time. After a stint as assistant designer at an advertising agency he moved on to a job at Linxfilm, an animated studio, in 1959. He had finally found his life calling.

After making a number of TV animated shorts for the studio, Ribas formed his own production company, Start Desenhos Animados, in 1966. His first international success came at the Venice Film Festival where he won an award for best animation in 1972. Following this, he entered the lucrative field of commercial animation with award-winning spots for Sharp electronics that were shown around the world. Beginning in the late 1970's, he also turned out many entertainment cartoons of short and medium length, including *The Rhinoceros,* another one of his award-winning films. Among the many honors bestowed on him, he was elected president of the Brazilian Association of Film Animators.

In 1997 Ribas released his first animated feature, *O Grilo Feliz e a Estrela Jovem* ("The Happy Cricket and the Young Star"), on which he had been working for the past 12 years. A singer and composer, the happy cricket puts on a show with his mate Young Star; dramatic conflict is supplied by the villain Maledetto who tries to abduct Young Star. As in all fairy tales there is a happy ending. "My aim is to entertain children," the artist recently declared, "while teaching them notions such as respect for others, friendship, solidarity and, above all, freedom."

A.M.

RICHARDS, FREDERICK T. (1864-1921) American cartoonist born in Philadelphia, Pennsylvania, on May 27, 1864. F.T. Richards studied art at the Pennsylvania Academy of Fine Arts under Thomas Eakins and later at the Art Students League in New York City. Richards's ambition was to be a cartoonist, and when his earliest submissions to *Life* were accepted, he was that. From 1889 to his death he was a regular staff member. Richards also drew for *Collier's Weekly* in a lightly political vein and retained newspaper affiliations through the years with the *New York Herald (1901-02)* as well as the *New York Times,* the *New York Evening Mail* and the *Philadelphia Press.* In 1912, he joined the *Philadelphia North American* and remained there until he died. In politics, Richards was a Progressive.

His style was jolly and inoffensive. In the early years at *Life* he would frequently attempt hard-hitting editorial slams, but his overall outlook was too benevolent. Richards drew the monthly and annual roundup of news topics for *Life* that he inherited from Attwood and relinquished to Sykes, a fellow Philadelphian. Richards drew with rough, short pen lines, and somehow all his figures looked roly-poly.

Serious art was his favored avocation; he was exhibited at the Paris Exposition of 1900 and produced two folios of color prints, The Royal Game of Golf and Color Prints from Dickens, as well as a book, *The Blot Book.* Richards died of a heart attack at his drawing board on July 8, 1921.

R.M.

RICHTER, HANS (1888-1976) German animator, painter and filmmaker born in Berlin, Germany, on April 6, 1888. After art studies in Berlin and military service in World War I, Hans Richter, attracted by the Dada movement, went to Zurich. Together with Viking Eggeling he created a new syntax of animation, making use of techniques borrowed from painting and the graphic arts. He was one of the first to paint directly on film stock, opening a whole field of experimental animation that is still going on today.

Richter's most notable films are those of the immediate post-World War I era: *Prelude* (1919), *Fugue* (1920), *Rhythm 21* (1921), *Orchestration of Color, Rhythm 23* (1923), Rhythm 25 (1925) and *Filmstudie* (1926). His films were much admired by the Surrealists and are still being studied today for their fusion of rhythm, form and motion.

Like many other film animators, Richter later turned to live-action moviemaking, with such avant-garde experiments as *Vormittagsspuk* ("The Breakfast Ghost," 1928), *Everyday* (1929) and *Sturm iiber La Sarraz* (1930). In the 1930s he worked on commercial and industrial films throughout Europe. Emigrating to the United States in 1941, he made a number of avant-garde films, including the celebrated *Dreams That Money Can Buy* (1946). He also taught cinema at New York City College. Richter was a distinguished painter whose works were exhibited in galleries throughout the world, and a theorist who wrote several books, including *Filmgegner von Heute-Filmfreunde von Morgen* ("Film Haters of Today-Film Fans of Tomorrow, Zurich, 1931) and *Dada: Art and Anti-Art* (New York, 1965).

Hans Richter died on February 1, 1976, in Locarno, Switzerland, where he had retired.

M.H.

RICHTER, LUDWIG (1803-1884) German graphic artist, painter and cartoonist born in Dresden, Saxony, on September 28, 1803. The son of a respected minor printmaker, Carl August Richter, young Ludwig worked in his father's studio until an admiring art publisher subsidized three years of study in Italy (1823-26). From 1828 to 1835 Richter taught drawing at an offshoot of the Dresden Academy, the art school attached to the world-famous porcelain works at Meissen (not far from Dresden). For the remainder of his life he was a professor at the Academy itself.

Ludwig Richter, chapter heading for "Rüberzahl," a German folktale.

It was not until 1835 that Richter shook off his perpetual reminiscences of Italy to become forever after the beloved archetypical delineator of German (particularly Saxon) folk life. At the same time, his major interest shifted from painting to book illustration, especially for the publisher Georg Wigand. Over the years Richter was to produce some three thousand drawings for about three hundred volumes, not to mention several print portfolios. His activity as an illustrator is intimately associated (whether casually or not) with the concurrent rebirth of the German wood- cut in the spirit and technique of Diirer and the Renaissance masters (as opposed to the previously dominant wood engraving of the Bewick school).

In this vast output of Richter's, humorous and gently satirical illustrations are to be found side by side with sentimental, fairy-tale and purely scenic ones. These appear with greatest frequency in the numerous popular almanacs and songbooks to which he contributed. Recollections of odd human types he had known as a boy kept cropping up in his depictions of tradesmen, street entertainers and self-satisfied burghers enjoying the most harmless of pleasures on their nights out; in general, his city scenes were more often subjects for caricature than the countryside and forest views for which he is justly famous, but which, like his religious imagery, he took quite seriously.Richter's most outspoken satire appeared in a series of 24 drawings of 1849 called Musenkldnge aus *Deutschlands Leierkasten* ("Tones of the Muses from Germany's Barrel Organ"); here he parodied Goethe's Sorrows of Werther and the typical romance with a medieval setting, employing a true cartoon style not found in the bulk of his work. *Musenklange* has been praised as a worthy anticipation of Busch.

Richter's eyesight, which began to trouble him in the 1850s, became so feeble by the early 1870s that he had to abandon his career. He died in Dresden on June 19, 1884.

His autobiography, which does not extend beyond 1847 (the year in which his wife died), is highly regarded as a work of literature.

S.A.

RICHTER, MISCHA (1912-) American cartoonist born in the Ukraine, Russia, in 1912. Mischa Richter immigrated to the United States with his parents in 1924. The family settled in Taunton, Massachusetts. Richter was educated in Boston at the English High School, where he proved an intellectually adept and highly artistic student. He won scholarships to both the Boston Museum Fine Arts School and the Yale School of Fine Arts, and he graduated from the latter in 1934. His early attempts at a career in commercial art were not especially successful, but he was fortunate enough to get a job through the Work Projects Administration. Future readers of the *New Yorker* were also fortunate, for it was while working for the WPA that Richter found his instincts for cartoon art overcoming his inclination toward serious or fine art. He sold his first cartoon to *Cavalcade* in the mid-1930s and soon followed with sales to the *Saturday Evening Post.* In the early 1940s Richter began to refine the style that by the latter half of the decade made him one of the top cartoon artists in America, and a regular contributor to the *New Yorker.* His early cartoons in the *Post* reveal a bland executor of simple ink-line caricatures lacking any personal stamp; in the early 1940s, his drawings began to take on bold lines, like those of Peter Arno and George Price. Even his signature underwent transformation from a simple, printed "Richter" to the sweeping script favored by Arno; the quality of his cartoon ideas also improved noticeably, probably thanks to his increasing contact with other *New Yorker* artists.

Richter specializes in the comedy of manners and the absurdist reversal. His is the sort of cartooning in which the caption and the art are so interrelated that their humor is not easy to describe. One must, for example, see the glassily determined expressions of the people pouring out of an airplane and galloping off across the field in order to truly appreciate the information one onlooking attendant is giving another anent this bizarre behavior: "Seventeen major European cities in twenty-one days." Similarly, one conventionally dressed businessman to another as they wait for the morning train among a number of young execs, hip and hirsute: "I feel like a damn fool." To achieve his effects, Richter employs a very precise and disciplined approach and has been known to do a single drawing twenty times before arriving at a satisfactory result.

A published collection of Richter's early cartoons appeared under the title *This One's on Me* in 1945, and he is well represented in the *New Yorker*'s 50th anniversary album of drawings. He was also the author of *Strictly Richter,* a daily gag panel that King Features began syndicating in 1946 and that lasted into the 1960s. Now well into his eighties, he still does an occasional cartoon for the *New Yorker* where, along with Saul Steinberg, he is held in high regard as one of the early contributors to the glory days of the magazine.

R.C.

"Corona Corona."

Mischa Richter. © Dave Breger.

RICKARD, JACK (1922-1983) American cartoonist and illustrator born in Rochester, New York, on October 8, 1922. Jack Rickard (pronounced with the emphasis on the second syllable) decided in grammar school that he wanted to be a cartoonist. At the time his goal was to be a sports cartoonist or staff illustrator for a newspaper. He studied art as much as he could in high school but earned more fame as a drummer with a local band than as a cartoonist. It was the height of the big band sound.

After high school, Rickard served in the U.S. Army in both the European and Pacific theaters of war. However, he was not one of the published cartoonists of the war, though he did sketch when he was able.

With support from the GI bill, he earned a degree in commercial art from Rochester Institute of Technology in 1949. He then studied art at the Art Workshop School in New York City. There he studied under illustrator David Stone Martin and award-winning children's book artist Ezra Jack Keats. He worked briefly as a freelance artist in Rochester before he returned to New York City in about 1953 to join the advertising art studio of Fredman-Chaite. About that time Rickard began freelancing color cover paintings and black-and-white line art for the men's adventure and western magazines published by Magazine Management Company. Most of his career has been as a freelance artist-cartoonist.

Rickard has done a good deal of work for *Mad* magazine—a relationship that developed out of necessity. He also drew a short-lived comic strip created and written by Mel Lazarus of *Miss Peach* and *Momma* fame. The strip, entitled *Pauline McPeril,* was syndicated by the Publishers Newspaper Syndicate and at one time appeared in over a hundred newspapers. The svelte blond heroine with a penchant for perils such as spying behind the iron curtain became a permanent victim of the consolidation and failure of several New York City newspapers in 1967. The strip was published for about a year and a half.

Major motion picture companies have sought Jack Rickard's art and *Mad*-style caricature for innumerable movie posters, beginning in the 1960s. He has created the posters for many Peter Sellers movies, including the first, classic *Pink Panther* film. Other recent films include *A Touch of Class*, starring Glenda Jackson and George Segal, and Harry Belafonte's *Uptown Saturday Night.* (Interestingly, *Mad* cover artist Norman Mingo also has a distinguished reputation for painting movie posters, especially for many Marilyn Monroe movies, including Bus Stop.)

Jack Rickard was really a painter who blended classical illustration and caricature techniques to bring life to his movie posters and *Mad* magazine covers. He preferred to blend tones of gray to create his figures rather than outlining them in ink. His *Mad* covers were crisp and in the tradition of *Mad* covers established by Norman Mingo. Jack Rickard signed his *Mad* covers with his initials only. He died in July 1983.

B.C.

RIGAL, ANDRÉ (1898-1973) Born in Paris in 1898, André Rigal is one of the unsung pioneers of French animation. After finishing high school he went to the Paris School of Fine Arts where his studies were cut short in 1918 when he enlisted in the French Army, serving in the artillery corps in the last months of World War I. Demobilized in 1920, he joined the staff of Publi-Ciné, the first French studio of animation (it had been founded in 1919 by Robert Collard, a.k.a. Lortac). There he learned his craft from the illustrious veteran Emile Cohl himself.

In 1928 he left to start his own studio, dedicated to turning out comic strips as well as animated cartoons; that same year he created his best-known cartoon character, a crusty old salt called Cap'taine Sabord, for the boys' weekly, *Pierrot*. The series proved short-lived, and in 1933 Rigal went back to animation full-time, producing a weekly one-minute cartoon, *France Bonne Humeur* ("Good-Humored France") as a complement to the Gaumont film newsreel, *France-Actualités*. This humorous look at current events was to last for many years, only ending with the German occupation of France in 1940.

That year Rigal came briefly back to comics with a revived Cap'taine Sabord, but he returned to animation a few years later, notably releasing three *Cap'taine Sabord* cartoons in 1942-43: *Cap'taine Sabord appareille* ("Cap'taine Sabord Sails Off"), *Cap'taine Sabord dans l'ile mystérieuse* ("Cap'taine Sabord on Mysterious Island"), and *V'là le beau temps* ("Good Weather Comin' "). After France's liberation in 1944, American animated films, which had been banned under the German occupation and the Vichy regime, came back with a vengeance, and Cap'taine Sabord, enjoyable as he was, was soon eclipsed by Popeye. Rigal then turned to advertising cartoons, creating the famous Eskimo character that touted the Eskimo pies made by the Gervais company. His durable sea captain continued to appear desultorily in comics throughout the 1940s and 1950s and even spawned a short-lived illustrated newspaper sporting his name.

Ill health forced Rigal to retire in 1971, and he died two years later. Only after his death did his contribution to French animated cartoons receive its due.

M.H.

RIGBY, PAUL CRISPIN (1924-) Australian cartoonist born near Melbourne, Australia, in 1924. Writing in the international graphic arts magazine *Gebrauchsgraphik* in 1967, Ludwig Ebendh said: "Many so-called cartoonists resort to the same ruse as schoolboys who hide their lack of graphic talent behind grotesque exaggerations. These people are neither entitled to nor capable of creating the message of genuine caricature. For the cartoon is a very difficult form of graphic art which does not tolerate inferior work. And yet the sure mastery of the technique of drawing is merely a natural prerequisite." Paul Rigby is an artist who has mastered not only the technique but also the spirit of the cartoon.

Rigby was born in the Melbourne bayside suburb of Sandringham in 1924, and commenced to learn his craft at the Brighton Technical School. At the age of 15 he left school to work in a commercial art studio. In 1947 he left Melbourne, going west on his way to England, but he was offered and accepted a position as an illustrator in western Australia on the old Perth *Western Mail.* In 1952 he went to the *Daily News* as that paper's editorial cartoonist.

It was 20 years before he continued his journey to England, in 1969 joining the *London Sun*. In London Rigby experienced the great distinction of being given various cartooning assignments involving travel to China, the United States, the Soviet Union, Europe and Vietnam. He also worked directly for the Springer group of Germany and for the American *National* Star. Throughout this period his cartoons were being syndicated back in Australia. He returned to Australia and the Sydney *Daily Telegraph* in 1975, and in 1977 he moved to the United States to work for the *New York Post.* Today, after more than 20 years, Rigby is still drawing a daily cartoon for the *Post*'s opinion page.

The inevitable comparison is always made between Rigby's style and that of the English cartoonist Carl Giles. The similarities are natural; in the United States Pat Oliphant is experiencing the same form of flattery. Rigby's work produced in Australia, like that of Giles, has always been drawn to a "landscape" format-more wide than deep, using a complexity of figures in an appropriate

Picasso in Heaven
Paul Rigby. © London Express.

locale. And he exploits this format with his mastery of involved and dauntless perspective drawing. He has won five Australian Walkley Awards for the best editorial cartoon of the year, and there have been twenty or so books of his collected cartoons published since the first one in the 1950s.

V.L.

RIGHT AROUND HOME (U.S.) *Columbus Dispatch* cartoonist Dudley Fisher developed the idea for *Right Around Home* in 1937. He was then working on a weekly feature called Jolly *Jingles,* and he decided one day to draw one huge panel taking up the whole page and depicting what happens to a farm family when city relatives come to visit them for Christmas. It was so well received that Fisher dropped *Jolly Jingles* and devoted himself to his new creation, which got its definitive title not long afterwards. In January 1938 King Features Syndicate picked up *Right Around Home* for national distribution.

The two most striking characteristics of Fisher's panel were his bird's-eye perspective (looking downward at about a 45-degree angle) and the incredible crowding of his compositions. Working the whole scene into a single giant panel filling an entire newspaper page, Fisher crammed his characters into small, tight groups engaged in some activity or other in every corner of his panel. Gradually the action in the feature shifted from a rural to a suburban setting, centering more and more around such activities as barbecues, bridge clubs, car washes, etc. The principal protagonists of the hectic goings-on were the mischievous ten-year-old Myrtle, her family, pets and neighbors. Right *Around Home* had a cozy, homey, carefree flavor, and it enjoyed wide enough popularity to give rise to a spin-off, a daily strip called *Myrtle,* which King Features started syndicating in 1942.

Dudley Fisher died in July 1951. His feature, still bylined under the name of its creator, was taken up by Stan Randall and a succession of anonymous syndicate staffers; it managed to last into the 1960s.

M.H.

RIPLEY, ROBERT LEROY (1893-1949) American cartoonist and entrepreneur born in Santa Rosa, California, on December 25, 1893. LeRoy Ripley (the "Robert" was added afterwards) dropped out of high school and went to work to help his family. Having a natural talent for drawing (he had sold his first cartoon to *Life* at age 14), Ripley decided after a short-lived attempt at a sports career to turn to newspaper cartooning. He started as a professional sports cartoonist for the *San Francisco Bulletin* in 1910, later shifting to the *Chronicle* (at that time he used the pseudonym "Rip").

In 1913 Ripley was asked to illustrate actor Joseph Taylor's book of reminiscences, *Fifty Years of Footlights,* and took the manuscript to New York. While there, he was hired by the Globe as its regular sports cartoonist. One day

"Right Around Home." © *King Features Syndicate.*

Robert L. Ripley, first "Believe It or Not!" panel. © King Features Syndicate.

in December 1918, being at a loss for a suitable topic, Ripley decided to chronicle sports oddities on his page, which subsequently developed into the famous panel feature *Believe It or Not!* After the demise of the *Globe* in 1924, Ripley went to the *Evening Telegram,* and from there to the *Post.* In 1926 he published a collection of his panels that brought him a contract from Warner Brothers for 26 movie shorts, as well as international distribution of *Believe It or Not!* by King Features Syndicate.

In the 1930 Ripley embarked on a well-publicized worldwide tour in search of oddities of all kinds. For Chicago's 1933 Century of Progress Exposition he organized an exhibit of some of the artifacts he had collected, displaying them in his "Odditorium." He also had a popular program of radio broadcasts and made public appearances all over the world. Ripley is further credited with helping to establish "The Star-Spangled Banner" as the national anthem by pointing out in a 1931 Believe It or Not! panel that the United States lacked such a symbol of national unity and pride.

A true American original, Ripley was awarded a swarm of honors and distinctions for his various entrepreneurial exploits, including a number of foreign decorations and the title Fellow of the Royal Geographic Society of London. He died in New York on May 26, 1949. In 1961 Doubleday published his biography, Robert *Ripley,* the Modern *Marco* Polo, penned by fellow King Features columnist Robert Considine.

M.H.

RÍUS

See Del Río, Eduardo.

ROAD RUNNER, THE (U.S.) In 1948 Warner Brothers animation director Chuck Jones and his scriptwriter Michael Maltese decided to use in a cartoon the most basic of dramatic devices-the chase-without any adornment of plot or characterization. The result was "Fast and Furry-ous," wherein a scrawny coyote (*Canis lafrans)* was let loose in the Arizona desert in pursuit of a mocking road runner (*Geococcyx californianus*). The Coyote resorted to the wildest plans and constructed the most outlandish devices in order to catch his prey, but all in vain; his schemes backfired on him, crushing him under ten-ton boulders, flinging him into the path of oncoming trains and splashing him all over the desert landscape. The pace was unrelenting, and the similarity to silent slapstick comedy was further enhanced by the absence of dialogue.

(As a rest from his futile exertions, the Coyote also tried unsuccessfully to steal sheep from under the watchful eye of Sam the sheepdog, and he even crossed swords with Bugs Bunny. On one such occasion, in "Compressed Hare," after introducing himself as "Wile E. Coyote-Genius," he failed to capture Bugs with a giant electromagnet of his own invention, instead bringing down upon his head in quick *suc*cession a metal mailbox, an iron stove, a bank safe, a locomotive, a battleship and even the Eiffel Tower.)

Chuck Jones directed all the *Road Runner* cartoons up to his departure from Warners in 1962 ("Beep Prepared," "Gee Whiz-z-z-z" and "Lickety Splat" are among the titles). He was replaced by Bob McKimson and Rudy Larriva, who did not possess Jones's inexhaustible inventiveness. The series deteriorated further after it was

"The *Road Runner.*" © *Warner Brothers.*

farmed out to DePatie-Freleng in 1964, and it came to an end in the late 1960s.

The Road Runner, like other cartoon characters, enjoyed great success on the television screen (on some stations he even co-stars in *The Bugs Bunny/Road Runner Show*).The Road Runner and the Coyote appeared in games, puzzles and toys, and there was even a Road Runner car manufactured by Chrysler. They were also featured in comic books (in which the Road Runner became known as Beep Beep") published by Western (later Gold Key), starting in 1959.

M.H.

ROBIDA, ALBERT (1848-1926) French cartoonist, graphic artist and writer born in Compiégne, north of Paris, on March 14, 1848. Albert Robida started his career in 1866 with cartoons published in such magazines as Le *Journal Amusant, La Vie Elégante* and *Paris Comique.* A few years later he became one of the most prolific contributors to the noted satirical weekly *La Vie Parisienne.* Robida also pursued a career as an engraver and lithographer, and his works were exhibited in the Paris Salons of 1868, 1869 and 1870.

In 1873 Robida went to Vienna to work for the humor magazine *Der Floh.* He returned to Paris after a few months and founded his own magazine, *La Cari*cature, the following year. He produced a number of outstanding albums to which he contributed both text and drawings. In addition he found time to contribute cartoons to the leading French magazines of the day, including Le *Rire* and *Fantasio.*

Robida's works of science fiction and anticipation are especially remarkable: *Voyages Trés Extra ordinaires de Saturnin Farandoul* ("Saturnin Farandoul's Very Extraordinary Travels," 1879), *Le Vingtiéme Siécle* ("The Twentieth Century," 1883) and *La Guerre au Vingtième Siècle* ("War in the Twentieth Century," 1887) present a prophetic view of the society of the future, complete with space travel, television, cinema, tank warfare, etc.

Robida showed as much predilection for the past as he did for the future. He wrote and illustrated *Vieilles y Villes de Suisse, Vieilles Villes d'Espagne* and *Vieilles Villes d'Italie* ("Old Towns of Switzerland, Spain and Italy"), in which he lovingly depicted some of the most revered urban landscapes of Europe. He was also one of the organizers of the Old Paris exhibition at the 1900 Exposition.At the end of World War I Robida published *Les Villes Martyres* ("Martyred Cities"), a collection of stark and unforgettable drawings documenting the destruction of war. Robida died in Neuilly-sur-Seine on October 11, 1926. His son, Emile Robida-Boucher, was also a noted artist and engraver.

An artist of unusual genius and unparalleled fecundity, Albert Robida left behind an artistic legacy that has not been entirely inventoried to this day. His futuristic works alone put him among the top draftsmen of his time. His cartoons show the same tolerant amusement at the fads and follies of his epoch as do his fashion magazine drawings or his illustrations to the cookbooks of Brillat-Savarin and Edmond Richardin.

M.H.

ROBERTS, ERIC (1914-1983) The strips of Eric Roberts were never famous for their careful finish, but possessed a hurried look that stemmed from his earlier work as a gag artist for the popular magazines for adults. However many of his characters, especially those based on boys and their mischievous behavior at home, school and play, are well remembered. Some such as *Winker Watson,* a school strip he started in *The Dandy* in 1961, are still running, drawn by an excellent but unnamed impersonator some 15 years after his death.

Eric was born into a family of circus performers in 1914, and by the 1930's his cartoons began appearing with regularity in such weekly magazines as *Answers, Tit-Bits* and *The Passing Show.* In 1937 he spotted a now famous advertisement in the London newspapers, placed by the Dundee-based publisher, D.C. Thomson. Artists were required to send in samples, the object being the firm's expansion from boys' story papers to pictorial comics. Eric immediately created the six-picture strip *Podge,* about a chubby child always up to mischief. It was accepted instantly and appeared from No. 1 of *The Dandy* (December 4, 1937), earning Eric one pound a week.

When Thomson's launched their second comic, *The Beano,* in 1938, Eric did better. He produced three series: another boy hero, Helpful Henry, a full page about "Rip Van Wink," a 700-year old man who woke in modern Britain and caused no end of slapstick trouble, and "Good King Coke—He's Stoney Broke," about a penniless King and his naughty young Princeling sons.

After the war Eric joined *The Knockout,* published by the London-based Amalgamated Press, noted for being better payers than the Scottish company. His first strip, *Mike,* a reworking of *Podge* (he often used the same ideas), began as a half-page but was so popular with young readers that he soon moved to the full-color front page. Eric's cruder but lively art looked well in color. *Mike* ran for many years,

Albert Robida, fashion drawings.

later being reprinted in *Buster* and *The Big One* as *Smiler* (1964).

In 1947 Eric rejoined *The Dandy* with Smudge who, for a change, was a naughty little girl. She would later be reprinted in the same comic as *Hy Jinks* (1955). In 1948-1949 Eric contributed to many of the one-off comics published by Philipp Marx (*Glee Comic; Lucky Dip; Red Flash;* etc.). Then in 1953 he rejoined *The Dandy* yet again, producing *Willie the Wicked, The Wee Black Scallywag, Ginger's Super-Jeep, Willie's Whizzer Broom* and others. Once again the A.P. beckoned, and Eric drew an adventure serial about Sinbad Simms the Shark Boy for *Knockout* (reprinted 1964), and *Niblo Nibbs* for *Film Fun* (1960), reprinted 1967 in *Giggle*. Finally came the everlasting *Winker Watson* for *Dandy* (1961), and for the same comic his last strip appeared in *Dandy Annual*, September 1980. He died in 1983.

D.G.

ROBERTSON, WALLY (1892-1983) When Wally Robertson died in 1983 virtually the last link with the prewar British "penny comics" was broken. He spent a lifetime (and a laughtime) drawing nothing but funnies from 1914 to the 1970's, ending up doing lettering for speech balloons in girls' comics, and winning the Association of Comic Enthusiasts lifetime award of the Ally Sloper figurine to a standing ovation from his cartooning colleagues in 1980.

Walter Robertson was born in Glasgow on May 16, 1892, attending Queens Park and Woodside schools, and beginning working life as an apprentice to the Hill and Hodges Studio for Architects. Always a bit of an artist, he taught himself cartooning by imitating the work of his favorite professionals, Tom Browne and Phil May, making scrapbooks of their published work which he kept all his life. He submitted a few cartoons to local Scottish publications, and was first published in the D.C. Thomson women's weekly, *People's Friend*. He sent sample jokes and strips down to the Amalgamated Press in London, where his work impressed Fred Cordwell, editor of *Merry and Bright* comic, who sent him 4 pounds to pay his return fare to London for an interview. Cordwell gave him a staff job to draw a minimum of 12 pictures a week at a wage of 3 pounds. At the time, early 1914, this was a wage well above that of the average working man. Wally was put into the art room alongside such comic strip luminaries as George "Billy" Wakefield, Harry Parlett, and Freddie Crompton, whose work and freely given advice improved his style.

Wally began what was called "duplication," drawing other artists' characters when they were too busy, or absent with illness or on holiday. He became so adept at this approved form of imitation that most of his life on the A.P. comics was spent drawing other men's strips for them.

It was not until he returned to the A.P. comics after the Great War, which he had spent in the trenches drawing both serious and humorous sketches of life under bombardment, that he was given the chance to draw original characters of his own. Beginning with *Flossie and Phyllis the Flappers* in *Merry and Bright* (1918), he originated *Percy and his Pogo* for *Jolly Jester* (1921), *Sunny and Bunny* for *Funny Wonder* (1922), *Clara the Comical Cat* for *Sunbeam* (1925), the Scots hero *Andy Mac* (1926), *Thrifty Ted* (1929), *Fanny and Aunt Annie* (1930), *Professor Noodle's Nutty Notions* (1932), *Luke and Len the Odd Job Men* (1933), and many more, through to his last A.P. series, "Jingle College" in *Jingles* (1954). Among his many duplications were the cinema comedians "Charlie Chaplin," "George Formby," "Joe E. Brown," "Max Miller" and Sydney Howard" for *Film Fun*.

Let go by the A.P. where new and younger editors disliked his old-fashioned style, Wally, with Scottish determination plus talent, modernized his artwork and became a valued contributor to the irregular comicbooks of the period published by Gerald G. Swan. He also drew for *Lone Star* ("Walla the Cherokee") and *Space Ace* ("Rex from Planet X") from 1954 to 1960. His last strip was a parody, *Sheerluck Jones*, for the National Savings comic *Money Fun* in 1982. He died in February 1983.

D.G.

ROBINSON, BOARDMAN (1876-1952) American cartoonist, artist, teacher and muralist born in Somerset, Nova Scotia, on September 6, 1876. Boardman Robinson was educated in Canada and England and at the Massachusetts Normal School, receiving further art training at the Académie Colarossi and the Ecole des Beaux-Arts in Paris. At the turn of the century Robinson lived as a painter in Paris, then San Francisco, and in 1907 he joined the New York Morning Telegraph as staff artist and editorial cartoonist.

In 1910, the beginning of New York City's golden era of editorial cartooning, Robinson switched to the New York

—"What's the celebration about M's Milligan?" —"Sure, me boy's comin' home today. He was sentenced to ten years in the penitentiary, but he got three years off for good conduct." —"Ah! I wish I had a son like that!"

Boardman Robinson, 1915. © The Masses.

Tribune and soon exerted more influence on his profession than almost any other cartoonist over the years. With Robert Minor of the Pulitzer papers, Robinson explored the use of lithograph crayon as a means of shading on paper for editorial cartoons; Forain and Steinlen in France had used the medium to good effect. Visually, of course, the method simulated the look of actual lithography on stone and so was in a tradition that stretched from Daumier to Keppler. But in daily newspapers it was striking, and after Robinson and Minor, it remained a convention of editorial cartooning well into the 1960s.

Robinson on the Tribune was one of the country's most reprinted and influential cartoonists, but he left the Republican organ in 1914, reportedly over editorial policy-Robinson was swiftly moving closer to socialism-and because of his ardent opposition to the war in Europe. The next year he traveled to battle sites with John Reed, another Socialist, for the Metropolitan magazine, a Socialist journal.

In 1915-16 Robinson was on the staff of Puck, which was seeking to become an avant-garde journal in its dying days. He also drew for the Masses, the Liberator and Harper's Weekly until 1922. In 1922-23 he drew for the London Outlook in England.

About this time Robinson gradually left the sphere of partisanship and cartooning to pursue a career as a teacher and book illustrator; he instructed at the Art Students League in New York (1918-29) and was director of the Colorado Springs Fine Art Center (1930-47). Among the awards he received for his serious art was a gold medal from the Architectural League of New York for his murals, a genre in which he shone particularly in works for the RKO building in New York and the Department of Justice in Washington. His books include The War in Eastern Europe and Cartoons of the War (both 1916); and he illustrated The Brothers Karamazov (1933), The Idiot (1935), King Lear (1939), Spoon River Anthology (1941) and Moby Dick (1942). His work is featured in many museum and gallery collections.

Robinson not only pioneered the bold use of crayon shading in his newspaper work but was the leader of the group of editorial cartoonists who brought partisans hip to their spaces every day. Except for predecessors like Davenport, newspaper artists (their field only 10 to 15 years old when Robinson joined the Tribune) were generally vapid. Robinson's cartoons were invariably pointed and aggressive; he never hesitated to go to extremes to illustrate a strong message, but the artistic vehicle was always masterfully realized. Unfortunately Robinson's scores of imitators substituted shrill stridency for reasoned advocacy and used the crayon to hide their artistic deficiencies.

Robinson died on September 5, 1952.

R.M.

ROBINSON, HEATH (1872-1944) British cartoonist, illustrator and writer born at Hornsey Rise, London, England, on May 31, 1872.

Heath Robinson shares with Rube Goldberg the distinction of having entered the English language by name: people still talk of "a Heath Robinson invention" or call any

The Early Queuers. Mrs. Broadgusset to Mr. B. (an inveterate first-nighter):
"It's not that I mind waiting until the theatre's ready,
but suppose they change their mind and turn it into a town hall."
Heath Robinson. © The Bystander.

eccentric or humorously complicated contrivance "Heath Robinsonian." Yet the hundreds of cartoons Heath Robinson produced ridiculing the machine were but a small part of the output of a man whom John Lewis, in his 1973 book Heath Robinson, called "artist and comic genius."

Robinson's father, Thomas, was chief staff artist on the *Penny Illustrated Paper* (one of his cover drawings was of the famous Tay Bridge Disaster of 1879); his grandfather, also Thomas Robinson, was an engraver for the magazines Good Words and the *London Journal.* His older brothers, Tom and Charles, both became artists in their own right. He left school at 15 and entered the Royal Academy schools to study art. After three years he left to become a landscape painter, but with little success. He took a desk in his father's studio in the Strand and eventually contributed sketches to Good Words and the juvenile magazine Little *Folks.* In 1897 he received his first commission to illustrate a book, an edition of Hans Christian Andersen. Many more such commissions followed, until in 1902 he wrote and illustrated his first novel, a fantasy for children called *Uncle Lubin.* Unhappily the publisher, Grant Richards, went bankrupt.

The following year Robinson drew his first commercial work, advertising cartoons for the Lamson Paragon Supply Company. Advertising would prove a profitable second string, and as his Heath Robinsonian inventions developed, more and more commissions came from advertising agents and their clients. These cartoon absurdities originated in the pages of the Sketch, a superior weekly on art paper that went in for full-page "humorous plates." Later came similar pages for the *Bystander, Punch,* the *Humorist,* etc., and cartoons continued to alternate with meticulously illustrated books through the rest of his long and happy career. He died on September 13, 1944, aged 72.

Books: Fairy Tales and Legends (1897); *The Life of Don Quixote* (1897); *The Giant Crab* (1897); The *Pilgrim's Progress* (1897); *The Queen's Story Book* (1898); *The Talking Thrush* (1899); *Fairy Tales from Hans Andersen* (1899); *The Arabian Nights' Entertainments* (1899); *Poems of Edgar Allan Poe* (1900); *Mediaeval* Stories (1902); *Adventures of Uncle Lubin* (1902); *Adventures of Don Quixote* (1902); *Surprising Travels of Baron Munchausen* (1902); *Tales from Shakespeare* (1902); *The Child's Arabian Nights* (1903); *Rama and the Monkeys* (1903); *The Works of Rabelais* (1904); *Monarchs of Merry England* (1904); *The Merry Multi fleet* (1904); *Stories from Chaucer (1906); Stories from the Iliad* (1907); *W. Heath Robinson* (1907); *Stories from* the *Odyssey* (1907); *Twelfth Night* (1908); *A Song of the English* (1909); *Collected Verse of Rudyard Kipling* (1910); *The Dead King* (1910); *Bill the Minder* (1912); *Hans Andersen's Fairy Tales* (1913); *The Book of Heath Robinson* (1913); *Midsummer Night's Dream* (1914); *Water Babies* (1915); *Some Frightful War Pictures* (1915); *Hunlikely* (1915); *Peacock Pie* (1916); *The Saintly Hun* (1917); *The Art of the Illustrator* (1918); *Flypapers* (1919); *Get On With It* (1920); *The Home Made Car* (1921); *Old Time Stories* (1921); *Peter Quilp in Search of a Friend* (1921); *Quaint and Selected Pictures* (1922); *Humours of Golf* (1923); *Topsy Turvy Tales* (1923); *Incredible Adventures of Professor Branestawm* (1934); *Absurdities (1934); Balbus* (1934); *Book of Goblins* (1934); *Railway Ribaldry* (1935); *How* to *Live in a Flat* (1936); *How to Be a Perfect Husband* (1937); *How to Make a Garden Grow* (1938); *My Line of Life* (1938); Success *with Stocks and Shares* (1938); *How to Be a Motorist* (1939); *Let's Laugh* (1939); *Mein Rant* (1940); *How to Make the Best of Things* (1940); *How to Build a New World* (1941); *Heath Robinson at War* (1942); *How* to *Run a Communal Home* (1943); *Once Upon a Time* (1944); *The Life and Art of W. Heath Robinson* (1947); *The Penguin Heath Robinson* (1966); and *Heath Robinson* (1973).

D.G.

ROBOTECH (U.S.-Japan) The complicated origin of *Robotech* still generates arguments over which nations and creators deserve credit for it. Originally there were three separate Japanese TV animated serials: *Chojiku Yosai Macross* ("Super-Dimensional Fortress Macross"; 36 episodes, broadcast October 3, 1982 - June 26, 1983); *Kiko Soseiki Mospeada* ("Genesis Climber Mospeada"; 25 episodes, October 2, 1983 - March 25, 1984); and *Chojiku Kidan Southern Cross* ("Super-Dimensional Cavalry Corps Southern Cross"; 23 episodes, April 15, 1984 - September 30, 1984). All three were produced by the same studio, Tatsunoko Production Co., and all three were futuristic serials about humans defending their world from space invaders.

Macross was bought by Harmony Gold, a Hollywood-based TB distributor. But the American syndicated TV market wanted series of at least 65 episodes, and *Macross* had only 36. Harmony Gold consulted Carl Macek, an expert on Japanese animation. Macek advised buying Tatsunoko's two similar programs, and writing a new story to blend all three into a single serial of 85 episodes. Harmony Gold hired him to do the job. Macek originally planned to keep the Macross name, but the American license for the Macross robot vehicles had already been sold to Revell Toys, which was about to market them under the name Robotech, so that was used instead.

In the initial *Macross* generation, a gigantic derelict spaceship, the SDF-1, crashlands on Earth. When its alien Zentraedi enemy arrives looking for it, the SDF-1's automatic defenses blast them. Earth is caught in an interstellar war. *Macross* is a soap opera about three teens: Rick Hunter, a reluctant fighter for Earth's defense; Lisa Hayes, the commander of the SDF-1's human bridge crew; and Lynn Minmei, a civilian girl who Rick rescues and who later becomes a popular singer. In a subplot, Rick's buddy Max Sterling and the Zentraedi woman fighter Mirya fall in love and get married, signifying the basic unity of all space peoples.

In the *Robotech Masters* (*Southern Cross*), Max and Mirya's daughter Dana Sterling has grown to teenhood and entered the Robotech Defense Force. The Robotech Masters, builders of the now-destroyed SDF-1, come to Earth to reclaim its Protoculture power source. They need it for their own defense against a new enemy, the Invid. Earth and the Robotech Masters fight each other into mutual destruction, leaving Earth helpless when the Invid arrive.

In *Robotech: The New Generation* (*Mospeada*), Earth has been under Invid subjugation for decades. A liberating space fleet from the Earth colony on Mars is slaughtered. The only survivor, Scott Bernard, gathers a band of rebellious teens into a guerrilla army which fights its way closer to the main Invid base.

Robotech began syndication on March 1, 1985. It was so popular that Harmony Gold planned a completely new 65-episode sequel written by Macek, *Robotech II: The Sentinels*, continuing the adventures of Rick Hunter, Lisa Hayes, and Lynn Minmei. But the main sponsor pulled out shortly after production began. To salvage the animation completed for what would have been the first three episodes, it was released as an 80-minute video feature in 1988.

Carl Macek's *Robotech*, not the three original Japanese series, was released worldwide. The saga was novelized into a series of 18 American s-f books by "Jack McKinney" (Brian Daley and James Luceno) which have been reprinted over the years as serious s-f novels rather than merchandising tie-ins. A licensed *Robotech* comic book is still producing new issues in 1998. *Robotech's* popularity transcends the usual one- or two-season lifespan of most TV cartoon series.

F.P.

ROCKWELL, NORMAN PERCEVEL (1894-1978) American illustrator and cartoonist born in New York City on February 3, 1894. Norman Rockwell studied art at the

Chase School, the National Academy and the Art Students League (under George Bridgman and Thomas Fogarty). He made early sales of cartoons and illustrations to the Condé-Nast publications, the American Book Company, St. Nicholas and other juvenile publishers. In 1916 his major break came when he sold covers to the *Saturday Evening Post, Life, Judge* and *Leslie's*. From then until 1963, he was destined to paint 317 covers for the Post, and he also did hundreds of other pieces for the Boy Scouts of America (calendars and *Boy's Life* covers), for magazines (including *Look* after his *Post* days) and for advertising accounts. In his more recent days of revived popularity, his paintings were reproduced on plates, bells, canvas and many other media.

His work for *Life* and *Judge*—much of it during World War I and dealing with wartime and patriotic themes—was essentially cartoon material, although executed in oils. A Rockwell cover was captioned and usually humorous, as much a cartoon gag as any of the pen-and-inks or paintings in the interior of the magazines. Since these qualities carried over into his work for the *Saturday Evening Post*, it is not stretching definitions to say that Rockwell remained as much a cartoonist as an illustrator throughout his career. Most of his themes were humorous (though humor is not among the criteria of a cartoon). More to the point, he remained a one-idea situational artist (and not, by and large, an illustrator of stories), and in this sense he was a cartoonist.

Definitions aside, Rockwell captured for several generations the spirit of America—either as it was or as he wished it to be. His small-town folk with their everyday concerns really touched on universal themes and reactions. Rockwell's work will be evocative long after small towns and swimming holes and rural constables disappear—because things like family sentiment, a boy's springtime feelings and the humor of innocent encounters will remain.

R.M.

ROCKY AND HIS FRIENDS
See Bullwinkle Show, The.

RODEWALT, VANCE (1946-) Canadian cartoonist born to a ranching family in Edmonton, Canada, in 1946. Vance Rodewalt contributed ad cartoons to *The Roughneck*, a local publication, while he was still in high school. After studies in fine art he turned to cartooning for a living, drawing comic books for Marvel and humor cartoons for *Cracked* magazine. At the same time he tried his hand at editorial cartooning, and in 1970 the *Calgary Albertan* asked him to become the paper's regular political cartoonist. When the *Albertan* was bought by the *Calgary Sun* 4 years later, he kept the same position at the *Sun*. In the mid-1980s he moved to the *Calgary Herald*, for which he became the regular cartoonist in 1987.

As a political cartoonist Rodewalt has always mixed a healthy dose of good-natured humor and a winsome graphic style with sometimes acerbic commentary. While dealing mostly with Canadian concerns, his cartoons often take on a more universal meaning, as when he showed

Vance Rodewalt. © Calgary Herald.

Prime Minister Kim Campbell dressed as a witch-doctor ordering to "throw in more soldiers!" to the volcano-god of deficit. Another of his cartoons depicted a reform candidate running loose in a candy store full of goodies marked "perks" once he got elected to Parliament.

In addition to his daily *Herald* cartoons, Rodewalt, since 1988, has been turning out a newspaper strip called *Chubb and Chauncey* about a dog and a hamster. The feature is distributed by the Toronto Star Syndicate "all over the place, even Tasmania," according to its author. A versatile cartoonist, he has had two books of his cartoons published nationally. He has won Canada's National Newspaper Award in 1988, and he was elected president of the Association of Canadian Editorial Cartoonists in 1992.

M.H.

RODRIGUES, AUGUSTO (1913-1993) Brazilian cartoonist born in Recife, Brazil, in 1913. Augusto Rodrigues started his career in 1932, designing decorations at Percy Lau's commercial studio in Pernambuco (as Recife was called then). He later also did fashion drawings, cartoons and advertising art. In 1933 he began contributing editorial and political cartoons to the Diário de Pernambuco; the following year, with the help of a group of young artists who shared his outlook, he organized the first exhibition of modern art in Pernambuco. After working on the 1935 Centennial Exposition in Porto Alegre, Rodrigues settled in Rio later the same year.

Rodrigues's career as a political cartoonist flourished in the mid-1930s, with regular contributions appearing in such publications as *O Jornal* and the *Diário de Sao Paulo*; he also collaborated on *Fon-Fon!, Vamos Ler* and *O Cruzeiro*. During World War II his cartoons were widely reprinted throughout South America. After a short stay in Europe following World War II, Rodrigues settled down in Rio permanently. In 1948 he founded the Escolinha de Arte do Brasil; under his direction several exhibitions of Brazilian children's art were organized in Paris, London, Rome and Lisbon, as well as in Brazil. In 1961 he was made a member of the National Council of Culture. Rodrigues was president of a number of Brazilian art societies, and a permanent member of the jury of the American Biennial of Art.

Rodrigues combined a fine, almost lyrical style of drawing with a deep concern for the poor and downtrodden. He was one of the most respected graphic artists in Brazil today. He was working mainly as a painter when he died in 1993.

A.M.

RODRIGUES, VILMAR SILVA (1931-) Brazilian cartoonist born in Bagé, Rio Grande do Sul, Brazil, in 1931. In 1945 Vilmar Rodrigues moved with his parents to Rio de Janeiro, where he attended art school. In 1952 Vilmar (as he signs his work) had his first cartoons published in the daily Ultima Hora. He subsequently became one of Brazil's most prolific young cartoonists, with contributions to the magazines *Vamos Rir, O Riso, Revista do Disco* and *Esporte Ilustrado* (1953-56) and to the daily *O Mundo Portugues*.

In 1957 Vilmar began to do advertising art in addition to his cartooning work. His name appeared regularly in many Brazilian publications, including *O Cruzeiro, PifPaf, Diners, Jornal dos Sports* and *Correio da Manhá,* all of which prominently featured his cartoons, and in Ultima Hora, his first employer, for which he has also done a number of comic strips. Vilmar's cartoons have been published in foreign magazines such as *La Codorniz* (Spain) and *Il Travaso* (Italy). Vilmar has been the recipient of many awards and distinctions, starting with the first prize he won in a cartooning contest back in 1955. He worked for the Brazilian edition of *Mad* until the late 1990s.

A.M.

RODRIGUEZ CASTELAO, DANIEL (1886-1950) Spanish cartoonist, painter, writer and politician born in Reancho, Galicia, Spain, in 1886. Daniel Rodriguez started contributing cartoons to the leading magazines of his time in the early years of this century. His cartoons were widely exhibited in his native Galicia as well as in Madrid. Two landmarks in his career were the publication in 1931 of an anthology of Rodriguez cartoons, *Nos* ("We"), and the 1938 publication of *Milicianos* ("Republican Soldiers"). The 50 cartoons reprinted in *Nos* represent the most complete summation of leftist political cartooning in Spain since Goya; they are a cry against the destruction of rural life and a plea for the defense of the poor peasants of Galicia. *Milicianos* is an ardent apology for the Republican cause during the Spanish Civil War. In 1938 Rodriguez went into exile in Mexico. In 1941 he published an album of cartoons about the Civil War entitled *Meus Compañeros* ("My Comrades") and in 1945 founded the magazine *Galeuzca*. He was named a minister of the Spanish government-in-exile in 1946 and died in Mexico City in 1950.

In addition to his cartoon work, Rodriguez wrote many cogent articles on cartooning, art and politics. He was a chief administrator of his region, a director of the Galician Geographical Institute and a senior member of the Academy of Arts and Letters of Galicia. He traveled extensively through Russia, Cuba, Argentina and Mexico. His cartoons also helped forge a cultural renaissance in Galicia. One of the most interesting Spanish personalities of the first half of the century, Rodriguez excelled in all facets of his activities (cartooning, painting, literature, politics). His work remains closely tied to the history of his native Galicia.

J.M.

ROGER RABBIT (U.S.) The most successful animal cartoon character to come out of the Mouse Factory in recent years. Roger Rabbit first appeared in the 1988 film *Who Framed Roger Rabbit* (the title is often misspelled with a question mark at the end but actually does not sport one). Based on Gary K. Wolf's novel, *Who Censored Roger Rabbit?,* it mixed animation and live-action in a mystery yarn involving cartoon characters (or "Toons") purportedly living in a community of their own called Toontown. Suspected of the murder of his boss, Toontown owner Marvin Acme, Roger hires the flesh-and-blood (and flab) private investigator Eddie Valiant (played by Bob Hoskins) to solve the crime and exculpate him. After many a twist and turn Valiant succeeds in ferreting out the real murderer.

The blending of live action and animation was deftly handled, with Hoskins moving seamlessly among the Toons, who included the alluring Jessica Rabbit, Roger's wife and the victim's inamorata; the cigar-smoking Baby Herman; and Benny the Cab who could outrace the fastest sports car and outtalk the gabbiest cabby. (In an added touch Mickey Mouse, Bugs Bunny, Droopy, Dumbo, Woody Woodpecker, Betty Boop, Donald Duck and Daffy Duck all made cameo appearances.) An international team was assembled to produce the picture: Robert Zemeckis was the overall director while Richard Williams supervised the animation unit in England. *Roger Rabbit* was a clamoring success and the highest-grossing film of the year, while also winning four different Academy Awards.

The success of the movie caused Disney to plan a series of theatrical shorts starring Roger Rabbit. Beginning in 1990 these were shown the old-fashioned way, as curtain-raisers for the main feature ("Roller Coaster Rabbit," for instance, was screened along with *Dick Tracy*). Others in the series were "A Hare in My Soup," "What's Cookin'," "Herman's Shermans," "The Little Injun That Could," and "Wet Nurse." Most of them had to do with Roger babysitting Herman and the sundry catastrophes that ensued. Bob Minkoff directed most of the shorts and Charles Fleischer provided the voice of Roger Rabbit.

M.H.

ROGERS, WILLIAM ALLEN (1854-1931) American cartoonist and illustrator born in Springfield, Ohio, on May 23, 1854. W.A. Rogers attended the Worcester Polytechnic Institute but never graduated. He taught himself art (his mother had some of his sketches published in a Dayton, Ohio, newspaper when he was 14) before joining the staff of the experimental *New York Graphic*. On the *Graphic,* where he drew for its first issues while only 19, he assisted with news sketches and drew some cartoons in the company of later greats like C.J. Taylor, A.B. Frost, E.W. Kemble and Gray Parker. In 1877 he switched to the staff of *Harper's Weekly,* where he remained for a quarter of a century. Thereafter he drew daily cartoons for another 20 years for the *New York Herald*.

Rogers drew for other publications over the years; he was one of the first cartoonists on Life in 1883 and continued to contribute occasionally for another decade. *Puck* enlisted his services for the 1892 presidential campaign. He also drew cartoons and illustrations for *Harper's Monthly*, the *Century* and *St. Nicholas*. He illustrated the popular children's series of Toby Tyler books and authored *Hits at Politics, Danny's Partner* (1923) and *A Miracle Mine* (1925) in addition to his autobiography, *A World Worth While* (1922), a book crammed with reminiscences of America's great political, literary and cartooning figures. *America's Black and White Book* (1917) is his most notable cartoon collection, a compilation of his strident propaganda efforts to get America into World War I.

Rogers was a noted humanitarian and served as a director of the School for Disabled Soldiers; he also assisted in the establishment of Life's Farm, the pioneering Fresh Air Fund agency of *Life* magazine. For his prowar activities (in the New York and Paris editions of the *Herald*) Rogers was made a chevalier of the Legion of Honor. He died in Washington, D.C., on October 20, 1931.

W.A. Rogers achieved great success with what must be regarded as modest talent. His drawings, in retrospect, are models of awkward composition, uncertain anatomy and stiff, slashing, harsh pen lines and brushstrokes. Neither do his concepts place him in the vanguard of his contemporaries; it was only concerning the European war that Rogers's cartoon ideas distinguished themselves as anything more than assignments or partisan exercises. Similarly, his illustration work, the bulk of which revolved around the Spanish-American War and his excursions to the American West, is at best an adequate reflection and comes nowhere near the artistic insight of, say, Frederick Remington, who covered the same "beats."

But critical hindsight is no match for a half-century career during which distinguished editors and art directors constantly published Rogers or sought and reprinted his cartoons. It must simply be noted that the appeal of this man, who succeeded Nast on *Harper's* and whose style remained constant (the technical inadequacies of his 1870s cartoons are also present in his work of the 1920s), has been lost through the years.

R.M.

—No, señora. El niño no ha molestado. Se ha pasado toda la tarde entretenido en pasar a "comic" el trascendental discurso pol'itico de su esposo . . .

Sarafin Rojo ("Serafin"). © Serafin.

ROJO CAMAÑO, SERAFIN (1925-) One of the most important cartoonists in Spain, Serafin Rojo Camaño was born November 14, 1925, in Madrid. His family was staunchly Republican and during the Spanish Civil War they took refuge in Valencia, then the Republic's last capital, when the artist was 13; and that's where he learned everything about comics, cartooning and painting. His first professional job was for the children's supplement of the Valencian evening daily *Jornada* in 1941: it was a comic strip called *El Peque*, which he signed simply Serafin, which was to remain his pen-name for his entire career.

In 1943 he joined the staff of the best humor magazine in Valencia, *Jaimito*, to which he contributed a number of artful comic strips, including among others *Doña Tere*, *Don Panchito y su hijo Teresito* ("Mr. Frankie and his Son Terry"), *Saturnino Chiquiflauta* ("Saturnin Littleflute"), *Tip y Coll*, always using facetious names based on some personal trait. Later on he worked for the children's magazines *Pumby* and *Trampolin*; but comics proved not to be his favored medium and took up too much of his time, so little by little he left the field to devote himself to humor and editorial cartooning. He then devoted all his time to satirical, corrosive cartoons for the most daring magazine of the Fascist era, *El Codorniz*, where he garnered fame and not a few reprimands from Franco's censors.

Rojo has also worked in the book field, illustrating special editions published by Editorial Marte, but without ever abandoning his virulent brand of humor. A compilation of his artwork was published in book form by Editorial Planeta in the 1970s; and in 1974 he wrote and drew *Carmen Underground*, a satirical and erotic version of Prosper Mérimée's famous novel. He now lives in Madrid and is still on the job, working for all media, whether newspapers, magazines, or art agencies. Of late he has taken up painting and sells his work through galleries and to private individuals.

F.T.J.

PARECE QUE LA CLASE POLITICA ITALIANA ANDA BUSCANDO DESESPERADAMENTE A ALGUIEN NO IMPLICADO EN NINGUN CASO DE CORRUPCION
¿PARA HACERLE JEFE DEL ESTADO?
NO. PARA REIRSE
Romeu 93

Carlos Romeu. © Carlos Romeu Muller.

ROMEU MULLER, CARLOS (1948-) Spanish cartoonist born in Barcelona on May 17, 1948. The scion of a long line of textile craftsmen, Carlos Romeu soon discovered his interest was for cartoons, not fabrics, and he studied design and drawing while holding a variety of odd jobs, such as dishwasher and busboy. In 1972 he had his first professional work published in the major magazine *Nueva Dimension*, and from then on he became a constant and major contributor to almost every Spanish publication, from the movie magazine *Fotograma* to the erotic *Boccacio*. Soon he abandoned painting, engraving and sculpting, which he had practiced since childhood, to devote full time to cartooning. He has worked for the Spanish edition of *Playboy*, the satirical *El Papus*, the renowned French magazine *Charlie Mensuel*, and about 50 more publications of all natures and styles, without forsaking his trenchant irony.

Ever restless and enterprising, Romeu in 1976 founded the famous magazine *El Jueves*, which is still being published with great success, with a staff that includes Sanchez Abuli, Das Pastoras, and Juan Alvarez, all of them of the first rank in Spain. The following year he started two more magazines, *Matarratos* and *Muchas gracias*. His best known character, however, was created in 1975: it was Betty, a fun- and sex-loving girl whom he intended to be in answer to the saccharine girls featured in the publications of Editorial Bruguera. A few years later he came up with *Miguelito el facha* ("Little Mike the Fascist") which was turned down by *Diario de Barcelona* because of its daring intentions at the time, but was picked up by *El Pais*, where it is still appearing. Romeu has also worked for Catalan TV, for which he wrote about 800 scripts.

Romeu is a quiet man, of innocent mien, but with a sardonic sense of humor. He likes sports such as underwater fishing, rowing and sailing, but his favorite sports are *la siesta*, cooking and enjoying his title of Skipper. In addition to *Miguelito* and his other cartoons, in 1992 he became the star of the best-selling magazine *Muy Interesante*, and in 1993 he created a serial called *500 anos no es nada* ("500 Years Are Nothing"), for which he won the annual award for best cartoonist. Two anthologies of his cartoon art were published in October 1997.

F.T.J.

ROOBARB (G.B.) Roobarb, a big, sloppy, floppy (green) dog, bounced onto British television screens in 1974—and almost bounced right out of the screen, so lively was his animation. Drawn in a loose, large, ultra-simplistic, ultra-cartoony style, the crazy characters in Roobarb positively vibrate with the joy of life. So does everything else—the dog kennel, the house, the trees, the fence—all to the accompaniment of Johnny Hawkesworth's jolly music. Bob Godfrey, who designed and directed Roobarb, created it as the first television series to be drawn and colored entirely with Magic Markers. The thick, clumsy, but free-wheeling line of these felt-tipped pens contributed greatly to the style of the series, as well as enabling the 26 five-minute episodes to be brought in at an extremely low cost.

Roobarb the dog and his opponent, Custard the purple cat, whose main contribution is to laugh hysterically, not to mention the chorus of zany birds who cackle on the sidelines, began their adventures in a story called "When Roobarb Made a Spike." In the story the floppy simpleton sought to emulate his feathered friends by building himself a beak. A very basic logic formed the basis of most of Roobarb's adventures: seeing the wind "break" the autumn leaves from a tree, naturally he must gather them up on his claws and stick them back on to "mend" the tree!

Roobarb was created by Grange Calveley and filmed by Bob Godfrey's Movie Emporium. The stories were narrated by actor Richard Briers. A small number of books, jig-

"Roobarb." © Bob Godfrey.

saws and merchandising novelties was produced, including the Colour Knight series book When Roobarb Was Hot and the BBC Publications book Roobarb Annual. Artwork for these was by Graham Bingham. There was also a full-page comic strip series in the weekly TV Comic, drawn by Dennis Hooper.

D.G.

ROOSEVELT BEARS, THE
See Little Johnny and His Teddy Bears.

ROPS, FÉLICIEN (1833-1898) Belgian cartoonist, lithographer, illustrator, etcher and painter born on July 7, 1833, in Namur, Belgium. Félicien Rops started his career with lithographs satirizing various art exhibitions, the earliest at age 15: "Promenade Charivarique au Salon de 1848." These were followed by contributions to the Belgian edition of the French humor magazine *Le Charivari* (1852), to the student newspaper *Le Crocodile* (1853-1859) and to the ephemeral *Le Corsaire* (1853- 1854). In 1856 he founded his own political, social and artistic weekly, Uylenspiegel, which ran until 1861 and for which he drew almost 150 cartoons reminiscent of the style and themes of Gavarni and Daumier. He was also a frequent collaborator on *Le Charivari Belge*, later renamed *Le Grelot-Charivari Belge* (1854-1861). In addition, he illustrated many of the Symbolist poets' works (Baudelaire's *Les Epaves*, 1866; Mallarmé's *Poésies*, 1895 and 1899) as well as the novels of writers like Maupassant (1882) and Barbey d'Aurevilly (*Les Diaboliques*, 1883 and 1886).

Félicien Rops, "La Cocottocratie" ("Harlotocracy"), 1909.

Rops's *Till Eulenspiegel* cartoons reveal a healthy, earthy humor satirizing every aspect of Belgian life. His political and social drawings, by contrast, are those of a committed artist and have a haunting, violent appearance whether they deal with domestic problems or with foreign affairs (such as the battle of Sebastopol or the bloody repression of Poland by the Russians). Félicien Rops is most famous, however, for the erotic etchings that became more and more important in his work. These, in their depiction of women of easy virtue ("little witches" or cocottes), convey a mixture of sensual beauty and the macabre, of venal love and death.

"The so bizarre M. Rops," as Baudelaire called him, died in Essonnes, near Paris, on August 22, 1898.

P.H.

ROSE, CARL (1903-1971) American cartoonist born in 1903. Carl Rose's most famous cartoon was published only three years after his professional career as a cartoonist began. In December 1928, the *New Yorker* magazine published Rose's drawing of a curly-haired moppet with mother dining on what appears to be a light lunch. "It's broccoli, dear," says the mother. "I say it's spinach, and I say the hell with it" is the child's classic retort. The cartoon made spinach a catchword for anything unpleasant. However, in other cartoons, Popeye did much to restore spinach's good name by gaining super strength from the green vegetable. Ironically, Carl Rose did not write the gag line for his most famous cartoon. Author E.B. White, who did write the gag, remembers that the cartoon had been originally submitted with a different caption, long since forgotten.

Rose began his career in 1925, and the same year he sold cartoons to the *New Yorker*, also in its first year of publishing. His first *New Yorker* cartoon pictured a man trying to commit suicide, shown in mid-air after having jumped from a bridge. A stone was tied around his neck. Also in mid-air was a New York City taxicab. The driver called out the window, "Taxi, sir?" From then until his last cartoon appeared in the *New Yorker's* April 3, 1971, issue, over six hundred Rose cartoons were published.

From 1927 to 1929, Carl Rose also drew Sunday features and editorial cartoons for the New York World, and he was a political cartoonist for the *Boston Herald* from 1929 to 1932. Both his newspaper and magazine work often focused on social and topical subjects. For 20 years Carl Rose was the sole illustrator and an occasional writer for "Accent on Living," the *Atlantic Monthly's* section of light humor. He also contributed gag cartoons to *Collier's*, the *Saturday Evening Post* and, as he put it, "many-too many-others."

A collection of his cartoons entitled Bed of Roses was published in 1946. He also illustrated 50 books by other authors. Late in his career, under the pseudonym Earl Cros (the letters of his name rearranged), he illustrated *Our New Age*. This was a Sunday feature about the advances of science syndicated by the Publishers-Hall Syndicate.

Carl Rose's style was modified over the years from

Carl Rose, self-portrait. © Rose.

drawings with emphasis on loose, gray wash tones to a tighter, crisper rendering. The gag cartoons in Bed of Roses display an excellent sense of design and of the importance of variations in line. His use of large, solid black areas for structural as well as decorative purposes adds strength to the visual impact. As drawings, his magazine cartoons are much more interesting than the very competent but almost brittle tightness of his work in Our New Age. Possibly the scientific subject matter lent itself less to Carl Rose's drawing than the humanistic topics of his magazine cartoons. His last published New Yorker cartoon is a perfect example. A centaur observes as a sphinx tells a griffin, "You think you're the only one around here with an identity crisis?"

Rose died at age 68 at his home in Rowayton, Connecticut, after a long illness.

B.C.

Getting Punchy!

Hy Rosen. © Albany Times-Union.

ROSEN, HYMAN J. (1923-) American political cartoonist born in Albany, New York, on February 10, 1923. Hy Rosen was educated at the Philip Schuyler High School in Albany, the Chicago Art Institute and the Art Students League. Later he was a journalism fellow at Stanford University (1966); he also studied at the State University of New York at Albany. His artistic influences were Jerry Costello and Duncan Macpherson.

Rosen began drawing for his hometown paper, the *Albany Times-Union*, in 1945. His specialty is caricature, and through the years he has mixed his media, using a blend of pebbleboard, benday shading and, most recently, the doubletone paper now all but standard in editorial cartooning.

The independent-Democratic Rosen has had his work reprinted in many news periodicals through the years and has won top Freedoms Foundation awards in 1950, 1955 and 1960. The *Times-Union* now honors Rosen's institutional status in the city and respects his opinions by labeling his daily cartoon "As Hy Rosen Sees It."

In addition to his cartooning Hy Rosen is also a sculptor of some repute, having done a number of commissions for the city of Albany and the state of New York, including a bust of Christopher Columbus for the Bicentennial of 1992. In 1982 he penned an autobiography, *Do They Tell You What to Draw?* He is now retired.

R.M.

ROSS, AL (1911-) American cartoonist born in Vienna, Austria, on October 19, 1911. Born Al Roth, Al Ross eventually changed his surname, as he was almost bound to do considering that he has three brothers-Ben, Salo and Irving-all of whom are cartoonists and frequently contribute to the same magazines. In fact, in *Saturday Evening* Posts of the 1950s, one can sometimes find all four-signing "Ross," "Salo," "Ben Roth" and "Irving Roir' `-contributing gags to the same issue. Ross began his drawing career in 1935, having studied under William McNulty and Rico LeBrun at the Art Students League of New York. His first important sales were apparently to the *Post.* During World War II, he served as a member of the Committee on War Cartoons, established by the Society of Magazine Cartoonists in cooperation with the Office of War Information.

Of the cartooning Roths, Ross is easily the most interesting, as his frequent appearances in the *New Yorker* attest. This is so not only because of the sophistication of his

"Well, what are you staring at?"

Al Ross. © Collier's.

wit—above all a *New Yorker* desideratum—but also because, starting out as a rather derivative artist after the fashion of the day (a fashion shared by Bo Brown, Bob Barnes and Larry Reynolds), he has evolved his own distinctive and deceptively simple ink-line approach to comic art. His earliest panels for the *Post* in the 1930s reveal a stylist intent on depth and detail, working in washes that in no way differed from those of a dozen other contributors to that magazine. Gradually, during the 1940s (coinciding with his first appearances in the *New Yorker*), his work became simpler. As is frequently the case, the most obvious evidence of this transformation can be found in his signature, which changed from a simply printed "Ross" to the idiosyncratic semi-legible scrawl today associated with his work.

The deft, seemingly rapid and free lines that characterize Ross's art are at once crude and sophisticated—crude when they first strike the eye, but ultimately complex and vital as the "gestalt" of a work emerges. Take, for example, the uncaptioned *New Yorker* panel in which a giant computer resembling a high-rise is being attacked by swarms of figures armed in the classic "popular revolution" manner with pitchforks and other agricultural implements; it gives an unmistakable impression of movement and feeling. It is both amusing and a bit sobering-an effect due as much to the nature of the representation as to the keenness of the artist's perception.

Ross remains a regular contributor to the *New Yorker* and is well represented in its anniversary albums. For relaxation he paints seriously, perhaps putting to use some of that academic formalism from which his comic art style has thankfully strayed. Then again, his inspiration as a painter may be as distant from that tradition as a Mondrian. Certainly his cartoon style gives no clue.

R.C.

ROSSILLON, MARIUS (Ca. 1880-1946) French cartoonist and animator born in the south of France around 1880. Little is known about Marius Rossillon's early life. He seems to have moved to Paris in the early 1900s, embarking on a cartooning career soon after his arrival. Combining his love of horseflesh with the widespread anglomania of the times, he adopted the pseudonym "O'Galop" (literally "at the gallop") in his contributions to such satirical magazines as Le Rire and L'Assiette au Beurre. He also invented the character Père Bibendum for Michelin tires (the figure is still used as a Michelin trademark) and became one of the many colorful figures in the Montmartre district in the pre-World War I years.

O'Galop's humor was not very original, and his style was quite conventional. He would deserve only a footnote in the history of French cartooning were it not for his pioneering animation work, which has only recently come to light. As early as 1912 he made two social reform cartoon films, *Le Circuit d'Alcool* ("The Path of Alcohol") and *Le Taudis Doit Etre Vaincu* ("The Slums Must Be Vanquished"). After World War I, in which he served, he came back to animation with a series of cartoon fables (*The Tortoise and the Hare, The Fox and the Stork* and others). With the coming of sound, O'Galop, like so many other early animators, left the field to devote himself to newspaper cartooning. He also painted watercolors and is fondly remembered by all who knew him. He died at his country home in Carnac on January 2, 1946.

M.H.

ROSSO, GUSTAVO (1881-1950) Italian cartoonist and illustrator born in Turin, Italy, in 1881. Gustavo Rosso was an ardent admirer of Gustave Doré, and in deference to him he signed his work "Gustavino" ("little Gustave"). As a young man he contributed cartoons and illustrations to publications in Turin and Milan. Rosso illustrated his first book in 1908 and was later to illustrate numerous other books (Dickens, Mark Twain, Alexandre Dumas). He also worked for a number of magazines but chiefly for *Il Corriere dei Piccoli*, doing many story and cover illustrations. He is best known for his *Il Dottor Faust*, which he drew in comic strip form; it was published in the comic weekly L'Audace in 1939.

Rosso was a very able craftsman whose world, reflecting "eternal childhood" (in Antonio Faeti's words), was one of fable, fantasy and adventure. He died in Milan in 1950.

S.T.

ROTH, ARNOLD (1929-) American cartoonist born in Philadelphia, Pennsylvania, on February 25, 1929. Arnold Roth graduated from Central High School and attended the Philadelphia College of Art. He began freelancing cartoons in 1952. Roth was copublisher and editor of *Humbug* magazine in 1957-58 and drew the Sunday feature Poor

We tend to overindulge in our ultimate escape from real life—
we call it "work."

Arnold Roth. © Punch.

Arnold's Almanac for the *Herald-Tribune Syndicate* from 1959 to 1961. Since then he has freelanced cartoons, ideas and illustrations to *TV Guide, Punch, Sports Illustrated, Holiday, Playboy, Saturday Evening Post* and many other magazines. He has won numerous illustrators' and art directors' show awards and several category prizes from the National Cartoonists Society. He served as president of the National Cartoonists Society in 1984-86 and received the NCS's Silver T-Square Award in 1995.

Arnold Roth is one of the most inventive and original American cartoonists in decades. His style is almost reminiscent of Searle's but is more disciplined and avant-garde. His Almanac was an inspired comic masterpiece that suffered poor promotion and is remembered devotedly by a large Roth cult. In recent years his cartoons—line drawings and washes shaded beautifully—have appeared with increasing frequency in *TV Guide* and *Sports Illustrated*. And he is in *Punch* so much that many readers on both sides of the Atlantic think he is British. His freedom and lunacy in concepts, as well as freshness and native humor in delineation, mark him as among the most progressive of contemporary American humorous illustrators.

R.M.

ROUNTREE, HARRY (1878-1950) British illustrator and cartoonist born in Auckland, New Zealand, in 1878.

"If you want to be happy, know animals." This was the motto of Harry Rountree, who drew some of the most delightful furry and feathery creatures ever to adorn children's books, comics, cartoons and advertisements. For many years his merry mice sold the wares of the Cherry Blossom boot polish company.

He was educated at Queens College, and his first professional artwork was as an apprentice to a lithographic printer. He designed labels for jam jars. He went to England in 1901 and soon began to contribute cartoons to *Punch*, the *Sketch* and other illustrated weeklies of the day. His drawings were collated and published yearly in *Harry Rountree's Annual* from 1907, and his color work began to center on the juvenile market under the direction of S.H. Homer, editor of the high-class children's magazine *Little Folks.* His comic strip work began in 1919 when the Amalgamated Press originated an unusual half-size comic weekly, *Playtime.* Rountree drew the full-color covers and the full-color center spread strip, which (curiously) retailed the pictorial adventures of Mickey Mouse. He was made president of the London Sketch Club, and died on September 26, 1950.

Books: *Child's Book of Knowledge* (1903); *Book of Birthdays* (1906); *Uncle Rem us* (1906); *Harry Rountree's Annual* (1907); *Little Robinson Crusoes* (1908); *Alice in Wonderland* (1908); *Transformation of the Truefitts* (1908); *The Wonderful Isles* (1908); *The Magic Wand* (1908); *The Young Gullivers* (1908); *The Fortunate Princeling* (1909); *The Enchanted Wood* (1909); *The Forest Foundling* (1909); *Golf Courses* (1910); *The Dolomites* (1910); *Magic Dijon* (1911); *Tales from Woods and Fields* (1911); *Adventures of Spider and* Co. (1912); *Four Glass Balls* (1912); *The Poison Belt* (1913); *Bevis* (1913); *Animal Tales* (1914); *My Best Book of Fairy Tales* (1915); *Rountree's Ridiculous Rabbits* (1916); *Rabbit Rhymes* (1917);*Art of the Illustrator* (1918); *Dicky Duck* (1919); *Arkansaw Bear* (1919); *Pinion* and *Paw* (1919); *Trail of the Elk* (1922); *Tootles and Timothy (1922); Dramas of the Wild Folk* (1924); *Fairy Tale Book* (1924); *True Zoo Stories* (1924); *Me and Jimmy* (1929); *Wonderful Adventure* (1929); *The Pond Mermaid* (1929); *Birds Beasts and Fishes* (1929); *Caesar (1930); Ronald Rupert and Reg* (1930); *Animal Rhymes* (1931); *Beetles and Things* (1931); *Jungle Tales* (1934); and *Wag and Wig* (1947).

D.G.

ROUSON, JOHN (1908-) American cartoonist born in London, England, in 1908. John Rouson loved to draw as a child, and his talent was encouraged by his parents. After a stint at art school and some college studies he trained for the banking profession, but the Depression intervened. After doing all kinds of odd jobs as barman, soccer player and errand boy, he decided in desperation to send some of his cartoons to the *Sunday Express* in London; these were accepted. It was the mid-1930s, and John Rouson had finally found his niche.

Rouson later joined the art staff of the *London Chronicle* and created two weekly strips in the late 1930s: *Shop Act*, which was set in a department store (it was syndicated for awhile by King Features in the United States), and a feature about Gracie Fields titled *Our Gracie*. He also did theatrical caricatures for the *Bystander* and later added two more weekly strips (both silent) to his workload: *Little Sport*, a sports strip, and the self-explanatory *Boy Meets Girl*. When World War II broke out, Rouson enlisted in the Royal Navy as a seaman and finished the war as a lieutenant commander in 1946. All during the war he managed to mail in his weekly installments of Boy Meets Girl.

Back in civilian life, Rouson found that the British newspaper market had shrunk. After a one-year stay in Paris, during which he developed *Little Sport* into a daily strip, he went to New York in 1948. There he contributed caricatures to the *Herald-Tribune* and gag cartoons to *Collier's*, *True* and other magazines. In the 1950s General Features picked up *Little Sport* for syndication; Rouson later added *Boy and Girl* (a two-panel strip on the model of Boy Meets Girl), *Little Eve* (a woman's strip which he signs "Jolita") and *Ladies' Day* (a gag panel) to his roster-which makes him one of the busiest cartoonists around today. An adequate, rather plodding artist, Rouson is noted here less for his contributions to the cartooning arts than for his sheer doggedness and staying power.

M.H.

John Rouson, "Boy and Girl." © General Features Corporation.

RUBRIQUE À BRAC, LA (France) After the discontinuance of *Les Dingodossiers,* which he had been drawing on scripts by René Goscinny, Marcel Gotlib decided to produce his own weekly panel broadly modeled on *Les Dingodossiers.* The series was entitled *La Rubrique à Brac* (which can be freely translated as "The Odds-and-Ends Column"), and it debuted on January 11, 1968, in the pages of *Pilote.*

If anything, this new panel (usually spread over two full pages) was even more sardonic in its humor and more savage in its commentaries than its predecessor. Gotlib was no longer hindered by somebody else's captions and could give free rein to his anarchistic and iconoclastic inventiveness. His parodies of current happenings, contemporary television shows and hoary fairy tales were as rollicking as they were nerve-grating. No modern folly or idiocy escaped his merciless pen: fatuous talk-show hosts, self-important movie stars, harebrained athletes and conniving politicians all got their comeuppance in Gotlib's wild and chaotic drawings, punctuated by a variety of outrageous puns and insidiously subversive captions.

When Gotlib decided to abandon *La Rubrique à Brac* in December 1972 in order to strike out on his own, the loss of the panel was much lamented. Many of the pages were later reprinted in a series of albums published by Editions Dargaud.

M.H.

RUGE, JOHN (1915-) American cartoonist born in Faribault, Minnesota, on October 2, 1915. Although raised in the heart of America's largest Scandinavian community, John Ruge is, at least to judge from his work, anything but the stereotypically dour and taciturn Norseman (once again suggesting the limited utility-to non-cartoonists, anyway-of stereotypes). Ruge was trained at the prestigious Art Students League of New York during the 1930s, when that institution was one of the main forums of the social realism school of artistic expression. He received a thorough grounding in the principles of his craft and became not only a fine pen-and-ink caricaturist but a watercolorist of the first order as well. It is the blending of this mastery of technique with a keen wit and a strong social sensitivity that makes the best of Ruge's work something more than the usual gag cartoon.

Ruge sold his first drawing to *Collier's* in 1936 and soon made sales to the *Saturday Evening Post* and the *New Yorker;* he thus launched a career that would ultimately find his work in periodicals from *Family Circle* to *Playboy*—a diversity that is in itself a notable achievement. During this distinguished career, Ruge has not hesitated to mix opinion with humor. Thus a panel in late 1940, even as the newly reelected FDR was again pledging American neutrality; it shows three members of the German General Staff discussing their futures over dinner. "Oh," announces one, "Buenos Aires is all right, but I have my heart set on a little place in Connecticut." Particularly striking is Ruge's ability to crystallize meaning. For example, a four-panel piece in the *New Yorker* (1965) shows a billboard picture of a classic gray-haired granny holding out a sample of "Mrs. Heimer's Pies" and being altered by sign painters into a hip modern matron, hair tinted and fashionably styled, shilling for the "New Improved Mrs. Heimer's Pies." A better illustration of the cosmetic image of old age characteristic of the 1960s and 1970s could hardly be found. And for those who might wonder what an artist of Ruge's gift has to offer a magazine like *Playboy,* attention is directed to the smashing watercolor in the June 1978 issue.

John Ruge. © Look.

Ruge originals can be found in the personal collections of Presidents Kennedy and Truman, former senator Stuart Symington, Bernard Baruch and many other public figures of the past four decades. In addition, the artist holds the prestigious Award for Distinctive Merit presented by the Art Directors Club.

R.C.

RUSHTON, WILLIAM (1937-1996) William George Rushton, known to his friends as Willie—and eventually to everyone else thanks to radio and television—was one of the finest, funniest, and at times cruelest cartoonists in England. One of the modern school satirists, his work could be sharp and caricatured, and charming and colorful, for he drew weekly cartoons for the famous satirical magazine *Private Eye* as well as wrote and illustrated delightful books for children.

Willie was born in London on August 18, 1937, and died with sudden shock to all on December 11, 1996. He continued to "live" for some while, thanks to a number of episodes of his popular radio series, a comedy quiz game entitled *I'm Sorry I Haven't a Clue.* As well as a radio star, he appeared frequently on television, in the game show for cartoonists *Quick On The Draw,* and even toured the theaters in a two-man stage show, *Two Old Farts in the Night,* in partnership with Barry Cryer, scriptwriter and comedian.

Educated at Shrewsbury School, he chummed up with Richard Ingrams, who was one day his junior. Together they wrote and edited the school magazine *The Salopian,*

Willie providing the cartoons. This partnership would last the two 13-year-olds through life, for in 1961 they would jointly found *Private Eye*. The magazine still runs and in 1997 published a Special in tribute to Willie. *Rushton in the Eye*, 40 pages of his best work including a detail from "The Crew of the Good Ship *Private Eye*," a painting from 1988 showing the staff as old-time sailors and including such notables as Peter Cook, Ian Hislop, and Barry Fantoni.

After army service (1959) Willie joined Ingrams to illustrate his underground magazine *Mesopotamia*, and his first stage performance proper was as Lord Fortnum in Spike Milligan's play, *The Bed Sitting Room* (1962). From this he won a TV spot in David Frost's satirical/topical series, *That Was The Week That Was*. Many small parts in plays, films and TV series followed, but he never stopped drawing. A regular job was illustrating articles by Auberon Waugh after the death of cartoonist Nicolas Bentley in 1978. Thus apart from *The Eye*, he now featured weekly in *Literary Review* and more frequently in the *Daily Telegraph*. His work was predominant in the fine *Private Eye* art exhibition held at the National Portrait Gallery in 1996, organized by his cousin Tony. Fortunately he lived to attend the opening.

BOOKS: *William Rushton's Dirty Book* (1964), *I Didn't Know the Way* (1966), *How to Play Football* (1968), *The Day of the Grocer* (1971), *Sassenach's Scotland* (1975), *The Geranium of Flut* (1975), *Superpig* (1976), *Pigsticking* (1977), *Unarmed Gardening* (1979), *Reluctant Euro* (1980), *The Filth Amendment* (1981), *Great Moments in History* (1985), *The Alternative Gardener* (1986), *Marylebone Versus the World* (1987), *Spythatcher* (1987), plus many books by other authors which he illustrated.

D.G.

RUSSELL, BRUCE (1903-1963) American cartoonist and Pulitzer Prize winner born in Los Angeles, California, on August 4, 1903. Bruce Russell was educated at public schools and attended the Los Angeles Polytechnic High School, where he drew for the Poly Optimist and the school annuals. After receiving mail-order training from the Federal and W.L. Evans cartooning schools, he continued to draw for his college papers at UCLA (including the humor magazine The *Pelican)* as well as contributing cartoons to Los Angeles newspapers on a freelance basis.

In 1925 Russell obtained a position with the *Los Angeles Evening Herald*, where he worked on sports cartoons, editorial cartoons, theater drawings, news sketches, photo retouching and crossword puzzle art for two years, after which time he switched to the *Los Angeles Herald* for similar duties. In 1933 he became its chief political cartoonist and remained there until his death on December 18, 1963.

Between 1930 and 1932 Russell, under the name Bruce Barr, drew the comic strip *Rollo Rollingstone* for the Associated Press; it was his constant ambition to draw a successful strip. In addition to his 1946 Pulitzer for an early Cold War comment, Russell received the Sigma Delta Chi award in 1948, 1950 and 1951, and the National Headliners award in 1949.

Russell's drawings are honest—definitely old school in style, but always a forthright presentation of strong message. He drew with a supple pen and brush and produced beautiful crayon shades with his grained board. Most

Bruce Russell. © Los Angeles Herald.

closely resembling Vaughn Shoemaker's work, his caricatures could be very comical, but he could also emulate the Tribune school of pantographing faces realistically.

R.M.

RUTTMANN, WALTER (1887-1941) German animator and filmmaker born in Frankfurt, Germany, in 1887. Walter Ruttmann studied architecture but soon displayed a talent for painting and music. He was attracted to the Dada movement at the end of World War I, and he started experimenting with animation in 1918. From 1920 to 1925 he produced four stunning works of animation simply titled *Opus I, Opus II, Opus III* and *Opus IV*, which showed the mesmerizing motions of odd shapes and forms made from real objects that Ruttmann had hand-colored for stronger effect.

Ruttmann's other notable achievements in animation include "Der Falkentraum" ("The Falcon's Dream," a sequence in Fritz Lang's 1924 film saga *Die Nibelungen*) and the 1925 Traumspiel ("Dream Play"), a vaporous evocation of forms and shadows. Ruttmann also assisted Lotte Reiniger on her silhouette film *The Adventures of Prince Achmed* (1926).

In 1927 Ruttmann made the very successful documentary *Berlin, Symphony of a City*, and he was subsequently lost to animation. His credits as a documentary cinematographer include *Melodie der Welt* ("The Melody of the World," 1929), *Stuttgart* (1935) and *Dflsseldorf* (1936). He also made propaganda films for the Nazi regime, notably *Deutsche Panzer* (1940).

Walter Ruttmann died on July 15, 1941, from complications after a surgical operation in Berlin.

M.H.

Ss

SABU TO ICHI TORIMONO HIKAE (Japan) *Sabu to Ichi Torimono Hikae* ("Detective Stories of Sabu and Ichi") was an animated television series based on the comic strip of the same name created by Shotarō Ishihomori. It is a graphic dramatization of a genre of novels traditionally popular in Japan, "detective" stories set in the Edo period of Japanese history (1600-1867).

Sabu is a young teenage boy who becomes an *okappiki* ("detective") for the feudal government. Assisted by his sidekick, Ichi, Sabu solves cases by the time-honored method of capturing the bad guys, but the story takes on complexity and interest through the thorough development of character and a loving attention to seasonal changes and historical detail. Ichi, moreover, is a middle-aged blind man who, before joining Sabu, was a masseur and also an expert swordsman. Inspiration for his character clearly came from the popular *Zattoichi Monogatari* ("Blind Swordsman") movie series. Together, Sabu and Ichi pursue the cause of justice and help protect the interests of the merchants and common people in a feudal society where they are the underdogs.

Sabu to *Ichi Torimono Hikae* initially appeared in the first edition of the biweekly magazine *Big Comic* in April 1968 and ran for 84 episodes. Its lyric quality, combined with excellent draftsmanship and an almost cinematic approach, netted it the 13th Shogakkan award for comics in 1968. The animated version began running on NET television on October 3, 1968, and lasted for 52 black-and-white episodes, each episode 23 minutes long. It ended in September 1969. It was unique in that it was the first television animation series for adults to be aired in Japan, and it was produced by the joint efforts of three companies; Toei Dōga, Studio Zero and Mushi Productions. Sadatsugu Matsuda was in charge of overall direction, and Akiyo Sugino was in charge of animation. The final product represented a faithful recreation of the aesthetic beauty in the original comic, using both full and limited animation to excellent effect.

F.S.

SAEKI, TOSHIO (1945-) Japanese cartoonist and illustrator born in Miyazaki Prefecture in 1945. Toshio Saeki is generally regarded as an avant-garde cartoonist and is noted for his often bizarre, beautifully graphic pictures. Between the ages of 4 and 23, Saeki lived in the Osaka and Kyoto area, but, following in the footsteps of countless artists and cartoonists before him, he moved to Tokyo. One year later, in 1970, he independently published *Saeki Toshio Gashō* ("The Toshio Saeki Picture Collection"), which later led the Agureman Company to put out a work of the same title.

Following this success, Saeki was very active and appeared in *Young Comic, Hanashi no Tokushū, Playboy* (Japan), *Hei bon Punch, Erotchika* and *Mantoppu,* among others. He is particularly noted for his somewhat surreal depiction of demonlike figures that appear to have materialized from another subconscious world to crack our civilized veneer. An excellent example is his well-known cartoon of a bridal couple in traditional Japanese wedding dress, with the groom standing and the bride seated. Although they are maintaining perfect decorum, behind the bride is a clinging, half-naked demon/monster with one hand slipped into the bride's kimono. Whether this represents her mother-in-law, whom the bride must soon confront, or her ghost is left up to the viewer.

In February 1971 Saeki put out his second collection, *Saeki Toshio Sakuhinshu* ("The Collected Works of Toshio Saeki"). Since then he has continued illustrating and working on a series of ten color posters entitled *Watakushi no Marilyn Monroe* ("My Marilyn Monroe"). Like Suehiro Maruo, whom he clearly influenced, Saeki is more of an "artist" than a "cartoonist," and he has exhibited widely. At a recent exhibition at the city of Kyoto, he was described as a "modern ukiyo-e artist, who conveys to the modern world the erotic and grotesque esthetics so popular in the Edo period." Reflecting his popularity as an artist, his book *Saeki Toshio Yogakan* ("The Tashio Saeki Collection of Goblin Pictures"), published in 1992, retailed for almost 100 dollars. One of his more recent collections is *Jimushi* ("The Idiocy Bug"), issued in 1995, with a sequel following in 1996.

F.S.

SAILOR MOON (Japan) *Bishojo Senshi Sailor Moon* ("Lovely Young Woman Warrior Sailor Moon") began as a comic book serial by Naoko Takeuchi in the girls' monthly magazine *Kakayoshi* in 1990. It was an instant hit. Takeuchi's stories are being kept in print in paperback collections, currently up to volume fifteen.

The weekly half-hour TV cartoons, produced by Toei Animation Co., debuted on March 7, 1992. They were presented as a series of programs of about 40 episodes each, as an excuse for dramatic changes among the action figures and toys based upon them. So *Sailor Moon* segued through *Sailor Moon R, Sailor Moon S, Sailor Moon SS* (or *Supers*), and finally *Sailor Moon Sailor Stars.* The TV series culminated with the 200th episode, on February 8, 1997. There were also some *Sailor Moon* animated features.

Fourteen-year-old Usagi ("Bunny") Tsukino is a kind-hearted but scatterbrained junior high school student. She rescues a cat from a group of delinquents. The cat, Luna, is an agent of the Moon Kingdom, on Earth to search for the missing Moon Princess Serenity, and to prevent evil energy vampires of the Dark Kingdom from draining the life-force of Earth's humans. Luna gives Usagi a magical hair brooch/tiara which transforms her into Sailor Moon, to battle the monsters.

The original formula was that the monsters grew in power until, around every eighth episode, Usagi (and her growing band of "Sailor Scouts") would finally be outclassed. Just then, she/they would meet a new friend with a similar latent power, whom Luna could turn into Sailor Mercury, Sailor Mars, Sailor Jupiter, and Sailor Venus. Thus they could maintain parity with the agents of the Dark Kingdom's Queen Beryl, all extremely handsome but sinister young men named after cold gemstones: Jadeite, Nephrite, Malachite, etc. The Sailor Scouts were also aided by a mysterious male teen, Tuxedo Mask. The Sailor Scouts were eventually revealed as the modern reincarnations of the Moon Kingdom's ancient knights, and Usagi herself was the reborn missing Princess Serenity. Queen Beryl and her minions were defeated, to be replaced by all-new supernatural adversaries in sequel story-arcs.

The attraction of *Sailor Moon* is that it enables young girls to fantasize themselves as powerful as their brothers' macho superheroes, without losing any of their femininity. Usagi and her junior high girls' club (Amy Mizo, Rei Hino, Makoto Kino, and Minako Aino) can giggle and talk about clothes and boyfriends like ordinary teens, then transform into superheroines in costumes which are lovely fashion designs based on Japanese schoolgirls' uniforms. Their confrontations are often parables of issues which adolescent girls must address, such as to be cautious of handsome boys' smooth talk, and other attractive temptations.

Sailor Moon is popular around the world, especially in Europe and Latin America. In North America, 65 TV episodes wee produced by DIC for syndication in August (Canada) and September (U.S.) 1995, out of the first 72

"Sailor Moon." © Toei Animation.

"And this is Rachel—our head girl."

"Saint Trinian's." © Ronald Searle.

Japanese episodes, omitting those with overly-Japanese ethnic elements or too much violence. Names were Americanized (Serena instead of the sexist Bunny; Raye for Rei) or simplified phonetically without keeping their double meanings (Jedite and Neflite, losing the affinity with gemstones). *Sailor Moon* picked up a devoted following which was not large enough to justify DIC's producing more episodes, despite a 1996 media-publicized "Save Our Sailors" Internet campaign which claimed 30,000 signatures.

F.P.

ST. TRINIAN'S (G.B.) "Observe those typical English Roses, the Girls of St. Trinian's, a nightmare synthesis of Roedean, Heathfield, and Wycombe Abbey," wrote D.B. Wyndham Lewis in his foreword to the first hard-cover collection of the cartoon saga, *Hurrah for St. Trinian's,* published by Macdonald in 1948. The "typical English Roses" sang up for themselves in the words of the old school song:

Maidens of St. Trinian's,
Gird your armour on.
Grab the nearest weapon,
Never mind which one!

With words by Sidney Gilliat and music by Malcolm Arnold, the chant (with its school motto, "Get your blow in first!") first impinged on the public ear in *The Belles of St.*

Trinian's, the first film to feature Ronald Searle's incredible school and its equally incredible inmates—young girls who were scraggy, scruffy and spotty in the Junior School who suddenly burgeoned into bosomy, stocking-topped seniors, apparently overnight.

The first St. Trinian's cartoon (although not labeled as such) appeared in *Lilliput* magazine in October 1941, the second came in 1946 (after a gap in which the cartoonist was a POW in Japan), and the remainder spasmodically between 1957 and 1962. The first book, although titled for the nationally famous (by 1948) educational establishment, was by no means devoted to the extracurricular antics of pupil and tutor. Later, hardback reprints of Searle's magazine cartoons were dominated by the girls, however: *Back to the Slaughterhouse* (1951), *The Terrors of St. Trinian's* (1952) and *Souls in Torment* (1953), which was supposed to be the end of the saga. Professor C. Day Lewis wrote a farewell dirge: "It is my melancholy task, as the last surviving Governor of St. Trinian's, to announce the closure of this famous, nay, this unparalleled school." However, in the words of Kay Webb, wife and anthologizer of the artist, this "turned out to be an abortive effort to pension them off," and she compiled the definitive *St. Trinian's Story* in 1959. This handsome souvenir volume included contributions by such as Bertolt Brecht, John Dankworth, Michael Flanders, Robert Graves, and James Laver.

The films inspired by the cartoons, and always graced with Ronald Searle's credit titles, began with *The Belles of St. Trinian's* (1954). They were produced, directed and often written by Frank Launder and Sidney Gilliat, established comedy filmmakers on the British scene. Alastair Sim played the headmistress, Miss Millicent Fritton, and her scapegrace brother, Clarence. Blue *Murder at St. Trinian's* (1957) starred Sim again. *The Pure Hell of* St. *Trinian's* (1960) introduced Irene Handl as Miss Matilda Harker-Packer, and the last outing, *The Great St. Trinian's Train Robbery* (1966), shot in Eastmancolor, featured Portland Mason as Georgina and Elspeth Duxbury as Veronica Bledlow.

D.G.

SAJTINAC, BORISLAV (1943-) Yugoslav cartoonist and animator born 1943 in Belgrade. After graduation from the Academy of Fine Arts in Belgrade, Borislav Sajtinac started his *career* as a humor cartoonist on such publications as *Jez* and *Kerempuh* in Belgrade. He began working on animated films in 1966, contributing to such cartoons as *In Love with Three* Cakes and Pardon, as well as to the feature-length *The Conference of Animals*, produced by Gloria-Linda Film in Germany and released in 1969.

In 1967 Sajtinac joined the fledgling Neoplanta Film animation studio in Novi Sad, releasing *The Analysis* the same year. In collaboration with Nikola Majdak he brought out *The Spring of Life* (1969), a tale inspired by the works of the Serbian baroque painter Hristofer Zerafović. *Everything That Flies Is Not a Bird* (also 1969), a neat little satire on intolerance and repression, followed. The 1971 *The Bride and Temptation* further consolidated Sajtinac's stature in the animation world. In 1973 *Wie Sind Wiele* ("We Are Many"), produced in Germany, seemed to sum up

Borislav Sajtinac, "All That Flies Is Not a Bird." © Neoplanta *Film.*

Sajtinac's achievements in its neatness and terseness. All his subsequent films from 1980 on have been made in Germany, including *Der Meister* ("The Master"), the feature-length *Everything that Flies Is not a Bird* (an extension of his 1969 short), and *Harold und die Geister* ("Harold and the Ghosts").

One of the most original artists working in the animation medium, Sajtinac once stated that his films are "living stories about living persons in living surroundings who are transformed into cartoon characters in order to achieve a universal appeal." His works have won many honors in Belgrade, Locarno, Mamaia, Tampere, and other places.

M.H.

SALAS MARTINEZ, ARMANDO (1946-) Spanish cartoonist born January 30, 1946, in Marta de Ortiguerra, a little town in the province of Galicia, in northwestern Spain. Armando Salas since childhood displayed a love of drawing and comics, with a special fondness for comic strips and humor cartoons. Very soon he was sending his cartoons to magazines and daily newspapers, while taking classes in drawing. He also studied banking and got a job in a bank, which allowed him to dedicate his afternoons and evenings to cartooning.

Salas's contributions to the cartoon medium are many and varied: he was one of the first, if not the first, to bring eroticism to Spanish publications in the form of semi-nude girls, an eroticism tempered with irony and sarcasm, and this during the darkest years of the Franco dictatorship. In 1967 he began drawing professionally for the newsmagazine *Diez Minutos*, and also for *Comic Camp, Comic In*, a fanzine dedicated to the study of comics where he created Saturday, an ironic take on Sunday, a popular comics character created by Victor de la Fuente. A little later he contributed editorial cartoons to the daily *Pueblo*, and he joined the staff of the daily *El Correo Gallego* and that of the magazine *Doblon* in 1970. That same year he started contributing to the TV journal *Todo Television*, and he also created a syndicated panel series, *Don Teleneco*, in which he satirized "couch potatoes" before the term was invented. He began working for the daily *Ferrol Diario* in 1972, and a year later he contributed cartoons to *Heraldo Espanol*, the most important paper in the province of Aragon.

For the comics magazine *El Globo* he created his most

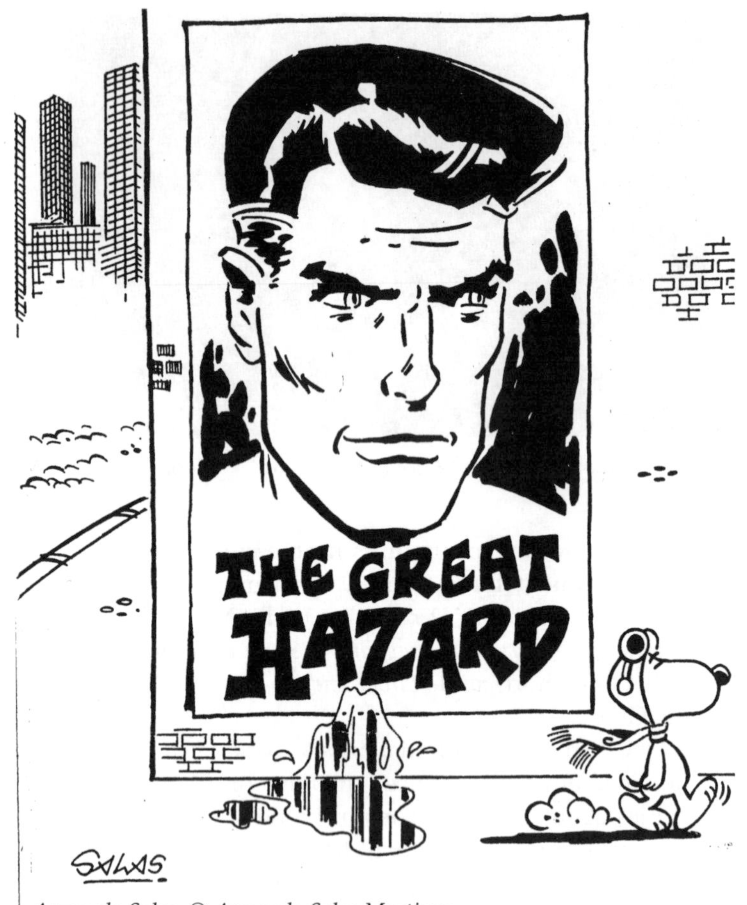

Armando Salas. © Armando Salas Martinez.

famous series, *El Eden*, renamed *Adan* for publication in book form. This cartoon series was a satirical view of Adam and Eve, in which Eve, a blonde in the Marylin Monroe mold, appeared in bikini. Sensual, provocative and sexy, how this series passed the censors no one knows! While working in several mediums, he also created another cartoon series, *Jauja y Colas*. Another successful series came out in 1981: *Merlina*, about a female wizard who was beautiful, sexy and ready for anything. Less than six months later *Merlina* was also published in book form.

This fabulous artist, whose work reflects his love for the best American and Spanish artists, is publishing today in *Telenovela*, and occasionally in *Comicguia*, the oldest Spanish journal devoted to the study of comic art in Spain. A fan of the late American cartoonist Frank Robbins, Salas has dedicated a number of cartoons to him.

F.T.J.

SALLON, RALPH (1899-1991) British caricaturist born in Warsaw, Poland, on December 9, 1899. Perhaps the last of the great traditional caricaturists in British journalism, Ralph Sal Ion was born Raphael Zielun. His family brought him to London at the age of four, and he attended Crouch End School, leaving at 14 with a scholarship to Hornsey School of Art. He stayed only one term, however, leaving to earn a living working in a factory. He served as a clerk in the army during World War I, then continued clerking in civil life until 1922. He traveled to South Africa on a government scheme and there began to draw professionally.

He contributed caricatures to a local African newspaper until he returned to London in 1925 to further his art. After a term at St. Martin's School of Art his tutor advised him to abandon academic art study for a commercial career built on his natural ability to caricature. He was taken up by R.J. Minney, later a screenwriter and film producer, then the editor of *Everybody's Weekly.* For this magazine he drew personality caricatures and sporting celebrities from 1926 to 1945. He retained his African connections by drawing a weekly caricature for the paper *East Africa* (1930-39).

Sallon's newspaper caricatures began with the *Daily Mail* (thumbnail portraits for the book reviews), continned in the *Daily Express, Daily Herald* (1943-48) and finally in the *Daily Mirror.* He was on the staff of that newspaper from 1948 to his retirement in 1964, and he continued to have a desk there and to contribute caricatures as required, which was often. His portrait caricatures decorated the walls of the Press Club, the Wig and Pen Club, El Vino's and most newspaper offices in London. "I draw character, not physical perfection," he says, "but I never demoralise my subject. I'm simply honest. I draw what I feel." He continued to contribute caricatures to the Jewish Chronicle until 1991, a 61 year run! He was awarded the MBE in 1977, and died on December 9, 1994, aged 95.

D.G.

SALUDOS AMIGOS (U.S.) In 1941, at the urging of a State Department eager to further the Good Neighbor policy, Walt Disney went to South America and brought back material for four animated shorts. They were tied together by live-action footage and released as a feature in 1943 under the title *Saludos Amigos.* The first animated sequence had Donald Duck fighting an ornery llama on the shores of Peru's Lake Titicaca; the second, "Pedro the Plane," starred a game little airplane carrying the mails over the Andes; then came "El Gaucho Goofy," in which Goofy displayed his skills on the pampas; in the last sequence, Aquarela do Brasil," Donald and a new character, the parrot José Carioca, made merry in the streets of Rio at Carnival time.

Saludas Amigos was the first of Disney's package films,

Donald Duck as an American tourist at Lake Titicaca in "Saludos Amigos. " Walt Disney Productions.

(so called because they did not revolve around a single character like Snow White or Pinocchio, or have a central theme such as the musical program of Fantasia, but consisted of several fragments, not necessarily all animated, strung together by a more or less tenuous thematic or narrative thread). *Saludos Amigas* was a charming and unpretentious film, and it met with much success both in Latin America and in the U.S. It also introduced two Latin hit songs, "Brazil" and "Tico Tico," and its mood was generally upbeat and optimistic, as the times required. Each of the animated sequences was later released as an independent short for movie houses and for television.

M.H.

SAM (G.B.) "Sam, Sam, pick up thy musket/Go on, lad, just to please me . . ." So spake the Grand Old Duke of Wellington, but Sam Small would have none of it. "He knocked it down,/Reet then, he picks it oop,/or it stays where it is on the floor."

The discussion of the ups and downs of Sam Small's "moosket" formed the basis of a perennially popular monologue written by Marriott Edgar and declaimed on stage, radio and record by Stanley Holloway. Sam was brought to the screen as an animated cartoon hero by the veteran British producer-director Anson Dyer in 1936. Tremendous publicity surrounded the initial announcements: "New Competitor for Mickey Mouse," headlined the *Daily Mail* on September 5, 1935; "British Colour Cartoon!" They might have said "First British Colour Cartoons," for the Sam series was the first to be made on a regular production schedule for cinema *release.* The color system used was the Dunning two-color process, which critics found "very bright, but not garish, the lines clear, and the mobility smooth and copious."

The first film, *Sam* and His Musket, was trade-shown in October 1935 by Reunion Films, who handled the distribution. It was followed by *Alt! Oa Goes Theer?* in April 1936. The next pair came along in November 1936, the distributor changing to Associated Producers and Distributors: *Beat the Retreat* and Sam's *Medal.* The final two *were* taken on by Sound City Distributors: *Drummed* Out and *Gunner Sam* in February and May, 1937. Production throughout was by Dyer's Anglia Films, and the series was supervised by another veteran animator, Sid Griffiths. Stanley Holloway narrated and spoke for Sam, and the music was by Wolseley Charles. Technical background to the series, with color reproductions from cels, formed a six-part sequence of articles by Dyer in the monthly magazine *The Artist* (1936).

D.G.

SAMBOURNE, EDWARD LINLEY (1845-1910) British cartoonist born in London, England, on January 4, 1845. The artist who inherited the weekly *Punch* cartoon from Tenniel, Linley Sambourne was the son of a prosperous City merchant; he attended the City of London School and Chester College. At the age of 16 he was apprenticed to a firm of marine engineers at Greenwich. Although an untrained artist, he reached such perfection that David Low claimed "he evolved a style which for sheer purity of line and solid correctness of draughtsmanship has not been excelled among British artists."

Sambonrne was perhaps the first cartoonist to attempt the "photographic" accuracy of artwork that would be reborn in the comic strip work of Frank Hampson. He kept a reference library of pictures that, at his death in 1910, numbered one hundred thousand items. Sambonrne was also proud of being able to draw a perfect circle freehand, and he drew his figures from the naked body before clothing them. His first cartoon, "Pros and Cons," was published in Punch in April 1867, and he was elected to the Punch Table in 1876. He took over the secondary spot known as the "Cartoon Junior," graduating to the major cartoon on Tenniel's retirement in 1901. He also designed and painted furniture.

Books: New History of Sanford and Merton (1872*); Military Men I Have Met* (1872); *Our Holiday on the Riviera* (1874); *Our Holiday in the Scottish Highlands* (1876); *Modern Arabian Nights* (1877); *Venice from Childe Harold* (1878); *The Royal Umbrella* (1880); *Society Novelette* (1883); *Sherryana* (1886); *The Water Babies* (1886); *Friends and Foes from Fairyland* (1886); *The Green Above the Red* (1889); *Real Adventures of Robinson Crusoe* (1893); *New London* (1895); *Papers from Punch* (1898); and *Three Tales from Hans Andersen* (1910).

D.G.

SANCHIS AGUADO, JULIO (1942-) Spanish cartoonist born in Picasent (Valencia, Spain) on October 10, 1942. Julio Sanchis had a love of drawing from earliest childhood and his first teacher, a man of great artistic sensibilty, helped him develop his natural talent. On his teacher's recommendation he joined Academia of San Carlos in Valencia, but because of his father's opposition he had to leave school after one year despite his desire to become a cartoonist.

While holding down an office job, Sanchis at 14 had a cartoon accepted by the comic magazine *Jaimito.* Later he was asked by the Picasent Cultural Club to illustrate a lecture about Martin Luther King, and still later he became a contributor to the Club's journal *Razones.* In 1957 he discovered Angel Villena's cartoon anthology, *Caricatulogio,* and was hooked forever on humor. He focused his line and sharpened his concepts and, as "Harca," he continued to freelance cartoons from Picasent until 1973 when he got married and moved to Valencia.

In 1975 he began contributing to Olimpiada Internacional del Humour, an annual event taking place in Valencia during which the best cartoonists of Spain exhibit their work. The year 1975 was especially fruitful for Sanchis, since that was when he started working for *Levante* and *Pueblo,* two important Spanish newspapers. From that time on he has freelanced cartoons to almost every newspaper in Spain. He has also collaborated to periodicals such as *La Golondriz* and *Almanaque Vermot,* as well as to to TV-Aitana, illustrating several of their shows in the 1980s.

Sanchis has exhibited at most of the major cartoon shows, including those in Bordighera, Italy; Knokke-Heist, Belgium; Saint-Just-le-Martel, France; Omiya, Japan; and Haifa, Israel. He has been the recipient of a number of

Carlo Santachiara. © Santachiara.

prizes and awards in the 1980s and 1990s. He is currently president of FECO (Federation of European Cartoonists Organizations).

F.T.J.

SANDERS, WILLIAM WILLARD (1933-) American cartoonist born in Tennessee in 1933. Bill Sanders attended Western Kentucky University on a football scholarship. In 1955 he went to Korea with the army and drew cartoons for *Stars and Stripes,* and in 1957 the paper hired him as a civilian cartoonist and sportswriter in Tokyo. Sanders left Japan in 1959 and took a job as cartoonist for the Greensboro (N.C.) *Daily News;* in 1963 he switched to the *Kansas City Star*. He changed papers again after another four years, going to the *Milwaukee Journal,* where he remains today. His cartoons were syndicated by *Field Newspaper Syndicate.* He retired to Ft. Myers, Fla., in 1990.

Sanders's style has reflected the dominant styles in the field during his career: Herblock, Conrad and most recently Oliphant. He uses toned paper and occasionally mixes pen, brush, benday, Craftint and crayon.

Sanders is one of the most stridently left-wing cartoonists in America, though he once defined his limits by drawing a series against student bomb-throwers. At the same time he was suspended without pay by the Journal for drawing anonymously for an underground radical newspaper.

R.M.

SANTACHIARA, CARLO (1937-) Italian cartoonist, illustrator and sculptor born in Reggiolo, Italy, on November 27, 1937. Carlo Santachiara took an interest in art at an early age and started contributing cartoons to the humor magazine *Il Travasa* in the 1950s. In 1965-66 he was the recipient of a number of cartoon awards; in 1967-68 he drew a satirical comic strip, Sordello (on the model of Jules Feiffer's feature) for the monthly magazine *Linus.*

Santachiara abandoned cartooning in 1969 in favor of lithographs and bronze sculpture. His works in these fields have been favorably received. He currently teaches at the Art Lyceum of Bologna, his adoptive city. Santachiara returned briefly to political cartooning in 1975. He has also illustrated a number of books and magazine stories.

M.G.P.

SARG, TONY (1882-1942) American cartoonist, puppeteer, author and designer, born in Guatemala in 1882. Tony Sarg,

—Irate Captain: "I say, Corporal Jenkins, have you seen my baggage about anywhere?"
—Jenkins: "Yes, sir. She's talking with the Colonel over there!"

Tony Sarg, 1917. © Judge.

who eventually adopted America as his home, traveled as widely as his appeal eventually spread. He was a universal jolly man and a favorite on all continents. Educated in Germany, self-taught in art, he sold his first cartoons to the London Sketch and entered the advertising field in England. It was in London that he became intrigued by marionettes, following the great Holden to all his performances to learn the tricks of the trade. Later Sarg himself became a premier marionette designer and craftsman.

Arriving in America in 1914, Sarg made an immediate impact by illustrating the enormously successful magazine story (and best-selling book) *Speaking of Operations* by Irvin S. Cobb. He also experimented in the nascent animation field-even his panel cartoons seemed to be alive and drew brilliant full-page cartoons for *Puck* and *Judge*. Sarg's later credits include the design of the huge balloons for the Macy's Thanksgiving Day parades in New York City, books for both children and adults and designs for a wide assortment of commercially manufactured products.

His cartoon style was amazingly easy and matched the mood of some of the merriest work of Heath Robinson and Bateman in England. Sarg's specialty was bird's-eye and worm's-eye views of congregations of people on street corners, boardwalks, etc. Perspectives were flawless, and anatomy was consistently accurate, animated and amiable. Good humor permeated every corner of his busy cartoons. He also, when drawing specially for books of cartoons or designing cartoon jigsaw puzzles, showed a flair for color work.

R.M.

SARGENT, BEN (1948-) American political cartoonist born in Amarillo, Texas, on November 26, 1948. The *Austin American-Statesman* cartoonist, unlike most of his young contemporaries, shuns doubletone shading effects, using instead meticulous old-fashioned crosshatch techniques and scratchboard.

Ben Sargent. © Austin American Statesman.

Sargent received no formal art training but instead studied journalism at Amarillo College, University of Texas (1970). His artistic influences include Jack Patton, *Dallas News* cartoonist of the 1920s, who drew a series of history strips studied by the succeeding generations of Texas schoolchildren. He was also inspired by *MAD* magazine cartoonists Will Elder, Jack Davis, Don Martin, Wally Wood and others.

Entering the industry as a reporter for the Corpus *Christi Caller-Times* in 1969, Sargent then drew for the Long News Service (1969-71, 1972-74). He served stints with the American-Statesman (1971-72) and United Press International (1972) before joining the American-Statesman as permanent political cartoonist in August 1974. He was awarded a Pulitzer Prize in 1982. His work is now distributed by Universal Press Syndicate.

A self-proclaimed populist cartoonist, Sargent displays a solid compositional grasp and mastery of his unique media—all coupled with freshness and forcefulness of ideas. He is now considered one of the major cartoonists in America.

R.M.

SARKA, CHARLES NICHOLAS (1879-1960) American artist and cartoonist born in 1879. Charles Sarka was one

Miraculous. Englishman (reading): "KEEP OUT—THIS MEANS YOU!" Bah Jove! How did they know I was coming?"

Charles Sarka, 1905. cJudge.

of the great contributors to American pen-and-ink technique, although he, like another major exponent, Gibson, ultimately abandoned it for other media.

Sarka began drawing editorial cartoons in Chicago during the Spanish-American War; they were neither clever nor particularly well drawn, and they dealt mostly with local subjects. After a stint in San Francisco, however, Sarka moved to New York and bloomed. He started his career as an illustrator for Cosmopolitan and joined the staff of Judge.

He did some lithographic color cartoons for *Judge,* but his best work was in the black-and-white mode. At first his new work-in cartoons, illustrations and spot drawings-was trendy, with the swirling, decorative look being explored by others like Will Crawford, E.N. Clark, Joseph Clement Coll and Rudolph Dirks (who, around the turn of the century, found stylistic respite from *The Katzenjammer Kids* in drawing for *Judge).* Sarka's work soon began to transcend playful experimentation and develop into a style mature with texture and emotion. Shading swirled to carry the reader's eye through the picture, and there was an exciting boldness of design in all his work.

Sarka's production might have been greater were it not for a wanderlust that carried him to corners of the earth from Tahiti to Iceland to Morocco. His companions often included artists Thomas ("Pop") Hart and Rudolph Dirks-whose work was also interrupted occasionally by these travels. Charles Sarka frequently wound up drawing upon these travel experiences for his illustrating and cartoon assignments; "This was my art school-to travel and paint: to paint and travel." This passion for painting led him eventually to abandon the pen for the watercolor brush. Before his death in 1960 he became a life member of the American Watercolor Society.

R.M.

SATO, SANPEI (1929-) Japanese cartoonist born in Nagoya, Japan, on September 11, 1929. Sanpei Sato was raised in Osaka. Like most schoolboys of the time, he was mobilized to work in a factory durihg World War II. Drawing had always been his hobby, and he dreamed of attending art school in Tokyo at the end of the war. However, poverty and his father's opposition made this impossible, and instead he entered the dyeing department of the Kyoto University of Industrial Arts and Textile Fibers to learn a trade that bore little relation to the type of art he longed to study.

In comparison with other artists in Japan, Sato entered the cartooning field rather indirecily and without training. In 1950, so the story goes, he graduated from the university and applied for a job at the Daimaru department store in Osaka, submitting his résumé in cartoon form. Though it was his first cartoon work, he was actually accepted. Later, during boring orientation lectures, he further improved his skills. He first contributed to the company magazine and in 1953 began appearing in the newspaper *Shin Osaka* on a weekly basis with his *Osaka* no *Musuko* ("Osaka Son"). In 1957, after seven years at Daimarn, Sato quit his job and left for Tokyo to work as a professional cartoonist. He was heavily influenced by editorial cartoonist Taizo Yokoyama and became noted for his strong

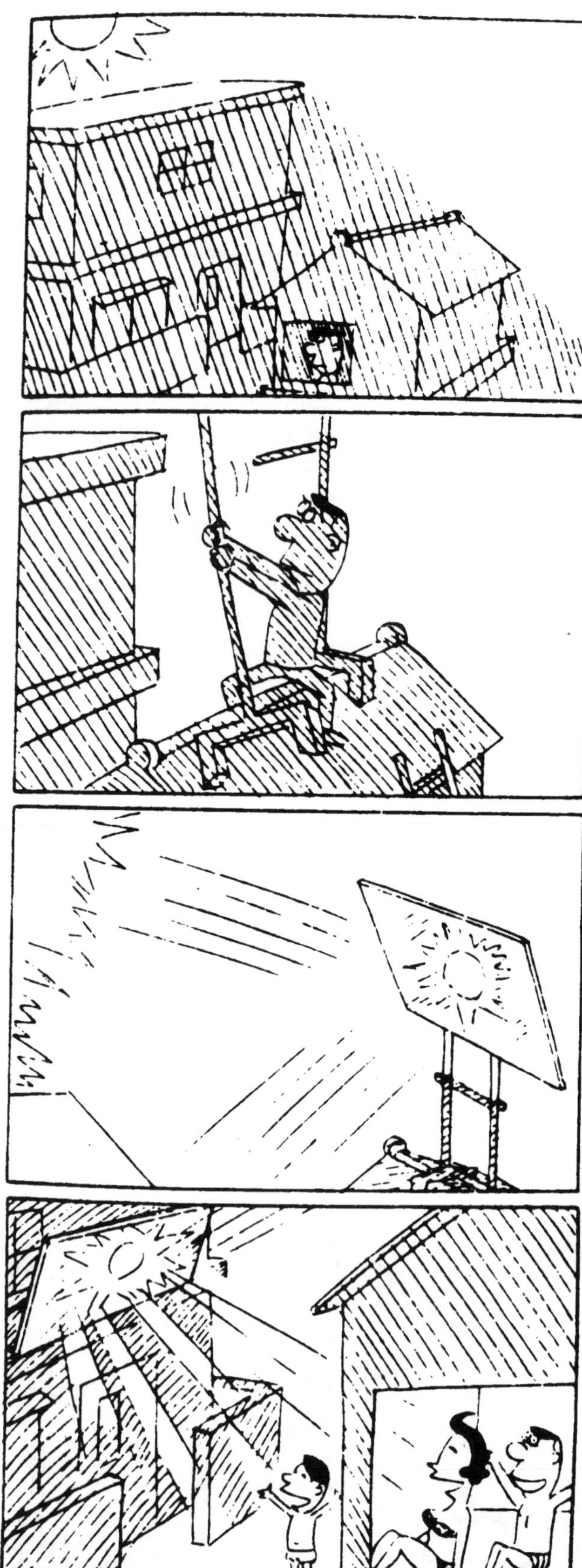

Sanpei Sato.©Asahi Shimbun.

satire, as in *Ossu Messu* ("Male-Female"), which ran in the *Sankei* Sports newspaper in 1957-58. This was followed by *Yangu Madamu* ("Young Madam"), which appeared in the newspaper *Key* in 1959, and *Instanto Madamu* ("Instant Madam"), which began in the evening edition of the *Sankei Shimbun* in 1961.

Asa Kaze Kun ("Young Morning Breeze"), his first long

work (30 frames), appeared in the weekly Shukan *Manga Sunday* from 1963, and *Fujisantara* (both a name and pun involving Mount Fuji) started in the evening edition of the *Asahi Shimbun* in 1965. These two works are perhaps most representative of Sato, and they solidly established him in the field. Because of their themes, he became known as an artist who wrote for the average "salaryman" (white-collar worker). In 1966 he received the Bunshu cartoon award, and thereafter his output soared, with a string of new pieces such as *Ranchikun* (1964-68), *Hanabei* (1966-67) and *Yūhikun* (1968-). Sato depicts the trials and tribulations of the everyday office worker's life and often includes biting political satire—an excellent formula for success in overwhelmingly middle-class Japan. *Fujisantaro* won the Bungei Shunju Manga Award in 1966, and was serialized for 26 years, only coming to an end in 1991.

F.S.

SATONAKA, MACHIKO (1947-) Japanese comic book artist and cartoonist born in Osaka, Japan, in 1947. Both prolific and precocious, Machiko Satonaka today ranks among the most popular and best-selling creators of comics for young girls and women. As early as seventh grade, Satonaka had resolved to become a comic book artist; she spent her free time devouring the works of big-name artists like Osamu Tezuka, Shirato Sanpei and Shōtaro Ishimori, and her allowance buying pens, pencils and paper to create her own stories. Her zeal soon paid off; at the age of 15, her *Pia no Shōzō* ("Portrait of Pia"), a romantic vampire story, won her the 1964 Kodansha award for new artists. The following year she dropped out of high school and moved to Tokyo, where she commenced work as a professional.

Since then, Satonaka has not only made herself famous but has also made a major contribution to the development and sophistication of her preferred genre: shojo *manga*, or comics for young girls. Today she writes consistently on themes of love, both requited and unrequited, and adapts herself to a variety of ages and readers, so that her following ranges from elementary-school girls to secretaries and even includes some men. Her skilled draftsmanship and mastery of human psychology have added to the interest her work generates, for the genre is generally beset by a chronic lack of both. Satonaka's strength lies in the diversity of the plots she manages to create. Her romances are skillfully interwoven with subjects such as racial discrimination, Vietnam, Nazi persecution of the Jews, and leukemia.

Most of Satonaka's works are full-length stories numbering in the hundreds of pages when compiled: *Lady Ann (1969), Hanayame Sensei* ("Teacher Bride," 1971), *Ashta Kagayaku* ("Shining Tomorrow," 1972) and *Hime Ga Yuku* ("Hime Goes Forth," 1973).The last two won her the fifth Kodansha Shuppan Bunka award (children's division) in 1974. *Ashta Kagayaku* is a romance drama beginning in Japanese-occupied Manchuria before the end of World War II; it depicts a love that survives in spite of constant upheaval and tragedy. *Hime Ga Yuku,* on the other hand, is a comedy starring a young girl whose name happens to be a pun on "Snow White."

In 1972 she also collaborated with Shinji Mizushima (one of the best-selling sports comic book writers today) to produce *Yakyūkyō no Uta* ("Saga of Baseball Mania"). In addition to her *manga,* she has been active in the 1980s and 1990s against censorship and organized a protest against Disney for lifting parts of Osamu Tezuka's *Jungle Tatei* in the making of *The Lion King.*

F.S.

SAWANT, SURESH (1942-) Indian-born Suresh Sawant's interest in cartoons developed when he was about eight years old; he drew pictures on the floor of his home, which family members respected by stepping over them, especially when the themes were religious. After finishing his schooling, with no clearcut goal in sight, Sawant met famed Indian political cartoonist Bal Thackery, his idol, who in 1963, gave the young man his first public exposure by publishing one of his cartoons in *Marmik,* the humor magazine.

Most of Sawant's career was spent at the *Times Of India,* where he began as a clerk/translator and after 8 months, moved to lettering assistant on the new *Indrajal Comics.* He remained with *Times of India* publications for 24 years, during which time, he drew gag and strip cartoons for the children's magazine *Paraj, Economic Times, Evening News of India,* and *Blitz.* He left the organization in 1988 when the *Times of India* enforced its exclusive use policy. For most of his stay at the premier publishing house, Sawant had sent his work to other periodicals under the pen-name of Shresh.

Working solely on a freelance basis since 1988, Sawant draws about 100 cartoons of all types monthly, which he sells to businesses, syndicates, newspapers, magazines, and television. A large portion of them goes to *Blitz.*

Sawant's cartoons are noted for their sophisticated and subtle gags and their social consciousness themes. He was the first Indian to draw cartoons on eco-social issues on a regular basis.

J.A.L.

SAWKA, HENRYK (1958-) Henryk Sawka was born in Poznan, Poland in 1958. From 1985-90, he drew political cartoons for *Itd* ("Et cetera"), a students' magazine, before having his own page of cartoons called "Photoplastikon," in the weekly newsmagazine *Wproste* ("Direct").

Working freelance, Sawka also draws political cartoons that appear from time to time in two other magazines and about 10 to 20 newspapers; his monthly output averages 30-50 cartoons. Sawka is popular throughout Poland, partly because of his relentless attacks on politicians, based on the premise that he should "attack the prime minister not because he is good or bad, but because he is the prime minister."

Most of Sawka's cartoons employ line drawing solely, done with pen and ink; his full page in *Wproste* incorporates some gray wash.

J.A.L.

SAXON, CHARLES D. (1920-1988) American cartoonist born in Brooklyn, New York, on November 13, 1920. Charles Saxon attended Columbia College, receiving his

"We know what happens to bad little boys who won't eat their cereal, don't we?"
Charles Saxon. © Saxon.

A.B. in 1940. His first job was with Dell Publishing Company; he served in the editorial offices of its various magazines until 1943, when he went into the army. Discharged in 1945, he returned to Dell, becoming editorial director of the special features department there, and then editor in chief of Modern Screen and ScreenStories, two of the company s more popular entries in the pulp field. During this period, he also served as the cartoon editor of This Week magazine. Saxon was the last editor of the long-running "girlie" magazine *Film Fun.*

His career as a freelance cartoonist began in the 1940s with contributions to publications like the *Saturday Evening Post* and *This Week,* and came into full bloom in 1956 when he was named a staff cartoonist at the *New Yorker.* This enabled him to leave Dell and devote him- self full time to a career in commercial and cartoon art. In both capacities he has been quite successful. His cartoons have appeared in many magazines, his paintings have frequently graced the covers of the New *Yorker,* and he has been presiding artist and creative force behind graphic and animated ad campaigns for commercial accounts such as Xerox, American Express and American Airlines, and public service accounts such as the United Nations.

Saxon works in ink, pencil and watercolors. He has been' described as a disciplined craftsman who begins with an idea-not so much a line drawing as a suggestion—which he then refines and polishes until, out of perhaps twenty renderings, he chooses the one he will submit. His drawings, relying on the very finest of lining, have such a grace and fluidity that one can easily take them for granted. They show the stylized ease of the best commercial art, guided by an insightful intelligence. Saxon takes his humor from a world most of us can identify with; yet he presents it to us in a form that, for subtlety and relevance, easily ontstrips the run of commercial art. He even manages to introduce irony into his ad art—and irony is not a quality ordinarily associated with Madison Avenue. Among his works, those employing the multi-paneled "scenes" approach to cartoon art stand out. They are not strips in the sense of telling a story, but rather a series of thematically related drawings upon such subjects as "The Country Life" or "The Day the Trains Stopped Running," which as tableaux of comic art are Saxon's own contribution to the field. Looking at a Saxon drawing is often a bit like looking into some gently sarcastic version of the wicked queen's mirror-do we really look that silly?

Among Saxon's honors are an award for animation at the Venice Film Festival (1965), a gold medal from the New York Art Directors Club and an honorary degree from Hamilton College (1972). His cartoons have been collected in *Oh, Happy, Happy* (n.d.) and *One Man's Fancy* (1977) and represented in the *New Yorker's* 50th anniversary album of drawings and Great Cartoons of the World, 1969-71. He has also illustrated numbers of books. Charles Saxon died in December 1988.

R.C.

SAZONOV, PANTELEIMON (1895-1950) Soviet graphic designer and animator born in Moscow, Russia, on May 28, 1895. Panteleimon Sazonov studied law at Moscow University from 1913 to 1917, but his studies were interrupted by the Russian Revolution. Using his talent for drawing, he went to work as a studio graphic designer and later as a theatrical set designer. In the mid-1930s Sazonov went into animation as an assistant to Aleksandr lvanov; among other cartoons, he worked *an Kvar*tet, the undistinguished 1935 version of a Krylov fable that Ivanov was to remake with greater success in 1948. In 1937 Sazonov directed his first film, *No Biting Here,* followed by *An Uninvited Guest* (1938), also from a Krylov fable. From then on he concentrated on fables, fairy tales and children's stories. His most interesting efforts were *A Tale About Emile* and *The Cat's House* (both 1938), The *Tale of the Priest and His Servant Balda* (this cartoon, released in 1939, was a watered-dawn version of a film Tsektianovsky had planned earlier) and *Vile Persons* (1941).After turning out propaganda films during World War II, Sazonov returned to entertainment animation in 1949 with *The Hunter's Rifle,*

Panteleimon Sazonov, "The Cat's House."

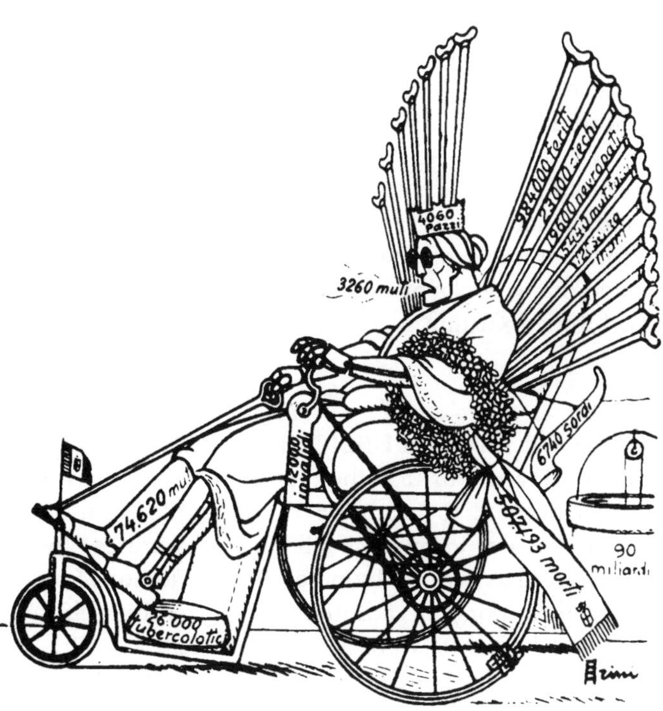

The Victory Chariot, 1919

Giuseppe Scalarini. © Scalarini.

which was followed by *The Builder Fox,* released shortly before his death in Moscow on October 3, 1950. Sazonov was a skilled if uninspired craftsman. His son, Anatoly, and his daughter, Tatiana, have also been active in animation.

M.H.

SCALARINI, GIUSEPPE (1873-1948) Italian cartoonist born in Mantna, Italy, in 1873. Fresh out of art school, Giuseppe Scalarini started his remarkable cartooning career in the last decade of the 19th century on the Socialist daily *Avanti!* and the anticlerical weekly *L'Asino.* Scalarini is unanimously regarded as Italy's major political cartoonist. He exercised great political influence in the first two decades of this century and during the few years when the Fascist regime "tolerated" freedom of the press. In his neatly drawn and incisive cartoons he captured some of the most dramatic moments in Italian history.

The ecclesiastical authorities, militarism, censorship, the war-mongering bourgeoisie and Fascism were among the targets Scalarini attacked with great eloquence and immediacy. His cartoons rarely pictured joy, hope or victory; though deeply convinced of the need to fight for change (he spent many years in prison during the 20 years of Mussolini's dictatorship), Scalarini always preferred to depict the cruel, malevolent face of the traditional enemies of the working class. He may have forced his caricatures, but it is indisputable that his grotesque and vehemently ferocious cartoons in many ways reflected reality.

Scalarini drew cartoons for publications other than *Avanti!* and *L'Asina,* notably *Merlin Cacai* and *Il Sacialista* (both of Mantna), *Pasquina* (Turin) and *Italia Ride* (Bologna). He also contributed to the foreign publications *Simplicissimus* (Munich) and *Lustige Bláffer* (Berlin). His nonpolitical cartoons appeared in *Carriere* dei *Piccali* and *La Damenica del Carriere* in Milan. After World War II, Scalarini resumed his career as a political cartoonist for the Socialist publication Codino *Russo,* remaining there until his death in 1948.

C.S.

SCARFE, GERALD (1936-) British caricaturist and political cartoonist born in London, England, in 1936. The cartoonist virtually responsible for the recent renaissance of the caricature tradition in English political art, Gerald Scarfe "shows a Swiftian hate for the human state by having his characters as skull-like and skeletal, or fat, flabby, and overlapping in greasy folds," according to an acknowledged expert, Michael Bateman, in his book *Funny Way to Earn a Living* (1966). "The human functions are called on to show a political mess of politicians as pigs, crawling over each other and defecating."

Scarfe's caricatures shock: his drawing of the beloved Winston Churchill in his last days in the House of Commons was done for the *Sunday Times* magazine cover but rejected. His drawing of Prime Minister Harold Macmillan as a prostitute (during the scandalous Profumo affair) was not only rejected by W.H. Smith, the United Kingdom's leading bookseller (it was for the cover of *Private Eye Annual),* but an article about Scarfe and the drawing was rejected by the Sunday Observer and caused the resignation of John Berger, the newspaper's art critic and writer of the article. His caricaturing career is riddled with such regular rejections that to list them would be tiresome. And yet young Gerald Scarfe's first drawing was published in *Eagle,* the comic weekly for boys, where it won a prize.Gerald Scarfe spent an asthmatic youth in long absences from school. He studied art at the St. Martin's School of Art and then attended the London School of Printing. After his debut in *Eagle,* he drew cartoons freelance for the *Daily Sketch* supplement, *Cartoon Sketch* and then *Punch,* where violence first began to creep into his work. Soon it took over, and Scarfe found happier response to his hideous symbolism in *Private Eye,* a magazine dedicated to satire and iconoclasm. Soon America recognized his talent, and his drawings appeared in *Life* and *Esquire:* for the latter he drew a picture story about the Berlin Wall. Visits to America affected him sufficiently for

Gerald Scarfe. © Punch.

"Grandfather, to whom do you leave your beard?"
Filiberto Scarpelli. © Scarpelli.

him to write, direct and animate a computerized cartoon of his experiences for BBC television. He has illustrated several books, and in 1968 published his own *Sketches from Vietnam.* He has animated sequences for the Pink Floyd film *The Wall* (1982). His many later books include *Father Krissmass and Mother Claws* (1985), *Safety Scarfe* (1986), *Seven Deadly Sins* (1987), *Lines of Attack* (1988), and *Scarfeland* (1989).

D.G.

SCARPELLI, FILIBERTO (1870-1933) Italian cartoonist, illustrator and writer born in Naples, Italy, in 1870. Filiberto Scarpelli drew his first cartoons in the 1890s for the satirical weekly *L'Asina* and for the Socialist daily *Avanti!* His work displayed an incisiveness and bite worthy of a Daumier or Caran d'Ache. At the turn of the century he began his long career as chief illustrator for the children's weekly *Giornalino della Damenica,* where he had to temper his irony.

But Scarpelli never forgot that he was first and foremost an editorial cartoonist. He collaborated assiduously on *Il Travasa delle Idee* (literally "The Transfusion of Ideas," later called simply *Il Travaso).* This humor weekly was founded in Rome at the beginning of the century and survived, through many vicissitudes, for more than sixty years. In *Il Travaso* Scarpelli gave free rein to his sense of irony and his subtle humor. During the years of the Fascist regime, Scarpelli did not express any opposition, but neither did he stoop to the heavy-handedness and insulting tone shown by other cartoonists of the time towards opponents of the regime.

Scarpelli died in 1933. He was eulogized in an obituary in *Il Travaso* that read in part: "An indefatigable worker, he spent long hours drawing or writing for the enjoyment of children and adults." In addition to his cartoons, Scarpelli wrote a number of juvenile stories and novels and illustrated many books by authors ranging from Cervantes to the brothers Grimm.

C.S.

SCÈNES DE LA VIE PUBLIQUE ET PRIVÉE DES ANIMAUX (France) In 1839 the French publisher Pierre-Jules Hetzel decided to commission Grandville (Jean-Ignace-Isidore Gérard) to produce a book of caricatures illustrating short texts written by noted French authors. Some of the contributors, in addition to Hetzel himself (who signed P.J. Stahl), were Honoré de Balzac, Alfred de Mnsset, Charles Nodier and Jules Janin. The book was titled *Scènes de la Vie Publique et Privée des Animaux* ("Scenes of the Public and Private Life of the Animals"), or *Les Animaux* for short. It was first issued in weekly installments between November 1840 and December 1842 and was later republished in a two-volume edition.

The entire enterprise was meant as a satire on contemporary society, mores and institutions. The illustrations depicted a variety of animals—from beetles to elephants—engaged in the most incongruous occupations. The chap-

"Scènes *de la Vie Publique et Privée des Animaux," half-title* page.

ters bore such titles as "Heartaches of an English Cat," "Memoirs of a Crocodile," "Animals as Doctors," "The Philosophical Rat" and "Journey of an African Lion to Paris" and offered amused glimpses into the manners, concerns and morals of the time. Grandville's vignettes were nothing short of inspired; he drew his animals straightforwardly, in the minntest and most realistic detail, and his humor was the more excruciating for being so literal.

Les Animaux is widely regarded as one of Grandville's masterpieces, and it has remained constantly in print over the years, a testimonial to the bizarre genius of the artist.

M.H.

SCHABELITZ, RUDOLPH F. (1887-1959) American cartoonist and illustrator born on Staten Island, New York, in 1887. R. F. Schabelitz studied in Munich and at the Art Students League in New York and sold his first illustration to *Harper's Weekly* in 1902, at the age of 15. Soon he was a frequent contributor to *Cosmopolitan, Redbook* and *Harper's.* The 1910s were Schabelitz's most active period as a cartoonist; he had many sales to *Life* and was a mainstay of *Judge*'s staff (he drew there into the 1920s), with many double-page spreads to his credit. Schabelitz later turned to oils and more individualistic illustration work for the *New York Daily News.* He died at his home in New York on July 2, 1959.

Schabelitz was a penman who utilized bold, slashing lines and rigid crosshatches, sometimes at the expense of the texture or subtlety he could have achieved with a more fluid line. In short, his cartoons, though pleasant, were simply derivative; he was one of dozens of "poor men's Gibsons"—at the time a stock-in-trade, as lesser magazines couldn't procure the services of Gibson himself. To Schabelitz's credit, his work in this genre was as strong as that of his contemporary, James Montgomery Flagg, whom he seemed to rival at one point.

R.M.

SCHADOW, GOTTFRIED (1764-1850) German sculptor, printmaker, art educator and author, and cartoonist born in Berlin, Prussia, on May 5, 1764. Gottfried Schadow, one of the greatest artists ever connected with Berlin, is best remembered for such sculptural works as the now destroyed quadriga (1795) on top of the Brandenburg gate, the monumental cast-bronze statue of Blütcher (completed in 1819) and his exquisite marble portraits. Though his work as a Berlin cartoonist is less well known, it places him alongside Dörbeck, Hosemann, Schördter and Menzel.

The son of a master tailor, Schadow studied at both the royal sculpture studio and the Academy in Berlin. As a student he executed prints that were already of excellent quality, and his instructor, Tassaert, advised him to confine himself to graphics because he was too nearsighted to be a sculptor! In 1785 Schadow eloped and lived in Italy for the next two years. Back in Berlin, he did designs for porcelain figures until he was named director of the royal sculpture studio in 1788, after Tassaert's death. He traveled to Sweden, Russia, Denmark and France to immerse himself in the latest sculptural techniques. In 1805 he became the rector of the Berlin Academy, and its director in 1815. After 1821, when his sight became especially weak, he devoted himself almost exclusively to drawing.

Among Schadow's humorous works are several prints from the 1780s: satires on the French siege of Gibraltar in 1783, on the lowering of the coffee tax in Berlin in 1784 and on the "factory" production of revolutionary prints in Paris in 1789. In the period of the Napoleonic Wars, Schadow did 11 prints attacking the French emperor (because of local censorship, Schadow signed these "Gillray, Paris"). Unlike most of the German anti-Napoleon prints (including those of Voltz), Schadow's were too subtle, allusive, complex and devoid of brutality to become really popular.

When a local art publishing firm, Gropius, began commissioning humorous lithographic scenes of Berlin life in the 1820s, Schadow furnished five of the very best (1827 and 1828) in the series Berliner Witze ("Berlin Jokes"). Schadow's drawings and prints of the 1830s also include such witty items as a human- figure alphabet and scenes in inn gardens and art galleries.

Gottfried Schadow died in Berlin on January 27, 1850. (His son Wilhelm, also an artist, left his teaching post at the Berlin Academy and went to Düsseldorf, where, together with Schördter and others, he made that city's Academy one of the artistic centers of Germany.)

S.A.

SCHAEFER-AST, ALBERT (1890-1951) German cartoonist, illustrator and printmaker born in BarmenWuppertal, January 7, 1890. Everything about Albert Schaefer-Ast was eccentric, even his name. Born Albert Schaefer, he added the tag when his signature his initials, plus *f* for fecit—was mistakenly read as *Ast.* What's more, there was a notorious miracle worker in Germany at the time (about 1920) who not only was really named Ast but was a shepherd *(Schäfer)* as well. To add to the muddle, *Ast* means "bough," and the cartoonist lost few opportunities of making verbal and visual puns on all this.

Indeed, even though his highly personal drawing style—a sophisticated black-and-white interpretation of the draftsmanship of children, folk artists and "primitive" tribesmen—is universally pleasing, a knowledge of the German language and culture is almost indispensable for a thorough appreciation of his pictures and captions, which are full of puns and allusions and are often weird literal depictions of metaphors and folk sayings. Humorous fabulous beasts of his own creation also abound in his oeuvre, which is highly rated by art historians. Like Grosz and just a few other modern German satirical artists, Schaefer-Ast is seriously regarded as more than a "mere" cartoonist.

After studying art in Düsseldoff from 1906 to 1912, Schaefer-Ast began contributing cartoons to numerous magazines: *Jugend* (1912-14), *Die Berliner Illustrierte* (1921-33), *Uhu, Die Wache, Die Dame,* the children's journal *Der Heitere Fridalin* and so on. As early as the 1920s he was also publishing witty print portfolios in a variety of media, but the real breakthrough came with his 1932 volume *Bilderbuch fár Kinder und Solche, Die Es Werden Wollen*

("Picture Book for Children and Those Who Want to Become Children"). His rise to fame was soon interrupted by the Nazi seizure of power; his art branded as "degenerate," he was refused permission to work for three years and subsequently allowed only limited freedom of expression as a journalistic draftsman. In 1943, bombed out of his house in Berlin, he moved to his pet-filled summer home on the Baltic.

The end of hostilities saw a change in his fortunes. In 1945 he was appointed professor of graphics at the Weimar Advanced School of Architecture and Fine Arts. He resumed his career as a cartoonist, working for the Berlin magazine *Ulenspiegel,* and issued a respectable number of new books and portfolios until his death in Weimar on September 15, 1951.

S.A.

SCHIAFFINO, GUALTIERO (1943-) Italian cartoonist born in Camogli, Italy, on April 27, 1943. Gualtiero Schiaffino studied law for a time but dropped out of school in the early 1960s. He contributed his first cartoons to the Communist daily *L'Unita* in 1968, while working as a commercial artist for an advertising company. In 1970 Schiaffino (who signs "Skiaffino") received an award at the Bordighera Humor Salon and won a competition organized by the daily *Paese Sera.* His comic strip *Santincielo* (literally "Saintinheaven") began publication in *Paese Sera* in 1973, transferring the next year to the monthly Eureka. That same year Schiaffino gave Santincielo its obverse, *I Diavoli* ("The Devils"), a strip drawn in "negative" (white on black) and obviously located in Hades.

Schiaffino, one of the most prolific of contemporary Italian cartoonists, is a regular contributor to a number of daily newspapers (*Il Lavora, Paese Sera, Il Secolo XIX,* etc.) and magazines *(Eureka, Urania, Segretissimo, ABC).* His cartoons have also appeared in Brazil, France and Germany. He is the recipient of many awards, both for his cartoons and for his comics. For two years (1975-77) he edited *La Bancarella,* at first a weekly supplement to a Genoa daily newspaper, later an independent monthly. In 1975 an anthology of Schiaffino's Santincielo strips was published under the title *La Presa per il Culto* ("Power through Worship"), followed in 1977 by a collection of his political

". . . And then women are not fit for the priesthood: they are too frivolous and birdbrained."
Gualtiero Schiaffino ("Skiaffino"). © Editoriale Corno.

cartoons, *Lei Non Sa Chi Sono Dio* ("You Don't Know Who God Is"). Since 1980 he has been devoting most of his time and talent editing a priodical aimed at teachers.

C.S.

SCHLESINGER, LEON (1884-1949) American film producer born in Philadelphia, Pennsylvania, in 1884. Leon Schlesinger dropped out of school at age 15, and his love of the stage led him to take a job as an usher in a Philadelphia theater. He moved to Chicago, where he held positions as cashier and later treasurer of a theater. He was press agent and manager for road shows and vaudeville acts, and in the mid-1910s he started his long association with the movies, first as a salesman and later as foreign sales manager of the old Metro Corporation. He came to Hollywood in 1922 as West Coast sales manager for Agfa Films.

In 1925 Schlesinger founded the Pacific Title and Art Studio, which he later sold. It was Jack Warner who suggested in 1930 that he enter the animation field. Schlesinger followed the advice and started producing animated cartoons for Warner Brothers that same year. Looney Tunes (to which he later added Merrie Melodies) was the overall title of his first cartoons, beginning with Sinkin' *in the Bathtub.* Starting with a staff of six, the Schlesinger studio employed over two hundred people ten years later.

An ardent racetrack devotee and dedicated gambler, Schlesinger seldom tampered with his artists' work, and this resulted in a loose, good-natured, rowdy style that was a far cry from the discipline of the Disney studio. Many critics have denied Schlesinger any creative distinction, but some credit must attach to the man who produced such series as *Porky Pig, Bugs Bunny* and *Daffy Duck* and nurtured the talents of (among others) Hugh Harman, Rudolph Ising, Friz Freleng, Bob Clampett, Tex Avery, Frank Tashlin and Chuck Jones.

Leon Schlesinger sold-out to Warners in 1944 and briefly worked as a producer for Columbia Pictures. He died at Cedars of Lebanon Hospital in Los Angeles on December 26, 1949.

M.H.

SCHLITTGEN, HERMANN (1859-1930) German cartoonist, illustrator, printmaker and author born in the village of Roitzsch, Saxony, on June 23, 1859. Hermann Schlittgen was one of the chief contributors to the great Munich humor magazine *Fliegende Blätter* in the last part of the 19th century; Eduard Fuchs, in *Die Karikatur der Europäischen Völker* (original edition 1903), considered him the most talented German cartoonist of the day.

Schlittgen's father was a day laborer. Both the boy's parents died in a cholera epidemic when he was 7, and he went to live with an uncle. In 1873, not quite 14, he entered the Leipzig Academy of Art, and by the age of 17 he was already selling drawings to magazines and achieving independence. Even after moving on to the Weimar Applied Art School, he continued to contribute to the Leipzig humor magazine Schalk. In 1880 Schlittgen arrived in Munich; there he settled, pursuing his studies at

The Salon-freethinker
Hermann Schlittgen, 1896.

the Academy (he later attended the Académie Julian in Paris as well) and joining the staff of the *Fliegende Blätter.*

All the staff artists of the *Fliegende Blätter* (which, founded in 1844, was already exhibiting some of the inflexibility of old age) had their particular genres, to which both the editors and the readers expected them to adhere. In Schlittgen's own words (from his very readable autobiography, *Erinnerungen,* published in 1926): "My field was the elegant world, with its gentlemen and ladies, officers, playboys, confidence men and all the types that revolve around them: servant girls, soldiers, orderlies and cabbies." Schlittgen's military drawings were highly admired by such a demanding connoisseur as Bismarck himself.

In later years Schlittgen did occasional work for *Die Gartenlaube* and the *Berliner Illustrierte Zeitung,* but he expressed no interest when approached by the New York *Harper's Monthly* and the *London Graphic.* Later, disillusioned by the reactionary artistic policies of the *Fliegende Blätter* and its editors' constant criticism of all contributors except the sacrosanct Adolf Oberländer, Schlittgen began to do some drawing for the new *Simplicissimus* (1896), which offered unusual freedom and potential to its artists. But after he had submitted just a few drawings to the great new Munich magazine, the *Fliegende Blätter* objected to the divided loyalty. Schlittgen stayed where he was and regretted it. It is curious to reflect that he might be much better known today if he would or could have accepted those other offers.

Schlittgen was also a minor painter and was briefly associated with one of the splinter Secession groups of the late 19th century, along with Slevogt, T.T. Heine, Trübner and Corinth. At the age of 61 he retired from the *Fliegende Blätter* and devoted himself to painting. He died in the Bavarian town of Wasserburg on June 9, 1930.

S.A.

SCHMIDT THE SPY (G.B.) "Such is the fear of a Zeppelin raid that the womenfolk have taken to living under ground." This was the text of the first message to Berlin from Schmidt the Spy, datelined London, England, 1914. He wrote it from his vantage point in a handy dustbin (embossed "Made in Germany"), and the readers of the weekly humorous paper *London Opinion* laughed and took Herr Schmidt to their Hun-hating hearts. For the incident depicted by Alfred Leete showed a dusty skivvy sticking her head out of a coalhole, in converse with a coalman who had just shot his load! The following page of the collected messages of *Schmidt the Spy,* as published in book form in June 1915, showed our Hun hero, disguised in "drag," reporting, "The Indian Army has arrived in London, and its officers are to be seen carousing in the streets of the West End." Leete's cartoon showed three "nigger minstrels" bnsking outside a saloon bar! Schmidt the Spy, the first cartoon character of World War l, even hit the cinema screen. Phoenix Films, specialists in comedy productions, produced *Schmidt the Spy* in April 1916, with Lewis Sydney portraying the bespectacled, bristly, moustachioed master of disguise.

Alfred Leete was born in Thorp Achnrch, Northamptonshire, on August 28, 1882. His farming family moved to Weston-Super-Mare, where they sent young Alfred to Kingsholme School. He studied art at the Weston School of Science and Art. His education ended at the age of 12, when he became an office boy to a Bristol architect. There he acquired a working knowledge of perspective and assisted his employer's freelance sketching of Bristol buildings for a local newspaper. Preferring humorous work, Leete bombarded the London papers with cartoons, and his first was accepted by the *Daily Graphic* when he was 16. The following year he exchanged architecture for furniture design and freelanced cartoons to the local comic, *Bristol Magpie.* He went to London but at first met with little success, save for a few sketches for *Ally Sloper's Half-Holiday,* at five shillings apiece. With the launching of *London Opinion,* his luck turned, and then came a series for *Pick-Me-Up, Play Titles Travestied,* which ran for eight years. But his most famous work was not a cartoon: it was the classic "Kitchener Wants You" recruiting poster. He died on June 17, 1933.

D.G.

SCHOLZ, WILHELM (1824-1893) German cartoonist and painter, born in Berlin, then capital of Prussia, on January 23, 1824. Wilhelm Scholz holds one of the great career records among German cartoonists: 42 consecutive years (most of them as sole illustrator) on the most important German political satire magazine of the second half of the 19th century, the Berlin- based *Kladderadatsch.* (The magazine itself had a record of uninterrupted publication from 1848 to 1944!)

The son of a minor official, Scholz was able to attend the Berlin Art Academy for only a short while before his father died; he then had to turn to commercial art for a living. He made a name for himself in 1847, when about a hundred of his cartoons were published in an album spoofing the major Berlin art exhibition of the previous year. The Revolution of 1848 saw a lively outcropping of liberal humor magazines, and Scholz contributed to the short-lived *Krakehler, Freie Blätter, Berliner Grossmaul* and others, besides illustrating political posters.

Bismarck and Napoleon III painting dark pictures of each other.
Wilhelm Scholz, 1869.

His work did not appear in the equally new *Kladderadatsch* (the name was humorously onomatopoeic, representing the crash of a falling object) until its second issue. Scholz, however, was already familiar with its publisher, Albert Hofmann (who had brought out his 1847 volume) and, through political club life, with its editors, David Kalisch, Ernst Dohm and Rudolf L6wenstein, and once on the staff, he was a fixture for life.

In *Kladderadatsch's* first decades, the pictorial matter was generally subordinate to the text, more illustrative than truly inventive; nor can Scholz's style honestly be called suave or polished. Still, he displayed boundless energy and all the imagination that the situation demanded. As 19th-century events unfurled, the two giants in Europe, from the point of view of a German political cartoonist (although Scholz attacked social problems as well), turned out to be Napoleon Ill and Bismarck, and Scholz became famous for his treatment of them. In the case of Bismarck, he reflected the ambivalent attitude of the liberals toward the man who was finally achieving German unification, though at the cost of civil liberties; Scholz created many of the "trademarks" and visual metaphors that were to be used for decades as standard representations of Bismarck.

The artist had many other interests and hobbies that made him a charming member of the Berlin society of his day. In the 1850s, for instance, he designed witty theatrical costumes for local productions, and in the 1870s he hobnobbed with the Berlin musicians who championed the advanced cause of Wagner. Scholz died in Berlin on June 20, 1893.

S.A.

SCHRÖDTER, ADOLF (1805-1875) German cartoonist and painter born at Schwedt an der Oder on June 28, 1805. Schrödter's father, a commercial artist, died when Adolf was very young, but the boy's artistic vocation was already determined. *By* 1820 he was enrolled at the Berlin Academy. A humorist throughout his career, Schr6dter became known in the 1820s for his outstanding comic lithographs of Berlin life, particularly the two series *Berliner Volksszenen* ("Scenes of Everyday Life in Berlin") and *Charakteristische Fuhrwerke* ("Typical Conveyances").

When the artist and professor Gottfried Schadow left Berlin for Düsseldoff in 1829, Schrödter followed him and started to paint oils, but even in this medium he specialized in parodies and witty genre and fantasy scenes. His finely executed etchings done at this time, with their intricate wreathing vines, gained him the sobriquet "King of the Arabesque." In 1840 he married Alwine Heuser (1820-92), who became known in her own right as a flower painter.

Also during his Düsseldorf years, Schrödter was an important contributor to the *Düsseldorfer Monatshefte*, probably the best German humor magazine after Munich's *Fliegende Blätter* in the 1840s and 1850s. Supported by the liberal industrialists of the Rhineland, the *Manatshefte* was even more radical and more addicted to personal satire than the Bavarian periodical.

By the late 1840s, Schrödter was discouraged with German affairs and had lost his verve. In 1848, planning to emigrate to the New World, he got as far as London when his love of country brought him back to Germany, specifically to Frankfurt am Main. In this city, where a pan-German constituent assembly was being held in the wake of the revolutions that had swept across Europe in February and March, Schrödter was inspired to compose what the art historian Eduard Fuchs called "one of the most outstanding creations in political caricature of all time": *Thaten und Meinungen des Herrn Piepmeyer* ("Mr. Piepmeyer's Deeds and Opinions"). These studies of an ambitious political opportunist with no mind of his own are also an important milestone in the history of narrative art and the prehistory of the comic strip.

In 1859 Schrödter was called to the Karlsruhe Polytechnicum, where he taught freehand drawing until shortly before his death on December 9, 1875. Influenced by Dürer (Schrödter did marginal illustrations to several books in the style of Dürer's prayer book for Maximilian I), as well as by Holbein, Callot, Chodowiecki and very probably Töpffer, Schrödter in turn influenced a number of younger German artists, including Hosemann and Menzel, who in his youth did lithographs after works by Schrödter.

S.A.

Herr Piepmeyer practicing oratory.
Adolf Schrödter.

The car pool: "I was speeding down to the police station to buy tickets for the policemen's ball before they are all gone."
John Schuffert. © Army Times.

SCHUFFERT, JOHN H. (1919-) American cartoonist born in New Castle, Pennsylvania, on December 19, 1919. Jake Schuffert is the U.S. Air Force's most famous and popular cartoonist. As a child he endlessly copied drawings from the newspaper comics. His own favorite, and the greatest influence on his work, was Bill Holman's Smokey Stover. One can see the influence in the skinny legs and big stomachs of the characters in Jake Schuffert's cartoons. His cartoons first began appearing during the Berlin airlift in 1948.

Schuffert joined what was then called the U.S. Army Air Corps in late November 1941, just a week before Pearl Harbor and America's entry into World War II. He had graduated from high school a year before and "just hung around for a year." On December 31, 1962, he retired from the U.S. Air Force as a chief master sergeant, the most senior enlisted rank. He is now a civilian employee in the audiovisual department of Bolling Air Force Base, Washington, D.C.

During World War II, Schuffert was a radioman and gunner on B-24 Liberator long-range bombers. He flew 50 missions over Africa and Europe before "we were clobbered over Ploesti and managed to sputter as far back as Yugoslavia." With others from the crippled aircraft, he parachuted to safety, and with the help of partisans he was able to return to the American forces. He served the rest of the war in the Pacific theater. Most of his cartooning during the war was for his own amusement; he also painted innumerable pinup girls on the sides of aircraft, including his own bomber, *Pistol-Packin' Mama.* Schuffert was on active flying duty for 14 years of his air force career. In 1948 he was a radio operator on General William Tunner's aircraft while the general commanded the Berlin airlift.

When not flying, Jake Schuffert drew cartoons for the regional command newspaper *Taskforce Times*. The wide-circulation air force weekly tabloid *Air Force Times* soon began publishing his panel cartoons. He's been with them ever since as a weekly feature, now reaching over 400,000 military men and their families. The panel at first appeared without title and was named No Sweat during the Korean War. He was also a staff artist with *Stars and Stripes,* the most important of all American military newspapers, during the Korean War. *Air* Force Times, which is a civilian commercial enterprise has also published four paperback collections of *No Sweat* that have sold about 150,000 copies each. In 1966 the *Airman,* the official air force public relations slick magazine, began publishing a full page of his gag cartoons under the title *It Counts for Thirty.* In 1973 the title was changed to *Here's Jake.* He continued to draw his panel *Here's Jake* through Operation Desert Storm in 1991. Though now semi-retired he plans to go on cartooning "until he's assigned to that big Air Force hanger in the sky."

Jake Schuffert's style is loose, with characters grossly exaggerated in true big-foot fashion. He often uses Craftint paper for his benday patterns in shading. He was the first military cartoonist to receive the Pat-on-the-Back award from the Joint Armed Services Office of Information.

B.C.

SCHWIND, MORITZ VON (1804-1871) Austrian painter, graphic artist and cartoonist born in Vienna, Austria, on January 21, 1804. Not until the early 1820s, after the death of his father, a diplomat attached to the Austrian court, was Moritz von Schwind able to follow his inclination and study art at the Vienna Academy. At the same time he began to draw for magazines and became part of Franz Schubert's circle, which included Schwind's lifelong friend, the composer and conductor Franz Lachner. In 1828 Schwind moved to Munich to study the art of historical fresco painting with the illustrious Peter van Cornelius, and it was this aristocratic and somewhat arid genre that brought him his major commissions through the years; Schwind's paintings were to cover walls and ceilings in the Munich Residenz, Karlsruhe, the Wartburg and the Vienna Opera House.

Nevertheless, he was always interested in caricatures and cartoons, and he created some memorable ones. As early as 1824 he did an excellent lithographic series called *Verlegenheiten* ("Embarrassing Moments"), and in Karlsruhe in the 1840s official pressure was brought to bear on him because of his liberal political cartoons. However, his genius in this area did not flower fully until he moved to Munich in 1847 to become a professor at the Art Academy. From 1848 to 1858 he furnished numerous fine cartoons for Braun and Schneider's *Fliegende Blätter,* by far the best German humor magazine of the time. These cartoons included political items (slaps at the reactionary rulers of Austria and at Bavarian king Ludwig I's infatuation with Lola Montez), fantasy drawings of animated trees aud objects à la Grandville, social satire, and such tours de force of draftsmanship as the 18-image series depicting a trio of acrobats in the most intricate poses.

For Braun and Schneider's less satirical, "folk-style" picture series *Münchener Bilderbogen,* Schwind's exquisite

Der Teufel und die Katz

Düstere Ahnungen durchbebten Mausbeisias Busen; sie sah bald, aber zu spät ein, daß sie einem Ungethüme das Leben geschenkt, welches jetzt offen die Larve wegwarf, grinsend die Peitsche über ihr schwang, und sie in Netze zog, aus denen kein Entrinnen mehr war

In einer finstern stürmischen Nacht erscholl aus Mausbeisias Hause ein entsetzliches Wehgeschrei, und man will gesehen haben, daß ein grauenhaftes Gespenst, so einige für den Teufel selbst gehalten, die Katze durch die Luft davon geführt habe

Moral.

Nimm keinen Teufel in dein Haus, auch wenn er noch so klein wäre, denn er wird dir über den Kopf wachsen und dich verderben.

Moritz von Schwind, illustrations for a fairy tale, 1847.

work included the 1847 series *Herr Winter,* in which he created the enduring visualization of the German *Weihnachtsmann* ("Father Christmas"), much as Nast was later to crystallize the American image of Santa Claus. The comic masterpiece of Schwind's later years was an unusual pen drawing in honor of his old friend Lachner. The "Lachner-Rolle" of 1862 was a single strip of paper over forty feet long on which Schwind celebrated Lachner's entire life and musical career in a protocomic-strip style reminiscent of Töpffer's work, though much more brilliantly drawn. Schwind died in Munich on February 8, 1871.

S.A.

SCISSORS SKETCHES (U.S.) An important cartoon series that reflected the contrast between British social customs and cartooning styles and those of the United States, *Scissors Sketches* debuted in the pages of *Life* with the issue of February 6, 1896, and ran through the issue of April 30, 1896.

The series very cleverly combined actual figures from various cartoons by *Life's* Charles Dana Gibson and Punch's George Du Maurier; the competent inbetween work was evidently done by a *Life* staffer. The series subtitle was "Anglo-American vignettes- introducing a new mechanical process by which the familiar creations of two widely different schools of illustration are forced to meet and exchange views." In addition to the contrast in styles—Gibson's art was slicker and more lithe, Du Maurier's reminiscent of woodcut reproduction-the captions dealt with the rivalry between American and British society by touching on such themes as marrying for a title, the English sense of humor, etc.

The cartoons were signed "Scissors, del." (*delineavit,* "he wrote"), an amusing *nom de plume* that at the same time rendered unto Scissor the things that were Scissor's.

R.M.

SCORFIELD, EDWARD SCAFE (1884-1968) Australian cartoonist born in North Shields, England, in 1884. In 1925, the *Sydney Bulletin* brought Ted Scorfield from England, primarily to express the *Bulletin*'s editorial policy. Scorfield, an ex-soldier who was with the Engineers at Gallipoli and later a draftsman with a Newcastle-on-Tyne shipbuilding firm, was a freelance artist in London at the time. He had been selected by David Low, then working in London, as the best applicant among the English artists who had responded to a *Bulletin* advertisement for a leader cartoonist.

"Take no notice of them blokes, choom.
You'll be jist like one of us in no time."

Ted Scorfield, 1940. © Sydney Bulletin.

Scorfield first drew cartoons on his shipping-company desk and regarded Phil May as his ideal. It was May who, on returning to London in the late 1880s after three years as a Bulletin staff artist, had devised a radical new approach of dash and simplicity. Although Scorfield soon developed his own personal drawing style, May was always his inspiration. Like the other political cartoonists of the *Bulletin*—Norman Lindsay, David Low and Percy Leason—Ted Scorfield drew a large number of joke drawings during the 36 years he stayed with the *Bulletin.*

Scorfield's draftsmanship is hard to fault. His original and distinctive comic style was expressed with pen and drybrush, a technique whereby the artist partly dries his inked brush on paper before applying it to his drawing. The effect, which is similar to crayon on a grained paper, requires skilled control. Scorfield used it perfectly for his strong, rugged, interesting drawings of political comment, for his humorous cartoons of the city slums and the outback farm and for his favorite subject-animals, especially dogs.

The Bulletin had declined in influence since the 1930s; perhaps because of this decline the principal reference works have neglected Scarfield, although he was acknowledged in the massive ten- volume 1958 edition of the *Australian Encyclopedia.* Two collections of his Bulletin joke drawings were published in book form, *A Mixed Grill* (1943) and *A Mixed Grill No. 2* (1944). He was the last of the practicing Australian cartoonists working in the tradition and challenge of sound drawing. Scorfield's books record many examples of his superb draftsmanship and his significant contribution to Australian graphic humor. Ted Scarfield retired in June 1961 at age 77. He died in 1968.

V.L.

SCRAMBLED HISTORY (U.S.) Utilizing historical figures is a ready-made device for cartoonists, and one done to death by magazine artists around the turn of the century. But in 1924 the redoubtable Ralph Briggs Fuller played perhaps the cleverest variation on the theme with his *Scrambled History* for *Judge.* In the series, always rendered in wash and running a full page, two famous figures met in ironic, ridiculous or embarrassing situations. Fuller skillfully wrung all he could from the rich potential, and his artwork was always detailed and superb.

Beginning with the issue of February 2, 1924, Paul Revere meets Lady Godiva, William Tell shoots an apple being dropped by Isaac Newton onto Barbara Frietchie's head, Nero fiddles as the Liberty Boys march, Washington passes Cleopatra's barge on the Delaware and Samson saves the day at Waterloo. Other misalliances followed: Lucrezia Borgia and Richard the Lion-Hearted; Ponce de Ledn and Methuselah; King Solomon, Brigham Young and their respective wives; the Queen of Sheba and Ben Franklin; St. George, the Dragon and Noah's Ark; Jonah and Chris Columbus. The series also featured Sir Walter Raleigh covering up Salame's seventh veil, Delilah getting after the Smith brothers, Horatius at the Brooklyn Bridge, Al Jolson in the Roman Coliseum, W.J. Bryan with the Omar Khayyams, George M. Cohan charging up San Juan Hill, King Canute surrounded by bathing beauties, Babe Ruth disabling a battery at Bull Run, Henry Ford encountering Ben Hur, and Ben Turpin staring dawn the lions in Daniel's den.

Unfortunately, the series was never compiled in book form; Fuller remains one of the most prominent unanthologized American cartoonists.

R.M.

SCRAPPY (U.S.) *Scrappy* was one of several series produced by Charles Mintz and released by Columbia in the 1930s. "Yelp Wanted" is the first recorded title, and it introduced the chief protagonists—the feisty little bay named Scrappy and the pup he had rescued from its tormentors. Scrappy's girl friend, Betty, joined the proceedings a short time later.

The series was clearly aimed at young children, and the plots were very simple. The titles say it all: "Scrappy's Auto Show" (1933), "Scrappy's Dog Show" (1934), "Scrappy's Ghost Story" (1935), "Scrappy's Side Show" (1939), etc. Mintz (or someone at his studio) must have had a science fiction streak in him, accounting for such entries as "Scrappy's Television" (in 1934 yet) and the innovative "Scrappy's Trip to Mars" (1938).

Some of the directors who worked on the series, such as Art Davis, Sid Marcus, Harry Love and Dick Huemer, later went on to better things. After Mintz's death in 1939 the studio was taken over by Screen Gems/Columbia, and the *Scrappy* cartoons were discontinued.

M.H.

SEARLE, RONALD WILLIAM FORDHAM (1920-) British cartoonist, painter, designer, author, animator and creator of St. Trinian's, the world's wickedest school for girls, born in Cambridge, England, on March 3, 1920. Ronald Searle studied art at the Cambridge School of Art (1935-39) while working in a solicitor's office. He was fired from the latter for drawing on the briefs.

His first cartoon, sent on "spec," was published in the *Cambridge Daily News* when he was 15. He became a regular contributor and dedicated his collection *Hurrah for St. Trinian's* to "Morley Stuart, 30 years Editor of the *Cambridge Daily News,* who published my first 200 drawings." Within a year or two Searle was having cartoons accepted by many magazines of that prewar period: *Lilliput, Men Only, London Opinion* (which featured him in its profile series by Percy V. Bradshaw, "They Make Us Smile").

Ronald Searle. © Searle.

Nineteen when World War II broke out, Searle went into the Royal Engineers. He was able to continue his art in the camouflage section before being sent to Singapore in 1941. One month later capitulation made him a prisoner of war, and for three and a half years he continued to sketch his experiences through the terrible times of the Changi Railway and Changi Gaol. Demobilized in 1946, he returned to England and married Kaye Webb, an assistant editor of *Lilliput.* The 300 drawings he had made during his incarceration, often with inks made from dyes and an any scrap of salvageable paper, were successfully hidden from his captors' eyes and brought home to farm an exhibition and a book.

In the postwar period his highly individual style of cartoaning became popular with both magazine editors and advertisers alike, and his posters for Lemon Hart rum, etc., became instant classics. America became interested, and major magazines including *Holiday, Life* and the *New Yorker* commissioned him to illustrate covers and special travel features. His Punch cartoons date from 1949, and he joined the staff in 1956 as a theatrical cartoonist. He began designing far films in 1957, and an experimental animated cartoon he made in America received 11 awards. In 1960 he was invited by the United Nations high commissioner for refugees to visit camps in Austria, Greece and Italy, and draw his impressions.

In 1961 Searle decided to live permanently in Paris, France, where in 1973 he became the first foreign artist to have an exhibition of work at the Bibliothèque Natianale. In 1975 a major documentary film, *A Step in the Jungle,* was made about him by BBC television, truly justifying the remark made on the nine-year-old Searle's school report in July 1929: "Drawing and Painting, V. Good Indeed." Now well into his seventies Searle is as active as ever. As he laconically stated in his bio to the 1996 edition of the National Cartoonists Society Album, "Began freelancing in 1935 and...still at it."

Books: *Forty Drawings* (1946); *Le Nouveau Ballet Anglais* (1947); *Hurrah for St. Trinian's* (1948); *The Female Approach* (1949); *Back to the Slaughterhouse* (1951); *The Naked Island* (1951); *An Evening at the Larches* (1951); *London So Help Me* (1952); *The Terrors of St. Trinian's* (1952); *John Gil pin* (1952); *Souls in Torment* (1953); *Looking at London* (1953); *Modern Types* (1955); *The Rake's Progress* (1955); *Merry England* (1956); *Paris Sketchbook* (1957); *The Big City* (1958); *USA far Beginners* (1959); *The St. Trinian's Story* (1959); *Russia far Beginners* (1960); *Refugees* (1960); *The Penguin Ronald Searle* (1960); *Which Way Did He Go?* (1961); *A Christmas Carol* (1961); *Oliver Twist* (1962); *Great Expectations* (1962); *Escape from the Amazon* (1964); *From Frozen North to Filthy Lucre* (1964); *Searle in the Sixties* (1964); *Exploring London* (1965); *Those Magnificent Men in Their Flying Machines* (1965); *Searle's Cats* (1967); *Hello, Where Did All the People Go?* (1969); and *Secret Sketchbook* (1970).

D.G.

SEAVEY, DAVID EARLE (1936-) American editorial cartoonist and artist born in York, Maine, on August 26, 1936. Raised in Rochester, New Hampshire, David Seavey received a scholarship to attend the School of Visual Arts

David Seavey, 1976. © *National Observer.*

in New York after winning first prize in the 1954 National Scholastic Art Competition. In 1961, Seavey joined the staff of the new Dow-Jones national news weekly, *National Observer.* The independent cartoonist remained there as staff artist until its demise, contributing a steady flaw of striking editorial cartoons and illustrations; the *Observer's* format frequently gave him broad areas to fill. In the late 1980s Seavey was appointed the titular editorial cartoonist for *USA Today*.

Seavey has been influenced by Heinrich Kley, Norman Rockwell, Albert Darne and Walt Kelly. The common factors in all these artists-technical brilliance, humor and commentary-are easily recognizable in Seavey's editorial drawings.

R.M.

SEIBEL, FREDERICK OT'TO (1886-1969) American cartoonist barn in Durhamville, Oneida County, New York, on October 8, 1886. Frederick Seibel was educated in local schools and studied art in New York at the Art Students League from 1905 to 1907; among his teachers in New York and elsewhere were Kenyon Cox, Howard Pyle and Albert Sterner. Seibel entered the art field in 1911, taking a jab with an advertising agency in Utica, New York; in 1915 he moved to the Utica *Herald-Dispatch.* The next year Seibel began a ten-year stint as editorial cartoonist an the *Albany Knickerbocker-Press,* where he and his mascot (a bespectacled little crow bearing a resemblance to the cartoonist) attracted attention. The much-reprinted Seibel switched to the *Richmond* (Va.) *Times Dispatch* in 1926 and remained there until a year before his death an June 18, 1969.

Seibel only occasionally used crayon shading; the bulk

Under the Mistletoe.
F.O. Seibel. © Richmond Times-Dispatch.

of his work was rendered in impressive, strong, lush pin strokes. He had a master's sense of shading and spotted blacks very well. The mascot was a holdover from the days when practically no political cartoonist was without one; Seibel was a bridge between that era and Oliphant's later reintroduction of the gimmick.

R.M.

SEM
See Goursat, Georges.

SEMPÉ, JEAN-JACQUES (1932-) French cartoonist, poster artist and set designer born in Bordeaux, France, an August 17, 1932. Jean-Jacques Sempé began his career in 1950, first contributing drawings to the local weekly *Sud-Ouest Dimanche* under the pen-name "Drô," then, under his own name, to *Ici Paris, France-Dimanche, L'Express, Punch, Elle, Life, Sports Illustrated,* the Op-Ed page of the *New York Times,* etc. His publicity posters include ChryslerSimca, Shell and Au Printemps. He has also done several animated cartoon commercials for a French candy company (1962).

Most of Sempé's work has been reissued in albums, more or less on an annual basis. The most important and funniest are *Rien N'est Simple* ("In France, Nothing Is Simple," 1962), *M. Lambert* (1965), *Des Hauts* et *des Bas* ("From Highs and Laws," 1970) and *L'Ascensian Saciale* de *M. Lambert* ("Mr. Lambert's Social Climb," 1975). He has also collaborated with René Goscinny (of *Astérix* fame) on a series of books relating the amusing adventures of Young Nicolas and his friends (1960-64).

Like Dubout, Sempé is fascinated by crowds, not, however, far their hilarious confusion but as minuscule nanentities lost in a cavernous department stare, at the terrace of a café, on a long waiting line or at the bus stop at rush hour. His characters are pompous, phony intellectuals, unhappy husbands and wives forever dreaming of killing one another, presidents happy to be loved by crowds rushing for the subway entrance, *nauveaux riches* who have not quite forgotten their petty origins. Even children have something of the naughty if not downright nasty, as with the kid who makes the ugliest and most disgusting faces in a mirror, until the last drawing reveals not a mirror but a picture of his parents. His cartoons all have a beautiful balance among protagonists, setting and action, with the right dramatic buildup for maximum suspense, impact and euphoric explosion of laughter.

Jean-Jacques Sempé has exhibited his work in museums and art galleries all over the world and received numerous prizes. In 1988 French critic Jérome Garcin said of him: "Paragon of elegance, as refined in life as he is in his albums, Sempé is slowly taking the road toward that smiling misanthropy to which, without fanfare or pronouncement, the last irreducible opponents to the leveling of art and soul are pushed against at the close of this century."

P.H.

SENATOR SOUNDER (U.S.) Gluyas Williams's early contributions to *Life* were well received, but his desire for a reputation was helped immeasurably by a cartoon series he introduced shortly after joining the staff. Senator Sounder was in many ways a holdover from his days on the *Harvard Lampoon,* where he wrote as much as he drew.

Jean-Jacques Sempé. © Samedi-Soir.

Sounder started in *Life's* issue of May 27, 1920, in a six-panel cartoon entitled "If Senators Talked at Home As They Do in Congress"; the senator was not named yet, but the Sounder prototype pompously extolled the merits, demerits, ramifications and patriotic imperatives of having a second cup of coffee as his wife progressively sank into a deep sleep. On his next appearance, in the July 22 *Life,* he was accompanied by a biographical blurb wherein he was christened. On August 19 a "campaign biography" appeared, and thereafter the full-page six-panel cartoon came out regularly. On January 13, 1921, Williams took to the typewriter and began ghosting a weekly column by Senator Sounder on Washington doings. Each column was filled with illustrations that displayed, by the way, Williams's unfailing talent for caricature- Senators Lodge, Borah and Johnson were frequently present, as was President Harding.

Sounder was an overblown know-nothing who could ramble far hours on subjects of no interest to anybody; he completely misinterpreted the major currents of political and social thought; he committed frequent blunders, such as thinking that applause intended for a colleague was meant for some idiot pronouncement of his own. Williams's brilliant pen portrayed him as a flamboyant orator in frock coat and pince-nez.

The series proved popular and even got Williams an abortive assignment to cover Washington from the capital itself for the Hearst newspapers. In 1924 it began appearing with less frequency and was probably no longer written (only illustrated) by Williams. Sounder's last august jeremiad, on October 9, 1924, was a rousing denunciation of that year's presidential campaign-he failed to get the nomination himself.

Apart from its outstanding caricatures and real humor, the series has great value today as a consistently clever satirical examination of the postwar "normalcy" period.

R.M.

SENESI, VAURO (1955-) Italian political cartoonist born in Pistoia on March 24, 1955, better known by his Christian and art name Vauro. He started his career on the pages of the graphic humor magazine *Help* (1976 and 1978) and then contributed to *Linus, Satyricon* (1981), and *Zut* (1987).

Since 1985 he has been the editorial cartoonist of the newspaper *Il manifesto* which describes itself as a "Communist daily". In the 1990s he has contributed also to the satirical periodicals *Cuore* (1994), *Il clandestino* (1994-1995) and *Boxer* since its beginning in 1997. Vauro's political satire is based on single panel cartoons and on comic strip pages. His graphic sign is simple and swift, but effective. His satire is often outrageous. It has been said that "Vauro's cartoons are like a belch...healthy."

Vauro has illustrated Bucchi's book *Mille e non più mille,* and part of his graphic work has been collected in book format: *Cotti e mangiati* (1986), *La satira alla guerra* (1991), *Vita e morte della DC* (1992), *Foglio di via* (1993), *Il papa è morto* (1997).

In 1996 he was awarded the Prize Forte dei Marmi for Political Satire.

G.C.C.

Vauro Senesi ("Vauro"). © Vauro Senesi.

SENNEP
See Pennès, Jean.

SENYA ICHI NO MONOGATARI (Japan) *Senya Ichi no Managatari,* released in English under the title *A Thousand and One Nights,* is a feature-length adult animated cartoon made in Japan by Mushi Productions. First released in June 1969, this full-color 130-minute film was produced by Osamu Tezuka, then president of Mushi Productions. Tezuka also wrote the script in conjunction with Ichia Fukuzawa, with the avowed goal of creating "Animerama'—an animated film that adults could enjoy. This and other works earned Tezuka the title "God of Manga" after his death.

The plot is actually an amalgam of several stories from the *Arabian Nights* ("Ali Baba and the Forty Thieves," "Sinbad the Sailor" and others). Strains of the *Odyssey* and the Old Testament are also apparent. Aldene, the protagonist (whose face is amusingly modeled after that of Jean-Paul Belmanda), arrives in Baghdad destitute, only to fall madly in love with a beautiful slave named Miriam, who is being auctioned off that day. During a freak sandstorm he seizes his chance and kidnaps the girl, but after one blissful night with her he is seized and imprisoned. He finally escapes, and many adventures ensue; Aldene becomes wealthy, becomes Sinbad and also, amazingly, becomes king of Baghdad. In the interim, Miriam dies, but not before bearing a beautiful daughter named Jalice—unbeknownst to Sinbad. Sinbad nearly falls into an inces-

"Senya Ichi no Monogatari." © Mushi Productions.

tuous relationship with his own daughter, sees his kingdom literally crumble and, as Aldene once mare, strikes out to make a new life.

Notwithstanding same weaknesses in the plot, *A Thousand and One Nights* is a surprisingly beautiful, erotic and at times hilarious cartoon with outstanding color artwork and composition. It also makes excellent use in places of animation mixed with live-action shots. The score is superb. The opening scenes of Aldene trudging into Baghdad to a rock beat are particularly dramatic and beautifully timed, with music composed by Isao Tamita to create an atmosphere of sensuality and anticipation. Credit should also be given to the film's chief animatar, Kazuko Nakamura.

F.S.

SERAFIN
See Rojo Camano, Serafin.

SERVAIS, RAOUL (1928-) Belgian animator born in Ostend, Belgium, on May 1, 1928. Raaul Servais's father had built up a small film library, and the young boy became entranced by Charlie Chaplin shorts and *Felix* the Cat cartoons at an early age. His love of drawing led him to enroll at the Royal Academy of Fine Arts in Ghent in 1946, and he graduated four years later with the highest honors.

Servais's first foray into animation came in 1946, when he made a short called Ghost Story under the direction of his teacher, André Vermeiren. In following years he produced three mare films, the popular *The Sandman* (1951), the more avant-garde *Parallel* (1952) and *Painter's Hodgepodge,* a documentary. After a fruitless trip to England in search of animation work, Servais came back to Belgium and in the next years devoted himself to drawing and painting, with modest success. In 1955 he worked as assistant on Henri Storck's film Le *Trésor d'Ostende* ("Treasure of Ostend"). But Servais never lost his love for animation, and he released his most significant work to date in 1960: *Harbor Lights,* which won a number of awards. Thus encouraged, Servais followed with The *False* Note (1963), *Chromaphabia* (1965, an interest- ing experiment with color), *La Sirène* ("Mermaid,"1968) and Goldframe (also 1968).

Servais further asserted himself with a series of stunning films that he produced in the 1970s, notably *To Speak or Not to Speak,* a somber allegory of totalitarianism (1971), and *Operation X-70* (1972), a dark parable of nuclear annihilation. In recent years Servais has also made a number of advertising cartoons, including the prize-winning *La Sclérase Calcaire* (1975). He was head of animation an Jacques Kuprissanaff's feature-length film *L'Amour en Liberté* ("Love at Liberty," 1978), and he teaches animation at his old alma mater in Ghent. Among his latter films the most notable are *Le Big Bang* (a political satire, 1987), and especially *Taxandria,* his first first feature-length animated

Raoul Servais, "Goldframe." © Servais.

picture, a surrealistic tale combining legend and political allegory which took him ten years to complete (1984-94).

Servais's films have wan countless awards and distinctions, and he himself is one of the most respected figures in European animation today.

M.H.

SETH, VIJAY N. (1944-   ) Vijay N. Seth, more commonly known as "Vins," was born March 10, 1944, in New Delhi, India. One of India's most prominent cartoonists, Vins is equally at home drawing illustrations, painting, or lecturing to art students, the wide spectrum of jobs necessitated by the scarcity of full-time cartooning positions in India. His work has appeared in dozens of Indian and European periodicals, including *Reader's Digest* and *Nebelspalter*.

Vins knew in high school that he wanted to be a cartoonist; he was further inspired upon receiving an "A+" in a cartooning correspondence course out of Westport, Connecticut. His first published cartoon appeared in *Caravan* in 1965, while he was a student at the Sir J.J. School of Art in Bombay. About the same time, he began submitting a weekly pocket cartoon to *Himmat* where he was staff cartoonist for 17 years. An agreement Vins had with *Himmat* allowed him to submit cartoons to other periodicals, and from 1978-1982, he did gag cartoons for the Swiss tabloid *Treffpunkt*. After leaving *Himmat* in the early 1980s, Vins contributed regular political and pocket cartoons to the daily *Indian Express* (1983-1987) and corporate gag cartoons to in-house magazines of leading industrial companies (1985 - present).

To make a living through a multitude of sources, Vins employs diverse styles, techniques, and materials, most recently, charcoal and pastels. His works often are deceptively casual, easy-on-the-eye cartoons that avoid captions and detail, expressly to appeal to a larger segment of the common mass audience. Inspired by Virgil Partch (VIP), even to the extent of using a similar pen-name, Vins has been likened to McLachlan of *Punch* fame.

J.A.L.

SEUSS, DR.
See Geisel, Theodore.

SGRILLI, ROBERTO (1899-1985) Italian cartoonist and animatar born in Florence, Italy, in 1899. After graduating from high school in 1906, Roberta Sgrilli started his career as a cartoonist and illustrator far several publications in his native Tuscany. He later contributed cartoons to national publications such as Bertoldo. In the 1930s he transferred to Milan and started working far *Il* Corriere dei *Piccali*. Beginning in 1936, he drew a comic strip, *Farmicchina* ("Little Ant"), that was strongly inspired by Walt Disney's *Silly Symphonies*. Sgrilli's style was fresh, cheerful and full of movement, and these qualities helped set him apart from the numerous Disney imitators who were springing up all over Italy at the time.

In 1940, with the Disney cartoons progressively disappearing from Italian screens, Sgrilli was asked to pro- duce in Agfacalor an animated short for domestic consumption; this cartoon, titled *Anacleto e* la *Faina* ("Anacleto and the Marten"), was released the next year. It told the amusing tale of a mother hen and her chicks (the black one was named Anacleta) threatened by a ravenaus marten whose feraciausness equalled that of Disney's Big Bad Wolf.

"Attention squad! By four to the parade!"
(To hear Gigino, you'd think he was commanding an army.)
Roberto Sgrilli. © Sgrilli.

In addition to cartoons, comic strips and animated films, Sgrilli also drew many book and magazine illustrations. He is best noted in this respect for the illustrations adorning the covers of a great many schoolchildren's notebooks. He retired in the mid-1970s and died in 1985.

S.T.

SHANKS, BRUCE McKINLEY (1908-) American cartoonist born in Buffalo, New York, on January 29, 1908. Raised in Buffalo, Bruce Shacks secured a jab with the *Buffalo Express as* a capyboy-cartoanist just after graduation from high school. Two years later he became a regular cartoonist far the *Buffalo Times,* and four years later, in 1933, he joined the *Evening News,* where he remained as political cartoonist. He retired from full-time cartoaning in 1974 and freelanced about one cartoon a month to the *News* from his home in Florida until his retirement in the 1980s.

Shanks's cartoons are rendered in brush and ink, with crayon shading on grained paper. The influence of Vaughn Shoemaker is much in evidence, although Shanks's products are drawn a little mare stiffly, with a firmer line and less detail. Among his many awards (Freedoms Foundation, Christopher, National Safety Council) is the Pulitzer Prize of 1958 far work done the previous year.

R.M.

SHAVER, JAMES R. (1867-1949) American cartoonist born in Reed's Creek, Arkansas, in 1867. J. R. Shaver studied at the St. Louis School of Fine Arts and the Drexel Institute of

Blind Man's Bluff
Bruce Shanks. © Buffalo Evening News.

Philadelphia. Beginning around the turn of the century, he began appearing in *Life* magazine, an association that was to continue for nearly thirty years. At the same time, his one-panel pen-and-ink cartoons were staples of the humorous columns in *Scribner's, Century, Harper's Monthly* and *St. Nicholas.*

Shaver's style was invariably one of scratchy pen lines in seeming disarray, although they blended for a total shading effect-the look achieved by Franklin Booth with his pen, but with far less discipline in the case of Shaver. Shaver seemed to take up the mantle of Michael Angela Woolf at the turn of the century; the great majority of his drawings featured street urchins and ragamuffin city kids. They were less personal than Woolf's and certainly less hauntingly compelling; they also lacked the wise-guy attributes of Percy Crosby's creations in the next generation. But they were real and realistically portrayed; like the *Peanuts* crew, they seldom shared their panels with adults, which gave a special-world atmosphere to the weekly cartoons. In the 1920s, *Life* frequently ran the crasshatched drawings over two pages, in a way vitiating the concentrated look that reduction otherwise brought. Around the same time, Shaver also did occasional covers, again an kid themes.

Shaver died on December 23, 1949, at his residence in New York's Chelsea Hotel.

R.M.

Where Danger Hurts
James Shaver, 1900. *© Century Magazine.*

SHEN TIANCHENG (1946-) A self-taught cartoonist, Shen Tiancheng was born in Shanghai in 1946 and was a worker in the Shanghai Steel Plant before starting his career as a cartoonist in the year that the ten-year "Cultural Revolution" was finally ended (1977). When the news of the arrest of the "Gang of Four" spread, thousands of cartoons pointing at the crimes committed by the infamous four were created and posted in the streets. Shen was among the many enthusiastic "artists" who took part, and since that time his interest in cartooning has never flagged. After he had published over 1,000 cartoons in various media, his talent was discovered by Hong Huang, then editor of one of the most authoritative newspapers published in Shanghai, *Wenhui Bao.* Since 1983 Shen has been working as its art editor.

As with most of the cartoonists in China, the topics of Shen's cartoons involve political satire or societal humor. In that respect the comparison between the two most famous cartoonists in Shanghai, Shen Tiancheng and Zheng Xinyao, is very instructive. Shen's work is still rooted in the traditional belief in China that cartooning should be based on life, albeit presented in an abstract, stylized way. His cartoons reflect real facets and events from reality, but with an unexpected punch line. In contrast, most of

Outside Exeter Hall: animal spirits.

W.J.A. Shepherd. © Punch.

Zheng's work is filled with much imagination and exaggeration, and its source may be found in dreams but never in real life.

H.Y.L.L.

SHEN TONGHENG (1914-) Under the penname Stone, Shen has been known as an active cartoonist immediately after he graduated from Shanghai Xinhua Art School in the summer of 1937, the year when the Sino-Japanese War broke out. He and other cartoonists persisted in agitating the Japanese invasion by organizing the Salvation Cartoon Propaganda Team to mobilize the masses in the cities and villages when the Team passed through from Shanghai to

Shen Tiancheng. © Shen Tiancheng.

年年一厚本
——谁说我长年不翻书？

沈同衡

Shen Tongheng

A thick volume every year —
"Who says I never ~~(turn book-pages!")~~ read books!"

Shen Tongheng. © Shen Tongheng.

the South and ended up in Hong Kong. Shen's cartoons were made in different media, depending on the circumstances, such as wood carving, large cloth, wall painting and leaflets. His cartoons were exhibited in Moscow in 1939 and republished by the Soviet *Literature Journal*. In 1945, Shen with Ye Qianyu, Liao Bingxiong and others organized the famous "Eight-Person Cartoon Exhibition" in Chongqing. At the same time, Shen edited the only existing cartoon publication named "Weekly Cartoons" in Chongqing, which actually resumed the function of the professional publication of the Chinese Cartoonist Association that was established in 1936.

During the Civil War of 1945-1949, Shen was the leading organizer of the underground "Cartoon Study Group by Workers and Students" against then the Guomindang government. The Group began in early 1947 in Shanghai, and Shen and some other well-known cartoonists—Ding Cong, Mi Gu, Yu Suoya, Zhang Wenyuan, Tao Mouji and Hong Huang—were the "teachers" for the "students" and the "lectures" were held in a very irregular manner. When the government censored and closed all the publications by the Communists, the Group tried to publicly advocate the anti-government movement by the only available means—cartoon exhibitions. The first such monthly exhibition was held in April 1948, in which 60 cartoons were made by the Group members and exhibited in tours of schools, universities and workers' unions, which gave great inspiration to the visitors. The second exhibition in May, however, was distributed by the Guomindang government and three student leaders were arrested and later sentenced for participating in the exhibition. This was the

"She wrote a letter to her congressman, and, well, there he is!"
Barbara Shermund. © Collier's.

well-known "Shanghai Cartoon Event" in Chinese history.

Shen, an active and well-respected cartoonist from the 1930s, was wrongly labeled as a "Rightist" in 1957 and expelled from his editor position at the *People's Daily*. After that time, Shen was forced to stop cartooning. In the "Cultural Revolution", he and his entire family were removed from Beijing to a farm in Xinjiang, where his right of having a pencil was taken away. In the late 1970s, he was able to return to Beijing, and he resumed cartoon activities, cartoon theory research and writing, and also the leadership in several professional organizations including the presidency of the Chinese Press Cartoon Society, until the time he became paralyzed in the early 1990s.

H.Y.L.L.

SHEPHERD, WILLIAM JAMES AFFLECK (1867-1946) British cartoonist and comic strip artist born in London, England, an November 29, 1867. "J.A.S." was the familiar signature to the cartoons and strips drawn by William Shepherd, one of the first English cartoonists to specialize in anthropomorphism, or "humanized animals."

After ordinary schooling, Shepherd studied art, and in particular caricature, under the tuition of the Victorian caricaturist Alfred Bryan. Attracted to animals, he spent three years at the zoological gardens in Regent's Park, emerging as a full-fledged animal painter and a Fellow of the Zoological Society. In 1891 he contributed the first of his *Zig-Zags at the Zoo,* a pictorial humor feature running to several pages of the *Strand Magazine.* An immediate success, *Zig-Zags* became a monthly feature and blossomed into a short series of animated cartoons produced by Kine Komedy Kartoans far Phillips Philm Phables in 1919. Other strip series he created were *Animal Actualities, Fables* (a fully developed visual strip in Strand, 1896) and The *Arcadian Calendar.* For awhile Shepherd served as a staff artist on Moonshine, a humorous weekly, and contributed cartoons to *Judy* and *Cassell's Magazine.* Then, in 1893, he received the call to *Punch* and served as a staff cartoonist on that illustrious weekly for 40 years. In 1911 he was awarded a gold medal at the International Exhibition of Humorous Art at Rivoli, Italy. His mare serious work was represented in an exhibition of his watercolors at Paterson's Gallery in May 1928. He died on May 11, 1946.

Books: *Zig-Zags at the Zoo (1895); Tommy at the Zoo* (1895); *Zig-Zag Fables* (1897); *Who Killed Cock Robin* (1900); *The Frog Who Would A-wooing Go* (1900); *A Thoroughbred Mongrel* (1900); *Uncle Remus* (1901); *Wonders in Mansterland* (1901); *The Donkey Book* (1903); *The Arcadian Calendar* (1903); *Old De- dick's Tales* (1904); *Funny Animals and Stories About Them* (1904); *Nights with Uncle Remus* (1907); *Three Jovial Puppies* (1908); *Life of a Foxhound* (1910); *Jack's Insects* (1910); *Zoo Conversation Book* (1911); *Badley Head Natural History* (1913); *Story of Chanticleer* (1913); *Jack's Other Insects* (1920); *Sang of the Birds* (1922); *A Frolic Round the Zoo* (1926); *Idlings in Arcadia* (1934); *and Animal Caricature* (1936).

D.G.

SHERMUND, BARBARA (1910?-1978) American cartoonist born in San Francisco, California, around 1910. Barbara Shermund received her art training at the California

School of Fine Arts, where she studied painting, sculpture, etching and design. In those days, one headed east rather than west to find fame and fortune in the world of art; no exception to the rule, Shermund moved to New York City. She repeatedly told herself that she did not intend to stay, but she nonetheless managed to eat up the money earmarked far her return trip and was forced to look for a jab. She first worked far the *New Yorker* doing spot illustration, department headings and covers. Her entrance into the field of cartooning came, she said, the day "I was told to write lines under my drawings." In Dale Kramer's *Ross and the New Yorker,* Shermund is remembered as a "pretty girl not long in from California (who) had a firm grip on the young ladies of the Jazz Age"—undoubtedly because she was one of them.

Although she was a contributor to all the major periodicals of the 1930s and 1940s, it was in the *New* Yorker that Shermund's swift, effortless grace of line and attention to detail came to maturity. Her work was almost breathlessly "feminine," reflecting the milieu of the young, pampered, usually upper-crust, at times spoiled and almost always boy-crazy flapper (Shermund's two female contemporaries, Alice Harvey and Helen Hokinson, also injected this quality into their work, each in her own way). In this, her ear proved as apt as her eye. Thus the two slender, long-limbed ingenues riding their bikes along a park lane or country road as one explains her tactics in what a colleague (James Thurber) was pleased to call "the war between men and women": "Then l wrote him an awfully nasty letter but, you know, cute."

As of 1972, Shermund was still a regular contributor to King Features Syndicate, though her art no longer showed the facility and inspiration that characterized her best work for the *New Yorker.* She died in 1978.

R.C.

SHERRIFFS, ROBERT STEWART (1907-1961) British caricaturist and cartoonist born in Scotland in 1907. Robert Sherriffs studied art and heraldic design at the Edinburgh College of Arts, but realistic representation of figures and landscapes meant little to him. His special fascination with design and ornament reduced faces and figures to patterns, and through this technique he developed a new and intriguing style of portrait caricature. Coming to London, he spent his time visiting theaters and cinemas and caricaturing the stars he saw; within a month he had sold his first "decorative caricature" to the Bystander, an upper- class weekly. His subject was film star John Barrymore.

A chance meeting with writer Beverley Nichols obtained for Sherriffs (as he always signed his work) the chance to supply caricatures for Nichols's series of celebrity profiles for the *Sketch,* another glossy weekly. After illustrating Marlowe's *The Great* Tam*burlaine,* Sherriffs was engaged by the *Sketch* to supply regular caricatures for their theater and film criticism pages (1932-39). On the sudden death of Arthur Watts, their regular cartoonist and illustrator, Radio Times commissioned Sherriffs to take on the task of supplying five cartoons a week. He held this job for five years, parallel with his *Sketch* stint, until World War II called him into the tank corps.

After demobilization, Sherriffs joined Punch as a film caricaturist, a job which he held for 13 years, until his early death. He was never to achieve his ambition of drawing a wordless novel in 300 pictures. An exhibition of his film caricatures was held at the National Film Theatre in 1976. His one book was *Salute If You Must* (1944).

D.G.

SHIMADA, KEIZŌ (1900-1973) Japanese cartoon and comic strip artist born in Tokyo, Japan, on May 3, 1900. Keizō Shimada was almost entirely self-taught, but he did receive some instruction from one of the great early Japanese cartoonists, Rakuten Kitazawa (1876-1955), and he spent a short time as an art student in the Kawabata School of Illustration. At the age of 17 or 18, Shimada went to work as an illustrator for the *Manchō News.* From 1937 to 1942 he worked on the staff of the *Mainichi News* as a cartoonist. He then switched to Shogakkan, a famous publishing house, where he became a regular staff artist. After World War II, Shimada created Dōga Productions, an animation studio in Tokyo. Besides acting as president of Dōga Productions, Shimada was also chairman of the Tokyo Jido Manga Kai ("Children's Cartoon Association of Tokyo"). He died in 1973.

Shimada's name is closely associated with that of Suiho Tagawa. Both men are best remembered for their pioneering efforts in the field of Japanese children's cartoons during the years before World War II. Although Shimada did not seriously begin to produce children's cartoons until after his 40th birthday, his works—such as *Han-chan Torimono Chō* ("The Memoires of Little Han the Detective"), which appeared in *the Mainichi News* in 1937; *Bōken Dankichi* ("Dankichi the Adventurer"), which ran in *Shonen Zasshi* ("Young People's Magazine") from 1933 to 1939; and *Kariko no Boken* ("The Adventures of Kariko"), which also appeared in *Shonen Zasshi*—were landmarks in the field of children's cartoons.

It might be said that Japan's present children's comic book industry, which boasts some weeklies with a circulation of two million, is indebted to the pioneering efforts of Keizō Shimada. Until he began to produce cartoons and comics for the entertainment of young people, Japanese cartoons had been intended largely for adults. Many varieties existed, such as the politically inspired proletarian cartoon, the humorous social satire and the artistically inspired *ero* and *guro* (erotic and grotesque) cartoons, but Shimada, along with Tagawa, introduced simple adventure comics complete with heros, villains, crises and happy endings. These cartoons won a new, younger readership that is still devouring comics today.

J.C.

SHIRVANIAN, VAHAN (1925-) American cartoonist born in Hackensack, New Jersey, on February 10, 1925. Like many other cartoonists, Vahan Shirvanian did not study art formally, instead taking his bachelor's degree in English. Yet his development as an artist, if not positively accelerated by a parallel study of literature and language, certainly proceeded apace; in 1946, at the age of 21, he sold his first cartoon to the highly prestigious *Saturday Evening*

Vahan Shirvanian. © Saturday Evening Post.

Post, at that time the preserve of some of the best and most widely known cartoonists in the United States. Recognition followed this initial success rapidly, and today the list of periodicals to which Shirvanian contributes is a roll-call of all the most important showcases. His work appears (or has appeared) regularly in the *New Yorker, Playboy, Penthouse, Saturday Review, Look, Life, Time* and the *New York Times,* to mention only a few. He has won the respect and acclaim of his fellows and was named Best Magazine Cartoonist of 1962 by the National Cartoonists Society, of which he is a leading member. Now in his seventies, he still turns out his entertaining brand of cartoons from his studio in New Jersey.

Working mostly in simple line and washes, Shirvanian adapts his art to a broad range of humor—from an intellectual's fascination with the cybernetic society (e.g., a complex machine with buttons for *on, off* and *maybe* or a television that informs prospective viewers that it will present nothing worth seeing that evening) to the more ribald visions that characterize his contributions to *Playboy* and *Oui* (like the tarted-up young thing who informs a large dog with bedroom eyes, "Let's get one thing straight, Bruno. I got you for protection, not for companionship"). While the overall quality of Shirvanian's work is uneven, he is undeniably (and frequently) capable of a whimsical lyricism that ranks with that of the very finest practitioners. Take, for example, the *New Yorker* rendering of a man standing under a starry sky, hands thrust deeply into his pockets, staring into the distance with baffled abandonment while his wife, in nightdress, calls from the lighted doorway of the house behind him, "Come to bed, Ridgely. If your boomerang were going to return, it would have come back hours ago." To those of us who have waited, similarly bereft, for the return of our vanished "boomerangs," such a drawing literally speaks volumes.

These days Shirvanian devotes himself to working for *Playboy* and *Penthouse,* which he likens to "coming home after a hard day's work and playing tennis—great relaxation" after years of the apparently more restrictive regimen of magazines like the *New Yorker.* In addition he has branched out into comic strip art with the commencement of a syndicated strip for King Features in the spring of 1979.

R.C.

SHOEMAKER, VAUGHN (1902-1991) American cartoonist and Pulitzer Prize winner born on the South Side of Chicago in 1902. Vaughn ("Shoes") Shoemaker was educated in the Chicago public schools up to the first year of high school, when he dropped out and worked various jobs. For awhile he was a lifeguard, and in that occupation he met a woman, later to become Miss Chicago and still later his wife, who encouraged him to aspire to higher vocational goals.

He enrolled in the Chicago Academy of Fine Arts and took a job as an office boy at the *Chicago Daily News* in 1919; within six months he was eased out of the academy for lack of talent, but he remained at the paper. In 1922 the *News* cartoonist Ted Brown and his assistant both quit to join the staff of the *New York Herald Tribune.* Shoemaker was hastily drafted to draw the day's editorial cartoon and continued to draw the daily cartoon for nearly 30 years, winning two Pulitzers in that time. Seven years after leav-

"Now, I'll show you how you should have done it."
Vaughn Shoemaker. © Chicago Daily News.

ing the Academy, he returned—as an instructor! Through the years his pupils included the likes of Bill Maul-din, Cal Alley, Charles Brooks and Ed Holland.

In 1951 he resigned from the increasingly liberal *News* and moved in a trailer to Carmel, California, continuing his daily cartoons to one hundred clients via the Herald-Tribune Syndicate. In 1962 he also became chief editorial cartoonist of Hearst's *Chicago American* until Wayne Stayskal assumed more duties and the paper became *Chicago Today* before merging with the *Chicago Tribune.* He retired in the 1970's and died on August 19, 1991.

Shoemaker's style is one of old-time flavor and good spirit. He is reputed to have contributed the Q. to John Q. Public, and for years his harried Common Man was a symbol as recognizable as Uncle Sam; he belonged to Shoemaker as much as to anyone since Opper. His cartoons were executed in pen and crayon with generous use of cartoon conventions like beads of sweat, motion lines and stars of pain. His pen lines were supple, and there was an air of informality that masterfully camouflaged his technical control and methodical shading. On occasion he drew in a style of handsome realism.

For all the visual delights and up-front humor, Shoemaker drew some of the most powerful statements in the history of the political cartoon. His best periods were before World War II, when he rallied against European threats and American intervention, and during the Cold War, when his cartoons formed a virtual textbook of Western anticommunist rationale. He won his Pulitzers for cartoons during each of these periods.

For years he produced *Batch of Smiles* and dozens of spot drawings a week for the "More Truth Than Poetry" column in the *Daily News.* He won Freedoms Foundation gold medals every year from 1949 to 1959, the National Headliners Award of 1945 and numerous National Safety Council awards; he was awarded an honorary LL.D. from Wheaton College in 1943 and anthologized seven times in history-of-our-times formats.

Shoemaker early dedicated his life to Christ and was a founder of the Christian Businessmen's Committee and chairman of the Gospel Fellowship Club of Chicago. He sought (and succeeded) to reflect his concern for righteousness in his cartoons. His work remains as some of the finest cartooning ever produced in America.

R.M.

SHŌJI, SADAO (1937-) Japanese cartoonist born in Tokyo, Japan, on October 30, 1937. While Sadao Shōji was in the first grade, the war resulted in his evacuation to mountainous Yamanashi Prefecture, and it was not until his second year of junior high school that he returned to Tokyo. After graduation from high school he prepared for college for one year and then entered the Russian literature department of Waseda University in Tokyo, where he achieved the dubious honor of being enrolled for five years before dropping out. While still in school, however, he joined the now famous Manga Kenkyu Kai ("Cartoon Study Club"), which at the time also included Shunji Sonoyama, Kineo Shito and Hosukē Fukuchi.

Although Shōji was heavily involved with cartoons while in school and had works appear in various magazines, it was not until he began writing *Shin Manga Bungaku Zenshū* ("Complete Collection of New Cartoon Literature") and *Shōji-kun* ("Young Shōji") in 1967 that he really attracted attention. Today these remain his most representative works. *Shōji-kun,* which ran in *Manga Sunday,* deals with a relatively common theme in modern Japanese cartoons and literature—the pathetic existence of the average white-collar worker in a hierarchical company. The hero, amusingly, has the same name as the artist; his primary interests in life are women, food and getting promoted, but he is generally thwarted in all three areas. Other works by Shōji in the same style include *Sararyman Senka* ("A Speicial Course for Salarymen"), *Asatte-kun* ("Mr. Day-After-Tomorrow"), and *Tanma-kun.* In 1997 he had over 90 collections of his works in print.

Shōji continues to draw actively for a wide spectrum of weekly and monthly magazines. He claims to have been heavily influenced by Sanpei Sato.

F.S.

SHŌNEN SARUTOBI SASUKE (Japan) Following upon the success of *Hakujaden* ("Legend of a White Snake") in 1958, the Toei animation department created a second feature-length cartoon, *Shōnen Sarutobi Sasuke* ("The Adventures of a Little Samurai"). It required over a year in production and was released in 1959. Although *Shōnen Sarutobi Sasuke* had a purer Japanese theme than *Hakujaden,* it too was designed for the world market and was distributed worldwide by contract between Toei and MGM at an export price of $100,000. It was first commercially released outside Japan in December 1960, showing in Manila, Hong Kong and Singapore.

The hero, young Sarutobi Sasuke, was based on a legendary character of the same name who may have been active during the Warring States period of Japanese history (15th and 16th centuries). His primary claim to fame was that he was a master of the Kōga school of *ninjitsu* (the art of being a "secret agent," involving all sorts of esoteric and martial skills, including the power of invisibility). The story was first popularized at the beginning of the 20th century, and aspects of the character were adapted from the Chinese classic *Saiyuki.* It was also made into a comic strip by Shigeru Sugiura. In Toei's version, however, Sarutobi Sasuke is represented as a youthful Robin Hood/Superman who, aided by a host of cute animals, constantly battles the forces of evil.

Shōnen Sarutobi Sasuke was an ambitious and expensive effort that utilized 256,486 drawings and a small army of personnel. Taiji Yabushita, the director responsible for other famous Japanese animation classics (*Hakujaden, Ukare Violin, Saiyuki,* etc.), was in charge of direction, and the screenplay was adapted from a story by the late novelist Kazuo Dan. *Shōnen Sarutobi Sasuke* took a Grand Prix award at the 1959 Venice International Children's Film Festival. It was also the world's second wide-screen animated cartoon (Walt Disney's *101 Dalmatians* was the first).

F.S.

SIÈVRE, MARTIN
See Coelho, Eduardo Teixeira.

SILLY SYMPHONIES (U.S.) *Silly Symphonies* is the collective title that was given to a series of inspired and inspiring cartoon shorts produced by the Walt Disney studios throughout the 1930s. Actually, the first cartoon in the series was released in 1929 with the overblown billing "Mickey Mouse Presents a Walt Disney Silly Symphony." This was the famous *Skeleton Dance* that blended animation and music (an original composition by Carl Stalling, with some bars of Edvard Grieg's "March of the Dwarfs" thrown in for good measure).

The *Silly Symphonies* plodded along in 1930 and 1931 without equalling the success of *Mickey Mouse,* but in 1932, *Flowers and Trees,* the first animated cartoon filmed entirely in color, created a sensation (and earned Disney an Academy Award). More color shorts followed: *King Neptune, Babes in the Woods* (both in 1932) and *Father Noah's Ark* (1933); the greatest success in the series came in 1933 with *The Three Little Pigs,* a thoroughly enchanting version of the old tale. It too won an Oscar, helped along by Frank Churchill's hit tune, "Who's Afraid of the Big Bad Wolf?" More cartoons came out year after enchanted year: *The Tortoise and the Hare* (another Oscar winner), *The Wise Little Hen* (in which Donald Duck made his first appearance) and *The Grasshopper and the Ants* (1934); *Who Killed Cock Robin?* and *Music Land* (1935); *Three Blind Mouseketeers* (1936); *Woodland Cafe* and the Oscar-winning *The Old Mill* (1937); *Timid Elmer* and *The Practical Pig* (1938), among many others. After 1940 the *Silly Symphonies* title was abandoned, although Disney continued to produce cartoon shorts.

Among the many artists who worked on the *Silly Symphonies,* mention should be made of the inimitable Ub Iwerks (who animated *The Skeleton Dance* and several other titles in the series), Albert Hurter (whose work on *The Three Little Pigs* proved pivotal), Ferdinand Horvath, Arthur Babbitt and Dick Huemer.

Although they never equalled the *Mickey Mouse* and *Donald Duck* shorts in popularity, the *Silly Symphonies* were sparkling little gems that will long endure. Like most other Disney cartoons, they were adapted into book form and, starting in 1932, they were also made into a Sunday comic feature (drawn, most notably, by Al Taliaferro).

M.H.

The first Silly Symphony, "Skeleton Dance." © Walt Disney Productions.

"Well, you may be able to spot some bears, but I doubt it."
James Simpkins, "Jasper." © Maclean's.

SIMPKINS, JAMES N. (1920?-) Canadian cartoonist born around 1920. James Simpkins grew up in Winnipeg, Manitoba. For several years he attended art school in Winnipeg, and during World War II he served in the Canadian army. On release in 1945, he began doing artwork for the *Beaver* (the Hudson's Bay Company magazine) and the National Film Board of Canada. As a staff artist for the NFB for 16 years, he produced filmstrips for school use, and after leaving their regular staff, he continued to freelance for them. Simpkins's work also includes gag cartooning and book illustration. In 1955 he submitted a design for a hockey stamp that was used by the Canadian Post Office Department. In the last ten years, Simpkins has had cartoons appearing regularly in the *Medical Post* and has also done some advertising work.

Simpkins's most familiar creation is Jasper the Bear. Starting in 1948, Jasper appeared regularly in *Maclean's Magazine* for over 24 years. Peter Newman, in an introduction to one of the published collections of Jasper cartoons, calls the bear "the Quintessential Canadian: using his wits (because he has few other weapons) . . . muddling through the most difficult situations with a kind, self-deprecating good humour that manages to salvage his self-respect, if little else." Jasper finds himself in a variety of situations involving people who come holidaying into his environment. Occasionally, outside events dramatically penetrate Jasper's world, as when the trans-Canada

David Simpson © Tulsa Tribune.

pipeline was built through his cave or when Jasper, looking down on people constructing a Bomarc missile base, commented to his woodland friends, "I wish we could do something before they become extinct."

Jasper has been used by the Boy Scouts and has appeared on greeting cards and on bear warning posters in parks. He is also well represented in Jasper Park, Alberta, where his effigy is used in many ways. In the late 1960s and early 1970s *Jasper* was a Sunday comic strip distributed by Canada Wide Features. Currently, it is a panel syndicated by GLP Features to weekly newspapers across Canada. Most Canadians are familiar with Jasper the Bear. As Simpkins once said, "I thought I had created a new cartoon character. Now I know I was trapped by a bear."

D.K.

SIMPSON, DAVID K. (1946-) American political cartoonist born in Elkton, Maryland, on July 7, 1946. Dave Simpson received no art training but acquired an M.A. in English. His early cartooning influences were from the staff of *MAD* magazine, and he reports that his outlook was fashioned by television.

As editorial cartoonist of the *Tulsa Tribune* since 1971 (syndicated part of that time), Simpson has attracted attention with his handsome, witty cartoons. His style is purely derivative and reminiscent of Oliphant, MacNelly and especially Mike Peters. Simpson draws in a horizontal format and employs single-tone shading as these other artists do. Like many of the 1970s latter-day antiestablishmentarians, Simpson labels himself a mugwump.

R.M.

SIMPSONS, THE (U.S.) The Simpsons made their first appearance in 1987 in the form of 3-minute animated segments that were part of *The Tracey Ullman Show* broadcast over the Fox Television Network. These vignettes soon gained wide popularity, to such an extent that Fox in late 1989 aired *The Simpsons Christmas Special*, followed on January 14, 1990, by a weekly prime-time program called simply *The Simpsons*.

Probably the most critically-acclaimed cartoon show of the decade, *The Simpsons* showcases the outlandish escapades of "a normal American family in all its beauty and horror," according to one commentator. The principals include the loutish and balding Homer, a blue-collar worker at a nuclear-power plant and the putative head of the household; his wife Marge, the family peacemaker and the owner of the world's most impressive blue beehive hairdo; their two daughters, the six-year-old Lisa, the brains of the family, and the infant Maggie, always seen with a pacifier in her mouth. The most prominent of the Simpsons, however, is the ten-year-old Bart (an anagram for "brat"), a juvenile subversive whose anti-social sayings ("Don't have a cow, man," "Eat my shorts," "Underachiever, and proud of it") have passed into the language and become emblazoned on T-shirts.

With its lumpy and barely adequate animation, the show relies heavily on verbal humor, most of it supplied by the characters' creator, Matt Groening. Set in the typical (?) American town of Springfield, the action not only satirizes all the usual TV sitcom cliches but also offers a snide commentary on contemporary American society and values. Situations have involved cases of kidnapping, mayhem and skulduggery, not to mention Bart's flights into high adventure as the caped and masked avenger known as Bartman. The winner of two Emmy Awards to date and the object of a vociferous cult following, *The Simpsons* has enticed many celebrities to do "voice cameos" for some of the incidental characters. These "guest voices" have included Michael Jackson, Ringo Starr, Tony Bennett, Danny DeVito, and Michelle Pfeiffer; and when Lisa uttered her first word ("Daddy"), it was spoken by Elizabeth Taylor.

The most beloved dysfunctional family in America even received Presidential criticism during the 1992 campaign, when George Bush compared them unfavorably to the Waltons, the heroes of a 1970's television show set in the Depression era. "Hey, we're just like the Waltons," retorted an indignant Bart. "We're praying for the end of the depression, too." By now a national phenomenon, the show has unleashed a flood of merchandising, including ubiquitous T-shirts, dolls, toys, beach towels, posters, watches, and hats. There is also a line of comic books published by Groening's company, Bongo Comics.

M.H.

SINÉ
See Sinet, Maurice.

SINÉ MASSACRE (France) *Siné Massacre* was a short-lived extreme left humor magazine published by French cartoonist Siné (Maurice Sinet). It was originally a weekly (for 7 weeks), and there was a single monthly issue; the publication ran from December 20, 1962, to March 1, 1963, increasing its number of pages from 4 to 8 (weekly) and then to 32 (monthly). While Siné himself contributed most of the drawings, he was also assisted by other cartoonists, chief among them Strelkoff, Cardon and Bovarini.

Like *L'Assiette au Beurre* of the early 20th century, this magazine, except for the first two numbers, dealt with a weekly theme: it treated French refugees from Algeria *(Pieds noirs)* as assassins and torturers; it illustrated select-

Maurice Sinet ("Siné"). © Siné

ed quotations from the laws regulating the press; it compared life's daily spectacle to the sadistic blood-and-gore Grand Guignol; it graphically presented *l'amour* in its most unromantic, tasteless and venal aspects. The last weekly vilified the Roman Catholic clergy, especially the Pope, who was shown walking on wooden crucifix-crutches, being revived by watching a nun dancing the cancan and being exterminated by an all-purpose vermin spray. The final issue (no. 8) bludgeoned every segment of middle-class society, De Gaulle in particular, as if each artist were vying to be the most scabrous, the most shocking, the most malicious in his presentations.

At the same time, many if not most of these drawings are funny, perhaps because of the bizarreness of the depictions; they not only jeer fearlessly at all our sacred cows, they also massacre them in the most anarchic (albeit warped) manner.

P.H.

SINET, MAURICE (1928-) French cartoonist, poster artist and set designer born in Paris, France, on December 31, 1928. After his secondary and technical schooling, Maurice Sinet became a singer with the vocal group Les Garçons de la Rue (1946-48). He turned to cartooning in 1949, contributing artwork to all major newspapers and weeklies that publish graphic humor: Paris-Match, Le Canard Enchaîné, Elle, France-Soir, L'Express, Satirix and from time to time the American Horizon. He has added a number of additional publications to his roster in the 1980s and 1990s, including *Le Matin, Vogue,* and the Belgian *Le Point.*

Under the pen name "Siné" he is justly famous for his drawings of cats and political and social events, most of which have been published as albums (also in the United States): *Complaintes sans Paroles* ("Laments without Words," 1956), *Portée de Chats* ("Litter of Cats," 1957), *Dessins de L'Express* ("Drawings from *L'Express,*" 1961), *Dessins Politiques* ("Political Drawings," 1965 and 1972), *CIA* (1968), *Je Ne Pense Qu'à Chat* ("I Think Only About Pussy," 1968), etc. For a few months (December 1962-March 1963) he published his own magazine, *Siné Massacre,* a rabid extreme left publication which attacked everything from De Gaulle and imperialism to love.

His cat cartoons are charming, to the point and comical, with the pun expressed in the clear linear sketch as well as in the brief caption: *chat laid* ("ugly cat") makes a play on the word *chalet;* a *chat val* is a cat with the typically stupid and empty face of Chaval's characters. On the other hand, his political and social commentary often shows a bent toward sick and cynical gallows humor, and Siné is not afraid to use lots of red ink to stress the blood and gore. His victims can be a colonialist being eaten by smiling representatives of the Third World; a mean-looking, black-robed priest with sharp teeth and outstretched bat wings having a stake driven through his heart, again by a smiling person; or a nice old lady giving candy to a legless cripple whose gestures resemble those of a begging dog.

Cruelly insistent and scurrilous in his hatred for the establishment (even the Communist newspaper will have nothing to do with him—"I am too much of an anarchist for them"), he has become increasingly acid over the last 15 years. Yet Siné, who has been compared to Jules Feiffer and Virgil Partch, remains the uncontested leader of the new generation of politically committed and active French cartoonists, both for his acerbic sophistication and for his zany wordplays. Now entering his seventies, he has lost none of his pugnaciousness. "I like my humor bloody, violent, aggressive, provoking," he declared in 1981. "I think we must give people a jolt."

P.H.

SINFONIA AMAZÔNICA (Brazil) *Sinfonia Amazônica* (known as *Symphony of the Amazon* in the United States) was the first feature-length animated film ever produced in Brazil; released in 1953, it was a labor of love directed and animated almost single-handedly by Anelio Latino Filho.

Despite his obvious debt to Disney (and especially to the "Aquarela do Brasil" segment of *Saludos Amigos*), Filho was able to develop an original work based on old Indian folktales and legends. Color was used to good effect, and the animation, while clumsy in parts, had a suitably primitive and folksy air about it. The music, comprised of popular songs and extracts from classical works by Villa-Lobos and others, formed an integral part of the picture and served to underscore the visual impact.

Sinfonia Amazônica was a valiant—and on the whole successful—try at producing an animated film of genuine Brazilian spirit and flavor.

M.H.

SIRIO, ALEJANDRO (1890-1953) Argentine cartoonist and illustrator born in Oviedo, Spain, on October 26, 1890. Alejandro Sirio immigrated to Argentina in 1908, settling in Buenos Aires. He worked for a time as cashier in a department store and studied art in the evenings. Manuel Mayol, then director of the humor magazine *Caras y Caretas,* asked the young Sirio to join his staff as a cartoonist in 1910. Around the same time Sirio also worked for *Plus Ultra* as a cartoonist and illustrator. In 1924 he became editorial cartoonist for the daily *La Nación,* a position he occupied until his death. In 1926 and 1931 Sirio made

George Sixta. © The Sport Eye.

study trips to Europe. Upon his return from the second, in 1932, he started his collaboration with *El Hogar,* to which he contributed a number of witty creations in the form of panels and humor strips.

Alejandro Sirio also illustrated many books by Argentine and foreign authors. He taught illustration at the National School of Fine Arts in Buenos Aires, held many exhibitions, received a great number of awards and distinctions, and was president of the Association of Argentine Graphic Artists. He died in Buenos Aires on May 6, 1953.

A.M.

SITO, TOM (1956-) American animator born in Brooklyn, N.Y., on May 19, 1956. While attending the School of Visual Arts and the Art Students League (both in New York City), Tom Sito went to work as an assistant animator on the critically acclaimed *Raggedy Ann and Andy* feature. Later he went on to Nelvana Studios in Toronto, Canada, as a senior animator on *The Ring of Power* (originally titled "Rock and Rule"). Other prestigious productions he worked on in various capacities in his early career have been such animated feature films as *Starchasers* and *The Secret of the Sword,* and well-received television specials like *Gnomes* and *Ziggy's Gift,* for which he received an Emmy Award for Best Animation in 1982.

That same year he settled in California, where he directed such Saturday-morning TV shows as *Shera, Princess of Power* and *Ghostbusters.* A senior animator and storyman at Walt Disney since 1987, Sito has worked on some of the studio's most noteworthy features, including *Who Framed Roger Rabbit, The Little Mermaid, Beauty and the Beast, Aladdin, The Lion King,* and *Pocahontas.* Listing his influences as Richard Williams, Shamus Culhane, and Ben Washam, he has evolved a fluid, streamlined style as is evident in his storyboards.

One of the most talented and articulate artists in the animation field, Sito is known for his strong views on his craft. "As I see it," he wrote in 1986, "animators will no longer be able to draw the same character for thirty years or more, but will have to diversify if they want to survive;" to which he added, "Studying your art or your field is not enough, it is only the beginning. You must be a student of the world and bring something original and personal to your art." This has led him to teach animation at the University of Southern California, and to lecture widely in the United States and abroad.

M.H.

SIXTA, GEORGE (1909-1986) American cartoonist born in Chicago, Illinois, on March 13, 1909. George Sixta went to school in his native Chicago. While in high school, he took night classes at the Chicago Academy of Fine Arts, where he worked under Everett Lowry (1927-28). In 1929 Sixta joined the art staff of the *Chicago Times,* contributing gag cartoons, illustrations and spot drawings, and building a steady reputation as he went. In 1941 he created a newspaper strip, *Dick Draper, Foreign Correspondent,* which he abandoned a few months later to join the U.S. Navy.

Sixta was serving in the public relations office of the Department of the Navy when he sold a gag panel to the *Saturday Evening Post* in 1944: titled *Rivets,* it was about a frisky mutt whose well-meaning but clumsy affections usually created havoc around him. Discharged from the navy after the war, Sixta went back to freelancing cartoons and created two more panels, *One for the Book* and *Hit or Miss.* In 1953 Publishers Syndicate took over *Rivets,* which began syndication as a regular newspaper strip. Sixta devoted most of his energies to the feature which he turned out up to the time of his death in January 1986.

Sixta has had a long career as one of the steady and dependable, if unspectacular, journeymen cartoonists who make up the backbone of the profession.

M.H.

SI YEOO KI (China) *Si Yeoo Ki* ("The Westward Pilgrimage") was written by Wu Tcheng-en in the 16th century. An allegorical novel of epic and mythic dimensions, it has long been a classic of Chinese literature, and it has been adapted to the stage, the opera and comic books, as well as animated cartoons.

One such adaptation occured in 1940, at the height of the Sino-Japanese conflict. Based on an isolated episode in the long, involved narrative, *The Princess Iron Fan* was the work of Wan Lai-Ming, China's most distinguished animator, in collaboration with his brothers, Wan Ku-Chan and Wan Chao-Chen. In the 1960s Wan went back to *Si Yeoo Ki* with a two-hour feature released in two parts (1962 and 1965), *Trouble in the Kingdom of Heaven;* the screenplay was by Wan himself, assisted by Lee Ke-juo, and the animation was done by Tang Cheng.

The feature retraced the very first episodes of Si *Yeoo Ki,* where the monkey-hero of the tale, Souen Wu-Kong, proclaiming himself the Celestial Emperor, wreaks chaos and turmoil on the kingdom of Heaven before a new republican order is finally established. (The ending, doubtless dictated by ideological and political considerations, is sharply at variance with that of the original tale, in which Buddha has the troublesome monkey chained to the Mount of the Five Elements.)

The action in the film is admirably handled, and the use of color nothing less than stunning; the characters are well delineated, and the animation is excellent, albeit conventional. The cartoon caused a stir (and won several prizes) when it was shown at the 1965 Locarno Festival. If an astute distributor were to bring it to the United States, there is no doubt that *Trouble in the Kingdom of Heaven* would enjoy a tremendous success.

M.H.

SKETCHES OF LOWLY LIFE IN A GREAT CITY
See Woolf, Michael Angelo.

SKUCE, THOMAS LOUIS (1886-1951) Canadian cartoonist born in Ottawa, Ontario, on July 6, 1886. Lou Skuce began his cartoon career on the Ottawa *Journal.* He was an active athlete, playing rugby and hockey, and he won five Canadian paddling championships, as well as world honors in paddling. His background in sports helped him turn out detailed, accurate cartoons for the sports page. From

Max Slevogt, 1897.

Ottawa, Skuce went to the Toronto *World*, where he drew political and sports cartoons.

After serving in the psychological warfare branch of the National Defense Department during World War I, Skuce worked on several newspapers in Toronto in the 1920s and 1930s. He was art editor of the *Sunday World* for 14 years. In 1927, he drew the comic strip *Cash and Carrie* for the Bell Syndicate and also ghosted for other cartoonists. In 1928 he created the short-lived *Mary Ann Gay* for United Press Features. During the 1920s and 1930s he drew cartoons for *Maclean's Magazine* and the *Canadian Magazine* and did advertising cartoons for various companies. His cartoon symbol, which appeared in many of his works, was a goose with a strange-looking hat perched on its head at a rakish angle.

From the mid-1930s until his death, Skuce was a freelance cartoonist. He developed the "cartoonagraph," a machine that projected onto a screen the freehand drawings he made. He performed at the Adelphi Theatre in London, the Roxy Theatre in New York and many Canadian movie houses. His cartoonagraph was put to work during World War II to promote Victory Bond sales. While in New York, Skuce became interested in both playwriting and acting. His work in these fields led to his involvement with the American Guild of Variety Artists, and he later became chairman of its Toronto chapter. One of his better-known plays was *Bill of 13*. Skuce's largest-scale work was a series of murals for the Toronto Men's Press Club illustrating vignettes of club life and humorously depicting the evolution of the printed word from the Stone Age to the era of giant printing presses.

Skuce died at age 65 on November 20, 1951. At the time, a packet of his cartoons for a new series was in the mail, on its way to the Bell Syndicate in New York.

D.K.

SLEVOGT, MAX (1868-1932) German painter, illustrator and cartoonist born at Landshut, Bavaria, on October 8, 1868. Max Slevogt ranks high in the small group of really first-rate German artists for whom humorous art was not the final goal but a brief professional phase and continuing accompaniment to their careers.

Slevogt's father was an army officer who died of a wound received in the Franco-Prussian War. After a boyhood spent in Würzburg, Max attended the Munich Academy and also made study trips to Paris, Italy and Holland between 1889 and 1898. Painting was always one of his major concerns, and by the late 1890s he had moved out of the murk of Munich academicism into an impressionism that was strongly influenced by Van Gogh and Cézanne but that gradually became a more and more personal synthesis of light and color.

However, the storyteller in Slevogt was simultaneously crying for release. Happily, the beginning of his career as an illustrator coincided with the founding of the two outstanding Munich art magazines *Jugend* and *Simplicissimus* in 1896. For *Jugend* Slevogt drew satirical comments on the Boer War and the Boxer Rebellion; for *Simplicissimus* he illustrated poems by Wedekind and Liliencron and did a series of swift, Kley-like pen sketches wittily acknowledging the power of femininity in the scheme of things.

In 1901 Slevogt moved to Berlin. After his illustrations for *Ali Baba* (1903) he quickly became the foremost book illustrator in Germany, using a versatile and dazzling lithographic technique. Like his best paintings, these pages seem to both absorb and radiate light. Other major illustrated books were *Lederstrumpf* ("Leatherstocking," 1910), the autobiography of Cellini (in Goethe's translation, 1913), the history of Cortez's conquest of Mexico (1918) and an album of musical excerpts from Mozart's *Magic Flute* with the artist's marginal illustrations (1920). Several children's books appeared with pen drawings and pen lithographs by Slevogt, including *Rübezahl* in 1909 and Grimm tales in 1918; others had woodcuts after his drawings, including *Kinderlieder, Tierfabeln und Märchen* ("Children's Songs, Animal Fables and Fairy Tales," 1920).

Countless occasional drawings made for friends

Jiří Sliva. © Jiří Sliva.

throughout his life testify to Slevogt's continued interest in cartooning. Moreover, he was a close friend of the famous historian of humorous art Eduard Fuchs, whose portrait he painted in 1905. Other artistic ventures included reportage at the front in 1914, instruction at the Berlin Academy in 1917, stage design in Dresden in 1924 and truly delightful frescoes executed in the 1920s. Slevogt died at his home in Neukastel, in the Rhine-Palatinate, on September 20, 1932.

S.A.

SLÍVA, JIŘÍ (1947-) Jirí Slíva was born July 4, 1947, in Pilsen, Czechoslovakia (now the Czech Republic). He graduated with honors from a mechanical engineering technical school where he studied metallurgy, but he did not pursue that vocation. Instead, he helped to organize a popular music group on the model of the Beatles. After that Slíva attempted to satisfy his yen to study philology or literature and enrolled in the Prague College of Economics, where he learned English and German, wrote poetry, played in the orchestra, and translated in the area of futurology studies. He joined the Institute of Philosophy and Sociology and worked 8 years as a futurologist, at the same time he nurtured his interest in the arts, writing poems and songs and illustrating them with his paintings and drawings.

His first cartoon appeared in 1972. Seven years later, after the Mlada Fronta Publishing House had shown an interest in his work, he left behind life as a scientist in favor of one as an artist. Since then, he has freelanced as a book illustrator and created black-and-white cartoons and drawings and color lithographs. He has been a steady contributor to the Swiss satire magazine, *Nebelspalter*, to the op-ed page of the *New York Times*, and other periodicals and a many-time winner of international cartoon awards such as "Golden Hat" (Knokke Heist, Belgium), "Palma d'Oro" (Bordighera, Italy), and a special prize of the Cuban government. His work has been visible in dozens of one-man exhibitions throughout Europe; he has illustrated more than 25 books, at least 5 of his own anthologies, and much Czech advertising.

Slíva's artistic proclivities resolve around surrealism and its Czech version, "poetism" or "magical realism". His cartoons are easily recognized by their use of mixed metaphors (e.g. the Mona Lisa family of Mona, Charlie Chaplin, and Mickey Mouse) and depictions of mechanical instruments that go awry or are placed in strange contexts, and the bizarre and grotesque. The gramophone of "His master's voice" fame, Charlie Chaplin, and clowns feature in a number of Slíva cartoons.

J.A.L.

SLOAN, JOHN (1871-1951) American artist and cartoonist born in Lock Haven, Pennsylvania, on August 2, 1871. John Sloan was educated at the Central High School of Philadelphia and at the same time took night courses at the Philadelphia Academy of Fine Arts under Thomas P. Anshutz. In his student days he earned money and trained

At the End of the War.—St. Peter: "I've got a full house!"
—The Devil: "You lose. I've got four kings!"

John Sloan, 1914. © The Masses.

himself by designing calendars and lettering diplomas; in 1892 he joined the art staff of the *Philadelphia Inquirer,* three years later switching to the Sunday supplement staff of the *Philadelphia Press.* For the *Press* he drew various strips, panel cartoons and comical puzzles, continuing the latter well after he left the staff in 1903 to paint in New York. Sloan did not abandon the pen entirely, however, for he soon became an illustrator of some demand, along with his friends William Glackens, Everett Shinn, Rollin Kirby and Ernest Fuhr—whose styles he approximated.

In 1912, when he became art editor of a new magazine, the *Masses,* Sloan again plunged into cartooning. Now, as a Socialist (he had run for elective office on the party ticket) and an ardent propagandist (though he soon lost his attraction to radical politics), he drew fiery cartoons that graced the covers and interiors of the weekly. Perhaps more important, as editor he gathered a group of cartoonists (and artists recruited to cartooning) the likes of which have never been brought together before or since in American journalism. In terms of freshness of approach, artistic excellence and strength of opinions, the group Sloan attracted was unique. It included Art Young, George Bellows, Robert Minor, Glenn O. Coleman, Stuart Davis, Walt Kuhn, Maurice Becker and others.

Around the same time, Sloan was part of another group, with overlapping membership, that was to shape the rest of his career and the course of American art. "The Eight" was a loose collection of progressive artists who shared aesthetic views, mounted many exhibits and promoted younger artists. Led by Robert Henri, the members included Arthur B. Davies, George Luks, Ernest Lawson, Everett Shinn, William Glackens and Maurice Prendergast; the 1913 Armory Show was one result of their efforts. As the years passed, Sloan increasingly busied himself with purely artistic pursuits and eventually abandoned cartoons as he became a major force in etching and oil painting. He died at his home in Hanover, New Hampshire, on September 7, 1951.

Sloan's cartoon style was at first loose and almost sloppy, but his strips and panels were full of humor, action and character; their composition was very handsome. In the latter part of his career as a cartoonist and illustrator, his work took on a look also achieved by certain of his contemporaries—a look that Wallace Morgan was to use to good advantage in later years—featuring bold, parallel, stiff brushstrokes and monochrome shading. As a political advocate, Sloan was an effective concept man.

R.M.

SLUČAJ . . . (Yugoslavia) In 1960 Zagreb Film produced a series of animated cartoons in the mock-mystery genre for American producer Sam Bassett on scripts by Phil Davis; since each and every film started with the word slučaj ("the case of"), the cartoons came to be known as the *Slučaj* (or *Case*) series. In all, 26 *Slučaj . . .* cartoons were produced, in two separate series of 13, in 1960 and 1961.

Nikola Kostelac supervised the production of the series, which starred a fumbling police inspector forever being undone by schemes of his own invention (an early prefiguration of Inspector Mask). Among the best entries in the series are those that Kostelac himself directed, with Milan Blažeković and Zdenko Gašparović as his animators; "The Case of the Eggless Hens" and "The Case of the Missing Matador" are probably two of the wittiest. The whole thing, however, was not up to Zagreb's standards, and it was accordingly unsuccessful.

M.H.

SMIES, JACOB (1764-1833) Dutch illustrator and cartoonist born in Amsterdam, the Netherlands, on June 11, 1764.

Holland had given Europe lessons in caricature and humorous art since at least the late medieval period, the 17th century being especially rich in funny genre scenes that are still models of their kind; but by the late 18th century the tradition had dwindled into the feeble "Dutch drolleries" scoffed at by the great English cartoonists of the day, and Dutch wit seemed permanently stifled by learned allegories and pomposity. At the outset of the French Revolution, the journal *De Lantaarn* briefly cast a new glow thematically, but not yet artistically.

It was Jacob Smies who first freed the modern Dutch cartoon from many of its shortcomings, adding vigor and real observation to its line and general style, and taking all sorts of everyday events and all classes of the population as his subject matter. Strongly influenced by such English masters as Rowlandson, he depicted popular dances in drinking places as well as classical concerts among the worldly. He poked fun at the learned societies of Amsterdam and at such current fads as phrenology. The lectures of Kant, the first balloonists in Holland, Napoleon's retreat from Russia—all were grist to his mill. At about the same time as Chodowiecki and Ramberg in Germany, he parodied the characters and manner of Greco-Roman art—or, more precisely, its contemporary neoclassical reincarnation—prefiguring the "scandalous" *Histoire Ancienne* series of Daumier. Fantasy (and even a touch of allegory) was not totally absent from his oeuvre

The New Heavyweight Challenger
Dorman H. Smith, ca. 1938. © New York American.

(one satirical item shows the chemical manufacture of children), but it never got out of control. Most of the abovementioned subjects appeared in the form of prints, sold either as contour engravings or filled in with colors applied by hand; they are effective both ways.

Smies was also very active as a book illustrator, and he was most particularly associated with Arent Fokke Simonsz, a humorous philosopher and prolific writer; two of their many collaborations were *Iets over Alles* ("A Little Bit About Everything") and the seven-part *Boertige Reis door Europa* ("Humorous Journey Through Europe"), which contains fictitious anecdotes about highly placed persons of the day. Other important books illustrated by Smies were *Leerzaam Onderhoud Tusschen een Vader en Zyn Kinderen* ("Instructive Conversation Between a Father and His Children," 1801) by H. Essenberg; *Avondstonden voor de Jeugd* ("Evening Hours for Young People," 1801) and *De Wereld in de XIXe Eeuw* ("The World in the 19th Century," 1803). Smies died in Amsterdam on August 11, 1833.

S.A.

SMITH, DORMAN H. (1892-1956) American cartoonist born in Steubenville, Ohio, on February 10, 1892. Dorman Smith was educated in the public schools of Columbus, Ohio, and secured his first job, in a steel mill, at the age of 20. After taking the Landon correspondence course in cartooning, he got his first artistic job drawing ads for the Jeffrey Manufacturing Company in Columbus (1917-19).

Smith became an editorial cartoonist for the *Des Moines News* in 1919 and in only two years moved to Cleveland, where he became chief editorial cartoonist for the Newspaper Enterprise Association—and immediately thereby one of the most widely distributed of his profession in America. In 1927 he switched to the Hearst papers and drew for outlets in New York, Chicago and San Francisco until 1941, when he returned to NEA. He remained there, alternating with the young John Fischetti during the last years of his career, until his death on March 1, 1956.

Smith is remembered for the exuberence of his cartoons; he drew on a very large scale and filled his drawings with enormous doses of animation, excitement, action, sound effects and labels. In this regard he was happily old-fashioned, and his cartoons presented strong opinions lucidly, unencumbered by crowded panels and busy crosshatch shading. Smith won awards for his watercolors as well as for his cartoons. His books were largely instructional in nature and include *101 Cartoons, Cartooning* (a course) and *First Steps to a Cartoon Career.*

R.M.

SMITH, JEROME H. (1861-1941) American cartoonist and illustrator born in Pleasant Valley, Illinois, in 1861. As an Illinois farmboy, J.H. Smith raised western horses and traveled west himself at the age of 18, joining the silver rush in Leadville, Colorado. After drifting—the fate of many Wild West emigrés in the last years of the frontier—he returned to Chicago in 1884 and attended art school.

J.H. Smith's first published illustrations appeared in the short-lived Chicago weekly the *Rambler.* His cartoons caught the attention of the reconstituted staff of *Judge,* then

Jerome H. Smith, 1910. © Judge.

gearing up and being financed to compete full-scale with *Puck.* Smith joined the *Judge* staff in New York in 1887 and became a major contributor; his cartoons were as numerous as Grant Hamilton's or Zim's in those early years. His subject matter ran the gamut of jibes (*Judge*'s targets seemed more ethnic and rural than *Life*'s or *Puck*'s), but his specialties were society drawings and western cartoons. His popularity was evidenced by the many book illustrations he made while contributing heavily to *Judge;* Bill Nye books were his most notable works.

In 1889 Smith was sent by *Leslie's Weekly,* the sister publication of *Judge,* to the West to record visual impressions for a series of western articles. The West was his love, and his on-the-spot drawings of cowboy and Indian life are excellent. The following year Smith traveled to Paris for art study but returned complaining that an old dog couldn't learn new tricks. His cartoons for *Judge* thereafter became less frequent as he was once again drawn west by his love of the frontier.

Smith traversed the West in many capacities: mining, cattle herding, stagecoach driving and freighting. He finally settled down in British Columbia and married a part-Indian woman. "Retired" to a life of painting, he achieved a moderate success and reputation for his western oils. Sometime after the turn of the century, Smith was in Chicago again as a cartoon teacher; he was Nate Collier's admired instructor there.

The cartoons of J.H. Smith—except those during his later years, which showed an economical, polished look—were busy, scratchy Victorian illustrations-with-captions. His figures were homegrown and agile but never as com-

"This is your President speaking."
Robert Gray Smith ("Graysmith"). © San Francisco Chronicle.

fortable to look at as those of similar development (Zim or early Opper). He was, though, in many ways a true representative of the school he led, at least in terms of output: the pre-Gibson penmen who claimed no specialty of subject but mastered the basics of early photoreproduction and supplied the secondary humor magazines with their staples (Smith's work occasionally appeared in magazines such as *Texas Siftings* and *Truth*). He died in Vancouver, British Columbia, on March 7, 1941.

R.M.

SMITH, ROBERT GRAY (1942-) American cartoonist born in Pensacola, Florida, on September 17, 1942. Because his father was in the air force, Robert Graysmith (as he signs his work) never lived for more than two years in any one location when growing up; most of his youth was spent in the Orient. Graysmith attended the California College of Arts and Crafts in Oakland between 1960 and 1965, spending the following year as a copyboy on the *Oakland Tribune.* He then became a cartoonist, drawing editorial cartoons for the *Stockton Record* for three years and switching to the *San Francisco Chronicle* in September 1968. In the mid-1970s Graysmith contributed to *Crazy* magazine.

Graysmith's work is squarely in the contemporary style but is marked by a fierce individuality; he is one of the freshest political cartoonists working today, and his concepts are among the most forceful. He is reprinted often, no doubt due equally to the appeal of his cartoons and to the publicity efforts of the perspicacious Stanleigh Arnold, whose Chronicle Features syndicates them. The cartoonist has recently changed his name legally to Robert Graysmith, in part a professional tip of the hat to Herb Block's "Herblock," and in part an acknowledgment that "Bob Smith, cartoonist" lacks a certain flair. His distinctive and distinguished political cartooning would alone have precluded any recognition problems, however.

Robert Graysmith (he had his name legally changed at the end of the 1970s) turned to freelance activities in 1983. In recent years he has become best known for his true-crime books about unsolved murders; these have included most notably *Zodiac* (1986), *The Sleeping Lady* (1990), and *The Murder of Bob Crane* (1992). He has also illustrated works by others and still turns out an occasional cartoon or two for the magazine market.

R.M.

SMURFS, THE (U.S.) *The Smurfs* was a popular Saturday-morning cartoon show based on a popular Belgian comic strip. Pierre Culliford, signing his work "Peyo," created the winsome little blue creatures as incidental characters in his medieval mock-epic, *Johan and Pierlouit*. The Schtroumpfs (as they are called in the original) gained their own series in 1960 and went on to conquer the world.

The Hanna-Barbera studios brought the Smurfs to television (on NBC) in 1981. Only a few changes were made in Peyo's original concept: the members of the happy tribe were increased from 100 to 103, and they were given names reflecting some particular trait, in the fashion of the dwarfs in Disney's *Snow White*. There were Hefty, Clumsy, Vanity, Brainy, Grouchy, Lazy, and so on, not including the Smurfette, the only female of the group and its *femme fatale* by default; all of them under the benign authority of Papa Smurf. Feeling the need for some human characters, the producers brought in Peyo's Johan and Pierlouit (Peewit in the American version) in 1982. Baby Smurf arrived in 1983, followed by Grandpa Smurf in 1986.

The paradisiac life of the Smurf village would have been complete had it not been for the evil sorcerer Gargamel who was forever trying to ensnare the elves in order to further his sinister designs (such as changing lead into gold by adding six Smurfs to the molten metal). Fortunately for his enemies, Gargamel was hindered in his schemes by his inept apprentice, Scruple, and by his highly excitable brown cat, Azrael, who would meow in expectant glee at the most inopportune moments and give away the game to the alerted Smurfs.

In parallel with the show there were a number of television specials. *The Smurfs' Springtime Special* and *The Smurfs' Christmas Special* were both aired in 1982. Then came *My Smurfy Valentine* (1983), *The Smurfic Games* (released in the Olympic year 1984), and *'Tis the Season to Be Smurfy* (the last one, in 1987). *The Smurfs and the Magic Flute,* a Franco-Belgian animated feature, originally produced in 1975, was released in the United States in 1983.

The Smurfs won many Emmy Awards for "Outstanding Children's Entertainment Series," starting in 1982. The show concluded its long run in 1990.

M.H.

SNAPSHOTS IN HADES
See Hell.

SNARK, THE
See Wood, Starr.

SNEGUROTCHKA (Russia) Veteran animator Ivan Ivanov-Vano produced a number of feature films over the years, most of them adaptations of fairy tales or traditional Russian stories, and all of them much the same. The 1952 *Snegurotchka* ("The Snow Maiden") is representative

"Snow White and the Seven Dwarfs." © *Walt Disney Productions.*

of Ivanov-Vano's output and has the advantage of a fairly interesting screenplay.

The coming of spring awakens the lovely but loveless Snow Maiden from her long slumber. Her heart filled with longing, she receives from her mother, Spring, a garland in which is hidden the irresistible power of love. Under its spell the Snow Maiden falls in love with Misgir, a merchant's son, but is destroyed by the Sun, who strikes her down out of hatred for her grandfather, Frost. Nothing stops the onrush of love, however, and the forbidding countryside is transformed into a haven of songs, flowers and happiness.

Using elements of both the original story by A.N. Ostrovsky and the opera by Rimsky-Korsakov, the film moves at a steady, if somewhat slow, pace. The animation, done at the Soyuzmult'film studios in Moscow, is capably handled; the color is stunning though a bit cloying in places, and Rimsky-Korsakov's music adds immeasurably to the conventional story line. All in all *Snegurotchka* provides an enjoyable experience. (The film can be seen from time to time on American television.)

M.H.

SNOW WHITE AND THE SEVEN DWARFS (U.S.) Never a man to rest on his laurels, Walt Disney decided in 1934 to initiate his most ambitious venture: a feature-length animated cartoon that would stand on its own merits rather than take second billing to the main feature. The subject Disney chose was from one of his favorite fairy tales, the Grimm brothers' *Snow White;* by the end of 1934 the story had been well plotted out, and actual animation work began the following year. Finally, after a host of technical, financial and production problems had been overcome, at a cost of $1.5 million, *Snow White and the Seven Dwarfs* opened to a star-studded audience in Hollywood on Christmas week, 1937.

The film stayed fairly close to the original tale, although most of the grislier scenes in the Grimms' story were eliminated (the scene of the Queen transforming herself into a witch remained, however, and Disney's detractors were to lambaste him for years to come for the trauma this sequence allegedly inflicted on children). In contrast Disney gave prominence to the Seven Dwarfs, each of whom is a fine study in caricature: Dopey, Sleepy, Sneezy, Grumpy, Happy, Bashful and Doc fully justify their names. The animals who befriend Snow White in the forest also received extended treatment. Of the human characters the Queen was masterfully portrayed, and Snow White also proved adequate, albeit a little too sweet; her Prince Charming, however, remained a cardboard cutout, and is the only disappointment of the picture.

The scenes were enchanting and often dazzling (Snow White's flight through the forest, the dance with the dwarfs, the ballet of the forest creatures, etc.), and the animation all but flawless. The story was further enhanced by the masterly use of color and by Frank Churchill's tuneful songs, especially "Whistle While You Work," "Heigh-Ho," and "Some Day My Prince Will Come."

Snow White achieved spectacular popular and critical success, and received a special Academy Award in 1939, in the form of one big Oscar and seven little ones, from the hands of Shirley Temple. With this film Disney had proven—against all his critics—that a full-length animated feature was both economically and artistically viable, and he thus ushered in a new era in film animation.

Snow White has remained a popular property for Disney to this day. In 1983 a syndicated television special, *The Fairest of Them All,* was broadcast to salute the rerelease of the animated feature; and in 1987 the self-explanatory *Golden Anniversary of Snow White and the Seven Dwarfs* aired on NBC-TV.

M.H.

SOLOT, FRANÇOIS (1933-   ) French cartoonist born in Paris in 1933. Self-taught in art, François Solot (who signs simply "Solo") contributed his first drawings to the weekly *La Presse* in 1951. A couple of years later he started col-

François Solot. © *Solo.*

laborating as a freelancer to a variety of French publications, from the left-leaning *Combat* to the humorous *Marius*, without breaking his stride (or changing his highly idiosyncratic, almost abstract style).

Very soon Solo specialized in caricature, and his subjects have ranged from movie stars like Kirk Douglas and Sylvester Stallone to world politicians such as Ronald Reagan, Valéry Giscard d'Estaing, and Yasser Arafat. In all of his drawings he combines an uncanny sense of recognition with the least number of lines. The same spareness can be found in his humor and especially in his political cartoons, which he draws with particular aggressiveness. "After a drawing is done, a great amount of pressure is released," he once admitted. Among the outlets for his caricatures and cartoons have been such diverse French periodicals as *Le Canard Enchainé, Témoignage Chrétien, Révolution, L'Humanité, Libération,* and *Les Nouvelles Littéraires*. His cartoons have been collected in about a dozen books so far.

In addition to cartooning, Solo also draws postcards, posters, record jackets and T-shirts; in collaboration with his wife he also creates games and crossword puzzles. His cartoons have found their way into a cabaret act he performs solo (no pun intended) or with actor friends. Despite his professed contempt for comics, he has produced several comic stories, mostly for educational publications.

Solot is equally known for his activities in favor of the cartooning profession. He has edited and/or published a number of magazines devoted to comic art; particularly notable on this score is *Caricature et Caricaturistes*, which he started in 1989. He is also the author or editor of several books on the subject, especially the remarkable *5000 Dessinateurs de Presse et Quelques Supports* ("5,000 Newspaper Cartoonists and a Few Vehicles"), which he edited and published in 1996. A ten-year long labor of love, it constitutes an invaluable reference source to anyone interested in French cartooning from Daumier to the present.

M.H.

SOPKA, LJUBOMIR (1950-) A rare combination of shrewd commentary and droll pictorial humor characterizes the work of Ljubomir Sopka, a Serbian artist and illustrator whose trenchant social and political cartoons have regularly graced periodicals and books throughout Eastern Europe since the 1960s. Born in 1950 in Novo Orahavo, he has been dedicated to the art of cartooning since his childhood—he determined to become a professional when he was 15 and published his first cartoon in a national periodical 2 years later—but was compelled by economic pressures to undergo a more conventional training.

He graduated from the Serbian naval academy and later from law school in Novi Sad. Before he was 30 he served as legal counsel for a publishing firm, worked as an art editor of textbooks and a newspaper reporter, and published 3 volumes of short stories in Serbian and his native Ruthenian, but he never lost sight of his aspirations of a career in cartooning. He returned to school in 1980, studying art and graphic design at the national school of art in Belgrade. After graduating, he worked for a time as an animator with Zagreb-Film, the largest motion-picture studio in Yugoslavia.

Ljubomir Sopka. © L. Sopka.

Sopka has contributed illustrations and cartoons to the newspapers of his country and throughout Europe during his entire varied career. By the middle 1980s, he was one of the most prolific and best-recognized artists in Yugoslavia. A successful book illustrator and designer, he has been an active member of UPIDIV, the Designers Association of Vojvodina, since 1987, and has been a frequent exhibitor at its art gallery in Novi Sad, the capital of that region of Serbia. He has also been honored with solo exhibitions of cartoons and picture-book illustrations in Zagreb and elsewhere in the former Yugoslavia, as well as abroad. His work has received numerous honors, including the annual Cartoon Award from the Vojvodina Journalists Association and a special certificate at the International Salon of Anti-War Cartoons in 1985, prizes at the annual International Cartoon Gallery Competition in Skopje, Macedonia, in 1986, 1988, and 1995, and honors in Belgrade in 1987 and 1988. In 1991 he received the first prize at the Serbian-Japanese Society Cartoon Competition in Belgrade, and was co-winner of the 1995 *WittyWorld* Logo Competition in the United States.

Sopka's animated and visually compelling graphic style is in the classic tradition of the gag cartoonist, reflecting a sure technical control and a whimsical spirit. But it is his distinctive insights into social, psychological, and political realities that have earned him his reputation. Employing images and making points that transcend the cultural limits of his Eastern European background, he pillories bureaucracy, hypocrisy and the absurdities of everyday life in contemporary society. As a writer in *WittyWorld*

International Cartoon Magazine noted in 1997, "Ljubomir Sopka offers us not only a window into the life of a particular place and time but the deeper and more universal perceptions of a unique creative mind."

D.W.

SOREL, EDWARD (1929-   ) American cartoonist born in New York City on March 26, 1929. Ed Sorel attended Cooper Union, receiving his diploma in 1951 and going to work for *Esquire.* In 1953 he left *Esquire* and joined with two Cooper Union classmates, Milton Glaser and Seymour Chwast, to found Push Pin Studio, an innovative enterprise that became highly influential in the commercial and graphic art worlds. Sorel left Push Pin in 1956 and went to work for CBS, remaining there until 1958, when he decided to go into freelance work. During the 1960s he progressed steadily and had soon achieved a position in the first rank of political cartoonist-illustrators. In 1967 he placed *Sorel's News Service* with King Features. This political feature lasted until 1970.

Sorel's artistic perceptions were shaped by the Depression and by the intense political ferment of the World War II and Cold War environments in which he grew up. His earliest political satires—*How to Be President* (1960), *Making the World Safe for Hypocrisy* (1961) and *Moon Missing* (1962)—were relatively mild, possibly because his targets were men like the bumbling Eisenhower and Nelson Rockefeller, with his almost laughable bomb-shelter mania. But when civil rights and Vietnam became the great issues of the 1960s, Sorel began more and more to resemble those artists to whom he traces his artistic lineage—Goya, Gillray, Rowlandson and Daumier. His work for *Esquire* and particularly for *Ramparts,* the glossy monthly that served as the New Left's answer to *Time,* became angry, and his partisanship ever more pronounced.

Edward Sorel. © Sorel.

The Optimistic Pessimist.
—"It's hard luck, but you never agree with me on anything."
—"Just as well. If I did we'd both be wrong."

David Souter, 1923. © Sydney Bulletin.

Sorel's style does not rely on the linear caricature associated with the modern political cartoonists—Herblock, Oliphant, Mauldin, Osborn; rather, it is reminiscent of the work of the European masters and of noted 19th-century Americans like Nast and Bellew of *Harper's*—a trait common to the young artists coming out of the Push Pin Studio school of cartooning. It is a style particularly suited to the biting opinions it often represents. Sorel provides a test case in this regard; as his views grew stronger, his artistic representation of them became more refined.

Sorel contributes his political satire to various national publications like the *Realist, New York* magazine and *Rolling Stone;* he also does a weekly panel for the *Village Voice.* Much of the best work from his later period has been collected in a volume entitled *Superpen* (1978). In 1970-71, Sorel's work toured Europe as part of a Push Pin Studio retrospective, including a premiere viewing at the Louvre in Paris. He also had one-man shows at the Graham Gallery in New York City (1973) and at the New School for Social Research, also in New York (1974). In the conservative political climate of the eighties and nineties, Sorel seems to have abandoned the angry political satire so typical of his Vietnam Era work, concentrating instead on editorial illustrations for articles, some of which he also writes, for a range of general interest periodicals, including *Forbes, Esquire, GQ, American Heritage,* and *The New York Times Book Review.* Since the early 1990s, he has also been a regular contributor of cover art and editorial illustrations to *The New* Yorker. He has received awards from the Society of Illustrators and the Art Directors Club of New York and was given the Augustus Saint-Gaudens medal by his alma mater, Cooper Union. He has also won a Society of Illustrators Gold Medal (1983) and the 1990 Newspaper Guild's "Page One" award for his editorial cartooning. He is a member of the American Institute of Graphic Arts and the Alliance Graphique Internationale.

In addition to his success in the field of caricature, Sorel has gained a reputation as an illustrator of children's books; among his credits in this area is a 1962 *New York Herald Tribune* award for the illustration of *Gwendolyn the Magic Hen.* His own children's book, *The Zillionaire's Daughter* (1989) won the 1990 Hamilton Fish Award, given by the Society of Illustrators.He is also noted within the field of commercial art for his work in advertising and for numerous book illustrations and record album covers.

R.C.

SOUTER, DAVID HENRY (1862-1935) Australian cartoonist born in Aberdeen, Scotland, in 1862. In the *Bulletin* newspapers early development, artist contributors were slow in coming, but gradually in the 1890s a renowned band of artists was attracted to its pages. In one decade artists such as D.H. Souter, Frank Mahony, George Lambert, Percy Spence, A.H. Fullwood, Fred Leist, B.E. Minns, Alfred J. Fischer, Alf Vincent and Ambrose Dyson (the older brother of Will Dyson) established the Australian black-and-white tradition of hard-hitting humor which made Australia, in the second half of the 19th century, one of the most important centers of black-and-white art in the world.

Of these artists the best remembered today is D.H. Souter, who for over forty years had at least one drawing in every edition of the *Bulletin* and who put his own price on his drawings from the time he started contributing his work in 1892. At the age of 18, he joined the staff of the *Bon Accord* in his birthplace, Aberdeen, Scotland; then, after working in Natal, South Africa, for five years, he went to Australia in 1886. His beautiful, decorative pen work, drawn with exceptional grace of line, showed the early influence of art nouveau, a sinuous and flowing style that originated in Belgium and England and was designed to break with previous decorative tradition.

Within a few weeks of the outbreak of World War I Souter was drawing his large, full-page war cartoons for the *Stock Journal.* These cartoons displayed outstanding passages of drawing and pen work; avoiding any black masses and aids like mechanical tints, Souter preferred built-up tones and textures, sometimes being almost machinelike in the weight and spacing of his pen lines.

Souter's humorous themes in the *Bulletin* were never other than domestic in character: usually dashing women scoring a point or two off the male, be he boyfriend or husband. Despite their grace of line, his drawings were strong on the printed page—large black solids complementing fine, firm pen lines. Souter's superb compositions and groupings were helped by the inclusion in every cartoon of the well-known Souter cat, which, it is said, originated as the result of his furbishing an accidental inkblot on one of his drawings. Some of these wonderful cat studies are pictured in his *Bush Babs,* a collection of nonsense rhymes and jingles written for his young children, then illustrated for publication as a book in 1933.

There was a mind behind Souter's work. His humor was sophisticated, knowing, often wise but never harshly cynical. David Souter was also a reflective writer of verse, stories, plays, an operetta called The *Grey Kimono* and art criticism for the *Bulletin,* its sister publication the *Lone Hand* magazine, *Art in Australia* and other publications.

V.L.

SOUTH PARK (U.S.) Some years ago when *Sesame Street* became a huge hit with young children, it was thought that no show could target a younger audience. Then came *Barney and Friends* to prove the pundits wrong. Likewise, when Music Television's (MTV) *Beavis and Butthead* were dubbed princes of grossness, it was felt their dubious honor was secure. This has also been proved wrong. Enter the world of *South Park,* which the March 23, 1998 *Newsweek* touted as "the coolest schoolyard craze since MTV's *Beavis and Butthead* introduced eight-letter words like "ass-munch" into the prepubescent vernacular." (The eight-year-olds in *South Park* prefer to stick with four-letter words.)

Nine *South Park* half-hour episodes were aired by cable television's Comedy Central from August to December 1997. In those 6 months, one million T-shirts and $30 million in merchandise with *South Park* characters have been sold. Comedy Central immediately ordered 20 new episodes.

Created by twentysomethings Trey Parker and Matt Stone, who met as students at the University of Colorado-Boulder, *South Park* is a classic example of crude animation used to illustrate U.S. Senator Daniel Moynihan's theory of "deviancy downward". Senator Moynihan created the phrase to describe behavior that is now acceptable but a decade ago was unacceptable.

The four main characters in *South Park,* Kyle, Cartman, Kenny and Stan, attend third grade in South Park, Colorado, the so-called alien visitation capital of the

"South Park." © Comedy Central.

United States. The supporting characters include Wendy Testaberger, Stan's would-be girlfriend, whom he throws up on everytime they are close; and Chef, a priapic school cook with very verbal hots for Kathie Lee Gifford.

When *South Park* premiered, Comedy Central distributed a poster which sums up the principle behind the show, "Alien Abductions, Anal Probes & Flaming Farts. South Park. Why They Created the V-Chip."

The four foul-mouthed grammar schoolers debuted in animated short by Parker and Stone in 1995 about an evil Snowman terrorizing a town. They then starred in a video Christmas card commission for $1,200 by Brian Graden, then a Fox television development executive. *The Spirit of Christmas* was a five-minute animated short Graden gave to his industry pals. It featured the kids teasing Kyle because he's Jewish and Cartman because he's fat. Then Jesus and his antithesis Kringle, a.k.a. Santa Claus, fight it out kung-fu style. The video became an underground bootleg hit.

South Park is beyond low-brow. It is no-brow humor. It's also, according to the March 28-April 3, 1998 *TV Guide*, "one of the most sophisticated shows on TV these days - and cable's highest-rated series." Senator Moynihan has a point when *TV Guide* declares vomiting, racial slurs, farting, a kid in a Hitler costume at a school Halloween party, and a literal talking piece of human excrement in a Santa hat named Mr. Hankey, to be "sophisticated". Some 5,000 construction paper cutouts were used to animate the pilot. The low-tech look is now animated high-tech on computers with a staff of over 60 people. Gross is the name of no-brow humor. Money is the aim. Comedy Central claims that this is an adult cartoon broadcast late at 10 p.m. so grammar school kids can't see it. In the age of video and the Internet, they are fooling nobody. Comedy Central is owned by entertainment giants Paramount and Warner Bros.

Children are cute but they can be mean. *South Park* isn't *Peanuts*. Co-creator Trey Parker summed up his concept in a February 19, 1998 *Rolling Stone* interview. "Kids are malicious little fuckers." In each episode Kenny is killed in a horrible way. "Oh my God, they killed Kenny," is the cry. Optimistically this cult of grossness can't last forever. *South Park* will eventually be an embarrassing blip on the history of American animation.

B.C.

SOUZA, CARLOS ESTEVAO DE (1921-) Brazilian cartoonist born in Recife, Brazil, in 1921. Carlos Estevao (as he signs his work) studied art first in his native city, then in Rio de Janeiro. In the early 1940s he began contributing to *O Cruzeiro* and *Diretrizes;* later he worked for *Diário da Noite* and *O Jornal.* A man of many talents, he also works in advertising and commercial art and has drawn a number of weekly panel features, such as *Dr. Macarra, Antes e Despois de Casamento* ("Before and After Marriage"), *Ser Mulher* ("To Be a Woman") and *Preguntas Inocentes* ("Innocent Questions"). In 1961 he took over the famed feature *O Amigo da Onça* ("The Two-Bit Friend") upon the death of its creator, Pericles Maranhão.

In addition to his work for Brazilian publications, Carlos Estevao contributes to *Il Travaso* (Italy), *El Dibujo Humorístico* (Spain) and other foreign magazines. He is also a caricaturist.

A.M.

SPADGER ISLE (G.B.) This cartoon combination of comic strip and splash panel à la *Casey Court* started life as a full-page feature in the *Wizard,* number 126 (February 14, 1925). It was then entitled *Spadger's XI,* the name of the backyard football team captained by the towheaded Spadger (Cockney for "sparrow"), a half-pint hero in a turtleneck sweater, black shorts and, apparently tights. S.K. Perkins, the original artist, drew their adventures as the left-hand page of a center spread of strips printed in red and blue, the comic section of a weekly story paper for boys. The format was a short strip of four panels leading to a climax in the form of one large-scale epic cartoon depicting Spadger and his "Eleven."

Originally confined to the football field, Perkins was soon forced to expand into all kinds of fun: fishing, skating, farmyard, etc. Finally, the gang was taken on by a Scottish cartoonist, Chick Gordon, who solved the ideas problem by sending Spadger and his pals on a world tour: they played havoc, rather than football, in a different country every week. Football became so rare in the series that from number 425 (January 31, 1931) the title was changed to *Spadger Isle.*

The gang had by now disappeared, to be replaced by a fat old sea dog called Skipper Sam, settled once and for all on a tropical island. The island was peopled by a fairly uncivilized bunch of "Nigs," as they were known, and Spadger and Sam set out to bring them the delights of civilization in the best British comic style: boat races, the derby, pancake day, Christmas dinners with circular, custarded puds; any and every event in the calendar was grist to Spadger's mill. The war saw the Nigs sandbagging the Isle against the Nazis—in full color.

The shrinking of the *Wizard* due to paper shortages moved the feature to the colored cover (October 28, 1939). Spadger and company stayed put after the war and continued their now somewhat outdated adventures until 1956, when their sudden disappearance is thought to have been due to the death of their artist.

D.G.

SPAHR, JÜRG (1925-) Swiss cartoonist born in Catania, Sicily, on February 1, 1925, of Swiss parents. Jürg Spahr

Jürg Spahr ("Jüsp"). Nebelspalter.

went to school in Catania but was sent to high school in Switzerland. After graduation from law school in 1948, he worked for awhile as a consultant for corporations and financial firms. The love of drawing he had developed in grammar school never left him, however, and in 1950 he decided to make cartooning his lifelong career (he had contributed occasional cartoons to magazines as early as 1945).

Using the pseudonym "Jüsp," Spahr embarked on a busy career that has included illustration and advertising work in addition to cartoons. He became a regular contributor to *Nebelspalter* and the *Nazional Zeitung* with a popular string of gag cartoons, doing editorial cartoons for *Wir Brückenbauer* at the same time.

Jüsp's cartoons are simple in line and direct in meaning; they are often captionless and rely on telling details in order to make their point. They have earned the artist a number of awards, including the Dattera d'Oro and the Palma d'Oro at the Bordighera Cartoon Festival (1962 and 1968, respectively). From 1978 to 1994 he was curator of the Museum of Caricature and Cartoons in Basel, Switzerland.

M.H.

SPANG
See Spangler, Frank M.

SPANGLER, FRANK M. (1881-1946) American cartoonist born in Springfield, Ohio, in 1881. Frank ("Spang") Spangler studied art in public schools and for a short college term, but seeking a career in newspapers, he secured a job in the art department of a local paper. By 1905 he was offered the post of editorial cartoonist with the *Montgomery* (Ala.) *Advertiser.* Except for a period before 1912 when he headed the art department of *Grit* (a weekly newspaper published in Williamsport, Pennsylvania), the transplanted Northerner was a famous fixture in Montgomery, where he remained, cartooning, until his death in 1946.

Spang was a powerful idea man and executed his cartoons in a dark, brooding crosshatch and / or crayon style. His caricatures could be realistic or grotesque. It was always evident that he was self-taught, but his overwhelming talent for clearly presenting strong opinions, coupled with a native sense of humor, made his work notable for 41 years. Spang was a highly individualistic cartoonist and deserves to be anthologized.

R.M.

SPARGO, DONALD NICHOLAS (1921-) British animator-writer-director born in Birmingham, England, on March 16, 1921. Nicholas Spargo was educated at Handsworth Grammar School and went on to study architecture at the Birmingham Art School, being articled to a local architect in 1938. As a member of the Territorial Army, he was called up in 1939 and served as a radar instructor throughout the war while freelancing joke cartoons and story illustrations for the monthly magazine *London Life.* Always intrigued by the animated cartoon (he had attempted to make a home movie out of toilet paper at the age of six), he contacted Disney director David Hand when Hand came to England to set up the Gaumont British Animation studio at Cookham in 1946. By studying the book *The Art of Walt Disney,* Spargo learned how to construct a storyboard and sent Hand a pictorial scenario based on a favorite Welsh legend. The result was immediate: Hand procured Spargo's early release from the army and assigned him to the story department under Ralph Wright. An "economy" series was devised by using more camera movement than is involved in animation. It was called *Musical Paintbox,* and Spargo worked on it. One of the first entries, *Wales,* used his Welsh legend storyboard: "The Devil's Bridge" (1949).

After Ralph Wright's departure, Spargo became story supervisor at GBA until the studio closed. One of his unproduced storyboards was turned into a comic strip, *Legend of the Lincoln Imp,* which ran in the weekly children's paper *Eagle* (1951). This led to a return to press cartooning, and *Spargo* ran a weekly strip called *Spargo!* in the *Sunday Empire News,* drew a weekly topical cartoon for the *Sunday Graphic* and scripted strips for the children's comics *Comet* and *Sun.* Then came a call from Halas and Batchelor and a return to animation via the story adaptation of George Orwell's *Animal Farm* (1954).

Around this time England was preparing for the birth of commercial television, and the J. Walter Thompson agency opened a television department. Spargo's storyboard for a Persil commercial was not only accepted, but he was asked to make it. With his wife, Mary, who had worked with the Royal Navy film unit, Spargo set up a studio in his home village of Henley-on-Thames, and soon 25 people were working for Nicholas Cartoon Films. Among his many television commercials was the first British cartoon to win an award at Cannes, *Cheese Baby.* In 1962 a new style of cartoon was created in *The Arnold Doodle Show,* a weekly 15-minute "advertising magazine." By keeping his animated cartooning a "cottage industry," and thanks to continuing sponsorship from the Central Office of Information, Spargo has weathered several severe economic depressions. Recent work includes *Duel* (for Shell, 1962), *Genius Man* (1967), the *Joe and Petunia* series (1971), *Disgusted Binchester* (for the Race Relations Board, 1974), *Supernatural Gas* (1975) and *And So Do You* (for the Nigerian government, 1977). Later films include *Willo the Wisp* (television series, 1981) and *The Story of the Devil's Bridge* (1989).

D.G.

SPEED BUMP (U.S.) In 1993 cartoonist Dave Coverly from Indiana won first place in the Boston Comic News Cartoon Contest. The resulting publicity brought his work to the attention of Creators Syndicate, and *Speed Bump* was launched shortly thereafter. *Speed Bump* was so well received it won the National Cartoonists Society award for Best Syndicated Panel for 1994.

Coverly says in regards to *Speed Bump,* "Basically if life were a movie, these would be the outtakes." He also claims to draw only what he finds personally funny. The success of the daily panel resulted in a Sunday color comics being added.

Blessed with a style not too dissimilar in look from *The*

Fortunately, cooler heads prevailed.

"Speed Bump." © *Creators Syndicate.*

Far Side, Coverly's off-beat humor and the look of the strip made editors feel comfortable. When *The Far Side* ended in 1995, *Speed Bump*, now in over 200 newspapers, was a major beneficiary.

While off-beat, *Speed Bump* is not as weird as the panels *Bizarro* or *The Quigmans* or the comic strips *Zippy the Pinhead* or *The Fusco Brothers*. But it does have its moments. For example, captioned "Why Fixed Dogs Hate to Use the Locker Room", the square panel shows two dogs showering and soaping up. One dog says via word balloon to the other, "Gee, Larry, why are you wearing your bathing suit in the shower?" In another daily panel captioned "Really, Really Missing the Point", the hand of God descends from a cloud pointing for Adam and Eve to leave the Garden of Eden. Adam looks up to heaven and says, "...can I have a doggie bag for the rest of the apple?"

Off-beat animals and humans, usually both captioned and with word balloons, are presented in a straight forward pen-and-ink style with shading and crosshatching but no benday patterns. The Sundays are a continuation of the square panel theme and have not yet taken advantage of the artistic opportunities offered by more space.

Word play, de rigueur for an off-beat panel, is a frequent them. Sumo wrestling, for example, becomes pseudo-wrestling. Funny, off-beat without being so wild it scares editors, *Speed Bump* brings Dave Coverly's sense of humor to the head of a pack of panels looking to become the next *The Far Side*.

B.C.

SPEED, LANCELOT (1860-1931) British cartoonist born in 1860. Artist, illustrator, animator, Lancelot Speed was the first major talent in the history of the British cartoon film. He was at the peak of his fame as a book illustrator and magazine artist when Arthur Moss Lawrence, the barrister behind the scenes of a new film company, Neptune, hired Speed as artistic adviser on settings and costumes. Speed's qualifications were high. He was famous for his careful historic illustrations, which ranged from the 1897 edition of Bulwer's *The Last Days of Pompeii* to his own version of *The Legends of King Arthur and His Knights* (1912).

The declaration of war quickly turned Speed's attention to animated cartoons, an idea he had been privately experimenting with since 1912. On Friday, October 2, 1914, less than two months after the declaration, the Neptune Company showed Speed's *Bully Boy No. 1.* The advertisement described it as "a Series of Lightning Sketches of incidents in and comments on the war, which are distinctly novel and fascinating."

Using mixed techniques (including the undercranked camera to show his hand and pen at work, cutout cardboard figures and other devices), Speed aimed at releasing a new ten-minute cartoon every other week, but after eight editions the project collapsed, along with Neptune Pictures. In 1917 Speed began again, releasing through William Jury's Imperial Pictures. His first, *Tank Pranks* (1917), caused a commotion for its depiction of the German "secret weapon." Then came *The U Tube;* in 1918, *Tommy Atkins* and *Britain's Effort;* and in 1919, *Britain's Honour.*

After the war Speed returned to animation as "technical adviser" for *The Adventures of Pip, Squeak and Wilfred* (1921), a long series of cartoon one-reelers adapted from A.B. Payne's famous *Daily Mirror* strip for children. These were cheaply made and poorly animated, using the dated "cutout" techniques of a bygone age. It was Speed's last contact with animation. He died on December 31, 1931, better remembered for his historical illustrations than for his somewhat prehistoric animations.

D.G.

SPEEDY GONZALES (U.S.) The last memorable creation to come out of the Warner Brothers animation studio, Speedy Gonzales was sprung on an unsuspecting public (in a cartoon of the same name) by director Friz Freleng in 1955. The short was well received and even earned an Academy Award in its category, which prompted Warners to start a *Speedy Gonzales* series.

Speedy was a facetious, flamboyant Mexican mouse whose slow speech and south-of-the-border accent hid a quick wit and an ability to move at supersonic speed. Like Mighty Mouse, he played the role of Robin Hood for countless mice threatened by some dastardly cat; unlike Mighty Mouse, however, speed and inventiveness were his sole weapons, and he never resorted to physical force. His favorite victim was the hapless Sylvester, whom he delighted in outwitting at every turn until the browbeaten feline hoisted a white flag in abject surrender (the 1959 "Here Today, Gone Tamale" is a good example). In "Snow Excuse" Speedy took on (successfully) another Warners regular, the cunning Daffy Duck.

The *Speedy Gonzales* series did not last long (like the rest of the Warners animated productions, it disappeared in the 1960s), but it was pleasant and imaginative, demonstrating that the artists and writers at the studio had not lost their touch, even at that late date.

M.H.

"Speedy Gonzales." © Warner Brothers.

SPIKE AND TYKE (U.S.) As one critic observed, all animated cartoon bulldogs seem to be named Spike. Two of these Spikes, however, stand out: the nemesis of Warners' Sylvester the cat, and the even more famous Spike of the MGM studio.

That Spike, who made his first appearance in the 1941 "Dog Trouble," was Tom's tormentor in the *Tom and Jerry* cartoons; the bulldog would always get the best of the cat, despite Tom's frenetic efforts to get rid of him (the aptly titled "Pet Peeve" is a good example of this constant tug-of-war). The character of Spike, with his roughhewn manner and bullying demeanor, apparently appealed to Tex Avery, who put him into some of his most celebrated cartoons, such as *Counterfeit Cat* and *Ventriloquist Cat.* Spike was best used by Avery-as a foil to the phlegmatic Droopy in such gems as "Wags to Riches," "Dare-Devil Droopy" and "Droopy's Good Deed."

"Spike and Tyke." © MGM.

Meanwhile, back at the old *Tom and Jerry* series, Spike had acquired a pup named Tyke, on whom he outrageously doted. Teaching him the tricks of the canine trade, he would sick his offspring on the hapless Tom in cartoon after repetitive cartoon ("That's My Pup," "Love That Pup," "Pup on a Picnic," etc.). The father-and-son team became a regular fixture at MGM, and they were given their own *Spike and Tyke* series in the early 1950s. Dog-and-cat stories remained the dominant theme of the cartoons, as in "Scat Cats," in which Spike and his pup fought off the neighborhood cats while the master was away. Never as popular as *Tom and Jerry, Spike and Tyke* disappeared when the studio closed its doors in the late 1950s.

A *Spike and Tyke* comic book was sporadically issued by Dell Publishing Company from 1953 to 1961.

M.H.

SPITZWEG, CARL (1808-1885) German painter and cartoonist born in Munich, Bavaria, on February 5, 1808. The son of a wealthy merchant and local political luminary, Carl Spitzweg never had to worry in later life about earning his bread by pen or brush, but when he was young his father insisted he learn a "solid" profession—in this case, pharmacy. Mentally exhausted after his long course of study and apprenticeship, Spitzweg was sent off for a rest cure at a spa in 1833. It was there that a chance encounter with an art teacher revealed his own artistic vocation and resulted in introductions to leading Munich painters.

Spitzweg was too old for regular study at the Academy, but he observed the old and new masters diligently and picked up many technical tips from his newfound artist friends. He also made several European study trips around 1850—to London, Venice and especially Antwerp (where he was decisively influenced by the old Dutch and Flemish genre painters), and to Paris (where the living art of Delacroix and Diaz became crucial elements in his painting technique). From that time on, Spitzweg became from the technical point of view a sort of gifted pre-Impressionist, while his subject matter was a special blend of South German *Gemütlichkeit* and his own personal taste: whimsical interiors, street scenes and landscapes peopled by poets, scholars, soldiers, monks, booksellers, picnickers and harmless eccentrics. Unlike many of his academic contemporaries, Spitzweg has never fallen out of favor with connoisseurs of painting.

But even without his witty paintings Spitzweg would have to be placed high on any list of German humorous artists. As early as the 1830s and 1840s he was submitting cartoons to the *Fränkische Blätter* and *Nürnberger Trichter* (both in Nuremberg) and other magazines. He contributed to the famous *Fliegende Blätter* from 1845 (its second year) to 1868, working on such longer or shorter series as *Freikorps Wachtstubenfliegen* ("Flies in the National Guard Guardhouse"), *Bilder aus dem Leben auf der Strasse* ("Pictures from Street Life"), *Grosses Keroplastisches*

Kabinett ("Large Cabinet of Wax Figures"), *Naturgeschichte* ("Natural History," equating human types with animals) and *Monumente* (in which he proposed civic monuments for the inventors of the bootjack, the frock coat, the rebus and the polka). His *Fliegende Blätter* cartoons also included theater, opera and concert parodies. In 1913 an album called *Spiessbürger und Käuze zum Lachen* ("Humorous Philistines and Eccentrics") gathered together most of these cartoons.

Spitzweg's verse and his personal correspondence with his few chosen friends are also great sources of fun. Although he died in Munich on September 23, 1885, a new Spitzweg discovery was published as recently as 1962: a witty scrapbook of favorite recipes that is a surprisingly modern combination of calligraphy, collage and handwork in various media.

SA.

SPORTS OF ALL NATIONS (U.S.) Rea Irvin was one of the most prolific and influential cartoonists of his day. His many series explored varieties of the absurd, and his stints as art editor of *Life* and especially of the *New Yorker* served to bring new talent to the fore and give direction to American magazine cartooning. *Sports of All Nations* is perhaps the most representative of his cartoon series for *Life.*

The cartoons—full pages in wash—take a banal subject and happily twist it to ridiculous ends. Like later literary humorists, particularly Benchley and Thurber (who were admittedly in his debt), Irvin could take a common misconception and run to fantastic lengths with it; he would play endless variations on a theme while remaining just on the borderline of logic and sanity. Thus, *Sports of All Nations* visited Germany, where stereotyped Teutons bobbed for pretzels in a pool of beer. Playing "crack the whip" was revealed as a dangerous pastime in the Swiss Alps. Valentine's Day in Italy meant the kiss of death—the delivery of which was a popular sport in Irvin's travelogues. Other diversions included spelling bees in Wales and a squad of carpenters decoying woodpeckers for the manufacture of bird's-eye maple.

The series began on October 17, 1912, and ran intermittently through the mid-1910s in *Life.* Often two cartoons ran in the same issue. Irvin's poster style made the cartoons attractive, and his visual flights of fancy were no less exciting than the cerebral variety. The cartoons are still zany and fresh today, and this series, like *Meetings of the Sceptics' Society,* and many of Irvin's others, cries for republication.

R.M.

SPY

See Ward, Sir Leslie.

STAINO, SERGIO (1940-) Italian cartoonist born at Piancastagnaio, near Siena, on June 8, 1940. He earned a degree in architecture but never entered the profession: he first preferred teaching and only later on he devoted himself to cartooning.

In 1979 he started his contribution to the monthly *Linus* creating a character named *Bobo.* The protagonist is between 30 and 40 years of age, partially bald-headed, bearded, bespectacled and has put on weight like those who appreciate cooking and lead a sedentary life. Politically left-inclined, Bobo is always torn between middle class longings and revolutionary yearnings which never come true. Being married and a father of two daughters, Bobo has to cope with the feminism prevailing in his family and to control his subconscious, atavistic macho attitudes. His critical conscience speaks through his old friend, nicknamed Molotov, who is still loyal to a strict version of Communism. Bobo's contradictions are largely autobiographical and mirror those of the 1968 protest movement generation in Europe, a generation which has by now become completely integrated into the Establishment. The character's experiences parallel the slow change of the former PCI (Italian Communist Party) into the present PDS (Left Democratic Party) which draws inspiration from Social Democratic Party's ideals. Bobo's "sociological adventures" take on a variety of formats - from the single-panel or multi-panel cartoon to the traditional comic strip. The character has appeared on several periodicals, such as the dailies *l'Unità, Il Messaggero* and the weeklies *Satyricon* and *Sette* (pullout of the *Corriere della Sera*).

In 1986 Staino launched and edited up to 1988 *Tango* (the weekly satirical supplement of the PCI official daily, *l'Unità*): the target was the remains of Stalinism within the PCI.

Staino has illustrated some advertising campaigns, has been the artistic director of the Teatro Puccini in Florence, and has also directed two movies: *Cavalli si nasce* (1989) and *Non chiamarmi Omar* (1992).

A good deal of Staino's cartoons have been collected in book format: *Berlino amore mio* (1981), *Bobo* (1982), *Bobo nel-*

Sergio Staino. © Sergio Staino.

l'anno del sorpasso (1984), *Tempeste* (1992), *Amori* (1993), *...150, la Coop canta* (1994), *Famiglia mia...*(1995).

In 1984 Staino was awarded the Prize Forte dei Marmi for Political Satire.

G.C.C.

STAMATY, STANLEY (1916-1979) American cartoonist born in Dayton, Ohio, on May 21, 1916. Stan Stamaty studied at the Cincinnati Art Academy and sold his first cartoons to the *Saturday Evening Post* at the age of 20. Thereafter, for three decades, his cartoons appeared regularly in major gag markets, from the *Post* to the Dell magazines. His work has been included in major anthologies such as *Great Cartoons of the World* and *Best Cartoons of the Year.* Stamaty's style relies on simple line work, sometimes strengthened by varieties of gray in wash. His most famous creation is the Happy Fireman, spokesman for Fire Prevention Week; the character has appeared on many posters and in countless brochures. He died in September 1979.

Clara Gee Kastner, Stamaty's wife, is an accomplished cartoonist (with series of teenage cartoons for Scholastic Publishers to her credit) and an artist in many media; both she and her husband now teach art in the Elberon, New Jersey, area. Their son Mark Stamaty is an incredibly inventive and funny illustrator of children's books and did brilliant double-page cartoons for New York's *Village Voice* until 1997.

R.M.

STANNY, JANUSZ (1932-) Janusz Stanny was born in 1932 in Warsaw, Poland. He studied at the Akademi Sztuk Pieknych in Warsaw, under the tutelage of Henryk Tomaszewski, and received his diploma in 1957.

A teacher at the Warsaw Academy of Art, Stanny specializes in graphics and satirical cartoons and illustrations for books, newspapers, and magazines. For a number of years, he illustrated children's books. His satirical illustrations, which appear regularly in one of Poland's largest dailies, *Gazeta Wyborcza*, and in *Cultural News*, caricaturize the hard and tough features of common working people. Stanny said that in these works, he tries to capture the "funny beauty" of the workers, all the while sympathizing with them. More generally, he said his cartoons are not meant to change the world but to show the world as it is, and in the process, to make a few people smile. In his children's illustrations, Stanny tries to teach children to have a sense of humor and to acquaint them with the poetic way of seeing the world. His work has been exhibited widely, including in Poland, Argentina, Russia, Italy, and Slovakia.

J.A.L.

"Think, man, THINK!"

Ralph Steadman. © Punch.

STAR BLAZERS
See Uchu Senkan Yamato.

STEADMAN, RALPH (1936-) British caricaturist born in Wallasey, Cheshire, England, in 1936. Ralph Steadman is a caricaturist of the modern English school nurtured by the satirical magazine *Private Eye.* Educated at Abergele Grammar School in North Wales, whither he was evacuated during World War II, he showed no particular aptitude for art. He worked in Woolworth's, an aircraft factory and an advertising agency before national service in Devon. There he took the correspondence course offered by the Percy V. Bradshaw Press Art School, but he preferred to copy the style of Giles. Further art study at the East Ham Technical College and the London School of Printing and Graphic Arts led to a staff job at Kemsely Newspapers. For three years he drew cartoons for the *Sunday Chronicle,* including the strip *Teeny,* the adventures of a teenage girl.

On the advice of Leslie Illingworth, he gave up the grind of staff cartoonist for freelancing and began to sell to *Punch.* He began to paint unusual covers for this then-traditional magazine but achieved regular rejections for his unorthodox cartoons. The *Daily Telegraph* accepted his caricature work, and the deliberately iconoclastic *Private Eye* eagerly accepted his more outrageous drawings. Steadman illustrated his first children's book in 1964, *Fly Away Peter,* written by strip cartoonist Frank Dickens (creator of *Bristow*). Many similar commissions followed, the most controversial being his grotesque version of Lewis Carroll's much-loved fantasy, *Alice in Wonderland.*

Books: *Fly Away Peter* (1964); *Love and Marriage* (1965); *Where Love Lies Deepest* (1966); *The Tale of Driver Grope* (1966); *Alice in Wonderland* (1967); and *Ralph Steadman's Jelly Book* (1967). To date he has drawn and illustrated a total of over 75 books. Among his recent titles mention should be made of *Between the Eyes* (1984) and *The Grapes of Ralph* (1992). His awards include the Victoria and Albert Book Award (1973) and the BBC Design Award (1987).

D.G.

STEIG, WILLIAM (1907-) American cartoonist and illustrator born in New York City on November 14, 1907. William Steig attended the City College of New York (1923-25) and then studied at the National Academy of Design (1925-29). In 1930 he submitted some of his work to the *New Yorker,* and editor Harold Ross liked it enough to hire him as a staff cartoonist for the magazine. In addition to the *New Yorker,* he has contributed comic art to many of the mass-circulation magazines of our times.

Steig refers to himself as a humorous artist, probably because of his continuing interest in more formal styles of

"Mother's not very intelligent, but I think you'll like her."
William Steig. © Look.

representation. He works in watercolors as well as ink wash, and his watercolors can be found in the permanent collection of the Brooklyn Museum. Steig is also a wood sculptor whose pieces were featured in one-man shows at the Downtown Gallery in 1939 and at Smith College in 1940 and today are in the permanent collections of the Rhode Island Museum in Providence and the Smith College Museum in Northampton, Massachusetts.

Steig has been an exceptionally durable figure in the field of cartoon art, but hardly a static one. His early work for the *New Yorker* was formal in style and strong in the elements of depth and perspective, perhaps due to his parallel involvement in the plastic medium of wood carving. At first realistic, his style began to shift in the 1930s toward caricature and the flat, nondimensional conventions of comic art. A fine example of his exploration of this mode is a set of primitive, deliberately childish panels from the *New Yorker* entitled "A la Recherche du Temps Perdu"; here he renders recollections apparently from his own childhood in a fashion inspired by Proust. It is a wonderful piece, both as art and as concept, and it is the sort of work that marks Steig as one of the truly thoughtful and innovative artists in a field where being funny need not be the only objective. Like his colleague Steinberg, Steig depends a great deal upon pure style. This is not to say, of course, that Steig is not a funny cartoonist; but in recent times he has shown an increasing tendency to abandon the standard format of cartoon and related caption in favor of small, winsome drawings in the expressionist mode.

Collections of Steig's work, both serious and comic, include *About People* (1939), *The Lonely Ones* (1942), *All Embarrassed* (1944), *Small Fry* (1944), *Persistent Faces* (1945), *Till Death Do Us Part* (1947), *Agony in the Kindergarten* (1949), *The Rejected Lovers* (1951) and *Dreams of Glory* (1953). He is also an award-winning creator of children's books, including *Sylvester and the Magic Pebble* (1969), which won the 1970 Caldecott medal; *Dominic* (1972), which won the 1973 Christopher medal; *Abel's Island* (1976), a Newberry honor book; and *The Amazing Bone* (1976), a Caldecott honor book. Steig's twenty-fifth book, *Grown Ups Get to Do All the Driving* appeared in 1995, and at age 90, his output, which to date has included 1,650 drawings and 117 covers for *The New Yorker*, shows no signs of flagging.

R.C.

STEIN, ENRIQUE (1843-1919) Argentine cartoonist and lithographer born in Paris, France, on October 4, 1843. Henri Stein (he later hispanicized his first name to "Enrique") graduated from the Association Polytechnique de Saint-Denis. He settled in Argentina in 1866, and in 1868, after holding down a variety of odd jobs, he joined the staff of *El Mosquito*, a magazine that had been founded five years earlier by fellow Frenchman Henri (Enrique) Meyer. Stein rapidly rose to the position of editor, and in the early 1870s he bought the publication from Meyer. Stein was the principal artist of *El Mosquito*, for which he drew countless political and humor cartoons, as well as illustrations, until the magazine closed down in 1893. He later worked for other publications, including *La Presidencia* and *Antón Perulero*. His style, inspired by Daumier and the French caricaturists, greatly influenced the course of Argentine cartooning in the late 19th and early 20th centuries.

Stein was also a noted book illustrator and a lithographer of great talent. He left many portraits, including the famous series of portraits of Argentine presidents. Stein exhibited widely throughout Argentina; in later years he taught art at the Argentine Military College. He died in Buenos Aires on January 17, 1919.

A.M.

STEIN, ULI (1946-) Uli Stein was born in Hannover, Germany, in 1946 and named Ulrich Steinfurth. As a cartoonist he later changed his name to the shorter Uli Stein. Uli Stein grew up in Hannover and decided to become a teacher. Therefore he studied in Berlin and Hannover and, after graduation, became a public school teacher of German, biology and geography. He gave up teaching in 1972 in order to work as a freelance press photographer. He also started writing for newspapers and for radio. For 6 years he wrote the satirical texts for a daily late night broadcast on Saarländischer Rundfunk. His penchant for humor and satire led to his rediscovering an ability to draw. So he began drawing gag cartoons, cartoons of black humor, satirical cartoons, critical reports, art for advertising, and post cards. In 1977 he got his first regular cartooning column in the ladies' magazine *freundin*.

Other magazines started asking for his contributions. Among them *Neue Revue*, *Stern*, *Hannoversche Presse*,

Bunte, Playboy and *Hör Zu*, the largest TV guide-type magazine in Germany. For *Hör Zu* Stein created the character of Hörbert, who from 1975 to 1997 was featured on page 3, the opening humor page of *Hör Zu*. The lines Stein supplied Hörbert with more often than not were absolutely hair-raising puns. But they were fun. Apart from the cartoons, Uli Stein also supplied many other humorous features to *Hör zu* and other magazines. For instance photographic cartoons, puns realized as photo montages, or photos of crazy inventions. He also wrote text features, among them, of course, all kinds of puns.

Uli Stein is one of the most visible of entertaining cartoonists in Gemany. His characters, especially his crazy penguins, appear on all kinds of stationery and clothing. Stein's artwork may not be the most graceful around, but it is highly effective and to the point. And it has that deceivingly simple look that attracts large audiences. But, most important of all, the cartoons are funny because Stein is not only a cartoonist but an excellent writer and humorist as well. Apart from oodles of merchandise and publication in the press, Stein's cartoons have been published in book form ever since 1984.

W.F.

Uli Stein, self-caricature.

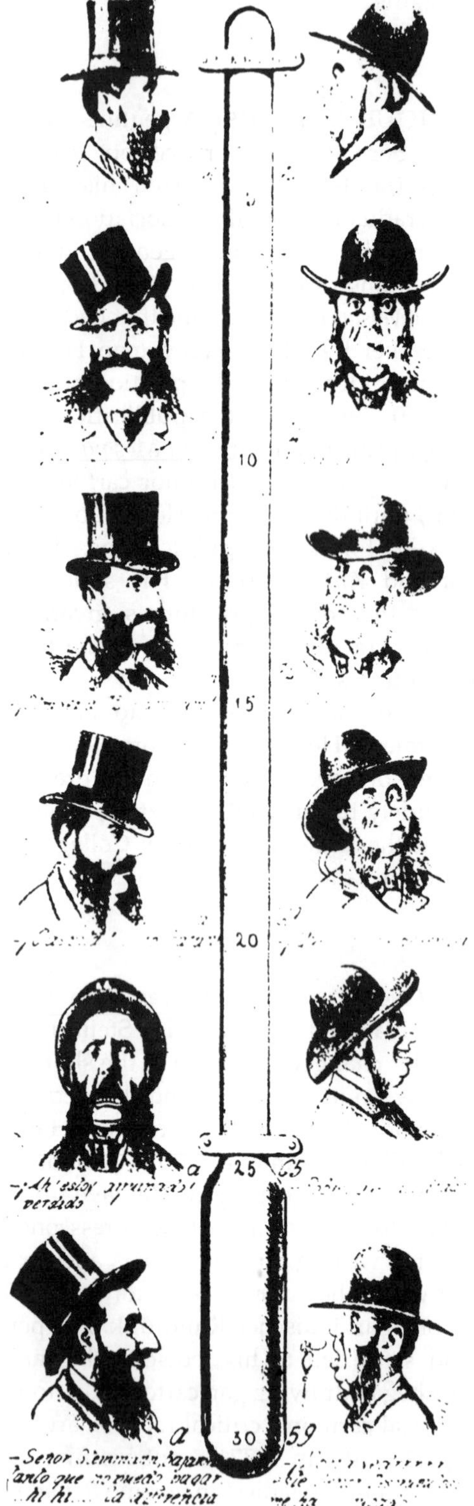

Enrique Stein, 1876.

STEINBERG, SAUL (1914-) American cartoonist and graphic artist born in Romanic-Sarat, Romania, on June 15, 1914. Saul Steinberg graduated from Bucharest High School in 1932 and went on to the University of Bucharest as a student of philosophy. In 1933 he moved to Milan, Italy, and entered the Regio Politecnico as a student of architecture. Between 1936 and 1939, while studying there, he became a contributing cartoonist for the Italian magazine *Bertoldo*. Receiving his doctorate in 1940, he began to practice architecture in Milan. In 1941 he left Italy, a fugitive from Fascism, stopping first in the Dominican Republic, then moving on to the United States in 1943. Naturalized as an American citizen the same year, he immediately joined the U.S. Navy, serving until 1945. After his discharge he took up graphic art as a career, quickly rising to prominence in the field.

Steinberg has won wide popular esteem as a result of his contributions to the *New Yorker*, beginning in the early 1940s; his credentials as an artist have been steadily reinforced by the highest critical acclaim and by one-man exhibits in such prestigious showcases as the Museum of Modern Art in New York (1946), Stedelijk Museum in Amsterdam (1953), Galerie Blanche in Stockholm (1953) and Galerie Maeght in Paris (1973). He is also represented in the permanent collections of the Metropolitan Museum and the Museum of Modern Art in New York. Published collections of his work include *All in a Line* (1945), *The Art of Living* (1949), *The Passport* (1955), *The Labyrinth* (1960), *The New World* (1965) and *The Inspector* (1973).

The foundation of Steinberg's artistic style appears to lie in the surrealism of the early Giorgio di Chirico. As critics have pointed out, however, there is virtually no movement in 20th-century art, from Cubism to pop, that he has not parodied in his own inimitable way. In fact, parody as a potentially wordless language capable of being universally heard and understood is an important element in Steinberg's work. This universality would be meaningless,

Saul Steinberg, 1942. © Liberty.

of course, in the absence of a style distinctive enough to capitalize on it, and this is where Steinberg's gift for the pictorial pun elevates him to true originality; he has indeed invented a language that anyone can understand, yet a language far more complex than those international symbols warning travelers to avoid drinking the water or to refrain from smoking. One's comprehension of Steinberg's achievement is continually laced with wonder as one discovers a world of expression so timelessly obvious, yet so new and unexpected.

The sheer inventive genius of Steinberg's work is staggering. He travels in so many different directions, often simultaneously, that one must see to truly understand—which is, of course, the precise intention of the artist. Take, for example, his use of music staff paper in such a way as to incorporate the bars into his own work so that, except for reference bars left at the top or bottom, one might not be aware that the surface has been marked (a smile in the direction of "conceptual art"?); or his execution of "television" images by series of tiny, tightly massed ink lines that duplicate the visual patterns of telecommunications media (a humorous nod to the pointillists?); or his unique ability to define through pure visual representation, as in his rendering of the phrase "Who did it?" in block letters, with the characters of *who* pushing over the characters of *did*, under which the characters of *it* lie crushed . . . while the question mark looks on with an indefinably yet indisputably curious attitude. In the tradition of the mathematician or Esperantist, then, Steinberg offers a universal language. But in comparison to the relative erudition required of the user of numbers or words, Steinberg's only literacy requirement is a pair of eyes.

Saul Steinberg is arguably the most original and influential of modern cartoonists. He has garnered every possible honor and distinction for his works. In 1978 a Steinberg retrospective was held at the Whitney Museum in New York City, and an exhaustive catalogue was published for the occasion by Knopf. While his output has considerably decreased in the last decade, Steinberg at century's end is still an awesome presence in his field—although his field may be hard to pinpoint exactly. As he himself has said, "I don't belong to the art, cartoon or magazine world, so the art world doesn't quite know where to place me."

R.C.

STEINIGANS, WILLIAM J. (1883-1918) American cartoonist born in New York City in 1883. For practically his whole career—except for contributions to the humorous weekly magazines around the turn of the century—W.J. Steinigans was employed by the *New York World*; he joined the staff as a cartoonist at the age of 19. For the magazines, and for the *World* at first, Steinigans specialized in dog cartoons, but he soon abandoned single-panel drawings for strips. Among his best-remembered features are *The Bad Dream That Made Bill a Better Boy, Splinters the Clown* and *Mr. Hubby.* His drawing style was wistful and breezy, a bit like that of his young compatriots Billy Marriner and Gene Carr. His panels were open—he seldom used solid blacks—and populated by animated dogs and kids.

Steinigans, who was never in good health, moved to California around 1913 and worked for his paper by mail; there he remained, except for several trips to Arizona, until his death in Los Angeles on January 25, 1918.

R.M.

Our Bourgeois Citizens:—"What are you laughing about?"
—"I was just thinking if the Missus saw us."

Alexandre Steinlen, 1901.

STEINLEN, ALEXANDRE (1859-1923) French cartoonist, lithographer, illustrator and poster designer born in Lausanne, Switzerland, on November 10, 1859. At 19, Alexandre Steinlen went to Mulhouse in eastern France to work as an industrial designer in a textile factory. From there he moved to Paris in 1882, joining the crowd of artists and writers around Montmartre's Le Chat Noir nightclub, and contributing to the journal of the same name the amusing series *Les Mésaventures du Corbeau Pochard* ("The Misadventures of the Tippling Raven") and the highly successful *Pages de Chat* ("Pages of Cats"). He collaborated on dozens of papers and magazines, among them *Le Mirliton,* using the pen name "Jean Caillou" *(caillou* means "pebble," and *steinlen* means "little stone" in Swiss German), *Le Croquis, Le Gil Blas Illustré, Le Chambard Socialiste* (under the alias "Petit Pierre"), *Le Rire, Le Petit Sou* and *L'Assiette au Beurre.*

In 1910 Steinlen founded the short-lived *Les Humoristes* with a group of 12 famous cartoonists (Forain, Willette, Léandre, Veber, etc.). In addition to painting a fresco in the Taverne de Paris and designing posters for singer Yvette Guilbert, he illustrated Aristide Bruant's collection of songs, *Dans la Rue* ("In the Street," 1889-95), Anatole France's *Crainquebille* (1901) and several of Maupassant's novels (1902). His own books included *Des Chats: Images sans Paroles* ("Cats: Images Without Words," 1897), *Contes à Sara* ("Tales for Sara," 1898), *Croquis de Temps de Guerre* ("Wartime Sketches," 1919) and *Des Chats et Autres Bêtes* ("Of Cats and Other Beasts," 1923). Alexandre Steinlen died in Paris on December 14, 1923.

Steinlen's social and political cartoons depicted with much bitterness the pain, suffering and poverty of the downtrodden and disinherited, of workers (particularly miners), abandoned children, tramps and prostitutes. They were drawn with compassion and strength as well as a heavily sentimentalized realism that earned him the nickname "Millet of the streets." Along with Forain, Steinlen influenced a whole generation of American cartoonists.

P.H.

STEPHENS, HENRY LOUIS (1832-1882) American cartoonist born in England in 1832. Henry Stephens was one of the most prolific woodcut cartoonists of his day and specialized in political themes. He drew for *Harper's Weekly* and the Frank Leslie publications before founding *Vanity Fair* magazine in 1859, with his two brothers. *Vanity Fair* was one of the most consistent and successful of the scores of American comic sheets in the woodcut era, although it lasted only to 1863. The English proclivities of its founders—anti-Lincoln, anti-black and ever so mildly pro-South—did not foster its popularity in Civil War America (even with the Copperhead sentiment in New York).

Stephens continued to work and surfaced as the chief artist of *Punchinello,* a comic magazine said to have been financed by William Marcy Tweed and other Tammany Hall bosses in 1870. It had a distinguished list of contributors (presumably the talent could be bought) but lasted only nine months. Later, for *St. Nicholas* and the *Riverside* magazine, Stephens drew cartoons and illustrated children's stories. His books included *Aesop's Fables, The Death of Cock Robin* and *The House That Jack Built,* all, obviously, for children, and the earlier *Comic Natural History of the Human Race,* published in Philadelphia.

Stephens was versatile, prolific and, when he wanted to be, acerbic. He died, blind from diabetes and beset by its other complications, at the age of 50 in Bayonne, New Jersey, on December 12, 1882.

R.M.

STERNER, ALBERT (1863-1946) American cartoonist and artist born in London, England, on March 8, 1863, of German-born American parents. Albert Sterner studied art on a scholarship at King Edward School in Birmingham and came to the United States in 1879, only to cross the Atlantic again soon thereafter to study in Paris at the Académie Julian and the Ecole des Beaux-Arts.

Back in America, Sterner worked in Chicago as a painter, etcher and lithographer before establishing a New York studio in 1885. After a first sale to *St. Nicholas,* he sold cartoons to *Life* and cartoons and illustrations to the *Century, Art Age, Collier's* and *Harper's.* His cartoons were illustrative, handsome and self-confident. Sterner had a mature sense of composition and a wonderful command of pen and shading techniques (aided, no doubt, by his experience in preparing woodcuts for engravers several years before). Many of his locales were drawing rooms; the subjects were as dignified as his art.

Sterner taught in some of the best art schools—the School of the National Academy, the Art Students League, and the New York School of Applied Design for Women. Among his many distinctions, he was named to the National Academy, was a founder of the Society of Illustrators (and its president in 1907 and 1908), was commissioned to paint portraits of many prominent people and has work hanging in many museums.

His awards include an honorable mention at the Paris Salon, a bronze medal at the Paris Exposition of 1900, a silver medal at the Berlin International Exposition, a gold medal at Munich (1905) and the National Academy of Design Award (1935). Sterner died on December 16, 1946.

R.M.

STO

See Tofano, Sergio.

STOP

See Morel-Retz, Louis-Pierre.

STORNI, ALFREDO (1881-1966) Brazilian cartoonist born in Santa Maria do Livramento, Rio Grande do Sul, Brazil, on November 4, 1881. Alfredo Storni founded several humor magazines in his native state, including *O Bisturi* in Rio Grande in 1899 and *O Gafanhoto* in Santa Maria da Bôca do Monte a few years later. Starting in 1906, he also contributed cartoons to the Rio magazine *O Malho.* Discouraged by the failure of his publishing ventures, Storni moved to Rio in 1907. For many years he was *O Malho's* most prolific contributor, mainly doing cartoons of a topical or humorous nature but also drawing some of the magazine's covers (this latter activity became more frequent after 1918).

Storni drew a number of comic strips for the children's weekly *O Tico-Tico,* starting in 1908, and freelanced cartoons to the magazines *Filhote* (from 1909 on) and *Careta* (1922-36). Indeed, there are few Brazilian magazines that have not boasted at one time or another the signature of Alfredo Storni. In addition Storni occasionally turned out editorial cartoons for daily newspapers (the *Correio da Noite,* notably) and did a number of book and magazine illustrations. He is best known, however, for his long tenure in *O Malho,* where his witty cartoons were enjoyed by several generations of readers. Storni died in Niteroi, near Rio de Janeiro, on March 21, 1966.

A.M.

STREETS OF NEW YORK, THE (U.S.) Though not as searching as the tenement cartoons Michael Angelo Woolf was to draw later in the decade, *Puck*'s series *The Streets of New York* provides students of the city with a revealing view of urban life and, through satire, of its problems. Students of cartoons can also trace the development of one Frederick Opper, as he was the major artist for the series, which ran intermittently in *Puck* between 1881 and 1886. The series was mainly his (he even included himself in the half-page cartoon of May 31, 1882), although Graetz, Gillam, Woolf and Zimmerman contributed other cartoons. Opper's style progressed from crude and broad to illustrative and refined during its run.

The cartoons were always on *Puck*'s interior pages and in black and white. They were mainly humorous, with such gags as a deliveryman's horse eating hay from the wagon in front (May 30, 1883) and a suicide turning into an advertising stunt (August 8, 1883). Sometimes they provided what must have been realistic glimpses of city life: swarms of Germans crowding the sidewalk on a warm night on Avenue A (July 5, 1882) or the horrors for pedestrians of pipe-laying (November 1, 1882). Occasionally the series probed deep into social conditions, as in Graetz's devastating half-page "The Gospel unto Sinners," where the police shove the poor out of a church entrance so women in finery can enter (April 19, 1882), or Woolf's "Homes of the Microbes," a simple and brilliant depiction of squalor, mud, dead cats, liquor shops and overcrowding (April 1, 1885).

The series deserves to be collected and reprinted along with other early views of urban life as seen by American cartoonist-observers.

R.M.

STRUBE, SIDNEY (1891-1956) British cartoonist born in London, England, in 1891.

"Never let it go until you are satisfied—and never be satisfied!" This was the motto of Sidney Strube, for 36 years the king of Fleet Street cartoonists, with an unrivaled record of employment on one newspaper, the *London Daily Express.* Strube started his artistic career by drawing technical advertisements, after an apprenticeship as a designer of overmantels for a firm off the City Road. Tiring of drawing technical electricals for the trade press, Strube signed on at the John Hassall School and immediately felt at ease under the genial tutelage of the leading humorous poster designer of the day. Encouraged to extend his caricaturing capabilities, Strube took some specimens to the *Conservative and Unionist* at Hassall's suggestion. The editor immediately bought four cartoons for ten shillings apiece. Strube was made!

Setting up a freelance studio with Hearn Scott, Strube began supplying a weekly full-page cartoon for *Throne and Country* (1910), which paid him a full guinea a week. One day they turned down what Strube regarded as his most brilliant effort. Incensed, he left it at the editorial office of the *Daily Express* and next morning saw it published in that newspaper. Within a few weeks he had signed on as a staff cartoonist, exclusive, on a two-year contract. He remained with the *Express* until he retired, 36 years later.

Of all the cartoon characters who emerged from Strube's pen during those six-a-week years for England's leading daily, none was more endearing than the Little Man. This symbol of the average man went to the hearts of the *Express* readers, who eagerly turned to the center leader page each day in the hope of seeing their hero in action—or perhaps *reaction* is more the word. The Little Man was more a sideline commentator than a "doer" until World War II, when he donned his tin hat and his air raid warden's armlet and symbolized Britain at bay against all comers. His downtrodden datedness wore out his welcome, however, and his bowler hat, pince-nez, celluloid collar, rolled umbrella, tailcoat and striped pants were outmoded symbols by the time Carl Giles and his common man's gritty Granny moved in to take over.

Books: *Cartoons from the Daily Express* (1927-28); *Strube's Annual* (1929-30); *100 Cartoons* (1931-35); and *Strube's War Cartoons* (1944).

D.G.

STRUWWELPETER (Germany) For Christmas 1844, the Frankfurt physician Heinrich Hoffmann, who had a couple of unspectacular books of verse to his credit and had had no art training whatsoever, wrote and illustrated a little book for his three-year-old son. Hoffmann was drawing upon his experiences with frightened child patients, whom he would calm by telling and sketching funny little tales about just such difficult children as they were. He showed his book to his crony Dr. Löning, who, together with J. Rütten, had recently founded the Frankfurt publishing house Literarische Anstalt.

The manuscript was faithfully copied by the Anstalt's lithographers, and the lithographs were hand-colored. The book, called *Lustige Geschichten und Drollige Bilder mit 15 Schön Kolorirten Tafeln für Kinder von 3-6 Jahren* ("Merry Stories and Funny Pictures, with 15 Beautifully Colored Plates, for Children from 3 to 6") and signed Reimerich Kinderlieb (*Reimerich* is a combination of "rhymer" and "Heinrich"; *Kinderlieb* means "child-love"), was published in 1845 in an edition of 1,500 copies that was sold out in a month. It contained only 6 of the later canonical 10 stories, and the boy with wildly unkempt hair and long uncut nails—Struwwelpeter (variously known in English as "Slovenly Peter" and "Shock-headed Peter")—came last in the book. Today only 5 complete copies of this first edition are known; the one in the New York Public Library (Spencer Collection) was acquired in 1933 for $1,000.

It was not until the fifth edition that Hoffmann's name appeared on the book (an intermediate credit had been "Heinrich Kinderlieb"), that Struwwelpeter appeared at the beginning instead of the end (children had clamored for him especially) and that all ten characters or groups of characters were finally present: Struwwelpeter; cruel Friedrich, whose whipped dog turns upon him; Pauline, who plays with fire and is burnt to a cinder (this was to be the fate of Busch's *fromme Helene*—and indeed, Hoffmann's stories, drawings and doggerel couplets are all direct ancestors of Busch's much finer efforts); the three bad boys who laugh at a little blackamoor and are dipped into ink by the giant Niklas; the Sunday hunter (the only protagonist not a child) who is attacked by the rabbit he has been stalking (a theme harking back to the Middle Ages and ahead to Bugs Bunny); Konrad the thumbsucker, whose thumbs are cut off by the bogeyman exactly as his mother warned (can mothers lie?); Kaspar, who refuses to eat and dwindles away; Philipp, who squirms at the table and is buried under the whole meal; Hanns, who won't watch where he's going and falls in the river; and "flying Robert," carried off by his umbrella. Hoffmann was seriously aiming at inculcating moral precepts by means of these little adventures.

Late in the 1850s, the author, apparently no longer satisfied by his extremely primitive but charming first drawings, created an entirely new manuscript of *Struwwelpeter;* reproduced by wood engraving instead of litho, it is the basis for all subsequent editions. In 1876 the Literarische Anstalt published the hundredth edition, which included an anniversary page depicting Struwwelpeter with beautifully combed hair! By 1925 there had been almost six hundred German editions.

Translated into numerous languages, the book became familiar to children everywhere. It has often been parodied ("political Struwwelpeters" have regularly appeared in Germany since 1849, and there was one published in London in 1899). Musical pieces have been written about the characters, including a comic opera produced in London in 1900.

S.A.

J.H. Stuart, cover for "ABC," 1921. © ABC a Rir.

STUART, JOSÉ HERCULANO TORRIE DE ALMEIDA CARVALHAIS (1888-1961) Portuguese cartoonist born of Scottish ancestry in Vila Real de Trás-Os-Montes, Portugal, on January 7, 1888. José Stuart's studies were irregular. In high school he failed in the subject of drawing. Around 1909 Stuart began working as an illustrator for *Suplemento Humorístico do Século, Má Língua* and *Ilustração Portuguesa,* and he also published drawings in *A Sátira, O Gorro, O Zé* and *O Pardal* after the fall of the Portuguese monarchy in 1910.

Stuart went to Paris in 1913 and lived in Montparnasse, where he joined other Portuguese artists, such as Santa Rita Pintor, Almada Negreiros, José Paxeco and Sousa Cardoso. He succeeded in his Parisian period, publishing drawings in *Gil Blas, Excelsior, Le Journal, Pages Folles, Cri de Paris, Le Rire, Le Sourire* and *L'Assiette au Beurre.* However, unable to submit himself to the discipline of a contract, he finally broke off with his French editors and returned to Portugal.

Stuart then began a period of intense activity, publishing cartoons in *Papagaio Real* (1914), *Riso da Vitória* (1919), *Abc a Rir* (1921-32), *Corja* (1924), *Ilustração* (1926), *Sempre Fixe* (1926-46), *Magazine Bertrand* (1931), *Magazine Civilização* (1931) and all types of publications—weeklies, daily newspapers, posters, programs, postcards and book covers. His participation in youth journalism was very important. His main creations in this field were the characters Quim and Manecas, heroes of a comic strip that started in *Século Cómico* in 1915, in which Stuart began using balloons and onomatopoeia (devices that were not very common in Europe at that time). The other youth magazines that published his works were, mainly, *Abczinho* (1921), *O Carlitos* (1922), *Sportsinhos* (1925), *O Senhor Doutor* (1933), *Tic Tac* (1933-36) and *Pajem* (1952). The last humorous magazines that published his drawings were *Os Ridiculos* (1945), *Cara Alegre* (1951) and *Picapau* (1955).

Stuart's activity as an artist suffered because of a bohemian life that led him to waste his talent and branch out into other fields. In 1954 he held his only individual exhibition, which had little significance. He died in the Hospital Santa Maria in Lisbon on March 3, 1961. Stuart's paintings are at present scattered among private collections. His vast work, which captures beautifully the life and character of the people of Lisbon in the 1930s and 1940s, is still far from being catalogued. In his honor there is in Lisbon a little street named after him.

C.P.

STUCK, FRANZ VON (1863-1928) German painter, printmaker, sculptor and cartoonist born in Tettenweis, Lower Bavaria, on February 23, 1863. Franz Stuck (the *von* came in 1906, when the then hallowed painter was knighted) was the son of a miller. In 1882 he went for the first time to Munich, which was to become his permanent home (the grandiose villa he designed for himself there at the height of his fame was a noted showpiece). From 1882 to 1884 he studied at the Munich Arts and Crafts School, moving on to the Academy in 1885.

To earn money while studying, he did commercial art and sold cartoons to the local humor magazines *Allotria* and *Fliegende Blätter*. These cartoons, characterized by remarkable draftsmanship, won him his first fame. They depict students carousing mindlessly, fat bourgeois and peasants visiting the Pinakothek, and—already—the allegorical figures Stuck was so fond of. The masterpiece of this early cartoon period was the series of illustrations for the magazine story *Hans Schreier, der Grosse Mime* ("John Shouter, the Great Actor").

In the first half of the 1880s, Stuck had drawn vignettes for the famous art publisher Martin Gerlach, contributing, for instance, to the design album *Allegorien und Embleme*. In 1887 Gerlach published a comparable book by Stuck alone, the extremely well received *Karten und Vignetten*, containing designs for menus, invitations and the like. Humor was an important feature of this volume, emphasized on the title page, and even though it was chiefly exemplified by frolicsome putti (forecasting the archness of Stuck's later work), there were also such items as a popular scene at the races and a peasant couple dancing.

In 1889 Stuck began to achieve fame as a painter. Influenced by Böcklin, Diez and Lenbach, Stuck acquired a virtuoso technique that made the surfaces of his pictures rich and scintillating, but his subject matter gained him the disapproval of the young and a long general oblivion in his old age and after death. He chose to chronicle the amours, sports and sundry everyday doings of—centaurs and fauns! His hundreds of only slightly varied canvases combine these insipidly precious themes with pronounced realism in the rendering. The humor is now ponderous. Fortunately, his numerous preliminary drawings (made directly from completely human models) join great freshness of vision to their immense skill, and glints of the old cartoonist occasionally come through.

In 1893 Stuck helped to found the artists' group known as the Munich Secession (he designed well-known posters for their shows). He became a professor at the Munich Academy in 1895. He died at Tetschen (now Děčín, Czechoslovakia) on August 30, 1928.

S.A.

SUBURBAN RESIDENT, THE (U.S.) *The Suburban Resident* was the creation of Frederick Burr Opper in the pages of *Puck* magazine. Reacting to and lampooning the phenomenon of suburbanization, Opper introduced the diminutive and harried Suburban Resident in 1889. At first nameless, Opper's suburbanite was usually pictured as sad-eyed, mousy and bespectacled. His home was usually in the outer reaches of Brooklyn (much of which was rural in those days) or in "Loneliville, N.J." He had the "bundle habit," riding home each night along forlorn commuter rail lines with packages and bags from the city. He delighted in the sounds, smells and sights of the country—although sane observers could only recognize cacophony, stench and barrenness.

Opper used his Suburban Resident in single-panel cartoons and multipanel back-page drawings in color throughout his tenure at *Puck*. Eventually his character assumed a name, Howson Lott (a poor pun), and this character survived to Opper's comic strip days; *Howson Lott* ran intermittently in the Hearst papers, except for a five-month stretch in 1910 when it appeared every Sunday. The theme here was similar: city friends would visit the Lotts for a quiet respite in the country, only to be driven away by the farm noises, animal smells, mosquitoes, rural oafs, etc.

The Suburban Resident, when considered as a whole, constitutes a remarkable study (albeit a parody) of suburban life and social migration in Victorian and turn-of-the-century America. Ironically, Opper himself became a suburbanite in the late 1890s when he moved to Bath Beach in Brooklyn; he later settled in New Rochelle, New York, another commuter community.

R.M.

SUDARTA, GERARDUS MAYELA (1946-) G.M. Sudarta has spent his three decades of cartooning with one newspaper, the Jakarta-based daily *Kompas*. His association with the paper began in 1967 when he contributed gag cartoons. Since 1969, he has served as *Kompas*'s political cartoonist, averaging two cartoons a week. He also draws caricature to accompany stories and works with the *Kompas* culture foundation in its efforts to preserve Indonesian traditional arts. When his political cartoons use words, Sudarta includes a stock character, "Oom Pasikom," who has become popular in his own right.

Besides his *Kompas* work, Sudarta has contributed political and gag cartoons to *Prisma, Merah Putih, Penyebar Semangat*, and other Indonesian magazines, and once a month, his cartoons about Japanese life in Indonesia appear in Tokyo's *Mainichi Shimbun*. Considered Indonesia's most prominent political cartoonist, he captured the top award for opinion cartooning given by the Indonesian Press Association 5 years running before being made ineligible when selected as a judge for the award.

A master at indirect criticism during the long and repressive Suharto regime, Sudarta uses traditional puppet (*wayang*) characters, well known to the public for their qualities of frankness or slowness, to get his points across. He hopes through his political cartoons, to bring situations to the surface in order to create dialogue which might lead to improvements or solutions. But he warns that he must

Gerardus Sudarta. © Kompas.

be careful, making sure a dialogue continues between critics such as himself and those being criticized. Sudarta believes, "We need cartoons which draw a smile for all. A smile for the one being criticized, so he won't be angry; a smile for the society which feels repressed in its aspirations; and a smile for the cartoonist who feels no worry of being put in jail."

J.A.L.

SUGIURA, HINAKO (1958-) Born on November 30, 1958, in Tokyo as the daughter of a kimono manufacturer, Hinako Sugiura became interested in the lifestyle of the people of the Edo Era (mainly 18th and 19th centuries) during her student days at Nippon University, College of Fine Arts. She studied intensively to become a historian, specializing in the Edo Era, but to express her interests in a different way until she became a professional in that field, she began drawing cartoons and sent them to *Garo*. Her first work was published in 1980. *Gasso* ("Joint Funeral"), a fine study of the life, works and mentality of ukiyoe artists, was met with high praise.

Sugiura drew extensively, and her works include: *Eimosesu* (1980), *Nipponica Nippon* (1980), *Sarusuberi* (1982) and *Furyu Edo Suzume* (Fantastic Days of Edo Era) (1987). With her four volumes of *Hyaku Monogatari* (A Hundred Horror Stories) in 1994, Sugiura retired as a cartoonist. Although the eight-volume *Complete Works of Sugiura Hinako* was published in 1996, Sugiura is now a full-fledged historian, a commentator on television and a major book reviewer. She also reveals her exceptional talent in her essays on the Edo Era.

All the stories of Sugiura's comics are set in the Edo Era, a time in Japanese history in which she thinks the common folks were most lively. Drawing with brush strokes in the traditional Japanese painting style, Sugiura vividly recreates the lifestyle of the people who, she believes were able to carry on a more humane life than in the modern age. A clever blend of humor and authenticity, Sugiura's works are appreciated by historians as well as the common reader.

K.O.

SUGIURA, YUKIO (1911-) Japanese cartoonist born in Tokyo, Japan, on June 25, 1910. Yukio Sugiura graduated from middle school in 1929 and began his study of cartooning under Ippei Okamoto.

Sugiura is considered one of the "old guard" of Japanese cartoonists. As in the case of Hidezo Kondo, another famous elder statesman of the Japanese cartoon world, his career spans the period in which Japanese cartoons underwent the greatest changes. Sugiura was one of the founding members of the Shin Mangaha Shudan ("New Cartoonists' Group"), an association of young cartoonists who lobbied during the years before World War II for greater access to major Japanese newspapers and magazines. In 1940, Sugiura became one of the staff members of the Shin Mangaka Kyōkai ("Association of New Cartoonists") and produced most of the social satire cartoons for its publication, *Manga* ("Cartoon"). When the war broke out, *Manga* was forced to print only those cartoons deemed "supportive" of official policy, but Sugiura

Yukio Sugiura, a World War II satirical cartoon attacking food-hoarders and black marketeers. © Bakusho.

was able to slip in a few cartoons critical of wartime injustices.

After the war, Sugiura became a staff member of the revived *Manga* and built a reputation as an "erotic" cartoonist who depicted life in the new cafés, cabarets and strip clubs in occupied Japan. His style has always been light and gentle, with frequent use of background shading, but the themes of his work were never less than direct, particularly when he dealt with the seamier aspects of life in postwar Japan. Sugiura drew for many of the short-lived comic publications that sprang up just after the end of the war, such as *Comet* and *Manga to Dokusho* (both of which appeared in 1946); but his most lasting contributions include *Hanako-san, Atomic Obon, Kokayoshi Korako* and various cartoons drawn for the magazines *Shukan Tokyo* and *Tokyo Chaki Chaki Musume.* In 1956 Sugiura received the second Bunshu cartoon award for his cartoons of social satire and parody entitled *Karufūryū Hakusho* ("A White Paper on Simple Elegance"), which appeared in the magazine *Manga Dokuhon.* He is now retired.

J.C.

SUISHIN OYAJI (Japan) A three-to-four-panel Japanese cartoon created by Ichio Matsushita, *Suishin Oyaji* ran in the magazine *Asahi Graph* from the autumn of 1940 to the end of the war in 1945. The hero of the cartoon was a small but wiry company president known for his tremendous vitality and bustle, and each episode showed him admonishing his workers to increase production, reduce waste and keep morale high. The spirit of *Suishin Oyaji* (which can be translated roughly as "Mr. Promotion") matched the official philosophy of the times: the little company president did his utmost to see that his firm achieved its full production potential, which was exactly what the Japanese government wanted every citizen to do.

Though cartoons in wartime Japan were in reality propaganda tools, Suishin Oyaji did have his more human moments. When his exhortations seemed to have an effect, he would sometimes exclaim with a tear, "M—men, you h—have made me very h—happy." *Suishin Oyaji* is probably best remembered as one of the major vehicles of the wartime slogan "No matter what, we shall succeed!" It was a classic example of how Japanese cartoon art, which had been so innovative and expressive in the 1920s and 1930s, became thoroughly colored with nationalistic themes after the start of the war in China and the Pacific.

Ichio Matsushita, the artist, was born in Nagano Prefecture on April 23, 1910. He graduated from the journalism department of Meiji University and studied under Rakuten Kitazawa. Later he worked as a cartoonist for the *Jiji Manga* ("Cartoon Times") and the *Maiyū Shimbun* ("Evening News"), where he drew political and social commentary cartoons. Ironically, he also had a hand in the founding of *Karikare,* a cartoon magazine highly critical of the establishment, but he was later converted to the militarists' cause. During the war he not only created *Suishin Oyaji* but was also active in producing propaganda cartoons that were distributed over the Southeast Asian front to weaken enemy resistance. After the war, Matsushita created the Komikku Manga Kenkyu Kai ("Comic Cartoon Institute"). He continues to work actively in cartoons. Other representative works include *Hoshi Kara Kita Otoko* ("Man Who Came from the Stars"), *Aka Zukin* ("Red Hood") and *Ten Ten no Techan.*

J.C.

SULLIVAN, PAT (1887-1933) American cartoonist, animator and producer born in Australia in 1887. Pat Sullivan worked briefly as a cartoonist on a number of Australian newspapers before moving to London at the age of 20. While there, he reportedly worked on a number of comic features, including *Ally Sloper.*

Sullivan moved to New York in 1914 and tried his hand (not too successfully) at drawing comic strips. In 1915 he entered the animation field, learning his craft in the studio of pioneer animator Raoul Barré. Sullivan's first effort is said to have been animation titles for Metro Pictures. By 1916 he was producing animated shorts (usually half a reel) for legendary distributor Pat Powers, releasing through Universal Pictures. A number of these cartoons were based on Sullivan's comic strip character Sammy (sometimes spelled Sammie) Johnsin; these included "Sammy Johnsin Slumbers Not," "Sammy Johnsin at the Seaside" and "Sammy Johnsin Magician." *Trials of Willie Winks, Nervy Nat Has His Fortune Told* (based on a James Montgomery Flagg character) and *Motor Matt and His Fliv* (on which Sullivan's talented animator Otto Messmer received credit for the first time) were some other noteworthy 1916 releases.

In 1917 the Sullivan Cartoon Comedies (as they were officially called) lost Otto Messmer to World War I, but Sullivan continued with such replacements as Will Anderson and George D. Clardey. Some of the titles of that year were *Barnyard Nightmare, Cupid Gets Some New Dope* and *Young Nick Carter, Detectiff.* Also that year Sullivan launched a short-lived series of *Boomer Bill* cartoons featuring a sailor; but his most momentous effort was *Tail of Thomas Kat,* the prototype of *Felix the Cat.*

Origin of the Shimmy
Pat Sullivan, 1919. © Pat Sullivan.

With Messmer's return from the war in 1919, the Sullivan studio went into high gear; Felix the Cat became the most popular cartoon character of the 1920s. Sullivan left the animation chores in care of Messmer and other gifted artists (including, ironically, Sullivan's former boss, Raoul Barré). With the income his cartoons and clever merchandising generated, he indulged his tastes for high living, horse races, boxing bouts, fast cars and attractive women. After the mid-1920s he seldom set foot in his own studio. He died of cardiac arrest in New York on February 16, 1933. By that time, owing to his refusal to bear the extra expense that sound would have entailed, he had lost his leadership of the animation field to Walt Disney.

Sullivan dominated animation in the 1920s. He was responsible for bringing to the screen the first cartoon character to win worldwide popularity. Yet his artistic achievement remains clouded; while he did have a hand in the creation of his cartoons (at least prior to 1925), he never exercised the kind of direction and story control later shown by Disney. It is nonetheless undeniable that Sullivan is one of the most important figures in American (and world) animation.

M.H.

SULLIVANT, THOMAS S. (1854-1926) American cartoonist born in Ohio in 1854. Raised in Germany, T.S. Sullivant

No Time to Waste. —Mrs Farmer: "If I offered you a job would you refuse it?" —Weary Willie: "No, lady; I couldn't spare de time. I'm simply rushed ter death refusin' offers uv jobs."
T.S. Sullivant, 1904.

returned to the United States to study at the Pennsylvania Academy of Fine Arts; in his late twenties, his cartoons began to appear in minor humor publications. His first major sale was to *Puck* magazine in 1887, on the recommendation of A.B. Frost.

Sullivant's early work showed him to be an unsure imitator of the prevailing style of realism, tight cross-hatching, etc. But in the early 1890s he blossomed in the pages of *Life,* most likely under the personal supervision of editor J.A. Mitchell, himself a cartoonist and a sagacious spotter of talent who was also wisely coaxing the likes of C.D. Gibson, Will Crawford, Hy Mayer, Art Young and others from obscurity to individualized recognition.

There was a cartoonist for *Life* named MacNair whose exaggerated heads may have been an inspiration to Sullivant—or perhaps F.M. Howarth's stylized figures in *Puck* might have planted the germ. It is also possible, of course, that Sullivant's artistic eccentricities were wholly native. In any event, in the mid-1890s the cartooning world awoke to Sullivant's genius just as the public relished his highly individual—philosophically and graphically—world view.

As he may have borrowed (the point became irrelevant), others now borrowed from him: Charles Dana Gibson drew one cartoon with characters straight from Sullivant's inkwell; Will Crawford for some time drew figures reminiscent of Sullivant's; J.S. Pughe, in *Puck,* kept Sullivant derivatives on reserve when he switched styles for variation's sake.

At the turn of the century Sullivant switched the majority of his work to the pages of *Judge* magazine, where he had greater scope and occasional use of color. Here, between 1900 and 1903, the best work of his career was done. For *Judge* he reveled in his calculated exaggerations. His was a wonderworld of funny animals, bizarre realities, altered perspectives and outrageous character types—principally the Irish, Jews, Negroes, tramps and farmers. Beneath all his visual fun and playful tampering with reality was an absolutely stunning knowledge of things as they should be. Sullivant was a superb draftsman, and his grasp of shading, perspective, anatomy and construction of physical objects was flawless. Since he was in complete control of his creations, his work was all the more intriguing: everything that was wrong was still somehow right.

The omnipresent talent-hunter William Randolph Hearst lured Sullivant from *Judge* to design top strips for his Sunday comic sections and draw political cartoons for the *New York Journal.* These were, predictably, brilliant—at least in artistic execution—but Sullivant left Hearst around 1906. It is reported that he went to Europe to study.

In 1911 he returned to the pages of *Life,* where he remained until his death. His work was still wholly his own, and he remained popular (Sullivant was heralded as one of the magazine's major stars in the 1920s, when Gluyas Williams, Percy Crosby, Maxfield Parrish, A.B. Frost, Benchly and others vied for attention), but the almost supernatural zip of the early years was gone. In the early 1920s he drew a series of political cartoons for *Life;* the lines betrayed his advancing years and the subjects simply were not the old assortment of special Sullivant surprises. The animals remained, but the chorus of ethnics was gone. Though he was still a cartoonist above the average, at the end of his career Sullivant's vision had turned conventional. He died in 1926.

Sullivant's original drawings, always huge, betray as much scratched-out area as inked lines—he evidently agonized over just the right shadings and lines. One anecdote, delivered entirely facetiously, no doubt, has it that Frederick Opper commented during one of Sullivant's correction scratch-out marathons, "If Tom Sullivant scratched his head as much as his paper, he'd draw better cartoons!" Of course it was merely a jibe; Sullivant, even today, with the dearth of reprinted Sullivant material, remains a major inspiration to cartoonists. No less a cartoonist than Walt Kelly worshipped his genius.

R.M.

SUNFLOWER STREET (U.S.) *Sunflower Street,* the creation of Tom Sims (writer) and Tom Little (artist), started in 1934 as a daily panel for King Features Syndicate. In 1939 Sims went on to write the *Thimble Theater* strip, and by 1940 Little remained as sole author of the feature. *Sunflower Street* was unusual in that it had an all-black cast of characters (its closest antecedent was E.W. Kemble's *Blackberries*). Although not devoid of stereotypes, *Sunflower Street* was far from being a funny-paper *Amos 'n' Andy.* The people in it—the gentle but shrewd Pap Henty, the sagacious Granny Lou, the white-bearded Mr. Native, the ne'er-do-well Cousin Bobo, the panel's children, Eenie, Meenie, Miney and Moe—had real character and much charm. The pace was relaxed, and the humor always low-key.

Nothing really disturbing ever happened on Sunflower

Susie, Granny Lou and Eeny
"Sunflower Street." © King Features Syndicate.

Street, and its critics have pointed to that fact as proof of the panel's failings; but the same omission also characterized most small-town features of the 1930s and 1940s. Little poured a great deal of heart into *Sunflower Street,* as well as many fond remembrances of his rural Tennessee childhood. It was therefore with great reluctance that he finally discontinued it in 1949, due to falling readership.

M.H.

SUOMALAINEN, KARI YRJÄNÄ (1920-) Finnish cartoonist and graphic artist born in Helsinki, Finland, on October 15, 1920. Kari Suomalainen is by far the best-known political cartoonist in Finland today. His cartoons and comic strips have been published since his high school days in the mid-1930s. British influence could be seen in his early cartoons, and his comic strips were very American in inspiration. Intending to become a painter—he still paints occasionally—Kari (as he is usually known) dropped out of high school to attend the University of Arts, the alma mater of so many famous Finnish cartoonists.

Kari wrote and illustrated suspense stories and drew covers for pulp novels. During World War II he worked in the documentation and propaganda section of the army, drawing pictures of the war and making pinup illustrations. In 1951 he became the editorial cartoonist of *Helsingin Sanomat,* the largest newspaper in Finland, and this has remained his main occupation ever since.

A staunch conservative from the beginning, Kari has often aroused hard feelings and sometimes provoked other political cartoonists to counterattack in their cartoons. On the other hand, his drawings hang on the walls of many of the politicians he has satirized. Kari belongs to no political party; he is best described as a populist who denounces big government and political parties and often voices the sentiments of "the man in the street." He rarely touches upon world affairs, but his works in this vein are included in the book *Verdicts on Vietnam.*

Kari has also written plays and published several books, including *Kakarakirja* (1959 and 1977), *Löysin Lännen* ("I Found the West," 1960) and *Sotakuvia* ("War Pictures," 1963). A collection of his cartoons, *The Christmas Street,* was published in English in 1964. In Finland these collections have come out almost yearly, the first being *Karin Parhaat* ("Kari's Cartoons") in 1953. His cartoons have been published in such magazines as *Tuulispää, Pippuri* and *Viikko.* He is the only Finnish recipient of an American National Cartoonists Society award (1959). He has also received many other international and Finnish awards. He retired in the 1990s.

J.R.

In the Manner of Da Vinci:
(The People's Artist Kari had become the Court Portrait Painter.)
"How do I feel? Just like a man who has lost a gold mine."

Kari Suomalainen. © Helsingin Sanomat.

"Superman." © DC Comics.

SUPERMAN (U.S.) The fantastic success enjoyed by the Superman comic books ever since the character's first appearance in 1938 prompted Max Fleischer and Paramount to attempt an animated version of the adventures of the "Man of Steel." The first *Superman* cartoon, directed by Max's brother Dave, was released in 1941 and proved successful enough to give rise to 16 more episodes, produced between 1941 and 1943.

The Fleischer brothers succeeded in preserving the naive but winning spirit of the original creation. The characters of Clark Kent and Lois Lane were cleverly transposed to the new medium; if anything, Superman's amazing feats appeared even more awesome on the screen, as spectators saw him actually leap over tall buildings, outrace a speeding bullet or stop a powerful locomotive. World War II intervened in the filming of the series and provided the Man of Steel with foes more suitable than the motley lot of villains he was used to fighting. Japanese and Nazis were made short shrift of in such entries as "Superman in the Japoteurs" and "Superman in Secret Agent." The series was wildly popular and might have continued had not soaring production costs and financial difficulties forced Paramount (which had taken over the Fleischer studios in the meantime) to discontinue the venture in 1943.

Superman was one of the very few successful straight-adventure cartoon series. The artistic quality of the cartoons was due to Max Fleischer's tight rein on production (before his departure in 1942), the inspired direction by Dave Fleischer (and later by Seymour Kneitel and Isadore Sparber) and the excellent layout and design.

Superman was again the protagonist of a cartoon series (this time for television) in the 1960s; the program was aimed, however, at the Saturday morning kiddie audience and was only a paltry reflection of the scintillating Fleischer shorts. Superman is currently appearing on TV again, along with other DC supercharacters, in *Superfriends,* a Saturday morning cartoon program. Following the success of the *Superman* movies in the 1980s, CBS again aired a *Superman* TV series in 1988-89, without great success. In 1996 a new *Superman* animated show started TV syndication in the wake of the popularity of the *Lois and Clark* program.

M.H.

SURVAGE, LEOPOLD (1879-1968) French painter and artist born Leopold Sturzwage in Moscow, Russia, on July 31, 1879. Survage attended the Moscow School of Fine Arts, from which he graduated at the turn of the century. Greatly impressed by the work of the modern French painters and disillusioned by the failure of the 1905 Russian revolution, he went to Paris in 1908 and studied at the studio of Henri Matisse. The first exhibition of his paintings took place in Paris in 1912, and he was soon part of the coterie of artists that included the likes of Picasso, Braque, Léger, Modigliani and others.

Between 1912 and 1914, Survage made a series of color paintings that he called "rhythm-color symphonies in motion"; he intended to have them put on film, thereby bridging the gap between painting and the cinema. Although nothing came of his efforts because of the advent of World War I, Survage's contribution should not go unnoticed. He proved to be the first theoretician of abstract animation, and his work paved the way for other painters (Léger, Man Ray, etc.) who would successfully follow in his footsteps. His theories have now come to be regarded as seminal in the development of avant-garde animation.

Survage abandoned his pioneering work in animation in the early 1920s and devoted the rest of his life exclusively to painting. He died near Paris on October 31, 1968.

M.H.

SUTENEKO TORACHAN (Japan) One of the first quality animated films to be produced in the wake of the devastation of World War II, *Suteneko Torachan* ("Little Tora, an Abandoned Kitten") was created and directed by Kenzo Masaoka in 1947, with production handled jointly by Nihon Dōga and the educational film department of Tōhō. It was a two-reel talkie, and the first in a series of four *Torachan* films, followed by *Torachan to Hanayome* ("Little Tora and the Bride," 1948), *Torachan no Kan Kan Mushi* ("Little Tora, the Dry Dock Worker," 1950) and *Torachan no Bōken* ("Little Tora's Adventures," 1955).

Suteneko Torachan was a gentle, slowly paced but beautiful film that served to lift the spirits of Japanese children at a time when they were often worried about where their next meal would come from. It was a time when war orphans still wandered the streets, and little Tora, an abandoned kitten, provided a pleasant focus for a happy resolution of their plight. In the cartoon, Tora, freezing on the streets, is picked up by the family of young Mikě (all personified as cats) and given so much love and attention that Mikě becomes jealous and runs away with Tora. The film then depicts their adventures as they travel and play before finally returning home.

Suteneko Torachan has an almost timeless quality to it. It transcends the realities of Japan in 1947: Mikě's family leads a life and lives in a house that most children can only dream about. The film contains a minimum of violence and negative emotions, progressing with an almost operatic quality and little dialogue. The music was composed and conducted by Masa Hattori. Interestingly, one episode depicting little Tora and Mikě caught in a violent thunderstorm is very similar to a scene in Walt Disney's *Fantasia,* although *Fantasia* was not released in Japan until 1955. Apparently the animators saw a private screening of a reel that had been captured by the Japanese army in Singapore during the war and derived their inspiration from it.

Suteneko Torachan was one of the last films created by Masaoka, but the *Torachan* series paved the way for Toei Dōga, the animation branch of the Toei company, which was created from Nihon Dōga artists and today is a leader in the animation field.

F.S.

SUYAMA, KEIICHI (1905-1975) Japanese political cartoonist and cartoon historian born in Nagano Prefecture, Japan, in 1905. Upon completing his basic schooling, Keiichi Suyama moved to Tokyo and entered what is today known as the Tokyo University of the Arts. In 1925, while still at the university, he began actively participating in the Nihon Mangaka Renmei ("Japan Cartoonists' Federation") and the Nihon Proletariat Geijutsu Renmei ("Japan Proletarian Art Federation"), drawing cartoons that were highly political and ideological in content.

As did many of his compatriots, Suyama became a protégé of Masamu Yanase, the most famous political cartoonist of the time. In 1928, he entered a collection of his cartoons, *Tōma o Oikaese* ("Drive Back Tom"), in the first exhibition of proletarian art held in Tokyo; after graduation from school, he submitted what is still regarded as one of his most representative works, *Ajita Purokichi* (a pun on the words *agitator* and *propaganda)* to the *Musansha Shimbun* ("Proletariat News"). *Ajita Purokichi* was a well-received, humorous psychological expression of proletarian heroism. Suyama also contributed cartoons regularly to magazines such as *Tokyo Puck* and *Nap,* but he was increasingly banned by the government. Following the example of Yanase, Suyama became a member of the Japanese Communist party in 1933, but with increased government repression of Communists and anyone opposed to Japan's growing militarism, he met with the same fate as his men-

新しきピラミッド　ファシズムの正体　須山計一「東京パック」
The Real Face of Fascism. Lèon Blum (French premier) to Mussolini: "It's a new kind of pyramid."
Keiichi Suyama, 1936. © Tokyo Puck.

tor and was arrested that year.

After spending two years in prison, Suyama was released and found himself in a changed world where political cartoonists were not only unable to find magazines to print their works, but where their actual lives were in danger. Suyama turned increasingly to less dangerous pursuits like oil painting, and when peace finally came he began chronicling the history of Japanese cartoons. In the postwar years he produced books such as *Manga no Rekishi* ("History of Cartoons," 1956), *Nihon Giga* ("Japanese Comic Drawings," 1961) and *Teiko no Gaka* ("Resistance Artists," 1970). In addition, his *Nihon Manga Hyakunen* ("One Hundred Years of Japanese Cartoons") and *Manga Hakubutsushi* ("A History of Cartoons") remain the most authoritative books on Japanese cartoons today. Keiichi Suyama died in April 1975, one of the most respected elders of the cartoon world.

F.S.

SUZUKI, SHINICHI (1933-) Japanese animator and film director born in Nagasaki, Japan, on December 4, 1933. From the time he could walk, Shinichi Suzuki was an aspiring cartoonist; by junior high school he was contributing to local magazines. Upon graduation he began working for a printing company, and during this period he claims to have seen Walt Disney's *Bambi* and *Snow White* more than forty times each.

In 1953 Suzuki moved to Tokyo and began living in the now legendary Tokiwaso apartment building, along with many struggling young cartoonists who are now famous. While employed in a design workshop, he drew cartoons for magazines. His big break came in 1956, when Ryūichi Yokoyama's Otogi Productions was formed and he was hired as an animator. In 1963, after gaining valuable experience at Otogi, Suzuki joined Shōtaro Ishimori, Fujio Fujiko, Fujio Akatsuka and other comrades from his days at Tokiwaso to form Studio Zero and produce television animation and commercials.

A very modest man, Suzuki has concentrated on quality rather than quantity in his career. While with Otogi Productions, he animated films such as *Fukusuke* (1957); *Hyōtan Suzume* (1959); *Otogi no Sekai Ryoko* ("Journey into Fantasyland," 1961), a compilation of animated cartoons made by Otogi Productions staff members; and *Purasu Go Man Nen* ("Plus 50,000 Years," 1962). The last work, a short, is considered one of his most representative and is a fine example of his sharp wit. At Studio Zero, Suzuki has both animated and directed television cartoons such as *Osomatsu-kun* (1965), *Parman* (1966), *Umeboshi Denka* (1968) and *Kayo Manga Series* (1970). In 1974 he created a video cassette animation entitled *Kyūyaku Seisho Monogatari* ("Stories from the Old Testament"), and in 1976 he made a humorous short called *Hyōtan* ("The Gourd"). Most recently he assisted on the animation segments of Osamu Tezuka's film *The Pheonix* (1978).

In the 1980s and 1990s Suzuki has continued to work on a wide variety of films, ranging from shorts such as *The Bubble* in 1980 to the popular TV series *Warau Serusuman* ("The Laughing Salesman"), based on a comic book of the same name by Fujiko Fujio (A), in 1992. He has also become more international in his outlook, producing two films for the Asia/Pacific Cultural Center for UNESCO, *Mina Smiles* in 1993, and *Mina's Village and the River* in 1998. Both of these were codirected by the famous Malaysian cartoonist Lat, and the latter picture was produced in Thailand. In addition Suzuki has branched out beyond traditional animation and created several short works for the Japanese TV channel NHK, using unorthodox materials such as stones, branches, cloth, and sand.

Suzuki is reknowned for the clear lines and realism of his animation. His hobby used to be playing the trombone, but he says he has had to quit. In crowded Tokyo too many people complained of the noise.

F.S.

SUZUKI, SHŪJI (1927-) Japanese cartoonist and children's book illustrator born in Tokyo, Japan, on September 24, 1927. Shūji Suzuki (who uses the pseudonym "Shinta Chō") graduated from a technical school in Urata, Tokyo. Chō's early interest in cartoons led him to work first for a tiny affiliate of the *Mainichi* newspaper in Yurakucho, Tokyo. In his free time he often frequented a bar in the Ginza where he met cartoonists of the Dokuritsu Mangaha ("Independent Cartoonists' Faction"). This group was first formed in 1947 by five artists to promote their own work, with Koh Kojima playing a central role. It was a loose association of starving friends who strove for new and unorthodox styles rather than for graphic perfection, and it opposed the art establishment. By 1955, when Chō joined, its membership had increased to over twenty and included the likes of Yōji Kuri and Yōsuke Inoue (today prominent avant-garde cartoonists in their own right).

In 1956 the Dokuritsu Mangaha published the magazine *Gamma,* in which Chō began running his works (having by then quit his newspaper job). With a unique, gentle style showing the influence of Paul Klee and James Thurber, Chō soon attracted attention. When *Gamma* collapsed, he began working independently, and in 1959 he garnered the 5th Bungei Shunju award for cartoons with his *Oshaberi na Tamagoyaki* ("The Gossipy Fried Egg"). Chō's other awards include the 14th International Cartoonists Salon award, Il Prefetto de Imperia, in 1961; the Tokyo Illustrators Club award in 1966; and the International Andersen Prize in 1975. Representative published works include *Umi no Bīdama* ("Sea Marbles") and *Sanbiki no Raion no Ko* ("Three Lion Cubs"). Among his later works special mention should be given to *Dobutsu Are Are Ehon* ("Illustrated Book of Animals' That and That") and *Konna Koto te, Aru Kashira?* ("Do Things Like This Really Happen?"). Additional honors include the Grand Prix Award for Illustrated Books in Japan (1990), and the Sankei Children's Publishing Culture Award (1994). Also in 1994 he was awarded the prestigious Order of Culture Medal with Purple Ribbon in recognition of his contributions.

Shinta Chō is one of the more influential and amusing cartoonists in Japan today, contributing frequently to magazines such as *Bunshun Manga Dokuhon.* He is also active as a children's book illustrator, and his gentle characters with their big noses are particularly popular. One excellent example of his humor is an untitled piece that appeared in *Bunshun Manga Dokuhon* in September 1970; it shows a huge skyscraper that has drooped to the ground (covering four pages), with a surprised little character on the top floor who has spilled his spaghetti dinner out the window.

F.S.

Kamikaze: "Where's Premier Kodama's home?"
Yoshiji Suzuki's "Weird News Commentary." © Suzuki.

SUZUKI, YOSHIJI (1928-) Japanese cartoonist born in Tokyo, Japan, on September 26, 1928. Yoshiji Suzuki is a prominent cartoonist who works in the popular Japanese genre known as *fūzoku manga,* or cartoons that deal with everyday subjects. In his childhood he was often ill, which may have contributed to an early interest in art, particularly oil painting. Towards the end of the war he was mobilized, as most boys were, and worked in a factory as a lathe operator. Later, when peace came, he entered what is today called the Tokyo University of Agriculture and Technology, graduating in 1948. Just when he was about to join a company, however, he was diagnosed as having a heart ailment, which led to an abandonment of all existing plans. Indirectly it was also a determining factor in his career, for while recuperating he often read the cartoons in the *New Yorker* magazine at the American Cultural Center in Kawasaki. The *New Yorker* was his first introduction to cartoons and stimulated him to read further; he thereupon became so enamored of the art form that he resolved to become a cartoonist.

Suzuki soon began submitting his own cartoons to a variety of magazines. In 1952, with other cartoonists like Minoru Saka and Tsugio Yoshizaki, he formed the group Manga Epoch, and the next year he made a formal cartoon debut in a newspaper. He did not, however, gain much attention until around 1955. In 1962 Suzuki joined the now famous Manga Shūdan ("Cartoonists Group") and afterwards began turning out a series of works such as *Pepē no Pēsuke, Keroriko-chan, Kizape, Yoshiji no Shūkan E Nikki* ("Yoshiji's Weekly Picture Journal") and *Sanwari-kun.* In 1969 he received the 15th Bunshun cartoon award. Most of Suzuki's works are simple, one-page, often one-panel humorous cartoons. *Sanryu Byōin* ("Third-Class Hospital"), from his series *Nani ga Okoruka Wakaranai* ("No One Knows What Will Happen"), shows a hospital on fire; while a nurse is quickly evacuating the babies, the pregnant women who are in the hospital to give birth are evacuating a terrified doctor on a stretcher. He is clutching the hospital safe in his hands.

Suzuki's cartoons are often lighthearted pokes at the everyday absurdities of life, but they sometimes contain topical social criticism couched in humor. One of his most serious attempts at social commentary thus far has been *Suzuki Yoshiji no Kiza Geba Jihyo,* which consisted of one-panel cartoons with extensive narration; one of his most humorous themes in the past has been the Japanese inferiority complex towards Westerners and how to cure it. His simply drawn characters tend to be very genial but not altogether bright, which multiplies the humor in the nonsensical situations he so often depicts.

In 1969 Suzuki received the 15th Bungei Shunju Manga award, and in 1996 he was finally awarded the prestigious Order of Culture Medal with Purple Ribbon in recognition of his achievements.

F.S.

SVANKMAJER, JAN (1934-) Czech animator and filmmaker born in Prague on September 4, 1934. Jan Svankmajer attended the School of Applied Arts in Prague and the Academy of Performing Arts from 1950 to 1955, studying puppetry and graphic design. He initially worked as a painter, sculptor and engraver before going into animation with his first film, *The Last Trick* (1964). Having found his calling, he went on to make over 30 more films over the next three decades.

Svankmajer came into his own in the early 1970s with such acclaimed animation works as the 1971 *Jabberwocky,* based on his life-long admiration for Lewis Carroll, and the 1972 *Punch and Judy,* in which engravings and illustrations from old newspapers came to life. Also in 1972 he made *Leonardo's Diary,* animating the drawings of Leonardo da Vinci. Following the crushing of the "Prague Spring" by Soviet troops in 1973, he was classified as a subversive and went into forced idleness for seven long years, during which he practiced collage and worked out different animation schemes for further reference.

Returning to the animation scene in 1980, Svankmajer embarked on two of his most ambitious projects to date, a full-length animated film, *Dimensions of Dialogue,* in which drawings, collages, puppets, and various other techniques of animation were all used to create a world of dreams (and nightmares), where a head danced unattached, an Arcimboldo-like face made up of tomatoes, cabbages and lemons spouted nonsense poetry, and clay figures kissed and melted. This was followed by *Alice* (1988), an 84-minute reverie on themes from Lewis Carroll again.

In the United States Svankmajer is best known for his *Faust,* a full-length 1994 film that pulled out all stops in its hallucinatory retelling of the medieval legend, mixing stop-action animation, object animation, puppets, and rotoscoping of real people. *Faust* earned its creator many awards and even a profile in the *New Yorker,* which called him "Kafka's heir." Since that time the artist has occasionally worked for the U.S. market, even making spots for MTV; but despite offers from abroad he prefers to work in the Czech capital because, as he says, "Prague does possess a certain quality of magic." Calling himself a "militant surrealist," he devotes his spare time editing a Surrealist magazine.

M.H.

SWORDS, BETTY (1917-) American cartoonist and illustrator born in 1917. Betty Swords studied art at the University of California at Berkeley, graduating in 1938. She entered the Academy of Advertising Art in San Francisco to prepare for a career as a fashion designer but abandoned this intention upon her marriage and subsequent nomadic life as a government geologist's wife in the South and Southwest, far from the fashion markets. Coming by chance upon a handbook for writers, she discovered that cartooning was a commercial art form that could be practiced anywhere. Undaunted by the apparent rarity of female cartoonists, she began drawing and submitting her work to various publications. Her first success was long delayed; when it came, it was a "ghost" piece for the *Saturday Evening Post* in the name of Martha Blanchard, a freelancer. In 1955 she made her first sale under her own name to King Features Syndicate, and a few months later to the *Post.*

Swords's fashion background is evident in her attention

"I remember Charles as more the quiet type."

Betty Swords. © California Monthly.

to dress, sweeping lines and the posed attitudes of figures. Apart from that, the chief influence on her work was *New Yorker* cartoonist Richard Taylor, whose primer, *Introduction to Cartooning,* helped her a great deal as a would-be cartoonist, and with whom she maintained a longtime correspondence. She utilizes pencil roughs, then finished pen-and-inks via the light table. As a fashion designer, she started out using brushes but switched to pen and has recently adopted felt-tips as her preferred cartoon media. Besides the *Saturday Evening Post,* her work has appeared in *Look, Good Housekeeping, Redbook, Ladies' Home Journal, Changing Times* and *Modern Maturity.* In addition to cartoons, she paints seriously and has sold some of her canvases. She does fashion illustrations, creates art for ad campaigns, both print and animated, and does magazines and book illustration. She also writes humorous material, from short gag fillers to longer articles she illustrates herself.

A late-blooming but outspoken feminist, Swords has dedicated herself to eradicating the sexist humor in cartooning, that which relies upon clichéd images of women—the dumb sexpot, the shrew, the battle-axe. To this end, she illustrated the Male Chauvinist Pig Calendar for 1974, and she hopes through such gentle ridicule to lay to rest someday the whole spectrum of misogynist humor. It is her conviction that the great cartoonists have not all been motivated by bile, misogyny or warped perceptions of the world, and that there is a need for the gentler sentiments in the field of cartoon art. A cartoon from *Changing Times* expresses both these convictions rather nicely; it shows an older couple watching a female candidate speak on television as the husband complains to his wife, "Sure,

Genoa's Job
Charles Sykes, 1923. © Philadelphia Ledger.

you'll vote for her just because she's a woman—and you know she's running against a brother Elk!" In the 1980s she also became a lecturer and college instructor on humor and cartooning on several university campuses in Colorado. She is now retired.

R.C.

SYKES, CHARLES HENRY (1882-1942) American cartoonist born in Athens, Georgia, in 1882. Charles ("Bill") Sykes was educated at the Drexel Institute, graduated in 1904 and freelanced for two years as a cartoonist. His first regular assignment was for the *Philadelphia North American,* preceding Herbert Johnson as the paper's editorial cartoonist; this was followed by stints on the *Williamsport* (Pa.) *News* and the *Nashville Banner,* where he preceded Carey Orr as the city's star cartoonist. In 1911 Sykes returned to Philadelphia to draw political and sports cartoons for the *Philadelphia Public Ledger* and became the *Evening Ledger's* first cartoonist after its reorganization in 1914. He was to be the paper's only cartoonist, and he retired when the paper went out of business early in 1942. He died a short time later.

From 1922 to 1928 Sykes was the regular editorial cartoonist for *Life,* executing a weekly political drawing, full page and usually in wash. Also, he inherited the weekly and annual cartoon roundup of news subjects upon the death of F.T. Richards.

Sykes had one of the most amiable styles in all cartooning His perspectives were unique, his anatomy precise and his shading almost theatrical. No matter what the subject, his cartoons were usually funny, with figures delightfully distorted. When his characters register delight, surprise or anger, it is hard to conceive that any more emotion could have been poured into them. In his early newspaper days he used unusual patterns of coquille board that allowed interesting effects; he was just as adept, later, at getting such effects from crayon and wash.

R.M.

SYLVESTER (U.S.) Sylvester, the quintessential scaredy-cat, made his appearance—unnamed—in the 1942 Bob Clampett cartoon "A Tale of Two Kitties." He lost no time in chasing (unsuccessfully) Tweety Pie the canary, whose first reaction to the encounter was the immortal cry "I taut I taw a puddy tat." Their duel continued in such hilarious entries as "Kitty Kornered" and "Tugboat Granny," as well as in "Tweety Pie" and "Birds Anonymous" (the Oscar winners of 1947 and 1957, respectively). For all his troubles Sylvester invariably ended up with the short end of Granny's umbrella whacking him over the head. (It should be noted here that the cat now named Sylvester was referred to as Thomas in the earlier cartoons.)

The fall guy of the Warners menagerie of funny animals, Sylvester always managed to get into trouble. In "Scaredy Cat," he repeatedly saved Porky Pig's life only to have his intentions misinterpreted by an enraged Porky; and in "Here Today, Gone Tamale," he was the butt of Speedy Gonzales's fast tricks. Then, in some of the zaniest entries in the *Sylvester* series ("By Word of Mouse," "Hop, Look and Listen," "Slap-Hoppy Mouse," "The Mouse That Jack Built," etc.) he ran afoul of Hoppy, a baby kangaroo that the witless cat kept mistaking for a giant mouse. (Every time the cowardly Sylvester ran away from Hoppy, his precocious son, Sylvester Jr., would exclaim in despair "My father—afraid of a little mouse! Oh, the shame of it!")

Friz Freleng, Chuck Jones and Robert McKimson were the directors who most felicitously handled the *Sylvester* cartoons. Credit is also due Mel Blanc, who gave body and tone to the feline's sputtering diction (Blanc could inject infinite variation into Sylvester's favorite exclamation, "Sufferin' succotash!").

"Sylvester." © Warner Brothers.

From 1948 to 1984 Sylvester has been featured in a comic book titled (oh, the shame of it!) *Tweety and Sylvester.* He fortunately was restored to first billing status again in *The Sylvester and Tweety Mysteries,* a Saturday-morning cartoon show that began airing on the WB Network in 1995.

M.H.

SZABO, JOSEPH GEORGE (1950-) American cartoonist, editor and publisher born in Budapest, Hungary, on February 4, 1950. After studies at the Hungarian School of Journalism, Joe Szabo started his career as the art director of the weekly magazine *Nok Lapja,* a position he held from 1975 to 1978, later becoming the managing editor and editorial cartoonist for the daily *Magyar Nemzet.* Unhappy with the restrictions put on his freedom of expression by the oppressive Communist regime, he fled the country with his whole family in 1979. Temporarily settling in then-West Germany, he applied for and eventually received permission to emigrate to the United States, where he arrived in 1981.

In the U.S. Szabo has traversed the whole spectrum of graphic art activities, being at times (and often simultaneously) designer, illustrator, art director, and photographer, but editorial cartooning remains his one true love. His freelance cartoons have graced the pages of the *Philadelphia Inquirer* and the *Philadelphia Daily News* (to which, for a time, he contributed two cartoons a week), the *Los Angeles Herald-Examiner*, Paris's *Le Monde*, Barcelona's *El Pais*, and publications from Rome to Tokyo; and these have won him numerous awards.

Szabo's cartoons are economical, even austere, drawn with only a few lines ("Two reasons for this," he says, "I am impatient and I try to keep the drawing clean and easily understandable"), and they very rarely use captions or speech balloons. For these reasons they make their point tersely and directly. One cartoon, for instance, depicted the American delegate slamming the door on Unesco (after President Reagan had pulled the United States out of the organization) while the letters "U" and "S" fell from the institution's name. In addition to his cartooning duties he has also edited, for a brief time in the 1990's, a panel feature called *Carousel*, to which editorial cartoonists from all parts of the world contributed.

In 1987 Szabo realized a long-held dream with the publication of *WittyWorld*, an international cartoon magazine, which he terms "the first magazine serving the entire cartoon world on a wide international scale." The publication is indeed international in scope and outlook, numbering about 60 foreign editors as of 1996. In its pages there have appeared articles on every facet of cartooning in virtually every region of the globe, and these have been complemented by the publication of a number of books on topics of international significance anthologized in cartoons.

M.H.

Joe Szabo. © Joe Szabo.

SZECHURA, DANIEL (1930-) Polish animator born in Wilczogeby, Poland, on July 11, 1930. Daniel Szechura graduated from Warsaw University with a degree in fine arts in 1955. He worked as a set designer and also made a number of award-winning amateur films. In 1960 Szechura joined the Se-Ma-For Studios of Film Shorts in Lodz, directing *Conflicts.* This was followed in 1961 by *The Machine,* an animated collage based on 19th-century drawings. Szechura produced more animated satires in the next few years: *The Letter* (1962), *The Armchair* (1963), *First, Second, Third* (1964) and *The Graph* (1966) are the most memorable.

Aside from a couple of cartoons he produced for the *Adventures of Sindbad the Sailor* series, Szechura's later films have grown increasingly somber and introspective. The 1968 *Hobby* depicted a woman engaged in the activity of capturing men and putting them in cages; the 1973 *Arena* is a gray-toned film full of foreboding and unresolved conflict. *The Journey, The Lumber Room* and *King Popiel,* to mention a few more recent cartoons, also partake of this sense of loneliness and entrapment. Szechura has received countless awards for his cartoons, including prizes at Kraków, Warsaw, Mar del Plata, Paris, Oberhausen and Mamaia.

In the 1980's he turned increasingly to magic and legend for inspiration. In 1983 he completed his masterpiece in this occult vein, *Diptych: Morgan le Fey I* and *II.* A surrealistic montage of haunting images, *XYZ,* followed in 1987, along with a number of lesser projects.

M.H.

SZEP, PAUL (1941-) American cartoonist born in Hamilton, Ontario, Canada, on July 29, 1941. Paul Szep graduated from the Ontario College of Art in 1964 and worked as a fashion illustrator, graphic designer, book illustrator and newspaper staff artist. He began his political cartooning career when he came under the heavy influence of the Canadian Duncan Macpherson (their styles are hardly discernible). In 1966 Szep joined the *Boston Globe.* He has won, among other honors, the Sigma Delta Chi award of 1973 and the Pulitzer Prizes for 1974 and 1977. He has also received honorary doctorates from Worcester State College and William Penn College; since 1987 he has been an occasional political commentator on public television.

Szep's style is characterized by erratically varying brushstrokes and seemingly uncountable and obtrusive wrinkles, crosshatches and texture lines. His cartoons for the *Globe* are among the nation's most left-wing in intent.

R.M.

Paul Szep. © Boston Globe.

SZEWCZUK, MIRKO (1919-1957) Austrian editorial cartoonist and illustrator born in Vienna, Austria, in 1919. At the age of 17, Mirko Szewczuk's talent for drawing was ignited by his discovery of the work of Olaf Gulbransson. The famed *Simplicissimus* cartoonist's flowing linear style exerted such an overwhelming influence on the young Viennese that after some years of searching for an identity, Szewczuk swung to the other extreme and turned to painterly techniques, with heavy shading and busy backgrounds.

World War II found Szewczuk in Berlin, where he did drawings for the magazine *Die Woche*. In 1945, he moved on to Hamburg. There the former publisher of *Die Woche*, now co-publisher of the newspaper *Die Zeit*, offered him a job as editorial cartoonist that decided Szewczuk's career. In his four years on *Die Zeit*, his reputation steadily advanced, especially after his editor in chief, Richard Tüngel, persuaded him to return to the linear style that suited him so well (Szewczuk even went back to study, at the Hamburg State Art School). His linearity now became a thoroughly personal instrument; he worked with simplified, jagged contours, heightened as necessary with areas of solid black or intense crosshatching, with a refined sense of composition and figure placement.

In 1949, still in Hamburg, Szewczuk transferred his services to the newspaper *Die Welt*, continuing on its staff until his premature death in Hamburg on May 31, 1957. His cartoons were generally severe condemnations of political and social inequities, lashing out against militarism, heavy taxation, hoarding, unfairness in housing, and the yearning for the "good old days" of the Third Reich. The tense situation of a divided Germany placed between the two world powers obviously preyed constantly on his mind.

In addition to numerous powerful editorial cartoons, many of which appear in various anthologies and in the posthumous 1957 book published by Die Welt in his memory—*Einsichten und Aussichten* ("Insights and Prospects")—Szewczuk authored three volumes: *Meine Tochter Ilona* ("My Daughter Ilona," 1950, describing adventures with his baby girl), *Stars und Sterne* (celebrity caricatures, 1955) and *Szewczuks Kleines Welttheater* ("Szewczuk's Little World Theater," 1957). Moreover, he did illustrations and covers for a dozen other books written by people as diverse as Heinrich Böll and Damon Runyon.

S.A.

SZYK, ARTHUR (1894-1951) Polish-American cartoonist, illustrator and miniaturist born in Lodz, Poland, in 1894. Arthur Szyk studied fine arts in Paris and Kraków. His studies were interrupted by World War I, and he fought in the Russian army; after the 1918 Brest-Litovsk armistice, he joined General Sikorski's Polish army and fought against the Bolsheviks.

Szyk started his career as a cartoonist and caricaturist in Warsaw in the early 1920s. His cartoons were well received, and his fame led him to Paris; there he illustrated a number of books, including *The Book of Esther*, Gustave *Flaubert's La Tentation de Saint Antoine* and Pierre Benoit's *Le Puits de Jacob*. In 1934 he was sent by the Polish government to the United States, where his works were exhibited in the Library of Congress in Washington and in many museums around the country. Upon his return to Poland he was commissioned to do a series of miniatures on the American Revolution, and the Polish government presented them as a gift to President Franklin Roosevelt in 1938.

The outbreak of World War II found Szyk in England, and he put his pen in the service of the Allies, drawing many cartoons for British newspapers and magazines. In 1940 he went to the United States, where he continued to draw cartoons savagely satirizing Nazi leaders and the Nazi regime (these were later collected in a 1941 book titled *The New Order*). Szyk is probably best noted for the striking covers he did for *Collier's* (chiefly on war themes) and for the cartoons he drew for such newspapers as *P.M.* and the *New York Post.* He was also a calligrapher of the first order, working in the tradition of the illuminated manuscripts of the Middle Ages, as in the elaborate Declaration of Independence he executed for the State of Israel in 1948. Arthur Szyk died of a heart attack in New Canaan, Connecticut, on September 13, 1951.

M.H.

Arthur Szyk, caricature of the Axis leaders, 1943. © Szyk.

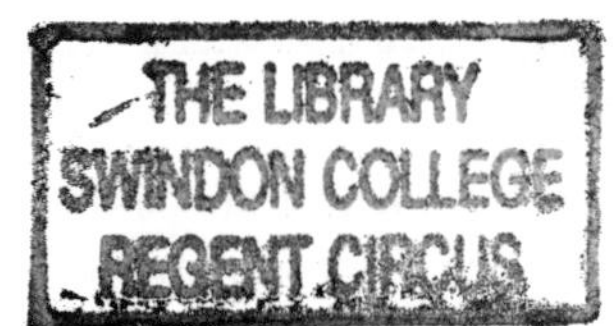

Tt

TABAKA, MALGORZATA (1948-) Malgorzata Tabaka was born March 18, 1948, in Silesia, District Katowice, Poland. Her early childhood interests in drawing prompted Tabaka's mother to enroll her in art classes at the Palace of Youth in Katowice; later, she graduated with an art degree from a university in Torun. Her first position had nothing to do with cartooning as she worked in the county office for art conservation. Nevertheless, Tabaka drew feverishly in between maintaining her job and nourishing her growing family. In fact, she chose drawing over painting because it required less space and time.

As her portfolio filled, Tabaka sent some cartoons to the newspaper *Trybuna Slaska* in Katowice, which published them in 1976. After that, her work appeared on a frequent basis in many Polish magazines, including *Polityka, wprost, Radar, Zycie Literackie, Szpilki,* and others, and in exhibitions in Poland and abroad. She has been honored with Poland's highest award in satire, "Zlota Szpilka."

Tabaka's cartoons are distinguished by their treatment of the nonsensical elements of situations and ideas, their subtle, non-aggressive, and refined satire, and their light artistic touches. From her youth, she has transformed the mundane and the paradoxes of life into drawings that have been called graphic metaphors. Tabaka uses wordless cartoons whose power of expression lies in the nuance—the movement of the mouth, the direction of a glance, the tiny spot of color stressing the meaning of a metaphor. She describes her style as "quick reaction," necessitated by the demands on her time by family and other obligations: "My cartoons are like jazz, which I enjoy; they are easy, not heavy, improvised, on-the-spot."

J.A.L.

TAGAWA, SUIHŌ (1899-1989) Japanese artist and cartoonist born in Tokyo, Japan, in 1899. Suihō Tagawa is a sixth-generation descendant of a long line of Tokyoites. His true family name is Takamizawa. He studied in the design division of the Nihon Bijutsu Gakko ("Japan School of Art") and eventually became caught up in the turbulence of the Shinko Bijutsu Undo ("New Art Movement"), which was popular during the 1920s. There he worked with such New Wave artists as Tomoyoshi Murayama (1901-), a playwright-producer who became the founder of the Dada-inspired art movement called Mabuo. During this time, Tagawa produced a number of Dada-influenced wood-block prints, but he had little success earning a living with his art. He finally took part-time work as a comic in *yose,* the Japanese equivalent of a vaudeville house. It was his job to warm up the audience before the main acts came on stage.

Eventually Tagawa found work as an illustrator and adult cartoon artist for magazines published by Kodansha, one of the largest publishing houses in Japan. In 1928 he produced his first cartoon strip for *Shōnen Kurabu* ("Young People's Club"). Titled *Medama no Chibichan* ("Little Eyeball"), it continued for two years and was followed by another Tagawa cartoon called *Shinshu Sakuranosuke.* His masterpiece, *Nora Kuro,* a comic strip with a simple, lovable canine hero, was published in 1931, and for ten years Tagawa's popularity grew with each episode.

Tagawa has often been criticized for fanning the flames of fascism with *Nora Kuro*'s military setting and its preoccupation with Japanese expansion into the Asian continent; and he has admitted that there are some elements of imperialism in his work. But the fact that *Nora Kuro* has retained its popularity to such an extent that it was reprinted with great success as *The Complete Nora Kuro* in 1976 speaks for its merits as simply an entertaining and enjoyable cartoon. Tagawa also produced an adult comic strip called *Taco no Ya-chan* ("Little Ya, the Octopus"), which was again well received by his readers.

Tagawa was active as an "elder statesman" of Japanese cartoons and comics until his death at age 90 on December 12, 1989. He is best known, however, for the wartime comic strip *Nora Kuro* and for the influence it had on most of today's popular Japanese cartoonists.

J.C.

TAGUCHI, BEISAKU (1864?-1903) Japanese cartoonist born in Tochigi Prefecture, Japan, probably around 1864. As a young man, Beisaku Taguchi traveled to Tokyo and began to study Western art and cartoon drawing under Kiyochika Kobayashi, one of the early leaders in the development of the Japanese cartoon. After his apprenticeship, he joined the staff of Kobayashi's *Marumaru Chinbun,* one of the earliest Japanese illustrated humor magazines, and became its editor in the early 1890s. The *Marumaru Chinbun* was printed with the facilities of the *Chuo Shimbun* ("Central News"), one of the major newspapers of the period, and this afforded Taguchi the opportunity to meet important political figures and newsmakers. He used this vantage point to observe the events of the day and produce topical cartoons focusing on current trends. His most powerful drawings appeared around the turn of the century. Generally they showed the popularity of labor unions and the need for new labor laws. Taguchi's cartoons became less and less humorous as they depicted the growing violence in worker demonstrations and the contrasting arrogance of the Japanese courts.

It has been said that Taguchi's political cartoons tended to be a little too abstract, and his design skills have also been criticized. As an artist, Taguchi may not have had as much talent as Kiyochika Kobayashi, but as editor of one of the earliest successful cartoon magazines, he deserves recognition. He made a sigiiificant contribution to the journalistic development of Japanese cartoons. He died in 1903, still active as a political cartoonist.

J.C.

TAILANG, SUDHIR (1960-) Born in Bikaner, India, February 26, 1960, Sudhir Tailang had a successful cartooning career when other children his age had only play on their minds. He became interested in funny drawings at age six and was published regularly in all major Indian newspapers since he was ten. His dream had been to be a medical doctor, for which he prepared with a bachelor's degree in biology from the University of Rajasthan. In 1982, he received a masters in English literature from the same university and then joined the *Illustrated Weekly of India* as a trainee cartoonist. Throughout all those years, he freelanced cartoons to dozens of periodicals, including *Filmfare*, *Economic Times*, *Evening News*, and *Science Today*.

Tailang's first full-time assignment was as staff cartoonist for the daily *Navbharat Times*, from which in 1989, he moved to his present position as staff political cartoonist for the *Hindustan Times*. Enthralled by all dimensions of comic art, Tailang draws acerbic political cartoons, a daily pocket cartoon, *Here and Now*, illustrations, and caricatures for the *Hindustan Times* and its sisters, sculpts caricatures of politicians for exhibitions, and helps administer the *Hindustan Times* annual cartoon contest. He has also created a series of short, animated cartoons, socially educational in nature, for the national television system, *Doordarshan*, and a two-part animated documentary on the history of cartooning worldwide and in India.

Indian politicians are Tailang's favorite targets. As he said, "Jokers in politics are my stars; most of the politicians in India are working full-time for the cartoonists, not the people." Tailang prefers uncluttered cartoons, with details removed to keep focus squarely on his main protagonists. He added, "I am not here to show my prowess as another Michaelangelo; my main aim is to convey an idea with clarity." Most of these ideas come when he is on the toilet, reading newspapers, in the local square (Connaught Place) observing people, and at the zoo, because, he said, many of the politicians he draws look like animals.

J.A.L.

TAINSH, DOUGLAS EDWARD (1921-) Australian cartoonist born in Sydney, Australia, in June 1921. A comic artist who favors watercolor wash for his cartoons, Douglas Tainsh is a one-time shearer's roustabout and bush worker, soldier and television scriptwriter. Tainsh studied painting for seven years before traveling overseas, where he had his work published in such English magazines as *Punch, Everybody's, Men Only, Strand* and *Lilliput*, as well as in the American and French press.

In 1955 the Melbourne *Argus* published a refreshing and original comic strip written by the nationally famous short-story writer Alan Marshall and drawn by Tainsh. A daily strip feature, *Speewa Jack* was about an old up-country character, a spinner of tall tales. It expressed much of what is today the Australian's conception of himself; this self-image, like that of all peoples, is the part-truth that lies between the part-myth and part-legend. After the *Argus* failed in 1957, *Speewa Jack* was continued in the *Age* newspaper for a few weeks. The paper's editors thought that the strip was developing too many slang Australianisms, put too much emphasis on drinking and was a bit on the vulgar side.

Douglas Tainsh has also created another up-country character, Cedric, a wily, battling "swaggie," or outback tramp, who usually wins out in most situations, thanks to his native wit and resourcefulness. Tainsh's *Cedric,* with its echoes and overtones of the Depression years, has retained its popularity with readers of the national weekly magazine *Australasian Post* for the last 25 years.

V.L.

TAKEDA, HIDEO (1948-) Japanese cartoonist born in Osaka, Japan, in 1948. As soon as he received his master's degree from Osaka University, Hideo Takeda plunged headlong into the then unpopular field of black humor with a privately published book of cartoons entitled *Madame Chang's Chinese Restaurant* (actually the title has no bearing on the contents). These cartoons dealt with sadomasochistic relationships and with physically handicapped people, a subject still taboo in Japanese comic art. One of his recurrent characters was a man sealed in a giant egg about to hatch. Working with felt-tip pen, Takeda created a disturbing world in which humans, animals and insects coexisted, as in the real world, but with marked shifts in emphasis and perspective.

Becoming known as the Japanese Charles Addams, Takeda soon published a second book, *Yogi* (again the title has no relevance to the subject), and held exhibitions in various art galleries. In 1976 he won the Bungei Shunju cartoon award for his series of full-color serigraphs entitled *Monmon,* which hovers on the threshold of fine art. Here Takeda dwelt with irreverent humor upon *irezumi,* a Japanese style of body tattooing; the artist literally transformed the tattooed men into objects devoured by their tattoos in little dramas enacted just below the skin.

Other works by Takeda include *Opera Glass* and *Altamira.* In addition to cartoons he has created reliefs and three-dimensional works. In 1993 he had an exhibit in the British Museum. In 1988 he also won the Japan Cartoonists' Association Award for Excellence.

F.S.

Hideo Takeda. © Takeda.

TAKITA, YŪ (1932-1990) Japanese cartoonist born in Tokyo, Japan, on March 1, 1932. Yū Takita became interested in cartoons after graduating from high school in 1950. He studied under Suihō Tagawa, creator of the famous *Nora Kuro* series. In 1951 he entered university but withdrew after a year and made his debut as a professional cartoonist in *Manga Shonen.* Thereafter, while continuing to draw, he also worked as a sign painter for bars and cabarets.

In 1956 his *Kakkun Oyaji* series was published by the Tokyo Manga Publishing Company and soon proved a success. Several works followed, with an emphasis on entertaining children. In 1962 his *Ashigaru* was released in the now famous magazine *Garo,* and this provided him with the opportunity to develop his own creative style. *Terashimacho Kidan* ("Adventures in Terashimacho"), a semiautobiographical story of his childhood in Tama no I, appeared the same year and was an immediate success. It is a somewhat sentimental and lyrical account of a childhood spent in an industrial neighborhood, with full attention paid to the small details of everyday life. Takita followed with a string of works on a similar theme, and in 1971 the *Takita Yū Shu* ("Collected Works of Yū Takita") was issued. In 1974 he was awarded the 20th Bungei Shunju comic prize for his *Enkabashi Hyakukei* ("One Hundred Views of Enka Bridge"). Other representative works include *Shukabashi Hyakkei* ("One Hundred Views of the Bridge of Bitter Laments"), *Showa Yume Zoshi* ("Dream Tales of the Showa Period"), and *Uramachi Serenade* ("Backstreet Serenade").

Takita continued to produce series that stressed the everyday community life of the common people, and his drawings, with their somewhat loose, somewhat abstract lines, placed a heavy emphasis on the minutiae of ordinary surroundings. The overall effect was one of nostalgia. One particular device that Takita had developed and employed skillfully was to draw little pictures in the balloons that would normally house words, thus cleverly suggesting specific thoughts indirectly. In 1987 Takita won the Japan Cartoonists' Association Grand Prix award for *Uramachi Serenade.* He passed away in 1990.

F.S.

TALBURT, HAROLD M. (1895-1966) American Pulitzer Prize-winning cartoonist born in Toledo, Ohio, on February 19, 1895. Harold Talburt was educated in local public schools and was employed as a soda jerk and sign painter before joining the staff of the *Toledo News-Bee* as a reporter on the first day of 1916.

On the *News-Bee* he came to the attention of Negley Cochran (father of J.R. Williams's assistant and successor), who had helped cartoonists Sidney Smith and Walter Wellman with their careers. It was 1919, and Talburt had drawn some sketches at Jack Dempsey's training camp before the Willard fight. Cochran encouraged Talburt's cartooning, and when he went to Washington in 1921 to set up Scripps-Howard's Washington bureau, he sent for Talburt. In 1922 the latter became Scripps-Howard's "chief Washington cartoonist" from his desk at the *Washington Daily News*—no small feat considering that other artists syndicated by the news organization included Dorman H. Smith and Herblock.

"They laughed when I sat down to play."
Harold Talburt, 1952. © New York World Telegram and Sun.

Talburt won his Pulitzer in 1933 and was president of the Gridiron Club in 1947. He retired in 1963 and died on October 22, 1966. His drawing was wonderfully old-fashioned, all his figures rounded and in a comic style. Talburt used pencil and thick grease crayon for a soft but busy look to his cartoons; his work is full of exaggeration, labels and motion.

R.M.

TANTTU, ERKKI (1907-198?) Finnish cartoonist and illustrator born in Viipuri, Finland (now Vyborg, USSR), on October 4, 1907. Erkki Tanttu (formerly Lydén), a largely self-taught artist, has achieved excellent results in pen-and-ink drawing and in woodcuts, which are a very Finnish form of artistic expression.

Tanttu was 19 years old when he began to earn his living by drawing. His teacher at the Helsinki University of Arts in 1929-30 was the famous cartoonist "Topi" Vikstedt. Tanttu also studied in Munich for awhile. Up to 1945 Tanttu did layout and illustration work for the publishing houses WSOY and Hakkapeliitta. During World War II he drew humorous cartoons that were used to fight black marketeering and boost fighting morale. After the war he started his career as a freelance cartoonist and illustrator.

His first collection of humorous illustrations of Finnish proverbs (*Sata Sananpartta*) came out in 1945; now there are a dozen such collections which have sold over two hundred thousand copies. With good reason Tanttu has been called the most popular artist in Finland. His latest book, *Woodcuts,* was published in 1967. In all Tanttu has

Erkki Tanttu, 1950. © Tanttu.

illustrated almost seventy books, among them Aleksis Kivi's Seven Brothers and other classic novels, as well as children's books. Tanttu's cartoons, which seldom deal with political topics, can be seen in magazines like *Pippuri* and *Tuulispää.* He created his long-lived comic strip, *Rymy-Eetu,* in 1930.

Tanttu was president of the Graphic Artists Union until 1970. His works are on permanent display in many museums. His art is as solemn, quiet and grave as the man himself. He has received many awards for his books, and in 1972 he was named an Honorary Professor. He died in the late 1980s.

J.R.

TARZAN (U.S.) In addition to being the hero of countless novels and stories, Tarzan has also starred in a number of animated cartoons, all of them for television and all of them on CBS. The first *Tarzan, Lord of the Jungle* show aired on September 11, 1976. (Ironically it had been preceded by a number of years by a cartoon parody, Jay Ward's *George of the Jungle,* which was seen on ABC in the late 1960's.)

Filmation was the producer of the CBS series, and Don Christensen directed in a crisp, clear, no-nonsense way. Despite limited animation, each episode provided a vivid and dynamic spectacle, as Tarzan battled evil white hunters, mad raiders, and rescued lost safaris. The drawings were pleasantly rendered in a style reminiscent of Russ Manning who was turning out the *Tarzan* newspaper page at the time. Despite all these efforts, Tarzan lasted only for one season, as the show came to an end in 1977.

In 1978 it was decided by the powers at the network that what the Lord of the jungle needed was an infusion of superhero adrenalin. As a consequence *Tarzan and the Super 7* made its appearance in 1978, co-starring the jungle hero with an odd assortment of old and new characters, which included Batman, Web Woman, and Hercules, among others. The show was ill-conceived and folded the next year.

The character was too popular, however, for the network to just abandon him like a discarded toy. Thus CBS and Filmation tried again in 1981, teaming up the apeman with a couple of Western justice-fighters in the cumbersomely named *The Tarzan/Lone Ranger/Zorro Adventure Hour;* and again their brainchild did not survive the one-season curse, being terminated in 1982. (For the record it should be noted that through all these avatars, Tarzan's voice was provided by solid, dependable Robert Ridgely.)

M.H.

TASHLIN, FRANK (1913-1972) American cartoonist, writer and filmmaker born in Weehawken, New Jersey, on September 19, 1913. Frank Tashlin started his cartooning career in the early 1930s as a freelance artist signing himself "Tish-Tash," then went to work with pioneer New York animator Amédée Van Beuren. In 1933 he moved to California, which had replaced the East Coast as the center of animated cartoon production. He worked as an inbetweener at Warner Brothers but disliked the autocratic ways of the studio boss, Leon Schlesinger. He moved over to MGM, where he worked as a full-fledged animator on Ub Iwerks's *Flip the Frog* series. Around the same time he started drawing a newspaper panel titled *The Van Borings,* also under the pseudonym "Tish-Tash."

In 1935 Tashlin went back to Warner Brothers, working on their Merrie Melodies and Looney Tunes cartoons. He directed a number of *Porky Pig* shorts, already developing his famous style of having household items, pieces of furniture and other inanimate objects come to life, usually with explosive results. In 1940 the ever-restless Tashlin became the head of the Columbia animation unit, where he originated the classic *Fox and Crow* series ("The Fox and the Grapes," based on an Aesop fable, was the first in the series). After a brief stay at the Disney studios, Tashlin returned again to Warners and in the mid-1940s was one of their more imaginative directors, with such gems to his credit as "Plane Daffy," "The Unruly Hare" and "The Case of the Stuttering Pig."

By that time Tashlin had already decided to go into live action: his first association with feature films came as a scriptwriter on a Bob Hope-Jane Russell romp, *The Paleface* (1948). His first assignment as a film director was, naturally enough, on *Son of Paleface* (1952). He then became one of the more skilled directors of the Jerry Lewis-Dean Martin comedies, and later of some of the best of Jerry Lewis's solo vehicles. His credits include *Artists and Models, Hollywood or Bust, Will Success Spoil Rock Hunter?, The Man from the Diners' Club, Bachelor Flat, Who's Minding the Store?* and *Caprice.* Tashlin died in Los Angeles on May 7, 1972.

Frank Tashlin was a very gifted animation director, and he later transferred his skills to the staging of hectic comedy scenes in live-action films. Sequences such as Danny Kaye frantically fighting off the assaults of a computer gone berserk in *The Man from the Diners' Club* or Jerry Lewis sailing over acres of floor coverings, merchandise displays and bemused customers in a rowboat in *Who's Minding the Store?* are indisputably derived from the conventions of the animated cartoon. A number of magazine articles have been devoted to the career of Frank Tashlin, and he himself wrote and illustrated a lovely little fable, *The Bear That Wasn't.*

M.H.

TATOOED MAN, THE (U.S.) One of the most important and effective symbols in American political cartooning lasted only the length of one presidential campaign. In 1884 the Republican candidate, James G. Blaine, was portrayed by *Puck*'s cartoonists as a sideshow attraction, nearly nude and tatooed with his many political sins. The able researchers Hess and Kaplan have discovered two earlier uses of the tatoo motif by *Puck*'s founder, Joseph Keppler, one in 1875 for *Leslie's* (on U.S. Grant), and one in 1876 for the cover of *Puck*'s ninth issue (on the figure of Columbia). This, however, does not disprove Eugene Zimmerman's claim in Book VI of his cartooning course (1914) that the basic theme of the 1884 version was suggested to Bernard Gillam by the German humorist Carl Hauser. It is likely that in the editorial session Keppler recalled the device and recommended it for one particular cartoon.

In any event, the 1884 Tatooed Man series of cartoons became the hit of the election—Democrats ordered thousands of reprints—and catapulted Gillam to his greatest fame. The first depiction of Blaine was on April 16 as one of 31 figures in "The National Dime-Museum—Will Be Run During the Presidential Campaign." His political sins were Bribery, the Mulligan Letters, Guano Statesmanship (referring to a soured business venture), Northern Pacific Bonds, Bluster and Anti-Chinese Demagogism. It was a lusty double-page spread. On May 7 Gillam followed up with "Love's Labor Lost," a back page in color showing Blaine's managers, Phelps and Reid, attempting to eradicate the tatoos with sandpaper and pumice. Keppler's center spread the following week seemed to add tatoo color to Blaine's face as an afterthought. Opper followed on May 21 with the Tatooed Man as Pied Piper. The metaphors were mixed, but the public—the Democrats and reformers, at least—loved the association *Puck* made.

It was an unbeatable combination. On June 4 the editorial columns first made note of the motif, and the center cartoon for that day was one of the most famous ever printed: "Phryne Before the Chicago Tribunal," a parody of a popular academic painting by Gérôme. Blaine was stripped to his underwear (and a quack-remedy "magnetic pad" then in vogue) before a group of influential Republican delegates and leaders. This was the high point of the cartoon attacks, although Blaine was portrayed thirteen times more this way until election day, and twice afterwards, all but three times by Gillam. Other symbols heaped on Blaine besides the magnetic pad (mocking his vaunted magnetic personality) included a cabbage leaf (casting doubt on the stated reason he missed a campaign appearance), rusty armor (recalling Ingersoll's description of Blaine as a "plumed knight") and a feather plume with the name of Gail Hamilton (the ghost writer of his recent autobiography).

Blaine lost the election, and by common consent *Puck*'s cartoons were a strong factor (so was MacDougall and Gribayedoff's cartoon in the *World*). It has been recorded that Blaine wanted to sue the magazine. Zimmerman records that the savage and successful cartoons were also the undoing of Gillam's association with *Puck.* At the height of their popularity he sought a salary advance and was refused. In his disaffection he decided to accept an invitation (and part ownership) from W.J. Arkell, who was buying *Judge* with Republican money. Allegiance meant little to Gillam, who actually voted for Blaine after his merciless onslaught! Zimmerman, who had done most of the coloring on the *Tatooed Man* series, also left for *Judge* the following year.

One other icon related to this election should be noted: the Independent New Party, represented by a handsome, strapping lumberjack type. Clad in a red shirt and ready to clear away old timber, this young man was *Puck*'s pox on both parties. The nomination of reformer Grover Cleveland obviated the necessity for a third-party movement, so the lad never got anywhere except as an allegory for a dream. He was drawn, mostly by Keppler, between 1882 and 1885. Other cartoonists outside of *Puck* never picked up on the theme.

R.M.

TAYLOR, CHARLES JAY (1855-1929) American artist born in New York City on August 11, 1855. C.J. Taylor was educated in the New York public school system and received art training at the National Academy, the Art Students League and schools in London and Paris. Later in his career he earned an LL.B. from Columbia (1874) and was honored with an honorary M.A. from Middlebury College (1911).

Taylor was among the original staff artists on America's first illustrated daily, the *New York Graphic* (1876), and drew for the early issues of *Life* magazine, the first major black-and-white cartoon weekly. When he joined the staff

A cartoon by C.J. Taylor.

of *Puck* in 1886, he was already a veteran of wide fame and influence. On *Puck* he became a major fixture, drawing elegant line cartoons and illustrations as well as colored political lithographs. At the turn of the century he abandoned contract work to freelance for *Life* and *Judge,* and for *Punch* in England.

His first book was *The Taylor-Made Girl* (1888), and a deluxe book of drawings, *England,* was issued in 1899 by R.H. Russell. Other illustrated books include *Short Rations* (1898), *Poems with Music* (1898) and *Partners of Providence* (1907). His most notable illustration work, however, was for the light short stories of H.C. Bunner, including the memorable *Short Sixes* (1894), *More Short Sixes* (1895), *Made in France* (1896) and *The Suburban Sage* (1897). The Bunner books are tales compiled from *Puck,* and they display Taylor's versatility.

Around 1910 Taylor laid down the pen to become chairman of the department of painting and illustration at the College of Fine Arts of the Carnegie Institute in Pittsburgh. For his noncommercial art Taylor received honorable mention at the 1901 Pan-American Exposition, and his work was exhibited at the National Academy, the Society of American Artists, the Pennsylvania Academy of Fine Arts, the Art Institute of Chicago, the Paris Salon, the Chicago World's Fair (1893) and the Paris Exposition (1900). Taylor died in Pittsburgh on January 19, 1929.

C.J. Taylor remains one of the greatest of America's unremembered cartoonists. His influence was vast; his was a confident, lyrical pen line mastered just at the time when the introduction of photoengraving techniques freed artists from woodcutters' interpretations. That Gibson was influenced by the "Taylor-Made Girl" is obvious, at least in a thematic sense, and Taylor's forays into pictorial whimsy marked him as the artistic cousin of his friend A.B. Frost.

For all his society drawings, his beautiful depictions of the emerging emancipated American woman and even of rural and ethnic themes, Taylor was at his best in delineating middle-class couples in everyday scenes, usually leaning towards romantic and pastoral settings. He stands as a chronicler of the Sedate Nineties—of courtship, bicycle rides and boating afternoons. With breezy but well-orchestrated pen lines that became wispier through the years, he achieved evocations that were equalled but not surpassed by other cartoonists and illustrators. It remains for Taylor to be rediscovered for his influence and intrinsic merit.

R.M.

TAYLOR, RICHARD D. (1902-1970) American cartoonist and painter born at Fort William, Ontario, Canada, in 1902. Showing an early talent for art, Richard Taylor began to study under Harry Britton in Toronto at the age of 12. He attended the Central Technical School of the Ontario College of Art and Design. His first earnings as an artist came from what seems today an odd source—coloring magic lantern slides for Sunday schools. His first success as a cartoonist was in the Toronto magazine *Goblin* in 1927. In 1932 he became a freelance commercial artist, and in 1935 he was named a staff cartoonist at the *New Yorker.*

Taylor was the creator of an imaginary world called

"Mrs. Bristow, won't you just leave us to our own devices?"
Richard Taylor. © Collier's.

Frodokom, upon which he based a whole series of paintings, and his cartoon art shows the influence of this sort of imaginative temperament. There is an individuality to his large-eyed, heavy-lidded characters that makes one think of fairy tales and other worlds; it stamps his work immediately, be it a cartoon or an ad for Sanforizing.

From his bold, unbroken line and the solidity of his composition, it would appear that Taylor worked almost exclusively in watercolors. There is, even in the black-and-white reproductions in the *New* Yorker, something colorful about Taylor's art. One feels inclined to add some pink to the cheeks and a light blue to the eyes of his characters. But for all its fairy-tale quality, his cartoon art frequently occupies itself with the grotesque (a portly woman in a butcher shop excuses herself to a hanging beef carcass she has just bumped into and which, in shape, she resembles) and the ribald (Taylor's own evocation of the rape of the Sabines has one of the soon-to-be-violated women winking at another maiden over the shoulder of her captor).

Taylor was a prolific artist both within and outside the cartoon field; his unpublished watercolors were featured in a show that toured a number of American cities in 1941. He was also represented in international watercolor exhibits at the Chicago Art Institute and the Brooklyn Museum, and his works were shown at the Modern Art Society of Cincinnati (1941), the Metropolitan Museum of New York (1942), the Whitney Museum in New York (1943), the DeYoung Museum in San Francisco (1943) and, along with William Steig's, at the Flint, Michigan, Institute of Arts (1943). His paintings are included in the permanent collections of the Museum of Modern Art in New York, the Boston Museum of Fine Arts, the Albany Gallery of Fine Arts, the Wichita Museum and in a number of private collections. A published collection of Taylor cartoons appeared in 1944 under the title *The Better Taylors.* He also illustrated a number of books.

Richard Taylor died in May 1970.

R.C.

TENNIEL, SIR JOHN (1820-1914) British cartoonist and illustrator born in Kensington, London, England, on February 28, 1820. John Tenniel, "the Olympian Jove of cartoonists," as he was called by F.G. Roe in *Victorian Corners,* died on February 25, 1914, three days away from

John Tenniel, comment on Crimean peace negotiations, 1856.

his 94th birthday, with a record of 2,000 *Punch* cartoons, 38 illustrated books and a knighthood (1893).

A self-taught artist, Tenniel duly attended the Royal Academy schools but quickly left, dissatisfied with their teaching methods. However, he exhibited at the Royal Academy from 1837, when he was only 16, and 5 years later executed his first book illustrations for *The Book of British Ballads* (1842). His first cartoon was drawn in the days before the term changed its meaning; in fact, it was submitted to the very competition (a fresco design for the Houses of Parliament) that changed that meaning. In 1850 editor Mark Lemon invited Tenniel to join *Punch* as chief cartoonist, in tandem with John Leech. He stayed with that weekly for 50 years, retiring on December 31, 1900. His first work therein was art for the title pages to volume 19 and the political cartoon "Lord Jack the Giant Killer" (February 1, 1851). His most famous cartoon, "Dropping the Pilot" (March 1890), depicted Prince Bismarck, the German chancellor, leaving the ship *German Empire.* He also drew for other periodicals such as *Good Words* and *Once a Week.*

Tenniel's art is still familiar today through the happy fact of his having illustrated two books that became world classics of children's literature, *Alice's Adventures in Wonderland* (1865) and *Through the Looking Glass* (1872). His depiction of Lewis Carroll's fantastic characters is immortal.

Books: *The Book of British Ballads* (1842); *Undine* (1845); *Aesop's Fables* (1848); *Dramatic Scenes* (1857); *The Gordian Knot* (1858); *The Silver Cord* (1860); *Parables from Nature* (1861); *Lalla Rookh* (1861); *Cartoons from Punch (1864); Ingoldsby Legends (1864); Arabian Nights' Entertainments* (1865); *Alice's Adventures in Wonderland* (1865); *Ballads and Songs of Brittany* (1865); *Poetical Works of Poe (1866); Legends and Lyrics (1866); Juvenile Verse and Picture Book* (1866); *Tales of a Wayside Inn* (1867); *Mirage of Life* (1867); *Punch on Pegasus* (1869); *Christmas Books* (1869); *1001 Gems of English Poetry* (1871); *Through the Looking Glass* (1872); *Historical and Legendary Ballads* (1876); *Mother Goose Nursery Rhymes* (1877); *Mother Goose's Melodies* (1878); *Parables from Nature* (1880); *Cartoons by Sir John Tenniel* (1901); *Life and Work of Sir John Tenniel* (1901); *Alice in Wonderland Paint Book* (1940); and *Sir John Tenniel* (1948).

D.G.

TERRY, HILDA (1914-) American cartoonist born in Newburyport, Massachusetts, on June 25, 1914. Hilda Terry was interested in art as a child. After school and a factory job, she left home for New York City in 1931 "to see what this art business was all about." She did patent drawings, portraits and fashion art until she sold her first cartoon to the *New York American* newspaper in 1935.

While in New York City, Hilda Terry met cartoonist and illustrator Gregory d'Alessio. The couple married in 1938. Terry has written, "After one year of marriage (I) had learned enough about cartooning to go out and sell to the *New Yorker, Saturday Evening Post,* and *College Humor."* Her drawings of teenagers were a regular feature in the *Saturday Evening Post* and generated wide response from readers. In 1940 King Features Syndicate received word from its supreme commander, William Randolph Hearst, to hire Terry.

Her first attempt at a strip was turned down. She turned for advice to Cliff Sterrett of *Polly and Her Pals* fame. He encouraged her, and on December 7, 1941, the day of the Pearl Harbor attack, *It's a Girl's Life,* starring Henny and

"Now, now, Mama, daughter's got to start shaving SOMEtime."
Hilda Terry. © Dave Breger.

Penny, began syndication. In 1944 the name of the daily panel and Sunday page was changed to *Teena.* The strip was published until 1964.

The teenage girls that Hilda Terry drew were thin and linear. Her daily panel emphasized control of line in the Russell Patterson style, but with the end result being a wistful teenager instead of a mature, full-bodied woman. Solid black areas were artfully used to provide contrast in the design.

When *Teena* ended syndication, Terry found herself typecast. "After 23 years with *Teena,* I wasn't surprised that people believed I could draw only teenage girls," she stated. Instead of remaining artistically stagnant, Terry returned to school. She learned varityping and took computer science courses. She also worked with an electronics inventor, and before becoming a cartoonist she had worked in a radio tube factory. Now she was trained to become one of the foremost creators of animation for huge, sophisticated, computerized scoreboards in stadiums and arenas.

Other cartoonists may draw work to be interpreted on scoreboards. None, however, have Hilda Terry's unique background in writing, cartooning and computer science. She has said, "I'm unique because I can work directly with the computer. No one would miss me, but no one can replace me yet. I know shortcuts and function as three different people simultaneously." Her work involves traveling to the major centers of American professional sports, where she is often referred to by teams like the Kansas City Royals as their "computer lady." She is now retired. Since the death of her husband, Gregory d'Alessio, in 1993, she has taken up spiritualism.

As a cartoonist, Hilda Terry has always been a pioneer. In the field of syndicated comics, where successful women cartoonists are the exception rather than the rule, she enjoyed a long career. Now she is possibly the only cartoonist so intimately involved with the newest technological cartooning medium.

B.C.

TERRY, PAUL (1887-1971) American cartoonist born in San Mateo, California, on February 19, 1887. Paul Terry grew up in San Francisco, where he got his first art training at Polytechnic High School. He started out as a newspaper cartoonist on the *San Francisco Chronicle* in 1904, then went on to the *Call.* In the ten-year period preceding 1915, he drew for *Life* magazine and worked on an assortment of newspapers, ending up on the *New York Press* and producing a short-lived comic strip for W.R. Hearst.

Terry's first animated cartoon was *Little Herman,* a five-minute short for which he was paid the munificent sum of $405. During World War I, Terry produced a series of animated films on surgical technique, started *Farmer Al Falfa* in 1916, and in 1919 joined Paramount. He created his famous series *Aesop's Film Fables* (the first being "The Cat and the Mice") in 1921.

In 1928 Terry decided to strike out on his own: he joined Audiocinema, where he was given a free hand, but the firm was wiped out by the 1929 crash. Doggedly Terry and his partner, Frank Moser, went ahead, and in 1931 they released their first independently produced cartoon,

Paul Terry's most famous cartoon characters. © Terrytoons.

Hungarian Goulash, which was also the first of the Terrytoons. The Terrytoons were to give rise to many famous characters like Dinky Duck and Rudy Rooster. But Terry's most famous creations came out during and just after World War II, starting with the *Mighty Mouse* series ("The Mouse of Tomorrow," 1942), a rodent version of *Superman.* This was followed by *Heckle and Jeckle* ("The Talking Magpies," 1946), featuring a pair of rascally birds, and by *Little Roquefort* (1950), about yet another mouse, eternally at war with the cat Percy.

In 1955 Terry (who had bought out Moser in 1936) sold his backlog of cartoons to the Columbia Broadcasting System and went into semi-retirement, devoting most of his time to painting watercolors. He died on October 25, 1971.

Paul Terry is one of the unsung pioneers of early animation. While he was never an authentic creator of the caliber of Disney or Fleischer, he did contribute significantly to the nascent medium of animated film. He is credited with perfecting the method of cel animation, which consists of superimposing a set of translucent celluloid papers over the background drawing, with the artist inking in only the necessary changes in movement of the characters, thus cutting drawing time by about eighty percent (this technique is still in use today). Terry received a number of honors and distinctions during his long career, and in 1952 a retrospective exhibition of Paul Terry cartoons was held at the Museum of Modern Art in New York City.

M.H.

TESTU, ROGER (1913-) French painter and cartoonist born in Bourges, in central France, in 1913. After studies in

Roger Testu ("Tetsu"). © Tetsu.

the humanities, Roger Testu first embarked on a career as an abstract painter, then as a figurative painter and watercolorist, both with scant success. Only after World War II, in 1951, did he enter the cartooning profession at age 38 (as "Tetsu," an anagram of his name) with drawings published in the weekly *Noir et Blanc*. The success was immediate. "It worked right away," the artist declared in 1980. "I believe I brought in something new [to the French cartooning scene]: people who have known this period...tell me that it had the same effect as a small bomb."

Tetsu is a master at what the French call *humour farfelu* ("off-the-wall humor"). In spirit and style he resembles Chaval; but while Chaval's world is gray and resigned, Tetsu's is black and despairing. The critic Jacques Sternberg praised Tetsu's "intuition of the absurdity of daily life" manifest in the cartoonist's drawings—drawings often bereft of any caption and legend, mute witnesses to the bleak happenings they portray. In one instance a convict has his guardian angel carrying his ball and chain for him; in another a puppet master admonishes the bickering dummies he animates with his feet. His characters—mostly male—have sad, long faces and stooped silhouettes, as if they were carrying the world on their shoulders—which indeed they do.

In the course of his long career, Tetsu has contributed cartoons and drawings to most major French publications, from the dailies *Paris-Presse* and *France-Soir* to the monthlies *Le Monde et la Vie* and *Lectures pour Tous*, from humor magazines like *Le Rire* and *Satirix* to sober-sided periodicals such as *La Vie Catholique* and *Jours de France*. He has also published in foreign magazines that include *Le Soir* in Belgium and *Il Travaso* in Italy. Many of his cartoons have been collected in book form and he has held exhibitions of his works throughout Europe. Additionally he has written a number of short stories, not all of them humorous. For all these activities Tetsu has been awarded many honors, and in 1983 he was made a Knight of Arts and Letters.

Now in his eighties he continues to turn out drawings and cartoons, although he has reduced his output somewhat.

M.H.

TETSU

See Testu, Roger.

TETSUWAN ATOM (Japan) *Tetsuwan Atom* ("Astro Boy"), Japan's first television cartoon serial, was aired on Fuji television on January 1, 1963, and ran for 192 episodes until December 31, 1966. Produced by Osamu Tezuka's Mushi Productions,it was a resounding success, not only in Japan but around the world. The series was based on Tezuka's comic strip of the same name, which ran for over ten years in the monthly magazine *Shōnen*. Each TV episode lasted for 24 minutes and was in black and white.

Atom, the protagonist, was a very special robot created by a Dr. Temma in the year 2003 (or on April 1, 2013, according to his fan club). Dr. Temma had unlimited funds and the best brains in Japan at his disposal. His son had been killed in a traffic accident, and Atom therefore became a surrogate—but no normal son was he. He had a 100,000-horsepower atomic motor for a heart, acomputer brain, super ears, searchlight eyes, a rocket propulsion system in his legs and a machine gun for a tail. He could easily tell good and bad people apart, translate over sixty languages and fly. He had a photographic memory and lived on a diet of uranium. He also had emotions, however, and was capable of crying, sometimes enough to put out fires (as in episode number 85).

Other regular characters were Dr. Ochanomizu, a lovable but high-strung scientist devoted to Atom; Uran, Atom's robot sister; Cobalt, Atom's robot younger brother; and Hige Oyaji, a moustached schoolteacher type who provided comic relief. Atom lived in a "family" environment complete with adult guardians, and through him viewers were able to see inherent human weaknesses as well as Atom's attempts to help mankind. In each episode Atom aided people by defeating an endless array of enemies, but as opposed to the rather simplistic themes of U.S. superhero cartoons, he also provided valuable and sophisticated insights into human character. Although he was a robot, Atom was nonetheless guided by very strict robot principles (ten, in fact) that ranged from absolute service to mankind to never hurting or killing men to not going overseas without permission from his parents (creators).

Tetsuwan Atom remains a classic of Japanese animation, and an entire generation of Japanese youth was literally raised on it. It has been shown in over twenty countries around the world (on NBC-TV in the United States), and its popularity is such that its creator, Osamu Tezuka, is planning an entirely new series in the near future. (It came out in full color in the 1980s.)

In the United States the English version was so skillfully produced by Fred Ladd that millions of young Americans had no idea they were even watching "Japanese animation." In the 1990s, with the boom of popularity of "anime," many of these now-adult fans are going back to "Astro Boy," as it was titled, and enjoying the series in a new light on video, often sharing the experience with their own children. Whether in Japan or overseas, the character of Atom has transcended the era in which it was created, and with the aid of videos and merchandise, has become a universal favorite.

F.S.

THAT'S JAKE (U.S.) Since beginning national syndication by Tribune Media Services in 1985, *That's Jake* by Jake Vest has carved a niche as the home of good ol' boy country humor. It's published as a daily panel plus Sunday page.

A copy editor for the *Orlando Sentinel* newspaper in Florida, Jake Vest incorporates his love of bluegrass music, golf, and "Southern culture" into his panel. Vest grew up in Forks of the River, Tennessee, and attended the University of Tennessee, Knoxville, where he was staff artist on the student newspaper. While in the Army he drew for *Grunt,* the unofficial magazine of the Army in the Pacific area.

Vest claims he discovered he was a "hillbilly" when he found himself in a platoon with 125 guys from New Jersey while serving in Korea. In *That's Jake,* the protagonist, a good ol' boy comfortable with his beerbelly, is never shown without his ten-gallon cowboy hat. Although nationally syndicated, *That's Jake* is in many ways a regional strip with the bulk of its sales to newspapers in the south and west, such as the *Denver Post* and *Houston Chronicle.*

In one panel, while driving in his pickup truck, past a "Ristorante", Jake comments, "That's a shame, ain't it. They didn't know how to spell restaurant, but they were too proud to call the place a diner." Drawn in pen and ink with some crosshatching but no benday, Vest uses sight gags infrequently, relying mostly on a combination of dialogue balloons and captions underneath the panels.

That's Jake has been collected in two anthologies, *If You Didn't Want Grits, How Come Your Ordered Breakfast?"* and *Croissants Act Like Biscuits in Paris, Tennessee.*

There's true grit in *That's Jake,* a comic panel that rejoices in down-home country humor and makes no apologies about doing so.

B.C.

That's Jake

'I wonder what they do with all that caffeine once it's been removed.'

"That's Jake." © Tribune Media Services.

THOMAS, BERT (1883-1966) Welsh cartoonist born in Newport, Monmouthshire, in 1883.

"Arf a mo', Kaiser!" was the caption to one of the most famous cartoons in British history. Bert Thomas whipped it off in ten minutes flat—a scribbled sketch showing a typical Tommy Atkins pausing to light his pipe before marching off to war. It caught the spirit of the times like no other cartoon, the cheerful Cockney spirit in the face of awful adversity. It was drawn for the *Weekly Dispatch* in 1914, for that newspaper's fund to provide the British troops with tobacco and cigarettes. It worked wonders and was reprinted enough times for Thomas to have retired—had he charged a royalty! It collected at least £250,000 for the campaign, nothing for Thomas. Nor, curiously, was Thomas a Cockney.

Bert Thomas was one of 7 children of Job Thomas, a sculptor, and at the age of 14 he was apprenticed to an engraver in Swansea. He soon began to sketch for a living, however, and came to London to work in an advertising agency. He quickly became the art director, and in his spare time he dashed off joke drawings for the many weekly papers and comics of the day, among them *Pick-Me-Up* and *Ally Sloper's Half-Holiday.* Soon he was the political cartoonist on *London Opinion.* Came World War I, and Thomas enlisted in the Artists' Rifles, executing England's largest-ever poster, a gigantic cartoon for the war savings campaign that all but covered the face of the National Gallery. After the war he began cartooning jokes for *Punch* and by the end had contributed over one thousand to that paper alone.

It was after the war, too, that Thomas's style developed into the one he is best remembered by. Abandoning the pen, he deliberately used an old, matted brush on the rough surface of a Whatman board to produce an "instant" speed technique. He also developed an interesting two-color cartoon series for the *Sketch,* reproduced in red and black. His untidy line was especially good at capturing Cockney life and laughter, and he illustrated readers' contributions to the *London Evening News,* under the heading "Cockney War Stories," through the 1930s and into World War II. He died on September 6, 1966, at age 83.

Books: *War Cartoons from London Opinion* (1919); *Sea Whispers* (1926); *In Red and Black* (1928); *Meet These People* (1928); *500 Best Cockney War Stories* (1930); *Candid Caddies* (1935); *Cartoons and Character Drawing* (1936); *Nazty Nursery Rhymes* (1940); *Fun at the Seaside* (1944); *Fun on the Farm* (1944); *Podgy the Pup* (1945); *Mixed Bag* (1945); *Fun in the Country* (1946); *Fun in the Town* (1946); *Playtime* (1947); *Toyland* (1947); *Trip on a Barge* (1947); *Railways by Day* (1947); and *Railways by Night (1947).*

D.G.

THOMPSON, BERYL ANTONIA (1918-1970) British cartoonist born in Melbourne, Australia, in 1918. Both Antonia Thompson (as she preferred to be called) and her brother, Harold Underwood, were artistic children. They came to London from Melbourne in the late 1920s, and Beryl went from school to the Royal Academy. Her success as a fashion artist prompted Harold to return to his art studies after a start in business. He began to publish cartoons signed "H. Botterill" in the *Bystander* and then contributed to a new weekly, *Night and Day.* By the mid-1930s he had so much work that he began to pass his rough sketches over to his sister to finish. In 1937 they formed a team, and as "Anton" (an abbreviation of her name), they evolved a new outline-and-shading technique for line cartoons.

This new style, partly designed to replace the wash work they had been using for the glossy magazines, pleased *Punch,* and by 1939 the "new" cartoonists were a great success. World War II, however, interfered; Harold was called into the navy. Antonia, her surname changed by marriage to Yeoman, carried on, as rough ideas continued to arrive by mail from her brother overseas. After the war, the partnership continued, but for a number of years before her death in June 1970, Antonia was on her own, and she acquitted herself with great credit.

D.G.

THOMPSON ST. POKER CLUB, THE (U.S.) The fledgling *Life* magazine had more than luck to account for its initial success; some of New York's most prominent black-and-white artists (many of them veterans of the *New York Graphic)* filled its pages. Among early literary contributors were such respectable names as Brander Matthews, James Whitcomb Riley and Henry Guy Carleton.

Carleton, *Life*'s first drama reviewer, pitched in with other duties on the small staff, and on April 17, 1884, the first minutes of *The Thompson St. Poker Club* appeared (unsigned, as they were always to be). Thompson Street was then the black section of New York City, and the series purported to give accounts of the poker confabs of such characters as Cyanide Whiffles, Thankful Smith and Deacon Trotline Anguish. Of course, they were raucous, cheating, murderous affairs, but reported in an understated manner such as a society reporter or punctilious secretary might use. The effect was hilarious.

The series became enormously popular, running into the following year and inspiring a book collection. Its success was no doubt due as much to the cartoon illustrations of E.W. Kemble as to the text. Kemble was then relatively unknown, but his marvelous handling of very funny situations and his sympathetic depiction of blacks (even in broad caricature) was as masterful as in his maturer years. As *The Thompson St. Poker Club* attracted attention, Kemble's cartoons vindicated the judgment of Mark Twain, who had just engaged Kemble to illustrate several books, including *Huckleberry Finn* and his *Encyclopedia of Humor*

.R.M.

THÖNY, EDUARD (1866-1950) Austrian cartoonist and painter born in Brixen, Austria (now Bressanone, Italy), on February 9, 1866. One of the great veterans of the Munich satirical magazine *Simplicissimus,* Eduard Thöny was on its staff from its first year to its last (1896-1944). The son of a Tyrolean sculptor of sacred images, Eduard was sent to study art in Munich at the age of seven. When the time came for him to enroll in the School of Applied Art, he was refused admission because of a technicality, and so he attended the Academy instead, thus changing his whole future. During his long student years he was already drawing for such magazines as the *Berliner Modewelt,* the *Münchener Humoristische Blätter* and the Munich *Radfahr-Humor.*

His ambition was apparently to become a historical painter of military scenes, for he went to study in Paris with the great horse painter Edouard Detaille and then studied uniforms and equipment in French and German

Inopportune: "When we're on the street, please drop your eternal nagging and quarreling. What have we got a home for?"
Eduard Thöny, 1921. © Simplicissimus.

collections. But when he returned to Munich in 1896, it was to become a permanent staff member of the new *Simplicissimus,* for which Thöny was eventually to do some four thousand drawings. In 1908 he acquired a house (renovated for him by the architect-cartoonist Bruno Paul) at Holzhausen on the Ammersee in Bavaria; burned in 1944, it was later rebuilt, and he died there on July 26, 1950.

Aside from his work for *Simplicissimus,* Thöny illustrated several volumes of poetry and fiction, and even for that magazine his work was varied, including witty studies of all classes of society, from eccentric Bavarian peasants to the nouveaux riches and profiteers. But he remained true to his early training in that his specialties were military, and especially cavalry, subjects. A major portion of his work satirizes the duty-obsessed, self-important but circumscribed young officers of Prussia and other parts of Germany. His drawing style, always impressive, was quite academic at the outset, became more fluid and alert with the years, but never partook of an outright "cartoon" quality.

Thöny's separately published albums included *Der Leutnant* ("The Lieutenant"), *Der Bunte Rock* ("Military Life"), *Gemischte Gesellschaft* ("Mixed Company") and *Vom Kadetten zum General* ("From the Cadet to the General"). His drawings were often the object of "the sincerest form of flattery," for Thöny imitators were legion in many countries.

S.A.

THURBER, JAMES GROVER (1894-1961) American cartoonist and author born in Columbus, Ohio, on December 8, 1894. A playground accident cost James Thurber his right eye at the age of six, and he was left to depend upon one steadily weakening eye until he became totally blind in his mid-forties. He entered Ohio State University in 1913 as an English major but did not graduate. Unable to serve in the army during World War I, he finally managed to get overseas in 1919 and was stationed in Paris as a code clerk for the State Department. Thurber married in 1922 and returned to Columbus the same year. He got a job as a reporter for the *Columbus Dispatch,* where he remained until 1925, when he and his wife went back to Paris. There he took a job with the Paris edition of the *Chicago Tribune.*

"It's a naive domestic Burgundy without any breeding, but I think you'll be amused by its presumption."
James Thurber's most often reprinted cartoon, 1937. © The New Yorker.

At a salary of $12 a week, it wasn't long before the City of Light became a very dim place indeed, and the Thurbers returned to the United States.

This time they settled in New York City, where Thurber found employment with the *Evening Post* and began to lay siege to the offices of the recently launched *New Yorker* magazine, a sophisticated weekly that, under the editorship of Harold Ross, boasted some of the finest and most innovative artists and writers of the day as regular contributors. (It should lift the spirits of every budding writer to know that Thurber received 20 rejection slips before getting his first acceptance.) In 1927, through the intervention of the magazine's "Talk of the Town" editor, E.B. White (whom Thurber had met socially), he was hired as a member of the *New Yorker* staff. However, through some odd turn of events, he found himself titled "managing editor" and given purely administrative duties. Fortunately for the history of American humor, this placement blunder was soon rectified, and Thurber got himself transferred to the "Talk of the Town" department as a contributing editor. Soon he and White were turning out the sort of material that became emblematic of the *New Yorker* style. Many pages would be required to discuss Thurber's contributions to comic literature, which rank him among the Olympian humorists of the English language. But almost as enduring were his contributions to the field of comic art.

It is said that someone once castigated editor Ross for publishing a "fifth-rate artist" like Thurber; whereupon Ross stoutly defended Thurber, affirming that he was in fact a "third-rate artist." What, then, can be said of Thurber's drawings? By none of the ordinary aesthetic criteria can they be judged successful. The fact is that a half-blind man simply created and used without apology his own standard of expression—and it worked. Perhaps it worked because it seemed to communicate none of the technical mastery that ordinarily separates the artist from the rest of us. And yet, no one has ever succeeded in duplicating the Thurber style, which for all its otherworldly simplicity is as intricate as any of the mannered, traditional modes. If discipline and an identifiable style—realism, impressionism, etc.—are the bases of art as we normally think of it, the bases of Thurber's art were an absolute freedom from convention and an almost furious whimsy. It was "art" originating in and defined by the unique temperament of one individual.

The best metaphor for Thurber's drawings is the Rorschach blot—ink-line dumplings or amoebas with which the only appropriate free association is laughter. Consider his rendering of "A Group of Miscellaneous Creatures" for the *New Yorker*. Can one deny, can one even doubt, that a "tantamount" looks like that fuzzy arboreal creature Thurber presents to us? Isn't it clear that if we were only to put on our aqualungs and descend into the lake, we would encounter the "qualm," the "glib" and the "moot" exactly as the artist depicts them? Has there ever been a more perfect representation of the shy "bodkin," a more convincing portrait of the seldom-seen "chintz"?

Much has been written of the misogyny in Thurber's work, the recurrent theme of the battling sexes. To deny this strain in his humor would be foolish and shortsighted, but to dwell on it seems equally inadvisable. The

Thurber cosmos is a varied place, one part of it no more significant than another. This is true of both his writings and his art, and especially his art, where tenderness between men and women can often be seen. To suggest otherwise distorts the essential keenness of his perceptions and dims the brilliance with which he captured them.

A list of Thurber's publications is hardly necessary here, but among his better-known illustrated collections of writings are *The Owl in the Attic and Other Perplexities* (1931) and *The Seal in the Bedroom and Other Predicaments* (1932). He was also the author of a *New Yorker* memoir, *The Years with Ross* (1959). He was awarded honorary degrees by Kenyon College (1950), Yale (1953) and Williams College (1951), and he received countless appreciations and awards for his art and written humor. Thurber's works have often been adapted to the stage, the animated cartoon and the TV screen.

Thurber left the permanent staff of the *New Yorker* in 1933 but continued as a frequent contributor for many years thereafter. He died in New York on November 2, 1961, of complications following serious surgery.

R.C.

TIM
See Mitelberg, Louis.

TIMOTHY
See Birdsall, Timothy.

TINGLEY, MERLE (1921-) Canadian cartoonist born July 9, 1921, in Montreal, Canada. After one year at the Valentine School of Commerical Art in Montreal, Tingley joined an engineering firm as a draftsman in 1939. War interrupted his career, and in 1942 he enlisted into the Canadian Army where he worked on several service publications as a cartoonist. His contributions were so appreciated that upon his return to civilian life he landed a job with the *London* (Ontario) *Free Press* as their editorial cartoonist in 1947.

Ting—as he signs his work—enjoyed a long and harmonious career at the paper. His cartoons were done in a broad style reminiscent of old-time cartoonists such as John McCutcheon and Bill Ireland and a great attention to line. He liked to draw a worm—a reminiscence of his draftsman days—in his cartoons, and the creature, nicknamed "Luke Worm," became a favorite with the readers. He paid close attention to local concerns, but he also extended his commentary to include Canadian and international issues. This aspect of his work is the one best known to American readers, as many of his cartoons were later reprinted in U.S. publications. His comments had a conservative bent to them, and he often took stands against government and big labor.

One of Ting's major concerns is for the environment. After the Three-Mile Island accident one of his cartoons depicted Death roasting a barren globe over a nuclear reactor; in another cartoon a nuclear survivor exclaims to his irradiated family, "Well, thank God... the neutron bomb left our home intact!" His almost 40-year long career

Merle Tingley ("Ting"). © Merle Tingley.

at the *Free Press*, one remarkable for its consistency and absence of malice, came to an end in July 1986.

Ting has kept busy since his official retirement. He still turns out a weekly political caartoon which he syndicates himself. A 1994 two-panel cartoon drawing a hilarious (if painful) parallel between the British landing with guns drawnon the beaches of Normandy in 1944 and their landing on the far side of the Channel Tunnel 50 years later wielding wallets and credit cards was particularly well received in Canada and abroad.

M.H.

TINTIN (Belgium) In the years following World War II Hergé's *Tintin* was inarguably the most popular comic strip in Europe; it was featured not only in newspapers and magazines, but also in books, toys and games. It was only a question of time before *Tintin* would be brought to the screen.

In 1948 Studio Misonne in Brussels released a full-length puppet film, *Le Crabe aux Pinces d'Or* ("The Crab with the Golden Claws"). Drawn from the *Tintin* book of the same title, it proved unsuccessful. After a hiatus of almost ten years, Raymond Leblanc, publisher of the *Tintin* weekly magazine, decided in 1957 to produce a series of *Tintin* animated cartoons for French television. The series was well received, the cartoon being more suited to the character than the puppets had been, and it was followed by a second group of cartoons in 1960. All the *Tintin* shorts closely followed Hergé's comic strip stories.

Thus encouraged, Leblanc commissioned the artists at his studio, Belvision, to embark on a feature-length animated cartoon. This was *Tintin et le Temple du Soleil*

"Tintin et le Temple du Soleil." © *Belvision.*

(*Prisoners of the Sun* in the English version), released in 1969. Among the cartoonists who worked on the feature were Bob de Moor, Nic Broca and Robert Flament. Jacques Brel composed several original songs for the film. *Tintin et le Temple du Soleil* had been adapted from previously published material; the 1972 *Tintin et le Lac aux Requins* ("Tintin and the Lake of Sharks"), on the other hand, was based on Hergé's original screenplay, with virtually the same personnel. Hergé's death in 1983 interrupted the making of more *Tintin* films. In the early 1990s, however, Nelvana in Toronto, Canada, produced 39 new cartoon episodes of *Tintin* that were shown all around the world (in the U.S. they were broadcast on HBO).

The cartoon Tintin remained faithful to Hergé's characterization: a resourceful, energetic adolescent, he embarked on his adventures with brio and enthusiasm. As in the comic strip, he was flanked by his frisky fox terrier Milou (Snowy in the English version), the cantankerous Captain Haddock and the absentminded Professor Tournesol (Calculus). His cartoon adventures are entertaining if predictable, and the animation is adequate. (It should be noted that *Tintin* has also been adapted to live-action films, but these do not concern us here.)

M.H.

TIPPIT, JACK (1923-1994) American cartoonist born in Texas on October 19, 1923. Presently best known among readers for his continuation of the popular juvenile daily panel gag feature *Amy,* Jack Tippit was raised in Panhandle country, attending Texas Tech and Syracuse University. A magna cum laude graduate, he saw action in World War II with the U.S. Air Force as a B-24 pilot in the Pacific and did gag cartooning on the side. Later a successful contributor to such magazines as *Look,* the *Saturday Evening Post* and the *New Yorker,* Tippit continued his air force career through the Korean war and is presently a full colonel in the reserves, having served in the meantime in the Office of the Secretary of the Air Force, Washington.

In 1960 he took the Register and Tribune panel feature *Amy* from the ailing hands of Harry Mace, its creator and Tippit's friend. Tippit worked on the panel for four years until Mace's untimely death in 1963 and carried it on afterward. Creator of a two-panel gag feature, *Doctor Bill,* in the early 1960s, Tippit also originated the weekly gag feature *Family Flak,* which runs in the nationally distributed *Family Weekly.* Winner of the Best Magazine Gag Artist awards in 1963 and 1966 from the National Cartoonists Society, and of the Best Syndicated Panel Artist award for *Amy* from the NCS in 1960, Tippit is also a past president of the NCS. He also drew the *Henry* newspaper strip from 1979 to 1983. He died at his home in Wilton, Conn., in October 1994.

B.B.

TISNER
See Artis Gener, Aveli.

TITTLE, WALTER (1883-1966) American cartoonist and painter born in Springfield, Ohio, on October 9, 1883. Walter Tittle studied art under Robert Henri and William Chase, and around 1905 he began selling cartoons and illustrations to *Harper's, Scribner's,* the *Century* and, principal among the comic journals, *Life.* For *Life* he drew numerous pen-and-ink interior cartoons and cover paintings.

Tittle's pen-and-ink style was an annoying pastiche of everything Gibson was supposed to be, as seen through an erring eye; Gibson's methods and delineations were copied but only captured superficially. Tittle's themes were Gibson's, too: society drawings, boy-and-girl stuff, embarrassing situations. Gibson's imitators were legion, but Tittle was one who seemed never to graduate.

His pursuit of serious art was obviously more successful. He took up etching and drypoint in 1917 and portraits soon thereafter, executing a distinguished series for the Washington Naval Disarmament Conference in 1921. Among his many distinctions were the National Arts Club Award of 1931, the Printmakers International Award in 1932 and the Chicago Society of Etchers Award, presented at the Century of Progress Fair in 1934. Tittle died, active in several fields of art, in Carmel, California, on March 27, 1966.

R.M.

TOASPERN, OTTO (1863-ca. 1925) American cartoonist and painter born in Brooklyn, New York, on March 26, 1863. Otto Toaspern was a graduate of the Royal Academy of Fine Arts in Munich (1888) and became a genre and portrait painter in America; he also taught at the National Academy. As a cartoonist and illustrator he drew for *Harper's, Century, Ladies' Home Journal* and several European periodicals, but chiefly for *Life.*

Toaspern's specialty was crayon over grained paper, producing the stone-grain look—an interesting effect in the late 1890s, when lithography was losing favor with cartoonists. Ironically, his shaded drawings were hits in the photoengraved *Life,* especially against the rigid pen-and-ink cartoons that surrounded them. He concentrated on caricatures, a nascent art form, and was best known for the full-page studies, *Life's Interviews,* in which *Life's* little cupid would sternly interrogate an invariably cowering public figure. He revived this series of the 1890s briefly in *Life* in the early 1920s; he died about 1925.

R.M.

TOBEY, BARNEY (1906-1989) One of the most prolific gag cartoonists in American magazines, Barney Tobey entertained a large public with his genial humor for over five decades. A regular feature of such national periodicals as *Collier's* and *The Saturday Evening Post* during their heyday, his work began to appear in the *New Yorker* late in the 1930s and continued to be one its most popular features until his death.

The cartoonist, who signed himself B. Tobey, was born in 1906 in Manhattan, the son of a Russian immigrant who worked as a pushcart salesman. He showed an early talent for humorous art, and during his years at Evander Childs High School he wrote and drew a comic strip called *Ambitious Ambrose* for the school paper. His skill at more conventional draftsmanship earned him a scholarship to the New York School of Fine and Applied Arts, where he studied for a year before accepting a job as an artist with the city's largest advertising agency, Batten, Barton, Durstine & Osborne.

Tobey's work as an advertising artist gave him an opportunity to exercise his imagination, and the antic turn it frequently took led him inevitably to try his hand at the magazine cartoon market. His efforts met with considerable success, and after 6 years with BBD&O he felt secure enough to give up his job and take the plunge as a freelance. He later took some classes at the Art Students League, but his bland, rather conventional graphic style never changed much. He became a contract artist with the *New Yorker*, which over the years published more than 1,200 of his cartoons and numerous illustrations, including four covers. Tobey illustrated several children's books and frequently did theater posters and book covers.

Tobey was to become something of an icon as a survivor of the flourishing post-World War II cartoon industry, and he received exhibitions at such venues as the Metropolitan Museum of Art, the Museum of the City of New York, and the Grolier Society. In 1976 he had a solo show in New York's Nicholls Gallery, which prompted *New York Times* art critic John Russell to write, "With some cartoonists, the caption helps the drawing along. With others the drawing raises hopes which the caption doesn't fulfill. With Tobey, the two are in perfect equilibrium." Four years later, a collection of his work, *B. Tobey of The New Yorker*, was published by Dodd, Mead & Co.

Tobey relied on many of the conventional subjects of the humor of his time. In one *Collier's* cartoon, a tactless child at a dinosaur exhibit observes, "I guess this takes you back almost to your childhood, doesn't it, Grandpa?" In another, a man showing an urban apartment to prospective tenants points out hopefully, "If you're fond of birds, there's a pigeon that walks around on that roof every day." Never an innovator in either style or content, Tobey neither cut very deep nor departed far from reality, but presented an engaging picture of everyday life. His work made gentle fun of the traditional foibles of his middle-class audience, and his long career earned him a place among its favorites.

D.W.

"Tobias Knopp." © EOS Productions.

TOBIAS KNOPP (Germany) *Tobias Knopp, Abenteuer eines Junggesellen* ("Tobias Knopp, Adventures of a Bachelor"), a 100-minute animated film based on the drawings of 19th-century cartoonist Wilhelm Busch, was produced in West Germany in 1950. The director, Gerhard Fieber, used only black-and-white stock in order to remain faithful to the flavor and the spirit of the old master's cartoon stories.

Tobias Knopp, a swinging bachelor, decides it is time for him to get married. In the course of his nuptial quest he goes through a number of adventures and has several encounters with potential brides and former girl friends. The film is a recounting of these episodes, each with its own subtitle ("A Shady Co-Worker," "The Rustic Celebration," "The Game Field," etc.). In the end Tobias meets the girl who will become his wife, and the film concludes on this happy note.

Tobias Knopp is a charming feature, full of ingenuity and wit, with graphic effects and flowing lines directly traceable to the original (and masterly) drawings of Wilhelm Busch.

M.H.

TOFANO, SERGIO (1886-1973) Italian cartoonist, filmmaker and actor born in Rome, Italy, on August 20, 1886. Sergio Tofano (as he was known to theatergoers), or "Sto" (as he was known to his many readers), received a law degree in 1909 but decided to go into acting instead. He joined the theatrical company of Ermete Novelli. His act-

Sergio Tofano ("Sto"), "Signor Bonaventura." © Corriere dei Piccoli.

ing career did not prevent him from pursuing a cartooning career at the same time, with many contributions to the Turin humor publication *Il Numero* (1914-23) and to *Il Giornalino della Domenica.*

In October 1917 Sto created the celebrated comic strip *Il Signor Bonaventura* for *Il Corriere dei Piccoli.* This strip was so successful that Tofano played the character on the stage in 1927 and directed a movie based on his creation in 1942. He directed several more films thereafter, including the 1943 *Giamburrasca,* in which he inserted an animated sequence. *Il Signor Bonaventura* ran uninterruptedly until 1955 and was revived in 1970. Tofano, who adapted his strip to the stage a second time in 1953, drew his feature up to the time of his death on October 28, 1973.

S.T.

TOLES, THOMAS GREGORY (1951-   ) Editorial cartoonist Tom Toles has spent his life within a few miles of his birthplace, but his work has brought him a reputation that extends throughout the country. Born in Buffalo, New York, on October 10, 1951, the son of a professional writer, Toles majored in English at the State University of New York in his native city. With no plans for making a career in art, he worked on his campus newspaper, *Spectrum,* as graphics director, and upon graduating in 1973, took a job with the Buffalo *Courier-Express* as a staff artist. By 1980 Toles had become the paper's graphics director.

Toles' skill at caricature, which had found expression on the pages of the *Courier-Express,* led the paper to offer him the post of editorial cartoonist that same year. Although he had never considered such a career and, as he recalled, "not having a clue as to how to do political cartooning and not much of a desire to do it," he accepted the challenge. From the beginning, he determined to retain his personal integrity and intellectual independence in his work. "My goal," he has stated, "has been to align the cartoons as closely with my own thoughts and personality as possible."

Toles' thoughts and personality are far-ranging and reflect a deep engagement, especially in issues of environmentalism and consumerism. A success from the start, his minimally drawn cartoons were among the most popular features in the *Courier-Express.* When that paper ceased publication in 1982, Toles received offers from others around the country but accepted that of *Buffalo News.* His audience was not long limited to his hometown, however; less than two weeks after he began with the *News,* Universal Press Syndicate began distributing him nationally. The next year, Universal reported that Toles was "the fastest growing syndicated editorial cartoonist in the country today," and by 1985 his work was being carried in 110 newspapers.

That year his first collection of cartoons, *The Taxpayer's New Clothes,* appeared. Later volumes, including *Mr. Gazoo* (1987), *At Least Our Bombers Are Getting Smarter* (1991), and *My Elected Representative Went to Washington* (1993), continued to comment shrewdly on the government and society. Applauded for his trenchant wit as well as for the distinctive structure and style of his cartoons, Toles has been credited with "brash originality and incisive social understanding" and ranked "among the funniest cartoonists in America" (*Comics Journal,* February, 1992). His many honors include more than 20 Page One Awards from the Buffalo Newspaper Guild between 1971 and 1982, a First Place in the John Fischetti Editorial Cartoonist Competition in 1984, the Golden Apple Award for Excellence in Educational Journalism in 1984, and the Pulitzer Prize in 1990.

In 1993, Toles introduced *Curious Avenue,* an insightful series described as a "sharp-edged comic strip that reads like a collaboration between Charles Schulz and Ingmar Bergman" (*WittyWorld,* Autumn/Winter, 1994). Like his editorial cartoons, this penetrating examination of the world of childhood reveals the same keen wit and originality of vision that have brought Toles to the top rank of American cartoonists.

D.W.

Tom Toles. © Buffalo News.

TOM AND JERRY (U.S.-1) Not to be confused with the later MGM series of the same name, these cartoons were produced by the Van Beuren studio and distributed by RKO. The first Van Beuren *Tom and Jerry* cartoon short, "Wot a Night," was released in the summer of 1931.

The Van Beuren series was a throwback to the earlier days of animation when most cartoon characters were human, and especially to *Mutt and Jeff,* which it resembled in many respects. Tom and Jerry were two young ne'er-do-wells (one blond, the other brunet) perpetually at odds

"Tom and Jerry" (1), from a tracing by I. Klein. © Amédée Van Beuren.

"Tom and Jerry" (2). © MGM.

with each other but emotionally inseparable. Their misadventures took them to all kinds of climes, and they adopted any number of roles—aviators, explorers, mountain climbers, etc.—although they were seen to best advantage as hobos, the occupation dearest to their hearts. Some of the more notable entries in the series were "Polar Pals," "Jungle Jam" and "Swiss Trick" (all 1931); "Plane Dumb" and "Rocketeers" (both 1932); and "Happy Hobos" and "Phantom Rockets" (both 1933). Like most Van Beuren productions, *Tom and Jerry* did not last long: it was discontinued in the mid-1930s. John Foster, George Stallings, Frank Sherman and Frank Rufle directed most of the cartoons; and Joe Barbera (who later co-created the MGM *Tom and Jerry*) was one of the writers.

M.H.

TOM AND JERRY (U.S.-2) The inseparable duo made up of Tom Cat and Jerry Mouse was created by that no less inseparable duo of animators, Bill Hanna and Joe Barbera, in a 1939 cartoon entitled "Puss Gets the Boot." The names Tom and Jerry may have been inspired by similarly named cartoon characters in a series produced by Amédée Van Beuren's studio in the early 1930s, for which Barbera wrote several stories.

The *Tom and Jerry* cartoons (which were produced by MGM under the aegis of Fred Quimby) were instantly popular. Their whimsical atmosphere, frenetic motion and choreographed violence were more in tune with the times than Disney's shorts, and they very soon started chipping away at Disney's almost unbroken monopoly on the Academy Awards. Starting in 1943 with the timely title "Yankee Doodle Mouse," *Tom and Jerry* received no less than four Oscars in a row, for "Mouse Trouble" (1944), "Quiet, Please" (1945) and the classic "Cat Concerto" (1946), with Tom as a concert pianist and Jerry intent on disrupting his performance of Liszt's Hungarian Rhapsody no. 2. Three more Oscars were added in following years: in 1948 ("The Little Orphan," in the course of which a small orphan mouse joins Jerry in outwitting Tom), 1951 ("The Two Mouseketeers," in which Tom and Jerry carry their feud to the court of Louis XIII) and 1952 ("Johann Mouse," a charming tale set in the Vienna of Johann Strauss).

The theme of *Tom and Jerry* was fairly simple: Jerry would run afoul of Tom for one reason or other, and a frantic chase would ensue, in the course of which Tom would be bashed over the head, crushed under a safe, crunched between two trucks, only to spring to life for more of the same treatment. Sometimes a twist would be provided, as in "Dr. Jekyll and Mr. Mouse," with Jerry transformed into a killer mouse and Tom the object of the pursuit.

When the MGM animation studio closed its doors in 1957, Hanna and Barbera went on to bigger (but not necessarily better) things. In the late 1950s and early 1960s Gene Deitch did a second series of *Tom and Jerry* cartoons. Produced in Prague and distributed by MGM, these cartoons (of which "The Tom and Jerry Cartoon Kit" was the most notable) were too slow and predictable. MGM then called on veteran animator Chuck Jones to produce a third series; in many of the Jones-directed *Tom and Jerrys* (which ran until MGM closed down the unit in 1969), the cat and the mouse became partners instead of adversaries, and much of the fun and spirit of the old cartoons was lost. In 1976 Hanna and Barbera went back to producing *Tom and Jerry* cartoons for television, but these are only pale imitations of their early masterpieces. In 1993 the characters were brought to the big screen in *Tom and Jerry: The Movie*, a pointless exercise in the course of which Tom and Jerry not only spoke but sang as well. The characters' offspring have been appearing since 1995 on the Cartoon Network in the *Tom and Jerry Kids* show.

Tom and Jerry have decorated towels, chewing gum cards and vitamin tablets, and they were successfully featured in hundreds of comic books from the 1940s on.

M.H.

TOMASZEWSKI, HENRYK (1914-) Polish cartoonist, illustrator and poster designer born in Siedlce, Poland, on June 10, 1914. Henryk Tomaszewski attended the Academy of Fine Arts in Warsaw from 1931 to 1936. He started a cartooning career that same year, but his activities were interrupted by World War II. After the end of the war in 1945 he resumed work as a graphic artist (mainly drawing posters) and as a cartoonist for the resurgent Polish press.

While Tomaszewski is best known for his posters (he has won many prizes for his work in this field, and in 1968 he co-founded the Warsaw Poster Museum), his achievements as a cartoonist are just as impressive. His cartoons, full of the fantasy and sense of mystery that characterize surrealistic drawings, tend to deflate pomposity and to expose—but in a gentle, insouciant way—the absurdities of modern life. Never overtly political, they nevertheless exhibit a sharp critical tinge. Tomaszewski received a special prize for his satirical cartoons from the magazine *Przeglad Kulturalny* in 1960. An anthology of his cartoons, *Ksiazka Zazalen* ("The Book of Complaints"), was published in 1961. Unlike many of his colleagues specializing in "black" humor, Tomaszewski refuses to give up on the human race. "Let us not be led into going mad" is one of his favorite exhortations.

Widely regarded as the greatest living graphic artist in

Poland, Tomaszewski has received countless honors and awards; his works have been exhibited in Poland, Eastern and Western Europe, the United States and Latin America. He *is* also a noted illustrator of children's books and has designed stage sets and costumes. He has been a professor at the Warsaw Academy of Fine Arts since 1952 and is an honorary member of the Royal Society of Art in England. A book-length study of the artist by B. Kwiatkowska was published in Warsaw in 1959. His work is on permanent display at the Warsaw Cartoon Museum (opened in 1983). His son Tomasz is also a cartoonist of repute.

M.H.

TOMINAGA, ICHIRŌ (1925-) Japanese cartoonist born in Kyoto, Japan, on May 20, 1925. Ichiro Tominaga works in the genre known as *fūzoku manga,* or cartoons dealing with everyday subjects. Although he has had no formal art training, his cartoons are a humorous burlesque of human relations for which he draws inspiration from his own varied personal experience. When Ichiro Tominaga was five, his father died, and as a result his early childhood was a period of considerable flux. He found consolation in comics, however, and was a particular fan of Suihō Tagawa's *Nora Kuro.* Early in life he also developed two avid interests that have continued to sustain him and serve as a source of creative reference: movies and Japanese *kayōkyoku* ("popular songs"). They have, he claims, become his tranquilizers in life. He sings constantly and is convinced that singing is the key to his excellent health. In the spring of 1943, so the story goes, he sailed off for further schooling in Taiwan (then a Japanese colony), and when an accompanying ship was torpedoed by a U.S. sub, he was ordered to ready his valuables in case it was necessary to abandon ship. Tominaga grabbed his popular song notebooks.

Tominaga spent over three years in Taiwan, but not all in school. Soon after arriving, he was drafted into the military and had his education disrupted. At the end of hostilities the school automatically issued him both a diploma and a teaching certificate as a consolation, for when the Chinese Kuomintang troops arrived on the island he was reduced to utter poverty and starvation, like all the other Japanese. Finally repatriated to Japan in 1946, he worked making charcoal for two years until fired for giving it away. He then worked as a schoolteacher until 1951, when he began contributing cartoons to magazines and newspapers.

Tominaga was highly impressed by Kenji Ogiwara's *Nihon Igai Shi* (1948) and saw no reason why he too couldn't produce something along the same lines. Stimulated by the idea, he moved to Tokyo and by 1957 had become very serious about cartooning. In addition to drawing for children's books, he began contributing cartoons to magazines such as *Modern Nihon* and *Yomikiri Kurabu.* Yukio Sugiura, the creator of *Atomic Obon,* and an elder statesman among cartoonists, gave Tominaga a valuable assist to his career by introducing him to the magazine *Manga Sunday.* The result was *Gon-san* (1964), a humorous work depicting a young college student. Since then Tominaga has firmly established himself in the field with classics such as *Ponkotsu Oyaji* and *Chinkoro Nēchan,* as well as *Interi Nēchan, Pico, Hana no Ketchonta, Tonkachi Oyako* and *Ichiro Ninjakō.*

Tominaga's cartoons and comics are fast, full of action and short on words. His humor is often somewhat violent and sexual, which has led to criticism from certain quarters in Japan. He revels in the unexpected, and his characters tend to be run-of-the-mill, average people, as opposed to slick urban sophisticates. His women are invariably old hags. Tominaga shows great versatility in his formats, which vary from one-panel cartoons (as in *Bikkuri Zone*) to pictures with narrative (as in *Kappa Den*) to 4- to 18-panel comics. His characters are simply drawn in a style found frequently in this genre, featuring intentionally abbreviated lines and background and a maximum deformation of facial features.

After 1975 Tominaga began appearing regularly on the popular TV show *Owarai Manga Dojo* ("The Funny Manga Dojo") and achieved true household recognition, not just as a cartoonist, but as a "celebrity." In 1986 he received the Japan Cartoonists' Association Grand Prix award; in 1992 he was granted the coveted Order of Culture Medal with Purple Ribbon.

F.S.

TOMITA, EIZŌ (1906-1982) Japanese cartoonist born in Nagoya, Japan, on January 2, 1906. Eizō Tomita was a man of diverse talents who has shown remarkable flexibility in adapting his styles and subjects to the changing times. After dropping out of the Osaka University of Foreign Studies, Tomita worked as a reporter for the *Osaka Shimbun.* At the same time, he began studying art in his spare hours and also wrote a novel entitled *Nettaigyo* ("Tropical Fish") that won him a literary award from the *Sunday Mainichi* newspaper. Later he moved to Tokyo, where he continued working as a reporter and writing; he also produced plays and drew cartoons.

As war approached in Japan and the environment turned chilly for outspoken cartoonists, Tomita came out in support of government policies, like many others, and eventually was employed as a cartoonist by the government. It was therefore not until the war ended that he really bloomed as a cartoonist in his own right. Since childhood one of his ambitions had been to become a poet and wander around the world. He finally had an opportunity to actualize this dream when he toured the United States in 1954, doing ink sketches of scenes that struck his eye, such as the cabarets, gay bars and artists' colonies of Greenwich Village in New York. His experience was recorded in a travelogue entitled *San Doru Amerika Ryokō* ("The Three-Dollar American Journey"). He later toured the capitals of the world, a trip which resulted in *Sekai no Yoru wa Boku no Mono* ("Nights of the World Are Mine," 1961).

With these two works Tomita in effect achieved his aim of becoming a traveling poet, for his pen sketches are really little poems that stand on their own. One well-known example, Rōba no Shi ("Death of an Old Woman"), shows a fallen New York matron in front of a posh hotel; an epauletted doorman fends off gawkers while her poodle stares on in utter confusion. Ironically (given some of his wartime positions), Tomita's style and the scenes he

Creative Fever
Roland Topor. © Topor.

depicts have often led to his being referred to as a "decadent" cartoonist in Japan today. He died in 1982.

F.S.

TOPI
See Vikstedt, Toivo Alarik.

TOPOR, ROLAND (1938-1997) French cartoonist, graphic artist and writer born in Paris, France, on January 7, 1938, of Jewish refugee parents (a fact the artist always stresses in his interviews). After completing his studies at the Ecole des Beaux-Arts in Paris, Roland Topor founded "Mouvement Panique" with the Spanish playwright Fernando Arrabal in 1960. Since 1961 Topor has had his drawings exhibited in art galleries from Paris to New York, from Chicago to Amsterdam. He has also published several novels (*Le Locataire Chimérique, Princesse Angine*) and a collection of short stories (*Four Roses for Lucienne*).

It is as a cartoonist, however, that Topor is best known; his first cartoons appeared in the satirical magazine *Hara-Kiri,* but he has contributed cartoons to a great number of magazines in France, the United States and throughout the world. His cartoons have been collected into books published in France and elsewhere. Topor has also collaborated with René Laloux on several animated cartoons, including *Les Temps Morts* ("Dead Times," 1964), *Les Escargots* ("The Snails," 1965) and the award-winning *La Planète Sauvage* (1972).

While continuing to publish his drawings and cartoons through his latter years, Topor expressed his deeply held convictions in every possible area of creative endeavor. He wrote and worked for the stage, producing *Batailles* ("Battles") with Jean-Michel Ribes in 1983., doing the design and backgrounds for Francis Poulenc's opera *Les mamelles de Tirésias,* also in 1983, staging puppet shows, and directing new productions of classic plays. At age 59, and after four decades of practicing what a French commentator called "humor with an axe," he died of a cerebral haemorrhage in his Paris studio on April 16, 1997.

Roland Topor is at the forefront of French (and international) cartooning. He is a master of black humor and blends the most far-out and disturbing images into a deceptively classical style. His work has received the highest praise from such cartooning luminaries as Ronald Searle and Saul Steinberg. Michel Melot, curator of drawings at the Bibliothèque Nationale in Paris, wrote that "Roland Topor is not only an original draftsman but a researcher who bursts out of the traditional bonds of thought." Top or has received countless awards and distinctions in his triple capacity as cartoonist, animator and writer. It is likely that he will forever remain a man of many parts. In an interview with Joseph Szabo in 1994 he unequivocally declared, "I don't want to be reduced to a single function. I don't like specialization."

M.H.

TORII, KAZUYOSHI (1946-) Japanese cartoonist born in Aichi Prefecture, Japan, in 1946. Kazuyoshi Torii, perhaps alone among the many comic book and cartoon artists in Japan today, can claim to have cornered the market on children's comics dealing exclusively with scatalogical themes. He apparently had a very normal childhood, growing up in a middle-class *sarariman* ("salaryman") family and exhibiting a strong interest in comic books from an early age. Among his favorites were those created by Osamu Tezuka and Tsunayoshi Takeuchi. After dropping out of high school, he went to seek his fortune in Tokyo at the age of 19. After a stint on an animation staff, he hired on as a member of Fujio Pro, the company head-

Kazuyoshi Torii. © Torii.

ed by Fujio Akatsuka (creator of the popular *Osomatsu-kun* and *Tensai Bakabon* strips).

Torii debuted as a professional cartoonist with *Toiretto Hakushi* ("Professor Toilet"), which first appeared in *Shukan Shonen Jump* (a weekly comic) in 1969 and to date has appeared in over 350 issues. It remains his most representative and best-known work, although Torii also does other series, such as *Uwasa no Tenkai* ("Tenkai the Notorious"). *Toiretto Hakushi* is a series involving a gang of small children led by Professor Toilet, who, as his name implies, is an expert on anything scatological or outrageous. In nearly every issue the gang is involved in mischief that may consist of curing someone's constipation with a broomstick or diagnosing a friend's indigestion but always involves defecation and the toilet.

Though cartoons with similarly bizarre themes have appeared in the West, their audience has tended to be underground and adult. Torii's *Toiretto Hakushi,* however, is specifically aimed at children and runs in a weekly with a circulation of over two million. Protest, moreover, has been minimal. The artist nonetheless claims to have broken a certain taboo in Japan. He notes that while Fujio Akatsuka was a pioneer in children's comics with his humorous treatment of money and theft, and while Go Nagai set a precedent for sex and voyeurism for children with his *Harenchi Gakuen* series, he himself has created a new genre all his own—*unko,* or "shit" comics. Cleverly drawn, with their outrageous themes, Torii's cartoons are indeed a child's wildest scatological fantasies. His characters, moreover, fulfill what modern Japan's studious children most lack—the need for wild abandon.

In 1997 Torii was featured in Mitsunari Oizumi's book *Kieta Mangaka* (2) ("Cartoonists Who Have Disappeared (2)"), as an example of a formerly famous, now largely forgotten artist; but in that same year a website appeared devoted to Torii, and a CD entirely dedicated to *Toiretto Hakushi* was released, indicating a strong nostalgic feeling for the strip among now grown-up fans.

F.S.

TOURNACHON, GASPARD-FÉLIX (1820-1910) French caricaturist and photographer born in Paris, France, on April 6, 1820, to a well-to-do family of printers and booksellers. After the lycée and a few years in medical school, Félix Tournachon abandoned his studies to work for small newspapers like the *Journal des Dames et des Modes* and finally, in 1839, for his own journal, *L'Audience,* where he wrote theater reviews. Following a student fad to end words or names with "dar," Tournachon became Tournadar, and in 1842 he began to sign his articles simply "Nadar."

It was not until the end of 1845 that he turned to caricature work, mainly for satirical papers (*Le Corsaire-Satan, La Silhouette, Le Voleur*); he reached a high point in his budding career with the January 1848 caricature of the comic actor Grassot in *Le Charivari.* After the Revolution of 1848 he worked for several papers, especially for *La Revue Comique,* in which he created the type of the reactionary, "Mossieu" Réac, and for Charles Philipon's *Le Journal pour Rire,* where he contributed timely caricatural reviews of important events and personalities from 1849 to 1862. Many of these, poking fun at people like Dumas, Gavarni and Daumier, appeared in a series entitled *La Lanterne Magique* starting in 1852.

Nadar's first great success came from his publication in March 1854 of four giant lithographs, the *Panthéon Nadar, a* vast catalogue of 249 of the most influential movers and shakers in letters, arts and music (e.g., Hugo, Baudelaire, Ingres, Berlioz). This grotesque collection of caricatures, dedicated to a gentleman of the year 3607, depicts in the craziest and most astonishing manner not only the physical but the psychological idiosyncrasies of the all-too-willing victims. It is a witty and energetic satire in which Nadar himself appears with an astonished, almost naive face. A second *Panthéon* printed as a bonus supplement to *Le Figaro* came out in 1858 with 270 personages (some of the first collection's celebrities were replaced by new ones).

Increasingly, however, Nadar turned to photography, then in its infancy, while still contributing sketches dealing with everyday life; but he finally gave up cartooning altogether in 1865. As a photographer he captured the essence of most of the greats of his time. It was, as a matter of fact, in his studio at 3, boulevard des Capucines, that the first exhibit of Impressionist paintings was held in 1874. By then, he had also become a fervent advocate of the lighter-than-air movement, going as far as to fly in his own balloon, *Le Géant,* in 1863—a trip Daumier depicted in one of his lithographs: "Nadar Raising Photography to the Height of Art."

Nadar died a wealthy and illustrious man on March 21, 1910.

P.H.

TOURTEL, MARY (1870-1948) Children's cartoonist supreme and creator of the *Daily Express*'s incredibly popular character Rupert Bear, Mary Tourtel was that rarity in cartoon art, a woman, particularly considering her published works date from the end of the last century.

Born Mary Caldwell in Canterbury in 1870, one of a family of 13 children, Mary's father was a stone mason and stained glass artist who worked for Canterbury Cathedral. Her eldest brother, Edmund Caldwell, was a well-known animal artist; he illustrated the book *Jock of the Bushwold.* Another brother, Samuel, followed their father's artistic footsteps in the stained glass field. Mary herself, a scholar at the Simon Langton School, later attended the Sidney Cooper School of Art, eventually winning a gold medal.

In 1896 Mary married Herbert Bird Tourtel from Guernsey in the Channel Islands. Educated at Trinity College, Cambridge, he would eventually become a subeditor for the London *Daily Express*. Meanwhile Mary embarked upon a career as an illustrator for children's books. Her first two titles were in the series *Sunday Dumpy Books for Children,* and were *A Horse Book* and *Three Little Foxes,* published by Grant Richards in 1897. From the beginning, her love for animals was obvious in her choice of subjects. By 1900 she was drawing for the children's monthly magazine, *The Girls' Realm,* and in 1902 came illustrations for *The Humpty Dumpty Book,* a book of nursery rhymes.

With the brightening of the world following the end of

the Great War, newspapers were introducing more artwork and features for the children of their readers. Her husband, working on Express Newspapers, influenced the editor of the newly started *Sunday Express* into giving Mary a chance. She introduced a weekly series of single drawings entitled "In Bobtail Land." This was immediately popular, and soon a daily drawing began to appear in the parent newspaper: "When Animals Work" (March 31, 1919). This humanized Mary's favorite animals, and introduced Mr. Monkey the Dentist, Miss Squirrel the School Mistress, and Mr. Fox the Barber. The following year R.D. Blumenfield, impressed by the rival *Daily Mail* 's introduction of Charles Folkard's *Teddy Tail* and seeking a children's character of his own for the *Express*, asked sub-editor Herbert Tourtel to see if his wife could devise a new daily serial hero. In consequence, Mary drew the six-week serial, "Little Lost Bear." The star was, of course, Rupert; born November 8, 1920.

Although followed by a different serial, Rupert's impact on young readers was such that their demand brought him back for a further adventure, and finally the series that has run to this very day. The first book reprint, published by Thomas Nelson, was entitled *The Adventures of Rupert the Little Lost Bear*; there would be many more. Mary's husband, who wrote the rhymes that sometimes appeared under the pictures, died in 1931 in a German Sanatorium. Depressed, Mary continued her work, cheering up when the children's feature introduced the Rupert League, a club for readers with a splendid (and very collectible) badge. Members received Rupert Birthday and Christmas cards every year. Later came *Rupert Annuals* in color, and Mary's final serial, *Rupert and Bill's Seaside Holiday*, concluding June 27, 1935. Although Mary never drew again for publication, Rupert was taken over by Alfred Bestall, and on his death by other artists. She died of a stroke on March 15, 1948.

D.G.

TOY STORY (U.S.) The Disney organization has always been at the technological vanguard when it comes to animation. To stay a step ahead of the competition it perfected in the 1990s, in association with the computer-software company Pixar, a new method of animation blending traditional cartoon drawings with computer technology. The studio had experimented with computers as early as *Tron* (1982), but the results had proved disappointing. In this new process, called "computer-assisted imagery," hand-drawn storyboard sketches delineate the film's progression; then an animator recreates the scenes on a computer by duplicating the sketches through a computer model; and finally other animators flesh out the outlines, adding texture, lighting, color, and visual effects. This technique culminated in the 1995 *Toy Story*, in which the toys moved with the precision associated with computers and the freedom enjoyed by cartoon characters.

John Lasseter, who directed the feature, conceived of it as basically a buddy picture in the course of which two antagonistic personalities unite in the face of a common threat. In this case the two adversaries turned friends were toys both vying for the attention of their owner, six-year-old Andy. Woody was a pull-string cowboy (voiced by Tom Hanks) who resented being replaced in Andy's affections by the breezy space hero Buzz Lightyear (speaking through Tim Allen). When they found themselves thrown into the world outside their familiar surroundings they had to join forces and fight their way back to Andy's bedroom.

The action was depicted with meticulous care, and the characters were believable both as individual personalities and as toys. This amalgam of computer-generated graphics and traditional animation was an almost total success, due to the seamless teamwork between animators and computer technicians. "Animation is still filmmaking frame by frame," Lasseter later declared. "Computers are just tools. Computers don't create anything. The artists do, using computers."

In recognition of his pioneering work in the field, Lasseter was awarded a special Oscar in 1996 for "the development of an inspired application of techniques that have made possible the first feature-length computer-animated film."

M.H.

TRAVIÈS DE VILLERS, CHARLES-JOSEPH (1804-1859) French cartoonist and lithographer born in Winterthur, Switzerland, on February 21, 1804, Charles Traviés studied art first in Strasbourg, then in Paris with the famous François Heim. Using the shorter "Traviès" for his pen name, he actively collaborated on Philipon's *La Caricature* and *Le Charivari,* and later on *L'Artiste, La Silhouette* and others.

Traviès's real popular success came in 1830 when he

Mayeux climbing the greasy pole to reach for a cabinet portfolio. *Charles Joseph Traviès de Villers.*

launched his acerbic *Facéties de M. Mayeux* ("Mr. Mayeux's Jokes"), a series of more than a hundred vignettes portraying Mayeux—a middle-aged and hunchback dwarf, simian and ugly, cynical and vain, more lecherous than gallant—engaged in all kinds of professions (journalist, judge, businessman, etc.). This deformed and impudent outcast cheapens and debases everything and everyone he comes in contact with, whether he is painting a pretty woman whose dress pattern is the same as his smock's or helping a good-looking servant girl across a narrow bridge and saying, "I'm French, my good girl, I'm French, for God's sake!" Yet, by constantly deriding himself, he also bitterly attacks those hypocrisies, vices and loose morals that right-minded, respectable bourgeois want to hide from others and above all from themselves.

Other Traviès drawings deal mainly with political personalities or events: an 1831 lithograph shows a patriot being bludgeoned to death by a mob of paid "false workers"; pro-government newspapers are personified as prostitutes accompanied by their pimps in drawings done in 1833 in collaboration with Grandville. Traviès also satirized middle-class people and values in numerous series: *Types Français* ("French Types," 1835), *Moeurs Commerciales et Industrielles* ("Commercial and Industrial Mores") and a comprehensive five-volume collection, *Les Français Peints par Eux-mêmes* ("The French Portrayed by Themselves," 1840-42).

If at times the quality of Charles Traviès's art is rather average and uneven, especially in his early political satires, the *Mayeux* drawings are superb and positively inspired. It is no wonder that Baudelaire and others were such great admirers of his work.

After seeing the excesses of the Second Empire, Traviès, a misanthrope all his life, ended in complete despair. He died in Paris on August 13, 1859.

P.H.

TREDEZ, ALAIN (1929-) French cartoonist born in Berck, a resort on the English Channel, in 1929. Alain Tredez at first contemplated a career in the foreign service, but during his military service in the parachute corps, he discovered he had a knack for drawing funny pictures. He sold his first cartoons at the age of 19 to a number of weekly and monthly publications: these cartoons (which he signed "Trez") were all of a humorous nature, allying a good gag sense with an open, almost lackadaisical line. They didn't bring their author much fame or money, however, and to supplement his income the artist wrote and drew more than a dozen children's books in the 1950s and 1960s.

After a short partnership with fellow cartoonist Jean Dejoux in the early 1960s, he finally hit it big in 1972, when he started contributing a daily political cartoon for the evening newspaper *France-Soir*. In this avenue Trez found both his style and his *métier*. Whether they show President François Mitterand striking a martial pose in a paratrooper outfit complete with sidearms at the start of the Gulf War and declaring, "We gonna rumble!," or former Soviet Premier Mikhail Gorbachev losing a poker hand to a cagey Boris Yeltsin (holding several aces up his sleeve), his drawings are devastatingly funny without losing any of

FRANÇOIS MITTERRAND S'ENGAGE DANS LA GUERRE DU GOLFE (**TREZ**, 1991)

Alain Tredez ("Trez"). © Trez.

their charge. A compilation of his most popular political cartoons has been published annually since 1982.

Trez has contributed cartoons to virtually every publication in France, as well as to *Punch* in England, *Pardon* in Germany, and *Life* and *Playboy* in the U.S. He is the recipient of many professional honors and awards.

M.H.

TREES AT NIGHT (U.S.) No more unlikely combination in cartooning can be imagined than the Art Young of the mid-1920s and the *Saturday Evening Post.* It was nevertheless at that time that the conservative *Post* editor, George Horace Lorimer, through humorist and associate editor Tom L. Masson, requested a cartoon series from the fiery Socialist. That the combination worked well is testimony to Young's amazing versatility; even in the turbulent days of World War I, when he was arrested for sedition, Young was able to produce purely humorous gag spots—and very funny ones at that.

For the *Post,* among other, later series, Young produced the immortal *Trees at Night* cartoons. They ran for more than a year, usually every other week. Most often rendered in wash, these chilly and interesting cartoons were sometimes anthropomorphic, sometimes character studies—for trees, in Young's eyes, had an abundance of character. They were inspired by the countryside near Young's little home in Bethel, Connecticut, on Chestnut Ridge behind Nashville Road Extension. "My conception of trees showed them as fantastic, grotesque, humanized or animalized, with trunks, limbs and foliage tossed in gayety or inert and solemn against the night sky," he was to write in his autobiography. The cartoons were collected and published by Boni and Liveright in 1927.

R.M.

TREZ
See Tredez, Alain.

TRIER, WALTER (1890-1951) German cartoonist, illustrator and painter born in Prague, Bohemia (then part of the Hapsburg empire, now in Czechoslovakia), on June 25, 1890. Walter Trier's good-natured, uncomplicated, fanciful but never puzzling cartoons and illustrations were among the most popular in the Germany of the 1920s and 1930s. They celebrated tranquil love, innocence and simple joys. The writer Erich Kästner, with whom Trier was associated as illustrator and friend for over 20 years, has called him the 20th-century Spitzweg.

At the Munich Academy, Trier studied under Franz von Stuck, who had been a fine cartoonist in his youth. During these student days Trier sent drawings to *Jugend* and *Simplicissimus.* In 1910 he was called to Berlin to work on *Lustige Blätter.* In the years that followed he worked regularly for periodicals published by the gigantic Ullstein Verlag: *Die Dame, Uhu* and *Der Heitere Fridolin* (a children's magazine); in 1926 he published three Fridolin tie-in volumes, *Fridolins Siebenmeilenpferd* ("Fridolin's Seven-Mile Horse"), *Fridolins Harlekinade* ("Fridolin's Harlequinade") and *Fridolins Zauberland* ("Fridolin's Magic Land").

It was as a specialist in illustrating for children that Trier worked with Kästner on the writer's first and most famous children's book, *Emil und die Detektive* ("Emil and the Detectives," 1927), and later on such novels as *Arthur mit dem Langen Arm* ("Arthur with the Long Arm," 1931) and *Das Verhexte Telefon* ("The Bewitched Telephone").

Trier was a connoisseur and collector of puppets and other folk toys, and his collection accompanied him on the many forced journeys of his later years. In 1922 he did color illustrations for a book about toys (*Spielzeug*) that has been regarded as his artistic masterpiece.

Hitler's rise drove Trier out of Germany in the early 1930s and then out of Austria in 1938. For about ten years after that, Trier lived in London, where he did monthly color covers for the magazine *Lilliput.* In the late 1940s he moved to Canada to be near his married daughter. Living in a mountain home near Collingwood, about a hundred miles from Toronto, he continued drawing for magazines and also did advertising art. He died in his mountain retreat on July 8, 1951.

S.A.

TRIPLÉS, LES (France) Published as a full page in color in the French weekly *Madame Figaro* magazine, *Les Triplés* ("The Triplets"), a stylish humor feature, was created by Nicole Lambert in 1983 specifically for *Madame Figaro*. The cast is not named except for the family pet, Toto, a French bulldog. The mother is blonde, sexy and very fashionable. The father's presence is implied but he is never seen. Rather the children's grandfather is featured from time to time. The children, two boys and a girl, are the core of humor in the feature with both their comments and sight gags. They are blonde preschoolers who are into everything. Toto, the dog, who communicates with thought balloons, is also often a source of humor.

Nicole Lambert who studied at le Arts Decoratifs and les Beaux Arts in Paris brings a very personal artistic style to *Les Triplés*. She calls it a "bricole" (literally "do-it-yourself") technique combining pencil, watercolor, air brush and pastels. She wants each cartoon to be "a little world of its own". Her carefully designed harmonies of color add to the overall soft polished look of her art. The family in her feature is upper class and the artwork helps reinforce this ambiance which is that of *Madame Figaro.*

A number of *Les Triplés* books have been published reprinting the art from *Madame Figaro.* As Nicole Lambert changes her perspective and design from week to week from dividing the page into thirds or a serpentine of numerous images to a single picture, the books are visually livelier than ones which lack such a high design quality. A short live action *Les Triplés* film is being made by Just Jaeckin.

Besides *Les Triplés*, Nicole Lambert has written and illustrated two books about the customs of childhood in Europe. Her *Petits Français* ("Little Frenchmen") is a major work continuing her studies of childhood in the different regions of France.

Les Triplés is uniquely French in mood. Its humor is occasionally raucous as the three kids enjoy being exuberant with youthful energy. However, none of the children are in the *Dennis the Menace* mode. This is not a dysfunctional family. Mother, though occasionally a bit exasperated by her triplets' antics, is always in charge.

B.C.

TRNKA, JIŘÍ (1912-1969) Czech animator born in Pilsen, Bohemia, in the Hapsburg empire (now in Czechoslovakia), on February 24, 1912. The son of a plumber, Jiří Trnka briefly studied art in high school, then turned to puppeteering in 1929. From 1935 to 1938 he managed his own puppet theater. The years of German occupation (1938-45) were hard for Trnka, who had to support himself by working at odd jobs and giving occasional puppet performances.

After the end of World War II Trnka set up the animation section of the nationalized Czech cinema and became its first head of production. His first cartoon, *Grandpa Planted a Beet,* completed in 1945, did not show great originality; the following year, however, saw the release of the more personal—although still "Disneyfied"—*The Animals and the Brigands* and especially of *The Devil on Springs* (also known as *The Chimney-Sweep*), a savage satire in which the traditional violence of the cartoon is turned against the hated German occupiers. Trnka's later cartoons did not rise to such heights: The *Happy Circus* (1951) was a cute tale of the big top, *Grandpa's Three Misfortunes* (1952) a slight fable, and *The Two Frosts* (1954) a charming but confused parable. After that last effort Trnka abandoned the animated cartoon in favor of puppet films.

Trnka had never lost his love for the puppet theater, and as early as 1947 he had directed the puppet film *The Czech Year.* This was followed by an Andersen tale, *The Emperor's*

Archangel Gabriel and Mother Goose
Jiří Trnka. © Barandov Studio.

Nightingale (1948), and *Song of the Prairie,* a western parody (1949). Other puppet films of note directed by Trnka include *Old Czech Legends* (1953), *Brave Soldier Schweik* (1954), *Midsummer Night's Dream,* from Shakespeare's play (1955), *Cybernetic Grandmother* (1962), *Archangel Gabriel and Mother Goose* (1964) and *The Hand* (1965).

Although he is best noted for his puppet films, Jiří Trnka also deserves recognition for his original and personal work in cartoons. He has received more than a score of awards and prizes for his animation work from organizations around the world; and his passing in 1969 (occasioned, it has been said, by the Soviet invasion of his country) was much lamented.

M.H.

TROG
See Fawkes, Walter Ernest.

TRUDY (U.S.) *Trudy* is a cartoon panel created by Jerry Marcus in March 1963 and distributed (both weekdays and Sunday) by King Features Syndicate.

Trudy and her husband, Ted, lead an exemplary life in the suburbs, threatened only by the shenanigans of their son, Crawford. While Ted is the typically harried husband and father, Trudy finds time for reflection, sarcasm and self-improvement. She can be in turn romantic ("I'm going to the beauty parlor—now, remember, Ted, the girl that walks in here in a couple of hours from now will be *me,* your *wife."),* thoughtful ("What wine goes best with a husband who hates fish?") or wryly perceptive ("I know you're not listening when you get that idiotic *attentive* look on your face!"). While she usually manages to stay a step ahead of the rest of her family, she is sometimes outwitted

"Why can't you READ yourself to sleep like everyone else?"
"Trudy." © King Features Syndicate.

by Crawford and friends, and even Ted occasionally stands up to her ("Here we are," he declares at one point, putting a record on the turntable, "Music to Nag By.").

A warm and unpretentious feature, *Trudy* is drawn in a simple, ingratiating style. The panel enjoys a fairly wide circulation, and several collections have been issued in paperback form by Fawcett publications. Termed by its syndicate in 1996 "a humorous sendup of marriage, parenthood and nosy next-door neighbors," *Trudy* is still going strong after more than three decades.

M.H.

TSEKHANOVSKY, MIKHAIL (1889-1965) Soviet animator born in Russia on May 26, 1889. Mikhail Tsekhanovsky's art studies were interrupted by World War l, and he did not graduate from the Moscow Art Institute until 1919. He started his career as an illustrator but went into animation in the late 1920s. In 1929 he made the first Soviet sound cartoon, *Posta* ("Mail"), a remarkably innovative little film based on a book by Samuel Marshak. This highly successful effort was followed in 1931 by *Pacific,* set to Arthur Honegger's "Pacific 231," and later the same year by the allegorical *Gopak.*

Tsekhanovsky then set to work on his most ambitious project, *The Tale of the Priest and His Servant Balda,* a full-length animated opera on music by Dimitri Shostakovich. It was scheduled for release in 1934. In the meantime, however, the composer got into trouble with the authorities, and the project was cancelled (alledgedly on Stalin's direct orders). Tsekhanovsky followed Shostakovich into disgrace; he was demoted to in-betweener and worked in utter obscurity on other people's films. He resurfaced as a director only in 1940 with the slight, if winsome, *Tale of the Foolish Mouse.*

During World War II Tsekhanovsky turned out propa-

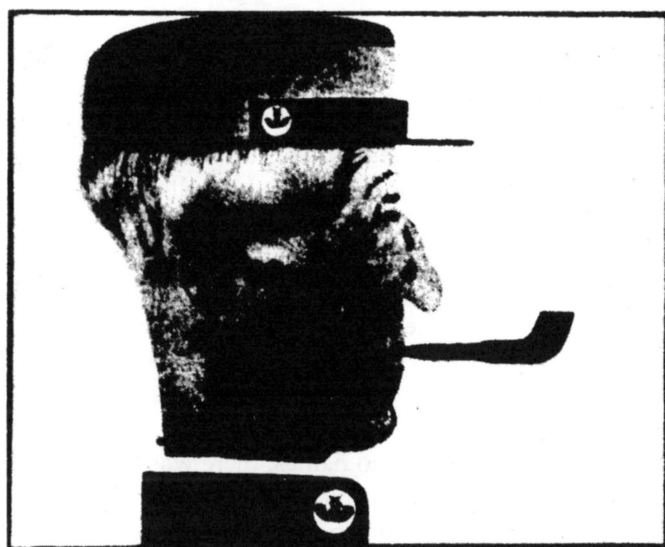

Mikhail Tsekhanovsky, "Posta."

ganda works. He went back to entertainment cartoons in 1945 with *Telefon.* There followed *The Seven-Colored Flower* (1949, from a story by Chekhov) and *The Fisherman and the Fish* (1951, after Pushkin). *Kashetenka* (1952), *The Frog Queen* (1954) and *The Girl in the Jungle* (1957) were more conventional cartoons intended for children; but in *A Tale of Chapaev* (1958) the artist again asserted himself through the use of flat drawings and flat colors to suggest the quality of posters coming to life. Toward the end of his life, Tsekhanovsky lost some of his powers of imagination and sought refuge in folktales, directing (often with the assistance of his wife) *The Legend of the Saracen's Will* (1959), *The Fox, the Beaver and Others* (1960) and *Wild Swans* (1963), a feature-length animation film from a Hans Christian Andersen story. The 1964 remake of *Posta* was the last cartoon Tsekhanovsky did; he died soon afterwards, on June 22, 1965.

Tsekhanovsky was one of the foremost Soviet animators. His cartoons were bold and imaginative, and his pioneering efforts in the late 1920s and early 1930s helped establish Soviet animation as an artistic as well as an entertainment medium. As film historian Jay Leyda stated in his remarkable study of the Soviet cinema, *Kino* (1960), "If (Tsekhanovsky's) *Tale* had been finished, the Soviet animated cartoon of today might look very different."

M.H.

TSUCHIDA, YOSHIKO (1948-) Japanese cartoonist born in Musashino, Tokyo, Japan, in 1948. Yoshiko Tsuchida is somewhat unique among cartoonists in Japan, not because she is a woman, but because she draws a gag strip in *shōjō manga,* or comics for young girls. In Japan, particularly because of the consciousness of sex roles, girls' comics tend to be peopled by extremely serious, romantic, starry-eyed, Caucasian-looking characters. Tsuchida's specialty is the exact opposite. Her cartoons generally have homely characters that perform the outrageous, and for this reason she has been labeled a "female Fujio Akatsuka."

Upon graduation from high school, Tsuchida worked for Fujio Pro (Akatsuka's company) as an assistant, at first concentrating on more serious, conventional girls' comics. Later she discovered that she had a knack for gag comics, and in 1967, at the age of 19, she came out with *Harenchi Kun* (an untranslatable adjective describing a young boy intent on mischief and curious about sex). After leaving Fujio Pro she concentrated entirely on humorous works, turning out *Yoshiko Desu! Waratte Itadakimasu!!* ("This Is Yoshiko! Laugh!") and others, such as *Kimidori Midoro Aomidoro Neba Neba Neba Ko. Tsuruhime Ja-!* ("It's Princess Tsuru!"), which first appeared in the comic *Margaret* in 1973, is Tsuchida's most famous work. Though the name implies a beautiful princess, Tsuchida's Tsuruhime is an uncouth, ugly, outrageous little one with the top of her head shaved, and she is universally disliked and feared as the terror of the castle. Moreover, everything she does goes wrong, but the servants are forced to endure her in good faith.

Tsuchida naturally absorbed a great deal of Fujio Akatsuka's humor while working at Fujio Pro, but even as a child she was an avid reader of young girls' comics, and a true fan of Osamu Tezuka and Shigeru Sugiura. As with many artists who do nonsense or gag strips in Japan, the features of her characters tend to be highly abstract and distorted in order to achieve maximum comic effect.

In 1990 Tsuchida's *Tsuruhime Ja-!* was animated for television, thereby gaining an even broader audience. A prolific artist, she has produced many other works, including

Mattanashi! Yoshika wa OL ("The Awaited! Yoshiko's an Office Lady"), serialized in a young men's comic magazine. She is also active as an essayist. She has won the Japan Cartoonists' Association Award for Excellence for *Tsuruhime Ja-I.*

F.S.

TURGEON, JEAN (1952-) French-Canadian cartoonist born in Quebec City on June 28, 1952. Jean Turgeon settled in Montreal. Aside from a few contributions to the magazines *Photo-Journal* and *Echo-Vedettes,* he did most of his early cartoon work for the semi-underground publication *L'Illetré* (1969-70), which published his cartoons of social protest. Signing himself "Gité," Turgeon gave *L'Illetré* one full page of monthly cartoons for a year.

In 1969 Gité started working with the publishing group Perspectives. In collaboration with his brother, the newspaperman and writer Pierre Turgeon, he contributed not only cartoons and covers, but also most of the humorous illustrations accompanying the articles in the magazines *Perspectives* and *Perspectives-Dimanche.* For these magazines he also created a comic strip, *Le Joueur de Hockey* ("The Hockey Player"), in 1972, and since 1978 he has been drawing a weekly panel, *Le Sondage de la Semaine* ("The Weekly Opinion Poll").

From 1973 to 1977 Gité contributed humorous illustrations and an occasional cartoon to the major Canadian magazine *Week-End.* He now contributes sporadically to daily newspapers such as the *Montreal Star* and *Le Courrier de St.-Hyacinthe* and to magazines such as *L'Actualité* and *Toronto Life.* He has also done a number of book covers. This relatively young artist certainly shows a great deal of promise and can be regarded as heir to a long tradition of quality and experimentation in the field of cartooning in Quebec.

S.J.

Jean Turgeon ("Gité"). © Perspectives.

"Must be a soldier!"
"The Two Types," 1944. © Eighth Army News.

TWO TYPES, THE (G.B.) "The Two Types are as much a part of the pattern of this war as the bulldozer, the Bailey Bridge or the Flying Bomb. They could not have emerged from any other war, and when this one is over they will disappear into the anonymity of the well-brushed bowler hat and tightly rolled umbrella." Thus Cyril James, in his introduction to *The Two Types by Jon,* a World War ll collection of cartoons published by the British Army Newspaper Unit, Central Mediterranean Force, "for the fighting men of all ranks and Services in this theatre." The book is subtitled *Being the Saga of the Two Jaunty Heroes Who Have Given Us the Best Laugh Since the Campaign Began.*

The Two Types had no names; there was the Fair Type, with his black beret and blond moustache, and the Dark Type, with his battered service cap and black moustache. They were both officers of the Eighth Army and fought their way through to victory, remaining true to their very British breeding, blue blood, and baggy sheepskins, suedes and corduroys, however hot the sun or the shooting. As James predicted, an attempt to adjust them to the demobilized joys of "Civvy Street" failed to gel, although the *News Chronicle* ran them for awhile as a pocket cartoon.

"Jon," who won the M.B.E. for his creation of *The Two Types* and his contribution to army morale, was really William John Philpin Jones. A Welshman born in Llandrindod Wells in 1914, he studied at the Birmingham School of Art for three years and then joined the *Western Mail* as a cartoonist. Moving to London, he joined an advertising agency just before the war, then volunteered for the Coldstream Guards, being commissioned in 1940. He was assistant military landing officer in Sicily, Salerno and Anzio before rejoining the British Army newspaper unit. The first *Two Types* appeared in the *Eighth Army News* on August 16, 1944, spread to *Crusader* on October 15 and to all editions of *Union Jack* by November 7. Their image continues in Jon's long-running pocket cartoon series for the *Daily Mail,* which carries the title *Sporting Types.* His books include *The Two Types* (1945) and *The Two Types* (1960).

D.G.

TYTLA, VLADIMIR (1904-1968) American animator born in Yonkers, New York, in 1904. Vladimir (Bill) Tytla started his cartooning career at John Terry's studio in the early 1920s. He later moved to the more prosperous studio of Paul Terry (John's brother), where he worked as an animator on *Aesop's Fables*. In 1934 Tytla went to Hollywood and joined the Walt Disney studio. A member of the inner circle among Disney cartoonists, Tytla developed and animated, in collaboration with Fred Moore, the Seven Dwarfs in the *Snow White* feature, animated and directed on *Pinocchio* and supervised the "Night on Bald Mountain" sequence in *Fantasia*. Tytla is also credited with the creation in 1941 of Dumbo.

When the famous strike at the Disney studio broke out in 1941, Tytla joined the strikers. After the settlement he went back to work for Disney (his credits as animator include *Saludos Amigos* and *Victory Through Air Power,* both released in 1943), but he left late in 1942. Back east, Tytla worked first for Terrytoons as a director of animation,. later joining Paramount, where he directed many *Little Lulu, Little Audrey* and *Popeye* cartoons. In the late 1950s Tytla turned to television and directed more than a thousand cartoon commercials. In 1960 he opened his own studio, William Tytla Productions, which produced public relations and educational films in addition to commercials.

One of the unsung artists of the animation medium, Vladimir Tytla died in his home in East Lynne, Connecticut, on December 29, 1968.

M.H.

Uu

UCHŪ KAIZOKU CAPTAIN HARLOCK (Japan) *Uchū Kaizoku Captain Harlock* ("Space Pirate Captain Harlock") was the first major solo creation of cartoonist Akira "Leiji (Midnight Samurai)" Matsumoto, who had produced the art design and the 1974-75 comic book novelization of TV producer Yoshinobu Nishizaki's *Uchū Senkan Yamato* (Space Battleship Yamato). Matsumoto's *Space Pirate Captain Harlock* comic book series (1977; collected in 5 volumes) was less important by itself than for the TV and theatrical animation which it inspired. The *Harlock* comic book also introduced a female counterpart, Emeraldas, who was spun off into a separate comic book, *Queen Emeraldas* (1978; 4 volumes). Matsumoto achieved greater popularity with his *Ginga Tetsudo 999* ("Galaxy Express 999") 18-volume comic book series and its TV and theatrical animated adaptations, in which both Harlock and Emeraldas made brief appearances.

Toei Animation Co. initially produced *Space Pirate Captain Harlock* as a 42-episode weekly TV serial, broadcast from March 14, 1978, through February 13, 1979. The enigmatic Harlock (his first name is never revealed) is a charismatic "good guy" rebel who keeps alive the spirit of freedom and adventure in the decadent Solar society of 2977. He flourishes the flamboyant costumes and Jolly Roger of Earth's Spanish Main, and has even built a rococo galleon's sterncastle onto his spaceship, the *Arcadia*. Harlock is introduced as preying only on government cargo ships which transport liquor and narcotics from the other planets to keep Earth's masses sedated and docile. But the Mazons, a warrior race of alien plant-women, are scouting the Solar System for invasion. Their agents strike by terrorist assassinations of Earth's leading scientists, which they blame on Harlock. Harlock must fight both to clear his name, and to rally a defense force capable of defeating the Mazons and their Queen Rafflesia.

This TV space-adventure serial and Harlock's appearances in the 113-episode *Galaxy Express 999* (1978-1981) TV series and two theatrical animated features kept his popularity high enough to generate a separate *Harlock* theatrical feature and a second TV series. Both retold the events in the first TV series more somberly, replacing the Mazons with more Nazi-like aliens similar to those in the *Space Battleship Yamato* series. The theatrical feature, *Waka Seishun no Arcadia*; a double entendre meaning both "My Arcadian (Innocent) Youth" and "My Youth in the (Spaceship) Arcadia" (July 1982; an epic 130 minutes), tells how the young Harlock, an embittered veteran of the Solar Federation's defeated space navy, returns to a conquered Earth and gradually organizes a resistance against its cruel Illumidas overlords. He has the help of Emeraldas and of Tochiro, his best friend from the Federation Navy and the engineering genius who designs the super-raider *Arcadia*. This movie was followed 3 months later by a 22-episode TV sequel (October 13, 1982 - March 30, 1983) *Waka Seishun no Arcadia; Mugen Kido SSX* ("My Youth in the Arcadia: Endless Frontier SSX"), popularly known just as *SSX* (the heading on the Illumidans' reward posters for Harlock, Tochiro and Emeraldas), which tells the exploits of the three after they escape from Earth in the *Arcadia* and spread the revolt to other conquered planets in the Illumidas Empire.

The original *Space Pirate Captain Harlock* animation series was popular throughout the world, especially in French-speaking countries where Harlock was known as Albator. Significantly, both French Québec and the U.S. produced their own *Albator/Captain Harlock* comic books based upon Toei Animation's versions rather than translating Matsumoto's moody and less dramatic original manga.

F.P.

UCHŪ SENKAN YAMATO (Japan) *Uchū Senkan Yamato* ("Space Cruiser Yamato") is the title of a comic book, a television animation series and a full-length animated feature film. Yoshinobu Nishizaki wrote the original story, which in 1975 was made into both a comic strip (by Matsumoto Reiji) and a television series. The television series was produced by the newly formed Academy Company with Yoshinobu Nishizaki, as was the feature film, which was released in 1977. The film version of *Uchū Senkan Yamato,* though little more than a splicing together of the television series, fired the imagination of the Japanese public and spawned a multitude of related toys, T-shirts and book bags.

Uchū Senkan Yamato is an extremely romantic science fiction film. In the year 2199, Earth is under heavy atomic attack from the evil forces of the planet Gamilus, and humans have been forced to live in underground strongholds. Just in the nick of time, however, word comes from the benevolent planet Iskandall of a "Cosmo Cleaner D," the only machine in the universe capable of decontaminating Earth and saving it. Alas, Iskandall is 148,000 light-years away and surrounded by the enemy. Undaunted, Earth's forces convert the World War II battleship *Yamato* (of all things) into a spaceship capable of making the journey and send 114 picked men with her on a nearly suicidal mission to obtain the Cosmo Cleaner. After innumerable battles with the enemy, during which the *Yamato* begins to look like a pile of scrap, the mission is accomplished and Earth is saved.

Uchū Senkan Yamato's popularity appears to be the result of its unusual mix of uniquely Japanese romanticism and subtle nationalism. In this regard the theme is highly original: with Earth's back literally to the wall, the *Yamato* becomes a sort of Noah's Ark savior ship. In real life the *Yamato* was of course the ill-fated giant battleship on which the hopes of Japan rode; it was sunk by Allied air power in 1944 with all hands on board. The name *Yamato* (which can also stand for "Japan") thus connotes a national, almost religious mission against overwhelming odds. By cleverly linking this to a science fiction theme in which the *Yamato* actually succeeds, the film taps a vast reservoir of latent romanticism.

The art and design of *Uchū Senkan Yamato* were handled by Reiji Matsumoto, and Yoshinobu Nishizaki provided the overall supervision. Two years were required in production, and a 98-minute shortened version dubbed in English was shown at the Cannes Film Festival and distributed in the United States and other countries. On the whole *Uchū Senkan Yamato* has excellent color and contains some breathtaking scenes but is weak in editing. The original comic book version actually has a far more coherent plot.

Uchū Senkan Yamato was so popular that it led to five or six feature sequels (whether one counts the TV features that were also released in theaters). The 1978 sequel titled *Saraba Uchū Senkan Yamato* ("Arrivederci Yamato") had one of Japan's then most popular singers, Kenji Sawada, performing the hit theme song. In this film the ship's fate seemed finally sealed as the Yamato was used in a spectacular kamikaze run on the enemy, thereby saving the Earth for a "final" time. Commercial pressures, however, caused *Saraba Yamato* to be followed by yet more questionable features.

With its broad popularity, *Uchū Senkan Yamato* helped trigger the enormous boom in animation in Japan that occurred in the 1980s. It also helped spark the popularity of Japanese animation overseas. In the United States the television series was re-edited and shown under the title *Star Blazers*, which earned a considerable cult following. A further sequel was released in Japan in 1980-81 and seen in the U.S. as "The Bolar Wars" (the Bolar Fedration was an alien coalition of planets). A remake, titled *Yamato 2520*, came out in Japan in 1996 as a direct-to-video release.

F.S.

UNCLE OOJAH (G.B.) Uncle Oojah, the outsize elephant in striped pajamas, was the most popular pachyderm of pre-Babar days. He made his first appearance under his real name, Flip-Flap the Great Oojah, in the *Daily Sketch* on Febrnary 18, 1919, in a "Children's Corner" cartoon and serial written by Flo Lancaster (Florence Wallis), a prominent children's writer of the period. Curiously, neither Miss Lancaster nor Oojah appears in Brian Doyle's *Who's Who in Children's Literature* or Margery Fisher's *Who's Who in Children's Books*, despite their enormous and long-lived popularity.

The format was that of a serial text illustrated with a single panel cartoon that was drawn by Thomas Maybank. From January 22, 1923, the panel turned into a strip cartoon series, although Oojah had already appeared in a weekly strip from October 8, 1921, when the first comic section in British newspapers, *The Oojah's Paper* (which changed title to *The Oojah Sketch* from its second issue) began. This four-page comic continued to April 22, 1922, after which it was reduced in size.

Later the title changed again, to *The Donjeroo Sketch*, which combined the names of Don, Jerrywangle and Oojah. Don was a boy who was the only human character in the series. His partner in adventure was Snooker, a black puss-in-boots, while Jerrywangle was Oojah's naughty nephew (an elephant, of course). The first book version, *Oojah House*, was published in June 1922, and that Christmas the first of many *Oojah Annuals* was published. These continued after the newspaper series was dropped, and later editions were drawn by H.M. Talintyre.

Books: *Oojah House* (1922); *Oolah Annual* (1922); *Oolah's Treasure Trunk* (1926); *Uncle Oojah's Annual; Uncle Oojah's Big Annual; Uncle Oojah's Travels* (1938); *Uncle Oojah* (1944); *Uncle Oojah Books* (1946); *The Oojah Annual* (1948); and *Uncle Oojah Annual* (1951).

D.G.

UNGERMANN, ARNE (1902-1981) Danish cartoonist and painter born in Copenhagen, Denmark, in 1902. A member of the artists' association Grønningen, in Copenhagen, Arne Ungermann was a cartoonist and illustrator at the daily *Politiken*'s weekly magazine from 1930, and a coeditor from 1946 to 1952. Among his most well-known contributions is the charming comic strip *Hanne Hansen* (with captions in verse), about a stolid, unruffled young maid in

Arne Ungermann. © Ungermann.

a snobbish upper-middle-class family. He has also done cartoon-like vignettes and illustrations for editorials and book reviews, plus political and social satire in the daily *Politiken.*

Overflowing imagination, a bold drawing style and a rare sense of humor place him in the top rank of Danish artists of his kind. Internationally known as the illustrator of *Nils All Alone, Candide,* the *Decameron* and Hans Christian Andersen editions, Ungermann has won several prizes at Scandinavian children's book competitions. He died in Humleback on February 25, 1981.

J.S.

URDA MARÍN, MANUEL (1886-196-?) Spanish cartoonist born in Barcelona, Spain, in 1888. Manuel Urda started his career in 1909 with cartoons in the Catalan magazines *En Patufet* and *Follet.* He also freelanced cartoons to the Madrid publication *Monos.* In 1917 Urda began his long association with the weekly comic magazine *TBO,* of which he became one of the main cartoonists and comic strip artists. He also produced animated cartoons for advertising in the 1920s and 1930s.

Urda's subjects were as simple as his graphic style: both could be easily grasped by children, who constituted his principal audience. His drawings were schematic, and his humor chiefly visual. Urda died, in more or less total oblivion, sometime in the 1960s. He deserves to be remembered for his long and prolific career in cartoons.

J.M.

URUSEI YATSURA (Japan) There have been many teenage-themed comedy comics since *Harold Teen* in the 1920s. Most have employed the humorous fantasy of exaggeration of adolescent awkwardness and naïveté to an implausible extreme, but have otherwise been basically realistic. Rumiko Takahashi created both a career and a new genre when, at 21 years in 1979, she began *Urusei Yatsura* in the weekly *Shonen Sunday* boys' cartoon magazine.

Ataru Moroboshi is the star goof-off of Tomobiki High School, never studying and chasing every pretty girl in school. But he becomes a computer's randomly-chosen representative of humanity when a huge spaceship arrives from the planet Uru, and their leader announces that they are about to enslave Earth unless our champion can defeat their champion. Their champion is Lum, the Uru leader's daughter; a cute 16-year-old with horns who can fly and give off 100,000-volt electrical shocks when she gets upset. When Ataru wins the contest by an unexpected trick, Lum considers it as a proposal of marriage. Instead of leaving with the other aliens, Lum insists on moving in with the Moroboshis to be near her "fiancé". She enters Tomobiki High as an exchange student. Then, gradually, Lum's outerspace friends begin filtering in. It becomes "in" among the alien teens to move to Earth as exchange students. Gradually everyone adjusts to the new status quo.

Urusei Yatsura is a comedy on many levels. Geopolitical: the "aliens" and "humans" are obvious metaphors for the Euro-American culture and the Japanese. The aliens are raucous but friendly; gauche but too powerful to ignore. (Lum always addresses Ataru by the English endearment,

"Urusei Yatsura." © Rumiko Takahashi/Shogakuken.

"Darling".) However, Takahashi misses no opportunity to show that the Japanese are just as boorish and crass as the alien "slobs" who they complain are moving in and ruining the neighborhood.

Mythological: the aliens are also personifications of mythological and folkloric characters, usually Japanese, in sci-fi trappings. Lum and the Uru-ites with their little horns are traditional *oni* or demons; powerful but stupid and easily tricked. Lum's friend Yuki, a teen princess from the frozen planet Neptune, is an ancient Japanese snow goddess. There are also parodies of Western stereotypes such as cowboy heroes and costumed superheroes. Later stories introduce outright fantasy characters such as ghosts and shape-changing foxes; by then both *Urusei Yatsura*'s cast and readers accepted them without a blink.

Pop-cultural: Much of *Urusei Yatsura*'s humor is built around turning these mighty mythological beings and foreigners into the teen readers' peers. More is derived from the human teens' adaptation of the aliens' science (magic) to their adolescent concerns, as when Ataru uses an Uru photocopier to duplicate himself so he can chase several girls at the same time. The dialogue relies heavily on contemporary teen slang; the title *Urusei Yatsura* is itself a multi-level slang pun sometimes translated over-simplistically as "Those Obnoxious Aliens".

Takahashi's cartoon was serialized as a series of weekly comic book short stories in *Shōnen Sunday* from 1979 through 1986. These were collected into 36 volumes which have been continuously in print in Japan, and translated into many foreign editions. Animated cartoon adaptations began as a TV series in 1981, and encompassed 218 TV episodes, six theatrical features, and 11 direct-to-video releases by 1991.

Urusei Yatsura also brought fantasy "out of the closet" and made it a natural part of adolescent social life. Previous fantasies such as *Sabrina the Teenage Witch* had presented the young space alien or sorcerer as posing as a normal teen among unsuspecting schoolmates, using his or her sci-fi devices or magic powers in secrecy. In *Urusei Yatsura,* half the cast is openly alien and they allow all the normal teens to share their powers. The popularity of *Urusei Yatsura* quickly led to imitative "tributes" in Japan and many countries. American examples include *Ninja High School, Galaxy High School,* and *Teenagers from Outer Space,* in comic books, TV cartoons, and role-playing games.

F.P.

USELESS EUSTACE (G.B.) The only day since 1935 when the familiar, fat, round, bald (save for three lone long hairs) face of Useless Eustace failed to put in an appearance in the *Daily Mirror* was the day he applied for a job as the Invisible Mender. Being useless, Eustace made himself invisible! Otherwise, the fat little fellow in black jacket and bowler hat had amused readers more than eleven thousand times before he suddenly slimmed, grew a long nose, changed his headgear and was signed "Maddocks." That happened when his creator, Jack Greenall, retired in 1975, after forty years of daily drawings. (Many consider that the "character" went out of his cartoon character with him.)

Useless Eustace was born on the morning of January 21, 1935, in the wake of one of the least successful strips the *Daily Mirror* had ever run, *The Mulligans.* The artist, Jack Greenall, had drawn strips for many magazines over the years, including *Pa, Ma and the Boy* in *Pictorial Weekly* (1929) and *Mr. and Mrs. Penn and the Nib* in *Ideas* (1933). He had also drawn for children's comics: *Cruiser Ben* in *Sparkler* (1934) and *Betty and Her Boy Friend* in *Jolly Comic* (1935). But not until he abandoned strips for a daily joke about a regular character did he hit the public funny bone. Eustace, with wife Winnie and son Walter, was basically a suburban middle-class clerk, but Greenall had the knack of putting him into any job, trade or profession suitable to his gag line. Thus, Eustace became a sort of symbolic comedy Everyman, particularly during World War II. He would be a soldier one day, a sailor the next, a pilot the third and a submariner the fourth, not to mention his civil defense duties or the Home Guard!

Useless Eustace is unique in British cartoon history in that, for reasons unknown and untraceable, the first and last letters of its captions are traditionally used by clubs and charities all over the country as the basis for sweepstakes. Cynics who disapprove of Greenall's very basic "comic" style consider this side effect to be the paper's only justification for continuing the series! *Useless Eustace* books have been published in 1945 and 1947.

D.G.

Vv

VALLÉS TORNER, JOSEP-MARÍA (1947-) Spanish cartoonist born in Barcelona, Spain, in 1947. J.M. Vallés spent the first 14 years of his life in a religious school, a fact he now claims as "his first humorous act." He later went to the University of Barcelona in order to study law and economics but dropped out of school in his first year. In 1965 Vallés contributed his first cartoons to the humor magazines *Tele-Cómico* and *Matarratos;* he later also drew for *Bel, Jano* and *Garbo.*

Vallés joined the staff of the satirical publication *Hermano Lobo* in the late 1960s. In 1973-74 he worked for the magazines *Mundo Joven* and *El Papus* (voted the best European humor magazine of 1976), as well as for the daily *El Noticiero Universal.* He presently also collaborates on *Por Favor* and *Muchas Gracias.* In 1976 Vallés published a book of cartoons, *Cuarenta Años de Balde* ("Forty Years for Nothing"), a summation of the Franco years. He has also contributed humorous drawings to a number of books, such as *Diccionario Politico* and *Historia de España.* In the 1990s two more collections of his cartoons were published: *Viñetas de Espana* ("Cartoons from Spain") and *Nuevas Viñetas de espana* ("New Cartoons from Spain"). He also wrote *La Madre que nos Pario,* an obscene Spanish expression that might be translated as "The Mother Who Bore Us All."

Vallés is one of the most representative cartoonists of his generation. His humor, chiefly of a political and polemical nature, attacks sexual taboos, politicians of the left and right, and social institutions. His cartoons are so bare that he has often been accused of not knowing how to draw, but his characters come alive in spite of the lack of formal draftsmanship.

J.M.

"You give me your money, I lend you my experience. Voila!"
Felix Vallotton, 1901.

VALLOTTON, FÉLIX-EDOUARD (1865-1925) Swiss cartoonist and painter born in Lausanne, Switzerland, on December 28, 1865. Félix Vallotton studied art at the Académie Julian in Paris and, upon graduation, decided to remain in the French capital, where his whole artistic career developed. In the 1890s Vallotton worked mostly in the woodcut medium, turning out fine portraits of noted artists of the day and subtle compositions of Parisian life. His style found its best expression, however, in the many illustrations and cartoons that he contributed to French humor and satirical magazines from 1894 to 1903: to *Le Rire* (1894), *Le Courrier Français, Le Sifflet* and *La Reine Blanche.* He later developed a terse, striking style influenced by Japanese *ukiyo-e,* which contrasted spots of solid black volume with white, flat backgrounds: in this technique he showed himself as one of the precursors of modern cartooning.

Vallotton's best works appeared in the anarchist publications of the turn of the century: *Le Cri de Paris* (for which he worked from 1897 to 1899), *Le Canard Sauvage, Les Temps Nauveaux* and especially *L'Assiette au Beurre,* which published his famous series of 22 lithographs titled *Crimes et Châtiments* ("Crimes and Punishments"), castigating with rare violence the excesses and injustices of the ruling class. In 1904 Vallotton left cartooning and devoted his talents to painting. His landscapes, interiors and nudes are strongly patterned in lines laid out with sharp precision.

Félix Vallotton is best remembered as a cartoonist, the originator of graphic "black" humor, and one of the most gifted practitioners of the art of cartooning. He died in Paris on December 29, 1925.

M.H.

VALTMAN, EDMUND (1914-) American cartoonist born in Tallinn, Estonia, on May 31, 1914. Ed Valtman sold his first drawings, cartoon illustrations for a children's book, at the age of 15. Later he studied in private studios (1936-

Dilemma
Edmund Valtman. © Hartford Times.

39) and at the Tallinn Art and Applied Art School (1942-44). Valtman was a cartoonist when the Soviets overran his homeland in 1940; he was forced to quit and instead worked as a draftsman. When the Germans occupied Estonia in 1942, he became a political cartoonist for *Eesti Sona* until 1944; then, with the Soviet reoccupation, Valtman fled. After the war he spent four years in a displaced persons camp in Allied-controlled Germany and moved to America in 1949. In 1951 he secured a position as political cartoonist for the *Hartford Times;* he has since remained in Hartford, syndicated for many of those years, drawing his powerful political cartoons.

Not surprisingly, Valtman brings a European look to his cartoons, which are often horizontal in format. He generally eschews crayon shading, icons and symbols. Instead he draws gags as vehicles for his political statements and relies more on humor and irony than on traditional caricatures of public figures. His compositions are solid, and his concepts usually devastating; Valtman's indictments of oppression and tyranny could be collected as a textbook on liberty. One of his cartoons (anti-Castro) was chosen for the Pulitzer Prize in 1962. He has received many other awards and has been exhibited widely. He listed himself as still active in the 1997-98 edition of *Who's Who in American Art.*

R.M.

VANDERBEEK, STANLEY (1927-1984) American animator, filmmaker and fine artist born in New York City on January 6, 1927. After dropping out of college, Stanley VanDerBeek briefly engaged in farming and just as briefly worked as an assistant on a local television station before deciding to strike out on his own as an independent artist. His first work of animation was *What Who How* (1955), which incorporated the clever use of collages with exposed film. This was followed by *Mankinda* (1956), in which animation was directly applied to celluloid, a technique VanDerBeek calls "time painting."

In the 1960s VanDerBeek did a number of politically committed films, including *Achoo Mr. Kerochev* (1960), *Summit* (1963) and especially an antiwar movie titled *Breathdeath* (1964). All three were a further refining of his "time paintings." At the same time VanDerBeek continued to experiment with drawn animation in such efforts as *The Life and Death of a Car* (1962) and *Fluids* (1965). Later he experimented with computerized animation (*Collideoscope,* 1966) and developed the "moviedrome," a device of his own invention which allowed him to project multiple images on a screen simultaneously.

Not content to be one of the most original and innovative artists currently working in the animation medium, VanDerBeek was also a painter, sculptor and calligrapher of repute. Two of his experimental films, *Science-Friction* and *Newsreel of Dreams,* were included in the groundbreaking "The American Independent Cinema" show at the Whitney Museum in New York in 1984. He died of cancer on September 19, 1984, in Columbia, Maryland.

M.H.

VASILEVSKI, ANE (1947-) One of the best known and most prolific cartoonists in Eastern Europe, Ane Vasilevski began his career as a cartoonist in 1960. He was born on August 21, 1947, in Brezno-Tetovo in the Federal Republic of Macedonia, then one of the constituent republics of Yugoslavia, and since the dissolution of that Balkan state in 1993, an independent nation. A graduate of the Pedagogic Academy in Skopje, Macedonia's capital, he was already a seasoned cartoonist by the time he left school, having published his first cartoon at the age of 13 in the Skopje newspaper *Trudbenik.* Since that auspicious beginning, he has produced a steady stream of trenchant graphic commentary and humor in newspapers and magazines not only in the Balkans but in the many republics of the former U.S.S.R. and in Poland, Bulgaria, Rumania, Slovakia, and the Czech Republic in Eastern Europe, as well as in Belgium, France, the Netherlands, Italy, Greece, England, Turkey, Iran, Korea, China, Japan, Cuba, Mexico, Canada, and the United States. A staff member of *Osten,* Macedonia's national satire magazine and one of the oldest and most honored humor magazines in Eastern Europe, he has been a regular contributor since 1966 and also frequently appears in *Jez,* its Serbian counterpart, published in Zagreb. Collections of his work were published in 1980 and 1988, both entitled *Koso Gledano* ("Viewed Obliquely").

Vasilevski has held a pivotal position in Macedonian cartooning for many years, both as a creative artist and as an administrator. A founder and the first president of the Macedonian Association of Cartoonists, he has also long served as the director of the World Cartoon Gallery, an international venue for the presentation of comic art in Skopje. In association with his wife Ruszika, who serves as art manager of the Gallery and secretary of the Association of Cartoonists, he organizes the prestigious annual cartoon competition in Skopje and the festival that accompanies it. His work has been presented in many solo exhibitions throughout the former Yugoslavia, in Sofia and Gabrovo, Bulgaria; Bratislava, Czechoslovakia; Petrosani, Rumania; in Moscow, Teheran, Istanbul, London, Paris, Brussels, Amsterdam, Athens, Montreal, and Buenos Aires. Among the many honors he has received are awards from competitions in Knokke Heist, Belgium (1981); Akshekir, Turkey (1982); Havana, Cuba (1984, 1988, 1991, 1993); Edinburgh, Scotland (1984, 1985); Istanbul, Turkey (1985, 1991, 1992); Mexico City, Trento, and Belgrade (1988); Budapest (1990); Tokyo (1990, 1992); and Seoul (1992, 1993). He took the PJER Award, Macedonia's equivalent of America's Pulitzer Prize for cartooning, in Skopje in 1989, and the First Prize for Graphics in Anglet, France, in 1992.

The cosmopolitan perspective of Ane Vasilevski finds expression in his work for numerous international organizations; he is the Macedonia editor of *WittyWorld International Cartoon Magazine* and was a founding member of the Federation of European Cartoonists' Organizations (FECO), of which he serves as Vice Chairman. He has been responsible for exhibitions of the work of his countrymen in Turkey, Albania, Bulgaria, Rumania, Greece, France, and Italy, and his own cartoons are distributed internationally by Creators & Writers Syndicate of New York City. Most often targeting official bureaucracy, corruption, and greed, his witty and gracefully executed drawings transcend local reference to make shrewd observations on the absurdity of everyday life.

D.W.

VAURO

See Senesi, Vauro

VEBER, JEAN (1864-1928) French caricaturist, cartoonist, designer and lithographer born in Paris, France, on February 13, 1864. The son of caricaturist Eugène Veber, Jean Veber studied first with the painter Maillot, then at the Paris Ecole des Beaux-Arts, where he was Cabanel's pupil. He started his career in 1890, when he decorated the Paris city hall and the Guinguette nightclub, as well as designing various Gobelins tapestries. All of these show the influence of Bosch's and Bruegel's freewheeling and exuberant style. He contributed drawings to several satirical journals, in particular *Le Rire, Gil Blas Illustré,* and *L'Assiette au Beurre.*

Although Veber never achieved great artistic stature, he obtained several *succès de scandale:* in 1897 his "La Fête de Robinson," better known under the title "La Boucherie" ("The Butcher Shop"), was rejected by the jury of the Salon des Artistes because it portrayed a butcher resembling Bismarck selling human heads; in the 1908 "Vision d'Allemagne" ("Germany's Vision") he satirized Kaiser Wilhelm II riding in the Taurus Mountains of Turkey; and a series of bitterly realistic drawings depicted the life of the Boers imprisoned in "reconcentration camps" in the British Transvaal, with official War Office reports as captions. This Boer War series was released in a special issue

The Progress of Science: "The Boer prisoners have been gathering into large enclosures where they have found peace and quiet for 18 months. A wire netting with an electric current running through it is the most healthful and secure kind of fence. It allows the prisoners to enjoy the view outside and thus to have the illusion of freedom" (official report to the War Office).
Jean Veber, 1901.

of *L'Assiette au Beurre* (September 28, 1901) and temporarily banned by the French government, which wanted to sign a mutual defense pact with Great Britain.

His work was published in the albums *Bataille de Dames* ("Ladies' Battle"), *Les Maisans Ont des Yeux* ("Houses Have Eyes") and *L'Ivrogne et Sa Femme* ("The Drunkard and His Wife"), and the illustrations he did for his brother Pierre's articles appeared in *Les Vebers* (1892-95). Finally, his haunting lithographs were edited posthumously under the title *L'Oeuvre Lithographié* (1931). Jean Veber died in Paris on November 28, 1928.

P.H.

VERDINI, RAOUL (1899-1981) Italian cartoonist and illustrator born in the Marche region of Italy in 1899. Raoul Verdini started his career as a draftsman for the National Railway System but soon abandoned his job in favor of cartooning. In the early 1930s he joined the staff of the humor magazine *Marc' Aurelio* and contributed many gag cartoons. He also worked briefly as an animator, notably on the first (black-and-white) animated version of *Pinocchio* (1936). After World War II, Verdini was one of the founders and editors of *Il Merlo Giallo,* a satirical maga-

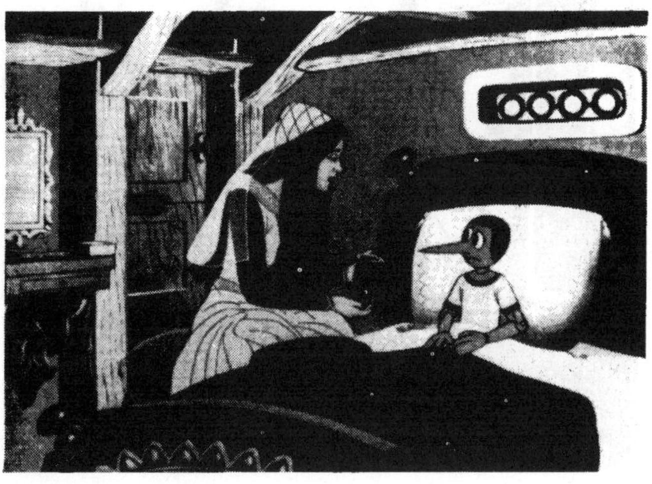

Raoul Verdini, "Pinocchio," 1936. © CAIR.

zine, and also collaborated regularly on the left-wing weekly *Vie Nuove,* for which he did editorial cartoons. His drawings packed a strong polemical charge; he delighted most in depicting the interior minister, Mario Scelba, invariably represented with a helmet on his head, a night-stick in his hand and sometimes a rifle slung across his shoulders to highlight the "repressive" violence of Italian police.

At the same time Verdini worked for *Il Pioniere,* a children's magazine that the parties of the left tried to oppose (without much success) to the Catholic *Il Vittorioso* and the conservative *Il Corriere dei Piccoli. For Il Pioniere* Verdini created, among others, the character Cipollino, protagonist of a picture story in verse. In this feature, a group of humanized vegetables (Cipollino, Pomodoro, Ciliegino, Carotino, etc.) representing vices and virtues enacted themes of everyday life in a series of rustic little fables. Verdini currently draws for children's periodicals such as *Miao* and *La Via Migliore.* He died on December 4, 1981.

C.S.

VERNET, ANTOINE CHARLES HORACE (1758-1836) French caricaturist and painter born in Bordeaux, France, on August 14, 1758. The son of famous marine painter Joseph Vernet, "Carle" Vernet (as he signed his work) was sent to Rome at an early age to study art; he came back to France around 1780, settling in Paris and pursuing a career in painting. His works, usually gay, exuberant city and court scenes, were well received by the elegant society of his time, and in 1788 Vernet was admitted to the Academy.

During the French Revolution his sister Emilie was guillotined, and Vernet's outlook became gloomy and pessimistic. He regained his *joie de vivre* with the advent of the Directoire regime (1795) and devoted his talent to caricaturing the manners, institutions and personages of the times. During the days of the Empire (1800-14) he resumed painting and became famous for his battle scenes (notably for his *Battle of Morengo,* much praised by Napoleon himself).

With the restoration of the French kings in 1815, Vernet went back to drawing humorous and satirical scenes and soon found himself hailed as one of the founders of the French school of cartooning. An inveterate lover of horseflesh, Vernet was also noted for his spirited drawings of horses and horse races. He died in Paris on November 27, 1836.

M.H.

VICKY
See Weisz, Victor.

VICTOR, F.
See Gillam, F. Victor.

VIE EN IMAGES, LA (Canada) Created by Jacques Gagnier, a commercial artist who later turned to political cartooning, *La Vie en Images* ("Life in Pictures") debuted on February 6, 1944, in the Sunday edition of the Montreal daily *La Patrie.* It was a cross between the illustrated Sunday page and the conventional panel. *La Vie en Images* provided a lighthearted comment on subjects of topical

Carle Vernet, "An Office Clerk Getting Groomed."

"La Vie en Images." © La Patrie.

interest, on the mores of the times and on events close to the hearts of Montrealers. Using a versatile and free layout (sometimes the entire page was filled by a single panel, sometimes the composition was close to the comic strip technique), Gagnier treated all kinds of topics, from traditional themes like women and fashion to the minute rendering of daily Montreal life. A number of Gagnier's Sunday pages were collected into an album, *La Plume au Vent* ("Feather in the Wind," 1946).

On June 1, 1947, Gagnier signed his last page, and the panel was taken over the following week by Paul Leduc. In his often crowded pages Leduc dealt with more general themes (progress, travel, etc.) and at times even turned the feature into a conventional gag panel. *La Vie en Images* came to an end in May 1956 and was replaced the following month by a topical-interest panel, *Un Peu d'Actualité* ("A Few Current Events").

S.J.

VIEIRA DA CUNHA, ATÔNIO BELISÁRIO (1896-1956) Brazilian cartoonist born in Cachoeiro do Itapemirim, in the state of Espirito Santo, Brazil, in 1896. After some art studies, Antônio Vieira went to Rio in 1912. That same year he had his first cartoon published in the Rio newspaper *Correio da Noite.* He specialized in caricatures of famous personages in the arts, the theater and politics, signing either "V. da Cunha" or "Belisário."

In addition to his work for *Correio da Noite,* Vieira contributed to many other publications, among them *A Rajada, A Tribuna, Gazeta de Notícias, A Nação, Diário de Notícias, D. Quixote, O Dia, A Manhã* and *O Malho.* In 1914, in partnership with his colleague Fernando Correia Dias, he founded the Apolo publishing company. He was also a noted art critic whose many articles were published in magazines and newspapers throughout Brazil. He died in Rio in 1956.

A.M.

VIGNETTES OF LIFE (U.S.) A weekly color page of seven to eight gag drawings centered on a new theme of domestic American life each week, *Vignettes of Life* was introduced as a Sunday magazine feature of the *Philadelphia Public Ledger* early in 1924, going into national syndication at the same time. A color imitation of *Among Us Mortals,* W.E. Hill's earlier weekly black-and-white gag page for the *New York Tribune,* the *Ledger's Vignettes of Life* was initially drawn by the gifted Frank Godwin. Godwin, a staff artist for the *Ledger,* also drew full-page thematic anecdotes for the *Ledger* magazine section cover (also syndicated to other newspapers for Sunday magazine use), and illustrated magazine fiction for the same publication.

Godwin left *Vignettes of Life* to investigate continuity comic strip work in such features as *Connie* for the *Ledger* on November 13, 1927; the artist most popularly associated with *Vignettes of Life,* J. Norman Lynd, took over the weekly feature on November 20. Previously employed as a spot gag cartoonist by the Bell Syndicate, Lynd had a touch for the familiar life patterns of the American middle class. *Vignettes of Life* blossomed under his sensitive and richly humorous handling, its readers easily recognizing the mildly caricatured but not unflattering portraits of themselves Lynd presented every week.

A large book collection of Lynd's work was published in 1930 under the *Vignettes of Life* title by the Reilly and Lee Company of Chicago. Widely syndicated by the 1930s, the Lynd work continued to appear under the *Ledger* aegis until 1938, when Lynd was signed by King Features to do a weekly half-page anecdote feature identical to *Vignettes of Life,* titled *Family Portraits.* The *Ledger* entrusted the *Vignettes* feature to Kemp Starrett for awhile longer, and Lynd continued *Family Portraits* until his death a few years later.

B.B.

VIKSTEDT, TOIVO ALARIK (1891-1930) Finnish cartoonist born in Viipuri, Finland (now Vyborg, USSR), on June 12, 1891. Toivo Vikstedt (better known as "Topi"), the grand old man of Finnish cartooning, died young but had a remarkable career, achieved great fame and taught a whole new generation of cartoonists.

Vikstedt studied in Viipuri and Helsinki, later went to Copenhagen, Germany and Italy (1912-13) and then to Paris. He had an exhibition of his own in Viipuri as early as 1910, and he won many prizes in postcard, stamp and cover contests, beginning in 1913. From 1914 to 1917 he ran an art studio, Kolmikko, the first of its kind in Finland. He then worked as a freelance illustrator and advertising artist and drew cartoons (which he had already done during the czarist period) for the important humor magazine *Tuulispää* He later became editor of *Kerberos* and also did cartoons for *Arena, Garm, Joulukärpänen* and *Lucifer.* Prohibition was one of his favorite subjects.

Before Vikstedt, illustrations for Finnish book covers were rare, and he opened the way to poster art in Finland and was a pioneer in advertising as well. He also did caricatures, heraldic design, miniatures, decorative paintings and murals. In 1923 he illustrated Aleksis Kivi's *Nummisuutarit* ("The Shoemakers of the Moor"). The famous cartoon character Mustapartainen Mies ("the Black-Bearded Man") was also his creation.

Vikstedt was the first professor of graphic art at the University of Arts in Helsinki. A very skilled draftsman, he was one of the founders of humor cartooning in Finland. His works display a lusty humor rather than sharp satire, and even in his more serious pieces he introduced many humorous touches. He often worked in pencil in preference to pen and ink.

Toward the end of his life Vikstedt also designed the books of two publishing houses—Otava, and Söderström and Company. His death from a heart attack on May 6, 1930, was blamed on overwork. A memorial album of his cartoons, *Topin Pilakuvia,* was published in 1935. Memorial exhibitions of his works were held in Helsinki in 1935 and 1967.

J.R.

VILLON, JACQUES
See Duchamp, Gaston.

VILMAR
See Rodrigues, Vilmar Silva.

VINCINO
See Gallo, Vincenzo.

VINS
See Seth, Vijay J.

VIP
See Partch, Virgil.

VIVIANO, SAM (1953-) Born in Detroit, Michigan in 1953, Sam Viviano traveled to New York City to seek success as an illustrator following his 1975 graduation from the University of Michigan. He arrived in New York with a friend-of-a-friend letter of introduction to Harvey Kurtzman, then cartoon editor at *Esquire*. While Kurtzman couldn't use his work, he referred him to the art director of *Mad magazine*. At the time, *Mad* had a full roster of cartoonists. Unless one of the *Mad* guys died or retired, there was no room for anybody new.

Viviano quickly found work in 1976 in youth-oriented publications put out by *Scholastic Magazine*. He did covers and spot illustrations, much of it in full color, for *Dynamite* and *Bananas*. Growing up in Michigan he had been a voracious comic book reader. Carmine Infantino was his favorite comic book artist. In comic strips, he was influenced by Roy Crane and Al Capp. He especially liked how Crane combined humor and adventure. He also read *Mad* as a kid.

While still doing freelance illustration and computer graphics, Viviano is today best known as a veteran *Mad* cartoonist. His first chance at *Mad* came in 1980 when cover artist Norman Mingo retired. Mingo was the first person to ever create a full color cover for *Mad* with the picture of Alfred E. Neuman, the "What Me Worry" kid on it. Viviano was assigned painting the cover of *Dallas's* wheeler-dealer, J.R. Ewing, shooting a gun off in the side of a person's head. A flag comes out the other side with Alfred on the flag. The issue proved a low-seller. Viviano didn't receive another job from *Mad* until 1984.

Sam Viviano, self-portrait.

Although he does a variety of art for *Mad*, Viviano is best known for his parodies of movies and television shows. In 1984 his second job for *Mad* was a parody of the hit movie *Ghostbusters*. Editors and fans liked what they saw. In 1998, Viviano was selected to draw the parody of all-time box office smash hit *Titanic*.

Mad, especially under the leadership of the late Bill Gaines, operates as a family. Viviano feels he became a real *Mad* regular by 1987. He has occasionally done covers such as the one featuring the California Raisins and another with President Bill Clinton and Vice President Al Gore as Beavis and Butthead. He also did the computer graphics for a cover where Batman's signal beam of light is transformed to show Alfred E. Neuman's face.

Mad remains cutting-edge humor for a specific age group and is indeed a coming of age experience for many worldwide with the magazine published in many foreign language editions. Viviano's style with caricatures of the actors' heads slightly larger than they should be for their bodies is his take on the *Mad* school of caricature. He uses sepia ink instead of black for drawing the parodies to give his work a different look. The artwork is busy and contains lots of noodling. For example, the parody of the TV show *Ellen* showed copies of the gay magazine *The Advocate* around Ellen's apartment, long before the star of the series publicly used her gayness as a theme on the show.

B.C.

VOLTOLINO
See Lemmi, Lemmo.

VOLTRON: DEFENDER OF THE UNIVERSE! (U.S.-Japan) Many animated cartoons have been retitled and edited when released in foreign countries. *Voltron*'s claim to fame is that it was the first original creation made from two entirely separate works.

The raw material for *Voltron* was two Japanese TV animated serials. *Hyakuju Oh Go Lion* ("Go Lion, King of a Hundred Beasts") consisted of 52 episodes, broadcast weekly from March 1, 1981 to February 24, 1982. It was followed directly by *Kiko Kantai Dairugger-XV* ("Dairugger-XV, the Armored Fleet"), 56 episodes shown in Japan from March 3, 1982 through March 23, 1983. Both were produced by Toei Co., Ltd. (Toei Co., Ltd. is a different studio than Toei Animation Co., Ltd.) and both were space-adventure serials created around giant-robot toy marketing concepts. The Go Lion giant robot consisted of 5 ("go" is the Japanese word for "five") small lion-robots which fastened together into one giant robot in the form of an armored knight with a stylized lion-head helmet. Dairugger-XV was a single giant robot made from 15 individual interlocking vehicles; 5 for land travel,5 aquatic, and 5 aerial. "Dairugger-XV" was an exercise in wordplay, made from the Japanese "dai" (big), and the English "rugger" (a rugby player); and there are 15 players on a rugby team. Neither the giant-robot toy nor the adventure had the slightest connection with rugby; but who cared?

World Events Productions, an American company, licensed both programs to turn them into a single 125-episode program for the American syndicated TV market. As rewritten by Jameson Brewer, both series were united in a futuristic space age settled by the human-dominated Galaxy Alliance, which maintained interstellar peace through its defense force, the Galaxy Garrison.

The *Lion Force Voltron* adventure, which introduces the robot, was the more popular, both in America and in the original Japanese *Go Lion*. The Galaxy Garrison sends 5 teenaged Space Explorers to the distant planet Arus, outside the Galaxy Alliance, to investigate its legendary secret weapon, the Voltron super-robot. Arus has recently been conquered by the brutal reptilian armies of planet Doom, despite the heroic defense of its Voltron defense team. The Galaxy Garrison fears that Doom's tyrannical King Zarkon may become truly invincible if he adds the Voltron to his military arsenal. The five explorers (Sven, Keith, Lance, Pidge and Hunk) discover that an Arusian resistance force led by Princess Allura is still fighting a guerrilla war against Doom's occupation army. They join the Arusians as allies, recover the 5 hidden separate robot lions, and become the new Voltron fighting team. When Sven is wounded in action (he is killed in the Japanese version), Allura becomes the fifth teammate. The 5 face escalating battles against the robeast (robot-animal) battlecraft of King Zarkon and his son/commander, Prince Lotor. This *Lion Force* sequence was so popular that World Events Productions commissioned 17 new episodes from Toei Co. to extend the story. After the final defeat of Zarkon, the grateful Arusians give the Voltron technology to the human heroes so the Galaxy Garrison may build its own robots.

In the V*ehicle Team Voltron* serial, set several years later, the larger and more complex 15-component robot is the first of the Galaxy Garrison's new Voltron-class fighters. The Vehicle Team (the robot and its large crew) is sent in the research ship *Explorer* to locate new habitable planets for humanity. However, the Galaxy Alliance's enemy, the Drule empire, also needs new planets since its homeworld is becoming uninhabitable from environmental destruction. Rather than conduct its own search, the Drule emperor orders his space fleet to trail after the *Explorer* and occupy the worlds that it finds. Action is divided between the natural perils faced by the Vehicle Team explorers on strange planets, and their battles in their separate vehicles or combined into the Voltron robot against Drule's poachers. One factor that lessened *Vehicle Team's* popularity was the confusingly large cast of 15 Voltron pilot-explorers plus the *Explorer*'s support crew, with none standing out as did *Lion Force*'s 5 heroes.

Voltron: Defender of the Universe! first appeared as a 90-minute TV special in 1983, then began regular syndication in September 1984. It may have been coincidence, but transforming-robot toys were the major craze during the 1984 Christmas gift season and *Voltron* received much of the credit for setting it off.

F.P.

"Voltron." © World Events Productions.

VOLTZ, JOHANN MICHAEL (1784-1858) German printmaker, illustrator and cartoonist born in Nördlingen, Swabia, on October 16, 1784. Although he was in no way a great artist, circumstances and his own industriousness made Johann Voltz (also spelled Volz) one of the great creators of German iconography, both serious and humorous, in the first half of the 19th century. His most highly esteemed efforts date from the years of Germany's resistance to Napoleon in the early 1810s.

The son of a schoolteacher, Voltz had to work for a year as a buttonmaker until his urge to draw overcame all opposition. Mainly self-taught, he was apprenticed to a minor artist in Augsburg from 1801 to 1805, then worked for an art dealer there until 1808. After disappointments in Munich, in 1809 he moved to Nuremberg, where he formed a valuable and lasting connection with the art publisher Friedrich Campe. Now commissions began to pour in, and Voltz's future was secure. He was eventually to do some 4,000 drawings for at least 57 publishers in Germany, Switzerland and Holland (19 of the German firms being located in Augsburg and 11 in Nuremberg). His popularity and influence were immense. In 1812 he returned to his native city of Nördlingen, where, except for an Augsburg interlude from 1824 to 1827, he remained until his death on April 17, 1858.

Leaving aside Voltz's book illustrations (including almanacs and children's books), his costume studies, his thematic cycles (trades, five senses, ages of man, etc.), his single-sheet illustrations of German classics, his religious and historical subjects and serious treatments of current events, his portraits, views, animal studies, designs for coins, crests and games, his oil paintings and watercolors (all these done between 1805 and 1857), we can divide his specifically humorous works into two parts: at least 31 satires on Napoleon, which were among his most famous pieces (these, of course, ceased in 1815); and about 80 satires on politics and other subjects, done between 1811 and 1832.

The last-named group includes humorous prints about fashions in clothing and hairstyles, attacks on war profiteers, lampoons on the Congress of Vienna and the general obscurantism of the Metternich reactionary age, spoofs on journalists and a series of 32 *Krähwinkliaden* (done during his Augsburg interlude in the 1820s). "Krähwinkel" is a typical benighted German small town (the often-used name comes from a famous play by Kotzebue); in Voltz's series, the foolish townspeople continually take figures of speech in a strictly literal sense.

Three sons and a daughter of Voltz became artists in their turn.

S.A.

VUKOTIĆ, DUŠAN (1927-) Yugoslav cartoonist and animator born in Bileća, near Dubrovnik, Yugoslavia, on February 7, 1927. Dušan Vukotić studied architecture at the University of Zagreb. He started on his cartooning career in the late 1940s as a regular contributor to the satirical magazine *Kerempuh,* the stepping-stone of many of Yugoslavia's top animators. In 1951 he was made head of his own animation unit, releasing through Duga Film; there he created the character Kićo, a feisty little government inspector, in such cartoons as *How Kićo Was Born* and *The Haunted Castle at Dudinić.*

When Duga Film went out of business in 1952, Vukotić made a number of advertising cartoons in collaboration with Nikola Kostelać. In 1956 he went back to entertainment animation with *The Playful Robot,* which received many awards. Then he established himself as a master of the cartoon medium with a series of three satirical cartoons he directed in 1957-58: *Cowboy Jimmy,* a spoof of movie westerns; *Concerto for Sub-machine Gun,* a takeoff on gangster films; and *The Great Fear,* a parody of the horror genre. More cartoons followed, the more notable being *Piccolo* (1959), *Ersatz* (the Academy Award winner of 1961) and *Play* (1962).

Vukotić then turned to live action with *The Seventh Continent* (1966), a children's film, and to animation mixed with stock footage in the disturbing *A Stain on His Conscience* (1968). He returned to pure cartoon animation with two delightful little comedies, *Opera Cordis* and *Ars Gratia Artis* (1968-69). *Gubecziana* (1973) was again a blend of animation and documentary footage that depicted the world of *naïf* artists, while *The Grasshopper* (1974) was an unpretentious little cartoon fable.

The major figure in Yugoslav animation, Vukotić has received more than one hundred awards and distinctions. His cartoons have been honored at festivals around the globe, and he is the first foreign cartoonist ever to receive an Oscar for animation. His work helped establish Zagreb Film as a major animation studio, and though his star seems to have waned somewhat in recent years, he remains one of the undisputed masters of the form. In addition to his work as an anemator, he has become politically active in his native Croatia.

M.H.

Dušan Vukotić, "Concerto for Sub-Machine Gun." © *Zagreb Film.*

VYNÁLEZ ZKÁZY (Czechoslovakia) One of the most imaginative and successful attempts at blending animation with live action, this feature-length film was produced by Karel Zeman in 1957. *Vynález Zkázy,* literally meaning "The Diabolical Invention," was released in the United States under the title *The Fabulous World of Jules Verne.*

Freely adapted by Karel Zeman himself and his coscenarist František Hrubin from a number of Jules Verne stories, Vynález Zkázy is an enchanting parade of adventures, plots and counterplots. In the film a scientist, Professor Roch, invents an explosive of unprecedented powers, only to be kidnapped along with his assistant, the engineer Hart, by the ruthless pirate Artigas. Brought to Artigas's hideaway, an uncharted island, Hart uses the explosive to destroy the island and all its inhabitants. Only Hart and his girl friend, Jena, escape: Roch himself is buried under the ruins, along with his deadly invention.

Vynález Zkázy has become a classic of both the animated film and the science-fiction cinema. In it, Zeman was able to preserve the flavor of the old Jules Verne illustrations as well as the atmosphere of the novels. In her book *Kiss Kiss Bang Bang* (1968), the usually hard-to-please Pauline Kael enthused: "Like Méiès, Zeman employs every conceivable trick, combining live action, animation, and puppet films. For many scenes several film strips are printed on one film strip. The variety of tricks and superimpositions seems infinite, and the spectator can't help wondering how the designers, the animators, miniature-makers, and photographers have worked their magic. . . . There are underwater scenes in which the fishes swimming about are as rigidly patterned as in a child's drawing. . . . There are more stripes, more patterns on the clothing, the decor, and on the image itself than a sane person can easily imagine, and the painted sets are a triumph of sophisticated primitivism."

Vynález Zkázy has received countless international awards, from the grand prize at the Brussels International Film Festival to the Crystal Star of the French Film Academy.

M.H.

Ww

WAIN, LOUIS WILLIAM (1860-1939) British illustrator and artist born in Clerkenwell, London, England, on August 5, 1860. Known throughout the world as "the Cat Man" because of the funny-faced felines that became his trademark, Louis Wain had little formal education, preferring to study music and the arts. He studied at the West London School of Art (1877-80) and became a teacher there in 1881. After a year or so, he became a full-time commercial artist, joining the staff of the *Illustrated Sporting and Dramatic News* in 1882. In 1883 he drew his first cat. From that point on, cats began to dominate his life as well as his art, until in time he became president not only of the National Cat Club but of virtually every other feline organization imaginable. His yearly collation of cat cartoons, *Louis Wain's Annual,* first appeared in 1901 and continued every Christmas for many years. These annuals are now much-prized collectors' items.

Wain often used strip techniques, beginning with the pictorial narrative "Our Cats: A Domestic History," one of his early pages for the *Illustrated London News* (1884). His cats caught the eye of the publisher Macmillan, who invited him to illustrate a children's book, *Madame Tabby's Establishment* (1886), by "Kari." Many book and magazine commissions followed, with cartoons and strips for children gradually taking precedence in the weekly paper *Chums, Boys Own Paper,* and the *Playbox* supplement to *Home Chat.* Trips to New York came in 1907 and 1910 with consequent comic work, the series *Cats About Town* and *Grimalkin.*

In 1917 Wain went to the Gaumont studio to experiment with animated cartoons, but the projected film *Pussyfoot,* if completed, was never shown—unless it was the short film entitled *The Golfing Cat,* which received some scant showings in August 1917. On August 11, 1925, the *Daily Express* carried the tragic headline "Louis Wain's Plight: Famous Cat Artist in Pauper Asylum." The newspaper's rival, *Daily Graphic,* launched an appeal which met with an instant response. Nine years later the *Express* ran another headline: "Louis Wain Still Draws Cats but His Studio Is an Asylum." He died on July 4, 1939. Headlined the *New York Tribune:* "Wain dies at 78: Drew Pictures of 150,000 Cats."

Books: *Madame Tabby's Establishment* (1886); *Our Farm* (1888); *Dreams by French Firesides* (1890); *Old Rabbit the Voodoo* (1893); *Miss Lavemouse's Letters* (1896); *Puppy Dogs' Tales* (1896); *Comical Customers at the New Stores* (1896); *Jingles, Jokes and Funny Folks* (1898); *Pussies and Puppies* (1899); *The Dandy Lion* (1900); *Cats* (1901); *Louis Wain's Annual* (1901-21); *All Sorts of Comical Cats* (1902); *The Louis Wain Nursery Book* (1902); *Fun and Frolic* (1902); *Ping Pong Calendar* (1903); *Kittenland* (1903); *Comic Animals ABC* (1903); *Louis Wain Kitten Book* (1903); *Louis Wain's Baby Picture Book* (1903); *Louis Wain's Dog Painting Book* (1903); *Louis Wain's Cat Painting Book* (1903); *Louis Wain's Cats and Dogs* (1903); *Louis Wain's Summer Book* (1903); *With Louis Wain to Fairyland* (1904); *In Animal Land with Louis Wain* (1904); *Funny Favourites* (1904); *Kits and Cats* (1904); *Claws and Paws* (1905); *Cat Tales* (1905); *Louis Wain's Animal Show* (1905); *Louis Wain's Summer Book* (1906); *Adventures of Frisky and His Friends* (1907); *Mephistopheles* (1907); *The Kings and the Cats* (1908); *Full of Fun* (1908); *Cats Cradle* (1908); *Holidays in Animal Land* (1909); *Two Cats at Large* (1910); *The Happy Family* (1910); *Such Fun* (1910); *Cats at School* (1911); *The Cat Scouts* (1912); *In Story Land* (1912); *Louis Wain's Happy Land* (1912); *Louis Wain's Painting Book* (1912); *Louis Wain's Father Christmas* (1912); *Happy Hours* (1913); *A Cat Alphabet* (1914); *Tinker Tailor* (1914); *Daddy Cat* (1915); *Little Soldiers* (1916); *Little Red Riding Hood* (1917); *Cinderella* (1917); *Merry Times* (1917); *Cats at Play* (1918); *The Story of Tabbykin Town* (1920); *Pussyland* (1920); *Tale of Little Priscilla Purr* (1920); *Tale of Naughty Kitty Cat* (1920); *Tale of Peter Pusskin* (1920); *Tale of the Tabby Twins* (1920); *The Teddy Rocker* (1921); *The Pussy Rocker (*1921); *The Kitten s House* (1922); *Charlie's Adventures* (1922); *Louis Wain's Children's Book* (1923); *Daddy Cat* (1925); *Souvenir of Louis Wain's Work* (1925); *Louis Wain's Animal Book* (1928); *Louis Wain's Great Big Midget Book* (1935); and *Louis Wain: The Man Who Drew Cats* (1968).

D.G.

WALES, JAMES ALBERT (1852-1886) American cartoonist born in Clyde, Ohio, in 1852. After basic schooling the young James Wales removed to Toledo and Cincinnati, where he decided to learn the art of woodcutting cartoons and illustrations. Eyestrain, as well as the public's evident lack of interest in his prints, prompted him to seek a career as a newspaper artist. After failing to secure steady employment in Cincinnati, he took his art portfolio to Cleveland, where he was hired by the *Leader.*

Several years later Wales moved to Chicago, where he covered the campaign of 1872 with his sketchbook for the *Leader.* The next year he moved to New York. He accepted a position on *Leslie's Weekly* and on *Wild Oats,* next to another Ohio native, Fred Opper. Working for the *Weekly* was Joseph Keppler, founder of *Puck,* who was impressed by Wales and hired him to draw for *Puck* when he was assembling an art staff eight years later. In 1875 Wales went to London, where he drew for *Judy, Illustrated Sporting and Dramatic News* and the *London Illustrated News.*

By 1881 Wales was feeling his wild oats and sought to establish a rival to *Puck,* generally Republican in nature. He gathered a staff of such veterans as Thomas Worth, Frank Beard and Frank Bellew and newcomers like Grant Hamilton and D.A. MacKellar. The new weekly, *Judge,* limped along until the election of 1884, when partisanship placed a premium on anti-Democratic cartoons. But business and staff problems soon led Wales to sell his share of *Judge* to a combine fronting for the Republican party, and when Bernard Gillam and Eugene Zimmerman left *Puck* as new part-owners of *Judge,* the restive Wales, after some drawing for the *World,* returned to *Puck.* This trade-off occurred in late 1885, and Wales was a welcome and comfortable fixture again at *Puck.* But fate unfortunately intervened just a year later, when a heart ailment felled him at the age of 34. He died on December 6, 1886.

Wales was a competent pen-and-ink artist who never seemed to be fully comfortable with lithographic stones. His colors were frequently drab, and it is likely that he applied them himself (Keppler had younger staffers such as Zim help with colors). In any event Wales did have a faculty for forceful presentation of ideas and was an effective partisan—whichever party he happened to be boosting at a given time. His best-remembered cartoon may be the "15-14-13 Puzzle" (1880), which capitalized cleverly on a little game then popular; in it, Senator Roscoe Conkling is as frustrated by the arrangement of presidential candidates as the public was by the proper placement of the 15 squares. It was a classic cartoon and made Wales's career.

R.M.

WALKER, ALANSON BURTON (1878-1947) American artist born in Binghamton, New York, on November 19 1878. A.B. Walker was educated at Buffalo Central High School in New York, from which he graduated in 1894. He later studied art and received a B.A. degree from the University of Rochester (1897).

Walker thereafter studied at the Art Students League in New York City, and when he left in 1901, he began contributing to magazines. For years his principal markets were *Life, Harper's* and *Scribner's;* his brother, William H. Walker, was *Life's* chief editorial cartoonist at this time.

A.B. Walker drew in an extremely simplified style of rather stiff pen lines, with elementary shadings using parallel lines or basic crosshatches. His humor was gentle and situational; the caption largely carried the gag, and the art was a restrained, amiable accompaniment. Early in his career he drew large, full-page, involved cartoons, but he quickly evolved to a format of a few figures, often standing on a plane tableau-style.

During World War I Walker drew some sharp and effective propaganda cartoons, and in the 1920s and 1930s he contributed frequently to *Judge* and *Ballyhoo,* where his reserved style balanced the freewheeling abandon of a new generation of cartoonists and gagmen. He died on January 22, 1947.

R.M.

WALKER, RYAN (1870-1932) American cartoonist born in Springfield, Kentucky, on December 26, 1870. Ryan Walker was educated in the public school system of Kansas City and received artistic training at the Art Students League in New York. His first professional work appeared in the *Kansas City Times* (1895-98). Between 1898 and 1901 he was the chief cartoonist on the *St. Louis Republic,* where he carried much of the burden for the colored supplements, and where a youngster named George McManus did his first work under Walker's direction. In 1901 Walker moved east and drew for the *Boston Globe* for a year, at the same time freelancing to such New York markets as *Life, Judge,* the *Bookman* magazine, and the *Times* and *Mail* newspapers.

Walker experienced a conversion to radical leftist politics about this time, and most of his future work was devoted to Socialist and Communist causes. The International Syndicate of Baltimore distributed his political material between 1904 and 1911, and until 1917 he featured Henry Dubb as a character representing the Common Man. He was also a prominent contributor to the leftist magazines produced in Girard, Kansas, including *The Appeal to Reason* and the *Coming Nation.* He followed Robert Minor as political cartoonist on the *New York Call* (1916-21), a Socialist paper. Between 1924 and 1929, Walker was the art director and rotogravure editor of the nonpolitical, sensationalist *New York Graphic.* From 1930 until just before his death on June 21, 1932, he was the creator of the *Bill Worker* cartoons in the Communist *Daily Worker.*

Ryan Walker was one of a band of politically conscious cartoonists of the 1910s—artists committed, for varying lengths of time, to leftist causes. His art style was not theirs, however; he was no technical relative of Minor or Robinson. Rather, his art was of a purely humorous vein. His lines were wispy, almost like those of Clare Victor Dwiggins. His concepts could sometimes be harsh and devastating but more often were good-natured. When he aimed elsewhere, he usually seemed to be straining. Some of his cartoons were effective propaganda vehicles, however, and Walker even experimented with the Socialist Realist crayon. Evidently a gregarious fellow, and well liked by his contemporaries, Walker was for years the official cartoonist of the Lambs Club in New York.

R.M.

WALKER, WILLIAM H. (1871-1938) American cartoonist born in Pittston, Pennsylvania, on February 13, 1871. William Walker, whose family moved to Kentucky, studied at the University of Kentucky in 1888 and 1889 and then at the University of Rochester until 1891. From 1891 to 1893 he was a student at the Art Students League in New York.

In 1894 Walker began contributing to *Life* magazine, and in 1898 he joined the staff of *Life* as a personal favorite of editor J.A. Mitchell. Some of his earliest cartoons there were vicious denunciations of the Spanish-American War, dovetailing with the magazine's editorials. Walker, whose brother, A.B. Walker, was also a mainstay of *Life's* art staff, was the magazine's major editorial cartoonist through the 1920s. Theodore Roosevelt, of course, was a favorite subject, and Walker, like *Life,* supported Woodrow Wilson. However, he later got in some good slams against Wilson's leadership before and during American participation in World War I. In 1918, in perhaps his most famous cartoon, he predicted the rise of a militant, rearmed Germany "in 20 years or so."

Walker's style was always stiff and, almost an insult when nestled among other comic masterpieces in *Life*'s pages, appeared hurried and rough. Many cartoons were elaborate, but there was a persisting awkwardness; one gets the impression that he was never quite comfortable with his thick, scratchy pen. Still, he was Mitchell's favorite, and his cartoons reflected many of *Life*'s editorial policies through the years.

In 1924 he retired from *Life,* with Mitchell gone and a new staff of bright artists in its pages. Walker became a landscape and portrait painter and died at his home in Flushing, New York, on January 18, 1938.

R.M.

WANG DAZHUANG (1936-) Wang became first known in Shandong Province when he started to publish cartoons, as a freelance, at the age of 17. However, 2 years later, after one of his cartoons was criticized as "satirical of the socialist system" in 1957 by the local authorities, no newspapers dared to accept his cartoons for publication, which cut off his income resource. In order to make a living, in 1959 he moved to work in Harbin, the capital city of Heilongjiang Province. Since then he has worked at the provincial television station as Art Editor and then Senior Editor. Many television shows that he created and directed won awards locally and nationally.

In addition to his cartooning in the 1950s in Shandong, Wang continued to create cartoons in the early 1960s, mainly on international political topics. During the "Cultural Revolution" (1966-1976), cartooning was stopped in the whole of China. The third time Wang started over again in cartooning was in 1980, when his cartoon entitled "3 x 0 = 0" won the Best Creation Award issued by the *Humor and Satire* magazine in the same year, which was regarded as the highest award in the profession. Wang's cartoons were introduced internationally by publishing in journals that were distributed around the world, such as *People's China* and *China Reconstruct*. His works were included in publications in Japan and Hong Kong as well. As a member of many national and provincial professional organizations and also president of the Heilongjiang Cartoonist Association, Wang has been mentioned in many biographies nationally and internationally.

Being both cartoonist and TV show creator, between 1987 and 1995, Wang alone created a large television special series show, *Zhongguo Manhua Daguan* ("An Overview of Chinese Cartoons"). It has recorded the complete history of Chinese cartoon development over the past one hundred years or so. The total length of the show is about 9 hours divided in 36 segments. It has included the interviews of over 100 best and famous cartoonists, systematically describing how the contemporary cartoon creation in China has been affected in each historical period since the early 20th century, and it has introduced the professional organizations and cartoonist publications in China. Such a large documentary television show about cartoon art and development has been the first one successfully done in China as well as in the world.

H.Y.L.L.

WANG FUYANG (1935-) From early childhood, Wang loved cartoons and imitated many of them when he was a high school student. In 1950 he studied art in the Northeast China Luxun Art Institute and was assigned, after graduation, to work as art editor in a newspaper in Beijing. However, just as he started his career with success, the "Anti-Rightist" movement in 1958 destroyed many people, mostly intellectuals, including Wang. Wang's "crime" was that he tried to protect one of the best cartoonists, who was wrongly labeled a "rightist". Thus, Wang was robbed of his rights to his life and career choices. He was expelled from Beijing and was assigned to one of the remotest and poorest areas, Qinghai, and spent more than 20 years there. During that time, his right to cartooning was taken away, and the golden time of his life was wasted by working as a physical laborer in a forsaken place thousands of miles northwest of Beijing.

Wang Fuyang. © Wang Fuyang.

After the "Cultural Revolution" ended in 1976, Wang was rehabilitated and returned to Beijing. He has been working at the *Beijing Evening* as editor as well as being the editor of *Humor and Satire* (of the *People's Daily*). His cartoons won many awards and he was elected to the board of directors of the Chinese Artist Association and deputy director of the Chinese Cartoonist Commission.

Wang's early cartoons were all lost after he was removed from his position in Beijing. Nowadays, perhaps due to his personal experience in those terrible years, Wang's cartoons often contain light criticism and much humor, while reluctantly touching on politically related matters. Topics in Wang's cartoons are usually correlated with ordinary daily life, such as pollution, low-quality merchandise, and red tape, etc.

His cartoon, *Landslide*, criticizes the consequence generated by those who do not pay any attention to piled-up urgent projects, quite a common occurrence in China. In one cartoon, an officer is dozing at his desk, while the documents marked "urgent" are piling up beside him, until all of a sudden, the pile collapses upon his head.

Another cartoon's title in itself is very humorous: "Husband-Brand Sweater—Flexible in length." It is borrowed from a well-known expression in China that a husband will survive only if he can be flexible to his wife's demands. This cartoon mocks the low-quality goods, which are a common problem in China. The sweater, in Wang's cartoon, becomes so long when it is soaked by rain, that it shrinks too short after it is dried in the sun.

H.Y.L.L.

WARD, SIR LESLIE (1851-1922) British cartoonist known as "Spy," born in 1851. A great *Vanity Fair* caricaturist, second only to "Ape," Spy began contributing full-color chromolithographic caricatures to that magazine from 1873. Leslie Ward was the son of the historical painter E.M. Ward and was educated at Eton. He entered the Royal Academy schools in 1871, where his studies led him toward serious portraiture. Although he had a natural gift for caricature, it was not the be-all of his life and work, as it was with the man he was to replace.

Ward was introduced to Thomas Gibson Bowles, editor and publisher of *Vanity Fair,* by the painter Millais. He was promptly taken on the staff as Carlo ("Ape") Pellegrini's deputy, being given those subjects whom Ape did not choose to caricature himself. Among these personalities were Professor Owen and Anthony Trollope, both caricatured during Spy's first year. As photography came to replace portraiture in the popular press, Ward's work lost the lively comment of caricature and became little more than a colored photographic likeness.

Natural Selection
Leslie Ward ("Spy"), caricature of Charles Darwin in "Vanity Fair," ca. 1885

"Remember that cup of sugar you borrowed last November?"
Leonard Warren, 1965. © Cincinnati Enquirer.

Leslie Ward was knighted in 1918 and wrote a volume of illustrated recollections, *Forty Years of Spy,* in 1915.

D.G.

WARREN, LEONARD D. (1906-1991) American political cartoonist born in Wilmington, Delaware, on December 27, 1906. L.D. Warren graduated from Camden High School in New Jersey in 1925 and considers high school art teachers and his parents as the only influences on his career and artistic development.

Warren was an editorial cartoonist for the *Camden Courier-Post* (1925-27) and then moved across the river to draw feature, sports and editorial cartoons for the *Philadelphia Record* for the next 20 years. In 1947 he accepted a position at the *Cincinnati Enquirer,* where he remained until his retirement in 1973.

The recipient of many honors through the years, Warren has received Freedoms Foundation awards from 1949 through 1973, three Reuben award nominations from the National Cartoonists Society and the National Headliners Award for 1961. His gallery showings have included the Art Academy of Cincinnati, the Metropolitan Museum of Art in New York and the National Portrait Gallery in London. Warren's cartoons received honorable mentions from the Giornate Mediche Internazionale in Verona, Italy, and the Third World Cartoon exhibition in Skopje, Yugoslavia. His work was syndicated in the United States from 1951 to 1974, and between 1960 and 1964 his work appeared in *Tarantel Press* in West Berlin. He continued to draw a weekly local cartoon for the *Enquirer* until the mid-1980's. He died in 1991.

L.D. Warren's cartoons are among the handsomest and most pleasingly stylized in the history of political cartooning. His sense of humor balances his meticulous handling of anatomy and perspective and his wondrous grasp of his media, brush and crayon.

R.M.

WATKINS, DUDLEY DEXTER (1907-1969) British comic strip artist, illustrator, cartoonist and painter born in Manchester, England, on February 27, 1907. As a baby, Dudley Watkins was taken to live in his mother's hometown of Nottingham. His artistic talent emerged at an early age: in 1917 he painted the entire procession of the Nottingham Historical Pageant, and the picture was exhibited at Nottingham Castle. It attracted much comment, and the "schoolboy genius" was acclaimed in the *Nottinghamshire Guardian.* He was photographed for the *Children's Newspaper* (July 26, 1919), and the story was picked up by the national *Sunday Express* (June 1, 1919) under the headline "Clever Boy Artist." Dudley studied at the Nottingham School of Art, where the beginnings of a cartoon quality were noted by a local reporter: "A good deal of his work appears to be founded on the lines of Tom Browne."

Watkins's first published cartoons appeared in the *Beacon,* the staff magazine of the Boots Pure Drug Company, in March 1923. His first job was in the window display department of that local firm. His strips and cartoons appeared monthly until December 1923, when he left work to become a full-time student at the Art School. A representative of the Scottish publisher D.C. Thomson visited the school seeking new talent and was told of Watkins by the principal, Mr. Else. Watkins went to the Dundee offices of Thomson's on a 6-month trial and stayed for 44 years, becoming their star artist.

His first work for Thomson's was to illustrate stories appearing in their chain of weekly boys' papers; the first of these was "The Boy with the Jungle Voices" in *Adventure* on October 3, 1925. He also illustrated stories and articles in the magazines *Weekly Welcome, Topical Times* and *Red Letter,* and the newspapers *Sporting Argus, Sunday Post* and *Evening Telegraph,* before settling down in the boys' field with *Rover, Wizard, Hotspur* and *Skipper.* For the *Sunday Post* he drew *Oor Wullie* and *The Broons* from 1936, but it was not until the creation of the new Thomson comics *Dandy* (1937), *Beono* (1938) and *Magic* (1939) that Watkins changed to strip technique. His creations *Desperate Dan* and *Lord Snooty and His Pals* and his adaptation of Hal Roach's *Our Gang* are British comic classics. Many other characters followed: Mickey the Monkey in *Topper,* Ginger in *Beezer,* Tom Thumb in *Bimbo,* plus the picture serials from *classic* novels such as *Treasure Island* and *Oliver Twist.* These ran as weekly pages in the *People's Journal* from the mid-forties and were reprinted in full color in *Topper* and finally as hardback books.

At his peak, working from home (a beautiful house he designed himself), Watkins produced more than eight full-page strips each week, plus extra pages for annuals. He also drew, free of charge, a monthly strip, *William the Warrior* (later called *Tony and Tina),* for a small-circulation religious magazine for children, *Young Warrior.* A deeply religious man, Watkins often gave illustrated talks to children at Sunday schools, and at one time he held down a regular life class at the Dundee Art School. His paintings, produced for his own pleasure, fill the walls of his home; they are as brightly colored as his comics, and peopled with characters as cheerful as his cartoons. As the only Thomson cartoonist allowed to sign his name, he is remembered with affection by millions of his readers. He died in 1969.

Books: *The Broons* (biannual from 1939); *Oor Wullie* (biannual from 1940); *The Story of Kidnapped* (1948); *The Story of Oliver Twist* (1949); *The Story of Robinson Crusoe* (1950); *The Story of Treasure Island* (1950); *Adventures of William the Warrior* (1961); *Tony and Tina the Twins* (1966); *More About Tony and Tina* (1967); and *Tony and Tina Again* (1968).

D.G.

WEBB, PAUL (1902-?) American cartoonist and illustrator born in Towanda, Pennsylvania, on September 20, 1902. Paul Webb grew up wanting to be an illustrator and greatly admiring the work of Wallace Morgan. He took his art training in the 1920s at the School of Industrial Arts and the Academy of Fine Arts, both in Philadelphia. While in school he won scholarships that allowed him two summer-long trips to wander throughout Europe. His art training was interrupted by a time at home caring for his ill mother. During this time he began freelancing magazine cartoons to the old *Life*, the *New Yorker, Judge, Collier's,* and *College Humor* magazines. Once *The Mountain Boys,* which Webb had created in 1934, became popular, the feature took all of the cartoonist's time.

In the 1930s, *Esquire* syndicated the feature to newspapers. Two collections of *The Mountain Boys* were published

"Junior! For Heaven's sake, turn down that radio."
Paul Webb. © Collier's.

in that period: *Comin' Around the Mountain* (1939) and *Keep 'em Flying* (1941). In the mid-1960s, Paul Webb briefly drew his hillbillies for Columbia Features Syndicate. A paperback collection entitled *The Mountain Boys* was published at that time.

Paul Webb is now semi-retired. He devotes part of his time to giving humorous after-dinner speeches on the banquet circuit; his topic: "A Few Ill-Chosen Words About Nothing in Particular." Nothing has been heard from him in the past dozen years, and he may be dead.

B.C.

WEBER, HILDE (1913-1995) Brazilian cartoonist born in Waldau, Germany, in 1913. After her secondary schooling, Hilde Weber worked as an apprentice in a graphic arts studio in Hamburg in 1930. In 1933, with Hitler's rise to power, she emigrated to Brazil, later becoming a citizen. She first settled in São Paulo, where she painted street scenes and also designed stage sets and scenery. In 1949 Hilde (as she signs her work) moved to Rio de Janeiro. She established herself as the editorial cartoonist for *Tribuna de Imprensa,* a position she filled energetically from 1950 to 1962. Starting in 1956, she also contributed cartoons to *Estado de São Paulo,* and weekly caricatures to the magazine *Visão.* Her drawing style, simple to the point of sparseness, is widely admired by young cartoonists. She now resides in São Paulo, to which she returned in the mid-1960s.

Hilde has received many honors, including a first prize for political cartooning for the Latin American section from the California Newspaper Association (1961) and a gold medal for cartoons from the Brazilian Press Association (1962). Her works have been exhibited in many cartoon shows, and she has also had several one-woman shows, principally in Rio and São Paulo. She worked as a political cartoonist for *O Estado de Saõ Paulo* in the 1980s. She died in 1995.

A.M.

WEBER, ROBERT (1934-) American cartoonist born in Baltimore, Maryland, on June 26, 1934. Bob Weber studied cartooning at the School of Visual Arts in New York in 1953 and worked for a couple of years as a technical illustrator in Baltimore before scoring with gag cartoons in the major New York markets. Starting around 1959, Weber became a mainstay of the *Saturday Evening Post, Look* and many other magazines. At the same time he sold gags to major strip artists and assisted on Dick Cavalli's *Morty Meekle/Winthrop* strip.

In 1965 King Features comics editor Sylvan Byck employed his successful formula of converting gag cartoonists into strip artists and launched Weber's *Moose Miller.* This strip, a kind of American answer to *Andy Capp,* concerns a boorish suburbanite devoted to avoiding work and mooching off his neighbors. Weber's style in *Moose Miller* and his magazine gags is one of the funniest in modern American cartooning. He draws enormous noses and feet-and the unlikeliest bandaged props; every line on the horizon is warped, wilted or winding. This, combined with Weber's zany humor, gives a total effect of old-fashioned fun, broad characterization and slapstick. After more than 30 years *Moose Miller* is still going strong. Weber's son, Robert Weber Jr., is also a cartoonist and the creator of the very successful *Slylock Fox.*

R.M.

WEED, CLIVE (1884-1936) American artist born in Kent, Orleans County, New York, in 1884. When Clive Weed was a youngster his family moved to Philadelphia, and it was there he attended high school. Aspiring to a career in serious painting, he went to the Pennsylvania Academy of Fine Arts and studied under Thomas P. Anschutz, graduating in 1903. Further study in Paris followed. Back in America, however, Weed became a newspaper cartoonist and prospered on a succession of papers. The *Philadelphia Record* ran his editorial cartoons in 1910, and he then switched to the *Philadelphia Press* in 1911-12. The *Evening Sun* lured him to New York in 1913, only to lose him later in the year to the *Tribune.* These years (1913-15) were probably the most distinguished of his career—he and the great Boardman Robinson were the *Trib*'s one-two punch, and Ding Darling appeared frequently, as well.

When Weed left the *Tribune* it was to return to Philadelphia, where he drew for the *Public Ledger* until 1918, then becoming the cartoonist of the *New Republic* magazine. He freelanced on *Collier's* and the *Nation* as well, and from 1921 to its demise the following year he was *Leslie's Weekly*'s editorial cartoonist. At the same time—and until the end of the 1932 elections—Weed was the regular political cartoonist on *Judge.* He joined the *New York World* just before it folded, and thereafter, until his death on December 27, 1936, he cartooned for King Features Syndicate. Other work during Weed's career included monthly cartoons for *Farm and Fireside* and spot work for *Collier's,* both in the 1920s, and illustrations for columns by his best friend, Don Marquis, and for columns and a book by Edward Anthony.

"Whatcha got in that bag?"
Clive Weed, 1929. © New York World.

Weed drew with a heavy grease crayon—he was one of the earliest to do so—but was often extremely sloppy and careless with it. When the "mud-stick" school was criticized, therefore, he was a chief defendant; but at his best he drew with the finesse of a Rollin Kirby. Weed was a liberal Republican throughout most of his career and could summon effective arguments as he attacked and defended by pen. On *Judge,* however, his concepts became formularized. He attacked Prohibition, censorship and the KKK, and while these subjects would seem like heaven-sent gifts for a political cartoonist, in Weed's hands they became as predictable and hackneyed as the proverbial drive-safe cartoons of a later generation. Weed was, like a good newspaperman, a devotee of speakeasies, and this, together with the lack of a demanding environment on *Judge,* probably made his stint there an amiable semi-retirement. He even began to substitute a series—*Noble Decisions,* satirizing asinine court findings—for editorial cartoons, which was a comedown for an effective partisan, especially during a time of moral crisis. In the 1930s, however, his old fire returned, and his cartoons were reminiscent of the outstanding work done for the *Tribune* before World War I.

R.M.

WEG
See Green, William Ellis.

WEISZ, VICTOR (1913-1966) British cartoonist and painter born in Berlin, Germany, on April 25, 1913.

"Vicky is a genius," Randolph Spencer Churchill said in his foreword to *Twists,* a collection of Vicky cartoons from the *Evening Standard.* Part of the genius of "Vicky" (as Victor Weisz always signed himself) was that he was born in Berlin and did not come to Britain until he was 22 years old, yet he was able to so absorb the British way of life and politics that he became the most famous newspaper cartoonist of his period, chosen by Lord Beaverbrook as successor to the mighty but retired David Low.

Victor Weisz, a Hungarian citizen, studied art, but his father died when the boy was 14, and he had to leave school to support his family. His first cartoons were caricatures of current personalities, which he sold to various newspapers in Berlin. With the rise of the Nazi party in 1929, he turned to political cartooning, which necessitated his emigration to England in 1935.

His first regular newspaper cartoon work was for the *News Chronicle:* he joined the staff in 1941. Dissension over one of his cartoons caused him to resign, and he joined the *Daily Mirror.* He added a weekly cartoon to his workload in 1952, for the political journal *New Statesman,* and in 1958 left the *Mirror* for the *Evening Standard,* continuing the Beaverbrook tradition of employing a left-wing cartoonist on a right-wing newspaper. He was a spare-time painter and exhibited at the Lefevre Gallery and the Modern Art Gallery. His view of life was generally somewhat pessimistic (he once said, "I find it difficult to draw a cartoon praising anyone"), and he committed suicide on February 23, 1966.

Books: *Cartoons by Vicky* (1944); *Nine Drawings by Vicky* (1944); *Aftermath* (1946); *Let Cowards Flinch* (1947); *The Editor Regrets* (1947); *Up the Pole* (1950); *How to Be a Celebrity* (1950); *Stabs in the Back* (1952); *Meet the Russians* (1953); *Pilgrim's Progress in Russia* (1959); *Vicky's World* (1959); *Evening Standard Cartoons* (1960); *Twists* (1962); *Home and Abroad* (1964); and *Vicky* (1967).

"—then I would go to the country, before the next wave of inflation, and run on sterling—and start preparing an emergency autumn budget." (N.B. Not being an economist, I speak, of course, purely as an expert.)

Victor Weisz ("Vicky"). © London Evening Standard.

D.G.

WEJP-OLSEN, WERNER (1938-) Danish cartoonist born in Brønshøj, Denmark, on January 7, 1938. Originally educated as a journalist, Wejp-Olsen, whose pen name is "WOW," was bitten by the cartoon bug at an early age. He created his first family humor strip while he was still in grade school. But he had to wait until the ripe age of 17 for his first cartoon sale to a major Copenhagen newspapers—a newspaper that sold a record number of copies the day of WOW's debut in 1955. By the following year WOW was syndicating his cartoons all over the world. Before he was 27 he had launched his first comic strip, *Peter and Bonzo,* a humorous adventure featuring a boy and his dog. He kept this highly successful feature going while he served as comics editor for PIB, one of the largest newspaper syndicates in Europe.

In 1972 WOW decided to work full time as a freelance cartoonist. With Jørgen Sonnergaard, he coedited *Comics,* a most important comics anthology that aroused interest in newspaper comics and the artists who drew them. At the same time, he took over the popular Swedish satire strip *Felix.* By 1975 he had added *Fridolin and Company* to his list of creations. It is a comic strip about teenagers and the pitfalls of the generation gap and appears in Denmark's biggest Sunday newspaper.

Werner Wejp-Olsen ("WOW"). © Wejp-Olsen.

His ideas for cartoons usually reflect a fresh and funny look at today's family. "This subject intrigues me," WOW says, "because there haven't been many that really reflect the big changes in domestic life—changes like working mothers, more independent kids and senior citizens that are often more alert and active than their juniors." His *Granny and Slowpoke* (1975-76), an American strip, dealt with the new family, and his latest effort, the humor strip *Amalita and the Maestro,* debuted in 1978. Since the 1980s he has been devoting much of his time writing and drawing his weekly feature, *Crime Quiz,* distributed by Asterisk Features. He now resides partly in Copenhagen, partly in Massachussetts, constantly shuttling between two continents.

Besides working with the funnies, WOW is extremely industrious as a cartoon supplier to major European newspapers and magazines. His drawings are clean, nice to look at and, most important, always funny.

J.S.

WENZELL, ALBERT (1864-1917) American cartoonist and artist born in Detroit, Michigan, in 1864. Albert Wenzell studied art in Detroit, and later in Munich and Paris. He arrived in New York in 1890 and led a school of high-fashion oil-painting illustrators and cartoonists. He became a fixture in *Life,* where society cartoons were a staple, and distinguished himself from the horde of Gibson imitators—his society cartoons were always paintings, rendered in gray tones.

Wenzell entered the field just as halftone engraving was being perfected. *Life* gave him good exposure, with full- and double-page spreads. The gags were often insipid, sometimes anticlimactic under the ambitious (sometimes overambitious) paintings. His work was frilly, shiny, glittering and, ultimately, tragically superficial. He sought humanity and universal statements among "the 400" while other cartoonists and artists were looking to the streets and hearths.

His serious work did mature, and Wenzell won distinction and prizes at the Pan-American Exposition in Buffalo in 1901 and at the Louisiana Purchase Exposition in St. Louis in 1904; he also executed murals in a classical vein. Wenzell died in Brooklyn, New York, on March 4, 1917. A book of his cartoons, *The Passing Show,* contained many cartoons from *Life.*

R.M.

WEP
See Pidgeon, William Edwin.

WERNER, CHARLES G. (1909-1997) American Pulitzer Prize-winning political cartoonist born in Marshfield, Wisconsin, on March 23, 1909. Chuck Werner attended high school in Oklahoma City and college at Northwestern University in Evanston, Illinois, but never received any art training beyond a correspondence course. His influences were the great political cartoonists of the day, especially Ding Darling and Daniel Fitzpatrick.

Werner began his career in cartooning as an artist-photographer for the *Springfield* (Mo.) *Leader-Press* in 1930. He switched in 1935 to the *Daily Oklahoman,* where he remained until 1941 as chief editorial cartoonist. It was there that he earned a Pulitzer Prize in 1938 for his commentary on the "death" of Czechoslovakia. Werner was the youngest recipient of the Pulitzer to that point.

Before the merger of the *Chicago Sun* and *Times* in 1947, Werner served a seven-year stint as chief cartoonist of the latter. Since 1947 he has been the political cartoonist of the *Indianapolis Star.* He is an independent conservative, and his cartoons forcefully continue in their traditional format; a rough-cut and freewheeling crayon style is his trademark. He retired in 1994 and died at his home in suburban Indianapolis in July 1997.

Werner's other awards include a Sigma Delta Chi in 1943; the National Headliners Award in 1951; National Highway Safety Award of 1970; and nine Freedoms Foundation awards.

R.M.

WESTERMAN, HARRY JAMES (1876-1945) American cartoonist born in Parkersburg, West Virginia, on August 8, 1876. After study at the Columbus, Ohio, Art School, H.J. Westerman joined the art staff of the *Ohio State Journal* in

Charles Werner. © Indianapolis News.

1897. From 1901 on, he cartooned exclusively, appearing in many periodicals besides the *State Journal.* His social and sentimental cartoons were syndicated by McClure, he drew the *Dickenspiel* strip (also written by George V. Hobart and illustrated by Opper and Kemble), and he was a major fixture on *Puck* in the mid-1910s. His books include *A Book of Cartoons* (1902), in which he seemed destined to become another McCutcheon, and *The Young Lady Across the Way* (1913), which continued in *Puck* as an immensely popular series. He died on June 27, 1945.

Westerman's style, when he drew political cartoons and utilized the crayon, could approach the power of a Minor or Boardman Robinson; he was a Democrat. But usually his cartoons were good-natured, dealing with childhood and small-town themes, aiming for a chuckle or a feeling of affinity. He was indeed closer to McCutcheon than to Minor. He drew most often with a pen and lightly shaded his cartoons on coarse paper, and his work was pervaded by a warm good humor.

R.M.

WHITE, CECIL (1900-199?) Australian cartoonist born in Auckland, New Zealand, in 1900. By any standards Cecil ("Unk") White would be included among the best four or five comic draftsmen ever to work in Australian journalism. White, a New Zealander, immigrated to Sydney from Auckiand in the early 1920s to freelance with the *Bulletin, Melbourne Punch, Beckett's Budget* and other publications.

From his earliest work he maintained a deep respect for traditional draftsmanship. After working for a few years in Sydney, he furthered his relentless ambition to draw correctly by studying in Paris, returning to Australia and submitting to the *Bulletin* his domestic and rural humor and his wonderful comic drawings of cows. It was his drawings of animals that brought him a world public in the pages of the London *Tatler,* the *Bystander* and the *Sketch.* When Will Dyson was working in Australia in 1925, he said that Unk White was the most hopeful urchin he had encountered in the Australian nursery.

White's originality with the pen was matched in later years when he developed a most competent facility with the drybrush technique, displaying magnificent freedom, briskness and quality of line and earning a deserved reputation as one of Australia's outstanding black-and-white artists. During World War II, Unk White published three books of his joke cartoons, four children's books, and his *Diggers,* a collection of drawings depicting the Australian soldier. He traveled to New Guinea to draw with the Royal Australian Air Force and went on to Japanese waters with the British navy.

After the war, syndication of foreign material into the Australian press hit local artists hard: syndicated joke drawings, comic strips and political cartoons left little room for the home product. When *Smith's Weekly* ceased publication in 1950, and when the *Bulletin* changed hands and format in 1960, opportunities for Australian artists narrowed to a frightening degree. Unk White did no more cartooning but concentrated on illustrating books, drawing noteworthy buildings in Australian cities. His first was *Sydney Sketch Book.* Unk White died in the early 1990s.

V.L.

"Sorry, sir, but there were no kangaroos about."
Cecil White ("Unk"), 1943. © Sydney Bulletin.

WHITMAN, BERT (1908-1991) American political cartoonist, comic strip and comic book artist born in Brooklyn, New York, on July 27, 1908. Though he had no formal art training, Bert Whitman admired the work of political cartoonist Dorman H. Smith and others and taught himself to draw. At the age of 16, in 1924, Whitman began to work for the *Los Angeles Times.*

A steady succession of editorial and political cartooning jobs followed: he worked for the *Detroit Mirror* (1929-32); the *Detroit News* (1932-36); *Ken* magazine (1936-38); the *Cincinnati Enquirer* (1938); the *New York Post* (1944-48); the *Miami Herald* (1948-52); the *Stockton* (Calif.) *Record* (1952-69); and since 1969 as political cartoonist for the *Phoenix Gazette.* In 1938 he took a seven-year respite to work in comic books, and while on the *Post* he also drew *Debbie Dean,* a comic strip that utilized plots of social significance and commentary.

Whitman has won many honors, foremost among them 20 consecutive Freedoms Foundation awards. The politically conservative cartoonist draws in a simplified style, with loose brushwork and breezy composition leaving his ideas uncluttered. He retired in 1982, and died in 1991.

R.M.

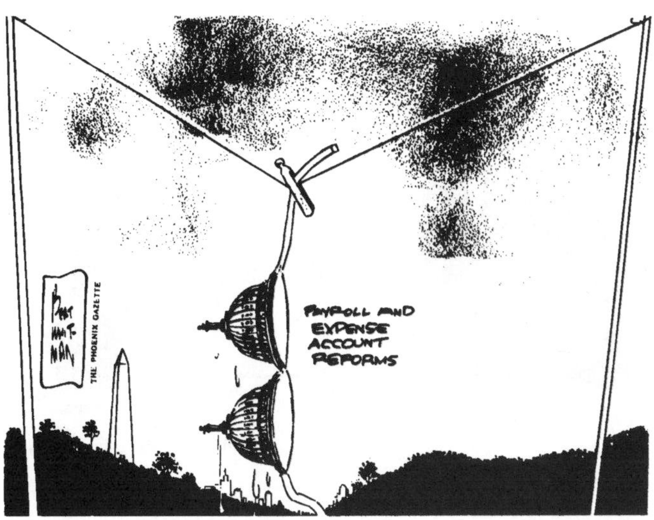

Wash Day
Bert Whitman. © Phoenix Gazette.

WICKS, BEN (1926-) Canadian editorial cartoonist born in London, England, on October 1, 1926. At age 14, Ben Wicks left school and began work. His art training came during this period, when he attended Camberwell School of Art for two weeks. World War II saw Wicks in the army, starting in the infantry and finishing up his service managing a swimming pool. Leaving the army, Wicks began practicing the clarinet in the evenings. After six months, he started his career as a professional musician with several bands, spending a year in Europe entertaining the troops and making numerous trips with a band on the liner Queen *Elizabeth II.* One bandleader decided to fancy up the stand by printing the names of the musicians on cards. He changed the name of his clarinetist to that of another well known clarinetist, and Wicks, whose name was Alfred, became Ben.

In 1957, Wicks and his wife emigrated to Canada. Living in Calgary, Alberta, Wicks held a variety of jobs and finally joined the army as a musician. With afternoons free, he bought a *Writer's Digest,* started drawing and submitted his work to the highest-paying magazine. The *Saturday Evening Post* bought one of his cartoons. Soon he was doing editorial cartoons for the Calgary *Albertan,* and these also appeared in numerous other western papers.

An offer from the Toronto *Telegram* brought Wicks east in 1966. His work was also carried by the Los Angeles Times Syndicate, and Wicks drew 15 cartoons a week—8 for U.S. papers and 7 for Canadian papers, leaving one for each editor to omit. (He has an uncanny knack of anticipating news several days in advance, so when his work is printed it often relates to the headlines of the day.) During this period he also drew a weekly strip, *Captain Squid,* for the *Weekend Magazine,* and a weekly drawing for the London *Observer.* His cartoon work took him to such places as Africa during the Biafra-Nigeria civil war and California during the Sharon Tate murder trials. Since 1975, his work has been syndicated by the Toronto *Sun.*

After regular guest appearances in radio, Wicks became a television personality with a weekly interview show, *World of Wicks,* for Global Television. After five seasons of conversations with people ranging from Ingrid Bergman to Colonel Sanders, his series ended in 1975. In the same year, Wicks began *The Outcasts,* a satirical political comic strip. The New York News Syndicate first spoke to him about doing this type of strip, and it led to a double-identity feature—the leading characters resemble the political leaders of either the United States or Canada, depending on the country in which the strip appears.

In 1976, *Ben Wicks' Canada* was published. The book was an equal balance of photo, cartoon and text material. A satirical look at Canada from a British perspective, it sold fairly well, but some Canadians took offense at some of the material in it. Wicks has written numerous articles that have appeared in various publications. He once said, "I don't think political satire is portrayed brutally enough in North America," and his approach has led to his being the highest-paid Canadian cartoonist. He also feels people take most things in this world much too seriously. He was named to the Order of Canada in 1986.

D.K.

WICKS, RANDY (1954-1996) American cartoonist born October 10, 1954, in Belmond, Iowa. Already a working cartoonist at age 16, Wicks drew editorials for the *Kanawha Reporter* in his native Iowa for three years before attending Iowa State University and then going on to the California Institute of the Arts from which he got a B.F.A. in film graphics in 1980. Upon graduation he became the titular

"Come to think of it, where were you the night of the Watergate incident, Pat?"

Ben Wicks. © Toronto Sun.

Randy Wicks. © The Signal.

cartoonist for the *Newhall Signal* in Valencia, Calif., later also doubling as the paper's art director.

Wicks's cartoons were direct and to the point. Never vicious they could be unsparing in their pungency. One 1987 cartoon showed party girl Donna Rice modeling No Excuses Jeans, while a discomfited Gary Hart appeared with "no excuses, no jeans" in front of potential voters. In addition to presidential hopeful Hart, Presidents Ronald Reagan and George Bush, Surgeon-General Everett Koop, Colonel Oliver North of Iran-Contra fame, and many other politicos and would-be earth-shakers have been pilloried by his merciless pen.

A simple, uncluttered style characterized Wicks's cartoons. As he stated in a 1988 interview, his intention had always been "to become a cartoonist who utilizes one's talents to express opinions on daily controversial subjects—an editorial cartoonist." This he did with a dry wit, a sharp eye for society's foibles, and a sense of humor that helped him keep his perspective (as well as his sanity) during the 16 turbulent years he served on the *Signal,* until his untimely death from a heart attack on August 3, 1996.

M.H.

WIDOW AND HER FRIENDS, A (U.S.) Following his immensely successful series The *Education of Mr. Pipp,* Charles Dana Gibson brought *A Widow and Her Friends* to the pages of *Life; it* was probably second only to the *Pipp* series in popularity and stands as the definitive statement of his idealized version of American womanhood.

The cartoon series, all double-page spreads, debuted on October 4, 1900, and dealt with the emotional adjustments of a fresh—and young, handsome and increasingly assertive—widow. At the beginning of the series she contemplates devoting her life to the church but is dissuaded by friends. She disagrees with her doctor's prognosis, deciding "to die in spite of Dr. Bottles." Soon she is pursued by a variety of admirers, from dashing Gibson Man to paunchy bore to foreign fop. In succeeding weeks she leads the parade of suitors, always, whether riding, hunting or dancing, a step better and a step ahead of the lot. In a surprise ending, the crew sadly observes from a distance that she has finally joined the church after all; garbed in a white habit, she is surrounded by her new admirers, a group of children.

The Widow was the supreme Gibson Girl: impervious, athletic, ravishing, proper, self-willed and superior. Her attitude was fiercely independent but always with the magical touch of winsomeness that only Gibson could provide. In his choice of a widow Gibson found a formula for bypassing the innocence that would have been out of place in this particular worldly heroine. If her demeanor, dress and effect did not truly mirror young American womanhood of the day, the Widow certainly inspired a generation to emulation.

A Widow and Her Friends ran 24 nonconsecutive weeks until July 4, 1901.

R.M.

WIJESOMA, W.R. (19(?) -) The granddaddy among Sri Lanka's 5 political cartoonists, W.R. Wijesoma began his career as a proofreader at the *Times of Ceylon*, in the country's year of independence, 1947. Because of the scarcity of cartoonists slots on the country's few dailies and the embeddedness of veteran artists such as Aubrey Collette and G.S. Fernando, Wijesoma had to ease into a cartooning position very slowly.

In 1953, he drew Sri Lanka's first pocket cartoon, *What a Life*, followed soon after by *Tikiri Tokka* (Tiny Nook), also a pocket cartoon, in the Sinhalese daily *Lankadipa*. Wijesoma also created *Sittarapati* (4 frames, each on a different news item), when the editor of *Lankadipa* requested a regular cartoon.

It was much later in 1968 that he had a solid place on a newspaper, hired by Associated Newspapers as the *Observer* cartoonist. Simultaneously, he contributed political cartoons to the evening *Janatha* and Sunday *Silumina* both in Sinhalese, and a pocket cartoon to the *Daily News*. But in 1973, the government confiscated Associated and Wijesoma found himself unwillingly promoting the government line.

Thus, when Upali Wijewardene invited him to join the newly-established Upali Group in 1981, Wijesoma readily accepted. He has remained at Upali, drawing *The Island*'s daily political cartoon, featuring his common-man character, "Punchi Singho". He has also contributed other cartoon features, including *Jest a Minute* and *Politikka,* to newspapers, and has collected some of his works into a published anthology and at least 9 exhibitions.

Independent in outlook and knowledgeable about a range of topics, Wijesoma has used his cartoons to blast government officials, at the same time, he has enlightened readers with his allusions to East and West classics, religious scriptures, foreign pop music and film, or political philosophies. His cartoons have generated death threats against him, especially during a 1989 insurrection.

J.A.L.

WILKE, RUDOLF (1873-1908) German cartoonist born in Braunschweig, Germany, on October 27, 1873. Brief as his career was, Rudolf Wilke was internationally acclaimed in his lifetime as one of the most powerful talents associated with the Munich satirical magazine *Simplicissimus.* His style was a highly personal blend of the patterned composition of the French Nabis (he had studied at the Académie Julian in Paris in the early 1890s) and a proto-expressionist treatment of the human figure not unlike that of Schiele or Kokoschka.

He turned his attention to the poorer members of society, taking as his spokesman for sanity a sort of philosopher-tramp, and reserving his most pointed barbs for the gymnasium or university professors who saw life in terms of dry scholastic studies and who harped on a return to the "healthier" Germanic primitivism that was preached in some circles (and was later to irritate George Grosz as well). Every type of hypocrite appalled Wilke; one of the pictorial series on which he worked, *Gemütsmenschen* ("Sentimentalists"), laid bare the falseness of many social poses. Another subject that fascinated him was a type of prematurely old child, already dead to the sensory pleasures of existence.

When the Munich art magazine *Jugend* was founded in

Calculation: —"It's a sin and a shame, Mary, that so few people go to church nowadays."—"That's all right, old man. Then our sort will get a bigger share when God distributes his rewards."
Rudolf Wilke, 1900.

1896, Wilke joined its forces, but from 1899 until his untimely death in Braunschweig on November 4, 1908, his work was chiefly for *Simplicissimus.* His influence as a draftsman outlived him, and the eminent German art dealer Paul Cassirer bought the bulk of his estate, putting on a large Wilke exhibition in 1917. Separately published Wilke albums included *Gesindel-Album* ("Rabble Album," 1908) and *Skizzen* ("Sketches," 1909).

Wilke had two artist brothers, the painter and commercial artist Hermann Wilke (born in 1876) and the competent cartoonist Erich Wilke (1879-1936), who worked for *Jugend, Simplicissimus* and *Lustige Blätter.* Rudolf Wilke's daughter, Charlotte Gmelin-Wilke (born in 1906), and his son, Ulfert Wilke (born in 1907), also became painters. As director of the University of Iowa Museum of Art, Ulfert mounted an important centennial show of his father's work in 1973.

SA.

WILKINSON, GILBERT (1891-195-?) British cartoonist and illustrator born in Liverpool, England, in October 1891.

The cartoonist with the most undecipherable signature in the business was Gilbert Wilkinson—yet everyone knew his name. "He makes up for the mystery of his writing with the mastery of his drawing," quipped Percy V. Bradshaw in his chapter on Wilkinson in *They Make Us Smile* (1942). "There is no humorous illustrator of today whose work gives a greater impression of speed and spontaneity." But Bradshaw, an artist himself, was able to point beyond those hasty jags of pen and splats of wash to the years of painstaking draftsmanship that lay concealed beneath them. "He simplifies now with such confidence because he has such sound knowledge of drawing."

As a boy, Gilbert Wilkinson was saved from drowning in the Mersey by his elder sister. The family moved to London, where he was a student at Bolt Court and Camberwell art schools and duly endured a seven-year apprenticeship with a firm of color printers. From 1915 to 1919 he served with the London Scottish as a lance corporal (unpaid) and was then invalided to a military hospital. There he began sending cartoons to the popular pictorial papers of the period: *Passing Show, London Opinion, Punch.* He became the cover artist for *Passing Show* when that paper blossomed into two-tone gravure colors, then made the switch to full color. In this medium he produced a weekly color painting of such superb impressionistic quality and vigor that his name became a household word.

America, where he had published many wash cartoons for *Judge* and *Life* and story illustrations for *Cosmopolitan,* lured him with offers to become cover painter for the *Saturday Evening Post,* but he preferred to stay in London. *Passing Show* became *Illustrated,* and Wilkinson painted on; then a change of policy coinciding with the outbreak of World War II moved him to a newspaper in the same publishing group, Odhams Press. The *Daily Herald* became the platform for his daily gag, *What a War,* which eventually, with peace, became *What a Life.* He died some time in the late 1950s.

Books: *A Christmas Carol* (1930); *What a War* (1942, 1944); and *What a Life* (1946, 1948).

D.G.

WILKINSON, SIGNE (1951?-) Born in Wichita Falls, Texas, in the early 1950s, Signe Wilkinson moved about with her parents before settling in Paoli, Pennsylvania, where she spent her childhood. In 1972, she received a BA in English from a university she does not mention because it was "pretty wretched". Instead, Wilkinson acknowledges a more meaningful enrollment at the Pennsylvania Academy of Fine Arts, beginning in 1976 or 1977.

The 1970s, in Wilkinson's words, were a "mess, a mosaic of jobs, education, and all sorts of things." Shortly after college, she worked as a stringer for the West Chester (PA) *Daily Local News,* where she found out she liked the newsroom atmosphere, and in late 1973, went to Cyprus to help set up a housing project for Turkish Cypriots under wartime conditions. In the latter 1970s, while still enrolled at the Academy of Fine Arts, Wilkinson worked on and off for 4 years at the Academy of Natural Sciences, where she did layout, graphic design, and some exhibition work.

Her cartoon career commenced on a freelance basis in the 1970s at the *Daily Local News,* after which *The Nation, New York Times,* and other publications used her work. For a brief time, she substituted for cartoonists at the

Signe Wilkinson. © Philadelphia Daily News.

Philadelphia Inquirer and *Philadelphia Daily News*, before receiving a position as cartoonist for the *San Jose*, (CA) *Mercury News* in 1982. Three years later, Wilkinson joined the *Philadelphia Daily News* as staff cartoonist, her current position.

Wilkinson's very sharp pen earned her the Pulitzer Prize for editorial cartooning in 1992, the first woman to receive the coveted award, and the dubious title of "attack Quaker," bestowed upon her by a former editor. Syndicated by Cartoonists and Writers Syndicate, Wilkinson nevertheless draws a large proportion of cartoons on Philadelphia politics, as well as non-political subjects. She said the latter are important because "most readers care about them—race, guns, abortion, etc.—and go ballistic over them, and I am interested in these topics too."

J.A.L.

WILLEM
See Holtrop, Bernard Willem.

WILLETTE, ADOLPHE (1857-1926) French cartoonist, decorator, painter and lithographer born in Châlons-sur-Marne, France, on July 31, 1857. After studying at the Ecole des Beaux-Arts in Paris and participating in various art exhibitions, Adolphe Willette embarked on a cartooning career and contributed to most of the important humor magazines, especially to *Le Chat Noir* (from 1881 on), *Le Courier Français* (1885-1908), *Le Triboulet, Le Rire* and *L'Assiette au Beurre* (1901-09). He also founded his own ephemeral journals, *Le Pierrot* (1888-89) and *Le Pied de Nez.* Many of his drawings have been released as albums: *Pauvre Pierrot* ("Poor Pierrot," 1887), *Chansons d'Amour* ("Love Songs," 1898), *Oeuvres Choisies* ("Selected Works," 1901), *Cent Dessins de Willette* ("100 Drawings," 1904) and *Sans Pardon!* ("No Excuse!," 1914-17). He also illustrated his autobiography, *Feu Pierrot! 1857-19 . . ?* ("The Late Pierrot! 1857-19.. ?"), published in 1919.

In addition to publicity posters, Willette painted several Montmartre cafés and dance halls (Pierrots and Colombines dancing on Paris rooftops at Le Chat Noir, and the seven deadly sins at the Fernand Xau mansion) as well as the staff room of the Paris city hall. He also did a set of designs for Gobelins tapestries ("Hello to Paris").

Whereas his political and social drawings (his series on the Boer War, the English repression of the Irish uprising or German atrocities during World War I) are stark and haunting, his Montmartre sketches are full of poetic charm and grace. They present young women who, like Gavarni's pretty *grisettes,* are not shy about showing a little cleavage or a well-turned leg from under lacy petticoats. Their inherent ingenuous sexiness and gentle naïveté made these cartoons (such as the one called "Mimi Pinson, You Will Go to Paradise," in which Mimi is seen kissing a horse harnessed to a cab) extremely popular. Willette's favorite character, however, was definitely Pierrot, the artist and moon lover, who goes from one adventure to another. These cartoons are drawn in the "cinematographic" black-and-white tradition of other

"Look, a drawing by the artist I sentenced yesterday!" (Magazine titles: "The Toilets," "The Underpants" and "The Bowwow.")
Adolphe Willette, 1903.

Chat Noir contributors (e.g., Caran d'Ache and Steinlen) and depict a dreamworld reminiscent of Watteau's.

Adolphe Willette died in Paris on February 4, 1926.

P.H.

WILLIAMS, GLUYAS (1888-1982) American cartoonist born in San Francisco, California, on July 23, 1888. Gluyas Williams attended Harvard University, where he wrote and drew cartoons for the *Harvard Lampoon.* He graduated in 1911 and later studied fine art at Colarosi's in Paris. According to legend it was Williams, as editor of the *Lampoon,* who convinced fledgling cartoonist Robert Benchley to try his hand at writing. A childhood tour of the art capitals of Europe had inclined Williams toward art, and the success of his sister Kate Carew, America's first major female caricaturist, attracted him to cartooning. (Carew drew strips, including *The Angel Child,* and did theatrical caricatures for the *New York World,* which sent her to Europe during World War I to sketch society notables.)

After his Paris studies, Williams served as art editor of the *Youth's Companion* magazine and then joined the staff of the *Boston Transcript* as a cartoonist and caricaturist; he at once attracted national attention with his work, which even then displayed a handsome and severe economy of line. Towards the end of World War I, Williams sold his first work to *Life.* For *Life,* as on the *Lampoon,* he both wrote and drew, although the frequency of his text pieces (mostly the incisive *Senator Sounder* political spoofs) declined in direct proportion to the increased output of another newcomer, Robert Benchley. Williams became a fixture on *Life* magazine, drawing many series and full- and double-page cartoons. His style, marked by sophistication and a distinguished reserve, was slightly reminiscent of Rea Irvin and Caran d'Ache.

When the *New Yorker* was founded in 1925, Williams at first resisted invitations to contribute and remained with *Life.* Later, after Harold Ross rejected a Williams submission because of a lack of physical humor, Williams rejected the rejection, sending it back with a lecture on humor that Ross claimed revolutionized his outlook and molded the *New Yorker* style. Williams drew for both magazines until 1930 and then did his cartoons exclusively for the *New Yorker.* However, he did illustrations for other magazines and for many, many books (by Edward Streeter, Corey Ford and others). For John Wheeler's Bell Syndicate Williams for years produced the daily panel *Suburban Heights,* featuring Fred Perley. Williams's own books include *Fellow Citizens* (1940) and *The Gluyas Williams Gallery* (1957). He died in February 1982.

Seldom in the history of cartooning has there been an artist as much in command of his media as was Gluyas Williams. Technically his pen line was confident, attractive and reproducible, his figures comical but anatomically perfect, his use of perspective unerring. Conceptually his characters were strong, his choice of themes humorous, ironic and critically mature, his moods evocative and familiar. Williams seldom used tones but spotted blacks in seas of white and supple lines. His balanced drawings were often full of dozens of figures and dealt with such subjects as family reunions, vacation resorts, commuter trains, boardrooms, banquets and (in dozens of Benchley books and hundreds of his stories) the harried Little Man.

R.M.

WILLIAMS, RICHARD (1933-) Canadian animator born in Toronto, Ontario, on March 19, 1933. Richard Williams is one of several "sons of the British Empire" who contributed to the mother country's rebirth as an international force in the animation world. His parents were both artistic and encouraged young Dick to draw from the age of two. Despite their divorce when the boy was five, he continued to enjoy art and was inspired to enter animation by his first viewing of *Snow White and the Seven Dwarfs.* At the age of 15 young Williams cashed in his savings and visited the Disney Studios in Burbank, California. He was treated to a tour of the studio and encouraged by Dick Kelsey, who advised him to learn drawing properly before venturing into animation. Accordingly Williams paid his own way through Ontario College of Art by freelancing artwork for advertisers. At the end of his studies, he returned to the Disney Studios, this time as an employee.

"The distinguishing aspect of suburban life is the commuter."
Gluyas Williams.

Richard Williams, credits for "The Charge of the Light Brigade," 1968. © Dick Williams Associates.

Somewhat disillusioned by the Disney methods, Williams spent awhile in Spain before landing in London in 1955. Determined to make his own cartoons, he went to work for George Dunning at TV Cartoons, animating commercials by day and his own film by night. He emerged from three years of Spratt's Top Dog, Guinness stout and Mother's Pride bread with a 30-minute cinemascope cartoon, *The Little Island* (1956). This symbolic, funny story of three characters, Truth, Beauty and Goodness, who should live in harmony and do everything but, was an enormous critical success but failed to break even at the box office. Supported by more commercials, Williams made the shorter, less ambitious but funnier cartoon *Love Me Love Me Love Me* (1962). Narrated by comedian Kenneth Williams, it was the story of loved but unkempt Squidgy Bod and unloved but kempt Thermos Fortitude. This time success was both critical and financial, and Williams was able to open up his own studio, Richard Williams Animation Ltd.

In addition to commercials for Volkswagen, Cresta, Smarties, Yellow Pages and many more, Williams has designed cartoon titles for many feature films, including *What's New Pussycat* (1965), *The Dermis Probe* (1966), *A Funny Thing Happened on the Way to the Forum* (1966), *The Spy with the Cold Nose* (1967), *Casino Royale* (1967), *The Charge of the Light Brigade* (1968) and *The Liquidator* (1968). He made an animated background (*The Apple Tree*) for the live theater and won an Academy Award for his TV special based on the Charles Dickens novel *A Christmas Carol* (1972). This led to his direction of the feature-length *Raggedy Ann* (1977) from Johnny Gruelle's series of children's books, made by the publishers Bobbs-Merrill. True to his own love for "traditional" animation, Williams used veterans Grim Natwick and Tissa David on the film (he had earlier brought Natwick and Art Babbitt to London as teachers for his animation staff).

While Williams's successes have been many, he has perhaps more unrealized projects than any animator in history. *Circus Clowns, I. Vor Pittfalks, Confidence Man* (1965), *Diary of a Madman* (1966), *Nasruddin* (1968) and *The Cobbler and the Thief* have all been started, none completed. The latter, however, did see projector-light in 1995, completed by other hands under the title *Arabian Knight*. His biggest success, however, was his directing of the animated sequences of *Who Framed Roger Rabbit* (1988).

D.G.

WILSON, GAHAN (1930-) American cartoonist born in Evanston, Illinois, on February 18, 1930. Gahan Wilson graduated from the Chicago Art Institute in 1952 and settled into a cartooning career after what he describes as "a brief stretch as an airman."

Wilson's weird cartoons depict the strange doings of no less strange creatures with green skin, bulging eyes and hypertrophied heads. Though not to everyone's liking, they have won him a devoted coterie of fans. Published mainly in *Playboy*, his cartoons have been anthologized in a number of collections, including *Gahan Wilson's Graveyard Manner* (1965) and *The Man in the Cannibal Pot* (1967). Wilson has also written a number of fantasy and science fiction stories, and he does a review column for *Fantasy and Science Fiction* magazine.

In addition to drawing the trademark cartoons for which he has become justly famous, Wilson has also made several forays into the world of comics. From the late 1970s to the mid-1980s he drew *Nuts*, an unromanticized comic strip about a small child facing the hostile world around him, for the *National Lampoon*. In 1990-91 he adapted two anthologies of Edgar Allan Poe stories and poems for the Classics Illustrated comic-book series; and he also was a contributor to *The Big Book of Freaks*, published by Paradox Press in 1996. As he explained to an interviewer for *Publishers Weekly*, "I've always had an innocent affection for the ghostly and the macabre."

M.H.

WILSON, ROWLAND BRAGG (1930-) American magazine gag cartoonist and animator born in Dallas, Texas, on August 3, 1930. Rowland B. Wilson grew up in Dallas and began cartooning and drawing in high school. He attended the University of Texas in Austin for four years, earning a degree in fine arts in 1952. Work toward a master of fine arts degree followed at Columbia University in New York City. He did most of the course work but never completed his masters project painting.

In graduate school, Wilson supported himself doing gag cartoons for the *Saturday Evening Post, Collier's, Look* and *True* magazines, to mention a few. Drafted by the U.S. Army, he served from December 1954 to December 1956, drawing classified charts. "I worked a lot in the service

Cossacks riding over the hill to meet the train.
Rowland Wilson, "Trans-Siberian Express." © Pushkin Vodka.

with a Leroy lettering set, and it was really 1957 before I got myself together with my own art. I took a couple of months and created a portfolio. In doing it I arrived at animation as the thing I was really interested in," remembers Wilson.

With his portfolio, Wilson joined Young and Rubicam advertising agency in 1957. He did conceptual drawings for print ads. During this same time he was also freelancing magazine gag cartoons; his full-page color cartoons in *Esquire* began appearing about 1958. They were later published as an anthology entitled *Don't Fire Until You See the Whites of Their Eyes.* The book jacket illustration showed the British troops charging up Bunker Hill with dark glasses on. In the late 1950s and early 1960s he was published in the *New Yorker*.

Frustrated at Young and Rubicam because he did no finished pieces of art on his own designs, Wilson quit his job as an art director and went freelance in 1964. The ad work was demanding enough that he could no longer submit cartoons regularly to many different magazines. As *Esquire* phased out full-page cartoons, Wilson began selling full-page color cartoons to *Playboy* about 1966. In 1967 he did a syndicated strip for the New York News-Chicago Tribune Syndicate entitled *Noon.* "The name of the main character was Noon Ringle, an unemployed cowboy in a dying small Texas town in sort of modern times," Wilson remembers. The strip was syndicated for only six months. This experience helped Wilson decide to go into animation at last.

By 1968 he was designing animated films on a freelance basis. "The ad agencies literally forced the animation studios to start letting outside designers like myself do some work," he says. Also about this time he was contacted by an ad agency to begin his now-famous full-color, full-page ads for national magazines. ("What's my life insurance company? New England Life, of course.") Over 40 of these ads have been published nationally.

From 1973 to 1975, Wilson worked in London, England, at the animation studio of Richard Williams. Upon his return to New York City he freelanced and then joined Phil Kimmelman and Associates, an animation studio doing mostly advertising work. Wilson's animated film *The Trans-Siberian Express* won a first prize at the Third International Animation Festival in 1975. He still contributes cartoons to *Playboy*. In the 1980s he moved to California, where he has been working mostly in animation, especially for the Disney studio.

Rowland B. Wilson considers cartooning to be "picture writing." To him the design is the real fun of cartooning, and this shows in his *Playboy* and New England Life Insurance work. His style stresses three-dimensionality, using color not just to be decorative but to help define the spatial relationships in the cartoon. "I look at drawing as a series of contrasts between straight and curved lines plus light and dark areas," he says. True to this concept, his drawings all have an element of tension in them.

B.C.

WINNIE THE POOH (G.B.) "Here is Edward Bear, coming downstairs now, bump, bump, bump, on the back of his head, behind Christopher Robin." And so, on October 14, 1926, the children of Great Britain were introduced to an endearing and enduring character, "a bear of little brain."

"Winnie the Pooh and the Honey Tree." © *Walt Disney Productions.*

Winnie-the-Pooh (originally never appearing without his hyphens) was created by *Punch* contributor and popular poet A.A. (Alan Alexander) Milne (1882-1956), based on the battered teddy bear belonging to his own son, the original Christopher Robin. Edward Bear's change of name came when the child was taken to the London Zoo to see an American black bear named Winnie. He conjoined the new name to Pooh, the name of a swan he had met, and rechristened the stuffed doll (purchased from Harrod's store as a first-year birthday present) "Winnie-*ther*-Pooh." Pooh, as he was called for short (which he was), lived in a house in a forest under the name of Sanders (literally "under"!), and went on many an adventure with his chums Piglet, Rabbit (and his friends and relations), Eeyore (a donkey with a loose tail), Kanga and Roo, Owl and Tigger—all of whom were based on toys belonging to Milne's young son.

Delightful and funny as Milne's prose and verse are, life was given to Pooh and pals by the lovely line (and later color) of Ernest H. Shepard (1879-1976). His delicate but delightful sketches illumine the adventures and are as tightly linked with Pooh-Bear as are Tenniel's with Alice. Shepard, son of an architect, began cartooning for *Punch* in 1907. He is also renowned for his illustrations for Kenneth Grahame's classic children's book, *The Wind in the Willows.*

It was Shepard's depiction of Pooh that Walt Disney used as inspiration for his series of three animated cartoon productions: *Winnie the Pooh and the Honey Tree* (1965, director Wolfgang Reitherman), *Winnie the Pooh and the Blustery Day* (1968, director Reitherman), and *Winnie the Pooh and Tigger Too* (1974, director John Lounsbery). The second cartoon won an Academy Award. Pooh's voice was that of Sterling Holloway.

Books: *Winnie the Pooh* (1926); *The House at Pooh Corner* (1928); *The Christopher Robin Birthday Book* (1930); *The World of Pooh* (1958); *The Pooh Story Book* (1967); and *The Pooh Painting Book* (1968).

D.G.

WINNIE THE POOH (U.S.) Having abandoned production of most of its shorts, the Disney Studio in the 1960's concentrated instead on making a number of medium-length cartoons (called "featurettes") in order to hone the skills of their younger animators before they went on to work on full-length features. Such a featurette was *Winnie the Pooh and the Honey Tree* based on A.A. Milne's classic children's stories, which was released in 1966.

Many of the familiar characters appeared in this adaptation: Winnie the gluttonous bear, his donkey friend Eeyore, Roo the kangaroo, as well as Piglet, Rabbit and Owl, not to forget their human child companion, Christopher Robin. The film was a success, helped in no small measure by Wolfgang Reitherman's snappy direction. Reitherman also directed the next Winnie cartoon, *Winnie the Pooh and the Blustery Day* (1968). With the addition of the bouncy Tigger (who was absent in the first outing) it proved to be an even bigger hit, and even won an Academy Award. A third Winnie cartoon, *Winnie the Pooh and Tigger Too,* directed by John Lounsbery, came out in 1974. (These three films were later compiled into a theatrical feature, *The Many Adventures of Winnie the Pooh,* released in 1977.)

To date *Winnie the Pooh and a Day for Eeyore* (1983), directed by Rick Reinert, is the last film in the cycle to hit the movie screens. The roly-poly bear continued his cartoon adventures on television, however. *The New Adventures of Winnie the Pooh* was broadcast on the Disney Channel and later on ABC, from 1988 to 1992, and won an Emmy; and in-between there was *Winnie the Pooh and Christmas too,* a TV special that aired on ABC in 1991. Winnie the Pooh also starred in comic books and in a newspaper strip that lasted from 1978 through the 1980's.

M.H.

WIRGMAN, CHARLES (1833-1891) English journalist, artist and cartoonist born in England in 1833. Charles Wirgman spent the last 30 years of his life in Yokohama, Japan, working as a foreign correspondent for the *London Illustrated News. He* was one of the founding fathers of the modern Japanese cartoon. The significance of Wirgman's contribution lies in the nature of the man himself: Wirgman was foreign, spoke English and was involved in the political affairs of the day. Japan was undergoing rapid modernization and was thirsting for foreign knowledge and insight. Wirgman's cartoons were exotic and timely enough to arouse great interest among progressive Japanese.

Wirgman spent his early years as a military man, but after his discharge he became a journalist and was sent to Yokohama in 1857 to report on Japan's reentry into world affairs. The same year, Wirgman began publishing *Japan Punch,* a British-style humor magazine that made fun of the Western governments and capitalists who were rushing to Japan to gain political influence and profit. *Japan Punch* was a monthly periodical written in English and distributed only among the English-speaking foreign residents in the Yokohama area. In fact, its original circulation was only 200. But the magazine achieved instant popularity among the Japanese as well and became the model for numerous other Japanese humor magazines: *Nipponchi* (1874), *Marumaru Chinbun* (1877) and *Tokyo Puck* (1905).

Wirgman's life was filled with the kinds of experiences that made Meiji Japan (1868-1912) a period of tremendous social change. Soon after his arrival in Yokohama, he witnessed a bloody attack on the British legation by disgruntled samurai. His watercolor painting of the scene is now an important cultural treasure in Japan *(Night Attack in the Eastern Zen Temple,* 1861). He also drew such historic scenes as the murder of the English consul, Baldwin Byrd, and the execution of his murderer, and he witnessed the Meiji emperor's coronation ceremony in Edo in 1868. As a journalist, Wirgman found himself in the middle of most of the major political events in Meiji Japan. His illustrations of these events, which appeared in *Japan Punch* as political and satirical cartoons, served as models for a new generation of Japanese cartoonists. Among the many Japanese artists and illustrators who trained under Wirgman were Goseda Hōryū (1827-1892), who studied Western-style painting, and Kiyochika Kobayashi (1847-1915), who became one of the major cartoonists of modern Japan.

Wirgman married a Japanese woman and adopted a Japanese name, Wakuman. He had one son, whom he named Ichirō. He died on February 8, 1891, and was buried in the Yamate Cemetery for Foreigners. The inscription on the headstone reads (in Japanese) "In memory of Charles Wirgman. . . . a fellow of infinite jest."

J.C.

WITZ, IGNACY (1919-1971) Polish cartoonist and illustrator born in Lvov (then in Poland, now part of the Soviet Union) on March 20, 1919. Ignacy Witz attended the State Institute of Art in Lvov, graduating in 1939. He began to freelance cartoons to various Polish periodicals as early as 1937, and in 1938 he designed his first posters.

During World War II Witz served in the Russian and Polish armies. He resumed his career in 1944 and soon established himself as one of Poland's foremost cartoonists, with contributions to many Polish and foreign periodicals; he also began a long and distinguished career as a book illustrator (over the years he illustrated more than one hundred books). In 1951 he became a lecturer in graphic art at the Warsaw Academy. Many of Witz's cartoons were collected in book form, and he had no fewer than 26 one-man shows in Poland and 15 abroad (in Prague, Sofia, Budapest, Berlin, London and Vienna, among other places). He won many prizes, including the 1957 Polish-Soviet Friendship Society Prize. Witz died in Warsaw on July 7, 1971.

Witz's style was much in the tradition of German expressionism, and he made his points in his drawings rather than in their captions. His humor remained rather wooden and was not on a par with his excellent draftsmanship.

M.H.

WOLF, FRITZ (1918-) German cartoonist born at Mühlheim in the Ruhr district of Germany in 1918. Fritz Wolf (whose early pseudonym was "Lupus") studied at the Folkwang Art School in Essen. In 1949 he began doing commercial art for the *Neue Tagespost* in Osnabrück and moved into the political cartoonist's chair on that same paper in 1954. During the later 1950s and the 1960s his horizon expanded, and his work was seen in the *Allgemeine Sonntagszeitung,* in the *Bremer Nachrichten* (Bremen), *Der Mittag* (Düsseldorf), *Die Welt* (Hamburg) and the *Kölner Stadt-Anzeiger* (Cologne).

Wolf is represented in such important collections of political cartoons as the two omnibus anti-Adenauer albums *Konrad Sprach die Frau Mama* ("'Konrad,' Said Mother," 1955) and *Konrad Bleibst du Jetzt zu Haus?* ("Konrad, Are You Going to Stay Home Now?," 1963). In 1965 he did a solo flight on the subject of the controversial and seemingly perpetual chancellor, with the title *Adenauer: ~~M~~Sein Leben* ("Adenauer: ~~My~~His Life"). Here pictures add a sarcastic comment on the running first-person captions, which summarize Adenauer's career as he would have told it himself—if he had been his own worst enemy.

In 1966 Wolf extended his scope to include the two highest-ranking Germans of the moment, Chancellor Erhard and President Lübke. Together with Erhard Kortmann, who assembled the embarrassing and ludicrous captions from actual speeches and interviews of these statesmen, Wolf produced *Ich der Kanzler: Professor Erhards Barockes Poesiealbum* ("I the Chancellor: Professor Erhard's Baroque Poetry Album") and *Sauerland Bleibt Sauerland: Heinrich Lübkes Goldiger Zitatenschatz* ("Sauerland Will Always Be Sauerland: Heinrich Lübke's Gilt Treasury of Quotations"—Sauerland being a geographical designation of South Westphalia). These are genuinely hilarious books, Wolf's cartoons putting just the right "wrong" interpretation on the already incredible pronouncements of the mighty. He has received many awards and his work has been featured in a number of exhibitions. One of his regular features, *Cartoons from the Provinces,* which is published in the magazine *Stern,* has well over seven thousand entries by now.

Wolf works in a pleasantly loose and comfortable pen style (at an earlier stage it was somewhat scratchier) that makes good use of solid black areas where an accent is required.

S.A.

WONG KEE-KWAN (1955-) Born in Hong Kong, Wong Kee-Kwan, known professionally as Zunzi, studied arts at the crown colony's Chinese University from 1974-1978, a transitional period in China politics that sparked much intellectual ferment on campus. Zunzi credited this period with developing some of the fearless ideas he puts in his cartoons. After graduation, he worked briefly as a print journalist, teaming with friends to bring out two short-lived political magazines, and as a secondary school teacher. In 1980, he became a political cartoonist at *Ming Pao Daily News,* where he has remained.

Considered Hong Kong's best known political cartoonist, Zunzi submits biting cartoons on Hong Kong internal politics and broader China affairs to mainly Chinese-language newspapers and magazines. His publication credits include *Next Magazine, Economic Times, Hong Kong Economic Journal, Pai Shing,* and *Asiaweek.* He is respected by Hong Kong readers for his courage, outspokenness, and political savvy; Zunzi characters say what many Hong Kong people think but dare not speak. Among his major topics have been the 1997 return of Hong Kong to China, about which he drew more than 2,000 cartoons, Deng Xiaoping, and China's human rights and corruption problems. Zunzi's cartoons also benefit from his deep commitment to research; to prepare for some cartoons, he supplements his reading with interviews of common people on the topics featured. That research interest is also reflected in his study of the history of cartooning.

To achieve his primary aim of conveying important political and social messages, Zunzi relies on simple line drawings and witty dialogues in lively cartoons that have been said to have a movie-like feel to them.

J.A.L.

WOOD, JAMES ARTHUR, JR. (1927-) American cartoonist born in Miami, Florida, on June 6, 1927. Art Wood moved to Washington, D.C., at an early age. He served with the navy in World War II, becoming a staff cartoonist on *All Hands* magazine and *SEA,* the service syndicate. After the war he attended Washington and Lee University (where his roommate was John Warner, later a U.S. senator), graduating in 1950. Wood immediately secured a cartooning job with the *Richmond Times-Dispatch.* He remained there until 1956 and then moved to the *Pittsburgh Press,* leaving in 1963. Since then, although he still freelances occasionally to other outlets, he has been director of information for the U.S. Independent Telephone Association. In this capacity he handles public relations, edits publications and draws cartoons for a variety of functions.

"I'm speaking for the consumer."
Art Wood. © Wood.

Wood's drawing style is reminiscent of Seibel, Hungerford and Herblock but is distinctive and full of animation. He streamlines the labels and complicated symbols out of his cartoons and draws with crisp brushstrokes and crayon shading. The conservative-leaning cartoonist also owns one of the largest collections of original cartoon art in the world. In 1995 he finally realized his dream of a permanent home for his collections, when the National Gallery of Caricature and Cartoon Art opened its doors in Washington, D.C., with himself at the helm.

R.M.

WOOD, STARR (1870-1944) A popular joke cartoonist of the early 20th century, Starr Wood, who usually signed his work "The Snark", was looking quite old-fashioned by the late Twenties and early Thirties, although he still remained a quite prolific contributor to certain magazines and weeklies. One paper which used him a lot was *The Winning Post*, a sporting weekly, and for many years *The Winning Post Annual*, published every Christmas, featured his cartoons throughout. This became *Starr Wood's Annual*, and featured his artwork even more - he was the editor, of course.

Starr Wood was born in London on February 1, 1870, and was privately educated. His first employment was as an apprentice to a Chartered Accountant when he was 17, but his hobby interest of sketching soon began to dominate his life, and in 1890 he began a full-time freelance career as a cartoonist and black-and-white illustrator. Speedily successful, he soon would found his own magazine, a quarterly illustrated that ran from 1898 to 1900. Later came *Starr Wood's Magazine* (1910), and eventually his own Annual.

Wood contributed to most of the popular magazines of his period, beginning with *Puck* in 1890, and following with *Fun* (1892), *The Sketch* (1893), *Judy* (1895), *Pick-Me-Up* (1895), *The Idler* (1896), *Chums*, a boys' story weekly (1896), *Parade* (1897), *The English Illustrated Magazine* (1898), and the famous *Punch*, from 1900 to 1914, after which he seemed to concentrate on sporting jokes. However, his pictures of "bright young things," the girls of the Twenties, were very popular. He died at his home in Hertfordshire in 1944, and is one of the most forgotten cartoonists today.

D.G.

WOODBRIDGE, GEORGE CHARLES (1930-) American cartoonist and illustrator born in Flushing, New York, on October 3, 1930. George Woodbridge grew up in the Bayside area of Queens, New York. At the time this New York City borough was quite rural, and he worked on farms as a part-time job.

He graduated from Newtown High School in 1948, after taking as many art courses as possible in school. The following year he entered the U.S. Army. Although he was technically an infantryman, Woodbridge's cartooning often brought him special assignments doing illustration. A number of his cartoons were published in the *Army Times*, a civilian-owned weekly tabloid with worldwide circulation.

After being discharged from the army in 1952, he used the GI bill to study illustration at the School of Visual Arts until 1956. Woodbridge had not read comics as a child. Instead his heroes were the great illustrators: Howard Pyle, Frederick Remington and N.C. Wyeth. However, many of his friends at the School of Visual Arts were avid comic strip and book fans. One friend from these days is Nick Meglin, now an associate editor at *MAD* magazine. In the 1950s, Meglin suggested that Woodbridge submit work to *MAD*, and soon he was a regular contributing cartoonist. Now, after four decades, he is still a proud member of "the usual gang of idiots" (as they term themselves) at the magazine.

"I've never considered myself a cartoonist," says George Woodbridge. "I think I'm too realistic. The stuff I do is more humorous illustration. The more it relates to history, the more effective it is." Recognizing his special talent for parodying historical periods in cartoons resplendent with accurate costumes and detail, *MAD*'s editors often use his art for pieces such as "A *MAD* History of Medicine." His distinct style of humorous costumed characters is sometimes similar in mood to slightly jazzed-up military uniform and costume prints. Working in line and wash, Woodbridge gives historical drawing a verve and vigor rarely found in parodies. He has illustrated two original *MAD* paperback books, *MAD's Cradle to Grave Primer* (1973) and *MAD'S Guide to Leisure Time* (1976). He has also illustrated the first volume of a planned six-volume series of *American Military Equipment* by Col. Frederick P. Todd, one of America's leading military historians in the field of uniforms and equipment.

During the United States Bicentennial celebration, George Woodbridge served in the Corps of Light Infantry of the Brigade of the American Revolution. The brigade was a group that authentically recreated military units of the American Revolutionary War and restaged important battles. As president of the brigade from 1973 to 1977, Woodbridge was in effect its commander during the Bicentennial celebration. This is hardly the sort of thing one would suspect of a *MAD* cartoonist, but it points out the strength of the magazine, based on the diverse interests of its nucleus of freelance artists.

B.C.

WOODMAN, BILL (1936-) American cartoonist born in Bangor, Maine, on October 30, 1936. Finishing high school in his hometown in 1954, Bill Woodman enlisted in the U.S. Navy and served until 1957. Upon leaving the service, he attended the Phoenix School of Design. He then moved back east and settled in New York City, there to complete his art training with "one course at Pratt and a couple of courses at Visual Arts."

That Woodman is a man with his own way of doing things is apparent not only from his cheerfully admitted lack of formal training but also from the manner in which he broke into the field. As he reports of his first sale, "I had to take the publication to small claims court to get paid." Still, his learn-by-example technique eventually paid off. By the early 1960s he was selling regularly to men's magazines like *Dude, Gent* and *Cavalier,* as well as to more sophisticated outlets like the *Saturday Review, Writer's Digest* and the *New York Times.* The 1970s has found his work appearing in the most prestigious showcases—the *New Yorker, Playboy, National Lampoon* and *Esquire.* Despite a fire that destroyed his studio and his files in the 1980s, Woodman has remained a steady and entertaining purveyor of cartoon humor to this day. He has also written and/or illustrated a number of children's books throughout the 1980s and 1990s.

Of course, the most convincing evidence of Woodman's individuality is his work. Like the very best cartoons of his older colleagues—Koren, Price and Addams—a Woodman drawing is immediately identifiable. His humor is informed by a gentle irony, and his uniquely rude, deliberately naive, minimally detailed style is perfectly suited to the task of making that humor visual—down to the highly idiosyncratic signature he affixes to each piece. His world is that of a laughing Kafka, an upside-dawn place where alarm clocks with painfully sincere faces sing "Oh, what a beautiful morning" to bedfast grumps, where benevolent-looking bears with "just doing my job" expressions protect the creatures of the wood by waylaying hunters and rendering them *hors de combat* as they emerge from a lodge hosting the annual Hunters' Breakfast. In fact, a recurrent theme in Woodman's work—perhaps deriving from his north-woods boyhood—is the war between men and animals (and fish), a conflict in which he is firmly and happily on the side of the animals. Somehow, it is also characteristic of Woodman that he is willing to endorse his favorite medium by its commercial name—the Pentel Rolling Writer. "I like the Zen in them," he reports.

As might be expected, Woodman belongs to no professional organization and isn't really sure whether his work has ever been shown in an exhibition or requested for a permanent collection. On his chosen métier: "I'd say that cartooning is fun to do; I suppose it's work, but I have problems defining work." One is tempted to hope that Bill Woodman never solves this particular problem.

R.C.

WOODY WOODPECKER (U.S.) Woody Woodpecker made his first appearance as a supporting character in an *Andy Panda* cartoon. The redheaded, shrill-voiced bird with the cackling laugh received star status in 1941 and rapidly became the best known and the most popular of Walter Lantz's animated creations.

Unlike Bugs Bunny, who had to be provoked into retaliation, Woody was a pesky creature who could be moved to wild outbursts of aggression and mayhem without the slightest excuse. Using his bill as an attack weapon, he would swoop dawn on dumbfounded car attendants, slow-moving bank clerks and the citizenry at large just because they stood in the way of a free meal or a quiet snooze. Two good examples of Woody's manic behavior are "The Reckless Driver" (wherein the woodpecker wrecks a test examiner's offices simply because he is refused a driver's license) and "Dippy Diplomat" (in which Woody not only pilfers the meal prepared for a visiting diplomat by his hapless adversary, Wally Walrus, but heaps untold indignities upon his victim to boot).

Woody's most resourceful enemy was Buzz Buzzard, the all-purpose crook who, no matter what villainous role

"Woody Woodpecker." © Walt Lantz.

he happened to be playing—pirate captain, highway robber, shyster lawyer—always ended up being foiled by the feisty woodpecker. Gabby Gator, the Florida alligator forever trying to lure Woody to his lair as a meal, fared no better. A latecomer to Woody's lengthening roster of foes was Professor Dingledong, who appeared variously in the guise of a taxidermist ("How to Stuff a Woodpecker"), a rocket engineer ("Round Trip to Mars") and a clockmaker ("Calling All Cuckoos"). Late in his career Woody acquired a nephew, Knothead, and a niece, Splinter, to whom he often spun tales of the Woodpecker forebears ("Three Little Woodpeckers," a retelling of the famous "Three Little Pigs" tale, is perhaps the most notable of these later cartoons).

Woody's high-pitched laugh (supplied by Lantz's wife, actress Grace Stafford) was his trademark, and it found its way into the "Woody Woodpecker Song," which enjoyed great success in the late 1940s. The *Woody Woodpecker* series continued to be turned out by Walter Lantz, although at a diminishing rate and with diminishing humor, up to 1973, when the studio closed down. The *Woody Woodpecker* cartoons—directed most notably by Jack Hannah, Paul J. Smith, and Sid Marcus, and released through Universal—have been revived on the televised *Woody Woodpecker Show.* There have also been countless *Woody Woodpecker* comic books published since 1947 by Dell, and later by Gold Key.

M.H.

WOOLF, MICHAEL ANGELO (1837-1899) American cartoonist born in London, England, on August 27, 1837. Michael Angelo's father, Edward Woolf, was a talented musician and artist who brought his family to America shortly after his son's birth. The younger Woolf quickly evidenced a talent for drawing and at a young age became an illustrator, contributing woodcuts to the popular monthlies. For some years before the Civil War he turned aside from the drawing board and became an actor.

After the war Woolf returned to illustration and cartooning and was soon one of the most published of such artists. He was an early staffer on the *New York Graphic,* but feeling the need for formal training, he went to Paris and received regular art instruction under Edouard Frère. Upon his return to America, Woolf painted in oils and even exhibited a canvas *(How It Happened)* at the National Academy. But he turned most of his attention to cartooning and sold to *Puck* and its lesser imitations before securing a regular berth on *Life* immediately after its inception in 1883; he also appeared frequently in *Judge* until the time of his death.

Mike Woolf was the American cartoonist who pioneered the social cartoon—not in the sense of dwelling on society's fads and fancies, as many of his contemporaries did, but by depicting social problems, the life of the tenements, the uncomfortable scenes of drunken fathers and shoeless children. Throughout the early part of his career the cartoons were purely humorous, mocking the pretensions of gutter kids and laughing at the eternal forbearance of immigrant wives. But later the pathetic themes entered: Woolf aimed for the conscience as surely as for the funny bone.

Only rarely did Woolf editorialize outright—such as when Father Knickerbocker chides those who combined to contribute fifty thousand dollars to the starving of Armenia when wretched conditions prevailed in New York's Mulberry Bend. Perhaps his most effective comment was the dialogue-free "Empty Stocking"—a neglected, raggedy waif crying on Christmas night in an empty tenement room. Not only did Woolf foreshadow an army of cartoonists in the following decades who dealt with social problems, but he was clearly the first popular graphic artist to pioneer the themes being explored by the naturalists of literature like Howells and Crane. Where Riis went with a camera, Woolf had been with a pen.

OUR NATIONAL BIRD AS IT APPEARED WHEN HANDED TO JAMES BUCHANAN MARCH 4 1857
THE IDENTICAL BIRD AS IT APPEARED A.D. 1861.

Michael Angelo Woolf, 1861.

Needless to say, he also led the way—though not always in treatment—for creations such as *The Yellow Kid.* Woolf's art should be noted as carefully as his thematic preoccupations. Even in woodblock days his work was delicate and wispy. His shading consisted of thin parallel lines, with an infrequent reliance on crosshatching. Children were obviously his favorite subject, and they were always portrayed sympathetically. Later in his career his pen line became firmer but just as light. His drawings were powerful statements delivered in fragile packages.

Woolf was a favorite with fellow cartoonists and was widely mourned after his death of heart disease at the Brooklyn home of his sister on March 4, 1899. He was a giant who is unjustly forgotten today and deserves recognition. A collection of cartoons, *Sketches of Lowly Life in a Great City,* was published posthumously by Putnam's in 1899.

R.M.

Barsqualdi's Statue: Liberty frightening the world.
Bedbugs Island, N.Y. Harbor (only authorized edition).

Thomas Worth, 1884.

WORTH, THOMAS (1834-1917) American cartoonist born in New York City in 1834. Thomas Worth is a fascinating figure in the history of American cartooning, an artist who was in on the birth of several important media and genres—and not just by chance. His considerable talents make him worthy of study for more than being in the right place at the right time.

Worth was an art student at the Wells studio in New

York. He later became the most prominent of Currier and Ives's humorous artists in the period of that lithographic firm's greatest popularity. He designed hundreds of prints (always letting lithographers transfer them to stone), many of which hung in windows, shops, saloons, hotels and parlors. His most popular series was *Darktown*, chronicling the deeds and misadventures of minstrellike black folk. His farcical riding subjects were also collected. In the early 1870s Worth was the first major cartoonist to contribute regularly to the *New York Graphic*, America's first illustrated daily paper. A decade later he was a mainstay of the new *Judge* magazine (he also drew for *Truth*, another rival of *Puck*, a few years later). And in the late 1890s he was one of the first artists to draw cartoons for William Randolph Hearst's *American Humorist* newspaper comic supplement. He later drew for other papers and dabbled in the strip genre.

Thomas Worth thus pioneered in many areas of cartooning, excelling at every turn. He did not shy from difficult subjects. He seemed compelled to draw scenes crowded with people and animals, all in colorful, bustling action. He died in 1917 and deserves more recognition today.

R.M.

WORTMAN, DENYS (1887-1958) American cartoonist born in Saugerties-on-Hudson, New York, on May 1, 1887. Denys Wortman was educated at the Blair Academy from 1903 to 1904, and at Stevens Institute of Technology from 1904 to 1905; familial pressures directed the youngster toward a career in engineering. He studied at Rutgers the next two years before he decided to follow his own inclinations and enter art school. He studied at the New York School of Fine and Applied Art until 1909.

"We gotta get busy. Summer's nearly over and we ain't put in our supply of boy friends for all winter."

Denys Wortman, 1935. © United Feature Syndicate.

More study and freelance drawing occupied much of the next ten years, until Wortman landed a position on the art staff of the *New York Tribune*, assigned to do feature illustrations. In 1924 he joined the *World*—it was in its glory days then—and continued to draw for the *World* and for the reorganized *World-Telegram and Sun* until his retirement in 1954. At first on the *World*, then for the *New Yorker*, *Collier's* and the *Saturday Evening Post*, Wortman did illustrations of a general nature, but he hit his stride when he inherited the *World*'s long-running standby, *Metropolitan Movies* (it had been done by Gene Carr, Paul Rehse and Rollin Kirby, among others).

Wortman elevated the panel cartoon to its highest plane. With his grease crayons and genius, he assumed a place next to Daumier, Goya and Hogarth as cartoonist-social commentator. Wortman, however, never had a cause or grudge. Everyday life was his theme, and much of his genius lies in the modesty of his approach. His most popular recurring characters, interestingly enough, were tramps. Not only did the character types intrigue him as a cartoonist with a six-day-a-week deadline, but the free spirit and visual possibilities of locales and figures delighted him. Thus Mopey Dick and the Duke were born.

"I prefer to draw my man in an old suit of clothes," he once wrote, "because not only do his patches allow me to make almost any number and variety of lines I choose at the most important places, but all the rest of his suit has become a very part of him. On the other hand, a new suit of clothes demonstrates only the tailor's art, and the creases that are in it, and the wrinkles that are not, are designed specifically to make the man look like something he is not."

His panel was syndicated by United Feature as *Everyday Movies;* it garnered enough respect to be collected in its entirety by the Metropolitan Museum of Art and the New York Public Library. Wortman was also elected to the National Academy. As a painter, he was exhibited in the Armory Show, the National Academy and the Society of Illustrators, where he served as president for two years beginning in 1936. Wortman also painted a scene of Washington's inaugural journey that hangs in the New Britain, Connecticut, Museum of Art. He himself portrayed Washington in a reenactment of the journey over several states in the 1930s.

His ink-and-crayon drawings—crowded, loose, sympathetic—are masterpieces of observation and execution. He deserves a major reprinting of most of his work. Wortman died on Martha's Vineyard, Massachusetts, on September 20, 1958.

R.M.

WOW
See Wejp-Olsen, Werner.

WRIGHT, DONALD (1934-) American artist born in Los Angeles, California, on January 23, 1934. Don Wright moved with his family to Florida as a young boy and "fell into cartooning." Seeking to follow the path trod by many

Don Wright. © Miami News.

earlier greats, he took a job as copyboy; but the *Miami News* never let the teenager graduate to the art staff because of the prospect of his being drafted. He became a photographer instead, one of the *News*'s best, and was eventually drafted in 1957. In December 1958 Wright left the service and returned to the *News* as picture editor—a fitting piece of justice for the art department. Matters were further set straight when Wright resigned a short time later and the *News*, pleading for his services, offered to run some Wright cartoons. By 1963 Wright had transformed one or two editorial cartoons a week on local issues into a regular berth on the editorial page.

Wright's political cartoons are now among the most widely reprinted in the nation, and his style one of the most derivative (or copied, depending on who defines the chickens and eggs). The liberal cartoonist draws with a fine brush line, uses toned shading and, acknowledging a debt to Fischetti, works in a horizontal format. His cartoons are masterpieces of composition, and he utilizes humor well as a weapon in his advocacies. He won the Pulitzer Prize in 1966 and the Sigma Delta Chi award in 1978, and he lists the Overseas Press Club award among his many other honors. Having retired from the *News* in the mid-1980s, he now draws for the *Palm Beach Post*; his cartoons are syndicated four times a week by Tribune Media Services.

R.M.

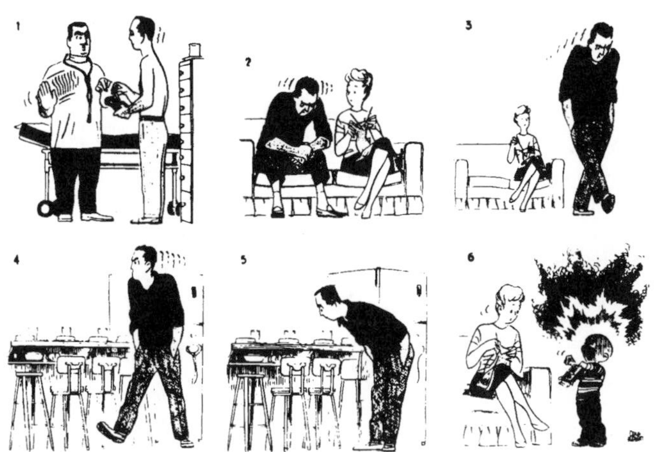

Doug Wright, "Nipper." © Weekend.

WRIGHT, DOUG (1917-1982) Canadian cartoonist born in Dover, England, on August 11, 1917. Doug Wright attended King's College in Wimbledon, where he did not get along with his art teacher. After becoming a commercial artist at age 18, he emigrated to Canada in 1938 to work in the art department of Sun Life Assurance.

Working as a navigation instructor in the Royal Canadian Air Force during World War II, Wright began having his cartoons published in the station magazine. Noting the positive reaction of the airmen to his cartoons, he decided to go into cartooning. After his discharge, Wright went to New York with his samples and was told to go home and get experience on the local papers. In 1948, Wright began his professional cartooning career on the *Montreal Standard*. In the same year Jimmy Frise died, and Wright was chosen to carry on the *Juniper Junction* strip. This strip continued until September 1968, when the paper that had jointly shared the strip, the *Family Herald*, folded.

Wright's work has been featured in both of the major Canadian weekend newspaper supplements. The strip *Nipper* in the *Weekend Magazine* was about a bald-headed young lad and his antics within his family. This cartoon family, with an additional child, transferred to the *Canadian Magazine* in 1967 under the new title *Doug Wright's Family*. Two books reprinting these strips have been published. In addition to his weekly strip, Wright has done advertising work and editorial cartoons, first in the *Toronto Telegram*, and later twice a week in the *Hamilton Spectator*. He died in late December 1982.

Wright's work has been seen by a large percentage of the Canadian population over the last 30 years. While his own three sons are now too old to supply any inspiration, Wright's cartoon family of two strange-looking boys and their harassed parents continues to amuse many readers across the country.

D.K.

WRIGHT, LARRY (1940-) Political cartoonist and comic-strip artist Larry Wright was born in 1940 in Youngstown, Ohio. The son of a reporter on a local newspaper, he has been a member of the Fourth Estate since his youth. He drew a comic strip for his high-school paper and weather cartoons for his father's newspaper while still in his teens.

Larry Wright, "Wright Angles." © United Feature Syndicate.

After his tour of army duty in Asia, where he served as a Chinese interpreter from 1958 to 1961, he remained for 4 years as news editor and political cartoonist of the *Okinawa Morning Star,* for which he drew the comic strip *Uncle Milton* from 1961 to 1965.

Back in Ohio with his Japanese wife, Wright took a job as a copyreader for the *Detroit Free Press,* where he remained from 1965 to 1976. During that time he revived *Uncle Milton* in 1967 and the next year created *Needlescope,* a weekly feature with no continuity or recurring characters. In 1974, *Needlescope* was renamed *Wright Angles,* acquired a regular cast of characters, and became a daily and Sunday gag strip. When Wright accepted the post of editorial cartoonist with the *Detroit News* in 1976, he carried *Wright Angles* with him, and United Feature Syndicate began distributing it in August.

Wright Angles deals with the middle-class suburban family of Tom and Nancy Kane and their children Joey and Sharon. Conventional in setting and situation, it is rather more acerbic than most of its competitors, reflecting the critical eye of the political cartoonist; Tom's employer, the town's mayor Orwell Twit, for example, is the editorial cartoonist's ideal of corrupt, incompetent small-town pol.

It was the character of Motley, an ironic and cynical cat introduced in 1977, that became the star of the strip. Worldly-wise, when Motley overhears Tom's plan to have him fixed, he reflects, "He'd better be talking about a bribe!" The popularity of Motley, who has taken his place with George Gately's Heathcliff and Jim Davis's Garfield among the most popular comic-strip felines in the country, led Wright to create another cat-based feature, *Kit 'N' Carlyle,* in 1980. Distributed by Newspaper Enterprise Association from December, the six-day-a-week panel feature deals with a single girl, Kit, and her innocent kitten Carlyle. The new feature provided a distinct contrast with *Wright Angles;* where Motley coolly manipulates his family and dreams of new furniture to scratch and new rats to eat, Carlyle is still learning the ways of the world and needs frequent naps because, as he explains, "Being cute all the time takes a lot out of you."

In 1982, Wright published a volume of cat caricatures entitled *Celebrity Cats,* and his two strips have each generated a collection: *Kit 'N' Carlyle* (1983) and *Motley the Cat from "Wright Angles": Round Up the Usual Cat Suspects* (1988).

Despite Larry Wright's growing popularity as a cat-cartoonist, his reputation as a political commentator has not been eclipsed. Widely syndicated throughout the country, his daily editorial cartoons continue to reflect a keen eye for social and political wrongs and a caustic wit in revealing them. The National Cartoonists Society awarded him the plaque for Best Editorial Cartoon in 1980.

D.W.

Yy

YABUSHITA, TAIJI (1903-1986) Japanese animator born in Osaka, Japan, in 1903. In 1925 Taiji Yabushita graduated from the photography department of what is today the Tokyo University of the Arts, and in the same year he joined the developing department of Shochiku Urata Studios, where he studied color processing under Rin Masutani. In 1927 he was hired by the Social Education Bureau of the Ministry of Education and was placed in charge of film production.

Drafted into the army in 1944, Yabushita was sent to the Philippines but survived to return to Japan three years later and join Nihon Dōga as an animator. During this period he was able to study under such noted figures in Japanese animation as Kenzo Masaoka, the creator of *Chikara to Onna to Yo no Naka* (the first talkie animation in Japan). Eventually he was promoted to director of the company. In 1955 he dramatized and produced *Ukare Baiorin* ("Happy Violin"), a children's story with considerable fantasy appeal. The success of this work apparently prompted Toei Motion Pictures to sign on the Nihon Dōga staff and create their own animation department.

In 1956 Yabushita became director of animation at Toei, and his first production was *Koneko no Rakugaki* ("Kitten's Doodlings"), an amusing black-and-white piece. In 1958 he produced the now famous *Hakujaden,* based on a Chinese classic, and with this success he became the producer in charge of Toei's feature animation. Thereafter he turned out such works as *Shōnen Sarutobi Sasuke* (1959), the story of a youth, based on Japanese history; *Saiyuki* (1960), based on a 16th-century Chinese classic; *Shinbaddo no Bōken* ("The Adventures of Sinbad the Sailor," 1962); and *Shōnen Jakku to Mahōzukai* ("Jack and the Witch," 1966).

Taiji Yabushita, "Hakujaden" ("Legend of a White Snake"). © Toei.

In 1967 Yabushita left Toei and eventually became an executive with the Nihon Dōga corporation. He also served as a lecturer at Tokyo Design Gakuin's department of animation, providing budding animators with the experience and knowledge he had accumulated over the years. He received awards both for his long years service to the film industry and for his contributions to education. After long service as an educator he retired in the early 1980s and passed away in 1986.

F.S.

YAMAMOTO, SANAE (1898-1981) Japanese animator and producer born in Chiba Prefecture, Japan, on February 6, 1898. Along with Kenzo Masaoka, Sanae Yamamoto is one of the pioneers in Japanese animation. He witnessed the growth of the industry from scratch. Yamamoto began working in animation at the age of 19 as an assistant to Seitaro Kitayama, one of the first artists to work in the medium in Japan. Learning on the job while creating mostly government-commissioned animation, Yamamoto quickly became enthralled by what was then an experimental field.

In 1923 the earthquake that devastated Tokyo killed Yamamoto's mother and brother, but it only strengthened his will to work. In 1924 he independently produced his first animated film, *Ubasute Yama* ("The Mountain to Abandon Old Women"), which also became the first film in Japan to receive a commendation from the Ministry of Education. In 1925 he produced *Ushiwakamaru* ("Ushiwakamaru, the Brave Little Samurai") and then began creating films at the rate of two a year, often using a folktale or educational theme. His other well-known films include *Kyōdai Koguma* ("Sibling Bear Cubs," 1932) and *Tonochan no Itazura* ("Little Tono's Tricks," 1934).

During the war Yamamoto made animated films for the Imperial Navy, but with the end of hostilities he embarked on a new phase of his career—planning and producing feature-length animation. In 1945, with other animators such as Kenzo Masaoka and Yasuji Murata, Yamamoto helped found Shin Nihon Dōga, but two years later Yamamoto and Masaoka broke away and formed Nihon Dōga, which produced works such as *Suteneko Torachan* ("Little Tora, an Abandoned Kitten," 1947). Yamamoto became president of Nihon Dōga, and under his direction more than ten films were produced. In 1956 (Masaoka having meanwhile retired), the entire company and its animators were taken over by the Toei company and became its animation department, today known as Toei Dōga. Toei has since become the leader in Japanese animation, in large measure due to the work of Sanae Yamamoto. (Yamamoto himself died in 1981.)

F.S.

Equal fertilizer distribution by Prime Minister Tanaka.

Masamu Yanase. © Musansha Shimbun.

YAMBO
See Novelli, Enrico.

YANASE, MASAMU (1900-1945) Japanese political cartoonist born in Aichi Prefecture in 1900. Masamu Yanase was perhaps the most feared political cartoonist of his day. In his short life he was exceedingly prolific and fiercely dedicated to the cause of the masses.

In 1914 Yanase moved to Tokyo, where he studied watercolor and oil painting. In 1920 he joined the staff of the *Yomiuri* newspaper as a cartoonist. From the beginning his interests were eclectic: he helped start a futurist movement, joined a Dada group called Mabuo and came heavily under the influence of George Grosz, a revolutionary German cartoonist. By 1925 his direction had become clearer, however, and he joined the Nihon Proletariat Bungei Renmei ("Japan Proletarian Literature Federation"), thereby launching his career as an agitation-propaganda cartoonist.

Yanase was an admirer of Robert Minor of the *Daily Worker,* the U.S. Communist party newspaper, and his cartoons soon adopted the same inflammatory style, depicting wholesome, muscular laborers and fat, corrupt bosses. The growing militarist faction in the Japanese diet, Japan's capitalist bosses, and even her prime ministers were not spared the satire of his pen. His work ranged from cartoons to posters to a comic strip entitled *Kanemochi Kyoiku* ("The Education of a Rich Man"), which was an ideological version of George McManus's *Bringing Up Father* and ran in the magazine *Yomiuri Sunday Manga* in 1929. That same year he also published a book on his idol, Minor

Yanase gradually made himself a more conspicuous target for the militarists, who were growing daily in strength. In 1931 he became a member of the Japanese Communist party and published more and more political cartoons in the party news sheets. This inevitably led to his being caught in the 1932 suppression of the Proletariat movement in Japan and arrested by the police. After prolonged torture he was sent to prison at Toyama, and while he was there his wife died. In a reflection of the degree to which the authorities feared him, he was allowed out of prison only long enough to attend her funeral.

Upon release from prison (Japanese fascism was always more benign than its German counterpart) Yanase traveled to Peking several times, sketching the everyday scenes he saw there. As the war increased in severity, however, he was in effect prohibited from drawing cartoons. Prevented from working in his usual medium, he returned to oil painting and traveled around rural Japan, eventually holding an exhibition in Tokyo. In a final twist of fate, Masamu Yanase was caught in an air raid on Shinjuku on May 25, 1945, on his way to visit his children, who had been evacuated to the countryside. His body was found amidst the rubble several days later. He was 45 years old.

F.S.

YARDLEY, RICHARD QUINCY (1903-1979) American cartoonist born in Baltimore, Maryland, on March 11, 1903. Yardley was educated at the Friends School and the Maryland Institute and joined the news department of the *Baltimore Evening Sun* in 1923. It was not until 1934, when

". . . But to forgive is divine."

Richard Yardley. © Baltimore Sun.

1. "Did I ever tell you about the time when I caught an octopus alive? Well, it wuz this way: Me and Spike Marlin went ashore in Madagascar, and all of a sudden a big octopus jumps outer the water and comes at us!——

2. —— He puts two o' his flippers around each of us and holds up tight, and with the other two he goes through our pockets. That ding busted critter fishes a bottle o' booze from me pocket and a pipe full o' 'baccy outer Spike's.——

3. —— Then he starts in ter have a gay old time—and all the time huggin' me and Spike tighter 'n a python!——

4. —— Whew! Boys, that wuz an excitin' half hour. That thing flipped us around like we wuz nothin' at all—and gettin a worse jag all the time.——

5. —— By and by the booze gets the best o' him, and he falls asleep. Then we ties all the dem critter's flippers in knots and double knots.——

6. —— So when he wakes up he 's clean helpless. And, jumpin' jibbooms, what a head he had! We chucked him inter the boat and rowed him ter the ship. Yessiree, we sold him ter a museum, and he 's alive yet."

"The Yarns of Captain Fibb," 1909. © Judge.

Yardley switched to the *Morning Sun,* that he became a regular political and commentary cartoonist; in 1949, upon the retirement of Edmund Duffy, his title became editorial cartoonist. Since 1966 the *Sun* has carried his cartoons, although others' work now alternates with his. Under the name "Quincy," Yardley for years did *Our Ancestors,* a panel syndicated by the Newspaper Enterprise Association; his cartoons have also appeared in the *New Yorker* and the *Reporter.* He retired in 1969 and died ten years later, in November 1979.

Yardley has one of the most unique and engaging styles in American editorial cartooning history. It is an amalgam of childlike lines, simple shadings, remarks by "mascots," labels and other very personal paraphernalia. His cartoons are charming without sacrificing lucid commentary; he seems to center on situations rather than issues or transitory headlines.

R.M.

YARNS OF CAPTAIN FIBB, THE (U.S.) There is hardly an outlet for turn-of-the-century American cartoonists where one does not find the work of C.W. Kahles represented. Kahles's magazine work for *Puck, Judge* and *Life* was copious—and at the same time he drew a full load of Sunday strips. (In 1905-06 he produced eight different Sunday features a week while supplying panels to the weekly magazines!)

As good as any of his strips—and a cartoon series in itself—was the outstanding *Yarns of Captain Fibb,* which Kahles did for *Judge* (1905-10). The series usually appeared in six sequential panels, running either a half-page or full page in black and white, or in color on the back page of the magazine. At this time *Judge* was doing direct color separation, so the color cartoons must have been from Kahles's originals, and they show imaginative use of the palette.

The format was that of an illustrated tall tale, often a narrative seemingly told to children. Fibb was an ancient mariner with a short white beard and a slicker hat, as well as an enormous imagination. In one tale about kindness to dumb animals, some whales he kindly fed reciprocated by using their spouts to quench a shipboard fire. In another tale, a mermaid's retinue included a seahorse, a sea cow and a cat fish, as well as a dog fish that proceeded to attach itself to the seat of the captain's pants.

Except in *Judge's Caricature* anthologies, there seems never to have been a reprint collection of this amusing series. *The Yarns of Captain Fibb* was later published in the Swedish magazine *Veckan* and provided cartoonist Victor Bergdahl, then a novice, with the inspiration for the famous *Kapten Grogg* series of animated cartoons.

R.M.

YASHIMA, TARŌ (1908-1994) Japanese cartoonist born in Tokyo, Japan, in 1908. Tarō Yashima, originally named Jun Iwamatsu, might be called the American equivalent of Tokyo Rose. He graduated from the Tokyo Bijutsu Daigaku (Tokyo University of Fine Art), where, as a student, he built a reputation as a talented creator of proletarian cartoons. In 1940 he traveled to New York to see the World's Fair and was unable to return to Japan after the bombing of Pearl Harbor. In 1943 he put his cartooning skills to work and published an account of his life in Tokyo in an illustrated book called *The New Sun,* which was printed by the Henry Ford company. The book contained drawings critical of the restrictions and pressures that were brought to bear on artists in Japan before the war, and it was probably this aspect of his work that caught the eye of the American military. After seeing the book, the Office of Strategic Services and War Information hired Yashima to produce cartoon propaganda that was distributed on the Pacific front.

Most of the famous Japanese cartoonists, such as Rakuten Kitazawa and Ichio Matsushita, were involved in the production of propaganda cartoons that were printed in English and distributed on the battlegrounds in hopes of lessening the morale of the Allied troops. Pictures of a "GI's girl friend back home making love with the guy next door" were a common propaganda tool. But when similar anti-Japanese cartoons appeared in American propaganda publications like the Japanese-language *Mariana Nippō* ("Mariana News") and on leaflets dropped from airplanes over battle zones, the Japanese were baffled. How did the Americans produce such "Japanese-looking" cartoons? The cartoons, of course, were Yashima's pen-and-ink drawings.

Yashima never returned to Japan but settled in Los Angeles with his wife, who had accompanied him on his visit to the United States before the start of the war. After the war, he drew political cartoons for a California Japanese-American newspaper called the *Pacific Citizen.* He retired in the 1970s and died in 1994.

J.C.

YATES, FLOYD BUFORD (1921-   ) American cartoonist and editor born in Samson, Alabama, on July 5, 1921. Floyd ("Bill") Yates studied cartooning through the W.L. Evans Correspondence Course and sold his first cartoon in an *Open Road for Boys* magazine cartoon contest. At the University of Texas, Yates was editor of the campus humor magazine. With national freelance sales under his belt, he moved to New York in 1950 to draw magazine panels and edit cartoon magazines for Dell. He soon became a mainstay of all major gag markets. In 1960 King Features took on his strip about an absentminded inventor, *Professor Phumble,* which lasted until 1978. Before and during that time, Yates worked on other magazines, illustrated books, drew comic books, wrote gags for other artists, worked in advertising and drew twice-weekly editorial cartoons for the *Westport News* in Connecticut.

Yates has a pleasant "big-foot" style with looser lines than are usual in that school, and well-spotted blacks balanced with an effective use of white space and shaded areas. His gags are always fresh, and he seems never to resort to clichéd themes or situations. In 1978, upon the retirement of Sylvan Byck, Bill Yates became comics editor of King Features Syndicate. He resigned that position in 1988; since that time he has been turning out the *Small Society* daily panel, and in 1990 he assumed the writing of the *Redeye* newspaper strip.

R.M.

"You're deliberately paying attention just to confuse me."

Bill Yates. © Saturday Evening Post.

YELLOW SUBMARINE (G.B.) The first animated cartoon to cash in on the Beatles craze was an international effort: King Features Syndicate put up the financing, George Dunning's British studios took care of the production, and German designer Heinz Edelmann was brought in to supervise the artwork; the Beatles themselves provided four new songs; and the whole enterprise was called *Yellow Submarine* and released in 1968.

The plot of the film—the Beatles embarking on a holy crusade against the Blue Meanies aboard the Yellow Submarine—was flimsy. The action was essentially made up of nonsequential and sometimes happenstance events that were disjointed to the point of incoherence. The commentary provided by the principals, and the Beatles' songs, were used to plug the holes in the story.

Edelmann's designs were brilliant and sometimes dazzling, but the baroque quality of the drawings and the

"Yellow Submarine." © King Features Syndicate and Subafilms.

visual intensity of the colors finally worked to the detriment of the picture as a whole. As Mike Barrier summed it up in a 1970 review in the magazine *Funnyworld,* "*Yellow Submarine* is the apotheosis of the quarter-century-long revolt against the Disney school of animation, and it's an empty shell."

Yellow Submarine will be remembered, however, for its wild experimentation with color and form, and for some of the best songs the Beatles ever wrote, especially "All Together Now" and the title tune.

M.H.

YING TAO (1925-) Born in 1925, Ying has been involved with cartoon art as early as 1949. Among his countless published cartoons, his main interests have always been political caricature of international topics. However, due to the changed situation in China, the tone in his cartoons has been obviously changed since the 1980s, which became more friendly with light humor in comparison to those created in the 1950s and early 1960s.

During the 1950s and early 1960s, under Mao's "class struggle" guiding thought, the entire nation was engaged in one political movement after another led by the Communist Party of China. Major newspapers, such as *People's Daily* which Ying has been working with, were the important organs for disseminating the Party's policies and guidelines for either domestic or international affairs. Thus, Ying and other cartoonist editors followed the newspapers' guidance in their cartoon creation, with no way of finding out whether the issues were truly reported by the Chinese media or not.

In those years, the main targets were the United States and other Western powers, sometimes other events occurring in the world. One such example was Ying's cartoon

Ying Tao. © Ying Tao.

"It's okay, Yogi—he's on a leash!"

"Yogi Bear." © Hanna-Barbera Productions.

entitled "People are the Owners of the Country", reflecting accurately the point of view of the Chinese government. The cartoon was based upon the uprising in Hungary in 1956 against the Soviet surrogation. The cartoon, following exactly what the Chinese media reported, showed the event as "counter-revolutionary" in which "the bourgeoisie" intended to take back the power they had lost after Soviet tanks crushed the uprising and Soviet troops occupied the country.

Ying also worked as the art editor of the *People's Daily* in addition to turning out his own cartoons, and in that position he had the important duty of helping promising amateur cartoonists to perfect their style, especially in the pages of the *People's Daily*'s comic supplement, *Humor and Satire.* In this respect he has been most instrumental in the rebirth of Chinese cartooning after the Cultural Revolution.

H.Y.L.L.

YOGI BEAR (U.S.) Yogi Bear first appeared in a segment of the *Huckleberry Hound Show,* produced for television in the late 1950s by Hanna-Barbera. The gluttonous and resourceful plantigrade became so popular with viewers that, in 1958, the series' sponsor, Kellogg's, commissioned a weekly 30-minute program of Yogi Bear cartoons, which they placed in markets of their choice. Only in 1961 did *Yogi Bear* start as a regularly scheduled program on the ABC network.

A denizen of "Jellystone National Park," Yogi had only one aim in life: to satisfy his ravenous appetite. By hook or by crook he would relieve unsuspecting tourists of their picnic baskets, displaying a high degree of cunning and inventiveness in the operation, from lying dawn in front of passing cars feigning injury to lassoing barbecued chickens and honey cakes from atop a tree. Yogi was accompanied in these exploits by the diminutive and sorrowful

Boo-Boo, whose gloomy countenance was in sharp contrast to Yogi's brazen demeanor. Yogi's most constant adversary was a park ranger whom the bear delighted in outwitting at every turn, proving that he indeed was, as he steadfastly maintained, "smarter than the average bear."

The *Yogi Bear* show ran until 1963 and then went into wide syndication. In 1973 ABC began a Saturday morning show, *Yogi's Gang,* which lasted into 1977. A theatrical full-length cartoon, *Hey There! It's Yogi Bear!,* was produced in 1964. A *Yogi Bear* comic book has been continuously published since 1959, and a newspaper strip since 1961. Yogi has also starred in a number of TV specials, notably *Yogi's Great Escape* (1986) and *Yogi and the Invasion of the Space Bears* (1988). These were greeted with a sufficient measure of success for the character to be revived in his own weekly show, *Yo, Yogi!,* which lasted only for one season (1991-92).

M.H.

YOKŌ, TADANORI (1936-) Japanese illustrator, cartoonist and philosopher-purveyor of pop religion born in Hamakura Prefecture on June 27, 1936. Although Tadanori Yokō straddles the line between cartoons and illustration, he is often referred to as an avant-garde cartoonist. He exhibited great artistic talent at an early age, winning several prizes at exhibitions before he graduated from high school in 1955. After working for two advertising institutes, he left for Tokyo in 1960, joining a firm called Tokyo Design Center. Four years later he quit to begin working independently and hold exhibitions in Japan, and by 1966 he was able to enter several of his works in an exhibition of posters at New York's Museum of Modern Art. As a result, articles on his work appeared in both *Time* and *Newsweek* magazines, establishing him as a prominent artist in the poster field.

In 1970 Yokō was in charge of the Textile Pavilion for the Osaka World's Fair, and he designed all its displays; in the same year he starred in a movie called *Shinjuku Dorobo Nikki* ("Diary of a Shinjuku Thief"). He has won a string of awards, both in Japan and internationally, and his travels around the world have helped give his works a more cosmopolitan flavor than is often found in Japan, a fact which has in turn contributed to his popularity outside Japan.

Yokō is extremely prolific, and his cartoon pictures often appeared in magazines like *Asahi Journal* and *Hanashi no Tokushu.* During 1966 a particularly notable series ran in the latter; it parodied prominent public personalities, including a blood-spattered Yukio Mishima and Ken Takakura. Yokō often works in wood-block prints, and the influence of the old masters is readily apparent in his pictures, although their themes and use of color are decidedly modern. Often they have a pop art quality and liberally employ montage and collage. Such techniques have helped Yokō win commissions to create record jackets for rock groups such as Santana.

In the 1980s, Yokō has extended his activities to writing books on religion as part of a growing Japanese movement to revive interest in native spiritual traditions such as Zen Buddhism. Ironically, this movement at times appears to be trying to replant U.S. hybrid forms of Zen and Tantric Buddhism in modern industrial and agnostic Japan. Yokō's books include *Indo E* ("On to India," 1977) and *Wa Ga Zazen Shūgyōki* ("My Journal of Zazen Training," 1978). Yokō's interest in religion has increasingly influenced his work, often resulting in an Indian/psychedelic flavor. A beautiful book titled *100 Posters of Tadanori Yokō* was published in 1978, and it includes his most representative posters from the past decade.

Mieru Mono to Mienai Mono ("The Seen and the Unseen," 1992) and *Yokō Tadanori Spiritual Pop* (1994) are some of his more recent works. In the meantime he has also continued his art work, with exhibitions of his work held widely around the world. No matter what medium Yokō works in, whether it be books or design or collage, he has been extremely popular, especially among young people. Today he is one of Japan's most internationally recognized artists.

F.S.

YOKOI, FUKUJIRŌ (1912-1948) Japanese cartoonist and children's comic book artist barn in Tokyo, Japan, on September 25, 1912. After graduating from the prewar Japanese school system Fukujiro Yokoi studied under Rakuten Kitazawa, the famous and influential cartoonist who started the first Japanese cartoon magazine, *Tokyo Puck,* in 1905. In 1932 Yokoi, in conjunction with other aspiring or already famous cartoonists like Hidezo Kondo, Ryuichi Yokoyama and Yukia Sugiura, founded the Shin Manga Shūdan (today known as the Manga Shūdan, or "Cartoonists' Group"). He also began contributing cartoons to the magazine *Shōnen Kurabu* around this time and quickly evidenced a talent far drawing children's cartoons.

As World War II approached, Yokoi was mobilized, but upon being sent to Corregidar he fell ill and spent two years being shuttled around various field hospitals. In 1943 he was finally repatriated to Japan, where he continued to draw cartoons. Like most cartoonists at the time, he supported the war effort, but his work usually consisted of comical little sketches designed to increase worker productivity, as in *Tsuigeki Shacho* ("President Pursuit"), which ran in the weekly magazine *Shūkan Mainichi* in 1945. With the end of the war Yokoi's work took on new dimensions, and he began contributing social commentary cartoons such as *Ie naki Hitobito* ("Homeless Persons") and *Shokunashi Hitobito* ("Unemployed Persons") to the magazine *Van.* One cartoon that appeared in the February issue of *Van* in 1947, during a period of severe inflation, showed three little children making play money. The caption read, "Gosh, how many more zillion-yen notes do you think we should make?"

It was with the comic strip *Fushigi no Kuni no Putchā* ("Putchā in Fantasyland"), which ran in *Shōnen Kurabu* in 1946, that Yokoi truly made his mark, however. This was a clever little science fiction number that became the idol of children everywhere in postwar Japan. It offered the hope that science would solve the world's problems, and in depicting a world with no army and no nuclear power it appealed strongly to prevailing sentiments. This masterpiece was soon followed by a string of others, such as *Bōken Tarzan* ("Tarzan's Adventures") and *Bokkuri Boya no Bōken* ("Bokkuri Boy's Adventures"). Unfortunately, the strain of hard work proved too much for Yokai, and he died an December 5, 1948, at the age of 35.

F.S.

YORK, ROBERT (1909-1975) American cartoonist barn in Minneapolis, Minnesota, in 1909. Robert York was educated at Drake University, and it was while in Iowa that he received cartooning pointers from the legendary Ding Darling. Later he studied at the Chicago Academy of Fine Arts and was again assisted in his cartooning efforts, this time by Carey Orr, Vaughn Shoemaker and Gaar Williams. Through the efforts of Orr, York became Carl Ed's assistant on the *Harold Teen* comic strip and landed a job on the *Chicago Tribune,* although not as a cartoonist. In the mid-1930s York took his first jab drawing editorial cartoons, for the *Nashville Banner;* within a year he switched to the *Louisville* (Ky.) *Times,* where he remained to draw liberal-oriented cartoons and win a Pulitzer Prize (1956) in the process.

York's style was one of incredible informality. Although he occasionally used brush and crayon, most of his cartoons were rendered in simple pencil, with loose, sketchy lines serving as fluid outlines for his figures. York retired in 1974 and died in May of the next year.

R.M.

YOUNG, HENRY ARTHUR (1866-1943) American cartoonist barn in Monroe, Wisconsin, in January 1866. Art Young was raised in Monroe and studied at the Chicago Academy of Design, the Art Students League in New York (under J. Carroll Beckwith and Kenyon Cox) and the Académie Julian in Paris. His first jobs were with the *Chicago Evening Mail* (news sketches on chalk plate), the *Chicago Daily News* and the *Chicago Tribune;* he made his first sales in 1884 to the *Nimble Nickle,* a Chicago trade journal, and to *Judge* magazine.

During the Chicago World's Fair Young drew for the *Inter-Ocean* of that city and then contributed to some of the very first color comic pages in American newspapers.

—"What's he been doin'?"—"Overthrowin' the guvment."

Art Young, 1925. © Daily Worker.

Young had contributed to the *Pall-Mall Budget* in London and was later to draw for *Cosmopolitan* and the Hearst papers in America, but the 1890s saw his primary development in the pages of the humor weeklies *Puck, Judge* and *Life.* He was one of the first artists to freelance to all three simultaneously, and although some (like J.A. Mitchell and Heywood Broun) later characterized his style as old-fashioned, in retrospect his bold lines and economical shading seem a refreshing respite from the woodcut-type cartoons and Gibson-like crosshatch nightmares by which he was surrounded.

The first decade of the century was one in which Young's cartoons not only became distinctive for their mature style and popularity but began to sharply reflect his growing political awareness and his resultant swing leftward. For *Life* and *Puck* more than for *Judge,* Young's cartoons became increasingly satirical. Naturalism in literature found its match in cartoons as Young and a growing number of contemporaries took their themes from the slums and overcrowded factories. *Life,* itself flirting with socialism, gave Young free rein, and *Puck* provided full double spreads in color.

Soon Young was art editor of the *Masses,* and a contributor to the *Liberator,* the *Nation,* the *New Leader,* the *Coming Nation, Appeal to Reason,* the *Dawn* (a Leigh Danenberg antiwar paper), the *Call* (a New York Socialist daily paper), the *Big Stick* (a major national weekly of strong socialist bent, with Theodore Roosevelt as a contributing editor), various IWW publications, and his own paper *Good Morning* (May 1919 to October 1921). In short, Young was in the forefront of a very active left-wing movement in American arts and letters in the 1910s. Unlike others (Boardman Robinson and John Sloan, far example) he did not lose interest in politics; unlike Max Eastman he remained left-wing, becoming a Communist and drawing for papers like the *New Masses,* not socialist but Stalinist.

What is most remarkable about Young, his audience and his editors is not only that a man of such radical views—one who was on trial for treason during World War I—could simultaneously maintain an output of humorous, inoffensive gag cartoons, but that magazines like the *Saturday Evening Post* could cheerfully and prominently run them. And if the *Post* was a symbol of the establishment, then William Randolph Hearst must have been pure anathema—but Young drew for him, too, in his radical days.

In his later years he drew less, grew a little bitter about life and the tide of the times (although our wartime assistance to Russia buoyed him) and was a constant advisor to young radicals and young cartoonists. He wrote books (including two autobiographies) and published a collection of the best work of his career, drew far obscure journals and studied his craft, writing essays on cartooning and entries for encyclopedias. He died in Bethel, Connecticut, at his home on Chestnut Ridge Road, on December 29, 1943.

It would be difficult to find a figure in American cartooning who mare personified the craft, the function, the essence of political cartooning than Art Young. The neglect into which he has fallen today does nothing to diminish the fact that his work stands among the best, inferior to none. He had a remarkably amiable line that served his humorous cartoons splendidly but made his devastating political onslaughts all the more striking. This contrast kept him apart from the Minors, Ellises, Grappers and Burcks, whose inevitable crayon smudges primed the reader for a predictable left-wing polemic. Young streamlined and simplified; he seldom used the crutch of symbols and labels. His capitalists were fat and his workers were gaunt, but Young conveys a sense of honesty, a sense that (unlike many of his fellows) he wasn't just drawing propaganda icons but was portraying the world as he really saw it. His compositions were strong, his lines fluid, his spotting of blacks and use of shading flawless. Many, many famous cartoons attest to his mastery of both the gag panel and the political broadside. That he has not been anthologized today is a tragedy far cartoon and political historians.

Books: *Hell up to Date; Snapshots in Hades; Hiprah Hunt's Journey Through the Inferno; Art Young's Inferno; Trees at Night; On My Way; Art Young: His Life and Times; The Best of Art Young; Thomas Rowlandson; Authors' Readings;* and others.

R.M.

Zz

ZAC, PINO
See Zaccaria, Pino.

ZACCARIA, PINO (1930-1985) Italian cartoonist and animator barn in Trapani, Italy, on April 23, 1930. Pino Zac (as he prefers to be called) completed his high school studies in Rome, where he later attended the School of Architecture. He left college to design puppets and in 1950 created *Il Gatto Filippo* ("Philip the Cat"), a comic strip based on one of his puppet characters. Accepted by the daily *Paese Sera,* it was the first Italian comic strip to be published in a national newspaper and ran until 1958.

A restless soul, Zac in the meantime went to Poland, where he drew cartoons far the magazine *Spillky* (1955); he then moved to Berlin, where he designed sets far the Berliner Ballet. Leaving far Paris the next year, he illustrated a number of books and initiated his collaboration an the satirical weekly *Le Canard Enchaîné* with a great number of editorial cartoons criticizing every aspect of the social structure. In this period he also authored four cartoon books, *Rouge et Noir* ("Red and Black"), *Pretesti* ("Pretexts"), *La Cambiale* ("The Promissory Note") and *Questo Popolo di . . .* ("That People of . . .").

Back in Rome, Zac tried his hand at animation; his first cartoon short, *Welcome* to *Rome* (1959), was well received and much awarded; it was followed by *L'Uomo in Grigio* ("The Man in Gray") the next year. After a brief interlude in London, Zac returned to Rome and animation in 1962. *Man, Superman, Poor Man* (1962), *Registered for Life* (1963) and *Postage Stamp* (1965) were witty shorts that further established his reputation. In 1967 he went to Prague to work on the feature-length *Il Cavaliere Inesistente,* a combination live-action and cartoon film that was not released until 1969, after many vicissitudes. In 1973 Zac drew a special issue on the pope far the French magazine *Satirix* and received a suspended sentence for his pains.

Zac has also contributed comic strip series to the monthly *Eureka (Orlando Furioso, Kyrie e Leison)* and published cartoons in such foreign periodicals as *Le canard enchainé* in France and the Belgian *Pourquoi Pas?* His works have been collected in a number of books, and he has received many awards and honors for his satirical drawings as well as for his animated cartoons. He died at his home in Fontecchio in 1985.

L.S.

ZE'EV
See Farkas, Ya'akov.

ZEMAN, KAREL (1910-1989) Czech animator and filmmaker born in Ostromer, Bohemia, in what was then part of the Austro-Hungarian Empire, in 1910. After a successful career as a commercial artist and designer, Karel Zeman starting working on puppet films alongside Jiří Trnka right after World War II, realizing *Summer Dream* in 1945 and *The Horseshoe* in 1946.

In 1947 Zeman brought to life the most famous cartoon character in Czech animation, Pan Prokouk ("Mr. Prokouk"), a somewhat befuddled but game little man imperturbably facing every kind of improbable circumstance. The character slowly developed in a series of shorts, from *Pan Prokouk Jede na Brigadú* ("Mr. Prokouk Leads a Brigade"), *Pan Prokouk Uřaduje* ("Mr. Prokouk Bureaucrat") and *Pan Prokouk v Prokušeni* ("Mr. Prokouk's Temptation"), all of which were released in 1947, to *Pan Prokouk Filmuje* ("Mr. Prokouk Filmmaker," one of the funniest in the series, 1948), *Pan Prokouk Vynaléczem* ("Mr. Prokouk Inventor," a 1949 entry that prefigures Zeman's later use of science fiction themes) and *Pan Prokouk Detektiven* ("Mr. Prokouk Detective," 1958).

Zeman's first feature-length film, the fantastic *Poklad*

Pino Zaccaria ("Zac"), "Kirie & Leison." © *Editoriale Corno.*

Karel Zeman, "Baron Munchhausen," 1961. © Gottwaldov Studio.

Ptačiho Ostrava ("The Treasure of Bird Island," 1952) combined puppets with cartoon animation. Since then he has realized a number of outstanding films blending live action, puppets and every kind of animation imaginable; his *Vnyález Zkázy* ("The Diabolical Invention," 1957) is the most acclaimed among his later works, but *Cesta do Pravěku* ("Journey into Primeval Times," 1955) and *Baron Prăsil* ("Baron Munchausen," 1961), both in the same vein, are equally remarkable. After a distinguished career in live-action films Zeman came briefly back to animation with *Sindbad the Sailor* (1972) and *The Children of Captain Nemo* (1975), a theatrical compilation of cartoon shorts that he did for German television in the 1970s. In 1980 he realized *Karel Zeman for Children*, an anthology of selected extracts from his films. He died in Gottwaldow-Zlin on April 5, 1989. During his lifetime he had been literally showered with honors from film festivals around the world; and his passing was much mourned by the cinemagoing public.

M.H.

ZÈRE, AL
See Ablitzer, Alfred G.

ZHAN TONG (1932-1995) Born in 1932, Zhan had his first cartoon published when he was only 14 years old. Between 1952 and 1956, he studied at the Central Art Academy in Beijing, majoring in oil painting. However, his talent in cartooning was supported and directed by his teacher, Xiwen, a famous oil master in China. Zhan and some students organized a "Double Knife Society" creating cartoons in their leisure time, and had a chance to be instructed by the established cartoonists Hua Junwu and Mi Gu, etc. After his graduation, Zhan was assigned to the Shanghai Animation Film Studio, the only such studio in China at that time, and worked there as art designer, script writer and director, until he passed away in 1995.

Animation films made by Zhan number more than 50, and his cartoons published in different media were countless. Among animators that won prizes nationally and internationally, Zhan was the one who successfully made the first paper-cut film in China in 1956, and was the first one whose cartoons won the prize at an international competition held in Germany in 1980. Zhan was among the group of pioneers, from 1988 to his last day, who experimented cartooning in traditional Chinese brush-and-ink. His art work collections include *Chinese Fairytales*, *Zhan Tong's Cartoons for Children*, and *Zhan Tong Cartoon Selection*, etc.

Together with Zhan, two other men's names should be mentioned. One was Xu Jingda (1934-1087), and the other was Wang Shuchen (1931-1991). All three worked in the same Shanghai Animation Film Studio, and all of them

郎君出门早早回，日出走来日入息；
路上残花莫要采，家中牡丹正在开。

Zhang Guangyu. © Zhang Guangyu.

were famous for the animated images and numerous cartoons they created. For such similarities, they were known as "Three Sword-bearers", a metaphor meaning that their drawing pens were like sharp weapons pointing toward evil in society. Wang had one cartoon selection published after his death, and Xu did not have any personal collections of art work left behind, due to his sudden death. But all three men and their achievements will always be remembered.

H.Y.L.L.

ZHANG GUANGYU (1900-1964) As an important figure in Chinese cartoon art development, Zhang was known as an excellent artist in the 1920s before his cartoons became popular. In his earlier artistic career, he worked as a Peking Opera stage designer and an illustrator of calendars, cigarette packages and magazine cover pages. In 1934, when China was under the attack of foreign powers, he resigned from his well-paid artist position in the advertising department of a British-American tobacco company, and with others started his own publishing company (he was the manager), which published five different cartoon journals at the same time. With those publications, one of his goals was to provide a nurturing soil for young cartoonists' growth. Since then, Zhang kept cartooning until the end of his life. His younger brother, Zhang Zhengyu, was also a good cartoonist and the two brothers worked together for some time running the cartoon publications.

Zhang's cartooning topics were mainly political due to the political situation in China in the early half of his lifetime. Living in Shanghai, he experienced a life in a society of semi-colony and semi-feudalism. The masterpiece of Zhang's cartoons was the color series entitled "The Traveling in the Western World", whose topic came from a famous ancient novel. Its contemporary political content attacked the government's ruling class and revealed the people's bitter lives at the time.

Based on his background and training as an artist who used to paint with details and heavy colors, Zhang was a pioneer for decorative cartooning. His personalized style in cartoon creation was strongly influenced by such a decorative art design, especially in his later creative period after the 1930s. His art development was also a result of absorbing Chinese folklore and traditional art and literature. His *Folksongs & Art Collection* published in 1935 was a combination of his talents and artistic techniques. Such talent was also found in his work of the late 1950s: in his cartoons that were under the watchful eye of the Chinese Communist Party's, and in his design for what was then the best known animation film, *Monkey King.*

H.Y.L.L.

ZHANG YAONING (1951-) Of his cartooning peers of the same age group in cartooning, Zhang is among the best. Since his birth in the early 1950s, painting was his favorite thing to do. In the elementary school, he got 4 years of systematic training in painting in the Children Palace, which laid a solid foundation for Zhang in his future life, although one's life was not dominated by an individual but by the government in those years. He spent

Zhang Yaoning. © Zhang Yaoning.

7 years in a remote village in Northwest China, where there was no electricity. In the daytime he worked in the fields with the peasants. Only at night under oil lamp did he enjoy his life by persisting in painting.

After 7 years of struggling, Zhang was able to go back to start a new life in his birthplace—Beijing. However, his artistic talent was recognized when he was transferred to work as art editor at the *China Daily* in 1980. The newspaper has provided him with more knowledge and also opportunities for self-improvement. He studied for 3 years in the Beijing Educational Institute majoring in Fine Arts. That was the time Zhang began cartooning. Since his first cartoon was published in the *China Daily* in May 1981, Zhang has published more than a thousand cartoons domestically and internationally. His cartoons with a wide range of topics were often seen on the *People's Daily, Chinese Youth News, World Women Review,* and journals in Hong Kong, Japan and the United States. Some of his works were selected in cartoon collections published in China and Japan.

Zhang's work was also chosen many times by cartoon exhibitions held in China as well as abroad: Chinese Cartoon Exhibitions in China in 1987, 1988, 1991 and 1993; China Art Grand Exhibition in Hong Kong in 1990; the Second International Cartoon Exhibition in Japan in 1990; and the International Cartoon Exhibition in Brazil in 1992, etc. His works were awarded in 1987, 1991, 1992 and 1993. Upon his success in cartooning, he was highly recognized by the professional organizations and readers as well. It was a rare case to entitle him, at the age of early forties "Senior Editor" by one of the most important dailies in China (*China Daily* has been the only one English newspaper published and distributed worldwide). In 1995, his first cartoon collection in Chinese, *Focus & Plane,* was published by Waymont International Publication, New Jersey.

H.Y.L.L.

ZHENG XINYAO (1958-) Born in Shanghai in 1958, Zheng Xinyao began his cartooning career as an amateur in 1978, and since that time his large output of modern humorous cartoons has gained him much fame. In the 1980s he became the art editor of *Xinmin Evening,* a nationally distributed newspaper, and his cartoons there have been published and have won many awards not only in China, but abroad as well, notably in Japan, Belgium, and

Zheng Xinyao. © Zheng Xinyao.

France.

Zheng's cartoon collections published in recent years show him drawing more or less in a style absorbed from what he had learned from cartoonists in the West. As soon as these cartoons appeared, they caused some argument and disagreement among the Chinese professionals, since from the time of the People's Republic's founding some 30 years before, humor cartoons were regarded as "non-proletarian" art and as such were not allowed in China. In this respect Zheng may be considered not only one of the best among the new generation of Chinese cartoonists but also as a pioneer who established the popularity of the modern humor cartoon in China.

H.Y.L.L.

ZHUANG XILONG (1949-) As a native to Shanghai and a self-taught cartoonist, Zhuang has been the art editor in one of the most advanced cities in which youngsters wished to live—Shen Zhen (Guangdong Province). Shen Zhen was a backward little town but it was rapidly developed into a center of the economic reform in today's China since the early 1980s. In 1983, Zhuang began his editor's duty at the *Shen Zhen Special Economic Zone News*, and published several thousands of cartoons in the newspaper that he edited as well as in others across the country.

Zhuang's cartoons are mainly of a humor found in daily life. His artistic styles consist both of Chinese traditional brush-and-ink painting, and in the Western way of cross-hatching. By looking at Zhuang's many cartoons and comparing them with others', one of his noteworthy aspects is the attention and patience he has put in to his creation. Unlike other cartoonists, mainly the younger generation to which Zhuang belongs, whose cartoons look as if the cartoonist is always in a hurry, the artwork rough and imperfect, Zhuang's cartoons, on the contrary, were always made in a painstaking, detailed style.

As humor cartoonist, art editor, and editorial cartoonist for the newspaper in question, Zhuang drew each of his cartoons as if it were a report on daily happenings. Topics including red tape, low-quality merchandise, misuse of government funds, and so on, were presented realistically by way of exaggeration and humor. In the cartoon, "Please save God", an air balloon basket has written on it: "customers are God". Two men inside the basket are scared and sweating because the balloon is leaking air through several holes. The catching line is what is written on the balloon: "untrue advertising".

Zhuang's first cartoon collection was published by Sichuan Art Publishing House in 1989 which selected his work between 1979 and 1989; and his later work was published by Hunan Art and Literature Publishing House in 1996.

H.Y.L.L.

ZHUKOV, NIKOLAI NIKOLAEVICH (1908-1973) Cartoonist, illustrator and painter born in Moscow, Russia, on December 2, 1908. Nikolai Zhukov studied at the School of Industrial Arts in Nijni-Novgorod from 1926 to 1928, and in Saratov from 1928 to 1930. He first came to prominence with children's cartoons; his treatment of children was realistic but understanding. His cartoons were later published in book form.

During World War II Zhukov worked on a front-line newspaper and also contributed to *Pravda*. In 1943 he became director of the M.B. Grekov Studio of Military

救救上帝

Zhuang Xilong. © Zhuang Xilong.

Artists. He also illustrated books and designed posters. After the war he devoted himself mostly to painting (usually watercolors) but still turned out a cartoon or two on occasion.

Zhukav was awarded the Order of Lenin as well as many other Soviet distinctions. He became a corresponding member of the Academy of Arts in 1949, and was made a People's Artist of the USSR in 1963. He died on September 24, 1973, in Moscow.

M.H.

ZIEGLER, JACK (1942-) American cartoonist born in New York City on July 13, 1942. Jack Ziegler was educated at Fordham University, where he received his bachelor's degree in communications arts. He has had no formal art training. His first cartoon sale was to the *Saturday Review World* in 1972, and his work first appeared in the *New Yorker* in February 1974. Other publications to which he has contributed include *Esquire,* the *New York Times, Cosmopolitan, National Lampoon, Writer's Digest, TV Guide, Oui* and *Rolling Stone.* His first cartoon collection, *Hamburger Madness,* was published by Harcourt-Brace in 1978.

That Ziegler would be a successful cartoonist was obvious from his first (and personally well-remembered) *New Yorker* panel, in which a heavenly assembly-line superintendent, confronted by mooing ducks pouring out of his machines, is shown worriedly on the phone: "Hello? Beasts of the Field? This is Lou over in Birds of the Air. Anything funny going on at your end?" The sheer inventive genius of this idea and its bold ink-line rendering immediately stamped the artist as a young man to be reckoned with. And indeed, his subsequent work in the gag cartoon genre has more than confirmed this initial promise.

But Ziegler has not been content to stay within the usual format. He has recently initiated a new approach in which the drawing relates to the descriptive caption rather than vice versa, as is usually the case. It is a subtle distinction and therefore does not readily lend itself to explanation. Certainly it must derive in large part from Ziegler's training in communications, for the intent of these pieces is definitely to convey attitudes, emotions or ideas via the caricaturist's technique. The closest analog among current artists—although the similarity is only in intent—would seem to be Jules Feiffer. One of Ziegler's efforts along this line presents the following bit of Newspeak: "Long after losing the election, Fred Gort continued to campaign, thus making a mockery of those reporters who called him the 'I don't care' candidate." The drawing shows a slightly insane-looking but conventionally dressed man making an impassioned address in an empty hall.

Ziegler is a member of the Cartoonists Guild and has served that group as treasurer (1976-79). His work has been featured in exhibitions at the Bethel Gallery in Bethel, Connecticut (1977), the International Tennis Hall of Fame in Newport, Rhode Island (1977), the Washington Art Gallery in Washington Depot, Connecticut (1978) and the Nancy Roth Gallery in Katonah, New York (1978), among others. In addition to his cartoons Ziegler in the 1980s and 1990s has illustrated and written several children's books.

"Ziggy." © Universal Press Syndicate.

"I try to do cartoons that are hopefully funny, rather than clever," he declared in 1990.

R.C.

ZIGGY (U.S.) Cartoonist Tom Wilson had been a successful greeting card artist for a number of years when he decided in 1966 to draw a syndicated comic strip. *Ziggy,* as it was called, was repeatedly turned down; in 1968 Wilson put a number of previously rejected and some original *Ziggy* cartoons into a little book, *When You're Not Around,* published by the American Greetings Corporation. Jim Andrews, the editor of Universal Press Syndicate, happened to came upon the book and liked it; by 1970 *Ziggy* was established as a daily panel distributed by Universal Press, later adding a Sunday page.

Ziggy (who was an elevator operator in the aborted version) is now a little character with no particular status in life—and no particular talents either. He is well-meaning, ill-adjusted and naturally incompetent. He sprays his armpits with shoe polish, squeezes toothpaste out of the wrong end of the tube and rolls himself up in the window shade. He is so unlucky that his wall calendar only shows Friday the 13th, and so bland that even his mother doesn't recognize his voice on the phone. In short, he is a modern-day Everyman completely overwhelmed by our mass civilization.

Ziggy is a very endearing feature, and its diminutive hero goes through countless contretemps not unlike those experienced by his readers. As Wilson himself once stated, "I want the reader to became directly involved with Ziggy, both by identifying himself with him and with what he has to say." Judging from *Ziggy*'s popularity in the United States and abroad, it can be said that Wilson has been very successful in this endeavor. Not only does Ziggy appear in newspapers, but his likeness can also be seen on greeting

Little Mary Patrzkopp: "Gosh what a nifty hoofer that Maxie is!"
Heinrich Zille, 1923. © Simplicissimus.

cards, posters, and note paper. The feature has been reprinted in numerous books, and has been adapted into two animated specials (one of which, *The Thief Who Never Grew Up*, received an Emmy).

M.H.

ZILLE, HEINRICH (1858-1929) German cartoonist and painter born in Radeburg, Saxony, on January 10, 1858. Heinrich Zille's family, which came to Berlin in 1867, was extremely poor; for years his father languished in debtors' prison while his mother supported the children with home crafts. In 1872 the artistically gifted youngster, who had been impressed with cheap reproductions of Hogarth prints, began learning lithography as a trade. With his earnings, he paid for two evening art lessons a week with Theador Hosemann, the genial depicter of Berlin popular scenes, who encouraged young Zille to become an independent observer of proletarian life. Zille soon extended his practical knowledge to all sorts of art printing; in 1876 he entered the employ of a printing plant, where he was practically enslaved until his success as an artist finally released him for full-time creativity in 1907.

Around the turn of the century Zille began exhibiting in art shows and contributing cartoons to *Ulk*, the *Berliner Tageblatt, Lustige Blätter* and *Jugend.* A brief but fruitful association with the Munich satirical magazine *Simplicissimus* commenced in 1909. In his thousands of drawings, Zille celebrated the poor people of Berlin—the very old and the very young, the criminals and the prostitutes, the pleasures of Sunday bathing at the suburban lakes, the fearfully overcrowded slums, the occupations and the perilous idleness of the streets and courtyards—neither as a judge nor as a Jeremiah, but as a patient, humorous and understanding chronicler.

Although official recognition was slow in coming—his 1924 nomination to the Berlin Academy caused great disgust in some quarters—few artists have been so sincerely loved as Zille was by his rightful audience. During his lifetime, popular songs were written about him, charity costume parties were held in his honor, and outstanding films about proletarian Berlin were shot with the conscious intention of bringing his drawings to life on the screen. Zille and the ambience he chose to depict (his *Milljöh,* as the Berliners say) are a living force even today.

From 1915 on, he published a number of albums, including *Rund um Berlin* ("All Around Berlin," 1921), *Berliner Geschichten und Bilder* ("Berlin Stories and Pictures," 1925), *Rings um den Alexanderplatz* ("Around the Alexanderplatz") and *Vier Lebensalter* ("Four Ages of Man," 1929). He died in Berlin on August 9, 1929.

S.A.

ZIM
See Zimmerman, Eugene.

ZIMMERMAN, EUGENE (1862-1935) American cartoonist born in Basel, Switzerland, on May 25, 1862. Eugene Zimmerman's parents moved to America when their son was young, and he was educated in the public schools of Paterson, New Jersey. He was employed variously as a farmhand, baker and sign painter. In 1882 he joined the staff of *Puck,* although at first he simply ran errands; before his first cartoon was published the following year, he had served as Joseph Keppler's assistant, finishing portions of his lithographs and coloring most of them. This training stood him good stead, for "Zim" (as he signed his work) was to became a consummate master of the crayon, bath on the stone and for shading effects on paper. His pen-and-ink style blossomed at the same time, and he became the technical cousin of Opper in the sense of broad exaggeration (in fact, Opper became more sedate in his renderings as Zim grew wilder) and deft subject treatment.

In 1885 Zim left *Puck* for *Judge,* receiving a percentage of ownership in the reorganized magazine for so doing. On

Took him too literally: —"Now, all ready, sir!
Try to look and act natural." —"De-e-e-lighted!"
Eugene Zimmerman ("Zim"). © Judge.

Judge Zim was a fixture for a solid 28 years and contributed panels into the late 1920s. He remained a leading political cartoonist into the Taft years and was the premier black-and-white artist of the staff. Off the magazine, Zim illustrated many of Bill Nye's stories, wrote several manuals on the art of caricature and cartoons, and ran the Zim Correspondence School of Cartooning, Comic Art and Caricature in Horseheads, New York. He also wrote a column, "Homespun Foolosophy," for *Cartoons* magazine and organized the American Association of Cartoonists and Caricaturists in the 1920s. Zim died at his home in Horseheads on March 26, 1935.

Zim was a cartoonist of overwhelming competence, one of the preeminent American cartoon craftsmen of all time. In an age of largely reserved and tight drawing styles, his cartoons were always free and crammed full of character, emotion and movement. In the 1890s he abandoned the crosshatch technique and worked in broad, thick, lush strokes, no doubt inspired by his use of the lithographic crayon on stone.

His nonpolitical cartoons were genre drawings; seldom did he picture the rising middle class or average urbanite. Instead, his subjects were mostly hoboes, Negroes, Jews and Irishmen. He also drew a healthy dose of kid cartoons. After awhile the captions seemed to be of secondary importance, and his cartoons became character studies. He excelled at character types. In politics he was a lifelong Republican and until 1912 frequently drew on political subjects. As a partisan, though, he was more the amiable opponent than the vitriolic foe. In fact, all his cartoons—editorial and purely comic—were imbued with a sense of charm and humor. Their vitality and good will speak to us over the years, and students of comic art continue to marvel at Zim's easy mastery of his media and his subjects.

R.M.

ZIMNIK, REINER (1930-) German illustrator and author born in Beuthen, Upper Silesia (now Bytom, Poland), on December 13, 1930. After becoming a journeyman cabinetmaker in rural Bavaria after World War II, Reiner Zimnik attended the Munich Academy for five years (he still lives in Munich). While a student there, he wrote and illustrated a modern book of fables called *Lektro.* This won him immediate fame, enthusiastic offers from publishers and opportunities to draw on television (most of his later books originated on the small screen).

By the time Zimnik was 25, he had two more children's books to his credit: *Jones der Angler* ("Jones the Fisherman"), which combined the tranquility of fishing in the Seine in Paris with a story of world travel; and *Der Bär und die Leute* ("The Bear and the People"). Among his subsequent titles for children and adults (some translated into a dozen languages) are: *Die Trommler für eine Bessere Zeit* ("The Drummers for Better Times"); *Bills Ballonfahrt* ("Bill's Balloon Ride"), in which toy balloons waft a little boy's bed over a vast landscape, just as Winsor McCay's rarebit eater soars aloft in his bed in one famous nightmare sequence; *Der Kleine Millionär* ("The Little Millionaire"), an interplanetary Christmas story; and *Professor Daniel J. Koopermans' Entdeckung und Erforschung des Schneemenschen* ("Professor Daniel J. Kooperman's Discovery and Investigation of the Snowman"), a picture story about a hunt for the Himalayan yeti. There are at least eight more.

Zimnik has also occasionally illustrated books written by others, such as Jennika Ulrici's *Das Ist Zubunt* ("That's Zubunt"). In these verses, Zubunt is an imaginary man suffering from shortsighted stubbornness and irascibility; the title, if written *das ist zu bunt,* means "that's going too far!" Zimnik has radio plays to his credit, too. In 1961 he won a prize entitling him to work and study at the Villa Massimo in Italy.

By 1973, feeling that for all his success, book illustration was nevertheless too commercial an enterprise, Zimnik was turning increasingly to "free" drawing, using the same understated, scratchy, sketchy pen technique as in the past. He specifically requests not to be called a cartoonist, but a satiric-poetic draftsman. He proclaims a love for people in general but is not interested in political art or journalism, which he considers a trap; he believes that very few editorial cartoonists are sincerely committed to a cause, and that those who are, like George Grosz, quickly burn themselves out in its service. His career has continued on a steady course over the years, and now nearing 70 he is still as active as ever.

S.A.

ZIRALDO
See Pinto, Ziralda Alves.

ZLATKOVSKY, MIKHAIL M. (1944-) A political cartoonist of Russian, Mongol, and Jewish blood, Zlatkovsky was born August 21, 1944, in the Central European part of the Soviet Union, in the small village of St. Christopher. Although very different from most of his western counterparts, his cartooning career took shape in the usual Eastern European way. After several years of work in another field, it developed out of a relatively well-paid and highly respected professional career. He was a graduate of the Moscow-based Nuclear Physics Institute with a Masters degree in applied physics, and for 6 years, had been preparing his Doctor of Science thesis, when on an October day in 1971, he suddenly quit all research and became a freelance artist/cartoonist.

He immediately started participating in international cartoon competitions, and simultaneously, winning prizes. His work quickly became well known for its craftsmanship and particularly strong originality that was feeding on the sad themes of the Soviet socialist reality, as well as basic human fallacies and human rights issues. He has probably become the cartoonist who has won the most prizes -he has to date received 143 prizes. About 40 of them are grand or first prizes. The international recognition he built by entering over 200 cartoon competitions and winning prizes at most, paid off nicely in 1992. In a survey, conducted by *WittyWorld International Cartoon Magazine,* his worldwide peers, considering both art and ideas, voted him the best overall cartoonist in the world. Although a bigger portion of the votes came from his homeland and other Eastern European countries, it is still significant that from virtually oblivion, Zlatkovsky sud-

MIKHAIL M. ZLATKOVSKY/Soviet Union

Mikhail Zlatkovsky ("Zlat"). © Zlat.

WittyWorld International Cartoon Magazine, No. 10, Winter/Spring 1991

denly found himself on a list ahead of such superstars as MacNelly, Mordillo, Searle, Oliphant, Adolf Born, Watterson, Sempé, Steadman, Topor, Hergé, and Steinberg.

There was a huge irony to his success, though. While many of his above mentioned colleagues were millionaires, Zlatkovsky, who in this survey was topping them all, was making only about the equivalent of one hundred dollars a month.

After over two decades of freelancing and taking art director positions in national publications, in the early 1990s, he decided to try his luck in the United States. His efforts to break into the New York and California markets mainly failed because of the tremendous cultural contrasts he encountered. His ideas proved to be too intellectual and abstract, and his themes too sad, even depressing, for the American culture. Five years later, he was back in Moscow, where now he was flooded with job offers and was soon named president of the First International Moscow Cartoon Competition in post-Communist Russia.

Even beyond his unmatched number of international prizes, Zlatkovsky's list of accomplishments and recognitions are very impressive. His satirical illustrations are collectibles today. He founded and presided over the first cartoonist association of the former Soviet Union. He is an honorary member of the French Academy of the Humorous Art (1991), The Russian Academy of Great Art Authorities (his translation) (1992) in St. Petersburg. His interest in a variety of art genres such as fine art, illustration, commercial art, animation, and sculpting, made him a very well-rounded artist.

Zlatkovsky's successful international performance became a natural source for invitations to preside over and / or be a member of cartoon / art juries among others in Skopje, St. Petersburg, Rostov, Anglet, Istanbul, Budapest, and Kazan.

His professional association memberships include the Artists Union of the former USSR, the Union of Russian Journalists, and the Graphic Artists Union of Moscow. His one-man shows graced the galleries of Belgium, Canada, Estonia, France, Italy, Malta, Poland, Russia, Turkey, and the United States.

J.S.

ZUKAS, STEPAS ADOLFO (1904-1946) Cartoonist and graphic artist born in the village of Dubelin, near Anikshchiai, in Lithuania on November 5, 1904. Upon graduation from high school in 1923, Stepas Zukas enrolled in the Kaunas School of Art, where he earned his degree in 1929. He soon became involved in the revolutionary movement trying to undermine the newly independent Lithuanian Republic. In 1933 he helped establish the satirical monthly *Sluota* ("The Broom"), for which he worked first as cartoonist, then as editor in chief in 1940 and 1941. His cartoons were published in a collection entitled *Faces and Masks* (1939).

Stepas Zukas actively helped in the establishment of Soviet power in Lithuania. From 1941 on, his works were for the most part savage attacks on the invading German armies and an the Nazi regime. He died in Kaunas on May 6, 1946.

M.H.

ZUNZI
See Wong, Kee-Kwan.

Appendixes

Glossary

Select Bibliography

Notes on the Contributors

Appendixes

A. Pulitzer Prize Winners
B. Sigma Delta Chi Award Winners
C. Academy Award Winners
D. Cartoons in Japan
E. Animation in Japan

Appendix A

Pulitzer Prize Winners

The Pulitzer Prizes were established to recognize excellence in literature and journalism. A Pulitzer for editorial cartooning was created in 1922. Here is the list of winners since that year.

1922 Rollin Kirby
1923 no award
1924 Jay Darling
1925 Rollin Kirby
1926 Daniel Fitzpatrick
1927 Nelson Harding
1928 Nelson Harding
1929 Rollin Kirby
1930 Charles Macauley
1931 Edmund Duffy
1932 John McCutcheon
1933 Harold Talburt
1934 Edmund Duffy
1935 Ross Lewis
1936 no award
1937 C.D. Batchelor
1938 Vaughn Shoemaker
1939 Charles Werner
1940 Edmund Duffy
1941 Jacob Burck
1942 Herbert Block ("Herblock")
1943 Jay Darling
1944 C.K. Berryman
1945 Bill Mauldin
1946 Bruce Russell
1947 Vaughn Shoemaker
1948 Rube Goldberg
1949 Lute Pease
1950 James Berryman
1951 Reginald Manning
1952 Fred Packer
1953 Edward Kuekes
1954 Herblock
1955 Daniel Fitzpatrick
1956 Robert York
1957 Tom Little
1958 Bruce Shanks
1959 Bill Mauldin
1960 no award
1961 Carey Orr
1962 Edmund Valtman
1963 Frank Miller
1964 Paul Conrad
1965 no award
1966 Don Wright
1967 Pat Oliphant
1968 E.G. Payne
1969 Giovanni Fischetti
1970 Tom Darcy
1971 Paul Conrad
1972 Jeffrey MacNelly
1973 no award
1974 Paul Szep
1975 Garry Trudeau
1976 TonyAuth
1977 Paul Szep
1978 Jeffrey MacNelly
1979 Herblock
1980 Don Wright
1981 Mike Peters
1982 Ben Sargent
1983 Dick Locher
1984 Paul Conrad
1985 Jeff MacNelly
1986 Jules Feiffer
1987 Berke Breathed
1988 Doug Marlette
1989 Jack Higgins
1990 Tom Toles
1991 Jim Borgman
1992 Signe Wilkinson
1993 Steve Benson
1994 Michael Ramirez
1995 Mile Luckovitch
1996 Jim Morin
1997 Walt Handelsman
1998 Stephen P. Breen

Appendix B

Sigma Delta Chi Award Winners

Each year Sigma Delta Chi, a professional association of journalists, bestows awards in a number of categories, including editorial cartooning. Here is the list of the winners since the inception of the awards.

1942 Jacob Burck
1943 Charles Werner
1944 Henry Barrow
1945 Rube Goldberg
1946 Dorman H. Smith
1947 Bruce Russell
1948 Herbert Block ("Herblock")
1949 Herblock
1950 Bruce Russell
1951 Bruce Russell Herblock
1952 Cecil Jensen
1953 Giovanni Fischetti
1954 Calvin Alley
1955 Giovanni Fischetti
1956 Herblock
1957 Scott Long
1958 Clifford Baldowski
1959 Charles Brooks
1960 Dan Dowling
1961 Phil Interlandi
1962 Paul Conrad
1963 Bill Mauldin
1964 Charles Bissell
1965 Roy Justus
1966 Pat Oliphant
1967 Eugene Payne
1968 Paul Conrad
1969 Bill Mauldin
1970 Paul Conrad
1971 Hugh Haynie
1972 Bill Mauldin
1973 Paul Szep
1974 Mike Peters
1975 Tony Auth
1976 Paul Szep
1977 Don Wright

Appendix C

Academy Award Winners

In 1932 the Academy of Motion Picture Arts and Sciences (AMPAS) established a new category: short subject (animation).The first award, in the form of the fabled statuette better known as Oscar, was bestowed the next year for the best animation short released in 1932. Here is the list of all the Oscar-winning animated films since 1932 (it should be noted that not all animated shorts are cartoons).

1932 Flowers and Trees (Walt Disney)
1933 Three Little Pigs (Walt Disney)
1934 The Tortoise and the Hare (Walt Disney)
1935 Three Orphan Kittens (Walt Disney)
1936 The Country Cousin (Walt Disney)
1937 The Old Mill (Walt Disney)
1938 Ferdinand the Bull (Walt Disney)
1939 The Ugly Ducking (Walt Disney)
1940 The Milky Way (MGM)
1941 Lend a Paw (Walt Disney)
1942 Der Fuehrer's Face (Walt Disney)
1943 Yankee Doodle Mouse (MGM)
1944 Mouse Trouble (MGM)
1945 Quiet, Please (MGM)
1946 The Cat Concerto (MGM)
1947 Tweety Pie (Warner Brothers)
1948 The Little Orphan (MGM)
1949 For Scent-imentall Reasons (Warner Brothers)
1950 Gerald McBoing Boing (UPA)
1951 The Two Mousekeeters (MGM)
1952 Johann Mouse (MGM)
1953 Toot, Whistle, Plunk and Boom (Walt Disney)
1954 When Magoo Flew (UPA)
1955 Speedy Gonzales (Warner Brothers)
1956 Magoo's Puddle Jumper (UPA)
1957 Birds Anonymous (Warner Brothers)
1958 Knighty Knight Bugs (Warner Brothers)
1959 Moonbird (Storyboard, Inc.)
1960 Munro (Rembrandt Films)
1961 Ersatz (Zagreb Film, Yugoslavia)
1962 The Hole (Storyboard, Inc.)
1963 The Critic (Pintoff)
1964 The Pink Phink (DePatie-Freleng)
1965 The Dot and the Line (Chuck Jones)
1966 Herb Alpert and the Tijuana Brass (Storyboard, Inc.)
1967 The Box (Brandon Films)
1968 Winnie the Pooh and the Blustery Day (Walt Disney)
1969 It's Tough to Be a Bird (Walt Disney)
1970 Is It Always Right to Be Right? (Bosustow and Adams)
1971 The Crunch Bird (Ted Petok)
1972 A Christmas Carol (Richard Williams, England)
1973 Frank Film (Frank Mouris)
1974 Closed Mondays (Vinton and Gardiner)
1975 Great (Bob Godfrey, England)
1976 Leisure (National Film Board, Canada)
1977 Sand Castle (National Film Board, Canada)
1978 Special Delivery (National Film Board, Canada)
1979 Every Child (National Film Board, Canada)
1980 The Fly (Pannonia Film, Hungary)
1981 Crac (Société Radio-Canada)
1982 Tango (Film Polski, Poland)
1983 Sundae in New York (Motionpicker Productions)
1984 Charade (Sheridan College)
1985 Anna & Bella (CineTe, Netherlands)
1986 A Greek Tragedy (CineTe, Netherlands)
1987 The Man Who Planted Trees (Canadian Broadcasting Co.)
1988 Tin Toy (Pixar)
1989 Balance (Laurenstein)
1990 Creature Comforts (Aardman Animations, England)
1991 Manipulation (Tandem Films)
1992 Mona Lisa Descending a Staircase (Joan C. Gratz)
1993 The Wrong Trousers (Aardman Animations, England)
1994 Bob's Birthday (Snowden Fine Animation, England)
1995 A Close Shave (Aarman Animations, England)
1996 Quest (Tyrone Montgomery and Thomas Stillman)
1997 Geri's Game (Jan Pinkowa, Poland)

Appendix D

Cartoons in Japan

Japan today is a nation where cartoons and comic books have assumed a cultural significance unparalleled in the rest of the world, and it is therefore not surprising that the art form originated as early as the eighth century, during the Nara period of Japanese history. Doodlings and amusing sketches found in the Horyuji temple in the city of Nara are believed by most scholars to be among the first examples of Japanese cartoon art.

Several hundred years later, during the late Heian period, a series of four scrolls known as the *Chōjūgiga* (literally, "Humorous Pictures of Animals and Birds") was drawn by a disaffected artist-monk who used the comical antics of monkeys, frogs and rabbits to parody the religious hierarchy and establishment of the time. Scrolls were an important medium, and in cartoon format they reached a certain zenith in the Kamakura period (1192-1333), with such classics as *Jigoku Sōshi* ("Hell Scrolls"), *Yamai Sōshi* ("Disease Scrolls") and *Gaki Sōshi* ("Hungry Ghost Scrolls"). Such scrolls were related to the Buddhist cosmology of the time and were sometimes burlesques, sometimes grotesque pictorial narratives.

During the Edo period (1600-1867), artistic works that had hitherto been the property of the aristocracy and clergy became widely available due to the rise of the merchant classes and the new mass-production techniques of the wood-block masters. This was especially true of *ukiyoe*, or "floating world" block prints by masters such as Hiroshige Ando and Hokusai Katsushike, whose works are priceless today. Lesser-known artists produced everything from pornographic works to humorous caricatures of reigning Kabuki actors.

The arrival of Commodore Perry and his black ships, and the start of the Meiji era in 1867, marked not only an end to Japan's self-imposed isolation but a virtual revolution in all aspects of society, including cartoons. Under the influence of foreigners like Charles Wirgman, an Englishman, and Georges Fernand Bigot, a Frenchman, Japanese cartoonists quickly absorbed Western journalistic techniques of satire and parody. Wirgman, who published and wrote for the English monthly *Japan Punch*, is regarded as one of the founding fathers of cartooning in Japan. His influence contributed to the establishment of such Japanese magazines as *Maru Maru Chinbun* (1877), which in turn provided an outlet for artists like Kinkichiro Honda (1850-1921), whose cartoons satirized the social changes Japan was experiencing. *Tobae*, a magazine founded with the aid of Bigot in 1888, attracted numerous talented artists, among them Shisui Nagahara, Fusetsu Nakamura and Beisen Kubota.

In 1905 Rakuten Kitazawa, a giant of Japanese cartooning, ushered in a new era by founding *Tokyo Puck*, a weekly color cartoon magazine, and one of the first devoted to political and humorous cartoons. In 1912 Emperor Meiji died, and Japan entered the Taisho period, which saw a flowering of Japanese political and artistic freedom. Newspapers, now solidly modeled after those of the West, enlisted cartoonists to liven up their pages, men like Ippei Okamoto and Shigeo Miyao, who drew political and social commentary cartoons. A new genre, cartoons for children and the family, also sprang up (*Nonki na Tōsan* or "Easy-going Dad") in the *Hōchi Shimbun*, for example, and four-panel cartoons became an established tradition, paving the way for actual comics later on.

With the growth of democracy in the 1920s came the increasing politicization of cartooning. Influenced by the success of the Russian Revolution and the worldwide momentum of Marxist ideology, Japanese cartoonists began to view the world around them in a different light. In 1925 the *Musansha Shimbun* ("Proletariat News") was founded, and it provided a forum for the "propaganda-agitation" cartoons of such artists as Masamu Yanase, Keiichi Suyama and Fumio Matsuyama. On the other hand, a faction led by Saseo Ono depicted modern scenes of "decadence" and "eroticism," while Keizō Shimada produced immensely popular cartoons and comic strips for children.

The 1930s dawned innocuously enough in Japan, but there was also a growing conservative and militaristic trend. In 1932 a number of prominent cartoonists, including Hidezo Kondo and Ryūichi Yokoyama, banded together to form what became known as the *Manga Shūdan* ("Cartoonists' Group"), one of the most influential organizations of its kind. Such associations were part of a long tradition in Japan. Their purpose was to help artists publish their works, but they often became factional and self-serving, sometimes even making it difficult for upcoming artists to break into the field. While Manga Shūdan was exploring humor, left-leaning cartoonists (and progressives in general) were gradually being eliminated through arrest, repression and ostracism. By the end of the 1930s, the militarists were in full control, and as war erupted in China, virtually all Japanese united—willingly or under coercion—behind what was to be the lost cause of the century.

As war spread to the Pacific and involved the United States and Britain, many cartoonists went to work for the army or navy (at times at the front), creating propaganda cartoons and leaflets designed to demoralize enemy troops. Often these bordered on pornography, and many are quite humorous in retrospect. Notable during this period were Hidezō Kondō, who portrayed Roosevelt with fangs, and Tar(Yashima, who became a reverse "Tokyo Rose" by drawing propaganda cartoons for the U.S. Army.

The end of World War II marked a rebirth of artistic and political freedom and produced a plethora of subjects for cartoonists to depict. Taizō Yokoyama, Kenji Ogihara and other fresh talents got a start in new or revived publications, such as *Van* and *Manga,* while the old guard either adapted to new conditions or, in the case of those who had been persecuted, came out of hiding and prison to draw in progressive magazines like *Kumanbachi.* In the newspapers, such four-panel cartoon/comics as Machiko Hasegawa's *Sazae-san,* which dealt with the daily life of the average person, became immensely popular.

In 1955 the establishment of cartooning awards by major publishing houses such as Bungei Shunju, Shogakkan and Kodansha gave further impetus to a growing movement and helped launch the careers of Shinta Chō, Noboru Baba and others. A host of young artists with a totally new, nonideological, often bizarre sense of humor also appeared, among them Yōsuke Inoue, Ryūzan Aki and Yōji Kuri. Some of these, led by Koh Kojima, founded the Dokuritsu Mangaha ("Independent Cartoonists' Faction") in 1956. As Japan's middle class burgeoned in a booming economy, yet another new school of cartoonists, including Sanpei Sato and Sadao Shōji, emerged to portray the trials and tribulations of the average white-collar worker, or "salaryman."

At the same time, the success of major comic book artists like Osamu Tezuka and Sanpei Shirato who drew long, narrative comics with "cinematic techniques" began to affect the cartoon industry and eventually changed its nature completely. The ranks of cartoonists drawing one-panel or four-panel cartoons rapidly shrank, leaving a minority overshadowed by the explosion of either graphic "story comics," or *gekiga.* In a reversal of the U.S. pattern, sales of comics magazines skyrocketed during the 1960s, and their readership expanded from children to adults as the old form of cartoons increasingly became the domain of purists.

Little distinction exists in the Japanese language between cartoons and comics. *Manga,* a general, inclusive term, corresponds roughly to "whimsical or amusing pictures," and *gekiga,* which was coined in the postwar period to describe the newer, more realistic story comics, means "action or dramatic pictures." Today, weekly comics magazines such as *Shūkan Shōnen Jump* ("The Weekly Boys' Jump") have circulations in the millions (Jump peaked at over 6,000,000 in 1996) and top artists earn some of the highest annual incomes in the nation; in fact, nearly forty percent of all published books and magazines in Japan today are actually comics. Given this situation, which has no parallel elsewhere in the world, it is little wonder that single-panel cartoonists find it more lucrative to do longer works. With no equivalent of the *New Yorker* in Japan today, many cartoonists are also comic book artists or, in the case of more avant-garde figures, illustrators.

Single-panel cartoons occasionally appear in magazines, however, and are frequently shown at exhibitions or published independently as collections. The vertically arranged four panel cartoon or strip is by far the most popular form of "short" cartooning today, and is a staple feature in all omnibus-style comics magazines, as humorous filler between long stories. In the 1980s, in particular, this four panel genre experienced an explosion in popularity with the emergence of artists such as Hisaichi Ishii and Masashi Ueda, both of whom became minor industries in and of themselves. In addition to appearing in comics magazines, they wound up working as the regular cartoonists for the coveted spot of the traditional four panel family comic strip that appears on the second to the last page of most national newspapers.

In the United States and Europe, the political cartoon on the editorial page of a newspaper often packs more punch than the editorial itself; by contrast, political cartoons in Japan in the postwar period tended to have a rather anemic quality to them, both in terms of art work and impact. They were long continued by such veterans as Taizō Yokoyama in the *Asahi*, Fumio Matsuyama in the Communist party's *Akahata* and Ryōsuke Nasu in the *Mainichi*; but these cartoons themselves were of such small size as to lose their impact, and they did not adequately represent the existing pool of younger, better talent. The reasons for the demise of this genre were complex, ranging from economic and cultural factors to the fundamental political apathy of the Japanese public, and to the wartime history of repression. By 1997, the state of political cartooning in newspapers had improved somewhat, with artists such as Sunao Hari working in the *Asahi Shinbun*, and Saburo Yutenji in the *Yomiuri Shimbun*. In magazines, the European-influenced Norio and the black-humor specialists Shōji Yamafuni also did increasingly interesting work.

The field of cartooning has expanded so much today that it is no longer necessary for artists to belong to specialized associations in order to be published, as was often the case in the past. Virtually anyone with original ideas can find an outlet somewhere, although many artists do belong to the Japan Cartoonists' Association, which has nearly 500 members. One of the most dramatic changes in the postwar period has been the entry of women in the comics and cartooning field. There are around two to three hundred magazines that carry comics and cartoons in Japan today, and probably half of them target female readers; the majority of cartoons and comics for females are created by female artists. In the seventies women such as Moto Hagio, Keiko Takemiya, Yumiko Ōshima, Riyoko Ikeda, and Machiko Satonaka helped raise the level of comics for girls to a level of sophistication arguably surpassing those for boys. In the '80s and '90s women such as Rumiko Takahashi, Shungicu Uchida and Akimi Yoshida managed to transcend "girls'" or "womens'" comics genre and achieve a true mass audence that included many males. Nonetheless, in the fields of shorter cartoons and political cartooning, in particular, women still lag far behind their male counterparts.

In the late 1980s and the decade of the 1990s, the huge size of the Japanese comics industry began to be felt around the world, with popular titles exported in translated form to Southeast Asia, Europe and the United States. In large part, however, these comics have piggy-backed on the popularity of Japanese animation. Furthermore, while Japanese narrative comics have been highly successful overseas, this has not been true of either the shorter comic strips or political cartoons. Nonetheless, the members of the Japan Cartoonists' Association, for example, have been actively promoting exchanges with counterparts in Asia and other parts of the world, in the form of exhibits, visits, and information interchange.

Given the incredible diversity of cartoon genres in Japan and the huge reservoir of untapped talent, it is to be hoped that in the future more encouragement will be given to those artists who wish to draw single-panel cartoons, especially editorial cartoons. It is also to be hoped that more Japanese comic strip artists, and more social-satire or political cartoonists, will take an active interest in creating an international audience.

Frederik L. Schodt

Appendix E

Animation in Japan

The roots of animation in Japan can be traced back more than a thousand years if one considers indigenous art forms that approximate the movement of characters. Starting in the 11th century, for example, illustrated schrolls were read slowly by unrolling from right to left, with changes in time and place indicated, if not by text narration, by carefully placed visual devices such as floating clouds or naturalistic elements like cherry blossom leaves. *Chōjūgiga,* in particular, bears an uncanny stylistic resemblance to the anthropomorphic animation so popular in early 20th century America. Later media that predate film also include *kami shibai,* or "pictures with storytelling"; *kage-e,* or "shadow puppets"; and paper lanterns that cast shadow pictures.

In the strict sense of the word, however, animation did not really begin in Japan until the early 20th century. Fascinated by J.R. Bray's early cartoons, which arrived in Japan around 1915, animators such as Oten Shimokawa, Jun-ichi Kouchi and Seitarō Kitayama began producing their own films. These three men in turn trained others, who brought the art form to a level of sophistication rivaling that of the West. In 1924 Sanae Yamamoto produced *Ubasuteyama* ("The Mountain to Abandon Old Women"), and in 1927 Yasuji Murata created *Tako no Hone* ("Octopus Bones"); both works dealt with uniquely Japanese themes.

The 1930s saw a burst of activity in animation, with outstanding creations by such artists as Kenzō Masaoka, Noboro Ōfuji and Mitsuyo Seo. Masaoka made a giant contribution to the art form with his *Chikara to Onna no Yo no Naka* ("Strength, Women, and the Ways of the World," 1932), which was Japan's first "talkie." Ōfuji worked increasingly with silhouette animation, and Seo gave new significance to the use of music with his *Nora Kuro Nitohei* ("Nora Kuro, the Second-Class Private," 1935).

During World War II, virtually without exception, Japanese animation films were used for propaganda purposes and to further national solidarity. Creativity was naturally given a rather low priority. Nonetheless, in 1943 the first feature-length animation in Japan, Mitsuyo Seo's *Momotaro no Umiwashi* ("Momotaro's Brave Navy"), was made at the request of the Japanese Imperial Navy, and Masaoka created *Kumo to Chūrippu* ("Spider and Tulip"), today generally regarded as one of the all-time classics of Japanese animation. Both of these films had a huge influence on pioneer animators who came of age in the postwar period and helped establish the modern industry. As soon as the war ended, Masaoka, Yamamoto and Murata banded together to form Shin Nihon Dōga, an animation production company. This later became the nucleus of Nihon Dōga, where the Torachan series was produced from 1947 to 1955, and eventually of Toei Dōga, today one of Japan's biggest producers of animated cartoons.

Toei Dōga's first production was Yasuji Mori's *Koneko no Rakugaki* ("Kitten's Doodlings," 1957), a charming color film. The next year Toei embarked on the production of feature-length films with the intention of finally making animation a solidly commercial and even exportable commodity. First in the series was *Hakujaden* ("Legend of a White Snake"), directed by Taiji Yabushita. *Hakujaden* utilized the talents of some of the top animators in Japan, and its success resulted in other feature-length films, such as *Shōnen Sarutobi Sasuke* ("The Adventures of a Little Samurai," 1959).

In the early 1960s, several new production companies were established, including Ryūichi Yokoyama's Otogi Productions and Osamu Tezuka's Mushi Productions. *Otogi no Sekai Ryokō* ("Journey into Fantasyland," 1962) was a compilation of shorts by the staff of Otogi Productions. *Aru Machikado no Monogatari* ("Story of a Certain Street Corner"), created by Mushi Productions in 1963, won the praise of critics for its expressionism and excellent use of music. The early 1960s also saw the advent of animation for television. *Tetsuwan Atom* ("Astro Boy"), by Mushi Productions, was Japan's first television series; using the more economical "limited," instead of "full" animation, it ushered in a new era of mass production. In addition to proving enormously popular in Japan, it was exported to the United States and shown on NBC. *Atom's* success spawned a variety of imitators and competitors and heralded a new age of diversity, though much of the new output was of lower quality. It also paved the way for the much later popularity of Japanese animation overseas.

In 1965 Mushi Productions came out with the first color animated serial for television, *Jungle Tatei* ("Jungle Emperor"), based on Tezuka's comic book of the same name; two years later, nearly all television animation was in color. Like "Astro Boy," *Jungle Taitei* was exported overseas, and it is widely believed by many today to have been an inspiration for Disney's 1994 hit, *The Lion King*. In Japan, sports themes also became highly popular on television. In 1969 Toei set a precedent by using a rotoscope (trace machine) to produce *Tiger Mask,* cashing in on the wrestling craze then sweeping Japan, and in 1970 Mushi Productions animated the comic book *Ashita no Joe* ("Tomorrow's Joe"), a boxing story. Other, newer production companies soon became active in television animation. Tatsunoko Productions released *Minashigo Hutch* ("Orphan Hutch"), a fantasy starring a bumblebee, and Tokyo Movie created the action-filled *Lupin III.*

Science fiction also became a popular theme, with *Tatsunoko's Kagaku Ninjatai Gotcaman* (shown in the United States as *Battle of the Planets*) appearing in 1972, and Office Academy's *Uchu Senkan Yamato* ("Space Cruiser Yamato," or "Star Blazers") in 1974. The latter series proved so popular that it was later made into multiple animated features.

Television animation based on folktales has also been popular, as evidenced by Group Tac's *Manga Nihon Mukashibanashi* ("Japanese Folktale Cartoons"). At the end of the 1970s, the giant warrior "robot" space fantasy, *Mobile Suit Gundam,* first shown on television, was turned into multiple theatrical features and spawned a huge merchandising industry for toy models among other goods. In the late 1980s and up to 1997, director Hayao Miyazaki assumed the mantle worn by Osamu Tezuka as the central figure in commercial animation, creating theatrical features of remarkable originality and depth, starting with the now-classic *Nausicaa* in 1984 and culminating with the 1997 blockbuster hit, *Monomokehime*. Along with Katsuhiro Otomo, the creator of *Akira,* he became the best known animation director in Japan, as well as overseas.

In the 1980s, the commercial Japanese animation industry exploded in size, not only because of its long incubation as an extension of the gargantuan comics industry, but because of the rapid diffusion of videotape recorders, which dramatically increased the number of viewers. Not only could people watch favorite shows whenever they wanted to; they could analyze and appreciate them better. As a result, an entirely new animation industry was spawned—the so-called OAV, or "original animation video"—which allows works to be commercially animated that were never broadcast on television or shown in theaters. With the synergy produced by linking the comics and animation industries, and the merger of both into a giant merchandising machine that generated billions of dollars in revenue from sales of related goods, animation, or "anime," also became very profitable, and at the end of the nineties was increasingly regarded as the shining hope of Japan's otherwise struggling "software" export industries.

Many of the main creative thrusts in Japanese animation still originate outside the domain of television. Before Osamu Tezuka's Mushi Productions folded in 1973, it produced several unique feature-length animation works specifically designed for adult audiences. One of these, *A Thousand and One Nights* (1969), represented a pioneering use of eroticism in the medium. Some comics artists, such as Katsuhiro Otomo, have continued the tradition established by Tezuka, of pushing the boundaries of the animation within the context of commercial works. Otomo, who began as a brilliant and highly successful manga artist, today also directs or produces commercially successful theatrical animation (such as the well-known *Akira*), and several of his theatrical works—such as the omnibus style *Robot Carnival* and *Memories*—have an experimental quality to them.

Elsewhere, independent animators who create mostly short works remain active but they are still plagued by low budgets, lack of access to the mass media, and a scarcity of forums in which to air their creations. In recent years, however, several Japanese experimental animators have received considerable exposure overseas, in animation film festivals and special shows of animation shorts that show commercially in theaters. In the eighties, for example, American audiences frequently had the opportunity to view the late Osamu Tezuka's *Jumping* and *Broken Down Film,* as well as shorts by Renzō Kinoshita, Sadao Tsukioka, Yōji Kuri, and Kihachiro Okamotō. In Japan, newcomers to the industry, as well as veterans such as Shin-ichi Suzuki and Taku Furukawa, continue busily working.

Domestically, experimental animators in Japan have been aided by the activities of ASIFA-Japan, the branch of the world wide International Animated Film Association, and—especially in the late eighties and early nineties—by the late Renzō Kinoshita and his wife Sayoko, who worked hard to establish links with the international animation community, and who were a major force behind the establishment of the prestigious Hiroshima Animation Festival.

Animation in Japan today faces the same problems that beset the field in the United States and Europe—the high cost of labor for commercial productions and the lack of funds and outlets for independents. On the commercial level, one of the most striking recent developments has been the internationalization of the industry, with increasing cooperation in the production stage between the United States and Japan, and the growing practice of subcontracting basic work to Korea, China, and Taiwan in order to cut down on costs. On the independent, experimental level, the tendency of directors and animators to be diverted into the more lucrative field of television commercials remains a problem. Nonetheless, Japan has today become the animation capital of the world, and like manga, or Japan's gargantuan comic book industry, the animation industry has achieved a massive size. With huge blockbuster commercial hits like the first-TV-series—then-theaters-then-national-phenom *Evangelion* (directed by Hideaki Ano, and estimated to have indirectly generated over 30 billion yen of revenue) or the feature *Mononokehime* (Hayao Miyazaki) in 1997, an entire generation of Japanese is growning up on animation. As a result, today many of the best and brightest young minds in Japan dream of becoming not doctors or lawyers, but animators. In the near future, therefore, we may expect further great things of animation in Japan.

Frederik Schodt

Glossary

Glossary of Cartooning Terms

animated cartoon A series of drawings photographed on film and shown like a motion picture. The animated cartoon is the most popular as well as the most widespread form of film animation.

animation The technique of giving the illusion of movement to inanimate objects (drawings, puppets, clay figures, etc.). The term can be used to describe either the process itself or its result on the screen (e.g., *Fantasia*).

Animation: Ryan Larkins's "Walking." © National Film Board.

anime Japanese word for animation, by extension a cartoon film following Japanese conventions of narrative or style.

animation director The person responsible for all the different steps (story development, storyboarding, sketching, inking, etc.) that go into the making of an animated cartoon.

animation producer The person responsible for all the business decisions (budgeting, format, time allotment, promotion, etc.) that are ancillary to the production of an animated cartoon.

animation studio A company set up with the express purpose of producing animated films. An animation studio can be an independent company producing animated films for release through major film companies or film distributors, or it can be the animation arm of a major film studio (e.g., MGM or Warner Brothers).

animator 1. A person who develops the key drawings for an animated cartoon. **2.** By extension, anyone (animation director, inker, in-betweener, etc.) who contributes to the process of making an animated cartoon.

ASIFA Association Internationale du Film d'Animation (International Association of Animated Film), an organization composed of animators from around the world and devoted to the promotion of animated films.

background A setting against which action takes place. In animation, backgrounds may be either drawn or painted on paper with animation cels placed over them, or directly executed on the cels.

background man An animator who draws or paints the backgrounds of an animated cartoon.

balloon An outlined area typically connected to or pointing toward the mouth of a cartoon character. The balloon is

Somewhere in France
THEY MAY TURN FRANCE INTO GERMANY BUT THEY'LL NEVER TURN FRENCHMEN INTO GERMANS
LA BONBON

The balloon in print cartoons: Vaughn Shoemaker. © Chicago Daily News.

generally used to convey dialogue but can also enclose a variety of signs and symbols. A widespread convention of the comics, it is used sparingly by magazine and editorial cartoonists but is a common device in newspaper panels (e.g., *The Days of Real Sport, Ziggy*). The balloon was widely used as a dramatic device in early animated cartoons, reflecting the comic strip background of many of the pioneer animators; after 1920 it was largely replaced by the intertitle, derived from the movies. The advent of sound cartoons made both balloons and intertitles obsolete.

benday (or **Ben day**) A transparent screen, usually dotted or crosshatched, pasted over a drawing to add shading (named after Benjamin Day, the inventor of the process). Common in the comics, this technique is not as widely used in panel cartoons.

caption 1. A line or lines of type (usually dialogue) set underneath a cartoon drawing. **2.** Synonym for legend.

caricature 1. A drawing of a person in which particular or unusual characteristics are emphasized to the point of ridicule or grotesqueness. **2.** A style of drawing that exaggerates the unique characteristics, mannerisms or features of a person. (For a detailed discussion of the art of caricature, see the essay "Caricature and Cartoon: An Overview" in this encyclopedia.)

A caricature: Leon Tolstoy by Olaf Gulbransson.

The balloon in animated cartoons: Raoul Servais's "To Speak or Not to Speak." © Servais.

cartoon (from the French carton, a sketch or study on pasteboard) A drawing of political, satirical or humorous intent, containing, usually within one frame, a self-explanatory scene or composition, often accompanied by a caption or legend.

cartoon film An animated film in which cartoon drawings are used; an animated cartoon.

cartooning The art of drawing cartoons.

cartoonist An artist who draws cartoons.

celluloid 1. A transparent sheet on which an animation drawing is traced (most often referred to as a cel or cell). Despite its name, it is usually made not of celluloid (which is highly flammable) but of cellulose acetate or clear plastic. **2.** The animation drawing itself.

collage The technique of pasting cutouts or preexisting material (paper, cardboard, money, etc.) on a drawing or painting. Collage can be used in both print cartoons and animated cartoons.

copperplate An illustration obtained by engraving or etching on copper. The copperplate was the most prevalent form of printing in the 18th century and was extensively used by the early cartoonists.

cutout An object (usually a drawing) cut from paper, cardboard or other soft material and placed over a cel. Animation of cutouts is achieved by slightly altering their position after each photographic exposure. Cutouts can be hand-painted if desired.

distributor A company or company division set up to release independently produced films (including animated films) to movie theaters (for example, Paramount Pictures was the distributor of the animated cartoons produced by the Fleischer studio).

drypoint An engraving made directly on a copperplate by means of a sharp needle, without the use of acids (hence the name).

editorial cartoon A cartoon meant to illustrate or amplify a point, whether political, satirical, social or rhetorical.

feature A cartoon appearing in a newspaper or magazine and having its own continuing title (e.g., *Believe It or Not!*, *The Family Circus* and *Berry's World*).

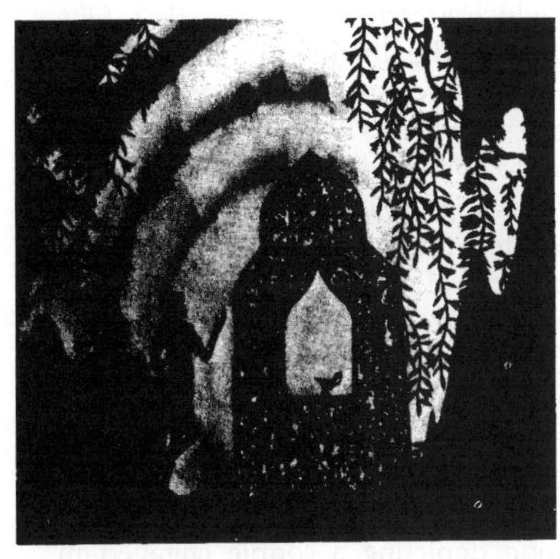

A cutout: "The Adventures of Prince Achmed," 1926. © Lotte Reiniger.

GLOSSARY

Why Call Them Sportsmen?
An editorial cartoon: Jay ("Ding") Darling. © Outdoor America.

feature film A theatrical film, usually fictional, that is over 3,000 feet in length. Animated films are usually measured in terms of duration rather than footage; thus, an animated cartoon is said to be a feature film if it lasts for 60 minutes or more.

Featurette An animated film between 30 and 60 minutes in length.

film animation Any animation process realized on film. All modern animation is film animation; it represents the application of cinematographic techniques to the graphic or plastic arts. In the case of an animated cartoon, drawings must be prepared in series, with minute variations in their positioning. The succession of drawings is photographed by a movie camera frame-by-frame and then projected on a screen, where the illusion of movement is created.

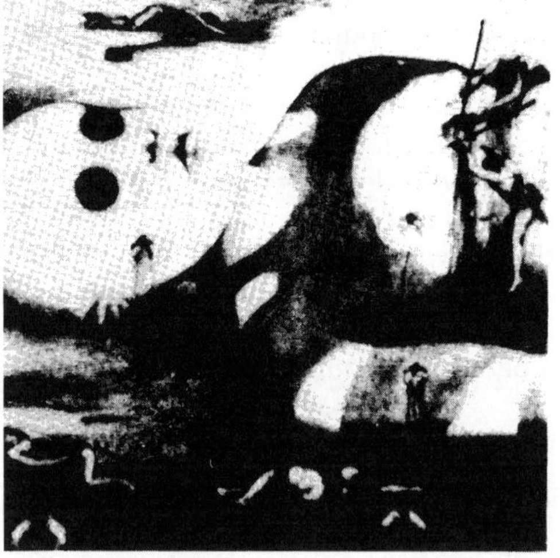

A feature film: "La Planète Sauvage." © Films Armorial.

film cartoon Synonym for animated cartoon.

frame 1. The space in which a cartoon is enclosed. **2.** One picture on a strip of film. **3.** The different components of a cel drawing (characters, backgrounds, fore grounds, cutouts, etc.) that are assembled to be photographed by a movie camera in order to appear in a single frame of film.

frame-by-frame The cinematographic process of creating an animated film by separately photographing each frame (or cel). When the succession of pictures thus obtained is projected on a screen (at a speed of 16 frames a second for a silent film and 24 frames a second for a sound film), the illusion of movement is visually perceived by the spectator.

gag cartoon A cartoon whose only intent is to amuse, without any satirical or editorial implication.

he/she cartoon A cartoon depicting a couple engaged in witty or sardonic repartee.

humor cartoon Synonym for gag cartoon.

"Paris has its good points, ma'm, but you haven't lived until you've seen Dallas."
A gag cartoon: C.E. Martin ("CEM"). © Collier's.

in-between A drawing between two key positions in an animated cartoon.
in-betweener A person who draws in-betweens (also called an assistant or junior animator).
inker A person who traces drawings on cels.
inking The tracing onto cels, in ink, of the outlines of animation drawings.
intertitle A printed text giving narration or dialogue and positioned between frames of a silent film to explain or advance the action.
joke drawing (British) Synonym for gag cartoon.
key A drawing in an animated cartoon of the principal positions in a sequence of movements. Keys depict those points at which any part of a character or object starts, stops or changes directions.
key animator A person, often, simply called an animator (def. 1), who draws the keys in an animated cartoon.
layout 1. The distribution on a flat surface of the different elements of an illustration or cartoon. **2.** The design of an animation scene, including colors, positions of the characters, cel levels and camera movements.
legend 1. A text, usually descriptive, placed above a cartoon drawing. **2.** Synonym for caption.
limited animation The technique of giving only a partial illusion of movement to animated objects or figures (eye and lip movements only, for example).
lithography The process of reproducing illustrations engraved and inked on a stone surface. Perfected by Aloys Senefelder in Bavaria in 1796, lithography gradually replaced the copperplate process as the prevailing method of printing cartoons during the 19th century.
mini-short An animated short one minute or less in duration.
multiplane A special device (perfected by Ub Iwerks) for photographing different levels of cels with one exposure of

A mini-short: "Happy End." © Zagreb Film.

the movie camera. The multiplane consists of a number of layers of glass on which cels can be positioned, and which can be placed underneath the camera lens at varying distances. This gives an animation scene a more realistic feeling of perspective and depth.

NCS National Cartoonists Society, an American association of cartoonists.

package film A film, animated or otherwise, consisting of separate segments linked together by transition scenes and/or narrated text (e.g., Walt Disney's Saludos Amigos).

painter A person who applies paint on an animation cel or directly on film to obtain a color effect.

panel 1. The space enclosing a cartoon; synonym for frame (def. 1). **2.** A cartoon having a separate and continuing title and appearing daily or weekly in a newspaper. Panels traditionally appear on the same page as comic strips. A *multi-panel* cartoon is a cartoon that uses two or more panels (def. 1) to make its point. It differs from a comic strip in that one or more of the constitutive elements of comics (balloons, continuity, permanent cast of characters, etc.) are missing. A *single-panel* cartoon uses only one panel to make its point.

peg system A system devised by Raoul Barré to insure the correct positioning of animation drawings (and later of animation cels) by the use of register pegs.

picture story A story told mainly by means of pictures, with a narrative text printed underneath each picture.

political cartoon A cartoon whose main intent is to comment on a political personality or situation.

print 1. A reproduction of a cartoon or illustration by a printing or photoprinting process. **2.** A positive copy made from negative film.

print cartoon A cartoon reproduced in any of the print media (as opposed to an animated cartoon).

register holes Holes punched in animation paper and/or cels to correspond to register pegs.

register pegs A device placed in the camera gate to insure the exact positioning of every drawing or cel in an animation film.

rotoscope A device (patented by Max Fleischer) used to convert a live-action shot into a series of animated drawings. The process itself is called *rotoscopy* or *rotoscoping*.

A multi-panel cartoon: Alberto Fremura. © Il Resto del Carlino.

series A succession of cartoons (print or animated) linked together by a permanent cast of characters or a similar situation.

short (or short subject) A theatrical film, animated or otherwise, that is 30 minutes or less in duration (as opposed to a feature).

silent film A film in which only pictures have been recorded (as opposed to a sound film).

silhouette film An animated film made with jointed cutout figures.

single-frame 1. Synonym for single-panel. **2.** Synonym for frame-by-frame.

sound film A film in which sound has been recorded in addition to pictures, by means of a sound track.

sound track The narrow band or bands along one side of a motion picture that record dialogue, music, sound effects, etc.

speed lines Lines added to a series of animated drawings to give a heightened impression of speed when projected in quick succession on the screen.

sports cartoon A cartoon whose subject is sports.

storyboard A board used to display in proper sequence the sketches and layout of an animated film.

synchronization The process by which the movement of animated drawings is matched to the accompanying sound or music.

syndicate An organization that handles the distribution of individual features (panels, cartoon series, comic strips, etc.) to subscribing newspapers.

theatrical A film produced for showing in a movie theater.

tracer Synonym for inker.

transparency Synonym for celluloid.

wash 1. A technique for creating cartoons or illustrations by means of a brush and ink diluted with water. **2.** A drawing obtained by this technique.

woodcut 1. A printing process in which a block of wood (usually pear, cherry or beech) is cut along the grain, leaving in relief the lines and surfaces to be inked for impression on paper. **2.** A drawing obtained by this technique.

wordless cartoon A cartoon using only a drawing to make its point.

zincography A printing process in which an illustration or cartoon is directly engraved onto a sheet of zinc by means of chemical inks.

A sports cartoon: L.D. Warren. © Philadelphia Record.

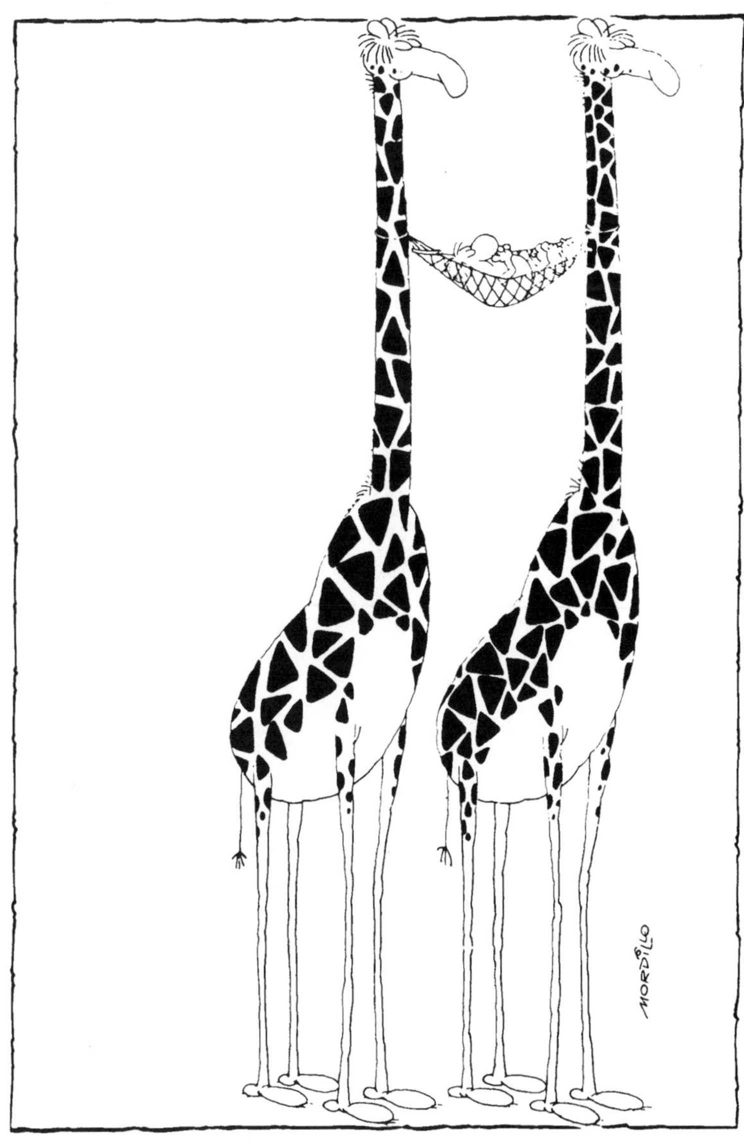

A wordless cartoon: Guillermo Mordillo. © Mordillo.

Select Bibliography

The literature on cartoons and cartooning is immense, spanning two centuries. Only the most significant or comprehensive books, those dealing with some general aspect of cartooning, have been included here. Technical works, how-to manuals, press releases and promotional pieces have been omitted, as have biographies, monographs and anthologies devoted to individual cartoonists. Similarly, articles have been selected on the basis of general appeal or interest, though a few dealing with particular artists or features have been included where they also contain a more general discussion of the field.

To facilitate further research, this bibliography is divided into two categories, works on print cartoons and works on animation. Each category is further subdivided, listing books first, then articles and essays.

Print Cartoons

Books

Appelbaum, Stanley, ed. *French Satirical Drawings from l'Assiette au Beurre.* New York, 1978.
—, *Simplicissimus.* New York, 1975.
Becker, Stephen. *Comic Art in America,* New York, 1959.
Bénézit, Emmanuel. *Dictionnaire Critique et Documentaire des Peintres, Sculpteurs, Dessinateurs et Graveurs.* 8 vols. Paris, 1976.
Blum, André. *La Caricature Revolutionnaire.* Paris, 1917.
Bradshaw, Percy V. *They Make Us Smile.* London, 1942.
—, *Lines of Laughter*. London, 1946.
Breger, David. *But That's Unprintable.* New York, 1955.
Brisson, Adolphe. *Nos Humoristes. Paris,* 1960.
Champfleury, Jules-François-Félix. *Histoire de la Caricature.* 4 vols. Paris, 1863-85.
Chase, John. *Today's Cartoon.* New Orleans, 1962.
Cole, William and **Thaler, Mike**, eds. *The Classic Cartoons.* Cleveland, 1966.
Columba, Ramón. *Qué Es la Caricatura?* Buenos Aires, 1959.
Craven, Thomas. *Cartoon Cavalcade.* New York, 1943.
Crouse, Russel. *Mr. Currier and Mr. Ives.* Garden City, N.Y., 1930.
Davies, Randall. *Caricature of Today*. London, 1928.
Dell'Acqua, Amado. *La Caricatura Politica Argentina.* Buenos Aires, 1960.
Dessin d'Humour, Le. Exhibition catalogue published by the Bibliothèque Nationale. Paris, 1971.
Fielding, Mantle. *Dictionary of American Painters, Sculptors and Engravers.* New York, 1965.
Fisher, Edwin; Gerberg, Mort; and **Wolin, Ron,** eds. *The Art in Cartooning.* New York, 1975.
Fitzgerald, Richard. *Art and Politics.* Westport, Conn., 1973.
Fossai, Donnyos. *Antologia Brasileira de Humor. Porto Alegre,* Brazil, 1976.
Fuchs, Eduard. *Die Karikatur der Europäische Völker vom Altertum bis zur Neureit.* Berlin, 1901.
Geiger, Hansludwig. *Es War um die Jahrhundertwerde*. Munich, 1953. Geipel, John. The Cartoon. London, 1972.
George, Dorothy. *English Political Caricature.* London, 1960.
Getlein, Frank, and **Getlein, Dorothy.** *The Bite of the Print.* New York, 1963.
Gianeri, Enrico. *Storia della Caricatura.* Milan, 1959.
Gifford, Denis. *Run, Adolf Run: The World War II Fun Book*. London, 1975.
Gill, Brendan. *Here at the New Yorker.* New York, 1975.
Gowans, Alan. *The Unchanging Arts.* New York, 1971.
Grand-Carteret, John. *Les Moeurs et Ia Caricature en Allemagne, en Autriche et en Suisse.* Paris, 1885.
—, *Les Moeurs et Ia Caricature en France*. Paris, 1888.
Grose, Francis. *Rules for Drawing Caricaturas.* London, 1788.
Hausenstein, Wilhelm. *Vortrag über der Simplicissimus.* Munich, 1932.
Hess, Stephen, and **Kaplan, Milton.** *The Ungentlemanly Art.* New York, 1968.
Hiller, Bevis. *Cartoons and Caricature.* London, 1970.
Hoerschelmann, Rolf von. *Leben ohne Alttag. Berlin,* 1947.

Hoff, Syd. *Editorial and Political Cartooning.* New York, *1976.*
Hofmann, Werner. *Die Karikatur von Leonardo bis Picasso.* Vienna, 1956.
Horn, Maurice, ed. *The World Encyclopedia of Comics.* New York, 1976.
Image of America in Caricature and Cartoon, The. Exhibition catalogue published by the Amon Carter Museum of Western Art. Fort Worth, Tex., 1976.
International Pavilion of Humor. Catalogues to the International Salons of Cartoons (1968-).
Johnson, Lucy Black, and **Johnson, Pyke, Jr.**, eds. *Cartoon Treasury.* New York, 1955.
Kunzle, David. *The Early Comic Strip.* Berkeley, 1973.
Leguèbe, Eric. *Voyage en Cartoonland.* Paris, 1977.
Lima, Herman. *Historia da Caricatura no Brasil.* Rio de Janeiro, 1963.
Lindesay, Vane. The *Inked-In Image.* Melbourne, 1970.
Lipscyc, Enrique. El *Dibujo a Través del Temperamento de 150 Famosas Artistas.* Buenos Aires, 1953.
Low, David. *British Cartoonists.* London, 1942.
Lynch, Bohun. *A History of Caricature.* Boston, 1927. Reprint, Detroit, 1974.
Maurice, Arthur Bartlett, and **Cooper, Frederic Taber.** *History of the Nineteenth Century in Caricature.* New York, 1904.
Morin, Louis. *Le Dessin Humoristique.* Paris, 1913.
Murell, William A. *A History of American Graphic Humor.* 2 vols. New York, 1933 and 1938.
Nelson, Roy Paul. *Comic Art and Caricature.* Chicago, 1978.
Nelson, William, ed. *Out of the Crocodile's Mouth.* Washington, D.C., 1949.
Nevins, Allan, and **Weitenkampf, Frank.** *A Century of Political Cartoons.* New York, 1944.
Parton, James. *Caricature and Other Comic Art.* New York, 1877.
Peters, Harry T. *Currier and Ives: Printmakers to the American People.* Garden City, N.Y., 1942.
Piper, Reinhardt. *Nachmittag.* Munich, 1950.
Price, R.G.G. *A History of "Punch."* London, 1957.
Ragon, Michel. *Le Dessin d'Humour* Paris, 1960.,.
Roberts-Jones, Philippe. *La Caricature du Second Empire à la Belle Epoque,* 1850-1900. Paris, 1963.
Roth, Eugen. *Simplicissimus.* Hanover, 1954.
Rubiu, Vittorio. *La Caricatura.* Florence, 1973.
Shikes, Ralph E. The *Indignant Eye.* Boston, 1969.
Sinsheimer, Hermann. Geliebt *im Paradies.* Munich, 1953.
Spencer, Dick. *Pulitzer Prize Cartoons: The Men and Their Masterpieces.* Ames, Ia., 1951.
Sternberg, Jacques. *Un Siècle d'Humour Français.* Paris, 1961.
Suarès, Jean-Claude, ed. *Art of the Times.* New York, 1973.
Sykalin, S., and **Kremenskaia, I.** *Sovetskaya Satireskaya Pechat': 1917-1963.* Moscow, 1963.
Vené, Gian Franco. *La Satira Politica.* Milan, 1976.
Verechagin, B.A. *Russkaia Caricatura.* St. Petersburg, 1911.
Veth, Cornelis. *Comic Art in England.* London, 1929.
Weitenkampf, Frank. *American Graphic Art.* New York, 1924.

Articles and essays

Barshay, Robert. "The Cartoon of Modern Sensibility." *Journal of Popular Culture,* Winter 1974.

Battaglia, Roberto C. "Sentida Gráfico y Humanidad Son la Base del Dibujo Humoristico." *Dibujantes,* no. 2, 1953.

Becker, Stephen. "Cartoons." *Collier's Encyclopedia,* New York, 1974.

Bender, Jack H. "The Outlook for Editorial Cartooning." *World of Comic Art,* no. 3, Winter 1966-67.

Berger, Arthur Asa. "What Makes People Laugh?: Cracking the Cultural Code." **ETC.,** no. 32, December 1975.

Bertieri, Claudio. "Trent' Anni Dopo: *Il Bertoldo." Il Lavoro,* August 25, 1967.

Bojko, Simon. "Polish Humor and Satirical Drawing." *Arts and Artists,* September 1976.

Bordes, Georges. "La Politique Dessinée." *La Nation Européenne,* September 1967.

Carpi, Pier, and **Castelli, Alfredo.** *"MAD." Comics Club,* no. 1, April-May 1967.

Cebna'n, Julio. "La Nueva Frontera del Humor Español." *La Actualidad Española,* no. 729, 1965.

Chase, John. "The TV Editorial Cartoon." *Cartoonist,* January 1968.

De Luca, Michele. "Il Secondo Underground Italiano." *Comics,* May 1973.

Dennls, Everett E. "The Regeneration of Political Cartooning." *Journalism Quarterly,* no. 51, Winter 1974.

Devree, Howard. "It's Funny, but Is It Art? Steinberg's Cartoons." *New York Times Magazine,* September 8, 1946.

Dolbier, Maurice. "A New Historian of America: Comic Art." *New York Herald Tribune,* November 29, 1959.

Ebmeyer, Klaus U. "Cartoons." *Civis,* no. 7, 1967.

Hasley, Louis. "James Thurber: Artist in Humor." *South Atlantic Quarterly,* no. 73, Autumn 1974.

Kolaja, J. "American Magazine Cartoons and Social Control." *Journalism Quarterly,* no. 30, 1953.

Kunzle, David. "Two Hundred Years of the Great American Freedom to Complain." *Art in America,* no. 65, March-April 1977.

Marschall, Richard. "Mail Order Success: The Old Cartoon Correspondence Courses." *Cartoonist PROfiles,* no. 30, June 1976.

Mitgang, Herbert. "Reducing the Gods to Scale." *Art News,* no. 75, March 1976.

Ostrander, Sheila, and **Schroeder, Lynn.** "From Russia with Laughs." *World of Comic Art,* no. 3, Winter 1966-67.

Paine, A.B. "Origin of American Cartoon Symbols." *Harper's Weekly,* September 1908.

Pucciarelli, M. "Domenica con gli Addams." *Settimana Incom,* April 24, 1966.

Sandburg, Carl. "Cartoons? Yes!" *Cartoonist,* Summer 1957.

Schiefley, W.H. "French Pictorial Humor." *Catholic World,* May 1926.

Schroder, Peter H. "Unsere Welt im Zerrspiegel." *Die Welt,* June 16-17, 1967.

Seal, Basil. "Edward Lear e il Nonsense. *Linus,* no. 21, 1966.

Shelden, Florence H. "Drawing Power." *American Education,* no. 11, March 1975.

Smith, A.M. "Circus in Cartoons." *Hobbies,* no. 52, October 1947.

Stote, Amos. "Figures in the New Humour." *Bookman,* no. 31, May 1910.

Strelow, Hans. "Das Normale Ist das Absurde." *Frankfurter Allgemeiner Zeitung,* January 10, 1970.

Tarin-Iglesias, José. *"Cu-Cut y El Bé Negre." Gaceta de 1a Prensa Española,* no. 99, January 15, 1968.

Tubau, Ivan. "The Political and Satirical Cartoon." *UNESCO Courier,* no. 29, April 1976.

Worth, Sol. "Seeing Metaphor as Caricature." *New Literary History,* no. 6, Autumn 1974.

Animation

Books

Benayoun, Robert. *Le Dessin Animé après Walt Disney.* Paris, 1961.
Bryne, Daniel J. *Grafilm: An Approach to a New Medium.* London, 1970.
Cabarga, Leslie. *The Fleischer Story.* Franklin Square, N.Y., 1976.
Chevalier, Denys. *J'Aime le Dessin Animé.* Paris, 1962.
Collin, Philippe, and **Wyn, Michel.** *Le Cinéma d'Animation dans le Monde.* Paris, 1956.
Duca, Lo. *Le Dessin Animé.* Paris, 1948.
Edera, Bruno. *Full-Length Animated Feature Films.* London, 1977.
Fernandez Cuenca, Carlos. *El Mundo del Dibujo Animado.* Madrid, 1966.
Gianeri, Enrico. *Storia del Cartone Animato.* Milan, 1960.
Ginzburg, Semyon. *Rijsovamii Kykolni Film.* Moscow, 1957.
Goméz Mesa, Luis. *Los Films de Dibujos Animados.* Madrid, 1930.
Halas, John, and **Manvell, Roger.** *Art in Movement: New Directions in Animation.* London, 1970.
—, *Design in Motion.* London, 1962.
Herdeg, Walter, ed. *Film and TV Graphics.* Zurich, 1967.
—, *Film and TV Graphics* 2. Zurich, 1976.
Holloway, Ronald. *Z Is for Zagreb.* London, 1972.
Kinsey, Anthony. *Animated Film Making.* London, 1970.
Levitan, Eli L. *Animation Art in the Commercial Film.* New York, 1960.
—, *Animation Techniques and Commercial Film Production.* New York, 1962.
Lutz, E.G. *Animated Cartoons.* New York, 1923.
Madsen, Roy P. *Animated Film: Concepts, Methods, Uses.* New York, 1969.
Maltin, Leonard. *The Disney Films.* New York, 1973.
Manvell, Roger. *The Animated Film.* London, 1954.
Poncet, Marie-Thérèse. *Dessin Animé, Art Mondial.* Paris, 1956.
—, *Esthétique du Dessin Animé.* Paris, 1952.
Reiniger, Lotte. *Shadow Theatres and Shadow Films.* New York, 1970.
Rider, David. *The Great Movie Cartoon Parade.* New York, 1976.
Rondolino, Gianni. *Storia del Cinema d'Animazione.* Turin, Italy, 1974.
Stephenson, Ralph. *Animation in the Cinema.* London, 1967.
—, *The Animated Film.* London, 1973.
Thomas, Bob. *The Art of Animation* . New York, 1958.
Trinchero, Sergio. *Gli Eroi del Cartone Animato Americano.* Rome, 1972.
Zanotto, Piero, and **Zangrando, Fiorello.** *L'Italia di Cartone.* Padua, Italy, 1973.

Articles and essays

Barrier, Mike. "The Sons of Aesop." *Graphic Story Magazine,* no. 9, 1968.
Black, Ed. "Behind the Scenes at Walt Disney." *Cartoonist PROfiles,* no. 38, June 1978.
Brion, Marcel. "Félix le Chat ou la Poésie Créatrice." *Le Rouge et le Noir,* July 1928.
Chevalier, D.S. "Ouverture d'un Cours de Ciné-Peinture à Paris." *Arts,* October 31, 1947.
Culhane, John. "John Culhane's Motif-Index and Thesaurus of Gags." *New York Times Magazine,* March 7, 1976.
Disney, Walt. "Animated Cartoons." *Health Education Journal,* no. 1, 1956.
—, "The Cartoon's Contribution to Children." *Overland Monthly,* October 1933.
Duca, Lo. "Du Dessin Animé à la Plastique Animée." *La Nature,* no. 67, May 15, 1939.
Ford, Greg. "Warner Brothers." *Film Comment,* no. 11, January-February 1975.
Glover, Guy. "Nine Film Animators Speak." *ArtsCanada,* April 1970.
Halas, John. "Animated Film." *Art and Industry,* no. 43, July-August 1947.
Horn, Maurice. "Animation." *Collier's Encyclopedia,* New York, 1980.
—"Animation and Science Fiction." *Marvel Super Special,* no. 10, Winter 1979.
Hulett, Ralph. "Artist's Part in the Production of an Animated Cartoon." *American Artist,* no. 19, May 1955.
Jones, Chuck. "Diary of a Mad Cel-Washer." *Film Comment,* no. 12, May-June 1976.
Klein, Isidore. "Pioneer Animation Producer." *Cartoonist PROfiles,* nos. 25-27, June-September 1975.
Kneitel, Ruth F. "Out of the Inkwell." *World of Comic Art,* no. 2, 1966.
Knight, Arthur. "UPA, Magoo and McBoing Boing." *Art Digest,* no. 26, February 1, 1952.
König, Renée. "Analyse von Micky-Maus-Filmen." *Praktische Sozialforschung,* vol. 1, 1965.
Langsner, Jules. "UPA." *Arts and Architecture,* no. 71, December 1974.
Levinson, Richard M. "From Olive Oyl to Sweet Polly Purebread: Sex Role Stereotypes and Televised Cartoons." *Journal of Popular Culture,* no. 9, Winter 1975.
Low, David. "Leonardo da Disney." *New Republic,* January 5, 1942.
Macek, Carl. "From Little Nemo to Little Nemo." *Mediascene,* no. 21, September-October, 1976.
Maltin, Leonard. "TV Animation: The Decline and Pratfall of a Popular Art." *Film Comment,* no. 11, January-February 1975.
Manvell, Roger. "Animation." *Encyclopedia Britannica,* New York, 1976.
Petrucci, Norberto P. "El Dibujo Animado en la URSS." *Dibujantes,* no. 16, 1955.
Romer, Jean-Claude. "Les Mickey Mouse Cartoons." *Giff-Wiff,* no. 19, 1966.
Schmidmayer, Werner. "Animation für der Konsum." *Graphik,* no. 10, 1970.
Seldes, Gilbert. "No Art, Mr. Disney?" *Esquire,* September 1937.
Sullivan, Catherine. "United Productions of America: The Modern Look in Animated Cartoons." *American Artist,* no. 19, November 1955.
Thompson, Richard. "Meep Meep!" *Film Comment,* no. 12, May-June 1976.
Turner, Gerry A. "Artists Behind an Animated Cartoon." Design, no. 54, June 1953.
—, "New Horizons in Animated Cartooning: UPA Cartoons." Design, no. 55, January 1954.
Varlejs, Jana. "Cine-Opsis." *Wilson Library Bulletin,* no. 50, March 1976.
Verrall, Robert. "Making an Animated Cartoon: `The Romance of Transportation."' *Canadian Art,* no. 11, 1954.
Viazzi, Cesare. "Il Cartone Animato Nasce . . . a Genova." *If,* October-December 1973.
Weiss, William. "Terrytoons." *Cartoonist,* February 1967.
Zangrando, Fiorello. "Animazione a Strappi." *Eureka,* January 1979.
Zanotto, Piero. "Cartoons e Fantascienza." *Fantascienza Minore,* no. 1, 1967.
—, "I Disegni Animati." *Enciclopedia del Tempo Libero,* Padua, Italy, 1968.

An Additional Bibliography

Only books dealing with some important aspects of print and animated cartoons have been listed. Most are in the English language, but some foreign works of note have also been included. For a more comprehensive bibliography refer to John A. Lent's four-volume *International Bibliography* mentioned below.

Bendazzi, Gianalberto. *One Hundred Years of Cinema Animation.* Bloomington, Indiana: Indiana University Press, 1995.

Chiesa, Adolfo. *La Satire Politica in Italia.* Rome: Editoria Laterza, 1990.

Feaver, William and Ann Gould. *Masters of Caricature.* New York: Alfred A. Knopf, 1981.

Gifford, Denis. *British Animated Films.* Jefferson City, N.C.: McFarland and Co., 1987.

Halas, John. *Masters of Animation.* Topsfield, Mass.: Salem House, 1987.

Harrison, Randall P. *The Cartoon: Communication to the Quick.* Beverly Hills, Calif.: Sage, 1981.

Heller, Steven, ed. *Man Bites Man: Two Decades of Satiric Art.* New York: A & W, 1981.

Janocha, Bill and Mort Walker, eds. *The National Cartoonists Society Album.* Brooklyn, N.Y.: National Cartoonists Society, 1996.

Langlois, Claude. *La caricature contre-révolutionnaire.* Paris: CNRS, 1988.

Lent, John A. *An International Bibliography of Comic Art* (four volumes). Westport, Ct.: Greenwood Press, 1994-96.

Lucie-Smith, Edward. *The Art of caricature.* Ithaca, N.Y.: Cornell University Press, 1981.

Peary, Gerald and Dany Peary, eds. *The American Animated Cartoon.* New York: Dutton, 1980.

Petersen Teddy, Claude Seidel and Arne Sorensen. *Drawing the Line.* Copenhagen: AIDA, 1992.

Sloane, David E.E., ed. *American Humor Magazines and Comic Periodicals.* Wesport, Ct.: Greenwood Press, 1987.

Smith, Dave. *Disney A to Z.* New York: Hyperion, 1996.

Solomon, Charles. *The History of Animation* (revised edition). Avenel, N.J.: Gramercy, 1994.

Solot, François. *5000 Dessinateurs de Presse et Quelques Supports.* Paris: Te. Arte, 1996.

Zurier, Rebecca. *Art for the Masses.* Philadelphia: Temple University Press, 1988.

Notes on the Contributors

Notes on the Contributors

Maurice Horn

Maurice Horn, the editor of this encyclopedia, is an internationally recognized authority on comics and cartoons. He was co-organizer of the first exhibition held at a major museum, "Bande Dessinée et Figuration Narrative," at the Louvre in Paris. He also organized the exhibition "75 Years of the Comics" at the New York Cultural Center.

He has lectured on comics and cartoons at universities worldwide, and his European series of lectures in 1973-74 was printed in *Information et Documents*, the official publication of the American Center in Paris. He has written hundreds of articles on the subject for American and foreign magazines and has contributed to *Collier's Encyclopedia* and to *The International Encyclopedia of Communications*. He has edited a number of reprints of classic American and European comic strips, and has received many awards and honors in the field.

Many of the books he has authored or edited have become standard reference works in their field. In addition to *The World Encyclopedia of Cartoons*, he has edited *100 Years of American Newspaper Comics* and the multi-volume *Contemporary Graphic Artists*. He is co-author of *A History of the Comic Strip* and author of *75 Years of the Comics, Women in the Comics, Comics of the American West*, and *Sex in the Comics*. He is also the editor of the companion*World Encyclopedia of Comics*.

Stanley Appelbaum

Stanley Appelbaum was born in Brooklyn, New York, in 1934. He has always been interested in cartooning (his parents owned candy stores, and he got to read all the comics for free!).

Currently senior editor at Dover Publications in New York, he works on most of their art books, often supplying translations and introductions. For that firm, he has edited collections of the humorous works of the French illustrator Grandville and the Mexican printmaker Posada, extensive annotated anthologies from the major satirical art magazines *Simplicissimus* and *L'Assiette au Beurre*, and a number of titles dealing with the performing arts.

Bill Blackbeard

Bill Blackbeard, a Californian, has written a number of science fiction novels, as well as articles and stories on a variety of subjects. In 1967 he founded the San Francisco Academy of Comic Art, a unique institution devoted to the study and preservation of the comics and other forms of popular culture.

Blackbeard is the author of *Comics* (Houghton-Mifflin, 1973) and of many articles on the subject. Organizer of several exhibits of comic art in the Bay Area, he was a contributor to the Bicentennial exhibition, "A Nation of Nations," sponsored by the Smithsonian Institution in Washington, D.C. He coauthored *The Smithsonian Collection of Newspaper Cartoons* and was a contributor to *The World Encyclopedia of Comics* (Chelsea House, 1976).

Richard Calhoun

Richard Calhoun was born in Columbus, Ohio, in 1941. A lifelong cartoon addict, he did his graduate work at Columbia University (Ph.D., 1973), training as a social historian under the sponsorship of Professor David J. Rothman. This experience left him with an appreciation of cartoon art as social commentary as well as humor.

Calhoun is the author of *In Search of the New Old* (Elsevier, 1978), a historical inquiry into the changing image of the older person in post-World War II American society, and of a novel, *Dina* (Berkeley, 1978). He lives in New York City, where he is currently at work on his second novel.

Clube Poriuguês de Banda Desenhada

The Clube Português de Banda Desenhada (Portuguese Comics Club) was formed in the 1970s in order to research and preserve the works of Portuguese cartoonists, and to promote comic and cartoon art in general. The club organizers have written many articles and essays on Portuguese cartooning (always under the collective signature of the club), and they have also sponsored a number of cartoon exhibitions and shows.

Jared Cook

Born in 1949, Jared Cook was raised in Los Angeles. He became interested in Japan at an early age and has spent over four years there, primarily in Nagoya and Tokyo. He received his B.A. and M.A. in Japanese from UCLA and won a two-year scholarship from the Japanese Ministry of Education. Cook finds comic books and cartoons to be the most interesting form of Japanese popular literature (indeed, he spent most of his scholarship money expanding his collection, and most of his time reading comics).

With Frederik Schodt and a Japanese colleague, Cook formed Dadakai, a loose association that introduces Japanese comics and animation to the West and does translation work. Cook has appeared on national television in Japan numerous times in connection with his work in the comics and cartoon fields. For awhile, he taught Japanese at the university level, but he now works freelance as a translator and interpreter, primarily for Japanese cartoonists and animators.

Bill Crouch, Jr.

Bill Crouch, Jr., a Connecticut Yankee, holds degrees in art history and journalism. He began writing for *Cartoonist Profiles* in 1973. For that magazine he interviewed Harold Foster, Noel Sickles, and Norman Mingo (the first artist to paint Alfred E. Neuman in full color for the cover of *Mad*). He edited *Dick Tracy: America's Most Famous Detective* and coedited a series of five books about Pogo Possum with Mrs. Walt Kelly for Simon & Schuster. In addition he was a contributor to *The World Encyclopedia of Comics* and *100 Years of American Newspaper Comics*. He has also written scripts for syndicated comics and humorous comic books, specifically *Yogi Bear, Top Cat, Hong Kong Phooey*, and *The Flintstones.*

Giulio Cesare Cuccolini

Giulio Cesare Cuccolini, a native of Corregio (Emilia), studied at institutions in Italy, the United States, England, and France. He has been teaching at the University of Bologna, where he held seminars about comics and popular literature. He has written and lectured extensively on comics in Italy and abroad. He is a past president of Associazione Nazionale degli Amici del Fumetto, and has long been associated with the International Comics Salon in Lucca and with ExpoCartoon in Rome. He is also a contributor to *The World Encyclopedia of Comics*.

Wolfgang Fuchs

Wolfgang Fuchs, born in 1945, grew up and went to school in and around Munich, Germany. While attending university courses in American cultural history, journalism and communications, and English literature, Fuchs participated in a university project that led to his coauthorship of *Comics: Anatomie eines Massenmediums.* A number of assignments for television, audiovisual aids and articles followed.

Fuchs gained valuable experience in the comics field by translating a number of comics and editing a German *Peanuts* comic book. He has been a contributing editor to a number of journals devoted to comics and cartoons. In addition to his contributions to *The World Encyclopedia of Comics* (1976 and 1998 editions), some of his recent works have been *Comic Handbuch* and *San Francisco* (with Gerhard Muller).

Denis Gifford

The leading authority on British cartoons and comics, Denis Gifford became a professional cartoonist at age 14, turning out a number of cartoon series and comic strips for British publishers. He also edited several comic books and created the daily newspaper panel *Telestrip,* satirizing current TV shows.

In the 1960s, Gifford changed careers, taking up writing and show business. For BBC radio, he created a nostalgic panel show called *Sounds Familiar* (1966-74), followed by a television version, *Looks Familiar,* in 1972. Another of his brainchildren was the first panel game for cartoonists, *Quick on the Draw* (1974). He has written several books on comics and cartoons, among them *Discovering Comics* and *Stap Me! The British Newspaper Strip* (1971); *Run, Adolf, Run: The World War II Fun Book* (1975); and *The British Comic Catalogue.* Gifford is also the author of the acclaimed *British Film Catalogue* (1973) and was a contributor to *The World Encyclopedia of Comics* (Chelsea House, 1976).

Among his recent works have been *The International Book of Comics* and *American Comic Strip Collections.* He is also a major contributor to the revised edition of *The World Encyclopedia of Comics* (1998).

Hongying Liu-Lengyel

Hongying Liu-Lengyel was born in Beijing, China, and graduated from Anhui Univerity in Hefei in 1982. After marrying an American national in the mid-1980's she moved to the United States, where she received a Ph.D. in Communication from Temple University. She has written about 50 articles on comic art for various Chinese journals and a great number of book reviews on Chinese cartoons and comics for the U.S. publications *Wings* and *WittyWorld.*

She has lectured widely on the subject at Chinese and American universities. Among the books she has authored special mention should be made of *Chinese Cartoons as Mass Communication: The History of Cartoon Development in China* (1993). She also contributed to the 1998 edition of *The World Encyclopedia of Comics.*

Pierre L. Horn

Pierre L. Horn is professor of French at Wright State University in Dayton, Ohio, where he also holds the Brage Golding Distinguished Professorship in Research. He has written extensively on French literature and civilization, including biographies of Louis XIV and Lafayette. In addition, he has lectured on popular culture and contributed numerous entries to *The World Encyclopedia of Comics,* the multivolume series *Contemporary Graphic Artists,* and *100 Years of American Newspaper Comics,* and has edited the *Handbook of French Popular Culture.* He is also the advisor for the multivolume *Guides to the World's Cinema,* currently being published by Greenwood Press.

In 1978 he was decorated with the rank of Chevalier dans l'Ordre des Palmes Académiques by the French Government.

Bill Janocha

Bill Janocha is a feelance artist who has been studio assistant to Mort Walker on *Beetle Bailey* since 1987. He has contributed articles to *Nemo, Inks,* Comicana books and *Mad* magazine. Editor of the 1988 and 1996 editions of *The National Cartoonists Society Album,* Janocha helped with the development of the 1995 "Comic Strip Classics" U.S. postage stamps and with exhibitions for the Newspaper Features Council and for the International Museum of Cartoon Art. He was also a contributor to *100 Years of American Newspaper Comics* and to the 1998 edition of *The World Encyclopedia of Comics.* He has also served on the National Cartoonists Society's Board of Directors.

Serge Jongué

Serge Jongué was born on December 8, 1951, in Aix-en-Provence, France and received his M.A. from the University of Provence in 1973. The following year he went to Quebec and anchored a television series on Quebec comics and cartoons, in association with French-Canadian cartoonist Pierre Fournier. Since 1976 he has been an assistant director of the International Pavilion of Humor in Montreal.

Jongué has written a number of articles devoted to cartoons and cartoonists (including Charles Schulz and Guillermo Mordillo). He has helped organize several exhibitions of cartoons at the Pavilion of Humor and has lectured on the subject of comics and cartoons at the University of Quebec in Montreal.

Francisco Tadeo Juan

Francisco Tadeo Juan is one of the most noted scholars in the fields of Spanish cartoons and comics. He has collaborated to many periodicals in the field in Spain and abroad. He has been a contributor to such volumes as *La Historia de los Comics, Historia del Tebeo Valenciano,* and *Diccionario de Uso de la Historieta Española.* Since 1976 he has been editing *Comicguia,* a journal devoted to all aspects of cartooning in Spain.

Doug Kendig

Born in 1940, Doug Kendig was given a gift subscription to *Walt Disney Comics* at age four and has enjoyed cartoons and comics ever since. In 1972, after completing Master of Arts and Master of Library Science degrees, he began seriously building a research collection, with special emphasis on comic strips from the 1920s through the 1950s. Since then, he has issued a newsletter on comic strips and has done reference work on cartoons and comics for a number of researchers.

Kendig taught an undergraduate history seminar on the history of the comics and served as area chairman in comics for the Popular Culture Association, helping to organize presentations for the 1977 Baltimore and 1978 Cincinnati annual conventions. His background includes social work, teaching, the ministry and school librarianship. He is married, has three children and lives in rural Cassidy on Vancouver Island, British Columbia.

John A. Lent

Dr. John A. Lent, a professor at Temple University, has authored or edited 49 books, including *Asian Popular Culture* and his huge four-volume bibliography of comic art worldwide. He is chair of the Comic Art Working Group of the International Association for Mass Communication Research, the Asian Popular Culture Group of the Popular Culture Association, and the Asian Cinema Studies Society; he is also the editor of *Asian Cinema* and *Berita,* and the managing editor of *WittyWorld.* He has interviewed cartoonists and lectured on comic art on every continent, and was a contributor to *100 Years of American Newspaper Comics* and to the 1998 edition of *The World Encyclopedia of Comics.*

Lent's nearly 40-year career includes a Fulbright scholarship to the Philippines, directorship of the first academic program in mass communication in Malaysia, pioneering research in Asia and the Caribbean, and study at universities in Norway, Mexico, Japan, and India.

Vane Lindesay

Vane Lindesay was born Sydney, Australia, in 1920. He saw active service in the Australian army before being appointed to the art staff of the Australian Army Education Service magazine *Salt,* where he was senior artist. After the war he did advertising work in England and also worked in the theater, producing stage decor. Returning to Australia, he joined the Melbourne *Argus* newspaper and became head of the art staff.

For the past twenty years Lindesay has been prominent as a typographer and graphic designer in the publishing industry. He has won several design awards, including the Book Design Award of 1976. His black-and-white cartoon illustrations appear weekly in the magazine *Australasian Post,* where they have been published in every issue since 1954.

Lindesay is the author of *The Inked-in Image,* a survey of Australian comic art, and his book reviews appear regularly in the *Australian Book Review,* the literary quarterly *Overland* and Melbourne's daily newspaper the *Age.* He has written an extensive essay on the Australian-born cartoonist Will Dyson for *The Australian Dictionary of Biography,* to be published early in 1980 by the Melbourne University Press.

Augusto Magalhaes

Augusto Magalhaes was born in Rio de Janeiro, Brazil, in 1945. He came to the United States in 1967 to pursue graduate studies in journalism and art history at the University of California. While there, he contributed cartoons to several student and underground publications, using the pseudonym "Mag."

In the early 1970s Magalhaes began working as a translator and interpreter of Spanish and Portuguese. He also wrote occasional articles on South American cartoonists for West Coast publications and served as a stringer for several Argentine and Brazilian newspapers. He returned to Brazil in 1978 and is now working as a designer and copywriter for an advertising agency in São Paulo.

Richard Marschall

Rick Marschall has devoted his life to the study and collection of comic strips and cartoons. His collection includes more than 3,000 original drawings, bound runs of the early humor magazines, and voluminous amounts of published and unpublished miscellany about cartoons and cartoonists.

Born in 1949 in Ridgewood, New York, he started drawing cartoons at an early age and formed friendships with many cartoonists. He received degrees in American studies and history from the American University in Washington, D.C., writing his master's thesis on the early American humor and cartoon magazines. While in school, he began freelancing editorial cartoons to many of the nation's leading conservative journals.

In 1972 Marschall joined the staff of the Palisades Newspapers in Englewood, New Jersey, as a reporter and cartoonist. He shifted later in the year to the *Connecticut Sunday Herald* in Norwalk and served in the same capacities before becoming feature editor and magazine editor. Thereafter he did brief stints as associate editor of United Feature Syndicate and associate editor for comics of the Chicago Tribune-New York News Syndicate. In September 1975 he became comics editor of Field Newspaper Syndicate in Chicago, and he has been special projects editor for Marvel Comics since 1978. He was a contributor to *The World Encyclopedia of Comics* (Chelsea House, 1976) and edited *The Sunday Funnies* (Chelsea House, 1978).

Marschall has exhibited major portions of his collection and has spoken on the comics extensively, as well as having assisted on several books on the subject. His areas of specialization are early magazine cartoons, early humor strips, American illustration and the political cartoon. He credits his father's interest in cartoons with arousing his own passion for the field.

Alvaro de Moya

Alvaro de Moya is the foremost Brazilian authority on comics and cartoons. He has organized a number of important exhibitions of comic art in Brazil and South America and has lectured extensively on the subject in America and in Europe. He has been a member of numerous international juries. Among the books he has authored are *Shazam!, Historia da Historia em Quadrinhos,* and *O Mundo de Disney.* He is a contributor to *The World Encyclopedia of Comics.*

José Muntañola

Born in 1940, José Muntañola received his doctorate in architecture from the University of Barcelona in 1968. He was a research fellow at the University of California at Berkeley (1970-73) and received a postdoctoral fellowship from Berkeley in 1973. Since 1974 he has been teaching architecture at the University of Barcelona.

Cartoons are Muntañola's violon d'Ingres, and he has been interested in the subject from the earliest age (the noted cartoonist Joaquin Muntanyola is his uncle). He has written and researched a number of articles on cartooning and has also lectured informally on the subject.

Kosei Ono

Kosei Ono, the son of famed cartoonist Saseo Ono, is the foremost authority on cartoons and comics in Japan. He has contributed articles and essays to many publications in the field in Japan and abroad, has lectured extensively on the subject, and has organized a number of major exhibitions and manifestations in Tokyo and other venues in Japan and overseas.

Fred Patten

Fred Patten became active in comics fandom in the early 1960s, serving for four annual terms as Central Mailer of *Capa-alpha*, comics fandom's first amateur press association. He has written legthy articles on international comic art and edited the book-review section *Graphic Story Magazine* (later *Wonderworld*) in the early 1970s. This led to a specialization in Japanese *manga* and *anime*. Patten was co-founder of of the Cartoon/Fantasy Organization, America's first Japanese cartoon-art fan club. He authored or co-authored many articles on comics and animation for various publications. In 1997 and 1998 he was co-curator of a Japanese animation "festival within the festival" for the annual World Animation Celebration in Pasadena, California.

Maria-Grazia Perini

Born in Milan in 1943, Maria-Grazia Perini embarked on a journalistic career, first working for the daily *Il Corriere della Sera,* then for the monthly *Amica.* In the early 1970s she went to work for the publishing house Editoriale Corno, and from January 1977 to April 1978 she was the editor of the cartoon magazine *Eureka.* Since 1978 she has been working as an editor for Rizzoli in Milan.

Perini has written several articles on cartoons and cartoonists, and she has also lectured on the subject. She assisted Luciano Secchi on the Italian edition of *The World Encyclopedia of Comics.*

Jukka Rislakki

Born in Kuusankoski, Finland, in 1945, Jukka Rislakki now lives in Helsinki. He works as a staff writer at the foreign desk of the *Helsingin Sanomat,* Finland's largest newspaper. For many years he has also written commentary on comics and cartoons for the newspaper's cultural page, and he is a regular contributor to *Sarjainfo,* the organ of Suomen Sarjakuvaseura (Finnish Comics Society). He co-founded the society in 1971 and was its first president.

Rislakki attended school in Colorado in 1963-64 and received an M.A. in political science from the University of Helsinki, specializing in Latin American politics. He has also done some occasional cartooning for student newspapers and the like.

Carlo Scaringi

Born in Rome in 1936, Carlo Scaringi has been an editor on the daily newspaper *Avanti!* for the last twenty years. He also functions as the paper's television critic. He is the author of *Storia delle Olimpiadi* ("History of the Olympic Games," 1959) and has written numerous articles and essays on cartoons and cartoonists.

Scaringi has also written many radio broadcasts, including a radio drama on Copernicus and a series of 13 broadcasts, *Eravamo Cosí* ("The Way We Were," in collaboration with Sergio Trinchero). This series recalled in a semi-serious but not escapist way the customs, culture and society of the 1930s. The text of the programs was published by Nerbini.

Frederik Schodt

Frederik Schodt was born in 1950 in Washington, D.C., but has lived abroad most of his life, in Norway, Australia and especially Japan, where he has spent nearly eight years. He is familiar with the comics and cartoons of all three cultures but is most fascinated by those of Japan (in fact, he learned Japanese primarily by reading comic books).

Schodt's interest in animation and the comics blossomed in 1974 when he worked as a guide for Japanese tourists in Los Angeles. In that capacity, he attended Disneyland over seventy times in one year and one day actually saw Donald Duck eating a hamburger in the employee cafeteria.

In 1975, Schodt received a Japanese Ministry of Education scholarship to study translation and simultaneous interpretation in Japan. While working there as a professional translator in 1977, he formed Dadakai with Jared Cook and a Japanese colleague to introduce Japanese comics and animation to the West. In 1983 he wrote the definitive book on Japanese comics and cartoons, *Manga! Manga!* Since that time he has authored *Inside the Robot Kingdom: Japan, Mechatronics, and the Coming Robotopia* and *America and the Four Japans: Friend, Foe, Model, Mirror*. His latest work in the field is *Dreamland Japan* (1996).

Luciano Secchi

Born in Milan in 1939, Luciano Secchi embarked on an editorial and writing career in 1960. He has authored a great many comic strips, including *Maschera Nera* ("Black Mask"), *Kriminal, Satanik, Max Magnus* and the highly successful *Alan Ford,* under the pseudonym "Max Bunker." Under his own name, Secchi has written a number of essays on comics, cartoons and cartoonists, and he is also the author of many novels and short stories.

Secchi is currently general manager and editor of Editoriale Corno, an important Italian publisher of cartoons and comics. He has also been the leading light of *Eureka,* one of the most successful magazines in the field of cartooning. Among other activities, Secchi has written several scripts for radio and television and contributed to a number of Italian magazines and periodicals. For more information refer to entry in *The World Encyclopedia of Comics*.

Jørgen Sonnergaard

Jørgen Sonnergaard, a Danish editor and writer, was born in Copenhagen on April 27, 1936. After high school, he worked at the A.P. Miller Steamship Company and continued his education at Copenhagen Business Graduate School. In his spare time, he began working as a freelance journalist for Danish morning papers, wrote a handful of mystery stories for the weekly *Sondags-BT*, and gradually became involved with cartoons and comics.

He eventually left the steamship business and in 1959 became a feature editor of Presse-illustrations-bureau (PIB) in Copenhagen, where he remained until 1975. There, first as editor and then as vice president, he wrote gags for both new and established comics, working with many of Scandinavia's most talented cartoonists. Among the strips he has been co-writing for years are Vilhelm Hansen's *Rasmus Klump* (also known as *Petzi*) and Jørgen Mogensen's *Esmeralda* (also known as Lullubelle). In addition he does occasional political cartoons.

In 1975, when the Gutenberghus Group formed GPS (Gutenberghus Publishing Service), Sonnergaard became its executive editor, with responsibility for a portion of the Group's magazines and books in Scandinavia, Germany and England (Disney periodicals, comic pockets, children's books, *Popeye, Lone Ranger, Hägar,* etc.). He has been a member of the Newspaper Comics Council in New York since 1967, and he continues to contribute short stories and crime stories to major Scandinavian magazines under various pseudonyms.

Joseph Szabo

Joseph Szabo, himself a working cartoonist, is the editor and publisher of *WittyWorld,* the International Cartoon Magazine. he has written many articles on the subject of cartooning around the world, and has published a number of international cartoon anthologies.

Sergio Trinchero

Born in Rome in 1932, Sergio Trinchero is a journalist and author who has written countless articles and essays on the world of comics and cartoons. He has also written a number of books on the subject, including *I Fumetti* ("Comics"), *I*

Giornaletti ("Illustrated Newspapers") and *Gli Eroi del Cartone Animato Americano* ("The Heroes of the American Animated Cartoon").

Trinchero has also written for radio and television programs about cartoons, animation and comics, including *Gli Eroi di Cartone* ("Cartoon Heroes"), *Eravamo Cosí* ("The Way We Were") and *Supergulp.* A cartoonist and graphic artist himself, he has had many of his works exhibited in galleries and has won a number of awards for his writings as well as for his drawings.

Dennis Wepman

Dennis Wepman has taught English at the City University of New York and held the post of of cultural affairs editor of the *New York Daily News.* The holder of a graduate degree in linguistics from Columbia University, he is the author of twelve volumes of biography and has contributed to numerous publications in linguistics, literature, art, and popular culture, as well as to several standard reference books on cartooning. He has been a contributor to the multi-volume *Contemporary Graphic Artists,* to *The Encyclopedia of American Comics,* and to *100 Years of American Newspaper Comics,* as well as to *The World Encyclopedia of Comics.* He is the chief review editor of *WittyWorld,* the International Cartoon Magazine.

Indexes

Index A

Proper Name Index

Aa

Bb

Index A

Proper Name Index

Cc

Proper Name Index

Dd

Ee

Ff

Gg

Proper Name Index

Hh

Proper Name Index

Ii

Proper Name Index

Jj

Kk

Ll

Mm

Index A

Proper Name Index

Nn

Oo

Pp

Proper Name Index

Qq

Rr

Ss

Proper Name Index

Tt

Proper Name Index

Index B

Subject Index

Subject Index

Aa

Index B

Subject Index

Subject Index

Index B

Subject Index

Bb

Index B

Subject Index

Cc

Index B

Subject Index

Index B

Subject Index

Index B

Subject Index

Index B

Subject Index

Dd

Ee

Subject Index

Index B

Subject Index

Ff

Gg

Index B

Subject Index

Hh

Ii

Jj

Mm

Index B

Subject Index

Nn

Index B

Subject Index

Oo

Pp

Subject Index

Index B

Subject Index

Subject Index

Qq

Rr

Ss

Index B

Subject Index

Subject Index

Tt

Uu

Vv

Subject Index

Ww

Yy

Index B

Subject Index

Zz

Index C

Geographical Index

Geographical Index

Index C

Geographical Index

Geographical Index

Index C

Geographical Index

Index C

Geographical Index

Geographical Index

Index C

Geographical Index

Index C

Geographical Index

A History of Puck, Judge and Life

by Richard E. Marschall

A History of *Puck, Judge* and *Life*

The Graveyard

In an article in the *American Bibliophilist* in August 1875, Brander Matthews wrote that reviewing a history of comic journalism in America was like reading a "list of tombstones."[1] The condescension in academic and critical circles towards American comic art—now waning—was then actively shared by the general public. *Punch* and other European comic journals, however, were fairly popular in the United States, partly because of the widespread Anglophilia, Germanophilia and Francophilia of social, academic and cultural groups (more or less respectively) in the post-Civil War years. John Ames Mitchell theorized that the traditionally inevitable failures of American humorous papers were attributable to our "Puritan ancestors [who] alone should be held responsible." They taught Americans to have a contempt for art and humorous expression, Mitchell claimed, and their children had "no taste for leisure and no capacity for amusement. . . . literary things were luxuries."[2] Theodore Roosevelt summed up this viewpoint when he criticized the Puritans chiefly for their "tendency to confuse pleasure and vice."[3] No doubt the fact that America simply lacked for good cartoonists also played a role. After all, the European artists Hogarth, Daumier and Goya were also cartoonists.

Around 1870, tastes began to change. Mitchell once again offered an explanation, crediting the current aesthetic movement for the renewed interest in design and forms as manifested in architecture, bric-a-brac and other items of Victorian ostentation, all of which fostered a general regard for art.[4] Certainly, the popularity of Currier and Ives prints and the somewhat sudden emergence of Thomas Nast—a social and political force as well as an artist—had a part in the change of climate. More important, the economic and cultural revolutions of the late 19th century helped to create a market for the luxury of comic papers; America, flexing its muscles economically and physically, was now prosperous enough to sit back and take stock. This self-examination coincided with a new wave of literary maturity, a large part of which was humorous (Mark Twain, Petroleum V. Nasby, Artemis Ward, et al.). Finally, the printing and engraving industries had reached new levels of technical freedom and economy.

Among Brander Matthews's "tombstones" were such publications as *Frank Leslie's Budget of Fun, Wild Oats, Jolly Joker, Phunny Phellow, Punchinello, Vanity Fair, John Donkey, Mrs. Grundy, Yankee Doodle, Yankee Notions, Phunniest of Awl and Phunniest Kind of Phun* (one suspects merely from the titles that fate was kind in causing some early deaths). Publisher Frank Leslie was responsible for at least half of these ventures; and though many of them were short-lived, he deserves credit for bringing to the East Coast and printing, often for the first time, the work of such early giants as William Newman, Edward Jump, Frank Beard, J.H. Howard, H.T. Stephens, J. Bonker, Thomas Worth, Charles Green Bush, James Albert Wales, Joseph Keppler and Frederick Burr Opper.[5] Around the same time, the *New York Daily Graphic* was founded; it was the first paper in the United States to publish a daily cartoon.[6] On its staff were such future greats as A.B. Frost, E.W. Kemble, C.J. Taylor, C. Gray-Parker, Frank Bellew, C.G. Bush and William Allen Rogers.[7]

Many of these names we will encounter later: Joseph Keppler founded *Puck,* James Wales founded Judge, and Thomas Worth was widely popular for his Currier and Ives cartoons. Charles Green Bush, already a veteran illustrator at the time of the Civil War, was one of the ablest and funniest cartoonists America had yet produced. Frederick Opper went on to become America's most popular cartoonist, retiring in 1936 after creating *Happy Hooligan, Maud the Mule* and *Alphonse and Gaston* for Hearst, as well as thousands of cartoons for *Puck* and, in these early days, for the Leslie publications. A.B. Frost, of course, became a respected painter and illustrator; he is remembered chiefly for his drawings for the Uncle Remus stories. E.W. Kemble is remembered today for his illustrations for Mark Twain's books and in his time was also noted for his pickaninny kids.

There is not much evidence, then, to support Art Young's contention that "if you had taken the foreign-born out of America in the mid-nineteenth century, you would have taken out a large percentage of great value [to the comic profession]."[8] A few artists, such as William Newman, Thomas Nast, Matt Morgan (*Leslie's Weekly's* answer to Nast), Bernard Gillam and Joseph Keppler were foreign-born, but most of the early talents were native Americans, many from the Midwest.

By the 1870s the time was ripe for an indigenous flowering of comic magazines.

Notes appear on page 943.

"What Fools These Mortals Be!"

In 1882 a landmark was demolished on North William Street in New York City in order to make room for an approach to the Brooklyn Bridge. Though it was merely a dingy brick building of no particular architectural distinction, it deserves to be memorialized; for in its basement rooms began a minor revolution in publishing and a major revolution in American graphic humor. The central mover in these developments was Joseph Keppler, late of the Leslie publications. (For biographical information on Keppler and other figures mentioned here, see the alphabetical entry section of this encyclopedia.)

A word is in order about Keppler's artistic style, which was very influential in the early days of American cartooning. He belonged to the German school of cartooning, which was for all intents and purposes a synthesis of the English school, with its reliance on allegory, and the French school, whose hallmark was exaggeration.[9] Keppler was an able caricaturist who made extensive use of such sources as famous historical scenes, Wagner and Shakespeare for his cartoon ideas. When he left Europe, Sir John Tenniel was the leading cartoonist in England, Wilhelm Busch (Max *and* Moritz) was gaining fame in Germany, and Daumier ruled the French school; Keppler seemed to draw inspiration from all three. He was most at home on the lithographic stone (as his stiff woodcuts testify), and his drawings, at once gentle in execution and forceful in conception, showed an impressive command of anatomy, spacing and design.

At Leslie's, Keppler kept company with distinguished and promising comic artists (we find Opper doing a cover for *Wild Oats* in 1876). He soon became a star of the New York papers, and his fame bred restlessness and ambitious dreams. Determined to launch a cartoon magazine in New York, Keppler broached the idea to Adolph Schwarzmann, the business manager of the Leslie organization. Schwarzmann evidently was impressed with Keppler's talent and his past efforts and was convinced that a market for such a publication existed in New York. Accordingly, the two sought, and found in the person of Leopold Schenck, a third partner to handle the literary affairs of the magazine.[10] The result of their collective efforts was *Puck,* the first issue of which appeared in September 1876, in quarto, with text in old German script. *Puck's* main attraction lay in its cartoons, which were lithographed in black by the press of Mayer, Merkel and Ottman. Keppler's work was showcased throughout, particularly on the first and last pages and on a magnificent 21-inch-long center page. The magazine received many favorable notices and was an immediate success.

At this point, an up-and-coming playwright named Sydney Rosenfeld entered the picture. He had seen *Puck* and was so delighted by it that he convinced Keppler and Schwarzmann to expand their audience beyond the German-speaking population.[11] It was decided to publish an English-language edition with the same cartoons but with an entirely different text. Rosenfeld became the editor and chose the young Henry Cuyler Bunner as his assistant editor.

The first issue appeared in mid-March 1877, its sixteen pages highlighted by three Keppler cartoons, a Bret Harte poem, B.B. Valentine's first "Fitz-Noodle in America" installment, jokes, reviews and advertising. In spite of its brightness and optimism, however, the English *Puck* was notably unsuccessful. The two main supports that kept it alive were the health of its German sister and the "insistence of H.C. Bunner,"[12] who succeeded to full editorship early in 1878, after Rosenfeld left *Puck* in the first of several significant disputes.

Some signs of life appeared in the English *Puck* with the addition of color to the large lithographic plates. In those early days, they were colored in flat tones from wood blocks. Within two years of the first issue, as many as five colors, now all lithographically transferred, were in use. Color gave the magazine great visual appeal on the newsstands, and in spite of such continuing difficulties as the lack of artists to lighten Keppler's load (the interior pages of early issues contained mostly reprints of European cartoons), Keppler took a chance and doubled *Puck's* advertising rates on October 1, 1879. The gamble was successful, and thenceforth the sixteen-page magazine always had at least three solid pages of ads.

It is difficult to calculate *Puck's* circulation during the early days (the Audit Bureau of Circulation was not established until 1914), but the figures for some years can be estimated on the basis of advertisers' manuals and the like. Such sources indicate that *Puck* had achieved a quite respectable circulation of about 80,000 by the early 1880s. Regular features such as "Fitz-Noodle in America" (a parody on Englishmen), H.C. Bunner's "V. Hugo Dusenbury, Professional Poet," and "Answers to the Anxious" (a largely contrived letters column) gave *Puck* personality. By 1880, there was a healthy art staff as well. Keppler imported two old friends from Vienna, Carl Von Stur and Friederich Graetz. James A. Wales, an accomplished cartoonist, lightened the lithographic burden, and young Frederick Burr Opper added a real comic touch to the paper. *Flip,* a monkey series by the great Wilhelm Busch of Germany, ran in 1879. Freelance writers who contributed to *Puck* included Brander Matthews, who wrote as "Arthur Penn," and W.J. Henderson, who was to become Bunner's assistant in the mid-1880s.

In 1878, prosperity necessitated a move across the street from the dingy brick building to 8 North William, but two years later the establishment moved across town to 21-25 Warren Street, joined by the lithographers Mayer, Merkel and Ottman. Planning to settle there permanently, Keppler leased more floors on Warren and Murray streets, until *Puck* occupied twenty-two floors in all.[13]

In 1880, the English-language *Puck's* first presidential campaign, the paper lukewarmly supported Hancock and showed a great deal of respect for the new president, Garfield, especially in his fights against the Stalwarts. The editorials at this time were penned by the versatile Bunner, who was a fine poet and storywriter, a great essayist and a lucid commentator. His editorials remain interesting and readable today. Bunner carried a tremendous load in the pages of *Puck,* often writing not only editorials but essays, the "Dusenbury" feature, reviews, poems and jokes. He was also one of the great, if unrecognized, letter writers of his day and kept busy with freelance fiction assignments. W.A. Rogers remembered Bunner's "short but full life. . . . he lived as much in one year as most people do in two."[14]

In 1881, after another hot dispute, James Wales left *Puck* (to found a rival imitation, Judge), and an able English cartoonist, Bernard Gillam, joined the staff. Keppler and Gillam drew mostly on domestic politics, Graetz covered European affairs, and Opper did topical satire and social commentary. Mott computes that in 1883, an off-year for elections, sixty percent of the colored cartoons were on domestic politics, with another twelve percent on international relations.[15]

Puck's motto, "What fools these mortals be!," describes well the fearlessness and cynicism of its pages. But cynicism is often the last refuge of the idealist, and between jibes at the pastors Beecher and Talmage, at Mormonism and Edison and U.S. Grant, there were cartoons advocating civil service reform, tariff reform and charity for tenement dwellers. In 1882, the first year of massive voter support for civil service reform, a figure representing the "Independent New Party"—a young, handsome man reminiscent of the German Michel—made his first appearance, joining the ranks of such icons as the elephant, the donkey and Keppler's "Old Man Prohibition" (which was picked up in the 1920s by Rollin Kirby with great *success).*

Though *Puck* was now a respected journal of political opinion, it was the 1884 election that both made it America's foremost magazine of political commentary (with *Harper's Weekly*) and assured its place outside the graveyard fence. The Republican nominee that year was James G. Blaine, who over the years was the victim of some of *Puck's* most vitriolic barbs; and the Democrats nominated Grover Cleveland on a platform of civil service reform and just about every other ideal *Puck* cherished. The campaign was unprecedented for its smears and dirtiness, and *Puck* joined the fray with full-color, giant-sized vigor. From the staff came the idea of depicting Blaine as a tattooed man, his body covered with a multitude of political sins. Gillam's cartoons, and then Keppler's and Opper's, showing the candidate clad only in shorts, a quack-remedy "magnetic pad" and tattoos, were distributed by the thousands by the Democrats, and they firmly established *Puck as* a national magazine. Blaine's fatal loss of New York has been attributed to many things—including the "rum, Romanism, and rebellion" incidents, Mugwump defections, Jay Gould's Delmonico dinner (and the Walt McDougall New York World cartoon about it), Ben Butler and the *New* York Sun, and Theodore Roosevelt's reluctance to support the Republicans—but there is no doubt that *Puck's* consistently brilliant and effective cartoons played a large part in the Democratic victory. According to Draper Hill, Cleveland himself reportedly said, "*Puck*'s editorials and cartoons did more to elect me than any other influence employed in the campaign." *Puck* also benefited as circulation climbed to 90,000.

In all, 1884 was a prosperous year, and growing pains soon necessitated another move. A lot in lower Manhattan bordered by Houston, Mulberry, Jersey and Elm (now Lafayette) streets was purchased from the Sisters of Charity, and the Puck Building was erected in 1885. It still stands today, with its six and ten-foot-high statues of Puck, but its dirty lofts suggest little of the magnificence and importance of the 1880s building. It had an extensive "morgue" and library, and more steam lithographic presses under one roof than existed anywhere else in the world.[16]

The printing of cartoons with the lithographic process was a rather involved task. Using pen, brush and a thick, greasy emulsion, artists drew cartoons in reverse on the flat, smooth surfaces of 150-pound porous stones imported from Germany. A solution of gum arabic and nitric acid was then spread over the surfaces, eating into the stone except where repelled by the grease lines. The stones were rinsed with water, and the drawing left in relief was used to print the cartoons.[17] A separate stone had to be made for each different color. Fortunately for *Puck* fanciers, Ottman's presses (he went independent on the fifth floor of the Puck Building in 1885) were among the finest and most accurate in America.

In 1886 Bernard Gillam and Eugene Zimmerman left *Puck* to work for a revitalized Judge. James Wales returned but died a few months later; other cartoonists who joined the staff in 1886 were Charles Jay Taylor, once active on the old *Graphic,* A.B. Shults, so devoid of talent that one wonders how he found his way into *such* illustrious company, and Michael Angelo Woolf, who later drew social criticism for *Life* magazine (another *Puck* rival, founded in 1883). Graetz had returned to Austria, but freelancers were occasionally permitted to submit work, and among this distinguished group were A.B. Frost, E.W. Kemble, a young Charles Dana Gibson, C.G. Bush and painter E.N. Blue. By 1887 two more staffers had been added: Louis Dalrymple, who had a real comic style (if somewhat curious with regard to anatomical consistency), and Sid Ehrhart, whose style was clean and sophisticated. Both were destined to draw for *Puck* for more than fifteen years. The magazine was also acquiring an impressive literary staff in those years. Bill Nye wrote a couple of dozen pieces in 1884, and long-forgotten names like Manley H. Pike, Philip H. Welch, Thomas A. Janvier, R.K. Munkittrick, Williston Fish, Edward Mott and F. Marshall White brought prestige to its pages, as did Robert J. Burdette and James L. Ford.

All in all, *Puck* in 1887 employed 429 people, including a large number of young boys. The average salary was $25 a week; pressmen made $18 to $30 per week, artists and designers got $60 to $70 per week, and superintendents of departments earned $70 to $100 per week. *Puck* staffers worked 54 hours a week and were paid for overtime.[18]

Puck's contribution to the 1888 presidential campaign was a gigantic hat symbolizing Republican candidate Benjamin Harrison's notable lack of physical and statesmanlike stature. (Cleveland won again in popular votes but lost in the electoral college.) Another of Keppler's favorite targets in the Cleveland years was Joseph Pulitzer, an anti-Cleveland Democrat. Keppler's ribbing of Pulitzer went back to their days together in St. Louis, when he would end conversations with "Well, Joey, there's nothing else to do but go back to the office and draw your nose!"[19]

By the late 1880s *Puck's* most popular cartoonist after Keppler was F. Opper. Around 1886 his style had changed; crude exaggeration gave way to a sophisticated appearance, as reflected in *Puck's Opper Book,* published in 1889, and *This Funny World,* which came out the next year. He was a wonderful artist, very prolific, consistently clever, and popularly acknowledged as America's favorite cartoonist until the 1930s—first for *Puck,* and from 1899 to 1932 for Hearst, where he drew *Happy Hooligan, Alphonse and Gaston* and dozens of other titles. Art critic Thomas Craven found that Opper inspired and influenced American cartoonists of the 1940s and before more than any other artist.[20] His brightness and popularity were rivaled for awhile by Sydney B. Griffin, who joined the *Puck* staff in 1888 and was a funny and exceptionally competent cartoonist. Tragically, a stroke paralyzed his drawing hand in the early 1890s.

In spite of the efforts of its rivals, *Judge* and *Life, Puck* remained on top in terms of circulation, with a weekly readership of 90,000 as the new decade opened. In addition, it supported sister publications such as *Puck on Wheels, Pickings from Puck* and *Puck's Library,* which sold 60,000 monthly. Although its crusades were as vociferous as ever—especially for tariff reform and against unions and monopolies—Puck in the 1890s was devoting more space to fads and fancies, such as the bicycle craze and suburban living. F.M. Howarth joined the staff, and in his ten years he never drew a political cartoon. Short stories were featured and republished in book form. *Puck* had come a long way from its origins as a comic magazine with hard-hitting broadsides attacking people and institutions; it was now a sophisticated, clever and genteel paper.

The most prominent figure in this maturation process was the editor, H.C. Bunner. In the early 1890s he started writing short stories that ran as series in *Puck* and were republished as books: *Short Sixes, More Short Sixes, Made in France* (translations of Maupassant stories with American locales and situations) and novelettes such as *The Runaway Browns* and *The Suburban Sage*. These delightful tales remain bright and refreshing today. Bunner was in a class with O. Henry and Maupassant; certainly his contemporary sales and reviews equalled theirs. His works, illustrated by C.J. Taylor, F. Opper and Sydney B. Griffin, sold into the 1920s. He is a lost treasure waiting to be rediscovered by the reading public and literary historians.

One of the biggest events in *Puck's* career was the World's Columbian Exposition in Chicago in 1893. For this occasion, Keppler and Schwarzmann commissioned architect Stanford White to design a Puck Pavilion, which came to be one of the most popular exhibits at the fair. The public could walk through, observe the composition of the magazine and watch artists at work. At the pavilion the *World's Fair Puck* was printed from May 1 to October 30, 1893—26 issues in all, smaller in size than the New York *Puck,* and 8 pages in length. There was no politics (except for attacks on fair officials who wanted to close down on Sundays), and many pieces and cartoons were devoted to aspects of the fair.

Joseph Keppler was at the Puck Pavilion during most of the exposition but was very sick much of the time. For several months the pages of his magazine were empty of his work, and in early 1894, after a small flurry of drawings in the January issues, he died. The date of his death, February 19, was just a few weeks short of the 17th anniversary of the English edition of *Puck.* He left a great void, in terms not only of space but also of influence; he was the dean of active American cartoonists, and a genuine pioneer. To Keppler belongs the credit for founding America's first successful humor magazine, institutionalizing many classic cartoon conventions (such as Uncle Sam's beard!) and starting dozens of future comic geniuses on their way. Whether or not his ideas were original (a question raised by W.A. Rogers[21]), his impact was profound. His son, Udo J. Keppler, who had been an occasional contributor, ;now took on his father's load, signing his work "Joseph Keppler, Jr." Other new members of the art staff included Gallaway, F.M. Hutchins, Louis M. Glackens (brother of the painter William Glackens) and, for a short time in 1892 and 1893, William Allen Rogers.

Circulation dropped during the depression years of the 1890s, and another blow came in 1896 with H.C. Bunner's death at the age of 40, when he was in his prime. His output had been impressive, and his loss was soon felt in the pages of *Puck.* Under the new editor, Harry Leon Wilson, short stories disappeared, and there were more cartoons and jokes. Among the new artists were J.S. Pughe and Rose O'Neill, who was later to create her famous "Kewpies." Wilson, who wrote "Ruggles of Red Gap," added *such* names as Tom L. Masson, Edward L. Sabin, Carolyn Wells, Joseph C. Lincoln and Mrs. Wilson Woodrow to the literary roster.

In 1896 the Democrats nominated William Jennings Bryan for the presidency on a platform of free silver, which *Puck* abhorred. The Republicans ran William McKinley, whose high-tariff views were equally repugnant. While paying homage to President Cleveland and the symbolic Gold Democratic Party, *Puck* supported neither candidate that year; and its broad swipes at Bryan and McKinley were refreshingly reminiscent of the old Blaine days.

Although circulation rose again with good times and the publication of wildly patriotic cartoons during the Spanish-American War, an event that boded ill for *Puck* and for magazine cartooning generally had occurred in 1896. On February 16 of that year, the first *Yellow Kid* cartoon was published in the *New York World.* It not only introduced color (one of Puck's novelties) to the newspapers but also represented the birth of a new art form, the comic strip. Within five years, magazine cartoonists R.F. Outcault, F. Opper, F.M. Howarth, Rudolph Dirks, Carl Schultze, F.M. Follett, Billy Marriner, E.W. Kemble and others were enticed to the newsprint. This exodus naturally had a profound effect on magazine humor and depleted its artistic ranks; in the final analysis it was largely responsible for the death of the magazines.

In 1904 John Kendrick Bangs assumed the editorship and infused the magazine with new life. He came over from the same position on *Harper's Weekly* and was regarded as one of the nation's leading humorists.[22] *Puck's* literary flavor was improved by several serials and the works of Bert Leston Taylor ("BLT"), Franklin P. Adams ("FPA"), Arthur H. Folwell, Charles Hanson Towne and Arthur Guiterman. Although Opper and Howarth left for the Hearst newspapers, and Taylor and Dalrymple for *Life* and *Judge,* respectively, bright work was coming from the art department. "Kep" was drawing weekly, and L.M. Glackens was turning out many cartoons in his easy, clever style. Other major artists included Art Young, on his way to becoming a socialist; S. Ehrhart, in his third decade on the staff; Albert Levering, a facile illustrator; the Kewpies' Rose O'Neill, one of the first women cartoonists; Gordon Grant, later to be a noted marine painter; Will Crawford, a wonderful crosshatcher, and champion with Keppler, Jr., of American Indian causes; Leighton Budd, an early surrealist; Gordon Ross, later a respected illustrator of books; Grant Hamilton, on leave from Judge to draw anti-Theodore Roosevelt cartoons in 1904; and Fred Lewis and Frank Nankivell, each with an individual style. Although Bangs left within a year, the impetus of his changes continued under Arthur H. Folwell, who once again cut back on longer pieces of writing.

In 1908, as in the other two Bryan campaigns, *Puck* did not endorse any candidate but sat back and took potshots at all participants in the battle, including Theodore Roosevelt. The next few years saw a decline in quality, advertising and circulation, in spite of the resurgence of the Democratic party. Some drawings sparkled, such as those by A.Z. Baker and W.E. Hill, but it is evident that Keppler was not devoting much time to his cartoons; he was to retire shortly, to the disappointment of many, and devote himself to Indian problems. Meanwhile, *Judge* changed format and dropped politics in 1911; and its circulation, with that of *Life,* began to increase.

In 1914, *Puck's* owners, the Keppler and Schwarzmann company, sold the magazine to Nathan Strauss, Jr., of the Macy's department store fortune. More color pages were added, and the staff remained unchanged for a few months. Gradually old hands were replaced with newcomers like Raymond Crawford Ewer, who turned out during his year or so on the staff some of the most beautiful pen-and-ink cartoons in American art; Rube Goldberg, who was induced to do a dozen double-page cartoons; Percy Crosby, later of *Skippy* fame; and R.B. Fuller, the creator of the *Ooky Doaks* comic strip. There were some good moments in the magazine, but by and large old readers did not like the complete face-lift, and new readers were not attracted to an old title they had ignored previously.

In 1915 *Puck's* size was reduced, and color was eliminated except for occasional covers. The staff was talented and mildly avant-garde. Ralph Barton was doing sophisticated drawings and reportage from Paris. James Huneker wrote a brilliant column called "The Seven Arts," illustrated by C.B. Falls. George Jean Nathan reviewed drama, and John Held, Jr., drew some of his earliest cartoons in Puck's pages. The agile *New* York *Times* cartoonist Hy Mayer contributed, as did Tony Sarg and Ralphael Kirchner, but *Puck* found it necessary (or advantageous) to reprint old F. Opper cartoons as well. Other staffers were Hal Burrows, Louis Lang, Ray Evans, Lou Mayer, Rolf Armstrong and Everett Shinn.

Troubles continued, and in 1916 the management resorted to printing on cheaper stock. The same year, in hopes of rejuvenating sagging advertising and circulation figures, *Puck* opened all volleys for the presidential election. It was harshly partisan and intemperate and was most likely subsidized by the Democratic party. William Morris and Charles Macauley, both political cartoonists, at this time were imported to work on the campaign. *Puck* had been, like Wilson, against preparedness, but the paper did not hesitate to criticize "warlike" Republicans even when it, like Wilson, found it expedient to do an about-face on the issue.

For all its efforts, *Puck's* circulation continued to decline (no doubt its partisanship offended many readers), and in 1917, it was sold again.[23] The new owner was Hearst's International Magazine Company, which tried to spruce up the paper by adding literary stars such as Stephen Leacock, Bruno Lessing and Gustav Michelson. Alan Dale wrote on theater, and much of the text was littered with studio photos of actresses in poses and costumes that must have been more than slightly risqué for the day. Its star artist was the great Dutch cartoonist Louis Raemakers, supported by a number of Continental cartoonists and imitators who all drew in a style that was most decidedly a passing fad.

Readers rejected the superficial and European flavor of *Puck,* but the addition of cover drawings by the popular Penrhyn Stanlaws helped a little, and in 1917, the magazine became a bi-monthly. On the 41st birthday of the original Puck (fondly remembered but now discredited and shamed), in March 1918, it went to monthly publication. In that form too it was a failure and gave up the ghost in September 1918. The title *Puck,* with its masthead, was not transferred to a gravestone, however; Hearst used it as the masthead for his Sunday comic strip supplements in New York, Boston, Atlanta, Los Angeles and other cities. *Puck* the *Comic Weekly* continues today as the advertising vehicle of the Hearst comics.

Puck, in its days of splendor, was a landmark in American journalism-it pioneered a new type of magazine. It was a tremendous influence in politics (Boss Tweed once said, "The people can't read, but damn it, they can see pictures!"), easily the equal of *Harper's Weekly,* the *New York Sun* or *Times* or *Tribune,* and the *Louisville Courier-Journal.* And *Puck* had a profound impact on the American cartoon tradition—it nurtured cartoonists, set trends and established conventions. Perhaps most important, it created in the public a taste and desire for graphic humor, thus opening the door to all that followed.

VOL. XXI.—No. 533. NEW YORK, MAY 25, 1887. PRICE, TEN CENTS.

ENTERED AT THE POST OFFICE AT NEW YORK, AND ADMITTED FOR TRANSMISSION THROUGH THE MAILS AT SECOND CLASS RATES.

ON THEIR RETURN.

Red Shirt.—Heap poor-aw-style, heah.
Buffalo Bill.—Ya-as. That hawnsom 's weally the only wefreshing thing I 've seen, don'tcherknow?

PUCK,
PUBLISHED EVERY WEDNESDAY,
from the
PUCK BUILDING,
New York.
Publishers and Proprietors, Joseph Keppler.
A. Schwarzmann.
Editor, ... H. C. Bunner.

Wednesday, May 25th, 1887.—No. 533.

CARTOONS AND COMMENTS.

THE REPUBLICAN PARTY—or, at least, the conservative wing of the Republican Party, is having a pleasant little flirtation with Mr. Theodore Roosevelt. We mention the fact merely as a matter of news—or, rather, "society gossip"—and neither in sorrow nor in anger. Barring disparity of age, we can see no reason why the two parties to the flirtation should not be happy together. As far as Mr. Roosevelt goes, the party could not have a more desirable associate. Mr. Roosevelt is a virtuous young man with an agile intellect, great conversational ability, and a large assorted stock of lofty and amiable intentions. Though at times his temper is uncertain, he is never pettish for long.

* * *

Mr. Roosevelt started out, a few short summers ago, to reform politics and give us the blessings of pure government, and he would no doubt have succeeded in his enterprise had he not been frightened No blame should attach to him for this. He is young, probably of a nervous organization, and he is innocent, simple and confiding in character. Perhaps he was "rattled," as the boys say. At any rate, he meant to reform things; and the circumstances under which he retired permanently from the reforming business were exceptional. It was at the time of the last National Convention, and there was great danger that the Party would nominate for the presidency a man whose character can best be described as shady. Mr. Roosevelt went to the Convention as a delegate, and protested vigorously against the selection of that person. The person, however, was selected, and then Mr. Roosevelt was directed to support him. It is to be feared that the Party was harsh toward the young man. He was told that he would be cast out into utter darkness and exterior chill, and he yielded. We are pained to say that he was sulky for a few weeks; but he yielded, and supported the shady person as well as he knew how, until the election took place.

* * *

That, of course, was the time when his victory over his own angry passions ought to have been rewarded with a large slice of bread crowned with jam. But it so happened that the Party was defeated at that election, and there was very little bread and no jam at all to be dealt around. And, somehow, in the confusion, Mr. Roosevelt was forgotten and overlooked until, two years later, the Party found itself in great need of a man to run for the office of Mayor of New York—not to be elected, for that was impossible; but merely to run, so as to keep the Party before the public. Now, it was not easy to get a man for the job. No man cares to run for office for the barren honors of paying assessments and being defeated. But young Mr. Roosevelt, in his guileless ignorance of the world, thought it would be good fun to play at campaigning and oblige the Party. So he ran, and came in third in the race, with a wee sad little minority in his dainty grip-sack. And here came his first real enlightenment as to the coldness and cruelty of this hard world. He had known that he could not be elected: he said so—after election—but he had not expected to come in at the finish No. 3, several lengths behind a tramp apostle of Labor from the boundless west. He discovered that he had been basely sold out by his own paid agent, assigned him by the Party itself—that he had been delivered over to his enemies in the most shameless manner—betrayed in the house of his friends. He grieved deeply over this revelation of baseness: in fact, it was the persistent plaintiveness of his wailing that reminded the aged and forgetful Party of what she owed the young man, and moved her to welcome him once more to her palpitating bosom.

* * *

Be happy, Mr. Roosevelt, be happy while you may. You are young—yours is the time of roses—the time of illusions. You see not the rouge on the old cheeks, the powder on the wrinkled forehead. You are all right. Be happy. Do not let it annoy you if we smile. There is an oft-told tale of a Freshman at an inland college who began a letter to his father thus: "Dear Father: I am engaged to Miss Matilda Smith, of this town—" and who received in return a letter from his father beginning: "My dear son: Bless you! You need not tell me anything about it. I was engaged to Matilda Smith myself, when I was in my senior year, and I know just what fun you are having." Be happy, Mr. Roosevelt. You have read of Pitt, of Alexander Hamilton, of Randolph Churchill and of other men who were young and yet who, so to speak, got there just the same. Bright visions float before your eyes of what the Party can and may do for you. We wish you a gradual and gentle awakening. We fear the Party can not do much for you. You are not the timber of which Presidents are made, even if you were not, at present, disqualified for that office by the harsh law which decrees that the beautiful bloom of adolesence must be brushed from the cheek of manhood ere the doors of the White House open to the aspirant. But we fear that the Party will treat you even as her henchman treated you—the unsympathetic Cregan, whose standard of political morality she has now accepted as her own. For, Mr. Roosevelt, the Party is sadly changed from what she was a generation ago. The virtue went out of her when she stooped to an alliance with a conscienceless political trickster, who used public office for private gain.

From all parts of the country come reports that Decoration Day is not likely to be observed as reverently as it has been in past years. This is much to be deplored. We have no holier holiday in all the year than this that commemorates the cementing of our Union. It had its origin in a noble and patriotic sentiment, and its observance takes a form peculiarly fitting and beautiful. And at this time of all others, when un-American anarchy is taught in the streets and preached in public gatherings; when American workingmen submit themselves to a government of their own founding that does not recognize the laws of the land—at this time we should not fail to remind ourselves that our dead heroes of the last war fought for that true liberty that goes hand-in-hand with law.

We receive many complaints from regular readers of PUCK, that the paper is not to be obtained, or only with difficulty and after repeated application, on the news-stands in the Elevated Railway stations. We know that these complaints are well-founded, and an explanation is due to the readers of PUCK. The company which leases or sub-leases this valuable franchise from the city makes a practice of demanding from publishers a fee of $10 a week for exposing papers—that is, for selling them as they are sold on other stands. If the demand is refused, the contumacious journal is either not handled at all, or, if regular customers insist upon it, is kept for sale; but so hidden, in whole or in part, that purchasers can not readily see it. This fee we will not pay. The amount is trifling; but the principle is not. The charge is an out-and-out extortion; and we will not pay it, be it ten dollars or ten cents. In this determination we know that the friends of PUCK will gladly support us; and if they are further annoyed, we shall take what measures lie in our power to satisfy them and to protect our own interests.

HE DESERVED IT.

MRS. KILKILLEEN.—Afther mar-r-rchin' all day, wid th' Shixty-ninth viterans, it 's th' divil's own shame, childer, av yure ould man can't be dicorathed a little loike th' rist av thim sojers!

A COMING EVENT.

(During the twenty minutes' noon intermission, the young ladies of Madame Finisher's boarding-school discuss educational matters, and a luncheon of buns, éclairs, etc., sent in by a fashionable baker.)

EDITH *(munching a cream puff)*.—Oh, what a lovely spread! Nell, you 're the boss treater!

NELL.—Hear, hear! A graduate, and she says "boss"—

EDITH.—Oh, fudge; Madame is n't around!

NELL.—It 's a good thing she is n't, with these méringues in view.

EDITH.—That baker is a darling.

CLARA.—How does he get them in, any way?

NELL.—Why, he has an extra tray quite at the bottom of his basket, that no one suspects.

EDITH.—Yes; is n't it jolly? I would n't care a sou for the méringues if we were allowed to buy them.

NELL.—Edith, you are really depraved.

EDITH.—Oh, I just love to be fast!

CLARA.—
NELL.— } Oh, how perfectly dreadful!

CLARA.—Oh, girls; mama bought my graduation dress yesterday!

NELL.—Oh, what is it?

CLARA.—Indian muslin and valenciennes; just too lovely for any use!

EDITH.—I got mine last week. I 've a white silk slip, and an Irish point skirt over it.

CLARA.—Well, Connery told mama Indian muslin was quite *comme il faut* for graduation.

EDITH.—*Comme il faut* nothing. It may do well enough for your blonde infantile beauty; but I need something more substantial.

NELL.—Madame wants us to dress simply.

EDITH.—A fig for madame! I 'll wear what I like.

CLARA.—My dress is to have ten narrow flounces, edged with valenciennes—real lace, too; and the bodice is all lace inserting sewed together.

EDITH.—Just listen; and she calls that simple!

NELL.—The front of mine is all lace, too; and the back just quantities of soft, fluffy drapery.

EDITH.—Shall you wear sashes?

CLARA.—Oh, yes; mine is surah, five yards.

NELL.—Mine is awfully wide satin ribbon.

EDITH.—I think I 'll have moiré.

NELL.—Are n't you crazy for the evening to come?

EDITH.—Oh, perfectly wild!

CLARA.—I 'm to have quantities of flowers.

EDITH.—Madame wants us to have a "profusion."

NELL.—My brothers, and papa and mama each send me a bouquet, and sister May's fiancé says nothing short of a basket will satisfy him.

CLARA.—Each one of my cousins will send me a bouquet; and, of course, papa and mama.

EDITH.—Well, I am going straight to Klunder's, and order as many as I want.

CLARA.—Oh, I would n't do that for anything!

EDITH.—Why not? It 's no worse than boning every one you know for them.

CLARA *(haughtily)*.—I never "bone."

NELL.—Edith, you do have such a harsh way of putting things.

EDITH.—I don't care—it 's the way they are.

CLARA.—I 'm worried to death over my essay.

EDITH.—Oh, the essay is all right. Miss Barton took mine yesterday, and is going to look it over and touch it up.

NELL.—What is the subject?

EDITH.—"Is Civilization a Failure?"

NELL.—Goodness—what could you find to say about that?

EDITH.—Oh, I treat it humorously, you know!

CLARA.—Mine is "Watching and Waiting."

EDITH.—A lovely sentimental thing, I suppose.

CLARA *(with dignity)*.—Madame says it has many beautiful thoughts.

EDITH.—Oh, madame has got it?

CLARA.—Yes; she wants to revise it a little.

NELL.—Mine is the French essay, you know. "Mam'selle" is helping me on it.

EDITH.—Well, then, girls, we 're safe any way. I don't care a rap for the examinations.

NELL.—Why?

EDITH.—Oh, they 're to be private, you know; and we 'll be coached through all right.

NELL.—I hope so.

CLARA.—Oh, yes; madame says they will not be very severe, as she considers we have reviewed so often.

NELL.—I have to sing, you know.

EDITH.—Don't you dread it?

NELL.—Not a bit. Why, I have practiced all winter on my piece, and Prof. Staccato says I 've got every little shade now.

CLARA.—My drawing, "The Angelus," is to be exhibited, you know. Mr. Crayon took it home last night.

EDITH.—What for?

CLARA.—Oh, he thought the figures slanted a little, and the perspective was n't quite true, and the sky needed different shadings, otherwise it was lovely!

EDITH.—I shan't show my water-color.

NELL.—Why not?

EDITH.—Oh, there 's a castle in it, and it tips frightfully!

CLARA.—Could n't you call it the "Leaning Tower of Pisa?"

EDITH.—I might do that, only it 's a winter scene.

NELL.—I don't believe any one would notice.

CLARA.—No; put it in a lovely frame, and it 'll be all right.

NELL.—What are you going to have for a graduation present?

CLARA.—A sapphire bracelet. I 've been just sick for one.

EDITH.—I 'm going to have a diamond ring.

NELL.—And I—a saddle-horse.

EDITH.—Is n't it just lovely to finish, any way?

CLARA.—Yes, indeed. I am just crazy to come out in society.

NELL.—It is *such* a satisfaction to feel there is nothing more to learn.

PHILIP H. WELCH.

SPRING.

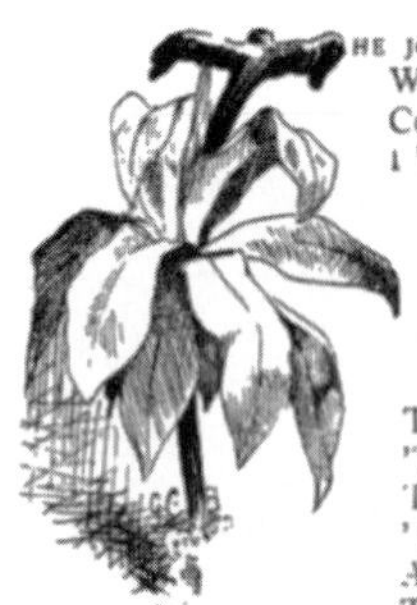

The johnny-jump-up now in Spring,
Will soon jump up and try again.
Come on, my John H. Jump, so bold,
I 'm waiting for you on the wold!
And when your head the sod shall prick,
I 'll walk with twirling walking-stick,
And twirl your head off double-quick;
While breaks yforth yfrom my throat,
This varying, various, changing note.

The bard the breath of Spring-time sips,
'Tis all he has, in faith, to sip;
The sage the warm gin cocktail nips,
'Tis all he cares in faith to nip;
And now the Baptist preacher dips
The converts in the icy slip;
"Click, slop!" the sugar-maple drips.

Where the snow still lies in the hedge-row down in the lane by the rill,
There the primitive oak and the boxwood—like myself and the little Lill—
Daily sigh for each other—they 'd die for each other—but the box wood stands in the shade,
And the love of the oak for the boxwood is not a thing for the latter which has what you might call paid.
So I love Lill, and my love dwarfs her, and hides her from the gaze of men—
But, oh, for one of Evarts's speeches, that I might expand into half an Aurora-Leigh Browning line more with my pen!

When oranges are all the fruit
The which my poet's purse can buy;
When lamb and mint and shad and peas,
And eke, the scarlet strawberries
Seem far removèd as the sky;
When, since I am no money-duke,
For me no cucumber will cuque;
And by the footman—which is I—
The rhubarb rides its barb right by—
Why, then, 'tis Spring,
And then I sing:

That, likely, if I went at work—
Au lieu de loaf and lurk and shirk;
If I would drop my silly pen—
Why, I might dine like other men!

Williston Fish.

Misconstrued.

Farmer Gidney.—I 've seen bees, 'n' wasps, 'n' hornits; but dum me 'f I ever seen one fitted with a sting like that afore! So, Boss!!

(N. B. —The Local Archery Club was practising in the next lot.)

NEW BOOKS.

Worth winning—A Jack Pot.

The monarch of dreams — A Welsh Rabbit.

Two gentlemen of boston — Sullivan and Kelly.

Factors of organic revolution —Italian Street Musicians.

The old house at sandwich—A R. R. Station.

Familiar short saying of great men—Dammit.

Lacked Originality.

He *(after morning service)*.—What did you think of the sermon this morning, Miss Breezy?

Miss Breezy *(of Chicago)*.—It seemed to me to lack originality. Why, some of the ideas advanced are old enough to have whiskers!

When sarah bernhardt buys material for a dress, she wants it all wool, but does n't care about its being a yard wide.

Comparing Notes.

Miss Strainer.—I 'm just through with trigonometry, and next week I review the differential calculus for the June examinations! How far are you advanced?

Mr. Harold.—I know how many apples John had if he had two and his father gave him one more; and I can knock a ball to short-stop before it touches the ground!

AN EMINENT CITIZEN.

He is a gentleman of about thirty-five summers, and he wears a plaid suit, a polka-dot shirt, a Lake George diamond-pin, and an air of insouciance. Observe the careless grace with which he stands on yonder street-corner, and receives the greetings of his many friends.

He seems to be enjoying rare popularity, does he not?

About every fifth man that comes along grasps him warmly by the hand and exchanges a few words with him.

That was Professor Giglamps, the great scientist, who left him a moment ago; the youth who is tremblingly addressing him now, and to whom he listens with ill-concealed impatience, is young Cashley, the dry-goods clerk around the corner; and the well-dressed, elderly man who is awaiting his turn to approach, is old Deacon Heavyboy, of the Church of the Everlasting Lugs.

Why is the society of the gentleman in the plaid suit so eagerly sought? Has he carved for himself a niche in the temple of Fame, and won a name that will go whooping down the Ages long after his heirs have done quarreling about his estate?

No, he has not. He has never done anything in particular to win the esteem and admiration of his fellow-men; but, nevertheless, he is in great demand just now. Wherefore? Why, because he possesses a straight tip on the Suburban.

F. A. Stearns.

We read of a condemned murderer losing hope, and he is the first of his kind who ever allowed such a thing to happen. It is all wrong for a murderer to lose hope, because it is the only thing that braces him up for the final ordeal.

THE LITERARY MOVEMENT IN TROMBONE.

IN THIS AGE of Pen and Ink every quarter enjoys a literature peculiar to itself, and a number of writers whose efforts constitute what is known as the literary movement of that territory. We have our California literature, our Southern literature, our Boston literature, our Pike County literature, our Eleventh Street between Sixth and Seventh Avenues literature, and what not!

It is very gratifying, to say the least, that there are as many brands of literature as of cigars, and that the man with a weakness for any particular quarter can satisfy his longing by investing in the novel of the specialist who covers it.

The horse thieves of the California days of '49 are lifted into realms of poetic ecstasy by reading "Tennessee's Partner," just as the London thieves in this country for their health are by "Oliver Twist," and the ex-slaves, waiting on tables in restaurants, are by the score of negro dialect romancers of the South.

But, to come to the point, we have lately been treated to a few brief histories of the literatures lingering about us; and these histories have been, strictly speaking, largely biographical; have given pictures of the subjects of the biographies, and have been noteworthy for telling us what they have done, and of the golden harvests promised.

Now we are going to give a brief history of the literary movement in Trombone, Dakota. This humble, little, out-of-the-way place, situated on top of a sand hill, miles from any railroad, is too modest to speak for itself. It is a place where one would scarcely turn for polite accomplishments; but, in fact, within its tumble-down precincts exists a little literary band whose members strike "deep notes" with "sure hands," and who have a "sincerity of purpose" which will, some day, see them sleeping with Theocritus.

It is pleasant to open this little list of biographical sketches with Emily Lumsden Skatts. Miss Skatts is the only daughter of a wealthy ranchman, and was educated under the eye of a governess, there being no good schools in that district. Her maternal grandfather was a Hindoo and from this relative, Hieronymus Bobo, she has inherited a natural love of all that is beautiful and luxurious, as will be readily seen by any one who reads her charming little book of essays and sketches recently gathered into book form, and published under the general title of "Lotos Blossoms." But perhaps her best efforts are those that deal with her present home, namely, "A Trombone Pastoral," "Skeetsy Wims's Baby," and "The Pine Top Ghost Club." These stories were written by their author without any idea of their literary value; and the world owes a debt of gratitude to the friend who chanced to read them, and advised her to submit them to a publisher.

Herbert Wickliffe Van Dusen was born and raised in Trombone. Having lost his parents at the age of six, he was taken care of by a ranchman who was a friend of his father. This kind-hearted man was not in a position to give his ward the education which his natural ability merited, and he was literally brought up in the saddle. With the exception of attending a district school one winter, Mr. Van Dusen never crossed the threshold of any institution of learning; but during this winter he learned to read. He became very fond of the poems in his reader, and the teacher, learning this, gave him for a prize a copy of "Scott's Poems." Thus equipped, he would ride about the ranch with the bridle in one hand and "Scott" in the other. He then began to dabble in verse, and having one day submitted a couple of his poems to the editor of the *Trombone Herald*, that kindly gentleman discerned a "golden promise," printed the poems, and gave the blushing author the position of reporter.

He then began to work in earnest, and poem after poem came from his pen only to increase his reputation. His "Trombone at Sunrise" is one of the finest bits of word painting in the language, and having sent a copy of it to Mr. Longfellow, that kindly old gentleman found time to write him a letter full of appreciation and encouragement.

Susan Dollinger Yandell is one of the most graceful and charming of Trombone's little literary band. She is not a native of Trombone, but has lived there since she was ten years old. Having been thrown from a horse at the age of twelve, she met with a misfortune which made it necessary for her to use crutches for life. This misfortune, naturally, caused her to avoid any exercise that required a great strain, and becoming sedentary, she first acquired the book habit, and then turned her attention to literature, as much for amusement as anything else. She is also a strong landscape painter. We frequently meet poet-painters and painter-poets; and, truly, Miss Susan Dollinger Yandell is both. Although she does not employ rhythm and rhyme, her writing is the essence and soul of poetry itself. Reuben Onslow, Esq., the proprietor of the Trombone House, gave her a neat sum to paint a picture of his establishment, with the stage coach at the door at the busiest hour of the day. Two of her pictures were also hung and sold at good prices in the Silver City Academy.

Anita Wiggery Primrose has been blind since the age of eight. But from her dark world she casts sunshine into this, and makes the flowers seem sweeter and the skies brighter. She loves to be rolled around in an invalid's chair, and when she is enjoying this daily pleasure she composes her poems, and on returning home recites them slowly to her brother, who acts as her editor. All her poems are characterized by a tender resignation that make them beautiful and sad. She is like the nightingale that sings in the dark, only to bewitch the hearer with her divine melody. Her poems, "Comfort in Sorrow," "Resignation" and "Above the Storm the Sky is Blue," all printed in *The Christian Soldier*, are full of chastened beauty, and show at once the hand and the heart of a poet. Her book, or rather booklet, entitled, "The Widow's Cruse and Other Poems" is one of the strongest first books we ever had the pleasure of reading, and some of the poems in it will go into the anthologies, and become favorites for all time.

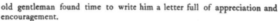

Trombone is justly proud of its literature and its makers, and, having such material, it is not to be wondered at. And we shall continue to look to this quarter patiently and lovingly for the fulfilment of that "golden promise" which is evident in the compositions of its every poet and story writer; and when that promise is fulfilled, as we have no doubt it will be, then will Trombone take its place among the literary centres of the United States, and be even as New York and Boston.

R. K. M.

THOSE NEW LONG-STEMMED EYE-GLASSES.

VICTOR *(tremblingly)*.—I *wuz* a leetle late wiv de tea, Missy Clemmis; but 'r don' see no 'casion fer ter sprung a razzer on yo' help!

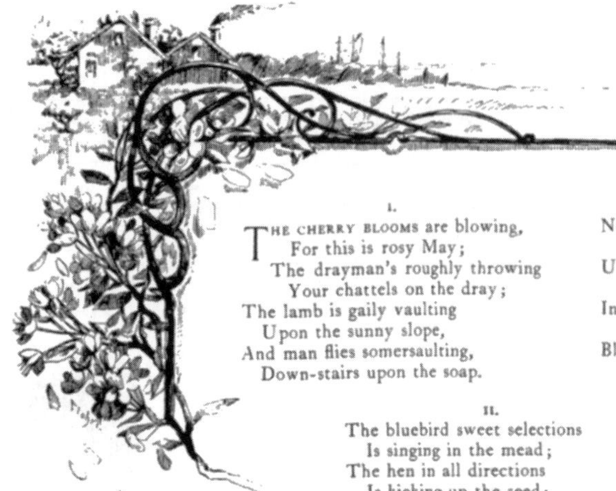

SOMETHING.

I.

THE CHERRY BLOOMS are blowing,
For this is rosy May;
The drayman's roughly throwing
Your chattels on the dray;
The lamb is gaily vaulting
Upon the sunny slope,
And man flies somersaulting,
Down-stairs upon the soap.

II.

The bluebird sweet selections
Is singing in the mead;
The hen in all directions
Is kicking up the seed;
And like a precious nugget
The buttercup doth shine,
Where Axminster and drugget
Are beaten on the line.

III.

Now windflower and arbutus
Light up the woodland rug—
Unlike the gyascutus,
The blithe potato-bug
In rapture eats the jimson,
Or any flower prim,
Blue, purple, pink, or crimson—
It 's all the same to him.

IV.

The housewife now is scrubbing
The stoop with vim intense—
The billy-goat is rubbing
His sides against the fence;
The dog is joyous rolling
About upon his spine,
And now it is consoling,
On lamb and mint to dine.

V.

Now May serenely blushes,
And joy 's each bosom's guest,
While sing the jays and thrushes
About the new-made nest;
And rapture 's the despoiler
Of every care and ill,
While Polly puts the broiler
To brown upon the grill.

R. K. M.

FOR OUR LITTLE READERS.

THE POET.

WHO IS THAT MAN Coming this way? Oh, he is a Poet. Why do you look so sur-pris-ed, children? Because he is fash-ion-a-bly dressed? You were under the im-pres-sion that All Poets wore clothes Cut in the style of the season before Last and had Long hair. Some of them do, but this gen-tle-man is not that kind of Poet. He wrote two sonnets this morning, and is Going to sell them for enough money to pay two weeks' Board. He is going to sell them to McDent & Co., for they Both sing the Praises of McDent's Un-ri-val-led Tooth Wash.

THE CLER-GY-MAN.

OH, CHILDREN, get onto this poor, Tired looking gen-tle-man who is ap-proach-ing! Do you Not feel sorry for him? *I* do. I feel so very sorry that I Would just like to Take his place for the Next three months. If I were per-mit-ted to Do so, what would Happen to me? Why, I should Go to Europe at the expense of an ad-mir-ing con-gre-ga-tion, and Stay until Oc-to-ber, and have Dead Loads of fun. I should Also be in receipt of about Seven hundred dol-lars per month Sal-a-ry. For the Weary looking gen-tle-man is a pop-u-lar cler-gy-man. Why does he look So tired, and why must he Go to Europe? Because, dear children, his Health is un-der-min-ed. He always is That Way at this season of the Year.

THE YOUNG TRA-GE-DIAN.

THAT CLOSELY SHAVEN GENTLEMAN, children, is a Young and Gifted Tra-ge-dian. How erect is his Car-ri-age, is it not? Observe with what hau-teur he flings a Coin to the son of It-a-ly who has just pol-ish-ed his boots. He is in Funds just now, and he has the Big Head. Next week he is to go on the Road at the Head of a Summer Snap. He im-ag-ines that the country is a-wait-ing his ap-pear-ance as a Star in Breathless Suspense, and that he is Going to make Big Money. In about a month he will be Back in the city ex-plain-ing that his failure was Due to beastly Bad man-age-ment. Must it not be Nice to be a Gifted Young Tra-ge-dian?

UNCLE WILLIE.

A DRY MEAL.

CUSTOMER *(at Sunday dinner)*.—What kind of liquor have you got, waiter?

WAITER.—I can give you some nice Adam's ale, sir.

CUSTOMER.—I don't care for ale. No wine, waiter?

WAITER.—There 's Crotonheimer, sir.

QUITE LIKELY.

CITIZEN *(to* NEW YORK GIANT*)*.—You will soon make a trip West, won't you?

NEW YORK GIANT.—Yes; before long!

CITIZEN.—Farewell trip, I suppose?

A WIFE'S ANXIETY.

MR. HAWBUCK *(of the New York Legislature)*.—I think I 'll run down to New York fer a day, my dear!

MRS. HAWBUCK.—What for?

MR. HAWBUCK.—Oh, jest to see what the town requires in the way of leg-islative statesmanship.

MRS. HAWBUCK *(anxiously)*.—Well, look out for them bunko-steerers, Josh, an' don't git lost!

OUT OF TOWN.

"I noticed your absence from your customary place in church last Sunday with some surprise," remarked the minister to Mr. Hendricks, who was out walking with young Bobby: "I suppose you were away from home?"

"Yes, sir," volunteered Bobby: "Pa was in Hoboken last Sunday!"

IN THE SMOKING ROOM.

DE LANCEY.—Would you mind changing your seat, sir?

PROFESSOR MILDMAY *(of the Suppression of Vice Society, who is stealing a quiet smoke)*.—Certainly not, sir!

DE LANCEY.—Thanks! On the trip out, I played with *another* party of these Boston business men who had "never been abroad before," and the clerical looking gentleman who sat just where you are, read his paper, my cards, and delight in the faces of his friends at the same time!

How It Works.

Walking Delegate.—Why does not yez quit? The Governor has given yez a half-holiday!

Voice in Fore Dirt.—Shure, we can have a half-holiday anny other day, fer the same price!

WHITE HOUSE NOTES.

Washington, May 16.—*(Special.)*—Your correspondent has received recently several letters from "Old Subscriber," "Constant Reader," *et. al.*, who complain because these dispatches contain none of those White House anecdotes which a portion of the daily press deals out so lavishly.

"Give us something about the private life of the White House occupants. Give us something funny about Hector," writes "Old Subscriber." Aye, aye, so we will, thou dear perennial bore! not only through love for thee, but also in recognition of the seeming popular demand for this class of news.

First, however, the writer must apologize to Puck's readers, if the following sketches of private life in the White House should contain one bright thought, or one line that is not insipid and impertinent. They are modeled after the aforementioned anecdotes in the daily press, and if they were *not* drenched with insipidity and impertinence, the reader might justly complain that the sketches were delusions and snares.

Finally, it may be stated that the items of news following were collected by an enormous expenditure—of imagination. Puck cares nothing for expenses, when it is a question of getting news for its readers:

* * *

Yesterday, Mrs. Cleveland went shopping. She entered a dry-goods store on Pennsylvania Avenue, and asked a saleswoman to show her some gloves. She examined a sample pair. They suited her.

"What is the price?" she inquired.

"Three dollars!" was the reply.

"Wrap them up!" said Mrs. Cleveland.

The gloves were wrapped up, and paid for.

And what did she do then? A novelist would, at this exciting juncture, digress into a verbose description of something or other, so as to prolong the agonizing curiosity of the reader, and thus chain the attention while he padded out his book to the proper size. But one of the rules in Puck's office forbids the use of such literary artifices, so—to the point at once.

After the gloves were wrapped up and paid for, Mrs. Cleveland took them, entered her carriage, and was driven to the White House.

Perhaps some obtuse reader may not be able to see the humor of this anecdote. If, however, he sees its insipidity and impertinence, the writer will feel proud of his imitative talent.

* * *

A very funny thing happened at the White House recently. One morning, while the President was breakfasting, the cook entered the room with agony depicted on every feature. He approached the President, as if to address him, but retired confusedly before opening his mouth. A few minutes later, he entered again, looking more determined, and, halting in front of the President, exclaimed:

"Mr. President, I have deceived you. I am an unhappy wretch. But I meant no wrong. I ordered pear preserves to be put on the table, and that miserable Sally put jam here instead. I did n't know it till a little while ago; and when I saw you eating jam for preserves, I knew you would think me the most deceitful wretch alive if you ever discovered what had been done."

"I knew it was jam," said the President quietly.

At this quaint, witty, picturesque reply, everybody in the room laughed heartily, and the cook stared admiringly.

W. L. Riordon.

The Excise Law.

"You are looking fine, Dumley, said Featherly, on Monday morning: "clear-eyed as a girl!"

"I'm feeling tip-top," responded Dumley: "never better in my life!"

"Nothing to drink yesterday, eh?"

"No; could n't get a drop. Is n't it a blamed outrage?"

A Feast of Reason.

"What do you do with all the newspapers the passengers give you?" asked a gentleman of a Third Avenue Elevated brakeman: "I see you have a quantity there under the seat!"

"Yes, sir," replied the brakeman: "I feed 'em to my goat. I 'm a Harlem man!"

DESPAIR.

Through the wooden spigot,
Maple sugar flows;
And the dewy lilac
In the garden blows.

Tangled water-cresses
Mat the crystal brook;
And the trout are madly
Snapping at the hook.

Little boys are playing
Marbles in the path;
And the morning-glory 's
Twining up a lath.

And the old book-keeper 's
Shivering with despair,
While his pen he 's wiping
On his dusty hair,

Thinking up a falsehood,
Shortly to appall
The firm, and gain the absence
For a game of ball.

Self-possession in a young woman is well enough for awhile; but she should n't keep it up too long.

There was a great mistake made in the anatomy of man. The backbone should have been on the stomach.

It is said that Mrs. Tennyson, wife of the ex-poet, can make good biscuits. She deserves a better fate.

Nothing in the way of fruit will upset a man's stomach quicker than a banana-peel.

The Glamour of the Footlights.

Scene in an Intelligence Office? Oh, no; it merely represents an average morning in almost any dramatic agency, and these are young ladies who want to go on the stage and play *Portia*, *Pauline*, *Juliet*, *Rosalind*, and a few other easy parts.

LITTLE ROOSEVELT!!! — THE

The old belated party knights
Equip their hero for the fray—

Yes, they who fought for equal rig
Through all the nation's darkest

LD PARTY MUST BE HARD-UP!

earlier steps would now retrace,
bring the spoilsmen's slavery back—

Their only objects pay and place—
Their champion—a jumping-jack.

CHANSON OF THE KNIGHT.

I'm one of the Knights of Labor,
I 'm going to do as I please;
Who thinks like me is my neighbor—
My doctrines?—for sample, take these:

On principle I despise work,
Supported by others I 'd be;
No "Heathen Chinee" or vile Turk,
A white man, all over—that 's me!

I think that the workman 's a fool,
Who in honest labor delights;
He refuses to be a tool,
He won't join the Order of Knights.

But, alas, he sticks to business,
Pays his way, while he runs himself;
If others did likewise, I tell you
I should soon be put on the shelf.

But while lots, who refuse to think,
Like cattle are driven or led;
I can count on plenty of drink;
They strike, they go hungry—I 'm fed.

For I am one of the Bosses—
Work not with my hands, but my jaw;
Thrive best on the workman's losses—
When he strikes, my money I draw.

I 'm one of the Knights of Labor,
I 'm going to do as I please;
Who thinks like me is my neighbor,
Who does n't, I 'll bring to his knees.

I mean what I say, by thunder!
Still business shall paralyzed be;
I 'll rule, if I 'm not kept under—
Jail only can paralyze me!

James Nye.

If the coach-dog should once get spotted fever, we fear it would be the end of him.

Complacency.

Miss Francis *(of New Haven, at the Myopia Hunt Ball).*—How these Boston women do dress, mama! There 's a train so skimpy that I can actually see the slipper-heels!

Mrs. Francis *(charitably).*—My dear, the longer you live the more you will realize that distilled molasses can never compete with the metallic cartridge as a provider.

The Inevitable Sculpin.

Cooley.—Give me a hand here, Perkins! I believe Filler 's got an attack of the delirium tremens!

Perkins *(who has just caught something new to him).*—Hold on to him! Perhaps I can catch the rest of his menagerie if you 'll give me time!

TO THE AMBITIOUS.

Young man, never despair in your early attempts at writing for the press. Henry Ward Beecher once offered to furnish regular letters to a certain publication at one dollar per letter, and his offer was refused. Suppose the manuscript you offer to your local sheet, in return for the paper for one year, is rejected, be not cast down. Mr. Beecher was finally paid as high as two hundred dollars per column for his work. Fancy that! Two hundred times as much as he once offered to work for, and yet was refused a chance.

The subscription price of your local paper is doubtless two dollars per annum. Strive on, and you may yet command four hundred dollars per column for the scintillations of your massive brain. Seize your pen and write how John Smith is shingling his barn. If your neighbor sneeze, or if your star Plymouth Rock hatches out fourteen chicks from a setting of thirteen eggs, use the wire. Let the world know the outlook for a big hay-crop in your locality, and whose baby has the measles.

Ferdinand Ward had no journalistic experience, yet he is said to now have a hand in the printing of one of the largest institutions in the State. If there be no hay, eggs, measles, babies, or other news in your neighborhood, try to be funny. It is very easy.

Clarence Stetson.

A Nice Climate.

Miss Waldo *(of Boston).*—You sometimes have very warm weather in Chicago, do you not, Mr. Breezy?

Mr. Breezy.—Occasionally; but last summer the weather was delightful. I don't think I sat down to dinner without my coat on more than two or three times during the entire season!

Miss Edith M. Thomas's poem, "The Crescent Moon," in the *Independent*, is evidently a parody on the famous lyric: "When this Old Hat was New." But, in all probability, she considered the above refrain sufficiently well known to be public literary property, and that it would be superfluous to acknowledge it in connection with the burden of her own sweet song: "When this New Moon is Old."

Getting Even.

Stranger.—What is the most powerful bomb you can make for me?

Anarchist.—Well, sir, give me money and time enough, and I can construct an implement of devastation which would shake the whole city of New York like a house of cards!

Stranger.—Would it make much noise?

Anarchist.—My dear sir, the concussion would be felt for hundreds of miles.

Stranger.—You don't say so! My friend, you can build me one of the machines, and have it done next Saturday night, if possible.

Anarchist.—Excuse me, sir; are you a Socialist?

Stranger.—Not to any great extent; but I live next door to a fashionable church with a bell-ringing sexton. I want to play a little joke on him when he starts the circus Sunday morning.

A Reasonable Price.

Customer *(to Boston Bartender.)*—How is it you charge me fifteen cents for whiskey, while the gentleman who just went out only paid ten?

Bartender.—You called for the best whiskey!

Customer.—Yes; but the liquor was from the same bottle!

Bartender.—I can't help that, sir! We charge five cents for the adjective!

COLERIDGE IS RULED OUT.

First Boston Girl. — We are tired of our Browning Societies. Let 's start another.

Second Boston Girl.—That 's so; and the Shelley Societies do not seem to be popular.

Third Boston Girl.—No; we must start something entirely new. How would a Walt Whitman Society do?

First and Second Girls *(in unison)*.—Oh, he would never, *never* do! He 's dreadfully improper.

Third Boston Girl.—Well, how would a Coleridge Society do?

First Boston Girl.—He 'd do; he 's written some lovely poetry, hasn't he?

Third Boston Girl.—Yes; he wrote "Kubla Khan," and ever so many sweet poems.

Second Boston Girl.—If he wrote "Kubla Khan," he won't do, either.

First and Third Girls *(in unison)*.—Why not?

Second Boston Girl.—Well, I 'll tell you. I read that poem yesterday; and he actually *(lowering her voice to a whisper)* says "pants," when you know any gentleman would say "trousers."

Third Boston Girl *(in consternation)*.—Does he, really?

Second Boston Girl.—Indeed, he does! Here is the quotation:

"And from this chasm with
ceaseless turmoil seething,
As if the earth in thick, vast
pants were breathing."

First and Third Girls *(in chorus)*. — That settles Coleridge's claim!

Second Boston Girl.—Yes; we 'll have to stick to Shelley, I 'm afraid.

King Kalakaua has twenty dancing girls retained in the royal service; and when he gets a little lonely over his wife's absence, two hundred light fantastic toes trip that loneliness away.

THE SAD FATE OF COUNTING NICK.

Have you ever heard the terrible tale
Of Nicholas Perkins Poppingale
Who counted himself to death?
He began by counting railroad ties,
And then he fell to counting flies,
I 'm sure it is n't any surprise
That he finally lost his breath.

A promising boy was little Nick,
But the counting fever made him sick;
I 've heard of it before.
When he took a step he counted that,
He counted the purring of the cat,
And counted the inches measured flat
Of everything he saw.

When he tried to play he had to stop
For he could n't keep up the count, and hop
As fast as other boys.
It 's hard to run and count your strides,
And count the other boys' besides;
And counting the pickets on sleigh-rides
Robs sleighing of its joys.

At every meal he counted each bite
Which sadly impaired his appetite,
And made him very thin.
He counted each cry the baby gave
When he went to sail, he counted each wave,
He counted the snores of his brother Dave
And the hairs on his grandma's chin.

It 's a pitiful tale and yet it's true;
And that counting boy was always blue,
I never saw him smile.
It 's all very well to count your cash;
But counting the winks of a friend's eyelash
Or the number of bites in a plate of hash,
Is really not worth while.

N. P. Babcock.

The water in Philadelphia is so dirty that before being used it has to be washed.

Repartee.

Sergeant-Major *(at inspection)*.—Your collar 's soiled, sir. Don't appear on parade in that condition again!

Private *(in a hissing whisper)*.—I 'm goin' to get transferred to your counter in the gents' furnishing department to-morrow, so it ain't likely I will.

PUCK.

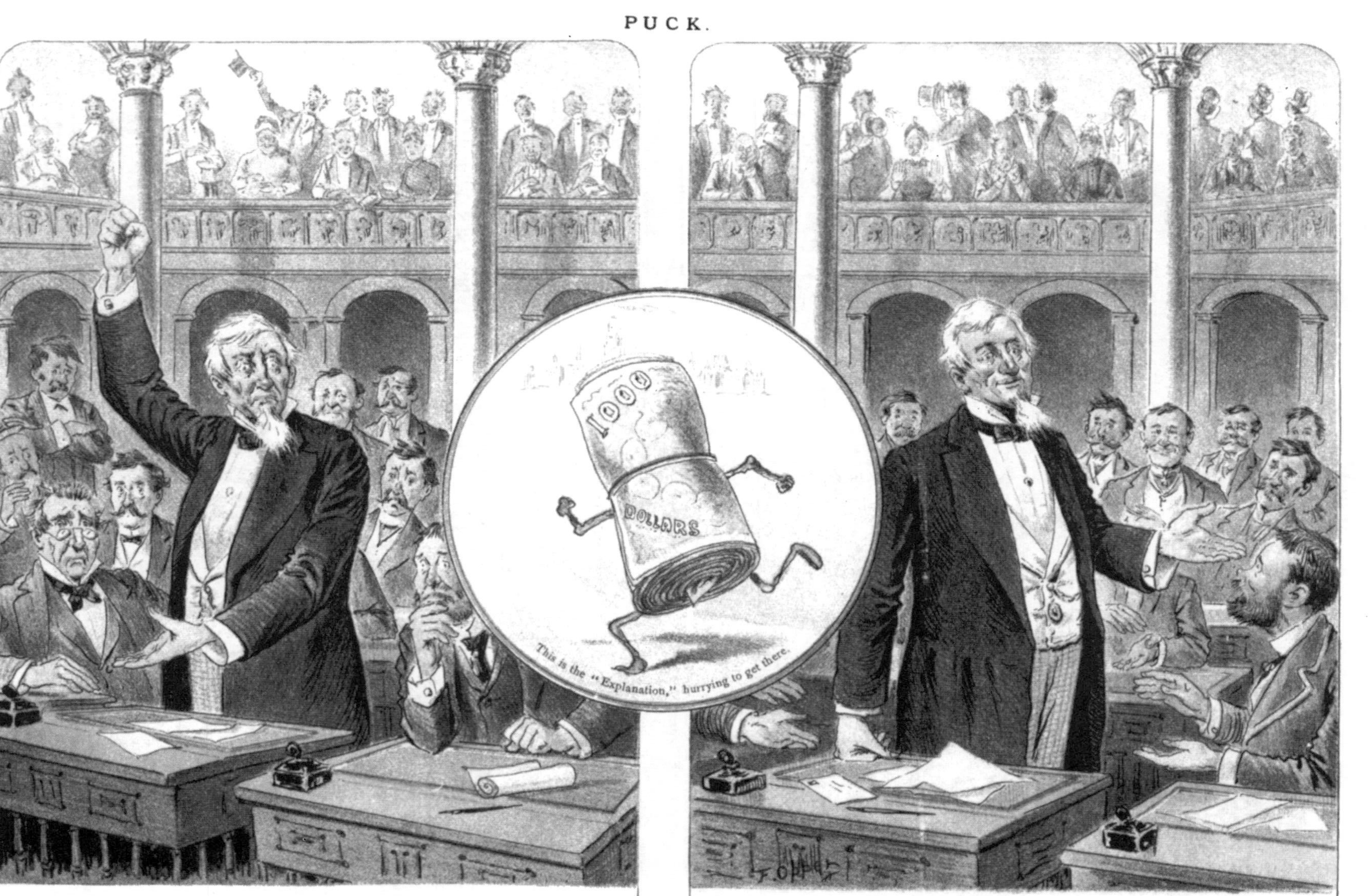

"Fellow-members of this august body, shall we permit that grasping and heartless monopoly, the Boodleville Construction Company, to get their bill through before we have received a satisfactory explanation of its real nature and purposes? Never! Our sacred duty to our constituents forbids!"

The next day.—"I feel that you will agree with me, gentlemen, that never in the history of this country has a more satisfactory explanation of any bill been given than the explanation which that courteous and public-spirited corporation, the Boodleville Construction Company, has given of this bill; and I say to you, gentlemen, that our sacred duty to our constituents requires us to pass it without delay!"

OUR LAW-MAKERS—THEY ARE ALWAYS OPEN TO CONVICTION.

"From the Bench"

The success of Puck tempted others to try similar experiments. Many imitators sprang up, most of them with the lithographic format of *Puck: Chic, Truth, Tid-Bits, Time, Texas Siftings, Rambler* and *Wasp*, a West Coast publication edited by Ambrose Bierce. One of these, of only slightly better quality than the rest, was *The Judge*, which first appeared on October 29, 1881. It was edited by James Albert Wales—who, it will be recalled, broke from *Puck* in a dispute midway through that year. Wales's partner and business manager was Frank Tousey, who dabbled in publishing and was part-owner of the American News Company.[24]

Though very weak in the literary area, *The Judge* had a creditable art staff. In addition to Wales, it included Livingston Hopkins, an Australian-born cartoonist, late of the *Graphic;* Thomas Worth, the popular creator of the *Darktown* cartoons for Currier and Ives; Frank Beard, a veteran of many defunct comic papers, and an inspiration to many budding cartoonists, including Frederick Opper; young E.W. Kemble, who was to be chosen three years later by Mark Twain to illustrate *Huckleberry Finn;* the venerable Frank P.W. Bellew, incorrectly identified by Mott and others as his son, "Chip" Bellew; and Grant Hamilton, who, after Wales, eventually became the chief cartoonist. The first issue contained this greeting and caveat:

> I have started this paper for fun. Money is no object; let sordid souls seek that. I have got all I want. If money *is* forced upon me through the enterprise, I shall found a hospital *or* a free beanery with it; my only object being to make people laugh and grow fat, so as to require more cloth for their clothes, in this way indirectly helping the manufacturing interests of the country. For my associates, I have selected men who have made you laugh before, either with pen or pencil, and I trust you will shake hands with them every week and be happy. I have not come in to crowd everybody else out, but only to make one more to assist the world to see the joyous side of life, and if I fail to please it shall not be for want of trying.[25]

The Judge was successful initially but was too much a carbon copy of *Puck* and too lacking in literary merit (nearly all the text was unsigned) to last. Philadelphians Albert H. Smyth (owner of the Saturday *Evening Post)* and Harry Hart put money into the magazine, but circulation did not pick up. It was the presidential campaign of 1884 that finally saved *The Judge*. First, it had been pro-Republican from its inception, so its cartoons found a ready market in that intensely partisan year. Second, and more important, *Life, Harper's Weekly* and especially *Puck* were all printing cartoons that helped the Democratic cause. These cartoons were receiving wide circulation and commentary, and leaders in the Republican party soon recognized that it would be beneficial to have a comic magazine of their own. Neither *Puck* nor any other magazine was owned or backed by a political party, but in a novel move, William J. Arkell was chosen to reorganize *The Judge* with substantial GOP money.

After the election, the magazine was completely overhauled, save for the retention of Grant Hamilton as a cartoonist. The rest of the staff left (Wales returned to *Puck*), the title was changed from *The Judge* to *Judge*, Bernard Gillam was lured from *Puck* with a partnership in the company, and young Eugene Zimmerman, a technical cousin of Opper, was also plucked from *Puck.* The typeface and composition were changed, and Arkell brought in Isaac ("Ike") Gregory of the *Elmira* (N.Y.) *Gazette and Free Press* as editor.[26]

With the second issue of 1886 (January 16) the new *Judge* made its debut, accompanied by a statement from Arkell: "This paper, under the new management, will be independent and American in its purpose and policy, . . . [employing] the wit of the philosopher rather than the coarseness of the clown."[27] The "independent" line was immediately repudiated by the dogmatic anti-Cleveland cartoons in that and succeeding issues, and the cartoons themselves were no more "philosophical" and no less "coarse" than those in *Puck* (to which the statement obviously referred). It might also be pointed out here that it was commonly known that while Gillam was drawing the coarse and savage

"Tattooed Man" cartoons for *Puck* in 1884, he was suggesting ideas to judge cartoonists and voting for Blaine!

In any case, by mid-1886, under Arkell's management (and probably due to bulk sales to local Republican organizations), circulation was up to 50,000.[28] Advertising increased proportionally, and revenue for the 1887 Christmas number (which sold for a quarter rather than the usual dime) reached $7,000.[29] In 1887 *Judge's Library* began publication, and in 1890 *Judge's Quarterly* first appeared. Both had large sales for years. *Judge* played a prominent role in Harrison's 1888 victory, issuing cartoons as tracts and publishing a pamphlet advocating the high tariff. Harrison later said, "*Judge* contributed more to my election . . . than did any other publication in the country, daily or weekly."[30] In 1891 the *Judge* company was prosperous enough to purchase *Frank Leslie's Illustrated Newspaper.*

Most of *Judge's* written pieces continued to appear anonymously, and the quality of this material was very low. Curiously, opinions were never expressed in the editorial columns, whose staples were one-or two-line jokes, insults and sarcasm. It almost seems that while *Life* tried to appeal to high society, and *Puck,* growing more sophisticated, aimed to please everybody, judge was meant for barbershops. Not that it was ever vulgar; merely that it could never with justice be accused of literacy. For years *Judge's* real showcase was its cartoons, and in this field it acquired many bright stars. J.H. Smith illustrated Bill Nye stories and was a cartooning teacher (of Nate Collier and others), and Emil Flohri was beginning his career; he was to remain on the staff for 25 years. Other cartoonists included Eugene Zimmerman ("Zim"), who was rapidly developing his amazing style of caricature; Bernard Gillam, who was to die in the midst of McKinley's 1896 campaign; his brother Victor Gillam ("F. Victor"), who created the "Full Dinner Pail" theme for McKinley; Grant Hamilton, who turned much of his attention to satirizing the passing scene; and newcomers F.L. Fithian and A.S. Daggy. Penrhyn Stanlaws drew the "Stanlaws Girl" in answer to *Life's* "Gibson Girl" and *Puck's* "Taylor-Made Girl" by C.J. Taylor.

The Full Dinner Pail and the Spanish-American War pushed *Judge's* circulation up to 85,000, where it remained until the 1907 panic.[31] The war provided a splendid opportunity for *Judge* to splash chrome colors over all its pages, give away American and Free Cuba flags, and employ flaps, foldouts and other devices while slandering the enemy. McKinley was a very popular president, and his successor, Theodore Roosevelt was perhaps the most popular in our history, so these were good years for the Republican *Judge.*

During the 1910s, in addition to the cartoonists named above, there was much talent in the pages of the paper (as well as a lot of amateurish work). The better artists included T.S. Sullivant, one of the geniuses of American cartooning history; Art Young, who was also drawing for *Puck* and *Life;* R.F. Outcault, who drew for *Judge* when he was not drawing *The Yellow Kid* or *Buster Brown;* George Herriman, who was later to create *Krazy Kat;* James Montgomery Flagg, whose *Nervy Nat* series was extremely popular; and C.W. Kahles, an early comic strip pioneer of *Hairbreadth Harry* fame. Some of the finest color printing of magazine cartoons was represented in Judge in these years.

In 1910 the company reorganized. Its name was changed to the Leslie-Judge Company, and the partnership with the GOP was dissolved. There were changes in the magazine as well. Politics was dropped completely in 1911, and the size of the pages was reduced. The *Puck*-like format was eliminated; the only color was on the cover of each issue. Many of the good cartoonists left, though Zim and Flagg remained. With average art and typically poor text, *Judge* nonetheless shot past *Puck* in circulation (it had always been ahead of *Life),* hitting the 100,000 mark in 1912 and remaining ahead. This development is especially curious since its guaranteed Republican readership had been set free. Moreover, it had little advertising and seldom went beyond 16 pages, while *Life* often had 100 pages or more per issue. Among *Judge*'s prominent cartoonists in these years were Carl Anderson, Frank Godwin, Ralph Briggs Fuller and Percy Lee Crosby (who were later to draw *Henry, Connie* and *Rusty Riley, Oaky Doaks* and *Skippy,* respectively); Johnny Gruelle of *Raggedy Ann* fame; Reginald Birch, who illustrated *Little Lord Fauntleroy;* and John Conacher, W.O. Wilson, C.W. Anderson, C.F. Peters, Lansing Campbell, L. Fellows and, of course, Zim. Cover artists included Flagg, Enoch Bolles and Rolf Armstrong.

In 1922 there was another shake-up as Leslie's went out of business. Douglas H. Cooke became publisher and editor in chief of *Judge,* and he chose freelance cartoonist Norman Anthony as his managing editor. For the first time in its history, *Judge* displayed some literary quality, with William Allen White writing editorials and Walter Pritchard Eaton reviewing books. Heywood Broun wrote on sports and movies, and George Jean Nathan was engaged to handle the theater column. Within a year, these writers (except for Nathan) left, but *Judge's* circulation had shot up to a quarter of a million.

One of the wisest things Cooke did was to give Norman Anthony free rein. Under Anthony, John Held drew for *Judge,* and its pages sparkled with the likes of Percy Crosby, Milt Gross, Dr. Seuss, R. B. Fuller, Jefferson Machamer, Gardner Rea, Crawford Young and G.B. Inwood—all of whom probably comprised the craziest magazine staff ever assembled, if *Judge's* constant inside jokes are any indication. In addition, Anthony had discovered S.J. Perelman writing for a college paper and contracted him immediately. Aside from Nathan, reviewers included Pare Lorentz on movies, Sidney Lenz on bridge and "Judge, Jr." on nightclubs. The magazine waged a major crusade against Prohibition through its editorial cartoonist, Clive Weed, and in the 19205 there was a long-running feature called "Here's How!," to which readers would send recipes for cocktails mixed from very unusual ingredients; two books were published from this column. *Judge* cashed in on the crossword puzzle craze and had nutty send-in contests like "Finish a comic strip" or "Give a sentence using the word *archaic"* (as, "We can't have archaic and eat it too").

In short, under Anthony and assistants Jack Shuttleworth and Phil Rosa, *Judge* was a funny magazine. *Life* was witty, but *Judge* was funny-so funny that the ailing *Life* and Charles Dana Gibson lured Anthony away in 1929 to edit that paper (after a year he was fired, and he soon started *Ballyhoo* magazine). Even if Anthony had remained on the staff, it would have been hard to be funny after 1929. Jack Shuttleworth became editor and had to contend with the Depression, falling subscriptions and failing advertisers. The revitalized *Life* and the successful *New Yorker* (born in 1925) were also at *Judge's* heels. At one point *Judge* dropped from fifteen cents to the prewar price of a dime, but in 1932 it went monthly at fifteen cents a copy. Many good artists and writers left; among those who remained were Dr. Seuss, Bill Holman (*Smokey Stover*), George Lichtenstein *(Grin and Bear It),* Reamer Keller and Frank Hanley.

In November 1936, *Life* magazine sold its title to Time, Incorporated, and *Judge* bought *Life's* subscription list and features. *Judge* then promised to be "bigger, better and brighter"—and at least it got a little bigger. It was enlarged from 36 pages a month to 52. From *Life* came much of the new format, the letters column, the reviews, Kyle Chrichton editorials, the "Are You Sure?" quiz, and cartoonists Don Herold, Ned Hilton, Robert Day and Chon Day. In 1937 came the boast "More than a million people now read *Judge,*" but it still seemed that nothing could pull it together. Advertising was scarce, and most of the good cartoonists had left to do newspaper comic strips (childrens' books in Dr. Seuss's case, books and scripts in Perelman's). *Judge* could not pay for good-material, and matters became so bad that in 1938 clips and reprints from old issues of *Life* and *Judge* were used. Through the 1940s it limped along on poor stock with a mediocre staff and more than a few "girlie" cartoons. One of its last issues, in October 1948, presented a reprint of a Norman Anthony piece, a page by Margaret Fishback and a transcript of a radio comedian's monologue. The advertisements in this issue included one for a crocheting book, a "3 cents a Day Hospital Plan," Foley Dog Supplies and public service spots.

The January 1949 issue was the last published. With a simper and a wheeze, *Judge* died. During its life, it seldom had real character or established rapport with its readers (as did *Puck* and, as we shall see, *Life),* but in its heyday it was an influential, powerful partisan voice. More important, it made its pages a showcase for some of America's greatest comic geniuses and cartoon artists.

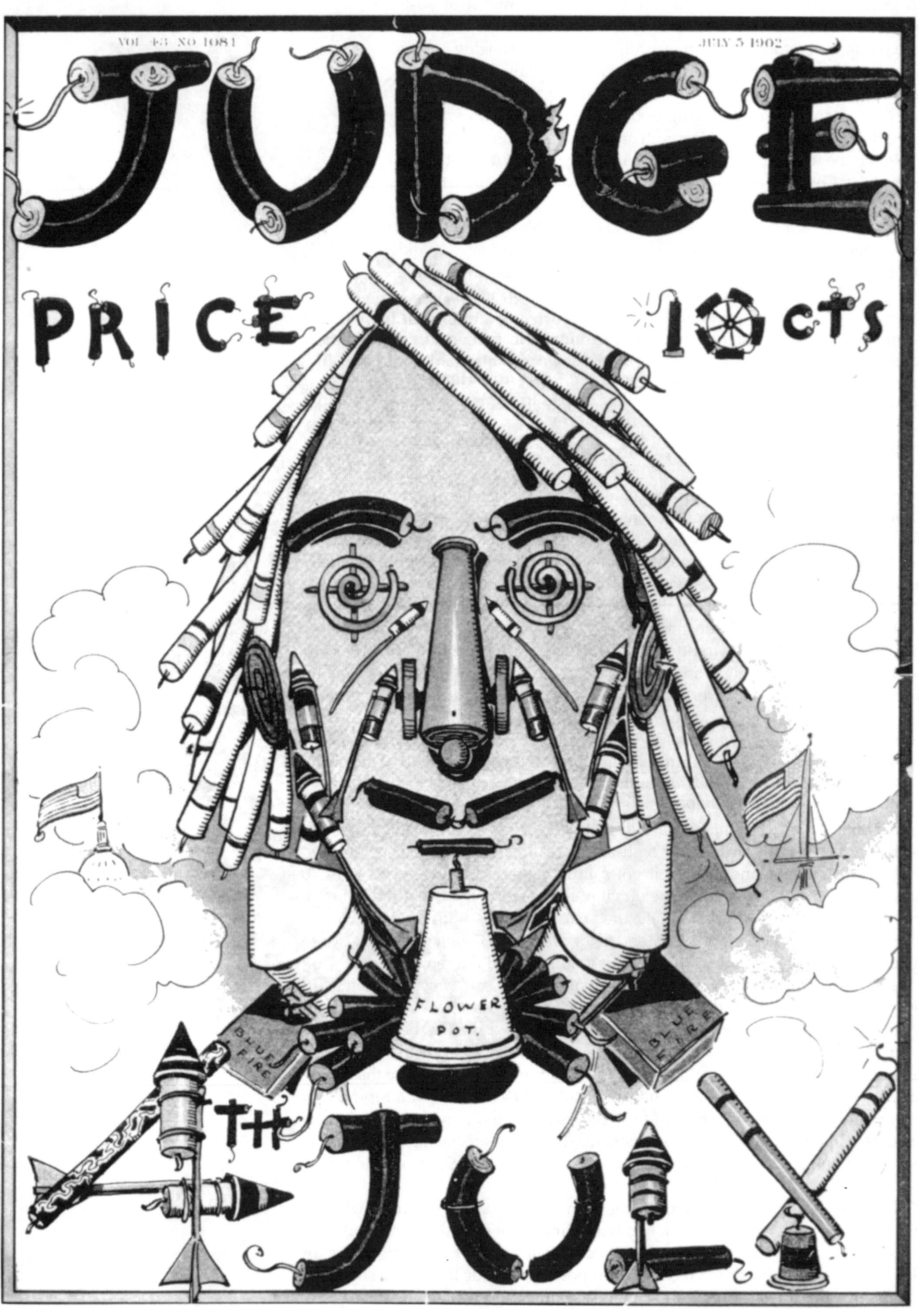
VOL 43 NO 1081
JULY 5 1902
JUDGE
PRICE
10 CTS
FLOWER POT.
BLUE FIRE
BLUE FIRE
4TH JULY

Judge

ENTERED AT THE POST OFFICE AT NEW YORK AS SECOND CLASS MATTER. COPYRIGHT 1902 BY JUDGE COMPANY. TITLE REGISTERED AS A TRADE MARK.

Sackett & Wilhelms Litho & Ptg. Co. New York

THE AMERICAN GIRL.

Here's the fair American
Girl, and she's a beauty.
When her sweetness is summed up
She is tutti-frutti.

She's a bird and she's a peach,
Also she's a daisy,
And the sort of witch that drives
All the nobles crazy.

But she wants no coronet
And no coronation.
She's a Yankee through and through,
Not for importation.

Judge

PUBLISHED WEEKLY
AT THE JUDGE BUILDING,
110 FIFTH AVENUE, NEW YORK.

Terms to Subscribers.

UNITED STATES AND CANADA IN ADVANCE.

One copy, one year, or 52 numbers	$5.00
One copy, six months, or 26 numbers	2.50
One copy, for thirteen weeks	1.25

Including the CHRISTMAS JUDGE.

FOREIGN SUBSCRIPTIONS—To all foreign countries in the postal union, $6.00 a year.

WESTERN OFFICE—*828-829 Marquette Building, Chicago.*

EUROPEAN SALES-AGENTS—*International news company, Bream's building, Chancery lane, E. C., London. Brentano's, avenue de l'Opera, Paris: Saarbach's news exchange, Mainz, Germany.*

CONTRIBUTORS must inclose a stamped and self-addressed envelope with all manuscripts, otherwise return of the latter when found unavailable cannot be guaranteed.

DRAWINGS and all contributions sent to the Art Department should have the sender's full name and address written plainly on each and every separate sketch. The accompanying joke or descriptive letter-press should in every instance be written upon its individual picture, and NOT upon a separate slip of paper. Inclosure of stamps to the full amount of postage is also required, to insure safe and prompt return of material not accepted.

THE ice-cream high-ball on the counter stands,
A pink-built joy, an evanescent boon,
And o'er it, beaming like the summer moon,
The wistful maid uplifts her lily hands.
Within her vision, as the drink expands,
She at it aims and darts the slender spoon,
E'en as the whaler does the long harpoon
That on the whale he like chain-lightning lands.
A surging melody then stirs her soul
And makes her fancies dance a rosy jig.
Her optics whirl, and she is quite on top
With ecstasy, suggesting rapture's goal,
Where now she dwells while pouring down that big
Long drink of which she doesn't lose a drop.

• • •

THE MAN in whom there is a fine stratum of undeveloped virtue and greatness is no longer called a rough diamond. He now enjoys the enviable reputation of being known as a rough lump of coal.

• • •

THE PRICES charged for seats at the coronation should place this imposing ceremony on a financial level with the Italian opera and the American prize-fight.

• • •

BIBULOUS PERSONS should not look upon the bowl too frequently on the Fourth lest they lose their heads and flee in terror when they see the snakes sizzle and whizzle out of the sky-scraping rocket.

THE HEAD that wears a crown does not lie uneasy if the owner has the forethought to hang it on the hat-stand before retiring. It may also be truthfully said that the feminine head does not lie uneasy that happens to wear a coronet.

• • •

FOR at least a little handful
Of swift years, flown here and there,
Edward Seventh's crowning glory
Hasn't been his topmost hair.

• • •

THAT ALL is not gold that glitters in a coronet will be thoroughly understood and appreciated by the impoverished peer who attends the coronation bedecked in a specimen hired from a theatrical costumer, that, in point of intrinsic value, is about on a level with an antique tomato-can.

• • •

BANG! bang! bangs the cannon—east, west, south and north—
To tell all Americans this is the Fourth;
And though they well know all the cannon's cute game,
They like it to tell them this thing just the same.

• • •

IT IS the opinion of a correspondent that the most expert and nimble Coney-island waiter will never spin down the aisle twirling a plateful of oxtail soup on his dexter finger with a grace and airiness so consummate as that which the duke of Marlborough will display when he glides to the front with the crown.

• • •

PERHAPS the brightest and most wildly picturesque fourth of July fireworks, as regards topsyturviness of form and general uniqueness of effect, will be those set off by the orator who, in his peroration, would at the same time stir the hearts of the people and do a little miscellaneous campaign somersaulting on the side.

• • •

THE BUMBLE-BEE goes on a spree; all day the nodding rose he sips. The lily jumps and bangs and bumps along the ripple as it rips. The high-ball beams and glints and gleams and lifts one to a rosy sphere. The peachy peach along the beach is now coquetting there and here. To beat the fates disintegrates the umpire 'neath the whirling bat; and now we glide and slip and slide as lively as the moonlit cat for mountain, sea and verdant lea, to leave behind the dusty town and get the fly alert and spry where old King Edward gets the crown.

• • •

WHIZZING the pin-wheel is heard, the ball of the candle is popping
Into the sky with a bang that fills the small boy with enjoyment.
Hissing the snake in the stars exudes from the petulant rocket—
Washington rides on his horse and smiles as he blazes in glory.

Bang! goes the pistol, and bang the hand of the banger a finger
Flips in the air with the bang that's drowned by his loud lamentation.
Next time the gun he'll eschew, and with the big union torpedo
Clip the bow-wow on the jaw and knock the tom-cat off the paling.

MAKING A NAME.

MRS. JUSTBLESSED—"We are going to name him Albert Edward, but we feel sure baby will make a name for himself before he is thirty."
UNCLE CRUSTY—"Yes; he'll be lucky if he doesn't have half a dozen aliases by that time."

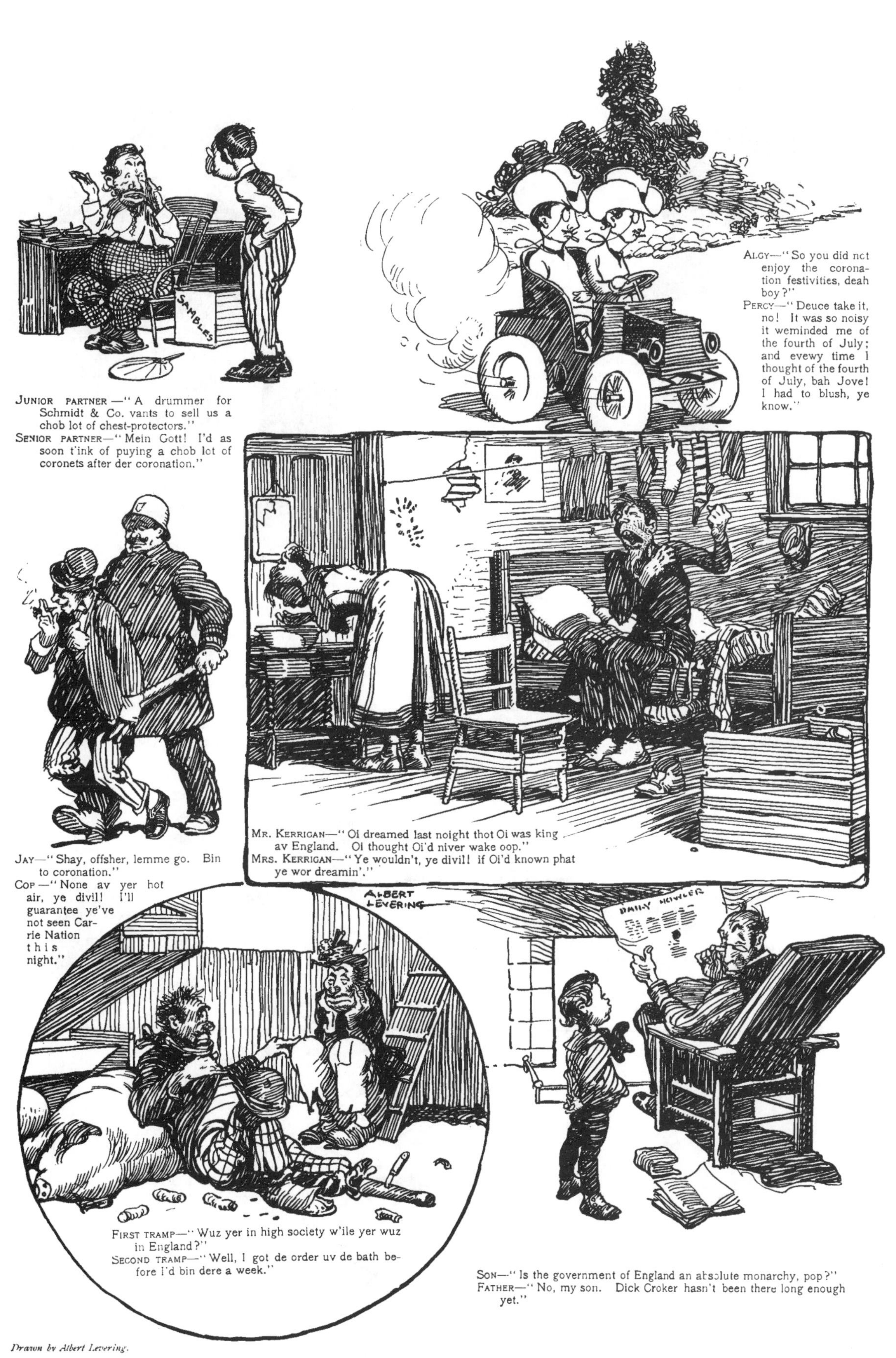

JUNIOR PARTNER—"A drummer for Schmidt & Co. vants to sell us a chob lot of chest-protectors."
SENIOR PARTNER—"Mein Gott! I'd as soon t'ink of puying a chob lot of coronets after der coronation."

ALGY—"So you did not enjoy the coronation festivities, deah boy?"
PERCY—"Deuce take it, no! It was so noisy it weminded me of the fourth of July; and evewy time I thought of the fourth of July, bah Jove! I had to blush, ye know."

MR. KERRIGAN—"Oi dreamed last noight thot Oi was king av England. Oi thought Oi'd niver wake oop."
MRS. KERRIGAN—"Ye wouldn't, ye divil! if Oi'd known phat ye wor dreamin'."

JAY—"Shay, offsher, lemme go. Bin to coronation."
COP—"None av yer hot air, ye divil! I'll guarantee ye've not seen Carrie Nation this night."

FIRST TRAMP—"Wuz yer in high society w'ile yer wuz in England?"
SECOND TRAMP—"Well, I got de order uv de bath before I'd bin dere a week."

SON—"Is the government of England an absolute monarchy, pop?"
FATHER—"No, my son. Dick Croker hasn't been there long enough yet."

Drawn by Albert Levering.

A FEW ALIEN REMARKS ON THE KING'S CORONATION.

JUDGE'S FAVORITES.

FLORA ZABELLE.

Twinkle, twinkle, little star—
Where the top is there you are.
At art's very topmost top,
Round the stage you gayly pop.

All hands shout both near and far,
"Twinkle, twinkle, little star,"
As you fly from town to town,
Wearing triumph's shining crown.

E'en the dude sighs with delight
When he buys you roses white,
"Twinkle, twinkle, little star;
All my peace of mind you jar."

You're of all the sweetest thing
While you caper, dance, or sing.
Yea, of all—for none we bar—
Twinkle, twinkle, little star.

HIS VACATION, PERHAPS.

"WHO is that gentleman who dodges and jumps so much whenever a fire-cracker is thrown near him?" asks the spectator.

"That," explains the native, "is Signor Alfredo de Caloric, the world-renowned fire-king, who was stranded here with his company last week."

WHAT, INDEED?

Cycler—"I see they are wearing peg-top trousers for bicycling this summer."

Old joaker—"Well, what could be more appropriate for a spin?"

A GREAT ATTRACTION.

FROM the Bowersville *Clarion:* "The committee in charge of the fourth-of-July celebration has decided not to buy any fireworks, but rather to purchase a ton of coal and burn it on the public square. This will make the puny celebration at Jamestown look like a fizzled squib when the matter of liberal expense is considered."

Drawn by L. F. Fithian. THE SENSATION.

BLEECKER—"Did you go to the coronation, old chap?"
BAXTER—"No; just went down and got in a Brooklyn-bridge crush, so as to get the sensation."

Drawn by C. J. Taylor.

THE TAYLOR-MADE GIRL.

MRS. SEASIDE—"How do you manage to keep the moths out of the beautiful dresses you leave behind?"
MRS. HIGHFLY—"Oh, I have two maids at home."

HER PICTURE.

I see your picture, fair Annette,
In all its dimpled loveliness.
By all your charms I'm quite upset
And captive held, I must confess.

My fancy conjures with your name,
Whose magic on me ever beams,
And dim your beauty makes the frame
That's builded of my brightest dreams.

NO 7.—JUDGE'S GALLERY OF FAIR WOMEN.

HIRAM PENNICK — OUR COUNTRY CORRESPONDENT "Takes his pen in hand"

Josh Mellun.

DAVIS JUNCTION, O., June 28th.

EDITER JUDGE:

Uncle Cyrus Whiffle is so's to be round agin. Cyrus says they ort to be a law to make auttymobiles run on tracks.

Josh Mellun 82 yers old celebratid his burthday tuesday fer last 9 yers Josh has turned a hanspring every birthday—but this time he givs it up owin to a cowbunckle on his neck.

Theres a good deel of talk in this part of Ohio bout the way the country is goin crazy over royelty.

Fust it wus that Princ Henery now its the King of England.

Levi Kink leedin citzen here says most of the royel famlys is humbugs & says if its true what he's heerd bout sum of them dukes, hangins to good fer em.

I made a speach in town hall here satday nite that shows you how the speerit that stured the boozums of our fourfathers haint ded yet as follers:

Feller Citzens: Sum famlys of ferrin lands has to be high up & others has to be low down. That's the way they been runnin things fer so long in them countries they dont kno no better. The Royel famlys that got to the top of the lader of fame as the poit says 2 hunderd yers ago is still up, & a good many on em wuld be keepin sloons er workin in cheez factrys if the peeple tuk a noshen to kick the lader out frum under em. In Ameriky the land of the free one man orto be az good az a nuther & a blame site beter if he fites fer his place & behaves hisself & has branes to back it.

If the rich city peeple wunt to pay fer dressin up 2 or 3 tony fellers in velvit close an sendin em over to a ferrin country fer to do plite bowin & scrapin front of a King thats a big gun caus his parunts wuz, wy let em do it but the U. S. Congres & the peeple of Davis Junction orto stick clost to the constitooshun & reklect that this nashun haint founderd on a monarky & is jest as much fer them that haint got pedigreez as them that has. The cloak of glory thats reddy made & dont hav to be paid fer wunt fit the Amerikan Egle. Cheers fer them that fites fer there fame but not a golblame cheer fer them that gets it fer nothin.

HIRAM PENNICK.

"Hangin 's too good fer 'em."

Uncle Hiram lectures his fellow-townsmen.

THE DESIGNATION SUITS.

"TOMMY," said the school-teacher to Tommy Taddells, "what do you understand by the term 'high explosives'?"

"Sky-rockets, ma'am," replied Tommy.

AT THE CORONATION.

King Edward—"My dear."
The queen—"My love?"
King Edward (anxiously)—"Is my crown on straight?"

Drawn by T. S. Sullivant.

MILKING-TIME.

MISS CITYBRED—"Little boy, don't you ever observe the holidays—the fourth of July, the king's coronation, or the sabbath for a day of rest?"
THE BOY—"Of course *I does*, but de cows *don't*."

Drawn by Gus Dirks.

CELEBRATING THE FOURTH IN BUGVILLE.

MR. SNAIL—"Aw, say! what are you all running away for? Didn't you ever see a snail before?"

DIS YERE'S INDERPENDENCE DAY.

TOOT de fish-horn, sonny—
Toot it, Pete, mah lam'!
Act like I feel funny?
Sho'ly, bub, I am
Antic as a colt at play—
Dis yere's Inderpendence day!

Git yo'r fire-cracks ready,
Light 'em sho' enuff;
Hol' yo'r han' right steady—
Dar, Jim, dat's de stuff!
Hear 'em bang an' hop away—
Dis yere's Inderpendence day!

Dinah! Sukey! Polly!
Beat dem tin-pan drums;
Dance like yo' feel jolly,
Cheer like army comes!
My ol' heart is light an' gay—
Dis yere's Inderpendence day!

MARY CLARKE HUNTINGTON.

A PERFECT IMITATION.

"HERE, sir!" I say angrily to the dealer; "that miniature volcano you sold me for my little boy's Fourth will not explode. We don't know whether it will go off or not. And yet you guaranteed it to be a perfect imitation of the real thing."

"Well," he answers insolently, "isn't it? They can't tell when the real ones are going to bust, either."

ONE REASON.

"PAPA," asked the little Peck boy, "why do they always have a lady to read the Declaration of Independence at the fourth-of-July celebrations?"

"Because," was the solemn answer, "the committee knows how foolish it would seem to have a man read it with his wife in the audience."

THE "POMP OF POWER" IN THE "PATHS OF GLORY" TO BE SEEN AT KING EDWARD'S CORONATION PROCESSION.

OH, HOW

UNCLE SAM—" Say, John, why are you shooti
JOHN BULL—" Because *I've* a crown, don't you
UNCLE SAM—" Because I'm *rid* of the crown."

ve

ENT!

rks?"

, Sammy, why are you celebrating?"

AMERICANS AT THE CORONATION.

THE papers have given accounts of the English preparations for the coronation of Edward VII.; of the tiara that Queen Alexandra will wear, of the one that Mrs. Bradley Martin has ordered, and many others, but of the distinctive American preparations it has remained for JUDGE to give the first account. American life will be adequately represented in all its wonderful diversity, representative men from all typical walks of life being chosen. American commercial interests will be represented by Russell Sage and Dr. Munyon. Mr. Sage, as the emissary of Wall street, will go as a jolly-good-fellow and typify gentlemanly conviviality. His robe will be of rich burlap, lined with genuine Baxter-street wool, and will cover most gorgeous undergarments consisting of tights spangled with coppers and a coat of costly canvas with richly hand-embroidered "L" cars in fleur-de-lis pattern. In one hand Mr. Sage will carry a penny bank and in the other a box for larger donations. His tarara will be even more gorgeous, beautiful, and costly than any yet described. Doctor Munyon will wear a grim look, and a magnificent plush robe of variegated colors adorned with appropriate mottoes. One hand will be raised dignifiedly, and in the other he will carry a box of pills to cure the London fog. His tarara will be even more gorgeous, beautiful, and costly than any yet described.

Richard Croker and Senator Hoar have been chosen as representatives of American civic interests. Baron Croker will appear in the first part of the coronation as an English gentleman and lord of a manor, wearing an appropriate mediæval costume, but by King Edward's special orders the coronation proceedings will be stopped to allow Hon. Richard M. Croker to change his costume and represent American civic interests; apartments in the bank of England have been especially set aside to allow of this change. Mr. Croker will wear a tarara even more gorgeous, beautiful, and costly than any yet described. Mr. Hoar, his companion, will wear a simple halo.

As representatives of American literature Harry Thurston Peck and Edward W. Bok have been most appropriately chosen. Mr. Peck will be attired in a garment suitable to the psychological moment, a bath-robe trimmed with forget-me-nots. In one hand he will carry a cigarette, and in the other an image typifying knowledge. His tarara will be even more gorgeous, beautiful, and costly than any yet described. Mr. Bok will be perfectly lovely in a robe of his own designing, the patterns of which will be published in the Ladies' Home Journal.

Following these will be a personage representing all that has gone before, and most that comes after. He represents at once American commercial interests, American literature, and the American drama—the redoubtable Major Pond. Mr. Pond will wear a linen duster and a silk hat. In one hand he will carry a green umbrella, and in the other a prospectus of King Edward's American lecture tour. His tarara, which he will carry under his arm, will be even more gorgeous, beautiful, and costly than any yet described.

The American drama will be represented by Charles Frohman, Ezra Kendall, and Richard Mansfield. Mr. Frohman will wear full livery, Mr. Kendall a Charles II. costume, while Mr. Mansfield will be attired in a magnificent negro-minstrel robe, modeled after one known to have belonged to Lew Dockstader. This part of the procession will be under the personal direction of David Belasco. Wigs by Levistein; robes by Rosenbaum; shoes by Mandlestein; mechanical effects by Goodbaum. Their tararas will be even more gorgeous, beautiful, and costly than any yet described.

American art will be adequately represented by Thomas Higgins, agent in southern Indiana for the Kalamazoo Photo-Enlarging Co., John V. Weeds, who sells spectroscopes, and George Jergerman, owner of the United States tin-type gallery at Ocean Grove. These three will wear silk robes of red, white and blue, with gilt stars as spangles. Mr. Higgins in one hand will carry a gilt frame with a sample of the work of the Kalamazoo Photo-Enlarging Co., and in the other his bicycle. Mr. Weeds and Mr. Jergerman will each carry a kodak. The tararas of all three will be even more gorgeous, beautiful, and costly than any yet described.

The American part of this picturesque and stately coronation procession will be brought to a close by a grand representation of American men of achievement. These will be headed by Mr. Carrie B. Nation, and followed by Thomas B. Reed, John L. Sullivan, Buffalo Bill, Richard Harding Davis, and Grover Cleveland. Mr. Reed will wear a purple robe with raglan sleeves. It will be lined with yellow silk. He will wear Scotch knickers. In one hand he will carry a Maine high-ball and in the other an apple from which he will take a bite at scheduled intervals. When one apple is eaten an attendant will hand him another. His tarara will be even more gorgeous, beautiful, and costly than any yet described. Mr. Sullivan will wear green tights, and the famous $10,000 belt as a tarara. Mr. Cleveland will wear a robe of fish net with two slash pockets quart-size, and pink tights, with two pockets quart-size. In one hand he will carry a fish rod and in the other a rare old decanter, known to have belonged to one of the Bourbons. Mr. Davis's costume beggars description. It is unique. It is unmatched. It is the limit. It is more gorgeous, beautiful, and costly than all the others. He will be photographed in it next week. His tarara also is even more gorgeous, beautiful, and costly than any yet described.

Hetty Green will represent American wealth, and will wear a green bombazine skirt trimmed with ham-colored passementerie and a shirt-waist of Swiss mull arabesqued with linen roses. She will wear a gargoyle on each shoulder blade and carry a pamphlet entitled "How to live on two dollars a week, with special directions for making a gallon of substantial lemonade with one lemon." Her tarara also is even more gorgeous, beautiful, and costly than any yet described.

H. R. HORR.

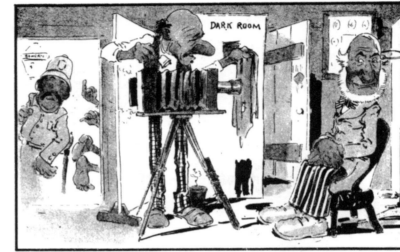

1.
THE BAD KID—"Hold yer breath, Mickey, till I put dese fire-crackers inside de machine, an' you'll see dat farmer guy do de 'loop de loop.'"

2.
FEENEY (*the cop*)—"Phat are youse kids doin' there?"
THE KID—"Dere's a man in dere tryin' ter commit sooicide."

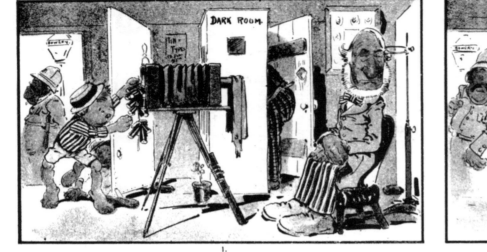

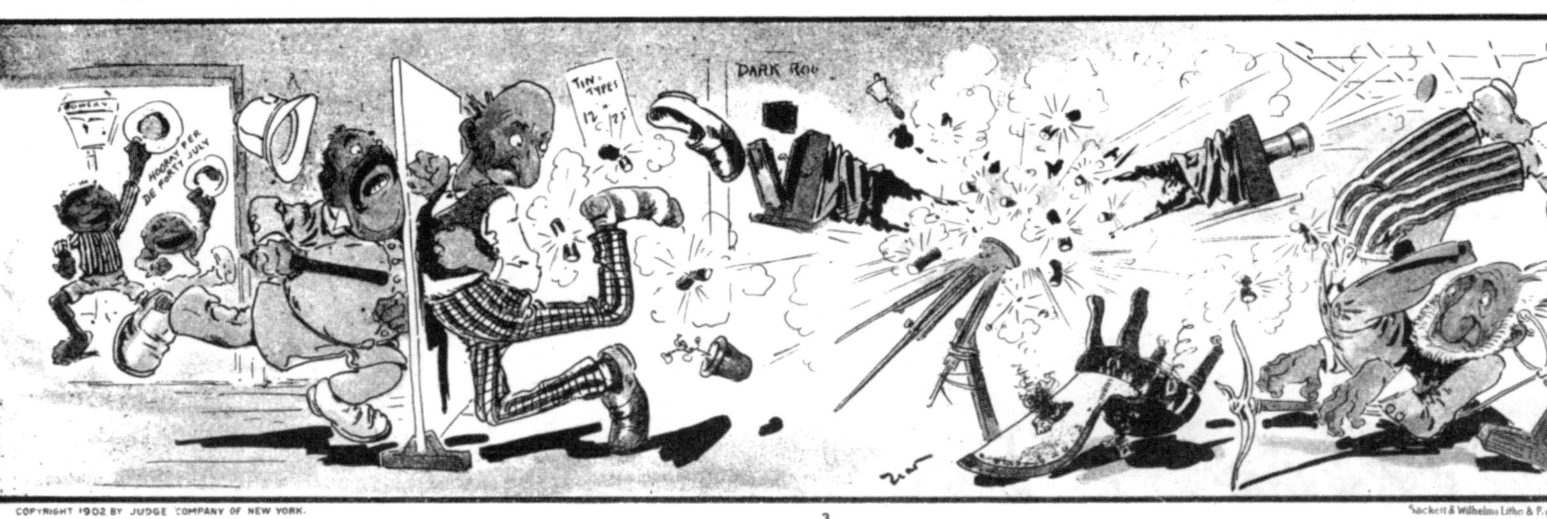

Sackett & Wilhelms Litho & P'g Co. New York.

3.
OLD HANK ZIPPET—"Jumpin' Jehosophat! 'Mandy 's right. I must have busted the machine by lookin' at it."

HE THOUGHT HE PUT IT OUT OF BUSINESS.

"Save a Little Place for Me"

LIFE—the perennial youngster—is up to his young-old tricks again—coming to the rescue of the harassed Christmas shopper. Rather thoughtful of him, isn't it, to offer his services just in time to solve the problem of the Unfinished List? LIFE is all set to go wherever he is wanted. And that means everywhere. From Main Street to Mayfair there isn't a home where LIFE would not be a welcome visitor fifty-two times a year. For when LIFE comes in at the door, worry flies out of the window. Think that over and remember that LIFE for a Friend Means a Friend for Life.

AND now, having made your decision, the coupon below will be found of enormous assistance. When you have filled it out and mailed it to us, we will send a Christmas card telling him—*or her*—what you have done.

Obey That Impulse **Life**

"While There's Life There's Hope"

The conditions that created a favorable climate for publishing ventures in the late 19th century and made possible the success of *Puck, Judge* and even the *Harvard Lampoon* loomed large in the mind of one John Ames Mitchell, an architect and illustrator of books, in the early months of 1882. In particular, it was while preparing a book of society cartoons and reflecting on the newest advance in means of reproduction—the process of zinc-etched engraving—that Mitchell formed an ambition to start a magazine. It was, he remembered, "one of those ideas that once in possession lays hold for victory."[32]

Growing more and more enthusiastic, but thoroughly without knowledge of printing, editing or managing a magazine, Mitchell turned for advice to his good friend Henry Holt, a publisher. Holt had toyed with a similar idea—that of publishing a bright, clever and attractive journal of humor, satire and reviews—but was too prudent a businessman to plunge ahead himself. He was, however, trying to convince Brander Matthews to start *such* a project, though Matthews at the time was hardly more than an amateur.[33] As it happened, Mitchell and Matthews had very different dreams in their heads, and the three friends parted company on the subject.

In addition to Mitchell's ignorance of how to accomplish what he proposed, there were other factors that invited pessimism. Chief among them was the very high mortality rate of humorous papers since the Civil War (Matthews was the reviewer who was moved to allude to tombstones). *Puck* had managed to survive through circulation, influence and sheer talent, but Mitchell planned to bypass color—*Puck's* selling point—and concentrate on the new photoengraving process of reproducing cartoons. The prospects for such an undertaking did not seem rosy, and his friends predicted another corpse for the journalistic graveyard.

But Mitchell had his ambition—and a $10,000 inheritance with which to further it. He persuaded Edward S. Martin, a Harvard friend who had helped found and publish the *Lampoon, to* cast in his lot with the venture. Martin was to remain associated with *Life* until its demise as a humor magazine. He wrote most of the editorials and was a prolific author as well. Like those of H.C. Bunner, Martin's editorials remain readable and interesting today—a rare quality. He expounded his views lucidly and logically, with humor and eloquence. As Mitchell wrote in 1908, "I can truthfully say of Martin that his civilizing influence has done much toward keeping *Life* from the gallows—the rest of us out of jail. . . . It is, perhaps needless to add that the moderation, justice, quiet humor, sanity and moral tone of (his) editorials have proved a benign influence toward counteracting certain pugnacious antics along the other pages of the paper."[34]

Martin now began a search for contributors, and the first steps were taken, but there was still no publisher. Finding one was no easy task, and Mitchell later described the kinds of arguments he encountered:

> "As I understand, you mean to give the public a periodical about half the size of
> *Harper's Weekly, Puck* or *Judge,* and yet you ask the same price for it. Now, *to* get that price, your smaller publication must be unquestionably better in quality, both artistic and literary. Have you secured the men whose work and reputation will assure you that position?"
> "No. The artists are not to be had."
> "And the literary men?"
> "The same with them."
> "That's bad enough. Is your own experience in journalism such as to warrant you in going ahead under such—peculiar circumstances?"
> "I have had no experience in journalism."
> "None whatever?"
> "None whatever."
> The man of experience indulged in a smile, but a smile of sadness and pity.[35]

Such exchanges notwithstanding, Mitchell remained convinced that America offered fertile ground for a high-quality black-and-white publication unlike any of the short-lived predecessors to which his attention was invariably directed when he broached the idea. Finally, after numerous attempts and many similar conversations, the Gillis Brothers press agreed to publish his magazine—with payment in advance. While hundreds of small problems remained, two large ones now loomed immediately: finding a man for the business department and finding a title for the magazine. Martin somehow secured one of his Harvard friends, Andrew S. Miller, who had worked for the daily *Graphic* and for a large advertising company. Again, Mitchell:

> One afternoon, about this time, Martin came into the studio and said in his usual quiet tone:
> "I have found him."
> "Whom?"
> "Our business manager. His name is Miller—Andrew Miller. I knew him at college."
> "And so you think he is equal to it?"
> "Well, he is young."
> "That's sensible. And he is not handicapped by any experience in the business?"
> "We must remember that if he were he would be out of harmony with his partners."[36]

Naming the paper was very important, and from many possibilities Mitchell and Miller selected *Life—"a* comprehensive title that left nothing out" and was properly philosophical.[37]

Mitchell, as managing editor, was ready as ever to roll. With Martin searching frantically for copy which seemed not to exist, and Miller for advertisements which must have had equally good hiding places, and himself in similar straits in the art department, he somehow produced the first issue on January 4, 1883.

> The first number bore the date of January 4, 1883. The others followed with confusing rapidity. Friday, the day we went to press, seemed to come around three times a week. The first number, probably from its novelty, sold reasonably well. The second issue showed a falling off. . . . Of the third issue, nearly all returned upon our hands. And when the returns of the fourth and fifth came in, the three anxious men who counted them made the blood-curdling discovery that the unsold copies outnumbered the edition printed! Six thousand had been issued, and there were six thousand two hundred returns. It seemed for a moment that miracles were being resorted to that *Life's* defeat might be quicker. A more careful examination, however, showed the extra copies were from previous editions.[38]

For six months the sales were almost literally nil. In spite of this, the redoubtable trio kept the weekly issues coming. Editor Mitchell attributes this feat to Miller's miraculous talent for convincing advertisers to buy space, which kept some revenue coming in. All the same, the situation remained rather grim for quite awhile. "It was alarming to reflect upon the number of intelligent Americans who got along comfortably without purchasing our paper," said Mitchell.[39]

Mitchell and Martin were not beyond performing miracles themselves. Mitchell recruited artists from the ranks of the *Harvard Lampoon,* some amateurish, some very good (including Henry McVickar and F.G. Attwood), and he found excellent cartoonists, some established, some just starting their careers: E.W. Kemble, whose exposure in *Life* attracted Mark Twain's attention; Palmer Cox, who became famous for his *Brownies;* and Charles Green Bush, later a great editorial cartoonist with the *New York Herald* and the *New York World.* Other early artists included W.H. Hyde, Charles Kendrick, W.A. Rogers (soon to succeed the great Thomas Nast at *Harper's Weekly*) and Gray-Parker. Mitchell himself drew many of the early cartoons.

Martin was having similar luck in the literary department. Besides his own essays and poems, which received considerable notice, he secured work from Brander Matthews, John Kendrick Bangs, James Whitcomb Riley, Tom L. Masson and Robert Bridges, who was later editor of *Scribner's Magazine.* Predictably, there was also a heavy assortment of Harvard talent.

Not until June was there a discernible increase in sales—and it was about time, considering the crude but obvious talent and the many favorable reviews from such sources as the *Critic,* the *New York Sun* and *Life's* rival, *Puck.* By August, though there were no profits, there were no more losses, and early in its second year *Life* passed the quite respectable 20,000 mark in circulation.[40] Mitchell had divided the concern three ways: he held a half-interest, and Martin and Miller each had a quarter.[41] *Life's* little mascot, a cupid, flew unassisted.

In its infancy, *Life* pledged to be independent in matters political and was held to its promise by the practical necessity of not offending any potential readers. Within these constraints, however, the irrepressible Mitchell and Martin remained neutral by attacking both Democrats and Republicans. By mid-1884, *Life* was solvent enough—and outraged enough—to join the fight against Republican presidential candidate James G. Blaine. Many Republican and independent journals also revolted against the scandal-ridden candidate, and *Life* was audacious enough to print a double-page cartoon showing a parade of independent and "mugwump" papers—including *Harper's Weekly,* the *New York Times* and *Puck*—all being led by *Life's* cupid! Perhaps Mitchell and Martin had Democratic tendencies from the start, but their support for Cleveland in 1884 marked the beginning of a definite Democratic bias in *Life* until the New Deal, with allowances for "vacations" during Bryan's campaigns.

Life was being noticed and gaining influence. Its appearance was now slick, no longer amateurish, and in 1886 Henry Holt started publishing the first dozen or so annual collections of drawings titled *Good Things from Life.* Another measure of its growth was *Puck's* changing attitude towards it. During the days of struggle, *Puck* had kind words for *Life,* but now that it was a strong competitor, *Puck* ran cartoons with stiff figures cut out of mail catalogues as parodies on *Life's* art and called the magazine "our esteemed black-and-white contemporary"; *Life* replied, addressing its elder as "our colored contemporary." In 1887 there was a battle between the two magazines over a cartoon *Puck* found in bad taste because it showed *Puck* in a gutter and Robert Louis Stevenson as a homosexual (January 6, 1887). *Life* answered that this was not what the cartoon was meant to represent, whereupon *Puck* retorted that its "younger brother" obviously hired cartoonists who didn't know what they were drawing. Ironically, *Puck* was negotiating at the time to contract this very cartoonist—a high honor. Fortunately for *Life,* the cartoonist preferred to stay where he was.

Just about one year before, in 1886, the same cartoonist had despondently climbed the stairway to Mitchell's office at 1155 Broadway to leave some drawings—drawings that had been rejected by a dozen other magazines. A few days later he climbed the stairs again to methodically reclaim his portfolio, expecting it to be accompanied by the inevitable rejection slip. Today, he declared, he would go home to Flushing, abandon his art and follow his father's advice by going into some "decent" business. He was led into Mitchell's office and waited in silence—a seeming eternity—while the editor examined the drawings slowly; through his beard, and with a twinkle in his eyes, he announced, "We're taking this one, Mr. Gibson."[42] Charles Dana Gibson had sold his first drawing to *Life* for four dollars.

The next week he returned with a portfolio full of drawings dashed off in a burst of confidence, but not one was acceptable. Mitchell saw his disappointment and took the 18-year-old Gibson to lunch. So began a warm relationship, a touching devotion (which, among other things, was what prevented Gibson from going to *Puck*), and a career that saw Gibson become America's most popular cartoonist, dictate fashion to a generation of men and women, and eventually take control of *Life* itself after Mitchell's passing.

Before long, Gibson was a weekly feature. He concentrated on drawing society subjects, and by the 1890s the "Gibson Girl" was on everyone's tongue. *Life* was on a lot of tongues, too. With its success came cocksureness, and commentary filled its pages as much as did humor. It attacked corruption, tariffs, monopolies, laborers, immigrants, Bostonites, the English, Jews, the *New York Sun* and the *New York World.* Other targets were society's "400," Christian Scientists, museum proprietors, Anthony Comstock and di Cesnola.

In 1887 Mitchell initiated the Fresh Air Fund for the Life's Farm program, which sent hundreds of tenement children to New York or Connecticut farms for two-week periods. This program continued for decades and always received generous help from public subscriptions.

By the mid-1890s *Life* was a major force in the magazine world, and fully respectable, in large part due to the Gibson Girl. Songs were written about her, her pictures were framed all over the land; thousands of girls dressed and carried themselves like the Gibson Girl, thousands of men shaved their moustaches, beards and sideburns and squared their shoulders. In this period of economic depression, Mitchell decided to "splurge" and employ halftone heliograph engraving. This method could accommodate washes, so that watercolors could be reproduced in grays in addition to the black-and-white pen-and-ink drawings—a boon to the "society artists," who preferred paint over pen-and-ink.[43] These artists, who spoofed the 400, the nouveaux riches and the fortune hunters, included Van Schaik and Albert Wenzel; holdovers from the early days who still dealt with these themes were W.H. Hyde and Francis Gilbert Attwood.

The art staff and list of contributors had expanded in the mid-1890s to include Oliver Herford, who often wrote essays or verse to accompany his wispy pictures; Albert S. Sterner, a painter and illustrator for the *Century* and *Harper's;* Frederick T. Richards, a comic artist who succeeded Attwood on the monthly commentary page after the latter's death in 1900; Charles Howard Johnson, an unpolished but prolific artist whose frequent appearances must have derived from a friendly prejudice on Mitchell's part; Michael Angelo Woolf, who drew cartoons of pathetic slum kids; Hy Mayer, whose unorthodox style belies his European training; F.P.W. ("Chip") Bellew, whose father was a pioneer American cartoonist, and who died prematurely in 1894; and T.S. Sullivant, noted for his wild exaggerations and outlandish animals, obviously a genius from the start. He drew for *Life* well into the 1920s.

Other cartoonists included A.D. Blashfield, who had by this time developed his shading technique and was turning out dozens upon dozens of the cupids that became *Life's* trademark; C.J. Budd, who was fond of superimposing photographs over his wash drawings; O. Toaspern, who employed a pebbleboard-and-crayon technique and was a masterful caricaturist; and the young James Montgomery Flagg, given at this time mostly to illustrated puns. There were also D. MacKellar, Ethel Johnson (the niece of C.H. Johnson), Winsor McCay, Carl Schultze, A.Z. Baker, Rudolph Dirks, Maxfield Parrish, McNair and Charles Broughton. On the literary side, "Droch" (Robert Bridges) was an excellent book reviewer who became editor of *Scribner's* late in the decade and was succeeded by J.B. Kerfoot. James Metcalfe's theater reviews became more and more outspoken, and Williston Fish and James L. Ford were bright additions.

Life's success was such that in 1893 Mitchell sought a new home for the offices. Land was bought at 19 West 31st Street in New York City, but right in the midst of planning, the depression hit. *Life* tightened its belt and continued to build until the plasterers went on strike, causing a loss of $20,000.[44] Finally, in May 1894, the staff moved into the Life Building, complete with a statue of its cupid. An incident that occurred in October illustrates the effect of Mitchell's personality and professional benevolence. On returning to his offices from lunch, the General (as he was called) found the staff and many contributors assembled around a gift, a bronze replica of the stone cupid outside; few eyes remained dry that day.[45] It was said that the only other editor who approached Mitchell in kindness was Richard Watson Gilder of the *Century.*[46]

On the commercial front, as *Life* did not rely on the novelty of color, it was not hurt too much by the advent of colored comic strips. Indeed, newspaper cartoonists such as Rudolph Dirks, Carl Schultze ("Bunny") and C. W. Kahles freelanced for *Life.* Editorially, *Life* stood by President Cleveland during his second term, depression and all, and abhorred the Populist movement and William Jennings Bryan. Though it had no love for William McKinley and his high-tariff policies, *Life* fought Bryan as savagely as any Republican journal. Its cartoons of him generally included stormy skies and a few anarchists in the background.

The Spanish-American War provided a good reason to heap criticism on McKinley. *Life* was violently anti-imperialist, anti-war (this war, at any rate) and anti-jingo. No Johnny-come-lately like Colonel Bryan, *Life* took a firm stand and remained consistent before, during and after the "splendid little war." It parted company with *Puck* and *Judge* on this issue and closed ranks with many of the Eastern liberal journals, notably the *Nation.* The "embalmed beef" scandal in the army gave *Life* yet another opportunity to lambaste McKinley and his secretary of

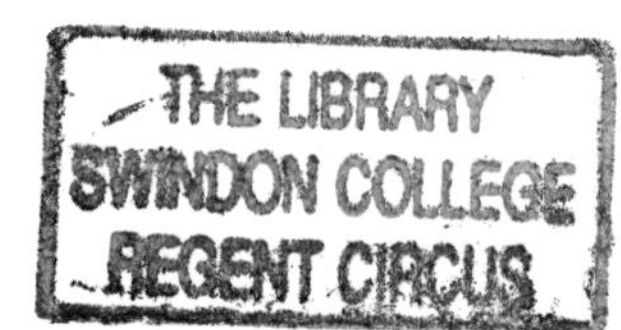

war, General Russell Alger. The ensuing struggles in the Philippines caused *Life* to compare the United States with the British in their Boer War (another atrocity in its eyes) and publish cartoons of Uncle Sam as bloody-handed murderer and modern Hun.

For all its opposition to expansion and Anglo-Saxon colonialism, it is evident from reading through its thousands of issues that *Life* considered the Anglo-Saxon races superior and viewed Western European culture, especially French culture, as the pinnacle of civilization. It regularly poked fun at Negroes, Irishmen and other ethnic groups, but it intended its jibes in fun, not maliciously. Such attitudes were in keeping with the times. The characters were stereotyped and satirized much as suburbanites and hippies are today. *Life* was serious, however, about its anti-Semitism, and the antipathy was mutual.

The Roosevelt years brought more new cartoonists to the magazine, as well as a new editorial flavor. It was the era of the Muckrakers, and reform was abroad in the land. *Life* had always been in favor of reform, whether of the civil service, the tariff or the monetary system. Now it turned its attention to trusts and social problems. The Fresh Air Fund was one recognition of urban problems, but now *Life,* along with millions of other Americans, began to see the government as a potential instrument for the reform of a broad spectrum of social ills. New cartoonists at this time included C. Allan Gilbert, who was famous for the still-popular picture of two stylish women sitting at a table, their outlines producing the general effect of a skull; Gus Dirks, the cartoonist of bugs; William H. Walker, an artist whose work was often unattractive, but who was a standby for years; his brother, A.B. Walker, who was neater and more economical with his line; Will Crawford, who produced marvelously crosshatched historical cartoons; Art Young, whose cartoons in this decade reflect his drift towards socialism; Orson Lowell, one of the better imitators of Gibson; an improved James Montgomery Flagg; and Walt Kuhn, later a great painter, then a cartoonist of birds and bugs.

Gibson, of course, was still there, and the period between 1900 and 1905 was his most successful. He had produced a wildly popular series entitled *Mr. Pipp* in 1899; he was elected to the American Institute of Arts and Letters that same year, and to the Society of Illustrators in 1902.[47] In 1904 the blossoming *Collier's* magazine tried to sign Gibson to an exclusive contract, but once again he refused to leave the General. Finally he signed an agreement to draw exclusively for *Life* and *Collier's* with the latter paying $100,000 for 100 drawings over the space of several years. Gibson later grew tired of the pen-and-ink work that had served him and his magazine so well, forsook approximately $75,000 per year, and went to Europe to learn how to paint.[48] *Life* certainly missed him but by no means collapsed. Its size increased with each issue, both from additional copy and from more advertising.

The biggest increase in the advertising columns was represented by cameras, liquors and especially automobiles. By 1908 each issue had dozens of car ads, many in color, and *Life* frequently put out "special numbers" with the humor focused on this phenomenon. Advertising was so heavy that in 1912 *Life* ran a Great Auto Race to see which manufacturer bought the most space in its pages. *Life* had quality ads and an upper-middle-class reading audience. Its commercial expansion, coupled with the addition of even more popular features (such as Wallace Irwin's "Letters of a Japanese Schoolboy"), led editor George Harvey of *Harper's Weekly* to declare in 1913, "The most successful 10 cent weekly is *Life.*"

At the same time, *Life's* social consciousness deepened. Around 1907 cartoons that were not meant to be funny began to appear. They were cartoons of gloom and pessimism, such as Art Young's "This World of Creepers—Afraid of the Almighty, the Unknown, and Themselves" or Balfour-Ker's "From the Depths," which shows a worker's fist emerging through the floor he and his enslaved comrades are supporting, on which dances a party of society people. Tom L. Masson, the brilliant managing editor, took on Ellis O. Jones, a Socialist, as contributing editor, and it was in these years that *Life* began its policy of publishing points of view different from its editorial stance.

In 1912, *Life* ably surveyed one of the most fascinating presidential campaigns in U.S. history. Martin was never more brilliant, lucid and fair in his essays. The magazine favored Wilson, though with some reservations; it preferred Taft's trust policy, for instance, to Wilson's and Roosevelt's. The traditional *Life* free-for-all reached new heights, with cartoons and essays for and against all the candidates.

Life's greatest success came in the years immediately preceding America's entry into the Great War. In 1916 issues ranged from 50 to 100 pages, and circulation reached 150,000.[50] (Although advertising was a boon, the magazine's strength always lay in its circulation. *Printer's Ink* magazine estimated that in 1893 *Life* made a profit of $100,000, one-third of it from circulation, which hovered between 60,000 and 70,000 until the early 1910s.[51]) All in all, the magazine was comfortable, mature and accepted as an institution by the public, even by those not included in its reading audience. Among its new cartoonists were Gedrge Penfield, Cory Kilvert, Will Rannels, Robert S. Dickey, A.O. Fischer, F.G. Cooper, R.B. Fuller, Percy Crosby, R.M. Crosby, Carl Anderson, Angus MacDonall, Victor Anderson, Paul Goold, Donald McKee and Paul Reilly.

When World War I broke out in Europe, John Ames Mitchell adopted it as the greatest crusade of his life, superseding Life's Farm, antivivisection ("If good for a horse, why not for a man?"), opposition to serums and inoculation, and all the rest. *Life* had always been Germanophobic and pro-French; that it had large sales in England probably had very little to do with Mitchell's position. Some contributors took anti-interventionist stands, but not for long (Ellis O. Jones was fired in 1916 for his pacifist views); Mitchell and Miller, through *Life* and along with Theodore Roosevelt and Elihu Root, were the earliest voices in favor of preparedness, and later of intervention. This stance prompted some savage cartoons against *Life's* erstwhile hero, Woodrow Wilson, for his weakness and vacillation before 1917. Mitchell threw his magazine's full weight behind the fight for preparedness, for the war effort, and against the amazing incompetency of the administration. His heart felt for the land where he had studied art for two long periods in his halcyon student days, and he established the French Orphan's Fund through *Life*. Immediately $200,000 was collected, and in 1918 *Life* supported 2,800 French children.

Sadly, the General died on June 29, 1918, some months before the German defeat. He had, however, lived long enough to see his other cherished dream, *Life*, become first a hope, then a reality, a going concern and a respected institution. He had not succeeded single-handedly, but he was always captain of the ship. He was involved with every page, every drawing; his mark was everywhere. That, in fact, was the problem that now confronted *Life:* the void was too great, there was no obvious successor. Charles Dana Gibson—once again drawing exclusively for Life—assumed the art editorship, which Mitchell had never relinquished, no matter what his other duties. For the interim, Martin and Metcalfe took control, and Metcalfe and Miller divided the duties of editor-in-chief, keeping *Life's* flavor more or less intact. E.S. Martin stepped in after two years to edit for another two. The reorganization of the company found Miller president (he had served previously as secretary and treasurer) and Metcalfe secretary; Masson continued as managing editor.

But Miller survived the General by only a year and a half, and the staff—that almost familial group of workers—was hit with the news that the Mitchell estate had put the magazine on the auction block. A new owner would not only bring inevitable changes in personnel but might also tamper with the institution.[52] After many conferences and much planning, therefore, the staff combined behind Charles Dana Gibson and went to the auction as a syndicate in 1920 to bid against agents for Doubleday, Page and Company, which was very interested.[53]

> There were critical moments at that sale. An attorney for Doubleday, Page bid strongly. His every offer was topped by Gibson. At last the attorney put the price up to $1,000.00 a share.
>
> "One thousand and one dollars," Gibson called.
>
> His rival hesitated, having reached the limit authorized by his instructions. He asked permission to wire Frank Doubleday at Palm Beach but the *Life* contingency, insisting that the sale must be consummated at once, managed to push it through at the last figure bid by Gibson.
>
> Charles Dana Gibson was the owner of *Life*, vested with the controlling interest by virtue of his own large contribution to the purchase fund. What a happy, suitable culmination it seemed! Here was another telling of the ever-thrilling American success story. The youth who had climbed the stairs of the

> old office in 1886 with a batch of crude drawings had in 1920 become editor-in-chief. To many, *Life* would not be *Life* without Gibson. He was *Life,* they said, but that was not true, for Gibson and the others who made *Life* always had served under the quiet, sterling command of "The General."[54]

The total price was one million dollars.[55] In another reshuffling at the top, Gibson was made president of the company. Le Roy Miller became secretary-treasurer, Frank de Sales Casey became art editor, and Martin served his two-year hitch as editor-in-chief.

Through all this confusion, the weekly was still coming out, now selling for fifteen cents. Just as Harding's "return to normalcy" didn't really bring a return to anything, so was it hard for *Life* to remain constant. In one sense, the changes were good, for many of them were due to the infusion of new talent miraculously appearing after the war. New signatures on *Life* cartoons included those of Rollin Kirby, brilliant *New York World* editorial cartoonist; Gluyas Williams, whose economy of line was to gain him fame as a Benchley illustrator; John Held, Jr., soon to be famous for his flapper cartoons; Percy Crosby with his *Skippy;* H.T. Webster, creator of *The Timid Soul;* and Norman Rockwell, painting his earliest covers. There was more of T.S. Sullivant's genius, and of course Gibson was active again, joined by A.B. Frost, E.W. Kemble, Russell Patterson, Edwina Dumm, Louis Raemakers, Rube Goldberg, Kerr Eby, Herb Roth and Charles ("Bill") Sykes, who did the weekly editorial cartoon. The literary staff also made impressive additions; new luminaries included Franklin P. Adams, Corey Ford, Montague Glass, Will Rogers, Dorothy Parker, Robert Benchley, Robert E. Sherwood, Ring Lardner, Marc Connelly and George S. Kaufman.

The magazine was tremendously clever and is entertaining even today—but the 1920s were not roaring yet for *Life.* From a circulation of nearly 500,000 in 1920, sales dropped to 227,000 in 1922.[56] In 1925 Andrew Miller's widow asked the courts to appoint a receiver for the company and set a "reasonable" salary for Gibson, who was said to be getting $30,000 a year for contributions and $20,000 as president. The suit was withdrawn immediately, but it had the intended effect of shaking things up. Editor's were coming and going; Louis Evan Shipman, Oliver Herford, Lucinda Flynn and Robert *E.* Sherwood all did stints between 1922 and 1929. Interestingly, the rival *Judge,* crude and cheaper-looking, was surging in sales. Evidently *Life* was too genteel for the speakeasy generation. *Life* wasn't changing, but life was.

A new format was tried in 1928 and flopped; *Life's* "Will Rogers for President" campaign attracted some attention, but to no avail. By 1929, sales had slipped to 113,000. Charles Dana Gibson turned over the presidency to Claire Maxwell.

It was Maxwell who lured Norman Anthony away from *Judge,* where he had been editor for five years and had turned it into a zany, successful sheet for the college crowd. Gibson assured Anthony that he was set for a long time and could have a free hand in revamping the magazine to make it turn the corner. On this basis, Anthony accepted the editorship. Aside from putting Gibson to work again and retaining E.S. Martin's editorials, Anthony threw tradition out the window. The accent was now on youth and drinking and New York's recommended night spots. The cartoons were wilder and more risqué, and the staff was interchangeable with that of *Judge,* including R.B. Fuller, G.B. Inwood, Frank Hanley, Dr. Seuss, Donald McKee, Paul Reilly and Gardner Rea. In addition, *Life's* whole format was changed as text took a back seat to cartoons.[57]

According to Anthony, sales during his first six months rose from 40,000 to 100,000.

> I was tickled to death; the advertisers were so sore they were using Absorbine, Jr. on themselves. *Life*'s dignity and tradition were being ruined; it was no longer a "high class" medium. What the ad boys were really sore about was the "editorial matter" in *Life* was attracting more attention than their ads which were no longer "framed" by nice solid columns of text. The fact that their ads were being seen by three times as many people didn't seem to enter their consciousness (as if they had any), and their howls of anguish could be heard way up in Maine where Charles Dana spent his summers.[58]

Finally, Anthony got the word that he was out; he immediately sued, claiming a verbal contract for $35,000 per year plus ten percent of the profits, which was what Gibson had offered. *Life* put up a fight but then asked Anthony to drop his suit, which he did.

Nevertheless, this episode probably hastened the inevitable demise. Bolton Mallory became editor for two years, and George Eggleston restored *Life's* conservative appearance, remaining until 1936, when it was gaining in circulation as a monthly. Gibson sold out his interest, but Edwina was drawing her delightful dog cartoons, and Marge spoofed society before going to the *Post* and *Little Lulu.* Percy Crosby kept *Skippy* going, and Milt Gross, Dr. Seuss, and Don Herold continued, each in his zany way. Frank Sullivan, George Jean Nathan, Robert Benchley and Dorothy Parker, along with the inevitable E.S. Martin, provided the literary humor and commentary. However, a new crop of cartoonists, including Garrett Price, George Price, Chon Day, Robert Day, Dorothy McKee, Ned Hilton, Richard Decker and Perry Barlow, was also drawing for the *New Yorker*, whose humor and popularity probably cut into *Life's* sales.

Life was now a quiet, amusing, conservative (it was anti-FDR) magazine once again on the upswing. Then, in 1936, its owners gave in to offers from Time, Incorporated, to buy the title. It was almost as if the old cupid, weary from the turmoil of the last dozen years or so, could no longer go on. Life's subscription and features went to the ailing *Judge*,[59] and its name to the proposed picture magazine. Henry Luce of Time paid $92,000 for *Life.* Ironically, Clare Booth, whom he had married the previous year, later told her husband that in 1933, as managing editor of *Vanity Fair,* she had urged her publisher to buy *Life*—then available for $20,000—and turn it into a picture-news magazine.[60]

What killed *Life?* Initially it was the fact that it relied too much on John Ames Mitchell. Then it was the fact that it vacillated between retaining its traditions and catering to a new audience. E.S. Martin seems to have felt that it was the passing of the old staff (he was sole survivor and wrote a eulogy in the last issue, November 1936), as well as the changing world—"a distracted world that does not know which way to turn or what will happen to it next."[61] Perhaps it was just that, having lived a long, busy, rewarding and happy life, it died a natural and honest death.

December
1925
Christmas
Price
25 cents
Life
My Lady's Stocking
RALPH
BARTON

Life
Christmas Number

OUTSIDE LOOKING IN

"I WONDER IF I COULD GET A JOB AS DEMONSTRATOR FOR THAT THERE BED?"

IN DARKEST AFRICA

First Monk: WHY IS MISS GAZELLE HIGH-HATTING EVERYBODY THESE DAYS?

Second Monk: OH, SHE'S BEEN THAT WAY EVER SINCE THE PRINCE OF WALES SHOT AT HER.

City Editor (on Christmas Day): GO UPTOWN AND INTERVIEW SOME OF THE POOR DEVILS WHO HAVE TO WORK AND CAN'T HAVE DINNER WITH THEIR FAMILIES TO-DAY. WRITE A GOOD SOB STORY, ABOUT A COLUMN AND A HALF. ON YOUR WAY BACK YOU MIGHT STOP AT A LUNCH WAGON AND GET HALF A DOZEN HOT DOGS. HAVE 'EM PUT PLENTY OF MUSTARD ON 'EM. I WON'T BE ABLE TO LEAVE THE SHOP ALL DAY.

CHRISTMAS IN TUDOR ENGLAND

SIR WALTER RALEIGH INTRODUCES THE CHRISTMAS CIGAR TO HER MAJESTY.

CHRISTMAS IN TUDOR ENGLAND

HENRY THE EIGHTH ADJUSTS THE MISTLETOE.

Mr. Common People: IF IT ISN'T MY OLD FRIENDS THE TRUSTS!
The Fat Boys: SH-H-H, NOT SO LOUD—WE ARE MERGERS NOW.

FLAMING YOUTH

"LEMME HAVE SOME OIL OF JUNIPER, MR. SQUILLS. I'M MAKIN' POP SOME GIN FOR CHRISTMAS."

The Unbreakable Doll—

—A Christmas Calamity

The Floorwalker: WELL, WHAT ARE YOU DOING IN HERE?
Little Girl: OH, NOTHIN'! WE'RE ONLY JUST MERELY LOOKIN' 'ROUND T' SEE IF THERE'S ANYTHING WE NEED FER CHRISMUS.

THE QUITTER
"SAY, FELLERS, IF HE DON'T SHOW UP IN AN HOUR OR SO, LET'S KNOCK OFF AN' GO TO BED."

THE THREE LITTLE ANTS

(Oh, you're not so smart, Mr. A. A. Milne!)

ONCE upon a time there were three little Ants.
They had lots of legs but they hadn't any pants.
They had no coats and they had no vests,
So they all caught cold in their legs and their chests.

They sent for the doctor and the doctor said,
"It's a wonder you haven't caught cold in the head;
Because, don't you know, if you don't wear cloze
You're sure to catch cold in your eyes and nose.

"And if you catch cold in your hands and feet
You catch pew-mony and you die toot sweet.
If you die toot sweet, why, you die mighty quick,
So you'd better buy cloze before you get too sick!"

Then they each gave a cough and they all gave a sneeze,
And they paid the doctor fifty-leven dollars, please;
And it made them gloomy and it made them sad,
For fifty-leven dollars was all that they had.

So they said, "Well! Well!" and they said "Gurk! Gurk!
We have no money so we must go to work,
Then we'll earn some money which will buy us vests
And coats and pants for our legs and chests.
Oh, we must have coats and we must have pants
Or we'll catch more cold!" said the three little Ants.

Then the first little Ant gave a pull and a push
And he climbed up Mister Bill Smith's rose bush;
He gave both his jaws six tweaks and two twiddles
And began eating rose leaves out in their middles.

Then Mister Bill Smith came along and said,
"If you eat all my roses my bush will be dead.
So please, Mister Ant, if you only will stop,
I'll pay you eighty million billion trillion sillion dollars
and a lollipop!"

Then the first little Ant said, "Thanks, Mister Smith;
I need some money for to buy cloze with,"
So he took the eighty million billion trillion sillion dollars in gold
And bought warm cloze, and they cured his cold.

Now the second little Ant began just at dawn
To build a house on Mister Bill Smith's lawn;
Then Mister Bill Smith came along and said,
"If you build that house my lawn will be dead.

"So please, Mister Ant, if you'll only stop,
I'll give you ninety million billion trillion sillion dollars and a lollipop!"
So the second little Ant took the ninety million billion trillion sillion
dollars in gold
And bought warm cloze, and they cured *his* cold.

But the third little Ant was a lazy little Ant
And he wouldn't work enough to buy a single pant!
He wouldn't work enough to buy a coat or a vest,
So he caught more cold in his legs and his chest.

And because he was lazy and wouldn't buy cloze
He caught a cold in his eyes and his nose;
He caught a cold in his hands and his feet,
Then he caught pew-mony and he died toot sweet!

So that is the story of the three little Ants
Who hadn't any coats or vests or pants.
They hadn't any coats or vests or pants,
And that is the story of the three little Ants.

Baron Ireland.

All in the Eye

"Say, I don't s'pose ya'd lend us a toy until after Christmas, I don't s'pose, would ya now? I want to kid a couple o' guys."

"The kid oughta be pleased with this, don't ya think?"

An Impression of Utop

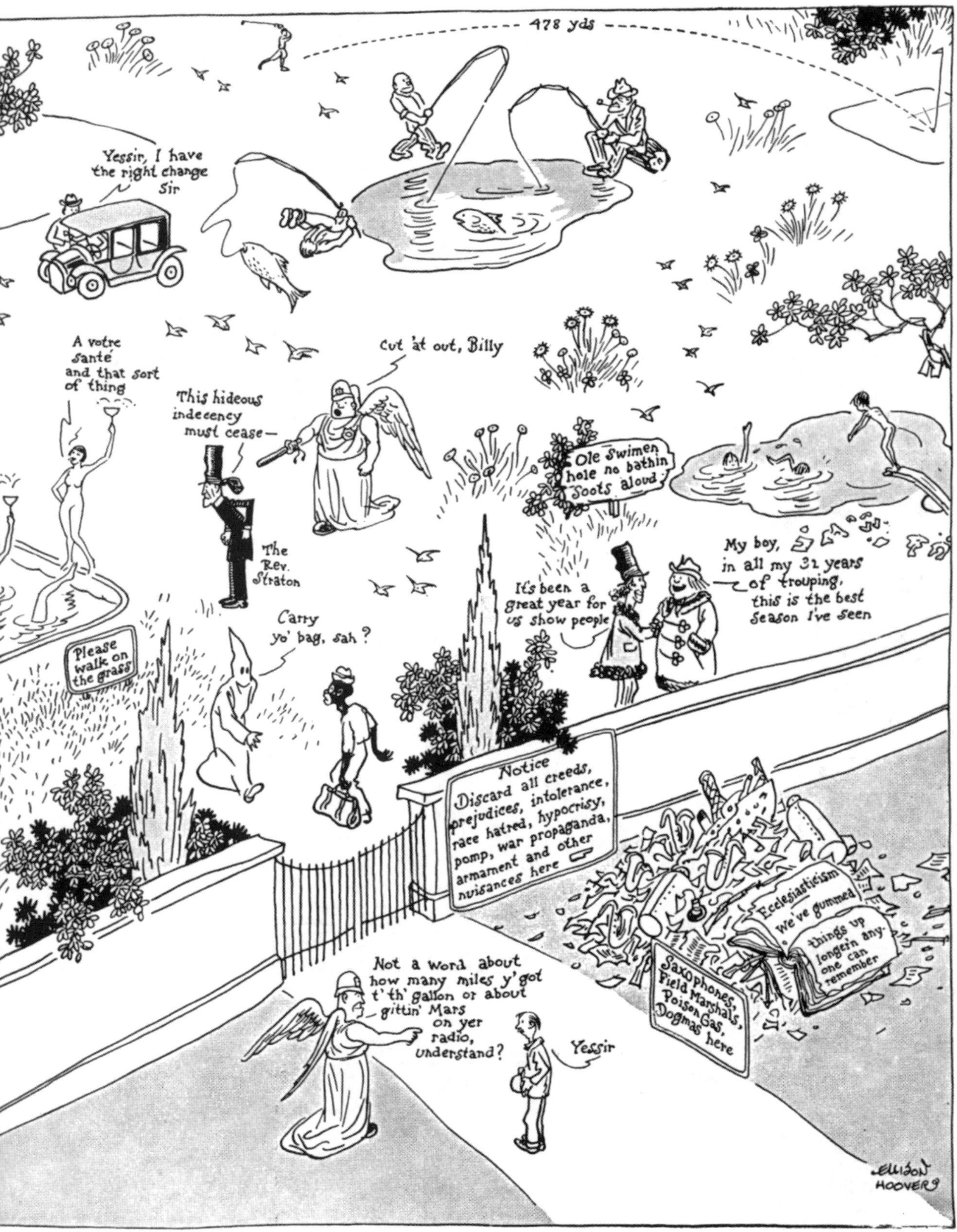

y One Who Has Never Been There

"NEVER MIND, KID, THERE'LL BE ANOTHER CHRISTMAS."

"MAMA, YA BETTER COME DOWN TO SANTY CLAUS—HE'S STEWED AGAIN."

"ANOTHER DAY 'N' ALL THIS'LL BE TAKEN AWAY. OH, WELL, THEY CAN'T TAKE WISHIN' AWAY FROM A BLOKE."

The Red Hand of Vengeance

THE judge asked, "Have you anything to say before I pass sentence on you?" The prisoner arose, bowed his head in thought for a moment, then said in a proud, grave manner:

Your Honor and gentlemen of the jury, it is true that I killed Isadore Gonnef, manager of the Rivialto Theatre. I held his head under the water in one of the gaudy fountains in his own theatre lobby.

That unfortunate evening I decided to see my favorite picture-star, Olivia Ostermoor, in her new film, "CHASTITY FOR CHINCHILLAS," playing at the Rivialto Theatre. I came early because I wanted to get home to bed at a reasonable hour.

The Rivialto super-magnificent augmented orchestra played a potpourri of airs from well-known Esthonian operas. George Cracknel, the finest organist in the world, obliged with "Love's Old Sweet Song," "The Rosary," "Kiss Me Again," and various other selections on the greatest organ in the world. Then the curtain went up on "In Old Heidelberg," an atmospheric prologue. The stage was packed with people in French peasant costume, bumping flagons of wine and singing a Polish folk-song. A dozen girls wearing wooden shoes came out and did a clog dance with their hands on their hips. No sooner had these finished than some girls dressed in kimonos came out, waved fans and did a Japanese dance. Other girls did a Russian dance. Four fat men in dress-suits sang, "The Radio Girl I Adore." They sang it singly, in pairs, as a trio and as a quartette. This led naturally into a Spanish dance and an Apache dance.

The curtain went down at last! But it went up again on a gentleman in overalls leaning against a rose bush and singing to a blonde lady leaning out of the window of a rose-covered cottage, "Roses Are Just a Little Bit Redder When I Love You." This was followed by a six-reel comedy, Larry Leatherneck in "Hot Potatoes."

Now the Classic Six, seven girls in lace curtains, favored with some dances of the old Greeks. Then came a man in a sailor costume who played selections from "Parsifal" on a saw.

My legs had gone to sleep, and I sat helpless while a lady in a silver robe led the audience in community singing. It was one o'clock and the last train to my home in Cranberry Bluffs had been gone fifteen minutes when the four-reel travelogue began. It was the record of a trip "Through the Mesopotamian Hinterland in a Kiddy-Kar."

About dawn, little Wilbur Whangdoodle, aged eight, the golden-voiced thrush of Union Hill, New Jersey, sang "Moonlight and Roses." An educational picture, "A Trip to a Primitive Etruscan Roller-Skate Factory," was just beginning when I managed to drag my paralyzed limbs from the seat and stagger out. An usher showed me the manager of the theatre standing near the fountain. The rest you know.

My only request is this: before I'm hanged, let me be taken to a bare hall, let me sit on a plain chair and see Olivia Ostermoor in "CHASTITY FOR CHINCHILLAS," without a prologue.

Robert Lord.

THE NIGHT BEFORE CHRISTMAS

"WAIT TILL THEY'VE ALL GONE TO BED, FELLOWS, AND WE'LL GO IN AND TRIM THAT TREE UP RIGHT."

Hesitation

"THAT daughter of mine wants a car of her own for Christmas."

"Are you going to give it to her?"

"I don't know. I doubt whether I can afford one that she'll accept."

Peace on Earth
Good Will
Men
AS FAR AS POSSIBLE WITHOUT JOININ
LEAGUE of NATIONS
THE SENATE

As Amended

DECEMBER 3, 1925 VOL. 86. 2248

"While there is Life there's Hope"

Published by
LIFE PUBLISHING COMPANY
598 Madison Avenue, New York

CHARLES DANA GIBSON, *President*
R. E. SHERWOOD, *Editor* CLAIR MAXWELL, *Vice-President*
F. D. CASEY, *Art Editor* LANGHORNE GIBSON, *Secretary and Treasurer*

AS Christmas comes, Peace and Good Will do not yet absolutely prevail in this world, but a good many things help observers to look towards them with some increase of confidence. There are several bright and cheering articles to hang on the Christmas tree. There is Locarno. It is premature to say that our world was saved there, but the spirit shown there was highly medicinal, and what was actually done there considerably helped matters. We cannot count up the practical results yet, but we have seen the effect on the spirits of men.

Europe is not cured yet, but at least Europe is convalescing. It is no comfort to the world to have the French involved in a war in Syria, especially as it is a war so destructive to ancient monuments and remains, but it is a comfort to have France, Britain, Italy, Belgium *and* GERMANY put in the way of agreement. That was done at Locarno and it is a whole Christmas tree in itself.

Of course, there are drawbacks to joy. The course of the United States in its dealings with the rest of mankind is not gratifying even to all the citizens of this country, much less to Europe. When Providence laid off so many of the old Battalion of Death from their mundane and political duties, with all the inscrutability characteristic of Providential action Borah was left on the job, and Borah seems not in favor of hanging much on the world's Christmas tree except receipted bills. Of course, there are others of his mind or worse, but that is no more than the ordinary course of human events. There are always impediments to being good or doing good, and if there were not, righteousness would turn flat to the taste, and we should doubtless be worse off than we are. How sport is to be kept alive when the devil is bound for a thousand years as the Bible forecasts is a curious query, but he is not bound yet and Borah and other survivals attest it.

AS a people we have two troubles in particular. They are both temporary. We are too rich and we are mean. At Buffalo the other day Methodist Bishop Thirkield of Chattanooga stopped talking about rum long enough to say that the United States was in peril from excessive wealth. "The burden of the world's gold," he said, "is upon us. The fact is that we are beastly rich." And that is considerably true. The farmers would not admit it, because the money flood has not overwhelmed them; but there is a money flood, at least there has been, and where it is, some effects of it are quite disagreeable, washing people out of their habits of life, sweeping them along into currents too deep for them, getting them infatuated with the idea that the chief end of life is to get money and spend it. All of that is disenchanting. All the lure of money, the yells of the people who are running to get it, the solicitations of the people who want to direct the uses of it—they are all tiresome and upsetting.

We have had to think too much about money, and too much about rum, which last has been forced upon our attention by the clamor about enforcement. However, rum, like money, is a passing evil. Being too rich is something that usually cures itself without much outside help; being persecuted for rum's sake may be good for us in the end, and probably is. It is still disputed whether the figure of Volstead or of the bootlegger is fitter to hang on the Christmas tree, but Bootlegger is holding his own.

THE churches still keep along. They squabble a good deal, clamor a good deal over theological differences, but pass the plate regularly, contribute liberally, and are on the whole in a fairly healthy state. It would be a bold observer that would call them Christian, but they certainly like the name and try according to their lights to deserve it.

It was remarked the other day that humanity is speculating freely about the job of the churches, what it really is and whether they are on it. A clergyman wrote to inquire what the job of the churches really is. He was told that it is primarily to locate the invisible world, explore it and get a steer out of it that will help in the conduct of life. Of course that is what the churches are for, and always have been, but it is quite likely to be news to many persons who pass the plate and to not a few who stand in a pulpit, and who seem to take little thought for the invisible and what may be drawn from it, and to concentrate their efforts on the promotion of righteousness, as they see it, by legislation and compulsion. That effort, now so prevalent, to produce by fiscal and political means results that can only be compassed by spiritual means is the worst stick in our Christmas stocking. Nevertheless, just as out of the war came a deep conviction that wars could not save the world, so out of the disappointing results of the struggle for the compulsory regulation of conduct is coming a better day for the other conception which thinks of righteousness as the fruit of an inward process; the fruit, not of restrictions, nor of padlocks nor of terror, but of freedom and of love, and of the teaching and the life that Christmas stands for.

That conception is gaining in the world. Hang it on the Christmas tree along with Locarno. *E. S. Martin.*

The Head of the Hou

Home for the Holidays

"Ah, don't cry, ma, ya singin' swell."

The Road to Yesterday

Mrs. Pep's Diary

November 1st Awake betimes, but with such a feeling of exhaustion that I was loath to quit my couch, and bawled loudly for service and stimulants from those about me, whereupon my husband, poor wretch, did say, Why do you not stop at home, for a change, and cease treating every invitation you receive as though it were a court command? So, there being somewhat in his words, I did telephone Marge Boothby not to expect me at the Madison, for Lord! better a luncheon of herbs in ease and contentment than to be getting into one's raiment three or four times a day as a fire horse leaps into his harness. This is the day of all the saints, on which I do usually go to church, but my fatigue so great that I did content myself with singing as much as I could remember of Hymn 176, and then fell a-pondering on what I should give my friends for Christmas, being strongly minded this year to dispense practical, desirable benevolences, for I had liefer myself be given a jar of pickles or conserve which adds to the pleasure of a repast than a tray or door-stop of uncertain æsthetic value. Helen Meacham in to see me, full of the opera's opening on the morrow, but I cannot summon the enthusiasm which once was mine, when the clothes Melanie Kurt wore as Sieglinde fairly kept me awake at night because of their unsuitability, and I doubt if I should ever step inside the Metropolitan again were it not for Elizabeth Rethberg, her voice thrilling me more than any I have heard since the days of Emmy Destinn. Helen has a new beau, it seems, and when I did ask her to tell me about him, she elaborated upon his distinction, which made me suspicious, so I said, Come now! What is wrong with him? and she responded, Oh, well! He has all sorts of letters after his name, but I rather wish his handkerchiefs and neckties were different, if you get what I mean, which I did, perfectly. Aroused myself by evening, and forth to supper at Larry Searles's, where all sorts of rag, tag and bobtail, some of them exceedingly stupid, too, and after attending at length to discourse which did not amuse me, I have concluded that there are two things in life of which I never wish to hear again, i. e., the details of a fire, and why an account was closed at any given shop.

November 10th A-talking with my husband at this and that, I did ask him if there were anything in his life which he truly regretted, and he did respond, after some reflection, that it pained him to realize he had never had a real New Orleans silver fizz, nor was ever likely to have one. And then we spoke, more seriously, of our Cousin Elsie, who always seems to get more out of life than is actually in it, the reason therefor being that if she cannot get a thing on which she has set her heart, she stops longing for it, and convinces herself that its achievement would have made her unhappy. Does not Bernard Shaw say that those who do not get their heart's desire are better off than those who do? He does indeed, and yet I cannot, in simple candor, see how a chinchilla cloak could work me any harm.... Out this morning to market, buying, through the sheer vision of the foodstuffs, more than we shall need for a week, plunging recklessly on alligator pears because their price was so much less than it is in our neighborhood, and remembering Ruth Roberts's tale of her introduction to them, how, visiting as a flapper in Honolulu, she could not get enough of them at table, and would purloin them from the console at night and eat them in her room with a shoe horn. Then to Mr. Hickman's, to see about my watch, which he tells me he can make go, thank God, and afterwards for a fitting on a gown of garnet velvet which I have ordered for evening wear, somewhat astonished to find that they had cut it down to my waist in the back, but they tell me that is the fashion now.... To dinner with Ethel Grant at a Russian place called Samarkand, finding there Irvin Cobb and Laura, Hewitt and Manie Howland amongst many others, also a Mrs. Barney with the loveliest profile that ever I saw in my life, and Sam so gay that it would not have surprised me had they put him out on the pavement, yet all, including myself, much amused with his antics. ...I set down, as a matter of record, that I am probably the only woman in New York who does not use a lipstick.

Baird Leonard.

American (in a London restaurant): SAY, JONES IS MY NAME. FROM EMPORIA, KANSAS. I WONDER, NOW, IS THERE ANY CHANCE OF GETTING A LITTLE REAL BEER?

Reciprocity

"OH, look, Charles," exclaimed the author's wife, "what a beautiful Christmas present I bought for you—a lovely set of lace curtains for the dining-room!"

"I anticipated your thoughtfulness, dear," said he, "and just see what I have got for you—a cunning little portable typewriter—for my desk!"

With No Maybe

MEPHISTO: What's your reaction to my proposition, doc?

FAUST: I'm absolutely sold on it, Old Boy! Absolutely sold! Show me the dotted line.

THE Rising Young Business Woman rolls down her stockings and goes to work.

MISTLETOE IS SCARCE BECAUSE IT TAKES SO LONG TO PICK IT.

The Hall of Fame

BILLINGS dashed into my office in great excitement.

"He's elected!" he exclaimed. "Just heard it over the radio."

"Who's elected?" I inquired.

"Jones—John Paul Jones. I'm so excited I can hardly talk. I've been sitting up getting the returns—"

"What election are you talking about?" I said.

"The Hall of Fame, of course," replied Billings. "I forgot to tell you, I was on the Jones campaign committee, making speeches on the street corner—"

"He was a great admiral," I said.

"Admiral nothing," said Billings. "He was one of the greatest little quarter-milers they ever had on the cinder track. You should have seen that lad in the Intercollegiate down at Philadelphia. How that boy could run!"

"I didn't know they had athletes in the Hall of Fame," I said.

"Sure," said Billings. "Didn't Ed Poe, the Princeton halfback, make it?"

"Who else was elected?" I asked.

"Some bird named Booth. He was the Actors' Equity candidate—"

"Booth? Never heard of him."

"Neither did I," said Billings. "There used to be a Sam Booth on the Keith Circuit who did a bicycle act—"

"What did they put him in the Hall of Fame for?"

"Well, it was a swell bicycle act," said Billings. "Still, he had a hard fight. He was running against a fellow named Walt Whitman—"

"Yes, I know," I nodded. "The bird that ran for District Attorney."

"That's the lad. He couldn't quite make the grade, though. The trouble with this Hall of Fame bunch is that they don't understand politics. What they need is a campaign manager, and buttons and slogans and things."

"Why don't you take the job?"

"I'm going to," said Billings. "I'm booming a fellow named Eli Whitney—"

"I don't think I ever heard of him."

"That's because you're plain ignorant. He's the lad who invented gin."

"Is that a fact?" I said. "Then he'll certainly get my vote."

"We're going to have banners, and buttons for the kids, and everything," said Billings. "We'll probably call on you for a contribution."

"Put me down for two cases," I said.

Newman Levy.

When the Last Christmas

Tree Has Been Cut Down

Advertising Man's Child (looking over his toys): AND ARE ALL THESE ARTICLES NATIONALLY ADVERTISED, DAD?

THE CHRISTMAS SPIRIT

"QUIT YOUR PUSHING OR I'LL SOAK YOU ONE IN THE JAW!"

IN YE GOODE OLDE DAYES

"YE RIGHTE SPIRIT."

"LOOKEY, FELLERS! ALL HE GOT WAS A SUIT O' CLOTHES."

"SANTA CLAUS USET TO BLOW IN FROM DE NORT' POLE IN A TWENTY-MULE-TEAM SLED, BUT I'M EXPECTIN' 'IM IN A AIRPLANE DIS YEAR."
"YE'RE CRAZY! HE BUNKS IN DE SALVATION BARRACKS!"

"I WANT OUR CHIMBLEY STRAIGHTENED OUT! SANTA COULDN'T GIT DOWN IT LAST CHRISMUS."

"IS YOUR NEW NURSE IRISH, FRENCH OR GERMAN, FREDDIE?"
"WELL, I THINK SHE'S BROKEN ENGLISH."

"BE SURE NOT TO DELIVER IT BEFORE CHRISTMAS MORNING, BECAUSE IT'S A PRESENT FOR FATHER. PLEASE SEND THE BILL TO K. PILKINGTON PELL, SAME ADDRESS—THAT'S MY FATHER."

Ye brave Knight
Ye Captive Maiden
Ye·Knight·Confoundeth·ye·Giant·
Ye·Knight·Bloweth·a·Blast·
Ye·Dragon·cryeth·a·Truce·
Ye·Dragon·maketh·merrie·with
ye·Maiden·&·ye·Knight·
Rodney Thomson

The Dragon's Christmas

A KNIGHT, with heavy armor laden,
Rode forth to free a lovely Maiden
Held captive by an awful Dragon
Whose tail alone would fill a wagon.

The brave Knight traversed wastes and antres; [1]
Confounding sundry bad Enchanters,
And Giants, too, of magic power,
He reached the Dragon's gloomy tower.

The good Knight blew his lusty bugle;
The Dragon glared like Barney Google, [2]
Displaying teeth designed for biting,
And groaned, "Aw, what's the use of fighting?

"I really do not want this Maiden,
Though she's a Peri [3] out of Aidenn. [4]
I steal these ladies, yes, but as to
The reason why,—a dragon has to.

"And since contention's out of reason
In this, the festive Yuletide season,
Come in and share my humble platter
And let's adjust the little matter."

"Now, by the poor, repentant Dismas!" [5]
The Knight replied. "You're right; it's Christmas,
The time for reconciliation,
So I accept your invitation."

On Christmas pudding primed with sherry
The Dragon, Maid and Knight were merry,
And emptied many brimming flagons
To "Peace on earth, good will to Dragons!"

Arthur Guiterman.

1. Shakespeare.
2. De Beck.
3. Moore.
4. Poe.
5. Apocrypha.

General Chorus: OH, BUDDY, GET SOMETHING ELSE! WE CAN'T DANCE TO THAT.

Fireman: HOW DID IT CATCH? ELECTRIC WIRE?
The Wife: NO, NO. MY HUSBAND, HE IS A BARBER, AND AFTER HE TRIMMED THE TREE HE STARTED TO GIVE IT A SINGE.

"It's all right, Santa—you can come in. My parents still believe in you."

WHY SHOULD CHRISTMAS BE A PERIOD OF GRATIFICATION TO CHILDREN ONLY, AND A SEASON OF SUPPRESSED DESIRES FOR ADULTS? FOR EXAMPLE, IF GRANDPA HAS WANTED A TOY ENGINE EVERY CHRISTMAS SINCE HE WAS NINE YEARS OLD, WHY SHOULD NOT GRANDPA HAVE A TOY ENGINE, GRANDPA SIZE, WITH A WHISTLE AND EVERYTHING?

MODERN PSYCHOLOGY TEACHES US WE SHOULD ALL HAVE WHAT WE WANT WHEN WE WANT IT. WHETHER IT IS GOOD FOR US OR NOT, SO UNCLE MARK GETS A BOUNCER SWING THIS HUMANITARIAN PSYCHOLOGICAL CHRISTMAS.

THE PSYCHOANALYST WOULD TELL US THAT FATHER'S ANNUAL PROTESTS AGAINST THE CHILDREN'S DRUM-BEATING HAVE REALLY HAD THEIR ORIGIN IN A HUSHED HUNGER FOR A DRUM OF HIS OWN, SO THIS YEAR HE GETS A BIG BASS DRUM ALL TO HIMSELF—TO BOOM ALL HE PLEASES ALL OVER THE PLACE.

AUNT MARTHA HAS NEVER PASSED A CHRISTMAS WITHOUT ENTERTAINING AN ALMOST PASSIONATE UNEXPRESSED DESIRE FOR ALPHABETICAL BUILDING BLOCKS. NOW SHE CAN HAVE THEM.

A Psychological Christmas

Suppressed Yuletide Desires of Adults Finally Gratified

UNCLE FRED'S SECRET LONGING HAS BEEN FOR A TOY TAXI WITH A REAL MOTOR. THIS YEAR HE GETS IT, RIDES DOWNTOWN IN IT AND TAKES IT RIGHT UP TO THE OFFICE.

UNCLE ARTHUR WILL BE A BETTER MAN IN EVERY WAY AFTER WHOOPING AROUND THE HOUSE FOR TWO WEEKS IN THIS INDIAN SUIT HE HAS CRAVED SINCE INFANCY.

UNCLE SIMIAN (SOMETHING OF AN INVENTOR) LONG AGO CONCEIVED A WHIMSICAL WANT FOR A TRICYCLE WITH A BOOK-RACK ATTACHMENT, AND HERE IT IS, THE ENVY OF ALL THE KIDS AND ALL THE SCHOLARS IN THE BLOCK. HE CALLS IT HIS PHILOSOPEDE.

AND MOTHER GETS A BIG, BEAUTIFUL DOLL ALL FOR HERSELF —WHICH LANCES A YEARNING THAT HAS BOILED WITHIN HER SINCE GIRLHOOD PASSED. DON'T YOU AGREE THAT IT WILL BE A FINE IDEA TO TAKE CHRISTMAS THUS OUT OF THE HANDS OF CHILDREN AT LEAST ONCE EVERY DECADE?

A Psychological Christmas

Instinctive Toy-Yearnings of Grown-Ups Relieved at Last

"OF COURSE, IT'S AWFULLY MESSY NOW, BUT THE PLACE SIMPLY HAD TO BE DONE OVER!"

An Even Deal

MRS. BARKER: Well, did you get many Christmas gifts?

MRS. HARPER: Yes, I got several lovely presents, and also some things from my husband's people.

"WE had quite a fire over at our house last night."

"Yes, my old man brought home a lump of coal, too."

The Postman's Merry Whistle

POSTMASTER-GENERAL NEW'S proclamation that there shall be no mail deliveries on Christmas Day appears generally popular, judging from the newspapers and the comment one hears. The only improvement we can suggest is that mail deliveries be also cancelled on the first of every month.

"OH, BOY! MAYBE I'M NOT GLAD MY DAD'S A STOCKING MANUFACTURER."

THE GAY NINETIES

CHRISTMAS MORNING AT JAKE'S PLACE DOWN ON THE CORNER, WHERE HOT TOM AND JERRYS WERE "ON THE HOUSE" TO OLD CUSTOMERS. THIS SESSION USUALLY LASTED UNTIL SOMEBODY'S LITTLE WILLIE ARRIVED WITH THE MESSAGE, "MAMMA SAYS PAPA IS TO COME RIGHT STRAIGHT HOME—THE TURKEY'S ON THE TABLE."

The Eleventh Hour

IN his dingy hall-bedroom the humorist lay starving. For sheer lack of inspiration he had written no jokes for months, and he had long since spent the money he had made on Calvin Coolidge's taciturnity and Henry Ford's terpsichorean ventures.

Suddenly his landlady—who from similar crises in the past was completely aware of his predicament—burst into the room, ecstatically waving a newspaper extra.

The humorist raised himself on one elbow and gave a glance at the headlines.

"Saved!" he gasped weakly, and fainted.

The Prince of Wales had fallen off his horse again.

FAIRY STORY—Once a young married man invited friends to a turkey dinner and said he would carve the bird himself, which he did very neatly.

Reflections

Puck, Judge and *Life:* there were attempts in the field before and have been attempts since, but these three magazines were the successful giants, each with its own unique story. *Puck,* the pioneer, early became an institution. Its staff was close-knit (although volatile) and was built around two geniuses, Keppler and Bunner. Non-staff contributors often climbed the stairs to the editorial offices with reluctance or apprehension, because the regular staff had practically become a legend in its time. The interoffice camaraderie is revealed by such things as the mock Opper-Bunner feud of 1884 and Keppler's many self-caricatures.

As *Puck* lived and breathed humor and cartoons, *Judge* was at first almost a side-effect of political maneuverings. Arkell managed it as a propaganda sheet, involving himself more in such efforts as hastily buying Mount McGregor in New York, opening it to U.S. Grant during his final illness, and trying to capitalize on its fame after Grant's death. However, in spite of its political motivation, its dearth of bright literature, and its many incompetent staff artists over the years, *Judge* had a great number of comic geniuses, such as Grant Hamilton and Zim, whose prints were extremely popular and hung in thousands of homes at the turn of the century. In its full-size, color heyday its immense popularity was probably due to its appeal to the rural unsophisticates, who comprised quite a large audience then.

While *Judge* spoke partisan politics and *Puck* was but one step higher in its commentary on political issues, *Life* was often obsessed with social, economic, religious and humanitarian affairs. Often a third to a half of its text was given over to essays and editorials. The other magazines had to cope with image revisions, such as smaller sizes (*Judge* in 1911 and *Puck* in 1915) and staff changes (for example, the dropping of a regular short story after Bunner's death in 1896, or Anthony's innovations in judge in the 1920s), but *Life* had the benefit of a half-century of uninterrupted ownership and an equally constant staff; changes such as color, halftones and longer fiction were therefore more easily absorbed.

As great as their individual significance is, the three papers share a number of characteristics. To today's scholar, they are an excellent reflection of American civilization of the day. Their primary purpose was to comment on the current scene, and the variance in their points of view has been noted. Thus, the cartoons that were consciously satirizing or commenting provide more valuable insights into the events of the time than charts, statistical graphs or treatises ever could. Not to be neglected—indeed, probably more significant—are the ordinary "humorous" cartoons. A respectable social history of America in this period could be traced in these cartoons of Kemble's Negroes, Sullivant's Irish immigrants, Keppler's workingman, Opper's suburbanite, Zim's rural people, Gibson's 400, Mike Woolf's slum kids, Art Young's malefactors of wealth, Gluyas Williams' harried family man. Humor cuts through pretense, and by exposing prejudices, fads, morals and life-styles, the cartoonist paints a unique and unrivaled portrait of his contemporaries. It should be noted that what may appear, in our basically humorless and hypersensitive era, to be bigotry or racism in early cartoons is most often innocent jesting; immigrant and minority groups were markedly less assimilated in those days, so they were obvious subjects for cartoons and were generally portrayed amiably, if stereotypically, without invective or hate.

Another great contribution, especially of *Puck* and *Life,* was the broad dissemination of liberal and reform ideas. As they were "popular" magazines and appealed to all segments of society, their influence was pervasive and profound. Art Young said that he "absorbed . . . many social ideas" from mugwump *Puck.* [62] W.A. Rogers reports that John Ames Mitchell wanted to find a way to balance *Life's* criticisms, satire and attacks so the magazine would not become too "cynical";[63] and the result was the Fresh Air Fund, a charitable institution that survives to this day. Many reforms—civil service, tariff, currency, railroads, armaments—were explained to a mass audience in sophisticated cartoons that were worth many thousands of tracts and speeches.

As forums for literary humor, the three magazines gave birth to three generations of American humorists. Bill Nye, Robert J. Burdette, John Kendrick Bangs, Franklin P. Adams, Robert Benchley and Gurney Williams, as well as scores of other first-rate, memorable humorists, rose to the top of a profession that was largely created by *Puck, Judge* and *Life.* They were the only long-running, successful humor magazines in American history. (The *New* Yorker deserves special study, but it has long since left the ranks of humor magazines.)

Puck, Judge and *Life* also brought the art form of the American political cartoon to a singular level of maturity. A synthesis of the French, English and German political cartooning styles with the American humorous tradition gave birth to an institution that nurtured Keppler, Gillam, Opper, Hamilton and other geniuses. This magazine dynasty was the father of the American newspaper editorial cartoon, with representatives such as Homer Davenport, McCutcheon, Rollin Kirby, John Sloan, Robert Minor, Daniel Fitzpatrick, Ding Darling, Mauldin, Herblock, Oliphant and MacNelly.

Last but certainly not least is the gift *Puck, Judge* and *Life* gave to America—a pantheon of comic geniuses. From the desert, as it were, of the 1860s and early 1870s, there arose scores of great cartoonists whose names need not be repeated here. J. A. Mitchell noted in 1889 that cartoonists had become more popular than painters.[64] For pure invention, brilliant criticism, fine perception and wonderful artistry, many of these artists deserve to be recorded prominently in the annals of American civilization. Often *Puck, Judge* and *Life* had interchangeable staffs, and many of their freelancers joined the ranks of the infant comic strip industry. It is fascinating to observe artists creating and defining a new art form, and the pioneers of comic strip art were all products of *Puck, Judge* and *Life.* For this, if for no other reason, these magazines deserve study and great honor.

Their day has passed, but their influence will never die.

Notes

1. August 1875, p. 199.
2. In *Scribner's*, December 1889, p. 728.
3. *Ladies' Home Journal*, October 1917, p. 119.
4. In *Scribner's*, December 1889, p. 729.
5. Stephen Becker, *Comic Art in America* (New York: Simon & Schuster, 1959), pp. 292-3.
6. Roger Butterfield, *The American Past* (New York: Simon & Schuster, 1946).
7. W.A. Rogers, *A World Worth While* (New York: Harper's, 1922), pp. 6-10.
8. Art Young, *On My Way* (New York: Horace Liveright, 1928), p. 250.
9. H.C. Bunner provides an interesting analysis in his introduction to Keppler's *Cartoons from Puck* (New York: Keppler & Schwarzmann, 1893).
10. Frank Luther Mott, *A History of American Magazines*, 1665-1835 (Cambridge: Harvard University Press, 1957), p. 521.
11. Ibid.
12. L. Draper Hill, "What Fools These Mortals Be!" (B.A. thesis, Harvard College,1 957).
13. *Supplement to Puck*, no. 521, March 6, 1887.
14. Rogers,*A World Worth While.*
15. Mott, p. 525.
16. *Supplement to Puck*, no. 521.
17. Ibid.
18. Ibid.
19. Hill, p. 14.
20. In his *Cartoon Cavalcade* (New York: Simon & Schuster, 1946).
21. *A World Worth While*, pp. 284-5.
22. Mott, p. 530.
23. Ibid., p. 532.
24. *American News Trade Journal*, June 1920, p. 13.
25. *Judge*, October 29, 1881, p. 2.
26. Mott, p. 553.
27. *Judge*, January 16, 1885, p. 2.
28. *American News Trade Journal*, June 1920, p. 21.
29. *The Journalist*, December 10, 1887, p. 3.
30. *Judge*, January 5, 1911, p. 4.
31. Molt, p. 554.
32. John Ames Mitchell, "How *Life* Began," *Life*, January 1893, p. 12.
33. Mott, p. 557.
34. "How *Life* Began," *Life*, January 1908, p. 15.
35. "How *Life* Began" (1893), p. 15.
36. Ibid.
37. Edward S. Martin, editorial in *Life*, January 4, 1923, p. 13.
38. Mitchell, "How *Life* Began" (1893), p. 14.
39. Ibid.
40. Mott, p. 558.
41. Martin, "*Life* Reincarnate," in the November 1936 supplement to *Life*.
42. Fairfax Downey, *Portrait of an Era As Drawn by C.D. Gibson* (New York: Scribner's, 1936),
pp. 48-53.
43. Mott, p. 564.
44. Mitchell, "As *Life* Runs On," *Life*, December 26, 1901, p. 553.
45. Ibid., pp. 552-3.
46. Downey, p. 50.
47. Ibid., p. 270.
48. Ibid., pp. 287-394.
49. Mott, p. 565.
50. Ibid.
51. Ibid., pp. 567-8.
52. Downey, p. 342.
53. *Life*, January 4, 1923, p. 4.
54. Downey, pp. 342-4.

55. Mott, p. 566.
56. Theodore Peterson, *Magazines in the 20th Century* (Urbana: University of Illinois Press), pp. 160, 59.
57. Norman Anthony, *How to Grow Old Disgracefully* (New York: Eagle Books, 1946), p. 100.
58. Ibid.
59. Peterson, p. 163.
60. James Playstead Wood, *Magazines in the United States* (New York: Ronald Press, 1956), p. 208n.
61. Martin, November 1936 supplement to *Life.*
62. Young, p. 122.
63. Rogers, p. 146.
64. Mitchell, in *Scribner's,* December 1889, pp. 735-6.

A Note on Sources

The primary sources for this study are the files of *Puck, Judge* and *Life.* It is absorbing material that takes the researcher back to the turn of the century almost by osmosis. Especially useful are the anniversary issues (1882, 1887 and 1902 for *Puck;* 1888, 1893, 1903, 1908, 1913, 1933 and the thousandth and two-thousandth issues of *Life;* and 1885, 1911 and 1938 for *Judge*), which discuss each magazine's own history.

Another useful magazine is *Cartoons* (Chicago, 1911-22), the files of which are full of cartooning anecdotes (such as Opper's remark about T.S. Sullivant's technique: "If he would scratch his head as much as his paper, he would be a better artist"). Articles bearing on this study can be found in the *American Bibliophilist* (August 1875), the *American News Trade Journal* (June 1920), the *Journalist* (December 10, 1887) and *Scribner's Magazine* (December 1889). Volumes exhumed from the "graveyard," especially Frank Leslie titles, also contain much of interest.

A very useful book is the third volume of Frank Luther Mott's *History of American Magazines,* 1865-1885 (Cambridge: Harvard University Press, 1957), which contains skeleton sketches of *Puck, Judge* and *Life* and offers a lucid discussion of the state of journalism in those days. William Murrell's two-volume *History of American Graphic Humor* (New York: Whitney Museum of Art, 1938) is a classic work on the origins of the American cartoon. Although it contains a few errors and could go into more detail in the second volume, which deals with *Puck, Judge* and *Life,* these are minor flaws. Murrell has done some splendid detective work on obscure points; the early days (etchings, wood-cuts, etc.) are covered thoroughly.

There are a number of books of reminiscences by staffers connected with *Puck, Judge* and *Life.* Most useful are W.J. Arkell's *Old Friends;* Norman Anthony's *How to Grow Old Disgracefully,* or *Anthony's Adversities* (New York: Eagle Books, 1946); James L. Ford's *40-Odd Years in the Literary Shop* (New York, 1921); Walt McDougall's *This Is the Life!* (New York: Knopf, 1926); Norman Rockwell's *My Adventures as an Illustrator* (Garden City: Doubleday, 1956); William Allen Rogers's *A World Worth While* (New York: Harper's, 1922); and Art Young's *His Life and Times* (New York: Sheridan House, 1939) and On *My Way* (New York: Liveright, 1928). Young's works, as well as those of Anthony, McDougall and Rogers, are eminently readable and revealing.

Especially useful was L. Draper Hill's "What Fools These Mortals Be!," which is on microfilm in the New York Public Library and was written in partial fulfillment of the requirements for a Bachelor of Arts in History (Harvard, 1957). Mr. Hill, himself an editorial cartoonist, was fortunate to be able to talk with members of Keppler's family and uncover much pertinent data. Gerard E. Jensen's biography, *The Life and Letters of H.C. Bunner* (Durham: Duke University Press, 1939), provides many insights into the workings of the *Puck* staff and into its leading "lit'ry feller." Fairfax Downey's *Portrait of an Era As Drawn by C.D. Gibson* (New York: Scribner's, 1936) is a good biography filled with Gibson cartoons. Albert B. Paine's *Thomas Nast: His Period and Pictures* (New York: Harper's, 1904) is useful when it discusses Nast's successors.

It is difficult to obtain general information from cartoonists themselves; George Price and Edwina (Dumm) had no vivid recollections since they drew as freelancers, not staffers. However, general histories of cartooning provide some background material. There are very few good works in this field; a substantial history *is* long overdue. Existing sources include Stephen Becker's *Comic Art in America* (New York: Simon & Schuster, 1959), which unfortunately devotes most of its space to contemporary artists; Joseph B. Bishop's *Our Political Dramas* (New York, 1904), which touches on editorial cartooning; and Roger Butterfield's *Our American Past* (New York: Simon & Schuster, 1946), which deals well with colored lithographic cartoons. Thomas Craven's *Cartoon Cavalcade* (New York: Simon & Schuster, 1946) has a section on 19th-century cartoons; Keppler's *Cartoons from Puck* (New York: Puck Press, 1893) has a short introduction by Bunner on cartooning traditions; and Frank Weitenkampf's *American Graphic Art* (New York, 1924) touches on *Puck, Judge* and *Life.* The same author also collaborated with Allan Nevins on *A Century of Political Cartoons* (New York: Scribner's, 1944).